Authors in the News

Biography News Library

Authors in the News

A Compilation of News Stories and Feature Articles from American Newspapers and Magazines Covering Writers and Other Members of the Communications Media

By the Staff of *Biography News*:

Barbara Nykoruk
Editor

volume 1

GALE RESEARCH COMPANY • BOOK TOWER • DETROIT, MICHIGAN 48226

Art Director: Susan Halbert
Assistant Art Director: Donna L. Hale

Editorial Researchers: Ann Evory, Judy Flintoff, Linda Gray,
Margaret Mazurkiewicz, Helen Merkrebs, Trenna Ruffner, John Schmittroth, Jr.,
Lori Smith, Marian Wiseman

Cover Design: Arthur Chartow

Library of Congress Catalog Card Number: 75-13541

ISBN 0-8103-0043-5

Preface

Authors in the News is an extension of a concept developed by the Gale Research Company in *Biography News,* a bimonthly publication featuring in-depth newspaper and magazine articles concerning persons in all lines of endeavor who are of widespread general interest.

The *Biography News* concept was simply that by means of clipping, arranging, indexing, reproducing, and binding newspaper and magazine stories about important and interesting people, a great deal of useful material could be preserved and made accessible. At the same time, the many hours devoted in some libraries to maintaining "personality files" could largely be saved.

The editors of *Biography News* frequently found, however, that after stories concerning men and women of general interest were selected, there remained much additional material in several categories which deserved preservation and circulation, but which could not logically. . .or physically. . .be included in *Biography News.*

One type of material which was of particular value, they felt, was that on authors, magazine writers, newspaper reporters and columnists, television writers, etc. Even though many of these people could not be considered as being of "general" interest, the criterion for *Biography News,* the interest shown over the years in Gale's *Contemporary Authors* and in similar publications suggested that this somewhat different type of material should be preserved in a special collection devoted to it alone.

Authors in the News is that collection. It is the first of an upcoming series of such special-category editions which constitute the *Biography News Library.* In this volume, users will find more than 500 pages of material from more than 50 newspapers and magazines on more than 350 significant authors and other personalities in all branches of communications, including some who previously appeared in *Biography News* and have been repeated here to round out the selection. The text has been adjusted in format, but has not been altered in content from its original publication.

It has not been the intention of the journalists who wrote the interviews and stories to produce a dry-even-if-factual biographical sketch. Rather, they have usually tried to present the living figure in a personal, intimate way, to provide information and insights which compliment rather than substitute for the usual biographical sketch.

Suggestions from users concerning content, format, or any other aspect of the publication are welcome. Please write to:

Editor
Authors in the News
Gale Research Company
Book Tower
Detroit, Michigan 48226

Surveyed Newspapers and Magazines

All material in the *Biography News Library,* of which this volume is a part, is used with the permission of the individual newspapers and magazines designated on each article. Rights to the further reproduction or use of the material are retained by the original publishers.

Newspapers

Eastern States

Buffalo Evening News
The Hartford Courant
Long Island Press
Newark Star-Ledger
The News American (Baltimore, Md.)
Philadelphia Bulletin
Philadelphia Inquirer
The Pittsburgh Press
Pittsburgh Post-Gazette
Portland Press Herald
Syracuse Post-Standard
Washington Star (Washington, D.C.)

Central States

Akron Beacon Journal
Arkansas Gazette (Little Rock, Ark.)
The Blade (Toledo, O.)
The Cincinnati Enquirer
Cleveland Press
Detroit Free Press
The Detroit News
The Grand Rapids Press
The Indianapolis Star
The Milwaukee Journal
The Plain Dealer (Cleveland, O.)
The Tulsa Tribune-World

Southern States

The Atlanta Journal and Constitution
The Columbia State-Record
Commercial Appeal (Memphis, Tenn.)
The Courier-Journal & Times (Louisville, Ken.)
Fort Lauderdale News and Sun-Sentinel
The Knoxville News-Sentinel
The Macon Telegraph-News
The Miami Herald
Press Scimitar (Memphis, Tenn.)
Tallahassee Democrat
Times-Picayune (New Orleans, La.)
Winston-Salem Journal-Sentinel (Winston-Salem, N.C.)

Western States

The Arizona Daily Star (Tucson, Ariz.)
The Dallas News
The Denver Post
The Fresno Bee
The Houston Post
The Oregonian (Portland, Ore.)
The Sacramento Bee
The Salt Lake Tribune
Seattle Post-Intelligencer
Star-Telegram (Fort Worth, Tex.)

Magazines

American Way (New York, N.Y.)
Atlanta
The Atlantic Monthly (Boston, Mass.)
Connecticut (Stratford, Conn.)
Cue Magazine (New York, N.Y.)
The Detroiter
Dun's Review (New York, N.Y.)
East West Journal (Boston, Mass.)
Editor & Publisher (New York, N.Y.)
Esquire (New York, N.Y.)
Family Weekly (New York, N.Y.)
Flightime (Los Angeles, Cal.)
Florida Trend (Tampa, Fla.)
Football News (Grosse Pointe, Mich.)
Forbes Magazine (New York, N.Y.)
Fort Lauderdale Magazine
Fortune (New York, N.Y.)
Freedom (Hollywood, Cal.)
Gold Coast Pictorial (Fort Lauderdale, Fla.)
Gulfshore Life (Naples, Fla.)
Hughes Airwest Sundancer (Los Angeles, Cal.)
Interior Design (New York, N.Y.)
Juris Doctor (New York, N.Y.)
Louisville Magazine
Mankind (Los Angeles, Cal.)
Nation's Business (Washington, D.C.)
New Engineer (New York, N.Y.)
Newsweek (New York, N.Y.)
New York Times Magazine (New York, N.Y.)
Palm Beach Life (Palm Beach, Fla.)
Palm Springs Life (Palm Springs, Cal.)
Pan Am Clipper (Los Angeles, Cal.)
Parade (New York, N.Y.)
Philadelphia Magazine
Pittsburgh Renaissance
Present Tense (New York, N.Y.)
PSA California Magazine (Los Angeles, Cal.)
Psychology Today (New York, N.Y.)
The Quill (Chicago, Ill.)
San Francisco
Sky Magazine (Los Angeles, Cal.)
Sport (New York, N.Y.)
Texas Monthly (Austin, Tex.)
Town & Country (New York, N.Y.)
United Mainliner (Los Angeles, Cal.)
Yankee (Dublin, N.H.)

Cumulative Indexing

The cumulative index which appears in each volume of the *Biography News Library* includes all entries from preceding volumes of the same title.

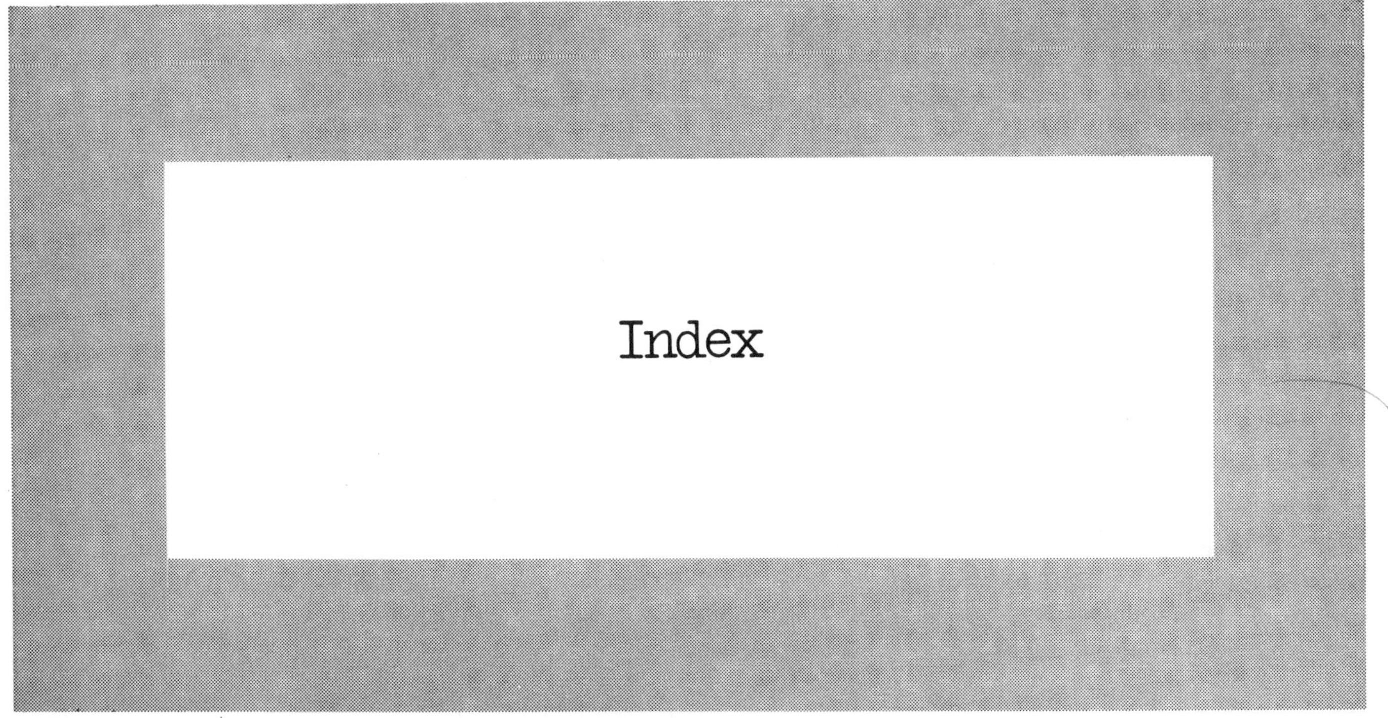

Index

Authors in the News

Master Photographer Ansel Adams Preserves Life's Beauty

By GENE ROSE
Bee Staff Writer

Photography has come a long way since the turn of the century when it was regarded as a craft and as an imitator of painting.

So says Ansel Adams, recognized as the foremost living photographer in the United States.

What he didn't say was that much of the credit for the eminence of photography as art lies with Adams' own efforts.

Adams, 72, shared his love of photography with Fresnans attending a reception in his honor last Sunday at the Fresno Arts Center.

"I'm as busy as ever," admitted Adams in a rare interview. "Besides appearances for my new book, I have a tremendous amount of printing to do.

"As a matter of fact, I'm not going to take any print orders after January, 1976. There's plenty to do."

His achievements have included a dozen books, two dozen one-man shows, countless articles, portfolios, four honorary doctorate degrees and over 50 years of photography.

"Art has changed — superficially, at least — in the 50 and more years I have related to it," Adams stated. "I have seen photography grow constantly from a shallow hobby, with very few exceptions, to a profound medium of expression and communication, accepted as a major art form and as a vital force in our culture."

The veteran lensman said there is no easy way to photographic excellence. He dismissed recent developments in automated cameras and other photographic equipment with little merit except to those whose photographic efforts are limited to visual documentations, or what Adams describes as a "visual diary" approach.

In response to the great number of young photographers climbing the photographic pyramid, Adams said he couldn't be too optimistic.

"I don't want to encourage them anymore," he said. "I just want to give them the facts of life. There is mean competition in the field and while there is always room at the top, there are very few at the top. I'd say about 95 per cent can't make it. Only 5 per cent have superior capabilities. But if the urge is great enough, he's going to do it."

When asked why he makes a certain photograph, Adams was less precise.

"I'm not an articulate person when it comes to explaining why I photograph a certain scene," Adams explained. "I can't tell you why. It is a subject of great importance to me.

"I look upon it as something that is an organized statement — the equivalent of what I felt at that particular moment. . it's the way I've seen it."

And what lies ahead for the famed photographer who has achieved more than most photographers ever dream about?

"I just hope I won't start going the other way, downhill," he grinned.

The bearded photographer said his health is good except for a little arthritis, which prevents him from getting to his beloved High Sierra where many of his early masterpieces were made.

Adams currently resides in Carmel.

Beyond his new, large format book "Ansel Adams," he said he hopes to present Portfolio 7, a collection of basically unknown prints by 1976.

While Adams is best known for his grand landscapes, he said he would like to be remembered as more than a nature photographer.

What perhaps is Adams' best claim to photographic excellence is his ability to conceive and execute clean and crisp images. There are no gimmicks, just fine photography. Not only does he have a highly sensitive and selective eye with tremendous visual awareness, but an ability to feel with his eyes, that is, to read the light. This coupled with a feeling for space and scale has enabled Adams to bring that special dimension to his very special art.

Although there are many assets in the Adams' retinue, the foremost figure belongs to his wife of 46 years, Virginia Adams.

Mrs. Adams, who accompanied the master lensman to his Fresno reception, said the family's aim in life has been to support its famous photographer.

"It's his world I'm interested in," she said. "His work is the most important part of my life. There is a tremendous reside of knowledge in this man, I'll do anything I can to help him."

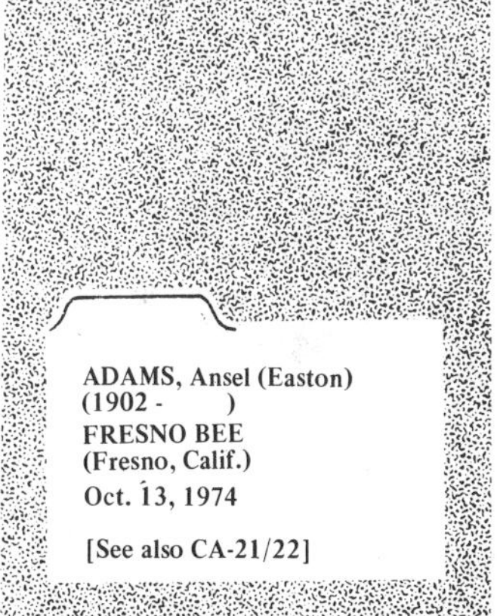

ADAMS, Ansel (Easton)
(1902 -)
FRESNO BEE
(Fresno, Calif.)
Oct. 13, 1974

[See also CA-21/22]

One of his two children, Fresno physician, Dr. Michael Adams, said he is very proud of his father's work.

"A lot of people ask me if I am a photographer," the younger Adams chuckled. "We each do our own thing. While I take a few family snapshots, I leave the serious photography to him."

Adams said he is especially pleased that his father is being recognized while he is alive.

"Most artists are never recognized until they are gone. He just loves this sort of thing. . .meeting people and talking about his work," he said.

Adams' work will be on exhibit at the Fresno Arts Center through Oct. 27.

In Publishing, This Is the Year of the Rabbit

By LESLIE CROSS,
Journal Book Editor

IN THE 1960s, it was hobbits. In the '70s, it's rabbits.

"Watership Down," the chronicle of a rabbit world, has been behaving like a very agile bunny indeed since its American publication last spring. Across the country, it has been bounding about the upper reaches of the best seller lists. On the campuses, its publisher reports, it is the only hard cover best seller. Even J. R. R. Tolkien's fantasies about Middle Earth and its jolly and diminutive hobbits didn't do that well, at least in hard covers, when they took the colleges by storm 10 or 15 years ago.

A movie is in the making. The paperback rights sold for more than $800,000, a record advance for a first novel before publication. The rabbits, it is certain, will be with us for a long, long time.

His Daughters Put Him Up to It

Not the least surprised witness to this publishing phenomenon is the author. A year ago, Richard Adams was a senior British civil servant — assistant secretary in the Department of the Environment, in charge of its clean air section. He made quiet trips from London to his cottage in the Berkshire Downs, where he studied plant and animal life, practiced bird calls and played "shove ha' penny" at the Crooked Billet pub. This year he has been shuttling across the Atlantic, signing incredible contracts, coping with the problems of international celebrity.

"Watership Down" had its origin in stories that Adams told his daughters, Juliet and Rosamond, to amuse them on long drives from London to Stratford-on-Avon, where they reveled in plays by his favorite author, Shakespeare. At the girls' insistence, he wrote the stories down.

But no one, it seemed, wanted to publish them. The publishers he approached told him that a 400 page novel about rabbits would never sell.

Adams was on the point of having "Watership Down" printed at his own expense when he came across a book published by Rex Collings, who had started his own firm after a career with Penguin Books. Adams liked it and looked up Collings' address in the London telephone directory. He sent him the manuscript. Collings agreed to take a chance on it. That was in 1970. Publishing tends to be a cumbersome business, and it was not until late in 1972 that the book came off

the press in England.

The first edition was a modest 2,000 copies. The reviews, however, were excellent; the Times of London hailed it "with trembling

ADAMS, Richard
(1920-)

MILWAUKEE
JOURNAL
(Milwaukee, Wisc.)

Sept. 1, 1974
[See also CA-49/52]

pleasure." "Watership Down," published as a juvenile, won the Guardian Award and the Carnegie Medal in England soon after its appearance. The American rights were up for grabs, and Macmillan of New York grabbed them. Macmillan intended to put the book on its juvenile list, but shrewdly changed its mind and published it as an adult title.

Though he was hardly prepared for the magnitude of his American sucess, Adams knew all along that he had a good thing going. Some reviewers have suggested that the book is too long and complicated for children. Adams scoffs at the notion. He prizes his many letters from children who have thrilled to the adventures of Hazel, Fiver and his other gallant rabbits in quest of a home safe from human land clearing crews. A good story, he thinks, is exactly that, without any age lines.

"As fast as you try to articulate rules for writing for children (or anybody else)," he wrote in a magazine article published a few weeks ago, "someone will triumphantly break them. What else did Lewis Carroll and Kenneth Grahame do? One can easily get so blinkered by the rules that one can no longer judge a book by the light of the heart."

No Whimsy for Welcomers

Adams is not a "literary type." Before he completed "Watership Down," he never wrote anything for publication. He has had a lifelong passion for English literature, though, and had a proper Oxford education. His daughters were born fairly late in his marriage, and he immersed them in the books and plays he and his wife loved. Juliet and Rosamond, who first heard the rabbit stories, are now 16 and 14, respectively. Their father is 54.

When Adams flew in for his New York publication, some American welcomers expected to see a gentle and whimsical soul bemused by the wonders of nature. On the contrary, he turned out to be feisty, with an almost pugnacious sense of propriety.

Back in England, he has been completing a second book, about a bear. He intends to call it "Shardik," and it will be about twice as long as "Watership Down." On weekends, Adams has been guiding tourists who come to inspect the haunts of his rabbits in Berkshire.

Then there are broadcasts and movie chores to attend to. The film version of "Watership" is being made, with animated figures, by Martin Rosen, an American producer in England. The American paperback edition of the book will be published by Avon.

At Thanksgiving time, Adams will be in America again to address the convention of the National Council of Teachers of English at New Orleans. The rabbits on the Down probably will not see him after that until snow flies.

'Rabbit' Writer Hops Into Limelight

By SYLVIA SACHS

Richard Adams is an Englishman — an English man of letters—and there's no mistaking that the minute you meet him.

He's different. We don't grow them like that around here.

From his reference to his "waistcoat," to his courtly treatment of the waiter at the Pittsburgh Hilton last night, to his request for proper English mustard, he is a delightful character out of all the English novels you have read and all the English movies you have enjoyed.

New Cult Figure?

Adams is in danger of becoming a cult figure as he starts his tour of the United States, having just arrived last Friday. But after talking to him for several hours, one has the feeling this won't happen.

Adams is his own man.

A recently retired civil servant from Her Majesty's Service, he has, at the age of 53, written a book which has all the chic reviewers running to their thesauri for adjectives of praise.

The book, "Watership Down," (Macmillan, $6.95) was written for his daughters from tales he spun for them on long drives from London to Stratford-on-Avon to see Shakespearean plays.

Written down at the insistence of his daughter, Juliet, the tales have evolved into a novel which has been taken up by the literati and is already being touted in advance review as a future classic.

Suffice it to say that one avant garde slick has already categorized it as "not for the lovers of Jonathan Seagull." It's in.

"My great passion is Shakespeare," said Adams last night. "It has been for 30 years. You know Alexander the Great was supposed to have gone to battle with a copy of Homer at his side. I took Shakespeare through 5½ years of war and read it under German fire.

"I have two daughters I love more than anything else in the world. I began reading them Shakespeare's plays when they were 5 or 6 at bedtime, and taking them to the plays for special grownup outings when they were quite young.

ADAMS, Richard

PITTSBURGH PRESS
(Pittsburgh, Penn.)

Mar. 20, 1974

"To pass the time on the 3½-hour ride from London to Stratford, I started telling them stories about a rabbit named Hazel, and one named Fiver. The stories came from my imagination and from my love of the countryside where I was born—Berkshire," Adams said.

Because he devoutly believes that today's children and young people are a "marvelous lot," more educated, more intelligent, more attuned to the world than any other generation, Adams wrote his book as he would have if he had pegged it for an adult audience.

His countryside is real and poetically described. His rabbit characters are distinct individuals, not cutesy parodies of human beings. They are true to the scientific knowledge of their breed.

Their story of a flight from a warren about to be destroyed, through unknown dangers, to a world where they can establish a viable society is as suspenseful and cliff-hanging as the same flight of humans would be.

Because of its animal characters, "Watership Down" has been compared to Orwell's "Animal Farm" or Graham's "Wind in the Willows.

Because of its plot of flight from man's encroachment, and its subplots of escape from a mindless "lotus land" and establishment of a good society, it has been touted as an ecological treatise or as "anti-facist."

"A lot of people have said this is a political fable or even a religious fable or a social comment," Adams said. "I promise you it is not a fable or an allegory or a parable of any kind. It is a story about rabbits, that is all.

'Leadership' Theme

"There is a certain theme, yes, a theme. Every book must have a theme," the author said. "This book is about leadership. Hazel, the rabbit, is a natural leader. He does not fight for it. He doesn't want it. He just kind of floats to the top.

"Hazel has a model. When I was in a parachute group in the war, we had a leader, a quiet chap who just walked about. His name was John Gifford. When there was [illegible]ble, John Gifford would always be there. We would all have done anything for that man."

Although he spent 25 years as a senior civil servant in the British government, Adams did not feel it ethical to discuss his work.

He was the chief of the Clean Air Division of England's Department of the Environment upon his retirement.

"I am a novelist now. I intend to spend the rest of my life writing," Adams said.

'More Vivid Than Daylight'

Virginia Hamilton and Arnold Adoff joke with their son Jaime

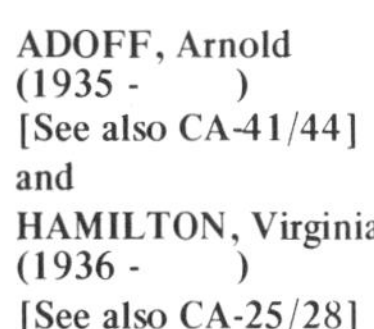

ADOFF, Arnold
(1935 -)
[See also CA-41/44]
and
HAMILTON, Virginia
(1936 -)
[See also CA-25/28]

CINCINNATI ENQUIRER
(Cincinnati, Ohio)

Jan. 5, 1975

By JUDITH WAGNER
Photographed
By TOM O'REILLY

Come with me if you love music and poetry and the enchantment that is childhood. Together we will visit a place, not so far away, where they are created, nurtured and brought to life.

We will shake hands with two productive writers with a vision of life to share. One is a widely acclaimed children's novelist; the other, a poet. We will ask them about their craft. We will listen and we will learn.

Yellow Springs, Ohio, in its outward appearance, is virtually indistinguishable from countless other college towns seen throughout the country.

We turn right, then left, passing old homes with neatly tended yards. At the very end of a dead end gravel road, we see a sleek redwood house which has high peaks, a deck and two patios. Large windows and sliding glass doors integrate interior and exterior. Despite its modern architecture, the house does not seem an intruder upon its antique surroundings.

With outstretched hands, Arnold Adoff comes out to greet us. He is a handsome man, tawny-complexioned and slightly stout. His voice booms in friendly rowdiness; his manner is gregarious.

Arnold Adoff is best known as an anthologist. He has edited more than a half dozen collections of poetry, most of which spotlight the works of young black poets or explore urban themes. Among his anthologies are "I Am The Darker Brother," "Black On Black," "City In All Directions," "Black Out Loud" and "It Is A Poem Singing InYour Eyes."

His first two original books for children have made a significant impact on children's literature. "MA nDA LA" is an innovative picture book for the very young and "Black Is Brown Is Tan" is perhaps the first children's book which deals squarely with the interracial family.

Mr. Adoff's newest work is "My Black Me." He describes it as "a beginning book of black poetry for the youngest child.

"We do not need any more white experts on black anything in this country," he states emphatically. "I am NOT an expert on black life or culture or even black poetry. I am a continuing student."

Mr. Adoff always insists on black artists to illustrate his works because he believes they can add a dimension which he, being white, could never create.

"I never write critical essays or articles on any aspect of black literature or life. I leave that to the many gifted, intelligent and qualified black writers and scholars," he explains. His eyes dart about the room as he talks. He shuffles restlessly in his easy chair. His hands are in perpetual motion, punctuating and accenting his remarks.

"I have been married to a black woman for more than a dozen years. I live within an extended and loving black family. I have two black children. But I can never, even for a minute, see the world through the eyes of a black or fully understand what it is to be black."

On this point his wife disagrees. Virginia Hamilton is among the most respected of contemporary writers of fiction for young people. "There are no boundaries on the imagination of a creative writer," she insists. "True, insightful portrayals of life can come solely from the imagination, rather than from the experience of the author. If a writer is good enough, sensitive enough, he can write about anything."

It was here in this rural Ohio community that Virginia Hamilton grew up. She was the fifth child born to Etta and Kenneth Hamilton. Her family was "dollar poor" in those days. "Franklin Roosevelt's New Deal hadn't touched our household nor much of the Miami Valley where the village lay."

Her mother's people had settled in the area before emancipation. The progenitor, a runaway slave, had come to the rich, fertile land, married and prospered. Through the generations, the family grew into the large Perry clan.

"I grew up within the warmth of loving aunts, uncles and cousins. Many of them and their children still live here, offering the same kind of extended family to my husband and my children."

THE ART of story weaving did not begin with Virginia. Her father, an outlander from Illinois, Iowa and points west, was a master storyteller, she says. "Having come from a Creole family that wandered the face of this country and Canada, he was always a traveling man, if only in his mind."

Her aunts and uncles, too, were apt to turn an afternoon into a time for fantasy and romance for the children of the Perry clan. "And my mother could capture a slice of fiction floating around the family and polish it into a saga."

Virginia Hamilton describes herself as "chronically overweight, foul-tempered, and given to alternate fits of depression and elation. I am a textbook neurotic who never sleeps. I love life, cherish freedom, and am prone to lazing around daydreaming and staring into space."

Despite her self-appraisal, she seems a warm, enthusiastic, cerebral person,

(Continued from preceding page)

always flirting with some amusement known only to herself. When her humor is made public, it is subtle, gentle and almost childlike in its ability to get to the meat of a subject. Her smile is elusive; but, once offered, it flashes happily, lighting up her eyes.

As she talks we perceive that she is playing a bit of a game with us — or perhaps with herself. "I'm fond of telling lies," she jokes. "I tell them about my age, my creations, my past and my husband."

Everything she says elicits a response from Mr. Adoff, who interjects himself into the conversation verbally or with expressions and gestures.

"As everyone knows," she explains with mock seriousness, "poets talk all the time. Arnold does. He is like a whirlwind, keeping things all stirred up and noisy.

"He's never boring, because he's always thinking up some outrageous new thing to do. He can juggle work on three or four books at once, build a grape arbor in the yard, give me extra help around the house when I have special pressures and spend hours of good time with the children. He is a whirlwind. . ."

He interrupts with an offhand remark and . . .

"You see," she continues, "I told you he never stops talking."

For as long as she can remember, Virginia Hamilton has been allowed to discover what she wanted and to learn what she could. "I was the baby in the family—bright, mind you, and odd and sensitive. My family realized early on that there was no changing me. I was born to live within my mind, to have thoughts and dreams more vivid to me than any daylight."

As she speaks, she often draws upon light and darkness for analogy. She claims to fear the night and its intrinsic darkness. Her father played his mandolin to conquer the night, she says. She conquers it "through the endless parade of figures that tramp across the reaches of my mind."

At the age of nine, young Virginia started her first work, entitled "The Notebook." In it she chronicled all the whispered, big-word mysteries of adult conversation. She wrote them down with care and exactness, planning to read them again when she was old enough to understand.

She lost "The Notebook," or merely forgot about it, in her enthusiasm for growing to 10. However, even now, as she creates characters like Geeder Perry, Junior Brown and Thomas Short, she remembers being nine and aching to solve the mysteries of grown-up talk.

As a teenager, Virginia discovered boys, yet pencil and paper remained her dearest friends. Her penchant for writing things down was recognized and encouraged throughout her high school and college days. She attended Antioch College, only a mile from her home, and then transferred to Ohio State University. After graduation she went to New York, only half-bent on becoming a writer of adult novels. To support herself, she worked part-time at bookkeeping, cost accounting and occasionally sang esoteric folk songs in a small night club. (She tells this softly, as if she is confiding in a friend of long standing. We believe her, even though she has warned us about her lies.)

It was through mutual friends that Miss Hamilton met Arnold Adoff, a bright, inquisitive teacher from the Bronx. He was teaching in Harlem, digging desperately for relevant materials to use in the classroom. He remembers:

ADOFF, Arnold
and
HAMILTON, Virginia

CINCINNATI ENQUIRER
(Cincinnati, Ohio)

Jan. 5, 1975

"When I first started to collect materials about and by black writers, historians and poets, it was not prompted by a conscious or political motivation. I simply needed materials which would speak to those children. I was teaching children who had grown up very much like myself: lower middle class from a minority. (Mr. Adoff's parents were Jewish immigrants.) We were not part of mainstream American society to which history and literature texts were directed."

Poetry has been a special love since his childhood. "I have always loved to collect it, to read it and to create it."

He makes grand gestures as he tells about his romance with the struggling young novelist. "It was Christmas day, 1958, when we first realized all the chemistry was there. The lights began to light up on Broadway. We were the black and white equivalent of Jeannette MacDonald and Nelson Eddy, Ginger Rogers and Fred Astaire, Doris Day and Rock Hudson . . ."

"Arnold!" she scolds.

He quickly slips in another: "Or Lois Lane and Clark Kent!"

She is put out; he chortles to himself.

"VIRGINIA was a fully liberated woman when I met her," he says. "She knew herself in a unique sort of way. From the very beginning, our marriage has been a 'share' contract. We both have demands on our time and talents, but we have been able to work it all out because we began on an equal basis. That's also why we have been able to revel in each other's successes, understand each other's disappointments and accept our professional differences of opinion."

Virginia Hamilton's first book met wide critical acclaim and achieved great popularity among the young readers for whom it was created. "Zeely" is set in a spot not unlike the Yellow Springs of the author's youth. Elizabeth (Geeder) Perry is swept away by her fantasies when she encounters statuesque Zeely Tayber, who is "deeply dark as a pole of Ceylon ebony," Surely, the handsome woman is a Watusi queen, the child concludes. Along the way to the story's satisfying and surprising conclusion, Geeder learns a lot about herself and the reader is right in the middle of it all.

The publication of "Zeely" was a happy accident. "The kind of thing that happens to you if you hang around New York long enough," Virginia says. "It all happened at a time when I was thinking of giving up writing, because I was having so much trouble breaking into the adult field. I thought my books were pretty good, but they surely weren't going anywhere. An old friend from Antioch College was working at Macmillan Publishing Company. She reminded me of a short story I had written in college and suggested that I make a book out of it. I worked over those 18 moth-eaten pages for quite a long time, but 'Zeely' was the result," she explains in her soft, casual way. She speaks slowly and intensely, but the words flow smoothly, without hesitation.

Since "Zeely," she has created other books for children. With a consistency in literary craftsmanship perhaps unequaled among her contemporaries, she weaves excitement, culture, a taste of history and the very essence of childhood together to make entertaining tales of mystery, fantasy and life itself.

Her fourth book, "The Planet Of Junior Brown," was selected as a Newbery Award honor book in 1972. It is a modern-day fable of courage and strength, centering around the capers of an overweight musical prodigy with a neurotic, overprotective mother.

"I was striving for a certain tone. The subject matter was unusual and I did not want to alienate the reader, so I stuck to a conventional structure. Once I got going on it, the story just seemed to roll out."

Of all her efforts, she is most satisfied with "Planet" from a literary point of view. "However, 'The House Of Dies Drear' is my favorite because it is so full of all the things I love: excitement, mystery, black history, the strong black family and the importance of the church."

IN "THE HOUSE OF DIES DREAR," young Thomas is obsessed with the idea of unlocking the secrets of the old house in which abolitionist Drear and two fugitive slaves had died. Thomas scours

(Continued from preceding page)

the labyrinth of tunnels in the old home which had once been a station on the underground railroad. As he unravels secrets from the past, he discovers his connections to that past.

Again, a union of the real from the author's past and the make-believe from her imagination becomes apparent. Yellow Springs is a smaller community than the one in which Thomas lives, but it, too, was important in the underground railroad system to Canada during the Civil War era.

"When I was a child, I knew that the large old houses here had once concealed running slaves — some of them my own ancestors. I needed to know how men, women and children could travel hundreds of miles on foot through enemy lands. I found out that they were brave and clever almost beyond belief. Perhaps with the book, I have touched them the way they touched me so long ago."

All the sights, sounds and imaginings of childhood wake up like a budding morning glory in "The Time-Ago Tales Of Jahdu." Mama Luke, who may be a composite of Virginia Hamilton's story-conjuring kin, picks stories from the air to entertain her young friend, Lee Edward. Her tales of Jahdu are filled with mystery, magic and animals, good and scary.

Only twice has she turned from fiction. In her biography of W.E.B. DuBois, she portrays the man she believes was most responsible for the changes in attitudes of black people toward themselves and their conditions in American society.

"Writing a book about the life and times of Dr. DuBois must have been in the back of my mind for half my life. My father ranted and raged against F.D.R. and his New Deal, against unions, against the war and ration stamps. But never did he allow a word to be spoken against the mysterious, marvelous Dr. DuBois and his Crisis magazine. He was a black man and a great man, who belongs to me and all those like me."

Her newest biography is "Paul Robeson: The Life And Times Of A Free Black Man."

Virginia Hamilton says she never remembers the initial idea from which her fiction is born. Usually, the title comes first. "When you are a professional writer, you just sit down at the typewriter and the creativity starts to flow. I decide what the characters will do and say as I go along. I never make any kind of an outline — it drains the spontaneity from the story."

Her characters, she contends, are not based on real people, but "I do take the atmosphere of known people, their emotions, and give them to my characters."

On the same subject, she states, "Though I reveal myself—my real self—only reluctantly, my readers must see that part of myself and my past which osmoses into my books."

Only once have the creative juices failed to flow on schedule. For more than a year, she worked every day on "M.C. Higgins, The Great." Deadlines passed, but the story eluded completion. "Something just wasn't right. I went over it and over it. Finally, it all went together and I think it's the best thing I have ever done. 'M.C. Higgins' was released by Macmillan in the fall."

The Adoffs spend mornings at their typewriters while Jaime, seven, and his sister, Leigh, 10, are in school. Afternoons are reserved for family activities. Virginia often returns to her typewriter during the midnight hours while the others sleep.

She works in a small office which

ADOFF, Arnold
and
HAMILTON, Virginia
CINCINNATI ENQUIRER
(Cincinnati, Ohio)
Jan. 5, 1975

overlooks the garden. Arnold's office is a helter-skelter section of an upstairs loft, which also houses Jaime's electric train. Scribbled notes are tacked here and there.

"Poetry is a vehicle for self-expression. However, the professional poet must go beyond self-expression to create a work of art," Mr. Adoff says, adding parenthetically, "Unfortunately, poetry is the least commercial of the art forms."

For "It Is A Poem Singing In Your Eyes," he solicited works from aspiring poets by sending flyers to schools, libraries and writing workshops across the country. In response, he received more than 50,000 poems. Some were from little children; others,from older writers with a glimpse of life to share.

"Each of the anthologies takes at least a year of hard work and research to put together. Then, I have to find a publisher who believes in what I have done, an artist who can add the black essence and a public who sees the need for reading black literature."

In their spare time, the Adoffs enjoy puttering in their gardens, potting plants to bring inside and "raising a little hell in town." Virginia has made her voice heard by serving on the Human Relations Committee and the Committee on Equal Education.

They do not feel social pressures because of their interracial marriage, nor do their biracial children have special difficulties. "We are not that exceptional in this community. Yellow Springs draws writers, artists, ecologists, socialists and other rabble-rousers like ants to a picnic," Virginia says with a smile.

Both she and her husband describe themselves as "homebodies at heart," yet they are obliged to be away more and more each year. "I don't know why writers are expected to be good public speakers," she complains. "I don't relish the idea of giving a speech, but once I get started I find it isn't so bad after all."

Arnold Adoff is more at home at the speaker's podium. "I think of myself as a pusher, a disseminator, of black materials. I seek out opportunities to tell college students, librarians, teachers and professors about my anthologies and the works of black poets, writers, educators and historians. I count on them to take this information to the place where it counts: to the children in schools and libraries throughout the country."

Arnold's current project had its genesis in the terror he and his family experienced as they huddled together for protection from the killer tornado which ripped nearby Xenia to shreds on April 3, 1974. "The wind was whipping around us, the rain roared down and the warning signals blasted in the distance," he remembers. "We were all children — Leigh, Jaimie, Virginia and I."

WHEN THE CRISIS passed, Mr. Adoff went straightaway to the typewriter to record his reactions to this freak-child of nature. "My poems tell the story from a child's point of view because I was a child then. I don't know if the book will sell. It's a rough piece of reality."

What advice do the Adoffs have for young writers?

Virginia Hamilton reflects on that for a long moment, but her husband jumps at the question: "Tell them to go sell used cars. There are enough of us out here struggling to get our work published as it is."

His mood changes. "No, tell them to listen to those who believe in their work and discount the opinions of those who do not see its merit. Tell them to keep at it."

Arnold Adoff plans to attempt a novel someday. "He has an innate capacity — a feel — for plot, characters and format," his wife says of him. "He does not think he is ready yet, so I don't question that, but when he is ready, I'm sure he will tackle it like a tornado."

"The white torna . . ." he fades out, realizing that his spouse has heard just about enough of his racial humor.

Of her own plans, she says, "I have lots more children's books to write yet. They're here in my head, and I'll have to work them out. Someday, I'd like to write some music, too. But most of all, I want to be a woman living to her fullest potential as a wife, a mother, a writer and a human being."

Again we believe her, even though she has told us about the lies. She beams a swift smile in our direction. She knows we understand.

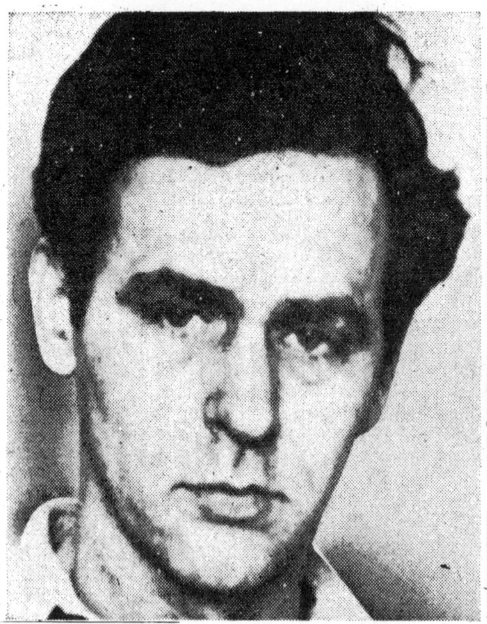

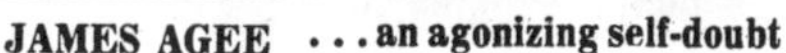

JAMES AGEE . . . an agonizing self-doubt

A Friendship That Molded Agee's Genius

By JUDITH KINNARD
Knight Newspapers Writer

On the morning of May 19, 1955, the friends of James Rufus Agee, a then little-known writer, assembled in the tiny chapel of St. Luke's parish in Greenwich Village.

His oldest friend and fellow expatriate from Tennessee, the Rev. James Harold Flye, read the burial service from the Episcopal Book of Common Prayer, then stepped to the head of the coffin.

"It is not the custom of this church to eulogize its departed," the aging priest said. "I want to say only that anyone who ever knew Rufus Agee will never forget him."

NINETEEN years later, those who have come to know the young author have spread far beyond the limited circle who knew him at 45, when he died of a heart attack.

An Agee legend, fed by a lack of recognition during his lifetime, has been passed along by a still-growing cult of admirers who are drawn not just by the power of his writing but also by the dark, brooding and ultimately destructive life he led.

Ever since the 1962 publication of "Letters of James Agee to Father Flye," hundreds of Agee's most fervent admirers have sought to learn more about him from the aging cleric who was his best known friend. The chronicle of their friendship itself is an incisive portrait of the artist in the American scene.

AGEE, James Rufus
(1909 - 1955)

AKRON BEACON JOURNAL
(Akron, Ohio)

June 30, 1974

NOW 89 and in failing health, Flye can be found these days in Greenwich Village, where he lives in church-owned property and still assists at St. Luke's services.

An arthritic knee makes such daily chores as grocery shopping or climbing the four flights to his apartment major undertakings.

With tenacity he has clung to the Village, where he has long been a familiar sight in his black suit and jaunty Fernandel hat.

It's the same kind of tenacity he showed as a young man from Florida who taught in a one-room school house for two years at $50 a month in order to earn enough money to attend Yale.

"If I left here," he contends, in a high, rather elegant voice, "I wouldn't be making any new contacts. I'd dry up."

DESPITE the physical infirmities, he can, with impressive precision, quote dates, or Agee, or Einstein as well as best-loved poems. And he still retains a deep-seated reverence for nature which he weaves into his conversation.

The fading afternoon sun illuminates the unwaxed floor piled high with papers, books and empty cartons of Saltine crackers.

Sinking into his wooden chair, Flye pauses thoughtfully. "In both of us there was the consciousness of much that we thorougly shared," he says of Agee's friendship. "One is that sense of wonder and mystery about the physical universe or about anything, and the repugnance to smug cocksureness."

THEIR LONG friendship began in the Summer of 1918 when Flye was a 33-year-old teacher at St. Andrew's School in Sewanee, not far from Agee's native Knoxville.

The small Episcopal school where he lived with his wife Grace in a cottage set in a thicket of trees and rambling vines was to be home for the next quarter of a century.

Rufus Agee, as he was then called, was a young boy of 9 whose father's death two years earlier had left the scars which were later to be probed in "A Death in the Family," his Pulitzer-prize winning novel.

"He was a charming, outgoing, intelligent and responsive child," explains Flye, who has often been called a surrogate father for Agee.

"SO WE had a lovely companionship and friendship that developed immediately. We would go walking down to look at the caves or the fossils in the coal seams."

Delving into the piles of papers, Flye burrows long enough to find a history paper, dated 1923 and written in a large scrawl.

At the end is a note which captures the dual nature of the relationship: "Goodbye forever, till next Fall," read the farewell. ("I'll see you at dinner.")

The next 36 years took Agee far from St. Andrew's through Phillips Exeter, Harvard, New York's literary world, Hollywood's film set, three wives and periods of deep depression and precarious health.

FLYE REMAINED one of the few constants. It was to him that Agee poured out his love of writing, his agonizing self-doubt, his outrage at all that was shoddy or false — especially in himself, his sense of failure.

"I take birthdays hard," he wrote on his 41st in late 1950. "Mainly a kind of melancholy about my life, a sort of personal Day of Atonement. And through the melancholy, a very deep sense of loneliness."

The feeling that he had done too little with his time became a constant theme. "Unless I learn some new holds or disciplines," he had written in 1940," I shall sooner or later break my heart or mind or both, without ever having done one thing I most wanted to or should have."

IN 1951, Agee had the first of a series of heart attacks. In a letter to Flye, he diagnosed the causes as: "Too much alcohol and tobacco, too little sleep, too much emotional, or nervous, or other strain and anxiety, or even just too much excitement."

Critics have mourned the excesses which resulted in his early death. They mourn the years spent as a journalist rather than a novelist.

Out of the years spent at Time and the Nation and Fortune, came a probing documentary book on the lives of Alabama sharecroppers, "Let Us Now Praise Famous Men," which is considered a major legacy and a journalistic classic.

But it was not until he was 40 that Agee wrote his first novel, "The Morning Watch," modeled on the years at St. Andrew's.

AND IT WAS not until after his death that "A Death in the Family" was published and began to create a broad interest in the writer. Tad Mosel's play, "All the Way Home," was based on the novel.

Several collections of Agee's prose, poetry, and film reviews have become available in later years.

"The short piece which begins 'Now is awareness,' " explains Flye, allowing some of the frustration to creep into his elegant speech, "would have served as the beginning of a very long, detailed autobiography of which 'A Death in the Family' would be four days."

In September of 1954, Flye had just completed a Summer stint at St. Luke's with long evenings spent in conversation or lusty hymn singing with Agee.

JIM AGEE took his oldest friend to the train station in New York for his journey to Witchita where Flye would serve as assistant priest for the next two years.

"It was in May, in the early, early evening about suppertime. I got a phone call from New York," says Flye, laying down his glasses.

"And it was David McDowell, an old friend of Jim's, and he said, 'Jim died this afternoon.' I got a night plane and had Jim's funeral from St. Luke's chapel.

"Considering what Jim thought of much of the clergy, I felt I owed him that," he finished, his eyes dimmed by the tears.

Has The Tarantula Escaped?

By Howard Schneider

ALBEE, Edward (Franklin III)
(1928-)

PITTSBURGH PRESS
(Pittsburgh, Penn.)

Feb. 3, 1974

[See also CA-7/8]

THE SAME YEAR he wrote "Who's Afraid of Virginia Woolf?," 1962, Edward Albee bought a small beach house on Montauk Point, not three doors down, on the ocean side, from Gurney's Inn.

In the years since, he has returned there often, to walk the beach alone, to swim, to play tennis, to read, to paint what he calls his "constructionist" paintings, and, most recently, to sit by an electric typewriter in an upstairs study and write his first new play in more than two years, "Seascape."

When he first arrived at Montauk Point at 34, Albee already was being hailed as a major new American playwright, as America's next Eugene O'Neill. His first full-length play, "Virginia Woolf"—the trenchant drama of an embittered middle-aged couple engaged in a war of verbal flagellation—propelled Albee from avant-garde notoriety to national prominence. Four years later, he won the Pulitzer Prize for "A Delicate Balance."

But that was seven years ago. Albee has written five plays since. None has evoked wide critical acclaim in New York. In 1971, after his last play, "All Over," about the family and friends of a great man who gather at his deathbed, a drama critic wrote, "In his latest play, we instantly recognize him (Albee) for what he now is—the club bore." Now, at the start of a new season that will see the premiere of "Seascape" (and the film version of "A Delicate Balance"), another critic has said, "Albee will try to prove it's not all over after 'All Over'."

Critics Are Leery

Very early in Albee's career, one observer said after watching one of his plays, "It's like opening a box of cracker jack and finding a tarantula." Has he mellowed with age, despite himself, as some of the critics have suggested? Has he let the tarantula escape?

"People talk softer in some of the more recent plays," he says quietly, "but they say angrier things. There was certainly as much rage in 'All Over' as in 'Virginia Woolf.' The fires haven't gone out at any rate." He looks up at the sky. "There's a very loud and angry play coming which will lead some idiots to say, 'Mr. Albee is back in fine fettle again.' It's called 'Substitute Speaker' and is either two or three plays away. The play is about how much pain we are allowed to exhibit before other people destroy us. That will cheer them up." Albee laughed.

He does not like to talk about his new play, "Seascape." "I despise the fact that critics spend most of their time telling their readers what a play is about. The whole notion of what a play is about—what does that mean? The play is about style, about a series of philosophical ideas and about a series of events. 'Seascape' is simply about a middle-aged couple at a beach. Suddenly, two giant sea lizards appear and begin a conversation. They take the couple back with them to the bottom of the ocean floor and later bring them up again. But the play's about a lot of things. It discusses evolution. It examines the relative social posture between lizards and people. And I'm not joking. And it examines the probability of a collective unconscious."

Albee cannot pinpoint where or when he first thought of the idea for "Seascape." "No, that's it. When I discover I'm with play, it's already happened. I'm toying now with the idea of doing a play about Attila the Hun or Genghis Khan. I don't know whether I will or not, but something has set me thinking. And ideas about such a play are already forming. But I don't know where they come from."

Adopted Into Wealth

Albee was born March 28, 1928, and two weeks later, he was abandoned by his real parents. He says he has never tried to uncover their identity. He was adopted by Reed and Frances Albee, heirs to the Keith-Albee vaudeville chain. He grew up in the Albee Tudor mansion in Larchmont, N.Y., surrounded by nurses, servants and tutors. By the age of 5, he was being sent in the family Rolls-Royce to Broadway matinees.

But he was also a self-confessed "problem child," rebellious and strong-willed. He dropped out of, or was expelled from, one school after another. "I did not write 'A Catcher in the Rye'," Albee once recalled, "I lived it." Finally, at 19, be broke with his parents entirely, took his books and his records and moved to Greenwich Village, where he would later first see the question scrawled in an alleyway: "Who's Afraid of Virginia Woolf?"

"We all run away from home," Albee says, staring into his swimming pool, "only I did it literally." For nearly 10 years, he drifted from one odd job to another—record salesman at Bloomingdale's, office boy, messenger for Western Union. He tried to write novels and poetry in the evening but failed. It was at the peak of despair one night, approaching his 30th birthday, that he sat down in the kitchen of his apartment and wrote a play that has subsequently been described this way: "About a pathetically lonely young man, orphaned at an early age by the premature death of his parents, and later shunned by society because of what psychiatrists referred to as a case of borderline sanity, a totally alienated failure bent on making contact with someone in the establishment—even if it meant dying in the proc-

(Continued from preceding page)
ess." Albee called the one-act play "The Zoo Story."

Despite the fact that he believes that each of his 14 plays—from "The Zoo Story" through "Seascape"—is unique, Albee does see a common thread running through all of them, a thread that may be the key to understanding his work. Over lunch two years ago, as he prepared for the season at Guild Hall, Albee said, "Just as all of Arthur Miller's plays are sociological, and O'Neill's psychological, all my plays were political.

"Subjects Of Plays"

"I find a political animal is not concerned merely with specific elections. The general politics of a government is concerned with its moral equilibrium, its philosophical principles . . . people who are passive and who are careless contribute to the decline of the system, especially in a democracy. It isn't the polling place where the decisions about a democracy, or any society, are made; it's the amount of honesty, dishonesty, the rationalization and escapism in a society as a whole. People still refuse to think, to act honorably with each other. They are still mean and vicious and these are the subjects of my plays."

It is a theme at which he hammers incessantly when he talks on college campuses. The "disengagement" of the population. The passivity of Americans drawn to a television set six hours a day. The religious, political and social structures that men have created to "illusion" themselves from the world and each other.

While none of Albee's major plays are built around "topical" political events, all are political. So while "Virginia Woolf" is about a married couple who fear love without illusion, it is also about the symbolic failure of their namesakes George and Martha (Washington). "The (fabricated) child," Albee explains, "represents the failure of the founding fathers to pass on the principles of the American Revolution." In "A Delicate Balance," when the character Dena is asked why she and her husband have suddenly and unexplainably abandoned their suburban home, she screams: "We were frightened." It is as good an epitaph as has yet been written for the 1960s.

"Specifics never interest me," Albee says, leaning back in his chair. "I'm more interested in the overtones or the underpinnings . . . the implications are more interesting than the events themselves. There's nothing interesting about Richard Nixon, for example. But there is something a great deal interesting about the state of mind of a population that has brought itself through shortsightedness and sloth to the particular point which tolerates and encourages things a Richard Nixon is capable of surrounding himself with. That's interesting.

"I'm more interested in examining—getting into people's heads and trying to change them so they don't cotton to that sort of thing. I would never write prop (propaganda) plays or tracts. There's a kind of collapsible quality with the stridency. Look at the works we cared so much about in the '30s, the political plays, the (Clifford) Odets and the other people. They're not good plays. They're naive. They're tracts. They yell. And they vanish. Because they're about specifics, about strikes rather than about the mentality that kills strikers."

Albee believes his plays will endure, and their greatest contribution will be to give playgoers of the future an accurate insight into the American mentality—far better than the newspaper headlines of the day. All of which leads at this point in Albee's career to inescapable irony.

Albee leans back, shuts his eyes for a moment and begins slowly. It is late afternoon and a cool breeze has come up off the ocean, and gulls can be heard in the distance.

"I don't know. I've found as a general rule that my plays have been received more intelligently outside of the United States." He half-laughs. "Take 'All Over.' It's been given a lovely production by the Royal Shakespeare Company in London; it's in its second year in Vienna, to packed houses. It's been successful everywhere but in New York City (where it ran for only 42 performances) . . . . I guess I do think of myself now as a European writer. I really do," and a note of wonder creeps into his voice, as if he were still having trouble believing it. "I mean, I obviously am an American writer, but I am a European writer at the same time."

Speaks As Critic

Albee feels that American audiences "want to be taken out of themselves rather than put in themselves," that there has been a retrenchment in the American theater since the late '30s, a fear of experimentation. He calls Joseph Papp, the director of the New York Shakespeare Festival and the recipient of large amounts of money for new, untried productions, "the misguided savior of the theater," and says he has not seen a good play since Samuel Beckett's "Not I" in 1972.

In the summer of 1972, Albee and his producer, Richard Barr, tried to bring their own brand of experimental theater to the Hamptons, at Guild Hall. The result was a financial and critical disaster. "We'd hoped we could ram that kind of thing through because we thought there was an audience out here," Albee says softly. "But when it came down to the crunch, the know-nothings, the reactionaries, the frightened, the entrenched, the established, ran us into the ground. The elaborate and large board of directors, the wives of the wealthy who considered Guild Hall their plaything. It is a boat which is not to be rocked. When they couldn't get us to change our program, there was a large telephone and whispering campaign against what was going on; that it was meant to be obscene and probably somehow terribly un-American and not the sort of thing we should have in our East Hampton community.

"If they want to have the kind of season they had this year, let them. Joan Fontaine reading the love letters of Elizabeth Barrett Browning. I just shrugged."

"Better As Craft"

Albee has much the same to say to the New York critics who now question his talent, and call him "finished." "My major concern is not to inspire the critics," he says evenly, without rancor. "The plays I've written since 'A Delicate Balance' are probably better as craft. Certainly they're a good deal more skillful and I suspect more mature and ultimately more interesting."

But under the recent critical barrage, has he never once questioned his own abilities, wavered, doubted? "I don't believe in thinking in those terms," he says, suddenly shouting over the drone of an electric power mower. "It's extremely dangerous."

Then Albee stands and walks over to the edge of the red brick pool deck which overlooks the Atlantic Ocean. After a few minutes, he talks about a dream he had in 1969 and had once written about. It had taken place on a beach by the ocean. Dusk rapidly turning into night. "I am with two or three friends, none of whom is anyone I can place on waking," he says. "We are lying about and perhaps we have a driftwood fire smoldering. It is incredibly quiet—rather as if all the sound had been turned off. And suddenly, it begins: An area of the eastern horizon is lighted by the fired explosion, hundreds of miles away, and no sound at all. Then another, perhaps to the west, no sound. Within seconds they are everywhere, always at a great distance.

"To the three or four of us on the beach, before our smoldering fire, there is no question as to what is happening: We are watching the end of the world. There is no time for terror; it is overleaped, and the suddenness is unimaginable as the silent bombs go off. It will be seconds before our own lives cease—or maybe we are already dead; perhaps that is why there is no sound."

Albee turns his back to the ocean, and reflects on the dream: "I think the ability to visualize the end of the world is probably a constructive step," he says. "To be able to be sort of sad about it. But there, you've got it out in the open and obviously are able to live with it . . . you take a chance every time you write, you risk your psyche, your mind and your career. But you've got to take the chance to find out what's in your head . . . I used to have a dream every year like the one I had on the beach. But ever since I wrote about it, I haven't had another. Writing does get things out of the system.

"And creativity," Edward Albee says, "is itself an act of optimism."

ALBEE, Edward (Franklin III)

PITTSBURGH PRESS
(Pittsburgh, Penn.)

Feb. 3, 1974

'. . .In the Front Door'

Staff Photo by Howard Walker

A. R. Ammons waits at a door to the Wake Forest library.

By Russell Brantley
WFU News Bureau

"I waited, worked. Now, by heavens, I've come in the front door. That's what it's all about, maybe."

A. R. Ammons' parents, who had more pride than money, probably would have approved of their son's stiff-necked attitude toward recognition. "I'm very proud. Caught it from them."

Ammons is 48 and it is only in recent years that he has been recognized as a major voice in American poetry. Some critics say he is the most important poet in the country today. He won the National Book Award in 1973 for "Collected Poems: 1951-1971" and his new work "Sphere: The Form of a Motion" is attracting about as much attention as America accords a new book of poetry. The first poem he remembers writing was when he was a 10th grader in Eastern North Carolina. "It was about Pocahontas. I don't remember it well."

Ammons is taking a year off from an endowed professorship at Cornell University and is working with young poets at Wake Forest University, an institution he graduated from in 1949 when it was a college in the town of Wake Forest and he was a general science major wondering what to do with his life.

One of his own estimates is that "it seems to me I've spent much of my life trying to renounce the role of poet." On the surface at least. He went to Wake Forest with the idea of becoming a doctor. His first job after graduating was principal of the public school at Hatteras. There was an interlude in California when he did graduate work and began to work more seriously at his poetry. Then, almost as if to disclaim such pretensions, he went to work for a New Jersey company that manufactured biological and medical glassware. He was in charge of sales at the beginning and wound up executive vice president. Hardly the sort of background one expects for a man who writes:

"I do the ones I love no good: I hold their pain in my hands and toss it in moonlight."

Ammons was born on a 50-acre, half-wooded farm four miles from Whiteville. He first went to school at the New Hope Elementary School which was two miles from home and close by the New Hope Baptist Church. "By 10 or 11 I was ploughing the fields. We had tobacco, a strawberry patch, potatoes, things like that." He also had the background for some of his early poems, including one titled "Silver" that was about a black mule "but I named her that because of 'Hi Yo, Silver.' "

When he was 18 he went in the Navy. On V-J Day he was on a destroyer escort in Leyte Gulf in the Phillippines. "Everybody broke out the searchlights. The night air was needled and riddled with searchlights." Ammons said a paperback anthology of poetry he read while in the Pacific prompted him to begin writing. When he came back the GI Bill helped send him to Wake Forest.

"I was a sort of cipher. I worked in a grocery store 16 hours a week. No one in my family had been to college before."

He met a teacher at Wake Forest, Phyllis Plumbo. He took her Spanish course one semester. They were married in November, 1949, after he graduated.

"While I was at Wake Forest I stayed on the periphery of things, not close enough to get trapped by it." Not getting trapped, meaning not being put in the positon of having to compromise his poetry, is a thing with Ammons.

"I never dreamed of being a Poet poet. I think I always wanted to be an amateur poet. When you have something else to do to earn money, you can do just what the hell you want to with your poems. A poem should be autonomous, not an instrument to success."

In 1953— nine years after he started writing poetry—Ammons had two poems accepted by the Hudson Review. In 1955 he took $480 of his own money and went to a vanity publisher who printed 100 copies. The book is titled "Ommateum," which is the Latin name for the compound eye of an insect. In five years 16 copies were sold. Ammons' father-in-law bought 50 copies and sent them to customers in South America and Ammons finally bought 30 copies from the publisher for $9. He kept two and gave the rest to friends. The book is a collector's item now and probably would bring $500 or more for a single copy.

The Ohio State University Press published "Expressions of Sea Level" in 1964. "It got a strong response. It was time. I had been sitting down in South Jersey all those years." That fall he went to Cornell as an instructor. Six years later he was an endowed professor but he is a peripheral member of the Establishment. He won't give public readings of his poetry. The idea unnerves him, although he could command fancy sums making public appearances. He doesn't wear ties and his clothing is nondescript except for a new Dobbs hat. He has been known to call Wordsworth "Mortimer Snerd" but he is exceptionally kind to the young poets who clamor for his time at Wake Forest.

His new book is a major work, "something I had been unconsciously working on for years. It's terribly ambitious and pretentious. You know how it is when there is a great deal of material at a committee meeting and somebody asks 'can you put that in the form of a motion?' That's what the second part of the title is about. You try to justify your pretensions." Did he think he did well with the new book?

"Yep, I think I did."

AMMONS, A(rchie) R.
(1926 -)

WINSTON-SALEM JOURNAL & SENTINEL (Winston-Salem, N.C.)

Dec. 1, 1974

[See also CA-9/10]

By Judy Flander
Star-News Staff Writer

Cleveland Amory began his career as president of the Harvard Crimson.

"After that, everything else has been down hill," he said yesterday, watching his interviewer for some sign of shock. Rewarded with an incredulous "Really?", Amory beamed in gratitude. Then he launched into a shaggy dog story about the one hill in his otherwise downward trip through life.

Like most shaggy dog stories this one does not benefit in the retelling; it was all about Amory's 25th Harvard class reunion and the verbal confrontation between a drunken classmate and the president of Harvard. The story was heavy on sarcasm and delivered with all the confidence of a veteran character actor.

Amory cheerfully admits that during a book interview he is purposely "on."

CLEVELAND AMORY, 56, has made a living out of good-humored sarcasm, irreverence, outrageous remarks and shooting holes through sacred cows. He is the world-famous improper Bostonian; he was drummed out of the social register for thumbing his nose at his equals (in three books, "The Proper Bostonians," "The Last Resorts" and "Who Killed Society?") and he got the Duchess of Windsor so mad she changed her mind about having him write her "autobiography."

For one who wants to be a character, Amory couldn't have chosen a better facade. He is tall, at least 6 feet 4, massive but not fat, and his wonderful wiry brown hair rises straight up from his head, no matter how ofter he smoothes it down. His smile is disarming.

He has joyously called his column in "Saturday Review/World," "Curmudgeon At Large," and the title is apt. But as curmudgeons go, Amory has at his center a soft heart. After carefully weaving one of his preposterous tales, he smiles broadly and fondly on one and all. He was really kidding and he doesn't want anybody to think he wasn't.

What Amory wasn't kidding about yesterday was his new book, "Mankind?" subtitles "Our Incredible War on Wildlife," in which he takes pot shots at all the great white hunters beginning with Buffalo Bill and continuing through president Theodore Roosevelt ("he killed anything he could get his hands on.") to the present sealkillers and whalekillers and grizzlykillers.

You have to be careful of everybody, he warned, "even those sweet little bird watchers at the Audubon Society." "John James Audubon may have painted birds but for every one he painted, he killed 100. His trip across the country was a bloody carnage."

AMORY ROLLED the bloody statistic off his tongue with relish. Ever since he saw a bullfight in Nogales, N.M. 17 years ago, he's been on the side of the animals. Even though he is a "Boston Episcopalian and everybody knows God is a Boston Episcopalian," he enthusiastically accepted the title of honorary vice president of the National Catholic Society for Animal Welfare. In 1967, he founded his own group, "The Fund For Animals."

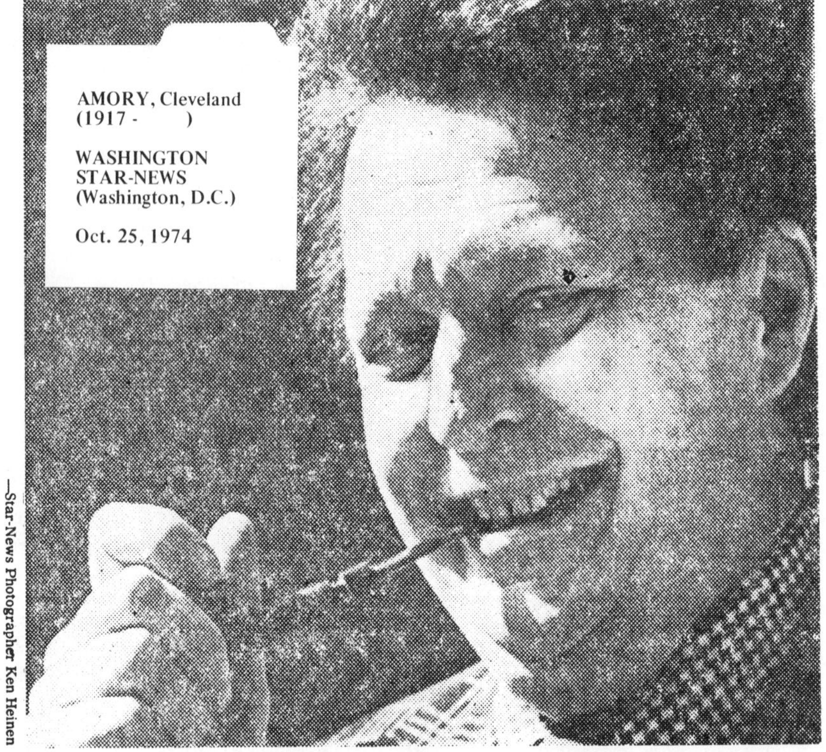

—Star-News Photographer Ken Heinen

Cleveland Amory

Besides his magazine column, he is chief critic for "TV Guide" and writes a syndicated newspaper column, "Animail." He and his wife, Martha Hodge Amory, have two Siberian huskies, huge black and white dogs with blue eyes, which they call Ivan the Great and Peter the Terrible. He wants to be sure you get the name switch: "They're purposely wrong, like mankind."

These days, Amory is beginning to feel dated. He told a young woman who works in his publisher's office that he hopes, despite all the extra meals during his book tour, "to stay as slim as Gregory Peck." "Who is Gregory Peck?" she asked.

The title of his column mystified one of the young women who works in the magazine office. "Such is the terror of these times, she asked what is a curmudgeon." Amory told her severely to look it up in the dictionary: "A word looked up is a word remembered."

Amory likes to start the story of his life with his "first rebellion." He was attending the posh Milton Academy and was slated for Harvard like his ancestors. His rebellion consisted of writing for catalogues to other colleges. "Father saw the one I got from Stanford, and he said, 'Bah!' so I went to Harvard."

HIS TILT with the Duchess of Windsor is another enormously satisfactory episode in his life, at least in the retelling.

Summoned to the royal apartment in the Waldorf Towers, Amory was told by the Duke that he was looking for someone with humor to help his wife write her autobiography, "because the Duchess is so witty."

The following week, Amory came back in typical style with what he thought was the perfect title for the book; "Untitled." The Duke and Duchess of Windsor were not amused. "There was stony silence," and the deal was called off.

The trouble with the humorless Dutchess was, Amory said, "She could never make up her mind whether she was more royal than royalty or was a democrat who got a King."

That wasn't the end of the Duchess. "Not to name drop," related Amory, "but I went all the way to Jamaica to ask Noel Coward how the Duchess of Windsor got her reputation as a wit." "In those circles, old boy," Coward told him, "it wasn't difficult."

JACK ANDERSON

'I would not publish a story that might endanger lives'

Jack Anderson, 51, muckraker and former Mormon missionary, writes the syndicated *Washington-Merry-go-Round* column, published in the *Herald* and other newspapers. Vacationing recently in Florida with his wife Olivia, Anderson was interviewed at the Diplomat Hotel in Hollywood by Rob Elder, *Herald* staff writer. Totally relaxed throughout the conversation, Anderson leaned back in a big leather chair, kicked off his shoes and chewed a toothpick as he talked.

You're described as a devoted family man, the father of nine children. You're a member of the Mormon Church, which in the minds of many people is associated with the simple life and with strong morality. Yet your friends would call you a muckraker, and your enemies say you're a scandalmonger, a man who makes his living by digging up dirt on other men. Isn't there a sort of Dr. Jekyll and Mr. Hyde quality about these two images? Doesn't your work conflict with your religion?

I think rather than producing conflict that my religion and my background have played a large part in what I do. In the Mormon philosophy the eternal struggle is not only between good and evil but between freedom and force.

I was brought up as a youngster to believe that the Constitution of the United States was almost a divine document, in the sense that it was a document of freedom. I was brought up to believe that public office, therefore, was a public trust and that those who abused it were people who should be exposed and removed from office. So I would think that this moralistic background has helped rather than conflicted with what I do.

A lot of people suspect that every headwaiter in Washington is on your payroll and probably half the bureaucrats are, too. Do you pay for information?

No. I go about it quite differently than I guess anyone else does. The FBI buys its information and I learned very early in Washington that their information was often tainted and unreliable because they buy it from an assorted collection of informants who quite often give them information just for the sake of the money. And when they don't have legitimate information they sometimes make it up. I think that this kind of information is far too unreliable for a newspaperman to count upon. And I just made it a rule not to pay for information.

I found that both the FBI and some of my fellow newspapermen believe that the way to get a story is to go to someone who hates the man involved or to find a disgruntled employe. My method is entirely the opposite: I seek out the idealistic, I seek out those who believe in our system of government, who believe in the public's right to know. I remind them that their salaries aren't paid by Richard Nixon or Henry Kissinger or their immediate superiors, but by the American people and that they have an obligation to these people to let them know about wrongdoing, inefficiency, mismanagement and corruption. And so, quite often, I find idealistic, high-minded people who are willing to work with us. Our biggest problem is that they often lack courage.

You've been criticized on the grounds that your standards of accuracy are loose, that you shoot from the hip. What's your answer to that?

Investigative journalism is high-risk journalism. We are breaking the ice and when you break the ice it's more difficult to see the whole iceberg than it is after the ice has been broken for you. But I completely reject the accusation that we are inaccurate. I've been in this business for 35 years, and there is no newspaper that I've ever worked on that's more careful in checking out its facts and contacting every possible source than we are. It's just that we are dealing with more sensitive material and so people are less willing to talk to us.

In 1972 you said in your radio show that Sen. Thomas Eagleton who was running for vice president had a drunk-driver record. Later you retracted that story. If it wasn't true, why did you use it, and if it was true why did you retract it?

I guess for the same reason that your paper and every other paper for 10 months published lies — lies told to you by the White House. You ran these lies, yet you had as much obligation as I do to make sure that you were being told the truth. The only difference was that my sources were unauthorized, while yours were authorized. I think your obligation to check out authorized sources is every bit as great as is my obligation to check out unauthorized sources.

In the Eagleton case, I did check out my unauthorized sources. I called one of the finest investigative reporters in Missouri, and went over a list of names and asked if these were reliable people, because you see, while I know the people in Washington, I don't know the people in Missouri. The reporter told me who was reliable and who wasn't, and we called a number of sources and these sources told us the story and we accepted what they told us. As a matter-of-fact, these sources have never backed down on the story, but they refused to say in public what they had told us in private.

Now I have a pretty strong rule. If we write a story that's damaging to another human being, we either have to back it up or we have to retract it. I therefore chose to retract, on the assumption that, since our sources wouldn't back up their story in public, they were misleading us.

Is there anything that you won't print? Where do you draw the line, for example, on what you will and will not write about a man's private life?

There are many things that we feel are none of the public's business. Generally, we won't write a story about a public man's private life unless his private life affects his public life. For instance, I had heard the drunk-driving stories about Thomas Eagleton for years before we tried to dig into them, because I wasn't interested. I knew that Thomas Eagleton was one of the best senators in Washington and it wasn't until he became a vice presidential nominee that I felt we had to examine the man's background a little more closely.

Another time, we wrote a story about the drunk driving of Sen. Paul Fanon for the simple reason that the charges against him were whitewashed in Arizona because he was a U.S. senator. Now I figured that Paul Fanon should have to pay the same penalty as any other citizen for drunk driving, and the final result was that Fanon went to jail — and I think he should have gone to jail.

Apparently you print information which has literally been stolen from government offices. How do you know that you might not be endangering national security by revealing something that might be part of a bigger picture?

I think that is a danger but a far greater danger is that the government withholds from the American people what it doesn't want the American people to know. The people own this country, and any time the people in government feel that they are above and beyond the law and that they can make decisions in our behalf without telling us about it, that becomes the great danger.

Unhappily, the government tends to hide almost everything that is embarrassing. Mistakes, misconceptions, blunders, corruptions — when anything like that happens, the government classifies it, because under

➡

ANDERSON, Jack
MIAMI HERALD (Miami, Fla.)
May 19, 1974

'The government hides almost everything that is embarrassing'

ANDERSON, Jack

MIAMI HERALD (Miami, Fla.)

May 19, 1974

(Continued from preceding page)

our system, censorship is intolerable. Well, a censored document is still censored no matter what the government chooses to call it. It is my duty and your duty to dig out anything that the government tries to hide from the American people. The press in a democracy is supposed to furnish the people with an alternative to the official version. Obviously we can't let them get away with censoring the news by substituting the word "secret" for "censored."

And because of this massive overclassification I have to use my own judgment. I don't pretend that I'm always right; sometimes we have agonizing discussions in our office on whether we should publish secret information. We publish it only when we consider it censored information.

We have to rely on our own judgment because massive overclassification is no classification at all. When your government classifies almost everything, then you might as well have no classification because we are forced to rely upon our own judgment. You see, under our system, the government does not own the news, the news belongs to the people. So when you talk about stolen documents — well, I'll tell you who has been doing the stealing: the government, because this information belongs to the public. And so it's the government that has been stealing the information from the people.

What's the toughest decision you've ever made about whether to publicize classified information?

I don't recall any particular story that I agonized over more than others. Generally, the decision is toughest if there's any reason to believe that this story is going to cost a life or endanger a life. I don't want to play God, so even though I think it may be information that the public ought to have, I would not publish a story that might endanger lives. As an example, I found out that we were preparing to bomb Haiphong and mine the harbor. I got those plans at a time when the President was telling the American people that the United States was winding down the war in Vietnam and that we had no intention whatsoever of expanding it. Well, I had an agonizing decision to make because these were secret military plans. So, finally, I published the fact that I had seen the plans and gave the dates so there could be no doubts in the mind of anyone in the government or among the readers. But I did not reveal the plans themselves because I didn't want to be a party to the shooting down of American bombers or the obstructing of American battle plans, however much I might disagree with those plans.

You've called for President Nixon to resign, and predicted that he'll be impeached by the end of the year Do you really want Gerald Ford in the White House?

Well, I think that it's time for us to go back to the law-and-order that the Nixon Administration preaches but ignores itself. I think this nation should be governed by law and that we must have order, and under our Constitution the President can be impeached. It's a perfectly proper thing to do when the President is guilty of failing to report crimes committed by his subordinates and of apparently helping to cover up those crimes. I say "apparently" only because the President hasn't yet been convicted, and we must assume that he's innocent until he's convicted. But there's no doubt in my mind that the President of the United States collaborated with Haldeman and Erlichman to cover up those Watergates. The evidence is so overwhelming that the impeachment clause in the Constitution is an entirely proper clause to invoke. If Nixon is impeached, then Gerald Ford becomes President because the vice president is the man who replaces the President under our Constitution and I wouldn't have it otherwise.

Now Gerald Ford is not my choice for President of the United States, but he happens to be vice president and he got there legally, by ratification of Congress. He's our legal vice president and if the President should be impeached, Gerald Ford should become President and I wouldn't have it any other way.

Do you ever worry that your story about Senator Eagleton's driving record was partly responsible for Spiro Agnew becoming vice president?

I don't think that my story about Eagleton had much to do with the election of Richard Nixon, and I don't think that any politician I've ever talked to believes that. It was quite clear what the result would be and Eagleton played no part or, at most, a very small part in the final result. That is still no excuse, and those of us who write about such sensitive events should take a lesson from the Eagleton affair to make doubly sure not only that our sources were giving correct information but also that they will back it up.

Whom did you vote for in that election?

I voted for George McGovern. George McGovern was not my choice for President of the United States but by November, 1972, I knew most of the facts about the Watergate scandal, and there was no way that, with that knowledge, I could vote for Richard Nixon.

You said earlier that you don't want to play God. But obviously you do make judgments day after day. Have you ever gone to a man and said, 'Look, you're thinking of running for public office, but I have information that convinces me, Jack Anderson, that you shouldn't hold that office. If you don't run, I will not use the information but if you do, I will.' Have you ever done such a thing?

I think that this is really not part of my business. I think it's my job to report what's going on, not to maneuver behind the scenes. There is only one exception that I can recall. This involved a man in a highly sensitive position in our government who was taking dope, thus making himself subject to blackmail. He was in such a high position that I laid the information before him. He confessed that he was taking dope and told me a long, tragic story on why he was taking it. He said he would leave the government if I would not publish the story, because of the great personal nature of his tragedy. I felt that this was the proper way to handle it; I therefore did not publish the story and the man did retire from the government.

But then, weren't you blackmailing him?

No. I didn't even go to his office with the idea of asking him to leave the government, I went there to get his side of the story. After he told me his side of the story he said that he would leave the government and he hoped that I would not publish the story I don't think I even told him what my decision would be. In fact, I agonized over it awhile, because it was a rather sensational story, and the man was so well known it would have made a front-page headline. But his tragedy was so personal that I felt that it wasn't really essential to the well-being of the United States to publish it. So I withheld the story.

You said earlier that you primarily get your information from the idealists in government, from people who believe the information belongs to the people. Isn't that a little simplistic? Don't people really come to you out of malice?

I was talking about the people that I seek information from, I'm not responsible for those who volunteer information to us. It's obvious that people who are disgruntled come to us with information. We get 300 letters a day, and I would say maybe a fourth of those are from people who have personal axes to grind. We continually get calls and visits from people who are disgruntled and who have vengeful motives. We are very skeptical about the in-

(Continued from preceding page)

formation they bring us, but if it is information that we feel the public ought to have we will investigate the story. We'll check it out and we'll certainly check *them* out, and if we can confirm the story from other independent sources then we will run it. But by the time we print the story it's *our* story and it doesn't really matter where it came from.

In the case of Sen. Tom Dodd, for example, when I first learned that he was violating the law, taking illegal money, I did, as a matter of routine, check his office employment list, and made a point of routinely contacting everybody who had worked for him to see what I could find out from them. In the course of doing that, we did come across with people who were disgruntled, and that I guess is about the closest I can recall seeking out someone. We weren't really looking for disgruntled people, we were just looking for anyone who knew what had been going on inside Senator Dodd's office.

You worked for, and often in the shadow of, Drew Pearson for 22 years, from 1947 until he died in 1969. During most of that time he was not overly generous about sharing the limelight with you. Wasn't this a little hard on your ego?

Yes. Very shortly after I became his chief investigative reporter, I decided that I should go off on my own. In fact, I actually approached *Parade* magazine and was hired by them. But then Drew thought it over and decided that my work was too important to the column to let me go so he called me back and offered me a partnership in the column. I said to him, 'If you make me a partner it may not mean too much to the readers and the editors, they've got to *know* that I'm a partner.' So Drew said, 'Well, I'll give you the by-line when I'm away, and eventually we'll share the by-line.' That's the only reason I stayed with him. I suppose ego had something to do with it.

How many people work for you now, and how does your relationship with them differ from what yours was with Drew?

I have six full-time reporters, and usually five or six interns, college editors who come to the office to work for a short period. I have also three secretaries. That's about the size of the staff.

I think that their relationship is more professional than mine was with Drew. Drew and I had almost a kind of father-son relationship. I think there was a genuine affection. I feel a genuine affection for my reporters, too, but I think that our relationship is more professional. I went out and looked for the best investigative reporters I could find and I came up with Les Whitom, whom I regard as the best investigative reporter in the United States. I haven't met all the investigative reporters in the U.S., although I have met many of them. But I know the records of most of them and I wouldn't trade Les for anyone.

Les and I have trained the younger men on our staff. They are all bright. We selected the best we could find and we had probably the best selection that you could find because so many young reporters want to work for us, and I can't tell you how flattered about that I am.

Britt Hume was one of your investigators, but he no longer works for you and there's some indication that perhaps there's ill feeling between the two of you. Is that true?

No. He does work with us. Britt is not full-time with us, and the only reason is that he's rather slow-paced and our pace was a little too fast for his comfort. He likes to spend a long time on one story. That's his method of operating but my reporters necessarily must juggle two or three stories at a time. Now, most of them have one long-range story that they'll spend two or three months on. But if that's *all* they did for two or three months, we wouldn't be able to put out the column.

So during the day they are handling routine stories, and then in the evenings or part of the day they are out working on their big one. I think Britt found it distracting to try to handle two or three things while he was concentrating on one big story. Now, there is no one better than Britt when he gets on one story. He's just a one-story man, and he stays on that until he's got it. So one day, he said he had rather write books and do magazine pieces, and just work part-time with the column. And this is exactly what he's doing. Right now he's doing some oil and gas stories for us. And he has written a book about the staff. I haven't read it yet, but I understand that the publisher was talking to someone in my office and said that if there is one thing wrong with the book it's that it is too adoring. So I think that when Britt's book comes out it will dispel any doubts.

You've talked about the enormous amount of work that you expect from your staff. What about yourself? How do you spend a typical day?

I get up around 7:30 and I usually do most of my writing in the morning. I sit down and write whatever I've gathered the night before or rewrite the best stuff that my staff has given me. I take the stories home every evening and each morning I sit down at home to do the column. I pick the best story we've got, and if there are any holes in it I'll call Les and say, don't you think we ought to check this out a little more carefully, or I'll make the call myself. Then when I'm satisfied I start work on writing the column. Sometimes it will take me until lunchtime so I stay home and work and have a sandwich, and come into the office after lunch. Other times I go in before lunch; in fact I quite often have lunch and appointments at the same time. I turn the story over to my secretary right after lunch to go on the wires, and then handle office appointments and other routine things. In the evening is when I do my real sensitive news-gathering, meeting people whom I couldn't see in their offices during the daytime.

How often do you meet these people on park benches, or go about terribly convoluted ways of making sure that you are not followed?

It depends on the source. Some of them like to play games, some of them enjoy the intrigue and if they want to play games I'll play games with them. Normally, I consider my own home or their home to be perfectly safe. My place is always buzzing with activity, cars all over the place, kids running in and out, and people can dart into my house without being noticed because there's a tremendous traffic going on there, mostly kids and their friends. So they come over or I go over to their place, or if they want to play games I'll play games. And if I have any feeling that I'm being followed, it's simple to shake the tail, simply get into an elevator in a hotel and get off on the wrong floor. If anybody gets off with you you know you're being followed. You wait for him to go to his room, you just stand there in the hall until he's out of sight, then you walk up or down two or three flights and there's no problem. There's no way they can follow you if you don't want to be followed, no way for them to know into which room I go in a public building.

You obviously enjoy your work and you are very good at it. If you hadn't been a journalist, what do you think you would have been?

By golly, I've never thought about it. I started at the age of 12 writing for newspapers, and the only other thing that I've ever done — and I did enjoy it — was for a brief period during World War II. I was on a merchant ship as a cadet midshipman, and I had a great skipper who allowed me to help navigate the ship. I remember taking an old cargo ship, *The Cape Elizabeth*, into Calcutta on a moonless night. And I had a great time which lasted for seven or eight months, until I got my war correspondent credentials. I don't think I ever want to go back to sea, and that's the only other thing I've ever done.

ANDERSON, Jack

MIAMI HERALD (Miami, Fla.)

May 19, 1974

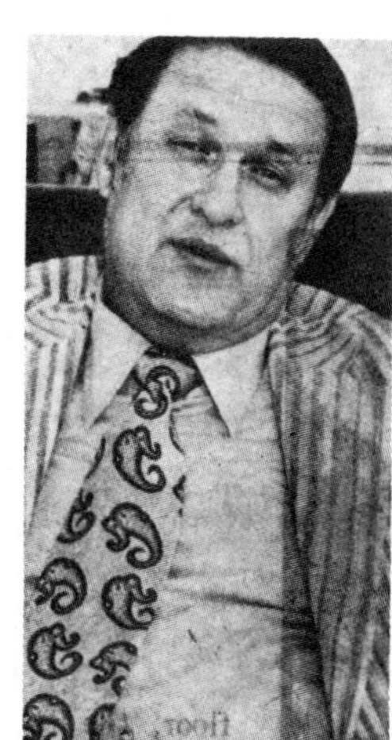

'We probably have the best staff you could find because so many young reporters want to work for us, and I can't tell you how flattered I am about that'

WRITERS WHO ALSO SPEAK GOOD STORIES

Biography News

ANDERSON, Robert (Woodruff)
(1917-)
[See also CA-21/22]
and
L'AMOUR, Louis (Dearborn)
(1908-)
[See also CA-4]
AKRON BEACON JOURNAL
(Akron, Ohio)

Oct. 27, 1974

By MIKE CLARY
Beacon Journal Staff Writer

When author Louis L'Amour finishes his next 40 books, he hopes he will have recorded in his novels the story of the American West. All of it.

He has written 62 novels and 400 short stories about the West, but L'Amour figures there is more to be said. The West, according to the author, is a gold mine of adventure.

Robert Anderson, on the other hand, wants to get back to the theater after striking gold with his first novel, called "After."

ANDERSON, who first found success as a playwright with "Tea and Sympathy" and "I Never Sang for My Father," received $250,000 for the film rights to "After." But the novel is not his medium, he said, and his next work will be for the stage, "where I have the ultimate approval over what happens."

Both L'Amour and Anderson were in Akron last week to plug their latest works, and in a joint appearance at the Press Club, they talked about their craft.

Anderson described "After" as the story of what happens to a man after his wife dies. It is autobiographical to the extent that Anderson's first wife did die of cancer in the 16th year of their marriage.

THE BOOK was well-received by critics after its appearance last Fall in hardcover, and is expected to sell well in paperback (Fawcett; $1.50).

Anderson acknowledged that interest in the book, which deals with a woman's battle with cancer, has been sparked by the recent mastectomies of Betty Ford and Happy Rockefeller.

In writing about a surviving husband, Anderson said he drew from his own expecience. "I can remember leaving my wife's hospital room about 11 p. m.," he said, "and walking out to the parking lot alone.

"I remember asking, 'Where is the help for me? I am a survivor, but I need help too.' "

Anderson, 57, is now remarried and lives in Connecticut.

L'AMOUR, whose latest paperback is "The Californios" (Bantam; $.95), turns out at least three novels a year and claims he could do much more. With 37.5 million copies of his books in print, he's closing in on Zane Grey and Max Brand.

But L'Amour bristles at the word "pulp" beside his work and is not overly fond either of "Western writer" beside his name.

And, indeed, L'Amour, a prodigious reader of Western histories, journals and diaries, is given high marks for honest and realistic treatment of people and places.

THIRTY-THREE of L'Amour's 62 novels have been turned into films, including "Hondo," "Heller in Pink Tights," and Shalako."

His energies now are being channeled into building an authentic Western town, circa 1865-1886, near Durango, Col., and completing a 40-book series tracing the history of three families from Europe to the West.

L'Amour proved himself an engaging oral story-teller.

He spoke of cannibalism, hanging, Indian tortures, Shakespeare-reading cowboys and the hardiness of the pioneers. Through all of the stories, L'Amour emphasized his admiration for "fighting men with a touch of romanticism," and his own reliance of history as basis of his tales.

"HISTORY has always outguessed you," he said. "As you study, you find that it has already happened, and happened more interestingly."

When at home in Los Angeles, L'Amour writes every day, for five to eight hours, with no fears that his story well will go dry. Like the pioneers he so admires — "they just kept coming, enduring"—L'Amour just keeps on writing.

FROM SUFFERING COMES NEW INSIGHT

ANDERSON, Robert
(Woodruff)

PLAIN DEALER
(Cleveland, Ohio)

Oct. 30, 1974

By Helen Humrichouser

One can't be too open in talking about cancer if distinguished playwright, Robert Anderson, is the judge.

"I feel a free discussion of cancer is very important," the New Yorker said in an interview with The Plain Dealer recently.

"Too many people still do not know or recognize the danger signs."

Anderson, author of "Tea and Sympathy", "I Never Sang for My Father", "You Know I Can't Hear You When the Water's Running," and the screenplay, "The Nun's Story," among others, has had so many literary successes it wasn't surprising that his first novel, "After," was widely acclaimed.

What is unbelievable or, as he says, "ghoulishly apt," is the coincidental timing of the release of his first paperback edition with the highly publicized surgeries of Betty Ford and Happy Rockefeller.

But because of that the paperback edition, released on Oct. 15, has had even greater impact than the hardback edition that came out a year earlier.

He has been inundated with letters from cancer patients, their spouses, friends, family and physicians.

The novel is, in part, biographical.

When asked which part, he answers: 'You'll never know. If I told you it was made up, you would feel cheated; if I told you it was real, you'd feel embarrassed, so all I say is that it isn't all fact."

But the suffering, anger, relief, guilt feelings and other emotions experienced by his characters are so accurate and sensitive, the book has become required reading in some medical schools to give phycians insight in the treatment of family survivors.

"After" is a love story of a couple after they discover, too late, that the wife has breast cancer and, subsequently, of his life after her death.

Anderson's first wife, Phyllis—a teacher-director, play agent and producer—died 15-years-ago

Her death followed a five-year bout with breast cancer, a fight they often appeared to be winning.

For two years after her death Anderson says he was unable to funtion properly as an individual or a writer. He went into analysis.

"My analyst once used a beautiful phrase: 'You are experiencing a guilt that denies what we are; which is, of course, a human being—falliable, needful, of limited saintliness."

Later, he was asked to speak to a large gathering of physicians at a medical school seminar on the emotional effects of death, both on the dying and on the survivors.

Anderson, also a lecturer and teacher, termed his participation in the seminar a "shattering emotional experience," which did nothing toward making him feel better.

But it was that experience which led him to write "After."

Until that time, I had wanted to do a book or to write something as a memorial to Phyllis; I had no idea what. I felt better after I finished the book."

Much of the response from the medical profession has been to thank him for the help the book has been to them in making them aware of the feelings of victims and their spouses.

One surgeon wrote: "I operate on people in these circumstances every day and never had any awareness of their private feelings."

The letters from others have been so personal and so heartbreaking that, for the first time in his career, Anderson is answering every letter.

Anderson emphasized the importance of all women knowing the self-examination procedure and of following it regularly from their early years.

"Medical science has discovered that if a woman starts early, she gets to know the contours of her own breasts so well it is easier for her to detect any differences."

One reason many physicians are extremely low-key about breast examinations is that the medical profession doesn't want to make women hysterical, he said, when asked why some do not suggest the procedure. Others seem indifferent.

A recurring question Anderson is asked is what should a husband do after his wife's surgery.

"I have to say it depends on the relationship. A lot depends on the woman. For instance, if she feels ugly and that she cannot be loved, a man can't overcome all of that alone. She has to help."

The American Cancer Society is using parts of his speech and his book in its literature. Paramount has bought the book (Fawcett Crest, $1.50) for a motion picture.

During his own struggle to live again, Anderson found that "the man needs to go away, the husband needs to come back; the man needs to move on to life, the husband is in love with death. The man seeks solace in sensation; the husband seeks comfort in remembering."

Even three years after his former wife's death, the lingering reluctance one feels to let go of a beloved one caught up with him once again—this time as he stood at an altar and exchanged vows with actress Teresa Wright. (They have been married 11 years.)

"It took enormous understanding and generosity on the part of my wife, Teresa, to take me on along with my ghosts," he said.

Mrs. Arceneaux's Novel Not Her Sole Occupation

ARCENEAUX, Thelma Hoffmann Tyler

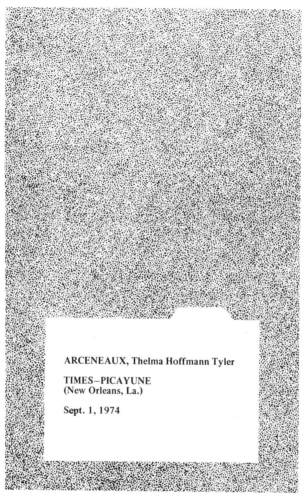

TIMES–PICAYUNE
(New Orleans, La.)

Sept. 1, 1974

By CLAIRE PUNEKY
(T-P Bayou Lafourche Bureau)

THIBODAUX, La. — In this historic city lives Mrs. Thelma Hoffmann Tyler Arceneaux, a lady with a great love for children who has raised 10 within her family and given a foster home to numerous others, who has had several careers — and finds time to write.

In fact, an historical novel by her based on the lives of Emmeline Labiche and Louis Arceneaux, actual couple from whom the poet Longfellow created his characters of Evangeline and Gabriel, has just come off the presses titled "They Emerged from the Shade."

Another work of history, "The Singing River," awaits publication. A book of her selected poems, "Reaching for the Unreachable," was published in 1970, and various works have appeared in periodicals.

Born Thelma Hoffmann in Thibodaux, she is of Acadian ancestry on her mother's side of the family and of German extraction on her father's side. Married and widowed twice, each time to a widower, she raised the two children of the first and the three offspring of the second husband.

In addition, she has five adopted children, raising the family count to 10.

She married Arthur Tyler of Columbus, Ohio, whom she had know in the days of World War II when she was employed by the Government of the United States in Washington, D.C. Five months later he drowned in a lake in Terrebonne Parish.

She and Junius Arceneaux were in school together as children. When they married they lived in a large two-story house which they filled with children, including the uncounted numbers to whom they gave a foster home. "At one time we had 27 of them," she said.

"He loved children." she said of this second husband who died died 11 years ago.

Alone now with her family of young ones, she took them on glorious camping trips around the country, into Florida, Colorado, the Smokies, and other interesting places, pitching tent at night and mapping out the next day's travel route.

Then this former teacher, assistant U.S. postmaster, and government worker decided she'd better go back to school when the children came home talking about "phonics" and "new math."

"I had to understand what they were talking about," she said, and decided to attend Nicholls State University in Thibodaux. There, encouraged by professor of English Dr. J. Maxwell Quertermous, she settled down to serious and productive authorship.

Housework is not to her liking. "I'm not a housekeeper," she said, calling it "useless work," and declaring that she does not want to spend her life doing it.

She does like to cook especially when people appreciate what she serves to them. Once she thought she had it made with two foster children who described everything she put before them as "good, until once they gave that word to a sandwich she prepared.

"That deflated me," she said, adding, "I thought they had been appreciating good cooking up till then.

"Her teaching career was primarily at Grand Isle, Labadieville and Folsom, with some substitute work in Lafourche Parish. She also had a career as assistant postmaster for some years at Grand Isle, a place she likes very much.

When World War II came along she went to Washington, and in addition to her employment there, she did considerable volunteer work, including teaching first aid to wardens and civilians.

She was a volunteer at Junvenile Court, work she found highly interesting, and also served in volunteer capacity at Georgetown Hospital.

She was a member of the National Security Women's Corps, first aid leader in charge of emergencies in the War Labor Building, and received a certificate for service to her country.

In Thibodaux, her love for children led her into organizing the first Girl Scout Troop here. "Some of my former Girl Scouts are now grandmothers," she said.

In the field of literature she holds membership in the Louisiana and Kentucky Poetry Societies, is in "Who's Who in International Poetry," has received awards in Europe for outstanding poetry contributions, is in a Ted Malone anthology and a recent one in Poetry Press.

The art work for her newly-published book was done by son Junius. There is another book, written when she was in her teens, which has never been typed.

the loner who wrote 'Sounder'

by PAM ROBINSON
Courant Staff

ARMSTRONG, William H.
(1914-)

HARTFORD COURANT
(Hartford, Conn.)

Nov. 25, 1973

[See also CA-19/20]

William Armstrong, author of 'Sounder', on the patio of his home in Kent.

At first glance, William H. Armstrong seems like a classic case of compulsive behavior. He's seen one movie "at least 10 times" and he's collected 482 books about Abraham Lincoln. He's soon to add the 483rd.

But Armstrong isn't driven by any neurosis.

He's viewed Academy Award-nominee 'Sounder' "at least 10 times" because he wrote the prize-winning book on which it is based. And he's an Abraham Lincoln fan since early childhood, using his collection to write his own book, 'Education of Abraham Lincoln' to be published by Coward and McCann in January.

Armstrong teaches ancient history and a course on how to study to ninth-graders at Kent School for Boys.

"I think I'll quit (writing) with 'Education,'," Armstrong said. "That was the only book I wanted to write. I always studied him and always collected books on him. I've been working on it for about 15 years."

His most recent work, 'The Mills of God," published by Doubleday in September is about the conflict between a boy and a man in an Appalachian setting. He says he's not exactly sure how he developed material for the story, but the title comes from a German author writing on retribution: "Though the mills of God grind slowly yet they grind exceeding small; Though with patience he stands waiting; with exactness he grinds all."

Even though the film, "Sounder," did not receive an Academy Award, Armstrong says ABC-TV has purchased the movie rights and is interested in turning the film into a series in its 1974-75 season.

He won the 1970 Newberry Medal for the book and the National Board of Review said, "It will do more to wipe out racial prejudice than any movie or TV show recently seen."

But Armstrong says the book, acclaimed for its insight about a poor black family in the South, could just as well have been written about any family of any origin.

"Except for one part of the book where the deputy sheriff makes a statement about being black, it could have been a poor white family," he said.

"Regardless of the trial or the ordeal, if there's a love or emotion deep enough, there's nothing that can destroy that. The movie stuck to my theme beautifully."

Hawaii honored him with the Nene Award, named after the state bird and given to authors of the most outstanding children's books. In addition, Scholastic Magazine selected the work for its young readers' book club. "Sounder" was part of a large manuscript he originally submitted in 1969 after it sat idle on a shelf for two years.

(Continued from preceding page)

Armstrong looks over the field in which some of his sheep are grazing. He owns 50 Corriedale sheep which he cares for in between teaching school and writing books.

Courant Photos by JOHN LONG

"One day I was out in my yard chopping some wood and my neighbor, Edmund Fuller, who's a reviewer for the Wall Street Journal, asked me what I was going to do with the wood. So I replied, 'How about trading the manuscript for this wood?' He read it and called me up and was very excited. He pointed out it wasn't one book but several. I sent it to Harper and Row's young readers' department. I got a phone call after a few weeks, asking me to come down to New York. So I went down to talk to one of the editors and she sat there, smiling and sort of twitching — I thought it was a nervous habit or something.

"So finally she said of the six editors who'd read

ARMSTRONG, William H.

HARTFORD COURANT (Hartford, Conn.)

Nov. 25, 1973

my book, 'They'd made a composite figure of you. Number one, you had to be a black man. Number two, you've suffered terribly in the South and you had a menial job at Kent and Number three, some English teacher had helped write the book and we'd be in trouble for giving you the credit.'

"I considered it a great compliment that I'd written that realistically.

"I sent it to the young readers' department because a friend of mine told me it was the kind of book librarians would talk about."

'The Sour Land' is a sequel to 'Sounder,' another part of the manuscript, but it contains just a single reference to the bestseller. Some of his other works include 'Barefoot in the Grass,' 'The MacLeod Place,' which deals with a man and his grandson trying to protect their farm from the machine age, 'Study is Hard Work,' 'Peoples of the Ancient World,' '87 Ways to Help Your Child in School' and 'Tools of Thinking.'

Armstrong studied at Augusta Military Academy and Hampden-Sydney College, graduating in 1936. He did graduate work at the University of Virginia and taught in an Episcopal school in Lynchburg, Va., before arriving in Kent in 1945.

He doesn't plan to change his routine in the future because of his books.

"I read a lot and feed the sheep and that's about it," he said. "I usually ride to the village just to see if the village is still there — I don't want it to change.

"I get away and visit other places just so I can appreciate Kent a little more, just enough to be anxious to get back."

He visited California and Toledo, Ohio this summer and spent a weekend in October addressing a conference of reading teachers at Findlay College in Findlay, Ohio.

Armstrong lives in a beautiful knotty-pine home on Skiff Mountain Road along the Housatonic River. He built the house in 1953 for his wife and three young children.

But 1953 turned into a year of mourning when his wife, Martha, died suddenly.

That left him with Christopher, then 8; David, 6, and Mary, 4, to raise without a mother or housekeeper. He began his schedule of rising early to start his day when he had three youngsters to feed and get off to school.

"You know, when you have tangles to comb out of your daughter's hair and vitamins rolling off the table you stop thinking," Armstrong rises at 3:45 a.m. to work on his literary projects.

"I think routine and schedule go alongside with Godliness," he said.

Religion is important to Armstrong.

"What else is there?" he asks. He grew up reading Bible stories in his Lexington, Va., farm and sometimes compared Biblical figures to those he knew.

A sign on his farm includes a quote from the Book of Ezekiel: "I seek out my sheep where they have been scattered in the cloudy and dark day." Religion, the earth and its beauty form themes throughout his works. Do his books reflect his life?

"I guess they do quite a bit. I'm a loner and some of the characters in my books begin to appreciate the quiet harvest of aloneness, the quiet symphony of creation and the earth, the quiet music of the earth — and its deep agony."

He bicycles to school each day, about a mile from his home. He spends his mornings in the classroom, his afternoons reading, chopping wood or feeding and caring for the 50 Corriedale sheep he maintains to 'mow' the grass that grows on the hilly land. His students are "very exciting people. They still want to learn and they haven't reached the point where they think they know everything, so there's great potential," Armstrong said.

"Every now and then, a student will bring a book in under his coat and come up to me after class and say, 'Sir, my mother saw the movie and would like an autograph.' Most of them aren't really aware I wrote it.

"I try to clear cobwebs out of youngsters' minds. Teaching is very exciting," he said, adding he almost became a journalist instead.

"My Greek teacher told me I was very immature and that I should teach for two years. I've been teaching for 30. It's really a great life, to work with young people." □

Jonathan and Richard: Catch Them if You Can

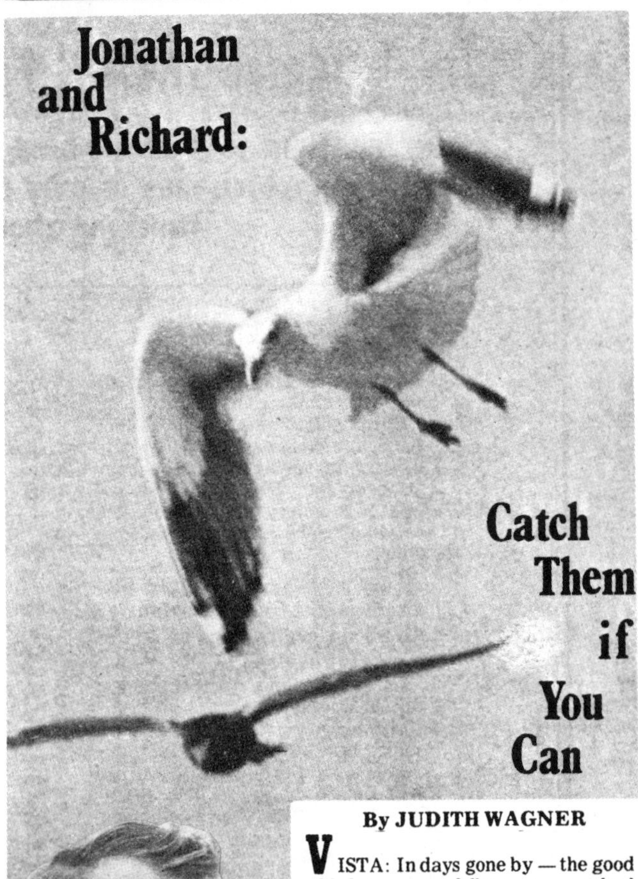

By JUDITH WAGNER

VISTA: In days gone by — the good old days, some folks say — we had heroes to believe in. Heroes who stood for important things, American things like courage, pride, the will to fight, power, strength, and winning. Heroes like Babe Ruth, Gen. Douglas MacArthur, Amelia Earhart, Eddie Rickenbacker, Rudolph Valentino, and Superman.

But somewhere along the way to 1974, many people have embraced gentler heroes. Heroes who stand for freedom of the spirit, self-fulfillment, commitment to some larger purpose, and caring. The flower children tied daisy chains and read poetry in the meadows. A philosophical beagle slept on the roof of his doghouse. He made us laugh and often made us think.

And now an acrobatic bird, created by author Richard Bach, has captured the imaginations of millions of Americans. To many of them, he says things worth hearing and symbolizes Man at his best.

"Jonathan Livingston Seagull, A Story" is an enigma, a phenomenon. Its success is astronomical and somewhat beyond the comprehension even of those who have believed in it from the start.

The first section of the story was first printed in "Private Pilot," a small aviation magazine.

Richard Bach

BACH, Richard David (1936-)	TOLEDO BLADE (Toledo, Ohio)	Mar. 24, 1974 [See also CA-11/12]

"I thought only fliers would understand Jonathan," Richard Bach says. "I sold the story to the magazine for $200."

The complete manuscript for the best-selling book was rejected by dozens of publishers before Bach finally found a kindred spirit in Eleanor Friede at Macmillan Company.

"She saw it right away. She told me then, 'Richard, this is going to be a book of the century. What is going to happen with this book is more than you can possibly imagine. Wait and see.'"

Miss Friede was right. The book has made Mr. Bach wealthy and famous.

"I was an obscure person who had the audacity to call himself a writer. Now I'm red hot. All because of Jonathan."

The ramifications of the book's success are widespread: there's the movie; Jonathan necklaces and T-shirts; and sculptures carved from wood, chipped from stone, and molded from plastic. They're red hot, too. And didn't someone start a Jonathan cult somewhere in Canada?

LISTENING: Just about everyone has an opinion. Here are some comments from area folks:

"What a sad commentary on our collective state of mind and being: that our needs for comfort, inspiration, and uplifting are so great that we must glean them from a trite piece of allegory."

"Nonsense."

"It reminds me of the parables my Sunday school teacher read from the yellowed pages of a religion primer."

"Not worth the effort it takes to discuss it."

"Ethereal, maybe even religious. An oasis of hope in a mixed-up world."

"Moving and inspirational."

"It's either a simple, imaginary story about a bird or a deep and beautiful song about life itself. But, I'm not sure which."

The reaction of critics and reviewers also has run the gamut. Some have compared the book to Saint Exupery's "The Little Prince" and Kahlil Gibran's "The Prophet." Others have said it is more like "The Little Engine That Could."

Publisher's Weekly called it "icky-poo." A magazine reviewer referred to Jonathan as "Horatio Alger in feathers" and concluded from the success of the book that "America's brains are addled."

A LOOK AT The Stars With Richard Bach: While there have been those who have proclaimed that Jonathan Livingston Seagull has had special significance in their lives, no one life has been more touched by the busy bird than that of Richard Bach.

For this man who loves to fly, there have been hard times — dismal times, when he had to take odd jobs to support his family and ward off the repossessors.

Even after the publication of his first books, "Stranger To The Ground," "Biplane," and "Nothing By Chance," his life remained unsettled. He left behind a long-time commitment to the First Church of Christ, Scientist, saying publicly that "organization can ruin anything." Before the publication of "Jonathan" as a book, he separated from his wife Betty and their six children, saying "I will never again live within the impingements of marriage."

Richard Bach's voice is mellow and his wit is quick and disarming. He asides to himself out loud, often calling himself by name. His conversation is rich with imagery.

He seems amiable, open, and bright — very bright.

Mr. Bach, how many copies of "Jonathan" have been sold to date?

Judith, I haven't checked for about 8 months. At that time it was something like 2½ million in hard cover and 6 million in soft. At first I had a high tolerance for the figures because they seemed to be proving something I already knew. Now I don't need the numbers any more.

In 1972 "Jonathan Livingston Seagull" broke all hardback records since "Gone With The Wind." How do you explain the success of the book?

Something invisible guides any idea into communication. Jonathan came in the '70s when people need to hear what he is saying to them. If I had finished the manuscript in the late '50s when I started it, the book probably would not have been accepted. People today are tired of reading about blood and gore and sex and violence. They prefer a story of hope and love.

Why do you think so many people have gotten emotionally involved with a seagull?

The lady has asked a hard one, hasn't she, Richard?

Jonathan is a crystal sphere in which we can see glimpses of our past and our future. He is true for anyone who finds him true. He believes in doing things that matter. He has his dark times and his bright times, just like all of us. To me, he is saying "I'm going to live the way I want to live, the way that is right for me. If you are going to destroy me for that, OK. But as long as I'm able I will follow my own direction."

What about all the themes which have been attributed to the story?

At first it was very difficult to accept the labels people tried to hang on the poor bird. They'd say he's a Buddhist, or a Christian Scientist, or a Roman Catholic I wanted to shout ➡

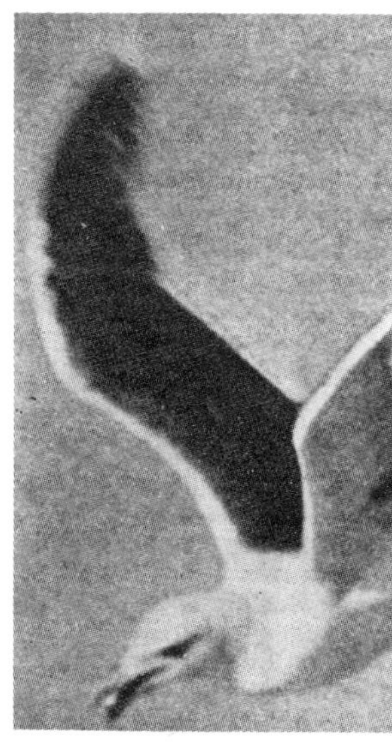

BACH, Richard David

TOLEDO BLADE (Toledo, Ohio)

Mar. 24, 1974

Photos by TOM O'REILLY, Blade Chief Photographer

(Continued from preceding page)

at them: "Leave the bird alone. Let him be what he is."

Then I finally got it through my head: Richard, Jonathan is not your property. He is who he is and he belongs to everyone.

Just who is Jonathan as you see him?

He is a crazy bird who does crazy things which may or may not be worth our thinking about.

One of the main problems is that some promoters have tried to peddle the book by saying that it is a story for everyone. That simply is not true. It is a story for relatively few people. People who see invisible things.

Lots of folks are taking this whole thing very seriously. Aren't you really laughing all the way to the bank?

If I am laughing, it is not smugly — not at anyone who has found something important in Jonathan. I might be laughing because I've proven a point to myself: if you believe in something, if it is really right, hang on. The world will catch up in time.

How fat are you getting from the spinoffs?

There she goes again, Richard.

Well, actually, I did a dumb thing. When I signed what I thought was a movie contract, I signed away the merchandising rights. My attorney tells me that I should eventually get a percentage, but so far I haven't realized a penny. I've got all the money I need anyway.

How come I'm paying for this phone call then?

(Laughter) You see, that's one of the reasons I have all the money I need.

You know, getting back to the watches and rings and dangles and bangles — I get a tightening of the lips when I see plaster wall plaques and plastic birds stuck on a wire. These put Jonathan in a cage when everything he stands for is free.

Is your sense of professional accomplishment diminished by the fact that the book has received precious little critical acclaim?

No. At first I was upset when I read bad reviews. I wanted to say, "Poor fellow, you really missed the boat, didn't you?" But now that doesn't matter either.

Book reviewers tend to be literary, very intellectual, and quite sophisticated. Jonathan is none of these things.

"Jonathan," the book, is the archtype Cinderella story. The depth of Jonathan's touch is as unique as the people who read his story. I wrote him for myself and for anyone else who finds special space for him in their lives.

How did you begin your writing career?

I sold my first story to the local newspaper when I was in high school, in order to get an A in journalism. But I began to think about myself as a writer when I was in the air force I felt impelled to tell what flight meant to me.

Actually, I hate to write. The process, you know. If I can avoid writing something, I know it's not right for me. But if something gets me by the collar and I just have to write it, then it will be pretty good. I've written a lot of things that I'm very happy with, even in retrospect.

I've read several accounts which say that "Jonathan" was dictated to you by a voice. Are you sharing your royalties with a ghost writer or a ghost gull?

I told the story of how "Jonathan" began to a reporter once and the thing got blown way out of proportion. If "Jonathan" did have a strange genesis, it is one which most any writer can understand. I was walking on the beach and I thought I heard a calm, serene voice behind me and to the right, saying "Jonathan Livingston Seagull." I don't know what I heard or what prompted me to think about seagulls at that particular moment. But I went back to my room and began to write very fast. Everything was just happening in my head — like having a dream when you're half awake. I got about ¾ of the way through and it stopped.

That was in 1959. I tried to finish it then. I played games with my conscious mind but I couldn't figure out what would happen to a seagull doing all that nutty flying, so I packed the manuscript away.

Eight years later, I awoke one morning about 5 and bang — there it was from the very flicker of a feather where I had left off.

There is nothing so mysterious about that. I rather think most every writer of fiction has had such an experience at one time or another. It really is kind of a miracle when you think about it — "Jonathan" took, all told, about four hours of actual writing time.

What has been the effect of this mammoth success on your personal life?

There are two parts of me. One wants to communicate my song to the world. The other is very jealous of my privacy. For a while I enjoyed press interviews and talk shows, but I try to stay away from them most of the time now. It frightens me when people recognize me out in public and I panic when people find out where I live.

Where do you live?

At the edge of a 30-foot cliff in Florida. You know, one of the main reasons I guard that secret is because so many people have so many ideas for how I ought to spend my new-found money. One man wanted me to give him $100,000 to start a Jonathan cult in Canada.

How do do you like the movie?

The film is a carnage. It is a great package of compromises, but it is not the disaster it was before the judge ordered them (Hall Bartlett) to change parts of the film. No one had a right to mess around with Jonathan like that.

How do you like all the bird jokes like it's a bird, it's a plane, it's supergull, or "If you like the book, you must be very 'gullible'" or . . .

Yeah, yeah. I know them all. When I hear a bird joke or read one in a review, I just eat a doughnut. It makes me feel better.

You know, the reactions to "Jonathan" would make a book in themselves. Some people tore the pages to shreds and sent them to me with X-rated reviews. Others wrote me letters saying that the book was their new Bible.

Were you trying to express a religious message?

Flying is my religion. It is my way of finding what is true. The concepts in "Jonathan" are nothing new, nothing original: where thought is, the body will be sooner or later. The idea also comes through that practice is incredibly important in everything we do. It's just an idea and we can play with it in our lives.

Do you see yourself as Jonathan Livingston Seagull?

No, I'm just one of his readers. I'm out there flapping away trying to get this living thing right. I'm not afraid to realize that what I see with my eyes is not real and that what is real is what I see in my mind. We are not doomed to nothingness; there is a higher level of existence.

Where do you go from here professionally?

I'd like to disappear and start all over with a new name just to see if it would all click for me again. But I guess I've gotten a bit too accustomed to the status quo for that.

My next book is coming together in pieces, in sparkles. I don't know just how they'll fit together yet, but they will in time. It will be another thoughtful book.

What about Richard Bach, the man? What makes you happy besides flying and writing bestsellers?

More than anything I enjoy finding someone I can talk to and listen to. There are not many of those people. And I like to play chess. If I meet someone whom I intuitively like, I say, "Let's play chess. After one game I'll know more about you than after hours of conversation."

What about your family?

My family? My family includes everyone on this earth who sees the same stars I see.

Goodnight, Richard. Oh, and Richard — I'm going to read "Jonathan" again and this time I'll try to listen better.

Good night, Judith.

Pair Of Pros

By Margaret Kreiss
Bee Staff Writer

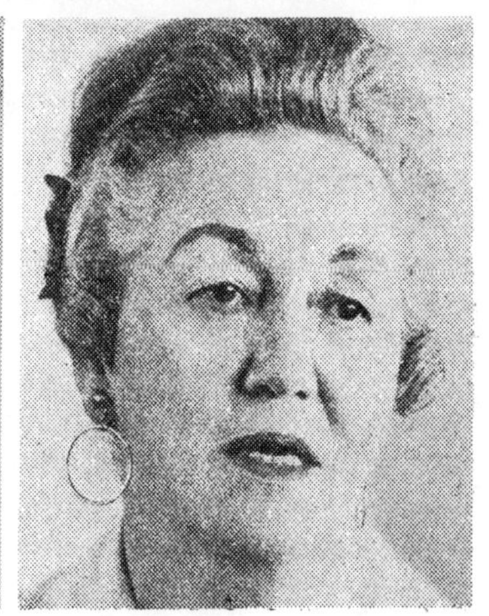

West Sacramento Authors Combine Work, Travel

BAKER, Al
and
BAKER, Marceil Genée (Kolstad)
(pseud. Marc Miller, Marc Baker, and Marsha Miller)
(1911 -)

SACRAMENTO BEE
(Sacramento, Calif.)

Mar. 5, 1974

IN THE A.A. Baker home in West Sacramento Baker thinks a lot about gold miners, claim jumpers and sheriffs. Mrs. Baker concentrates more on murderers and lovers.

Every morning the two of them go for a walk, stop at the El Rancho Hotel for breakfast and walk back to the house for four or five hours of steady writing.

He has written six Western novels and 250 short stories. She has produced 40 books, including seven mysteries and 25 romances. All of the books are hard cover. Thrown in for a grand total are her 15 paperbacks.

It's a good life. On mornings they are not walking around West Sacramento Al and Marceil Baker are strolling around some selected location such as Majorca off the coast of Spain or Guadalajara — two of their favorite places. Three months in either location usually yields a book for each of them. They like England, France and Portugal too. They take along current converters for their electric typewriters.

AL, FOR 20 years a business agent for the Amalgamated Transit Union (bus drivers) in California, Nevada and Utah, has been writing since 1947. He was reared in the Gold Run mining area and his father was in Alaska during the gold rush in the Yukon. He terms himself "an average writer turning out a couple of books a year." He owns an extensive research library dealing with Western Americana.

For more than a decade he wrote short stories for magazines such as Western Action and Popular Westerns which had an enormous circulation in the 1940s and' 50s. It was a time of magazine serials too and Al produced a few. A Western serial, "Digger John," ran for 10 consecutive years. Another, "Able Cain," ran for eight years.

WITTY AND LACONIC, with no vestige of the "litterateur" about him, Baker pointed out that accuracy in Western lore is imperative.

"If you have someone holding the wrong rifle, you hear about it," he said. "Sometimes the volunteer critics are wrong. Someone wrote me to point out there were no rim-fire cartridges in 1864 but there were. I have an encyclopedia on firearms."

Asked about techniques involved in writing Westerns, Al replied, "It's simple. The hero gets into three fights. He loses the first two and wins the third. Have you ever watched 'Mannix' on television? Check it out next week. The writers on that show follow the formula." He paused. "Of course, you have to know a few other things too." No doubt.

Marceil Baker is a fast writer. "Not that writing rapidly is a sign of superiority," she said. "Everyone has his own system. In four hours I complete 2,000 words. But everyone has his own system. Arthur Hailey spent two years in a New Orleans hotel researching and writing his book "Hotel." He told us that he writes for eight hours and produces 400 words. I cannot imagine how he could hang onto his story line. His wife says she can't either. But that is the way many writers work and you certainly cannot quarrel with success."

HER SUSPENSE novels are written under the name of Marc Miller. The romance books bear the names of Marc Baker or Marsha Miller. After writing short stories for several years she switched to books in 1956.

"Mysteries are more difficult to write than romance, " she said. "They have to be tightly plotted with no loopholes. Mystery readers are very quick to point out any fallacies. The stories are more of a challenge but the plotting is fun."

Plotting is something she did not bother too much about when she began her first book.

"It was what you would call a romantic Western novelette. Al told me to plot the entire book and diagram the chapters before I wrote a word. But I wanted to start typing right away. I ploughed ahead and believe it or not, up until the last 1,000 words I had no idea what the ending would be.

"But I guess I had a rare bit of luck. When the publisher sent me a check there was a note along with it saying, 'We accepted this story not only because the writing meets our standards but because we couldn't figure out what happened until the very end."

"I have to admit though that it was the only thing Al has been wrong about when it comes to writing and I have never been so foolish as to try my luck again."

THAT INDEPENDENT, creative writing for national markets is a lonely craft the Bakers agree.

"As a free lance writer I have eight or nine pieces out around the country at the same time," " Al said, "and I am usually working on a book too. Submitting manuscripts is like playing the slot machine. You don't know where they are going to land. You send some of them out again and if one editor doesn't like them another one usually does. A few of them ask for more and take everything you can turn out. But if there is a change in editors in a publishing house there can be a change in the writer's fortunes too, at least temporarily.

"Several years ago a New York publisher switched editors and I received 17 manuscripts back in the mail. That represented a lot of work. However, I watched the trends in the magazine and determined what it was that he wanted. I rewrote a few of them and sent some back in the original form during the following year and they were accepted. You never know."

The Bakers will be in New York in April to attend the Mystery Writers of America's "Edgar" awards dinner. Marceil is a member and the couple attends monthly meetings of the San Francisco chapter at Rocca's restaurant. The award is named for Edgar Allen Poe.

After that they will return to West Sacramento to pound out a few thousand more words and leave again late in the summer for Guadalajara.

"One of the fun parts of traveling," Marceil said, "is checking to see if any of our books are on the stands in the airport gift shops. We found four or five while we were in Palma and Majorca.

"We'll never make a fortune but we live as well as we wish to live and back in New York we have that most valuable asset of any writer — a good agent."

Romance Better Than Ever, Says Novelist Faith Baldwin

By ALAN D. HAAS
Sunday Group Feature

Romance is very much alive and thriving in America today, and it's still the course that the great majority of young Americans follow.

Who says so? Why, none other than that famous statistician of the heart, Faith Baldwin, author of hundreds of romantic novels and stories, the writer whose inspirational stories in women's magazines in the 1930's and 1940's helped to set the tone and the goal for an entire distaff generation.

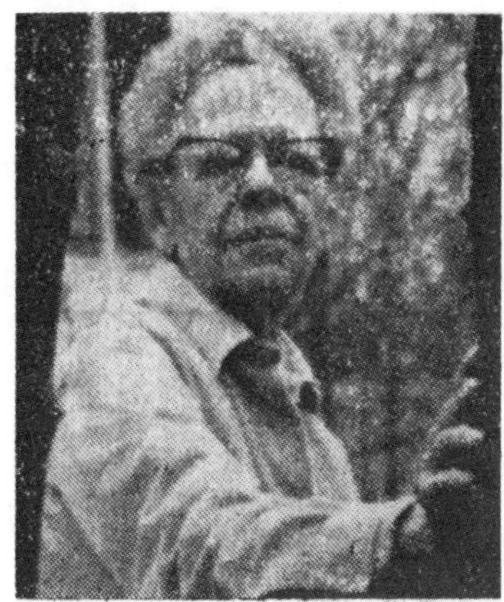

BALDWIN, Faith (1893 -)

CINCINNATI ENQUIRER (Cincinnati, Ohio)

Jan. 20, 1974

[See also CA-7/8]

AMERICA'S LEADING lady of hearts and flowers still turns out a romantic novel every year though she is 80 years old.

Romance, she claims, may have changed its outward signs a bit, but this generation of free spirits still reveres it — maybe even more than their parents.

"Love," which this 90-pound, sprightly, salty, great-grandmother defines as "when two people cannot imagine life without each other," remains the goal of the young "once they've acted out all their rebellions and tried everything else that modern society makes available."

That is not to say, Miss Baldwin points out, that romantic love hasn't lost some of its mystique since she was a girl. She feels that young couples today are less idealistic, more open, more aware of each other as individuals, and this she feels is all to the good.

"I GREW UP in the era of the flappers," Faith points out. "We had gin in hip flasks, rumbleseat love, unwanted pregnancies, and even sniffed cocaine. We tested all the moral strictures of our parents, too. But in courtship, women were still put on pedestals, bells were supposed to ring, lights flash. We swooned over poet Robert Browning bringing chronic invalid Elizabeth Barrett back to life through the magic of love. Women were all Sleeping Beauties to be awakened by a princely kiss.

"Some aspects of Victorian illusion still exist. Love makes us feel elated, we have difficulty concentrating, we have wild swings of mood from ecstacy to despair, we feel light-hearted and giddy, obsessed with the beloved, more alive. But nowadays the young are sensible enough to see that these manifestations of infatuation cannot be sustained over a lifetime. Tristan and Isolde meeting in secret in the forest has been replaced by the girl moving into her lover's apartment to share real intimacy."

Faith is aware that undying love which her own works often forecast is the stuff of fiction. "Once the heady excitement of passion wears off — and so it should — the lovers are set free to see each other as they are, fallible human being with quirks, faults and needs," she continues. "The new, liberalized attitudes needn't kill romantic love; in fact they may preserve it by enabling a young couple to enjoy a relaxed, tender, affectionate exploration and concern for each other without the burden of illusion."

Sitting in the modestly furnished living room of her unpretentious, 172-year-old, white frame house in Norwalk, Conn., attired in slacks, work smock, white socks and tennis shoes, Miss Baldwin, 80 years young, talks fondly of the American predilection for romance.

Today's young people — for all that they disavow it — are still romantics, Miss Baldwin believes. "The flower children sitting in the park, lyricizing with a guitar, are carrying out the wishes of their mothers that they be warm, gentle, caring, loving. Indian mysticism, Zen philosophy, the Jesus movement, all carry a message of abiding love, not really distant from the romantic ideal.

"When I was a child," she says, "wars brought forth patriotic fervor, bands playing, flags flying, soldiers marching off. And a kind of romance went with it all. The kids of this generation certainly don't view war that way. You might say they are just as romantic, but in a better and more meaningful way."

"What is this generation's view of life, then? It's never putting anyone else down, it's having black and chicano friends, it's remembering Kent State, it's working hard for a neighborhood improvement society, it's lending your friend a pad when he needs a place to stay, it's picking up beer cans at the beach, it's having two or less kids.

In short, a romantic is no longer someone who has an all-consuming passion for a one-and-only. A romantic is someone with a universal affection and respect for all human beings everywhere on the globe. In this sense, in the best sense, we are enjoying today a flowering of romantic love."

Miss Baldwin thinks that young couples today are striving to deal with the nitty-gritty of personal relationships, the art of communicating, establishing rapport, developing satisfactory mutual values. "All love involves conflict," she explains, "and that is what my books are about."

In her current novel, "No Bed of Roses" (Miss Baldwin has averaged at least one book a year since 1921), Katie Palmer, a liberated female, loves her job as a real estate saleswoman and wants to retain her independence, while her husband, Jeremy, a bookseller, wants her to quit work and start a family. A love triangle develops when Jeremy takes up with his beautiful assistant, but things work out in the end as they usually do in a Baldwin novel (Katie agrees to have one child).

"I write for women, primarily," she concedes, "but my characters have always been very modern. In the 1920's, a lot of people were shocked when I wrote about a girl who was pregnant but refused to marry her lover. (Try as she might, Miss Baldwin could not remember the title). "There's always sex in my books but I stop short of the bedroom door. I also stop short of four-letter words, although I know them all. I'm not sure a writer gains anything by using them."

Miss Baldwin denies that modern-day pressures and freedom are the roots of divorce. She feels that relationships are more likely to go on the rocks for traditional reasons, like financial difficulties, contrary viewpoints about raising children, inability to adjust to the other person's foibles, inability to communicate and so on. At one point in "No Bed of Roses," Jeremy says to himself, 'Why does she always have to do her nails when I'm playing Chopin?" More marriages founder over trivia than anything else, Miss Baldwin believes, suggesting that individuals have not yet learned to be sufficiently tolerant, understanding and accepting of each other.

MISS BALDWIN doesn't frown on the idea of a young couple living together before marriage ("after all, more than one in three marriages end in divorce anyway"). She thinks it's for them to discover what effect round-the-clock intimacy has on their ability to love each other. "A couple needs to learn that even love is not all powerful, all reliable, all forgiving, all understanding," she comments. "Love is a liaison between two separate people with individual needs and wants. It is an active, on-going process that requires much sacrifice, adjustment and commitment," is the way she puts it.

"Romantic love is constantly being tested in our daily relationships, and perfect harmony between two people is not possible. But a generosity of the spirit can leaven romance and keep it alive when both parties care deeply. Adult romance lives on after the melody fades, immature infatuation dies," she concludes.

Miss Baldwin sees certain trends in society today as anti-romance, in the sense that they devalue personal relationships. In this category, she includes pornographic films and books, sex without responsibility, female attire that is too revealing, the whole "group grope" movement.

"Pornography is boring," she feels, "it leaves nothing to the imagination. Why even back at the turn of the century a popular novelist named Elinor Glynn wrote so-called shocking books; people lay around on tiger skin rugs, women were lured to men's apartments and were sometimes even seduced. But nothing was made that explicit, nothing was offensive.

"When I was young I read the ribald classics, Bocaccio, de Maupassant, Balzac, etc., and they dealt heavily in sex, but the subject was handled with delicacy. These authors didn't reduce sex to a routine like scientifically brushing your teeth. They left the individual with constant hope of fresh discovery in a sexual partner."

Readers of Miss Baldwin's novels might be surprised to learn that she considers men more romantic than women, "in the sense that they have more illusions — including the ultimate illusion that they understand women. The distaff side is more practical, always planning for the future, worrying about the kids, etc. In America, both sexes grow older physically, but emotionally and spiritually they remain rather child-like, even naive. That's another reason why romance has such a strong hold on people in this country."

SHE WAS MARRIED to the same man, Hugh H. Cuthrell, for 33 years, raising four children (a daughter, Ann, still lives with her) becoming the grandmother of 10 and now is a great-grandmother. She became interested in psychic phenomena after her husband's death and is convinced that she communicated with him several times. Despite a cataract operation on one eye which has limited her sight, she still writes every day because, as she says, "I need the money, I never saved a cent."

Advancing age has not dimmed Faith's view of contemporary trends, and she heartily endorses most of the goals of women's lib. As Faith says, "Work is no bar to raising children effectively. I brought up four of my own with one hand in the spinach and one on the typewriter." Faith applauds women who seek personal accomplishment. "After all," she sums up, "the best relationships are between equals and that's where romance continues to flourish. It's more difficult to maintain between wage earner and housemaid."

Jose Balseiro Bridged the Gap Between Cultures

—Miami Herald / MIKE O'BRYON

BALSEIRO, Jose Agustin (1900-)

MIAMI HERALD (Miami, Fla.)

Apr. 29, 1974

By SANDY FLICKNER
Herald Staff Writer

Jose A. Balseiro slices with a letter-opener the still uncut pages of his copy of a book published in 1967, explaining that there is no need, really, to read — or look at — one's own books.

No, perhaps not, particularly when there were so many before.

But he turns, quite naturally, to those books to search for the particular passages that will help place the lectures and books, the travels and honors in perspective.

And Dr. Balseiro — poet, teacher, critic, cultural attache, musician — sums it all, simply: He tried to bridge the space between two cultures.

"Always I was trying to interpret the spirit of the U.S. to Spain and South America, and the spirit of the Hispanic world to the U.S., to students here."

Brought Understanding

HE WANTED to help two peoples understand each other.

The bronze plaque presented by "his grateful students" still hangs outside the office Dr. Balseiro occupied at the University of Miami, where he was a professor of Hispanic literature for 21 years. He left for the University of Arizona in 1967 to fulfill a promise to a man who had been one of his graduate students at the University of Illinois in the 1930s.

"I had told him over and over, 'Before I die, I'll come,'' Dr. Balseiro explains, laughing at how for six years he found family reasons — not excuses — why he couldn't leave Miami.

But wherever he taught, Mercedes Balseiro explains, he brought the students; as well as his associates, into his home.

"They were always with us, in the house day or night," Mrs. Balseiro explains. "It was wonderful to know them."

Dr. Balseiro, now 73, says he has, during the year and a half since his retirement and return to Miami, missed teaching "very, very much."

DURING THAT retirement he has continued to write poetry on his portable manual typewriter, agreed to edit a bicentennial book about Hispanic Floridians and the revolutionary movement, and lectured, specifically at Bryn Mawr, Yale, and the University of North Carolina.

And, about two months ago, he obtained the key to another office at UM, on the eighth floor of the library where he is now consultant for Hispanic literature.

But to the question of what else he might be doing during his retirement Dr. Balseiro offers an immediate apology:

"Unfortunately," he says, "I never had a hobby."

It is the singular, disarming humbleness of accomplished men

(Continued from preceding page)

or women, an apology that's incongruous with the still at the piano and violin; the musical compositions that have been performed in Carnegie Hall; the cultural missions for the U.S. State Department, in 1938; the 10 collections of critical essays, five books of poetry, three novels, and dozens of scholarly articles, all written in Spanish.

And it is incongruous with the awards and critical acclaim that have come for a half century, ever since his first book of literary criticism won the Spanish Royal Academy's prize for the best collection of essays published in 1925.

'Spanish, International'

IN THE 1920s a London Times critic wrote that "the originality of Senor Balseiro's criticism consists in the fact that it is both Spanish and international."

In the 1930s no less than Miguel de Unamuno credited Balseiro in his forward to "Abel Sanchez" as the man whose critiques brought him the Spanish-speaking people's attention and favor.

In the 1940s a South Atlantic Bulletin reviewer wrote that "Senor Balseiro, though a Puerto Rican by birth is not a Spanish-American critic examining the works of Spanish writers; rather he is an international scholar who knows no boundaries, and whose criterion is world literature."

He was described as modest at his earliest successes, and at his latest ones. In 1967 when the UM established the Jose A. Balseiro Award he insisted only that the winning essays never be about Jose A. Balseiro.

But Dr. Balseiro might have been a baseball player — having been, at the University of Puerto Rico, centerfielder and leadoff hitter with, it has been reported, a 300 batting average: "Oh, it was better than that," Dr. Balseiro says, grinning. "I was officially approached once, but to play baseball would have been heresy to my family.

And he was supposed to be a lawyer — chosen by his father, composer Rafael Balseiro, as the family's representative in the world of jurisprudence.

"I knew from this high" — Dr. Balseiro, seated, levels his palm with his chest — "that I was supposed to be a lawyer.

"So I studied law and I got my degree," he says. "I took the bar examinations and I passed them. And then I went to my father and said, 'Here's the diploma and the license. You keep it because I am going to Spain.'

That is when the pressure began, first from his godfather — the husband of his father's oldest sister — and then from another uncle who flashed an envelope in front of young Balseiros's face.

"I said, 'What is that?' and he said, 'This is the money for you.' I told him, 'No, that is the money if I open a law office, and I am not opening a law office so you may just keep it.'

'Do You Have Talent?'

AND THEN the godfather returned, to ask "Do you really think you have the talent for literature?"

"And I said, 'Absolutely, yes.'"

The family agreed that Balseiro could go to Spain and try for two years to write, and if he succeeded he could have his career in literature.

Within two years he had established himself, had his first book of poetry published, asked for and married Mercedes — whom he had met while she was a high school student and he at the University of Puerto Rico — and settled in Spain to write.

But there was no thought of teaching until, during a visit to Puerto Rico, Balseiro received a mysterious cablegram from the University of Illinois asking him to join the graduate faculty there.

He spent three years at the University of Illinois; then at the request of the University of Puerto Rico spent the next three years as visiting professor of Spanish literature; then at the insistence of the University of Illinois returned for three more years there.

He returned to Puerto Rico to devote himself to writing, and ended up serving one term as senator-at-large, an experience he shakes his head about, calling politics distasteful.

In 1946 he came to the University of Miami.

AND MEANWHILE, he became a cultural ambassador, an official and unofficial interpretor of the Americas in so many ways it is impossible to list all of them.

He served as president of the International Institute of Ibero-America Literature from 1955 to 1957, and was appointed a member of the consultative committee of the U.S. for UNESCO in 1959. He became a member of the U.S. Academy of Spanish Languages and the Puerto Rican Academy of Letters, and a corresponding member of the Spanish Royal Academy in Madrid as well as literary academies in Columbia, Argentina, and Mexico.

He had accepted his first state department mission in 1938 as official delegate to the First International Congress on Teaching Ibero-American Literature; in 1939 he represented the U.S. and delivered one of the two main lectures at the First Inter-American Conference on Libraries and Publications.

In 1954 he was chosen by the state department's International Exchange Program to lecture in South America.

In 1955 and 1956 he participated in the program again, delivering 51 lectures in universities and cultural centers in Spain and England. Later in 1956, at the invitation of the state department and the Department of Public Instruction of Puerto Rico, he gave 14 lectures in four Puerto Rican cities.

BALSEIRO, Jose Agustin

MIAMI HERALD
(Miami, Fla.)

Apr. 29, 1974

ON THOSE lecture tours he always offered at least a dozen possible lectures, allowing his audience to choose the topic. They were lectures explaining the philosophies and lives of musicians and poets, artists and leaders; identifying common influences and common bonds; tying two worlds together.

Now Dr. Balseiro mentions Franklin D. Roosevelt's "Good Neighbor" policy as the policy that began opening the U.S. to Hispanic culture and that culture to ours; and he calls John F. Kennedy's Alliance for Progress "a moment of hope, the summit of 20th century relations between the two continents."

But he would rather not speculate on whether that moment of hope slipped through our fingers.

He will say, sadly, that there were people in both hemispheres in the 1950s who didn't really want to understand each other, and that there are still such people now.

"But I would not want to say whether there is less understanding, or more understanding," he explains. "That would be getting into politics and I detest politics."

Instead he turns to a lecture he first wrote for a University of Miami audience.

"The nearer we approach our neighbors by the disinterested paths of art, literature, scholarship, and open-hearted friendship," he told his audiences on the 1950s, "the sooner will we demolish the prejudices that hamper the constructive development of human nature."

Formidable Collection

THAT IS still the way, he says, nor the Americas to look at each other.

His formidable — but uncounted — collection of books attests to Dr. Balseiro's own lifetime of looking at two cultures.

Some of those books are still in Spain, where his writing career began; some are in Tucson, where his teaching career officially ended. Some are in Westchester with his younger daughter Liliana Mees; some in Miami with his older daughter Yolly Buchmann; and some in his own study

The books — except for those with notes from such friends as H. L. Mencken and Karl Menninger, Robert Frost and Miguel de Unamuno — will go to the library where Dr. Balseiro's career as a cultural interpreter is continuing.

Know Your Talented Neighbor

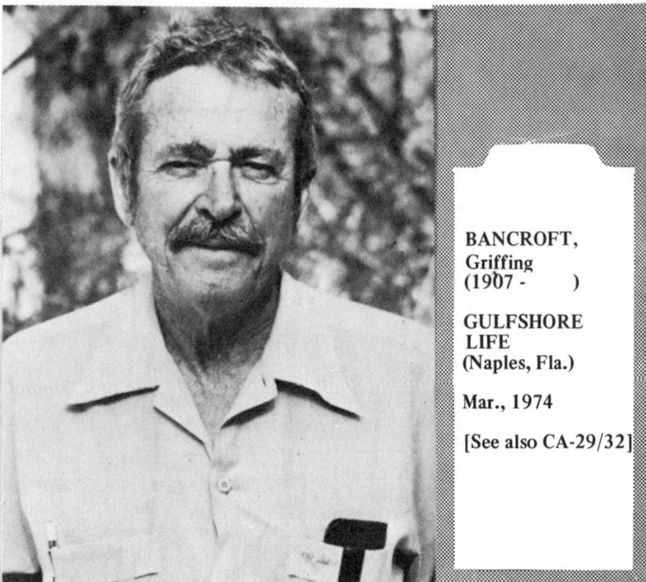

BANCROFT, Griffing (1907-)

GULFSHORE LIFE (Naples, Fla.)

Mar., 1974

[See also CA-29/32]

Reprinted from GULFSHORE LIFE magazine
published by Gulfshore Publishing Co., Inc., Naples, Florida.

By Leigh Plummer

There are many miles and many years from being No. 4 man on a boa constrictor feeding team at the San Diego Natural History Museum in the mid 20's to conducting bird watching tours in 1974 at the "Ding" Darling National Wildlife Refuge at Sanibel.

Yet that is the route trod in the last half century by Griffing Bancroft, veteran Washington correspondent, longtime radio commentator, authority on the American political scene, author of numerous books on birdlife, and winner of the Medal of Freedom – highest civilian award given by the Department of Defense.

Actually all this started almost a century ago. In 1849 to be exact. In that year Grandfather Hubert Howe Bancroft arrived in San Francisco – not to search for gold, but (1) a real estate business and (2) a reputation as the chronicler of the West.

Concerned that no one was recording the history of the western states, Grandfather Bancroft became the author of some fifty books about the western states, Alaska, New Mexico and the pioneers who settled those areas. Perhaps that fondness for writing carried through to his grandson.

But about that boa constrictor. Griffing Bancroft, Senior, was for many years Director of the San Diego Natural History Museum – a position which made him responsible for seeing that the boa constrictor ate regularly. And at times force feeding was necessary. Now boa constrictors don't bite but – if irritated, they wrap their coils, up to fifteen feet of them, around their annoyers.

The procedure, therefore, was to have a local market prepare a slug of meat. The No. 1 man would push the meat into the mouth of the snake being held open by No. 2 man. Operatives No. 3 and No. 4 stationed themselves along the length of the huge snake to hold him straight while the meat was being pushed down to the appropriate point.

There are many snakes on Sanibel but in his fifteen years there Griffing Bancroft, Jr., has not had to utilize his experience with any boa constrictors as at San Diego.

Rather, he has devoted himself to a continued study of birdlife – something which he had started with his father, a well known ornithologist as well as museum director. The father and son have enjoyed the honor of having two birds named after them – the Bancroft Yellow Crown Night Heron and the Bancroft Screech Owl.

But of more current interest are Griffing Bancroft's books. They are "Snowy – The Story Of An Egret" (McCall's); "Vanishing Wings – A Tale Of Three Birds Of Prey" (Franklin Watts); "White Cardinal" (Coward, McCann, Goeghegan); and "The Meaning Of Communism" (Silver Burdette). "Vanishing Wings" has been given the Junior Literary Guild Award and the Christopher Award For Young Adult books.

A 1930 graduate from the University of Chicago, Griffing Bancroft naturally gravitated – after a year's unhappy experience in the import-export business with a Mexican company, into the newspaper business at the depression pay scale of $15/week. Soon he moved on to Los Angeles with *International News Service* and a rewrite job on *The Herald Express.*

By 1938 he was covering the California State Legislature at Sacramento, thus introducing the young newspaperman to political writing, the second great love (after birds) of his life. The outbreak of World War II took him to New York, then to Washington with INS and *The Chicago Sun* as Washington correspondent.

When the government set up the Psychological Warfare Bureau, Bancroft became Director of News Operations in Algiers, Rome and Austria. One of the tasks of his group was to prepare leaflets printed in the appropriate language to be dropped to civilians in advance of the Allied Forces and to make broadcasts enlisting support of non-fascists as the war progressed.

Back in Washington in 1945, Bancroft rejoined *The Chicago Sun* bureau – covering Congress and politics in general. But radio beckoned and in 1948 the late Edward R. Murrow of CBS hired Bancroft to work with such luminaries as Eric Sevareid, and Howard K. Smith and Howard Reasoner, now news commentators for ABC.

The same year the Bancrofts built their first house on Captiva facing westward toward the Gulf. That house still stands but the Bancrofts sold it after a local storm washed away fifty feet of beach along a two mile stretch of Captiva and put their house right at the water's edge.

Since 1958 the Bancrofts have lived in a delightful home overlooking Roosevelt Channel on the east side of Captiva. Mrs. Bancroft herself a distinguished newspaperwoman who – for many years, wrote a column for the *Associated Press.* She is an accomplished painter and is active in art circles in Southwest Florida.

Mr. Bancroft served for two years on the Board of the Captiva Erosion Prevention District, is currently a Vice President of both the Sanibel-Captiva Audubon Society and the Sanibel-Captiva Conservation Foundation. He was one of the original members of the "Ding" Darling Memorial Committee and for two years was President of the Captiva Civic Association.

Today the Bancrofts lead a quiet life – Mrs. Bancroft with her painting, Griff with his writing and his bird tours which he conducts several days a week for visitors to the Island. His knowledge of birdlife can only be termed encyclopaedic. Which is what it should be. He spent most of his youth studying birds except when he was helping hold down that damn snake.

Photo by Eugene H. Mopsik

BANFIELD, Edward Christie
(1916 -)

PHILADELPHIA
INQUIRER
(Philadelphia, Penn.)

Dec. 1, 1974

The Professor Radicals Love to Hate

By PAUL TAYLOR

Edward Banfield is neither a racist, a fascist nor a Nazi; he does not want to starve the poor, oppress women or ressurect slavery; and nowhere is he on record as endorsing genocide.

These are hardly the sorts of testimonials which qualify their subject for sainthood, but this particular subject is not currently in a position to grumble about being damned with faint praise.

Banfield is a 57-year-old urbanologist at the University of Pennsylvania who has recently been elevated to the title of Public Pig Number One by what little remains of the radical movement on this country's campuses.

It is a position which entitles him to be shouted off stages whenever he tries to deliver a guest lecture; to be threatened physically; to have his classes at Penn disrupted by hecklers; and to be accused on radical broadsheets of transgressions against humanity which, by comparison, make Attila the Hun's handiwork look like the mischief of a choirboy.

He incurred all this wrath by writing a book entitled *The Unheavenly City* which holds that urban problems are both less serious and more intractable than is generally understood. It builds its case on the strength of some rather harsh observations about the lower classes who supposedly cause these problems and the upper classes who try to solve them.

It is an iconoclastic work, seeking to undermine virtually every popular assumption about the nature of our "urban crisis"—including the assumption that there *is* one. The book is written in deft and engaging prose, making it all the more infuriating to anyone smitten with the urge to undo the injustices of an imperfect society.

In Banfield's view, the "urban crisis"exists only in the mind's eye. Life for most city-dwellers has never been better—they live more comfortably and with more conveniences than ever before.

There remains, he concedes, some urban problems (crime, poverty, ignorance), but the irony is that while we perceive these problems to be getting more serious, they are in fact growing less serious. The paradox results from the constantly-rising standards our society sets for itself—a tendency which Banfield believes has dangerous implications for its general well-being.

What urban problems do persist are mostly inaccessible to governmental solution, he argues. They are created in part by the economic logic of metropolitan growth, which insures that there will be neighborhoods of relative deprivation (slums) in the center of a city, and in part by a phenomenon which Banfield has called "class culture." He divides all people into four (non-economic) classes, and defines each by its perception of the future: the spectrum travels from upper-class people who believe in a distant future and plan for it, through middle and working-class people, down to the lower classes, who live only for the moment and who cannot delay gratification.

Banfield considers the culture of the lower classes to be at the root of the most serious urban problems and doubts that this culture can be changed by "Great Society" legislation.

Indeed, instead of solving the city's problems, government policy has more often exacerbated them. Banfield cites compulsory high school education and minimum wage laws as two cases in point. The former, by forcing a lower-class child to suffer through an education for which he is ill-suited, will make him grow bitter and frustrated; the latter, by pricing menial jobs at an unnaturally high level and thereby encouraging more qualified applicants to compete for them, will place him at an economic disadvantage.

"If a ditchdigger's work is worth no more than $1.00 an hour," he writes, "and a 15-year-old dropout's work is worth no more than 50 cents an hour, these should be their wages."

To be sure, this is an unorthodox approach to easing the burdens of the poor, and it is small wonder that Banfield has achieved such notoriety among campus radicals. What is surprising, however, is the timing of that notoriety.

His book was published in 1970. The public debate over its merits—always lively, often acrimonious—was confined mainly to intellectual journals and seemed to have exhausted itself several years ago.

Now, suddenly, out of nowhere, Banfield is news again. He was shouted off-stage last spring when he tried to deliver a lecture at the University of Toronto, and the same thing happened a week later at the University of Chicago. Upon his return to Penn at the end of the academic year, he found hecklers waiting for him in his class there, too.

Banfield has managed to keep himself out of the line of fire for the past six months by retreating to the relative comfort and safety of his 300-acre Vermont farm. There, in a 1792 farmhouse whose front porch looks out over 20 miles of the Green Mountains, he spends his time en-

(Continued from preceding page)

tertaining weekend guests, preparing material for a new course he will teach next spring, gardening with his wife, watching the seasons change, and reflecting, every now and then, on the events of last spring.

"If these little troglodytes," he begins, warming to his subject, "want to misrepresent it (his book), there is nothing in the world I can do to stop them."

Banfield is a native Connecticut Yankee, a large, gangly man with outsized ears, a great big weathered face, grey, thinning hair and a disposition as rugged as his appearance.

How does it feel to be prevented from speaking? "How does it feel to be kicked by a mule," he shoots back. "I consider the source."

Banfield said that when the book was published in 1970, he expected a chorus of outrage from liberals and a strange sense of bedfellowship with radicals. "Here was a book which was saying that governmental solutions to our social problems aren't working," he said. "That's exactly what the radicals were saying. Our only difference is that I don't go on from there and advocate revolution. I thought that up to a point, anyway, the radicals would be with me."

It didn't work out that way. Both camps turned against the book — liberals for reasons that will be examined later; radicals because, in Banfield's view, they had begun to see their influence wane with the winding down of the Vietnam war, and they were scratching around for some new "program material" to hold their organization together.

"It always perplexed me that they choose me," he said. "I think they were trying to forge some sort of alliance between blacks and the working man, and by misrepresenting what I had written, they tried to paint me as the common enemy of both.

"Once you become useful to these people, they have a vested interest in keeping you in the news," he continued. "I suppose that accounts for this most recent outburst of incidents. They don't want to go to the trouble of trading you in for a new model.

"I wish you would be careful the way you write this," he said, tugging uncomfortably at his jaw, "because I don't want to give these bums the satisfaction of feeling that they have muzzled me. But it is true that I've canceled quite a few lectures as a result of their disruptions.

"I feel like a rat that is carrying fleas infested with the bubonic plague," he continued. "I really have no interest in making a profession of creating a row on campus after campus. I've got better things to do. Really, I wish I could just fade back into the wallpaper."

Banfield's first exposure to unfriendly student reaction to his book came during a lecture class on the cities he gave at Harvard, where he was a faculty member when *The Unheavenly City* was published.

"It was a big lecture course, maybe five or six hundred students," he recalled, "and I had gotten the reputation of having some snobbish and unorthodox ideas about cities. Every time I said something that students disapproved of, they would stomp their feet. It made a terrific racket. But back then, I always had the feeling it was all good-humored. There was really nothing nasty about it."

BANFIELD, Edward Christie

PHILADELPHIA INQUIRER
(Philadelphia, Penn.)

Dec. 1, 1974

Banfield left Harvard in 1971 for Penn, largely as a result of the wooing of Penn President Martin Meyerson, a close personal friend and collaborator on some earlier books.

"At the time I left Harvard," he said, "I think I could have gotten a job at just about any major university in the country. Well, I don't think there are too many schools around that would have me now. The experience of the late 1960s was terribly unsettling to many people in academia. They simply don't want any more provocative agents on campus."

If the radical assault on his work has scarred him, the liberal reaction has at least left some surface wounds.

Banfield prides himself in being a pure scholar; his book was received by the liberal community as being a political manifesto.

He lays part of the blame for the book's political reception at the feet of his publisher. The first printing featured a "quickie biography" of its author on the dust jacket which made reference to his service as chairman of a task force on urban affairs established by then-President Nixon.

Banfield lobbied with the publisher prior to publication to have the passage removed, but the advertising people at Little Brown Inc. sensed, correctly, that it would sell copies. The reference stayed in. "There is no question in my mind that the dust jacket got things off in the wrong foot," he said. "It helped define it as a political book."

It didn't help either, of course, that what the jacket said was true. Banfield did serve on a number of task forces in the late 1960s at the behest of Nixon, although he now discounts all interest in policy-making.

"When people are asked by a new president to advise them," he said, "they feel obliged to do so. I have never had the urge to be both a scholar and a policy maker. I don't want to be a John Kenneth Galbraith of the right. One career is enough for me."

Banfield's well-advertised involvement with the Nixon administration not only served to thrust his book onto center stage, but vastly magnified the threat it posed to liberal advocates of Great Society legislation.

The fears of these liberals were by no means idle. Not entirely by accident of history, Banfield's book was published at the absolute nadir of public confidence in liberal policy-making. After nearly a decade of Great Society legislation, there was no clear or convincing evidence that the billions of dollars spent on the cities had made any difference.

A new administration had just been voted into power, largely on the strength of a conservative, middle-American backlash against these social programs and Nixon's chief advisor on urban affairs, Daniel Patrick Moynihan, had just written an infamous memo which advised that a policy of "benign neglect" be taken towards the black urban ghettoes.

(Continued from preceding page)

The fear was abroad in the land that Nixon would move quickly to turn off the spiggot that had poured more than $75 billion over the last decade into the cities, using men like Moynihan and Edward Banfield (the two are close personal friends) as his philosophic underpinning.

But there was more at issue in Banfield's books than the comparative value of one set of social policies over another. The liberals themselves were reeling from a crisis of confidence, and Banfield's book represented a head-on assault on the most fundamental part of their doctrine—the belief in the malleability of society, its institutions and its people. These social environmentalists believed above all else in the possibility for change. All it would take was more money, more commitment, better programs. Along comes Banfield with his gloomy caveats about the limits of social policy—no wonder they felt attacked. "If Banfield is right," wrote an editor of *The Atlantic*," . . . the noblest efforts of the past thirty years have been wrong, what progress has occurred has been accidental, and only a 180 degree shift in sensibility can save us."

Not surprisingly, the liberals struck back.

He was called a "blame-the-victim" sociologist and accused of being callous, insensitive and emotionally dead. His ideas were described as "perverse," "wrong-headed," "irresponsible" and "propagandistic."

In this ocean of indignant reviews, there were some friendly islands. Irving Krisol, writing in *Fortune* magazine, called *The Unheavenly City* the "most enlightening book written about the urban crisis," and reviewers for *Time* and the *Wall Street Journal* were almost as effusive in their praise. But it was left to *Commentary* magazine, under the editorship of Norman Podhoretz, to discern the tendency among liberals to dismiss out-of-hand any perceptions about the cities which would dampen the impulse to reform.

"The utopians and the extreme environmentalists in the field of social policy," Podhoretz wrote, "having in the past ten years been given a chance to put many of their ideas into practice and having failed to deliver on one promise after another, are now attempting to discredit every rival school of thought in the field in the hope of fending off the discredit into which their own general point of view is deservedly falling, not only in the eyes of others but in their own eyes as well."

That is one explanation for the intemperate response accorded Banfield's book; there are others. The tone of the book seems to propose solutions to urban problems which are simply unheard of in a democratic society.

In a chapter on the nature of urban crime, for example, Banfield suggests that one way to effectively punish criminal behavior would be to give police the power of "curbstone justice"—the power to rough up a suspect at the moment of his apprehension. The rationale is that since most people who commit crimes are lower-class, and since lower-class people in Banfield's lexicon have no perception of the future, the threat of punishment being meted out at some distant date after lengthy court proceedings has no deterrent value.

BANFIELD, Edward Christie

PHILADELPHIA INQUIRER
(Philadelphia, Penn.)

Dec. 1, 1974

In the same chapter, Banfield entertains another proposal for auctioning off the babies of welfare mothers, and another which would incarcerate individuals who are believed to have a high propensity for crime. There would be varying levels of punishment, Banfield says. A person with a .5 probability of committing a crime would only have to report weekly to a parole office, while a person with a .9 probability would be sent to a penal village or work camp.

These are frightening proposals, and Banfield discusses them with a cool detachment. He concludes his chapter on the following note: "If abridging the freedom of persons who have not committed crimes is incompatible with the principles of free society, so, also, is the presence in such society of persons who, if their freedom is not abridged, would use it to inflict serious injury on others. There is, therefore, a painful dilemma . . . The question, therefore, is not whether abridging the freedom of those who may commit serious crimes is an evil—it is—but whether it is a lesser or greater one than the alternative."

What kind of man finds any dilemma at all in this formulation? Isn't there, between the lines of this detached logic, a yearning for a kind of totalitarian society which would not think twice about abridging the freedoms of those it believes to be dangerous?

"Absolutely not," says the author. "One of the things the book tries to point out, though, is that if you want democracy, you have to take the good with the bad. I'm perfectly happy to take the deal on those terms. But I'm just trying to show that its very difficult to improve things without short-circuiting fundamental principles of democracy. Again, to me, such short-circuiting is radically unacceptable. But I didn't feel the need to advance that opinion in the book. If you go through the whole book and try to red pencil all the value judgments, you won't find any. One or two maybe."

If there are times when his writing is infuriating, there are also times when it is deliciously rewarding. He is at his best when he is lamenting the rising standards by which our society has come to judge the quality of its urban life. As noted earlier, Banfield believes that urban-dwellers have never had it so good. But he compares the perception of the urban condition to the mechanical rabbit at the race-track which is set to keep just ahead of the dogs, no matter how fast they run. "Indeed," he writes, "if standards and expectations rise faster than performance, the problems may get (relatively) worse as they get (absolutely) better."

The question of course presents itself—just what is so terrible about rising standards? And the stock answer is: Nothing. They are the measure of a humane society—the spur which keeps our collective conscience from growing satisfied and complacent.

Banfield's answer is: that may be true, but if our society mistakes the failure to progress as fast as we ➡

(Continued from preceding page)

would like for the failure to progress at all, society might panic and resort to ill-considered resolutions that will only make matters worse.

Banfield illustrates his point with a discussion of the role of racism in American society. He believes racial prejudice has declined sharply in the years since the Second World War. While he acknowledges that it still exists, he believes its importance has been grossly magnified by the cult of rising expectations. The main disadvantage of the urban black today, he writes, is not racism, but the fact that "he is the most recent unskilled, and hence relatively low-income, migrant to reach the city from a backward rural area.

"Almost everything said about the problem of the Negro tends to exaggerate the purely racial aspects of the situation," he adds. Even black leaders who may understand that racism is no longer the chief obstacle facing their people cannot pass on that knowledge—the logic of their positions as black leaders prevents it.

And as for whites, particularly the middle and upper class whites who in Banfield's view have a distressing tendency to blame themselves for society's ills, racism is a satisfying explanation for the continuing economic disadvantages of blacks. It would be graceless, he notes, for whites to run the risk of under-emphasizing it.

The problem in all of this he says, is that by exaggerating the importance of racism, both whites and blacks set in motion a "reign of error" that eventually makes the exaggerated view a self-fulfilling one. "It is bad enough to suffer real prejudice, as every Negro does, without having to suffer imaginary prejudice as well . . . . In short, overemphasis on prejudice encourages the Negro to define all his troubles in racial terms."

* * *

Good, better, best
Never let it rest
Until your good is better
And your better best.

The Unheavenly City is really two books. One part—the part which drew the most criticism and provoked the most controversy—tries to debunk popular beliefs about the so-called urban crisis. The other part—a part which offers a far clearer window into Banfield's mind—is concerned with the way our society goes about defining its social problems and solving them. That is the subject Banfield has spent all of his adult life studying.

In Banfield's view, our biggest problem is that we are a nation of do-gooders. Not only that, he laments, but do-gooding has become a growth industry. If we really wanted to rid ourselves of urban riots and crime and poverty, we would resort to such drastic measures as incarcerating people likely to commit crimes and taking the offspring of poor people away from their parents. Our American democratic tradition, however, will not accept these extreme measures.

Nor will our country's do-gooding instincts accept lesser ones, Banfield complains. The idea that some people are not fit for formal education and should not be forced to waste valuable years in school, widely accepted in Europe, has no currency in this society. If our compensatory education programs do not work, the prevailing wisdom is that they are not good enough we must try, try again.

BANFIELD, Edward Christie

PHILADELPHIA INQUIRER
(Philadelphia, Penn.)

Dec. 1, 1974

These upper-class altruists who formulate these social policies are out for themselves, not the objects of their altruism. He draws an analogy to the remark about the distaste English Puritans had for bear-baiting: they opposed it not because of the suffering it caused the bear, but for the pleasure it gave the spectators. Today, he analogizes, the guilt-ridden member of the middle or upper class wants to improve the condition of the poor and downtrodden "not so much to make life better for them materially as to make himself and the whole society better off morally."

Altruism, in short, is this country's secular religion, and Banfield is not a believer. At the same time, however, he is a perceptive enough social observer to recognize that in the absence of this religion, the belief would spread that our society is not worth saving. And that, he feels, would be a far more dangerous state of affairs.

The whole of Banfield's thinking, then, deposits him unceremoniously in the darkness of a dead-end alley. The urge to reform is often counter-productive; but the absence of that urge is still worse.

Banfield himself seems to recognize his dilemma. Writing on another subject, he concluded: "In my judgment a sound program in the area of social policy would involve a radical devolution of federal activities to state and local government and, beyond that, of many public ones to competitive markets.

"Such a program is, however, incompatible with the nature of our political system, which is energized by the pressures that interests exert to get things from government. Since I believe that despite its evident faults this political system is vastly better than any practical alternative, I am in the awkward position of having to conclude that a sound program is really unsound."

What kind of man is it that does not subscribe to the religion of doing good? Richard Todd, writing about Banfield in *The Atlantic*, described him as "an alien contemporary mind (who) is able to survey the country and conclude that one of its most serious problems is the growth of an unreasonable ethic of hope and charity."

Banfield has said: "I wonder about myself. I try to feel the same things other people feel, but I don't. It seems that in everything I've done I've seen problems and no solution. So you wonder. Is that the nature of reality, or is it the personality of Edward Banfield?"

These occasional musings to the contrary notwithstanding, Banfield clearly believes his perceptions are being shaped not by his personality, but by reality.

While he admits to deriving a certain pleasure from "taking perceived truths, turning them around and looking at them in a different light," he also believes it is precisely this skeptic's perspective which makes him so qualified an observer of social reality.

"My satisfaction comes from the pure intellectual process of being an observer," he says. "That's really what its all about for me." □

Three Marias

By JORJANNA PRICE
Post Reporter
—Post photo by Manuel Chavez

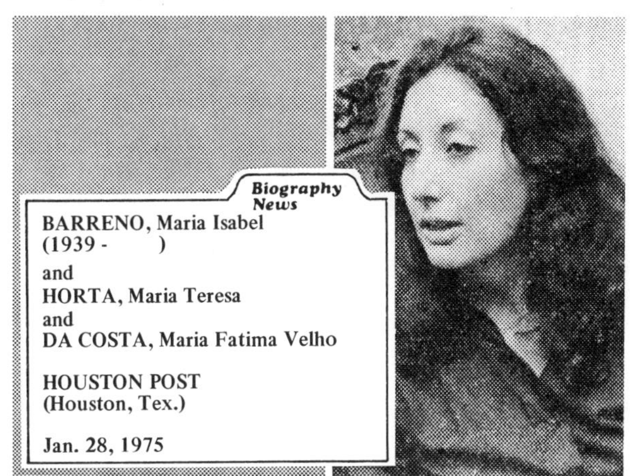

Biography News
BARRENO, Maria Isabel
(1939 -)
and
HORTA, Maria Teresa
and
DA COSTA, Maria Fatima Velho
HOUSTON POST
(Houston, Tex.)
Jan. 28, 1975

Maria Isabel Barreno

Maria Isabel Barreno is one-third of the team that published one of the most controversial feminist writings to date. Even a male reviewer has called it the best book written on the feminine condition and the frankness of the essays caused the Portuguese government to label it pornographic.

People are asking, after they read "The Three Marias: New Portuguese Letters," how did such a creative, uninhibited effort by three women come out of a country run by a dictatorship government unsympathetic to equality for women, and a society with mores very tradition bound?

Upon publication, the book was confiscated by the Portuguese government and charged as being an abuse to freedom of the press and an outrage to public decency. The authors were arrested and put through a year-long trial. In spite of the fact that news of the book was suppressed, women outside Portugal got word of the government's action and formed an international movement to protest the plight of the "three Marias" as the authors came to be known.

The story of how "New Portuguese Letters" was written and its authors freed is being told by Maria Isabel Barreno in her first tour of the United States.

The book is a compilation of letters, essays and poems the women wrote to each other trying to express their feelings about their sexuality and roles as woman, mother and wife.

It was just nine months ago, a few weeks after the overthrow of the military dictatorship, that Barreno and her co-writers were told they were free and encouraged by the judge to continue their literary efforts. forts.

Barreno, in Houston until Thursday, attributes the efforts of women outside of her country for bringing international attention to the trial and for shaking up the Portuguese government.

Because news was censored in Portugal, no one knew of the three Marias' situation until they smuggled a letter via a friend to France where a small but vigorous feminist movement had formed. French women began demonstrating on their behalf and soon others in Sweden, England and Germany took up pickets. A small group of Holland women took over the Portuguese embassy for 12 hours to press their point.

At a 1973 feminist conference in Boston, American women were told about the three Marias and that summer Houston women were picketing the Portuguese consulate.

"The Portuguese government began to know, began to hear of the effort," Barreno recalled. "From every part of the world they called Lisbon, some diplomat asking, 'But what can I do? Women here are demonstrating, passing petitions for the three Marias. The government became very upset."

The center of the furor began innocently enough. Barreno, Maria Teresa Horta and Maria Fatima Velho da Costa did not intend to write a book, they simply enjoyed intellectual discussions with each other. The three were good friends with much in common: All were in their early 30s, all were educated by nuns, all were married and the mothers of sons . . .

Barreno and da Costa worked as researchers for the National Institute for Industrial Research. Horta wrote literary reviews for a Lisbon newspaper. All of them had published books on their own.

Barreno suggested they transfer their thoughts onto paper. They agreed to meet at a home one evening and again for lunch each week. Get-togethers were somewhat "clandestine," Barreno said. "That was something the police were always looking for, meetings between people.

"We talked together a lot about when we were children, the meaning of writing, of being a woman, the oppression of women not only in Portugal but everywhere."

During the months they spent writing and comparing thoughts, new concepts opened up about themselves and women as a whole. Contrary to what society had told them, said Barreno, they found that women could work together and feel close.

"It was a very good way to work together, not only for the book but as a deep expression of what we can do together and create together. Already I was interested in feminism but only intellectually. I had the concept, but for the first time I could express what we can call sisterhood, the feeling when people are together. We really can do wonderful things."

When publishers learned that three Portuguese women had written a book, sort of a team effort, many were interested, that is, until they heard the book dealt with sexuality, politics and the oppression of women.

Finally, a woman who worked as a book advisor took the book to her boss and urged him to publish it. She argued for three months but finally the three Marias had a publisher.

The book was an immediate success. About 2,000 copies sold in the three weeks before government officials took it out of the bookstores. The women were arrested and had to borrow money from friends to raise the high cost of bail.

In the beginning, during the repeated police interrogations and the long months of waiting for the trial, it was frightening, Barreno remembers. The two working for the state department were told they would be fired if found guilty. There was the chance of a jail sentence or costly fines.

"But once the international fight began, our feelings changed completely," she said. "We were not afraid anymore. Even the government's behavior changed."

After all their experiences together, the three Marias are going different directions now and, ironically, are not as close as once.

Da Costa has dropped out of the group entirely. She never was sold on the women's movement, although during the police harassment and the trial she spoke as though she were close to adopting that philosophy. She is afraid of the bad image the movement has in Portugal, said Barreno, and believes the new government will banish the discrimination against women.

Horta is in Lisbon, continuing to write reviews and helping organize a women's movement there. New laws have been issued to guarantee women equal pay and equal opportunities with men but she still considers the system full of inequities.

Barreno recently completed a play based on the book with a Brazilian woman who helped the three Marias during their fight. While traveling this country she is recording impressions of American women she will use in future articles and she plans to finish a book she started three years ago analyzing the male-dominated culture.

While in Houston she will speak at Rice University Tuesday in 131 Biology Building at 8 p.m. and the University of Houston Wednesday at 8 p.m. in the Ft. Worth Room.

Rona Barrett

BARRETT, Rona

HOUSTON POST
(Houston, Tex.)

July 29, 1974

BY KATHY LEWIS
Today Asst. Editor

Ryan O'Neal once mailed her a tarantula.

Mia Farrow and a songwriter publicly dumped a bucket of champagne over her head.

Johnny Carson says she never has to ask for a steak knife in a restaurant—she can cut her steak with her tongue.

And at a presidential party Frank Sinatra offered a $1000 bill to anyone in sight, if they would toss her into the San Clemente swimming pool.

The woman they're all enamored with is Rona Barrett, the Hollywood gossip columnist.

Well, Rona has written an autobiography, "Miss Rona", where she supposedly tells all—only much of the embarrassing "good stuff" is about others—besides herself.

The opening line in Rona's book makes Washington's tell-all gal, Barbara Howar, sound like Mother Goose. Rona tells how one of Hollywood's top male sex symbols pleadingly propositioned her. Get this—his wife was sleeping 10-feet away.

Rona does tell of a number of propostions she's had— she describes many of them in language usually reserved for obscene phone calls—but that basically is not what the book is about. That opening line is a teaser.

It's mainly the sob story of how a fat, ugly, crippled Jewish girl finds success. (The adjectives are hers.) Rona had muscular dystrophy and as a child she once overheard the doctors say she wouldn't live another year.

The disease was arrested. Rona went on to start the Eddie Fischer fan club at age 14 and she climbed to bigger and better things—a syndicated column, fan magazines and television shows. She also moved on to a nose job, Rolls Royces and a Beverly Hills home.

Rona Barrett still isn't beautiful. But through the years she's done a number on herself. Inspite of gooey black mascaraed lashes—the look is glamorous.

When asked about the book, she says, "I just felt it was so important at this time to communicate on a totally different level. I wanted to lay my soul bear."

Rona doesn't think her book is part of the new female braggadocio. "Thousands of girls have had the same propositions made to them—males are males whether they are famous or not."

She puts down plenty of male egos in her book. During a poolside interview, she tells how Hugh O'Brian took off his swim trunks during the third question.

When asked about that episode, she sweetly says, "When Hugh looks into the mirror, he sees 3,000 Hughs. He thinks he's the only man in the world."

Rona uses some real names in the book—some are made up, these are usually her lovers. One, Mr. Washington, she describes as a cohort of Lyndon Johnson's.

"Everybody's playing a guessing game now. But I didn't do it for that reason. I just did it for legal reasons. In some cases invasion of privacy could have been claimed."

Those mentioned know who they are though. One exlover, whom she described very harshly, was only mad because she revealed his age. When his current young girlfriend found out, she exclaimed, "You're older than my father," says Rona.

Rona doesn't ignore her own ego in the book. She says she's replaced the Hedda Hoppers and Louella Parsons. "I am not like them though. They made moral judgments on the people they wrote about. I just chronicle what they do."

Rona's rules of good taste, which usually are not the same set used by the people she writes about, are this. Whatever it is—if the star is doing it publicly—it's fair game.

A couple of subjects are still touchy—drugs and homosexuality. More often than not, she avoids both. She says the cruelest thing that ever came out of Hollywood was the "false rumor" about two male personalities getting married—to each other.

"A group of Malibu homosexuals sent out phony wedding invitations.

Apparently, she doesn't consider impotency taboo. She doesn't mind telling you she thinks that's the reason for the break-up of a big Hollywood marriage.

Shs calls her big scoops—the Dyan Cannon-Cary Grant divorce, the Elvis Presley marriage, the John Lindsay party-switch. She believes people give up their private lives, when they become public figures.

"That is my whole argument. When you become a public person, you no longer are a private person. You can't use the press one day, then ask them to leave you alone the next."

Rona has a way of dropping teasers.

"Frank Sinatra dislikes women."

Then she backs up and says, "I don't mean to imply he's a homosexual, but he has no respect for women. That's why he comes out and lambasts me. "

Many of the items that once made gossip columns juicy, are now fairly tame. "The rest of the world has caught up with Hollywood. I am not saying everybody sleeps around or wife swaps, but it has become fairly commonplace. You rarely hear of paternity suits these days. In the fifties that was big stuff."

Rona was married for the first time last year. Her businessman husband, Bill Trowbridge, says of the book, "I'm proud of her. I don't think I could have been that open and honest."

Columnist Rona Barrett — She's No Hedda or Louella

By NANCY GREENBERG
Of The Bulletin Staff

YESTERDAY Rona Barrett, the syndicated television gossip columnist, was differentiating between a good news story and a crummy one.

"Barbra Streisand is your only bankable female star," she said, "so a good story might be that she was redoing the classic Judy Garland role in the remake of 'A Star Is Born.' Add to that the fact her hairdresser Jon Peters is poducing the flick, and well, you've got a real humdinger on your hands. As for a crummy story . . ."

"Tiny Tim will . . ." began Miss Barrett's husband, Bill Trowbridge, trying to be helpful.

'Really no News'

"No," Miss Barrett shook her head. "Tiny Tim's always human interest. I guess in a pinch I might say 'Robert Redford was seen walking down the street today.' Believe me, that's a big deal to some people. . . ."

Then the columnist in the platinum hair and false eyelashes looked absently across the KYW studio where she had just taped the Mike Douglas Show.

"You know," she said, "someday I'd like to get up in front of the damn TV cameras and say 'Greetings, folks. Today there really was no news.' "

The admission reflected the new candor of the 37-year-old columnist who has always been just as apt to comment on a starlet's messy housekeeping or dowdy wardrobe, as on her love life. Rona Barrett's latest scoop is Rona Barrett.

Joy of Sharing

The woman behind the magazines, "Rona Barrett's Gossip" and "Rona Barrett's Hollywood" — two publications which read exactly like they sound like they read — has discovered her own feelings and the joys of sharing them.

She has just written "Miss Rona," the autobiography which captures her childhood (fatness, ugliness, insecurity, underscored by a case of muscular dystrophy) and beyond. Beyond is mostly misery at the hands of men. It is a catalog of rejections, put-downs and one devastating break-down, ending on a quasi-upbeat note in the relationship with her present husband of 9½ months.

Higher Pinnacle

"Bill has turned out to be everything he seemed. "More," she writes in her last chapter. "But I'm still a manic-depressive. I am still someone who, no matter how high I climb, always sees a higher pinnacle."

BARRETT, Rona

PHILADELPHIA BULLETIN
(Philadelphia, Penn.)

July 12, 1974

"The pot," Miss Barrett yesterday discussed the rationale for her confessional," "could not afford to call the kettle black. Basically, I'm not a gossip, but if I'm going to pass on to the world what I hear, the world might as well know it all."

The TV personality is currently seen for 2½ minutes at the end of 50 nationwide news programs, none in Philadelphia. Her staff includes one person each in Washington and Europe, two in New York and five in Los Angeles, where she lives with her husband, a businessman from West Virginia.

Rona for Rona

Bill, a large, smiling hulk of a man explained, "I love Rona for Rona. There is a person underneath the personality. We rarely discuss gossip. In fact, if I want to know what's going on in Hollywood, I have to ask her."

"Nobody ever cared about me," said his wife. "Even the people who said, " 'Keep telling it like it is, baby,' had a need to think of me as bitchy. Nobody saw me for who I was — I wasn't just the next generation's Hedda or Louella. I was different and no one saw it.

"I am a truth-teller, not a gossip mongerer. I'll write that somebody has bad breath. I'm not interested in glamorizing the stars. I am a truth-teller and now the public will finally believe it when they see how I can write the truth about myself."

Truth Telling

In Philadelphia, Miss Barrett appeared much lower-key than she does during her tough 2½-minute segments. Dzspite heavy make-up, she was wearing a sporty three-piece outfit which looked like a navy tennis dress with a matching sweater.

Her truth-telling reached memorable heights on the television taping when a woman in the audience asked how she could reach Robert Redford and Miss Barrett walked up to her and whispered in her ear the directions to Sundance, Utah.

Then later, after discussing her break-down and rejuvenation, she smiled wanly and reported, "I don't go to as many parties as I used to . . . I've paid my dues, sweetheart."

Return of The Native

Story by MARK BOWDEN

John Barth disproves the notion that the typical 20th Century novelist is a social outcast or wild eccentric accessible only to friends and a handful of literary associates.

He started his writing and teaching career at Johns Hopkins in 1952, and after 22 years, six novels and a National Book Award he's back and apparently willing to talk to anyone he can squeeze into his schedule. He accepted a full professorship in the Hopkins English department last summer, taught a creative writing seminar during the fall semester and in January began a sabbatical year — part of the package that lured him back to his alma mater.

He is tall, almost gangly, but built solidly. His conversation is as loose and comfortable as his clothing — which is often a sweater and corduroy pants. "Bald as a roc's egg" (Barth's description of his persona in "Chimera"), except for the sides and back, with a bushy moustache and plastic glasses, Barth's appearance is as striking as his prose, but considerably less calculated.

He started teaching — a profession he says he's just as serious about as writing — while he was a graduate student in Hopkins' writing seminar. After receiving his master's degree he joined the faculty at Penn State, where he taught creative writing. In 1965 he moved on to the State University of New York at Buffalo, and in 1971 to Boston University.

"I have always been a full-time teacher as well as a writer," Barth says. "I find that teaching keeps me in touch with the world, and gives me the reassurance of a regular schedule.

"The academic life is a good one for a writer to live. All of my friends who decided to make a living in journalism, say, and do their own work in their spare time, found news work so exhausting in itself that they never had enough energy to work after hours.

"My teaching doesn't put so much pressure on me that I can't do my own work; in fact, it and my own work feed each other. And it frees me from financial pressures. Some contemporary writers, like John Updike, are under the gun to produce a commercially successful book every two or three years. I don't think I could write well under that sort of pressure."

Barth is a Marylander. Born and raised in Cambridge, he often uses the Eastern Shore as a setting for his novels. He even managed to work it into the mythical settings of his latest novel, "Chimera." "The Soft-Weed Factor," one of Barth's most ambitious and successful books, weaves a fictional history of Ebenezer Cooke — a contemporary of Capt. John Smith — into the history of Maryland's colonization.

Barth's father, John Jacob, was a judge in the Dorchester County Juvenile Court who found the time to run a small candy store called Whitey's.

"He started stocking paperback books when they first came out," Barth remembers, "and the family policy was that we could take the new books home and read them before they were put on the shelf as long as we didn't ruin them. I used to bring them home by the carton, and read them all. Mystery stories and adventure novels formed the bulk, but there was an occasional Dos Passos or Faulkner thrown in. It wasn't until much later though, that I recognized the few gems I had read among the piles of popular fiction: Dos Passos' 'U. S. A.,' for example, and Faulkner's 'Sanctuary.' "

Literature was then only a pastime for young Barth; his real passion was jazz. He played drums in a jazz band when he was in high school, and went to the Juilliard School of Music in New York the summer after graduation. But his plans for a musical career were dashed when he discovered that his talents didn't measure up to those of his classmates.

"I had to face up to it," he recalls. "It wasn't that painful, or even courageous, just dismaying and unequivocal." That fall he entered Hopkins on a scholarship.

Hopkins had a shaping influence on Barth. "I was fortunate enough to fall under the influence of three men, first-rate scholars and teachers, to whom I owe much of the way I look at things," Barth recalls. "George Boas, who still lives nearby Hopkins, was a philosophy professor who really formed my first definite ideas about art, literature and any number of things. I know that I find myself imitating Boas in my own lectures without even thinking about it.

"Another big influence was the late Leo Spitzer (a world-famous Austrian philologist who taught at Hopkins for 19 years). Pedro Salinas, though I had no idea at the time that he was the fine old Spanish poet he was, gave me a sense of nobilitity of a life spent in passionate dedication to literature. He was the first real live writer I had ever met."

But perhaps the most powerful influence the years at Hopkins had on Barth's future came outside the classroom.

"When I was an undergraduate here," he explains, "Hopkins was nice enough to let me file books in the library to earn money. Most ➡

"I think writing has gotten progressively more difficult for me," says John Barth, after six novels and a National Book Award. "I unconsciously set more and more complicated tasks for myself."

Photo by FRED G. KRAFT, JR.

BARTH, John (Simmons) (1930-)
NEWS–AMERICAN (Baltimore, Md.)
Mar. 31, 1974
[See also CA-1]

(Continued from preceding page)
of the time that meant having someone tell you to go back in the stacks and look busy. I worked over in the classics and oriental seminary stacks, and it was the long hours of reading back there that gave me my real literary education. I read mythology and folklore, and the old tale cycles like 'The Arabian Nights.'

"Another great source of liberal education was my job at the Chevy plant. I worked nights in the timekeeper's office and usually managed to get all my work done in about and hour and a half. There were no managers around that late, so I spent my time reading."

In his junior year Barth took a creative writing course that convinced him he wanted to be a writer, "even though the work I did for it was quite bad . . . If I look back at the things I wrote then and compare them, say, to the work a good first-year student turns in to me now, well, I was writing just barely C and D stuff. But by my senior year I was writing somewhat better.

"I knew by the time I graduated that writing was the main thing I cared about, and the only way I could think of to do it was to come back to Hopkins as a graduate student and teaching assistant. One often chooses a vocation out of a sort of impassioned lack of alternatives. That seems to be the way it is with most of my friends who write. You just don't see yourself doing any of the things other people do with their vocational time."

On writing days Barth is usually behind a desk in his Guilford home by 8 a.m. He carefully researches and outlines what he plans to write beforehand, and then composes the narrative in longhand inside an old Johns Hopkins folder that he bought at the university bookstore when he was an undergraduate. When he writes, Barth wears wax earplugs. He originally used them to shut out the sounds of a noisy household, but now they shut out the drone of traffic on Charles Street. His three children, all from his first marriage, are grown, and his wife Sheila is off early to teach senior English at St. Timothy's, so Barth works uninterrupted until early afternoon, or until he simply gets tired of sitting still.

"I use the old Hemingway trick of stopping while I still have my momentum," he says. "That way there's no trouble picking up on it the next day. I try never to stop when I'm stuck."

His fiction is not so much an impassioned emotional statement as a calculated plot to amuse and instruct. "The Sot-Weed Factor" is written in the style of a late 18th Century novel: lengthy, verbose, with an incredibly complicated plot that features such age-old fictional devices as mistaken identity, kidnappings and sea voyages. "Giles Goat-Boy," published five years later, is narrated by a computer, and its plot seems to have been constructed by one as well.

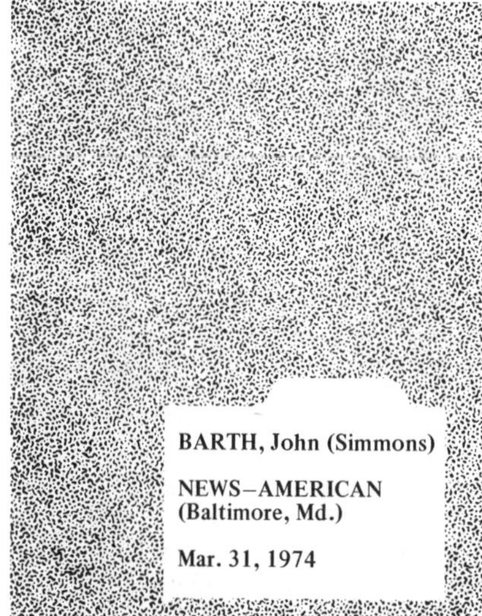
BARTH, John (Simmons)

NEWS-AMERICAN (Baltimore, Md.)

Mar. 31, 1974

Barth attacks his notions methodically; he is a master craftsman of a novelist with a wild imagination and an intensely satirical eye.

"I think writing has gotten progressively more difficult for me," he says, "because I consciously set more and more complicated tasks for myself. Perhaps this is because life seems much more complicated and multi-faceted to me in my 40's than it did when I was 30, and 20. My perception of the world around me gets more and more difficult to express, and my writing reflects it. Also I like to think that each one of my novels has been built on the one before it, and each task has been harder to execute.

"Now I find myself striving to cut through this ever-widening complexity to a sort of sweet simplicity — at least an attempt; you can get away with it if you're old enough. That was part of what I was trying to do in 'Chimera.' It's not uncommon to see a good artist get more difficult and obscure as he gets older. I would like to go the other way."

One critic has called Barth "the best writer of fiction we have at present, and one of the best we have ever had."

Barth's own favorites include; foreign authors Calvino ("Cosmicomics") and Gabriel Garcia Marquez ("100 Years of Solitude"), and five American contemporaries. "I admire John Hawkes and William Gass; Richard Brautigan is imaginative and thoughtful; and I enjoy Donald Barthelme's work and Thomas Pynchon's. Pynchon is one contemporary writer. I can read, enjoy, and come away with no clear idea of how he does it. His detailed knowledge of so many different things, from archeology to the least significant detail, is almost unbelievable."

Wondering aloud what he would have done with the last twenty years if he hadn't chosen to be a writer, Barth says, "If I were reincarnated with a whole new life to lead, and literature were excluded as a possibility, I think I would like to spend a life absolutely in the world. As it is my energies and activities are directed mainly toward projects of the imagination. It would be interesting to live a life where all my energy and activity would be directed outwardly, say in law or politics, and see how much I could accomplish.

Then he adds in all seriousness, "It would also be agreeable to be a ski bum."

John Barth, though he might look gawky poised at the top of a snow-covered slope, could probably coast through anything he chose to. do on the strength of his personality. He's just like his books — you just can't put him down.

Kin of Stowe Continues Fight

By CHET FULLER
Staff Photo—Bill Mahan

With his aging face framed by a striking white beard and the long strands of white hair on his head, he looks like something out of Biblical times.

John Beecher, the great-great nephew of the Abolitionists Henry Ward Beecher and Harriet Beecher Stowe, at 70 years old has seen a lot of America. He has seen her at her best and his bony chest would swell with pride.

He has seen her at her rock-bottom worst and it has made him ashamed that she could be so cruel.

Through it all, in his own way, he has worked and worked to make America better.

Beecher has been a journalist, novelist, publisher, civil rights activist, resettlement worker during the Depression, New Deal administrator under President Roosevelt, merchant seaman, college professor, rancher and poet.

Born in New York City in 1904, but moving with his family to Birmingham, Ala., three years later, he has spent his life championing unpopular causes, turning out fire-edged poems and work songs that have been the cries of the downtrodden.

He is no ordinary poet. He is no ordinary man and his long eventful life has been, by no means, ordinary.

Beecher has seen men beaten down by 12-hour shifts in Alabama steel mills where he worked as a boy and where he kept returning "to stay in touch with reality."

He has seen black sharecroppers when they tried to hide from attacks of the Ku Klux Klan. He watched the civil rights protests of the sixties along with the riots, and the moon landings of seventies.

He has kept a close eye on the changing face of this country and he has recorded the changes in his tough, compassionate poems.

"Birmingham was the toughest town in this country when I was growing up through the 1920s," Beecher says.

"I remember the time a railroad conductor there murdered his wife and children and threw them in the lake.

"Then he had the gumption to ride back through town on the train with his new woman. The people pulled him off the train and were going to lynch him but the town sheriff was a tough bird.

"He mowed down a bunch of the leading citizens with a Gatling gun he set up on top of the courthouse.

BEECHER, John [See also CA-5/6]
(1904 -)
ATLANTA JOURNAL Aug. 22, 1974
(Atlanta, Georgia)

"The others ran in horror. The next morning, the sheriff took the man out in front of the courthouse and hung him legally."

There was the time Beecher was blacklisted for nine years during the McCarthy era because he refused to sign a loyalty oath, which was found unconstitutional by the Supreme Court 17 years later.

But, at the time, 1950, he was fired from his job as a sociology professor at a California college because he refused to sign the oath.

He kept on writing poems, and when nobody would print them, he taught himself to print and did it himself.

Though he has paid his dues, he is still worried about the way this country is headed.

"I see impending catastrophe," he says, crossing his legs at the ankle so that the soles of his golf shoes with the spikes missing show.

"It is the same thing I saw before the Great Depression in 1929. I was in New York recently and saw elderly people on fixed incomes turning to pet foods to survive.

"The unemployment of black youth is out of all reason. How long can this go on without an explosive situation? They expect to live like human beings, too. But they have no chance for training or jobs.

"And white kids are very unenthusiastic about the kinds of jobs they can get. They're fed up with suburbia, but they don't have any concrete means of getting out of the rat race, only dreams.

"President Ford is the very essence of mediocrity at a time when we need genius and imagination," Beecher says.

"I'm sure he's good to his wife and kids and is kind to animals, but we need more than that. What have we got to look forward to? The stock market is like 1929. It's in a greater decline than it looks, because inflation masks it.

"And we're still turning out nuclear bombs and submarines, while cutting back help to orphans, widows, the blind and the poor. We can't afford them."

Beecher says the only things wants to do now with the time he has left is finish his autobiography and "leave a nest egg" for his wife, who he says is 21 years younger than he. "I've been married several times," he says.

The famous American poet William Carlos Williams has called him "a man who speaks for the conscience of the people."

Beecher has published nine volumes of poetry. His latest is "Collected Poems, 1924-1974," published by Macmillan.

He Calls Himself a Poet

By ROBERT STEINBROOK

AN AUTHENTIC American folk hero walked into The Bulletin's offices the other day.

John Beecher has been a steel worker, a rancher, a journalist, a printer, a chicken farmer, a New Deal administrator, a World War II seaman and a professor of English and sociology. But if you asked, he would call himself a poet.

He has fought injustices in Southern steel mills, served on the first integrated ship in the U.S. Navy, and been blacklisted for refusing to sign a California loyalty oath. But most importantly, he has captured in his poetry the stories and the language of America's common people, be they black or white.

Recently, Macmillan Co. published Beecher's "Collected Poems 1924-1974" and the author is finally getting a recognition denied him for the last 50 years. "If you have longevity, you may live to see yourself understood," he told an audience at the University of Alabama last March. Beecher is 70.

Birmingham, Ala., where Beecher spent most of his youth and first cast himself in a social activist role, declared last May 1 Beecher Day, and made him an honorary citizen of the town.

And within the academic and literary communities, some throw around superlatives like "the best poet the South has ever produced."

But not many years ago, Beecher recalls, he was viewed as a "demon with horns and a long tail" throughout the South, guilty of "high crimes and misdemeanors" for his championship of integration and workers' rights.

Beecher has written poems of everyday life, its injustices, its tribulations, its glories. He has written in the language of the people he writes about, eschewing indirection and metaphor to the chagrin of many critics unable to confront his poems on their own terms.

While Beecher's poems are often angry and violent, they are more fundamentally dedicated to a sense of love and trust necessary for the preservation of the original American ideals. He speaks of courage, freedom and human dignity as part of a continuing American revolution.

If a person ever was cut out for a lifetime of social radicalism, Beecher was. On his father's side, he was descended from Harriet Beecher Stowe, author of "Uncle Tom's Cabin." And on his mother's side he was descended from Irish nationalists. His grandfather was one of the original Molly McGuires, who dressed in women's clothes and used their shillelaghs to deal summary justice to British tax collectors.

Beecher's father, however, was a steel company executive in Birmingham, and his son's youthful ambition was to be president of United States Steel.

But that changed quickly. After Beecher was kicked out of the Virginia Military Institute at the age of 16 for refusing to inform on his roommates, his father found him a job in the open hearth furnaces of his steel mills.

Beecher recalls he was "fascinated with metallurgical processes involved in making

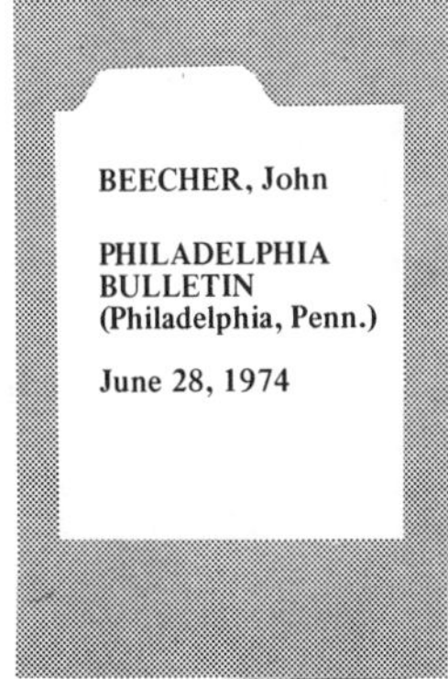

BEECHER, John

PHILADELPHIA BULLETIN
(Philadelphia, Penn.)

June 28, 1974

steel" but "indignant at the way people were treated there."

After a year studying engineering at Cornell, Beecher returned to the mills as a summer job. "Spontaneously, I started to write," he says. "I hadn't even heard of Marx or Lenin, but violent and revolutionary poems started coming out."

Some of his earlier poems are among his best. His "Report to the Stockholders" tells everything the board of directors never wanted in their annual report. His "In Egypt's Land," a long and moving narrative of a 1932 sharecropper's revolt in Alabama, captures much of the meaning of the civil rights movement.

Nearly a half-century later, now a visiting scholar at Duke University and hard at work on his autobiography, Beecher believes he hasn't changed "but the country has."

He notes that a dean he taught with at a black college in Alabama is now sitting on Birmingham's City Council. Of the South he says, "I find less racism down there than I do up here. The black man is not so frightening to the white man in the South because they have lived side by side all their lives."

For his vision of the good society, Beecher turns to the integrated ship he served on during World War II.

"It was a floating democracy, the kind of world we could have if men were free to develop all their potentialities."

By Clifford Terry

CONFESSIONS Of a Soap Opera Writer

Every day, Monday through Friday and sometimes on weekends, William J. Bell works himself up into a lather.

Bill Bell, with some justification, might object to that statement. He is the head writer for two network daytime television serials, and another little dig at the soap opera is, admittedly, somewhat gratuitous. They have been called dishpan dramas, washboard weepers and Procter & Gamble pap, and have otherwise been mocked with as much glee as front-yard plastic flamingos. In a series in *The New Yorker* about 25 years ago, James Thurber wrote of their radio predecessors: "A soap opera is a kind of sandwich. . . Between thick slices of advertising spread 12 minutes of dialogue, add predicament, villainy and female suffering in equal measure, throw in a dash of nobility, sprinkle with tears, season with organ music, cover with a rich announcer sauce and serve five times a week."

Their creators are quick to come to their defense. Irna Phillips, the Dowager of Duz, who has been responsible for such programs as *The Guiding Light, Another World* and *As the World Turns,* once stated in a magazine: "The truth is that every woman's life is a soap opera, and the inside story of every family would make a daytime serial. When people ask me why soap opera doesn't ever deal with a good, wholesome American family that isn't always in trouble, my answer is, 'Name two!' "

Bell also has heard it all. "I don't mind them being called 'soap operas.' It's such a generic term. Although we *do* prefer the more uplifting 'dramatic serials.' But then there's the cliche reaction by people who never watch the shows. It gets a little annoying, but after a number of years. . . Hell, I couldn't care less. Of course, everyone thinks you kill off someone every other day. I *did* have a death on *Days of Our Lives* earlier this year, and that was the first time in five or six years. I don't like to do it, but in this case it opened up the story. And God knows, death is a very real thing in living."

Besides NBC's *Days,* which he has been writing for eight years, he is also the co-creator (with his wife, TV show hostess Lee Phillips) and head writer of *The Young and the Restless,* the newest serial entry, which was launched by CBS last March.

Bell himself would be poor material for a daytime character. After all, how tormented can someone be whose favorite word is "nifty"?

For another thing, he isn't a doctor (even though he was, interestingly, a pre-med student). Neither is he a lawyer nor a small-town newspaper editor-publisher. On the soaps, if you're none of the above, chances are you're the town degenerate. Which also would be miscasting. A soft-spoken, gracious man of 45, Bell looks disgustingly clean-cut and youthful.

BELL, William J.
MIAMI HERALD
(Miami, Fla.)
Jan. 27, 1974

Bell is sitting in the study of his luxurious apartment, sipping coffee and keeping part of his attention on *Love of Life,* which is working things out on his color TV set. He is also reflecting about the Writers Guild of America strike that dragged on through the spring and summer of 1973, and the dialogue that was handled by non-union writers.

"The ratings went down during that period," he laments. "The caliber of the writing was pretty bad, the dialogue horribly diluted. Writing serials is a very abstract thing for many people to understand. Sometimes I have to sit at my typewriter for an hour or so before I can really crawl inside my characters. Each is as close to you as your family. You completely control their destinies: it's almost God-like. And suddenly, with the strike, your little family was removed from you. They were doing things and saying things that came as quite a shock."

Love of Life finishes up, and *The Young and the Restless* comes to bat. According to a Screen Gems press release, the serial combines "man-woman chemistry, young people and music." It deals with two families living in a Midwestern community, Genoa City (named after a town near the Bells' weekend home in Lake Geneva), and the head of one of them is, not surprisingly, a newspaper publisher. Stuart Brooks has four daughters, one of whom, Chris, is dating a member of the other family, the Fosters, whose nickname, heaven help us, is Snapper. Snapper, of course, is a medical student. Into the lives of the Brookses and the Fosters enters "a rather mysterious individual" named Brad Eliot, who, back in Chicago, is believed to be dead. (The mugger who bashed him was himself killed in the car he stole from Brad, and their identities were confused.) Brad Eliot's occupation back in Chicago: a neurosurgeon.

"It's very cliche to have the audience learn he really is a doctor," Bell admits good-naturedly. "But medicine and the law provide the most fertile ground for us, as opposed to something like the business world. Incidentally, I checked out the whole thing about the accident. About why someone couldn't identify the dead man from his teeth. It turns out that it's difficult to be positive if there's extreme facial damage. I don't blueprint all of that in the show, of course; it gets to be a little ugly.

"All three networks and Procter & Gamble were after me a long time to do another serial. On shows like *Days of Our Lives* — which is a successful, nifty program — we deal with families who are middle- and upper-class. Here, we have a very poor family, the Fosters. The father deserted them, the mother works in a factory — a tired woman but very nifty. I'm trying to do something different with them. I want to get

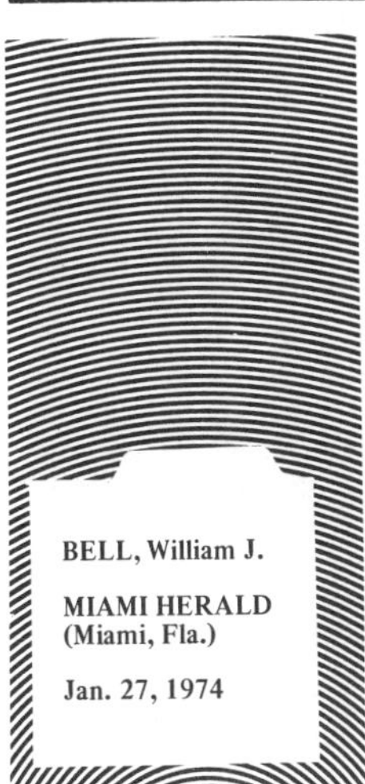
BELL, William J.

MIAMI HERALD (Miami, Fla.)

Jan. 27, 1974

(Continued from preceding page)

away from the melodrama, the enormous trauma, which has caused serials to be so caricatured."

Bell also says he is using music as a dramatic outlet, rather than just an organ-trilling segue to the commercials.

Perhaps a far more important reason for the new show, rather than displaying a family with less money and a script with more music, is the chance to help turn around the network's soap-opera image. "CBS has just kind of coasted along," writer Agnes (*One Life to Live*) Nixon once said. "Their audience has been getting older. They've been getting the Geritol crowd." Bell agrees that the CBS shows were starting to get old hat, that the characters were getting older, the young viewers couldn't identify, and this key consumer group (in their 20s and 30s) started switching over to the game shows.

"But CBS did research, and they were afraid of *young* in the title. There was some pressure to change it. Some thought the show was about hippies. Notice, however, that it is *The Young and the Restless* — not *The Young and Restless.* To me, 'restless' is an ageless word."

After Bell has checked his program and caught a little of *Search for Tomorrow,* he moves down the block to the neighborhood lunch counter where he stays roughly from *As the World Turns* to *Another World.*

"Many of the people who think daytime serials are mundane are the ones who are never exposed to them," he resumes over a martini on the rocks. "A lot of the shows are darn good. Maybe some *aren't* true to life. Personally, I hate melodrama. 'Dropping bombs,' I call it. I do not write melodrama.

"I think the appeal is that the serial offers a continuing story. You get to know these people as well as your best friend. You see them at their most intimate moments. Ideally, it's both identification with the characters — who must seem real — and a certain amount of escapism.

"For many years the underlying psychology was to write the episodes so that if you missed some, it wouldn't matter because the plot would be summarized. Many feel you should watch on Fridays, because that's when everything happens. I don't go in for repetition. I want to have something important happen in each episode, so that the viewer can't watch it casually every other day. Also, if you condense what happened previously, it sounds pretty trite. That's true of any literary work — whether the writer be Bill Bell, Irna Phillips or William Shakespeare.

"For instance, on *Days,* Laura conceived a child by her husband's brother. She was seduced by him, and it turned out later that her husband was sterile. Now, on face value, that sounds very sordid and immoral. But it was really fascinating. There really was love between these two people. And it was a story that made *Days of Our Lives.* About eight million people moved over from other programs. Later I got a six-page letter from some woman — as we seem to do with any sophisticated or unusual story — saying that it was *her* story and giving me all the intimate facts."

With the serials so preoccupied with murder, adultery, envy, hatred, malice and all uncharitableness, there is little time for anything else, such as race relations, government corruption, creeping pornography, higher bus fares, the price of hamburger, the energy crisis or tainted tuna fish.

Bell says he has been allowed to do the stories he wanted to with one exception — an interracial marriage. Obviously, though, he and other writers know what is expected of them by the sponsors and the audience, just as an editor of *Screw* wouldn't run Betty Crocker recipes. "I don't care what you're doing — maybe short of incest — it's how flagrant or not you are," Bell insists. "Politics? We have 10 shows in the can in advance, so even if you wanted to, you couldn't be that current. Besides, there are newspapers and TV news programs. Who am I, a storyteller, to subject an audience to more?"

With an occasional exception, the women on soap operas are housewives, more interested in schleping cookies than chasing a career. Those who do venture forth are often admonished by their husbands, as the serials — in their own hesitant manner — probe the psyches of male chauvinists. On *Search for Tomorrow,* a lawyer grouses, "I just can't get used to my wife working." On *Return to Peyton Place,* a husband suggests that his wife have another baby and give up running a local inn. "This place makes me feel alive," she protests. "I think you're jealous because this is important to me."

Such dialogue is unusual; sexism is another topic shunned by the soaps, which predictably has brought a rap by women libbers. Bell ponders the charge, then neatly skirts it: "I certainly think the liberated woman is very fascinating. I also think that to go totally that way on the serials is a mistake because most women are liberated in their own way — but it is a traditional way."

Besides avoiding controversy and biting the General Foods that feed them, soap-opera writers also have the problem of personnel changes. Performers die, take vacations, get pregnant — just last year, the actress who played Susan on *Days of Our Lives* switched to *General Hospital* for more money (and perhaps a neurosurgeon to be named at a later date).

Other times, the writer might decide that a performance is unsatisfactory, the actor is written out of the script, and a few weeks later the old character comes back — with a brand-new face. This brings a temporary big protest from those at home, but as one producer has remarked: "Our faithful viewers are a breed apart. They accept the ludicrous with the good, because they believe in the story."

Bill Bell himself became a believer as a schoolboy, when he'd go home for lunch and tune in *Our Gal Sunday, The Romance of Helen Trent* and *Life Can Be Beautiful.* He wrote in the early '50s, then switched to advertising (winding up as account executive for Sara Lee) but decided to drop cheesecake in favor of spicier fare. He joined up with Irna Phillips for 10 years, helping to write *The Guiding Light, As the World Turns, Another World* and *Our Private World.*

He switches over to a Bloody Mary and to what he considers irresponsible criticism of his trade. "Daytime is more than just sitting down and watching a show. My stance has always been, gosh, anyone who wants to review it, great, but please never on the basis of one show. It takes a week before an audience or a critic can see what these characters are all about, their interweaving stories, their dimensions.

"The cliche I keep hearing that really drives me up the wall is that we write down to the audience, to a 12-year-old mentality. People who perpetuate that belief are morons. That's just stupid. No one consciously writes to any level."

But this, too, he can shrug off. Not only is the money good — top writers reportedly earn six-figure incomes — but what you write is what you see.

"For a creative person, there is nothing else where, each day, what you've written comes to life. Imagine, beyond the money, the fulfillment that you feel. It can be good, or it can kill you if you compromise and let crap go through. There are some bad days when I talk back to the show, when I get physically upset. It comes back to haunt you. It's going to kick you right in the teeth. And it hurts. Oh Christ, it hurts."

They Just Sat and Talked — Suddenly It Was Best Seller

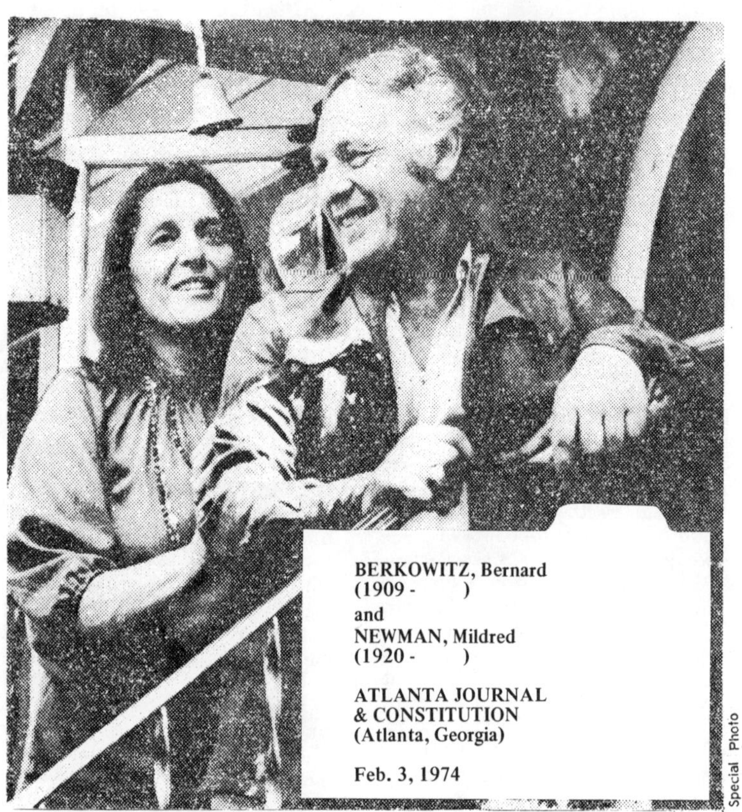

MILDRED NEWMAN, BERNARD BERKOWITZ SHARE THEIR JOYS
Without Intending to Write Book at All, They Now Have Best Seller

By EDITH HILLS COOGLER
Atlanta Journal Women's Editor

In this time of fuel shortage, the warmest place to be is within talking distance of Dr. Bernard Berkowitz and Mildred Newman.

They put out a glow like a Coleman stove.

This is incongruous because both are psychoanalysts, and it's a well-known fact that psychoanalysts and Brink's trucks just don't show what's inside.

VISITING ATLANTA, this husband and wife team explained how they just happened to write a 56-page best seller without even trying. Their book "How to be Your Own Best Friend" (Random House. $4.95.) has been a top seller across the nation for an eternity of weeks.

Part of the success of this slim volume of self-help is the fact that it actually is helping people—"Changed my life for the better!" That sort of response. But part of it is something the average reader couldn't know: The book is an extension of two perfectly attuned personalities.

Unlike Thoreau's observation about "most men," these two lead lives of quiet joy. In their marriage they are almost literally one person in the sense that she starts a sentence, he supplies the middle, and she contributes the end. There is no sense of interruption. Conversation flows smoothly, as if one person were talking.

They rarely use the first person singular. It's "we" most of the time.

"WE HAVE a very good friend, Jean Owen, who is a professional writer, and she was going to interview us and write a magazine article. She just asked questions—we had no idea she could do shorthand—and she kept saying, 'This is too good for a magazine article!'

"We were excited about what we were saying. We spent three days and three nights together in the country. It was just casual. Jean took books and books of notes, and just kind of organized and reorganized our philosophy and point of view that we had built up through the years.

"We paid a free-lance editor to edit it, but she squeezed out all the feeling. We said, 'Thank you, but no thanks.' And we took all her changes out.

"WE REALIZED that we didn't want anybody to touch it and change it and make all those 'wonderful' corrections, so we put our money into publishing it ourselves. It took all the cash we had—$20,000 for 20,000 copies.

"That was in 1971, and we had a distribution problem. The wife of a friend began to distribute the books right out of her own garage. So slowly we began to sell at first, then it became a sort of underground best seller."

Eventually they met a reader who told them that they really needed an agent, and who recommended a good one. Their agent arranged for established publishing houses to submit bids on the book.

"By then we were in a position to say, 'You can have this book, but you can't change even a comma in it.' Of course, Random House won with a $60,000 advance."

WHAT was in it for Jean Owen who made all those notes, and conveyed their sympathetic advice with admirable clarity to readers? At the start of it all, they were going to pay her $250, but . . .

"We told Jean, 'You can have the $250, if you'd like, but we know it's going to be a best seller, and you'd be better off to wait with us and take 20 per cent. You want to buy that house in the country? You're going to be able to buy that house in the country."

Jean now has the house in the country.

"We have given away 35 per cent of our 60 per cent to friends and our children—between this and Uncle Sam, we don't have much left, but that's all right. We're enjoying it."

Although the money isn't important to them, they revel in the letters from readers. They cherish those letters. You can't take those letters away from them for the simple reason that they've memorized the letters. Beaming at each other and at you, they will recite the letters.

Their favorite came from the vice president of a tie company, and never mind the cliche, "I would like to shout from rooftops how good this book is. But I went out and bought 35 copies and gave one to each of my salesmen, hoping that it would help them as much as it helped me."

THE BOOK consists of somewhat negative questions and opinions followed by reassuring, constructive replies. Here are a few examples of the authors' advice:

Happiness doesn't just come to you. You have to seek it. It's really inside yourself. Find the good things in yourself; appreciate yourself. Live up to your potential because you've got one. Don't put off doing the things you want to do. If you do something you're ashamed of, forgive yourself. You have in you the ability to treasure each moment of life.

And this time Miss Newman alone spoke (it'll be his turn next time), "I don't think most people need help, but I think many people do. The important thing is to be together with yourself. You can get together with yourself with help, or without it.

"To know who you are and what you need, and to be true to yourself is very, very important."

MILTON BERLE:

He made America cry 'Uncle' when he was 'Mr. TV'

By RICHARD CHRISTIANSEN

In 1948, when those four singers dressed in Texaco uniforms stepped onstage of the National Broadcasting Company's Studio 6B in New York, the revolution really began.

Surely you remember 1948, don't you? Well, perhaps not. That was 26 years ago, a generation or so back, and for many of you, it is now just a matter of history. But for those of us who were around then, 1948 was the year we discovered television, and the man who showed it to us was Milton Berle.

He was dubbed "Mr. Television" in those days, and nobody ever deserved the title more. Other popular shows (such as "Kukla, Fran and Ollie") and preceded him, and in future years there were to be more popular shows (such as "I Love Lucy"). But it was Berle who led the parade and brought television into our living rooms.

Indeed, we made him a part of the family. We called him Uncle Miltie.

In those early days of TV, Berle's "Texaco Star Theater," a one-hour show put together with comics, guest stars, crazy costumes, juggling acts, tap dancers and the omnipresent antics of Uncle Miltie, convinced hundreds of thousands of Americans that perhaps it was worth investing in a new television set.

* * *

With his manic energy, Berle literally swept the country, offering raucous, outlandish entertainment. It was primitive, oldtime vaudeville, but it was fun, and it demonstrated that television could provide us with something fresher than old British movies and panel quiz shows.

On Tuesday, Berle's night, movie theaters and nightclubs shut down. Appliance stores were jammed with customers who watched the show on demonstration sets — and then bought one of their own. A coin-laundry owner put in a TV set and advertised, "watch Berle while you wash."

And in Detroit, the water level in the city's reservoirs took a drastic drop from 9 to 9:05 P.M., when viewers, having finished watching Berle's show, went to their bathrooms.

Not everybody liked him. When I mentioned to a television director that I was planning a story on Milton Berle, he said, "Good lord, why? he's such a ham. I never liked him when he had that show anyway."

* * *

As a matter of fact, I wasn't that wild about him myself. His program never had the polish or wit of the old "Your Show of Shows," with Sid Caesar. It was much too crude, too corny.

But one week, on a visit to New York, I attended a Berle show in which a minor disaster occurred. It wasn't as bad as the time when Ella the elephant had dumped all over the stage in the middle of her act, but it was bad enough. The studio sound system went off for about 20 minutes of the show. Berle, left without a working microphone, had to mug crazily and pull out every kind of visual shtick he could think of in order to keep the show rolling.

He handled it beautifully, like the veteran vaudevillian he was, and when the program at last was off the air, he told the studio audience how sorry he was about the incident, and, for compensation, he gave them a few minutes of his best stand-up comedy routines. One had to admire the professionalism of an old pro.

In many respects, the new book, "Milton Berle: an autobiography" (Delacorte Press, $8.95) merits that same admiration.

* * *

Though written with the considerable aid of a professional writer, Haskel Frankel, the book is filled with gaucheries and crudities, making it read at times like true confessions. This is particularly true in those episodes recreating the blazing romance between Berle and "Linda Smith" (a phony name Berle uses to conceal the woman's real identity), the actress who bore their son — when she was married to another man, a Hollywood producer.

Take this exchange, for example, drawn from one of their bedroom scenes:

"Linda broke the silence. 'So, say something. What happens next with us?'

"I slipped an arm around her. 'We go on," I said. 'We make pictures and we make love. And that's us for now.' "

One senses, however, that, though such episodes may be embarrassing and banal, they reflect true Berle, an attempt by the author to exorcise all the old sins.

* * *

Of course, the book has plenty of very funny anecdotes culled from Berle's 61 years in vaudeville, theater, films and television. (There's an especially choice tale of how comedian William Demarest figured out a delightfully obscene method of wreaking vengeance on a talking bird act that was ruining his own routine).

But the overriding atmosphere of the book is one of pain. It's masochistic and exhibitionistic, perhaps, but genuinely felt nonetheless.

Berle lashes out at many persons who, he believes, did him wrong, including Al Jolson, a supreme egotist, and Frank Fay, the comedian whom Berle says he once flattened with a stage brace because of Fay's anti-Semitic remarks.

But the self-flagellation is worst of all. Berle hits himself for his addiction to gambling, for the failure of his two marriages to blonde showgirl Joyce Mathews, for the despicable way he sometimes treated his family and friends, for the consuming ambition that made him step on his fellow workers. He even tells us about his nose job and ugly feet (hammertoes).

He tells us that his father, Moses Berlinger, a sad, ineffectual man, was unable to hold a steady job and support his family. So it was Milton, who had won a Charlie Chaplin lookalike contest when he was 5, who soon became the breadwinner.

He was born in Harlem, not in a trunk. Yet by the time he was 13, he had already appeared in several movies including "Tillie's Punctured Romance," (with Chaplin) and he had his own act on the vaudeville circuit.

At 12, he had his first sex with a showgirl who whisked him into her dressing room for a quickie.

There were to be many women in Berle's life — chorus girls, starlets, secretaries and even the evangelist, Aimee Semple McPherson.

But the woman who dominated his life was Mama. Always Mama.

* * *

It was Mama who lugged him around from theater to theater, leaving her other three sons and a daughter at home with Papa. It was Mama who saw that he got the bookings. It was Mama who was forever out front in the audience, leading the laughter for his act. It was Mama who procured the girls for him when he was a teenager.

She was the essential showbiz stage mother, a woman who, out of love and vanity and desire, fulfilled her own quest for the limelight through her son.

Berle writes about her with a classic sense of love, hate, guilt and pride. To his friends in vaudeville, she became known as Queenie, the ruler of her son's world. She knew everybody in or connected with the business, including gangsters, and Milton even wondered if she could order a "hit" through her friendships in the mob. But he never asked her about it.

* * *

Sarah Berlinger, a former store detective, was amazing in her single-minded attention to her son's career.

She became so skilled in laughing it up for Milton's jokes that she had a cue sheet that noted when to start her high-pitched giggle for the jokes in his routine. Once, near the end of his monolog, he noticed that Mama was slamming her purse against a man in the audience who, she later said, was trying to molest her. When Milton asked her why she hadn't caused a disturbance earlier and thus stopped the man's advances, she replied, "I didn't want to miss my cues."

When she took a phone call from her son in a crowded hotel lobby, she would pick up the receiver and ask, in a loud voice, so that everybody could hear, "Is this my son, Milton Berle?"

Those were funny incidents, of course, but to Milton Berle, now 66 and looking back on his life with Mama, the whole thing seems terribly sad.

* * *

Here he is, for example, writing about himself when he was at the top of the heap in vaudeville — and desperately unhappy:

"The papers still wrote feature articles on us as the great mother-son team, love and sacrifice and all that crap, but, tied to a thirty-one-year-old man, the stories didn't read so touchingly anymore. While nobody said it to my face, I think we were beginning to turn into a bad joke. Or maybe I was beginning to take a hard look at us and see that the silver cord was turning into a silver noose that was strangling me with love and guilt."

The guilt has never left him. Writing about his relationships with his family, he notes:

"I say, looking back, that there's no one to blame, and yet harm was done. Not just me, but to my brothers and my sister. I think all the time that was spent on me and my career hurt the others . . . there must have been a time when they hated my guts. If I'd been one of them, I'd have hated me."

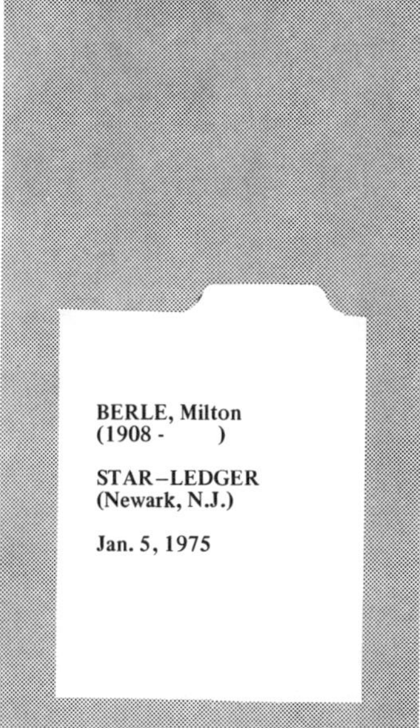
BERLE, Milton
(1908 -)

STAR-LEDGER
(Newark, N.J.)

Jan. 5, 1975

Fame Worries 2 Watergate Reporters

Bob Woodward — Bulletin Staff Photos by Joseph Tritsch

By JACK BOOTH
Of The Bulletin Staff

NEITHER looks like a millionaire, much less someone Robert Redford would play.

Carl Bernstein, 30, has long, scruffy hair and even scruffier shoes. His puffy face makes him look like he just got up. And he tends to fall down stairs.

Bob Woodward, 31, is better looking and better dressed. He looks like the Yale graduate he is. But even he needs a haircut.

Both look rather ordinary, which is just the opposite of what they have become since their Watergate stories began hitting the front page of the Washington Post last fall.

Their work won a Pulitzer for the Post. Their book, "All The President's Men" (Simon and Schuster), has topped the best seller list for the past two weeks. A film about them will star Robert Redford as Woodward.

They aren't quite millionaires, but they have a good start. The book advance was $55,000. "Playboy" bought the magazine rights for $30,000. The Book-of-the Month Club paid $105,000. The film advance was $350,000 immediately, with $100,000 more contingent upon success. And then there are paperback rights.

All that, as Woodward puts it, for "two police reporters with a background in that sort of reporting . . . who had the time — both divorced or separated . . . who had the support of the paper."

Only One Problem

There's only one problem. Investigative reporting may not mix with fame and fortune.

This week, for example, Woodward and Bernstein canceled some 19 interviews — many of them in Philadelphia — in order to follow the Supreme Court hearings on whether President Nixon should hand over tapes of 64 conversations to special prosecutor Leon Jaworski.

They also tried to cancel an appearance on William Buckley's "Firing Line," which had been scheduled to be taped at 11.30 yesterday morning at the WHYY-TV studios at 46th and Market sts. Only when the taping was moved up to 9.30 A.M. did they agree to appear.

During the taping, the two reporters exhibited considerable skill in turning pointed questions to their own advantage, prompting Buckley at one point to compliment them on their adroit use of euphemistic dodges.

Both were highly articulate, even in comparison with Buckley's witty and polished style.

After the taping, Woodward literally dragged Bernstein away from a crowd of admirers so they could get to the airport for 11.45 A.M. plane back to Washington.

On the way out the back door Bernstein fell down the steps — something he had almost done inside the building before the taping.

Joke About Fame

Inside the car, they joked about how fame and wealth has affected their lives.

Bernstein, who rode his "beloved Raleigh" bicycle on assignments until it was stolen the night of the Watergate indictments, bought a new bicycle. Woodward bought a new BMW sports car.

As for new apartments, Bernstein joked, Woodward bought a hotel.

"That is not true," Woodward said. "We live in the same places we did before."

"Obviously, it's changed our lives," he added.

"It has the potential of it and we're worried about that, to be very honest with you."

They worry, he said, "that we can't become reporters again. We get into the office and people want to interview us. The phone never stops ringing. It is absolutely impossible to do any work, or much work. We're anxious for it to settle down.

"I think you're always worried about anything that has the potential of trying to change your basic identity."

Identity Concern

"You perceive yourself a certain way," Bernstein said, "and you sort of say, 'Yeah, some changes are going to have to result, but I don't want to become another person or something like that.'"

The concern with retaining their identity surfaced again as they talked about Redford, an actor who is almost as famous for his individuality as he is for his sex appeal.

"He's not typical Hollywood in any sense of that word," Woodward said. "He's very, very sincere and dedicated. Wants to make a movie about newspaper reporting. And is just truly a great person in every sense."

"He's got a first-rate head," Bernstein said. "He's really a bright guy. Fun to be with, concerned about the same things in the movie that we're concerned about."

"Which is accuracy," Woodward filled in. "Doesn't like the hype."

"He doesn't want it to be some Batman and Robin trip that Hollywood does," Bernstein said.

"He's been married for 13 years," Woodward said. "Has a magnificent wife. A family. And that's hard to carve out that sort of life in the business he's in, and he's succeeded at it very, very well.

"He works hard, plays hard and rides his horses around all day — somebody who's got his life very organized and balanced. And for two people who don't have their lives very organized and balanced, that's really impressive."

"It's a great test," Bernstein said of their new celebrity status. "We can't predict how we'll meet it — unknowable.

Compatibility Shown

"We spend a lot of time in tarot card palors," Bernstein quipped.

During most of the interview, the two showed a high degree of compatibility, often filling in the end of each other's sentences. Bernstein joked incessantly.

Such compatibility was not always the case. In their book, which is written in the third person, they described their initial feelings about each other.

"It appeared that Woodward was also working on the story," they wrote. "That figured, Bernstein thought. Bob Woodward was a prima donna who played heavily at office politics. Yale. A veteran of the Navy officer corps. Lawns, greensward, staterooms and grass tennis courts, Bernstein guessed, but probably not enough pavement for him to be good at investigative reporting. Bernstein knew that Woodward couldn't write very well. One office rumor had it that English was not Woodward's native language."

"Bernstein," the book adds, "looked like one of those counterculture journalists that Woodward despised. Bernstein thought that Woodward's rapid rise at thePost had less to do with his ability than his Establishment credentials."

"We still mistrust each other," Bernstein said as he looked at Woodward in the back seat. "I'm not sitting in the front seat for nothing."

"We disagree on things, generally," Woodward said. "We have different opinions, some different values. Obviously there's some similarities. We both have better friends, but it works."

Humorous Moments

The book has moments of light humor, as when Bernstein picks up the "profoundly disturbing piece of information" that Jeb Magruder, a fellow bike freak, could be a Watergate conspirator.

At another point, Woodward, in an effort to buy time, offers to help Hugh Sloan clean house.

But basically the book reads like a detective novel as it follows the relentless efforts of the two reporters to uncover the conspiracy.

That effort, Woodward claims, wasn't nearly relentless enough.

"This is something we've never really talked to anyone about," he said. But in the first six of seven weeks after the Watergate burglary the whole story was there. We didn't realize it."

A lawyer for Ralph Nader, he said, called them and said he could positively identify one of the Watergate burglars as the man who attacked Daniel Ellsberg at J. Edgar Hoover's funeral in May of 1972.

They learned about street fights being staged at the Democratic convention in Miami, and they heard about Ehrlichman ordering Hunt out of the country. Yet they weren't able to tie it all together.

"When I read our book," Bernstein said, "I got through and said, 'Jesus, can't tell our head from our toes. I mean, there it all is.'"

BERNSTEIN, Carl (1944-) and WOODWARD, Robert Upshur (Bob) (1943-)

PHILADELPHIA BULLETIN (Philadelphia, Penn.) July 10, 1974

It's Write On for Reporter Bernstein

(Also see preceding article)
By JOHN DORSCHNER
Herald Staff Writer

In his Miami hotel room, Carl Bernstein was on the telephone, calling Information, trying to track down a source — for another Watergate story.

He was in South Florida Tuesday promoting the book he co-authored with Bob Woodward, "All the President's Men" (Simon and Schuster, $8.95), which has been on the best-seller lists for nearly two months. But between interviews, he was squeezing in a few phone calls.

THE BOOK has earned the two Washington Post reporters an estimated $500,000 each, but now, as they alternate visiting cities to plug the book, one stays in Washington to churn out stories.

"Why?" he asks, seemingly surprised at the idea that wealth might make them think of abandoning the newsroom. "I don't think that has anything to do with what we do. We're reporters. We've been on the story for two years. The story is very much there, and there'll be a lot of stories after the Watergate story.

"I don't know how to do anything else. I don't have too many marketable skills."

THE ONE skill he does have, however, is journalism, and he and Woodward have been given much of the credit for unraveling the Watergate coverup, especially in the summer of '72, when the burglary was receiving less attention than Nixon's march to an overwhelming election victory.

The investigation trail led Bernstein to Miami at least twice to question State Attorney Richard Gerstein and his chief investigator, Martin Dardis.

It was from Dardis that Bernstein learned of a cashier's check for $25,000, the first direct link between the burglars and the Committee for the Re-election of the President.

Both Dardis and Gerstein are miffed at the way they were handled in the book, and disagree with several statements.

"HE MAKES me out some kind of buffoon in the book," Dardis has said. "I picture Mickey Rooney playing my part . . . I just felt he should have given a little more credit."

Bernstein, in his hotel room Tuesday, replied. To Gerstein's description of him as having "the subtlety of a Marine drill sergeant," the reporter said, "I guess that's probably true." To Dardis' statement that he's "the most abrasive SOB in the world," Bernstein said, "I guess there are times when I can be. I don't like to be abrasive.

"I think there are times when you have to act in different ways to get facts. And to convince people to talk to you or to trust you or whatever . . . You don't go around being a method actor or something. You see what a situation calls for, and you use your head. Sometimes you're abrasive. As we described in the book, it was a frustrating day in Gerstein's office. (He waited most of the day in the reception room for Dardis.) It looked like we were going to have the s--- kicked out of us by The (New York) Times . . . So I did what I thought I had to do to get to see somebody."

Bernstein, after yelling at Gerstein and Dardis and their receptionist, did get to see the check. And that, said Bernstein, was "crucial information.

"THE FACT of the existence of their investigation . . . put more pressure on the Committee. And I . . . It's really one of the longest sections in the book. I can't think of a day in the whole book that's described as extensively as that.

"I mean, we would never have gotten anywhere if it weren't for them. At that point, the Committee was denying any connection with the burglars or the burglary whatsoever. That (the check) really firmly established it. So it was invaluable."

Tuesday, as Bernstein ate a room-service breakfast, the phone rang.

It was investigator Dardis. The conversation was short and amiable. Dardis said he wouldn't talk about the check or the frayed sportscoat that Bernstein described in his book (Dardis claims he doesn't own anything like it).

Dardis said he'd been sent a copy of the book by the publisher, but it wasn't autographed. He wanted a signed copy "for his grandchildren," and wondered if he could send his copy to Washington for signing. Bernstein told him not to bother —he'd mail down a couple of autographed copies.

RETURNING to his breakfast (he liked the fresh orange juice, grumbled about the quality of his corned-beef hash), Bernstein answered questions with measured hesitation, admitting he feels uncomfortable "on the other side of a notebook."

He is 30 now, with gray flecks in his long dark hair. Woodward is considered the "Ivy League" one of the pair. Bernstein, with his rugged face and long hair, is usually described as "shaggy" or "Neanderthal." He wore unpretentious wash-and-wear trousers.

He was separated when the Watergate investigation began. He is divorced now, and is living with Nora Ephron, a New York-based writer. "We're your typical New York shuttle-commuting couple," he said. "She comes down, or I go up there. I mean, we're not together all the time."

He still lives in the same apartment he found seven years ago ("a fun neighborhood; old, high ceilings") and still rides a bicycle to work (he doesn't own a car). He recently bought a Mercian bicycle, which retails for about $300, but that wasn't because of his new-found wealth. "I've always had good bikes."

THE BOOK'S success has been publicized, but Bernstein was cautious with figures. He said Simon and Schuster has printed 250,000 copies, and book dealers have ordered 185,000, but there's no accurate way of telling how many copies have been sold.

He's also hesitant talking about the money. "I don't think anybody can tell what ➡

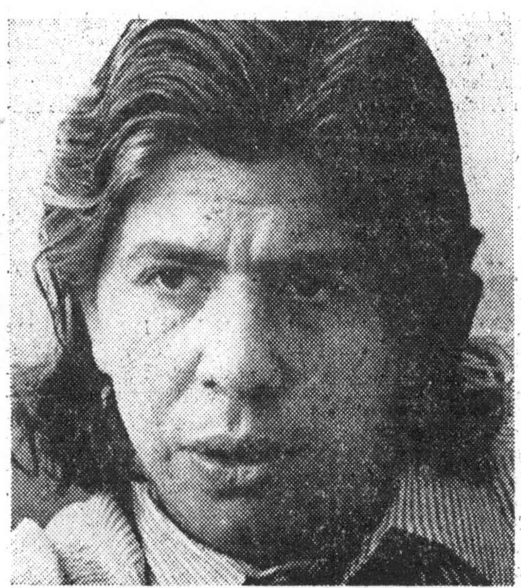

Bernstein

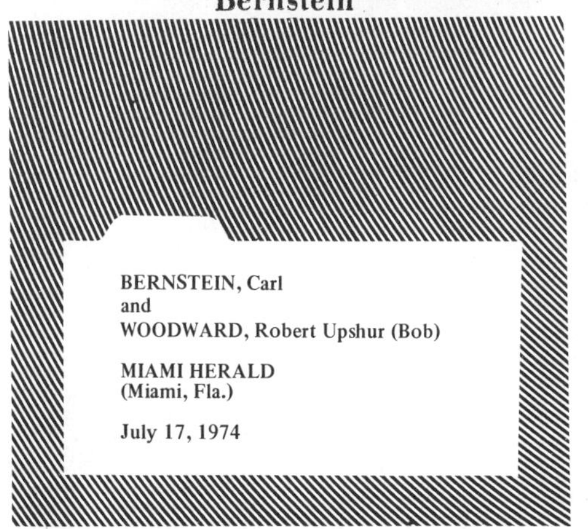

BERNSTEIN, Carl
and
WOODWARD, Robert Upshur (Bob)

MIAMI HERALD
(Miami, Fla.)

July 17, 1974

(Continued from preceding page)

the money is," but later he said "it's no secret" about the deals that were made, though the figures are often inaccurate.

They received $55,000 from Simon and Schuster for the hardcover advance, $500,000 from Warner Paperback Library (Simon and Schuster received another $500,000 from Warner), $25,000 from Playboy for two excerpts and $350,000 plus a percentage of the profits from Robert Redford for the movie rights (Simon and Schuster will receive 10 per cent of the movie money, too).

Their agent, David Obst, has said of the arrangements, "I'd do it differently today," but Bernstein noted that at the time none of them thought the book would be the overwhelming success it has been. "We were amazed at the size of the advance."

"AT THE TIME, October 1972, we intended to write an entirely different book, about the secret activities of the White House," inside information they'd learned while doing the Watergate stories. They had four chapters done when James McCord sent his letter to Judge Sirica.

"Then the dam broke, and of course at that point we didn't have any information that anybody else didn't have. So Woodward said, 'Look, let's write a book on our coverage of Watergate.' And I was adamantly opposed to it." Bernstein was worried that it would look like an "ego trip."

"Woodward said, 'Look, let me try to do the beginnings of a draft.' " That was the start. "I looked at it, said, 'OK, it needs a lot of work, but it seems to me that if we're going to do this, there's only one way ... We have to be totally honest about what we did, including the mistakes we made and including the ethical problems that we had to deal with, and didn't always deal with very successfully."

(THE ETHICAL problem that most bothered Bernstein was his attempts to interview members of the grand jury, which the judge had sternly warned against. "I think we were wrong. Period. And we didn't get any information," he said

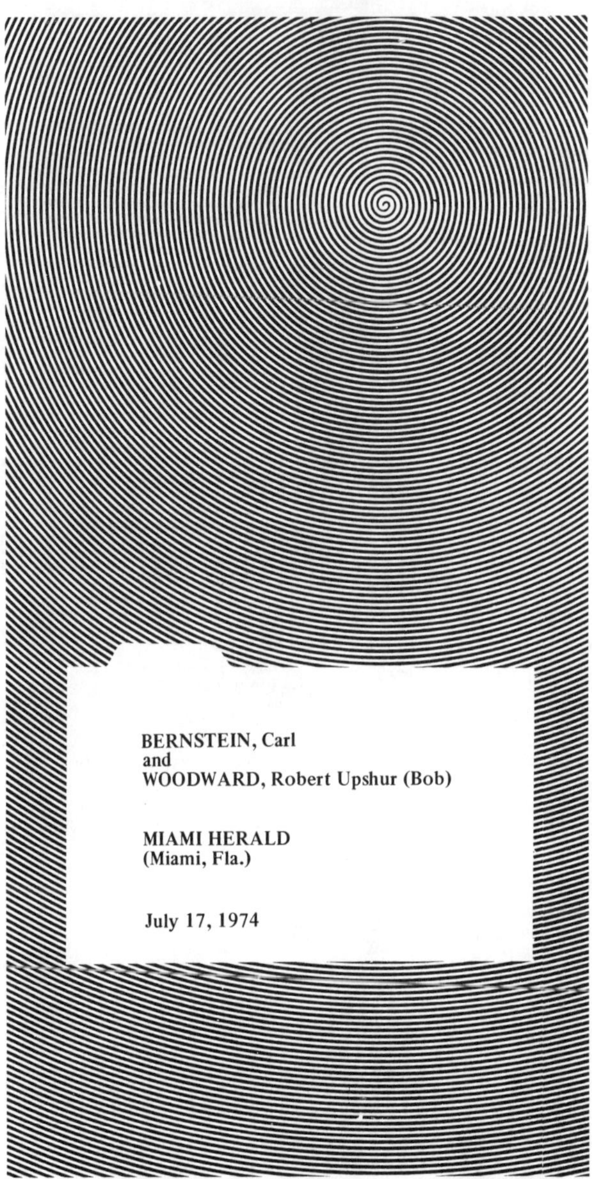

BERNSTEIN, Carl
and
WOODWARD, Robert Upshur (Bob)

MIAMI HERALD
(Miami, Fla.)

July 17, 1974

with an embarrassed laugh.)

After they found a publisher and an editor (Alice Mayhew), they charged ahead on the book. Woodward did much of the first draft, leaving gaps in the parts that had been mainly Bernstein's, like the trip to Miami. Then Bernstein rewrote or edited Woodward's writing.

"Bob's not the strongest writer in the world ... But he's very fast and he gets it all in," said Bernstein. "I sit there and redo stories half the night. I kind of have a thing about writing."

Whenever 50 or 75 typed pages were finished, they sent th^m to the editor.

IN DECEMBER 1973, Woodward and Bernstein took a suite at the St. Regis Hotel in New York City, and sat down with Editor Mayhew to discuss the 1,000-page draft. She wanted to cut roughly 40 per cent of it.

There was bitter fighting, between the reporters and the editor, and between Woodward and Bernstein. "About 10, 15 per cent of the cuts were restored."

Editor Mayhew, said Bernstein, is "a great conceptual editor. She's not the kind of editor that rewrites." All the writing and rewriting were done by the two reporters, he said, and then Ms. Mayhew edited heavily with a pencil.

Since the finished version came out, Bernstein has read the book once, on a transcontinental airline flight. "I have trouble reading the book."

The two reporters, he said, had "virtually every element of the story in hand by December of 1972, and we just couldn't put it together. We were kind of dumb on a lot of stuff."

THE WRITING style was another matter. "Bob likes to tell that he had this recurring nightmare, literally. The book was out and we had to go around and do this tour. And I would refuse to sign anybody's book unless I first made corrections on it. And it's kind of true."

It wasn't that Bernstein thought some facts in the book were wrong. It was only that he likes to keep rewriting his own copy, searching for the best words.

Though the two writers have fought bitterly over their Watergate stories, Bernstein said they plan to keep working together.

"It'd be crazy to say we're unaffected by it, because there's no way we can be. You have to do certain things, and live a little differently. People recognize you. You get stopped a lot.

"WE'RE NOT two obscure reporters on the metropolitan staff. We're two rather well-known reporters on the metropolitan staff ...

"We really like working together ... I think what we want to do is a kind of mix of things, some investigative, some life style stuff. It'd be absolutely crazy after Watergate to go out and say, 'Well, what's the next big story we can do?' It'd just be an insane approach. But on the other hand, you never know where a story's going to go until you report it."

Wendell Berry

BERRY, Wendell (1934 -)

COURIER–JOURNAL & TIMES (Louisville, Ken.)

Aug. 4, 1974

Photographed by JAMES BAKER HALL

By BRYAN WOOLLEY

EVERY TRIBE, nation and empire, no matter how urban, sophisticated or mechanized, is tethered, at some point, to the earth. The sustenance of us all, from the Australian bushman squatting on the sand to the American astronaut riding his capsule far beyond the pull of his home planet, is dependent on someone somewhere who drops a seed into the ground or serves as midwife to an animal.

"The farmers are the group that ties the society to the ground, that nourishes it and supports it. If the society is healthy, the farmers represent, to all other groups, and enact for all other groups, this essential connection. But our society is suffering, and our society is destructive, because not only do most people have no direct connection themselves to the land, but the people who *are* directly connected to the land are scorned as hicks and yokels. So they can't represent to the other people — and can't enact for them in any way that's useful and clarifying — that connection."

The man speaking is Wendell Berry, a farmer. He lives and works with his wife, Tanya, and his two children, Mary and Den, on a small hillside farm on the west bank of the Kentucky River in Henry County. As he speaks, bees are searching out nectar in his back yard and carrying it to the white wooden hives that stand on the concrete roof of the cistern. At the small barn down near the river, across the highway from the farmhouse, young Holstein calves bellow. Their voices are lost occasionally in the roar of a passing motorcycle or truck or boat.

Except for the machinery speeding by, the sights and sounds of the place awaken in the mind of Berry's approaching-middle-age visitor slumbering memories of small family farms that seemed large to childhood's eyes, in a different, drier region of America. Those farms are gone now, their small houses and big barns bulldozed or left to rot by the agribusinessmen who bought them. Gone, too, from the family-farm regions of the South and Midwest are most of the men who looked like Berry. He will turn 40 on August 5. His dark hair is beginning to gray. But his long body, clothed in khakis and work boots, is lean and strong. His bony face contains no element of softness, except the blue eyes, which have the inward look of farmers and poets and others who are accustomed to thinking long and alone. His voice is the slow drawl that farmers spread westward across the South a hundred and more years ago. Lately, their rootless descendants have carried it northward to city assembly lines and welfare rolls, where it is often understood mistakenly as a sign of laziness or ignorance. Some, perhaps, yearn to return to places like Henry County, where, among the hills and woods and riverbanks, their voices would blend better with their surroundings.

"The movement from the city to the country is a much more complicated and difficult movement than the movement from the country to the city," Berry is saying. "Farming — the use of the land — is a very complex and demanding discipline. And I think it could be argued pretty convincingly that a real back-to-the-land movement is not going to be accomplished in a family, say, in one generation. What we've done by the urbanization of our country people is take a farming tradition — or take a family succession, really — that went back to before history, and bring it to a stop. So the experience of generations of people has been cut off all of a sudden by the movement to the city. And in a generation, it's lost."

Berry is the fifth generation of his father's family and the sixth of his mother's to farm in Henry County, in the neighborhood of Port Royal. His father, John M. Berry Sr., although he went into the law, remains a farmer and a conservationist. He is the president of the Burley Tobacco Growers Cooperative Association. "I think the thing in his life that pleases my father most is the improvement that he has made in certain tracts of land," Berry says. "My father has always been motivated, as I have, by the thought of the small farmers, the family farmers, and what they mean to the country."

But Berry had to make that difficult city-to-country move. In his family, as in most other American families, the tie to the land is not as firm as it was in former generations. Wendell's younger brother, John Jr., is a lawyer and state senator. Although he is a conservationist and a spokesman for farmers in the legislature, he is not a farmer. His sisters are not farm wives. One lives in Anchorage, a bucolic suburb of Louisville, and the other in Philadelphia. Even Wendell, the eldest, went to the University of Kentucky to study literature, not agriculture, and, after earning bachelor's and master's degrees in English there, he joined the faculty.

He also became a writer. His books — three novels, four volumes of essays and five collections of poetry — and his essays in such various publications as The Hudson Review, The Nation, Organic Gardening & Farming and The Draft Horse Journal nearly all deal, in one way or another, with man and his relationship with the good earth. He meditates, especially in his novels and poetry, on man as a creature who springs from the earth, occupies a piece of its surface for a little while, and then returns to earth, leaving the place he occupied either better or worse than it was before his arrival. He sometimes writes in ➡

(Continued from preceding page)

anger. He attacks with hard, bitter logic the bloodless bureaucracies and corporations that methodically and enthusiastically displace people and destroy rich farmlands to build airports, dam rivers and destroy wildernesses for the sake of water-skiers; tear down mountains and poison waters for the sake of coal barons and energy-company plutocrats who are impatient to get richer. He adheres to the Jeffersonian faith in the worth of the common man and the values of the agrarian life, and he fears for the future of the country and the planet.

Many of our conflicts and problems would be more manageable, he believes, if so many people had not been removed from the countryside, if they and their animals had not been replaced by corporations and machines. We would be better off if so many of the wild places had not been destroyed. For in such places — from the days of the Old Testament prophets to the days of Thoreau and up to the present — man's truest insights into his own nature and his place in the universal scheme have been found.

Berry's own best insights have come to him on the farm, where he did not intend to live. "We started thinking about buying the place in the fall of '64," he says, "with the idea that we would use it as a vacation place, or a place to get away to. We started fixing it, and the next thing we knew, we were overhauling the house completely, and moved out here around the Fourth of July in '65. We've just kind of been getting in deeper ever since."

It is a real farm, not a writer-professor's country estate. Its chores include milking cows and currying horses and mucking out stalls and mending fences and mowing hay and all the other time-consuming, sometimes back-breaking, labor that family agriculture requires. But Berry and his family do not depend on it for their livelihood.

"We're getting our food out of it," he says, "and we're marketing more beef off of it all the time. But as an economic venture, this farm doesn't make much sense. Not yet, anyway. A lot of this farm was neglected for a good long while, and part of it was very badly abused by a developer who was attempting to make house-trailer sites on part of it. What fascinates me about this farm is the effort to take something that's been neglected and abused and make it productive; heal it up and make it good again. It's what people call 'marginal' land. I believe the marginal lands are probably going to be important to us someday. The most characteristic thing in our past was to take something that was virgin and abundant and half ruin it. I think that to take something that's been half ruined and make it productive may be the characteristic thing that we'll be doing in the future."

He walks over the trailer-site developer's abused acres with the pride and interest that only ownership can inspire, pointing out where brush must be cleared, where soil-holding vegetation has been planted, where a grove of walnut trees is being encc raged to thrive. He gazes from his hillside across the rain-swollen river and smiles. "It may not be the most productive farm in the world," he says, "but it's got the best view."

He made a deliberate choice to write about the world and its problems from a countryman's point of view, a perspective that he thinks is sadly underrepresented among the 40,000 or so new books published in this country each year and in its hundreds of periodicals. But it is not an easy point of view to represent, for there is so little rural culture remaining. "It used to be that a writer who wrote about rural things had a going concern to write about," he says. "As late as Robert Frost's time, when Frost came to know the New England rural countryside and rural people, they were a substantial continuous population with some sense of themselves as part of a going concern. In my time, rural life is under a terrible threat, and the population of the farms is dwindling. So I'm trying to live out a possibility that I believe in."

BERRY, Wendell

COURIER–JOURNAL & TIMES
(Louisville, Ken.)

Aug. 4, 1974

Berry did not make the transition alone. His wife, Tanya, daughter of Clifford Amyx, artist and recently-retired UK professor, had lived in the city all her life. "None of this would have been possible if Tanya had been a different kind of woman," Berry says. "She has made a country woman of the best kind. She's very confident and stable — much more stable than I am, and, I think, much more consistently and solidly supported by our values than I am."

A man who decides to live out of conformity with what is popularly considered to be the norm of his day, and then writes about that life, is bound to be interpreted by some of his readers as a guru of a "higher way," and by some others as a quaint eccentric. Both interpretations distort his intentions, Berry says. He emphatically rejects both roles and shies away from any publicity that might cast him in them. Disturbers of many of his Sunday afternoons are readers of his books and articles who regard his farm and his family as tourist attractions or objects of pilgrimage for organic gardeners and nature-lovers. Not long ago, Tanya walked into the house and told her husband there was a woman standing down on the highway who wanted to see him. "As I was coming down the steps to the road," he says, "she started making a movie of me. When I got to the road, she wanted me to say something for the camera. I was struck dumb. I wouldn't say anything to that damned camera. I don't *have* anything to say to a movie camera, because the assumptions that were running the camera were assumptions that I just can't speak to at all."

A culture that has taught people o expect instant gratification of all desires, he says, has sent a lot of people looking for one simple answer to all problems. "There are people who show up here on the theory that I've solved some kind of overwhelming modern question. And it's not so, you know. I'm as much involved in what's wrong as any- ➡

(Continued from preceding page)

body else. But if you publish things, if you say things in public about all these grave problems that are around us, you can very easily find that your privacy and your working time and everything else are being damaged by people who think they can get something from you that you can't give. What we've done is create a public that's terribly gullible and willing to live vicariously. There are people now, here and there in the country, who in some fundamental way have changed their lives. It's awfully easy for those people to pick up adherents, and it's very tempting to be a guru and sit down and instruct them. Well, it's more difficult than that. It's *got* to be more difficult than that, if anything good is going to come of it."

He also frets over the possibility that people — particularly the farmers who live around him, and actually make their living from the land — will think that *he* sees himself as an expert farmer or conservationist. Such a claim, he says, would be without substantiation, and, after some of his writings are in print, to remain unchanged forever in people's homes and on library shelves, he wishes he could take a razor blade to some of their pages.

"I'm not recommending anything to anybody," he says. "I think that I have authority to say what my experience has been and what I'm able to imagine. My authority to recommend behavior to other people is very slight, especially people that I don't know . . . . I think people resent having people that they don't know undertake to tell them what to do. I think that when my writing has undertaken that, either explicitly or by its tone, it's weak, and I dislike it strongly when it sounds like that. A big obligation that I feel as a writer is to keep trying to define the area that I stand in to speak, and what I have authority to say, and to keep my mouth shut when I don't sense that authority. I think I've slipped up fairly regularly. I think you could find in nearly all my books some passage where I've violated my own authority."

Then there is the danger that he will be dismissed as a mere oddity. Some of Berry's city and university friends consider him eccentric for wanting to live in the country at all, away from the repositories of culture, in what they consider isolation. And even some of his country acquaintances consider him odd, perhaps, for some of the ways he goes about living in the country, restoring on his farm and in his life elements that they consider relics of the pre-technological past. There is no flush toilet on the Berry place, for instance. A clean white privy stands in the back yard, and the wastes deposited there are used to make compost. There is no tractor, either. Berry works his fields and clears his woods with a beautifully matched team of draft horses. He has replaced exhaust-stink and engine-roar with the ancient commands to "Gee!" and "Haw!" and the beautiful flex of animal muscle.

BERRY, Wendell

COURIER–JOURNAL & TIMES (Louisville, Ken.)

Aug. 4, 1974

Berry acknowledges that such throwbacks to the past are oddities, but he does not consider them quaint or nutty. "I think that in certain respects my life has strayed rather widely from the modern norm. But I've never cultivated oddity for its own sake. I think most things I've undertaken that are kind of odd, I've undertaken because it was necessary in some sense for me to do them. I wish not to be helplessly dependent on others. Also, the changes that I've made in my life in the last 10 years have been to some degree motivated by my wish not to be living at someone else's expense. It's repugnant to me to feel that I'm using up in my life things that people who come along later will need to have in their lives. To try to quit doing that is much more difficult than it sounds. I'm using up what I'm sure is much more than my share of gasoline, for instance. I bought the horses, obviously, because I wanted to. I like to farm with horses. But one way to justify the use of horses on a farm of this size is that they don't use gasoline. When I'm using those horses, I'm not harming the environment, and I like that very much. The same for that composting privy out there, which I'm sure a lot of people would find the crowning eccentricity of my career. There's something very healing in the idea of that privy, that a broken circle has been mended there, that what came out of the land is being put back into it by means of that privy. It means that a certain part of our life that was potentially damaging to the world has been made useful to the world. I like that feeling. It doesn't mean that because of that I'm more virtuous than other people. It means that I have a practical understanding of the usefulness of that, and so I do it."

The people who visit Berry on an afternoon and use his privy cannot fully understand that. To understand the meaning of the privy, one would have to remain on the farm long enough to see the compost on the ground, the plants blossom and bear, their fruit eaten, the cycle of nature completed. And one of the reasons the planet is dying so rapidly, Berry says over and over again, is that most people in our society do not stay in a place long enough to observe the consequences of their ways of using the land.

Frequently in his more recent writings he uses the imagery of marriage — old-fashioned, till-death-us-do-part marriage — to describe the ancient, healthier relationship of man to the land. He explores the analogy at length in a wide-ranging essay, "Discipline and Hope." He muses on it poetically from a number of perspectives in a small volume of poetry called "The Country of Marriage." In "The Unforeseen Wilderness," an essay on Kentucky's Red River Gorge, where the governor and the Corps of Engineers want to build a dam, he states it negatively: "A man who would value a piece of land strictly according to its economic worth is precisely as crazy, or as evil, as a man who would make a whore of his wife."

We are the heirs of frontiersmen who held the whoremaster's view of the land. They moved onto virgin soil, denuded it, used it until it was exhausted, then moved on to more virgin territory — unlike their Old World forebears, who lived on the ➡

(Continued from preceding page)

same ground for thousands of years and, through care, kept it productive. The virgin land is gone now, but we still behave like our forefathers, and we compound their sins, seeking bigger and quicker profits than they, moving on faster than they, ignoring the long-term consequences of our actions.

"I don't think you know how well you're raising your children until you have a look at your grandchildren," Berry says. "I won't know how well I'm teaching my students until I have a look at my students' children. I won't know how well I've lived here until I get to the end of my life and I see whether my life has made it possible for another generation to live here. In some places, one generation has destroyed the possibility that another generation can live there . . . We have whole professional classes or groups that will move into a place and do whatever their thing is, and then move on to another place. And lots of our country is suffering badly from the activities of those people . . . . How would the Mellon family behave if they lived in their strip mines, or under one of them? That's of great interest to me, that question. I think that they would behave differently in Eastern Kentucky if they had to live there. If the people who own Eastern Kentucky lived in Eastern Kentucky, it would be a very different place."

The only corrective to the rape-and-leave policy of land use, he believes, is a marriage-like commitment to the place of your birth, or the place of your choice, whether it is in the country or in a city. "You forsake all others, and you make your fate the same as the fate of the place. And then, it seems to me, you'll get down to work and do some of the essential things that need to be done."

These thoughts began germinating in his mind more than a decade ago, he says, when he spent six months in Italy. "What impressed me more than anything else there was the countryside, the landscape, and how it had been used. You can't look at that landscape without realizing that generation after generation after generation has used it with the greatest possible care, and that great care has produced great skill, and that care and skill together have made a countryside that's very beautiful and very productive at the same time. That changed my feeling about the possibilities in the relationship between a man and a piece of land."

About the time that some American farmers were beginning to appreciate the land in that way — around the turn of this century — they were beaten down by unfavorable markets and began encouraging their children to leave the farms and seek their fortunes in the cities. The principal character of Berry's latest novel, "The Memory of Old Jack," is a member of that generation. He watches the world he loved fade slowly away.

Since that generation, such social upheavals as the Great Depression, migration to urban defense industries during World War II and mechanization of the countryside after the war have so stripped the countryside of its population that, Berry says, "We're coming down to some kind of deadline now on whether it's possible for a stable and hereditary farming population to survive in this country. It's reduced to where we can't spare anybody else . . .

"If you farm according to the laws of nature — that is, if you restore the fertility to the land that you take out of it in order to produce — you have the power, in any piece of land, of infinite productivity. And we've taken that infinite possibility and made it dependent on fossil fuels, for example, which are a limited supply, and maybe already *dangerously* limited. . . . This means that if something happens to the petroleum supply, on which we are dependent for both fuel and fertilizer, then we're probably in *terrible* trouble. Then we'll be dependent on some alternative supply of energy, which we could get from manpower if the society were differently organized. But we don't have that kind of manpower available, and we certainly don't have the manual skills that we would need."

BERRY, Wendell

COURIER-JOURNAL & TIMES (Louisville, Ken.)

Aug. 4, 1974

This is one of the reasons why the countryside is not being properly maintained — particularly on hilly, marginal land like Berry's. Machines, even while we still have the fuel to run them, cannot do everything. They cannot build and mend fences; they cannot build and repair barns, or doctor sick cows, or take the bees' honey from the hive. And the implications of the problem for the city-dweller go far beyond the cost of his groceries, or even the scarcity of them. When the farmers and their helpers left the countryside, they went to the cities, where the jobs were. Now many of them are standing in unemployment lines and living on welfare checks, while the farmers still left in the country cry for labor.

"We need a rural economy that would permit the necessary workers to live out here," Berry says. "And if we had been able to keep those people, obviously, the urban areas wouldn't be in so bad a shape because of the surplus of people — uprooted people, people who are not urban people to begin with."

It is a symptom of a society out of whack — a society that produces too many doctors of philosophy and not enough carpenters and plumbers and fence-menders; a society where certificates and diplomas are valued more highly than the ability to do an essential job well. And although Berry refuses to talk about what kind of future his 16-year-old daughter and his 12-year-old son dream of, he can quickly tick off his desires for them.

"I would like them to be capable of inexpensive pleasure. I would like for them to be able to amuse themselves just with the natural resources that are at hand. And I would like them not to be helpless. I would like them to be good at some kind of hand labor. And I would like them to understand the importance of excellence, of high standards. I would like them to understand what *good* work is, what the importance of it is and how to do it. I think something essential goes out of a person's character if he doesn't do some kind of work that requires him to hold himself up to high standards. It used to be that nearly everybody did."

Some people still do. There is this lanky yokel over in Henry County, for instance, plowing behind a horse, thinking poetry . . . □

It Was a Great Week for Authors

EVERYONE seems to be talking about Grace Paley lately, but few have seen her. But here she was, suddenly, in Milwaukee. In the flesh.

But not much flesh. She is a smiling, tiny woman with her hair drawn into a bun. Though one guesses that she might feel more comfortable in slacks, she wore a print blouse and a skirt. She has fine hazel eyes. She is the sort of person one would feel at home with as a neighbor. In the suburbs. In the city. Anywhere.

Grace Paley is one of almost a superabundance of authors who descended on the city last week. Three of them came for the annual dinner of the Bookfellows of Milwaukee, in connection with National Library Week. Another — Sol Stein, a publisher as well as an author (or is it the other way around?) — came on his own. By the week end, another large group of writers was here for a meeting of the Popular Culture Association.

Sol Stein

Grace Paley

Justin Kaplan

But in many respects, Grace Paley was in all likelihood the most unusual of all. In 1959, she published a book of short stories called "The Little Disturbances of Man." It did not have a large sale at the outset. But it made good friends. Their enthusiasm made it a collector's item. In 1968, a new edition was published. This spring another collection of stories appeared, "Enormous Changes at the Last Minute," and Grace Paley was a public as well as an underground celebrity.

* * *

The 28 stories in the two collections are not everybody's meat. They are in the nature of caviar and olives; if you like them, you like them very much. They are also thoroughly original and probably inimitable; nothing like them ever happened before.

Mrs. Paley made her way to Milwaukee from Thetford, Vt., where she has been living for several months. She is not an academic. She dropped out of Hunter College in New York at 19. Most of the time since then she has been a typist and a housewife. After her stories began to attract attention, she taught writing courses at Columbia University and Sarah Lawrence College. She considers herself an incorrigible New Yorker. Her stay in Vermont, the boyhood home of her second husband, Robert Nichols, has been on a sabbatical from Sarah Lawrence.

She'll be back in New York, at her apartment on W. 11th St. in the Village, when school reopens in September. Here she will rejoin the friends whose counterparts — large and small — populate her stories of the joys and sorrows of urban life.

Not that she puts real people into her stories. "I don't," she said on her Milwaukee visit. "As I wrote in my new book, everyone is imagined into life, except my father. But even he is imagined in a way, too. He's my father — but in another way he isn't."

Sometimes an actual event will suggest a story. One had to do with "The Little Girl," one of the flock of pubescents ("teeny-boppers," in the old phrase) who gather in the Village and its fringes to escape from middle class families. The broken body of the "little girl" was found at the bottom of an air shaft after an interracial sexual encounter. Had she been thrown from a window or had she jumped? Mrs. Paley doesn't know, but the horror of her story remains.

Mrs. Paley has sometimes been taxed for not having written a novel. One of her new stories began as a novel, but she felt it would be much better as a short story. And, as she acknowledged, the stories themselves interweave.

"Maybe there really is a novel in that book," she said. "Put it all together, and maybe you've got a novel. But I couldn't have done it any other way."

BIRMINGHAM, Stephen (1932-) [See also CA-49/52]
KAPLAN, Justin (1925-) [See also CA-19/20]
PALEY, Grace (1922-) [See also CA-25/28]
STEIN, Sol (1926-) [See also CA-49/52]

MILWAUKEE JOURNAL (Milwaukee, Wisc.) May 5, 1974

Grace Paley was born in the Bronx 50 years ago, the daughter of Isaac Goodside, M.D., to whom she pays tribute in "Enormous Changes" as "artist and storyteller." She has a daughter, Nora, 24, and a son, Daniel, not quite 23, by her first marriage, to Jess Paley. Her daughter lives in Vermont, her son in New York City, where he works in the public school system.

In her free time, Mrs. Paley has worked in the peace movement. She spent six days in jail on one occasion for sitting in the middle of a thoroughfare during an antiwar demonstration. She has visited Hanoi and Moscow with peace delegations, and spent six weeks in Chile with her present husband, a poet and playwright who studied literary developments in that country under the Allende government.

"I've been interested in all these things," she said, "but active? I don't think of myself as active. The important thing that is happening in this country is the work of young people. We older people have already made our own place."

* * *

Here Are Two Books to Watch For

A FEW years from now, people will be talking about a new biography by Justin Kaplan and another social history by Stephen Birmingham.

Kaplan, who won a National Book Award and a Pulitzer Prize in 1968 for his "Mister Clemens and Mark Twain," is already hard at work on a biography of Walt Whitman, the first full length study of that enduring poet of democracy in almost a quarter century. Birmingham, whose accounts of American society have led him through "the best people" in Yankee blood tradition and moneyed Jewish and Irish families, is ➡

(Continued from preceding page)

writing a book about a little known segment of the affluent population, black social leaders.

Between preparations for the Bookfellows' festivities,

BIRMINGHAM, Stephen
KAPLAN, Justin
PALEY, Grace
and
STEIN, Sol
MILWAUKEE JOURNAL
(Milwaukee, Wisc.) May 5, 1974

Stephen Birmingham

both writers talked about their works in progress.

Kaplan doesn't expect his book on Whitman to come from the press for four or five years.

Kaplan is a painstaking writer and researcher. He started his Mark Twain book in 1959 and delivered the manuscript in 1965. About a year later he began work on his second biography, "Lincoln Steffens." It was published this spring. The timing proved excellent — the life of the great muckraker of early 20th century journalism was published at the height of the Watergate scandals in a new era of muckraking.

Most biographers come to their craft through the purlieus of scholarship. Kaplan's path was different. From Harvard, where he had spent two years of graduate study after his baccalaureate, he went to New York to try his hand at writing and in publishing. He became an editorial assistant to Lincoln Schuster, a founder of Simon and Schuster. After five years of reading other persons' manuscripts as a senior editor of that firm, he left to write the Clemens biography.

"I moved to Cambridge," Kaplan recalled last week. "It was a gamble. I remember waking at 2 o'clock one morning and asking myself, 'What the hell am I doing? I've bought a house here and uprooted my family without anything really definite in sight.' I wondered whether I might be playing a hoax on myself."

But the book was published — by whom else than Simon and Schuster? — and went on to win its attendant honors and a large sale.

Biography, Kaplan believes, is a fine form for a writer and can be highly creative. In college, he wrote short fiction. Like many young writers, he found himself writing too much about himself (a fault that Grace Paley has found among her own students). To write about another person establishes a perspective that may have more satisfying results.

"Theoretically," said Kaplan, "it is possible to write a first rate biography about an absolute unknown. But, of course, the subject tends to take precedence — if you want to sell the book."

Kaplan thinks there is something of a pattern in his two published biographies and the one to come. "Mark Twain, Steffens and Whitman came out of a tradition of grassroots dissent and radicalism that is a fascinating part of the American background," he said. "I don't mean this in any partisan sense; people all over the political spectrum have shared in it. Whitman is an especially fine example, rising from a not very distinguished journalist to a truly great poet. There is something mysterious, almost supernatural, about this kind of development and flowering."

The Kaplan household in Cambridge is something of a literary workshop. His wife, a daughter of Edward L. Bernays, the pioneer in public relations, is the novelist Anne Bernays. She is completing a new novel, "Home Free," that probably will be published next year. She is also writing a book on psychoanalysis and feminism that will appear a year or so later. Her paternal grandmother, incidentally, was a sister of Sigmund Freud.

* * *

Stephen Birmingham's visit was somewhat in the nature of an exploration. When his book on the black upper crust is published, what will he do next?

"I've been wondering about brewing families," he confessed. "Do you think there's a book in them?"

Perhaps Uihleins, Pabsts and Busches had better beware.

His study of black society will deal with Johnsons, Yanceys and Greers, among others. The Johnsons are members of a Chicago family that publishes Ebony Magazine and books; the Yanceys are a medical clan in Atlanta; Edward Greer is a brigadier general in the Army.

Unlike some of the Irish who were the subject of his most recent book, "Real Lace," blacks of money and position usually stay out of the public eye. "They keep a low profile," Birmingham said. "That made the job especially interesting to me as a writer."

The Irish book did not please all Irish readers. (Birmingham, who grew up in Hartford, Conn., and lives in Westchester when he is not away for research or other projects, proclaims that he is Irish himself.) The Kennedys got only minor attention; comparatively, they were newcomers to the social scene and not in the same league as the McDonnells and Murrays of New York.

Last winter Birmingham took a trip to Paris. Aristotle Onassis invited him to fly Olympic — as a guest. Birmingham canceled his reservations on another airline and took off. On his way back, his flight was delayed at Paris. There was a great buzzing among the passengers. "*She's* coming aboard," they told one another; "all the first class space has been pre-empted."

As it happened, Birmingham got his first class seat, but a large section opposite it was reserved for Jacqueline Kennedy Onassis and her attendants.

"She glanced over and smiled," Birmingham said, remembering the scene. "Then she got up and came to my seat. I cringed."

"Mr. Birmingham," said Mrs. Onassis, "I enjoyed your book — particularly the part about the Kennedys!"

* * *

Sol Stein Has a Busy Time

SOL STEIN looked a bit tired as he bounded into The Journal's editorial offices the other morning, balancing two fairly hefty pieces of luggage.

"Twenty-two cities!" he said. "I've never done anything like this before."

Stein was in Milwaukee to promote his latest book, "The Living Room." A novel about a brilliant young woman who thought she had it made, it was reviewed on this page two Sundays ago.

Stein is one of the few publishers who write books on their own. Under an unwritten code in the book industry, "The Living Room" was published by Arbor House, rather than by Stein & Day, the firm that he heads with his wife, Patricia Day.

"The Living Room" is Sol Stein's third novel. The others were "The Husband" and "The Magician." "The Magician" had a huge sale; it was a major book club selection and has done well in paperback as well as in hard cover. All of them have had highly contemporary themes. The latest raises some questions about modern feminism. Stein is glad that women seem to like it.

Stein believes that fiction reading is coming back strongly. Of course, novels that find readers today are of a special type.

"I don't advise people to write novels," he said. "But if they do, I think there are three rules that are important now:

"First, a modern novel has to have an engine in it. It has to grab the reader in the first three or four pages.

"Second, dialog has to be done well. There's the dialog of the stage, the frothy Rosalind Russell sort of thing. I don't think that has much of a place in fiction today. Then there's the Paddy Chayefsky school — dialog as court reporting. I think this should be avoided, too. The contemporary writer's problem is to capture the essence of speech, not merely record it.

"Third, a novel should deal with the immediate scene."

As a publisher, Stein expects an autobiography by Marilyn Monroe to do extremely well. He plans to publish it in June. The manuscript takes the sex queen through her marriage to Joe Di Maggio.

"This isn't a piece of Norman Mailer fiction," he said. "This is the real thing. There are a lot of errors in it; we're leaving the book just as she wrote it.

"McCall's is running two pieces from it in July and August. And they've cleaned it up — copy edited it. Can you imagine doing that to Marilyn Monroe?"

A DAY IN THE LIFE OF JIM BISHOP

By Rob Elder

Jim Bishop always sleeps until 10 a.m. Then he wanders into the sun-buttered dining room of his Hallandale home, without shaving or dressing. "I come cruddy to the table, and with wrinkled bathrobe," he says.

It is a luxury he has earned. For 35 years in New York's dog-eat-dog publishing world, he worked as newspaper reporter, rewrite man, magazine editor. New York and his native New Jersey are still audible in his voice, and he still tells stories about who said what at the Stork Club. But he refers to that world as a jungle. He will never go back, he says. "This is where I want to be. This is where I want to die."

He sits at the head of the table. Breakfast is always the same: five cups of half-coffee, half-espresso, and a pack of Carlton cigarets.

He reads two newspapers, *The Miami Herald* and *The New York Times.* He takes his time, starting a typical workday at the pace most men save for Sundays. Not for nothing has the man written 2,716 syndicated columns and published 18 books which among them have sold more than five million copies.

At 66, James Alonzo Bishop still has all that abundant white hair. Yielding to fashion, he has grown longish white sideburns to go with it. His eyes are as blue as his hair is white. They read through black-rimmed bifocals. The face is well tanned and a little freckled and there are not many lines. Bishop smokes, like he writes and golfs, with his left hand.

Kelly, his wife, always has a coffee pot hot in the red-walled kitchen. She is a pretty strawberry blonde with a peaches-and-cream complexion. She was a secretary at the Diplomat when they met. Now she is his assistant. When Bishop interviewed John F. Kennedy at the White House, Kelly came along with her steno pad. She got facts he missed — like the color of the rug.

He was a widower with two grown daughters when he and Kelly were married in 1961. She too had two girls by an earlier marriage — Karen, now 21, and Kathi, now 19. He adopted them. They are a close family, and Karen and Kathi still live at home.

The house does not look as though a celebrity lives there. Bishop paid $52,000 for it in 1963, when he moved to Florida. It is a white stucco with dark red Oriental trim. A Lincoln Continental in the same shade of red is parked in the half-circle drive. There

is a swimming pool in back. The house is on an inlet of water in a neighborhood called Golden Isles, and Bishop used to keep a boat, but doesn't anymore. Vandals stuck a hosepipe in his cabin cruiser, and he lost his taste for boating.

Intruders would not get far now. Charliê Chan, 90 pounds of German Shepherd, is part of the decor. So are photos on the liv-

BISHOP, James Alonzo (Jim)
(1907 -)

MIAMI HERALD
(Miami, Fla.)

Sept. 29, 1974
[See also CA-19/20]

ing room wall showing the Bishops, Jim and Kelly, with two presidents, JFK and LBJ.

On the west wall of the living room is a piano. A small brass plaque says it was a gift from Bishop's father, John Michael. He was a police lieutenant in Jersey City. He used to do his police reports at home, at the dining room table. Watching, his son learned the minutely-detailed, minute-by-minute style of writing which became his trademark in best sellers like *The Day Lincoln Was Shot, The Day Christ Died,* and *A Day in the Life of President Kennedy.*

They and Bishop's 15 other books line the piano top. The first was *The Glass Crutch,* the biography of a reformed drunk. It was published in 1945, when Bishop was 38 and war editor of *Collier's.* It became a best seller within three weeks.

Others bombed. Who remembers *The Girl in Poison Cottage* or *The Murder Trial of Judge Peel?* Bishop's only novel, *Honeymoon Diary,* was an admitted disaster. According to the author himself, "It didn't sell to the number of relatives I have out of work."

Bishop's own favorite didn't sell. It was his second book, *The Mark Hellinger Story,* a biography of the Broadway columnist who helped Bishop get started at the *Daily Mirror.* When it was published in 1951, Bishop walked through snow to leave the first copy on Hellinger's tomb. It was inscribed: "To Mark: Take this off what I owe you."

With the Lincoln book, Bishop found his niche. "I wasn't trying to invent a new style," he says. "It just happened accidentally that I did." Next he wrote about Jackie Gleason and Jesus Christ, in that order. Lincoln remains his biggest book, selling three million hardcover copies in 16 languages. It was published in 1954. Twenty years later, it still earns Bishop $4,000 to $5,000 a year in royalties.

Seventeen of the 18 books on the piano are bound in rich brown leather with gold titles and marbled endpapers. One is too new to have received the special treatment. It is the just published *FDR's Last Year.*

The book recounts, day by day and sometimes minute by minute, the historic year (really 13 months) of April 1944-April 1945. Yalta. The winding down of World War II. Historic dealings among Roosevelt, Churchill, Stalin. Above all, FDR's own futile struggle against failing health.

The story of the sick president is told with sympathy. Bishop denies it is an empathy born of similar suffering. He is rarely ill. At five feet, seven and one-half inches and 173 pounds, he is fit. The Carltons add up to three packs a day, but they are his only vice. He drinks a little wine when out for dinner, nothing alcoholic at home.

After sitting over newspapers until about 11:20 a.m., he shaves with aerosol ➡

(Continued from preceding page)

cream and a double-edged razor and dresses and, three days a week, goes golfing. "A writer in his 60s must learn to get off his behind," he says. "It becomes therapeutic."

Bishop's regular golfing partner is Milton Goldstandt, a 78-year-old investment counselor. Goldstandt often wins. They play at the Diplomat or Aventura. Bishop averages 90.3. His best score is 82. In 1965 and in 1973, he had holes-in-one on the 145-yard eighth hole of the Diplomat course.

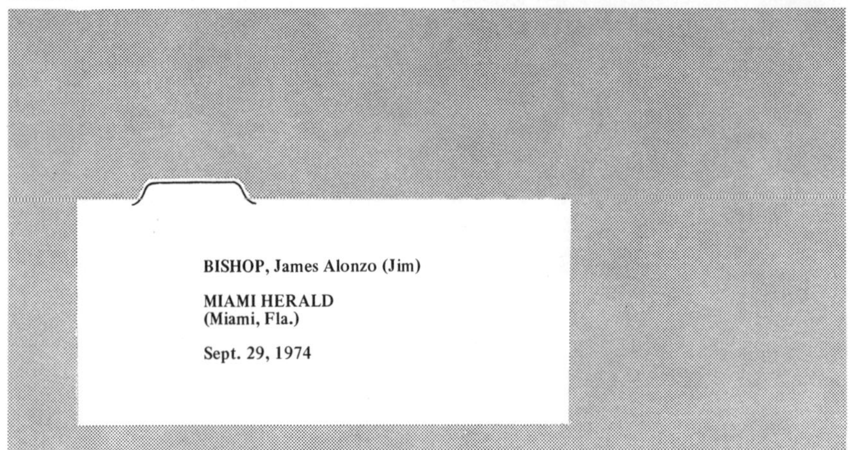
BISHOP, James Alonzo (Jim)

MIAMI HERALD
(Miami, Fla.)

Sept. 29, 1974

Between nines comes lunch: two kosher hot dogs with mustard, no buns. Another cup of coffee, his sixth for the day, and that's all. Bishop is a simple luncher.

By mid-afternoon he is back at the head of the dining table, going through his mail. It is copious. He divides it between two chairs. He answers the letters in one. Kelly will write "a nice letter" in reply to the others.

Bishop naps until 6 and gets up for the news. The big color television stays on during dinner. It is built into a wall of the living room. Bishop's place at the table is at the far end of the dining room. When there is something he wants to see, he races around the table and watches.

He goes to work after dinner. His work place is a pine-paneled study without windows or television. Reference books line all four walls, floor to ceiling. There are two encyclopedias, eight *Who's Whos,* 15 world almanacs and hundreds of *National Geographics.* There are books on history, biography, theology, medicine. There's a small Seth Thomas electric clock with roman numerals. There is a Sony tape deck. And there is a big blue Toshiba copier for which he paid $1,500. When he writes, Bishop sits in a gray metal straight chair and works on an old Smith-Corona portable. The typewriter is not electric.

Bishop says he has never sat more than 20 minutes waiting for an idea for a column. It usually takes him 45 minutes from start to finish. He writes on white Zipset paper with pink and yellow carbons attached. He does three columns a week, 950 words each. King Features distributes them to 200 newspapers, from Miami to Los Angeles. He writes each column at least nine days before it is published. So far he has turned out 2,716 of them.

There is no rewriting. "As a professional lazy man, I want to do it thoroughly and completely and correctly the first time around," he says. "I do not want the extra work of revising. To hell with that.

"I will not rewrite a sentence. When it's ripped out of the typewriter, Kelly gets it and scans it for errors and it goes to the publisher." At about 8:30 p.m., Kelly or one of the girls leaves for the Post Office with the completed column.

With the column finished, Bishop resumes work on "the next book," whichever that is at the moment. Right now it's an autobiography. For the *Day in the Life of* books he compiled sets of 25 notebooks for each book, one for each hour of the day, and one bibliography. As he uses the material in the notebooks, he X's it out with a pencil. He draws circles around the material that is not used. "I always try to have two and a half times as much as I need," he says.

Each notebook entry is coded. The code tells Bishop where he got the information. He will tell you that "I am not the best writer in America, but I am easily the most disciplined you ever met." Working on the books, he writes in 90-minute stretches, takes a break, goes back for more.

When possible, he tries to get fresh material from interviews. Doing this for the FDR book, he felt he was in "a race with death." People who were there are getting old, dying off.

"I think it will be the last book with fresh research on Roosevelt," he says. "These people just won't be around anymore."

When he interviewed them, he found his sources divided into two camps: "Franklin people and Eleanor people." The Eleanor people were still embittered about the President's long relationship with Lucy Rutherfurd. Bishop himself is more sympathetic: "It was not a dirty thing. It was a very sad thing, and it endured from 1915 until 1945.

"The reason I know is that my father left my mother for her best friend when I was 14 and he was gone 16 years and that was no affair."

The 690-page book is being reviewed as a serious and formidable work. Not all the critics are favorable. "It is difficult to judge," said one, "how much of the book reflects FDR and how much expresses Bishop." Another reviewer found that "it borders on history-as-soap-opera."

But Will Durant called it "a thorough and scholarly job." Benjamin V. Cohen, who was a close Roosevelt advisor, found it "a moving account." Bishop's fellow columnist, Jack Anderson, went so far as to say that "Bishop has long been one of my favorite writers and after reading *FDR's Last Year,* he has become my favorite author."

In *The New York Times Book Review,* Eric F. Goldman criticized Bishop's latest effort for "florid or maudlin" language and said it is "short on real efforts at analysis and long on an overdone you-were-there journalism."

But Goldman also found the book "thoroughly absorbing reading," and said it "should be and undoubtedly will be widely read." Coming from a Princeton history professor, that is no mean praise for an author who never went to high school.

Bishop is the first to admit his books lack critical analysis. That's deliberate, he says. "What I want to do is recreate something and make it happen again in your mind . . . this is the essence of the whole business."

Is it history or is it journalism? "I don't think most of us know when the hell we're crossing that line," he says. "All of it is history. It's a matter of how you want to relate it."

At 11 p.m., Bishop stops work and watches the television news. Then he goes to bed and reads until 2 a.m. A hospital table is his bedstand. It is piled with books and magazines, and scarred with cigaret burns.

Sometimes the reading is research for a book. Sometimes it is for pleasure. Always Jim Bishop reads as a writer, looking to see what another man in the same business has done.

He does not admire authors who write off the tops of their heads. He would assign Norman Mailer to that category. He says of Mailer: "He has this great talent, but he doesn't want to work at it."

Bishop likes to quote Ernest Hemingway: "We are all apprentices in a profession in which no one is a master." To Bishop, writing is not fancy rhetoric, it is hard, disciplined work. "You could make a first class writer out of almost anybody," he says. "Writers aren't born, they're made." He has a little analogy. "Writers are all target shooters. The best a writer can do is come close to the bullseye. It will never sing as you want it to."

At two o'clock the light goes out. Tomorrow will be another day of writing. Jim Bishop does not plan to retire.

"I could never fancy myself not writing." [T]

ROB ELDER is a Herald staff writer.

Picking Up Private Faulkner Pieces Isn't Easy

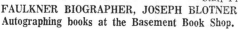

—Staff Photo.

FAULKNER BIOGRAPHER, JOSEPH BLOTNER
Autographing books at the Basement Book Shop.

By DON LEE KEITH

In 1930, when a magazine asked William Faulkner's agent for biographical information on the author, the writer replied:

"Sorry, I haven't got a picture. I don't intend to have one that I know of, either. About the biography. Don't tell the bastards anything. It can't matter to them I was born of an alligator and a nigger slave at the Geneva Conference two years ago. Or whatever you want to tell them."

Now, with Faulkner long since elevated to literary prominence, his quest for privacy has gone asunder, and the inevitable shroud of curiosity has surrounded the image of the man. According to his "authorized biographer," the task of piecing together the bits of Faulkner's life was no easy one.

Joseph Blotner, author of the massive two-volume "Faulkner: A Biography," says that while the mind of an artist almost always tends to be an extraordinarily complicated thing, this was especially true in Faulkner's case. "First, he was a writer in the truest sense, in my view, the greatest writer of prose fiction And second, he was a very private person.

"It was not my primary obligation to produce a theoretical biography, a structured analysis explainig what made Faulkner what he was. What he had to reveal, he did so in his art. My method of presenting his life was one of understatement. I tried to refrain from signposts, arrows that pointed to conclusions.

"The process of creation is so complex, yet a biography must try to follow it as closely as possible. Still, to present a systemized interpretaion asks more than one can achieve. In detailing Faulkner's works, it takes an awful lot of intelectual arrogance to say, 'Here's the way it happened.'"

BLOTNER, Joseph (Leo)
(1923 -)
[See also CA-19/20]
and
FAULKNER, William
(1897 - 1962)

TIMES–PICAYUNE
(New Orleans, La.)

Aug. 22, 1974

Blotner, a native of New Jersey currently a professor at the University of Michigan, says he found in his research that William Faulkner had been friends with more persons in New Orleans than in any other place he lived, with the exception of his hometown, Oxford, Miss.

"There were dozens of persons who had been friends with him here, and he had left vivid impressions on their memories, although the longest he lived here was for a six-month period. That was in late 1924 and early 1925, when he and his friend Phil Stone, a lawyer in Oxford, were preparing for Faulkner's trip to Europe, where they hoped he would so as Hemingway had done, you know, be able to live rather inexpensively, have plenty of time to write and build up a European following."

After living in New Orleans for six months, the author took his trip to Europe, returning to Oxford in December of 1925. For the following two years, he also spent time here, and he incorporated those experiences into his second novel, "Mosquitoes."

"While here," Blotner says, "he wrote a whole series for The Times-Picayune, mostly fiction, but some impressionistic sketches of the city. Years later, those pieces were collected and published as a book, but my guess is that he wasn't particularly anxious that they be published."

The biographer suspects Faulkner was probably paid about $15 each for the newspaper stories, which the author doubtless welcomed since he was living on the savings accumulated while he was the university station postmaster in Oxford. "When he was fired from that job, he said, 'Thank God, now I won't ever have to be at the beck and call of every sonofabitch who can buy a two-cent stamp.' But the firing was undoubtedly justified. The stories of his antics there are legion. The Rev. Mr. Hargis never got The Baptist Record on time. Once the university had supposedly sent out their catalogue to prospective students, but none were ever delivered. Somebody finally went down to the post office, and Faulkner explained that he had all the catalogues stored safely in the corner and was waiting for a stack to build up before he sent them out."

Blotner first met the Nobel Prize winner in 1957 when Faulkner became writer-in-residence at the University of Virginia, where Blotner was teaching. They established a close friendship which ended with Faulkner's death in 1962. Blotner was the only pall bearer who was not related to the Faulkners.

At the request of the Faulkner family, Blotner agreed to do the biography, and there began almost a decade of research and writing.

"Estelle (Faulkner's widow) had said, 'Tell the truth and shame the devil,' so there were very few things which the family asked me not to use in the book. And those were minor enough not to constitute an obstacle to the readers. As I would complete a chapter, I'd send a carbon to Estelle and Jill (their daughter) and they never asked me to change a thing."

The result was a manuscript of 3,000 typed pages, and when it was published by Random House in March, the two-volume set weighed eight and a half pounds. The first draft had actually been finished in 1969, but Blotner had to suffer through a number of delays in publication.

"The publishers took the book off production so they could print the Pentagon Papers. Not long after that, a close Faulkner friend, James Webb of the University of Mississippi English Department, was over at Rowan Oak, the old Faulkner house, to meet the Orkin man, and while he was waiting, he found a big box under the stairway. It was filled with various manuscripts and information which necessitated some rewriting of my book. Then, the New York Public Library located and purchased another load of Faulkner articles, and again, I had to do some rewriting.

"So, when somebody comes up to me now and remarks on how heavy my book is, I say that if I had it to do over, instead of it weighing eight and a half pounds, I'd make it maybe eight and a quarter."

UFOs Hold Authors' Interest

By BILL HUTCHINSON
Herald Staff Writer

Oh sure, you remember: It was last fall sometime and these two guys in Mississippi claimed they'd been picked up by a flying saucer that floated into a field near where they were fishing.

For a few weeks, UFOs were once again in the news — a Gallup poll taken at the time showed that 51 per cent of the population believed in them and 15 million Americans had actually seen one. But then the whole thing evaporated like a cloud of marsh gas when the President fired Archibald Cox and the nation turned to pressing terrestial matters.

RALPH BLUM wants to make sure that Pascagoula, Miss., and the UFO incident that profoundly changed the little town's character are not forgotten. For one thing, he and his wife have written a book, "Beyond Earth: Man's Contact with UFOs," which reexamines the unidentified flying object issue. But more than that, for purely academic reasons, they insist, the Blums would like to see UFOs removed once and for all from the lunatic fringe.

Pascagoula, says Blum, should have been a kind of turning point.

"Hell, all of a sudden flying saucers were hard news. People all over the country started to admit, yeah, they'd seen 'em too. Maybe these guys were on the level." (The two men, 42-year-old Charles Hickson and 19-year-old Calvin Parker, have passed every test thus far administered, says Blum.)

"Up to that point, I can't argue with the government's position of withholding support from this as a serious subject. But I think I'd have been forced to re-evaluate my position." Otherwise, he says, "an awful lot of sane, sensible people who wouldn't think to lie are suddenly either lying or hallucinating." Why not assume that they are simply telling the truth, he suggests.

"IT'S INCREDIBLE that people whose testimony on almost anything else would have been believed were ignored or dismissed or subjected to the most intense, subjective kind of examination . . . is that a nervous twitch, can he look me in the eye, what kind of family does he come from. Come on.

"We were talking about this with Margaret Mead and, as she said, anybody can fake a photograph. But when you've got 20 or 30 people giving you the same report, something is happening."

The Blums freely acknowledge that something is happening yet, like the Mr. Jones in Bob Dylan's song, they don't know what it is. They are not convinced that flying saucers exist. Nor are they convinced that they do not exist, however, and as long as some element of possibility remains, they feel that the subject deserves well-funded, comprehensive, scientific study.

Miami Herald / DAVE DIDIO

UFOs, they say, "intruded into our lives." Neither had given much thought to them before February 1973, when Cosmopolitan magazine suggested that Blum write a piece about flying saucers instead of the article on "Success in America" for which he had been contracted.

A novelist and freelance writer with impeccable educational (Harvard) and professional (The New Yorker, etc.) credentials, Blum had never been interested in UFOs. "What sane, right-thinking American man would be?" His British-born wife Judy vaguely recalls having read a brief article on the subject within the past decade, but the subject could hardly be considered of abiding concern to her.

WHILE RESEARCHING the Cosmopolitan article, however, Blum got caught up in the mass of evidence and counter-evidence that has for so long complicated the UFO question. He convinced NBC that the time had come for a serious white-paper investigation, timed to the Pascagoula developments. The network flew in camera crews, began to prepare an hour-long documentary, but then the Cox firing redirected its news department efforts.

Blum would not be redirected. He stayed on in Mississippi, enlisted the assistance of his wife, and completed the research that resulted in the recently published book.

The Blums will be in the Miami area for 10 days, and though much of their time will be spent promoting the book and talking with local UFO sources, they also hope to spend a week with friends and forget entirely about a subject that has come to engulf them.

"We're tired of it," says Blum. Quantitatively, the volume of material on UFOs is immense. Qualitatively, the material is confusing and contradictory. It's difficult, they admit, to avoid feeling frustrated by the fact that they are dealing in an area where nothing can yet be produced as irrefutable evidence.

Neither has ever seen a UFO. Blum doesn't care whether he does or not, while his wife would like to witness "a solid, recognizable craft at tree-top level because after all this I'd like to KNOW."

BEYOND THE question of their existence, the couple is interested in the sociological aspects of the UFO issue. "If these people are all lying, why are they lying," Blum wonders. "If they're hallucinating, what has caused them to have these hallucinations? This is certainly a legitimate area for behavioral study."

BLUM, Ralph
and
BLUM, Judy

MIAMI HERALD
(Miami, Fla.)

May 8, 1974

Author Fills 'History Gap' of Black Actors

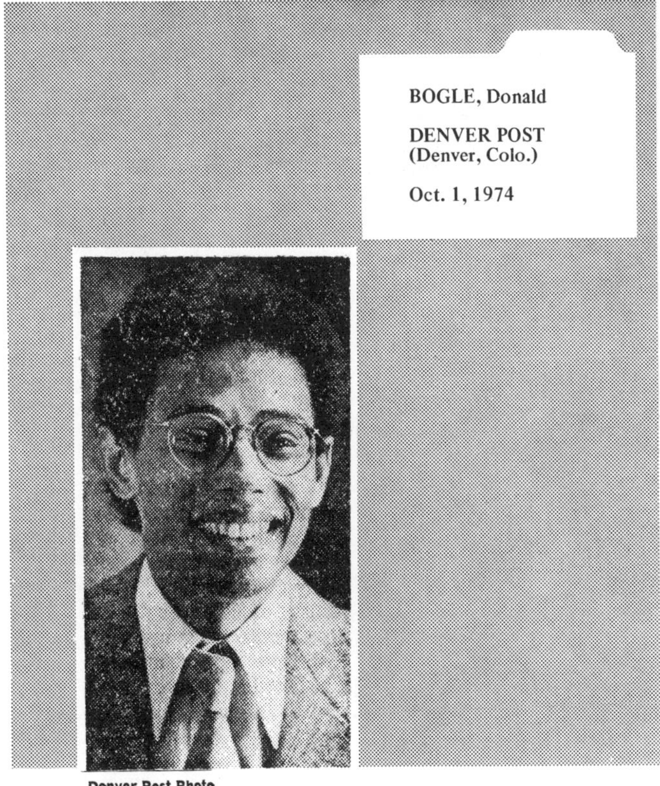
BOGLE, Donald

DENVER POST
(Denver, Colo.)

Oct. 1, 1974

Denver Post Photo

By ROBERT DOWNING
Denver Post Drama Editor

Donald Bogle is an intensely relaxed young author, not yet out of his 20s. He was in Denver Monday to help promote his first book, which has brought him a national reputation.

The book is called "Toms, Coons, Mulattoes, Mammies and Bucks."

"I have asked that my picutre be used on the cover of every copy of the book," Bogle says. "I felt everyone should know at once that it was written by a black."

"At first," Bogle says, "I thought some people — perhaps militants, might object to the title. Most have understood why I chose the title and once you dip into the book, you know it couldn't be called anything else."

As a history of black entertainers in this country, Bogle's work traces the rise of the race to prominence in the world of show business.

"When I was a schoolboy," Bogle remembers, "I didn't know there were any black actors." The lad grew up in a small town in Pennsylvania. "Then, when I was in high school, I happened to see the movie, 'Carmen Jones.' "

CHANGED LIFE

The picture changed the young man's life. He saw every film he could find in which black performers appeared. He learned all he could about these artists. Since he has almost total recall, he remembered most of what he saw and read.

Trying tro interview Bogle is a little like participating in an Olympic event. He lopes across a room. In any given corridor, he takes off as if he were on a 100-yard dash, clutching his overstuffed brief case, which is almost half his own size, and talking as he flies.

"What's in the brief case?" one is inclined to gasp. "Are you working on a new book?"

"Not yet," Bogle smiles — and he's 50 feet away, finding the newspaper's photographic room with a sure sense all his own, and already perched on a high stool, beaming into the lens when he is pinned down again by an inquiring reporter.

"When I'm not on tour for the book, I lecture on the history of black film at Lincoln University in Pennsylvania," Bogle reports — and the pictures have been taken and he's off to the elevators like a shot.

"Bantam makes all these appointments," he volunteers genially, glancing at his watch. In addition to dropping in at The Denver Post, Bogle was interviewed several times for television and radio during his single day in Denver.

After college, Bogle worked as a story editor for producer Otto Preminger.

"I was thinking about black actors in the movies all the time," he states. "I knew some of their work, not all. For instance, I had to be told that Dolly Wilson was the wonderful Sam in 'Casablanca.' I thought the name of that role belonged to Hoagy Carmichael."

That was Bogle's first traumatic experience relating to the work of blacks in films. When he was a staff writer for Ebony magazine, the second shock occurred.

"Gone With the Wind" had been reissued, and the young writer suggested a feature story on Butterfly McQueen who played Prissy in the movie. His colleagues promptly indicated that they considered most oldtime black actors to be toms and mammies, persons to be spoken about with disgust and condescension.

Bogle, recovering from this experience, felt this pointed to the fact that there really was no adequate history of black film in America. In fact, there was no history at all.

Instead of revealing the past and the people who participated in it, Bogle felt the early days of blacks in the movies needed to be defined and interpreted.

DIFFICULT TASK

This is when the young man set about writing his book. His research was exhaustive and difficult. From the printed page, from dozens of scrapbooks, and after examining hundreds of stills, Bogle finally graduated to the personal interview.

One by one, he tracked down black performers — stars, bit players, headliners, has-beens. Some of the actors refused to see Bogle. Others were helpful, but didn't wish to be mentioned by name. Then Mantan Moreland, Clarence Muse and Sidney Poitier came through for the writer. So did Robert Hooks. And King Vidor, the director, spoke of blacks in his famous films. Lorenzo Tucker helped, and Vivian Dandridge, the late Dorothy's sister.

Eventually, it became a problem for Bogle to decide who he should include and which players might not be in his book after all. He decided, at last, to deal with players on the basis of their importance to the history of blacks in motion pictures.

Bogle is informed, personable and communicative. His paperback book costs $2.25. With its penetrating text and its many illustrations, the book will become a collector's item.

"How many cities are you visiting on this tour?" Bogle was asked.

There wasn't a clear answer. The young author was already half way to east Denver looking for a cab.

Doubts of an animal cracker

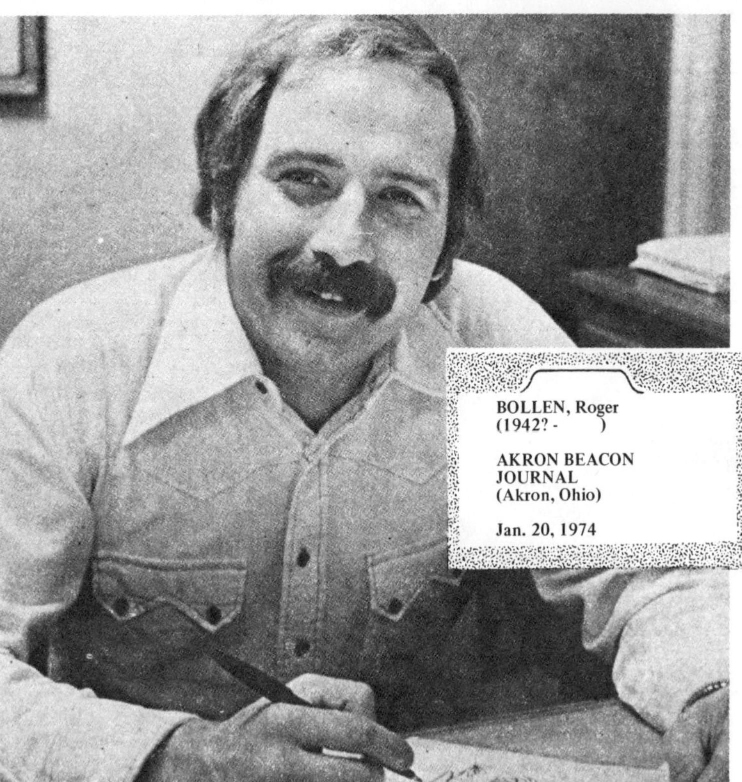

BOLLEN, Roger
(1942? -)

AKRON BEACON
JOURNAL
(Akron, Ohio)

Jan. 20, 1974

Bollen at the board.

By BOB DOWNING
Beacon Journal Staff Writer

"Animal Crackers" have sustained Roger Bollen for most of a decade now, but fears for survival reside still with the 32-year-old cartoonist who created the comic strip.

"The old comic strips like Nancy and Sluggo and Dagwood and Blondie will always be around," the mustachioed Bollen said. "The question is whether the public will allow strips like Doonesbury,' 'The Wizard of Id' and 'B. C.' along with my strips to be different — contemporary and not in the traditional mold of comic strips."

A Kent State University graduate, Bollen worked briefly for an Akron advertising agency. He currently has three strips sold nationally.

"THE NEW comic strips are contemporary and different. They try to reflect society as we see it. For that reason, I live with the fear that they'll never reach the top and never be super-popular."

Despite his fears, "Animal Crackers" is carried by more than 125 newspapers including the Beacon Journal; "Funny Business," a business-page comic strip runs in 400 newspapers, and his newest Western-based strip called "Catfish" is growing fast since its October beginning.

Bollen — who was raised in East Cleveland with dreams of drawing Bambi's and Dumbo's for Walt Disney when he grew up — reflected, "Generally cartoonists aren't exciting people. They're more like hermits.

"I wanted the independence and wanted to be my own boss," he said. "That's why I became a cartoonist. Besides," he quipped, "That's the only thing I know how to do."

WHEN HE is working in his plush Geauga County home, his 6-year-old, blond-haired daughter Milissa has learned to approach her father cautiously: "Daddy, are you thinking or drawing?"

Bollen explained his daughter's caution. "I can sit here with a blank sheet of paper in front of me forever if it's noisy. My wife Georgianna can't even iron when I'm trying to think," he said.

The brainstorming must be completed before the sketching begins, he says. And the drawing must be completed before the weekly deadline of 18 black-and-white comic strips and two Sunday color strips.

Bollen's friends include a seedy, buckskin-wearing Western scout named Catfish and a gaggle of assorted African animals in "Animal Crackers."

LYLE, a scrawny-looking, scraggly-maned lion, leads a crew of critters which includes a bitter, sarcastic dodo, a rebellious gnu and a bully elephant.

"The animals are real losers who see the ironies in life," Bollen explained. "They observe the foibles of man, commenting through sarcasm and innocent humor about things they really don't understand.

"African animals form a great platform for discussions, especially relating to ecology. But we called it conservation back in 1967 when the strip started.

"Good satire is successful through innuendo and implication," Bollen said. "You can't hit people over the head with the little points you're trying to make. You cannot preach and still hold the audience; they're too sophisticated for that. Comic strips are still a humorous medium and you have to work with that."

HE SAID he tried a nostalgia comic strip called "Ripple Falls" nine years ago. He was, however, unsuccessful in getting the series syndicated. The syndicates in New York suggested he try a business page strip and "Funny Business" was started.

Bollen says that of the cartoonists, he most admires the late Walt Kelly, who drew "Pogo" and Johnny Hart who draws "B. C." He said he designed "Animal Crackers" to fill a niche:

"There was 'Pogo' which was so sophisticated, profound and complex and the kiddies' comics like 'Bugs Bunny.' There was nothing in between,'' Bollen said. "That's how 'Animal Crackers' came into being."

Bollen, casually dressed in jeans and a blue work shirt, explained he draws the strips with felt-tip pens.

"CARTOONING is a highly specialized form of writing that really cannot be taught," he said. "You have to get the idea across with a limited number of words. The timing is crucial to the humor succeeding or flopping. Restraint is also important — you just cannot put too much into one strip."

Bollen added, "Most of my ideas just come from straining. I usually have to twist and sweat to come up with a good punchline. It's a demanding job and the punchline is the hardest part."

Saying he usually gets five fan letters per week, Bollen explained that he gets ideas from watching television news and reading magazines. "This way you keep abreast of trends, which may or may not be real in eight weeks when the strips finally appear."

Bollen, who admitted his dark-haired wife usually corrects his spelling and punctuation, said, "Under most circumstances, I think the job is 75 pct. coming up with ideas and 25 pct. drawing them out on paper — even though both are equally important.

"Cartooning is a very personal thing — either people like it or they don't. I just keep wondering if people will like the new image comic strips."

A sample from Animal Crackers

EXCUSE ME.. IS THIS
THE EASTBOUND LANE ?

'What Will They Do When They Find Out I'm Just Chubby Old Erma Bombeck From Dayton, Ohio?'

Photos by BRUCE SINNER, Blade Photo Director

BOMBECK, Erma
(1927-)

TOLEDO BLADE
(Toledo, Ohio)

Feb. 16, 1975

[See also CA-23/24]

By SEYMOUR ROTHMAN

For 20 years I rubbed elbows with the herculean heroes of the sports world. For 10 years I sat at the feet of glamorous stars of stage, screen, and burlesque. So how do I explain to my kids that my idol is a 47-year-old housewife-writer who doesn't even know how to spell Irma?

But that's a fact, and Erma Bombeck has my love letters to prove it.

You know Erma, of course. For one thing, she's the nation's No. 1 kindred soul. She does "At Wit's End," the hilarious life-with-dirty-laundry-dishes-and/or-kids column which has each American housewife feeling that she is writing her biography.

For another thing she appears three times each week in The Blade as well as 521 other newspapers in the United States and many more in Canada. That may not sound like much, but only if you are stone deaf.

The list of subscribers cover every large and medium city in the United States except New York. For some reason, the syndicate has been unable to sell Erma to a New York newspaper. It may be that she already appears in virtually every newspaper in the suburban areas for miles around.

In addition to writing for all those newspapers, Good Housekeeping magazine buys her prose every other month; Readers Digest and Today's Health reprint her columns frequently; she has three books in print and a publisher who's bellowing for a fourth; she is in demand as a lecturer, and there is a national TV talk show ready to welcome her aboard whenever she is available.

It is anyone's guess what sort of income this activity nets her, but it is large enough so that she finds it harder and harder to be funny about income taxes.

Being funny is a skill, but being funny the way Erma is funny elevates it to an art. Erma takes a sobering situation and laces it with funny lines to an acceptable philosophic conclusion. The philosophy generally is "Learn to enjoy frustration."

Of course, in such writing finding the situation is half the battle. Finding the philosophy is the other half. Getting the funny lines in between also is about 50 per cent of the battle — all of which adds up to 150 per cent and gives you some idea of the kind of a battle it is. But Erma, bless her, wins more than her share of them.

Erma writes things like: "For years I've been telling educators that they put their levys on the ballot at the wrong time of the year. If they had mothers vote during Christmas vacation not a levy in the country would fail." Any veteran parent of one or more kids knows immediately what she is driving at and agrees with her fully.

Or consider the column that started, "I didn't mind when my daughter's hair covered her eyes. I didn't mind when it hung longer than her hemline. But when I discovered it wasn't my daughter at all, but my son, I became alarmed." Couldn't you take it from there?

Erma's role in the column is that of a wife and mother who long ago has conceded defeat, but can't find anyone to surrender to. When you meet her in person, you get the idea that she's transferred this character to her real self.

On her lecture-visit to Toledo, for example, she displayed all the do-it-yourselfisms of a mother of long standing. We met for breakfast. She tried to carry her own travelling bag. She tried to pay for the scrambled eggs, and she worried that my coffee was getting cold.

It so happened that when Erma arrived in Toledo the evening before the lecture she was met by promoter Ken Shaw in his shiny new car, escorted to her motel, and then to the annual Ribs and Roast dinner.

Because Ken had to discuss an upcoming engagement of "Pippin" the following morning, Frank Fisher, the PR man, appeared in his beaten-up vehicle to deliver Erma to the Masonic Auditorium.

"Looks like I'm out and Pippin's in," Erma giggled, and jumped into the car as if it were her boy friend's. If success has spoiled Erma Bombeck, it's her secret.

While Erma has been writing funny stuff ever since she was Erma Fiste in Patterson Co-op High School in Dayton, O., getting well paid for it is something relatively new.

Erma's childhood was advantaged in one way. It gave her ample opportunity to learn to laugh at adversity. There was plenty of it around. Not only was she a depression baby, but her father died right in the middle of it. She was 9 at the time.

She went to Patterson so that she could work while in school, and took a job as a copygirl on the Dayton Herald, which now is the Dayton Journal Herald. The first of her funny columns appeared in type in the high school paper.

Erma upset the tradition of her kinfolk by finishing high school and going on to college, one year at Ohio U and then three years at the University of Dayton. She wrote funny stuff for the school newspaper and magazine, got a job in the women's department of the Journal Herald, and married Bill Bombeck.

Bill had been a copyboy at the same time Erma had been a copygirl. After high school he went into military service. After his discharge he enrolled at the U of D and wound up teaching at Centerville, O., High School.

Just about the time Betsy was born, in 1953, Bill moved into the Dayton school system and Erma left the newspaper to concentrate on motherhood.

Bill went on to get a master's degree and become involved in administrative education. Erma went on to have Baby No. 2, Andy, in 1955, and Baby No. 3, Matt, in 1959.

As any mother and Dr. Spock knows, what goes on with raising children you can write a book about, and the urge to write was strong upon Erma.

As Erma put it, "I'd reached the point where I was reading those 'address envelopes in your own home at a penny apiece' and wondering. Writing is writing."

Then one day in 1963 she collected her nerve and a few column ideas and presented herself to Ron Ginger, the editor of the Kettering-Oakwood Times, a weekly of 12,000 circulation. Housewife-columnists hold little attraction for editors, but Mr. Ginger, against his better judgment, agreed to $3 per week for her efforts.

Donald Wright, who now is editor, recalls that the general feeling was that this type of column is not for newspapers, but the reader response was such that the attitude soon ➡

(Continued from preceding page)

changed. As a matter of fact, the paper soon thought it was good enough to enter in the state newswriting competition and entered it twice. It didn't even win honorable mention.

"Erma called the column Zone 57' because that was her Zipcode number, and we learned to love her work and to love Erma. The column was so popular that quite a demand rose for her services as a speaker, and she escaped only by pricing herself out of the market," Mr. Wright recalled.

Only once was Erma called upon to write something besides her column.

"We asked her to cover a football game for us," Mr. Wright said. "She wrote a hilarious piece about the people in the stands, and handled the game itself in the final sentence That ended her reporting career with us."

Glenn Thompson, editor of the Dayton Journal Herald, saw Erma's work in the K-O Times and decided that it was too good for such limited circulation.

"Ginger was a friend of mine," Mr. Thompson said, "so I warned him that I was going to steal his columnist. He was pleased that Erma would be doing better. Erma and I reached an agreement for three columns per week at $15 each.

"It didn't take me long to satisfy myself that Erma could be funny three times a week. I then put together a batch of her columns and sent them off to Tom Dorsey at Newsday Syndicate. Almost immediately the syndicate called back that it was interested.

"Tom came to Dayton and had dinner with Erma and me, and Erma became a nationally syndicated writer. We could add her name to those of Milt Caniff, who does Steve Canyon,' and Phyllis Battelle who does 'Assignment: America, for national syndicates. They're out of Dayton, too."

Mr. Thompson now admits that his motive in selling Erma to a syndicate was not entirely altruistic.

"I was paying $45 a week for Erma. When the syndicate took her over I was able to buy her for $15." He chuckles at that.

Newsday had Erma in some 65 papers when the syndicate was taken over by the Los Angeles Times Syndicate in 1967. Erma had been working on a year-by-year contract with Newsday. When renewal time came along Erma found herself being courted by a number of syndicates who wanted to take her over.

"We all started romancing her," reports Robert G. Cowles, president of Field Newspaper Syndicate, which then was Publishers-Hall Syndicate. "There was literally a syndicate convention on her doorstep. She elected to come with us, and we tied her up with a long-term contract."

It's been a fine association all around. They love Erma as a person, as a professional, and as a profit-turner, and in a syndicate which has such hotshots as Sylvia Porter Bernard Meltzer, Allen Saunders, Johnny Hart, Mell Lazarus, Robert Cleveland, Earl Wilson, Herbert Block, Bill Mauldin, and Dr. Nick Dallis, to name a few, this is quite a love affair.

"We've been selling Erma as a women's page feature," Mr. Cowles said, "but we find more and more papers running her in other sections. One has her on the comic page, a number on the feature pages, and your Blade has her in the Peach Section. They found out before we did that she isn't strictly for women."

During the newsprint shortage a Kansas editor pulled the Bombeck column to save space, but reinstated it shortly afterward with a column to the subscribers apologizing for the move. He'd heard about it from the readers.

BOMBECK, Erma

TOLEDO BLADE
(Toledo, Ohio)

Feb. 16, 1975

Erma's column is edited at the syndicate by Mary Sharkey, who also is Mr. Cowles' secretary.

"Every once in a while Mary will break out into laughter, and I know that she's editing Erma," Mr. Cowles says.

All this success, which delights Erma, also frightens her.

"I keep thinking, 'What will they do when they find out I'm just chubby old Erma Bombeck from Dayton, Ohio? Will they take away my $100,000 house and swimming pool and the sprinkler system and my $495 worth of Dwarf Tiff grass?'"

These are among her proud possessions in Paradise Valley, Ariz., which is near Phoenix. Erma discovered Phoenix on a lecture tour and was determined to trade in the 30-acre farm in Bellbrook, O., (the family and long since moved from Centerville) for the sunshine and distant mountains of the valley.

It took a little doing. Bill had advanced from assistant principal to principal to supervisor of social studies in the Dayton school system over the intervening 20 years and wasn't in the mood for change.

See, if you have the idea that as Erma Bombeck's husband Bill is a candidate for charter membership to the Whistler's Father Club (along with Grampa Moses, Mr. Billie Jean King, and Gloria Steinem's boy friend) you are mistaken.

"I finally won him over by pointing out that the last three school levies had failed, and that if we moved he could take time off and complete work on his doctorate," Erma reports. "Also, he owed me a honeymoon which we could take."

Bill bought the idea, enrolled at Arizona State in Tempe, earned his doctorate and resumed his career as an educator-administrator in Phoenix.

"Being a character in Erma's columns has been no problem," Bill assured me. "She's been writing humor about the things around her as long as I can remember, and anyone around Erma must expect to be part of her funny world.

Few of his students have much awareness of his place in Erma's world. It is more commonly known among the parents. And, anyhow, who is going to chide the man who has power of pass or fail in his hands.

Erma appears to have no hangups about meeting deadlines. She's converted a part of the garage into a study where she works from about 8 a.m. to 2 p.m. Then she gets on with the matter of housing and feeding the family.

"I wash out a toilet bowl or two now and then just to keep humble," she explains.

Column ideas are collected on large yellow legal pads as they occur, and Erma expresses no fear that they will stop occurring.

"I use the 'cookie reward' system for incentive," she says. "I type my name at the top of the page and reward myself with a cookie. Then I decide on the subject matter and reward myself with another cookie. Every time I advance toward completion I get a cookie."

Erma produces 400-word columns for the newspapers, 1,500 words for Good Housekeeping, and whatever the publisher will accept for books.

"Among the neighbors is Bil Keane who draws 'Family Circus,'" Erma says. "He does in his cartoons what I do in my columns so we steal a lot from each other. We published a book together."

While she lives in Paradise Valley, Erma writes strictly from Dayton. The Arizona climate isn't typical enough for a homey column like "At Wit's End."

"You will notice," she says, "that every winter I cope with snow shovels and other problems of the season. I do them from memory. Who can be a typical mother in a climate like Arizona's?" ■

A writer who can escape: Off the world, onto the water

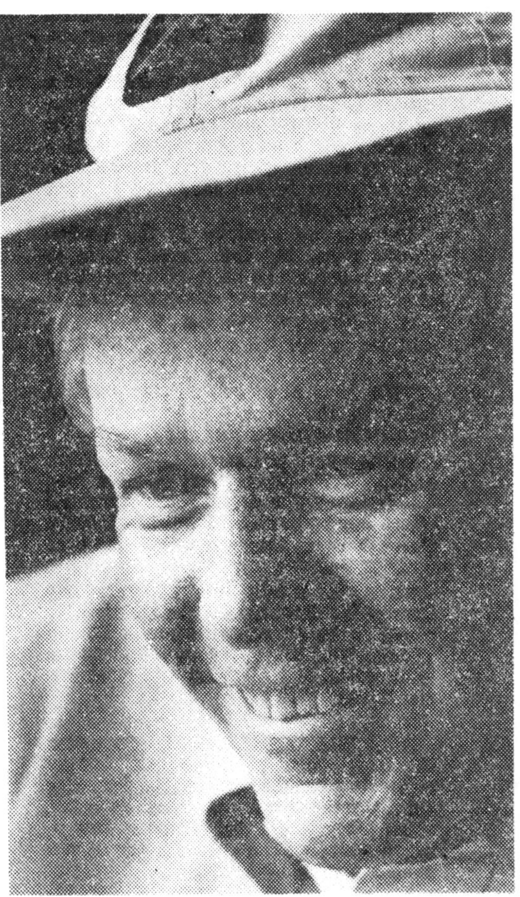

Staff photo by C. Thomas Hardin

By FRANCIS CHURCH

ARNOLD C. BRACKMAN is a noted authority on Southeast Asian affairs. He has won a number of book awards, the latest in 1970 from the Overseas Press Club. A former foreign correspondent for the United Press, he is a writer for such prestigious publications as The Economist of London and The New York Times.

But like many another American, when weekends arrive "Brack" Brackman likes to stop the world and get off — and onto the water. Donning the traditional long-billed hat with crossed-fish insignia, he becomes Capt. Moss Bunker (no relation to Archie: "I tell them I'm a cousin to Ellsworth Bunker, the former ambassador to Saigon").

Actually, the "captain" points out, Moss Bunker is derived from mossbunker, oily fish used for cat food and industrial purposes (known as menhaden in Southern waters). "Mossbunker are to the fisherman what fool's gold is to the prospector. When mossbunker show up, the sea boils with them, thousands on thousands of silvery backs. The novice fisherman baits up his line, goes through every maneuver to catch them. But mossbunker never go for a hook. The novice just sees them and goes home disappointed. Only a net or seine works."

CAPT. MOSS BUNKER has become an author, too, and the result is "Damn the Garbage, Full Speed Ahead: A Handbook on the Joys and Sorrows of Pleasure Boating" (McGraw-Hill. $5.95).

Writer Brackman was in town the other day to address the Louisville Committee on Foreign Relations. The next morning, Capt. Bunker put on his fishing cap, headed for a television studio to discuss the new book on a talk show, and still later sat over a cup of coffee and reminisced about his love affair with the water.

"Ever since I was a boy wandering along Long Beach on Long Island, I have been a fisherman. My wife is from the Amazon area of South America (specifically Surinan), and she's always fished, too. Our daughter naturally became interested. In fact, when she was 8 or 9 years old, in the days before Women's Lib, she entered a fishing contest in camp; the boys laughed, until she won the contest."

IN THOSE DAYS the Brack...the Bunkers went fishing in the large party boats that take groups fishing from seaport cities and towns. "Whenever we wanted to take off and fish, we simply got up at 4 a.m. and signed on one of those big boats."

But when the family got back from a sojourn in Southeast Asia in 1962, they ran head-on into one of the notable innovations of that decade, the transistor radio. Transistor radios on party boats? Yes. "I don't have anything against rock music. But we found that instead of offering a way of escaping, the boat was a bedlam of noise; that's not my idea of going to sea.

"At the same time, it was costing us more and more money. When we went to Montauk (the eastern tip of Long Island), the bill for the motel and all the other expenses was going higher and higher."

BRACKMAN, Arnold C(harles)
(1923 -)
COURIER JOURNAL & TIMES (Louisville, Ken.) Feb. 16, 1975
[See also CA-5/6]

So he looked to the classifieds in his favorite fishing magazine, and discovered what he wanted, a used 26-foot sport-fishing boat. "And I also found I was taking on maintenance and upkeep unimaginable to a landsman. I had to find my own fishing ground; no longer would the party-boat captain take me there."

THERE WAS more to come. "I had to become a mechanic. I had to study the weather, learn to operate a radio-telephone, get a license from the FCC, learn seamanship; one thing and another pyramided. The next thing I knew I was turning into a yachtsman instead of a fisherman. What's a yachtsman? Any dictionary will tell you a yacht is a boat used only for pleasure."

And it didn't take the captain long to encounter one of the realities of modern-day cruising. "On our first cruise we ran into a lot of garbage. Then a waterlogged object hit the propeller, and we were disabled. We discovered that in this technological age, one must damn the garbage, full speed ahead!" Hence the title of Capt. Bunker's new book.

THE NOVICE yachtsman will find that in reading the book, a lot of those early headaches will be eliminated. First off, there are useful rules to follow in buying the first boat (and the second and the third, and so on, for as soon as one invests in an 18-footer, he'll be ready to move up in a year or so).

He'll be able to read some of the weather signs, and perhaps save himself some heartaches on the water. Then the rules of the road, anchoring, cooking, charts, knot-tying and yards and marinas. While a lot of this material is more applicable to the coast than to the Ohio River or Kentucky Lake, many of the guidelines apply everywhere.

SUCH INFORMATION, much of it technical, becomes something of a bore in the hands of some authors, but not for one who enjoys it as much as Capt. Bunker. He sprinkles his advice with many an anecdote or footnote from history. In discussing knots, he reports: "Unfortunately, there is not enough credit to go around to the men who designed the first knot. The evidence is that in the beginning, when it came to knots and other things, people just did what came naturally. Thus, 5,000 years ago, Chinese sailors expertly belayed and spliced lines with the identical knots used by the Egyptians on the Nile on the other side of the world. When Columbus & Company hit the beach, they quickly established that they shared marlinspike seamanship (the art of dealing with rope), among other common techniques, with the Indians."

Putting it still another way, Capt. Bunker says one sort of goes into yachting backwards. "I'm more convinced than ever that one has got to be crazy to have a boat." But he makes that statement with a smile. For Capt. Bunker is also convinced that, though the purchase of a boat seems like a big investment initially, over the long term it's cheaper for family vacations than staying at motels.

"WE LOST a few years of fishing while we were learning yachting, but now we're back to fishing. I feel we have struck a happy medium." During the week his boat is tied up at a marina near New Haven, Conn., an hour or so from his home in Brookfield Center, Conn. On weekends it heads out into Long Island Sound for such unspoiled places as Block Island and Montauk Point.

"After these many years at sea," Capt. Bunker adds, "I have become a chicken of the sea. And the more you're out there, the bigger chicken you become. Just ask any doorman!"

Writer Criticizes Fantasy Fare

BRADBURY, Ray (Douglas) (1920-)

ARIZONA DAILY STAR (Tucson, Ariz.)

Sept. 28, 1974

[See also CA-4]

Ray Bradbury

By JUDY DONOVAN
Star Staff Writer

Science fiction writer Ray Bradbury is neither modest about his enviable writing achievements nor mild in his criticism of current film and television production.

"Most of the science fiction on television is pretty bad," he commented yesterday in a press conference at Braniff Place. He is here to address the annual joint conference of the Arizona State Library Assn. and the Arizona Assn. of Audiovisual Education continuing through today at the Tucson Community Center.

Bradbury said the early Rod Serling television productions were much better than today's TV fare, "mostly because they were written by me and my friends." The old Alfred Hitchcock shows were good too, he added.

"There is too much interference from producers who don't know what they're doing," Bradbury continued. "We have very few American fantasy writers who do science fiction at the same time. If I wanted to do a television series, I'd go to England and get writers and producers there because they're better."

He considers the movie version of his book "The Illustrated Man" a "disaster," but feels "Fahrenheit 451" was "much better."

Science fiction films have an unpredictable market, and the money is very tight, he remarked. "The people at the studios are basically morons when it comes to making decisions."

Bradbury's non-stop writing career, which includes "The Martian Chronicles," "The Golden Apples of the Sun," "The October Country," dozens of short stories, poems, plays, essays and films, had its tentative beginnings in Tucson, when he was a 12-year-old student at Amphitheater Junior High School in 1932. He wrote short stories and drew illustrations for them as well.

Bradbury also broke into radio production here, reading the Sunday Arizona Daily Star comics to child listeners. He said he was paid with free tickets to the local movies and went for "anything romantic with a fantastic flare, including all the horrror movies." The youngster saw "King Kong" three times.

"It turned out I had incredible taste, because all the old Buck Rogers, Tarzan and Prince Valiant comic books I saved are now the golden era comics of collectors," he said.

He doesn't fear running out of science fiction ideas because there's already plenty of "sci-fi" material in ancient history and "we're in a state of constant flux," he said.

The discovery of horse-training in Persia centuries ago, for example, was like a science fiction concept, Bradbury explained. It was a case of practicing an idea. When the idea works, it changes the course of history radically. Once the use of horses in combat became widespread, it meant the defeat of other forces, he said.

Life on earth will last only a few hundred years more, Bradbury believes. "Five hundred thousand years from now we'll all be living someplace else and looking back at Earth as the place where it all began," he said.

In matters of science Bradbury said he is "totally stupid."

"I can't tell you how to build an atom bomb and I don't even really understand how a car engine works. I'm interested in the impact of science on human lives. If you're too good a scientist, you're not a good writer," he added.

The Next Whole Earth Apocalypse

by Paul Ciotti

Stewart Brand was tired. When I went to see him at his shop in Sausalito he was slumped forward in his chair with his elbows on his knees. He had fallen behind schedule with the winter issue of *CoEvolution Quarterly* and he still had not yet recovered from what he was calling a "media flash" set off by the New York *Times* when they ran an article about the publication of his big *Whole Earth Epilog* and thereby attracted waves of reporters from *Time, Newsweek*, the national networks and right down the line.

"Let's wrap this up pretty quick," he said as I took a seat. It was not the sort of auspicious beginning for which a reporter might have hoped. Certainly I had not come all the way to Sausalito in the footsteps of so many other reporters merely to hear from Brand's own lips what he had previously told the *Times*. Yet if he didn't even want to respond to nuts and bolts newspaperman-type questions, he surely would not willingly throw himself into the more subtle and diffuse things I rather had in mind.

I started out conventionally enough asking Brand a few straightforward questions about *Catalog* sales, the Point Foundation and financial arrangements for *Epilog*. The *Whole Earth Catalog*, he said, sold some 1.3 million copies in 14 or 15 editions since it first came out in 1968. From this, it earned $1.2 million in profits for the Point Foundation (a non-profit corporation) which Point gave away so successfully that it went intentionally broke by the end of 1974, having gotten rid of both interest and capital. To publish the *Epilog*, Point then went $140,000 in debt ($25,000 of which was Brand's own money). By the end of this year, Point will have sold perhaps half-a-million copies, as well as another 100,000 *Catalogs*, which continue to move briskly. (Brand's deal with Point is that he gets 15 per cent of the profits from *Epilog*. If *Epilog* sells one million copies, this will bring him, he says, $100,000 over several years.)

Paul Ciotti, a frequent contributor to this magazine, wrote last month's article on Mensa and high intelligence.

As has elsewhere been reported, Brand started his impressively successful *Whole Earth Catalogs* in the summer of 1968 under the benign guidance of Dick Raymond at the Portola Institute in Menlo Park (the only Portola project which ever made money, says Raymond) and ended up a counter-culture folk hero a bit against his will. "Heroism is in scary repute . . .," Brand once wrote, "because some who stood charismatically tall have been shot down. I believe they asked for it, some of them. They came to rely too completely on audience and visibility until the vainglory showed and drew a bullet. If you sell your soul to the crowd, by and by they'll collect." On the other hand, fame has its uses, and at the end of the *Catalog* Brand printed a list of the ones he had noticed most. "It accelerates access, if you want access," he wrote. "You can hang around with famous people, which is fun sometimes. Your credit is good with strangers. It's never hard to meet people. It's usually easy to find work, make some money. If you've withstood fame there's some things you're strong at that you might not be otherwise." The important thing about it, though, is that it is mainly a matter of convenience for other people. Certainly, according to Brand, "there's no reason to take it personally."

BRAND, Stewart
(1938 -)

SAN FRANCISCO
(San Francisco, Calif.)

Jan., 1975

PAUL FUSCO

Stewart Brand: pointing out tools of independence.

In late 1969, Brand announced that he would suspend publication of the *Whole Earth Catalog* with a big fat issue for spring, 1971. As explained in the short history written by Brand for the *Catalog*, he was tired of working on the thing, somebody else could take it over now that he had shown the way, and, also (with a kind of Brandian whimsy) he was curious to know what would happen.

What happened was he found himself in a gold mine. Although Brand's intuitive decision to halt publication did not, according to Dick Raymond, turn on financial considerations, Brand could not have made a sounder business move had there been "seventeen vice presidents advising him."

The decision "was one of the great marketing inventions of all time," agreed ex-banker Michael Phillips, a former Point director who wrote a book about his experiences there called *The Seven Laws of Money*. "The Catalog," he wrote, "which might have sold over ten years at the rate of 100,000 or 200,000 a year, has sold over 1,100,000 in two years."

With the *Catalog* off his back, Brand was free to indulge in other fantasies. He bought land in Canada and built a house; along with the Point foundation he made a "misbegotten effort to liven up the UN conference on The Human Environment in Stockholm by sending over sundry poets, Indians, radical scientists and the Hog Farm traveling commune"; he spoke at New York's Lincoln Center in acceptance of the National Book Award prize for Contemporary Affairs (judge Gary Wills resigned in protest); and he put together a New Games Tournament in the Marin headlands just over the

(Continued from preceding page)

Golden Gate Bridge, a never quite fully-explained event (it had something to do with stopping war, Brand would later say) that drew some 4000 people, mainly on the strength of Brand's name and his not inconsiderable skill at using the media to his advantage.

Along about this time he also got back into full swing on something he had been thinking about since August, 1972 — resuming publication of the *Catalog*. He located a crab shack on a Sausalito pier, rounded up a crew and went back into the catalog business. Because of the fanfare surrounding his original decision to halt publication of the *Catalog* (he even held a demise party in the Exploratorium and invited 1500 people), Brand felt he owed his public some explanation. It appeared in the April, 1974 edition of *Harper's* Magazine, for which Brand edited the "Wraparound":

Some explanation is owed. In May, 1971 we ceased making Whole Earth Catalogs *forever sincerely enough on the expectation that someone would quickly come along and fill the niche better than we did. Well,*

1) They didn't;

2) The Last Whole Earth Catalog *continued to sell 5000 copies a week with increasingly outdated information;*

3) The North American economy began to lose its mind, putting more people in need of tools of independence and the economy as a whole in need of greater local resilience; and

4) After burning our bridges we reported before the Throne to announce, "We're here for our next terrific idea." The Throne said, "That was it."

Ever since 1968 Brand has been pumping out these newsprint catalogs telling folks where to get a good wood-burning stove, how to raise goats, where to find a windmill, plus a lot more having to do with education, communications, personal philosophy and cybernetics. Now people wouldn't go around handing over $5 bills for the *Catalog* unless they felt it would help them cope in one way or another with what Brand somewhat metaphorically describes as the apocalypse. And Brand himself could not have worked so long and hard on the whole project without having learned something more than how to put out catalogs.

It was, to my way of thinking, similar to the situation of those cancer patients who, upon learning that they only have a few more months or years left to live, suddenly and decisively take it upon themselves to make the fullest possible use of the time they have left. And so in a few months they arrive at a kind of self-knowledge that will probably be denied to the rest of us no matter how long we live. If Brand's greater vision really does see an apocalypse over the hill coming our way, his insights, like those of the cancer patient, ought to be correspondingly acute. Or so my theory ran.

Brand wasn't having any of it. I doubted that he understood much of what I was trying to explain in my inimitable and convoluted way. And to the extent that he did understand it, he appeared not to like it at all. I began again on another tack.

From your point of view, I told Brand, you have nothing to gain from talking to me. At best all you can hope for is a slightly garbled version of what you say appearing in print. And at worst there will be outright distortions. Besides, it isn't as if you need a reporter to make yourself clear to the world. You're a good writer yourself, if not a gifted one, and anything you care to write you can do perfectly well without any help from me.

Brand smiled. It was the one thing I'd said so far that he could agree with one-hundred per cent.

"What did you think of Tom Wolfe's book on Ken Kesey?" I asked. Brand was a bosom buddy of Kesey from the olden days and one of the Merry Pranksters Wolfe wrote about in *Electric Kool-Aid Acid Test*.

"There were a couple of mistakes in it," he said, apparently not sure what I was getting at. But otherwise the book was great.

That was my point. Brand, I felt, didn't want anyone snooping around in his private life. And on that we were agreed. But a kind of selective micro-biography on a particular subject need not be shamefully voyeuristic. Nor did it have to be any major project. What I had in mind was observing Brand at work and, if it seemed suitable, tagging along a bit on his daily routine. There was no thought that I would shadow him until a deep personal crisis transpired before my very eyes. Besides, it was the little things that either gave away the bullshit people (to use a Ken Kesey expression) or made you feel this was someone whose life held lessons worth knowing for your own. It was, I thought, a reasonable proposal, if Brand could spare the time.

BRAND, Stewart

SAN FRANCISCO
(San Francisco, Calif.)

Jan., 1975

Brand's present operation is run from a small warehouse (or large garage if you prefer) on the Sausalito waterfront. When I went to see Brand on a wet afternoon in late November, his shop was surprisingly quiet, though half-a-dozen people were busily at work on the winter *CoEvolution Quarterly* (same idea as the *Catalog* and *Epilog* but long articles rather than short blurbs). If you didn't count the occasional clatter of an IBM Selectric against the back wall, the loudest sound was the wind-up clock in the front office. "It is not the big happy communal operation that people think it is," I would later be told by one of the workers in the front office, Diana Barich. Barich is an old friend of Brand from the early days of the *Catalog* (and one of the few people ever to return a Point Foundation grant when she decided not to do what the grantors expected). "It's a job," she said. "You come to work in the morning and you go home at night." People don't expect that, she claimed, and when *Pacific Sun* printed a little notice last spring saying that Brand was firing up the editorial operation for the *CoEvolution Quarterly*, some 50 or 60 letters came in the mail, all offering to "do anything" just to work around Brand and the other staffers.

In person Stewart Brand has a long lean look about him that makes you think of a polar bear when he walks around in his brown overcoat and wool watch cap. At the moment, though, he was sitting in his little corner cubicle behind high card-board-boxed stacks of old *Quarterlies* and emergency food rations, wearing his standard blue denim shirt and jeans and, today, yellow sneakers. Although plainly bored by the mundane questions I have asked him thus far, Brand has been mostly forthright and direct about his financial affairs, but it was obvious he was not in a mood to talk about the kind of things for which I have really come to see him. As a result, I found that I didn't have anything like what I like to think of as my normal coherence when I tried to explain why I was there and what I was about.

"I don't understand what you're trying to do," he said at one point. Well, I wasn't surprised. If it was the sort of thing I could sum up in a nutshell I would have had it printed on my business card for people to read while we're shaking hands. It had rather to do with the whole thrust of Brand's *Catalogs*, the Point Foundation he has set up to give away the profits, and the "well-founded rumors" he so gleefully prints in the front of his *CoEvolution Quarterlies* in a section called "Apocalypse Juggernaut, hello."

"I don't know your work," Brand pointed out, which was true enough and a valid objection, though not an insurmountable obstacle. A far deeper problem was how I came across to Brand. "Tom Wolfe is a lot easier to talk to than you," he suggested at one point. Well, I didn't doubt it for a minute. But the fact of the matter was Brand was no great shakes as a charmer either. In any case, that was that. I hated to leave but there was no point to my wasting any more of Brand's time or mine. And I prepared to gather up my papers and put away my notebook. First, though, I had one final thought.

How about, I asked Brand, if I just hang around a bit to talk to some of the other people putting out the *Quarterly*, as he had earlier in the week agreed that I might? "They'd be flattered," he had said at the time. Now though, the idea seemed to have lost a bit of its luster. It would be okay, but I had to keep in mind that they had work to do. And also we just couldn't make the time limit on this thing completely open-ended.

"What did you have in mind?" I asked.

"An hour."

"I was thinking of more like the rest of the afternoon."

In the end Brand agreed, but I hardly came away feeling good about it. Before I went to see him I had imagined that we might enjoy each other's company. Instead we ended up bickering over straws. It was hardly the sort of insight I thought was out there when I began looking into my thesis three weeks before.

Self-Styled Author Jimmy Breslin Jives on New York, the Irish Etc.

—News American photos by Bill Perry

BRESLIN, Jimmy (1930-)

NEWS–AMERICAN (Baltimore, Md.)

Sept. 2, 1973

By Michael Olesker

The kid is writing one of those "What I Did Last Summer" pieces in school, only he's going outside of the accepted boundaries. He's writing about an old man who worked the stables at race tracks. And the words start pouring onto the paper. The kid can't write fast enough to keep up with his emotions.

And when he's finished, he walks proudly to the front of the room and hands his paper to his teacher. The teacher looks it over, and all she can say is, "Well. Just look at this handwriting. Do you call this penmanship?"

"No, sister."

Jimmy Breslin also doesn't call it an education. He sat in a bar downtown late this week, his tie open, his shirt undone, his hair all over the place, the reluctant businessman, and talked about growing up in New York City and not learning much in Catholic schools.

The school composition incident is recalled vividly in Breslin's new book, about an Irish Catholic cop in New York named Dermot Davey, called "World Without End Amen."

It is a novel, but it is about Jimmy Breslin and other real Irish Catholics, too.

"There's plenty of me in Davey. The thing with the penmanship, that was very common," Breslin said. "There are vast numbers of Irish Catholics in the city of New York, and out of all of them, they got maybe one or two writers in the whole place.

"The neighborhood where I grew up, we turned out maybe 30 policemen, 30 firemen, 16 fairly prominent felons, and some body and fender men open to practically anything.

"But guys with Irish Catholic names now write nothing but insurance policies or traffic tickets."

Breslin, 41 and fat, ex-sportswriter, ex-newspaper columnist, ex-political office seeker, author of "The Gang That Couldn't Shoot Straight" spoof of the Mafia, wrapped his hands around a glass of scotch and, for 90 minutes, talked.

He talked calmly, with plenty of casual cursing, but without reluctance

"I could have turned out like Davey," he said, "hating everybody blindly. But I started out as a copy boy on a paper when I was 18 years old.

"You throw a kid into a city room full of college educated Jewish kids and you let him grow up . . . man, they were talking sense. That's where the great ethnic game in the city of New York helps.

"You could even take a guy like Bobby Kennedy. I doubt he ever met a black person without a tray in his hands until he was 30. But he comes to New York, and that's all he talked about at the end. The man was transformed.

"With me, I think my education came in newspaper ciy rooms. And some whores helped. And hanging around Harlem bars. That was a great help to me."

But he would rather talk about things he does not like, which amounts to large numbers.

"I never had an easy day in the newspaper business," he said. "It's murder. You get short-sighted editors who want everybody to write the same way, and you wind up having to scream and abuse people and search for someone who can think and read.

"Most years, the Pulitzer should go to readers. And this is the worst year in the history of newspapers. They talk about the Watergate scandal, but hell, it was only two guys, nobody else.

"Without the Washington Post, it's nowhere. They tell me at this publisher's convention in New York, all the big shots were strutting around, really proud, pounding their chests over Watergate. But what did they do?"

Breslin started out writing sports. Today, but for an occasional reluctant sports magazine piece, he avoids writing about athletes.

"You find yourself covering the Kentucky Derby for the third time, and you realize there's nothing new to write," he said. "You gotta sit through a Sunday doubleheader, and you want to kill yourself. You get extra innings in there, and you're ready for an observation ward.

"And football is the worst of all. They're killing the game with this phony mystique, like telling people a guy needs the abilities of a brain surgeon to play left guard for the Baltimore Colts.

"They talk like a quarterback is so brilliant he can spot lumbar pneumonia at 40 yards. Hell, football is a game designed to keep coal miners off the streets on their days off.

"And they talk about Super Bowl VII, with the Roman numeral seven. It's like they're talking about the Roman Catholic Church already.

"So I had to get out of that. I wanted some day to write something serious. But it's hard to pursue when you're married with six kids. Great novels are fine, but who pays the phone bill while you're writing?"

He turned to writing a daily column for the old New York Herald Tribune, writing about politicians and people in the street, and about characters like Marvin the Torch, a professional arsonist, and Fat Thomas, a bookmaker.

"I'd write about crime and courts and civil rights most of the time," Breslin said, "and maybe once a week, to break the chain, I'd do one on Marvin or Fat Thomas. But the next thing you know, people are talking like that's all I did.

"They compare me with Damon Runyon, but that's not accurate. He really wrote about cardboard characters. They were charming and funny, and they were great for his time, but it's not me.

"The people I like are Murray Kempton, Toney Betts from the old New York Mirror, Joan Didion. Yeah, she writes the best sentences."

Author Tom Wolfe has chronicled those days on the old Herald Tribune where, Wolfe says, the New Journalism was born, in the writing of he, Breslin and others.

But Breslin says, "Life must pass me by. You can't dwell on the past. I can't remember the joint now. I got too many mouths to feed. If it was that exciting for Wolfe, then God bless him."

Breslin wrote a book on the old, inept New York Mets, called "Can't Anybody Here Play This Game?" while writing the newspaper column.

Then he wrote "The Gang That Couldn't Shoot Straight," a funny book about the Mafia that Breslin later looked back on and called "the work of a demented mind."

"I was doing some columns for Newsday, on Long Island, and there was this story about three innocent businessmen with their wives, who were having lunch in a restaurant and got shot by some Mafia guys by mistake.

"I got terrible conscience pangs, making these hoods look like funny guys. So I wrote in Newsday that the book was the work of a demented mind.

"But later, I hear they got the right guys. A friend of mine comes up to me and says, 'Don't feel so bad.' "

The latest book is dead serious. The Irish cop goes to Northern Ireland, falls in love with the same sort of society left-outs that he scorns at home. Breslin lived in Northern Ireland for several months while researching the book.

"There's no hope there," he said. "The only hope is to keep trying. But it's awful."

How does Breslin — the classic tough guy from Queens — stay angry, though, in the face of personal success?

"It's a problem," he said. "Success can ruin you. But you gotta keep hanging around the things that are outrageous. Also, I still live in Queens. The glitter of success is a little lost in a bowl of kid's oatmeal in Queens."

BRODSKY

Soviets' Suppression of Freedom Is Working, Says Exiled Poet Here

By Steve Aulie

Joseph Brodsky, regarded as perhaps the greatest living Russian poet, delivered a reading of six of his poems at Grand Valley State Colleges Friday night. Then, in a question and answer session, he told the audience the Soviet government's policy of suppressing freedom in Russia is working.

Brodsky said he was not surprised by the recent exile of Russian author Alexander Solzhenitsyn. Bordsky himself was exiled in 1972 at the age of 32, and now teaches at University of Michigan.

Discussing the Solzhenitsyn case, Brodsky, said, "Well, there's a lot of feelings. For myself it seems the logical thing in the process of the last half-century of spiritual castration of the people."

Brodsky added, however, "I think he'll manage."

Solzhenitsyn has gone to Norway to live on the royalties which have amassed from the sale of his books outside Russia.

THE RUSSIAN people do not yet know much about Solzhenitsyn's banishment, Brodsky continued. "I think they know more about my exile than about Solzhenitsyn's. I think they are confused Eventually, they'll know."

The elimination by the government of free-thinking people has not failed, he insisted.

"No, they try to remove it and they succeeded. The succeeded for more than half a century — killing people, exiling people . . . imprisoning them. The subject of this castration is 250 million people who are inhabiting one-sixth part of the earth's surface.

"It's quite simple, he continued. "In that country they treat people — this is almost a cliche — either as a slave or as an enemy. If you are neither of these, they don't know what to do with it.

"The government doesn't fear writers, but they fear there is some room in your mind that is not possessed by them. They don't have a moral alternative, and they know it. They try to suppress anyone who is trying to match them with a moral alternative."

BRODSKY SAID there are a "couple of thousands of people who are more or less not enslaved" in Russia and some intellectuals always will continue to speak out.

"Well, certainly they won't profit," the poet continued. "But free speech is something you can't suppress without a doubt. It doesn't depend on conditions, but on what is inside the people."

He insisted that he and other Soviet authors who have been at odds with the government should not be called "dissidents."

"We're not dissidents, we're writers. If we have any interest it is because we are writers. So please, stop talking about dissidents. Solzhenitsyn is interesting because his work is essential and he is a good writer. That's all."

Brodsky dropped out of school at 15, changed jobs many times, and wrote poetry until he was arrested in 1963 and labeled a "social parasite." He served 18 months of a five-year sentence at hard labor at a state collective near the Arctic Circle, and subsequently was confined in an insane asylum. After his release he worked as a translator of English works, and continued to write poetry.

"They just didn't like something about me," Brodsky said.

HIS REFUSAL to join any official writers' organization, his avoidance of Socialist themes and his periods of unemployment resulted in the ultimatum in 1972 that he either return to the asylum or leave the country. When he chose the latter, an American friend — UM Professor Carl Proffer — arranged the teaching position for Brodsky.

Proffer read English translations of the poems Friday night before Brodsky recited them in Russian. The poems, drawn from a recent publication, "Selected Poems by Joseph Brodsky," were entitled "Nature Morte," "Love," "Two Hours in an Empty Tank," "Anno Domino," "Almost an Elegy," and "The Presentation."

Brodsky declaimed the poems in a loud, clear and musical voice, standing with hands thrust in the pockets of his brown corduroy jacket.

BRODSKY, Iosif Alexandrovich (Joseph Brodsky) (1940-)	GRAND RAPIDS PRESS (Grand Rapids, Mich.) Feb. 24, 1974 [See also CA-41/44]

The musical rhythm of his poems was most striking, even to those who did not understand the language. One listener commented afterwards, "You're poetry is very rhythmic. Are you different from the majority of contemporary Russian poets, or is there more free verse in Russia as in this country?"

"There is no need yet to abandon form," he answered. Brodsky said most Russian poetry "has been and will be" characterized by the strong meters and rhyme with which he works. Brodsky said he sometimes worries that in exile he will forget the rhythm and sound of his language.

"WHY WRITE? Because I'm used to it," he said. "When writing a long time, you begin to exist in this realm of writing. Things occur to you and inevitably they are written."

Another listener commented that Brodsky's delivery reminded her of the "same sing-song" tone employed by Uri Yevtuschenko, a poet who has been allowed to remain in Russia. The comparison was not well-taken.

"I don't think you're correct . . ." Brodsky answered. Proffer interjected, "The only thing alike is they are both loud and somewhat dramatic. Yevtuschenko is much more histrionic," he said in defense of Brodsky.

Robert VasDias, poet in residence at GVSC, afterward described Brodsky's poetry as "Baroque" in its "elaboration on the figure." He added that Brodsky's high regard for the late American poet, Robert Frost, showed Brodsky's concern for traditional values in poetry writing.

Brodsky is a prolific writer. He soon will publish a 2,000-page collection of his poems. He no longer translates, however.

"I had been translating the dead people, now I teach the dead people," he said, laughed, adding that he translated only to earn money.

BRODSKY'S APPEARANCE at GVSC was one in about 60 such readings he had given in the last 18 months on college and university campuses around the country. He was invited to GVSC by Professor Christine Rydel, who first met Brodsky in Leningrad in 1970.

Russian Posy Throws Curve At American Poem Translator

A poet's life may be difficult: But it isn't easy being a translator, either.

George Kline, who translated Russian poet Joseph Brodsky's "Selected Poems," outlined a typical pitfall.

"Brodsky used the name of a Siberian wildflower in one poem," Kline said. "It translates in English as 'lion's jaw.' I took it literally and it worked very well."

What Kline did would be similar to a Russian's translating "snapdragon" to the equivalent of a fire-spouting monster.

"It was a very bad mistake," Kline said. "It got into a journal, I'm ashamed to say, but it didn't get into the book."

Miles Between Them

The hardships of translating are compounded when poet and translator are divided by thousands of miles.

Brodsky lived in Leningrad until 1972, when he was "invited," to leave the Soviet Union (in 1964-65, he spent 20 months in exile on a collective farm for "social parasitism").

He came to the United States and was poet-in-residence at the University of Michigan, then at Queens College, New York. Now he has a similar post at five New England colleges.

Communication between Brodsky and Kline is much easier, but Kline remembers when he'd have problems with a poem and send a message with a traveler to Russia. Months would pass before an answer came back.

The two men appeared onstage together last night at Carnegie Lecture Hall, Oakland, in a program sponsored by the International Poetry Forum. Brodsky read his poems in Russian, Kline the English translations.

BRODSKY, Iosif Alexandrovich (Joseph Brodsky) and KLINE, George L(ouis) (1921-) [See also CA-17/18] PITTSBURGH PRESS (Pittsburgh, Penn.) Oct. 31, 1974

Brodsky uses mythological references extensively in his poetry, as in the seperation of father and son in "Odysseus to Telemachus:"

. . . Telemachus, dear boy!
To a wanderer the faces of
all islands
resemble one another . . .
I can't remember how the
war came out;
even how old you are — I
can't remember.
Grow up, then, my Telemachus, grow strong.
Only the gods know if we'll
see each other again.

The poem has a deep and personal meaning to brodsky. Left behind in Russia is a son, 7 or 8 years old, who he will probably never see again.

"He was never married to the mother of his son," Kline said, "and she has since remarried. There is no way to get in touch with them. And the new husband by now will have adopted his son."

A second personal tragedy is Brodsky's seperation from his old and sick parents. He is their only child, and is trying hard to get them out of Russia for a visit.

Only 32, Brodsky already has a lot of life behind him.

His present concerns are with the education of American students.

Who's Telemachus?

According to Kline, Brodsky feels that in spite of the controls and distortions of education in the Soviet Union, Russian students have more of a sense of their own cultural roots, and of world culture.

"He's constantly shocked and outraged when the kids don't know the Bible — old and new testament — or Greek mythology," said Kline, who is professor of philosophy at Bryn Mawr College.

"Once at Ann Arbor, a student said, 'I'm sorry, Mr. Brodsky, but we don't know about Telemachus.' He called off the class and sent them all to the library."

Brodsky's own formal education stopped after eighth grade. He is mostly self-educated, but with the guidance of other poets and friends. ➡

(Also see preceding article)

THE UNDERGROUND LIFE OF A RUSSIAN INTELLECTUAL

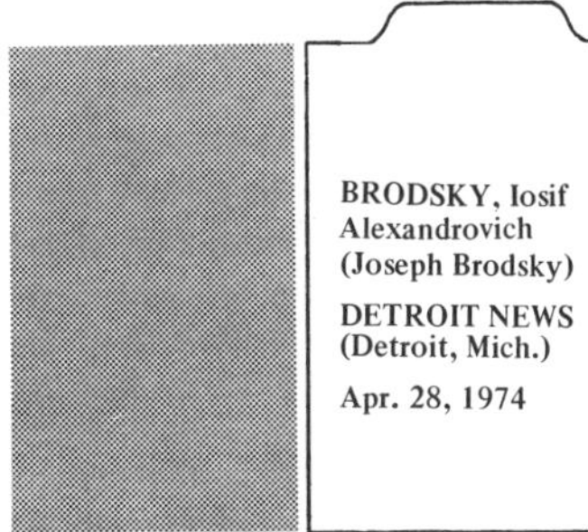

BRODSKY, Iosif Alexandrovich (Joseph Brodsky)
DETROIT NEWS (Detroit, Mich.)
Apr. 28, 1974

By JOHN GREEN
Sunday Magazine Writer

ANN ARBOR

When Joseph Stalin died, Joseph Brodsky was 13, a bright, searching and questioning elementary school student in his native Leningrad. Now 34 and banished from his native Russia, Brodsky lives the uneasy life of an exile, the poet-in-residence at the University of Michigan.

His voice, as does that of fellow countryman Alexander Solzhenitsyn, the Soviet writer who joined him in exile this year, speaks of a society in which literary independence is the mark of disloyalty.

He remembers clearly the day of the dictator's death.

"I was in school; they herded us all into the assembly hall, ordered us to get down on our knees, and the secretary of the party organization — a masculine female with a cluster of medals on her chest — wrung her hands and screamed to us from the stage, 'Weep, children, weep! Stalin has died.'"

Then, Brodsky recalls, the woman began wailing in lamentation.

"There was no way around it — we sniffled our noses.

"As for me...I did not weep."

His failure to weep was an early symbol of his independence of thought. It also foreboded his Odyssey through jail cells, mental hospitals, to a Leningrad courtroom, to the far north as an enemy of the state, an "idler," a "parasite." Finally, it was to bring him to a day in May, 1972, when the authorities, in desperation, simply told him to leave.

In an apartment near the U. of M.'s north campus, Brodsky, considered by some the finest poet writing in the Russian language, welcomed me with an open smile. Within minutes he was preparing a pot of coffee espresso, a Turkish blend laced with good strong spirits. Brodsky is a man or average height and build, with light brown, almost red hair. His English diction is spiced with strong Russian accents.

He wore dark blue jeans, a lighter blue shirt, sleeves rolled up. He is not at all the book jacket image of a Russian poet of darkly philosophic mien.

Because Brodsky was born a Jew there were some very bad times, and they began for him and millions of other Russian Jews during the almost paranoiac period of oppression that began even before Stalin died.

In Moscow the Jewish doctor's plot had already been invented by the heirs to the regime. In Leningrad Brodsky's father and mother were already making plans for the inevitable trip to the eastern regions.

The father, who had served throughout World War II as a journalist-photographer, was purged from the army. No work was to be found, and the family lived on the meager earnings of the mother.

Joseph, the only child, recalls that the family got rid of a piano, impractical baggage for such trips.

"I never could play it, anyway," Brodsky says.

But in the political confusion that filled the months and years after Stalin's death, the Brodsky family survived in Leningrad, where the poet's parents still live. They hope to visit him someday in this country, but chances of that happening do not seem bright. They are growing old, and Brodsky wonders if he will ever see them again.

"They have asked and been refused permission," says Brodsky. "The regime seems to like to make trouble for old people. It is a kind of police sadism, I think." This is one of the few notes of personal bitterness he allows himself.

The year after Stalin died Brodsky left school, and today he represents a monument to self-cultivated genius.

"I never got along with my teachers. I was always arguing with them. I read privately from Russian-German texts. In one of them I read a reference to 'unser fuhrer Stalin.'

"This is why I did not weep with other children that day. I would never weep for a fuhrer."

He grew up during the years when the cult of Stalin had reached deification levels. Brodsky recalls a school chum who was horrified to find a bug crawling over the face of the dictator in a book, fearing the consequences should a teacher happen to see such a desecration.

Brodsky's youthful insights were deepened by the Hungarian revolt that was crushed by the Soviets. "This was a great shock to me and to other young people."

Now in his mid-teens, Brodsky, in desperation and with the natural adventuresomeness of youth, had begun a long process of mental and physical escape from the oppressive society.

He applied for work with one of several geological expeditions whose purpose was to explore the hinterlands of the Soviet Union. So, for several months of the year there was the freedom of nothingness, living in tiny camp communities, trudging through forests and over frozen wastes collecting data on such matters as radioactive fallout from atomic testing.

"It was not unpleasant. The other workers, though not many, were a good sampling of society back in civilization."

The few months of the year spent in Leningrad, awaiting the following year's expedition, were devoted to self-education — and later, poetry of his own creation.

THE LONG lonely northern journeys were conducive to poetic thoughts, and at the urging of a fellow worker Brodsky began experimenting with meter and rhyme.

The experiments brought about his first arrest by the Leningrad officials.

"My poems, the early ones, were not very good, I think. They were not political, mostly about geological subjects."

But there was a strain of negativism running through them, and worse, bits of poetic phrases that raised the specter of ambiguity, of unsure interpretation. Quite naturally, Brodsky began seeking out other poets in Leningrad and his poems became, at first read, then enthusiastically published.

Published would not be the word for the underground dissemination of honest literature in the Soviet Union. It is called "Samizdat" publication, where one person receives a bit of literature, makes five copies, passes on the original to another, who makes his or her five copies, and so on.

In just such a way Brodsky later (1968) was to read Solzhenitsyn's "Gulag Archipelago," the explosive work that brought about that writer's banishment.

"I was visiting at a friend's house — in Riga, I think. At dark the friend took me out behind the house to a tree. He began to dig, and unearthed a metal box. Inside the box was the manuscript. I read it... It was the greatest book I'd ever read. Not a great work of art, mind you, but a documentary that really constitutes a sort of indictment on the order of the indictments for the Nuremberg war crimes."

Brodsky and his poetic thoughts were betrayed by a friend, an older man who had been arrested for carrying a gun, and who, remembering a previous stay in jail during which he had been beaten, talked to security authorities to save himself. That was in 1959. Brodsky was jailed, questioned, held without formal charges.

"Formal charges are a very big luxury in the Soviet Union."

By then, Brodsky, 19, had given up geological expeditions to devote himself to the writing of poetry, supporting himself with jobs of short duration — in a factory, as a janitor, anything that would keep him free of the cardinal Soviet sin of material non-productiveness and allow him the luxury of being a poet.

With warnings about his attitude, Brodsky was released. The process was repeated two years later and again in 1964.

By now Brodsky was recognized as a poet of some distinction among the secret Russian literary circles and, equally as important as it turned out, abroad. He had even translated Beatles songs and some of the "poetry" of Muhammed Ali, thus picking up the reputation of being a "Beatnik."

The final arrest came in February of 1964, the culmination of an investigation that began earlier with a campaign against him in the Leningrad newspapers, in readers' letters, which in the Soviet Union are more propagandistic than complaining. Brodsky recalls the period beginning with the assassination of President Kennedy as a particularly bad one for him and others in Leningrad.

"I was in Moscow to visit my girlfriend, and I returned to Leningrad on Feb. 11, 1964.

"On my return I was arrested and put into a mental hospital for examination."

This hospital stay was a particularly "bad time."

"It was obvious the regime had decided something drastic had to be done with me."

There were, says Brodsky, the undisguised attempts to rehabilitate, the injections with drugs that left the hands numb, the long questioning, the attempts at Pavlovian conditioning.

"I would be told that I was sick, and that the first requirement of good health is good sleep.

"After such questioning one finds it very difficult to sleep, just thinking about what had been said about sleep."

If any good can be said to have come from such an experience, it was that the mental hospital sojourn provided Brodsky with the material for one of his most ambitious works, the long dialog poem, "Gorbunov and Gorchako," which presents conversations among two mental hospital inmates and their keepers.

Then came "the trial."

BRODSKY HAS a transcript of his trial, thanks to a friendly member of the Leningrad Writers Union who wa present and took notes. It was subsequently smuggled out of the Soviet Union and translated.

The charge was brought under a state decree dealing with citizens who have no visible means of livelihood. For the regime, the writing of poetry did not represent a visible livelihood.

After explaining to the court his writing, including translations (which represent the main incomes of poets not in official favor), the following exchange occurred:

JUDGE: But in general what is your specialty?

BRODSKY: I'm a poet, a poet-translator.

JUDGE: And who said that you were a poet? Who included you among the ➡

(Continued from preceding page)

ranks of the poets?

BRODSKY: No one. Who included me among the ranks of the human race?

JUDGE: Did you study this?

BRODSKY: What?

JUDGE: To be a poet? You did not finish high school where they prepare.-..where they teach...

BRODSKY: I didn't think you could get this from school.

JUDGE: How then?

BRODSKY: I think it . . . (confused) . . . comes from God

For writing his poems, for reading them "at evening gatherings," and for being an "idler", Brodsky was banished to "a distant locality" for five years of enforced labor.

The pastoral peace of the northern wastes was for Brodsky what the briar patch was for Br'er Rabbit.

"I enjoyed it," recalls Brodsky. "At first we were cutting wood, then there was farming."

It was while in penal servitude at the state collective farm that Brodsky produced much of the poetry that is included in his latest recently published collection, "Selected Poems."

Friends kept the poet supplied with books, and he was able to hone his English. One trick was to make literal translations of the first and last lines of a stanza of English poetry, then reason out what was in between. The American, Robert Frost, became and remains a great favorite of Brodsky.

"As a matter of fact, during this administrative exile I lived 100 percent Frost poetry." Frost, too, notes Brodsky, found his own personal hardships reflected in nature.

Brodsky's trial and sentencing had created a stir in the west.

After 20 months he was released.

"Your own Dr. Edward Teller (father of the H-bomb) was instrumental in getting my release," says Brodsky. Teller and others made strong appeals to Soviet authorities to free the poet.

Brodsky returned to Leningrad, and turned to translations.

By the late 1960s Brodsky's known works had circulated widely and he was among those poets and writers who belonged to the secretive network of artists in Moscow.

W. H. Auden, the late U.S.-British poet, had arranged through literary contacts to write an introduction to a book of Brodsky's poems, which he had read in English translation. Auden, who welcomed Brodsky when he made a stop in Vienna on his exile journey in the summer of 1972, did, indeed, write the introduction, one of Auden's last published literary efforts. It appears in the Brodsky volume published in English this year

It was while becoming involved in such things that the shocker came for Brodsky.

"It became obvious to the regime that something even more drastic had to be done with me. Everything else had been tried — the whole spectrum of harrassment. But it was entirely unexpected."

DR. CARL PROFFER, a University of Michigan scholar in Slavic languages, was with Brodsky in his Leningrad apartment when the phone call came that day in May, 1972.

Proffer, who directs an Ann Arbor publishing house dealing in translated works, had known Brodsky for several years. He and his family made a point of taking a side trip to Leningrad to visit "Joseph" whenever they were in Moscow on publishing business.

"When Joseph got the call (from the ministry of visas) he was naturally afraid. It is highly irregular to get such a call."

When Brodsky returned later he told Proffer the unusual news. The ministry wanted to know why Brodsky had not accepted invitations to speak in Israel. Had Brodsky requested such a right, it undoubtedly would have been denied.

"When I told them I didn't want to leave the country, they told me, 'The hot part of the summer is coming,' and that I had better go." The alternative for Brodsky was another trip north to escape the "summer heat."

So with a single suitcase, the $100 in cash he was allowed to take, and leaving behind his parents and his poems (which he was forbidden to take, but which he had committed to memory), Brodsky set out for Israel via Vienna. Dr. Proffer had made arrangements to meet him at Vienna.

Before he left Moscow Brodsky, who has a love for his homeland entirely apart from any regime of the moment, wrote an appeal to Communist Party leader Leonid Brezhnev for the right to return eventually to the Soviet Union.

"I belong to the Russian culture; I feel a part of it," he wrote. "I feel bitter as I leave Russia. I was born, I was raised and have been living here, and I owe everything I have in the world to Russia. Everything bad that I have suffered has been more than compensated by the good. I have never felt that I have been hurt by my homeland."

The appeal went unheeded.

Proffer recalls the meeting in Vienna as Brodsky stepped off the plane.

"Joseph put up two fingers in the sign of a V."

Proffer, who has taken on the task of collecting all Brodsky biographical material over the years, stayed in Vienna to assist in escorting him to the United States. Proffer had managed to obtain for him the Poet-in-Residence post at the U. of M., appropriately the first to be established since Robert Frost himself filled it in the 1920s.

"There is no one in the Soviet Union to do it," says Proffer of his Brodsky work. "I happen to think that Joseph is one of the poets who will be read a couple of hundred years from now."

Brodsky, although unmarried, left a six-year-old son in Russia, who because of state rules was taken from him. The child bears a name unknown to the father.

When Brodsky applied through the U.S. consul in Vienna for permission to enter the country, he had to fill in long sheets of questions. Where he was to list relatives left behind in the Soviet Union, Brodsky wrote only two — his parents.

"No others?" asked the bureaucrat.

"Well, yes, I have a son, but he does not bear my name."

The consulate bureaucrat made a notation of the fact, saying, "One never knows. Things might change some day."

"Through all of my bad days it was the first time I felt like weeping," says Brodsky. It was the first official recognition of his fatherhood.

Brodsky sees this situation as a domestic-political triangle involving himself, the child and the regime. He develops the thought in a poem (one of his favorites). He uses the classic legend of Odysseus and his separation from his son, Telemachus, during the Trojan War. The poem, "Odysseus to Telemachus," is an imagined letter from the father to his son.

"Palamedes" of the legend is responsible for Odysseus' leaving home for the wars. In Brodsky's poem Palamedes may represent the regime that forces his own separation. The last stanza reads:

Grow up, then, my Telemachus, grow strong.
Only the gods know if we'll see each other
again. You've long since ceased to be that babe
before whom I reined in the pawing bullocks.
Had it not been for Palamedes' trick
we two would still be living in one household.
But maybe he was right; away from me
you are quite safe from all Oedipal passions,
and your dreams, my Telemachus, are blameless.

BRODSKY, Iosif Alexandrovich (Joseph Brodsky)
DETROIT NEWS (Detroit, Mich.)
Apr. 28, 1974

"For 50 years," says Brodsky, "the regime has practiced the spiritual castration of the people. Where the only opportunity for free enterprise is found in personal affairs, it is not surprising that adultery becomes widespread."

Nearly two years after his exile, Brodsky can put his life in a society hostile to the poet's spirit into perspective.

He does not consider himself a martyr, dislikes being cast in that role. How does he look upon the years of frustration and indignities?

"Yes, one's dignity is involved.

"But if one were to take seriously the role of being an enemy of the state, it would mean playing their game.

"For me, I think there was some selfishness involved in the way I was.

"There is a tradition of ethics among Russian poets. It has been so for centuries. We have never paid a great deal of attention to the reality of situations. This is difficult to explain. It is rather unfair to take advantage of situations such as imprisonment. Doing so creates an a priori indulgence.

"This is wrong and we try to avoid this kind of thing. It is so easy to set oneself up as the representative of good. 'I am in prison. They are evil, I am good, therefore I represent good vs. evil.'

"No, one can be a representative of good and still be a son of a bitch.

"So the thing is to behave as if nothing is going on. That is what irritated them. That was my game."

POETS IN EXILE do not plan very far ahead. Brodsky is enjoying his stay, and he feels that his teaching is important. "I feel that what I am doing is not unuseful."

He has traveled across the country, giving readings, meeting other poets and writers, and his official relationship with Soviet officials is nonexistent. For them he is a non-person. Some say that Brodsky's native language is showing signs of rusting from disuse. He denies it.

Occasionally, a student or a fellow poet will visit his apartment. While there is much to like about American society, Brodsky sees a lot not to like. He feels that Stalin and Hitler "burned society's moral bridges behind them," that their ways are winning out.

He sees much in U.S. society that provokes him.

Detente between the U.S. and Russia is one of the things that provokes. He sees it as a "big piece of cake" which was offered to the Soviet regime in order to convince them to stop supplying the North Vietnamese and thus help get U.S. GI's out.

Detente he also sees as the cause of the Mideast war. "Without detente the Arab nations would not have been able to predict U.S. response to the attack on Israel.

"Even though your Henry Kissinger is a knowledgeable scholar, I find among Americans a tragic lack of knowledge of history.

"You considered World War II merely a continuation of World War I. What was the cause of World War II? Wasn't it Poland? And World War II is over, and what has happened to Poland?"

Nor can Brodsky understand American socialist spokesmen.

"Robert Frost said it: 'Socialism has been based on bad arithmetic, where 2 comes before 1'— that is, where the masses come before the individual."

Although a non-political person, Brodsky says one of his duties is "to take the rings away from the red nostrils."

Brodsky joins colleague Solzhenitsyn in recommending a stance of noncooperation for those countrymen left behind.

"This is the only way. It is like an Italian strike, where one sits, and does not act."

Despite all of the development of mass communication, Brodsky believes the poet's dealing with the highest form of communication.

"Poetry deals with more essential things than does any other kind of communication. Its job is to provide for people the proper scale of their lives. Only a poet can do this. Philosophers, perhaps, but they use so many words." ■

By MARTHA LIEBRUM
Today Editor

Gwendolyn Brooks

She wrote about being black before it was considered beautiful

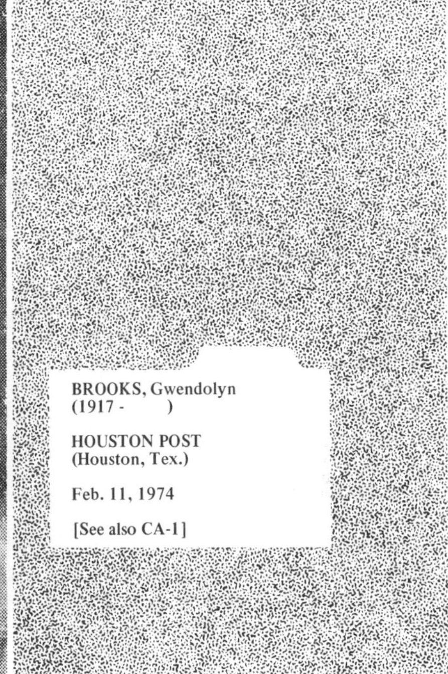

BROOKS, Gwendolyn
(1917-)

HOUSTON POST
(Houston, Tex.)

Feb. 11, 1974

[See also CA-1]

She wrote about being black before being black was beautiful.

"We real cool. We
Left school. We
Lurk late. We
Strike straight. We
Sing sin. We
Thin gin. We
Jazz June. We
Die soon."

(Copyright 1959 by Gwendolyn Brooks Blakely.)

And though she wrote and published and achieved success long before there was a Movement, Gwendolyn Brooks has survived as a heroine to new young blacks.

When she came to Houston last week to take part in a black awareness program at the University of Houston, she was met by eager students who wanted to know how she wrote, what inspired her, how she had been accepted back in 1945 when she was first published.

The fact that she achieved success before the Movement, and won a Pulitzer Prize and became poet laureate of Illinois even though she is black, make her an enigma to some of the young.

The younger generation of poets who tended to think of her as a "lady 'Negro poet'" decided in fact she was "beautiful" declared Don Lee in a poem about her.

She does not write violent militaristic poems, but she does record the black emotions, something she has been doing since she was 16, when she wrote her first "bitter" poem.

"Bitter is the word they use to describe poems written by blacks about the black experience," she said with a smile.

She began writing her first at age 12, she said, writing about "dandelions and clouds, love and death." She grew up in a Chicago home where music and poetry were part of the environment.

She discovered a writer's guide that told her where to send her work for publication and she tried all sort of women's magazines and the like with no luck.

"I was writing for the whole world, then," she says, "and by the time I was 16 I was thinking about maybe the back yard so they could be dug up years later and they would save the world."

That first bitter poem was written shortly after she was transfered to a predominatly white high school. The poem was called "To the Hinderer."

She finished school, married a writer and started her family.

At 28, busying herself with bringing up her son, she went to a writers conference and won a prize. A representative from a New York publishing house was there and asked her if she had enough to make a book.

So she rushed home and wrapped up a package of poems to New York.

The publishers wrote back that while the general poems "about nature, love, death" were very nice, they liked her "Negro poems." And would she get together enough to make a book.

She did . . . and then sent them to another publisher, who published them in 1945. In 1949, her second volume of poetry "Annie Allen" won her a Pulitzer Prize.

She has written several more books including an autobiography. It is some testimony to their timelessness that every single book she has written was checked out of the library when Today made an inquiry.

She spends lots of time now visiting campuses to speak, and plans several more books. She writes when she is inspired, getting inspiration from the daily news, she said.

She has seen a great change among black college students over the years.

She first saw what was going on in 1967, at a black writers conference, she said.

"There was such a churning. Young black people had changed. They were sassier . . . more upright. More inclined to take things into their own hands."

She had believed in a different way, she said, "I believed in the future of integration . . . you know, if we showed ourselves to be 'good' people it would work out.

"They believed that way They believed in using their hands and working among their own people

"And now I believe we need to get together, stop subscribing to white standards. The Afro was important — some people say it isn't any more—but I believe its time has not passed. And black studies are important."

She is not unduly disturbed at another more recent change among the black students—who were so energetic and "sassy" in the 60s.

"I see a good deal of apathy. A lot of interest in getting out of school getting that degree and moving out to a big job and a fancy house.

"But I think I haven't given up on you," she told the UH students. "I feel like you are just regrouping."

"I certainly cannot see them returning to the moods and tempers of years ago."

Though her poetry is often reprinted in women's rights publications, she is not a women's liberationist. She understands why women's liberationists would identify with her poetry, but she does not identify with that movement.

And she is opposed to it for black women. "I think we should not get embroiled in women's liberation. It is a dividing faction we don't need anymore dividing factions. It seems to me these women hate men so much.

"We need things that bring us together. Everywhere I go young girls confide to me that they are so worried that their young black boys are favoring white girls. They have the right idea, that they should be together. I favor black women and men getting married, and having children. Why not?"

She encourages kids wherever she goes to send their poetry for publication in the new black publishing companies. She herself has withdrawn from Harper and has her work published by a black publishing company.

She personally gives prizes to Illinois youngsters who compete in her poet laureate contests. She had been skeptical of the honor at first ("Would I have to write poems in honor of sanitary installations?") but she is especially fond of the title now. "Because I follow in the steps of Carl Sandburg, who was poet laureate of Illinois before me."

Author opens doors for others

She lives to help blacks

—News Photo by Alan D. Lawrence

MARIE BROOKTER — she wants others to "take my hand."

BROOKTER, Marie
(1934? -)

DETROIT NEWS
(Detroit, Mich.)

Oct. 24, 1974

By LUCILLE DeVIEW
News Staff Writer

The story of Marie Brookter's life as one of 12 children growing up on a Louisiana sharecroppers farm may be used to create a black version of television's popular Walton family.

Negotiations are under way for both a television series and a movie based on Mrs. Brookter's autobiography, "Here I Am — Take My Hand" written with Jean Curtis (Harper and Row).

"I am different from most black writers in that I had both a strong father and a strong mother who gave us a very happy childhood despite hard times," said Mrs. Brookter, who was in Detroit earlier this week to address the Women's Economic Club.

"My childhood ambition was fueled by love, not hate. There was warmth, encouragement and family pride. I was the first of the 12 children to graduate from high school and that was quite an achievement in those days."

SHE MARRIED soon after graduation and gave birth to a daughter, Carolyn (who is now a 23-year-old journalism major in college).

In 1952, Mrs. Brookter was working with her cousin, Lester Mitchell, getting Lousiana blacks registered to vote when he answered a knock on the door. She stood by horrified to see him shot to death in front of her.

She left the South determined to make his death meaningful by getting into the political establishment and "making a difference."

At the University of Chicago, she worked days and studied political science and constitutional law at night. She also began working in grass roots politics.

Eventually Mrs. Brookter became a press aide to John F. Kennedy in his presidential campaign; was credited as having a major influence on President Johnson for passage of the 1965 Voters Rights Bill; and was an advance worker in George McGovern's 1972 campaign.

THEN SHE WENT into television in Chicago and five of the documentaries she produced won Emmy awards. Most recently, she covered Watergate as a reporter for Encore magazine.

"Watergate was a good awakening for America," Mrs. Brookter told her Detroit audience. "We had forgotten the issues. Americans now will watch their candidates and listen to the issues and vote for people who will be responsive to their constituencies."

In an interview, she said her own choice in the next presidential election would be Arkansas' Democratic Gov. Dale Bumpers.

Asked why she worked for McGovern and not Rep. Shirley Chisholm of New York—who was also running for president — Mrs. Brookter said "Shirley didn't have a chance as a black woman in 1972."

MRS. BROOKTER attended Gerald Ford's first press conference after he became President and said she was "very happy to feel the difference in the air after the Nixon administration — it was invigorating."

But she said she was disappointed at Mr. Ford's pardon of Nixon.

She writes in her book of the heady days when she spoke person-to-person to presidents. In one incident, when she was consulted by President Johnson about a housing matter, she took the opportunity to talk tough to him.

She told him she had not approved of his nomination as vice-president; that his face reminded her in a negative way of the tenant-farm owner she had known when she was growing up; how her cousin had been murdered; and that Mr. Johnson could be the hope of her people.

ACCORDING TO HER account, Mr. Johnson was stunned and then said, "When you feel I'm being unfair or unjust with black people, or even if you feel I'm moving too slow, send me a note."

She said Mr. Johnson added when she was about to leave: "Marie, you are a good person to go to the well with."

Now widowed, Marie Brookter lives on Cape Cod where she is busy writing another book. She explains the title of her autobiography this way:

"In Chicago, a black congressman once told me he was No. 1 and other blacks had to look to him, he didn't have to look to them. He got in the door and shut it after him.

"HE WAS WRONG. I vowed if I ever got in the door I'd hold it open for other blacks. I did. When I started in TV in Chicago, I demanded black writers and I got them.

"As many hands were outstretched to me along the way, so do I proudly become a link in that chain of human kindness. I want to offer encouragement and love.

"That's why I call my book, 'Here I Am — Take My Hand.' "

Dr. Brothers On Bringing Up the Kids

BROTHERS, Joyce (Diane Bauer) (1927-)

SEATTLE POST-INTELLIGENCER (Seattle, Wash.)

Oct. 9, 1974

[See also CA-23/24]

—P-I Photo by Phil H. Webber

DR. JOYCE BROTHERS TALKED ABOUT CHILDREN

"They shouldn't develop sexist attitudes"

BY JANET GRIMLEY

If Dr. Joyce Brothers had followed the advice of a college dean, she wouldn't be a famous psychologist today. When she applied for her psychology doctorate at Columbia University, her entrance scores were so high she had to be accepted.

So a college dean called her into his office for a serious talk. She recalled, "He asked me to relinquish my spot in the class so a man could have it. He said I was being unfair to some man who would benefit more from the education than I would."

One wonders what that dean thinks today of his student. Dr. Brothers is one of the most quoted psychologists in the country, frequently appears on television talk shows, writes newspaper columns, magazine articles and advises several manufacturers on women's needs.

Se was in Seattle yesterday as a consumer attitudes consultant for Armstrong Tile Co.

Dr. Brothers said the education situation has improved considerably since her college days but sexism still is prevalent.

"It's enormously important that textbooks be changed because children pick up sexist attitudes from them. Some people think it doesn't matter, but it does. Children aren't dumb. They learn arthimetic and reading in school and they'll learn sexist attitudes, too.

"In non-sexist cultures, it's no big deal if a person is a man or woman. These cultures also tend to be less war-like than ours because the man doesn't have to show that he is big and strong and the woman weak and needing protection."

She believes a child should learn to be proud of what he is, "It's beautiful to be a man or it's fine to be a woman but we don't need all the artificial things society has built around these roles. Children repeat what they see and girls identify with their mothers and boys with their fathers anyway.

Children, no matter which sex, must have a positive attitude toward themselves."

She recalled that when she defended her right to be admitted to a doctorate program, inside she felt "terribly naughty. I was hot and flushed and felt I was wrong wanting that degree. But I did want it and I wasn't going to give it up. You know, women always used to assume they were wrong even when they weren't."

Dr. Brothers said the increased demands for equality between the sexes have made it easier for women to choose careers but some vocational counselors still try to channel women into traditional roles.

"I think our daughter was brought up non-sexist because her father and I developed an attitude of self-worth in her. He viewed her as intelligent and worthwhile and his feelings are crucial because he was the first man in her life.

"Because she identified in a positive way with him, she knew how to react to other men in her life."

Their only child is 21 and a medical student at Tulane University. Dr. Brothers has been married for 25 years and took five years from her career when her daughter was born.

'I feel strongly that the first few years of a child's life are so important that a parent should be there if at all possible. Those early years are vital. That is when a child needs security and consistency. If he has that for the first few years of his life, then he can learn to handle things with assurance.

"Day care is fine, and some mothers can find terrific people to watch their kids. But usually there are eight other kids around too. They all need attention and can't get it on an individual basis."

Dr. Brothers said she realized that some mothers had no choice but to work but the ones who could choose should think of their responsibility to their children.

"Because of improved birth control, no one has to have children unless they want them. I think women who want careers should consider not having children. Or they should plan to interrupt their careers for two to three years to stay home with the child."

She added that a father could just as well stay home with the child but usually the mother gets the responsibility.

A visit with Dr. Joyce Brothers

By JORJANNA PRICE
Post Reporter

Dr. Joyce Brothers is a handshaker. She came into the newsroom grabbing hands and when she left she stopped to brush those she had missed.

It's hard to believe this woman, a psychologist and columnist with a show business image, has time for such frivolities. Her projects are so numerous she can't remember them all when asked.

Among them: a newspaper advice column carried by 350 newspapers; a monthly column for Good Housekeeping; an appearance once a month on Captain Kangaroo to discuss children's problems with Bunny Rabbit and Mr. Moose; news commentary in a New York televison station; a morning information show on ABC every two weeks; plus lectures and tours.

In addition, she is producing her first movie and working on her fourth book.

Brothers was in Houston

BROTHERS, Joyce (Diane Bauer)

HOUSTON POST (Houston, Tex.)

Sept. 23, 1974

acting as consumer attitudes consultant for Armstrong Cork Co., one of three manufacturers she lends her counseling services to.

Brothers opens all of her own mail and usually writes the answers for her column on the back of an envelope she leaves for one of her two part-time secretaries to type up.

There are some new questions cropping up now for her to answer: inter-racial marriages is one. "It used to be the rarest of rare," she said. "Also, many, many more women have had it up to here with an impossible man and they are ready to make a break. Before they would put up with a man who ran around, they would rather live with half a man than take a chance on their own.

She also gets a good many letters from mothers concerned with daughters who move in with boyfriends. "We had the sexual activity among the young people for a while but not moving in. Now they're moving in with the pots and pans, the works.

In earlier days the psychologist would hear from men who felt their wives weren't interested enough in sex. Now, she reports, it's the other way around.

Through her college tours, Brothers gets a feel of the mood of young people. Right now, she says, they are angry and upset by the recent presidential pardon of Richard Nixon.

"They are turned off and unhappy about the decision," she said. "They think it's as unfair as anything could be."

How has this country emotionally survived the Watergate ordeal?

"Amazingly," Brothers thinks. "If you had asked before this happened, could America adjust to all these changes, it would have been another matter. But we are not in any way a sick country, not on the verge of a breakdown. We have arisen to the number of changes with a great ability. It shows the many strengths we have."

Going through a series of changes results in some differences, she explained. "It's never the same when a pendulum swings away and back. When you start at one point and come back you reach a different point. What really happens is a spiral, you start at one point and keep moving ahead.

"This new generation of college students is like the students of the 1950s," she said as an example. "They are self interested, interested in a career, preparing to join the establishment. But they're not like the 50s students because they will not accept things at face value. They are a good deal more cynical, more turned off on the political system."

(Also see preceding article)

The Brothers Approach: Sugar-Coated Psychology

By BILL HUTCHINSON
Herald Staff Writer

There is a Joyce Brothers in nearly everyone's high school class picture.

She's the one who looks as if she'd rather be on the rack than in front of a camera, surrounded by people who probably referred to her contemptuously as "The Brain." The shy girl who'd break out with hives when asked anything more personal than her opinion of the Hapsburg monarchs. The dedicated student who would have dissolved at any grade lower than an A.

Which, of course, she never got.

THE REAL JOYCE Brothers is still getting A's in whatever she attempts. And she is still almost neurotically inarticulate when cornered by a personal question.

"I rarely talk about myself on television or in public," she stammered late in her recent promotional day-trip to Miami. "I'm not very good at it, because I don't feel comfortable doing it.

"I'm not a natural talker. When I was a child, I was particularly conscious of it. Both my parents are attorneys and they used to talk circles around me. One of the things that drew me to psychology was that I thought, as a psychologist, I'd be able to just listen."

During the past 15 years, however, Dr. Brothers has managed to talk her way into international prominence as a sort of Mary Poppins for the psyche, a dispenser of advice and remedies made palatable by the large spoonful of sugar that is integral to her public personality.

SHE IS IMMENSELY popular, according to polls which consistently name her one of the most admired women in America, but to ask her why is to send her retreating into the sofa cushions of her Miami Beach hotel suite.

"I . . . really . . . don't know. I'm not . . . unless it's just that I am an honest person, not afraid to give direct answers even if they are unpopular, and people like that. In my wildest dreams I never expected such popularity, and it is certainly nothing I've ever sought.

"I'm not at all concerned with any sort of public image," she said, glancing past the publicist who accompanied her to Florida.

"I'm very serious about my work, but I'm not a very serious person. I don't have any vital message or golden words that must be said. I'm just having fun. If it's not fun, I don't do it. I promised myself 18 years ago when I went on 'The $64,000 Question' that if I won, I'd never again do anything I didn't want to."

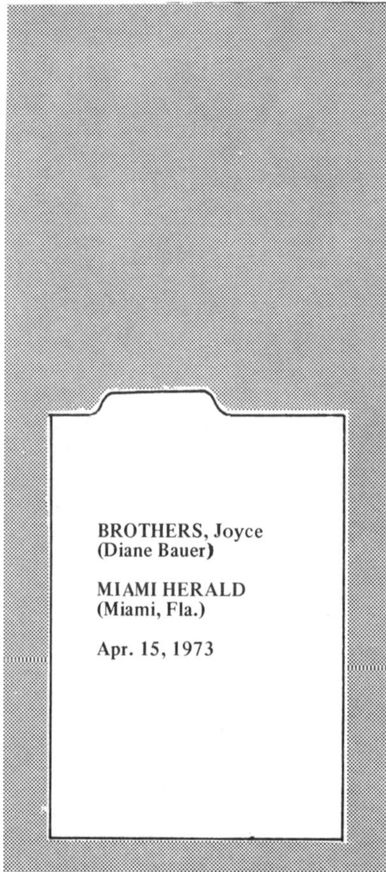

BROTHERS, Joyce (Diane Bauer)

MIAMI HERALD (Miami, Fla.)

Apr. 15, 1973

NATURALLY, she won. Appearing as a specialist on boxing, a field which she'd mastered solely because "it had enough oomph to get me on the program," she captured nationwide attention and gradually overcame the shyness that made initial shows a personal ordeal.

"I had a great motivation to be successful on the show: My husband and I were starving to death. He was an intern making $50 a month, and whatever we had we had to rely on our parents for. It was a very difficult situation, and a difficult time. The $64,000 seemed like such a hell of a lot of money. I hoped I'd just be able to win a Cadillac, which we could sell and live off of until my husband was in a position to support us.

"Later, when it was discovered that some of the shows were not completely honest, people were suspicious of the fact that I looked so calm and cool. (A grand jury investigation cleared her of any part in the quiz-fix scandal.) Actually, I was frozen, petrified with fear."

She thawed out gradually, "little by little, like a lobster being boiled," to the point at which, today, she no longer looks at the camera as if it were a bayonet.

Dr. Brothers still has difficulty realizing that her private life may be of some popular interest.

"I SWIM EVERY night and cook breakfast most mornings when I'm home and enjoy playing bridge and there has never been a moment in my life when I was not hungry. What else is there?

"I don't travel a great deal. I don't like to be away. My daughter is at Princeton now, so it's not her that's the problem. I prefer not to be away from my husband much. I don't trust him. I think women are wise not to trust their husbands in some circumstances. There's such a thing as situational infidelity. You know, a man goes off to a convention and watches television for the first couple of nights, but then he goes off in search of human companionship. We've been married 23 years, and I don't see any point in tempting fate.

"I enjoy learning things; it's a pastime for me. I have a good memory and was always a good student. I taught myself plumbing when I was in college, and can do my own electrical wiring, something that always fascinated me.

"I'm not very social. My husband's the social one. I prefer to just spend an evening with a few people, talking — you can learn so much that way. I don't like parties. For one thing, I don't drink. I just can't handle it, and there isn't much call for singing and dancing psychologists."

But if there were, Dr. Brothers would probably be at the head of the chorus line.

Comic Strip Superstar

Cartoonist Dik Browne with wife Joan, sons Chris and Bob and daughter Sally.

**by BILL CROUCH, Jr.
for The Courant**

What's six feet tall, bearded, 240 pounds, and inhales diet cola?

"Hagar the Horrible."

Wrong. "Hagar the Horrible's" creator, cartoonist Dik Browne of Wilton.

It is generally accepted that cartoonists draw themselves into their comic strips. Sometimes it happens subconsciously. However, the similarity in appearance of "Hagar" and Dik Browne is striking. The only differences are "Hagar" is shorter and drinks wine, beer or mead.

Browne, who with Mort "Beetle Bailey" Walker also does the syndicated comic strip "Hi & Lois," has created the most remarkable success-story in recent cartoon history.

In 18 months of publication, "Hagar the Horrible" has successfully pillaged the editorial offices of 600 newspapers worldwide. He is a comic strip superstar, read by millions.

"Hagar," a typical hard-working, barbarian businessman (sacking and looting), is primitive man with all modern man's problems.

"I'm going to start screaming when people start to analyze the strip," said Browne. "It's just the eternal struggle between man and woman and man and his world."

The world for "Hagar" is the ninth century. Competition is stiff for a Viking raider, and "Hagar" is away from home for long periods of time. His ample wife "Helga" blames these separations for all the trouble they're having with their son "Hamlet." The kid refuses to grow his hair a decent length, washes almost daily, reads books, wants to be the first Viking dentist, and is a never-ending source of embarrassment to his parents.

Their 16-year-old daughter "Honi" is unmarried and almost an old maid by ninth century standards. She has a ne'er-do-well minstrel for a boyfriend, wears armor and wants to go raid the English with her daddy. "Hagar" sees little future in either her boyfriend or her liberated career goals.

Harassed by competitors on the job and by his family at home, "Hagar" struggles on. Beleaguered as he may be, "Hagar" is still a Viking and his creator believes there's a little Viking in everybody.

According to Dik Browne, cartooning is one of the last true cottage industires. "Hagar the Horrible" and "Hi & Lois" are international products created by Browne and his sons Chris, 21, and Bob, 26, in the studio of the family's suburban Wilton home.

Though the phenomenal success of "Hagar" has overshadowed "Hi & Lois" in the past year, this strip is published in 600 newspapers and brought Browne into syndicated cartooning 20 years ago.

This combined total of 1200 newspapers makes Browne one of the big three of syndicated cartooning. The others are his partner on "Hi & Lois," Mort Walker of "Beetle Bailey" and "Boner's Ark" fame, and Charles "Peanuts" Schultz.

BROWNE, Dik (1917 -)

HARTFORD COURANT
(Hartford, Conn.)

Nov. 10, 1974

"Hi & Lois" is a family strip based on the affection between husband and wife instead of the more traditional bickering. Written by Mort Walker and drawn by Dik Browne and sons, the strip features your typical suburban family: one teenager, grammar school age twins, an infant who thinks like an adult, and a dog.

This year Browne received the National Cartoonists Society's "Reuben" award for being "Cartoonist of the Year" for the second time in his career. And to think he didn't even want to be a cartoonist.

Born and raised in New York City, Browne found the movies, especially comedies, more fasci-

(Continued from preceding page)

nating that the newspaper funnies.

"I was born in 1917," said Browne, "and grew up in the generation before comic books had been invented. Of the syndicated comic strips my boyhood favorite was 'Minute Movies.' However, I was extremely precocious about going to the movies. I have total recall on all the great silent comedies I've seen. I love Chaplin, Laurel and Hardy, and especially the Marx Brothers. Their movie 'Animal Crackers' has just been re-released for the first time in about 20 years. Do you know 'Sing Hurrah for Captain Spalding' from that movie? No? Let me sing it for you."

After the song, Browne continued recounting his boyhood years through various parochial schools and a year at Cooper Union.

"Cooper Union is an art school but I didn't really know what I wanted to become," said Browne. "Anyway it was in the Depression and I literally had to quit school and find a job in order to eat. My sister knew somebody at the old New York Journal and I was lucky enough to get hired as a copy boy. I was 18 and my salary was eight dollars a week."

If everything had worked out as Dik Browne planned, he would probably today be an award-winning reporter instead of a cartoonist. He claims he had all the desire to be a reporter but none of the talent needed for writing news stories.

"Newspapers back in the mid-1930s were unbelievable," said Browne. "When I entered the Journal's old office in lower Manhattan, I discovered a whole world I never knew existed. The city room was a mess with old newspapers thrown all over the floors. In the center sat the city editor and behind him was this big greasy guy cooking hotdogs at a grill. I couldn't believe it. Plus there's this midget who used to run the advance copy uptown to the Hearst offices buying a hotdog. And just as I walk in the city editor takes a New York phone book, throws it across the room and decks a copy editor with whom he had been arguing. It was fantastic."

Brown would soon end his career as "ace foreign correspondent of the future," when he was exiled from the newsroom to the art department.

BROWNE, Dik

HARTFORD COURANT
(Hartford, Conn.)

Nov. 10, 1974

"I used to doodle and the city editor knew it," he said. "The trial of the gangster Lucky Luciano was a big story but all cameras were barred from the courtroom. So the city editor began sending me to cover the tiral as the Journal's courtroom artist.

"I got to meet some very interesting people on that assignment and in fact I was taught to foxtrot by 'Stoneface Peggy'; a madam of some reknown, and her girls."

In 1941 Browne was thinking of getting married and when Newsweek magazine offered him more money than the Journal, he became its staff artist. Until he joined the Army in World War II, Dik Browne was the guy who drew all those newsmaps.

"Hi & Lois" generates a lot of mail and the most common response from readers is, "You must be peeking in our window."

Even with the tremendous success of "Hi & Lois," Browne was impressed by the belief of late cartoonist Rube Goldberg that an artist had to keep growing and taking on new challenges. "Hagar the Horrible" is the result of Browne's feeling. "It was time to do something new."

Many people wonder how "Hagar" got his name. It seems that Dik Browne likes to get up early, work, and then take a nap in the afternoon. When his children were in grammar school he would wake from his nap and trundle into the kitchen just as they were fixing themselves an after school snack. Upon seeing his father, Chris used to shout with glee, "Hagar the Horrible is here."

"The sentimental reasons for using 'Hagar' were just so great," said Browne, "that no other name seemed suitable."

Besides their two boys, Dik and Joan Browne also have a daughter Sally, 17, who is a senior in high school. This spring her 3.8 grade average earned her a place in the National Honor Society.

Sally is something special to the Brownes. Though Dik and Joan had always wanted a daughter, it just was never going to be. Over the years Dik has done a tremendous amount of work for Bishop Fulton J. Sheen. It was Bishop Sheen who suggested adoption as the way the Brownes' desire for a daughter could be realized.

"We adopted Sally when she was four," said Browne. "Her family had escaped from Communist China to Hong Kong and then her father died leaving a large family and Sally's mother pregnant with her. She was raised by Italian nuns in Hong Kong before she became part of our family. Her parents were Catholic and wanted her adopted by a Catholic family. When she arrived, she was a little girl with a big Red Cross identification tag on her coat who spoke no English and a little Italian, plus Chinese.

"She's the scholar in the family and a history buff. Two years ago she won the Daughters of the American Revolution's history award for her high school."

Dik Browne is a cartoonist whose achieved success many people only dream of. His strips are what's called "big-foot comedy" as opposed to the story strips best represented by another Viking, "Prince Valiant."

Story strips have been declared dead or dying by a number of writers. The most recent was a cover story in the New York Times Sunday Magazine that zeroed in on the problems of "Little Orphan Annie."

This point of view and the Times story in particular gripe Browne who thinks the appeal of the story strip is as real today as before the one-eyed monster, television. He commented that he felt The Courant had the right idea giving story strips half page format because they require more space than humor strips to be effectively displayed.

His first success with "Hi & Lois" came when he was 37 and his second with "Hagar the Horrible" when he was 56.

"Just remember," said Dik Browne, "Rube Goldberg was 80 before he became a sculptor. I can't even think of the marvelous projects that must be awaiting me in my future. When the time is right, they'll materialize."

Dr. Hilde Bruch

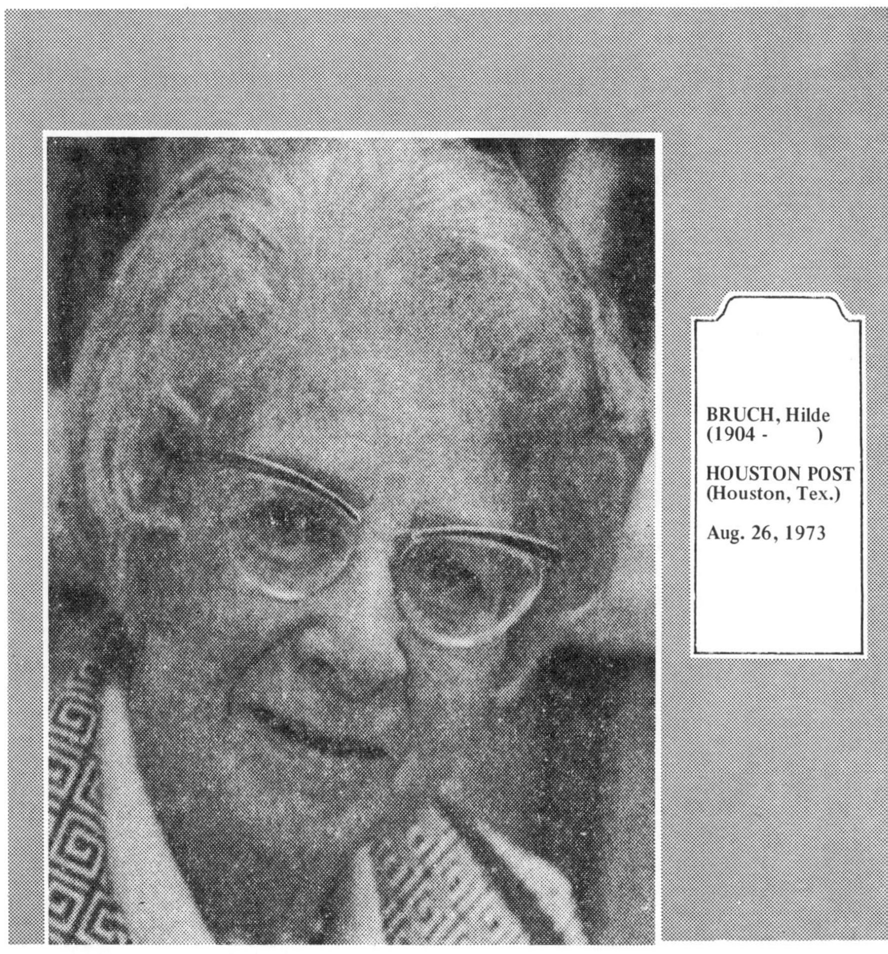

BRUCH, Hilde (1904 -)

HOUSTON POST (Houston, Tex.)

Aug. 26, 1973

By MIRIAM KASS
Post Medical Writer

One day in August of 1932 Dr. Hilde Bruch entered the dining room of Leipzig Children's Hospital as she had many times during her residency training in pediatrics.

It was the same familiar scene, yet it was different. The election had clearly reflected new strength for Adolph Hitler.

As she stood there before them, her fellow residents, they were suddenly silent.

She read the future of Nazi Germany. "I knew these people meant what they said."

FROM THAT day no one spoke to Hilde Bruch, a Jew.

In June of 1933 when she left Germany for England her own family members thought she was being overly cautious.

Most of those same relatives are now dead, victims of the concentration camps.

Hilde Bruch lives in Houston today, a world renowned authority on obesity and other eating disorders whose most recently published book is called "Eating Disorders/Obesity, Anorexia Nervosa and the Person Within."

SHE HAS come far, it would seem, from the small German town near the Dutch border where she was born in the early years of this century, a town where the only advanced education available for a bright girl was preparation for being a teacher.

Bruch is indeed teaching today—as a psychoanalyst and professor of psychiatry at Baylor College of Medicine.

She is a handsome, gray-haired woman, a presence who dresses smartly and with relish (she once thought of being a dress designer), who lives in a high-rise apartment overlooking the Texas Medical Center and drives a large cinnamon -colored Rolls Royce that seems to embody both her audacity and her devotion to quality.

A PROLIFIC author, she submits herself to a schedule of disciplined writing sessions. In leisure hours she consumes paperbacks almost indiscriminately.

Yet though the years have passed and the setting has changed, Hilde Bruch by her own description is very much the same as the girl who grew up in pre-World War II Germany.

Then as now she grasped reality with confidence, trusted her own perceptions, and was not afraid to act on them. She was convinced she could be best and was unwilling to accept less.

"I was not going to put up with the slightest implication of being a second class citizen," she recalls of that day in the hospital dining room. Her trust in her own observations saved her life.

YOUNG HILDE was 12 years old when she took the first decisive step toward what was to be her career. The winter was so cold one day that it was impossible for the children to study in their unheated school.

Instead, the class had gone to skate on a huge lake nearby. It was there that Hilde saw the bright red caps in the distance.

In the world of education where Hilde lived the colors and styles of caps students wore signaled the level and type of education they were receiving.

What caught Hilde's eye was not merely the red of the caps. It was the fact that the red caps adorned the heads of girls.

"I was a clumsy skater and a shy girl," she recalls today. But she made her way across the lake.

"I found out that they went to a school in a larger city where a girl could study anything she wanted."

SIX MONTHS later Hilde wore a red cap with a silver rim, studied Latin, mathematics and physics at the new school, "and I knew I was going to the university."

Through the end of World War I, a worldwide influenza epidemic which killed a third of the student body, through a dyssentary epidemic, the return of a defeated army, rashes of strikes and an inflation that dwindled her inheritance to an amount "that wasn't enough to buy a piece of bread," she persisted.

When she came to the United States after a year in England she was offered a position at the Babies Hospital of the Columbia University College of Physicians and Surgeons in New York City. She was asked to head the endocrine (hormone) clinic, the only clinic not already spoken for.

"NINETY PER cent of the children in the endocrine clinic were obese," she recalls. At that time it was widely assumed that obesity in children must be a glandular problem.

"Every fat child in New York was getting thyroid shots."

But not for long.

True to her searching nature, Bruch sought out the original article on Froehlich's Syndrome, one of the accounts on which the theory of hormone deficiency had been based.

The facts she found written there did not warrent conclusions that had been drawn, in her opinion. The further she investigated the more she doubted what was commonly held to be true.

In 1938 at a scientific meeting she spoke out, scrupulously documenting the fact that the obese children who came to her clinic were of ➡

(Continued from preceding page)

average or above average physical maturity—a finding inconsistent with thyroid or pituitary deficiency.

"EVERYBODY SAID, 'I'm so glad you said it. That's exactly what I felt,' and I asked them, 'Then why haven't you said it?' "

She felt like the child who pointed to the nakedness of the emperor when everyone else was acting as if he did, indeed, wear exquisite new clothes.

It was the first of many such challenges, including a proof that, contrary to assumptions, fat cells are chemically active and not inert.

But Bruch was doing more than questioning what was believed. She was also observing what was.

"I came up with the discovery that nothing was wrong with their endocrines," she says, "but something was very wrong with the way the mothers treated these children."

When it came to behavior Bruch was not qualified as an expert. She did not want to be a pediatrician dabbling in psychiatry. It was not the way of this woman who refused to be second class in anything.

So in 1941, Bruch went to Johns Hopkins for training as a psychiatrist and then went on to become a psychoanalyst.

LONG BEFORE family therapy was in vogue as it is today, she published the first complete family study on any topic undertaken from the point of view of understanding the child.

Again at Columbia, moving steadily up the academic ladder, Bruch published a book in which she urged upon parents her own skepticism of so-called expertise.

The book, called "Don't Be Afraid of Your Child," challenged the fads of both over-permissiveness and overstructuring of a child's life, urging parents to reject such generalized, mechanical approaches.

THE BOOK deals with the insecurity that is created by over-psychologizing attitudes," as she puts it.

"It doesn't make the slightest difference whether you hold the baby this way or that." she says. "What matters is how you feel about it."

As the years passed Bruch became widely known in private practice and in medical and lay literature, particularly for her interest in eating disorders.

In 1964, a clinical professor at Columbia, Bruch decided New York City was no longer the place for her.

"You could not go out at night there without being afraid," she felt. Fear was not her style.

SO WHEN she was invited to join the faculty of Baylor College of Medicine as a professor of psychiatry, she accepted. Once again. 30 years after her trip to America, she traveled hundreds of miles to a new place where she was a stranger.

It was here that she distilled years of experience and research in the meticulously written, recently published book, "Eating Disorders Obesity, Anorexia Nervosa and the Person Within."

"You can't explain obesity in terms simply of oral this and oral that," she says. "This is putting words in where there is a great unknown. There is much more involved even than the habits of eating, than food as a substitute for love."

HILDE BRUCH has concluded that many patients with severe eating disorders suffer from "the basic delusion of not having an identity of their own, of not even owning their own body and its sensations, with the specific inability of recognizing hunger as a sign of nutritional need . . .

"These patients act as if for them the regulation of food intake was outside their own bodies."

We assume that people are born able to recognize hunger pangs, but that is not so, says Bruch. Babies must learn to distinguish one form of distress or discomfort from another.

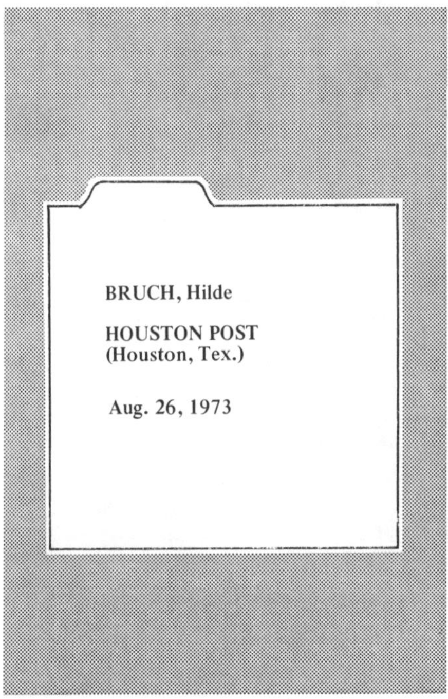

BRUCH, Hilde

HOUSTON POST
(Houston, Tex.)

Aug. 26, 1973

BY THE MOTHER'S response, by not confusing the child's needs with her own, by not confusing nutritional needs with other needs, she helps the child to "read" his own body's messages.

"If . . . a mother's reaction is continuously inappropriate, be it neglectful, oversolicitous, inhibiting, or indiscriminately permissive, the outcome for the child will be a perplexing confusion . . .

"Even more confusing . . . are the actions of a mother who is continuously preoccupied with herself; whatever a child does, it is interpreted as expressing something about the mother.

"IN SUCH A setting noneating may be equated with criticism of the mother, and eating as expressing happiness and love," Bruch says in her book.

Many such people are too perfect, almost robot-like in childhood, walking projections of their parents' desires. The obesity is only one aspect of the whole problem, which is that the person feels like a stranger in his own body, a creature controlled by a parent.

As Bruch came to understand obesity in this light, she recognized the same roots in a rare but intriguing problem called anorexia nervosa.

"The relentless pursuit of thinness through self-starvation, even unto death," is how she describes this condition, which she considers a mirror image of obesity.

Bruch calls anorexia nervosa "a caricature of what will happen when the common recommendation that reducing will make you slim, beautiful, and happy is taken too literally and carried out to the extreme."

BRUCH, WHO herself is naturally large-boned and full-figured, enjoys gourmet food, but eats with reasonable care to her diet.

She shuns the skinny ideal "that praises near emaciation as 'beauty' " and she thinks that the hostile regard of obesity "as a shameful evil" has helped turn obesity into a mental health problem.

There is a happy medium when a person is comfortable in his own body and is not obsessed with either devouring or avoiding food, Bruch thinks.

AS FOR the common belief that the only thing wrong with an obese person is a lack of will power, that is, perhaps, like saying the only thing wrong with an amputee is that he has no legs.

If a person is literally incapable of recognizing pangs of hunger or knowing when he is full, if he literally feels he has no control over his own body, how can he exert will power over a function that he cannot even recognize?

IN THERAPY, Brunch stresses, "you can't command will power, but you can help them understand the areas in which they misperceive things."

Therapists should not interpret to a patient with one of these eating disorders, in her view. What he needs least of all, she warns, is yet another person outside himself telling him what he feels.

Though she does not put it this way, Hilde Bruch would encourage the development in all people of those characteristics which have molded her own life. She would have them learn and heed their own perception and act with knowledge and confidence.

BUCHWALD, Art(hur)
(1925 -)

PHILADELPHIA
BULLETIN
(Philadelphia, Penn.)

Mar. 5, 1974

[See also CA-5/6]

He is an unobtrusive man, whose most distinctive feature is a smile—Art Buchwald.

Art Buchwald: For Whom Any Adversity Is a Profit

By NANCY DOHERTY
Special to The Bulletin

"I TOLD you never to call me at the office," Art Buchwald said when he picked up the phone.

But, he added, he says that to any woman who calls him at work.

He was reluctant to be visited in Washington.

"I don't really do anything. Other columnists go to the Hill every morning; I just come to my office, read the papers, make lunch plans, go to lunch . . . And anyway," he said in a mock whine, "I feel inhibited when somebody's watching me all day."

On the other hand, when he is on the road he likes company. Buchwald makes about 35 speeches a year; he says they account for almost half his income. He invited me to come along on the next trip.

Like a Peanuts Character

THE 9.10 P.M. train to Hartford was late. Buchwald put his suitcases down by a column in New York City's chilly Penn Station waiting room, lit a fresh cigar, and fretted. He looked a little like a Peanuts character bundled against the snow in his bulky beige car coat with a fuzzy hood and a baleful look on his full face.

Under the coat was a natty plaid suit and ➡

(Continued from preceding page)

bow tie. Rubbers hid his crinkly patent leather loafers. A couple of hours earlier he had taped the David Susskind show, and had been urbane, relaxed and very funny. Most of his conversation came from past or future columns; but lines that would just draw a smile when read drew laughs when Buchwald delivered them in his blunt New York accent.

Before the show he had outlined his schedule: A morning lecture and luncheon in Hartford, Conn. and an afternoon speech at the Yale Drama School. Susskind groaned in sympathy. "Don't you just hate it?" he said. "The middle-aged Republican ladies, the reception committee, the banal conversation?"

"Not really," Buchwald had replied contentedly. "I like meeting people I'd never meet otherwise."

What he hated was this: Late trains, cold drafts, no porters to take his bags. "Going first class — that's the payoff on these trips. I figure I owe myself the treat of a limousine ride and a good dinner," he had said in the station restaurant. But not even for $200 could he hire a limousine to take him to Hartford; there was no gas in the state of Connecticut. So he was, after eating a tasteless, overpriced meal, leaving without finishing his wine, for fear he would miss the train announcement.

No strangers spoke to him as he waited, although he got some curious glances when he talked about beating Henry Kissinger at chess. He is an unobtrusive man of middle age and medium height, whose most distinctive feature is a smile, a certain way his upper lip curls — from years, perhaps, of trying not to laugh at his own punch lines. Sometimes when people do recognize him they have second thoughts.

"Once a lady stopped me on the street," he said.

" 'Are you Art Buchwald?'

"Yes.

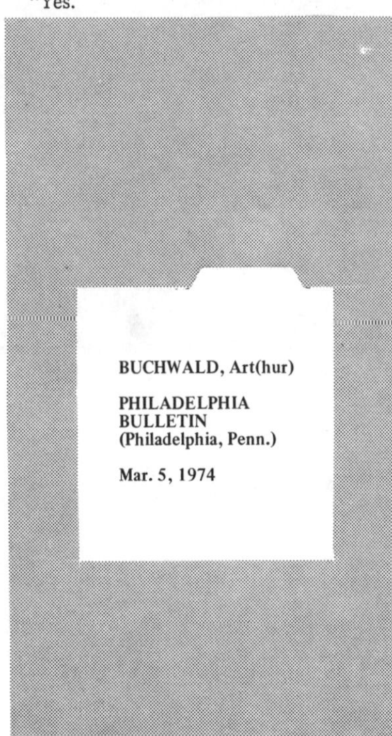

'It's Material'

" 'No you're not,' " she said.

He shook his head.

"Another time, a woman came up to me:

" 'Are you Art Buchwald?'

"Yes.

" 'Gee, you look just like him.' "

It was 9.25 and it felt as though Penn Station had turned off the heat to save fuel.

"Don't forget: any adversity is material for me," he said, stamping his feet to keep warm. "I can turn it into profit."

Finally the train did come. He settled into a plump orange chair in the club car, sipped a drink, looked around at the car's other occupants and pronounced himself content.

Buchwald hadn't grown up going first class. He spent most of his boyhood in foster homes in the Queens section of New York City. It was back then that he learned how to make the most of adversity.

"I discovered early in life I could make people laugh. My teacher would take me around to other classes and say, 'Look at the smile on this kid's face'."

"As a kid, I was very ambitious all the time. When I was 10 I used to stand outside the A&P on roller skates with my wagon. I had a sign that said, 'Buchwald's Service . . . 10 cents . . . We Deliver Everything But Babies.' "

When he was 17, Buchwald ran away from Queens and joined the U.S. Marines. After World War II, he went to Paris on the GI Bill.

But instead of attending a university, he became a stringer for Variety and a restaurant reviewer for the Herald Tribune.

Satirizing Politics

Inevitably, what he calls his "Jewish self-preservation humor" crept into his prose. By 1950, he was writing a satirical column three days a week on the international set for the Herald Tribune. His reputation was made.

When President Kennedy came into office in 1961, Buchwald decided to move to Washington with his Roman Catholic wife and three adopted children. There were dire predictions that he could never succeed satirizing politics, "but I had a feeling I just wouldn't bomb out."

Now his column, syndicated through the Los Angeles Times, reaches more than 400 papers in the United States (including The Evening Bulletin) and 100 abroad. Only Jack Anderson is more widely syndicated.

Ambition has taken him a long way. What he learned as a boy — that "people would always like me" — is now true of millions of his readers.

Organizations of every political stripe invite him to speak — from NOW (National Organization for Women) to the American College of Cardiology (for whom he is currently preparing a lecture entitled "cardio-vascular problems of the fourth estate").

His office is swamped daily with mail — invitations, manuscripts and requests, such as one from a Miami, Fla., sixth grade class that read:

"Dear Mr. Buchwald: We are writing a paper on the World Bank. Please answer the following 36 questions. We need it by Thursday."

"I'm a funny guy. People just don't get mad at me," he said as the train pulled into Hartford. He had said that earlier to Susskind. He would repeat it to reporters the next day. And, during those two days, he was as careful as a politician not to say anything on the record that might alter that image.

Coffee and Danish

The next morning Hartford was very cold, and Buchwald took a cab from his hotel to the capitol, a few hundred yards away. Gov. Thomas J. Meskill had invited him for coffee and danish and a chat with the local press before his speech. He strolled into the governor's reception room, took the cigar out of his mouth and said loudly, "I WANT GAS."

The secretaries looked up warily and then, recognizing him, tittered. One of them showed him into Meskill's office. For half an hour Buchwald stood placidly sipping black coffee and making wry remarks to the reporters, who seemed uneasy in the governor's presence. No one ate any danish.

Then an important-looking man with gray hair came to escort him to the Bushnell Hall across the street. Hundreds of heavily bundled people, most of them women, were hurrying in the doors. In the lobby two saleswomen from the local department store stood behind a table stacked with Buchwald's latest book, "I Never Danced at the White House." He joined them and began to sign the copies.

On Stage

He did a brisk business, and almost every woman who bought a book had to have a personal word with him. "You look so much younger in person" or "I read you religiously" they would say, reaching out to squeeze his arm, anywhere between the wrist and shoulder.

A few minutes after 11 Buchwald ambled onto the stage with his hands in his pockets. "Since you've been driving all morning to get here," he began, "I'll fill you in on the latest news. Richard Nixon is still President. (Laughter). "We learned today of the resignation of the President's friend, Bebe Rebozo. (Laughter) The White House has called a press conference for 4 P.M. to announce the appointment of a new friend." (Laughter)

Buchwald talked about everything from sex education to gun control legislation and his audience kept laughing. Then he moved on to a recent addition to his stock lecture, "A Watergate Slide Show."

About His Fee

In New Haven he stopped first at the home of his friend Robert Brustein, head of the Yale Drama School, to leave his bags. Brustein's wife, who was giving him a dinner party that night, was worried about the television repairman. "He's been upstairs working for three hours already," she said. "Bob will be furious."

A little later, Buchwald walked into Brustein's office "Listen, Bob," he said in greeting, "Norma wants to know if the TV man can stay for dinner."

While they talked an assistant came in to get his Social Security number, so they could send him his fee for the speech. "No, no," Buchwald said, pushing the form away. "I donate it to the school. I don't even want to know how much it was. Just tell me, is it enough to name a theater after me?"

Then, the 80 or more long-haired drama students crowded into a prop room, Buchwald gave a shorter version of the morning talk, and the slide show. They laughed, all in the same places.

"Everything emanates from the column," Buchwald explained, back in the car again. "These lectures, the books. I don't want to get involved with projects that would take time away from it."

But won't he someday get tired of having to be funny three days a week, he was asked. "I still get a kick out of seeing myself in the paper. If it got to be a struggle, if the thrill left, I'd quit. After doing this for 24 years, I have a feeling it may not happen.

"But who knows?"

He leaned back in his seat and drew on his cigar as the car turned up the hill to the Brusteins', where he would be the feted guest that night, in a house as lovely and elegant as any along those old streets of Rye and Scarsdale.

Pearl S. Buck: Controversial, Compelling

By ROBERT SCHWABACH
Of The Inquirer Staff

DUBLIN, Pa. — They buried Miss Buck here Friday morning, surrounded by children and trees. She loved children and trees.

She was a monument in life and is likely to remain so in death. There were the monumental novels, the fame and international literary reputation, the foundations and good works, the causes, the caring, the prizes—first the Pulitzer and then the Nobel Peace Prize. She was the first woman to win it.

Behind the graven image that can be found in the dictionaries of biography, the encyclopedias of literature, the inevitable graduate-school papers and doctoral theses that will imminently clutter up the stacks, is the missionary's daughter and the mother of two children, one of them retarded. She was, as her friend James A. Michener puts it,"a highly complex person."

She once remarked that Americans had a need to create idols if for no other reason than so they could then turn and tear them down again. She lived to fill the role and was not ignorant of her position.

FROM THE TESTIMONY of her friends, and some who were not friends, she could deal with people so warmly that they would, within minutes of knowing her, tell the story of their lives and reveal the most intimate details. When she was angered or merely annoyed she could cut someone up brutally.

She could be enormously distant and dignified in her image of "la grande dame," yet she had a sharp wit and was not above joking about herself.

When a friend told her that a magazine article had described her as a "rich, lonely old lady," she replied "I am old of course, but I'm not at all vain about it."

When two of her adopted daughters, teenagers, were about to go on dates one evening she admonished them to be home early. "What's the matter, mother?" one of them teased, "Don't you trust us?"

"I trust you as I would have trusted myself," she replied. "Be home early."

SHE DIED AT 80 and was by all accounts fully aware of the intellectual and social movements, the events, the fashions and the trivia of the time. When she was in her 60s, she learned to swim, and took diving lessons; in her 70s, she studied languages and furthered her music.

Michener and Greg Walter, the reporter who wrote an article which probably was the greatest single blow to her ego and her image, both agree that she was — without a contest — the most brilliant woman they had ever met. The public image of the idol hardly surpassed the reality.

SHE HAD HER darker side. It comes out in casual conversation with her friends and admirers — the shadowy image sometimes of a lurking wrath and vengeance, the Black Queen surrounded by her dark and moody courtiers.

"She surrounded herself," said one friend who did not want her name used in the press, "with sycophants and toadies, flatterers of the worst sort."

"SHE WAS A VERY WARM and friendly woman. But they would keep people from her, even sometimes old friends, and tell her things which were not true. The community came to think she was cold and withdrawn."

Walter says that the article he wrote (in Philadelphia magazine) about the Pearl S. Buck Foundation being used by certain directors for sexual perversion and personal gain was an effort to root the corruption out of something that was fundamentally good. "It was about these people around her, Theodore Harris and these others."

"She took it as a personal attack. She was enormously loyal. Now they're all still there — running the show up in Danby, Vt. (where she has a large estate and bought most of the houses in the very tiny village with a view into turning it into a handicrafts and arts center that would attract tourists.)"

Miss Buck accused Walter of writing the article as revenge for flunking her creative writing class at Columbia University.

She said he was motivated to do the article because Harris was a former dancing instructor and Walter had been abandoned by his mother, who was a ballet dancer.

THESE CHARGES weren't true, Walter says, but he made no reply to them. "I had tremendous respect for Miss Buck. She was tremendously intelligent, warm and good-humored.

"She was very kind to people and she helped me a lot. The article wasn't about her at all. It was about what had happened to the foundation and a noble cause.

"It was about Theodore Harris. His real name was Freddy Hair — he was from North Carolina where he was a dance instructor — and those others, but mostly about him."

Michener would not talk about that. He would only say that what was done sometimes did not detract from a person's work or what they were in other ways.

"I knew her in very trying times, under difficult situations," Michener says, "and she was sharper intellectually at her age than I am at my age.

"SHE AND I and Oscar Hammerstein used to hold a series of meetings on what the three of us could do to help black America, and out of that came adoption practices that helped a great deal and Hammerstein's work on better housing. She was always the dominant personality in those meetings.

"I don't think Oscar and I could be classified as dummies, you know, and she just ran the show."

That Pearl S. Buck in action was indeed something to see is agreed by those who knew her.

SHE WAS ABOUT 5 feet, 6 inches tall, heavy, with blue eyes and pale skin. Her hair was white and usually carefully done up. She wore jewelry often and dressed in conservative but expensive clothes.

"Her voice was soft and very clear," recalls a woman who served on the board of the Mental Studies Institute with Miss Buck. "You paid attention to everything she said. Partly because of who she was and partly because of her voice and her manner — she could be very gracious.

"But she always knew what she wanted and she usually got it. You could be discussing some problem, some issue at the Institute, and you know how your attention isn't always directly on all the time, how you sometimes let the discussion drift around you? She never did. The minute your argument faltered, she would be on it.

"She had great clarity of thought, and tremendous stores of facts and knowledge that she would throw at you. She knew exactly what she wanted and we always seemed to end up doing it her way.

"Oh, she could be swayed alright. But you had better be pretty sharp and really know your facts. Not many did."

BUT MISS BUCK had her soft spots. The problems of children of American and Asian blood, rejected by both cultures in her time more than now, would make her cry.

She deeply loved her nine adopted children and her two natural children and, like any doting mother, would continually tell friends and staff at the Foundation of the little funny things they did and said each day.

Mrs. Dorothea Sitley, who is on the foundation board, recalls that Miss Buck would laugh at these things and jokes on herself and had a kind of bubbling chuckle that was completely infectious.

Mrs. Pearl Wolfsohn, who takes care of public information for the foundation, recalls Miss Buck would never leave a car without first checking her makeup and her hairdo. "She was every inch a woman, you know."

Walter recalls that at parties in New York when he was a student she always came away knowing the most dramatic incident in the lives of everyone there.

"She liked to hear about people's lives," Mrs. Sitley says. "Everything made a story to her. She loved to make up stories about people.

"Sometimes she would write them down." ➡

(Also see preceding article)

Mystery Surrounds Pearl Buck's Will

Pearl S. Buck
... in Miami, 1967

BUCK, Pearl S(ydenstricker)
(1892 - 1973)
and
HARRIS, Theodore Findley
(1931 -)

MIAMI HERALD
(Miami, Fla.)

July 22, 1973

[See also CA-2; CA-41/44]

By GREG WALTER
Knight Newspapers Staff Writer

PHILADELPHIA — When author Pearl S. Buck died last March 6 at the age of 80, she left behind more than 80 books, hundreds of short stories and magazine articles, nearly 15 unpublished manuscripts — and a financial tangle that may never be completely unravelled.

That tangle — set forth in a complex series of trust agreements — appears to leave most of her estate to a 42-year-old former dance instructor to whom she devoted most of her time, her fortune and her affection for the last 10 years of her life.

Because of this, the validity of her will was challenged earlier this month by Edgar S. Walsh, 36, one of her seven adopted children, on the grounds that her often mysterious companion exerted "undue influence" on the way in which her substantial estate was distributed.

In his challenge, Walsh testified that Theodore F. Harris "alienated mother from me and the other children."

UNDER THE TERMS of Miss Buck's will and several trusts, Harris is to receive:

• **MORE THAN** $100,000 in a loan to be paid off by Miss Buck's estate.

• **ANOTHER $100,000** in real estate transferred by Miss Buck to a corporation owned solely by Harris.

• **ALL JEWELRY** owned by Miss Buck, with the exception of an engagement ring left to one adopted daughter.

• **ALL MONEY LEFT** over from a trust fund that leaves up to $4,000 annually to each adopted child — but which will not be paid to the children until Harris' $100,000 loan is satisfied.

• **ROYALTIES FROM** at least three books Harris allegedly wrote about Miss Buck and about himself.

Except for the value of the property and the $100,000 loan, little else is known about the value of Miss Buck's estate. Tangible assets, like Pennsylvania and Vermont real estate that she once owned, are gone.

What is known is that Miss Buck — from one book alone, "The Good Earth" — earned nearly $2 million in royalties and motion picture rights. Other highly successful novels, motion pictures and television sales earned her even more millions over a writing career that spanned more than 50 years.

It also is known that throughout most of her life, Miss Buck practiced the thrift, orderliness and a reticence to display personal wealth, habits imbued in her by her parents.

THE QUESTIONS to be asked by Walsh's lawyers will concern themselves with how much she earned, where it was spent and how much is left.

In 1963, she met Harris — then a dance instructor at the Arthur Murray studio in a Philadelphia suburb. For the next six years, through the Pearl S. Buck Foundation, she helped finance his expensive tastes in clothing, automobiles, jewelry, restaurants and travel.

Meanwhile, the Pearl S. Buck Foundation floundered under Harris's direction as president. It has since been reorganized and is operating without him.

In 1969, Philadelphia magazine published an article called "The Dancing Master," an expose of Harris' apparent incompetence and his attraction toward teenage mixed-blood Korean boys which the Pearl S. Buck Foundation was set up to help.

(Editor's Note: That article was also written by Knight Newspapers Staff Writer Greg Walter).

EVEN THOUGH Harris resigned in the wake of bad publicity, Miss Buck continued to finance his ventures and to defend him vigorously.

Included in Miss Buck's will is an in terrorem clause warning her heirs of the following:

"In the event that any legatee under this will contests the validity of any transfer made by me during my life to any person, corporation, trustee or foundation, then such legatee shall not be entitled to any distribution of my estate."

Shortly after learning she had terminal cancer, Miss Buck entered into a separate trust agreement to lend a Delaware corporation $100,000. At her death, Harris became the sole stockholder in the company. ➡

(Continued from preceding page)

THE ARRANGEMENT, in conjunction with the original trust, means that her heirs get nothing until the $100,000 she borrowed to give Creativity, Inc., is paid back.

In essence, the sum is a gift to Theodore Harris.

Miss Buck's lawyer, Gale L. Raphael of Newton, Mass., said that the trust arrangements dealing with his corporation were made by Harris.

Raphael is counsel to Creativity, Inc. He also is a trustee of the Pearl S. Buck 1971 trust under which her children will share in her literary earnings.

These facts place Raphael in a delicate position:

On the one hand, he must, by law, see that the trust is properly handled for the benefit of the heirs.

ON THE OTHER, he must protect the interests of Creativity, Inc., which are the sole interests of the man charged by one of the heirs, with exerting "undue influence" on Miss Buck's distribution of her estate.

Raphael contends that the estate is now small. He said he had prepared Miss Buck's tax returns for 1971 and 1972.

"The whole thing," Raphael said, "is a personal matter between Edgar Walsh and Mr. Harris. There isn't that much there to get excited about."

Walsh denies any personal motive directly involving Harris. He admits, however, that "there are practical considerations."

"But I have been turning it over in my head," he said in his Manhattan apartment last week. "I do question my own motives in the thing. But I think I know what they are essentially — and that is to get to the bottom of this thing. To find out why mother did what she did.

"She was totally blinded by Harris."

BUCK, Pearl S(ydenstricker)
and
HARRIS, Theodore Findley
MIAMI HERALD
(Miami, Fla.)
July 22, 1973

HARRIS HAS NEVER publicly discussed his involvement with Miss Buck. But he writes about it in a somewhat mawkish book about their relationship called "For Spacious Skies," the first of three books he is credited with writing.

In the book, published in 1968, Harris says of Miss Buck:

"In you I found a wealth of variety and I felt much the same as a prospector must feel when he strikes a new vein."

Theodore Findley Harris was born Fred Leon Hair Jr., on April 5, 1931, in Bamberg, S. C. His father was disabled by a stroke while Harris was still a youngster and his mother supported the family by working as a domestic.

Harris' childhood is hard to trace. The few neighbors who remember him say he was "always putting on airs," claiming descendancy from Robert E. Lee and conspicuously overmothered.

AT 17, ACCORDING to those who knew him, he was a young man with a driving ambition to "Make it." Little is known of him over the next 15 years except that he worked his way across the country as a dance instructor, traded his South Carolina accent for what might be best described as thespian English, and acquired enough charm to make him a popular dancing teacher.

By 1963, Harris' travels had taken him to the Arthur Murray dance studio in suburban Philadelphia where he was earning $100 a week.

Pearl S. Buck was living on her farm just a few miles away.

At 70, Miss Buck was a brilliant, quick and energetic person, as she was until a few months before her death. Since the death of her husband — one of the only persons with whom she was ever close — she had filled the lonely void by enrolling in language courses, swimming and diving lessons and studying the organ and, in 1963, taking dancing lessons.

Her call to the Arthur Murray studio set in motion a chain of events that would eventually embarrass her, separate her from her family — and yet, in some way, apparently bring her happiness.

AND IT IS HERE that the mystery begins.

In a matter of months, a close relationship had formed between Fred L. Hair and Pearl Buck. In 1964, Fred L. Hair legally changed his name to Theodore Findley Harris.

At the time, Miss Buck's prime charitable interest was Welcome House, an adoption agency she had organized years before. Harris, in late 1963, suggested that he organize a Welcome House Ball to raise money for the charity.

The board of directors of Welcome House apparently was not impressed with Harris, a fact that so angered her she established another charity, the Pearl S. Buck Foundation, set up as a Delaware corporation on February 3, 1964. Theodore F. Harris was listed as its president.

WITHIN SEVEN MONTHS, Harris had obligated the fledgling foundation to nearly $500,000 in expenses, including a $146,460 townhouse here and a Cadillac for himself.

A check of the foundation's 990-A Federal income tax form shows that the foundation took in just $6,800 in the same year. And a review of the foundation's books shows that in the same period of time Miss Buck gave it another $134,000.

The foundation's avowed purpose was to care for "Amerasians" — outcast Korean children fathered by American GIs.

One of Harris' first moves was to announce that the Arthur Murray organization had pledged to raise "a million dollars" by sponsoring balls at which Miss Buck would appear. She danced around the country at one fund-raising event after another — all promoted by Harris and the foundation.

As the foundation grew richer, Harris' position grew stronger but little was being done in Korea to help the children.

No one, it appears, had the heart to tell her that her dream was dying in its infancy because of the Harris mismanagement.

She was also apparently unaware of another facet of the problem:

There is the case of Chul Soo Park, a 16-year-old brought to America by Harris after Miss Buck untangled governmental red tape for him among Korean officials.

Chul Soo Park remembers: "I was so sad because I left my country the first night. (Harris) pretended he was like my father. He buy my clothes and teach me how to comb my hair and how to use hair spray. I remember that evertime Mr. Harris spray my hair, my hair was getting red.

ONE NIGHT ON the way to America he ask me about my father and I began to cry; he kissed me on the neck. When I would go to bed he would hold me in his arms. I did not like, but I thought this is the way American father treat his son."

In 1969, this and similar statements were published in the Philadelphia magazine article.

The resulting publicity brought about an order by the Pennsylvania Commission of Charitable Foundations for the Pearl S. Buck Foundation to suspend operations.

Miss Buck faced the press and television cameras and consistently denied that anything was wrong with the operation. She defended Harris completely, calling him "an honorable and honest man."

However, her board of directors ordered an audit. There was abundant evidence of mismanagement. Harris headed north to Vermont.

IN A FINAL GESTURE — perhaps to keep her dream alive — Miss Buck turned over 300 acres of Bucks County property and her 400-acre Vermont estate to the foundation.

After the collapse of the foundation (it has since been reorganized), Harris persuaded Miss Buck to invest in Danby, a pretty little town of 900 residents nestled amid old trees in the rough and rustic countryside of Vermont.

Miss Buck's Stratton Mountain home with its wide, unobstructed view, had gone to the foundation. She had either lost or turned away many of her friends because of her continued support of Harris. She was later to die in a house she had bought for him.

At 77, she was destined to live out her days in a tiny town she could not have loved as she loved the mountains. Protecting her from the world and the world from her was the same person who had, to one degree or another, betrayed her trust. A fact she chose not to believe.

Backstage on the Firing Line

His questions start slow, pick up tempo and fade into a rapid mumble

By Phil Garner

Photography by Steve Deal

A WAVE of wariness precedes the man. No one relishes the thought of being the foil for his bon mots.

"Mr. Buckley's a nice guy, really, especially off-camera," they said, with hopeful expressions.

In the studios of the Georgia Educational Television network, a buff, modern building set in a corner of the Atlanta Area Technical Vocational School, preparations were being made for the arrival of this Mr. Nice Guy. He would tape two "Firing Line" shows that afternoon — one with former Secretary of State Dean Rusk, the other with State Rep. Julian Bond and the Voter Education Project's John Lewis, both in on the founding of the Student Non-Violent Coordinating Committee.

Buckley's show, although recently imperiled by cutbacks of funds in the Public Broadcasting System, survived the threat and continues as one of the most popular adult programs on the public television network. The chief reason for its success is the image of its host, William F. Buckley Jr., as a mean and unrelenting interrogator of his guests — always on the most impeccably intellectual level. The technique is saved from the sadism that permeated the performances of such interviewers as the late Joe Pyne by the fact that Buckley's targets, or guests, are always persons whose own assumptions of power and importance make them valid subjects of the most critical kinds of examination.

But Buckley's infrequent public lapses from refinement into unrestrained verbal ferocity against his adversaries (such as his loss of cool against Gore Vidal in televised debates during the 1968 Republican Convention) have not passed without leaving an impression embarrassing to Buckley, who is himself a public figure vulnerable to critical examination.

As Buckley was flying to Atlanta from New York, Miss Barbara Piercecci, program promotion director for the state ETV network, was expectantly arranging for his visit. Nearly everything had been arranged — except for the ice.

BUCKLEY, William F(rank), Jr.
(1925 -)

ATLANTA JOURNAL
& CONSTITUTION
(Atlanta, Georgia)

Mar. 3, 1974

[See also CA-4]

"Have we got the ice?" Miss Piercecci asked someone on her telephone. "Fine. Good. Yes, I think everything else is set."

She hung up with a self-conscious grin.

The ice was locked in. So was the fried chicken. So was the wine. The latter item had produced a minor problem, since alcoholic beverages were not allowed through the doors of the studios. Special dispensation was granted for Buckley, whose favorite lunch, his producer had informed Miss Piercecci, was Kentucky Fried Chicken and white wine, chilled of course.

Warren Steibel, a pleasant, stocky New Yorker who wore an open-collared sport shirt and a sport coat and smoked cigars drawn from a bulging supply in his shirt pocket, produces "Firing Line," and has from its beginnings about seven years ago.

Buckley, said Steibel, was an easy guy to get along with. He would, for instance, make every effort in his visits to local stations all over the country to tape his shows, to tape promotional spots for local use, grant a reasonable number of interviews to local reporters, subject himself to press conferences, or any other reasonable request that would help out the locals who were accommodating him.

"There's only one thing," said Steibel. "He likes to be told ahead of time, you know, just to know what's going on."

Buckley had not been told that a reporter had asked to "follow him around" during his Atlanta visit. Steibel thought Buckley would approve, but explained he would try to collar him before the introduction. Merely a matter of fairness to Buckley, he indicated. No *faits accomplis,* however insignificant.

MISS Piercecci, Steibel, local ETV program director John Haney and the reporter met Buckley at the airport. His plane was late, delayed by fog, compressing the time left for Steibel to prepare for the tapings. Steibel become wary of a foul-up as passengers deplaned and walked off past him through the concourses and he still had not seen Buckley. Perhaps this was the wrong flight. Could he have missed the plane? Steibel stood on tiptoe to see over the bobbing heads.

"Okay," he said. "There he is."

William Buckley washed up with the last wave of passengers into the Delta Airlines rotunda, smiling as he spotted Steibel. He carried a flat portable typewriter in one hand and a small retangular leather suitcase in the other. The suitcase had sprung its seams at the bottom, and tips of shirts and underwear protruded. Steibel whispered brief explanations in Buckley's ear and then escorted him to the waiting delegation for introductions. Buckley warmly shook hands all around and explained to Steibel why he had been among the last off the airplane.

"I was seated next to a very nice elderly lady," said Buckley. "I had put my typewriter on my lap to do some work and she offered to hold my papers."

He seemed pleased with the happening. Whatever piece of conservatism her seat partner was writing now had as its co-conspirator a little old lady from somewhere. And he had helped her gather her possessions and on with her coat.

"So you're from The Atlanta Journal," Buckley said. "How are things with the empire?"

"The same," was the reply.

THE ride from the airport to the television station was unmarred by the need for repartee. Buckley chatted with Steibel about a home TV video tape viewer and recorder that Steibel had acquired for him in Japan. Buckley's wife, Pat, didn't like it. Some feature of it displeased her.

"When Pat doesn't like a part of something, she dislikes the whole thing," said Buckley.

Rolling up to the front of the studios, Buckley spotted the Georgia State flag, with its generous use

(Continued from preceding page)

of the Confederate battle flag, waving in the breeze.

"What flag is that?" he asked, facetiously.

Buckley was led, declining Haney's offer to carry his small case, inside the building and down a hall to the corner office of Dr. Richard Ottinger, the network's executive director. There he unzipped the cover of his typewriter, placed the machine on a low coffee table and fed some paper into it. Then he neglected it for a moment to meet a half-dozen network employes. Ottinger entered and welcomed him.

"I'm usurping your office, I believe," said Buckley.

"It's yours," said Ottinger. "Make yourself at home."

Buckley soon was left alone with his typewriter.

"Don't think anything of it if you're talking to him and all of a sudden he's excusing himself and he's off in a corner, typing," Steibel had said earlier. "That's the way he has to work, traveling as much as he does."

With Buckley in his corner, the others entered a conference room where lunch would be eaten. Miss Piercecci brought in a stack of boxed fried chicken dinners and two bottles of chilled white wine, some napkins and a corkscrew. She left and returned with a handful of newly purchased wine glasses.

BUCKLEY entered within a few moments and made straight for the fried chicken. Unceremoniously, he began eating while standing, chatting with the others, finding his wine glass and having it filled. A chicken wing was devoured first, washed down with wine, then a leg, then the breast, all interspersed with comments on a recent Public Broadcasting System function which Ottinger and Buckley had both attended. Buckley, judging from frequent returns to the subject, was most impressed with a final speech made by Bill Moyers, former press aide to Lyndon Johnson, and more recently a newspaper publisher and host of his own ETV show, "Bill Moyers' Journal." Several times, Buckley referred to the speech as "Bill Moyers' sermon."

Abruptly, Buckley apologetically excused himself from the room, "to write my introductions." Later he read them at the beginning of each taping session, defining his guests from his own perspectives: Dean Rusk, he would describe as " . . . the chief victim of the Viet Nam War," a phrase composed on the inspiration of a stomach full of Col. Sanders' best.

As Buckley had written his introductions, Steibel was regaling his luncheon companions with other tidbits from the PBS event. Buckley had turned down a suggestion, Steibel said, that as a part of the entertainment he conduct an interview with Sesame Street's "Big Bird."

" 'Big Bird?' " Steibel recalled Buckley's response. " 'Who's Big Bird?' "

"Well, he's the bird on Sesame Street," Steibel had said, possibly the hardest thing he'd ever had to tell Buckley.

But Buckley's wit does not allow tangents into buffoonery. The sense of value placed on decorum is no illusion.

Miss Piercecci had written what was intended as a clever little promo for Buckley to follow.

"We thought we'd have him with his back to the camera, a la Bob Newhart, you know, talking on the telephone," Miss Piercecci said. "He'd be saying something like, 'No, I never watch television, it bores me.' And then he'd pause and say, 'But there is one show I rather enjoy,' and then he'd turn around to face the camera and you'd recognize him as Bill Buckley, and he'd say something like, 'Firing Line, with me, Bill Buckley on such-and-such a day, and so forth.' But he wouldn't have any part of it."

Buckley and his nine brothers and sisters were reared by a father who instilled in them the desirability of standing on principal, eschewing absurdities whichever camp they came from.

"There was nothing complicated about Father's theory of child-rearing," a Buckley brother was quoted in a 1970 article in The New York Times Magazine. "He brought up his children with the quite simple objective that they become absolutely perfect."

A friend of William Buckley Jr., cautioned, however, "His public hostility is to the ideas, not the people."

WHEN Gore Vidal called Buckley a "crypto-Nazi" in the 1968 televised "debates," Buckley retorted with a straightforward threat of physical violence, coupled with a slur on Vidal's masculinity. The incident has embarrassed him ever since, even when he has been commended for it.

"In front of millions of people I lost my temper, and they admire it," said Buckley. "Can you imagine?"

Buckley's exterior reflects, as well, the rubbings of his early schooling in England and France, and at the Millbrook School in New York and his undergraduate years at Yale, where he graduated with honors in 1950. His tendency toward over-erudition in conversing with the guests on his show is something he claims to recognize and, partially, to regret. He envies, he said, the ability of some persons to state complex ideas in plain language. Buckley's questions tend to be long, comprised of introductory and background statements of fact and opinion, starting slowly in a deep, cultured voice, picking up tempo and losing volume until they degenerate into a rapid, faint mumble, leaving the interviewee frequently leaning out of his chair to catch the gist of the final, interrogatory portion.

DURING his first Atlanta taping session, with Bond and Lewis, the college students assembled for the audience, although seated literally at the feet of the host and his guests, could hardly hear the conversations. The guests as well as the host were extremely soft-spoken.

Buckley's first question, characteristically, sought out the most likely weaknesses in his guests' most cherished positions. It was, to paraphrase, whether enfranchisement of blacks and their increasing involvement in politics and government had brought the new justice and freedom predicted by persons such as Bond and Lewis. It was a question typical of most of his comments, reflecting his own subjective vision of how things are, hostile in the sense of challenging easy conclusions but, all in all, not unfriendly to his targets.

His subjectivity was more compatible with the stance of Dean Rusk, especially concerning justifications for the Vietnam War, allowing Rusk considerable room to defend himself against real or imagined misrepresentations of himself in the past.

The press conference which followed in the same studio was videotaped for use on a local ETV talk show, "Byline," hosted by Eugene Moore.

Moore had prepared an introduction, which he read to acquaint his audience with Buckley. Moore plunged immediately into his guest's exchange with Vidal, down to exact quotes. As he read, Buckley sat impassively, stonily.

A bit later, a reporter asked Buckley if he thought his outburst against Vidal was "the proper way to conduct oneself on national television."

"No, not at all," said Buckley. "And I examined the matter a year later in an essay, which I had hoped would be the end of it. And, in fact, it was. No one has brought it up again until today."

The quality of the questions asked of Buckley was limited by the nature of the event. One could quiz him on his opinions on current issues and get, at best, studied, conservative observations, most of which were already quite well known through his syndicated column, "On The Right," and through his magazine, "National Review." One could seek illumination of the man through personal questions, and get the limited responses of a person uncomfortable with self-descriptions.

ATLANTA Magazine editor Norman Shavin discovered that fact when he asked Buckley what reporters are wont to call a "two-part question."

"How do you see William Buckley," Shavin asked, "and with which figure in our nation's history do you most closely associate?"

Buckley looked puzzled and then annoyed. First of all he said, he was no good at introspection. Secondly he had never met any signers of the Declaration of Independence and could hardly identify with any of them. He simply could not answer the question, he said.

Shavin, apparently discouraged, possibly piqued, canceled a half-hour private interview with Buckley that had been set up for him for after the press conference.

Some of Buckley's better moments came in the spaces between planned events.

Seated with the reporters, waiting to read a promotion for the local network, he tapped his fingers impatiently and chatted.

"One minute," the floor manager announced.

Buckley tapped his fingers again, turned to a female reporter for a radio station and said:

"A minute can be a long time."

She agreed.

He paused, thinking.

"You can electrocute 20 people in a minute — I mean consecutively, of course."

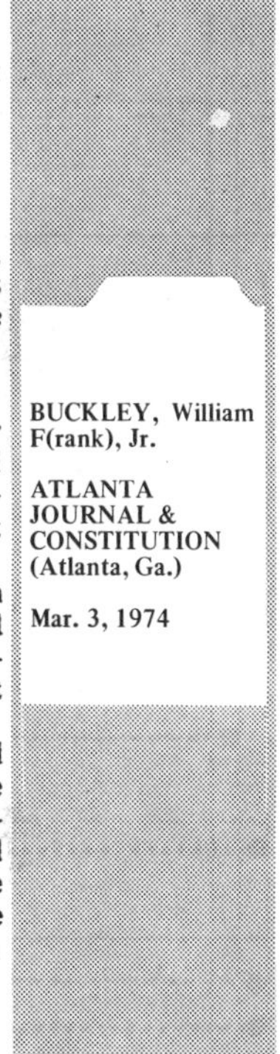
BUCKLEY, William F(rank), Jr.

ATLANTA JOURNAL & CONSTITUTION (Atlanta, Ga.)

Mar. 3, 1974

First Novel Cost Said Prohibitive

BURGESS, Anthony
(John Anthony Burgess Wilson)
(pseud. Joseph Kell)
(1917-)
TIMES-PICAYUNE
(New Orleans, La.)
Feb. 18, 1973
[See also CA-3]

By CHRIS SEGURA

Photos by William F. Haber, Times-Picayune Staff Photographer.

Whether over coffee on a stained college hangout table or gourmet food and wine at a famous uptown restaurant, the fare is literature, humor, music, personality anecdotes, and social philosophy for author Anthony Burgess and associates.

The creator of "A Clockwork Orange" ("It's not my favorite book and I really wish they'd think of me in relation to something else."), was in snowy New Orleans last weekend to deliver an address at Tulane University.

Burgess left the swirling snow and icy sidewalk and entered an overly-heated building for a cup of coffee with chicory.

At the table he dropped his too-thin coat on the booth seat. Later, again fighting the frigidity, Mrs. Burgess, a charming Italian woman, would gently chide him by saying, "Oh, Antonio, you didn't bring your fur coat.

"You didn't even bring your hat. I told you when you go to the South you should bring your fur coat."

They had encountered similar weather in South Carolina, she said.

But for the time being Burgess was warm with a hot cup of French coffee in one hand and a dark cheroot in the other. Both he seemed to enjoy with gusto, though his mind was on literature.

Current best Seller "Jonathan Livingston Seagull" was a "terrible book, just terrible" because it was a simplistic "sentimental, pretentious book" of heavy symbolism presenting a bird as "the emblem of man."

'Form Idea Not Bad'

The idea of the form of the book was not bad, he said. In fact Burgess has contracted to write a similar book with photographs dealing with "the human condition" as it is exemplified in New York City where the 54-year-old creator of 28 books is now teaching literature.

The book had already been advertised, he said, and was going to come out in May. A possible problem, he admitted, was the fact that he had not yet started the manuscript.

With an amused smile he compared this to a similar situation when Charles Dickens learned of an impending segment of a book he had serialized in a magazine by eavesdropping in a bookstore. Having heard from the proprietor the chapter was due to be published in a few days, Dickens hurried home and wrote it, Burgess said.

Unlike the "Seagull" pictures, Burgess said, his book would contain "sensible" photographs of life in New York.

And other popular works have even less to offer the literate mind, Burgess said.

The pot-boiling novels of Harold Robbins were "offensive, offensive. And he's an offensive man."

The extensive efforts of "Irving Wallace and the other Irvings" were simply "not serious, not serious."

Public's Tastes

But immediately after grimacing at the popularity of these novels, Burgess smiled and, while snubbing out a cheroot, said "But I'm fascinated by the tastes of the public.

"They want something pornographic and didactic at the same time. . .great wedges of information with lots of sex."

Last fall Norman Mailer, also speaking at Tulane, said "The novel is in trouble," Burgess was told.

The tall, thin writer brushed back a shock of reddish hair and said this was a current philosophical trend "but I believe there's still a lot of life left in the old novel."

Then Burgess digressed on Mailer's work, judging the pugilistic journalist-writer's first two books "The Naked and The Dead" and "Barbary Shore") as his best. The rest of Mailer's fiction had been "disappointing," Burgess said, but the quality of his journalism was unsurpassed.

"Some very good novels are being written and are going to continue to be written," Burgess said. "The trouble is they aren't going to be published."

Cost Prohibitive

He explained the cost of publishing a first novel was prohibitive.

"Publishers take books like first novels and some of my books and publish them but first they find a bad book that will sell and cover the cost. At least good publishers will do this."

But the prohibitive cost-return factor will continue to make it much more difficult to publish first novels, he said.

As a result a new movement of self-publication has begun on the U.S. West Coast. Young writers are photocopying their works and distributing them by the hundreds he said.

Burgess looks forward to the time when a typewriter will be converted into a machine capable of reproducing hundreds of copies of printed works. He said a major typewriter manufacturer had attempted this but the results were not satisfactory.

Aside from the publisher's cost aspect, the other most serious factor hampering publication of a first novel is the idealistic way it is written, Burgess said.

The trick, he said, was to follow the example of Shakespeare who sought to "appeal to a large audience . . . to cunningly try to appeal to all levels."

This way a writer could "trick an audience into listening."

Current Work

And what is Anthony Burgess writing currently? Apparently quite a lot, sandwiched in between a musical being produced in Minneapolis and destined for Broadway, and his teaching and lecturing chores.

He is working on two other musicals — one of them based on the life of Houdini — and yet another novel besides the one he hasn't started but must finish for a May publication date.

Burgess also anticipates writing a book in which he will use verse extensively. He feels there will be a resurgence of poetry in combination with prose.

"Verse will be read again," he says quietly but with the definite air of a prophet — as though the words were intended for the base of a statute of a bard with emphatic finger raised, punctuating words of wisdom.

This book could possibly be about the life of Napoleon, "with great chunks of verse" used to fill gaps in the famed general-statesman's life story. Heroic couplets and even Byronic stanzas would be used "as relief."

With a wistful expression he wished for a sort of new "Don Juan," by a modern poet like the great Lord Byron.

But before Burgess undertakes this effort he will have to "refurbish my verse skills," he said, by studying and practicing because creating lyrics or verse is "an exacting task."

Braves the Snow

Deciding the conversation could be continued enroute to a famous uptown hotel and restaurant, Burgess and his small entourage left the warmth and again braved the icy snow and an automobile drive through slick streets.

"We'll always think of New Orleans as having lots of snow. It's a pity," Mrs. Burgess said sort of dreamily from her place beside her husband. "It's really quite lovely though."

"Yes," Burgess agreed. "This thing happens to us quite often. We've never seen a windy Chicago. The skies are always quite blue and there's never any wind when we're there."

"Do you own a dog?" Burgess was asked abruptly (the rumor being that all English gentlemen are dog owners).

Actually he was very fond of dogs, Burgess admitted, but his hectic schedule prevented him from owning one at present.

The subject included, however, a veritable litany of animals the Burgesses have owned. The litany included mynah birds ("Mynahs speak very well; a bit parroty, perhaps, but also with a very humanlike quality), several types of dangerous and semi-dangerous reptiles, and at least one pet otter.

The otter and one of the snakes came to tragic ends.

The otter was bitten by a snake and died.

"Yes. This snake came to the back door and bit him . . . killed him," Burgess said.

Another snake, not the otter's nemesis, was killed by "one of the servants" in Malaya. The snake, a pet, was killed "because he (the servant) thought the snake was dangerous," Burgess said.

"I suppose he probably was dangerous," Burgess said, "but the servant never gave it a chance to demonstrate it."

Shakespeare

Once in the restaurant the topics of conversation turned to Shakespeare, then to race relations (after an explanation of Shakespeare's "dark lady"), then to wine.

Burgess selected the wine in an elaborate manner, informing his wife of his choice by the words "with your permission."

He toyed with the idea of ordering a $275 dollar bottle from the manager's private stock but decided he wouldn't, finally.

This prompted an anecdote about a friend who ordered a $1500 bottle of wine in a Paris restaurant.

It was wheeled out "amid cobwebs" and admiration, Burgess said, with the end result that the owner of the Paris establishment gave the bottle to the man tearfully and free of charge.

The proprietor explained he was overcome that a connoisseur thought enough of wine to order it at such a price and such dedication deserved to be rewarded in kind.

Burgess ordered Bordeaux and a light Rhine wine even though his wife "hates anything German."

The wine and the food were excellent, Burgess commented, even though he allowed the Bordeaux to be drunk before it had warmed properly.

"It was our fault," he told the waiter. "We were too eager."

The dinner conversation turned again to the novel.

Integrity a Must

A novelist must write with integrity, it was decided, but he must work "within the limits of the commission."

"Shakespeare took very bad plays and made them into very good ones. He certainly wrote within confines. He was very commercial."

But if everyone were to begin to publish all their works when technology provided a method, wouldn't there be even more second rate novels flooding America's market?

Burgess looked toward the ornate decor of the famous restaurant as though gazing into a vast distance.

"Well, I suppose what we need is a great patron," he said, "to inspire great works."

The conversation slackened. Possibly the diners were dreaming of great patrons and the works they would inspire.

"But this food is exceptionally good," Burgess said later. "It is such a pleasure to have a good meal after all the franchises. The food in America and the South in particular is so unfoully bad."

No Lawsuits for Sophy—Yet

—Journal Photo by Allan Scott

By JAMES AUER of The Journal Staff

DO SOME well known critics accept paintings as gifts from artists whose shows they have reviewed?

Do wealthy collectors occasionally arrange for the exhibition of paintings they own in museums of which they are trustees, in order to force up the market value of the works?

Has a major New York gallery ever been accused of tapping the telephone lines of a competitor?

Have important New York and London auction houses attempted in the past to manipulate the prices of works of art by concealing the fact that the works were "bid in" by a friend of the house after bidding failed to meet a secret minimum reserve price?

Has the effort to become "relevant" to the community harmed the scholarly and preservational functions of such museums as New York's Metropolitan and Washington's Smithsonian Institution?

The answer to all these questions, says writer and editor Sophy Burnham, is yes.

Inside Story

And so far the 39 year old author of "The Art Crowd" (David McKay $8.95) hasn't been sued by a single one of the critics, dealers, curators, museum directors, trustees and collectors she mentions by name in the book her publisher calls "the inside story of how a few rich and/or powerful figures control the world's art market."

In Milwaukee last week to address the Bookfellows' Eighth Annual Book and Author Dinner, Mrs. Burnham admitted she's been threatened with lawsuits by a number of art world figures who fancy themselves harmed by the "revelations" she serves up with relish in such chapters as "Do Critics Deal" and "The Princess of Power."

"I don't really want a suit," she told The Journal over an afternoon cup of coffee. "I'm not a reformer. I just find human nature so amusing and funny ... I'm amused by it all."

Even the reminder of hostile reviews (one magazine accused her of "cretinous philistinism") fails to dim the spirits of the slender, five-foot-four mother of two.

And the fact that one art world celebrity continues to send her letters in green envelopes decorated with pictures of creepy, crawly monsters seems not to bother her at all.

Manic Depressive

"I can never be serious for more than a few minutes at a time," she declared. "I sweep from exuberance to nihilistic despair. I'm manic when I have something to work on, depressive when I'm between projects."

The premise behind "The Art Crowd" began to emerge when Mrs. Burnham, a free lance writer, placed articles on the art world with New York magazine and Saturday Review. When a publisher suggested she expand her articles into a book, she hesitated at first, then agreed to go ahead principally because "nobody had ever asked me to write a book before."

The one accusation that does raise Mrs. Burnham's hackles is that "The Art Crowd" is "gossipy."

"It's a denigrating term," she said. "I did the entire book through interviews. I had to check every story with everybody else. I interviewed everyone."

She obtained the details of the firing of Bates Lowry as director of the Museum of Modern Art, for instance, from Lowry himself during a five hour interview.

Subsequently, she had Lowry's remarks transcribed and showed them to William Paley, president of the museum's board of trustees.

Similarly, some of her most devastating anecdotes were developed in the course of conversations with prominent art figures.

Her account of the dispute between critics John Canaday and Dore Ashton is supplemented by copies of memos exchanged between the two. And a court transcript adds substance to her chapter on the bugging of one prominent gallery by another.

"Just as in the Watergate," she said, "the response was one of puzzlement because they didn't get anything worth having. ... So it was all right."

What makes her angriest, Mrs. Burnham said, is not the fact that the artist is at the "bottom of the heap" in the art world, although this is, of course, disturbing.

It is "the lack of visual pleasure in the world . . .

"The art world is so pompous, so pretentious. ... Nobody ever says anything is junk because nobody trusts his eye."

BURNHAM, Sophy
(1936 -)

MILWAUKEE JOURNAL
(Milwaukee, Wisc.)

May 20, 1973

[See also CA-41/44]

The Metropolitan Museum of Art, she said, was unwilling to lift a hand to save two "landmark" townhouses across the street from demolition.

"But it was natural to do this because the whole system is built on money."

And does she, Mrs. Burnham was asked, expect "The Art Crowd," for all its scatter shot approach and occasional frivolity, to change the ways of the art world for the better?

"I do expect it to change things," she said. "And if things do change, it will be because people will have started looking at things differently."

He Rises At The Crack Of Noon ...And Works Backwards

BUSHMILLER, Ernest Paul
(1905 -)

PITTSBURGH PRESS
(Pittsburgh, Penn.)

June 23, 1974

[See also CA-29/32]

By Bill Crouch Jr.

ERNIE Bushmiller, who created, writes and draws the comic strip "Nancy," is the type of guy who can wear an ascot and get away with it.

This may not sound like much of an accomplishment until you think of all the famous and powerful men in the world who can't.

According to the last readership poll, "Nancy" was the Press' best-read comic strip. An interview with Bushmiller seemed the natural follow up. That was until Bushmiller's one major phobia surfaced.

"I hate to be interviewed," he said. "In fact, you might say I'm psychotic about it."

Once at the opening of a public park, Bushmiller refused to even speak into a local radio station's microphone. And he was a guest of honor.

Since "Nancy" is one of the top five syndicated comic strips in the world and appears in about 700 American and 100 overseas newspapers, success permits Bushmiller to indulge in his phobia. However, he sometimes makes exceptions and this is one of them.

"I'm always intrigued by the huge appeal of 'Nancy,'" says Bushmiller. "I guess there are kids all over the world and my gags being mostly visual there's no problem in understanding them."

A lover of word games and crossword puzzles, Bushmiller is very pleased that the "American Heritage Dictionary of the English Language" on Page 266 used a postage stamp-sized "Nancy" to illustrate its definition of the word "comics."

Cartoonist Ernie Bushmiller

However, he says, "If a gag I use for 'Nancy' can be set in type and stand by itself, it isn't worth drawing."

Many cartoonists have elaborate studios and a staff of assistants. Bushmiller works alone in a corner of the living room of his suburban Stamford, Conn., home. His "mini-studio" is a desk with art supplies on a bookshelf behind him.

"I get up at the crack of noon," says Bushmiller, "and do most of my work at night. It takes the newspapers and about 40 cups of coffee to get me started. But often I work until 2 in the morning."

He says his wife, Abby, usually watches television in the living room while he draws. They were married in 1930 and have no children.

Quiet is essential when he is thinking up gags, but if he is drawing late at night, he's addicted to the all-night radio talk shows originating in New York City.

Unlike many cartoonists, Bushmiller draws his strip backwards. He starts with the last frame that contains the gag or punch line and then fills in what comes before.

"I'm a very slow worker and a slow thinker," says Bushmiller, "and always late for my deadlines with the syndicate. When I draw, my lines don't have great flamboyance. 'Nancy' is the Lawrence Welk of the comic strip world."

Lawrence Welk of the funnies or not, "Nancy" and Bushmiller are becoming unique in the world of funnies and cartoonists. There is only a small group of cartoonists who, like Bushmiller, are still active and can trace their cartooning careers back to the 1920s. Among them are 81-year-old Hal "Prince Valiant" Foster and 73-year-old Chester "Dick Tracy" Gould.

Ernest Paul Bushmiller, a mere 69, was born in the Bronx on Aug. 25, 1905. Artistic ability was a family trait and his father had done funny chalk-talks at Tony Pastor's famous theater in the 1890s.

After grammar school and six months at Theodore Roosevelt High School, Bushmiller at 14 set out to earn his fortune. He answered two ads in the New York World. One sought an office boy for the newspaper itself and the other offered a similar position with Cunard Lines. Both wanted to hire him but he chose the newspaper.

Soon after he started as a copy boy at the New York World in 1919, he began evening art courses at the National Academy of Design.

Made A Decision

"All I learned to draw there was a plaster head of Dante," Bushmiller says.

He decided cartooning, not fine art, was what he wanted to do. At the World he was promoted to sweeper and general helper in the art department. This led to his first published artwork, the lines for a crossword puzzle. Down in the corner he carefully signed his initials.

"The World was the first New York paper to feature crossword puzzles and I became their expert crossword puzzle line drawer," Bushmiller laughs, however, his art career was under way.

For awhile he drew for the World's Sunday magazine, Red Magic. He and Arthur Nugent who now draws the syndicated "Uncle Nugent's Funland" (a children's game page), illustrated a game page of which escape artist Harry Houdini was editor.

Bushmiller was only 18 when he achieved syndicated success with the strip "Fritzi Ritz." He admits that initially "Fritzi" was an imitation of the then highly popular "Tillie the Toiler."

Fritzi was the leggy brunette poor little rich girl named by Meyer Marcus, comics editor of the World. Bushmiller drew her as a caricature of his fiancee, Abby Bohnet, in terms of her physical appearance. He himself appeared in caricature as her boyfriend, Phil. Today the curly-haired Rollo in the strip "Nancy" is the closest rendering of a self-portrait of Bushmiller appearing in the strip.

But how did "Nancy" start?

"You'd be surprised," says Bushmiller, "how many letters I get asking me who's Nancy? Where's her mother and father? What's the story on Sluggo? The problem is I don't know the answer.

"I started doing 'Fritzi' in 1922, and finally one week I simply ran out of ideas and gags. So I decided to have a niece drop by."

The niece was "Nancy" and Bushmiller's good friend, the late cartoonist Milt Gross, liked the character and suggested the little girl be kept in the strip. Milt Gross wasn't the only one who liked "Nancy"

"Soon editors around the country wrote United Features Syndicate and suggested that the strip be changed from 'Fritzi Ritz' to 'Nancy,'" remembers Bushmiller. Their advice was taken and "Nancy" became its official title in May, 1938.

"Sluggo was my answer to Nancy's need for a foil and I had to name him something. I picked Sluggo because he's a tough mug," says Bushmiller.

Bushmiller lived in New York City until 1952 when the late Alex Raymond of "Flash Gordon" fame talked him into moving to Connecticut's Fairfield County. Located in the southern tip of the state, it is the home of more internationally famous cartoonists than anyplace in the world.

"New York used to be inspiring and a great place to live," says Bushmiller, "but it's gone now. I haven't been to New York City in eight years or to my office at United Features in 12. In fact I renewed my contract with them by mail.

"I love the fact I don't have to commute anywhere. I look out my window at all the lawyers and executives hurrying to work in New York and laugh."

The Bushmillers' tastefully furnished home has the classic style of understatement. Prominently displayed in the living room are two superb watercolors by the late Herb Olsen.

The Olsen books on how-to-watercolor are considered among the best on the subject.

Prolific Reader

Many cartoonists of apolitical gag strips have little interest in journalism per se. Bushmiller is different. He revels in studying journalism and is a prolific reader.

In the slang of today, Bushmiller would be called an H. L. Mencken "freak." Mencken, the legendary editor of the Baltimore Sun, like Bushmiller was a man with tremendous personal style and success in his profession. However, he could see himself in perspective. He refused to let all the rough edges be worn away from his character. Bushmiller is the same.

The longevity and success of "Fritzi Ritz" and "Nancy" are amazing statistics in themselves. The only time Bushmiller was tempted to leave cartooning was in 1930 when he went to Hollywood to write gags for Harold Lloyd's film "Movie Crazy."

Asked what he would suggest to aspiring cartoonists, Bushmiller answered. "There's only one way to learn cartooning. It's like you can't go to school to learn to write a song. You just do it.

"I read humor strips when I was a kid and traced and swiped and developed my artwork. The gag of course comes first and is more difficult than the drawing part of cartooning."

Bushmiller, once the man-about-New York, has lost none of his wit but changed his life style to that of quiet country gentleman. Still, Ernie Bushmiller might be pleased that these autobiographical lines by H. L Mencken, almost describe him as well as Mencken.

"I delight in beef stew, limericks, burlesque shows, New York City and the music of Hayden, that beery and delightful old rascal! I swear in the presence of ladies and archdeacons. When the mercury is above 95, I dine in my shirt-sleeves and write poetry naked."

"Nancy" is an American original. So is Ernie Bushmiller.

Peeter Vilms

CAEN,
Herb (Eugene)
(1916 -)

SAN FRANCISCO
(San Francisco,
Calif.)

Feb., 1974

[See also CA-1]

The Real Herb Caen

by Susan Berman

HERB CAEN is stuck. He has tried to make his way to the exit ramp of industrial designer Walter Landor's glittery ferryboat for half an hour, but it's hopeless. There are 500 of San Francisco's beautiful people at Landor's party, many of whom Caen has invented, and they all want to get their few words in with him.

Caen, 56, and his third wife, Maria Theresa, 35, are glossy, spruced up, wearing just the right thing, saying just the right thing to just the right people, but they are a little tired.

After all, they've been to four other events in the last 36 hours. Gay Talese was here. Tomorrow it's Truman Capote. And there was the party for Peter Duchin and the dinner for Ginger Rogers, and Pierre Salinger and Ethel and Eunice are coming to town.

But it's no use. Herb Caen is in public; he will continue to give out smiles and be affable to everyone who blocks his path.

Up saunters a 40-year-old socialite decked out in a pirate costume gone high fashion, her mosquito-bite-sized breasts barely covered by a bead vest. "Have you met Sätty, Herbie?" she breathes.

"I don't believe that outfit, Linda," says Caen, all grins.

Robert Shields, the Union Square mime, one of Caen's more tiring creations, walks over. "There's the famous Robert Shields," says Caen to Shields.

"You made me famous, Herb." Shields says it with an air of utmost sincerity, but he appears to be trying to remember something. "I've been in your column 28—or was it 29—times. I still remember the first time you mentioned me."

Caen decides to switch him off before the gratitude becomes uncomfortable. "Say, Robert, when are you getting married?"

"At the end of the month, Herb. Have you met my fiancée?" Shields shoves someone who looks like a Pepsodent ad into Herb Caen's face. She smiles. She is dressed like Shields.

"You reviewed *Your Own Thing*, Herb, before I was in it, but it was a great review," she says, looking at Robert to make sure she hasn't committed a faux pas. He gives her a reassuring smile. Can't lose it for a minute with Herb Caen.

"Say, Herb, how would you like to be best man? I thought about asking you, but, uh, well . . . anyway, you'd look great in whiteface."

Caen's mouth creases into an even line. "Uh, I'll call you on that, Robert." Fat chance you'll get Herb Caen in whiteface. (And when Shields was married, much later, in Union Square, Herb Caen was *not* best man.)

Caen scouts around the ferryboat for his wife, finally gets her eye, takes her arm, steers her toward the off-ramp and starts to descend the stairs. He moves closer to his wife whenever their defensive line is threatened by a clever offense. It always begins, "Herb, you're just the person I'm looking for." At last they reach the last set of steps and finally descend them, looking like Marge and Gower Champion, gliding, gracious all the while.

A picture in Caen's office in the San Francisco *Chronicle* Building shows a young Herb Caen listening to the sounds of a distant cable car through the tracks. He looks happy, perhaps because he is to some degree responsible for making the cable cars of San Francisco one of the nostalgic wonders of the modern world.

This is the office that Mr. San Francisco, three-dot columnist Herb Caen, occupies, the center of his existence, 1000 words a day, six days a week. The search for Herb Caen starts and ends with his column, because that is where his allegiance lies.

The desk is clean, organized, a bit boring. The memorabilia isn't what you could call funky either. There is a picture of a young Herb Caen with his assistant and their mutual idol, Benny Goodman. Alongside is a photo of the same trio, 35 years later. Across from Caen's desk is a filing cabinet with bound copies of The Column going back some 33 years. Except for the three and a half years he spent in the Army, he has never missed a day—a truly incredible feat in this business.

Names have changed in The Column. Goodwin Knight has become Ronald Reagan. Mayor Joseph Alioto has replaced former Mayor Roger Lapham. Peace and ecology take up space once devoted to Nob Hill blondes and brunettes. But the meat of The Column hasn't changed: scoops, gossip, puns, nostalgia, fog, little old ladies, and always three dots . . .

Immaculate as his office, the Three Dot Man sits behind his desk. His corduroy jacket is perfect; the Gucci shoes sparkle, his curly brown hair flips just so over the very upper tips of his ears. He is slightly tan and a little pink-cheeked from tennis, looking for all the world like the incarnation of the word "fit."

His thin, six-foot frame tries to hang ➡

(Continued from preceding page)

loose, but is always a little tense. The most prominent feature of his face is his nose, which is long. He walks lightly and quickly, at times with an almost feathery grace. He is usually smiling.

The phone never stops ringing, but most calls have until recently been screened by Jerry Bundsen, his aide for over 30 years, a former press agent.

(Bundsen quit, amicably, last month to pursue other interests, though he plans to continue to gather items for Caen from, as he puts it, "the outside." Bundsen's office next door, was an extension of Caen's hand, which was likely to press Bundsen's phone line at any moment to check a fact.)

Of the two Herb Caens, the outer person, who is easier to understand, is in his office today.

Through the door comes a Maharishi disciple, unannounced. Caen is accessible, gentle with him. "Keep an ear out for me at the retreat," he says as the boy leaves. Next comes Bob Moretti, Speaker of the California Assembly, who says he has been wanting to meet Caen. They talk politics—Caen the naive, Moretti the smooth.

Ask Herb Caen what he's all about, and he will look mystified. "Look, there's just not that much here. I'm sorry to disappoint you," he says, really meaning it, but looking a little hurt if you appear to believe him. "What can I tell you? I had a normal childhood, and got into this business. Sometimes I think to myself, 'why am I writing this stuff?' "

He gestures toward a letter from a woman who is canceling her subscription because Herb Caen doesn't write about San Francisco the way he did once. "How can I? San Francisco is still my lady, but now I see her warts. These people are just missing their youth." Caen says it in an understanding, gentle voice. He misses his youth, too.

There are stories of a young Herb Caen who always had a beautiful blonde on his arm, probably a model. He would play the drums at bars and musical events and sometimes stayed out all night. That Herb Caen wrote his column in the early morning, when the parties were over.

It is 11 p.m., a Grateful Dead concert at Winterland and Caen is glowing. He is Polk Street tonight — clean chinos, western shirt and a perky red bandana tied around his neck.

Caen has a beautiful person in town, author Gay Talese, who looks like a stiff, recently issued paperback. Mrs. Caen is early Berkeley — bare midriff, jeans, floppy suede hat. They are seated behind the Dead.

Herb Caen loves every minute of it tonight. "Look at it out there, it's just like the 'summer of love.' Look at the kids out there, all dressed up. Everybody looks so happy. There isn't much smell of pot; I wonder why." He is swaying to the grunts and lilts of the Dead. His wife is hunched over, staring at Jerry Garcia. "It's her favorite band," remarks Caen. Occasionally Bill Graham drops by. They exchange wisecracks, everybody smiles.

At Caen's suggestion, Talese gives a famous author's assessment of a friend: "Herb is successful because of hard work. He never misses a thing, and he's so curious about people. He wants to know everything about them . . . San Francisco is one city you can enjoy success in." Talese adds, a little wistfully, "It's not like New York, where you have to struggle to stay on top."

Then the Caens return, bend down, sort of envelop the smaller Talese and usher him off to his hotel.

CAEN, Herb (Eugene)

SAN FRANCISCO
(San Francisco, Calif.)

Feb., 1974

By noon of the next day, Herb Caen has spent a normal morning writing his column. Now he is keeping one of his lunch appointments. Lunch is an important source of items, and he never eats alone.

Today it's Vanessi's in North Beach, Caen dressed in a spiffy two-tone suit. Today is remember-old-San-Francisco-day, and he is eating with former Mayor George Christopher, Supervisor Al Nelder and car dealer Nick Geracimos. They called him to discuss a private matter, and now that it's over, they relax.

"You know, Herb, George never took a day off when he worked in the Mayor's office," says Nelder.

Caen agrees. George was a real workhorse.

"Look at these two South of Market boys, Herb. Didn't they make good?" asks Geracimos, bursting with pride.

"They sure did," says Caen, as Nelder goes into a discussion of what geographical districts are encompassed by "South of Market."

The bill comes. There is a fight over it, as usual. The outcome is uncertain, but Herb Caen, contrary to folklore, usually pays.

Lunch over, Caen jumps into his Mazda and heads for the office to answer some of those 1000 letters a week, those 200 phone calls a day, to check on some of those items.

Why did he go to lunch with the threesome? "It's important for The Column to know those people," he says, a little defensively, and he looks into the distance.

Perhaps he is thinking of how all this started—the constant hordes of people who want something, the constant good humor he maintains without visible effort, his constant worry The Column will slip.

Friends say Herb Caen fears if the items aren't fresh every day, his readers will desert him. Once he wrote a column on the respect he feels for the average reader's intelligence, that readers are so smart "they may be in danger of breeding themselves into extinction." Caen truly feels this, is always afraid readers will get bored.

He is a people-lover and, according to his sister, Estelle Barrett, always was one. Herbert Eugene Caen says he was conceived when his parents visited the Panama-Pacific International Exposition in July, 1915. He was born the next year in Sacramento. where his father, Lucien Caen, a French Jew from Alsace-Lorraine, was in the wholesale liquor business.

His German-born mother sang Schubert at family gatherings. The Caens came to Sacramento to give their children a solid, middle-class life, and they succeeded.

Herb was a plump, affable baby, who liked people and wanted to be liked. His mother was a hard-driving woman who insisted both children take piano lessons. Estelle went on to become a fine classical pianist who studied at Juilliard. Herb gave it up for another love, baseball.

In high school, Caen wrote a column in the school paper signed "Raisen Caen," drove a shiny Model T and was seldom without a girlfriend. But it was the Depression, so Herb joined the sports staff of the Sacramento *Union*.

At the age of 20, he was hired by Paul Smith, then only 27 himself, the editor of the *Chronicle*. He wrote a radio column that lasted two years before starting The Column, then called "It's News to Me."

Herb Caen adopted the three-dot style originally popularized by the late Walter Winchell. (They met once in New York's Stork Club, and Winchell told him, "Here's the kid who imitates me best." Caen took it as a compliment.) Another element of the Winchell style, which from time to time draws criticism, is Caen's occasional "blind" or unattributed item. A recent example: " A highly charged name in Peninsula electronics has left Wife No. 4 to return to No. 3, which is slightly confusing to the seven children involved."

Caen left the *Chronicle* for a tour in the Army. He also switched to the *Examiner* for eight years before returning to the *Chronicle* in 1958. Estimates vary, but somewhere around 30,000-50,000 subscribers switched papers with him.

Herb Caen now makes about $75,000 ➡

(Continued from preceding page)

a year plus a generous expense account for his column, which is also syndicated to six other newspapers (*The Orange Coast Daily Pilot* in Costa Mesa, the Las Vegas *Review Journal*, the Houston *Chronicle*, *The Columbian* in Vancouver, Washington, the *Star Free-Press* in Ventura, and the Honolulu *Advertiser*), and another $10,000 for his books. (Top scale for most newspapermen in San Francisco is $15,600 or so.)

Herb Caen doesn't like to talk about himself, but he will comply, under repeated assaults, trying all the while to squirm into another topic. "I remember my childhood as mainly wanting to succeed," he says, pulling the words up from deep within. "I just don't know what I can tell you about me that would be interesting. I just write a column. That's all."

Caen is now at his home away from the office, Enrico's, where all his favorite cafe society friends hang out. He is modest and a little embarrassed when he gets a lot of attention. But he loves *some* attention, needs people to stimulate him and doesn't know quite how to react to it. And he's always a little scared that it's The Column they're after, not himself.

Today he has taken a back table, but it's useless. He is a magnet. Women encased in makeup, 10 years postdeb, drop by. Poet-author (*The Beard*) Michael McClure sits down. "I enjoyed that dinner at your house, Michael," says Caen.

McClure just smiles. He is mourning the death of Louis Leakey, the anthropologist. "All those discoveries," says McClure. "What a man."

"I know." Caen warms to the subject. "Somebody named Louis Leakey should live to be 84; they shouldn't just die," says Caen, the subject of age making him, as usual, slightly melancholy.

He tries a few wisecracks to change the subject, cocks his head to one side, gestures with his right hand—but can't shake off Leakey's death. "You know, Michael, 69 doesn't seem so far off to me anymore. I guess it's still a long way off for you."

McClure assures him that 69 is getting within seeing distance for him too, looks a little uneasy and withdraws.

Caen takes care of his business and heads homeward to a small house in Pacific Heights. Here he resides with Maria Theresa and their seven-year-old son, Christopher.

The inner man isn't reflected in his home, either. The house is decorated like many other Pacific Heights homes—rugs on the wall, fancy trappings, artwork. There is a well-stocked bookcase attesting to the fact that Caen is a print junkie, his seven books strewn within (his latest is for children, *The Cable Car and the Dragon*, written in two hours after he got the idea).

He walks into the living room, mixes a drink, then into the kitchen where he can gaze on a small, very green backyard. Denise Minnelli Hale telephones, asks for his wife, and she takes it upstairs. Something smells good in the oven; Caen comments that Maria Theresa is a very good cook.

He looks a little uncomfortable, as if he doesn't quite know what to do when alone, when there is no one to reflect. "When I woke up this morning, I felt sick. And I realized it was the war. I want to write about the war, but I get letters. People want to hear gossip. They say, 'Stick to what you do best.' What am I supposed to do?"

Nobody denies The Column's influence in show business, but even in political matters Herb Caen has considerable impact. Some City supervisors credit him for helping rally opposition to the U.S. Steel highrise waterfront project, which was eventually shelved. Congressman Philip Burton and Assemblyman Willie Brown say favorable references in The Column have helped win voter support. Jerry Mander, a former advertising and public relations man, says, "There is no one that makes an idea acceptable like Herb does. He taps our unconscious in his writing and can really mold public opinion."

Caen's frequent jabs at Mayor Alioto are usually ignored, but at the Opera recently he was approached by Mrs. Angelina Alioto, who said, "Are you with us or against us?"

He recalls, "That was before her daughter pulled her away, saying, 'Mother, are you crazy?' "

His enemies hate Herb Caen. Interviews with some of them show they pretend to ignore his column but admit to reading it. They can usually paraphrase every comment made about them. Walter Shorenstein, the high-rise king, sat in his office. On the walls were pictures of Hubert and Muriel and a letter from LBJ. Saying he is not afraid of the columnist, Shorenstein added, "Herb Caen? I'd better not comment."

Herb Caen often prints retractions, and he has lost two lawsuits. When he disclosed that a local chiropractor was a cabbie by night, it was invasion of privacy. And he libeled Mustang Ranch's Joe Conforte when he accused the Nevadan of bugging the walls of his house of prostitution. Rumors also persist that Caen has betrayed personal confidences in his constant search for items.

For years, Caen's private life was secondary to his column, and his first two marriages ended in divorce. His vacations are searches for that one more item. And perhaps the inner person, elusive and well-guarded, has suffered. The people he says are his six best friends don't pretend to understand any of his complexities.

Some express amazement that a man who appears to be caught up in the social whirl, who appears to be the little boy from Sacramento who landed in the big city, can write with such sensitivity.

"I remember once when he got drunk, he said, 'So little paper, so little paper' " says a friend, novelist Herb Gold, referring to the fact that Caen had so much to say and so little space in his column. Another friend confesses to spending many hours with Caen and knowing little of his background.

Caen seldom loses his temper, doesn't even seem to have one. The only time he can ever remember being really upset was when a former houseboy burned his box of item-smashers by mistake. (Item-smashers are leftovers from the column, stored for future use. On that day, Herb Caen lost 500 of them and says he felt disconnected.)

He really is stickily sentimental on occasion, and he is capable of writing a column on Senator John Tunney, which ends, "But for today he is just another troubled American," looking at it six months later in embarrassment.

And he is truly happy when he meets a feisty little old lady, when the fog envelops him, when the occasion calls for another "I love San Francisco" column. "He has the lyrical soul of a poet with all that nostalgia," says Gold.

Herb Caen is extraordinarily sensitive to a touching story, but he saves all the intimacy for his column. Perhaps the most interesting column would be the one he will never write, the one on himself.

Herb Caen is in Trader Vic's today. He is discussing opera with the maitre d', Hans.

"Hans is the most cultured maitre d' I know," he says, ingratiatingly, looking softly at you to make sure you forgive him this.

The beautiful people come to his table, all with news of the latest party, of another celebrity coming to town.

Caen looks tense for a moment. That look is familiar and seems to say: the people here at Trader Vic's are going to continue to come over, and I am going to continue to write about them, and as the years go by, I am going to get older, and there is nothing I can do about either fact.

Then a new person comes over to the table. Caen's curiosity is aroused, and conversation flows. After all, there might be an item . . . □

CAEN, Herb (Eugene)

SAN FRANCISCO
(San Francisco, Calif.)

Feb., 1974

Cain, 82, Still Writes Of Faithless Sex

By LARRY SWINDELL
Knight Newspapers Writer

From years gone by, when I was an impressionable youth and often saw him around Hollywood, I remembered a huge gnarled oak of a man, and wondered how he'd look now.

The scene was Washington's Sheraton Park Hotel, the event was the American Booksellers Association convention, and James M. Cain was one of the interviewees in a line-up dominated by nonwriters ranging from Brooks Robinson to Tom Eagleton to Jimmy Hoffa.

So Cain was this year's literary token figure, as Henry Miller was last year. Annually the ABA trots out a Grand Old Man, and Cain would qualify. He was 82 July 1.

MOST OF THE reporters were unborn when Cain was mining his best-remembered ore. Indeed, he is a throwback to a vibrant age of American fiction, which he influenced enormously despite the anonymity of his long afterlife. He still influences writers who have never read or heard of him. He knows this, and isn't displeased.

He's writing again, and that's why he's on display; Mason & Lipscomb, a relatively new house, is publishing a new Cain novel called "Rainbow's End" this Fall.

"The title sounds valedictory but I'm working now on another book, about a love affair. At the moment it's called 'The Cocktail Waitress' and a funeral starts it," Cain said.

CAIN'S stories and novels were little triumphs of innuendo, usually dominated by the sex impulse. But sexual satisfaction was not the catalyst for his melodramatics. Rather, it was sexual hunger, with built-in literary fringe benefits of tension and suspense.

Cain's protagonists are never standard hoods but are likable yet vulnerable men, almost always driven to crime (most often murder) by a calculating woman. Sex motivates the Cain anti-hero; money is what goads his women.

James Mallahan Cain became a newspaperman (the old American) all of 57 years ago. After service in World War I he switched to the Sun and earned the friendship of H. L.

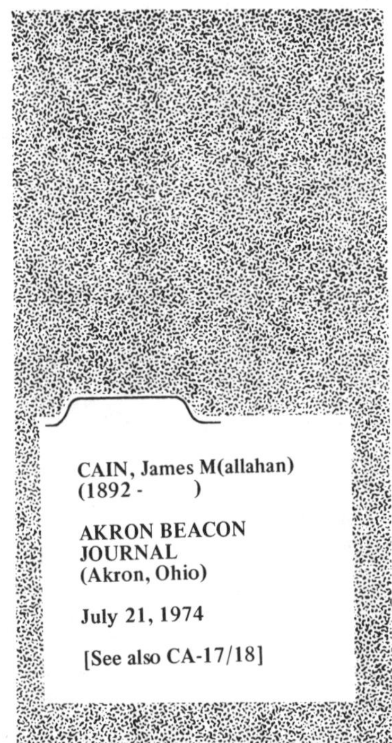
CAIN, James M(allahan)
(1892 -)

AKRON BEACON JOURNAL
(Akron, Ohio)

July 21, 1974

[See also CA-17/18]

Mencken, who later published Cain's first story ("The Baby in the Icebox") in the American Mercury.

CAIN WAS a late-starting novelist, already into his 40s when "The Postman Always Rings Twice" was issued in 1934, a sensation. Then came "Double Indemnity," "Serenade," "Mildred Pierce" and other works lesser known, but richer-textured, such as "Galatea" and "Mignon."

Mencken cited Cain as the founder of the "hard-boiled school" of American fiction that perhaps finds its best expression in the Raymond Chandler legacy.

Cain was more rough-and-tumble, his characters more pathetically low-life, or critically weak where Chandler's say, were strong.

For many years Cain was thought unfilmable because his stories and characters behaved beyond the limits of the movie production code. And the man wouldn't compromise.

IT WASN'T until 1944 that Billy Wilder broke through with a terrific film of "Double Indemnity." Ironically, Wilder's collaborator on the script was Raymond Chandler; while Cain, at the same time, was providing a screenplay for the Arabian hijinks of Maria Montez and Jon Hall.

Suddenly Cain was very filmable indeed, and very rich — which only increased his debt potential as he dispatched alimony to a succession of wives. Finally, "The Postman Always Rings Twice" was made in 1946 — a dozen years after its publication.

About half his life has been spent in Hollywood, but one senses he has little affection for the place, and perhaps it rankles him that his best known titles suggest movies rather than books.

Indeed, Cain is hardly read at all nowadays. Yet, consider what gets written today, and what gets read, and you see the hard-boiled school as a vital, ongoing experiment.

ON HIS own, he'd rather discuss what he's doing now. "The Cocktail Waitress," he said holds to his strong-woman theory. "Women run things in this world. And they rule the politics of this country, say by 99 pct."

But he's not oblivious to the Movement, and hints that women with ideals may be a new adornment to his octogenarian fiction.

He already seems vague about "Rainbow's End," which, you understand was written last year. How does it end? He's puzzled.

He finally remembers that in "Rainbow's End" he at least has deviated from the old Cain formula by allowing a "happy" ending. Or what sounds like one.

THE SEETHING sex is still there, but he's maybe old fashioned, even quaint, with the material. The hero, of course, is crazy for this girl. "Well, she teases him along, and I let him bathe her naked, yet he never gets her until the end of the book."

That's progress. In standard Cain, the fellow "gets his" for the climax and now he's getting hers.

What James M. Cain apparently would like to find at the rainbow's end is not a pot of gold, but a faithful broad. Write on, Big Jim.

Staunch champion for sexual civil rights

CALDERONE, Mary Steichen
(1904 -   )
LONG ISLAND PRESS
(Jamaica, N.Y.)
Apr. 28, 1974

In the years since 1964, Dr. Mary Calderone, director of the Sex Information and Education Council of the United States, has spearheaded a virtual revolution in liberalizing America's attitude toward sex education.

By PHYLLIS STEWART

Probably nobody in the world thinks about sex as much as Dr. Mary Steichen Calderone. Like a meteor, Mary Calderone suddenly rose from relative obscurity to become one of the most controversial figures on the American scene.

When the Quaker grandmother became director of the newly formed Sex Information and Education Council of the United States in May of 1964, she scarcely anticipated that within four years she would be accused of corrupting children and countenancing communism by the Rev. Billy James Hargis' right-wing Christian Crusade, the John Birch Society and their allies.

For Dr. Calderone and the other founders of SIECUS, their aim had been nothing more sinister than "to establish man's sexuality as a health entity."

According to their statement of purpose, this means: "to identify the special characteristics that distinguish (human sexuality) from, yet relate it to, human reproduction; to dignify it by openness of approach, study and scientific research designed to lead toward its understanding and its freedom from exploitation; to give leadership to professionals and to society, to the end that human beings may be aided toward responsible . . . assimilation of sex into their individual life patterns as a creative and re-creative force."

* * *

THIS HAS CONSISTED primarily of making available information to private individuals, professionals and the press through a newsletter and study guides on such subjects as premarital sex, masturbation, homosexuality and sexual moral values. SIECUS also provides speakers, organizes conferences and contributes to the sex education training of clergymen, doctors, psychiatrists and other counselors. And although the organization had not originally planned to become actively involved in school sex education, SIECUS was soon swept into it by a prodigious demand from school officials, who had no other place to turn for guidance.

An in the years since 1964, Dr. Calderone has spearheaded a virtual revolution in liberalizing America's attitudes toward sex education. In recognition of her achievements, she will be honored as "Woman of the Year" by the Hempstead Chamber of Commerce at a dinner-dance in Monti's Town & Country Restaurant on Wednesday.

"We have come very far and very fast during the past ten years," says the gray-haired woman whose straight-from-the-shoulder, no-nonsense answers to tough sex questions endear her particularly to youthful audiences.

"When we began, a scant 1 per cent of U.S. medical schools taught the subject of sex education; today 95 per cent teach it. This organization took sexuality out of the closet, out of the gutter, and placed it in the area of health where it properly belongs. It is now pretty well established that human sexuality is part of both physical and mental health. We are not beginning to move into the area of sexual civil rights.

"And with the old rules breaking down and temptations incessantly in front of our youth, I think it's essential that we give our young people sound grounding in sex.

(Continued from preceding page)

"BUT, TOO MANY people think that you complete sex education by teaching reproduction," she says thoughtfully. "Sex education has to be far more than that. Sex involves something you are, not just something you do. Children and adults must be taught to understand their sexuality so they can respect it, appreciate it, and use it properly at the right time in life.

"Our motive in sex education should not be just to prevent illegitimacy or venereal disease. It should also be the development of the personality of the individual, an integral part of which is sex."

At 69, Mary Calderone carries her height, 5'6", erectly and walks with vigor and bounce. Her conversation is punctuated with abundant physical animation, and her lovely blue eyes, deeply set in the dark shadows that characterize her face, sparkle with curiosity and candor.

Brusque, tough, she belies the extensive knowledge she has accumulated in a wide variety of areas by approaching questions with freshness and enthusiasm, leaving the distinct impression that during an interview she is rethinking opinions that she must have begun formulating in early adulthood. One can't help but appreciate her depth, spirit and open-mindedness.

In each year since the establishment of SIECUS, Dr. Calderone has traveled some 50,000 miles, often speaking several times a day to students, parents, teachers, physicians, pastor's and women's groups. The schedule could have tired a person half her age. And wherever she goes, she finds ignorance.

* * *

"YOU KNOW, THE MERE fact of being born with male or female sexual organs does not make you male or female," she says. "You must be programed. And you know, this is something very few people realize . . . that the child is psychologically oriented to heterosexuality or homosexuality by circumstances that apparently come together during the early years of life. Even though experts don't agree on what these circumstances are.

"Parents give a child his basic sex education through what they project as to their feelings about themselves, how they treat each other, how they treat the child. Parents first must accept their own sexuality, then they must accept a child's sexuality.

"So many people are marrying too young today. They are having children too young, before they have come to a full understanding of themselves. If a child comes before a couple has finished resolving their sexual identity, it will be as confused as they are.

"And the way parents treat a child in terms of its sexuality may result in homosexuality. Heterosexuality and homosexuality are opposite sides of the gamut. And it is important to realize that not all homosexuals are sick. There are ill homosexuals, just as there are ill heterosexuals: rapists, voyeurs etc. The problem is one of compulsive behavior.

"We have so many stereotypes in this society to overcome. People so refuse to learn the facts," she says angrily. "If people would lose their irrational fears, we would have a healthier race of people. Homosexuality is not a matter of looking different. Many of the most virile, masculine appearing men are homosexual, including a large percentage of professional athletes. The swishy stereotype is much in the minority.

* * *

"A POSITIVE FACTOR is that many young people are getting over these fears. We are in the middle of a sexual evolution, NOT a sexual revolution. The emergence of female sexuality is the major change, and people need to develop to their full potential as they are beginning to do now.

"I want to stress that young people are not promiscuous today. They're doing the same things today that we were doing 40 years ago, only it's more out in the open. Again people just don't want to hear the facts.

"Young people are beginning to realize that sex is more than something you do with someone in bed. Sex is not just for procreation; it is for mutual pleasure. Any close, intimate relationship . . . which doesn't necessarily have to include sex . . . takes time, it must be reciprocal, it must be fully trusting and the individuals concerned must delight in it. And if it is a sexual relationship, both parties must enjoy it."

Mary Calderone's qualities as physician, Quaker, grandmother of two and great-grandmother of one, make her a remarkable person. The daughter of world-famous photographer Edward Steichen (who created the celebrated "The Family of Man"), niece of the late poet Carl Sandburg, she has charismatic gifts of no small order and is a powerful and persuasive public speaker.

Born July 1, 1904 in Manhattan, she may have developed some of these traits through the pursuit of dramatics with Richard Boleslavsky and Maria Ouspenskaya. She studied dramatics for three years following her graduation from Vasser in 1925, where she majored in chemisty. Her career ambitions were temporarily abandoned in 1926, however, when she was married . . . a relationship that ended in divorce seven years later. Not long after, one of her two daughters died of pneumonia, plunging Dr. Calderone into an emotional crisis that was resolved with the help of psychoanalysis and the determination to pursue a career in medicine.

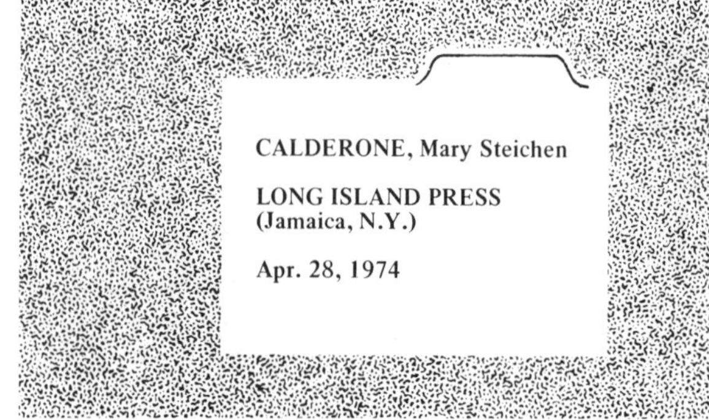
CALDERONE, Mary Steichen

LONG ISLAND PRESS
(Jamaica, N.Y.)

Apr. 28, 1974

SHE EARNED AN M.D. in 1939 from the University of Rochester Medical School and worked intermittently in the field of public health until she accepted the position of medical director of the Planned Parenthood Federation of America in 1953.

During her field work in public health, she met her present husband, Frank Calderone, also a physician, who at one time served as chief administrative officer of the World Health Organization and director of health services with the United Nations Secretariat. They have raised two children and make their home in Glen Head.

Although Dr. Calderone achieved wide recognition for her birth-control work with Planned Parenthood, she began to feel a deep sense of frustration with organizational policies that didn't allow her to develop programs of aid for people suffering from such sexual problems as impotence, frigidity and homosexuality. ("At least half of all married couples have some type of sexual problem.") This led her, with five fellow participants in a conference on family and religion, to form SIECUS, which operates out of a six-room office at 1855 Broadway in Manhattan.

A versatile writer, Dr. Calderone is the author of several books, a gourmet cook, an adept horticulturist and an accomplished sailor. She spends her vacations with her husband aboard a 60-foot schooner in the Caribbean and their home is a 175-year-old farmhouse on the North Shore.

With his wife Virginia, Caldwell looks ahead to more travel, more books, more observation of the human condition.

The Crack in Caldwell's Wall

By BETTY COOK Scene Staff Writer
Photograph by Richard Pruitt

There's this crack in the cowshed wall, see? And Tom, the spirit man, distiller of fine Georgia dew, likes to sit inside on a stool, looking out at the woods. "I come down here and sit and look," he says, "and I don't see nothing you can't see better from the outside, but that don't make a bit of difference . . . I don't know what it is, and it might not be nothing at all when you figure it out. But it's not the knowing about it anyway—it's just the sitting there and looking through it that sort of makes me feel like heaven can't be so doggone far away."

The wall Erskine Caldwell sits behind is invisible, but no less real than the one he built for Tom in 1935, in a book called "Journeyman." Now, from the closed, cool shelter of his mind, Caldwell looks out at you through hooded eyes set in a face clamped shut for privacy. He is not unkind. He is courteous, but the courtesy stretches thin across impatience if you block his view for long. At such times, if every word he speaks were a coin, you could starve to death waiting for enough to buy a sandwich.

You'd get little pity from Caldwell. He's seen hunger, tracked it through the woods of the world, watched it stalk and rule the carnival of losers who parade past the crack in his wall. He tells about them all, but not out loud. Words are too dear to waste on cheap conversation. He hoards them for the books that have made him one of the most-read, least-appreciated, money-makingest writers in the world.

For almost half a century Caldwell's works have been cursed, banned, deplored, denounced, exalted, vilified—and translated into 20 different languages. The play taken from his "Tobacco Road" set long-run records and is still being revived, most recently in Dallas' Theater Center. His notorious masterpiece, "God's Little Acre," is still legally banned in Boston. He has written 50 books in all, seen 60 million copies of them printed.

Here, now, briefly in Dallas for the "Tobacco Road" opening, he is waiting to get on with his fifty-first. But you are blocking his view. He endures your questions with grace, doling out syllables one at a time from some distance behind his wall.

Does he write his books from outlines?

"No."

When did he leave salaried work to strike out on his own as a writer?

"Don't know."

Where did he find the courage?

"Born that way."

"You are encountering Erskine," his slight, charming wife Virginia compassionately explains, "at a time when his mind is locked in a motel room with a typewriter."

They will spend the next six weeks, two months, however long they wish, moving from an arbitrarily selected point in Arkansas upward through the Midwest, traveling with three typewriters (once, when one broke down somewhere, they could not find a repairman; Virginia still pales at the thought) and many cartons of the fresh-ground peanut butter they eat on toast for breakfast. Clearly, he plans to write during the trip, but he will not admit it.

"We don't know what we're going to do," he says, jerking his head toward Virginia. "She's going to make illustrations."

"But she doesn't know what she's going to illustrate," Virginia shrugs. Perhaps to please her, per-

(Continued from preceding page)
haps to turn the talk from his book, he opens the wall a little.

"You're not permitted to stay too long in one place," he explains. "People get to know you too well. Lose too many friends that way." He almost smiles, but he is not really joking. The Caldwells have lived all over the country, never stopping over more than seven years in any single locale. Now, after almost that long in Dunedin, Fla., they are prospecting for a new site, a different region to settle in and study for a time. Out of some deep restlessness, Caldwell has been on the move for most of his life, tasting the life-styles of a dozen rough occupations. from professional football player to war correspondent. Wars have followed him. "We happened to be in Spain when the Civil War started," he says. "Then in China during the Japanese War, and in Russia when the German War broke out. Now that the wars are over, we go to Europe when we feel like it. Not just for pleasure—to work. Not hard work, nice work. Lecturing to university classes."

He has lectured to students on this continent too, from Puerto Rico to Alaska. What does he tell them? "I advise young writers to find a better profession than writing. Such as poultry raising—anything except trying to be a writer." Why? "Because it's heartbreaking to see students, hundreds of them, taking creative writing courses, intending to be a writer. I come along and tell them you can't make a living being a writer—forget it. Go be a poultry raiser." He nods with a gravity that may or may not be real. "I think I've helped a lot of people that way."

What about the people whose lives he has laid famously naked in his books—the water-blooded, string-fleshed country-poor whites and blacks he wrote about before exposing bigotry and numb misery became fashionable? Has anything helped them?

"Well, they've moved, you see, from the country to the city. That's what all the trouble is in ghetto life, now. It's different from the old days in the country, where people could get along a little bit—they could go out and cook milkweeds or something. In city streets you can't find any milkweeds to cook, or dandelions, or anything. So they depend on subsidy for a living, on welfare checks and charity. Whether that's an improvement or not, I don't know." He broods a moment, then goes on slowly, spending his costly words with care. "You see, as a society we're growing older, coming to different sociological levels, almost getting down to a peasantry. Some of the young people may be returning to it voluntarily, moving toward simplicity. But if we have a real hard depression, the people who live on credit will be bankrupt—that will be a different matter."

CALDWELL, Erskine

DALLAS NEWS
(Dallas, Tex.)

Sept. 15, 1974

And the moral climate that made his work the subject of sermons and court actions—has that changed too? He frowns.

"Morals are only customs, and customs never stay the same anyway, in any country. Take Turkey, for example. They grow poppies there for opium. We think that's bad—they don't. So that's all morals are, just the custom. The pendulum can swing around."

He believes communication has caused the pendulum to swing more rapidly. "We're losing our dialects," he observes, "because of the rapidity of communications. We're losing our southern accents, because everybody's trying to talk like Walter Cronkite. Walter is supposed to be the medium of America now, you know—who'll be next we don't know yet.

"All these changes, they're like the old domino theory. Once you break down a barrier, the next one's going down until you get to the last. Then you put up your dominoes again and start all over. The effect of the Supreme Court decisions on segregation, for example—there's no end to that 'til you get to the ultimate decision. Then we may turn around and go back again. Styles of thinking are like styles of clothing—they go from one extreme to another. But you see, civilization goes by eons, by centuries, not just by months or years. So it would take centuries to complete a cycle that will look very shortlived in retrospect. Of course, elements like wars can change the complexion overnight." He considers the prospect without joy. "When's the next war going to start? Nobody knows, but there will be another one, inevitably. There's always a war."

And does he have a place to go to wait out calamity? Caldwell shakes his head. "No. You need some land, and an uncle. An uncle can be about the best thing you have, I think, better than parents. Parents are subjective, an uncle is objective—he'll tell you the truth. I have no uncles left, so I don't know what I'd do."

He falls silent. The crack in his wall narrows again; he has spent too many words on you. Words are tools, planed boards and hard-driven nails to be structured into his carefully plain-styled prose. He needs them to describe what he discerns. By his own reckoning of time, Caldwell has been looking out at the woods, at the world, for mere moments. He's seen more than most people, but the scene keeps changing as he moves, the mystery is still there. And whatever passes for heaven still stands a far piece from his tight-focused range of vision. Still, it's like Tom said: "That's the Goddamnedest little slit in the whole world . . . I can't keep from looking to save my soul."

Neither can Erskine Caldwell.

(Also see preceding article)

Erskine Caldwell in Atlanta

Photograph by Floyd Jillson

By Phil Garner

THE furor in Georgia over his novels depicting life among poor whites in the South hardly touched Erskine Caldwell – not in 1938 when Atlanta censors attempted to suppress the stage version of "Tobacco Road," not in 1973 when he spent three days in Atlanta allowing himself to be used to promote the Alliance Theater production of the same play.

"Oh, Mr. Caldwell," cooed a patron of the theater at a reception, "how did you feel back then when you learned they'd tried to ban your play in Atlanta?"

"I didn't think much about it at all," said Caldwell. "I was too far removed from Georgia for it to matter."

And neither did Caldwell seem interested in attempts to compare the changed attitudes about his subject matter with the old attitudes.

He wrote about poor Southern whites, he said, because they interested him and he was a writer and writers should write about the things they know. He was once again in Atlanta, not to bask in a new atmosphere of enlightenment, but because the people of Georgia still interested him.

He was docilely punctual and kept all the appointments made for him. At the age of 70 he might have been expected to slow down, yet he continued meeting deadlines. He had written one book a year for many years and seemed nowhere near stopping. In January he had finished his latest novel, as yet untitled.

He and his wife, Virginia, were planning to drive to their home in Dunedin, Fla., a small town on the Gulf Coast north of Tampa. They were looking forward to the trip because both enjoyed seeing the countryside and the people.

Caldwell presented a dignified figure, tall and slender with a lined, long face that in some photographs resembled an older William Holden but in person seemed shorter and less firm. At the press reception, in a sea of raised eyebrows and bent elbows, he expertly hefted a bourbon on the rocks and drifted through the crowd, making easy small talk, Virginia on his arm. There were in the crowd a few old friends, but most of those who approached him with remembrances to share, he seemed not to remember.

One woman recalled as a little girl having known the author's father, a Presbyterian minister, when the family lived in Wrens, Ga., near Augusta, the locale of "Tobacco Road." But he did not remember her. Amid glass cases filled with African art objects and artifacts, the author confronted veiled segments of an obscured past and put himself on display.

LATER in the filled theater he was introduced from the audience. The performance of "Tobacco Road" which followed was well received, by the audience and later by Atlanta critics. The play, no doubt, was enhanced by the effect of the author's presence. The set sagged authentically upon the stage, each missing board in the house and well, the scattering of dried leaves on the porch roof, the shaky porch itself, the dusty red clay yard, (sneezers, beware, critic Howell Raines warned), all were immediately recognizable from real life. The actors projected convincingly.

Jeeter Lester and his family, all crazed by hunger and despair, stripped to the rawest instincts, careened toward the play's brutal end.

"We have our teen-aged son here to-

CALDWELL, Erskine

ATLANTA JOURNAL
& CONSTITUTION
(Atlanta, Ga.)

May 13, 1973

(Continued from preceding page)

night," a playgoer told a friend during intermission. "My wife and I were wondering if he could really understand the impact of the play, never knowing the times in which it was written."

Caldwell got to bed at 2 a.m., worrying about being on time for a breakfast appointment a few hours later. At 11:30 a.m. he still appeared a bit haggard and, although patient and polite, plainly restless. He had recently quit smoking, for one thing, and he hadn't been getting the sleep to which he was accustomed. Nonetheless he maintained his characteristic politeness with interviewers.

Yes, he agreed, Tobacco Road was history now and might well mean little to a youngster who had not been there.

"I didn't think of my characters as being bizarre," Caldwell said. "That was the era of the Great Depression, the early 1930s. It was ordinary life. It was natural and normal. Right now it would be unnatural and abnormal. A family like that, I doubt if any of them could read or write. If they could it would be unusual in that state of life."

CALDWELL had seen many productions of "Tobacco Road."

"Each performance is different," he said. "A lot of actors like to play the lead, Jeeter Lester. Some overplay it, either for the comic side of it or the tragic side of it. But this was more of a unit production and it was close to the feeling of the novel."

How, Caldwell was asked, does it feel to watch other people's interpretations of his characters?

"Sometimes they're a little bit different than your concept would be," he said. "Jeeter might not look like the Jeeter I had in mind. But they have to fit in with the original idea so that after a while you get used to it and accept it when you hear your own words coming out of their mouths."

Caldwell has not written of the poverty of the current decade.

"The landscape and the architecture are different," he said. "It would have to be a completely different story. There are pockets of poverty everywhere all through the South, especially in Appalachia – Tennessee, Kentucky, West Virginia. That kind of life always manages to get pushed into the background. But Tobacco Road was paved over 30 years ago. Things change."

Caldwell completed a new novel in January. The work is so fresh it has no title yet. He hesitantly talked about it.

"It concerns one person," he said, " a girl who grows up in a small town in the South. She has the usual problems with her parents, rebelling against them, running away, getting married, dropping out of college. She has emotional difficulty when she can't adjust to real life. She is a little girl who can't become a woman emotionally. She can't cope with it and she has to find a way to get killed. Finally, she does find a way."

Those annual novels are the result of ingrained work habits.

"I work from nine 'til five," Caldwell said. "Five days a week. Then as things go along, it stretches to six days, then seven days, even eight days a week. Usually I have to make myself stop."

His characters are composites, he said.

CALDWELL, Erskine

ATLANTA JOURNAL
& CONSTITUTION
(Atlanta, Ga.)

May 13, 1973

"It wouldn't interest me to write about real people. You must make people, build them, create them, in order to make fiction. A real person would turn out to be too thin. You'd soon run out of anything interesting. I have met a lot of people similar to my characters, however. I saw a lot of people similar to Jeeter Lester."

AS a boy, Caldwell had accompanied his minister father on visits to homes in the country. He also drove a country doctor on his rounds.

"I like Georgia life," said Caldwell. "I was born and lived with it. I like the atmosphere, the people and the scenery, the mountains, the red land, the pine woods. Albany (he pronounced it Albinny) is one of my favorite places."

Caldwell usually writes in motel rooms, frequently in one south Georgia town or another, without making his presence known to the townsfolk. Most recently he and Virginia holed up in a motel in Americus, where he relaxed between work sessions by strolling unrecognized through the city streets.

"My father very frequently would visit people much like the Jeeter Lester family," said Caldwell. "He would have visited Jeeter if he had really existed."

In the novel, Jeeter's daughter Ellie May, of marriageable age and disposition, lives at home, her beauty marred by a harelip. Jeeter frequently promises to take her to a doctor who can sew it up.

"I was with my father one time when he found one girl with a harelip," said Caldwell. "And he found a doctor who would operate on it."

His driving for the country doctor also yielded many other models.

"Sometimes we'd drive all day," said Caldwell, "visiting white and black families. They were always in financial or physical trouble. You learned a lot living in small towns those days before they became smaller versions of the big towns."

Caldwell never knows, when he begins a novel, how it will end.

"If I knew what the story was going to be," he said, "I'd be too bored to finish it."

The process of creation, as he describes it, begins almost as a daydream.

"Your mind begins to wander," he said. "One thing leads to another and it comes naturally."

BUT it didn't come so naturally for several years after the young man left his newspaper reporter's job in Atlanta and went to Maine to write fiction.

He spent five years writing short stories before the first one was published. He planted potatoes in the yard of his rented house and sold off the review copies of books sent him by a newspaper in Charlotte, N. C., for which he reviewed books at no fee.

The acceptance of that first short story opened doors and in 1933, his first novel, "Tobacco Road," was published.

In 1938 the Atlanta Board of Review tried to suppress the performance in Atlanta of "Tobacco Road," but a court injunction prevented the board's interference.

But efforts to censor Caldwell's works were not confined to his native South. In 1948 a similar court order was required to keep a New York censor's hands off his novel, "God's Little Acre." By then, Caldwell was established as the South's literary bad boy, the preacher's son who wrote of the seamy side of life. He was working on his next novel, "This Very Earth," still dealing with poor whites of the rural South. He had not, in 1948 been back to Georgia – except to pass through – in 10 years.

IN 1957 the Georgia Literature Commission banned "God's Little Acre," but lacked the powers to enforce the ban. In the same year, plans to make a film of the book on location in Augusta were scrapped when textile mill operators refused to allow the filming of the interiors of their mills. The film was made elsewhere.

By 1965, Caldwell was being invited to lecture at Georgia campuses and in 1969 he was honored by the Georgia Writers' Association for "four decades as Georgia's most productive and creative writer."

His most recent lectures in Georgia were given at Valdosta State College.

Caldwell's appearance at a luncheon meeting of the Atlanta Press Club, shortly before he was to return to Florida, drew a large turnout. Like most persons who communicate in print, he was ill at ease in the role of speaker. He related a few humorous incidents from his recent travels to Eastern Europe and retreated into the more comfortable format of answering questions from the audience. He lingered for a few moments afterward, autographing paperback copies of "Tobacco Road," which had been given out by his publisher.

Ahead lay a helicopter ride to a radio station, his last commitment in Atlanta before returning to Florida. He said he was looking forward to the long drive.

His traditional three-month vacation between books was almost over.

"I never have trouble getting an idea," he had said earlier. "The trouble lies in deciding which idea to pursue."

Creator of Heros

By **LINDA VIVIAN**

From the outside, the building is just another house on the quiet residential street. There is nothing unusual about it. Who would suspect that it is the home of dashingly-handsome pilots, wickedly-beautiful Oriental ladies, shifty-eyed thugs and assorted unsavory characters? They think nothing of waging wars, stealing, fighting and even murdering. On any given day this conglomeration of humanity flits from country to country wreaking havoc.

The neighbors are aware of the dastardly deeds that transpire in that house every day. So are 40 million other people.

The house is the studio of Milton Caniff, creator of the comic strips **Terry and the Pirates** and **Steve Canyon.**

Caniff is an amiable, modest man who has remained untouched by the fame of his characters. The many hours at his drawing board are spent with this credo in mind: "Draw for the guy who buys the paper."

He first began his career when he was in kindergarten. At least, he says that is when he became aware of what he was doing. "Nobody but my mother could have told me they were cartoons," he adds.

The son of a printer, Caniff whiffed that ink at an early age. By the time he was 13 he was working as an artist's apprentice on the Dayton *Journal-Herald* and his first cartoon, a panel, had been published in that newspaper.

During his high school years, Caniff continued his artistic pursuit by working on the school paper. He received a bachelor of arts degree in fine arts from Ohio State University in 1930. His college years sparked interest in yet another career — acting. A member of the University Players, Caniff had played the lead in its biggest production "Beau Kay."

His cartoonist-actor dilemma was quickly settled by veteran cartoonist Billy Ireland. "Stick to your inkpots, kid. Actors don't eat regularly," was his advice. Caniff has never forgotten.

Following his college graduation, Caniff obtained a position with the Columbus *Dispatch* and married his childhood sweetheart, Esther Parsons. Secure with a college degree and a job, he thought nothing could go wrong.

Nothing except the Depression. His security ended. But recalling Ireland's advice, he stuck to his drawings. For a while he did some free lance work. Then, toward the end of 1931, the Associated Press in New York offered him a job. He arrived in New York in the spring of 1932 and was given the assignment of drawing pen portraits of the thirty-some potential nominees for the 1932 presidential election. Soon there was an opening for an adventure strip — the beginning of the original **Dickie Dare**, which appeared for about 18 months.

"He was an adventurous young man and the prototype for Terry," Caniff recalls.

During this era the exotic adventure strips came into their own. Such features as Tarzan, Flash Gordon and Captain Easy transported the readers from their breakfast nooks to far-away places.

One large daily, the New York *Daily News,* did not have an adventure hero. Captain Joseph Patterson, the publisher, knew of only one man who could provide his paper with that magic draw. He hired Caniff in 1934 to create such a hero for him. Patterson not only wanted a handsome hero who rescued damsels in distress but also wanted the setting to be the farthest outpost of adventure — the Orient. Not much was known about China or Japan at that time, but that did not halt Caniff and his adventure-seeking publisher.

"I must have read every available word on the Orient," Caniff said.

Terry and the Pirates first appeared on October 19, 1934. The initial plot was not the epitome of originality — a trip upriver in search of an inherited gold mine. But the women were beautiful, the heroes fearless and the villains evil. Captain Patterson had his adventure.

Terry grew up in the strip. The forthcoming world problems were alluded to but never were actually defined. The basis of the strip was always adventure. Caniff drew Terry for some 12 years. He never owned the copyright on the strip or on any of the characters. He was, after all, just a hired hand.

CANIFF, Milton Arthur (1907-) PALM SPRINGS LIFE (Palm Springs, Calif.) Summer, 1972

With his contract at the *News* up for renewal in 1945, Caniff switched to Field Enterprises, publishers of the Chicago *Sun-Times,* to create a new strip. At Field he would have complete editorial control.

Steve Canyon, who was to become the most popular Air Force colonel, appeared on January 13, 1947.

This time Caniff obtained the copyright on his characters and the strip. Canyon is published in some 650 newspapers, translated into eight languages and available in 14 countries.

The strip is written and drawn in Palm Springs, sent to his assistant in Tucson, then to the background man in New York ("It's extremely important to have the background exact. A reader may *know* what the Rome airport looks like and we'd better know too.") and back to Caniff who mails it to Field Enterprises. A photostat is kept for his records.

Three days are required to do six complete daily strips and two days for a Sunday sequence.

"We work nine weeks ahead on Sunday and four weeks ahead on a daily," he revealed.

Caniff says he gets a lot of ideas from newspaper headlines. His readers also offer plot suggestions, "but I always politely refuse them. I have to carefully avoid using them even though they may be cute ideas; couldn't afford to accept their help because there is always danger of a lawsuit later on."

Steve Canyon is not entirely fantasy. His creator maintains vast research files. Books, models of airplanes, old mail-order catalogs and military hats from World War I to the astronauts' helmets — these are the basis of Caniff's research.

"I keep only photograph files and not artist's drawings. Their interpretation of a car, plane or clothing style is only that — an interpretation."

Cartoonist Caniff offers this advice to aspiring artists: "It's a tough business, there are fewer outlets today than when I started. If one is really determined, he should get a job as an assistant to someone and go from there. Cartooning is a big gamble, but it's worth it if you win. You can learn from everyone. At first I copied everybody I could until I developed this conglomeration of style into my own.

"In doing the story, try to have an ending in mind that you can lead up to through various paths. This is, of course, most important. It's very easy to end up in a pit. One sequence must end effectively so that you can lead easily into the next."

For Milton Caniff, Steve Canyon is a "good thing." He says he has no plans for retirement; that he will continue to do the strip as long as he is physically able.

"Why rock the boat by retiring and turning it (the strip) over to someone else? It's sabatoge to ruin a good thing," he said.

Caniff's day at the drawing board begins around 8:30 in the morning and lasts until 6 in the evening. He says he works at a steady "pitch, not a fevered pitch."

He is, without a doubt, the most honored cartoonist in the business. Awards include the Billy DeBeck Memorial Award of the National Cartoonists Society, which he received in 1947; the Air Force's Exceptional Service Award, their highest civilian award, presented in 1957; the first SEGAR (Popeye) award in 1971, and the highest honor ever bestowed by the National Cartoonists Society, the Reuben Award of 1971, saluting Caniff as the Outstanding Cartoonist of the Year. The list goes on and on.

"Heroes," it is said, "are created by popular demand." Milton Caniff, who once thought he wanted to be an actor, has stuck to his inkpots and filled that demand.

Cartoon Creator Stuck To Inkpots

CANIFF, Milton Arthur
THE STATE (Columbia, S.C.) Jan. 12, 1975

(Also see preceding article)

By JAKE PENLAND
Tempo Staff Report

Milton Caniff, whose adventure comic strip, Steve Canyon, is read regularly by an estimated 30 million persons, got some good advice during the depression year, 1932.

"Stick to your inkpots, kid," suggested Billy Ireland, staff artist of the Columbus (Ohio) Dispatch. "Actors don't eat regularly."

As a kid, Caniff was interested in both art and acting. As a Boy Scout he enlivened the summer camp daily newspaper with illustrations, a daily comic strip and other drawings. But also, at the age of nine, when his family was wintering in California, he did some acting in several two-reel movies and developed a taste for theatricals that never quite left him.

Caniff, born in 1907 in Hillsboro, Ohio, became interested in drawing because his father provided him with the materials. The father was a printer for a small weekly newspaper and often brought home paper trimmings from books and other printing jobs.

Young Milton also had a friend whose father, a paper hanger, gave the two his wallpaper samples. The boys covered the back of the samples with their drawings.

In the sixth grade Milton had a job delivering copies of two popular magazines, Life and Judge, both of which ran many cartoons. Milton read every copy before delivering it and began to experiment with drawings he hoped would some day sell.

The family moved to Dayton while Milton was still in elementary school. While in the eighth grade he took a correspondence course in cartooning and made volunteer drawings for the Boy Scout page of the Dayton Journal. That led to a job as office boy in the newspaper's art department.

While in high scool he drew a strip for the school newspaper, and continued his job with the Journal. By then it appeared that he was headed for a career as an artist.

His high school art teacher advised him to go to college rather than art school and "Soak up as much general education as you can." He enrolled at Ohio State and majored in fine arts. He also worked in the art department of the Columbus Dispatch.

Caniff was graduated from Ohio State in 1930, and he married his high school sweetheart. The depression caused him to lose his job with the Columbus Dispatch in 1932.

He submitted cartoon after cartoon to syndicates, they were all rejected, and he thought seriously of giving up drawing and trying his fortune at acting. It was then that Billy Ireland advised him to "stick to your inkpots, kid. Actors don't eat regularly."

Caniff headed for New York City with his wife, and he got a job at $60 a week with Associated Press. He drew mostly political cartoons and fashion sketches.

Al Capp worked in the same office and drew a strip called Mr. Gilfeather. Capp quit his job and young Caniff was invited to take over Mr. Gilfeather.

Caniff later started a new strip, Dickie Dare, about a boy who joined Robin Hood's band. The adventure strip came to the attention of Col. Joseph M. Patterson, publisher of the New York Daily News and head of the Chicago Tribune-New York Daily News Syndicate.

Patterson suggested that Caniff think up an adventure strip "So powerful that nobody could eat his breakfast without reading it."

The result was Terry and the Pirates, which made its debut on October 19, 1934. This one had every thing — handsome hero, gorgeous girls, bright dialogue and an absorbing continuity.

The Orient was chosen as locale for "Terry" and the cast of characters included sinister orientals and the Dragon Lady. Caniff found himself engaged in extensive research and he became unusually well-informed on that part of the world. The strip was a hit.

When World War II ended, Milton Caniff finally achieved his burning ambition — to own his own strip. He had created "Terry," but it belonged to the syndicate.

In 1947 Steve Canyon came into being, and Caniff owned it. The new strip was contracted for at the start by 125 newspapers, which is unusual. Today it appears in 650 papers and has an audience of 30 million.

Through the years Caniff has become probably the most honored cartoonist in the country. These honors include two honorary doctorates, several citations from the United States Air Force including its highest civilian honor, and awards from cartoonist organizations.

The success of Steve Canyon has brought him a handsome income and the personal satisfaction of knowing that his strip contributes to the morale of America's men in uniform.

In reflecting on his career, Caniff says he has "always admonished myself to write for the man in the bathroom, or the woman who is having her second cup of coffee after her husband and children have been sent off for the day.

"At these moments we are alone together and I bring to them an uninterrupted display of my wares. I am happy to have my reader alone for the few minutes each day during which we rendezvous."

In 1975, Milton Caniff is grateful for the advice he received way back there in the early part of the great depression of the 1930s:

"Stick to your inkpots, kid. Actors don't eat regularly."

Ex-Tulsan Mrs. Carnegie returns for visit

Dorothy (Mrs. Dale) Carnegie and H. Everett Pope (Tribune photo by Curtis Winchester)

By JACQUELYN BOUCHER
Of The Tribune Women's Staff

IN 1943 A YOUNG TULSA woman left her hometown to "broaden her scope" and make her mark on the hectic world of New York business. Her ambitions were realized beyond her wildest dreams and today she was back in Tulsa to tell about it.

Mrs. Dorothy Vanderpool Carnegie, wife of the late author Dale Carnegie, whose book "How to Win Friends and Influence People" has been inspiring people the world over, stopped briefly at the Oklahoma School of Business, Accountancy, Law & Finance to meet and chat with students.

In an interview with the Tribune before her appearance, Mrs. Carnegie, dressed in a gray wool pantsuit with fox collar, reminisced about her past life with her famous husband and spoke about several of her own current personal views.

A well-known writer in her own right, Mrs. Carnegie has authored two books, "How to Help Your Husband" and "Don't Grow Old, Grow Up," and she has carried on the operations of her husband's world-wide corporation since his death in 1955.

CARNEGIE,
Dorothy Vanderpool
(Mrs. Dale Carnegie)

TULSA TRIBUNE
(Tulsa, Okla.)

Oct. 8, 1974

AN EARLY advocate of working wives, Mrs. Carnegie said she does not consider herself a feminist in the traditional sense of the word.

"Anyone with a grain of sense knows that people of different sexes doing the same work should not be discriminated against because of their sex," she said.

"I am not in sympathy with the so-called feminist movement because I feel it is unfair to the majority of women who find it fulfilling and creative to be a housewife. I'm one of those people myself and I resent those who consider homemaking degrading or menial. No work is — as long as it's honest."

"It takes versatility and ability to perform as a wife and mother," she continued. "I'm an executive and run a large business and I love it — but I still love my family and my home. I thoroughly enjoyed raising my children (she has two) myself and I never would have dreamed of turning them over to a day care center, if they had existed at that time."

Mrs. Carnegie said she first enroled in a Dale Carnegie course at a local YMCA and later parlayed the Carnegie business skills she learned into a secretarial spot in the Gulf Oil Corporation's executive suite. She also used her newly-found knowledge to aid her in delivery of humorous talks at local men's civic club luncheons.

Apparently her ability impressed the Carnegie people because they offered her a promotional job in their New York office. There she met her famous husband, then 57 years of age.

"The course helped me the most in gaining confidence in myself and speaking before a group," she said. "It also humbled me, which I needed. I had been somewhat egocentric and the course inspired me to reevaluate myself.

What led her to New York 31 years ago?

"I was graduated from Tulsa Central High School and in those days my friends and I were very ambitious. We decided New York was the ideal place to work and would give us enough scope for our talents — or at least the talents we thought we had.

"Travel was more difficult then and I had hardly even been out of Oklahoma. But I had a good job offer from Dale Carnegie Institute and decided to take it."

ASKED ABOUT her fondest remembrances of her late husband, Mrs. Carnegie beamed.

"He was such a fun person to live with," she said. "He always was excited about life — a very happy and fulfilled person. He loved his family and enjoyed every second he spent with us.

"Even if you were a sourpuss, you couldn't help responding to Dale's enthusiasm.

"Just seeing him at breakfast was marvelous," she continued. "He always was bubbling over about something — especially his hobbies. He loved gardening and today I'm an avid gardener myself.

"All my memories are happy," said Mrs. Carnegie. "I love thinking about him."

After her visit at the local school, Mrs. Carnegie continued to Oklahoma City to speak at the Oklahoma Hospital Association annual meeting.

David Stansbury photo

Man of New York, Neshoba... and New Orleans

by Merikaye Presley

AS one might expect, Turner Catledge subscribes to The New York Times. He also takes the Neshoba Democrat.

The prestigious New York daily and the county weekly of Philadelphia, Miss., arrive regularly at his Garden District home, both carrying news of places he has lived, people he has known and events he has experienced.

Retired newsman Catledge, who at the zenith of his career directed the news content of the influential and powerful Times, first became enamored with the newspaper business in 1921 while working as "all-around man" for the Neshoba Democrat—setting type, soliciting subscriptions, selling ads and writing a variety of stories.

In the years between writing birth and wedding notices for the Democrat and becoming a Times editor, there were stints on other papers in Tunica and Tupelo, Miss.; Memphis; Baltimore; and Chicago.

In 1929, when Catledge was 28, The Times hired him on the personal recommendation of President Herbert Hoover.

Four decades later, he retired to New Orleans, the city which he says had fascinated him since childhood and which he now calls his hometown. Catledge jokes that he had five good reasons for settling here, then explains that all five were Mrs. Catledge, the former Abby Ray who is a native of New Orleans.

CATLEDGE'S Times career saw him advance from city reporter to Washington bureau member to chief news correspondent. Then he took a 19-month "sabbatical" to serve as chief correspondent and editor-in-chief of the Chicago Sun, returning to The Times to become national correspondent, assistant managing editor, managing editor, the paper's first executive editor and finally vice-president and a member of the board, on which he still serves.

Now more than two years removed from the day-to-day newspaper business, Catledge is a man satisfied with his life—present and past. Reflecting upon his newspaper career recently, he said, "I had a very good time. It was a very exciting, very interesting profession which I found very much to my liking. Life has been very good to me; my experiences have added up to a very fine total experience."

CATLEDGE, Turner
(1901 -)
TIMES–PICAYUNE
(New Orleans, La.)
Feb. 18, 1973

Catledge, smiling, said he personally found the newspaper business to be "tailor-made for an extrovert, a blabbermouth, a person who loves to pry into other people's business and tell about it" —characteristics he admits are his.

Later, not wishing to sound too flippant about the profession he firmly believes is a "noble calling," Catledge added that "a person who has a love for people, a knack for getting along with people, and an interest in what they are doing, starts out with something very valuable in the newspaper business."

Catledge's own exceptional ability to get along with all types of people, a trait acquired early in life, was undoubtedly a major factor in his success as a reporter and editor.

HIS friend and former colleague, Clifton Daniel, now associate editor of The Times, once wrote, "Mr. C. specializes in people. He is undoubtedly the most friendly, gregarious, convivial and popular editor of his generation in America . . . he is besought from coast to coast as a toastmaster, raconteur, commencement speaker, song leader and drinking companion."

Expressing another view, former Times reporter Gay Talese, in his book, "The Kingdom and the Power," wrote, "Catledge was probably the shrewdest managing editor of them all. While lacking (Carr) Van Anda's brilliance or the busy-beaver quality of (Frederick T.) Birchall, Catledge was their master when it came to handling men."

As a youngster growing up in Mississippi, Catledge set his sights on becoming a lawyer, greatly admiring attorneys' oratory in court and believing their sole function was to "rant before a jury." Conceding that he was something of a "showoff before people," Catledge recalled, "There were two types of people in Philadelphia who attracted my attention—preachers and lawyers. I found out very early that I was not cut out to be a preacher . . . although I'm sure that's what my mother wanted me to become."

After he was graduated with honors from Mississippi A&M (now Mississippi State University) in 1922, Catledge, who had worked summers for the Neshoba Democrat, was offered a full-time job running another newspaper owned by the same publisher, Clayton Rand. Lack of finances prevented any serious consideration of law school, and Catledge was obliged to become gainfully employed.

Many businesses in Philadelphia were owned and operated by his mother's family, the large Turner clan, and Catledge could have worked for any of them. But Catledge had a desire to succeed on his own and became the first member of the family to work on a newspaper, starting at a salary of $12.50 a week.

When that paper's crusading against the Ku Klux Klan eventually forced Rand to sell the paper, Catledge briefly worked for a bi-weekly in Tupelo before moving to Memphis "to try the big leagues of Southern journalism."

There Catledge had his first taste of big city reporting and decided that he wanted to make journalism a career.

THE transition from working on country papers as a jack-of-all-trades to reporting for a metropolitan daily was not entirely smooth. "I had some sinking spells at first," Catledge acknowledged.

"For one thing, I didn't realize how compartmentalized the news business was," he said. Catledge, used to doing everything on the Mississippi papers, simply asked for "a job" on the Memphis Press and was hired as a reporter. Had he been offered a choice, he says, he probably would have chosen to work in the print shop, where he felt at home among the type and presses.

On his first day, the city editor asked him to get an "add" on a story about a blizzard. In newspaper jargon, an "add" is an addition, or another page with more information, but Catledge had never heard the term. He only knew of one kind of newspaper "ad," and in his eagerness to please, he sold $130 worth of advertisements over the telephone before his editor realized what the zealous new reporter was doing.

(Continued from preceding page)

After five weeks on the Press, Catledge was abruptly fired with the suggestion that he would probably do better on the Memphis Commercial Appeal. Smarting with anger, Catledge marched over to the Commercial Appeal and into Editor C. P. J. Mooney's office and asked for a job.

Mooney, who soon became Catledge's hero, was impressed with the young Mississippian and offered him a job, but again it was touch and go before he was firmly established.

Once he filled in for an ailing society editor and pryed open her desk to look for news. He found a picture and information about a golden wedding anniversary party which a beautiful woman had hosted for her parents. He played the picture and story prominently in the Sunday society section, only to learn on Monday morning that the glamorous hostess was notorious in Memphis for another kind of entertaining.

DESPITE such blunders, Catledge had some lucky breaks, such as the time the Commercial Appeal's switchboard operator was sick and the paper was cut off from telephone communication because no one knew how to operate the switchboard—no one, that is, except the new reporter from Mississippi.

Back in Philadelphia, while just a youngster, Catledge had spent many nights manning the town's small switchboard, sleeping on a cot, waking to put through an occasional call or two. So in Memphis, Catledge stepped into the lurch, and a major crisis was averted. "Everybody was amazed," he remembers. "When the city editor walked in, my God, I was the man of the hour. Things like that happened to me all through my career."

Catledge's ability to touch-type, a novelty in those days, also stood him in good stead, as it did throughout his career. His ability to type rapidly without looking at the keyboard drew wondering stares from fellow reporters and attracted the attention of his editors. Even when he was on The Times, he was often called upon to type something quickly under deadline pressure, as it was (and still is) common for reporters to use the two-finger, hunt-and-peck method of typing.

Reporting was a tough, aggressive business in Memphis in the '20s. "No news source ever said 'no' to anyone from the Commercial Appeal," Catledge said. "If there was a closed door, we kicked it down, literally. That initial requirement for aggressiveness became a great asset for me later on."

Catledge admits that the tactics he used in Memphis would now be regarded as unscrupulous, indeed would not have been condoned in other cities at the time. One of Catledge's special talents was picture snatching. When there was a sensational murder, it was important to obtain pictures of the victim, family and accused, and Catledge would merely help himself to pictures he found on the walls or in drawers at the victim's home. And to insure that the competition did not obtain photographs by the same method, he made sure he left none behind. This questionable method of news gathering resulted in some near-libelous cases of mistaken identity.

LATER, when Catledge joined the Baltimore Sun, he introduced his picture-snatching technique there, but immediately gave it up after the Sun published a photo he obtained of a "dead" man which turned out to be the man's very alive brother. Reporting in Baltimore contrasted sharply with Catledge's experiences in Memphis, and he remembers his surprise at finding how "genteel" the Eastern press was.

One of the most significant stories Catledge covered in his career, not only in terms of magnitude then, but in benefits later reaped, was the Mississippi River flood of 1927. He covered the flood from Cairo, Ill., to the Mississippi Delta country, and when then-Secretary of Commerce Herbert Hoover came down from Washington to make a personal inspection of the disaster area, he needed someone knowledgeable about the disaster to serve as a guide.

CATLEDGE, Turner

TIMES–PICAYUNE
(New Orleans, La.)

Feb. 18, 1973

The Memphis mayor mentioned Catledge, and Hoover asked the young reporter to accompany him throughout the flood area. During those weeks, Catledge made a lasting impression on Hoover, so much so that Hoover wrote to the publisher of The New York Times suggesting that he hire the Memphis newsman.

Mentioning the incident in his book, author Talese made the following observation which Catledge later said was perceptive:

"Catledge had a wonderful way with men. Particularly older men. Particularly older men with power. This is a quality that perhaps cannot be learned but is inherent in certain rare young men who, partly because they are very bright and do not flaunt it, and partly because they are respectful and not privileged, confident but not too confident, attract the attention of older men, self-made men, and receive from these men much advice and help. The older men probably see something of themselves in these bright young men, something of what they were, or think they were, at a similar age. And so they help the younger men up the ladder, feeling no threat because these younger men are also endowed with a fine sense of timing."

FOR some reason, Times publisher Adolph Ochs did not act on Hoover's letter, and Catledge went to work for the Baltimore Sun. But in 1929, after Hoover became President, he had a meeting with Ochs and asked him why he had ignored his recommendation. This time, Ochs saw to it that Catledge was promptly offered a job.

It wasn't until years later that Catledge learned of his singular distinction of being recommended for his job by the President of the United States. Had he known at the time, he says he certainly would have held out for more than the $80 a week starting salary he received.

Although The Times had an impeccable reputation in 1929, Catledge remembers viewing it as "dull, stuffy, too gentlemanly." A standard joke among him and his fellow reporters was that a news event was covered by "10 reporters and one gentleman from The New York Times."

"The Times had a tremendous reputation," he said, "but it was not one to inspire an up-and-coming, Hell-bent-for-leather newspaper reporter." Nevertheless, heeding the advice of the Sun's managing editor and believing it to be a logical progression in his career, Catledge accepted the job.

He spent his last weeks at the Sun reading The Times, "trying to fall in love with it" and practicing the long, cumbersome sentences for which the paper was noted.

Later, as managing editor of The Times, Catledge was instrumental in changing the burdensome, wordy prose traditionally turned out by Times reporters. He urged shorter sentences, a more readable style and the translating of events into terms which related to the individual reader.

As a new Timesman, Catledge was aggressive, industrious and determined. Those traits did not go unnoticed by his editors, and within a few months, he was transferred to the Washington bureau.

Catledge, who had been interested in politics since he had hung around the county courthouse in Philadelphia as a youngster, found Washington exciting and became an excellent political reporter. He worked his way up to second man in the bureau, with the title of chief ➡

(Continued from preceding page)

news correspondent, and was in line to succeed Bureau Chief Arthur Krock, but Krock never realized his ambition to leave the Washington bureau and return to New York.

IT was Catledge who went to New York instead, after returning to The Times from the Chicago Sun. He was named assistant managing editor in 1945 and was groomed to assume the role of managing editor. "For the first seven years I was in New York, I yearned for Washington," Catledge recalled, "but when I went back to visit, I found that Washington had changed and my contacts were gone. It frightened me." After Catledge became managing editor at the end of 1951, he never looked back to Washington with any personal longing.

As managing editor, Catledge was credited with revitalizing The Times, with making it more readable, more interesting and a paper which people not only felt obligated to read, but one which they wanted to read.

"I don't deny any of it," Catledge, eyes twinkling, says today. "I wanted The Times to be absolutely necessary for anyone who wanted to be informed. When I came, The Times had already accomplished that goal. Then I wanted it to be wanted."

Under his editorship, the paper's advertising agency adopted the slogan: "The New York Times is much more interesting and you will be too."

"What I had to contend with was success," Catledge explained. "The Times was already successful without any effort to be interesting."

To accomplish his goal, Catledge confided in his reporters, told them where he was headed with the paper, what he hoped to accomplish. Writing styles became snappier, simpler. In a 1953 memo, Catledge said, "Brevity, simplicity and clarity are basically what we are striving for. We feel that the main news point of any story can be told in simple, short statements."

He warned his writers to guard against the "minutia" of reporting, the political infighting and procedural matters which rarely appealed to the average reader. "It was necessary to keep a reporter glued to the idea that he's telling what he knows to the reader in understandable terms," he said.

WHEN openings occurred on The Times, Catledge filled the slots with the brightest, most talented reporters he could find. He believes one of his greatest contributions was in advancing capable reporters to editor rank. Previously, most editors had moved up from the copy desks and had little or no reporting experience.

Catledge made other changes. He added to and expanded bureaus, introduced news analysis stories to the paper and broadened and enlivened society and cultural coverage. Lively, provocative feature stories were written.

A highlight of Catledge's career was a 1957 visit to Russia and a two-hour interview with Nikita Khrushchev, the first formal interview the Soviet leader had ever granted and a spectacular exclusive for The Times. The interview was reprinted in the Communist Party newspaper Pravda, and later was included in Khrushchev's book, "Khrushchev Speaks," a copy of which mysteriously appeared on Catledge's desk some years later. "Someone from the U.N. probably bootlegged it in," he said.

One of the most controversial stories printed in The Times during Catledge's tenure was the one in April, 1961, foretelling the Bay of Pigs invasion. Kennedy administration officials complained that publication endangered the national security, but Catledge said if he had it to do over again, he would have printed an even more detailed account and would have given it greater play. After that, his motto became: "When in doubt, print it."

CATLEDGE, Turner

TIMES–PICAYUNE
(New Orleans, La.)

Feb. 18, 1973

The New York Times was and is a powerful and influential news journal. "There's no question that it is the greatest paper in the English language—in any language," Catledge said. "It got that way as a purveyor of information, with goals of accurate information and fair presentation."

While the influence of a newspaper is hard to measure, Catledge believes government officials who read The Times are better informed and better equipped to make their decisions because they read The Times and are influenced by the news found on its pages. As far as editorial page influence is concerned, Catledge suspects that it may only influence those "who are already converted," those who already agree with The Times point of view.

As top news editor of what he says is the greatest newspaper in the world, Catledge said he didn't feel that he wielded any great power. "I never felt it emotionally," he said. "If I had been plucked up from Philadelphia, Miss., and placed in the executive editor's seat at The New York Times, it might have been different, but you come to these things gradually, day by day. Sometimes I could convince myself for a fleeting moment that my position was advantageous or powerful, but it never stayed."

IN 1968, after 17 years at the helm of the news operations of The Times, Catledge was named a vice-president and member of the board of directors. He was then 67 years old and began looking toward his retirement. Mr. and Mrs. Catledge bought a lot in uptown New Orleans and started building their "dream house," a two-story French townhouse which is a replica of their Manhattan apartment. Their architect went to New York to study the apartment, and designed the same floor plan for the New Orleans house, only switching the dining room and entrance foyer.

After living in the apartment for five years, the Catledges had arranged it exactly as they wanted it. "We wanted to take it with us—all of it," Catledge explained, so every piece of furniture and work of art was moved and positioned in exactly the same place. "The first morning we woke up here, we felt like we'd been here 10 years," Catledge said.

After their marriage in 1958, the Catledges had spent nearly every holiday and vacation in New Orleans and maintained an apartment in Claiborne Towers. New Orleanian Mrs. Catledge, the daughter of Byrne Ray, was the widow of George D. Izard. Catledge's first marriage to Mildred Turpin ended in divorce.

Prior to his retirement, Catledge spent as much time as possible in New Orleans supervising construction of the house. "The house became a catalyst for our retirement," he said. "We became impatient for retirement. When it came, it was a positive thing, a birth, a realization."

Catledge, who describes himself as a revolutionary because he is an advocate of change, said he has tried to view all change in his life in a positive vein. "Otherwise, you'd sink," he said. "When you're clawing your way up in life, you should never stop climbing, not just for economic or social reasons, but because you're bettering yourself spiritually, too.

"As much as I like to reminisce, I wouldn't want to return to the past. If you look over your shoulder too much, you'll fall into the ditch."

HISTORY buff Catledge says he feels he has lived through the most interesting portion of history to date. "The time I was on The Times (1929-1969) was the most newspacked era since the dawn of civilization," he said. "And the past 25 years have been the most newspacked part of this era.

"I've actually seen people walk on the moon through developments not even invented at the time I was graduated from college."

(Continued from preceding page)

After spending his entire career as a newspaperman, Catledge admits it hurts when a big story breaks and he is no longer in a position to experience it first-hand. "It hurts almost as bad to see an occasional shoddy or superficial job of reporting by a fellow reporter," he said. Acknowledging that he reads every newspaper with the critical eye of a former editor, Catledge said his pet peeve is unanswered questions or incomplete facts in a story.

Catledge said reporting has changed considerably since he started in the business. "It's much more responsible now," he conceded. "There is less showmanship on the part of the reporter. As wide as the credibility gap has become, I think the mission of the media is now better understood by the public.

"One thing that disturbs me," Catledge said, "is advocacy journalism or total reporting. I don't condemn it out of hand, but I think it's quite impractical because causes change so, and principles have a tendency to reverse themselves."

Catledge is disdainful of the super-tough, almost brutal questioning by reporters on televised news panel shows. "What you're after is information," he said. "These reporters are putting on an act."

Catledge's own method of interviewing was to ask a direct line of questions or to merely approach a source with the query, "What's new?" "Sometimes you have to challenge a person," he said. "Every news situation is different."

Catledge apparently found the less aggressive approach disarming and so did his subjects. National Recovery Act Administrator Hugh Johnson, the subject of a Catledge magazine piece, once wrote: "Turner Catledge has a baby face that masks a keen intelligence. He can ask the deadliest questions with an expression like the Age of Innocence."

Catledge believes the two greatest attributes a reporter can have are "an insatiable curiosity and a disposition to gossip—to tell and to entertain by telling." He says he acquired both these attributes growing up in Philadelphia, although the Turner clan was, as a whole, a reserved and quiet bunch. Iris Turner Kelso, a local television newswoman and Catledge's first cousin, developed the same reporter's instincts, he noted.

ALTHOUGH retired, Catledge today is still working hard. He spends one week a month in New York, attending The Times monthly board meeting and spending the rest of the week in the newsroom, serving in an advisory capacity and counseling reporters and editors.

Locally, he serves on several boards, including those of the N.O. Philharmonic Symphony Orchestra, the New Orleans Museum of Art, and WYES; he is a member of the Louisiana Council for Music and Performing Arts.

He was appointed by Atty. Gen. William Guste to the commission investigating the deaths of the students at Southern University in Baton Rouge, a task he said he approached as a reporter, first attempting to uncover all the facts before passing any sort of judgment or fixing blame. "Fixing blame is the easiest and cheapest thing in the world, and also the most useless," he commented.

During the past year, Catledge traveled over the country, raising $2 million for the American Press Institute's new headquarters building in Reston, Va. Additionally, he addresses journalism and civic groups throughout the nation and conducts seminars on college campuses.

One of his most common speech topics is the increasing attack by government on the news media, an attack which he says is "aimed at the very existence of the free press." Although he says the conflict between the press and government is inevitable and dates back to the days of George Washington, when that chief executive threatened to resign because of press criticism, Catledge believes the present administration has gone further in intimidating reporters than any other.

CATLEDGE, Turner

TIMES–PICAYUNE
(New Orleans, La.)

Feb. 18, 1973

Although his Times responsibilities and group memberships consume nearly all his time, Catledge has found some opportunity since retirement to do some writing. His autobiography, "My Life and The Times," was published in 1971, and he is considering writing a second book on a subject which interests him: the fate of Southern folklore in the face of the Civil Rights Movement. He is especially interested in investigating the disappearance of much Negro folklore, which he regards as one of that race's greatest contributions to American culture.

FOR relaxation, the Catledges play golf together, rising early and arriving at the New Orleans Country Club when the doors open. Mrs. Catledge loves gardening and their patio is surrounded by blooming camellias and azaleas. "I superintend," Catledge says.

Old Shep, the Catledges' mongrel dog obtained at the SPCA, has free run of the immaculate house and manicured gardens. "We paid $5 for him and have probably spent $500 making him happy," Catledge says of the part German Shepherd. Contending that mixed breeds make the best pets, Catledge says, "We wanted a mutt, so he'd appreciate a good home."

The Catledges are collectors of 20th century art, from impressionistic to very modern. They often present each other with works of art on gift occasions, and when in New York visit art galleries.

Catledge, who will be 72 March 17, occasionally returns to Philadelphia for a visit, but says, "Frankly, it's not very satisfying. Most of the landmarks I remember are either gone or submerged.

"The first time you go away from home, the whole town changes. When I first went away to college and came back, everything looked smaller, and nothing ever regained its size."

However, Catledge loves to get together with old friends and relatives and tell stories about the old days. "I have an almost total recall," he says, "and I'm afraid I'm a chronic, boring reminiscer."

He is regarded fondly in Philadelphia as the home town boy who became a celebrity. Catledge said he is touched that his fellow townspeople never forgot that he was "one of them."

"When they had the civil rights trouble down there, we were sending one wave of Times reporters after another there, and I think they were treated a little better than anyone else," he said. "Even when some of the reporters wrote stories that were critical of the people there, and they knew that I was directing their efforts, I don't think they ever associated me with it. Mississippians are tremendously loyal. They stick together."

Catledge, who has personally known Presidents, who has traveled around the world and met other heads of state, who has lived and worked in New York City and edited a famous newspaper, has never felt patronizing toward the people who stayed in Philadelphia, although he says they expect him to feel that way.

"It's touching the way they react," he said. "They say, 'You're one of us. You never talk down to us.'

"And I say, 'Why should I need to? Why, I wouldn't know how.' "

For all his years in the East working his way to the top of the competitive newspaper business, Catledge remains a Mississippian, a Southerner, a gentleman. His speech still bears a slight drawl and is full of the colorful expressions he picked up as a youngster in Philadelphia. On the wall of the study in his New Orleans home, among autographed pictures of Presidents, senators and generals, is a favorite watercolor of the Neshoba County Fair.

And, every week, Turner Catledge still reads the Neshoba Democrat.

AT HOME WITH HISTORIAN BRUCE CATTON

By AL STARK
Sunday Magazine Writer

FRANKFORT, Mich.

BRUCE CATTON, old Michigan boy and famous Civil War historian, lives up a hill outside this summer resort and port city on Lake Michigan. He likes to meet his visitors in town and show them the way to his home.

The way leads down a residential street and up past the high school, where a couple of young girls, shoes off, are lolling in the sun on the lawn. A little farther and there are fruit trees, their blossoms on view.

It has been a late spring. Catton has been in Frankfort just a week, having driven from his winter home, an apartment in Manhattan.

The temperature is in the high 70s, the sun is glorious, and the air is warm and yet fresh.

Beyond the high school and the orchard, you hit the blacktop road. In a few minutes the car moves down a trail through beech, wild cherry and ash trees. Out now into a meadow, furnished with a homemade park bench, then back into the trees and up to the house, a lovely white building with fireplace at the very top of the hill.

There are two chairs on the lawn at the back side of the house. Crystal Lake spreads below and beyond Crystal you can see the great sweep of the Lake Michigan shoreline — the whole face of the Sleeping Bear Sand Dune is there, the Manitou Islands and the blue infinity beyond.

Great questions are in the air, here as everywhere in the country. Watergate. The ecology. Others. But they seem easier handled here, where the birds flit from tree to tree in great excitement.

They say the system is in danger, but Sleeping Bear is always there. They say the earth is fouled, but here it is coming alive and turning green once again. They say we have never known such discouraging times, but young girls still want to be tanned.

Catton, 74, tall and erect and full of spice, stood up from his chair on the lawn, looked out over the lakes and said, "The winters are too hard for me here anymore, so I spend them in New York in steam heat.

"But, God, how I love it here!"

CATTON HAD brought a new writing assignment home which he will work on this summer.

CATTON, (Charles) Bruce (1899 -) June 16, 1974

DETROIT NEWS (Detroit, Mich.) [See also CA-5/6]

He has been commissioned by the American Association for State and Local History to write an historical book on Michigan in conjunction with the nation's bicentennial celebration in 1976. Similar books by other authors will be written about each state and the District of Columbia.

Catton also is working with his son, William B. Catton, a professor of history at Middlebury College in Vermont, on a general history of the United States. Eighty pages, Catton says, are in type, with 500 or so to go.

He has maintained his connection with American Heritage magazine, and he has other writing and television programs in the works.

"My son," Catton said, "is a trained historian. I'm a volunteer. I was an English lit major at Oberlin College. I didn't have a single American history course in college."

The noted Civil War historian laughed and said, "I like to say it is like being a National Guard officer when your son has graduated from West Point."

Catton, an old newspaperman, despite missing American history in college, won the Pulitzer Prize for history in 1954 for "A Stillness at Appomattox." That was the third of his Civil War trilogy, much of it involving the Army of the Potomac. The other titles in the trilogy are "Mr. Lincoln's Army" and "Glory Road," the bloody route from Fredericksburg to Gettysburg.

The gravel road you take up the hill to Catton's home is called Glory Road.

Catton smiles wryly. "Yeah," he says."We did that a couple of years ago."

The new Michigan book, he says, is going to be more impressions in essay form than formal history. Catton's last book, published a year or so ago, was called "Waiting for the Morning Train." It was recollections of his boyhood in Benzonia, just a few miles down the blacktop from his summer home.

"I told the association that I just wasn't up to doing a formal history of Michigan. I asked them if they'd go for something in the same general form of 'Waiting for the Morning Train' and they said that would be fine.

"I haven't outlined it yet, but I'm playing with the idea of Michigan as a crossing point. The idea that it has always been a way station. The early settlers, for instance, whose destination was China. They came to Michigan on the way, then crossed Lake Michigan. When they got to Green Bay, they thought it was Manchuria.

"But that's the general idea — that people and movements stopped in Michigan on their way somewhere else."

The American history book, which he is writing with his son, will explore the idea of the United States as birthplace of ideas and directions just beginning to spread throughout the world.

"It fascinates me that in the new nations of Africa they aren't following Karl Marx. They're following George Washington."

Catton paused a minute, then said, "But come on. I want to show you some things.

"There's a homemade Civil War monument in the cemetery at Benzonia that you ought to see. There's not another like it anywhere. And we'll go to a couple of other places."

PETOSKEY WAS Catton's birth-

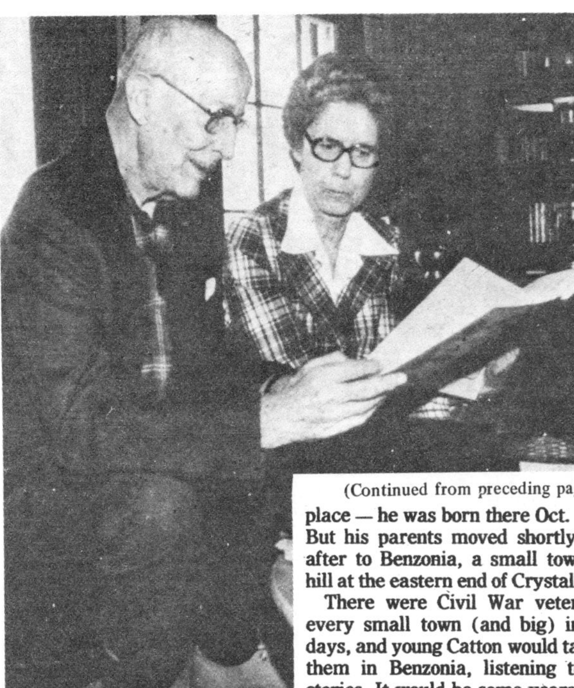

He lives with his sister, Barbara, and writes at least a paragraph a day.

(Continued from preceding page)

place — he was born there Oct. 9, 1899. But his parents moved shortly thereafter to Benzonia, a small town on a hill at the eastern end of Crystal Lake.

There were Civil War veterans in every small town (and big) in those days, and young Catton would tag after them in Benzonia, listening to their stories. It would be some years before he would sit down to write about their war, but that's where it all started.

"I think I had the impression then," he said as we drove toward the cemetery, "with all those old fellows around telling their stories, that the Civil War had been fought 10 miles east of Benzonia and just five years before I was born. I knew better than that, of course, but it seemed like that."

Catton would catch the morning train to college at Oberlin (the morning train, he said in his boyhood memoirs, is the one that carries you out into the world on the uphill side of life; the night train comes later, whistling another tune.) From Oberlin he went into newspaper work in Cleveland and Boston.

He moved to Washington during the Depression with Newspaper Enterprise Association and, when World War II broke out, he joined the War Production Board as director of information. He moved to the Departments of Commerce and Interior, serving as an assistant to Henry Wallace at Commerce.

In 1950 Catton faced a decision.

"I didn't want to stay in government," he said, "and I wasn't sure if I wanted to return to newspapers. I didn't know if I could go back to newspapering — I had a feeling I had been out of it so long I was out of step.

"I decided to become a big novelist. I started to write a big Civil War novel. I had never lost interest in the Civil War. I had talked with all those old veterans in Benzonia and I had read everything I could about the war.

"Now I was going to have my say in my big novel.

"Well, I got 200 pages down, and it was awful. Dreadful. I sat down one day and read it all over, and terrible, terrible.

"But the factual parts — where the armies were moving, when the battles were fought — that wasn't bad.

"So I scrapped the fictional parts and just wrote what I always wanted to write, the story of the Army of the Potomac.

"It was just as impromptu as that."

Catton steered his Buick into the town cemetery in Benzonia, turned down a lane, and parked.

"There it is," he said. "I can't imagine there's another like it."

The monument is about 4½ feet high and squat. It is a collection of field stones of various colors set in cement and across the top is a large slab of stone. The cement is rough, as if hands were used instead of trowels; the stones are from fields now full of wild flowers, fields the fallen never got back to see.

On the face of the monument is a plaque which announces that the monument was erected by the members of the E. P. Case Post 372 of the Grand Army of the Republic "in fraternal comradeship and loyalty to our comrades."

Catton said, "This has always meant something to me. The guys who put this up really meant it."

He shook his head, then said, "I was at a dinner party a few weeks ago and this woman was telling about her 13-year-old son. Apparently they had been in Washington and the boy had seen the Tomb of the Unknown Soldier and he had been very impressed. He told his mother, 'What a wonderful thing to die for your country!' and she told us at the dinner table that she had set him straight, and he didn't feel that way anymore.

"Set HIM straight?" Catton said angrily. "Someone ought to set HER straight! I'd like to tell the boys who put this monument up about her."

Then Catton shook the mood and said, "Now I have a suggestion. Let's drive into Frankfort and I will show you a place where they make a very fine martini."

THE PAC INN is on Main Street, two blocks from the foghorn at Frankfort Harbor. There are rooms upstairs and a dining room with pool table downstairs. There is a sign on the wall for the summer people that says "NO shoes, NO shirt — NO food or booze!" and another advertising the weekly jam session. There are paintings of two nudes on the walls, one sniffing trillium and the other preening. The waitresses look like schoolgirls, and all of them are buttoned up.

Catton wears both plaid shirt and pumpkin-colored cloth walking shoes, so he is served his martini promptly. All the waitresses know him, and they all stop to say hello.

"I figure I am lucky," he says, lifting his glass. "The Biblical thing is three-score and 10 years. Well, I am 74, which puts me four years to the good, and I've been drinking these and other things like them for many years."

He signals for another and says, "Yes, I'm ahead."

The talk turns to Catton's Pulitzer Prize, and he says, "You know, I got a National Book Award that same year, and they called ahead and said, 'Don't tell anyone, but you be in New York on a certain day at a certain place because you're getting a National Book Award.'

"Well, one of the people at the publisher's thought we had a chance for the Pulitzer as well, and I thought if it happened we'd get the same kind of advance word. Well, nothing. Then I saw a notice in the Washington Post — we were in Washington then — that the Pulitzers would be announced the next day.

"I thought, 'Well, that's that. Let's get back to work.'

"Then I got a call from some little girl working for NBC and she asked if I could be in New York the next morning to do five minutes on the Dave Garroway Show. I said yes, of course, and then I asked her what the occasion was and she said, 'Well, didn't you win a Pulitzer or something?'

"I told her I'd call her back. Then I called around and found out it was true. But that's how I found out — 'didn't you win a Pulitzer or something?'

"Boy, if ever there was a night to drink a bottle of bourbon, that was it."

On a coffee table at Catton's home is a book entitled "Pullet Surprises," the title inspired by a line meaning Pulitzer Prize in an essay by a 5th grade country schoolboy. Catton likes the line very much.

The waitress brought Catton a plate of perch. Then she stepped a few feet behind him, dropped a quarter in the juke box, and pressed the button for an Eddy Arnold record. Catton looked at her in mock displeasure and she said it wasn't her idea. She said the bridge club just around the corner had asked her to play music for them.

Catton looked and there they were, 12 of them, each with her hair just so, each eating a wedge of torte while the chairman passed out the tallies.

"God," said Catton, "things are going to be hot and heavy here pretty soon. We'd better get out of here."

BACK AT HIS house, Catton dropped the mail with his sister, Barbara, with whom he lives. She showed him a yellow wild flower she had put in a small vase.

The main room of Catton's home is furnished with books and with sofas meant for sitting. There is a sunny breakfast room at one end of the house and Catton's writing room is at the other end. The desk in the writing room is very neat for a writer, but then the writer had only been here a week and hadn't yet lunged into anything.

"I like to get something done everyday," Catton said, "even if it's just a paragraph. Something.

"I think that's important. I think you have to stick with it, keep hacking away. Otherwise, it's very hard to get back to it."

He looked out the big window facing the lakes, out over his magnificent view.

"Particularly up here," he said, with a good laugh.

"My sister and I have something we always say to each other when we drive up out of Frankfort and turn up the trail through the trees. One of us always says it:

"It's a long way from Park Avenue." ■

CATTON, (Charles) Bruce

DETROIT NEWS
(Detroit, Mich.)

June 16, 1974

AMBULATORY ANCHOR MAN

CHANCELLOR, John
MILWAUKEE JOURNAL (Milwaukee, Wisc.) Apr. 28, 1974

By MICHAEL H. DREW
of The Journal

NEW YORK, N. Y.

PERHAPS IT'S partly a residual of the Agnew attacks, but whatever the reason, most television anchor men seem unduly sensitive about their position and power.

Indeed, many have long objected to their public image as desk bound moguls, intoning the day's events in stentorian tones from steel and glass towers.

No network anchor man is concerned about this more than NBC's John Chancellor. Ask the 47 year old Chicago native about his job and he'll ruminate on campaigns he has covered, political and military.

In truth, Chancellor has spent a considerable part of his quarter century career on the scene of the story. Besides covering all but one presidential and off year election since 1950, he's served in NBC bureaus in Vienna, London, Moscow, Brussels and Berlin and reported on several wars and revolutions, including Cuba's.

"In 1972," he said proudly during a recent interview in his Rockefeller Center office, "I covered two space shots.

"I also went to China, Russia and Europe with the president and covered 10 primary elections. For the Wisconsin primary, I spent five days in Milwaukee.

"Over the years, I've been in Wisconsin hundreds of times. I guess the strangest trip was in 1951, when I was in NBC's Chicago bureau. President Truman had fired Gen. MacArthur and there were caravans for the general all over the country. TV was pretty new then and I rode with a cameraman on a plywood platform on top of a sedan, shooting 35 millimeter film.

"Motorcycle drivers were running into kids and two miles of soldiers came to attention when we rode past. I had soot all over my face.

"I started coming to Wisconsin as a Chicago kid, going to Wisconsin Dells. Wisconsin has had some terribly interesting politicians."

Chancellor attended the University of Illinois, served in the Army and worked for the Chicago Sun-Times from 1948-'50. He's been with NBC since, except for two years (1965-'67) as director of the Voice of America.

"I took the job kicking and screaming," he recalled at his desk, puffing on a pipe with his feet elevated. "Two presidents, Lyndon Johnson and NBC's, twisted my arm. I did it for two years on a nonpolitical basis and got out with my whole skin and reputation intact. I didn't have to shill.

"I learned how the government works from the inside and how much attention it pays to the press."

That information has helped him considerably since.

"I don't get as much contact with news sources as I like," he conceded, "so I keep my telephone going. I still have contacts in the State and Defense Departments. Before I was an anchor man I never got called back. When I identify myself to secretaries now and say 'I have to write about him tonight so I'd like to talk to him,' you'd be amazed at my call back rate."

Puffing away at that pipe in his book lined office, John Chancellor didn't look much like the sort of fellow who enjoys throwing his clout around. He's more professorial than reportorial, a charmingly avuncular chap with a sly sense of humor lurking around the conversational edges. Gray hair gives him a properly seasoned look. The even teeth, one suspects, are capped.

For three years in the early 1970s, Chancellor commuted between New York and Washington.

"I was on planes and trains so much that I collapsed and NBC said, 'Maybe you shouldn't do this,'" he recalled. "Also, it was costing them $150,000 to indulge my habit of seeing news sources in Washington. I have two teenagers, a girl, 15, and a boy, 13, and I wanted to be with them. So we all settled in New York last summer.

"I enjoy the priceless luxury of being able to walk to work. We were apprehensive about New York but we've always believed in living in the cities where I worked. We found New York safe, if you're prudent, and interesting, with a million things to do."

How well are the TV networks doing their news jobs?

"Okay, especially in the things that people must know, less well in other areas.

"We should do more investigative reporting, and maybe Watergate will prompt it. But it's tough on the national and international level and it's difficult when you need 800 words to make your point. Some of the best stories involve deeds and tax forms and even if we had three hours for them, we'd put people to sleep. I don't know what we'd have done if someone had dropped the Pentagon Papers on my desk."

Will Watergate, and Spiro Agnew's demise, lessen governmental attacks on the news media?

"No, now Ken Clauson of the White House staff, an intelligent man, is using a rifle instead of Agnew's shotgun."

What's his view on newscasting "happy talk"?

"Where it works, it's part of a good overall local operation. There's no sign of it on the networks so far. We're more serious fellows. The relentless 'happy talk' promises happiness and comfort, not 'a picture of the world upon which the citizen can act,' in Walter Lippmann's words."

How about Agnew's charges of eastern elitism in news judgment?

"We rely heavily on the Associated Press and UP and we have confidence and trust in them. The AP really sets standards, we're just the final transmitters. Walter Cronkite, Harry Reasoner and I were born within 400 miles of each other in the Midwest and there's not an Ivy Leaguer in the bunch. I read nine magazines and six newspapers regularly and get digests of papers from all over the country."

Despite his heavy newspaper diet, Chancellor sees faults in the print media.

"Too many small newspapers, not The Journal, are profit centers for the stockholders instead of instruments of journalism," he said.

There have been rumors that at least one network is considering expanding its evening news from 30 minutes to 60. His view?

"I'm against it and NBC has no such plans. About 25 days a month, half an hour of news is enough. If people watch local news and read The Milwaukee Journal with any care, which I devoutly hope, half an hour is plenty."

Chancellor says he writes at least half of what he reads, plus a daily radio essay. He hopes to teach a seminar at Yale University on American journalism history, with emphasis on the AP's development.

Should President Nixon resign?

"I'm all for having the case settled in Congress. His resignation would be a disservice and I don't want 45 million people to think the press and his enemies hounded him out.

"The most serious problem we're facing is a lack of confidence in our institutions and a lack of coherent sense of leadership on every level. It's a potentially explosive situation and the gloomiest time I can recall in my 25 years in the business."

How does he assess his profession?

"Journalism is a loose, unlicensed fraternity of men who get paid for their curiosity. Too many have lost the sense of fun and anger I saw in Chicago in the late 1940s and early '50s. In the words of an old Chicago Times editor, 'It's the newspaper's duty to print the news and raise hell.'"

Chris's Star Trek

By Judy Flander
Star-News Staff Writer
Sketch by Authors in the News

Chris Chase learned about acting from Lee Strasberg, grew up on television soap operas, was discovered by Vogue magazine, rediscovered by Stanley Kubrick, was Preston Sturges' "last protegee" and was discovered again by George Abbott. She's never played anything but leads or "best ingenue" parts.

So how come you've never heard of her? So how come she's not a movie star?

Chris Chase smiles her urchin smile. She's been in a lot of flops. She's easily bored, so she moves on to the next adventure without waiting for something to turn up.

"I've been so lucky, something always presents itself. I have an almost mystical feeling about it because so much of my life has been out of my control."

Right now you could call Mrs. Chase an actress "at liberty." But she's also an author, presently on tour peddling her first book, "How to Be a Movie Star or A Terrible Beauty Is Born" (Harper & Row, $6.95). It's a whimsical, partially true and hilarious story about how she didn't become a movie star.

It all started a couple of years ago when she quit acting. "It was a necessary breather. I just stopped. I had been playing ingenues for so long, I was bored with cracking my voice and trying to charm matinee ladies."

So she wrote a "funny piece advising out-of-work actors (a catagory into which most of her friends fall) about staying home and improving each shining hour by practicing how you're going to act and all the things you'll say when you get to be famous."

Seymour Peck, then editor of the New York Times' culture section, grabbed it and asked for more. Letters poured in. "I couldn't imagine the power of that newspaper," says Mrs. Chase. "A girl from Canada sent me a Tootsie Roll pop everytime I did a piece. She had to pay 5 cents duty on each one, the packages came stamped. One time she liked a story so much she sent me a whole box of Tootsie Rolls as a reward."

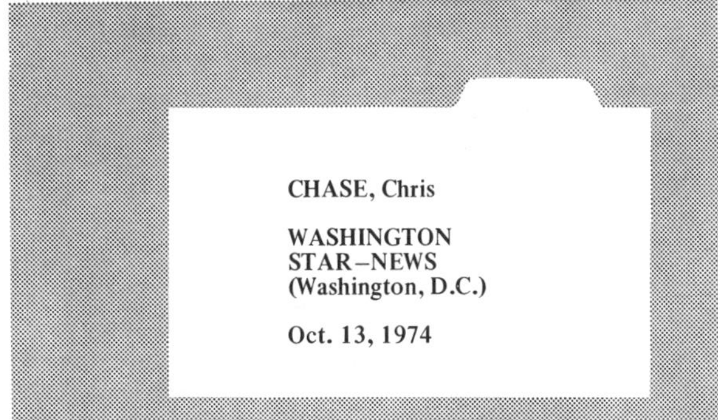

CHASE, Chris

WASHINGTON STAR-NEWS (Washington, D.C.)

Oct. 13, 1974

You can see why Mrs. Chase would have that effect on people. She looks like a waif. In person, she's fey, exuberant and funny. She's traveling with her husband, Michael Chase, who runs the TV network for New York State. ("Harper's paying for me and I'm paying for Mike; he's on vacation.") Chase's parents met as reporters on the Rocky Mountain News in Denver. His mother, Mary Chase, is author of the Pulitzer-prize play, "Harvey."

Chase tries to bury his nose in a book to be unobtrusive during the interview, but sometimes he can't resist and his head pops up.

Mrs. Chase is explaining why she "felt funny" about accepting an invitation to be on a book panel in Dallas. "Who would know me? Why would people want to buy my book?"

"She's a combination of insecurity, confidence and optimism," puts in her husband. "She worries about everything. She was afraid they wouldn't have any of her books in Dallas. I said, 'Honey, you can take some on the plane with you.' She said, 'How could I carry 1,200 of them?'"

Mrs. Chase says she finds book-peddling "degrading. We creep into bookstores to see if they've got it. We can't ask, we'd have to buy a copy."

But she has bought a copy. "I was walking by Rizzoli's on Fifth Avenue and there among all the art books and other lovely books was my little book. I rewarded them. I went in and bought a copy." But she was careful to hold the book out to the cashier with the back side down. Her picture is on it and she didn't want to be recognized.

"The awfullest thing about writing a book is you have to wait to find out if people like it, maybe three months. If you're in a play, you find out opening night if they love it or hate it. There's Clive Barnes sitting right out there in front."

Mrs. Chase wrote the book because she was asked — by eight publishers, bowled over by her pieces in the New York Times. It isn't that she's given up acting. "I certainly hope I don't die before some marvelous part comes along."

The trouble is, there are so few good parts for women. "Look how seldom Julie Harris works. Look at all those years Anne Bancroft worked before she got to play Gittel in "Two for the seesaw," that lovely play.

"Everybody wants to see Robert Redford kiss Paul Newman, I guess. All they have are movies with male pair-bonding starting with Peter Fonda in 'Easy Rider.' In most movies, women just don't exist unless as hookers."

Chris Chase has further narrowed her acting options by refusing to work out of town — "I wouldn't go for fear of being divorced by what's his name." — or do commercials. "What has it got to do with acting? It's selling." She's appalled that Lawrence Olivier is one of the renowned actors now doing commercials and she can only conclude he needs the money. "God knows. Oliver shouldn't have to do commercials."

Everybody wants to know if her book is an autobiography. She keeps referring to the "I" in the book as "that girl." The truth, she says, is "It's my life but I'm not that girl. The truth is, I don't tell anything about the way I feel, the books I read or the people I love. I'm not quite as dumb. I've been more successful."

Writing comes easily to Chris Chase. "I have no pretentions of being an intellect, so I don't take it seriously. But when I was acting, I always had the feeling I was up against Eleonora Duse."

Mysterious, but off the pedestal: A look at four first novelists

Kelly Cherry

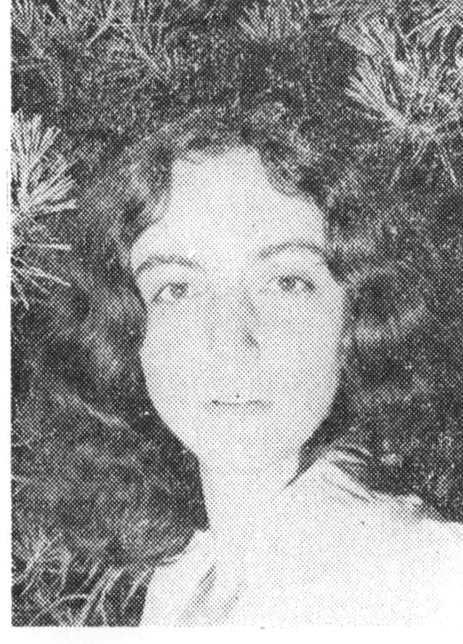
Susan Quist

Erica Jong

Eleanor Glaze

By DAVID MADDEN

"DAVID, how'd you like to meet the girl in the black raincoat?" asked George Garrett, grasping my elbow. "She's over there somewhere."

Somewhere among ordinarily attired folks I'd already met: Katherine Anne Porter, James Purdy, Peter Taylor, Hortense Calisher, Richard Wilbur, Leslie Fieldler, Diane Wakoski — participants in the 1973 Boatwright Literary Festival in Richmond, Virginia, now being partied in an old red brick mansion on Monument Avenue in the Fan District. From George Garrett, author of "Death of the Fox" but also of the movie, "Frankenstein Meets the Space Monster," I always expect the best and the least-expected.

What I got was not a girl in a black raincoat, but a young woman who wore very snugly the name Kelly Cherry.

I did remember "The Girl in the Black Raincoat" as one of Garrett's kite-flying antics, a collection of 41 stories and poems, variations of a theme, by famous and little-known writers.

"Once upon a time," Garrett tells us, "there was a real girl in a real black raincoat who attended my creative-writing class. She was a very talented girl, but she had to leave school. One of my students wrote a story about her." And one story led to another until the book came out in 1966, including a story by the girl herself.

A decade later, women writers are opening and sometimes taking off the black raincoat of male fantasy: Kelly Cherry wittily, button by button, in "Sick and Full of Burning" (Viking. 280 pp. $8.95). Susan Quist flauntingly, some say obscenely, in "Indecent Exposure" (Walker, 168 pp. $6.95) Erica Jong erotically, with a flourish, in "Fear of Flying" (Holt, Rinehart & Winston. 340 pp. $6.95). Eleanor Glaze esthetically, not so explicitly, in "Fear and Tenderness" (Bobbs Merrill. 453 pp. $8.95). Four first novelists, but also poets, ranging from 30 to about 39 in age; two are Northern Jews, two Southern WASPS.

SITTING at the dinner table at Lake Saranac, New York, the two women Fellows of the Fiction International Writer's Workshop looked, spoke, and thought very differently: Kelly Cherry, in a black raincoat, raven hair cut short now, Susan Quist braless in a t-shirt with a fantastic decal, long hair electric. Their novels just out, Kelly and Susan were jittery, awaiting reviews.

Visiting my workshop, Kelly was analytical (she'd just finished a year

CHERRY, Kelly
[See also CA-49/52]
QUIST, Susan
JONG, Erica
(1942 -)
GLAZE, Eleanor
(1930 -)
[See also CA-49/52]

COURIER JOURNAL & TIMES (Louisville, Ken.)
Oct. 13, 1974

in Minnesota teaching philosophy), but frenetic, her voice high, querulous. All during that week last June we shared an aesthetic, formalist approach to writing. Wide-eyed, insomniac, easily elated, quickly depressed, Susan, a dionysian, preached spontaneous combustion. When Erica Jong called to say personal problems would keep her away from edenic Lake Saranac, Susan and Kelly took over her workshops and students. Each had her own style to which different students were drawn.

The body auras they emitted clashed most visibly and vocally the night they read from their novels and their poetry, while rain on the lake and the boathouse roof and thunder forced us to draw our wicker chairs up to their feet.

Susan began with an archetypal image of the American adolescent girl: "Labor Day, 1958. The sun is shining. The sky is blue. The Annual Labor Day Pet Parade of Elmwood Park is about to begin. The band is tuning up. The dogs are barking. I am twirling my baton. I am 13 years old and the head majorette of Elmwood Park Elementary School. I am sweating under my white feather collar. I am wearing a 34 double-A brassiere. . . . I feel sad. I feel old. I am the head majorette. I am leading the Pet Parade. In my Maidenform bra. I put the silver whistle to my mouth. I bite it. I hold it fast between my teeth. Bitter. It tastes of metal. I blow. No hands. Taweeet, tweet. I lift my tassled foot. It begins."

THREE OF these first novels are told in the first person, inciting the reader in this healthy era of honest self-appraisal to insist on seeing autobiography, even where none is intended. In a replica of Susan's own handwriting, "Indecent Exposure" is ➡

He Is 'Father' Of Bugs, Tweety And Porky

Bee Photo

BY KATHEY CLAREY
Bee Staff Writer

When Bob Clampett graduated from high school he was offered a job with King Features at $75 a week. Instead, he took a job with Looney Tunes at Warner Brothers for $10 a week.

If he hadn t, the world may never have known Bugs Bunny, Tweety Bird or Porky Pig.

The creator of those well-loved characters, as well as Beanie and Cecil, was in Fresno yesterday to speak at Fresno State University. He traced the history of cartooning and puppetry, including 3-D animation, utilized film clips of his cartoon productions and manipulated his puppets from his Emmy award winning television show, "Time For Beanie."

Wearing a jacket sporting decals of his famous "children" and accompanied by his wife, Sody, Clampett took time out from his schedule to answer questions about his life and the characters he created.

Cecil, the lovable sea serpent, was the first, created out of an old sock when Clampett was a boy.

"I saw a movie where there were these long-necked prehistoric creatures and I was so excited I went home and made drawings of long-necked characters," he explained. "My mother helped me make the hand puppet out of the sock and I put on shows on my front porch. Cecil amused people from the beginning.

Born in San Diego, Clampett moved to Hollywood with his family a few years later. "That was when they shot the comedies in the streets," he recalled "And one day I watched Valentino at Paramount."

Undoubtedly influenced by his environment, he began drawing characters and making up stories to go with them He does not believe he drew any better or any worse than other children, but his parents did encourage him.

"That was very vital to me," he said. "My dad would even show some of my cartoons to his business friends."

Clampett began working for Warner s in 1934 and he helped draw the first Merrie Melody cartoon. When the studio conducted a contest among the artists to create an animal."Our Gang, Clampett came up with a pig named Porky and a black cat named Beans. (Yes, the name came from pork and beans.) A year later, in 1935, the first Porky Pig cartoon was released..

Three years later "Porky's Hare Hunt" introduced a wise-cracking rabbit or "wabbit" who usually went into a fake dying act. His name, of course, was Bugs Bunny. Other "stars" who were to come out of the Porky cartoons were Daffy Duck and Sylvester.

Tweety Bird, who was to get Clampett in trouble, made his debut in the early 1940s. He originally was a foil for two cats, but he stole the show from them when he said, "I tah I taw a putty tat. The trouble came when someone realized Tweety was a naked bird. So for his second feature Clampett had to put feathers on Tweety, making him a canary.

"I don't know why they never noticed Porky who just wore a coat and tie and no pants." Clampett said.

For all his successes, Clampett did admit he has had a few failures, characters who were tried out and never heard from again.

"I don't think of success when I'm giving birth to a character," he said. "I get excited and have hopes for its future. It's like having a baby.

"They do become very real. I'm constantly thinking up things they can do. I sometimes talk to them as if they are real persons."

When television came in, Clampett left Warner's to do a 15-minute puppet show called "Time for Beanie." Completely new and live each day, it ran 10 years, won three Emmys and spawned a television cartoon series, "Beanie and Cecil," which ran for seven years and is still playing in foreign countries.

And it brought good old Cecil to stardom.

"He is my favorite," Clampett admitted. "He s been with me longer than anyone else and I give him the edge, but Bugs is right behind him."

Clampett and his wife have been married 20 years and they have three children. Asked what it is like to be married to a cartoonist, Mrs. Clampett replied,

"It is a joy. I never have to worry where my laughter is coming from."

Together they run a studio in Hollywood which makes television commercials. She also helps coordinate his speaking engagements on the various college campuses throughout the country.

Clampett is amazed by the reaction he has been receiving from the students. "It's a wonderful thing to hear these college kids laugh as hard and in the same places as people did when I made the cartoons. I really enjoy going around to the universities. I learn more from the students than they do from me."

When students ask him why cartoons are so "punk" today, he replies, "They don't have charm or believability.

"I call the Saturday morning cartoons, 'walkie-talkies.' They walk a little and talk a little. There's no originality, no story.

"I believe cartoons should bring joy to the watcher and make him or her feel good."

Tha . . . tha . . . that's all folks.

Biography News
CLAMPETT, Bob
SACRAMENTO BEE (Sacramento, Calif.)
Nov. 15, 1974

Self-Educated Writers' Paths Meet

BY EDITH HILLS COOGLER
Atlanta Journal Women's Editor

When John Henrick Clarke was in elementary school in Columbus, blacks weren't allowed to take books out of the library.

But Clarke was an extremely enterprising black youngster.

Forging the names of prominent Columbus whites, he carried notes to the librarian: "Please give this boy the (name of a book) to bring me."

He got his books. And there is this to be said for Clarke as a boy, he did return them on time.

CLARKE left the South in 1933, attended high school in New York, and briefly attended college. But the greater part of his education came from studying at libraries. "At the library, you could read things the college would never assign you."

He became a writer. And recalling his early impressions of Columbus, he wrote a short story in 1939, "The Boy Who Painted Christ black."

Visiting Atlanta, Clarke recalled, "It was an innocent story about a child in school who paints Christ to resemble his father — black. The picture is on display at commencement and the superintendent of schools comes along and demands, 'Who authorized this!'

"THE principal defends the right of each person to interpret God in his own way. The principal puts his job on the line . . . and loses it. The superintendent appears as the villain.

"It was published in 'Opportunity Magazine' in 1940, and it was widely read throughout the country.

"Unfortunately I used the real names of the superintendent and the principal in Columbus, and they sued me. But I was out of work at the time and living in a $3.50-a-week room. I couldn't pay anything, so I apologized."

IF you're wondering how this off-beat character turns out, he turns out fine. He has just completed the formidable task of editing a two-volume book "World's Great Men of Color" by J. A. Rogers. Each volume in hardcover is $8.95 (Macmillan), and in paperback (Collier Books) is $3.95.

Clarke said, "Rogers was a Jamaican who came to this country in the early '20s. He had been through the 9th grade in the West Indies, the equivalent of about the 11th grade here — a good British education. Beyond that, he was self-educated.

"He was a lay historian and an extensive reader, such as I. And he spoke at least four languages.

"Someone told him early that he came from a people who had no history, the same as they told me when I was growing up in Columbus. He began to search, just as I did.

"HE BECAME a writer on the old 'Messenger' magazine edited by black socialists to get recognition, dignity, a whole new economic society for the blacks. It lasted from 1923 to 1928 and it would be considered conservative today.

"In the magazine he began a series of portraits of great black people in history.

"The final collection of these wasn't popular with the publishing companies of that time. The book was privately published in 1947. But the black academic community never gave him recognition during his lifetime — it was a natural snobbery which existed then because he didn't have the proper degrees.

"IN THE meantime, I was a scholar activist, writing and deeply preoccupied with the history of the Negro. In 1939 I discovered some of Rogers' privately printed books in the Harlem library. I not only read all of Rogers' books, but everything on black history I could get my hands on.

"Rogers and I were on a committee to raise money so that the Pittsburgh Courier, the major black newspaper at that time, could send a correspondant to Ethiopia.

"I kept up my friendship with Rogers until his death in 1966, and all along the way I was writing and editing. Since '62, I've been an associate editor of 'Freedomways Magazine' relating to civil rights movements throughout the world."

Clarke began to do well as a writer. His "Malcolm X" sold 125,000 copies in all. His "American Negro Short Stories" has sold over 150,000 copies through the years and is used in most black literature courses.

AND THEN, more recently, "Macmillan was listening to the great cry for black history, and finally got in touch with Rogers' wife and she said, 'You people neglected him while he was alive — it'll cost you $10,000 for the advance. She was an astute businesswoman. She wasn't that pushed for money, but was expressing her great respect for her husband."

The publishing house approached several distinguished historians and asked them

JOHN HENRICK CLARKE
Tricked a Library

to edit Rogers' biographies, but they turned down the offer. Clarke explained, "To edit this book is tantamount to legitimatizing Rogers whom they'd neglected during his life. Benjamin Quarles later relented as his statement on the cover shows."

Quarles statement: "A richly pioneering work that commends itself to all who are interested in black men whose lives have enriched mankind."

CLARK, who gladly accepted the job, explained that the book required quite a bit of editing. The original book covered a period which began in 3000 B.C. and ended in 1946.

"It needed to be brought up to date with introductions to every section. I didn't add any people to it, just new information. A lot of the people had died since Rogers wrote the book and I had to add death dates and a lot of information to make it valuable in teaching."

The title referring to "men" of color is a little misleading — a number of women are included. Rogers, in his own introduction to the biographies explains that with one exception, his criterion for including people in the book was that they have no less than an eighth of Negro strain. His research into her mixed ancestry qualified Cleopatra for inclusion.

Clarke said, "Cleopatra came into power at the time when Egypt had passed its prosperity, and she was legally married to both Caesar and Marc Anthony. The lineage came down from the woman, not the man. This is the distinction with African women, that very early they become inheritors of power. Logically both of these men had to marry Cleopatra, otherwise they could have no power in Egypt.

"Another myth about Cleopatra is that she died over Anthony. She loved him, but her great love and passion was not a man, but her country . . . when she knew Egypt would be reduced to a colony and there was nothing she could do to stop it, that's when she killed herself."

QUEEN Hatshepsut (c. 1500 B.C.) was engaged in a royal power struggle and at one point, she dressed in the royal robes, mounted the throne and declared herself Pharaoh of Egypt. She was popular as a ruler, but there was a certain masculine prejudice against her because she was a woman.

At this point she flatly declared that she was a man. After this, her sculptured portraits showed her with a male chest and beard. Clarke said that she actually wore a false beard.

Another interesting woman is Ann Zingha (1582-1663). She was known as the warrior queen of Matamba. To demonstrate her importance to the Portuguese, she had a serving woman get down on hands and knees and she used the woman's back as a seat.

When the audience ended, she left the woman on the floor saying, "It is not meet that the ambassadress of a great king should be served with the same seat twice. I have no further use for the woman."

In a subsequent war with the Portuguese, she had an army of amazon warriors by whom the enemy were terrorized.

ANOTHER colorful warrior queen was Zenobia (d. A.D. 272) who claimed descent from Cleopatra and who ruled a large area that included Egypt and Syria. She drank with her officers, rode horseback and personally led her heavy cavalry against Aurelian the Roman emperor.

More women warriors crop up in the story of Behanzin, 18th Century king in West Africa. He had an elite corps of fighters—5,000 women sworn to chastity and rigorously trained to fight. Part of their training was to charge barefoot upon an immense barrier of thorns. They also were required to kill bulls with their bare hands.

Rogers quotes another researcher, "Like the men, they fought nude to the waist."

CLARKE, John Henrick
(1915 -)

ATLANTA JOURNAL
(Atlanta, Ga.)

Apr. 8, 1973

A tough, but tender, heroine was Mary Seacole (d. 1881) a Jamaican, a nurse. Unable to get official British sanction to nurse during the Crimean War, she used her entire capital of $4,000 to buy medical supplies and push right out to the battlefields where she could be of the greatest help.

TODAY, Clarke finds academic acceptance more easily than Rogers did in his lifetime. Clarke, still without a college degree, is an associate professor in the Department of Black and Puerto Rican Studies at Hunter College, New York, and a visiting professor at Cornell University's African Studies and Research Center.

"I started at Hunter four years ago. Some of the students I'd taught at the community center said I was the caliber person to teach those subjects. And while I had no degree, I'd written 13 books and presented numerous papers on African studies at international conferences.

"It overwhelmed them and I got in on a waiver."

A Blue-Collar Walter Mitty

— GEORGE KOCHANIEC / Miami Herald Staff

"One of the waitresses I find hard to take asked me at one point today, 'Are you the boy who cuts the lemons?'

" 'I'm the man who does,' I replied.

" 'Well, there are none cut.' There wasn't a hint that she heard my point . . .

"In that moment, I learned the full thrust of those billboard ads of a few years ago that said, 'BOY. Drop out of school and that's what they'll call you the rest of your life.' I had read those ads before with a certain feeling of pride; education matters, they said, and that gave a lift to my field. Today I saw them saying something else. They were untrue in part; it turns out that you'll get called 'boy' if you have a Ph.D. It isn't education that counts, but the job in which you land . . ."

— From "Blue-Collar Journal: A College President's Sabbatical," by John R. Coleman, president of Haverford College, Philadelphia; BA, MA, Ph.D, author of seven books on labor and economics, chairman of the Federal Reserve Bank in Philadelphia.

By JANET CHUSMIR
Herald Staff Writer

So you talk about that. What can be done to change it?, you ask Coleman, the 53-year-old college president who worked as a ditch-digger in Atlanta, a sandwich-salad maker in Boston, a garbage man in a Washington, D.C. suburb.

And the tall, trim, rugged-looking man shifts uncomfortably in his chair. A couple of weeks ago, Coleman, who was guest speaker at the National Council of Jewish Women's luncheon Wednesday, could have given a pat answer. But that was before that dinner party in Philadelphia.

"Twice the waitress passed hors d'ouevres," he says. "Twice I took one, thanked her, without looking at her."

The third time, she said, "Hello, Mr. Coleman." And he looked at her face. And discovered "She'd worked in my home, six or eight times."

And so, if he who saw housewives shrink from him when he picked up their garbage, if he who so resented being called 'boy' could not see past the uniform to the person serving him, he despairs that the sensitivity will ever come to most of us.

He has learned some things, however, from his blue-collar work. He has learned how many other people want to do what he did. They, too, have their Walter Mitty dreams. Not dreams of bringing peace between Arabs and Israelis, or finding a cure for cancer. "Humble dreams like mine," he says.

His dream to live a different life was not because he was unhappy with himself or his job, or running away from Jack Coleman, he says. It was "curiosity to do something else." Doing something else helps him do what he does. He comes back with a different view.

Others can't chuck one lifestyle for another, even for the summer, because they don't have "the same luck I have."

His luck was being single. His marriage ended in divorce. His children didn't need him. His trustees didn't press him. If they had, he would have been forced to spend the time off doing "something respectable," he says.

Some of the things he learned at blue-collar jobs, he already knew. More than 20 years ago, in his dissertation, he wrote of the need for a grievance process so people in a subordinate position could safely and impersonally get their complaints heard.

Yet, when he was collecting garbage and was cheated out of an extra $10 bill, he was furious and frustrated that he had no recourse. It was different because he'd been "top dog," away from such things for a long time.

He has twice worked as a garbage collector. Last summer, he returned to the Washington suburb because the job he'd lined up in construction fell through. He laughs as he explains that there were no jobs in construction because the Federal Reserve system put interest rates so high. He's chairman of the Federal Reserve Bank in Philadelphia.

Second time on the garbage collecting job he was struck by "how many people want to do a job well, despite the abuse from the householders."

He attributes it to a new boss who showed appreciation for work well-done, a boss who could do the job well, too. "He'd practically eliminated absenteeism, which was a problem, and he'd eliminated liquor on the job. "What he was doing always was holding out expectations. Instead of knocking you down, he was holding out expectations above your level." People responded by reaching out

He finds he has more curiosity about the blue collar world. He wants to learn more about other people, all kinds of people. He's going back this summer. The friendships he makes supplement those he's made on campus. "They are different kinds of friends. I find them really rewarding as friends."

There are fewer differences between the groups in his two worlds than one would think, he says. "The same number of hangups, the same problems." But the blue collar workers are more open; they place fewer walls and defenses around themselves."

The biggest difference is not in the things people talk about in the faculty dining room or over a beer after a day digging ditches, he says. The difference is in the way they talk.

"Academia exhausts every topic, explores every nuance. We enjoy words, play with them very lovingly. I'm not convinced we add anything."

He is convinced, though, that there's too much questioning of "Where have all the leaders gone?"

He's trying to cut through "all the deep gloom" he finds everywhere he goes.

A large part of what's wrong, he says, is what's right. We're in trouble because expectations are so high""

There are racial tensions because everyone expects equal opportunity, which they should have, he explains.

There are men-women tensions because women have become aggressive; their expectations are high, which they should be. And that's threatening to the white male's supremacy.

What's bad, he says, is we're looking for a leader to take us out of poverty and despair and we re damning Jerry Ford because he isn't doing that.

"There's no Messiah. The truth is there's no big leader." If anything is to be done, it's going to be a lot of people in small ways. If you're going to bring that peace in the Mideast, he reminds, you'll have no time to help that ex-offender here in Miami find a job, no time to show an elderly person that someone does care.

We talk a lot, he says, about how we've lost control of our affairs. "Damn it, men and women never had control. We just talk about it more. On the job people talk how they're regimented, how they can't take pride in their work, see the end product.

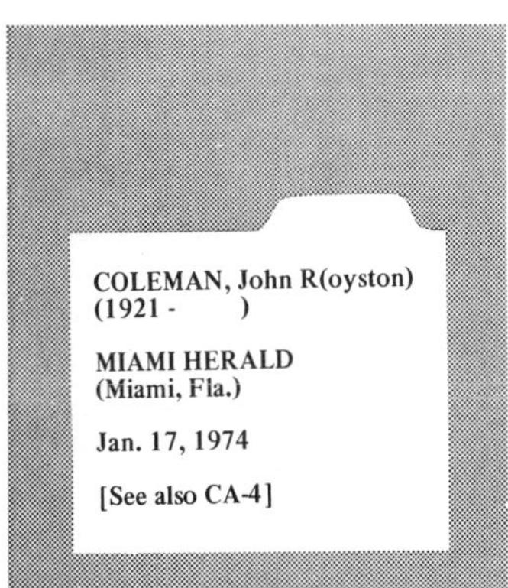

COLEMAN, John R(oyston) (1921 -)

MIAMI HERALD (Miami, Fla.)

Jan. 17, 1974

[See also CA-4]

Real-life 'Conrack' likes movie image

By TED MAHAR
of The Oregonian staff

"Well, it's pretty interesting to watch a movie made about your own life and wonder what's going to happen next," said Pat Conroy, whose autobiographical book "The Water Is Wide" was adapted into the movie "Conrack."

"Don't get me wrong, now," he said. "I liked the movie, and I would even if it had nothing to do with me. In fact, parts of it were a lot better than real life."

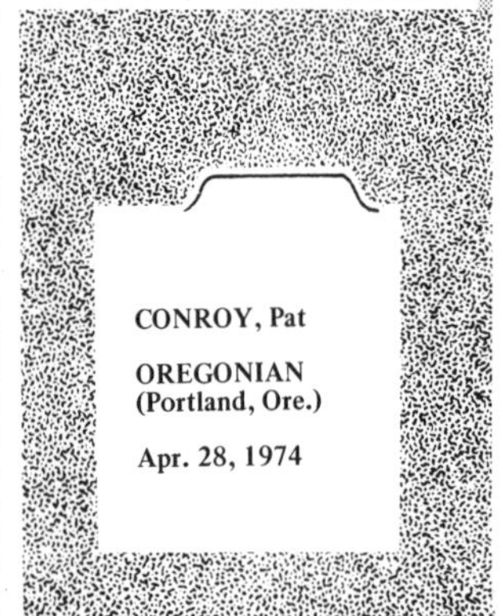
CONROY, Pat

OREGONIAN (Portland, Ore.)

Apr. 28, 1974

The book and movie deal with Conroy's academic year, starting in the fall of 1969 on a small, isolated island off the South Carolina coast. He attempted to teach near-illiterate black children how to get along in life and did so against the tradition of the school board which, he said, has actively — but perhaps unconsciously — been using the school system to keep the youngsters ignorant and safe. Conroy was fired at the end of the year.

Basically, that is the story the movie tells, but it adds details and subtracts some, like the fact that he got married during that year.

"My wife was sort of dreaming maybe Raquel Welch would play her," Conroy said. The movie ends with Conroy, whom his students called Conrack for just a few days rather than through the whole year, protesting his firing by driving a truck with a loudspeaker through city streets.

"I'd never even seen a truck like that until I saw the movie," Conroy said. The black woman principal of the school called him "Mr. Patroy" the first day, thereafter getting his name right. In the movie, she calls him that all the way through. "The wonderful world of Hollywood," Conroy says.

He met Voight during filming, but "Voight seemed kind of nervous, maybe because he'd read the book and saw the changes. Of course, if Gen. Patton had walked up to George C. Scott, it might have disrupted him, too. After all, an actor has to build the character in his mind, and meeting the real person might damage the performance without adding anything."

He wrote the book, he said, to vindicate his position.

"When you get fired like that, you have to do something. I couldn't get a job with the charges the school board leveled against me," he said.

He did not single out his local school board for special treatment.

"All school boards are alike whether in South Carolina or in Portland," Conroy said. "Coaches become principals, and teachers never do. Maybe they're too busy teaching. Then principals and coaches get onto school boards. This is why school superintendents tend to be so dumb; they were all coaches, too. Their ideas smell of the locker room. That's probably the reason they're interested in discipline instead of education. As long as the students are quiet, school boards are happy."

Conroy says he has gotten along well with teachers and that "principals think I'm Godzilla." When he left the island, the black principal took over all eight grades again, and the superintendent who fired him was rehired for another four years.

Conroy is now earning enough money to put his wife through law school and write another book, this one about the growing up of a military brat. His father is a Marine colonel "who got in all the wars from World War II through Vietnam.

"Dad loved Vietnam," Conroy said. "When he came back, he said he could hardly wait for the next one and that Vietnam was good because he ate well. When I was a little kid, I saw a Marine colonel cry when the Russian ships left Cuba. He'd missed his chance."

Conroy and his dad get along well, "because I'm the straightest of the seven kids — five boys. The others are outrageous hippies. I know dad'll cheer at the part in the movie where I get fired. When I was 18, just before I entered the Citadel military academy, my dad said, 'Son, you're a man now, and you can call me by my first name, Colonel.' He really brings the job home with him.

"But he's a great guy. My book will certainly be no assassination. We don't see eye to eye on things, but we really love each other. If it weren't for all that military crap in the Citadel, I would have joined the Marines, too," Conroy said.

He's glad the book and movie have had some success.

"Until that book came out giving my side, I was really the village Quasimodo," he said.

Pat Conroy's Move From School To Screen

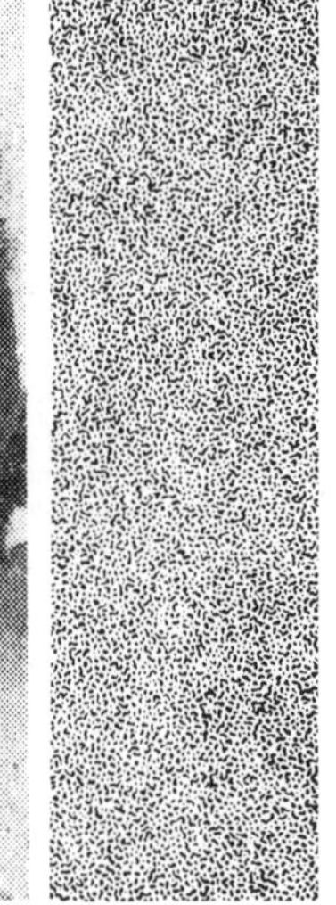

By TOM McELFRESH
Enquirer Film Critic

"My identity has been stolen, you realize."

His name is Pat Conroy. Teacher. Author. His first book — an intensely personal, biographical tome full of real names, "The Water Is Wide," has been made into a deeply-etched movie: "Conrack," which is full of the same real names. Jon Voight plays Conroy. The film is scheduled to open Wednesday at The Place, and shortly we'll come back to what the title, "Conrack," means.

CONROY, Pat

CINCINNATI ENQUIRER (Cincinnati, Ohio)

Mar. 25, 1974

Conroy's a big man. Tall, not particularly beefy. Not as beefy as the bio photo of him 20th Century Fox is sending around would suggest: It's shown herewith.

On my way to have dinner with him the other late night, I intercepted him walking up Walnut Street. Hands jammed in his pockets, a knitted cap pulled down tight over his straw-blond hair. A Southerner and just in from warmer climes he was not at all entranced with our chilly Cincinnati intimations of spring.

At dinner he ordered a real Southerner's aperitif, sippin' whiskey on the rocks — and talked about the paradoxes involved in seeing himself portrayed on the screen. He's 28 and a little young to be that intimately "immortalized."

"My identity has been stolen, you realize."

NOW, DON'T misread the above: Everything he said was laced with a little sly humor that explains a lot of things in the film. I'd joshed him about quite casually talking about things "I did in the movie" — mixing his own and the screen character's identity.

He spent a week on the film set. "Maybe I made him nervous," he said of his reserved conservations with Voight. Conroy went on, "I knew him no better after I met him than I did before. We do not write each other Christmas cards."

"Conrack" details Conroy's adventures as a white teacher in a sharply deprived all black school on an island off the coast of South Carolina. His 180-degree swing from a traditional set of ante-bellum Southern attitudes into a full scale integrationist eventually cost him the job.

The islanders speak a virtually incomprehensible dialect called gullah. Conroy said the kids many of them simply couldn't "hear" the word "Conroy," but heard it as "Conrack." Hence the title. Originally the islander woman who was principal of the school "heard" his name as "Patroy."

Though much of the detail was altered by the film's screenwriters — "That part's all Hollywood," he said of one character in the film — he is pleased with much of it. "There are," he said, "moments with the kids that I thought were very good. A smile here and there."

CONROY WAS married during the time he taught on the island. That's in the book, but was cut from the film. His wife, he said, took one look at the island and said she'd see him weekends in the closest town. "She liked," he said, "things like flush toilets."

She was unhappy about not having her character appear in the film, feeling, Conroy quoted her, "that perhaps Raquel Welch could have caught my innate sexuality."

Nowadays, Conroy lives in Atlanta, freelances magazine articles and is at work on another book, tentatively titled "The Great Santini." It's about his Marine Corps pilot father and the seven children who didn't turn out quite the gung ho militarists he's planned on raising.

(Also see preceding article)

'Conrack'

It All Started Because Teacher Was 'Teed Off' With The System

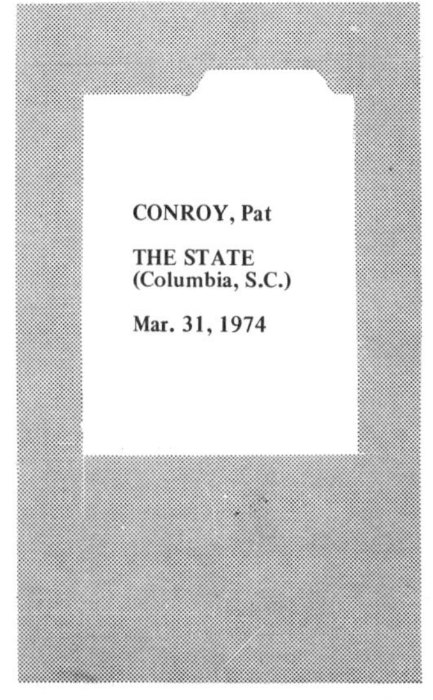
CONROY, Pat

THE STATE (Columbia, S.C.)

Mar. 31, 1974

By BILL McDONALD
Staff Writer

ATLANTA, GA. — The temptation, at first, is to call a Hollywood premiere a lot of schmaltz.

Everything seems so sugar-coated. The director, a genial cigar smoker, is always courting the press — (they can make or break) — and, at the bewitching hour in a packed movie house, he delivers the predictable verdict: .

"This is my best movie yet. No doubt about it. Both the script and the casting are superb. You're an idiot if you don't agree."

Then there are those cocktail parties where frivolity — and toasts — flow like champagne from Cinderella's slipper.)

Excesses, to be sure, but in the case of "Conrack," a Twentieth-Century Fox movie which premiered here a few weeks ago, it can all be forgiven, for the author , Pat Conroy, is a down home South Carolina boy who wrote the book ("The Water Is Wide") the delightful movie is based on.

Conroy, a graduate of The Citadel, told newsmen at the premiere he never dreamed of being a writer, as his lusty talent ran more toward verse; "I always wanted to be a poet," he said, "and I always boasted that I was the best poet that ever attended The Citadel."

Conroy's best-seller caused a stir when it was published: based on his year of teaching on Daufuskie Island, he had a lot of tough, hard things to say about (a) the school authorities in Beaufort, who later fired him; and (b) his black students, who were virtual illiterates.

The storm of protest has now subsided, and success, Conroy beams, has now turned his life into what he terms a "Disneyland."

And what of the movie which stars two veteran actors, Jon Voight and Hume Cronyn? Characteristically, Conroy's response is blunt: (And forever sprinkled with four-letter words.)

"I'm happy with the movie. To tell you the truth, I thought it was going to be a piece of junk. But I'm delighted with the essence. I'm totally satisfied."

Director Martin Ritt, who would have made his "Sounder" movie in Atlanta if it weren't for the bigoted reception he got here from an innkeeper, also agrees with Conroy: "It's got some great touches in it. I'm happier with it, in fact, than I was with "Sounder."

In the film, Conroy takes "Yamacraw Island" off the coast of Beaufort as his teaching assignment. (He had toyed, temporarily, with the idea of the Peace Corps.) His students, speaking a dialect, are unable to pronounce Conroy's name. Hence the name "Conrack."

Seated in the movie audience and watching Jon Voight on the silver screen was like watching a "foreign movie," Conroy admitted later. "It's hard to describe. When I see Voight it's hard to believe I ever went to Daufuskie. I feel removed from it — like it happened on Mars."

The film, costing somewhere in the neighborhood of $2 million, was shot on location in Brunswick, Ga. Daufuskie was turned down as a possible location, director Ritt said, because of transportation problems: there is no bridge to the island.

Too, there was no available housing on the island for the 50-member film crew.

"We were invited to Daufuskie," Ritt said, "but the logistics defeated us. There would be two hours of boat crossing each way — that's four hours. Too much wasted time."

Actor Jon Voight, he said, was chosen for the role of the gutsy idealistic school teacher not because he bears a physical resemblance to Conroy, the author, but because "he's a good actor."

"I knew he would have a strong commitment to doing this kind of film," he said.

Commitment? The word also applies to Conroy, a "literary light" at the tender age of 28. He is down-to-earth, unpretentious, yet he is ablaze with ambition. Already he is fast at work on a novel based on the Marine Corps and growing up in the South.

Conroy is a Marine Corps "brat," one of seven kids. His father, a strong-willed career Marine officer, seems to have had a very strong influence on his early life, which was spent traveling from base to base before finally settling in Beaufort.

Conroy speaks of his dad with awe: "He would make John Wayne look like a pansy." Yet it was not until a few years ago, he admits, that he felt any real stirring of filial devotion.

"Dad was a real (bleep) when I was growing up," he said in an interview. "I didn't really like him until about a year-and-a-half ago. He didn't relate to us kids. The Corps was it."

However, Conroy says his dad today counters such criticism simply by patting him (the author) on the head and saying, "I couldn't have done too much wrong — look how well you turned out."

"Dad thinks I'm a real business genius now," he laughed. "He belives I rigged the whole thing — the teaching bit — just so I could write a book about it."

Conroy says it took him six months to write the book. He was able to devote his full energies to it, thanks to a grant from the Ford Foundation. "That really saved my life," he said.

He also views the book as therapy: "I was tremendously teed off when I was fired," he said. "I was mad." (The school board fired Conroy for allegedly leaving his classroom without proper authority, insubordination and "unorthodox" teaching methods.).

Conroy, who now lives with his wife in Atlanta, says he's now discovering how difficult it is to write a novel because of the point of view Do you write it in the first person, or third person? He devours a book a day, almost, just to see how other writers do it.

"But I don't read too much of the modern stuff — mostly old classics: (When asked if he has a "major influence" in his writing, Conroy mentions Thomas Wolfe, a Southern novelist he says most young writers cut their teeth on.)

Despite the "implicit" criticism of his book of Beaufort school authorities, Conroy says he now feels no animosity. He can even joke about his return visits there: "We see each other, wave, act very pleasant. That's what I like about the South.'

Does he think he struck an effective blow for educational reform on Daufuskie, where, when he taught, his 21 students couldn't recite the alphabet, were unable to spell — and no one in the entire class had ever heard of Asia or knew the world was round?

Conroy shrugs his shoulders. He's philosophical. "I'd like to report to you that all of them got Rhodes Scholarships and are now living in England, but it just doesn't happen that way. I'd like to say, yes, there's been a great effect — but I really don't know that."

What it all boils down too, he says, is his unorthodox, frustrating attempts to teach kids who've been victimized by a System — a blind, senseless System.

Final score: Conroy, a handful of minor victories; the System, undefeated and still champion.

Other than that, he says, not too much can be said of his year on Daufuskie Island.

The Man Who Rediscovered America

By William T. Noble

A WANING winter sun filtered through the windows that overlook New York's Park Avenue and the north end of Central Park, illuminating the vintage oak, dark leather chairs, statues, paintings and floor-to-ceiling books in Alistair Cooke's study.

Cooke's desk faces the east so he can write with the afternoon sun over his shoulder. By turning he can peer down on the monumental traffic or muse over the comparative but often deceptive serenity of Central Park.

The study is warm and well-used. There is an eclectic collection of British and American memorabilia befitting the ex-Englishman who has been giving the United States a fresh look at itself.

Cooke is fairly tall and spare with the elegant look of a fragile piece of Wedgwood, or a country squire who spent a lifetime breathing the damp winds sweeping off a moor. His hair is as white as birch bark and his dark, inquisitive eyes beside a large aquiline nose look younger than his 64 years.

His voice and choice of words make an ordinary conversation sound like the reading of a poem by Lord Byron. In his deep blue suit and vest with brass buttons he looks as British as Anthony Eden.

Cooke traveled to America to write about it, and his assignment became a love affair. For 37 years he has made a Fifth Avenue living interpreting America for the British.

Radio Broadcasts

He has worked for such newspapers as the London Times and Guardian of England—papers that eschewed scoops and scandals but rejoiced in long, perceptive pieces. He also sent weekly radio broadcasts about America through the BBC.

His current TV series ("America: A Personal View," which runs biweekly through May 8) is in many ways a visual account of the things Cooke has been telling the English about America. It is his interpretation of American history without hysterics, doomsday predictions or sycophancy.

With Cooke as their guide, the British crew that previously directed and photographed Sir Kenneth Clark's "Civilisation" was in no danger of falling into an embarrassing quagmire as it hopped, skipped and jumped from one end of the country to the other. Example:

Producer Michael Gill told Cooke: "We can't photograph Valley Forge without snow. It won t be right. But there's no snow or ice. And there wasn't any last winter either."

Cooke: "There's a place in Massachusetts that looks just like parts of Valley Forge. And there's snow there. But don't comb the landscape. And watch out for Massachusetts oaks in backgrounds. They can't be found in Valley Forge and someone will spot the deception."

How many native-born Americans would have known that?

Despite his culture, Cooke is as unstuffy as George Meany and moves as charmingly among a poor Deep South congregation as he does among the dons of Cambridge.

No pedant, he does not talk down to his audience but tells it as he sees it in clear, concise, English:

"When we first played around with the idea of themes for the 'America' series (the series was originally intended for exclusive British viewing), such things as 'America and Business,' 'American Idealism' and 'Women in America' were discussed. Since I am temperamentally not a 'Whither America?' man, I lapsed into a coma of boredom within the first half hour and we abandoned that.

"Two days later I came up with a simple, staggering proposal to try and tell the history of the United States on TV in 13 hours."

For the next two years Cooke plunged even deeper into American history, mining little-known facts, chiding his former countrymen. ("I regret to say the British army of occupation showed the crassness of all armies of occupation") and telling about the agony of Civil War soldiers who had to bite the bullet when doctors severed mangled limbs without anesthetics. (President Lincoln embargoed shipments of chloroform to the South.)

For relaxation he "mooched around" his beloved New York, or retreated to his piano to skillfully ➡

(Continued from preceding page)

beat out New Orleans jazz.

Avoids Driving

Cooke, however, has not been Americanized to the extent that he understands football, or drives cars.

"American football is still as much of a mystery to me as the gymnastics of Zen Buddhism," he said, "and only doctors, cab drivers and maniacs drive cars in New York. I have not owned a car for 15 years and have never bought a new car in my life."

As a full-fledged American citizen, Cooke feels free to criticize his adopted land. And he does so, sometimes quite firmly.

In describing slavery in America, he says: "It was like a sore thumb sticking up through the Declaration of Independence." He also thought the country "got fat with pride" during the Wilson era.

"I always thought Americans were too obsessed with bathtubs," said Cooke changing subjects. "But during wars they crawled through mud without complaint.

"We are idealistic people and feel there are no limits to what can be done. It was common to hear years ago the expression that we lost China. Really we never had China to lose.

"Now there is a great deal of disenchantment with American capabilities. There has been a massive mistrust of American institutions since Vietnam.

"There also is a great apathy toward governmental scandals that years ago would have caused an uproar of protest. Today I believe people are so concerned with their own safety and problems with crime in the streets they don't have time to think or do anything about such things."

Meanwhile, he is savoring American life to the fullest.

His second wife, Jane, a painter, a war widow he married in 1946, shares his interests. They play chess, enjoy Mozart, Handel, Gilbert and Sullivan and New Orleans jazz.

Cooke has one son by his first wife, John, 32, of San Francisco. "He writes film scripts and manages a rock band," said Cooke. Mr. and Mrs. Cooke have a daughter, Susie, 23, and Mrs. Cooke has two children, Stephen and Holly.

"I am an Aristotelian," said Cooke, explaining his philosophy. "I do not truckle to Plato."

(Simply, an Aristotelian believes among many other things, that God is pure actuality, being the unmoved mover and unchanging cause of all changes. Platoism is a belief that the ideal state is aristocratic and made up of only three classes, the artisans, soldiers and philosopher-leaders.)

"America," believes Cooke, fulfills his Aristotelian beliefs about God and democracy. Unlike many foreigners who come here to work but never become citizens, he settled in as an American, accepting all of the responsibilities and rewards, of which he believes there are many.

One of the rewards was binding friendship with H. L. Mencken—an American as diverse from him in tastes and philosophy as Winston Churchill was from George Wallace.

"I was taking an American language course at Harvard," Cooke said "and of course, Mencken was the great living expert. I started corresponding with him and he invited me down to eat crabs. That's how our friendship started.

"It was astonishing that he liked me. I was the embodiment of everything he disliked. He distrusted Englishmen. He didn't like Methodists, and I was brought up a Methodist. He hated radio broadcasters, and that was to become my profession. As for golf, which is a passion with me, he said that everyone guilty of golf should be barred forever from holding any office in the United States."

Yet, for years and until his death, Mencken, the atheist, and Cooke, the Methodist, were the closest of friends.

"But one of my most exciting experiences was meeting Oliver Wendell Holmes (the Supreme Court justice who died in 1935 at 94). Here was a man who served in the Civil War and was wounded three times in some of the most classic battles of that event."

Colorful Writing

When Cooke met his first American Indian he wrote: "I was as tense as high C." His writing often is as colorful as his voice is honey smooth. His TV commentary is without a script or teleprompter.

As a journalist Cooke "mooched around" to such places as cranberry bogs, dockyards, farms, plantations. He studies the flora and fauna indigenous to each place as diligently as a scholar.

He also came to love the delightful eccentricities of Vermonters (a favorite state) and enlightened the English who Cooke once said "were abysmally ignorant of the United States."

He also moved easily into the drawing rooms of the rich and famous. He has interviewed presidents (a book of his interview with President Eisenhower and his relationship with Winston Churchill was published some time ago), and fell in love with California when he was there interviewing movie stars.

"California is a favorite state," he said, "but it is like a mistress who turned into a crone."

Years ago he spent almost an entire evening lighting Greta Garbo's cigarettes.

"Who are your favorite people?" I asked. "Of all the people you have met, who sticks out in your mind as the most impressive?"

"That is easy," said Cooke, listing the following in order:

1—Charlie Chaplin.
2—H. L. Mencken.
3—Adlai Stevenson.
4—Bertrand Russell.
5—Humphrey Bogart.
6—Frank Lloyd Wright.

Although they did not make his list, Cooke admires William Buckley, "a marvelous writer and a quality of logic," and Norman Mailer, "whose bloodshot writing has Shakespearean intensity."

The catholicity of his intellectual tastes and his almost complete Americanism is reflected in his list. The only true Englishman on it is Russell. Chaplin was an English citizen but lived most of his life in America.

Cooke told a story about the late Adlai Stevenson.

"When Stevenson was a guest at the White House and invited to sleep in the Lincoln room," said Cooke, "he paced the floor until the wee hours of the morning. He had such reverence for the memory of Lincoln he thought it would be a sacrilege to mess up the hallowed bed or disturb anything in it. Finally, he was overtaken by sleep and lay down on a small couch that would not show.

"But the joke was on Adlai. The couch was the only piece of furniture actually in the room when Lincoln was there. The bed had been brought in from elsewhere."

COOKE, Alistair

PITTSBURGH PRESS
(Pittsburgh, Penn.)

Mar. 25, 1973

Author: 'I'll Never Grow Old'

—P-I Photo by Dave Potts

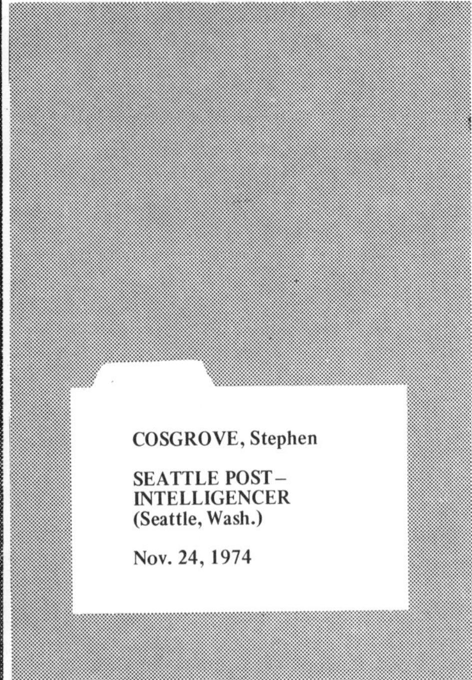

COSGROVE, Stephen

SEATTLE POST-INTELLIGENCER (Seattle, Wash.)

Nov. 24, 1974

BY JUDI MODIE

Stephen Cosgrove is a modern-day Peter Pan.

The author of "Wheedle on the Needle", "The Dream Tree" and a host of other children's books "still lives in a fantasy world, daydreaming the dreams" that eventually become his stories.

"I'll never grow old," declared the 29-year-old Bothell resident, and it is easy to believe him after hearing his ideas for future books.

Cosgrove is a storyteller in person, as well as on paper, and his ability to make his characters live is uncanny. A half-hour of listening to him talk about the "Wheedle" and suddenly, an individual begins to "see" the orange-colored monster with a red-blinking nose who sleeps on top of the Space Needle.

"I'm almost beginning to believe he's real myself," Cosgrove said. "When people ask me how the Wheedle is, I find myself answering, 'oh, he's fine, just fine.' But that's what happens when you live with your characters as I do.

"The Wheedle has become so much a part of my life, it's hard to remember when he wasn't there."

Cosgrove's world has been peopled with imaginative monsters and fanciful animals ever since he was a youngster growing up in Boise, Idaho. He describes himself as "almost an only child, so engrossed was I in the books I read" despite growing up in a family of four children.

His constant companions were the Brothers Grimm stories, the Oz books and a complete collection of Nancy Drew Murder Mysteries his mother had saved. "Sure the main character was a girl, but she had such interesting adventures. I loved them!"

Cosgrove's idea of fun was — and is — to curl up with a book on a rainy day "which isn't hard to find here in the Pacific Northwest so I've had plenty of chances to develop my imagination."

But at first he didn't write. He won a scholarship to Stephens College in Columbia, Mo., the first given by the all-girl school to a man, to study acting.

He gave up pursuing a career in the theater when it became "too political rather than fun," moved with his family to Everett and went to work for a cement mixing company.

Cosgrove started writing children's books after he got married. "I'm the gungho type," he admitted. "The moment we decided to have children, I went right out and checked on diapers and children's books.

"The diapers looked okay, but the children's books weren't. I didn't think, for example, that Dr. Seuss said anything and his drawings leaned towards the macabre so I decided to do something that would build a child's imagination."

Getting them published was something else. "I got offers, but each had a long waiting period before the books could go into productions. So I decided to publish them myself."

Cosgrove chuckled when he described a publisher's reaction to the idea. "They said it would be impossible to successfully publish children's books in the Pacific Northwest. I've been a life-long optimist anyway, so when they said it couldn't be done, I did it."

Now he has a daughter Jennifer, 3, a publishing firm — Serendipity Communications Ltd. — and seven books with seven more to be published next year.

His latest, "The Gnome from Nome," which tells the tale of a gnome who couldn't get warm, has been selected by the Bon Marche as a focal point for a month-long holiday program which eventually will benefit the Children's Orthopedic Hospital in Seattle and the Nome Receiving home in Nome, Alaska.

The Gnome will reign, with Santa Claus, over Toytropolis in the downtown Bon Marche from Nov. 29 through Dec. 24 in the form of a life-sized pixie who'll be on hand to greet children visiting Santa Claus. He'll distribute specially-designed lapel buttons and pose for pictures with Santa and the children.

Funds for the project will be raised through the Gnome from Nome Time Machine ride, which features animated scenes, sound effects and special lighting to parallel the story. It all begins in a sudden snow storm and ends in a feeling of happiness for two friends.

Cosgrove is delighted at the acceptance of his characters not only by the adults who buy his books, but children as well. "I think I've been able to successfully communicate with kids because I don't have any single key for reaching them.

"Children don't place any boundaries on their imaginations, so I don't place any on my own."

Remembering Noel Coward

By Vivian Matalon

Certainly he was witty, yes, and kind and generous and warm — indeed he was all of the things one has heard and continues to hear about Noel Coward. But at the risk of sounding capricious, it is his sadness that I remember more vividly than anything else.

BEFORE I MET Noel Coward, and after I had passed through the stage of dismissing him as "trivial," "old fashioned," etc, it was a frequent if somewhat idle speculation on my part to consider what would happen to "Private Lives" if it were performed for its "real reality." That is to say, what despair in the characters' lives made it impossible for them to speak to each other without being devastatingly witty. So it is possible that I was predisposed to detect sadness in him. On the other hand, maybe it was just a question of timing. I met him first in 1965 and he would soon be ill. If I had met him earlier, perhaps I would not have felt the way I did. I don't know.

I do know, however, that the moments with him that I cherish most nearly all took place in his dressing room at the Queens Theatre during the run of "Suite in Three Keys." He liked me to see each play at least once a week, go round in the intermission to say if I thought it was good so far, and then see him again at the end of the performance. By the time I reached his dressing room at the end of the play it would often be full of dignitaries of one sort or another and the pattern seldom altered. One of the great wits of the world was expected to go on being entertaining. After all, there he was and he was wearing a Noel Coward dressing gown, so on he would have to go.

He and I would obviously be unable to talk about the performance till the last joke had been made and the last visitor satisfied, but eventually it would happen and then one would observe the exhaustion and the relief and he would begin to remove the makeup figuratively and actually. It would be then that sometimes he would talk without a joke in sight. The conversation would be direct and sparse.

IT WAS ON one of these occasions that I brought up to him how dangerous I thought his pronouncements on acting were. You know the type: "Show me an actress who is real and I'll show you a crashing bore," "Learn the lines, dear, and don't lump into the furniture." I said that enough untalented actors held that view without having it reinforced by not only one of the most successful and gifted theatrical personalities alive, but one who as a performer worked in an absolutely opposite manner to the one he was recommending. I reminded him of the hundreds of times he would get depressed in rehearsal because "it doesn't feel true" or "does the reading of the letters seem real?"

On another similar occasion, I asked him directly about being Noel Coward, about the demands made on his wit, about being the center at all times of his particular group, and although he conceded that he often was (by then) wearied by it, even depressed by it, made lonely by it, he just as clearly wouldn't have wanted it any other way. I wonder though?

When we were trying to rehearse "Suite in Three Keys" in Switzerland, hoping that he would be well enough for the then February opening, the day came when he realized that we would have to postpone and we were all called in to his bedroom (Lilli Palmer, Irene Worth and myself) and were told matter of factly and professionally that he didn't think he was well enough to continue rehearsing. We said what we could, and Lilli and Irene left and I stayed behind. He looked at me and said, "I'm so sorry, so sorry that I've put you all out of work." I said whatever one says on these occasions; then he really startled me by saying, "Oh God, curse my aging body," and tears ran down his face.

To say that I was moved is almost a disrespect in the emotion that I felt and the emotion that motivated his lament. I think it was much harder for "Noel Coward" to concede that his powers were waning than it would have been for a writer actor called Noel Coward. It was also a much more shocking remark for me to hear from "Noel Coward."

ON THE subject however Noel Coward writer+actor. I can state categorically that he was the easiest, least defensive writer I ever worked with. He was jealous of nothing in his writing or at any rate in the three plays that made up "Suite in Three Keys." if it were agreed that a play was too long, he preferred me to do the cutting — "I'm too close to it" — and once that had been done we would go over the cuts together and probably debate points here and

COWARD, Noel (Peirce)
(1899 - 1973)

WASHINGTON
STAR–NEWS
(Washington, D.C.)

Feb. 3, 1974

[See also CA-17/18; CA-41/44]

there. it might take perhaps 10 minutes.

No other writer I've ever worked with has had as much objectivity. One of the three plays which is not being performed here was called "Shadows of the Evening." It's an ambitious play with some of his best writing, but it really doesn't succeed. The original version, however, was really poor Coward writing; the three characters are "brave and beautiful" and not remotely believable.

It was about 48 hours after I had met him that we got together to discuss the plays and I rather timidly said that I thought that "Shadows" needed quite a lot of re-writing. ' I know it does. Tell me what I should do." "Actually I've made a few notes," I said. "Just a minute while I get a pencil." We talked for perhaps an hour, I was a bit bemused to find myself giving notes to Noel Coward, who was actually writing them down. When I finished he thanked me, asked if he could take my notes with him to the Seychelles. He re-wrote the play there and on the first day of rehearsal handed me a little packet. He had bound my notes in a leather folder on the cover of which he had written "Vivian from Noel." He did the same for Irene Worth who independently had made notes on the same play.

To work with him as an actor was more complicated.He had a natural resistance to being told what to do, but a strong professional instinct made him listen. If I asked him to do something, the response in essence would be something like "I don't agree dear — let me try it" as one sentence. Then: "I don't like it — maybe I'll get used to it." Often he did, but if he didn't he would, after a couple of days, suggest an alternative. Often the alternative was better, but if I genuinely didn't like it, he would say a bit disagreeably "alright, alright, I'll do it your way," always polite; but I never though he enjoyed being directed.

ONE THING which he said in rehearsal I found amusing. He had been consistently revising the dialogue of a certain section. I mean not saying the words precisely as written. When I called him on it finally, he said again a bit disagreeably that he was saying just what was written. I showed him the script, and then he laughed and said "You know every good actor's instinct is to re-write th author even when the auth is himself." But he stoppe

However, all these events were more than seven years ago. "Suite in Three Keys" is now "Noel Coward in Two Keys" and it has been extremely interesting for me to observe the difference made to "A Song at Twilight" by not having a distinguished author playing a distinguished author. Maybe this is one more reason why my keenest memory of Noel Coward (leaving aside all feeling of privilege to have workd with him at all) is of an extraordinary gifted man trapped by his own legend. I am certain he would say that in thinking like this I am being a bore but I feel he would be wrong.

Fleur Cowles: she looks at life with gentleness

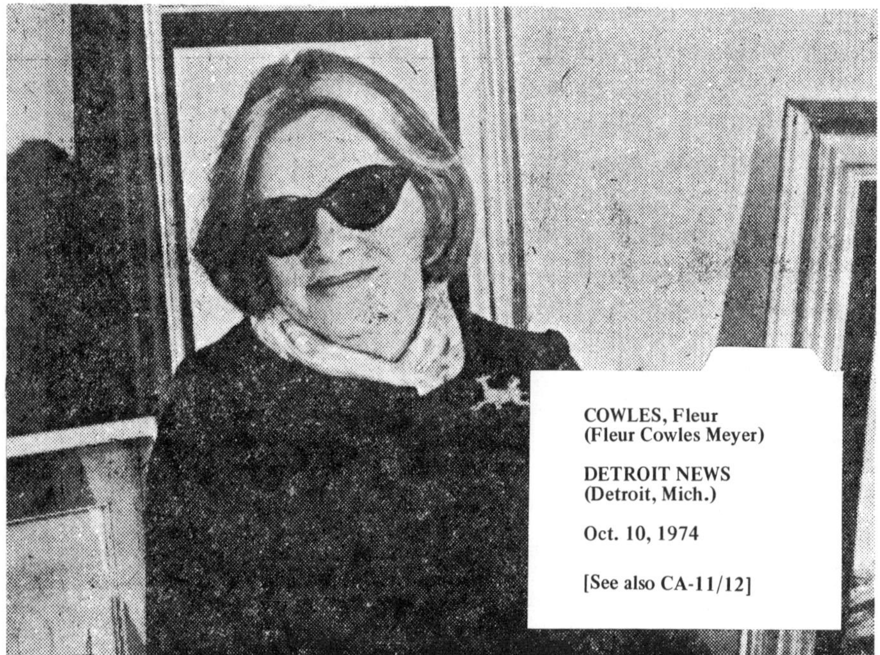
COWLES, Fleur
(Fleur Cowles Meyer)

DETROIT NEWS
(Detroit, Mich.)

Oct. 10, 1974

[See also CA-11/12]

—News Photo by Philip Webb

By CYNDI MEAGHER
News Staff Writer

Fleur Cowles is a quiet woman with a gentle vision of life.

She is a writer, an editor, a friend of great artists and good causes, a woman who has two homes in England and a restored seventh century castle in Spain and, above all, she is an artist herself.

But there is nothing grand about her manner — even when she discusses those who have taken her paintings of tigers, given them claws and ferocious expressions and turned them into wall paper or needlepoint designs.

"My animals are really quite tender," she says. "I paint them with gentleness, not to represent power and all the things that I hate. In my paintings the little things have power, the big things have none. I believe size shouldn't count."

Miss Cowles, who divorced American publisher Gardner Cowles and is now married to a Londoner, is in Detroit this week to open an exhibit and sale of her paintings in the Cranbrook Museum of Art, Bloomfield Hills. The exhibit-sale runs Oct. 14-Nov. 12.

She will be the guest of honor at a $150 a couple benefit dinner in the Museum Saturday night to be attended by some of Detroit's more powerful families. It is a tribute for her donation of a third of the sale's proceeds to the museum.

But yesterday morning she arrived at the Cranbrook Museum of Art in an immaculate but not very chic black pantsuit, her perennial dark glasses in place, to talk about her paintings and to meet museum officials and fundraisers.

The sale paintings — priced from $450 to $5,000 — were still just leaning against walls in the main museum gallery, but a dozen older Cowles paintings, loaned to the museum by friends of the artist, were displayed in a ground floor room.

The old and the new have an otherworldly quality: A giant tiger perched on a mountain guarding a minute town on the rocks below; a boy with birds caught in his tangled hair; a sad-eyed lion with a limp daisy dangling from his mouth; a green owl emerging from a green woods.

Miss Cowles says the boy was painted from a Gypsy boy she knows who does indeed spend hours watching birds. "I have seen him come out of a thicket covered with birds," she says.

He and his birds are the central characters in a book she is working on now, the third in a series of books featuring Miss Cowles' paintings. In each book, the paintings are woven together by a poetic tale written by Robert Vavra, an American living in Spain.

Like Miss Cowles, short-lived venture in an artistic magazine — Flair, which folded in the '50's, a year after she began it — her books contain cut-out windows which turn one painting into two, two into four.

The second book — "Lion and Blue" (Reynal and Company with William Morrow and Co., Inc.; $6.95) — comes out officially next week in New York but is already on sale at the Cranbrook Museum.

She says the books have led to the reproduction, and occasional mutilation, of her paintings in wall paper and needlepoint.

And it is easy to see why: They are bright and simply colored, with a friendly quality — just the thing to reproduce in tiny stitches and turn into a cushion or wall hanging.

"I have no snobbery about what happens to my work," Miss Cowles says. "But I like to have some control just so it is fitted to the purpose it's being used for."

She says one needlepoint canvas on the market is based on a painting she did with needlepoint in mind: "I have seen it done and that is quite all right. It can be quite beautiful."

But the others are not authorized.

She says five years ago she began copyrighting her paintings to protect them from borrowers.

"My animals are tender. When I see them with claws, I want to kill — and I am not a person who thinks of killing easily," she says. "It is supposed to be flattering, but it is really quite devastating."

Everywhere in her paintings are tigers, lions and birds. Only two of the 50 paintings in the show contain human faces, and she says she thinks she will "not paint many more of them — I prefer nature."

She says her husband attributes her love of painting wild cats to an Abyssinian pet cat she owned for six months.

She gently disclaims that notion, conceding only that "Abyssinians are not like normal cats. There is a suppleness to their bodies, and they are interesting. Mine used to stare at me for an hour."

Why did she chose to donate a third of her sales to the Cranbrook museum?

"I have many friends in this area I have known since back when I edited Look magazine (in the early '50's). And I have known about Cranbrook for a long time, too.

"Everybody abroad knows what I mean when I say I am going to have an exhibit at Cranbrook. This tiny little place is well-known in Europe."

As for donating a third of her sales, well, a woman able to restore a seventh century castle in a still-primitive area of Spain in less than five years probably doesn't need the money.

But more than that, she says, is her dedication to art.

"As an artist, my object in life is to have my paintings in museums. That is the final accolade. And anything I can do to feather the nest of a museum like Cranbrook's I am more than happy to do."

(Also see preceding article)

Fleur Cowles Still Has It

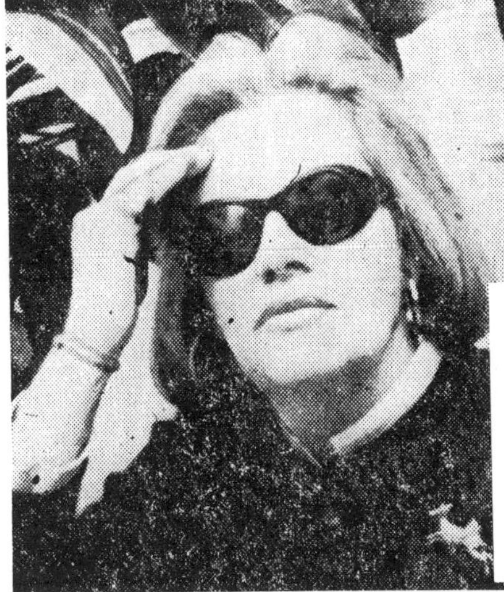

COWLES, Fleur
(Fleur Cowles Meyer)

DETROIT NEWS
(Detroit, Mich.)

Sept. 22, 1974

By JOY HAKANSON
News Art Critic

IN JANUARY, 1951, Fleur Cowles invited 14 cartoonists to illustrate a "smile-and-farewell" obituary for her magazine, Flair.

While the editor's remarks dealt briefly, almost casually, with "rising costs" and "imminent paper shortages," the illustrators took an upbeat view of what made Flair in only 13 issues an innovative, much talked-about magazine.

Some of the tricks which gave Flair its name included:

COVER CUT-OUT: A magician, for example, pulling strings of flags, rabbits, roses, birds and paper dolls out of the trademark hole in Flair's cover.

INSERTS: Paper pullouts and streamers providing group reading for a family of seven and a board meeting of eight executives.

STATUS: Upper-crust New Yorker using Flair-style cutouts in her sculpture, paintings, chairs, tables and clothing.

ELEGANCE: Stubby cars driving through the hole in Flair's cover and being transformed into sleek limousines.

If the tone of her last Flair editorial came across as lighthearted, Fleur Cowles admits now that she was "desperate" when the magazine folded.

"It broke my heart to see Flair die," she says.

TODAY, the creative energy that she once poured into publishing (she also was editor of the late Look Magazine) goes into writing and painting.

She has six books, including "The Case of Salvador Dali" and "Lion and Blue," the latter a new parable due soon.

By sheer perserverence and talent, Fleur Cowles has lived down the label of "hostess-painter."

Divorced from American publishing tycoon Gardner Cowles, she's been married to British lumber baron Tom Montague Meyer since 1955. She lives in London, has a 400-year-old farm in Sussex and a 900-year-old castle in Spain. Hers is hardly the denim-and-loft style of New York painters. Nor are her guests the wine-and-spaghetti crowd.

Visitors to the various Meyer (pronounced Meer) households include Prince Rainier and Princess Grace, Dame Margot Fonteyn, Lady Bird Johnson, actor James Stewart, and kings, queens, ambassadors and assorted celebrities from many walks of life.

The telephone operator in Sussex once called breathlessly: "Oh, Mrs. Meyer. There's a king on the phone but I didn't catch his name."

Although her reputation as Flair's creator might have opened doors, she had to prove herself in a highly competitive art world, where one critic admitted in print that he had come to her show expecting to see "chocolate box surrealism."

Her paintings fit none of the usual art classifications, although they have been called naive, surreal, realistic, literary and illustrative.

The truth is that Fleur Cowles is an original, who creates her own world on canvas.

This is what every good painter does, of course. Except that Miss Cowles' images — outsized flowers, oddly serene jungle cats, exotic birds and insects — seem almost startlingly out of step with the prevailing abstraction, conceptual art and experimentation with organic and industrial materials.

"I frankly prefer to create a world I'd like to see rather than paint the harsh realities around us," she says "So many creative efforts today stress rejection and contempt — a wild 'go' with gun, motorcycle and power tools."

SHE HAD always wanted to paint but didn't begin seriously until 1959, thanks to a shove from the late Venetian artist, Dominico Gnoli, whose family of poets, painters and writers is called "the Italian Sitwells."

Gnoli had been invited to the Sussex farm for a weekend. When he began to paint one afternoon, Miss Cowles asked if she could work with him.

"His condition was that I sit across the room so I wouldn't be tempted to copy," she says. "I borrowed some brushes and composed a still life with roses and shells."

She still remembers how Gnoli jumped up shouting: "You can't do that banal thing. I won't allow you to be so obvious."

When she explained that she was painting things she liked, Gnoli exploded that anyone who could dream up a magazine like Flair must have imagination and memories. "His advice was to create from ideas that already exist in my own mind."

Since that time she has drawn from a store of visual memories — the colors and contours of landscape; the way animals sit, walk and glide; movements of butterflies; the turn of a leaf, or the energy of flowers real and imagined.

Sometimes she changes the scale so flowers dwarf the animals. Or she's apt to insert one picture plane inside another to give a twist to illusion.

"I never draw, never compose, never have a plan," she says. "Memories and ideas just come pouring out as I paint."

She works in her lap even when doing five-foot canvases. She doesn't mind having people around while she's working, and she keeps to a strict three-day painting schedule at the farm in Sussex.

London time is devoted to writing. The new book, "Lion and Blue," which is a successor to the highly successful "Tiger Flower," will be ready for publication in mid-October, about the time she will be staging an exhibition of her art at Cranbrook Academy here from Oct. 12 to Nov. 10.

Prince Bernhard of The Netherlands wrote the introduction. Two paintings included in the book belong to Mr. and Mrs. William T. Gossett, the Bloomfield Hills friends who urged her to exhibit at Cranbrook.

"I'm doing about 40 new paintings for the Cranbrook show," she says. "Some are large, some are tiny and I hope to send a huge screen if I can get it done on time."

She has done other benefits: For the Seattle Symphony in 1970; for the San Fransico Zoo in 1972, and last year in New York for the Institute of the Facially Disfigured of which she has been a trustee for 20 years.

SHE CONSIDERS her style of collection a natural companion to her way of painting. "When I went abroad to live in 1955 I made two decisions: Never to buy anything for its name or label and never to hang a painting unless I knew or got to know the artist personally."

When she's traveling she looks for unknown artists because she believes this personal kind of patronage, if practiced on a large scale, could free talented painters "tied by insecurity to the salable art movement of the day."

Her own collection includes some great names, but only because there is a personal association. She owns several works by Braque, all canvases that she watched him paint during her many visits to his studio in Paris and his farm at Varengeville near Dieppe.

"All my Bombois primitives came to me during the years I called on him in his hideous little Paris house, bringing food, gossiping about art and putting up with his idiosyncracies," she says. "I was probably one of the very few people this old eccentric trusted before he died."

Other artists who did special paintings for Fleur Cowles include Picasso ("a powerful bull recalls a visit to his studio"); Rufino Tamayo ("one of his rare portraits of me in sepia and white"); Salvador Dali ("about whom I've written an authorized biography which took three years of checking to prove all his unlikely stories were true").

Collector Cowles' favorite discovery was Paul Dufau, an old farmer she found in France. He had been painting for 60 years, but never sold a work until she arranged a show for him at a top London gallery.

Other artists she spotted first were British Pop painter Peter Blake ("I picked him out of a London art class in 1955") and Dame Cosmy, an 80-year-old New Yorker ("working non-stop in her kitchen to record her Greek childhood").

She owns several Yugoslav primitives and particularly admires Bible pictures by the illiterate Raimundo d'Olivera, who painted on an island off the coast of Brazil.

"I adore naive paintings," she says. "A Margaret Mead of the year 2074 will have to think twice before ignoring the anthropological aspects of artists taking up their brushes all over the world, quite unaware of each other's existence, yet striking the same note in paint at the same time."

Fleur Cowles Meyer has been awarded highest honors by four governments — France, England, Greece and Brazil. Major museums have exhibited her paintings. The publishing world regards her as a legend for her trail-blazing use of magazine graphic arts. She's even had a rose named for her, an appropriately distinctive pink-beige flower.

Yet, she can become emotional about Flair and the fact that people still remember the magazine after so many years.

"During my exhibit at the Seattle Art Museum literally thousands of enthusiastic men and women brought copies for me to autograph, each describing how carefully it had been cherished," she says.

Flair isn't something that stopped with the magazine. Obviously its editor still has it.

Harvard Theologian Poses Christian Agenda

COX, Harvey Gallagher, Jr. (1929-)

GRAND RAPIDS PRESS (Grand Rapids, Mich.)

Nov. 9, 1974

Dr. Harvey G. Cox, Jr.

In the public mind, evangelical religion and political conservativism are one and the same.

But must a Christian choose between biblical tradition and radical politics? The two are not so different, says Dr. Harvey Cox Jr. There really is no choice at all.

For his audience at Calvin College Thursday night, Dr. Cox, a Harvard divinity professor, reconciled the two "choices" and outlined an agenda that modern Christians in America must act on.

The 44-year-old author, whose bestselling books are The Secular City, The Feast of Fools, and The Seduction of the Spirit, listed four misuses of religion today:

—The messianic attitude adopted by American Christianity that resulted in what Cox called the "American Civil Religion."

—The second-class status of women and the dominance of patriarchal patterns in most major churches;

—The burgeoning interest in Eastern, non-biblical religions in an attempt to find "a better answer;" and

—The failure to examine class conflict in a Christian context.

Cox criticized the American brand of "civil" religion because it identified one nation's people as special missionaries when the Christian gospel was addressed to all the world. "We've been had," Cox said, adding that civil religion has fragmented in the last few years.

On the status of women, Cox urged all churches to immediately open up full participation to women "in all layers and levels."

With civil religion splintered, Cox said, a new search is underway for a better idea, outside the western, biblical traditions. "It bothers me that it's such an easy switch from 'needing to convert everyone in the world' to 'everyone else has a better answer' ", Cox said.

The final item on the agenda, Cox said, is also the most difficult. "There is no society in the world to emulate," he said. "There are no models." He added he rejected portions of Marxist theory on religious and intellectual grounds.

But, he said, "Class conflict is real. There are enemies of the poor who have made them poor and want to keep them poor. The bible doesn't say people shouldn't have enemies; it says they should love them."

Cox's view of social action does not include "reformist" politics that merely reconcile class differences. He admitted a point will come when Christians should "exacerbate" and intensify the differences.

Cox pointed to Latin America where Christians are "deeply devoted to the gospel and equally devoted to the liberation of their continent. That's no surprise — people in bondage were the people who first responded to the gospel when Christ preached it."

Cox described his own fusion of political and evangelical traditions beginning with his varied religious background — bits of Pennsylvania Quaker, Conservative Baptist and "frontier revivalism."

"By the time I was 17 and joined the merchant marines," Cox said, "I had been genuinely saved at least twice that I can recall."

While touring eastern Europe after WW II in the marines, Cox developed a view of Eastern-Communist bloc politics. "By the time I got to college," he said, "I was a member of the New Left before the New Left was invented. But I was still committed to evangelical Baptist faith."

In 1948, when he campaigned for Henry Wallace's Progressive Party bid for the presidency, Cox said he was told by his peers in the Inter Varsity Christian Fellowship that "no Christian could possibly support that Pinko.

"I wavered between making a choice between the two. After the election, the party collapsed and Inter Varsity went on, but I was left with this rift in my soul," he remembers.

The schism was bridged and his present ministry is within a 12-family community at Cambridge that shares incomes, homes and property. "It's a small tiny, insignificant step," said Cox, "but more Christians should be taking them."

Sears Inspired Novelist in Harry Crews

CREWS, Harry
(1935 -)

MIAMI HERALD
(Miami, Fla.)

June 30, 1974

[See also CA-25/28]

By AL BURT
Herald Staff Writer

Harry Crews has decided maybe he will get off the freaks for a while. Maybe it is time to try something else. He is getting a reputation as a kinky guy. For seven novels now, a fascinating menagerie of freaks has crept out of his typewriter. Inside their heads, they have some normal ideas, but they are trapped by their outsides.

There are freaks of beautiful bodies, and freaks of incredibly misshapen bodies, but either way the burdens are too heavy. There are midgets and fat men and cripples mixed in with go-go dancers and sideshow entertainers and evangelists and physical culturists. They intertwine through a bizarre kind of counterpoint that produces unusual appetites and enterprising means of satisfying them.

In his new book, for example, Crews' hero is a deaf mute whose legs are so useless he ties them under the seat of his trousers. The young man lives in a gymnasium with an elderly weightlifter and two wasted boxers, and makes a living with a sensational hand-balancing act. Marvin may be the world's greatest hand-balancer. He can pirouette slowly on one finger, holding it for applause. But he is too grotesque to make the big-time. Ed Sullivan could not use him because his head is too big and square and his body is too ugly with his legs all tied up like that.

CREWS CALLS this parable **The Gypsy's Curse** (Knopf, $5.95) and it is a gem. Underneath the sex and hairy language, there is the anguish and pain of the freak who can live only by exploiting his freakishness. The Curse, for Marvin, is finding the perfect sexual partner for Hester, a blonde beach beauty looking for someone who will love her enough to kill her for being faithless. Even in perfection, Marvin loses. Again, a theme of unbearable cost in perfection and unbearable burden in imperfection. It is all very kinky.

"Not long ago," said Crews, "Playboy magazine sent word they wanted me to do something for them. The guy said they had a very kinky idea they thought I would like. Cocaine. They wanted me to write something about cocaine. I said, 'Aw, no, man. Do you know where I live? Not that. Maybe something else.' "

Crews paused for a moment, making his point. "Yeah. Oh, yeah. No question about it. I got a reputation as the guy who writes the kinky stuff. Somebody pretty soon's gonna call me up and when they do I'm gon' say, 'Yeah, but I want you to come down here and talk to me about it first' and then I'm gon' beat the s—- out of him. Somebody's gon' ask me if I don't want to go somewhere in a coverup in a carnival of freaks, you know, and watch a guy eat a live chicken, or something." He laughed.

CREWS, 39, looks a little like a primitive who has tried civilization and was unimpressed. He lounges about his lakeside cypress cabin, about 25 miles east of Gainesville, in faded jeans and wrinkled shirt and tennis shoes without

(Continued from preceding page)

socks. His hair is long. He has the expressive face of an actor and his hands leap about in emphatic gestures. He is a remarkable man who seems to speak several English languages, in addition to the one he writes so beautifully. He shifts roles, going from the Georgia farm boy to the boisterous ex-Marine to the philosophical recluse to the college professor.

Crews teaches a course in writing two nights a week at the University of Florida in Gainesville, and helps conduct a writer's conference once a year. But he lives and works here in the cabin, which has a fireplace, a couple of beds, a kitchen and a table in the back where sits the old Underwood standard typewriter on which he has written all seven novels, plus numerous short stories and essays. He has no telephone, either here or in his university office, and he will not permit mail delivery at home because he finds it distracting. His ex-wife and their son live in Gainesville.

"One doesn't mind the fact of the matter," said Crews, getting back to the business of freaks. "It's just the harping on it. All fiction is about the same thing. It's about a man doing the best he can with what he's got to do with. That's how I feel about it.

"I have to insist when somebody starts talking to me about freaks . . . That's not my word. We're all freaks, but just in different ways, most of us. To dwell on this business of the freaks and to dwell on what they call the Gothic novel offends me, yeah. I hadn't even heard of one until everybody told me I was writing 'em.

"ANOTHER THING they talk about me being a southern novelist. It's true I write in the South and it's true that's where my sense of place is and sense of people is and sense of language is. But hell, every writer has to have that. You know, some guys are in the Midwest, some guys . . . Norman Mailer's a New York Jew, you know, and he knows about that. John Updike knows about Pennsylvania and he's got that little town there . . .

"But even if those things are true, it seems to me sort of beside the point to harp on them. It doesn't demonstrate anything, it doesn't prove anything, it doesn't open anything up, illuminate anything. You know, I'm just not particularly fond of that.

"But I tell you, I have the feeling in me, and maybe it's just a feeling, I've had wrong feelings before, but I have the feeling that there is going to be some sort of departure in my work, that I'm going to do something else. I mean, I'm going to still write novels. Man, I started out to be a novelist. That's what I want to be. That's what I care about.

"I also like to write short stories, but unfortunately what you gonna do with them? Yeah, you can publish them in literary magazines, which is where all mine have been published, and they've been anthologized. You can publish them. But man, it gets back to audience and the rest of it. Short stories are hard to write. Hard to write as anything else. So what've you got? If you're lucky, you've got 1,900 or 2,000 readers. S— man.

"What I'm trying to say is, I think either the subject matter is going to change — and I don't know what I mean by subject matter because you know I got novels about boxers and sponge fishermen divers — I guess it's not subject. I guess it's more the form of the thing. Maybe that's what's going to change. I don't know. But I just have this feeling in me. Maybe I'll do two or three books of nonfiction."

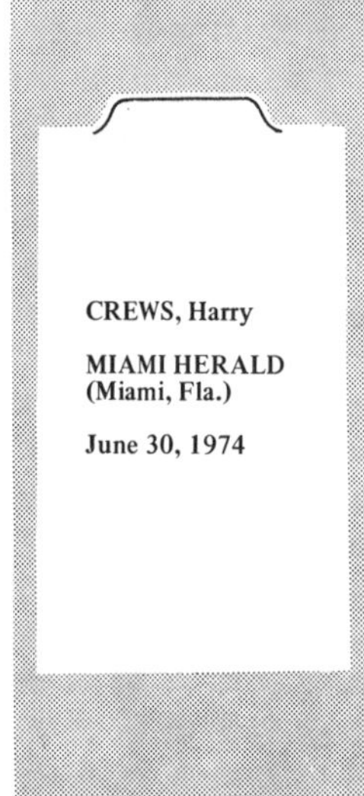
CREWS, Harry

MIAMI HERALD (Miami, Fla.)

June 30, 1974

The National Endowment for Arts, a federal project based in Washington, recently awarded Crews $5,000 to use professionally as he pleases. Two years ago, the American Academy of Arts and Letters gave him a grant of $3,000. "I like those grants, man," he said, smiling. "Yeah."

Crews has decided to use the money for an exploration of his own life as a boy in Bacon County, Ga. "It will be a biography of place. The focus will be me, autobiographical. It will be about those people up there and that time." It also would be his first book-length non-fiction. Whether it will be a conventional narrative, he does not know. "Something in my head resists that. But it can be nice, if it's done right."

The idea began last summer, when Crews spent seven weeks walking the Appalachian Trail from Georgia to Maryland, carrying along a photographer and a tape-recorder, collecting information and anecdotes. "I talked to people all along. You'd be dumbfounded, you'd be just dumbfounded at the stories that I got off that trail. Things that people told me and I heard and I saw. Really kinky, great things, right?" Part of that time, the description might have fit Crews himself. His hair grew down over his shoulders and he wore one golden earring.

CREWS TRIED to splice together his experiences on the trail with memories of his boyhood in Bacon County. But later, he decided that wouldn't work. Now, he plans to separate the two. The trail hike will be one story, and Bacon County another. He likes this better. The last couple of years, he has had this feeling that he needs to know more about himself and his beginnings. Going back to Bacon County will satisfy that urge.

"I think so. I think so," he said. He speaks rapidly, often in broken sentences, but the communication remains clear. "Yeah. For a long time I didn't know that. I grew to manhood without . . . Some of the language, you know. Some of the things we said. Things like, 'He's so stingy he wouldn't give you the steam off his s---.' A beautiful line, the steam off his s---. But the kids that always had bathrooms and things, they didn't . . . That must be a mystery to them when they heard it. Be out in the woods, or out on the ground, or even the outhouse. Hell, when it's freezing, it steams. You know, the ground's frozen. Very colorful, immediate, graphic, concrete language and those people, you know . . ."

The University of Florida has given Crews an indefinite leave of absence and he will go up to an uncle's farm in Bacon County (Alma, Ga.) and get reacquainted. "I want to talk to guys that knew my daddy," Crews said. "My daddy died when I was 18 months old. I never knew him. I grew up on faded photographs and, really, kind of legends. He was really a good man, but a strange man, a mean man, a lot of kinds of man. He died on the farm in the winter time, of a heart attack."

Although the language and the themes of his novels are not exactly what the rural folk in Georgia might find pleasant reading, Crews thinks the state has treated him well. In Bacon County, or over near his mother's present farm closer to Tifton, Ga., he has celebrity status. One reason for that may be, he thinks, that more have heard he is a writer than have read his writing.

"My mother only went to the second grade, and they just insisted she be on the board of the little library. Ma's never read a book, except the ones I've written. Only ones she's ever read. Takes her about six months to get through one of my books but she's one of the best readers I ever had. People find that strange. I mean, I've got a Baptist mother that's lived in the country all her life, one of those good women, and I don't mean that pejoratively, I mean that straight out, good women. She never blinks at anything that I've written. She's been around the block. She knows what's in the world. Doesn't bother her. She knows a word's a word, that it's not the deed or the fact, you know. No. Ma at one time is primitive enough and sophisticated enough to know that it's all magic, anyway, and that's the way she feels about it.

"She's dumbfounded, for instance, that anybody would pay you money to write something that wasn't true. You know. That really amazes her. When I wrote **The Gospel Singer** (the first novel), when I finished it, I called her up and said I sold it, I got this much advance, and so on. Later on, when I saw her, she said, 'Son, you didn't pass that off as the truth, did you? You didn't tell 'em that?' I told her, "No, Ma, that's not the gig.' "

Everything started for Crews in Bacon County, his love for the physical side of life, storytelling, his awareness of the perfections and imperfections of people, an annoying conscience, an insatiable curiosity, absorption with the unusual, a boiling kind of drive inside him to try new things, a battle with self-doubt, a compulsion to illuminate the whole thing.

"I got started in all this long, long before I ever had any notion . . . I was writing stories when I was just a little kid. I wrote 'em for my family and told 'em. I started telling 'em before I started writing 'em, for my friends. Mostly, with the exception of my brother, my playmates were black. You know, we were out on the farm. We used to get together and . . . I can tell you exactly how it started.

"THE WAY it happened, it started with Sears, Roebuck catalogue. We used to spend a lot of time looking at the thing and, among other things, here were all these perfect people. All these perfect people. Every- ➡

(Continued from preceding page)
body we knew was damaged, had sores on their legs and their fingers cut off, but here were all these beautiful, perfect people in this book and they were so well-dressed and they were obviously human. I would make up stories to account for the things they were doing. You know, 'See this man in the red coat, well this girl here's his daughter and she's gonna marry him on this page back here and he don't like him because he don't make his money just by standing there in that red coat. He's the deputy sheriff on the side . . .' So, anyway, I got into that."

Crews joined the Marine Corps at 17, served four years, and enrolled at the University of Florida. Predictably, he became restless and left for 18 months, but the burden of writing ambitions brought him back in 1958. Andrew Lytle was a writer-in-residence at the University of Florida, and Crews became first his student and then his disciple. "The only reason I've never dedicated a book to him is that I've never written anything I thought he'd want his name on. He's a demanding man," Crews said. The Lytle encounter was important to him.

One year of teaching junior high school English in Jacksonville, after graduation, sent Crews scrambling back to Gainesville for a master's degree. With that in hand, in 1962, he shifted to Broward Junior College in Fort Lauderdale, again to teach English. The year **The Gospel Singer** was published (1968) he returned to the University of Florida, where he has remained. Since then, a new Crews novel has been published each year. The others: **Naked in Garden Hills** (which he thinks was his best), **This Don't Lead to Heaven, Car, The Hawk Is Dying, Karate is a Thing of the Spirit** and, this year, **The Gypsy's Curse.**

"I wrote another book called **The Enthusiast** which I really liked a lot, at least I liked it a lot while I was writing it. I suppose it came out of my life in a way. It was about a guy that just everything he got into, he made a passion of. I got into karate and I did **Karate Is a Thing of the Spirit.** I got into hawks, I trapped and trained hawks and wrote **The Hawk Is Dying.** The books are somehow always after the fact. But anyway I wrote this book and it felt good the whole time I was writing it. But I never sent the damned thing off. Put it in a drawer. It just didn't work, finally. You know, you try to lie to yourself at first. It'll come back another time. The work is never wasted. Ten years from now, all that'll come back," he said.

Sometimes, something just works. The first time he drove to the farm near Tifton he got lost. He was working on **The Gospel Singer** then. He wandered into a town called Enigma, Ga., "I said God, that's where it happened. It's gotta be it. But I changed a lot of things around, like the highway, and the swamp. You know, I didn't want to p—- off the people in the town. I got nothing against them. But I did manage to do it."

NAKED IN GARDEN HILLS found its way into a phosphate excavation because Crews was driving from Vero Beach to Tampa, and wandered through Mulberry, the phosphate capital. **This Don't Lead to Heaven** came after a visit to a nursing home, during which he feigned sickness in order to leave quickly.

Despite the pace at which he drives himself, and his expanding interests (he has written and sold screenplays of two of his books and sold a third to the movies with the script to be done by someone else), teaching has never seemed a burden to Crews. He not only likes it, but in a way depends upon it to bring order to his life.

"No, it's not a burden. I'll tell you why. I guess the biggest reason is this. You get stuck when you're writing. Everybody knows that. You get stuck and you just don't know what to do, and it looks like the thing's gonna die on you. Maybe you've got three or four months in it. So you sit down . . . I work every day. I don't give a s—- whether I know what's coming next or not. I work. At least I sit at the typewriter. I tell myself, 'You go sit there three hours. You don't have to write anything. Just sit there.' So pretty soon you write something, just try something, and you find your way out. But sometimes it's bad, and you know it's bad. When that happens, at least me, I get really down on myself. I begin to doubt everything. I think, 'Hell, you weren't a writer to start with. Now you've got this charade. You really ought to . . . I just say terrible things to myself. Then, voila, I go to school.

"I LIKE to teach, see. That's the weird thing about it. I really do, I enjoy it. The students, they're honest, they'll run you up a tree. They won't take much phony stuff. I go in there and teach a sensational class. Just get in there and just wing and talk and get 'em excited and get all . . . When I come out of the class, I think, well, buddy, you might can't write, but goddam, you sure can teach.

"I've got a sort of theory in my head about that. I think every man ought to have more than one thing he does well. He doesn't have to get his bread by it, but if he's just really a good, competent, fine, amateur butterfly preserver or coin-collector or Sunday painter or bicycle rider or anything, so that he can go out there and get his head clean . . .

CREWS, Harry

MIAMI HERALD
(Miami, Fla.)

June 30, 1974

"You see, I don't think of writing as a job. I think of it as a, almost like an avocation. I would be writing novels if nobody was publishing them. I'd write novels if I had to send them out to sea in a bottle. I just know I would. So I really don't think of it as a job. At school, that's a job and it kind of gives direction to my life and, you know . . . I'm pretty bad to drink. As a matter of fact I will stay drunk on you for a while, from time to time. I would rather, all things being equal, I would rather not disappear into a bottle. It seems to me that's a cheap way to go. Having a job, having to go to the university, having students I'm responsible for, keeps me straighter than I otherwise would be. The hardest thing for me is to control my personal life so I can do the amount of work I want to do. I need to work. I have guilt feelings if I don't work, sourceless anxiety.

WHEN WRITING first draft material, Crews forces himself to sit at the typewriter three hours a day. Three hours at that stage exhausts him. Later, rewriting or revising, he might stay with it 18 hours. When he started writing **Naked in Garden Hills,** he had an idea and one line, "Wherever he was, it looked like he had been there forever." That started as the first line in the book, describing the fat man, but at the end could be found 200 or so pages back.

"When you've got that first page in the typewriter, of course, you been thinking about something for a long time, but you don't quite know what it means. There's a little bit of an idea in there. I start with a place and somebody and then I just try to know the story. All he needs to know is to be able to trust in his knowledge of craft and technique to discover the story.

"Robert Frost said all his poems ended in surprise and discovery — discovery for himself. You know, when he started out with a poem he really didn't have much at all. He talked about that little poem, 'Stopping by Woods.' He said, 'When I started that poem all I had was the first line, and so I then proceeded to try to write a second line in which I was consistent with the commitments made in the first. Then I wrote a third . . .'

"Well, that's the way I work with fiction. What apprentices don't understand is the important thing is not the f——— story. It's not any of that. The important thing is the writer whose perceptions all of this is being filtered through. The writer's vision of the world. It doesn't matter what he writes about. My writing will have a certain taste and a certain smell and a certain sound. Nobody's going to confuse Faulkner and Hemingway, no matter the story. I go on feeling when writing fiction. I don't give a rat's ass where the novel's going."

CREWS SAID he has learned more from reading Graham Greene, the British author, than anyone else. **Power and The Glory** is his favorite. "It's not so much the subject matter as the consummate skill. He's as accomplished a writer as I know, and both a popular and a critical success." He noted that Greene suffered the blackest kind of melancholy and depression. Both Greene and Crews have been accused of sacrilege in their books, a charge that bothers Crews.

"I wouldn't do that," he said. "I take all my books to be about the nature of faith. How does a man come to believe what he believes? How do you get to belief and how do you hold on to it? God, wife, job, whatever. I feel a sense of responsibility.

"Greene always insisted upon the right to portray the unbeliever as powerfully as the believer, the crippled and the halt as powerfully as he portrays the perfect. What most people want, out there in the suburb, is a papier-mache villain. A guy really powerful and really bad at the same time scares them. The devil in Milton's **Paradise Lost** came out heroic, saying it was better to rule in hell . . ."

Romantic, sentimentalized writing angers Crews. "Chekhov said learning to write is learning to murder your darlings. We've all got this kind of mush thing in us. We can't write about that. We've got to write about it the way it works."

The way it works, for Crews, is parable and metaphor. His darlings came out of the Sears, Roebuck catalog and he murdered them long ago. He trotted them out and brutalized them with truths that made people squirm. Now he will go back to Bacon County, Ga., where it all began, and turn that withering vision upon himself and his people.

Meanwhile, another novel percolates. "I'm going to call it **The Feast of Snakes,"** he said. "It's about these snake roundups. I went to one up in south Georgia not long ago. What's got me wanting to write the thing is the fact that here are these people catching these goddam rattlesnakes and they're eating them and they've got a beauty contest . . . People hanging on the wire and looking at the snakes. Lester Maddox was there and led us in a little hymn while he played his mouth harp and all this s - - -.

"Now, I want to find out what that means. Your ordinary ass on the street will say it don't mean anything, folks get together and they just eat the snakes. No, no, no, you can't s—- me. I watched those ladies. They want to eat some of that rattlesnake and they just been hanging on the pen looking at 'em where they're all writhing in there. And they get over there and the husband says, 'Aw, come on Dolores, just put it in your mouth honey. It's just like fried chicken.' I don't know what all that is, but I want to know. That's the kind of thing . . ."

Novelist mines a rich literary vein

Robert Crichton

Photo by Margaret M. Grieve

By MARK FINSTON

Everybody asks Robert Crichton about it. Everybody wants to know how come the paperback rights to his best-selling hardcover "The Camerons" brought the unusual figure of $700,001.

"Oh, that embarrassed me," says the gentle-seeming, articulate, tall (6-6), 49-year-old author. "It was to surpass some other previous record for such a sale. That's what the extra $1 was for. I've forgotten the name of the other book. Though it happened, what, almost two years ago, it's still the record for what is considered a novel."

Crichton, whose previous best-seller was "The Secret of Santa Vittoria," hasn't exactly let all this money cause him to overextend himself. He admits, half ruefully, half humorously, that, compared to himself, Jack Benny is a wild spendthrift.

* * *

"I was out walking with an editor just yesterday," he is saying in his book-lined, four-story brownstone house in the West 70s in New York. "I chipped through some solid ice in the sidewalk just to get a penny I saw stuck down there."

He says it rather quizzically, as if he doesn't quite believe it himself.

"If it were left to me, this house would have about eight pieces of furniture." (Fortunately, it isn't left to him. His wife, Judy, a TV producer, doesn't leave it to him nohow.) "When I go downtown, I walk. That's not for exercise. It's to save 35 cents on the subway. I never buy anything for myself. I never buy ANYTHING."

CRICHTON, Robert
(1925 -   )

STAR–LEDGER
(Newark, N.J.)

Feb. 12, 1974

[See also CA-17/18]

* * *

As you talk with Robert Crichton, you get the impression of warmth and humor. And something else. You get the impression that here is a man who enjoys seeing himself as somewhat more eccentric than he is. A lot of people do it. Not all are writers.

"When I got through with The Camerons', I wasn't very happy," he says. The 510-page book took him four years to write.) "I did the last 78 pages in one day. I was going to a party that night. My editor was to be at the party. I threw the whole pile of pages at him. I did it with such defiance! I couldn't remember for weeks and weeks how I ended the book.

"I know one author who got through with his book and decided to go to bed for 40 days. After 30 days, though, he wanted to get up."

Crichton smiles approvingly. He wouldn't go to bed for 40 days "because I'm a great walker of the streets," but it is apparent he admires someone who could make that decision.

"When a man finishes a book, words are his enemies. That's what Hemingway was quoted as saying. I remember I once sat down and spent an entire morning trying to write a coherent note to the milkman telling him we didn't want any more milk. I'd lost control of the English language."

* * *

"The Camerons" is a spellbindingly good story about the poverty of Scottish coal miners at the turn of the century. It started out as a portrayal of Crichton's own family; his grandfather was a Scottish coal miner who emigrated to this country. But by the fourth draft of the manuscript, Crichton's family had all but disappeared, to be replaced by totally fictional individuals.

Crichton's research even included descending into the mine where his grandfather once shoveled coal. The author sent a piece of coal home as a momento. The U.S. Customs people marked the lump "One Piece Sculpture-Modern." Friends of his four children dropped over to admire the "beautiful stone."

"Finally, the piece of coal dried up and fell apart," recalls Crichton.

* * *

The grandfather worked as a miner in Pennsylvania, but Robert's father went to New Mexico to cure a TB condition. The father, Kyle Crichton, from a sanitorium, started contributing vignettes on New Mexico life to publications — which started publishing them.

He married the daughter of an ex-governor of the Arizona-New Mexico territory; Robert was born in Albuquerque.

Ultimately, Kyle Crichton went to New York, became an editor at Scribner's, and started doing freelance articles; he contributed 80 stories a year to the old Collier's. The family lived in Queens ("Quite a culture shock," says Robert.) In 1935, at the height of the Depression, Kyle Crichton was earning $85,000 a year.

* * *

"My father had two rules," says Robert. "One was, 'Never check an interesting fact.' The other was, 'Make up your own dialogue — it's bound to be better.'"

Another move, this time to Bronxville. Robert did poorly in school.

"I was never under pressure to achieve anything at home," he says. "I flunked the 10th grade, and no one in my family even knew it."

Robert was sent to a Catholic prep school in Rhode Island — Portsmouth Priory. Always adept in athletics, he took schoolmate Robert Kennedy's place on the football team, and he also knew Kennedy at Harvard.

* * *

"Bobby was slow and small," says Crichton. "He was relentless as can be, though — he made the best of what he had. In practice, he kept trying to belt me for taking his place. We all felt he was going to become a monk. He was extraordinarily dedicated to the Church and its rituals. At Harvard he hung around with the football players. He gave absolutely no indication of any intellectual interest beyond sports."

After prep school — Crichton did very well — he was drafted, and was mustered out when enough mortar shells became embedded in him to classify him a disabled vet. With GI Bill money, he went to Harvard, majored in nothing ("They didn't make disabled vets major"), but took creative writing courses in which he did very badly.

He ran a chicken farm in Newtown, Conn. for a while, until a 1950 storm killed 80 per cent of his chicks. His father got him a job as a junior editor at "Argosy" ("It was a pretty good magazine then.")

"My re-writing of other authors was so heavy, they thought I better start doing the articles myself," he chuckles. "I was fired and re-hired four times. Maybe that's one reason I'm a writer — I couldn't hold a job doing anything else. They wanted me in at 9:30 in the morning. I think in two years I was only on time once.

"And I wasn't reliable. I once took an author's manuscript home to edit, and I lost it in a Third Avenue bar. To cover the loss, I invented my own article. My story was better, and I tried to sneak it through. this upset the real author."

* * *

He got married, started freelancing ("I knew a lot of people in the trade"), and began having children "one after another, though I was a great believer in Planned Parenthood."

Much of the time he was broke, then someone called and said, "Bob, you're a fraud in your own right. You're the man to do Fred Demara's story." Demara, the great imposter, became the subject of Crichton's widely-read nonfiction tome, "The Great Imposter," which was made into a movie starring Tony Curtis.

There are four Crichton children: Sarah, 19, a junior at Harvard, who wants to go to law school; Rob, 17, a basketball player at Brown, who also wants to go to law school ("I don't know where they got THAT"); Jennie, 16, a senior in high school, who wants to be a novelist, and who has written four novels, none of which she has yet permitted her dad to read; and Susie, 14, whose present ambition, according to her father, is to "help the world."

And Robert Crichton has a second cousin who is a well-known author: Michael Crichton ("The Terminal Man.").

* * *

"No one mistakes him for me," says Robert. "For one thing, he's taller. He's six-ten, I'm only six-six. We know each other, but we're not friends. He's the cool Crichton. I'm not hot, but I'm certainly not cool."

Robert Crichton is now "sorting things out" for his new project: A book about World War II, to be titled, "The Poor, Miserable, Rotten, Stinking Infantry." Crichton served in the infantry in 1941 and 1945.

* * *

A painful craftsman, who often does check interesting facts, he is now "getting close" to a first draft.

"I hope to get it done in six or eight months," says Crichton. "I can't see how it will take any longer, but it probably will. During the actual writing, especially if it isn't going well, I get very irritable. During 'The Camerons,' someone tape recorded me at a party. My irritability was astonishing. I don't know how anyone tolerated me."

And Crichton, who seems an eminently tolerable individual, appeared a bit proud of himself.

'Being a Critic Is 95 Percent Egomania'

Bulletin Staff Photo by Jack Tinney

"REVIEWING is a dream job: to see all movies and get paid for expressing your opinion — that's heaven."

By LESLIE BENNETTS
Of The Bulletin Staff

IT IS SAID that Elizabeth Taylor once broke down and sobbed when she heard what Judith Crist wrote about her. Grown men regularly bellow and rage over her opinions, and some take revenge in an icy snub—until their next movie comes out, when they flock to curry her favor once more.

Movie critic Judith Crist tends to grin and shrug at such consequences of her acid-

CRIST, Judith (Klein)
(1922-)

PHILADELPHIA
BULLETIN
(Philadelphia, Penn.)

Nov. 21, 1974

tongued pronouncements, as well as at other barbs.

The other night Mrs. Crist came to Cheltenham High School to speak at the Township's Adult School series. The packed audience of 1,500 remained respectfully attentive and delighted at all of Mrs. Crist's pungent comments—the more outrageous the better—except for one man who got up and demanded whether the critic's "many years of watching movies have left you so jaded that your perceptions are warped."

"It always puzzles me that people don't ask their dentist whether their perception of cavities is warped because they've seen so many," mused Mrs. Crist, who swears that she still thinks something wonderful is about to happen every time the lights go down and the music goes up for another movie.

"Sometimes the sensation doesn't last more than three seconds, but I still get the feeling," she added.

Mrs. Crist sees at least half a dozen movies a week, mostly in private screening sessions several weeks before the public opening. There is nothing the least bit private about her opinions, however—or her unrelenting enthusiasm for expressing them.

"Being a critic is 95 percent egomania," she says briskly. "You wouldn't be doing it unless you really believe, "I see'."

Of movies she doesn't understand, she adds, "' . . . and if I don't see, it's his fault."

Adjunct Professor

"It's a teacher-preacher complex. Anybody who teaches is a frustrated performer. So of course I loved the Today Show—it was Show Biz! And there were 4 million people watching me!" She beams.

Mrs. Crist, who is currently an adjunct professor at the Columbia School of Journalism (where she got her own master's degree), as well as movie reviewer for New York Magazine and TV Guide, was for 10 years the movie critic on NBC's Today Show, and for more than 20 years a reporter for the New York Herald Tribune.

"I always dreamed that if only I weren't fat and unbeautiful, boy, would I like to be Bette Davis—or Katharine Hepburn, with those cheekbones. I went on TV once locally, during a newspaper strike, and it was like wine."

With the power that she now wields, does she ever change her mind after she has delivered an opinion?

"Nah—I'm a stubborn old lady," grins Crist, who is 51.

Despite the didactic tone of much of her commentary, one of her more impassioned messages is a plea to all those apparent zombies out there to criticize right along with her.

"I talk about my own personal truth, but what I want is to share an awareness so people will react. I don't care if they disagree with me, but for god's sake, react! It's so quiet out there!

"It's time for people to start protesting this assault on their senses in all the terrible movies. The nuts always write in; the good guys never do.

"And what critics say has very little effect. Every critic has discovered that you cannot kill the bad. The best a critic can do is to push the good a little bit. People complain all the time about movies, but we're being given the sex and violence because we're buying the sex and violence. If they were not bought, they would not be manufactured."

Frequent Challenge

Mrs. Crist is exasperated by viewers who go to a movie and then look to the critic with "Now tell me what I'm supposed to think."

To the frequent challenge of, "What makes you a critic," she replies, "Essentially we are all critics—and I'm not being humble. All a critic does is to think."

What Judith Crist thinks of a large number of current films is that they're abysmal. "Many films today are not intended for anyone who can read or write," she says sternly. "Airport '75" is not intended for anyone over the age of 8. But we have many 8-y e a r-olds masquerading among us, as we all know."

There are few words strong enough to express all the dire things she thinks of a movie like "The Exorcist," a box-office smash. However, Mrs. Crist points out that movies are no longer the mass medium they were in the days when people went three times a week, whenever the fare at the local theater changed.

"That old assembly-line product has vanished, as film-making became highly individualized.

"This was traumatic to some moviegoers, who have operated on the assumption that all movies are for all people. No! All television is for all people. People are always asking, whatever happened to those wonderful old family movies. Well, they're on television now, in half-hour segments, every night of the week. And that's where the mass entertainment public has gone."

Although she stresses that it is television that molds our society today, rather than the movies where people go only irregularly, she adds, "Anyway, movies don't pervert society, whatever is in them. Movies are only a reflection of our society. What we are is what's reflected in movies. They even anticipated Watergate, with the endless films that glorified criminality on every level, all those rip-offs and capers."

Glories of Yesteryear

If the implications of today's movies are frightening, the glories of yesteryear were not all that healthy either. After commenting wryly on the unfortunate assumptions instilled in children brought on in movies in which relationships between men and women were abandoned to the blank mysteries of the "fade in/fa de out" at the crucial moment, Mrs. Crist adds, "It's a wonder any of us ever grew up to lead normal lives."

She feels it was foreign films which injected a desperately needed note of realism into American movies. "Suddenly we began to see things we had never seen on the screen before. One of the first things we saw were rotten teeth. It's rather horrifying to think that until about 1960 you never saw an imperfect tooth on the American screen," she remarks drily.

"And clothes even started looking as though the people had been wearing them — at least once before."

Mrs. Crist's clothes, it was noted in whispers by scattered members of the audience, almost looked as though she had slept in them. The famous movie critic and television personality was far frumpier than all but a few of the suburban matrons who had come to hear her. They, however, seemed wholly enchanted with her tart tongue.

Mrs. Crist, who lives in Manhattan in a roomy co-op apartment on the West Side, is married to Bill Crist, a public relations advisor for a nearY COLLEGE. She is also the mother of Steven, who is 18 and goes to Harvard. The Crists escape whenever possible to their weekend home, a geodesic dome in Woodstock, New York, where Mrs. Crist takes an eight-week vacation every year to "just vegetate."

"No television, no movies — and by the fourth week I start to get the shakes. I'm like an addict — I need a fix," she says cheerfully.

Staunch Defender

Although she deplores much of what she sees on the screen, Mrs. Crist has always been a staunch defender of anyone's right to see it, and an outspoken opponent of censorship. Asked what she thinks of the existing film rating system, she replies, "I think the whole system is absolutely asinine, because it's predicated on centimeters of pubic hair and frontal views and other such nonsense. Anyway, I think everyone should see a triple-X movie. You don't win by abdicating. You gotta know what you're going to contest."

She sighs. "And you've got to see 'Deep Throat' to see what we're down to defending. The day has passed when you arrived at the barricades clutching James Joyce's 'Ulysses.' You get there today and what you've got is 'The Devil and Miss Jones.'

"What I have been seeing in movies is scary. The movies are only signaling where we're all going. The day has come when everyone must function as a critic, and speak out."

CRONKITE
First a Newsman

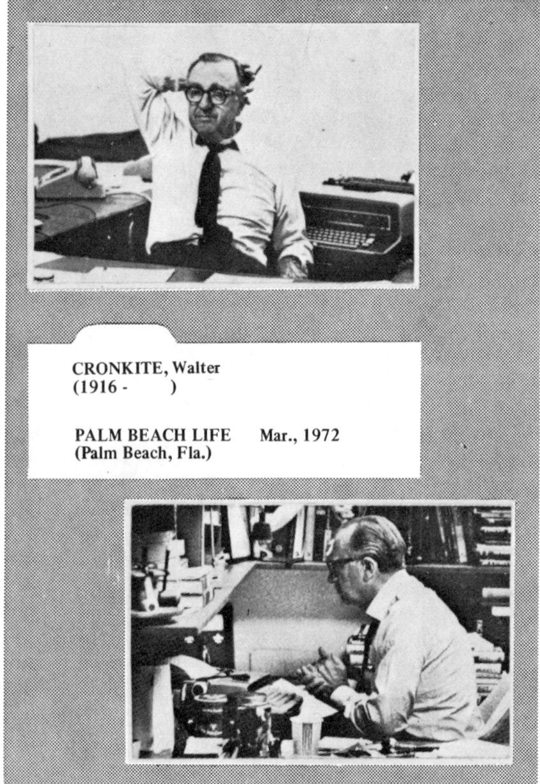
CRONKITE, Walter
(1916 -)

PALM BEACH LIFE Mar., 1972
(Palm Beach, Fla.)

By NANCY BELLIVEAU

A television writer for a national magazine, reviewing a recent CBS show hosted by Walter Cronkite, remarked somewhat facetiously that "Walter Cronkite again plays the role of Jehova, which was written for him by God." While this may be overstating the facts a bit, it is nonetheless true that as anchorman for television's longest running and most successful evening news show, Walter Cronkite has become somewhat of a national institution — the all- American father image, in living color each weekday evening. If Walter said so, it has to be true.

A major ingredient in Cronkite's phenomenal success has been his insistence on strict objectivity in the reporting of the news — to the point of refusing to do commentaries because he fears they might ruin his credibility with the public. This makes it all the more interesting to interview the man — to find out what thoughts lurk behind that dignified and generally unflappable exterior.

The setting for the interview — Cronkite's office in the CBS Broadcast Center on Manhattan's west side — belies the awe and respect he has achieved at CBS. It is a tiny, cluttered cubicle crammed with books, papers, trophies, autographed pictures of Cronkite with public figures (Agnew but not Nixon), models of Apollo space ships, and a few light touches — a statue of Snoopy in astronaut gear and an official "Spiro Agnew Hardhat." Two walls of the cubicle are mostly glass, looking out on the tiny, noisy newsroom where the evening shows are taped, and where Cronkite spends hours with his writers putting the program together. Cronkite, who spent the first half of his career as a newspaperman and UPI correspondent, insists that he is not a mere "conduit" for the news at CBS and accepted the title of "managing editor" for the evening show.

"It disturbs me," he muses, "that my newspaper friends were so critical of the title "managing editor" when I took it. They accused me of trying to play like I was still in the newspaper business. But this is precisely what I do!"

Cronkite assigns the television crews, has total veto of content, and edits every word that goes on the air — occasionally writing a story himself. He is such a perfectionist about the content of each show that he is busily rewriting, editing and changing the order of the news right up until the final moments before air time. One observer of a taping said that watching Cronkite during the last few seconds before going on the air is like watching a beautifully choreographed Apollo countdown. He sits behind his big desk, turning rapidly in all directions, grabbing copy, penciling in changes, conferring with his writers, and allowing makeup men to dab something on his forehead — without missing a beat. Then, as if by signal, he straightens his tie, runs a comb through his hair, and puts on his coat, with only a few seconds to go. And right on target, he whirls around to face the cameras to intone his famous "Good evening . . ."

In discussing the show, Cronkite admits that one of the most difficult parts of the job is deciding what news stories will be crammed into the half hour broadcast. "This is really the ultimate editorial discretion," he says. "People say we show bias in our reporting, and I disagree, but there is certainly an awful lot of individual discretion in what we put on the air." He lights up one of the innumerable pipes on his desk, leans back, and puffs on it reflectively. Cronkite is obviously onto one of his favorite topics: "You know, across the country, all editors seem to make the same judgments. On any given day you'll find the front page of the *Kansas City Star* is not that different from the *Baltimore Sun*."

The same is true for television news, says Cronkite. Often the order of news stories is the same for all three networks in one evening. (Cronkite has the advantage of personally monitoring the competition each night, for he tapes his show at 6:30 and NBC and ABC don't come on until 7:00). After a major presidential announcement he recalls the eerie sensation of seeing the same shots of the President on all three networks at the same time "with even the words of the President synchronized."

But what about the frequent accusation that New York television and newspaper journalists somehow constitute a "liberal Eastern press " with their own unique viewpoint that they are forcing on the rest of the country? "That would be easy to deny," muses Cronkite, "and I'm not sure it doesn't exist. But on the other hand, I'm not sure it wouldn't happen in Kansas City or Atlanta. Newsmen everywhere are inclined to be more liberal in their political philosophies, to be more concerned with people than institutions." Their common experiences make this true, guesses Cronkite. "They have seen the clay feet. They've seen the organizational brutality and callousness, in government, business, or social worlds, and as a consequence they become a little more cynical."

The press, he continues, is apt to react faster than the public to the fads of the moment and therefore to acquire a distaste for them much faster too. "For instance, the guys on the beat got pretty disgusted early on with the leaders for the dissident minorities. They seemed to have no programs but chaos and disruption." The liberalism of the press, insists Cronkite, is no more apt to lean far to the left than it is far to the right. "It is a true liberalism, not doctrinaire or hidebound, making up your mind on each issue and person as they come along. If this is a true liberal, then I guess I qualify as one."

Cronkite is annoyed by those critics who maintain that most press coverage is somehow slanted. "There's a ➡

(Continued from preceding page)

demagoguery on the part of those who attack the press," he says, "and all political parties, not just the current administration, are guilty." He points to the 1968 attacks of the Democrats after the conventions. "It's an attempt by politicians to transfer any lack of credibility on their part to those who are critical."

The public, maintains Cronkite, often agrees with these critics because they are responding more to the news and press reports than how they report it. "They just don't want to believe the worst — that things are as bad as they are," he says. "This war has done it. It's a terrible confrontation between duty to country and our consciences, and the press exposes that raw wound every day. The public doesn't want to believe My Lai, that American boys could do that sort of thing. So they fall back on 'we have got to follow our leaders . . . they know what is right.' "

CRONKITE, Walter

PALM BEACH LIFE (Palm Beach, Fla.)

Mar., 1972

One critical blast at the press, above all others, however, made Walter Cronkite lose his cool. And that, of course, was the famous speech of Vice President Agnew, to which many journalists felt Cronkite overreacted. "My strident reaction offended my friends in the press and government," admits Cronkite. "I hadn't played the game. You're supposed to walk out of the room with your arms around each other. You're not supposed to take this sort of thing seriously, and I did!"

He is annoyed at suggestions that he acted "naively" by saying what he did. "Hell, I've been used to criticism all my life. Why the first story I ever covered for the *Houston Press*, a politician stood up and pointed at me and ranted and raved against me for half an hour. 'There's that reporter from the *Houston Press* . . . see how he smiles at me?' " The Agnew criticism, insists Cronkite, was far different. At the root of his concern was the federal government's "life and death power" to issue licenses to broadcasters.

"I believe there is a serious danger in this country to free communication — and not from this administration necessarily, either. It's in the general structure, economic and political, of the news media." Cronkite explains that with newspapers becoming more and more monopolistic and broadcasters licensed by the government, there is very little in the ways of checks and balances on each other to maintain objectivity. "No matter how dedicated they are, newspapers are subject to all the mistakes and whims of a monopoly," he maintains. "And the broadcasters, who could be a monitor on those newspapers, are government licensed. What Agnew did was invoke the possibility that if you don't hew the line, higher authority will have to do something about it." Cronkite feels that as long as the government has this power, Congress will feel they have the right to investigate broadcasters. "And while the networks are big and powerful, the local stations, the small guy in Kansas City, are very beholden to their senators and congressmen."

This is not the first time in recent history that there has been a threat to press freedom, points out Cronkite. "In the early '50's, both Democrats and Republicans seriously considered a government 'press council' to judge and control what was said. "The journalists rose to the barricades on that one, and there was a great deal of debate within the profession. What annoys me about the written press this time, is that they won't come to the barricades with us."

Cronkite bristles at any suggestion that by responding to Agnew the way he did he proved he could "dish it out but not take it." "I was badly misunderstood by my colleagues," he says. "I think politicians *should* hit back every time, and straighten out the record if they can. For example, Johnson still thinks that the press brought down his administration . . . he is very bitter about it. I maintain we should be concerned only when the people being criticized suggest some type of controls over their critics." The Agnew attacks have had their effect, says Cronkite. "We're more inclined to wonder who is looking over our shoulders as we edit our copy. There is an awareness there."

What about the much-discussed "polarization" of the country that received so much attention before and after the Agnew speeches? Does he feel that his division between left and right is still a real problem in America? "I think it is on the decline," says Cronkite. "We've been through a trial by fire and everyone's a little winded. Many are realizing that violence doesn't settle anything. This is particularly true among the black leadership."

The quiet attitude of at least one group of Americans, however, does not leave Cronkite so benign. "It's kind of frightening what has happened to the youth," he says. "On the one hand, I'm glad of peace and quiet. But on the other hand, by golly, they have shown again that where we thought there was a genuine streak of idealism, they are typically human and responsive only to their own comfort." With the "hot breath of the draft" no longer down their necks, Cronkite feels young people are no longer as passionately involved. The low youth voter registration figures, for instance, he finds "depressing." Could it be that the young people have merely given up, having decided that nothing can move an impassive government?

"I find that attitude unrealistic," says Cronkite. "My feeling is that they are inclined to be concerned about their own little world, and when that was threatened, they got involved.

"The performance of the McCarthy followers in 1968 was abominable," he continues. "They were saying that if they couldn't promote their own man, they wouldn't work at all. They showed a total lack of understanding of what the democratic system is all about. I agree with the calls for reform. But the convention adopted some of them. Now the kids complain about Nixon, but they elected him! If they had just gone out and backed Humphrey, even though he was the lesser of two evils, he could have won."

In the long run, Cronkite thinks the so-called "youth revolution" may have some very positive effects in decreasing the polarization of American society. "Remember, there are a helluva lot of people who are parents of kids who have gone into a more liberal environment. I think this has tempered them. The "go and never darken my door again" attitude is really old hat today, if it was *ever* true. I think in most families the attitude is "gosh, Johnny is a good boy. If he believes this, maybe it has merit."

Walter Cronkite speaks very much from experience on this topic, for he has two daughters in their 20's — both married and away from home. The younger is an active conservationist and the elder is "fairly apolitical and turned off. But I see her changing. She is coming closer to the belief that you have to get in there and do something." This, says Cronkite, gives him reason for hope. "I haven't lost heart because of my disappointment over their present attitude."

Then he leans back with the mellow smile of a man who has covered many upheavals in his over 30 years as a newsman, "As a matter of fact," sighs Cronkite, "I'm glad for the surcease." □

(Also see preceding article)

CBS' trusted Mr. Cronkite

By MICHAEL H. DREW
of The Journal

NEW YORK, N. Y.

IN WALTER CRONKITE'S eight page CBS biography, a list of awards and honors takes up nearly two full pages. Time Magazine called him "the single most convincing and authoritative figure in television news." A survey by Oliver Quayle and Co. of public figures' "trust rating" found Cronkite the winner. Then there was the recent cartoon in Saturday Review/World in which a beleaguered TV viewer was clasping his forehead and shouting, "Anita, come quick! Walter Cronkite says the sky is falling!"

To be sure, there is a quality about this fatherly 57 year old, sitting across from me in his small office just off the "Evening News" set, that inspires confidence. "What is it?" I wondered aloud, and Walter Leland Cronkite Jr. seemed startled.

"Well, it's mainly longevity," came the reply, after a pause, "a successful culmination of hewing to the middle of the road without bias. Others are doing as good a job or better.

"But they do commentary and are classified as to ideological bias and that hurts them."

Is objectivity a daily problem?

"The biggest problem is keeping opinions from others' copy. I've been in this business 42 years and it doesn't weigh on me, it's automatic. Sometimes I have to ask myself, 'Do you really know that's true or is it an assumption?' And sometimes I'll do an analytic wrapup on a story, without comment."

Forty-two years. Apparently Cronkite is counting his reporting days on the school paper and yearbook in Houston, Tex., where his father was a doctor. He attended the University of Texas, worked on the Houston Post and, in 1937, joined the United Press. Cronkite spent most of the next 13 years with UP, covering several Allied invasions and, after the war, establishing bureaus and covering the Nuremberg trials.

In 1950, he joined CBS. For the last quarter century he has covered virtually every major American news event for the network — political campaigns, space shots, assassinations. (Another famed cartoon had a lady proclaiming firmly to her husband, "I just won't believe it until Walter Cronkite says so.")

That kind of responsibility could weigh heavily on a newsman. And as he talked slowly, in that familiar ringing baritone, feet up on his desk, a certain weariness crept through.

"I'm prepared to take a job with less pressure. When I leave this there are things I'd rather do than a daily column, like Eric Sevareid's. Perhaps a couple of documentaries a year on which I could spend some time."

There are pressures that Walter Cronkite would rather not talk about. To get into his office I had to pass between two standing armed guards, added since the Hearst and Atlanta kidnapings. Does he have a bodyguard?

"No, but I'd rather not talk about it because even that increases the nut quotient."

America's most respected newscaster was wearing a striped shirt and square horn-rimmed glasses. The hair is steel gray, the jowly face moderately flushed after two sets of morning tennis.

Cronkite's office is small but substantially appointed in walnut and leather with a boat painting and boat model (sailing is his favorite sport).

"Doing interviews like this," he was saying, "keeps me from making decisions that I should be participating in. As co-equal executive producer of 'The Evening News' I have ultimate responsibility for what goes on the air.

"I think we're doing our job about as efficiently as we can, or we'd be doing it better."

How about charges that network newscasts overlook the common people and their problems?

"We can't cover all segments simultaneously. Our job is to appeal to the greatest number of people most of the time. Special interests can be covered by other broadcasts and special publications."

Mention threats to press freedom and the mild mannered reporter (who resembles a younger Melvyn Douglas) turns into a fiery Superman.

"The danger is real and increasing. We're under considerable threat on several fronts. Though it's not likely that the press will lose its freedom, it doesn't take long for dictators to gain momentum. In two years, the Nazis took over the press.

"Government attacks have had their effect. Like any propaganda, if you say something often enough, some people will believe it. Also, people are sick to death of the news and we get blamed for it.

"Another big danger is one newspaper ownership in cities. Most are dedicated to the public good and don't let their position affect their judgment, but it does provide the opportunity for inadequate coverage.

"Newspapers are falling down in the same areas they blame broadcasters, with some incredible criticisms. They cite our commercials and then make readers chase through the ads by breaking up their stories.

"News 'holes' aren't as big as they should be, which gets back to papers' need for profits. The networks, by comparison, are puritanical. We could triple our ratings if we ran the sex murder stories which newspapers print, as circulation grabbers.

"They criticize our ratings' battles but before they all were monopolies they had circulation wars. In our fights, nobody is breaking up TV sets. Newspapers doll up their front pages with trivial pictures.

"I'd do away with the government's equal time and fairness doctrines. Some stations would have more virile coverage. We're one monitor of the press' inadequate coverage and we're under government control."

Though it was clear that he enjoyed his subject I led him back to TV's transgressions. How does he like "happy talk" chatter between newsmen?

"It denigrates the news and hurts our image. I should think that the public would be suspicious of stations that do it. Network news is more responsible and can afford to hold on to principles. I'm not sure that the public likes happy talk all that well."

Over the years he has interviewed the world's leading newsmakers and the results have led to several awards. What is his secret?

"You have to be conscious of the time available and the subject making sense; you make your questions clear so that the answers are distinct. If the interview isn't taped you must get right to the subject with hard questions.

"Actually, I'm the soft kind of interviewer, without the show biz quality of a Mike Wallace, who sometimes generates heat instead of light. TV's power is that we get to hear things right from the newsmaker's lips, to see them in action.

"It gave me a chance to meet, this year, people like John Dean, Archibald Cox, Leon Jaworski and Bebe Rebozo. There was no earth shattering impact in the content.

"It's important for me to get away on trips, like the presidential visits to Peking and Moscow. If I don't get assignments, I make speeches — about 20 or so a year — to get feedback on how people are feeling."

What new techniques are aiding networks?

"A minicamera which anyone can handle to tape on the spot or transmit back to the studio. It will make the cost of remotes cheaper."

Should President Nixon resign?

"I'd hate to see it. I think an impeachment proceeding would be preferable, though I'm not saying he should be impeached."

What are the most serious problems facing America?

"Divisiveness, which began in the McCarthy era.

"Lack of tolerance for dissent. The immediate problems are inflation and the lack of confidence in the administration."

Americans have plenty of confidence in Walter Cronkite. Richard Nixon and Co. would love to have his credibility.

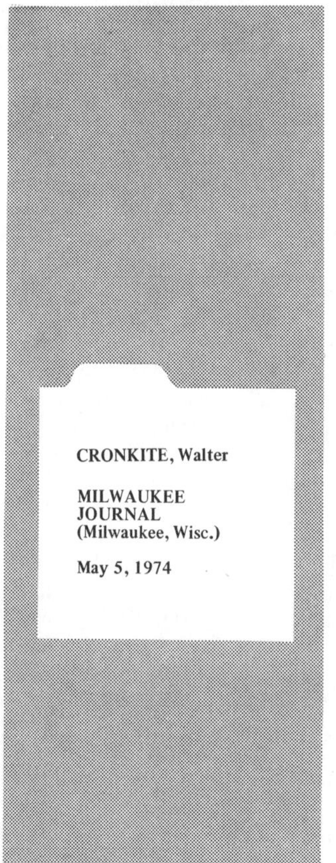

CRONKITE, Walter

MILWAUKEE JOURNAL (Milwaukee, Wisc.)

May 5, 1974

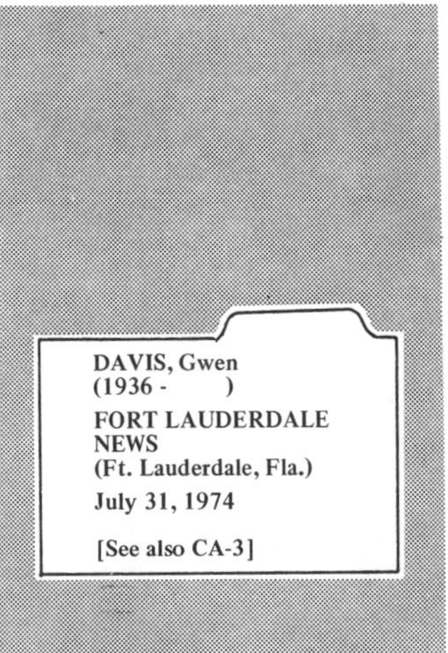

She's 'Gung-ho' About America

By RITA CICCONE

Staff Writer

Gwen Davis is a writer with a great sense of patriotism.

She admits to being a flag-waver and wears a replica of the American flag all the time. Even her selection of clothes tends to be red, white and blue.

"It's probably out to be so gung-ho about the government right now," Gwen said, in a telephone interview from her Malibu, Calif., home. "But I wear these colors because I really mean what they stand for. This is a time when popular faith is needed in the concept of this country. The concept is brilliant, only the execution is a mess."

Gwen's wild rash of patriotism came before the advent of Watergate and long before she started writing her newly released novel "The Motherland" (Simon and Schuster, $8.95), a brilliant story that takes a family from the Depression to the 1950s and deals with corruption in American politics.

She started the book in 1959 while getting her master's degree in creative writing from Stanford University, but she salvaged only 11 pages of that first draft for the released version. Meanwhile, she has written seven other novels, including the best-selling "The Pretenders," about New York's Beautiful People.

"The Motherland" was finally completed after her return from England where she and her family went in 1971 with the intention of living there "because I was disgusted with this country an all the apathy."

Gwen felt strongly about America in 1959, but she said things just seem to be going downhill and leaving the country was her answer for saving her sanity. Once back in the States, however, she began to feel that America was turning away from all the lies and darkness and returning to all the ways we were supposed to be.

"We might not be the best we could be," Gwen said, "but we're sure the best there is. We were on the verge of losing our freedoms and now we're going to get them back in time for the Bicentennial so it can be a real celebration. I think the founding fathers, instead of turning over in their graves, must be all around us, helping us get it together.

"Patriotism is getting better. What is happening in Washington right now, what is unfolding before us, is the greatest drama in history. And what makes it even greater is it is not being done with guns but with law. We're bearing witness to the survival of the best political idea any group of people ever had, which was the concept of this country and God."

Her sense of humor slips in as she details the idea of lower taxes, "for all, but as it turns out, only Nixon made out on that."

Gwen believes President Nixon will be impeached but she doubts the Senate will convict him.

"This is such a fantastic drama," Gwen said, "Only Congress could make it boring. I'm looking forward to going to Washington to host a talk show on a local television station. I'll be attending the debates and discussing them with other people on the show. From where I'm sitting, it appears everyone in Washington has too much information, too many facts and can't show the truth. It's like they can't relax their eyes. Unfortunately, the committee proceedings have become something akin to a locker room after a football game. I mean, when someone says 'Take it away, Jack' to John Chancellor, it reminds you of a sports arena atmosphere. I feel the whole business is much too serious to be treated lightly."

Gwen is a vivacious, funny lady who takes her country seriously. When her call came 15 minutes late from California, she explained she was sorry, but she couldn't seem to get her make-up on right. She moaned a little when questioned about her bio.

"Yes, it's all true," she said. "I was born in Pittsburgh and Oscar Levant did advise me never to admit it. I did go to Bryn Mawr and then to Paris to study music. I was filled with the dreams of Hemingway and Fitzgerald and resolved not to speak another word of English or mingle with Americans."

That lasted three weeks and she ended up selling Herald Tribunes in front of the American Express, hoping desperately to run into someone even slightly resembling an American, she was so lonely.

She sang in a Paris nightclub, played flamenco guitar in Spain, translated television shows from English to Americanized English in England and wrote songs and musical comedies.

Back in the States, she went to Los Angeles and worked in a nightclub, where a literary critic suggested she write a book about her experiences. That was the start of her writing career.

"I'm always amazed when I read my bio," Gwen said. "The whole time I was living my life, I thought I was missing it."

Much of the background for her new novel came from her grandfather, "who was a great storyteller and had all the fervor an Patriotism of all immigrants." For the financial dealings she drew on her experiences as a customer's representative on Wall Street.

"For the political party of the book I got a blessing," she said. "My best friend from Bryn Mawr is married to an attorney for the Pentagon. He is a noble Republican. I try to hear and I try to osmose, to pick up feelings, facts and history. What I write is a melange of all the emotions of my life."

Gwen is a registered Democrat. She says that does not sway her feelings about right and wrong in government.

"My next book will be non-fiction." she said. "I have such strong feelings about things that have happened to me in the past few months. For instance, John Dean moved in next door to me in California just before we moved to Malibu. The house we're living in now was used as a polling place in 1972. I had just been on a tour of the White House the week Agnew resigned. I'll be in Washington the week the impeachment vote reaches the house.

"All of the happenings seem to be an omen. If I'm a witch, I only practice white magic. Seriously, I do feel this country is on the verge of a spiritual renascence."

That fact, plus politics of this country, how to write an almost blazing first novel, and how to become your own woman are among the topics Gwen will be lecturing on around the country in the next few months.

"This wasn't something I planned," Gwen said. "But after 'The Motherland' was released, I started getting requests to speak before various groups. So many women have said they feel my book has given them great hope because it shows that a woman doesn't have to be what she thought she had to be."

Evelyn, in "The Motherland" is a dynamic protagonist a feminist before her time. Gwen says if Evelyn was living in today's world, she would more than likely be the head of General Motors, but only if she had the right connections.

"I think a woman in industry has got to find some way other than her charm, brilliance and ingenuity. Women still have something to prove, something to overcome.

"I suppose I am liberated. I'm married to producer Don Mitchell and we have two children, Madeline, 8, and Robert, 5. I've tried to bring the children up nonsexist but it's very difficult because they live in the world."

Gwen says she has developed "typewriter elbow," which is something like "tennis elbow" but she still hasn't written everything she wants to write or said all she feels should be said.

"I'm looking forward to getting to know many people across the country on my lecture tour. Hopefully, I'll be in your area during my travels. I want to share as much as I can with as many people as possible, and not just in books."

(Also see preceding article)

DAVIS, Gwen

PITTSBURGH PRESS (Pittsburgh, Penn.) June 14, 1974

GWEN DAVIS

Sonnet of love to family misinterpreted.

Kin, Friends Read Novel, Shun Author

By SYLVIA SACHS

Gwen Davis, Pittsburgh-born author of eight successful novels, now knows a heartbreaking truth learned some decades ago by another American novelist, Thomas Wolfe.

"You Can't Go Home Again," the title of a Wolfe novel, became a metaphor to illustrate that you can't write about a time, a place or a people that remotely resemble your own background unless you are ready to cut all the ties that bind you to that past.

"My family here isn't talking to me," Mrs. Davis reported, obviously shaken.

"Oscar Levant once told me never to admit I came from Pittsburgh," she rushed on. "But I never felt that way. My book is a sonnet of love to my native city and to my family.

"I love those people (her family) more than any other people in the world, just as I love Pittsburgh. I thought this was a free place in which to grow — that my family had dignity, humor and more love than any people I have ever known. They have always given each other so much love, so much compassion. It is a really beautiful family, the family I come from."

Mrs. Davis' latest book, "The Motherland," is the cause of her heartache. It is a big, sprawling, sometimes comic novel about a woman from a large Pittsburgh Jewish family who strikes out to achieve the materialistic goals of her generation. Now the book has raised the ire of her Pittsburgh relatives who take the portrayals as unflattering ones of themselves.

'Laid A Trap For Myself'

"People just don't understand what fiction is," Mrs. Davis moaned. "I laid a trap for myself with 'The Pretenders' (an earlier book) which was gossipy and was thought of as fictionalized fact. I don't write that way any more.

"In 'Motherland,' I wrote a saga of a family and an era. I thought, 'What better place to start it than in the city I love?' People don't understand that a novel is something you make up. Otherwise it would be on the non-fiction list. The characters I made up from Pittsburgh are a beautiful, loving family.

"It is not the Depression any more, but people still think that poverty is a sin," Mrs. Davis said, hitting the table.

"There is nothing wrong with not having money (like characters in the beginning of the book). That is the point of the book. The heroine gives up real riches she had here in Pittsburgh . . . she gives it up for money and politics and finance. And all she gets is grief.

"Cary Grant is a fan of mine. He bought five copies of the book and sent them over with his secretary to be autographed. He called me to discuss the book. He wanted to know where he could find a woman like Grandma.

"It is heartbreaking to me and really amazing. Everywhere I have gone since this book was published, people thought I was writing about their family. I have written about a universal family.

"And readers think the senators are the Kennedys and the rich men the Rockefellers. A girl I went to school with, one of the three richest girls in the world, isn't talking to me because she thinks she is in the book."

Still Defends Her Work

Crushed by her experience here when the family she always visited refused to see her, Gwen Davis still rises to the defense of her novel and fiction in general.

"We need fiction today because you can pretend the world is the way it is inside the book. You can have a few days away from today's horrors, like a vacation in another country."

But, she emphasized, a bit choked up:

"People must get over the notion that fiction is fact. They must also get over the idea that there is anything shameful in being any kind of minority group. The family in the book is not my family, except that I love them both.

"This is my farewell appearance in Pittsburgh," she said emotionally. "I feel like Sarah Bernhardt — or Sarah Heartburn, as my grandfather used to say."

Hearing her own words, rather melodramatic-sounding, she realized, she smiled and added, "But like Sarah Bernhardt, I can change my mind."

Yael Dayan: Quest For Normalcy

By KRISTY MONTEE
Assistant Living Editor

Staff photo by Henry Fichner

As former Israeli defense minister Moshe Dayan spoke before thousands of pro-Israel demonstrators in New York City Monday his daughter sat quietly in Fort Lauderdale, waiting her turn at the podium of the Plantation Women's Club.

Her father had come to speak of politics and war, to protest the United Nations' recent recognition of Arab terrorists.

Yael Dayan had come to talk of life and peace.

The Israeli author and journalist has lived war and politics for most of her 32 years. Her father is a charismatic war hero. Her mother, Ruth, has been actively involved in immigrant employment and Arab-Israeli relations. Yael herself has studied political science at Hebrew University in Jerusalem.

But she did not talk of politics on her 10-day swing through the country to raise funds for the United Jewish Appeal. Rather, Yael spoke of Israel's new struggle for normalcy in the shadow of war.

Born in a village near the seaport of Haifa, Yael now lives in a suburb of Tel Aviv with her two young children and her husband, a colonel in the Israeli army. A dark, quiet beauty, she doesn't share the piercing glance of her father. She speaks softly with authority and seemed slightly tired at this leg in her campaign.

As author of several novels and one book on the 1967 war based on her experiences as a war correspondent, she looks at the progress of her country with the mixture of warmth and detachment of a Sabra (a native Israeli.)

The recent influx of immigrants from all parts of the world has complicated war tensions in Israel now, she says. But while the worst is over, the real work has just begun.

"We have already accomplished the most difficult tasks," Yael said. "We have absorbed people from backward countries, one million Jews from Arab areas who came to us with nothing.

"Now we will spend the next 10-15 years homogenizing our culture."

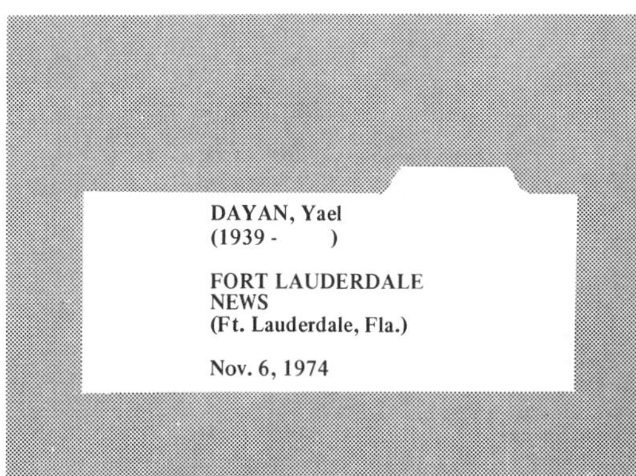

DAYAN, Yael
(1939-)

FORT LAUDERDALE NEWS
(Ft. Lauderdale, Fla.)

Nov. 6, 1974

Speaking before the Plantation Women's Division of the Jewish Federation later in the morning, Yael denied that there is a "mood of despair" in Israel now. People there are saddened by war, she explained, but Israel's social need now is not for war "but for life."

Yael picked up a newspaper and scanned a front page story of the New York rally where her father had spoken out against the U.N.'s decision to permit the Arab guerrilla Palestine Liberation Organization to take part in a Middle East debate next week.

Although war is a constant threat, Yael says Israel is striving to conduct life as usual.

"Tel Aviv is a large city, our cultural center like New York and people lead normal lives there now," she said. "Now, we're in a period of relative calm, of course, but even during the war you could still go to Tel Aviv and have a nice vacation if you were not emotionally involved. And people feel more secure there now than you would feel in Miami."

Yael thinks Israel's young people, who enlist in the army at 18 for an average of three years, are leaders in the quest for normalcy.

Their pragmatic approach to Israeli life, often misinterpreted as waning nationalism, is actually a stabilizing influence balancing the parents' emotionalism of their generation.

"There is no generation gap in Israel," Yael counters. "The only difference between the old and the young is they have different tasks."

Young Israelis are faced with building their new country, she explained, a job as important, but perhaps not as exciting as that of their parents.

"It is exciting in its own way but just not as glorious as before," Yael said. "I don't see it as a falling of enthusiasm on the part of the young in Israel. It is simply not as heroic to build up industry as it is to settle marshlands.

"The young people are just as strong in their devotion to Israel as past generations but they are directing their devotion to more prosaic needs."

One of the country's greatest social demands currently is accomodating the newly-arriving immigrants who must in many cases, must be helped to make substantial adjustments to their new way of life.

Yael claims it takes the average Russian immigrant two to five years to fully integrate into Israeli society. In addition to obvious culture and language obstacles, Russian Jews must learn to handle their first real freedom.

"Coming from a background opposed to personal initiative, they often do not understand the ways of a society built on initiative," she said. "Given sudden freedom, they can abuse it, such as the right to strike."

Immigrants often have a much less tolerant view of Arabs, particularly the Arab population still living in Israel. "We have lived with the Arabs and accept them but they tend to take an extremist view and see all Arabs as unknown entities they resent deeply."

For the American immigrant, the adjustments are of an entirely different nature Aside from learning to abandon many of the creature comforts to which they are accustomed, American Jews living in Israel must adjust psychologically.

"Israel as it is today is burdened with so many tensions," she said. "It is not a calm society and American immigrants must be prepared for a period of aloneness."

But despite a period of relative calm in the Mideast, Yael doesn't think peace is in Israel's near future.

She says total peace is still at least 10-15 years away and that it will not be possible without Israel having to relinquish some of it's new territories, particularly in the Sinai.

"It is not important what we give back," she said. "But rather what we get in return. We will not give at all if it means enduring constant belligerence."

She also recognizes the possibility of more disruption of life, a pattern she says Israel's young and old have simply learned to live with.

"We just want to live a normal life and that is not heroic in pioneer terms. But if people are called on to fight, they will do it and do it with enthusiasm."

An Embittered De Marco Tells Her Story

BY CHUCK THURSTON
Free Press Staff Writer

"And now," Fred Allen would say in his nasal New England tones, "the five De Marco Sisters." Then there would be a pause in the walk up Allen's Alley while the five little Italian kids, aged six to 17, sang a pop song of the '40s.

Arlene, the youngest singing De Marco then, is 36 now, the bitterly divorced mother of two girls. She writes trashy books to pay off old bills and to keep the kids in groceries and clothes. The first two novels, "Triangle" and "Make Believe Children," came out of her past and reflect her own rotten childhood and mixed-up adult life.

She was in Detroit recently to talk about her books, and her tumultuous, unusual life.

"Four of the five De Marco Sisters are divorced," she said. "Only Terry is happily married (to actor Murray Hamilton). The one De Marco brother, Billy, is a successful musician and song writer. Billy married the nurse he met when he had an appendectomy."

Arlene went through a stormy marriage with actor-director Keefe Brasselle. Twice, early in the marriage, she tried suicide. The first attempt was with pills.

The second time, almost a year later, Arlene was pulled back from a roof edge.

"It was in London," she recalled, "following a physical and vicious fight. Two people pulled me back. My feet were cut from whatever it is they use to make roofs in London.

"I think people mean it more when they try to jump than when they take pills."

The two daughters, Rosana and Melissa, now 10 and nine, came along after the rooftop episode.

Brasselle was earning about $75,000 a week with five television shows.

THEY LIVED high, with a houseful of servants and things like that. But in the late 1960s Arlene decided to change all the locks. No more Mrs. Brasselle for her and her daughters.

After that came a fast toboggan slide to welfare for Arlene and the girls.

"It is a man's world," Arlene said. "It's a man's world in fidelity. It's a man's world when you try to collect alimony. What is alimony anyway but child support?

"It's a man's world in the courts, too. You go into court to try to get some help and they give the other side a continuance. That means another six months."

Brasselle wrote a trash book based on his Hollywood experiences. Arlene's friend, the late Jacqueline Susann, wrote "Valley of the Dolls" and other works of pseudo-biographical art. These books spread like wildfire among people who played guessing games about which character was really Judy Garland, which was Cecil B. DeMille or whomever.

It occurred to Arlene that a book might be her ticket off welfare. She was running out of hockable mementoes from her marriage. Her first book, "Triangle," appeared in 1972.

"I do many things," she said. "I draw and paint and I'm still interested in music. I don't claim to be a writer or that my books are art. You can't write four-letter words and call it art. I write sexy, trashy books purely for the bread."

Arlene has strong ideas about raising her girls by herself.

"I broke up my marriage," she said, "to save the children. It is better for them to live with one sane person than two insane people. I have no use for these people who say they string along together for the sake of the children.

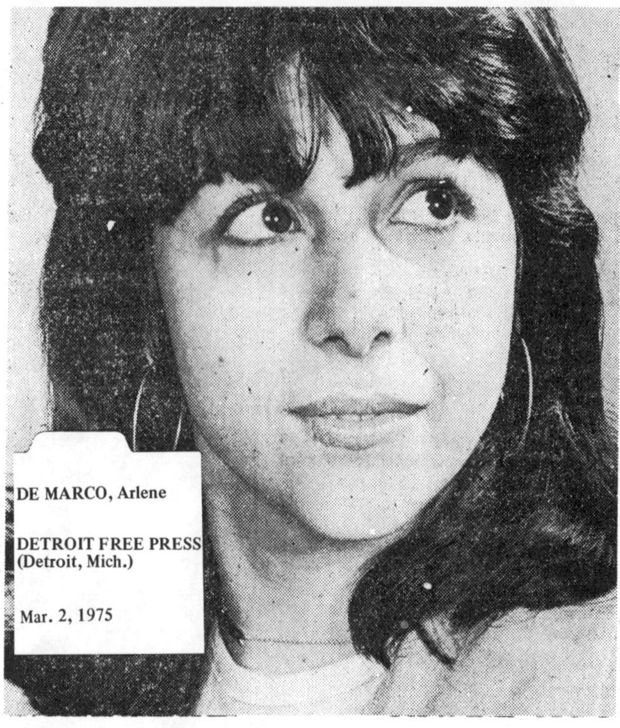

DE MARCO, Arlene
DETROIT FREE PRESS
(Detroit, Mich.)
Mar. 2, 1975

"They are setting up their children to be dope addicts."

ARLENE IS PROUD of her two girls. Rosana, a Girl Scout, won a dance contest this week while her mother was on the road plugging her second book. Melissa is a Brownie.

Though they are still broke, Arlene and the girls get along well enough and she has paid back every cent of the $279 a month welfare that she drew for two years.

The home life Arlene is building for her children is a long way from her own childhood.

Readers of "Make Believe Children" will find the De Marco parents in Mama and Papa Spinelli.

Papa De Marco made the De Marco Sisters act and went around selling the girls. Arlene, the youngest and cutest, was taken along to the agencies. She was five.

"People would put dollar bills in my pockets and I would have several when we got home. It was just plain panhandling.

"We got on the Fred Allen show when I was six," she recalled. "We were regulars until 1949."

In one of her books she says that the school for actors in Hollywood was taught on a very loose basis. The law required two hours a day and the hours were arranged at the convenience of the studios.

"I'm here to tell you," she writes in "Make Believe Children," "a ghetto kid today gets a better education than the most famous child stars ever got." Arlene said: "Both my girls are straight A students. How do you think I feel when they come to me with a math problem and I can't do it?

"We were on radio in the East, and it was just as bad.

"I never graduated from anything. Most of the time I was growing up we were on the road and took correspondence courses. The boys in Louis Prima's band did our lessons for us. How could we learn anything?

"WHEN WE were in New York we went to child-actors' school. It was like 'What's My Line,' sign in, sign out. That was all we had to do. Once I didn't go for 28 straight days. Nobody cared."

There were no playgrounds at correspondence school. The girls traveled in vaudeville, doing six shows a day. Vaudeville was mixed with movies in what were called "presentation houses." They played volleyball and roller skated on the stage behind the screen while the picture was on. Once they disrupted the movie when their shadows played across the screen from behind. After that they skated in the dark.

Outside entertainment was almost impossible so they watched the movie over and over. "I saw one picture 38 times."

Were these very young girls molested while growing up on a theatrical circuit that included vaudeville, sleazy nightclubs and smokers? Arlene ducks a direct answer, but refers to a scene in her novel where a movie producer holds young Kimberly Hudson on his lap while he masturbates.

Worse even than the lascivious men, homosexuals, grueling hours and skimpy education was the impersonal "show-must-go-on" syndrome the girls were up against.

Papa De Marco was hardly an ideal father, but he was all the father they had.

"He died on a Saturday," Arlene remembers, "and we had to do a Fred Allen show on Sunday. We were so programmed that I called him after the show like I always did to ask how the show went, forgetting that he was laid out."

Arlene De Marco today is an attractive lady who doesn't look all of 36. She is outgoing and outspoken and will talk about herself and her beliefs without hesitation.

A Hollywood nymph in her book has a phallic museum of the stars she has known. Arlene disclaims any knowledge of any such real collection, but says she got the idea from a stud who gave a sex rating to all the female stars. "I got an A," she added.

"One thing I won't do," she vows, "is a porno movie."

She won't marry again either. Date, yes. "I date and that is hard for the girls to understand. They say the other mothers in the apartment building don't go out on dates so I point out that there is a Mr. Feldman, a Mr. Murphy. There is no Mr. De Marco."

"Married men are more stable than single men," she said of her dating style. "I go out with the executive types. Single men are either spoiled or they're queer."

"Anyway, I don't date all that much. The main thing is the kids."

"Make Believe Children" has only been out a few weeks. It looks like it will make enough money to get the De Marcos out of their financial rut. What Arlene wants for her and the girls' future is more financial security. "Right now it's not so hot. We live from day to day."

A proposed book extolling the virtues of raising children in the suburbs has been put aside.

Instead, Arlene will write about another of her best known subjects, men. The title — "Loveable Frauds."

"Then I may do something about the courts," she promises from her reservoir of experience.

There is also a planned nostalgia record album with Ann, Gene, Gloria, Terry and Arlene De Marco getting together again to sing the old songs.

Meanwhile, don't worry about Arlene. She says she's neurotic, but she sleeps well.

Denker Play More Than Timely

DENKER, Henry
(1912 -)

WASHINGTON STAR-NEWS
(Washington, D.C.)

Apr. 19, 1974

[See also CA-33/36]

Sketch by Authors in the News

By David Richards
Star-News Staff Writer

Playwright Henry Denker doesn't want it thought that he is capitalizing on current events, and he has all the necessary papers to prove it.

His latest play, "The Headhunters," which is currently trying out in Knoxville, Tenn., before opening at the Kennedy Center at the end of the month,' tells the story of a dissident Russian author who returns to Moscow after seven brutalizing years in prison camp and discovers that speaking out is still more important to him than personal comfort.

Almost before you can say Solzhenitsyn, Denker has whipped out a neatly creased copyright form, dated April 1971, to show that he's not jumping on a bandwagon. "This is Washington," he says,"and I know you like to see these things in writing."

INITIALLY, Denker goes on to explan, he intended to dramatize Solzhenitsyn's "First Circle." By way of corroboration, he delves back into his pocket and pulls out a letter of inquiry, posted Oct. 1, 1968.

"But I never got the rights. I was told such a project might jeopardize Solzhenitsyn's life, or even send him back to prison. Well, a thought began haunting me — that maybe the better story for the stage was not 'First Circle,' which covers a period of 20 years, but what was happening to Russian dissidents in general. I began to jot down notes, collect clippings, talk to people. It's a long, slow process of building up until you're saturated. But suddenly, everything falls into place.

"We're inclined to think this is just a contemporary Russian problem," he declares with uncharacteristic force. "But Solzhenitsyn is just a fish the Russians throw us to relieve the pressure. Hell, this is a Yugoslavian problem, a Hungarian problem, a Czechoslovakian problem. I think I'm telling an exciting human story, but it's not about *one man.* There are thousands in this plight."

At 60, Denker is sliver-haired and baby-skinned. Dewlaps of pink flesh fold neatly over the collar of his gray suit. Not a trace of lint in sight. A burgundy handkerchief pokes jauntily out of his pocket. He could be a successful small-town banker, somebody's grandfather, your great aunt's accountant. Instead he writes what he calls "actuality dramas."

Some of them have been in play form — "Time Limit" (brainwashing during the Korean War), "A Far Country" (Freud and psychoanalysis) "A Case Of Libel" (the courtroom battle of Quentin Reynolds and Westbrook Pegler). Others have been novels, such as "The Kingmaker," which described, in thinly veiled terms, the take-over of Universal Pictures by MCA and the steady, shrewd rise of Ronald Reagan to the governorship of California. Denker also contributed 410 weekly sagas to "The Greatest Story Ever Told," which brought Jesus to the radio for 10 years running. "I treated that as 'actuality drama,' too.

"You see, just about everything I write is based on real events. I get stimulated by things that have really happened. They're more dramatic than anything you could make up. Some of the things I wrote in 'The Headhunters — and you've got to remember that this play was first done in 1970 at the Bucks County Playhouse — actually came about two or three months ago. But it's not prophecy. With given characters and a given situation, certain consequences are inevitable. It's almost mathematical."

THE Kennedy Center, of course, is delighted with the timeliness of the piece. Unlike Arena Stage, it has not always been on the breaking wave and has had to field charges in the past of being theatrically reactionary. Denker, however, feels otherwise.

"I wish people wouldn't talk to me about timing. A good play is a good play, regardless of the times. Anyway, there's no timing here — not when you consider all the changes and rewrites a play goes through. Not when a producer tells you he'll do the play if he can get a certain actor for the part, and negotiations drag on for months and months.

"Most of your playwrights today are writing novels — do you realize that? — because you don't have to wait around to cast a novel. A publisher won't call you up and say, 'Look, if we can't get John Jones to set your type, we won't do your book.' There are 6,000 novels published every year, and maybe 35 plays. You figure it out."

'Mind If I Kill You Off in Chapter Three?'

DENNIS, Ralph

ATLANTA JOURNAL & CONSTITUTION (Atlanta, Ga.)

June 30, 1974

By Phil Garner

Photography by William Wages

RALPH DENNIS was drinking a beer in a delicatessen in Virginia-Highlands when a large man pushed open the back door and limped in. He walked past Ralph's table and signaled "Hello." Ralph signaled "Hello" back.

"You written your chapter today?" the man asked.

"Nope," Ralph said.

The man went to the end of the bar and ordered a beer and a sandwich.

"That's Fred," said Ralph. "I killed him off in my last book."

"Does he know you killed him off?" I asked.

"Oh, sure," said Ralph. "I asked his permission. I see him all the time in here. I thought it was only fair. He said sure, go ahead."

Ralph always asks permission before he kills off a friend.

Ralph writes mystery novels with an Atlanta setting. He used to write serious stuff, but it wasn't getting published, except for some short stories years ago in little literary magazines. About a year ago he banged out a novel about a character named Hardman, a defrocked policeman who practices private investigation without a license, gets beaten up a lot, has an active-though-haunted love life, and has to kill people who are trying to kill him. Now Ralph's a published author again and working on the seventh in the series.

When he needs a character to fill in here and there, he models him after someone he knows. Like Fred.

FRED'S a good study, Ralph said. Like the other day, the owner of the delicatessen and his wife took one of those junkets to Las Vegas. Fred heard them planning the trip and gave the wife $10 and asked her to play the slots for him while she was there. Just play it till it's gone, he said. It was a nice gesture. Sure enough, she played the 10 bucks until it was down to a quarter. She plugged in the last quarter and hit the jackpot for $250, which she brought back and turned over to Fred, who's plowing it back into the bar receipts.

Ralph relishes little yarns like that. They reinforce his fatalistic side. After all, he was down to his last inspiration himself when he woke up one morning and started writing the first Hardman book, called "Atlanta Deathwatch." He hasn't exactly hit the jackpot yet, but he's making a living, and without having to work for somebody else. He even feels secure enough to gripe about how the editors are handling his books.

"I hate exclamation marks," said Ralph. "Somebody's always throwing in exclamation marks. I mean, if a sentence is strong, it stands by itself and it doesn't need all those exclamation marks." He doesn't have the manuscript so he can't point them out. Next time he's going to make a carbon.

Ralph lights up a cigaret and sips at his unaccustomed luncheon beer. I've upset his working rhythm, although he assures me it doesn't matter. When I'd telephoned him at his apartment overlooking Ormsely Park that morning, he'd sounded in a fog.

"Dennis, here," he'd said, accusingly. And then there had been a pause after I'd told him it was just me again. It had sounded like a struggle was going on. Lots of knocking and rattling. The line went dead for a second and then he came back on.

"It's that cat," Ralph explained. "Why is it cats like to sit in your face? Get out'a here!"

Ralph had turned aside a suggestion that I come over with a photographer.

"I'd really hate for anybody to see the place," he said. "I haven't cleaned it in months. There's trash and dirty laundry everywhere." He suggested lunch at the delicatessen instead.

Ralph has disciplined himself with a strict routine. He writes from 8 a.m. until 12:30 p.m., turning out about 10 pages a day. Then he goes downtown and has lunch in some sandwich shop. After that he walks to the public library where he browses through the stacks and finds a novel he hasn't read or one to ➡

(Continued from preceding page)
reread, reads through the newspapers and periodicals and watches girls, all this conscientiously until 4 p.m. Only then does he make his way to a favorite place to drink beer. On weekends he doesn't bother with the working.

This routine produces, in the course of a month, the first draft of a mystery novel and four surrealistic weekends. He takes another month, working the same pace, to rewrite and polish the draft into final form. That way, he turns out a book and eight surrealistic weekends in two months.

RALPH isn't making extravagant claims for his stuff as memorable fiction, but then again why don't you try writing a mystery novel sometime? It doesn't come easy or without discipline.

All the books in the Hardman series are set in Atlanta. Ralph uses the names of real streets and real landmarks such as the gold-domed state capitol building, City Hall, Underground Atlanta. The names of restaurants and bars and hotels are changed if he depicts them as harboring criminal activity. Otherwise they're used as they are. The Hyatt Regency Hotel, for instance, or Davison's department store (where Hardman buys new shirts when the old ones are bullet-ridden and bloody). Hardman, a sports fan like Ralph, watches the Hawks and the Falcons. Hardman's sidekick is a muscular, likeable black ex-Falcon player named Hump. Together, the salt-and-pepper pair move in and out of both societies, black and white, protecting each other from the racial bigotry found in each.

In the first book, Ralph drew his plot and characters out of the thin air., Then, when his publisher asked for a series of Hardman books, Ralph began basing his plots, loosely, on the germ of some actual event. His second book, "The Charleston Knife's Back in Town," is based loosely on the Ali-Quarry fight, which took place in Atlanta a few years ago and was followed by a party at which all the guests were stripped and robbed by bandits. In Ralph's version, the robbery was pulled by a group of youngsters who work at a Burger Hut.

Book number three is called "The Golden Girls and All." In that one, Ralph used a widely publicized theft of drugs from the New York Police Department evidence room and had it happen within the Atlanta Police Department.

"That one's probably going to get me in trouble," he said, figuring the Atlanta Police Department isn't going to like being associated with such incidents, even in fiction.

DENNIS, Ralph

ATLANTA JOURNAL & CONSTITUTION
(Atlanta, Ga.) June 30, 1974

Book number four is titled, "Pimp for the Dead." Ralph originally called it "The Sisyphus People," but the editors didn't go for the title. It's about the murder of a prostitute. Ralph used to sit near the window of a favorite beer bar on Peachtree Street near the 10th Street area and watch the girls pass back and forth with their clients. "You'd see 'em go up the street and back again, up the street and back again," said Ralph, "and it reminded me of the myth of Sisyphus, the guy who was doomed to roll this huge boulder up a hill and have it chase him back down again, over and over."

He saw the models for two main characters in "Pimp for the Dead" on a sidewalk in front of a loan office on Ponce de Leon one night as he drove by. "There was this girl and her friend on the curb, looking for business," Ralph said. "But her friend was a dwarf, a dwarf prostitute. It stuck in my mind and I used both of them in the book." That time, he didn't ask permission.

Book number five is called "Down Among the Jocks" and is set in the world of Atlanta's professional sports.

Number six is "The Stranger Kill." "Don't ask me what significance that title has," said Ralph. "The editors slapped it on."

The Ralph Dennis book in progress is called "Working for the Man," "the Man" being the name of a black underworld boss in the first novel.

RALPH began his writing career at the age of 18 by composing poems at night in the john of his Navy barracks. His first published work ran in the Virginia Quarterly under the title "Sampson on His Blindness and the Coming of Spring."

"I'd been reading a lot of Greek tragedy," Ralph explained. "You know, the kind of stuff you read when you're 18 and don't understand until you're 25?"

Out of the Navy, he enrolled at the University of North Carolina. Soon he entered a short-fiction contest. His story was about a group of sailors on leave in a red-light district. The prize had been put up by an elderly woman in memory of her daughter. Ralph won. When the donor read the winning story, she withdrew the prize. Ralph did get his $100, however. "I threw a great $100 beer party," he recalled.

In an honors class in creative writing, Ralph began an autobiographical novel about life in an orphan's home, where he had lived from age 10 to age 13. A visiting New York editor read his first chapters and told him her publishing house would take the book when he finished it. But the book was rejected and Ralph got his first taste of the vagaries of the literary life. Undaunted, he dropped out of school to rewrite the book. He took a job in the dietary department of a hospital. After two years of struggle he went back to school and entered a master's program in radio and television writing. He taught a while at Chapel Hill, then went to Yale to study playwriting. Later he returned to Chapel Hill to teach.

"But I just didn't like teaching," Ralph said. And he couldn't sell his book.

Ralph moved to Atlanta to write. He began working on another novel and finished it. "So far as I know, the only people who like it were my agent and me," said Ralph. He started another one. "One morning I got up and said, Hell, nobody's gonna like this one either. So I started writing a mystery novel. I was also working for local ETV, eighth-grader stuff, you know, like a 10-minute version of 'The Old Man and the Sea.' It was bad, so I quit. But I soon got broke, so I got another job, working for a law book publishing firm. About that time I sent my first Hardman book off to my agent and in two weeks they'd bought it.

"I kept my job and began work on the second Hardman book. I wrote a lot of that book on my lunch breaks, using the company's IBM electric typewriter. Finally my agent got me enough contracts to keep me in food and I quit my job. I've been writing the Hardman books ever since. Not very inspiring, I'll grant you, but it's a life."

JUST then an elderly man walked into the delicatessen. He was overweight and stooped, wearing a blue golf shirt, brown trousers and a rain hat. He waved at Ralph and went to the bar for a beer and to read his paper.

"That guy," said Ralph, "used to be one of the most successful gamblers in Atlanta. He made a pile. The woman behind the bar told me he'd been coming in here for years to drink a beer or two and she never really knew what his name was. They just called him by some nickname. So one day she asked him, she said, 'We don't know your real name. What if you're killed? Who would we notify?' Well, he didn't say anything and she thought she might have made him mad. But a day or two later he walks in for a beer and hands her a folded piece of paper. On it is his real name and the names and addresses of his relatives. It's behind the mirror over there right now."

Ralph paused and smiled.

"I used him in one of my books, too. He knows about it. The other day he came over and asked me if they might make a movie out of the book. I told him if they did, we'd get Rock Hudson to play his part. But he got real serious. He said, 'No, if they make the movie, I'd like to play myself.' "

Poet, Artist Blend Talents For Major Literary Coup

DICKEY, James (Lafayette) (1923 -)
[See also CA-11/12]
and
SHUPTRINE, Hubert (1936? -)

TOLEDO BLADE (Toledo, Ohio)

Oct. 20, 1974

By BOB TALBERT

With quiet southern charm and astonishing business acumen, some good ol' boys in Birmingham, Ala., have just pulled off the biggest publishing feat since Guttenberg moved the type.

Before the first copy of Oxmoor House's "Jericho: The South Beheld" hit the market last week, the southern firm had sold more than 80,000 copies of the book at $39.95 a copy. It takes no math genius to figure out that's well over $3 million tucked away in the coffers of the Progressive Farmer Co.

These books were sold by virtue of a preview of the book which appeared in Southern Living magazine and a mail-order coupon in the magazine, which is circulated to more than a million subscribers in 15 southern states.

* * *

But those good ol' boys pretty well knew they had a pair of aces back-to-back when they launched the project, the brainchild of Southern Living editor John Logue. The "aces" are author-poet James Dickey and artist Hubert Shuptrine, whose interpretive realism matched the same force that moves through Dickey's poetry-prose.

Logue says, "We wanted to do an art book, but not just another art book. The idea was to bring the finest writer and the finest artist together and let them create their own individual thing. A book of the scope that would have occurred had Ernest Hemingway and Cezanne done a book."

In Dickey and Shuptrine they have the modern-day Hemingway-Cezanne team. Logue says, "Hubert is gentle in his works and Jim is visceral. They hit it off from the first meeting, both having been long-time fans of each other's works.

"In my opinion about four things resulted in its becoming more than just a successful publishing venture. Obviously the talent of the two men was a necessity; Hubert's emergence as a force, as a figure-story painter. The decision was made to abandon the idea of doing the book along geographical lines and to use three divisions: The Land and the Water; Among the People; The Traditions' Web.

* * *

"And then came Jim's idea to name the book 'Jericho.' We wanted a title with all the mass and weight of a novel. Those elements merged to create a chemistry that permitted a book to come alive that was greater than even its separate parts."

Listen a moment to a transcript of Dickey's actual conversation concerning the title:

"Suppose we had something that completely oriented the South and we called it something out of the Bible, because to a lot of people, the South was and became and still is kind of a 'Promised Land.' And this is true of northerners that come down here who are almost invariably fascinated with it. Suppose we went back to our roots and our heritage and went even further back to what caused the heritage — to the biblical kind of reverence — to a 'Promised Land.' Suppose we call our book — suppose we call it 'Jericho.'

"I want the book to be an encounter. I do not want to let the readers off easily. Anybody that picks it up is going to get into the South in depth and in multifarious kinds of ways from the mountains to the lowlands — right?"

* * *

Right. It is an enormous experience. As you read the book, it reads you, totally capturing the subject and turning it on an artistic spit until the juices drip and the skin crackles. Your juices. Your skin.

The artist took three years and 25,000 miles in every crevice of the South, finding the faces and the feeling of Jericho. The author took time out from writing two novels — about the same people 25 years apart — and other projects to write "Jericho" which he says will be the book he's remembered for.

The first printing of the book is 150,000 copies, the largest printing of an art book in history, at an investment which Oxmoor's Les Adams says may be the largest investment in a book other than Bibles and encyclopedias. It cost $5 just to bind each book, which weighs seven and a half pounds.

* * *

Emory Cunningham, president of Progressive Farmer, caught the spirit of the project from the concept when he said, "If we don't sell a lot of books, and if we lose money on this book, it will be maybe the most valuable single thing we have done for the South since we started Southern Living magazine."

The people of Jericho have responded. So has the rest of the nation. For example, Frank Sinatra bought 500 copies to give as Christmas gifts. The Book-of-the-Month Club picked it as a January alternative, one of the few books they've picked that was not published in New York.

It is truly the South rising again.

'Jericho' unusual joint effort

DICKEY, James (Lafayette)
and
SHUPTRINE, Hubert

HOUSTON POST (Houston, Tex.)

Oct. 4, 1974

By CHARLOTTE PHELAN
Post Book Editor

The collaboration of Hubert Shuptrine and James Dickey on the big, beautiful volume called "Jericho The South Beheld" was just about as separate and independent as one could be—indeed, as if the artist and writer were working on different books.

"That's the way we wanted it," Dickey, who is now best known for his novel and film, "Deliverance," but who is also a widely admired poet, said here Thursday. "I really don't know how it all started, to tell you the truth."

Shuptrine, the artist, did, however. "They told me to travel around the South and paint, and 'in two and a half years we want to publish what you paint.' They told Jim the same thing."

"They" is Oxmoor House of Birmingham, Alabama, publishers of the magazines Southern Living and The Progressive Farmer, and they have achieved a significant milestone with "Jericho," a huge volume containing more than a hundred of Shuptrine's watercolors and sketches as well as Dickey's lyrical, affecting text.

Having committed themselves on this, their first major hardback edition, Oxmoor printed 150,000 copies, the largest first printing of any art book in publishing history. Moreover, some 80,000 of those were sold (at $39.95) through a preview excerpt and mail order form in Southern Living.

Neither could confirm a news wire item that Frank Sinatra had bought 500 copies as Christmas gifts, but Dickey shrugged and grinned. "Let's credit him with it."

"Anyway," Shuptrine said, going back to the beginning, "Jim took off and I took off. For the first year he didn't see my paintings and I didn't see any words."

"Our ideas changed and developed as we went along, but the objective always was to show what was unique and beautiful about the South. I think it has turned out to be the heart of the people," Shuptrine added. Then the artist suddenly changed the subject.

"Show them what's on your wrist," he said to Dickey.

"This is the compass Burt Reynolds wore in 'Deliverance,'" Dickey said, holding out his right wrist. "He said he wanted me to have it as a souvenir of the picture.

"He asked me if I had a watch and I told him I did. He said, 'All right. Wear your watch on your left hand and my old compass on your right. Then, you'll be the master of time and space.'"

One wondered when Dickey, who is writer-in-residence at the University of South Carolina, and Shuptrine finally turned the individual material over to Oxmoor for the book.

"When they started BINDING it," Dickey declared.

"No, we missed every other deadline, but the ultimate deadline. We made that one. Around Aug. 1 they said, 'Okay, you all have finished the book.' And I guess we had."

For Novelist Joan Didion, Success Came as a Surprise

DIDION, Joan (1934 -) [See also CA-5/6] and DUNNE, John Gregory (1932 -) [See also CA-25/28]

MIAMI HERALD (Miami, Fla.) Dec. 2, 1973

By JUDY KINNARD
Knight Newspapers Staff Writer

The Oak Room is a mammoth makeshift restaurant in the depths of the cavernous Philadelphia Civic Center. To reach it requires a seemingly endless passage through outsized hallways that form a vaguely threatening maze where the air becomes progressively stultifying.

Despite the regular occurrence of such functions as the luncheon meeting of 250 English teachers and the familiar odor of what must have been baked chicken still trapped in the halls, it is an alien landscape.

But Joan Didion is no stranger to alien landscapes. As a novelist and essayist she turned again and again to the environment — it's natural calamities, its wonders, its overwhelming influence on human behavior.

SO THE Oak Room seemed more fitting than some "Lions Meet Here" banquet hall for her rare speaking appearance before the teachers who were part of a national convention of almost 4,000 members meeting in Philadelphia.

"I'll talk about seeing myself, finding myself, finding a voice for the book," she promised. The speaking voice is hesitant, like a little girl too shy to be coy. "I can't talk about the book I'm working on now," she explained. "I haven't found that voice yet."

The physically frail, child-like woman leaned onto the podium so closely that the yellow light framing the pages on her lectern illuminated her small, intense face as well.

And for an hour, her eyes glued to the notes for the most part, Joan Didion gave her straightforward, occasionally amusing, openly professional, step-by-step account of writing "Play It As It Lays," the novel which thrust her into the national spotlight as a major American writer three years ago.

IT IS her writer's voice that is most familiar. That voice is a strong, highly personal and often terrifying viewpoint which lays open her subjects for meticulous dissection: a tragic marriage in her first novel "Run River," the Haight Ashbury flower-child invasion in the title piece of her journalistic collection "Slouching Toward Bethlehem" or the state of mind of a woman sucking at the underbelly called Hollywood in "Play It As It Lays."

At 38, she is a literary celebrity, her fame seasoned with a proper dose of controversy centering on a comparison of her reportorial skills, which are universally acclaimed, and her tragic novels (both probe the mind of a woman who allows a man to kill himself at the end) which are considered technically brilliant, but — in the case of the second — too morbid for some tastes.

She is birdlike. At 90 pounds, she seems constructed mainly of tendons and bones. She wears a delicate gold wire ring on her right hand like the band of a homing pigeon. More often than not, the thin hands are going through the ritual of smoking.

The cigarets and black-and-gold Chanel-style suit suffered for her Eastern visit give her a sophistication which washes away with a smile.

"IT CAME as a great surprise that this book made me so well-known," she explained later as she sipped a cup of consomme in a dingy green hotel room. "John (John Gregory Dunne, her husband) and I both thought it was good, but unlikeable."

John Dunne is her mainstay. He is a writer who has written several books of his own and collaborated with her on a now defunct column in the Saturday Evening Post and two screenplays. Almost 10 years ago, they left the literary world of New York where both had spent several years — she with Vogue and he with Time magazine — for her native California.

There they live in a bougainvillea-framed Southern California Spanish-style house on the cliffs overlooking the Pacific Ocean just north of Malibu, where the price of beachfront property is measured in thousands of dollars per foot of land.

There, sometimes in isolation, they write (as now while they are working on a new screenplay) and there, on other days, they serve as the nucleus of one of Los Angeles' numerous cafe societies, offering their beautiful view, a gourmet meal and good company to friends and Eastern visitors who gravitate there.

"WE'VE HAD enough time in 10 years to fight about everything we could possibly fight about," she said, her eyes gazing — as they often do — towards her daughter Quintana who is packing. "We're not given to rash personal moves, and we always know what each other is doing."

"John and I know that we're always working, even when we're not sitting at a typewriter," she continued. "Sometimes I go home to work and they say, 'why don't you go see your cousins?' "

Home for Joan Didion is still the broad plains of the Sacramento Valley where five generations of ancestors lived and sunk their roots into the rich soil.

"I come from California. I grew up on a lot of stories," she said. "And I bought the whole thing. Now I am trying to work through that — at this late date — in a new book which will be an extended essay about my family and myself."

THE WORLD of Hollywood whose chronicling has brought her fame and with which she confesses to have a love-hate relationship is to her "a great big game, a diversion, something that happens peripherally."

"I guess it won't be like that if Quintana becomes an actress like she plans," she said thoughtfully, facing her seven-year-old precocious child.

Joan Didion took Quintana home to Sacramento for her first birthday party. In an essay entitled "On Going Home" she wrote of her first child.

"I would like to promise her that she will grow up with a sense of cousins and of rivers and of her great-grandmother's teacups . . . would like to give her home for her birthday but we live differently now and I can promise her nothing like that. I give her a xylophone and a sundress from Madeira, and promise to tell her a funny story."

Quintana put on her coat, preparing for the return flight to California and explained why she wants to be an actress: "I want to be famous," she said simply.

Love, Hard Work Go Into Her Drawings

Courant Photo by Anthony Bacewicz.

Janina Domanska, at her drawing board, works on the illustrations for the new children's book she is preparing.

By ELEANOR SAPKO

Assistant Women's Editor

Being able to draw does not a children's book illustrator make.

And just knowing what children want to see, and then doing it, does not insure success, either.

Janina Domanska, who has intrigued children with her illustrations for 14 years, believes it takes instinct to make characters and scenes come alive in the minds of children. And it takes love—love for children and love for what you are doing.

"You don't even know when or how an idea comes to you," says the Polish-born New Fairfield resident. "It's impossible to explain. Something about a story will impress you unexpectedly, and you react. It is the realization of the idea"—getting it down on paper— "that is quite a discipline," she says. "You must spend time to build it, like building a house."

Miss Domanska's instinct for children's books must be very good, because she has worked for Macmillan Publishing Co. for the past ten years. Not bad for a woman who couldn't speak English when she came to this country in 1952, although she did speak Italian, French and Polish.

Miss Domanska, who lives with her husband, Jerzy Laskowski, proprietor of a Danbury book shop, and a dachshund, on five wooded acres near Candlewood Lake, is first and foremost an artist.

Born in Warsaw, she was graduated from the Academy of Fine Arts in Warsaw, where after World War II she received a prize that enabled her to go to Rome to study.

In fact, her painting saved her life once, she says. When Germany invaded Poland during the war, she, among others, was brought to a concentration camp in western Poland. "I always took my oil paints and brushes with me wherever I went, and in this camp I started to make sketches," she says in perfect English, with a heavy Polish accent.

A Polish doctor and his wife came to the camp and, impressed by her talent, the doctor told her he would lie to the German commandant, telling them she was a relative, if she would paint the portraits of his six children. The deception worked, and Miss Domanska stayed with the doctor's family until after the war.

She recently returned to Warsaw in triumph for a one-woman exhibition of her children's illustrations and paintings. While there, she appeared on Polish television and radio and was asked to leave her works on exhibition longer than the scheduled month. A Polish publisher wants to translate one of her books into Polish.

When the war was over, she left for Rome, where she stayed with her brother, studying painting and supporting herself by teaching painting. Her works were displayed in many Italian and international exhibitions, as well as being in private collections.

For four years in New York she worked as a textile designer, a job that didn't require a knowledge of English. When she had mastered the language, she began to walk the streets of New York, portfolio under her arm, showing her paintings to various magazines. The results were good: Harper's Magazine asked her to do some illustrations, as did The Reporter, a now-defunct publication.

An editor in the children's department at Harper's, who has since moved to Macmillan, suggested she should draw for children "because there were so many animals in my paintings," Miss Domanska says smiling. In 1960 she did her first book, a story she adapted from the Polish. Since then Miss Domanska has illustrated, or written and illustrated, more than 40 children's books.

When she began her career, Miss Domanska would "try to make harmony with the words of a book," illustrating exactly what the words on the page said. Then she discovered it was more exciting to "create a story behind the words." Children liked them more, too.

Thus in "Whizz!", a book of five simple limericks by Edward Lear, she has Lear's cast of characters crossing a bridge, one by one, until the bridge collapses from their weight and they all fall into the river.

But on the next page, the child will see that they haven't drowned after all, because Miss Domanska has painted the water only three inches deep. The following page shows the characters—including a cow, a gigantic bird, a bear, five very strange looking men and a little girl—all lined up, holding hands, like actors taking a curtain call after a play.

"An illustrator must work very hard," says Miss Domanska. At one time, years ago, she worked 14 to 16 hours a day, nights and weekends. "But I really like my work, or I wouldn't be able to do it.

"If you enjoy what you do, then children will enjoy it too."

DOMANSKA, Janina

HARTFORD COURANT
(Hartford, Conn.)

June 2, 1974 [See also CA-17/18]

A tribute to Picasso

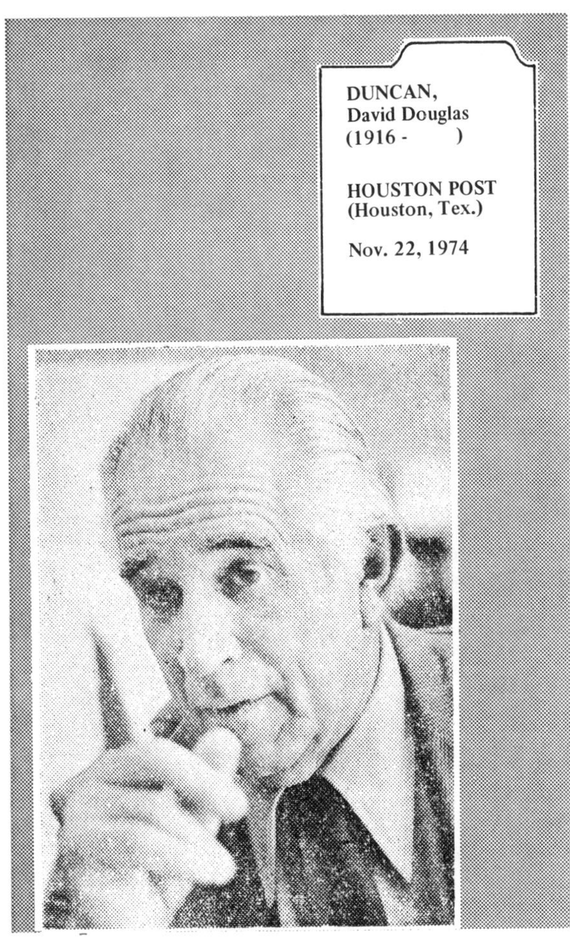

By CHARLOTTE PHELAN

Post Book Editor

David Douglas Duncan's new book about his old friend Picasso—it's called "Goodbye Picasso"—was a personal labor of love, quite literally from cover to cover.

Duncan quite simply made the book himself, the widely respected photographer said in a chat here Thursday, spending most of a year in Switzerland at his task.

Naturally, he took all of the photographs, both the black and white studies of the artist and the brilliant color portfolio of 108 paintings spanning 65 years. a number of them published for the first time.

"I did the text, designed the book, made the decisions on the format, chose the type face and the color ink and the cover. . ."

There could be no doubt about his pride in that binding, when he flipped back the black and white dust jacket to show its brilliant orange fabric imprinted in lavender.

That's pure jute from Bangladesh," he said of the burlap type material, "and I had it dyed to the color of one particular painting." With this he opened the spectacular volume to a Picasso portrait of a woman, dated 1937, and pointed to her beret.

"Then I took the lavender from the highlight of the beret for the lettering. You notice there is no author or publisher, that are usually on a book's spine, because this fabric could not take the ink of small type."

The publisher is Grosset and Dunlap, and it might as well be added right here that the price is $35.

The lanky Duncan is now 58 and graying but no less avid than he was when Picasso first welcomed him to his rambling and cluttered villa, La Californie, in 1957 and allowed the then world-traveled Life combat photographer to turn his sensitive Leicas on his art and personal habitat.

It was a friendship that lasted 17 years—until Picasso's death, of course—and became even closer, at least geographically, when Duncan (a native of Kansas City) and his wife built their own home in the South of France, at Castellaras, 14 years ago.

"I have said this before," Duncan said now. "I wasn't the best photographer nor the best reporter, but I was THE reporter and THE photographer who was there."

Withal, he has produced three books about the vital Spaniard many consider to be the greatest artist of this century— a black and white photojournalism study, "The Private World of Pablo Picasso," an art book, "Picasso's Picasso" and now the final tribute, "Goodbye."

"It's okay when you're shooting color reproductions if the guy is Raphael or Michelangelo or van Gogh, but Picasso was very much by my side when I was doing these," Duncan said in his uncommonly quiet speech and with one of his frequent smiles.

"We did sit side by side as I projected transparencies on a large screen to correct for color, usually absolutely without a word. I knew as well as he did when something went wrong.

"At first I was having one particularly bad problem, and I couldn't seem to eliminate it — a type of greenish gray or bluish gray kept creeping into my transparencies. I just couldn't figure it out.

"Finally, I found out in Switzerland what was wrong. I was using American Kodachrome film and sending it to Kodak in Paris for processing. They were treating it there as if it were French Kodachrome, and there is a difference in emulsions for the French film.

"When I switched over to Switzerland for processing— bam!—I was in business like that!"

He was indeed.

Picasso, Duncan: They Clicked

(Also see preceding article)

By NANCY GREENBERG
Of The Bulletin Staff

WHEN David Douglas Duncan was in town a few days ago to publicize his photo-memoir, "Goodbye Picasso," a newspaper photographer here observed that Duncan was wearing the same loden green corduroy sports jacket he had seen him wearing three weeks ago at a photography exhibit in Cologne.

In fact, the local photographer noted, Duncan was wearing the sports jacket three years ago when the two colleagues met for the first time.

"When I find something I like," explained Duncan when the coincidence was called to his attention, "something that's comfortable and simple — I just stick with it and eventually it becomes a part of me.

"Look," he pointed proudly to a large hole in the inside lining, "it's fraying but I'm still incredibly attached to it."

Duncan's verbal analysis of his intimate, 17-year-friendship with Pablo Picasso, who became the subject of tens of thousands of the photo-journalist's photographs gets about as complex as his analysis of his relationship with his sports jacket.

A major difference however, is that when it comes to the artist who was his neighbor in the south of France until his death last December, Duncan isn't as apt to point out the frayed parts.

"Picasso represented all the qualities I respected in men," Duncan, now 58, tells you. "He was compassionate and honest and natural. . .there was a purity about him that made you think of a primitive, except that he was totally cultured.

"I have no idea what he liked about me and to be honest, I can't really put a finger on the nature of our extraordinary rapport. But we clicked totally, in a way that is rare for human beings to understand each other. . Do you ask Juliet what she saw in Romeo?"

In February of 1956 David Douglas Duncan had finished shooting for "Life" in Afghanistan when he appeared at Picasso's villa in Cannes to give the 75-year-old master a ring he had made for him.

It was made out of an engraved strutting rooster, the kind Picasso had drawn many times.

"You know," Duncan smiles with pleasure, "I think he liked it — he really liked it. He had to wear it on his index finger, but of course, his fingers were thinner and finer than mine. ..

"Later, I found out people were always sending him gifts — Gucci shoes, a Lincoln convertible, Yugoslav wedding dresses — Yul Brenner once sent him a hat—but I think he really liked that ring. .You see, he's wearing it in some of the pictures. . "

The first time the two men met, Picasso was in the bathtub having his back scrubbed by Jacqueline Roque, the woman almost 50 years younger than he who later would become his wife.

DUNCAN, David Douglas
PHILADELPHIA BULLETIN
(Philadelphia, Penn.)
Nov. 4, 1974

The 'click' was instantaneous and though Duncan actually lived in an apartment in Cannes, he spent so much time at the villa during the late '50s, — sometimes shooting, sometimes not — people frequently presumed he was a houseguest.

"Goodbye Picasso" is his third book about the artist — Duncan is known also for his war photos and his work inside the Kremlin — and at $35, it has a cover cloth of Bangladesh jute loomed in England and dyed to match the scarlet background of Picasso's 1937 painting of a young woman photographed on page 140.

A comparison, however, indicates that the red of the cloth cover is not as deep as the real work. Duncan easily uses words like "intimacy," "rapport" and "love" in describing his relationship with Picasso but he shares no anecdotes — no wry, whimsical glimpses — that match the depth of his photography.

One must presume an intimacy between painter and photographer just to justify the massive invasion of privacy "Goodbye Picasso" represents.

It would seem that Duncan had to be a houseguest (and an invisible one at that) to capture the quiet moments between Pablo and Jacqueline, the looks of petulance, the looks of sadness, the clownish looks.

"I tell you frankly," says Duncan, "I wouldn't let anyone shoot me that much. He was simply totally uninhibited. For him, the camera just wasn't there. He was an incredible subject. . and of course, the trust between us was profound."

Trying to get Duncan to tell you what the two men talked about is like getting someone to remember a conversation they had with their postman a decade ago.

They never discussed art and rarely discussed politics except the photographer recalls, when he told Picasso that the communist party (of which the artist was an obscure member) didn't deserve him.

That such friends didn't discuss art and politics is conceivable; that they never discussed trivia is harder to believe. Duncan, however, insists "Picasso never discussed trivia" as if an admission to the contrary would cast an uncomplimentary shadow on his cherished subject.

Asked what they did talk about, Duncan says, "He was very interested in my travels particularly in Asia and inside Russia. . . Actually, sometimes I'd shoot him for days and not 50 words would pass between us."

Duncan paused. "There was his sheer manliness and gentleness — and that's how I like to think of myself. We were alike — Puritans by nature, compared to today's standards. We respected a certain courtliness and lived with a sense of decency — oh, sort of like Ernest Hemingway and that crowd. the sort of man you don't see much anymore."

"And Jacqueline — she was a lady, a thoroughbred. They wree companions for seven years before they were married and not once during that time — and I was shooting in hs bedroom in the early hours — did I ever see a nightgown lying around. A nightgown? Not a hairbrush or a bedroom slipper. Her discretion bordered on the mysterious. Her discretion. . ."

Duncan, who is talking quickly, now stops himself, as if he has committed an indiscretion in discussing Madame Picasso's fastidiousness.

For reasons which may never be clear to us — for reasons which, in fact, may be none of our business — David Douglas Duncan was admited to a genius's private world. In return for free reign with his camera, it seems, his sense of decency compels him to impose his own kind of discretion.

"We get angry at each other once," Duncan tells you somberly. "There was a house rule not to ask Picasso to sign anything but when my first book came out, I asked him to sign three lithographs for my editors and publisher.

"He became furious screaming that I was just like everybody else, that I just wanted to get things out of him." "I got in my car and mad as hell, drove to Rome.

"Three months later when I returned to his villa the lithographs were on the table where I left them only they had been signed and dated the night he exploded."

That story, Duncan points out, is to demonstrate Picasso's kindness, not his temperament.

Minstrel, Farmer, Weaver Of Spells

Photos by TOM O'REILLY, Blade Chief Photographer

By MEG CROSSGROVE
Blade Staff Writer

AFTER nearly 40 years, Max Ellison is a man who's finally made it.

Since 1934 when he left his rural home in Antrim County, Mich., at the age of 20, he's earned his livelihood as a stablehand, and has raised worms, been a hog farmer and a janitor, among other things.

Last March, he was the only American poet invited to participate in the International Poetry Festival sponsored by the Distinguished Visitors Program at the University of Massachusetts, and his fourth book, "Clean Livers of Antrim County, and Other Myths," co-authored with Judith Jebian, will be published in August.

His first collection of poems, "The Underbark," now in its sixth printing, was published at his own expense in 1969, and has sold 52,000 copies. "The Happenstance," in 1972, and "Double Take," in 1973, both were published by his own firm, Conway House.

Ellison, who says that although essentially he's always been a farmer he has also always been interested in writing, and "poetry just kept sneaking up on me." He wrote his first poem shortly after leaving high school. "I began to get some recognition as a poet about 10 or 12 years ago, but my work didn't begin to pay until about five years ago," he says.

From October to mid-June, he travels throughout the country in his Volkswagen — the gasoline shortage forced him to abandon his pickup truck — giving poetry readings, both his own work and that of others, with engagements in such places as Buffalo Gap, Va., and San Francisco.

He has spoken at 28 colleges and universities, before numerous clubs and organizations, and at elementary, junior high, and high schools. But his main target is to reach high school English classes and arouse an enthusiasm for and an interest in poetry. During 1972, he traveled 43,000 miles, and spoke in 125 high schools across the country.

"This is the way a poet becomes known," Ellison says. He recalls that the first time he was asked out of his home territory in Michigan several years ago, he paid his own expenses. Today, things are different. Readings at colleges and universities bring small fees, he says. "But they're mostly prestige engagements. The sale of my three books — that's my bread and butter."

Though his books are available at most book stores, he carries a supply of autographed copies when he is on the lecture circuit.

ELLISON is a man who speaks frankly, and sometimes abruptly, but his manner in conversation is forthright.

Recently, he was in Toledo to speak to English classes at Start High School. On such visits, he usually spends the day, and schedules readings during four class periods, allowing time for questions at the end. At Start, he held six sessions between 8:30 a.m. and 3 p.m., reciting and lecturing before 1,800 students and faculty members, some of whom returned a second time to hear him, according to a school official.

"He's not only a poet, he's an entertainer," Jim Epstein, Start's advanced placement English teacher, said, adding that, in looks, Ellison resembles the late Ernest Hemingway.

A man of medium height, with an unruly white beard, bright blue eyes, and a slight paunch, Ellison occasionally has been approached by some students who ask him if he's Santa Claus.

He takes such jesting with aplomb, and says it doesn't bother him, because if he can reach just one or two students in an audience and turn them on to poetry, it's time well spent.

Before a student audience, he is not patronizing, and talks "up," not "down," to his listeners, interspersing his readings with bits of conversation about his experiences, bits which lead him into the next selections. He speaks with sincerity, from long and deeply held beliefs, and while his manner is friendly, he is no patsy for the occasional disruptive student or two in the audience.

One time, two girls began whispering and giggling as he talked. "I stopped reciting. I looked at the girls and told them that I wanted them to hear the poem. Then I began again, reciting it directly at the two girls."

From his confident manner on the lecture platform, with his deep, resonant voice which can engulf an audience or sink to a whisper during his interpretations, one would never guess that, as a child, Max Ellison was terrified at the idea of speaking in public.

He was born on a farm in Michigan's Custar Township, near the small town (population 789) of Bellaire, tucked away in the hilly lake country of Antrim County, whose western boundary runs along the shores of Grand Traverse Bay in the northern part of the lower Michigan peninsula.

The third of the five children of Roy and Margaret Fuller, his family tree includes a literary ancestor. "My great, great, great grandmother, on my father's side, was the sister of Charles and John Wesley." (Charles Wesley was an 18th-century poet and hymn writer; John Wesley headed the Methodist movement.)

As a boy, he attended a former country school, Pleasant Valley, which was nicknamed Frog Holler. But his formal schooling ended when he left Bellaire High School after completing two years. "I'm a nonconformist, and I was bored with school. It was during the time of the depression," he explains.

About the time he entered high school, he began to concentrate on poetry, which he'd always enjoyed. "I was very shy as a youngster, and I began to memorize poetry to overcome my shyness."

As a first grader, he recalls, he was given a poem to recite at the school Christmas program, but burst out crying when his turn came. The same thing happened the next year, and he was never again asked to be in the Christmas program. After that, he says, things got to the point where he would freeze up whenever he tried to speak with anybody.

THE TURNING point came for him when he was 13 or 14. A visiting school official, unaware of the youth's problem, told Max that his own most difficult obstacle, which he had overcome, had been a dread of speaking in public. It was then that Ellison decided memorizing and reciting poetry might be a good method to conquer his problem.

ELLISON, Max

TOLEDO BLADE
(Toledo, Ohio)

Feb. 24, 1974

(Continued from preceding page)

A former schoolmate, still a Bellaire resident, has vivid recollections of Max reciting "Gunga Din" in those early days, a poem he still delivers today during readings. As a matter of fact, it was the first poem he recited in public, at the age of 18.

Thomas Hardy, James Whitcomb Riley, Carl Sandburg, and Robert Frost were among his favorite poets, and he memorized so much poetry that he could recite for two hours. Today, he says proudly, "I can recite for six hours without repeating a poem."

After leaving high school, he joined the Civilian Conservation Corps, and worked in the Wolverine area, south of Petoskey, Mich.

When he first struck out from his home country in 1934, Max headed for the Kentucky blue grass country. He got a ride as far as Toledo from Mrs. Florence Miley, a Toledoan whose family has owned property and spent summers at Lake Bellaire for many years, and she is acknowledged on the final page of his forthcoming book of poems and reminiscences, "Clean Livers of Antrim County, and Other Myths."

In Kentucky, he worked as a stablehand and groom at Calumet Farms, and also for horse trainer Marvin Childs at Almahurst Farm. For several years, he traveled around the country during the racing season working at various tracks. In 1941, he left the horses to take a job in a Detroit factory.

The following year, Ellison was drafted into the armed forces, served with the army's First Cavalry Division in the southeastern Asian theater, and was wounded three times in the Philippines campaign. Several of his poems memorialize the men and events of his World War II experience.

When the war ended, he returned to his native Michigan with his wife, Florence, whom he had married while in service, and their infant daughter. For the next 20 years, the family which grew to include another daughter and three sons, lived on a farm near Plymouth. "I raised horses. I had four or five mares and I bred trotting horses, which I sold as yearlings." It was there also, that he got into the hog business.

"Everything in my life has come by accident," he says, in briefly explaining this occupation. "I was employed for a time by the sporting goods department at Hudson's, in Detroit, to demonstrate tying trout flies. Many of the fishermen who came in wanted worms, so I began raising them. I needed garbage to feed the worms, got too much garbage, and began raising hogs. Eventually, though, my poetry began interfering with the hogs, so I let the hogs go."

About this time, the Ellisons decided to sell their farm so Max could devote his time to poetry. Florence enrolled in Wayne State University, and earned a master's degree in psychiatric social work. The family moved back to Bellaire, where she was employed by the Charlevoix-Emmert Intermediate School District. Today, she works for the Area Mental Health Clinic, in Petoskey, which serves four counties.

While Florence was working on her master's degree, Max worked on his poetry and at various part-time jobs. One winter, he worked at Schuss Mountain, a ski resort near Bellaire, loading chair lifts.

ELLISON, Max

TOLEDO BLADE
(Toledo, Ohio)

Feb. 24, 1974

HE ALSO spent three years as a janitor at the University of Michigan, working nights "to supplement the poetry." He was by that time earning small fees from speaking engagements during the day.

Max recalls, with a mischievous twinkle in his eye, a night at the university when he was cleaning a herbarium classroom; he drew a picture of the poisonous aminata mushroom on the blackboard, and added a bit of doggerel: "This mushroom so white and yummy/ is a bad one for the tummy."

Essentially a lyricist, much of Ellison's work takes the form of free verse and, whether writing philosophical poetry or light verse, his abiding love affair with nature and his lifelong ties to the rural environment are evident in his frequent use of nature objects both as subject matter and concrete images, from the convention of the moon to toads, an inchworm, or the mushrooms he delights in hunting.

Many of his poems are unnamed, he says. "I don't think a title for a poem is very important."

He also writes frequently of the common events of everyday life and the persons he has known in his rural home community. For example, "The Giving" was written on the marriage of a daughter; "Lines Written in Memory of a Neighbor," is, as the title implies, a reminiscence; "Nevada Larry Ellison," written after the death of a nephew in Viet Nam, is pure irony, while a light verse, untitled, bemoans in jest his wife's frequent late arrivals home after a day's work.

He has been compared to Robert Frost, and to a latter day Walt Whitman-Ralph Waldo Emerson combined. Often called the "Poet Laureate of Michigan," he has become so well-known in his home state that when a Kentucky friend, not knowing Ellison's address, wrote to him in care of Gov. William Milliken, the letter was forwarded. In 1970 at the governor's inauguration ceremony in Lansing, he was invited to read a poem praising the state of Michigan.

While about 70 per cent of his engagements now are outside his home state, he has been speaking in Michigan schools for several years under the auspices of the Michigan Council of Arts.

DESPITE his lately-found success and busy schedule, Ellison still finds time to speak, without fee, in schools and institutions for retarded children. "Many of them have IQs of less than 50, and I can communicate with them through certain sound poems like 'The Crossing.' " He then recites it. The subject is a simple One: a freight train slowly approaches a grade crossing, gathering speed as it moves along, and its movement is seen through the eyes of someone waiting for the train to pass. Max begins the recitation slowly, matter-of-factly, naming the various cars as they pass, and, as the train picks up speed, so does his delivery, the words finally running together until the last one — "caboose."

A few years ago, Max began to hold poetry readings in Frog Holler. One year, he "passed the hat" to raise money to send a local Little League player on a trip to the Chicago White Sox training camp in a western state. In succeeding years, contributions provided plane fares to send retarded children to the National Olympics for Retarded Children, and tuition for a college student. (The student later went on to earn a master's degree, and now teaches retarded children.)

As a lifelong non-conformist, Ellison has run into difficulties along the way, even in his home territory. A few years ago, one of his sons was sent home from Bellaire High School because authorities considered the boy's hair too long. Ellison sided with his son, and the boy stayed home and took a correspondence course through the University of Nebraska to keep up with his studies. The following year, after the U.S. Supreme Court had refused to review a Wisconsin case relating to hair styles and clothing, the youth returned to high school and graduated with his class.

Max now owns the acre of land called Frog Holler, where his boyhood school once stood. The site is hidden among the towering trees in the hills above Lake Bellaire, and a cottonwood tree has grown through the remains of the school's foundation.

And on summer Saturday nights, when word goes around that Max Ellison is in those parts, friends, neighbors, and vacationers from nearby lakes and resorts who can find their way through the rutted, twisting hill roads to the secluded glen, go and hear the "Pied Piper of Frog Holler" weave his spell around a campfire.

THE MAKING OF A BEST SELLER

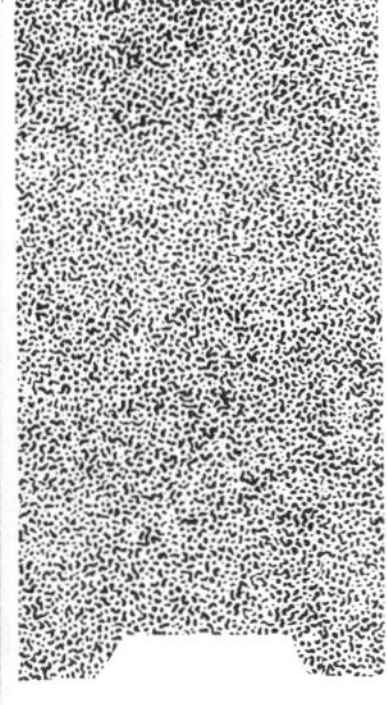

ERDMAN, Paul E.
(1932? -)

GOLD COAST PICTORIAL
(Ft. Lauderdale, Fla.)

Dec., 1973

BY OLIVER HANCOCK

Three years ago Bank President Paul Erdman was arresetd by the Swiss police and taken off to a castle prison in Basel where he was held for 10 months.

Today Best-Selling-Author Paul Erdman, initiator of a whole new mode of fiction (fi-fi, for financial fiction) is enjoying fame and fortune from his first novel, "The Billion Dollar Sure Thing" — published in Britain as "The Billion Dollar Killing."

He has moved to suburban Fort Lauderdale with his Swiss wife, Helly, and their two daughters, and is busy at work on his next two books, having sold the first to the movies. This fortunate turn of events is the sort of "switcheroo" he enjoys planting at the end of his novels. And it couldn't happen to a nicer guy.

For only in the eyes of the Swiss government, where money and banking are sacred, would Erdman be considered a criminal. His crime? Going broke.

As president of the Swiss branch of the United Bank of California he was responsible for a $25-million-plus loss. Actually his guilt goes beyond the embarrassment of this act, caused by employees who speculated in cocoa futures commodities. Erdman, a financial wizard when operating on his own, describes himself now as a poor banking administrator who naively relied on others' expertise in commodities. To cover up their losses, his Swiss junior executives compounded their speculations, attempting to hide both their losses and manipulations. It was the failure to admit and report these activities that resulted in arrests all around by Swiss authorities. As an American citizen Erdman was lucky enough to get off, posting a $125,000 "guarantee" which was hard to come by, since all his personal investments were wiped out in the bank failure. That amounts to bail, and Erdman won't be showing up for the trial, scheduled for this month.

The whole financial fiasco is described in chapter 14 of "Those Swiss Money Men" by Ray Vicker. London manager of the "Wall Street Journal," Vicker is also the man who put Erdman in touch with editor Burroughs Mitchell of Scribner's. He had heard that the ex-banker had been working on a novel while in prison and might have something to show.

And well he did. After five months of going stir-crazy (despite the rather comfortable prison quarters of private room and bath with privileges of ordering in food and wine) he needed something to kill time and challenge his mind. He decided to write a novel based on what he knew best — international finance.

Erdman brought an impressive background to the task. A graduate of the School of Foreign Service of Georgetown University and the University of Basel, he was author of many articles and two books on economics, one of them in German. He had served as an economist with the European Coal and Steel Community, as European representative of the Stanford Research Institute, and had been financial advisor to many foreign governments.

"The Billion Dollar Sure Thing" is not the story of his bank's failure and his imprisonment, however. Instead it deals with an international conspiracy to raise the price of gold and lower the value of the dollar. Swiss, Germans, British, Americans, Lebanese and Russians all figure in this "fi-fi" concoction. When published in the summer of 1973, it contained more truth than fiction. The price of gold had just hit the top and the dollar, the bottom, in the world market. It was all in headlines on the front pages of newspapers here and abroad.

"The people at Scribners have a good sense of humor and could see the irony in the whole thing," Erdman recalls. "I almost felt ashamed of myself."

Since then he and they have enjoyed seeing the book lead the best-seller lists all over the country, in addition to racking up countless foreign rights sales for publication in translation. Far from being stuffy in subject or approach, it has been compared to the work of Le Carre and Deighton. And one reviewer, Leslie Hanscom of "Newsday" credits Erdman with having invented a whole new mode of fiction — finance fiction which as fi-fi will take its place in library catalogues along with sci-fi.

"I think the James Bond era is over," says the author about his new twist to international intrigue. "People are sick and tired of the CIA and that stuff." But he admits that he jokingly refers to his second book as a sort of "Silverfinger," dealing as it does with the silver markets of the world financial scene.

As in "The Billion Dollar Sure Thing" it will jump from country to country introducing a large cast of characters who are depicted as types, rather than drawn in any real depth. This is intentional on Erdman's part, although he does see the necessity of a stronger hero emerging in novel number two. The lack of one in "The Billion Dollar Sure Thing," like the jumping from country to country, will present some problems for the movie version. Many locales will make the filming expensive; but the screenplay is in ➡

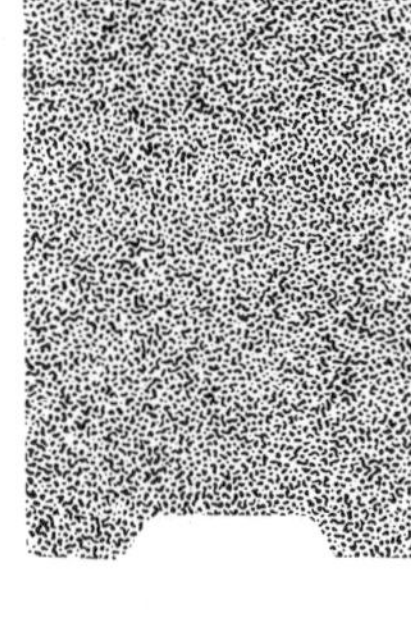

ERDMAN, Paul E.

GOLD COAST PICTORIAL (Ft. Lauderdale, Fla.)

Dec., 1973

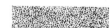

(Continued from preceding page)

the expert hands of Allen J. Trustman who wrote "Bullit." Erdman is confident it will come off well.

Besides the plush banking and government offices of Switzerland, Washington, London, etc., it will have some colorful exotic scenes. "My fat Arab, for example, is very close to types I've known," he says about the Middle Eastern monetary genius who deals with Westerners through interpreters in near medieval fashion from a dilapidated office near the bazaars of Beirut.

Rosen, the principal American in the book, is admittedly crude, "but there is nothing wrong with crudity," says the author. "It is the polished ones who are usually the sneaky ones. And the Swiss, for the most part, consider themselves a cut above the average mortal and expect you to respect that. My attitude is why? I should respect everybody equally."

This is the sort of statement which not only reflects his moral and philosophical atitude but open nice-guy approach to people. Although 41, Erdman's boyish manner and enthusiasm are disarming and his modesty and goodwill most appealing. This comes, perhaps, from the fact that he is the son of a Lutheran minister, the Rev. Horace Erdman, former execuive secretary of the Lutheran Church of Canada, now retired and residing in Fort Lauderdale. Born in Stratford, Ontario in 1932, Erdman grew up in the mid-west and attended prep school in Fort Wayne, Ind.

He met his Swiss-born wife at Georgetown. They moved to Basel where Erdman worked on his Ph.D. (summa cum laude) and enjoyed the fact that though he majored in economics he was able to hear lectures by such notables as psychologist Carl Jung and theologian Karl Barth.

But he will never return to Switzerland, thanks to their archaic system of justice. "It's a pity in a way I didn't go through the trial," he says "because you could write a marvelous book on the process of justice there — not necessarily fiction. The average American has no idea what his inheritance from British law means and the protection it affords," he states.

In Switzerland and other Western European countries, he points out, there is no habeas corpus, no charge necessary for arrest.

"But the worst feature is you are not in a position to build up a defense, especially where a bank is concerned.. And if you do, they prosecute you under the espionage and Swiss bank secrecy law. The prosecuting attorney decides what will be investigated. There are no cross examinations, they swear in no one, there is no defense nor witnesses," he explains.

"I did not exactly intend to attend the trial" he adds.

Some of this court material will doubtless appear in a future book. As it is, number two, still untitled but scheduled for publication next fall, moves from Iran to the Grand Canyon, Lugano, Turkey, Switzerland, San Francisco, Lichtenstein to Dubai. "It seems like a lot of jumping around," says Erdman, "but in the world of international finance everyone jumps around like that."

For many years Erdman jetted the world over and his home contains interesting mementos from his travels, many gifts from grateful governments. Erdman continues to serve as financial advisor for a few international groups, no individuals, and all by telephone. "I'm helping Southern Bell stay out of debt," he says, and adds, reflecting on his experience as a banking executive, "Now I believe strictly in organizations of one."

As for travel, he considers Western Europe "one big tourist trap," but enjoyed a trip through Eastern Europe "which is still an agricultural part of the world, full of peasants and all sorts of romantic things." Before moving to Florida the Erdmans lived briefly in England. "We enjoyed the English countryside. Everything was so green," he recalls, "with thousand-year-old oak trees in the back yard. It was beautiful, but the weather was lousy," says Erdman. "Of course, now when I tell people in New York that I live in Royal Palm Estates in Plantation they kind of edge away."

But he likes it here, and feels his daughters, Jennifer and Connie, European-trained young ladies who curtsy when they shake your hand, are receiving an excellent education at the Lutheran School in Fort Lauderdale.

The decision to move to South Florida was based in large part on providing a home base near the subject of his third novel — high finance in the islands of the Caribbean. "The book is blocked out," he says. "I've got the concept, but before I commit myself mentally I want to have a story." He expects that the British Cayman Islands, "where there are more banks than people" will figure in the story, and he plans to visit Haiti while he is doing research for the book.

"You must know exactly where you are going and will end up," he says. "If engineered correctly, the last 30 or 40 pages should be particularly exciting, with the surprise ending providing a switcheroo. I think readers enjoy having been misled."

"The Billion Dollar Sure Thing" has one of the best surprise endings in a long time.

As for the world money scene, does Erdman feel that Switzerland will continue to be a haven for foreign money? "Yes," he says. "For example there is a well-known courier service out of Geneva to Iran dealing in rials."

What concerns Erdman, however, is what he refers to as "bureaucratic symbiosis — the process through which big financial interests combine to clobber the little guy."

"The multi-national aspect is really most frightening," he says. "It seems in our society today, if you want to talk about bad guys, this is the type of force that can get to you and me most insidiously. It's hard to fight because it's outside any constraint of law. For example, IT&T would not dare do at home what it would dare do in Chile."

On the domestic financial front, he says: "We are now in the terrible aftermath of inflation caused by the Vietnam War, but it's going to run its course and hit a stable course."

Did he approve of Nixon's economic phases?

"If he had done phase one right, it could have been a good thing," says Erdman. "But as it was, it was a total bust, with prices going 15 to 20 percent higher.

"Mortgage money is going to stay very tight and very expensive for at least six more months," he predicts. "And the stock market, which has had a very nice run up primarily because corporate profits went up 20 to 30 percent, is not going to again next year.

"Profits are going to stagnate and the rate of growth is going to slow down. It won't be a recession with a capital R," says Erdman, "but a business slowdown.

"But I think that the fundamental economic factors in our free enterprise society are in the process of ironing themselves out," he says.

As for Florida? I think Florida will continue to boom," says the financial expert. "One investment vehicle which everyone throughout the world is pursuing is land, and especially warm-climate land. So Florida can't help but boom.

"And I think you are going to see German and Japanese capital coming in here and in the islands. It's inevitable."

It also seems inevitable that ex-banker turned novelist Paul Erdman will continue to write and prosper with his "fi-fi" books. For the moment, anyway, he seems to have cornered the market. ■

Author Tells How to Retire 'Side by Each'

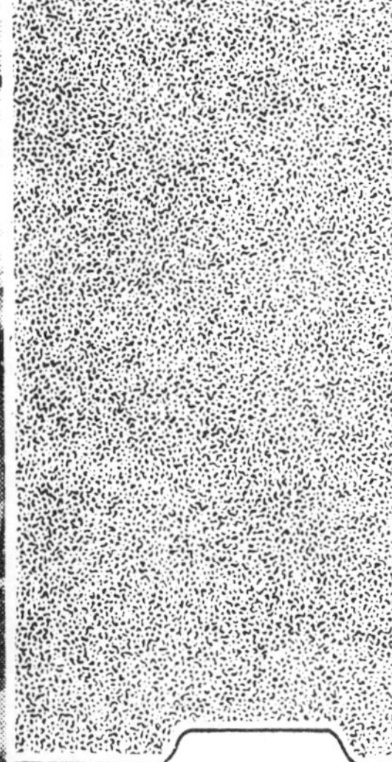

ETHRIDGE, Willie Snow (1900-)
MILWAUKEE JOURNAL (Milwaukee, Wisc.)
Feb. 3, 1974

[See also CA-17/18]

—*Journal Photo*

Author Willie Snow Ethridge likes to have her man around the house.

By Violet E. Dewey
of The Journal Staff

What happens when your husband retires? Will there be too much togetherness? Will it disrupt your life? What will he do? And what will you do?

Willie Snow Ethridge's husband retired not once but three times. She not only managed to cope but is very upbeat about the whole thing.

"Now he is really retired," she said, "and I find it perfectly delightful to have a man around the house. Mark knows how to spell and I don't. He knows a lot, and what he doesn't know he makes up.

"Retirement is full of challenges and excitement. It's like being born again."

Written 15 Books

Mrs. Ethridge, who has written 15 books, was in Milwaukee to talk about her newest one, "Side by Each." She will appear on the Milwaukee Public Library's "Critique" next Sunday on Channel 6, with repeats Feb. 14 on channel 10 and Feb. 15 on channel 36.

Mark Ethridge was publisher of the Louisville (Ky.) Courier Journal and Louisville Times when he first "retired" 10 years ago.

"When he was young, in his early 40s, he made a rule that everyone must retire at 65," said his wife, "and so when he got to be 65 he had to obey his own rule. But he stayed for two years as chairman of the board."

With many years of newspaper experience in various editorial executive jobs, Ethridge went back to work as editor of Newsday for two years, then retired again, Mrs. Ethridge said.

But he still wasn't ready for a life of leisure. He went to the University of North Carolina as a lecturer in journalism "for nine semesters. Then he got to be 70 and had to really retire."

Resists Move

At first Mrs. Ethridge was "horrified at the thought of moving away from Louisville and all the accouterments — a beautiful home, friends, being the wife of the publisher. But Mark wanted to be far enough away not to be able to look over shoulders. He thought everything would collapse, of course, after he left."

The Ethridges bought land in North Carolina, "where the paper would be 48 hours old before Mark saw it and he wouldn't be able to do anything about all those mistakes." Besides, "two sets of our children live in North Carolina and I didn't want to live with a passel of old people; one old man is enough."

Their 50 acres are on the edge of the sandhills, 22 miles from Chapel Hill and seven miles from Moncure, the post office.

Cleaning Land

"The land has never been lived on," said Mrs. Ethridge. "I clear land, grub out weeds and blackberry vines, saw down old elms and misshapen pines.

"One Christmas Mark gave me a power saw, a jar of perfume and long white kid gloves, a nice combination, I think.

"He's perfectly happy to let me do the digging and sawing. He's worked hard for 60 years — all newspapermen carry papers at 10 or 8 or 6 — and never had time to read books, just all the other newspapers and the Congressional Record. Now he reads and watches TV and answers the mail.

Make New Friends

"We go out some and entertain about once a month. We had to make new friends. I didn't want to draw myself in like a turtle. I didn't give up anything."

After their house was built and before Mrs. Ethridge started her gardening and to "make paths through the woods," the two new country dwellers thought they should watch birds as so many of their new friends did.

"We had a terrible time," said Mrs. Ethridge. "We got bird books and binoculars. We did work at it so hard. It bored us to death. You don't just learn to like it, like olives."

Writing Time

When the weather isn't good and Willie Snow Ethridge isn't outdoors hacking away at brambles or stamping down mole runs, she is at her desk from 9 a.m. to 1 p.m., writing. Then she and her husband relax with TV for a spell.

She has a cook-housekeeper and takes a turn in the kitchen only on weekends.

This is only the second time that she has "traveled with a book." This junket, paid for by her publisher, took her to Nashville, Milwaukee, Chicago, Akron and Cleveland.

"Side by Each," which deals with the Ethridges' life in retirement, may well be her last book, she said, because she has already said most of what she wants to say.

Earlier Books

Most of her books have been "informal essay autobiographical books," concerned with various experiences in her life. For example, "As I Live and Breathe" was about living in Georgia; "I'll Sing One Song" about life in Kentucky; "This LIttle Pig Stayed Home," a bestseller, about the war years. She also did books on travels with her husband on missions to Greece, Jerusalem, Turkey and Russia, two novels and two biographies.

Willie Snow started her writing career as a reporter. She met Mark Ethridge when she was a student at Wesleyan College in Macon, Ga., and he was so enthusiastic about journalism that she decided to study it. She did feature stories for the Macon Telegraph and after their marriage continued to do a column for the Telegraph "on what I was doing — with, I hope, a sense of humor." Out of this column grew her first book.

"It was successful," she said, "so I just kept on. I had had no intention of writing as a career, but Mark was so excited about newspapers that I had to do it."

The Ethridges have four children. Mark Jr., 50, also took up his father's career, and is now editor of the Detroit Free Press.

Eli Evans

No Alien in Promised Land

EVANS, Eli N.
(1936 -)

MIAMI HERALD
(Miami, Fla.)

June 18, 1974

[See also CA-45/48]

By ENA NAUNTON
Herald Staff Writer

It was 1950 in North Carolina and a family with a name shared by thousands of Welsh Protestants — Evans — was about to become the first family of the City of Durham.

The father, Emanuel "Mutt" Evans, running for mayor (a position he would hold for 12 years) was going out of his way to reveal his Jewishness, believing that "openness and pride were the best political means of battling anti-Semitism."

But his son, Eli, then a boy close to 13, harbored a secret thought as the result of a leaflet and whispering campaign that was part of the nastiness of politics. "I was glad," he confesses, "my name wasn't Goldberg."

Now, 24 years later, Eli Evans can say "I feel much more comfortable with myself now I know more of where I came from."

Journey South

THE DISCOVERY was made on a 7,000-mile pilgrimage through the South to research his book "The Provincials: A Personal History of Jews in the South," now into its third printing by Atheneum, having sold 10,000 hard cover copies since last September.

Someone once told Evans "We learn to be American by learning to hate what our parents came from . . ."

Evans doesn't hate it so much any more, although he remembers:

Fair-skinned, freckled, gray-hazel eyed, a son of the South, he remembers the shock waves when, walking home from school, he had a pamphlet thrust into his hand which read "One drop of Jew blood in your family destroys your white blood forever." It was signed by the Knights of the Ku Klux Klan.

He squirmed (still does, a little) that, although his was the prosperous First Family in his home town, living in a fashionable neighborhood, he could not swim in the restricted country club pool.

And, although he was invited to pledge the elitist Sigma Chi fraternity at the University of North Carolina, when he got to the fraternity house, as a freshman, another boy steered him aside and counseled that he pledge elsewhere for his own comfort, "being Jewish and all . . ."

Family Reunion

ACTUALLY, these were but sidelights to growing up in a big, successful family that was joyously Jewish and still is. About 30 relatives, under various names but still members of the Nachamson clan (the name of Evans's maternal grandparents) are in Miami Beach this week for a reunion in a city that Evans describes as "a Yankee enclave in the South."

It is for this reason that Miami, unlike Atlanta, New Orleans and Charleston, S.C., has no place in Evans's book of Jewish history in the South.

He traces the settlement of the Jews in some of the great Old South cities from the middle of the 18th Century. But Miami, he said, did not get its "tremendous influx" of Jewish population until after 1948.

'Yankee Enclave'

"IN 1948, There were about 40,000 Jews here and now there are about 180,000," Evans said. "It was too atypical even to be considered a Southern city any longer. It is a Yankee enclave in the South.

"But I have been told I missed a gold mine of material and there are many old families who are quite Southern in their roots . . . but that will have to wait for another book."

Meanwhile, he expects to work on transforming for television his history of the Southern Jews, from itinerant peddlers with packs on their backs to slave-owners, politicians and, more recently, to strong influences for racial integration. It is likely to be aired by one of the TV networks for the bicentennial celebration, but Evans won't say which network.

He will say what he discovered that bolstered his pride and gives a picture of what is to come in his portion of bicentennial memorials.

"I did not know (before the book research) of the roots of Jewish history in the South," said Evans. "I did not know there were more Southern Jews in Charleston in 1800 than in New York City. I did not know that 10,000 Jews fought for the Confederacy, as attracted to the tattered flag as the other white men around them.

"I did not know of the role the Jews played in the recovery of the South after the war. I came to feel that Jews were not aliens in the Promised Land but were blood and bones part of the South. And part of its history."

As for his family, his mother was "Hadassah's Southern accent," he said in his book and all her seven sisters were active in the Zionist movement.

THREE OF the sisters, Mrs. Leon Schneider, Mrs. S.T. Taylor and Mrs. Harold Wynn, live in the Miami area. Three of the sisters, including Evans' mother, married men who became mayors of their cities, Durham, N.C., Gastonia, N.C. and Huntington, W. Va.

Brought up in an atmosphere that always steered him to friendships with Jewish boys and girls and motherly hopes that he would marry a Jewish girl, Evans, at 37, has so far resisted marriage altogether.

He lives in New York and travels the country as a grants officer for the Carnegie Foundation, especially involved with grants to black law students. A graduate of Yale Law School, Evans doesn't even speak with a Southern accent any more.

HAS HE, who describes the assimilation of thousands of Jews into Southern and Christian ways of life, assimilated, too?

Hardly.

"I think the melting pot theory, such a poor philosophy in American life, is already proving to be a bad recipe for national reconciliation," he said. "That is the kind of statement that says to be American is to be bland. But Anglo-Saxons, Blacks, Cubans, Puerto Ricans, Jews, Mexican Americans have come to learn that to be an American is to be many things."

THE ROOTS from which a big family and a book on Jewish history in America's South came. Eli and Jennie Nachamson with their eight daughters and only son. All but Irene, second from right rear, and the parents, survive as the Nachamson clan.

Zoo World soft line on hard rock

President, publisher and editor at 25, Leslie Feldman (right) checks over a new issue of "Zoo World" with co-board member Arnie Wohl.
Photograph : Joe Elbert

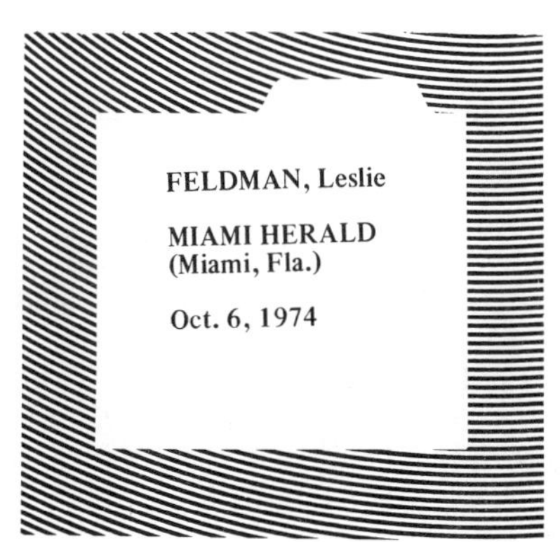

By James Trotter

On a hot summer's day in 1971, four young men sunbathing on a Fort Lauderdale beach agreed that they had talked long enough, and it was time to see if their idea would work. So they solemnly shook hands and went swimming — the first official act of *Zoo World's* board of directors.

For the uninitiated, *Zoo World* is not a journal devoted to wild life, but a Florida-based rock magazine geared to the youth market — and, like the better-known *Rolling Stone,* proof positive that rock and roll *can* be synonymous with financial success.

Launched on Jan. 27, 1972, with a capital of $25,000, *Zoo World* is this year projecting gross sales of $2.7 million. The first issue had a press run of 25,000 copies, all of which were given away free, as was the advertising space. Currently, the magazine is printing almost 300,000 copies per issue, and the staff has grown from five to 40, with another 60 receiving regular checks for free-lance services.

As one might expect, the prevailing mood is optimistic, tinged with that youthful aura of arrogance that seems to permeate the entire rock industry. "We *are* the music industry," claims Leslie Feldman, 25-year-old president, editor and publisher. "We do not intend to let anything stand in our way."

The *Zoo World* offices, located off Lauderdale's Oakland Park Blvd., are almost a caricature of what the rock music scene is meant to be. Long hair and beards are *de rigeur;* shirts are psychedelic and dark glasses frequently worn, presumably to cut down on the glare from the walls, which are papered with rock concert posters ranging from a semi-irreverent slogan about the Pope to a semi-obscene illustration of elephants copulating. Rock music drifts through the halls in a never-ending cacophony, and president-publisher-editor Feldman sets the style with blue jeans, Western shirt opened three buttons down from the collar, and platform shoes.

Nevertheless, despite the atmosphere and the pop nature of the magazine's contents, any good executive dressed in a Brooks Brothers three-piece would feel at home with Feldman and his board members as they talk of marketing concepts, motivational techniques, profit margins, success attitudes and other strictly non-rock subjects.

"If *Zoo World* had another name," quips Feldman, an intense young man of medium height and athletic build, "it would be *(Being in the) Black Is Beautiful.*

"The whole thing is attitude," he continues. "We didn't bring in a lot of professionals to tell us what couldn't be done. We emphasize what *can* be done with proper instruction and motivation. We took people who couldn't even paste-up a newspaper and told them they were artists. When we went national they became art directors."

For a man of his age, Feldman knows a lot about motivation. As a Miami newspaper boy, he won every carrier contest in the city. When he was 13, he had five other boys working for him. "I used to motivate them by taking them to ball games," he recalls. "If you're willing to work harder than your competition, you're bound to be successful."

Feldman's current competition is *Rolling Stone,* the formidable California-based music magazine which was printing issue No. 100 when the first copies of *Zoo World* rolled off the presses. However, unlike *Rolling Stone, Zoo World* does not contain political or social commentary, trading instead on a "clean and positive" approach to music. Feldman and the others look upon their publication as a partner to the music industry; an independent partner, but a partner nevertheless.

"We're *for* the music industry," says Steve Shor, the magazine's 25-year-old director of operations, and along with Feldman, Arnie Wohl and Sumner Wilson, one of its four board members. "We're not going to put the industry down. If something is too negative, we'd rather not print it."

"We *are* critical, but we don't put it in headlines," Feldman elaborates. "We're not a cutesy magazine where everything is puff. If an artist deserves criticism, we'll criticize. But we're not going to let an 18-year-old kid sit down behind a typewriter and blast a $400,000 project."

In contrast to *Rolling Stone,* noted for its uncompromising, straight-from-the-shoulder approach, there are no four-letter words in *Zoo World.* "We want the magazine to be so clean that a 15-year-old girl can take it home from school without her mother objecting," explains Shor. ➡

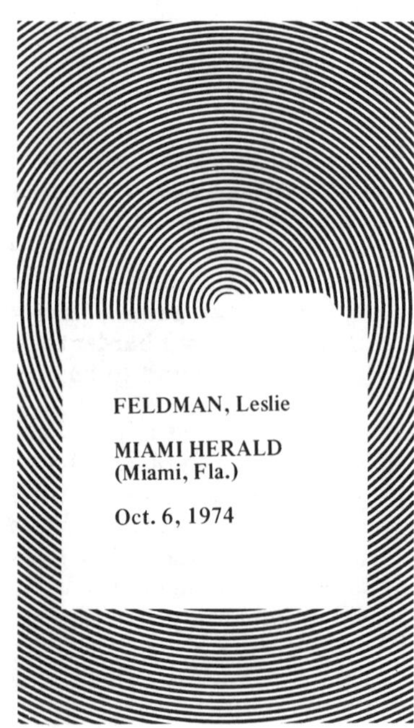
FELDMAN, Leslie

MIAMI HERALD
(Miami, Fla.)

Oct. 6, 1974

(Continued from preceding page)

Probably more vital to the magazine's success, however, is a shrewd marketing technique that directly links it with radio stations across the country. In each issue, *Zoo World* publishes some 80 different centerfolds, each one advertising the offerings of a rock station in a particular area.

The printing problems involved are immense, but so is the payoff; in exchange for an exclusive centerfold covering its prime broadcast area, the radio station is required to air an average of 25 one-minute advertisements weekly boosting the magazine.

In effect, the exchange agreement gives *Zoo World* a massive nationwide advertising campaign worth $1 million annually. "It's a pretty equitable deal," says Ron Shawn, director of the radio operation. "Ideally, we are looking for 110-125 radio stations covering 90 per cent of the major population areas in the United States. We have 80 of those stations right now."

The concept for the radio tie-in goes back to a time when Wohl and Shor were instrumental in putting radio station WBUS, at that time a progressive rocker on Miami Beach, on the air. "We had this idea that we could get to people's ears through radio and to their eyes through a newspaper," recalls Wohl.

At about the same time, Feldman, who had already had experience in various aspects of newspaper production, joined WBUS to produce *The Magic Bus,* an underground, counter-culture station. Soon, Feldman, Shor and Wohl were discussing ways to enter the music business on their own.

A cash offer was made for a Fort Lauderdale radio station, but was refused. "We missed on the radio station," said Wohl, "but we still felt like we had an idea. If we couldn't own a radio station, we figured we could at least put out a newspaper that was affiliated with one."

Soon after, a deal was made with Lauderdale's WSHE, and, with some trepidation on the part of its youthful staff, *Zoo World* was finally launched.

Immediately, the magazine ran into problems with Madison Avenue. The big New York advertising agencies "didn't want to recognize" that Fort Lauderdale was on the map. The same question was posed time and again: Why publish a rock magazine from Fort Lauderdale, as opposed to a giant music center like New York or Los Angeles? Each time, the same answer was given: "Fort Lauderdale is where we're from — and where we like to live."

"Slowly we gained, city by city," says Feldman. "In a short time, we had managed to affiliate the magazine with six radio stations across Florida. Then we made a deal whereby we could rent cars for a week without a mileage charge, and drove all over talking, discussing, bargaining. Often we'd turn the cars in at the end of a week with 3,000-4,000 miles on them. We gained city by city, and then we went back to New York and told them that we had the South tied up. So they said, 'Who the hell needs the South?' "

Finally, however, enough stations were showing an interest in the exclusive centerfold deal to induce Feldman and his associates to take the big gamble. With issue No. 29, dated March 29, 1973, *Zoo World* finally became a nationally-circulated publication.

If marketing is one problem, gaining reader support is quite another.

"Our main editorial problem is finding the time, energy and money to produce material with real backbone," says managing editor A. D. Penchansky. "It's a constant fight not to be overwhelmed by public-relations-oriented material. We try to keep the percentage steady in relation to the news we are actually digging out and presenting ourselves."

To provide nationwide coverage of the rock scene, *Zoo World* employs a staff of five in New York, five in Los Angeles and one in Chicago. But the heart of the operation remains in Fort Lauderdale, and Wohl contends that working out of South Florida is advantageous in dealing both with advertisers and with *Zoo World's* out-of-town employes. "When I come back to Florida I get rejuvenated. Now the account executives who once were saying, 'Where *is* Fort Lauderdale?', are saying, 'I wish I could live down there and get myself a tan.' "

To be 25 years old and heading a national publication is frequently a heady business. Recently, a representative of Bell & Howell, the electronics firm, called to ask about the price of inserting an ad in the magazine. Wohl cupped his hand over the phone and relayed the question to the others in the conference room. They discussed it briefly, then decided it would take some time to figure out.

"Tell them we'll get back to them," said Feldman.

"Yeah," said Shor, "Bell & Howell is just gonna have to wait."

There was laughter. The idea of making a big corporation wait is still new and funny.

"Our sights are high," says Arnie Wohl, "but one problem we have around here is dealing with reality. If we told our story to a lot of people they would think we were loonies."

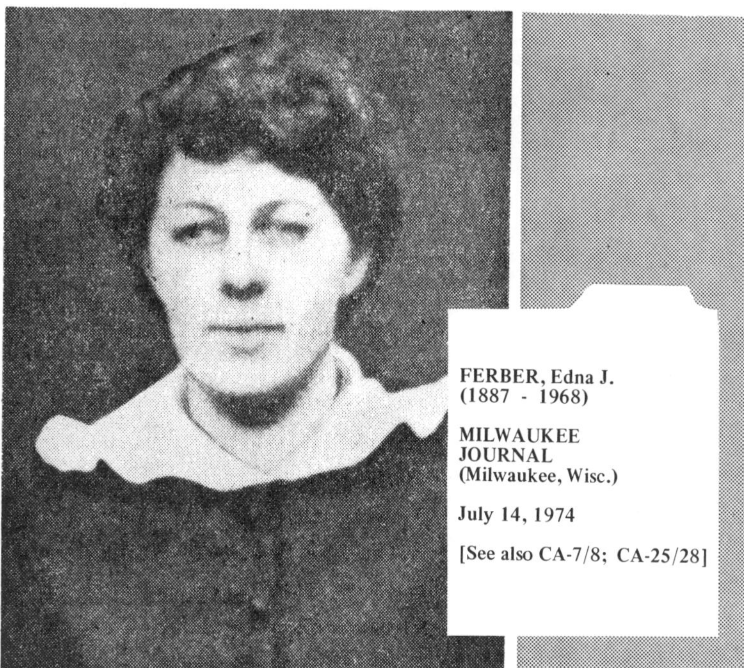

FERBER, Edna J. (1887 - 1968)

MILWAUKEE JOURNAL (Milwaukee, Wisc.)

July 14, 1974

[See also CA-7/8; CA-25/28]

Edna Ferber of The Journal staff

That 'Ferber House': Edna Didn't Like It

By LESLIE CROSS, Journal Book Editor

WHETHER it stands or is knocked to pieces by wreckers, one thing can be said for that decrepit house on N. Cass St.: Edna Ferber really lived there. She didn't live there long. It was not her favorite place. But she never forgot it.

Myths have a way of encrusting old buildings. Did one of the greatest careers in popular fiction begin under these century old eaves that pickets hope to keep in place? The evidence seems otherwise. For Edna Ferber, the house was a place of sickness. She went back to Appleton, where she had grown up. It was there that she began writing her stories and novels.

Edna Ferber was under 19 when she came to Milwaukee. She had been a reporter in Appleton. Her work there attracted the attention of Henry Colin Campbell, then managing editor of The Milwaukee Journal. Would she like to join The Journal staff? She took the earliest possible train and found herself in a new world.

When Milwaukee Was a German City

The year was 1906. Milwaukee was booming and full of news. It was also a city, in the new reporter's phrase of many years later, "as German as Germany."

In an autobiography published in 1938, "A Peculiar Treasure," Edna Ferber wrote about some of the experiences of her Milwaukee years. "Arrived," she related, "I made straight for a boarding house that had been recommended to me as cheap, clean, good. Kahlo's turned out to be a gold mine, for I used it, complete, in my first novel, 'Dawn O'Hara,' written four years later."

As to whether she went immediately to Kahlo's, the record is not clear. The Milwaukee City Directory for 1907 gave the address of "Ferber, Edna J., reporter, Journal," as 638 Astor St., which in time became 1220 N. Astor. For many years afterward that was the address of the Walther League Lutheran Girls' Home, where young women from out of town could find respectable and inexpensive temporary quarters.

But Kahlo's — "Hotel Kahlo" in the directories — enchanted her. It was not in the seemingly doomed building at 760 N. Cass St., but in a three story house on Jackson St., across from the old Milwaukee County Courthouse in what is now Cathedral Square. She described it in "Dawn O'Hara":

"I am living at a little private hotel just across from the court house square with its scarlet geraniums and its pretty fountain. The house is filled with German civil engineers, mechanical engineers, and herr professors from the German academy.

"On Sunday mornings we have pfannkuchen with current jelly, and the herr professors come down to breakfast in fearful flappy German slippers . . .

"Even the dog is a dachshund. It is so unbelievable that every day or two I go down to Wisconsin St. and gaze at the Stars and Stripes floating from the government building, in order to convince myself that this is America."

Alas, the tidy and gemutlich Kahlo's closed. On Cass St. a block east and a little to the south the young reporter found another room she could afford. It was in the house now marked for destruction. When Edna Ferber moved there it was grandiloquently called The Avon and Mrs. Bessie A. Haley was listed as its proprietor.

"For 25 years" Edna Ferber wrote in her autobiography of 1938, "I've tried to squeeze Ma Haley and Haley's boarding house into a book. They are too fanciful for fiction. My first room at Haley's was an attic room under the eaves and right out of an O. Henry story. The kitchen smells came up to it through the smokestack."

'Something Sinister' Hung Over It

Mrs. Haley, with her jewels and faded finery, seemed a phantasmal figure to her new lodger. "Though the house was definitely rich and even luxurious, there was about it something sinister. Really solid and even distinguished people lived there for months and years on end, yet unsavoriness pervaded its every corner . . . About it all there was a kind of whorehouse atmosphere."

And sometimes, just before the evening meal, there would be screams and shouts; "the chef, gone mad, would be chasing Ma Haley or one of his helpers with a cleaver or a carving knife."

Also, the food was bad. For a while, Edna Ferber escaped from it by moving with some friends to a furnished East Side house vacant in summer. But she had to go back. She felt weaker and weaker; soon she was seriously ill.

The Journal gave her a leave. She went back to Appleton. She never managed to return to her job. In all, she spent three and a half years in Milwaukee.

Recovering, she began to write fiction. Her Milwaukee years provided her first subject. Though "Dawn O'Hara" was not her personal story, she drew liberally on her friendships and struggles in Milwaukee in its construction.

Perhaps its most memorable character, a sports editor whom she called Blackie, was drawn from W. W. Rowland of The Journal, the Brownie of Wisconsin newspaper legend. In her autobiography, she wrote: "There came to me more knowledge, warmth and companionship from Wallie Rowland than from anyone I had known until that time. . . . I killed him in the book, but he is alive as I write this and, from all accounts, as vital and winning as ever."

After a lifetime of picturesque exploits, Brownie died in 1944. Edna Ferber died in 1968, at the age of 80.

From Appleton, she had moved on again to Chicago and New York. She was not a very approachable woman in her last years. She loved controversy but tried to conserve her energies for her work.

When her book "A Kind of Magic," an autobiographical sequel to "A Peculiar Treasure," was published in 1963, I visited her at her apartment at Park Ave. and E. 80th St. in New York. She was a tiny woman — smaller than I had thought she would be — with a radiant face and white hair. She talked about the issues of the day and about the Wisconsin of her girlhood — but not at length, for she kept a rigid schedule and had other engagements the same afternoon.

I had come to her apartment from Doubleday, her publisher, where I had been given a copy of her book.

"Let me sign it for you," said Edna Ferber.

She wrote, in the large, clear script that she had always used:

"To Leslie Cross of The Milwaukee Journal, as I, too, once was."

Glitter Hides the Real Fitzgerald

FITZGERALD, F(rancis) Scott Key (1896 - 1940)
FITZGERALD, Zelda Sayre (1900 - 1948)
SMITH, Frances Scott Fitzgerald (Scottie) (1921 -)
MIAMI HERALD (Miami, Fla.) Apr. 14, 1974

By JONATHAN YARDLEY
Herald Book Editor

So we beat on, boats against the current, borne back ceaselessly into the past.

That is the last sentence of F. Scott Fitzgerald's finest novel, **The Great Gatsby.** In 1974, with Fitzgerald's work at a new height of popularity, the words have acquired an unexpected irony.

The "past" of which Fitzgerald wrote is the dream world of American youth — the world into which, their dreams thwarted by cold reality, his characters were drawn or unconsciously retreated. His subject, as he wrote in **Gatsby,** was "the abortive sorrows and short-winded elations of men"—"the orgiastic future that year by year recedes before us."

Now, however, the "past" that Fitzgerald has come to represent is not a lost dream but a romantic nostalgic vision of the Roaring Twenties Fitzgerald is the latest entry in the nostalgia craze, and it looks as if he will be one of the most profitable. Nostalgia, however, is like a fun-house mirror: We see things not as they were, but distorted by time, hazy memories and our desire to rewrite the past to fit our current expectations and needs. We are creating a myth around Scott Fitzgerald, and in the process we are losing sight of the reality.

PARAMOUNT PICTURES, which paid Fitzgerald's estate $350,000 for the rights to film a third movie adaptation of **Gatsby,** makes no bones about its motives in doing so. According to Frank Yablans, president of Paramount, "We thought people were quite fatigued with the pressures of contemporary living and that nostalgia was a safety valve . . ." A few weeks after the film's release, the hunch has been proved a thumping success: In advance sales alone, the Robert Redford-Mia Farrow "Gatsby" has brought in more than triple its $6.4-million cost.

The movie is not the only money-maker in the burgeoning Fitzgerald fad. Something on the order of a million copies of Fitzgerald's books are expected to be sold this year in the United States — including an estimated 830,000 copies of **Gatsby,** most of them in the paperback editions published by Scribner's and Bantam. (The latter is pushing its edition as a movie tie-in.) Scribner's says that about 2,400 colleges make one or more of Fitzgerald's books required reading. In Britain, Penguin has just ordered a 250,000-copy paperback printing of **Gatsby.** And Scotty Fitzgerald Smith, Fitzgerald's daughter, is collaborating on a pictorial biography of her parents, to be called **The Romantic Egotists;** it is expected to be a best-seller immediately upon publication, probably this fall.

For Fitzgerald s estate, of which Mrs. Smith is sole executor and beneficiary, all of this is expected to add up to 1974 income in the high six figures, possibly seven. Fitzgerald, who had a tart appreciation of the ironic, no doubt would regard that with dour amusement — for in spite of his image as a high-living playboy, he had an unceasing money problem.

PART OF the reason was that Fitzgerald was utterly irresponsible with money; not merely did he spend money as fast as it came in, he spent money he did not have. But the larger reason was that he simply did not have much money. Of all his novels, only **This Side of Paradise** was an appreciable financial success. **Gatsby,** on which more than anything else his reputation rests, barely earned enough in hard cover sales to meet the $4,254 advance he received for it. Professor Matthew Bruccoli of the University of South Carolina, who has made a career out of Fitzgerald's work, estimates that he made no more than $60,000 from the book before his death in 1940, a figure that includes his share of the first movie sale.

To speak of Fitzgerald in terms of dollars and cents is not as demeaning as at first it may seem. For if he was obsessed with making ends meet—his invaluable **Letters,** edited by Andrew Turnbull, are filled with pleas for cash to editors and agents — he was also obsessed with money as a barometer of American success. Ernest Hemingway, who was incomparably nasty to Fitzgerald, used to mock him for it, as he did with extraordinary cruelty in a thinly-veiled reference in "The Snows of Kilimanjaro";

"He remembered poor Julian and his romantic awe of (the rich) and how he had started a story once that began, 'The very rich are different from you and me.' And how someone had said to Julian, Yes, they have more money. But that was not humorous to Julian. He thought they were a special glamorous race and when he found they weren't it wrecked him just as much as any other thing that wrecked him."

THE PASSAGE suited Hemingway's private purposes — Fitzgerald had been one of his early benefactors, and Hemingway had a perverse habit of turning against anyone who helped him — at the expense of the truth. Fitzgerald was indisputably fascinated by rich people, and no doubt he envied them their money, but he was always the outsider, the remarkably clinical and dispassionate observer. In the words of Nick Carraway, the narrator of **Gatsby,** Fitzgerald described himself:

" . . . high over the city our line of yellow windows must have contributed their share of human secrecy to the casual watcher in the darkening streets, and I was him too, looking up and wondering. I was within and without, simultaneously enchanted and repelled by the inexhaustible variety of life."

Like a number of other American novelists whose work has focused on the upper classes — notably John P. Marquand and John O'Hara — Fitzgerald was an outsider by circumstances of birth and rearing. He was born in 1896, not in the Northeast but in Minnesota. He was not an Episcopalian but a Catholic. His parents were not well-to-do but marginally middle-class.

When Fitzgerald entered Princeton in the fall of 1913, it was as an ambitious middle-class youth surrounded by haughty aristocrats. When, as a second lieutenant stationed near Montgomery, Ala., toward the end of World War II, he began to court the glamourous Zelda Sayre, her prominent parents viewed him with some skepticism. Zelda's biographer, Nancy Milford, describes their feelings: "Fitzgerald was a charming and attractive but uncertain young man: he had not graduated from Princeton, he was Irish, he had no career to speak of, he drank too much, and he was a Catholic."

He would always remain the outsider, and though he did like the high life, it was this persistent detachment that made him a genuine artist. Essentially, the Fitzgerald myth is built out of trivial apparatus: splashing tipsily with Zelda in the fountain at The Plaza, riding down Fifth Avenue perched on the roof of an automobile, wintering lavishly at the Riviera, hobnobbing with movie stars. Fitzgerald did all those things, but they say no more about the real Fitzgerald than all the bullfighting and boxing matches say about the real Hemingway.

Beneath all the public glitter of which the Fitzgerald myth is constructed, there was always — first and foremost — Fitzgerald the artist. No one knew that better than he. In 1924, when he was at the height of his brief celebrity, partying and carousing his way into the gossip columns, **he was nonetheless hard at work at his art. He was finishing The Great Gatsby, and he wrote a remarkably revealing letter about it to his editor, Maxwell Perkins:**

"In my new novel I'm thrown directly on purely creative work — not trashy imaginings as in my stories but the sustained imagination of a sincere yet radiant world. So I tread slowly and carefully and at times in considerable distress. This book will be a consciously artistic achievement . . ."

As William Styron has **commented, "Oppressively superficial as he may have appeared during the Twenties — and may have been in important respects — he never abandoned, even then, this stony, saving honesty and self-awareness."**

Gatsby is, indisputably, the best writing Fitzgerald did, though **Tender Is the Night** and a few of the short stories are very fine indeed. It is not a "great" book, for greatness demands far more breadth of

(Continued from preceding page) vision and accomplishment than Fitzgerald brought to any of his work. **Gatsby** is a miniature, but a very nearly perfect one. It is not a celebration of the rich, but a stinging satire of vanity and emptiness, and a mordant depiction of the rot that Fitzgerald saw eating away at the heart of the American dream:

"About half way between West Egg and New York the motor road hastily joins the railroad and runs beside it for a quarter of a mile, so as to shrink away from a certain desolate area of land. This is a valley of ashes — a fantastic farm where ashes grow like wheat into ridges and hills and grotesque gardens; where ashes take the forms of houses and chimneys and rising smoke and, finally, with a transcendant effort, of men who move dimly and already crumbling through the powdery air. Occasionally a line of gray cars crawls along an invisible track, gives out a ghastly creak, and comes to rest, and immediately the ash-gray men swarm up with leaden spades and stir up an impenetrable cloud, which screens their obscure operations from your sight."

It is that aspect of Fitzgerald which the sanitized legend neglects to take into account. Significantly, the quote which is featured in advertisements for the movie is not from the novel but from an Irving Berlin song: "Gone is the romance that was so divine." It is an invitation to recapture yesterday's romance, which is perfectly all right in itself but has very little to do with what Fitzgerald was up to in **The Great Gatsby**.

CERTAINLY the romance between Jay Gatsby and Daisy Buchanan is a lovely one, and Fitzgerald could write shimmeringly romantic prose. But romance, per se, is not the core of the book. It is the device Fitzgerald used to dramatize Gatsby's poignant failure to fulfill his dream:

". . . as I sat there brooding on the old, unknown world, I thought of Gatsby's wonder when he first picked out the green light at the end of Daisy's dock. He had come a long way to this blue lawn, and his dream must have seemed so close that he could hardly fail to grasp it. He did not know that it was already behind him, somewhere back in that vast obscurity beyond the city, where the dark fields of the republic rolled on under the night."

There, not in the story of Gatsby and Daisy, is the real romance in Fitzgerald's novel. He had a love affair with the American heartland, with "that vast obscurity" where people had not been spoiled by the tinsel of success. He wrote about it in a passage of surpassing beauty:

"One of my most vivid memories is of coming back West from prep school and later from college at Christmas time. Those who went farther than Chicago would gather in the old dim Union Station at six o'clock of a December evening, with a few Chicago friends, already caught up into their own holiday gayeties, to bid them a hasty goodby. I remember the fur coats of the girls returning from Miss This-or-That's and the chatter of frozen breath and the hands waving overhead as we caught sight of old acquaintances, and the matchings of invitations: 'Are you going to the Ordways'? the Herseys'? the Schultzes'?' and the long green tickets clasped tight in our gloved hands. And last the murky yellow cars of the Chicago, Milwaukee & St. Paul railroad looking cheerful as Christmas itself on the tracks beside the gate.

"When we pulled out into the winter night and the real snow, our snow, began to stretch out beside us and twinkle against the windows, and the dim lights of small Wisconsin stations moved by, a sharp wild brace came suddenly into the air. We drew in deep breaths of it as we walked back from dinner through the cold vestibules, unutterably aware of our identity with this country for one strange hour, before we melted indistinguishably into it again.

"That's my Middle West — not the wheat or the prairies or the lost Swede towns, but the thrilling returning trains of my youth, and the street lamps and sleigh bells in the frosty dark and the shadows of holly wreaths thrown by lighted windows on the snow. I am part of that, a little solemn with the feel of those long winters, a little complacent from growing up in the Carraway house in a city where dwellings are still called through decades by a family's name. I see now that this has been a story of the West, after all — Tom and Gatsby, Daisy and Jordan and I, were all Westerners, and perhaps we possessed some deficiency in common which made us subtly unadaptable to Eastern life."

THUS, IN the end, Fitzgerald did not glorify the world to which Hemingway thought he aspired; he renounced it. He saw it as "a night scene by El Greco: a hundred houses, at once conventional and grotesque, crouching under a sullen, overhanging sky and a lustreless moon." It is, indeed, a nightmare vision:

"In the foreground four solemn men in dress suits are walking along the sidewalk with a stretcher on which lies a drunken woman in a white evening dress. Her hand, which dangles over the side, sparkles cold with jewels. Gravely the men turn in at a house — the wrong house. But no one knows the woman's name, and no one cares.

"After Gatsby's death the East was haunted for me like that, distorted beyond my eyes' power of correction. So when the blue smoke of brittle leaves was in the air and the wind blew the wet laundry stiff on the line I decided to come back home."

FITZGERALD himself never did "come back home." After the publication of **Gatsby** in 1925, his fortunes began a steady decline. The unexpectedly poor sales of **Gatsby** wounded him severely, and more and more he retreated into alcohol. His marriage to Zelda, shaky from the start, became more and more difficult. Not merely were both of them drinking far too much, but their relationship became increasingly competitive. Years later, in a letter to Scotty, Fitzgerald wrote with remarkable directness about his work, his marriage and the conflict between the two:

"When I was your age I lived with a great dream. The dream grew and I learned how to speak of it and make

people listen. Then the dream divided one day when I decided to marry your mother after all, even though I knew she was spoiled and meant no good to me. I was sorry immediately I had married her, but, being patient in those days, made the best of it and got to love her in another way. You came along and for a long time we made quite a lot of happiness out of our lives. But I was a man divided — she wanted me to work too much for HER and not enough for my dream."

That letter is interesting for a couple of reasons. One is that it is is as vigorous an expression of artistic dedication as Fitzgerald ever permitted himself to make. The other is that it contains a remarkable amount of self-justification and bitterness, and neither was characteristic of Fitzgerald.

HIS ACCOUNT, in the letter, of the beginning of his marriage is simply inaccurate. The portrait he draws of a reluctant suitor is an utter falsehood: Fitzgerald pursued Zelda with single-minded ardor. And he rarely expressed such bitterness toward her. From her first mental breakdown until the end of his life he was kind

FITZGERALD, F. Scott
FITZGERALD, Zelda
SMITH, Frances Scott (Scottie)

MIAMI HERALD Apr. 14, 1974
(Miami, Fla.)

(Continued from preceding page)

and patient toward her with only rare exceptions, and after his death Zelda wrote: "He was as spiritually generous a soul as ever was . . . In retrospect it seems as if he was always planning happiness for Scottie and me. Books to read — places to go. Life seemed so promising always when he was around . . . Although we weren't close any more, Scott was the best friend a person could have to me . . ."

He was, in fact, the best friend any person could have. Beneath the image of the debonaire playboy was a man of almost infinite kindness and generosity and loyalty. Dozens of examples could be given, but perhaps the best is a letter he wrote to his close friends Gerald and Sara Murphy in 1937. Within two years, two of their three children died. At the death of the second, Fitzgerald wrote them what William Styron has called "one of the most beautiful letters of its kind that we have":

"Dearest Gerald and Sara:

"The telegram came today and the whole afternoon was so sad with thoughts of you and the happy times we had once. Another link binding you to life is broken and with such insensate cruelty that it is hard to say which of the two blows was conceived with more malice. I can see the silence in which you hover now after this seven years of struggle and it would take words like Lincoln's in his letter to the mother who had lost four sons in the war to write you anything fitting at the moment. The sympathy you will get will be what you have had from each other already and for a long, long time you will be inconsolable.

FITZGERALD, F. Scott
FITZGERALD, Zelda
SMITH, Frances Scott (Scottie)

MIAMI HERALD
(Miami, Fla.)

Apr. 14, 1974

"But I can see another generation growing up around Honoria and an eventual peace somewhere, an occasional port of call as we all sail deathward. Fate can't have any more arrows in its quiver for you that will wound like these. Who was it said that it was astounding how deepest griefs can change in time to a sort of joy? The golden bowl is broken indeed but it WAS golden; nothing can ever take those boys away from you now.

"Scott"

AT THE time he wrote that letter, Fitzgerald's fortunes were in almost total disrepair. Zelda was in a North Carolina hospital, where she would remain for the rest of her life. He had no money, and his only prospects were in Hollywood, where he would live out his last three years writing — or, between drinking bouts, attempting to write — screenplays. He received some comfort from a love affair with Sheilah Graham, the gossip columnist, and he continued to write devoted, attentive, thoughtful letters to Scotty; collected in book form in **Letters to His Daughter,** they are splendid reading.

Death, when it came in 1940, was caused by a heart attack, his second within a month. His health was not good in his last months, but he worked as diligently as he could on a novel that was to be called **The Last Tycoon.** He never finished it, but the incomplete manuscript suggests that it would have been work of the first order. Andrew Turnbull, in his superb Fitzgerald biography, makes the proper judgment: "Whether **The Last Tycoon** would have been his best novel we cannot know, but does it matter? The important thing was Fitzgerald's belief in his work and in himself . . . against great odds . . . and after long apostacy. The quality of a life can be more impressive than art."

Fitzgerald's life had many low moments, but it was a good life. He was not the dashing romantic of legend, though occasionally he played at the role, but a quiet and sensitive man of inordinate decency. If the current craze for his work leads people to explore his life and thus to find the true Fitzgerald, they will be richly rewarded — even if the man they find is not the one they had expected.

Scott and Zelda Fitzgerald's Montgomery, Ala.

FITZGERALD, F(rancis) Scott Key
FITZGERALD, Zelda Sayre
and
SMITH, Frances Scott Fitzgerald (Scottie)
COURIER-JOURNAL
& TIMES (Louisville, Ken.) Mar. 24, 1974

By KEITH RUNYON
Courier-Journal Staff Writer

MONTGOMERY, Ala.—Mrs. Eugenia Tuttle stood in Montgomery's Oakwood Cemetery, her eyes sad but her voice firm as she surveyed row after row of graves where soldiers of the Confederacy lie buried.

"We were brought up on the Confederacy. It meant more to us than almost anything else did," Mrs. Tuttle, now 72, remarked. She was trying to explain how her friend and contemporary, Zelda Sayre, felt about their native city.

It was here, 56 years ago in July, that Zelda Sayre first met Lt. F. Scott Fitzgerald of St. Paul, Minn., at a country club dance.

Fitzgerald was a soldier stationed at nearby Camp Sheridan. While paying only slight attention to his military duties, he was making quite a hit with the local belles.

He had arrived in Montgomery in mid-April 1918, after being stationed for several months in Ft. Leavenworth, Kan., and for a month in Louisville's Camp Taylor. In Louisville he finished the draft of a novel that he called "The Romantic Egotist," and he felt confident on the night he met Zelda Sayre that he would someday become a great novelist.

After the war was over and his romance with Zelda went through several traumas, Fitzgerald published his novel, by then retitled "This Side of Paradise." It took the nation by storm and launched his career as the fiction writer of "The Jazz Age," which he named.

Montgomery was to serve as the locale for many of his stories and portions of his novels, whether he called it by its true name or disguised it under others. And his wife would use it as the setting for her only published novel, "Save Me the Waltz."

They returned here periodically during their marriage, which began on April 3, 1920, eight days after "This Side of Paradise" was published, and lasted until Dec. 20, 1940, when Fitzgerald died of a heart attack in Hollywood at the age of 44. His wife died in a hospital fire in North Carolina eight years later at the age of 48.

Zelda spent most of the last 15 years of her life in Montgomery. During 1931, after years abroad and in New York, she, Scott and Scottie, their 10-year-old daughter, moved back to town and briefly set up residence in a large house at 919 Felder Ave.

Their stay there was short, however, since Scott left to write movie scripts in Hollywood, and Zelda soon suffered another nervous breakdown and was hospitalized in Maryland and North Carolina.

Later in the Thirties, she returned to Montgomery, and with her mother lived in a bungalow on Sayre Street, named for her ancestors, some of whom helped found Montgomery 150 years ago. (That home was torn down to make way for an expressway.)

Montgomery's only "official" monument to the Fitzgeralds is a tiny triangu-

(Continued from preceding page)

FITZGERALD, F(rancis) Scott Key
FITZGERALD, Zelda Sayre
and
SMITH, Frances Scott Fitzgerald (Scottie)
COURIER-JOURNAL
& TIMES (Louisville, Ken.) Mar. 24, 1974

These photographs of the late Mr. and Mrs. F. Scott Fitzgerald are from the earlier happy days in the lives of the writer and his bride, the former Zelda Sayre, before their love story became a tragedy. The pictures show Zelda, above, practicing ballet about the time she met Fitzgerald; the young writer, above, in a studio portrait; the Fitzgeralds, right, on their wedding day in New York City on April 3, 1920; Fitzgerald, upper right, as a soldier in World War I as he looked when he met Zelda, and, at lower left, a teen-aged Zelda on the porch of the Sayre family home, 6 Pleasant Ave., Montgomery.

Photos from the collection of Mrs. C. Grove Smith

(Continued from preceding page)

lar-shaped park adjacent to the house on Felder Avenue where they lived.

At the park's center is a small fountain, less than 6-feet tall, which can't help but to remind the visitor of the time in New York when the Fitzgeralds, then newlyweds, joyfully splashed about in the huge Pulitzer Fountain on Grand Army Plaza.

There are many other sites in this southern city that are associated with the writer and his wife, but it's unlikely that the Fitzgeralds would feel comfortable in the contemporary Montgomery — symbol of the New South with a population almost four times what it was in 1918 and with new industries and a latticework of expressways and interstate highways.

But if the city has changed physically, many of the people who knew the Fitzgeralds still live here, and their memories are filled with recollections of the days before life was cruel to them.

"Zelda was the most darlin' baby, and I loved her so dearly," said Mrs. Newman Smith, the former Rosalind Sayre, who

FITZGERALD, F(rancis) Scott Key
FITZGERALD, Zelda Sayre
and
SMITH, Frances Scott Fitzgerald (Scottie)

COURIER-JOURNAL & TIMES
(Louisville, Ken.)
Mar. 24, 1974

was almost 11 years old when her baby sister was born on July 24, 1900, in a house that has since been demolished on Montgomery's South Street.

Zelda was named for a gypsy princess who appeared in a novel that had delighted her mother, Minnie Machen Sayre, a Kentucky-born woman whose father had discovered Montgomery during the Civil War, when he represented Kentucky in the Confederate Congress.

Soon after Zelda's birth, her father, Alabama Supreme Court Justice Anthony Dickinson Sayre, moved the family of three other girls (Rosalind, Clothilde and Marjorie) and one boy (Tony) to a large but unpretentious house not far from South Street in the same residential section of Montgomery, which was perched above the Alabama River and known as "The Hill."

Zelda lived in that home until she went north to New York in 1920 to marry Scott Fitzgerald.

Today it is vacant. Local housing authorities have found its foundations cracking and posted "Condemned" signs on the rickety front door. But souvenir hunters pull down the signs as soon as the nails have fastened them.

A woman who lives in a very neat house next door to the old Sayre place (which has since been renumbered as 516 Pleasant Ave.) said that almost every day someone knocks on her door to find out if Zelda "really lived in that place next door."

And the visitor who enters through the unlocked back door of the Sayre place can find empty film wrappers that tourists have left scattered on the floor among broken glass and scraps of fallen plaster and wallpaper.

"The Hill," like the Sayre house, has seen better days. But with a little imagination, one can still picture how it looked in the years when Zelda slept in one of the two front bedrooms (no one now living can remember which one).

"We used to walk in the afternoons," said her elderly but still attractive sister, Rosalind. "Before Zelda could walk, I would take her out in my little box of a wagon for a ride. And Mama would watch for us.

"Our family sat on the porch and rocked. Zelda loved me and I loved her. She always went to me when she wanted anything, and I tried to keep her in good spirits," said Mrs. Smith.

Keeping Zelda's spirits high during her youth apparently was no difficulty, if the memories of her sister and friends are accurate.

"I was with Zelda all the time," said Mrs. Tuttle, her eyes turning toward the top of the beautifully carved staircase of the Pleasant Avenue house as she led a reporter through the place. "But Zelda was two years older and I couldn't do all the things she could do. She could swim better than anybody, she could skate better than anybody, and she was a tomboy and climbed trees."

Zelda used to spend the night with Eugenia Tuttle and sit up cutting out paper dolls. But Mrs. Tuttle remembered that she didn't like to stay very much at the Sayres', particularly if Zelda's father were at home.

"Frankly," she said flatly, "I was scared of Judge Sayre."

Rosalind Sayre Smith wasn't scared of her father, nor was her younger sister Zelda, but she said they were much closer to their creative, warm-hearted mother. "I won't say I was very close to him, because he never had very much to say. But he did have such a quiet voice and a wonderful mind."

Their mother was tender

It was their mother's great tenderness that dominated their lives, Rosalind Smith recalled.

Minnie Machen Sayre always spoke fondly of her "old Kentucky home." Her father, Willis Machen, was a Kentucky political figure for half a century—serving terms in the state House of Representatives and Senate, helping to frame a revised state Constitution in 1849, and sitting in the senates of both the Confederacy during the Civil War and the United States in 1872.

Leaving their handsome plantation at Eddyville, Ky., Minnie Machen attended finishing school in Montgomery, a city her father liked very much when he served in the Confederate Congress.

And she married a Montgomery lawyer, Anthony Dickinson Sayre, after her family prevented her from going on the stage —an ambition she never fully abandoned.

Zelda's talents encouraged

In little Zelda she encouraged her own artistic qualities, and she also gave the child a spirit of independence, according to Rosalind Smith. "Her ideas, even as a child, were interesting. She would draw pictures."

The schools where Zelda studied (Sayre Street Elementary, now called Chilton School, and Lanier High, now called Baldwin Junior High) are still standing in Montgomery.

Zelda's "soulmate" after she passed from the tomboy stage to young womanhood, was Mrs. Katharine Haxton, who also knew Scott Fitzgerald.

"I met Scott two weeks before Zelda did," said Mrs. Haxton, who was also a distant relation of the Sayres.

Fitzgerald was a dandy in his style of dress, Mrs. Haxton recalled.

"Scott was a nonconformist. During the war there were very strict rules about your uniform. Scott didn't do anything they told him to do. He wore judphurs that were exaggerated cream colored. He made them that way by putting salt on them and laying them in the sun to bleach. And he wore soft high boots, not like any Army boots anybody had heard of."

Around Camp Sheridan, his nickname was "High Pockets," and the girls at the country club saw why as he stood at the side of the room and watched them, his hands slipped into the pockets that were sewn parallel to his belt.

Before Scott came to town, Zelda used to meet the trains with the other young women of the town. "She was in a group of girls who ran a canteen at the train station. They went out and gave the soldiers coffee. It was called the Service League, but later became the Junior League," Eugenia Tuttle recalled.

Friends talk of her youth

Zelda's closest friends from girlhood days do not like to talk about the years when she returned, after Scott's death, and lived a solitary life with her mother on Sayre Street.

But she painted a lot in those years. Three of her paintings are in the collection of the Montgomery Museum of Fine Arts, but they aren't displayed. The museum's guides are willing to pull out the three canvases—one of tortured-looking ballet dancers, one of circus figures and another of delicate floating balls of blue in an aqua background.

Recollections 'astonishing'

Scottie Fitzgerald Smith, their daughter, now lives in Montgomery and is "astonished" to hear what the local residents remember most about her mother.

"Many people remember my mother as an athlete, far more than as a 'butterfly,'" she said. "Swimming, dancing and roller-skating—better than anyone else. That's what they remember most about my mother."

And if Zelda were alive, her friends maintain, she would tell others, as she once told Scott Fitzgerald, how much the city where she was born and the lost cause on which its heritage rested meant to her.

She wrote to Scott of that deep sentiment before their marriage when he was trying to make a living for them in New York:

"I've spent today in the grave-yard—It really isn't a cemetery, you know, trying to unlock a rusty iron vault built on the side of the hill. It's all washed and covered with weepy, watery blue flowers that might have grown from dead eyes . . . Isn't it funny how, out of a row of Confederate soldiers, two or three will make you think of dead lovers and dead loves—when they're exactly like the others, even to the yellowish moss? Old death is so beautiful—so very beautiful—We will die together—I know—Sweetheart."

➡

(Also see preceding article)

Fitzgerald's daughter recalls golden times, disputes escapades

LONG AGO STROLL — Of this photo of Scottie walking with her parents, she says, "My mother apparently loved to dress me up." She has written a book about the famous Fitzgeralds.

By WINZOLA McLENDON
Special Writer, The Oregonian

Her parents were symbols of the twenties. Their seemingly madcap adventures across two continents, while he wrote and she dabbled in the arts, were the essence that made the twenties roar. They celebrated and were celebrated wherever they went. They were the Fitzgeralds. Befitting their excesses, they died untimely deaths.

A heart attack in 1940 in Hollywood, at the age of 44, took advantage of hard-drinking F. Scott Fitzgerald's damaged body.

A hospital fire in 1948 in Asheville, N.C., consumed the life of once fun-loving Zelda Sayre Fitzgerald, who had found the world of mental hospitals after a series of breakdowns. She was only 48.

But their only child, Frances Scott (Scottie) Fitzgerald, remembers a childhood with them, so golden that today she wonders she isn't the "most rotten, spoiled person I know."

Scott she pictures as a giving, though protective, dad and Zelda as a loving mom who catered to extravagant whims.

For years, Scottie brushed off most inquiries about her parents, especially her mother. But now she is talking about their many sides, even the ones she was exposed to the least: Those that involved drinking and insanity.

The disasters came when she was a teen-ager, which, of course didn't make life fun, but "I cannot emphasize enough what a golden childhood I had," she said.

Imagine, if you will, she suggested, a little girl requesting a staged wedding and getting the request granted — on the French Riviera, complete with a honeymoon drive along the Mediterranean, the car festooned with fresh flowers and streamers.

Scottie is now the wife of Grove Smith, has a family of her own and homes in Washington, D.C., and Montgomery, Ala. Memories of her own early years are still close. They would not be easily forgotten.

She described Christmas, 1931, in Alabama, for example, when her mother constructed the history of mankind around the tree. A little electric train started its journey in Egypt and went on to Greece, Rome, the Crusades, the War of the Roses and so forth.

Comments Mrs. Smith, "She had made the Alps out of papier mache and there were palm trees sticking out of real sand, boats on a mirrored lake and soldiers marching and fighting their way across deserts and over mountains."

When she wanted a doll house, she said, her mother created one, a miniature replica of the home they lived in at Ellerslie near Wilmington, Del. Many of her dolls were also Zelda originals: "Some were works of art and I still have almost the whole court of Louis XIV. Inside his carriage were Louis and all his mistresses, the Three Muskateers, Cardinal Richilieu, all in gorgeous costumes."

Was there a favorite toy? Yes. It was the doll Monique. She says Scott bought it for her on one of his many trips to the Paris toy store, Nain Bleu (Blue Dwarf): "It was a fabulous store and of course he took me there so he could buy himself some lead soldiers at the same time he was buying me a doll. It was all a clever subterfuge, which was fine with me."

Scott, she explained, was intrigued with lead soldiers and would stage mock battles. Her mother would make a cardboard castle and the battlements, and there would be moats to flood. "It was magnificent; I was fascinated by it until the very end when historical necessity demanded the burning of the castle."

Along with the games and happy times, her parents had violent quarrels; but their daughter says that either she has a rotten memory or they took place when she was in bed.

"I don't think they fought as much as they are supposed to have, because in my opinion they stayed in love until the day they died. I don't think it was fighting in the sense of people who are hostile to each other — just fighting over conditions of their lives which frustrated them both."

As proof of their love, she notes the way Scott looked after Zelda when she was sick — tenderly and to the end. "The whole thing broke his heart," she declared.

The ordeal took its toll on Scottie, too.

She tells of witnessing, in 1932, Zelda's beauty fading and her general physical decline. Mrs. Fitzgerald was in a clinic in Baltimore, Md., undergoing treatment for her ongoing emotional problems, and Scottie visited her often. "It was a strain and so sad, because she began to look different as most people with mental illness do," she said.

Later, Mrs. Smith said, her mother was able to attend her graduation for the Ethel Walker School in Connecticut and met her boat when she returned from a post-graduation trip to Europe. She recalls that Zelda remained enthused about the glamour of New York and would mention how different the city had looked in her heyday. "But without regret. She never seemed sad that the good times were gone."

FITZGERALD, F(rancis) Scott Key
FITZGERALD, Zelda Sayre
SMITH, Frances Scott Fitzgerald (Scottie)

OREGONIAN
(Portland, Ore.)

Dec. 14, 1974

Mrs. Smith sees parallels between her parents' bad times and the bad times the country experienced. Zelda, she points out, had her first breakdown in 1929. As the economy depressed, America's appetite dwindled for the glamorous, rich people who populated Fitzgerald's books, which are experiencing another revival since the filming of his "The Great Gatsby."

"They were young and successful at the time of the boom, and then the stock market crashed at the same time everything was crashing for them personally," she said.

She says she liked her father's close friend, Sheilah Graham, and now sees her as a vital support to him during a most difficult period. "Without her, I can't imagine how he would have survived — Hollywood let him down

(Continued from preceding page)

so. . . "

Scott wrote dozens of letters to Scottie during her years at Vassar, filled with beautiful phrases, minute instructions and suggestions. Mrs. Smith smiles, "I just examined them for checks and important messages and threw them in my desk drawer because I was so annoyed with him. I wanted to lead my own life."

Among Scott's interferences:

-A warning against doing "anything rash like throwing away your honeymoon in advance."

-Objection to her writing under her own name, since "it does push me a little into the background" and "it calls attention to my being of my generation."

Perhaps Mrs. Smith can deal with her feelings for her parents publicly now because the inevitable pain has mellowed with time. But she still says she avoids what is written about them because "I don't like reading about some of the things they supposedly did."

Moreover, she insisted, "fifty per cent of what has been written about

FITZGERALD, F. Scott
FITZGERALD, Zelda
SMITH, Frances Scott (Scottie)

OREGONIAN
(Portland, Ore.)

Dec. 14, 1974

my mother and father has been sheer invention.

That does not mean Mrs. Smith is an ostrich. She readily admits that "there is no question but that my father's behavior was indefensible on many occasions. He seems to have had no tolerance for alcohol. But I do think his drinking must have been somewhat exaggerated. I don't see how you could turn out five novels, 160 stories and a lot of other writing if you were drinking as much as he was alleged to be doing."

Mrs. Smith is currently adding her own contribution to the literature about her parents, an autobiographical photo album called "The Romantic Egoists," edited with the help of Joan P. Kerr, a roommate from Vassar, and Fitzgerald expert Matthew Bruccoli, and published by Charles Scribner's Sons. Appropriately, it has a flamboyant price, $25. However, the contents tend to be realistic.

Mrs. Smith hints in the book that her parents' marriage was doomed at the start because her father needed a calming balance to his own inner turmoil. Also, Mrs. Smith said her father once told her that he thought Zelda, daughter of a prominent Alabama couple, didn't have the strength for the big stage, "might have been happy with a kind, simple man in a southern garden."

Mrs. Smith hasn't given up the thought: "Maybe she would have made out all right if she had stayed in the South. My purely amateur view is that if such strains had not been put on her she would probably not have cracked. But who knows?"

The Fitzgeralds: A Daughter's View

By LESLIE HANSCOM

FITZGERALD, F Scott
FITZGERALD, Zelda
and
SMITH, Frances Scott Fitzgerald (Scottie)

THE STATE
(Columbia, S.C.)

Dec. 29, 1974

If fate had ordained a long life for Scott Fitzgerald and he were alive today, he would be 73 years old. What is even harder to conceive of, the writer in whose work the young of the Jazz Age remain young forever would now be the great grandfather of twins. The twins, born this year, are the grandchildren of Scottie Fitzgerald Smith, the author's only child, the chief beneficiary of Fitzgerald's resurrection as a best-selling author and the living proof that children of the famous need not, contrary to the stereotype, be marked by psychic scars. To meet Mrs. Smith and be warmed by her serene normality is to be persuaded that the ideal way to grow up is to have two legendary come-aparts as your mother and father.

According to Scottie Smith, the most important legacy left to her by Scott and Zelda Fitzgerald is the memory of a blissful childhood. While Scott and Zelda live in myth for their adventures in upper class hooliganism — using the bathtub for gin and a public fountain for the bath — they abide in the memory of their daughter as conventional and loving parents. "People keep asking me," she said the other day, "why I don't write a book about them. The answer is that it would be a bore. All I can remember is being adored and treated like a doll. I was too young to be impressed by their friends. Hemingway, Ring Lardner, Sinclair Lewis — I wish I could remember them. Thomas Wolfe was just a very tall man."

Nevertheless, Mrs. Smith has done a book about Scott and Zelda. Called "The Romantic Egoists" (Scribners, $25) and put together with the help of two collaborators, Professor Matthew J. Bruccoli and Joan P. Kerr, it is a scrapbook of Fitzgerald memorabilia. Through photographs and press clippings, helped out by extracts from her father's writing which gave the book an air of autobiography, this tribute to two of the century's most glamorous worldlings sketches their lives from lucky beginning to dismal end. Few family albums could tell a story of such extremes of fortune. More vividly than the biographies do, Fitzgerald's press notices in the days of his early success reveal how unquestioningly he was accepted as the representative writer of the 1920's. Just as strikingly, the notices that appeared when he died in Hollywood in 1940 at the early age of 44 emphasize how totally he had outlived his fame.

In the days when Scott and Zelda were the typical Beautiful People, their daughter was too young to realize that English nannies, French governesses and villas on the Riviera were not the norm for every little girl. "Then when I was old enough to thrill to the glamor," said Scottie Smith, "they weren't glamorous any more." Zelda was in and out of mental institutions, winding up, in the years before she perished in a hospital fire, as a fundamentalist religious fanatic who wouldn't eat raspberries because she thought the Bible forbade eating a fruit that grew on thorns. Scott was an alcoholic hasbeen, hacking in Hollywood and carrying on with Sheilah Graham, a gossip columnist with a gamey past which she has since written about in a way that would have stunned Fitzgerald. In the words of his friend and executor, Judge John Biggs, Fitzgerald at his death left "the estate of a pauper and the will of a millionaire."

"I was able to stay on in college," said Scottie Smith, "only because Judge Biggs, Maxwell Perkins and Harold Ober (the last two, Fitzgerald's editor and agent respectively) gave me the money." Graduating from Vassar, the daughter of the forgotten author of "This Side of Paradise" and "The Great Gatsby" became a newspaperwoman, married, raised a family of three children and in due time turned into the engaging matron she is today, a grandmother in glasses and short bobbed hair of blondish gray. In the meantime, things were happening to her departed parents.

The rediscovery of Scott Fitzgerald has no parallel in American literature. Other forgotten authors have been re-established as classic writers; only Fitzgerald has been reborn both as a classic and as a best-seller. To the amazement of his daughter, he is especially popular with the young. "I don't know how they manage to identify with the young shieks and flappers of 50 years ago," she said, "but they do." This is gratifying to the heiress of the legend of Scott and Zelda for more reasons than one.

"Being Daddy's daughter," she said, "is a very well paid job." It isn't only the reveneus that flow in from television and movies. "I am always pleasantly surprised," she said, "when I get my $17.80 in royalties from the Hungarian edition of "Tender Is the Night" or my $14.50 for "Gatsby" in Serbo-Croatian. There's a translation of "Gatsby" coming out now in Korean. How do those people identify with the Long Island rich?"

When she thinks of her father in person, according to Scottie Smith, it is not in any way which relates to the legend. He comes back to her now as the teacher, the tireless nag in the cause of self-improvement. One section of the new book consists of letters written to Scottie in her college years: "I wonder if you've read anything this summer — I mean any one good book like 'The Brothers Karamazov' or 'Ten Days That Shook the World' or Renan's 'Life of Christ' . . ." But Fitzgerald had a very agreeable habit, according to his daughter, of sending along a check to offset the really reproachful letters.

The unhappy Zelda is remembered by her daughter, not as a woman destroyed by her husband's success, but as an artist confused by too many uncoordinated talents of her own. At the time of her first crack-up, Zelda was on the verge of her debut as a professional ballet dancer. In "Save Me the Waltz," she wrote a novel of more than passing interest. And Scottie Smith's new book contains a surprise. It is a portfolio in color of her mother's paintings, interesting enough to shed a whole new sidelight on the legend of Scott and Zelda.

(Also see preceding article)

The Most Envied Couple

By Roy Thompson

Staff Reporter

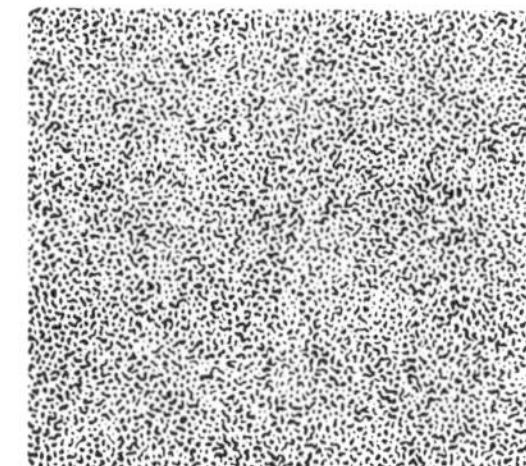

ASHEVILLE — F. Scott and Zelda Fitzgerald came to Asheville when the party was over.

The Roaring Twenties . . .

It may have been the longest, swingingest party ever pitched.

People danced the Charleston and sang "Ain't She Sweet?" and necked in rumbleseats and drank champagne out of pretty girls' slippers.

F Scott Fitzgerald . . .

Young, handsome and one of the hottest novelists of the decade.

He was also shy and introverted. He needed liquor to make him the life of the party.

He was insecure as a writer — even when he was on top. He thought he couldn't write without drinking.

Life for Fitzgerald was all partying and writing, so he found himself drinking most of the time.

He made piles of money, and he spent two piles for every pile he made.

Send tne bills tomorrow, Fitzgerald said, knowing there was no tomorrow.

Zelda Sayre Fitzgerald . . .

Young, beautiful and a non - stop party girl who was born in Montgomery, Ala., in 1900 — just the right time to be ripe for the Roaring Twenties.

She, too, had talent, but she didn't try to use it until later. Then it was too late.

She partied with her husband, and she drank to keep him company.

She, too, knew there was no tomorrow.

They were married on April 2, 1920. It was a kind of ribbon cutting for opening the Roaring Twenties.

Fitzgerald described the marriage as "the mating of the age." He said, "We are the most envied couple in America."

Every mirror on every wall told them they were the fairest of them all.

Wherever they went was the "in" place to be. If the Fitzgeralds passed through a place, it acquired instant chic.

The country spoiled them as if they were the only children the nation had.

Shortly after their marriage, they made a suicide pact. It was in keeping with the popular motto of the time:

"Live fast, die young and leave a beautiful corpse."

They would do this when they reached 35, they said, knowing that this was years away and tomorrow would never come.

Asheville . . .

Instead of getting drunk on bathtub gin, it got drunk out of its incorporated mind on land speculation.

Buy a lot for $500 and sell next day for $2,785. Buy another lot and sell in a week for $8,000. Buy a cow pasture with eight grand, draw a map and sell lots on non - existent streets for a quarter of a million bucks.

Anybody who couldn't make a fortune in real estate needed a keeper — and all the keepers were in real estate.

The sky was the limit. Every man a millionaire. There was no tomorrow.

Then, on a dark day in October in the last year of the Roaring Twenties, the bottom fell out, and there lay tomorrow.

The party was over.

It was followed by the longest and most dismal hangover of the century . . . the Depression.

The Fitzgeralds partied on for a time. From what they could see through their haze, this was no time to sober up and face reality.

But it caught up with them in time.

By 1935, the year in which Zelda was to have killed herself to avoid growing old (he was four years overdue at the time), even they knew the party was over.

Fitzgerald came here alone that year. He roamed the city like a homeless ghost. He moved from hotel to hotel, using different names at each. He never gave his real name. He didn't want people to know who he was.

Everybody knew.

Zelda came the next year. She was having mental problems, and he checked her into Highland Hospital for rest and treatment.

Fitzgerald closed their home in Maryland and moved into the Grove Park Inn.

He was broke. He owed large sums of money. He found that he couldn't write — even with liquor. And her bills were piling up.

Broke. And living in the Grove Park Inn. It was the most fashionable place in Asheville in which a man could be broke in high style.

Fitzgerald quickly became a favorite with people on the hotel staff. Big tipper.

The other guests didn't care for him when he was drinking, and he always was. The problem then was that he tended to call all Southerners "Farmers," and he did so in a loud voice.

At Highland Hospital, the doctors had decided that Zelda was schizophrenic.

The onetime Golden Girl — named for a gypsy queen in a novel her mother had read long ago — was still holding onto what youth remained to her. She held it in an iron grasp. Nothing ages a woman faster.

She was graying before her time. Her once beautiful complexion — one that Fitzgerald had sung praises to in many a novel — had gone gray and hard.

She was gaining weight. The figure a nation had admired was a dimly - recalled memory.

Whenever Zelda forgot and looked into a mirror, it no longer told her she was fairest of them all. It told her the party was over.

She had lost interest in clothes by this time, she who once had been queen of the fashion pages. The mirror now told her that hers was a lost cause. She had given up the fight.

She occasionally visited her husband for lunch at the Grove Park Inn, and they took isolated tables in dimly-lit corners when such was to be had.

People knew Fitzgerald. He still looked something like the face they had seen everywhere only a few years ago.

But could this dowdy, hefty woman be Zelda?

Fitzgerald was four years older than his bedevilled wife, but the years had dealt with him more gently — at least on the surface. The inner man was tortured by the conviction that he had brought about her breakdown.

He referred to her as "my invalid" and spoke of her to friends as "The Ghost of someone I once loved."

He clung to a slowly ebbing hope that she might one day recover. Then they could start the party again.

By the end of the Thirties, he had abandoned hope. He still wrote to her once a day, but he had gone to Hollywood, where he could still make money by writing, and he didn't visit her at the hospital the way he had.

Fitzgerald, too, had problems.

He blamed himself for her mental problems; he blamed her for his drinking. He had always had a reason for his drinking.

For a time he gave up hard liquor and went on a steady diet of beer. It took 20 bottles a day. He developed a pot, and this shook him, and he drank more to anesthetize himself against the pain of it.

He smoked constantly and ate seldom. When he ate, it was always the same menu: mashed potatoes and gravy.

He suffered from insomnia. He dreaded facing the darkness alone. He fought going to bed until he was near collapse. Then he knocked himself out with pills.

The beer was putting too much weight on him, so he went back to gin.

When anyone would listen, he told stories about having tuberculosis. No one knows why. He did not have tuberculosis.

He cried a lot.

Zelda was in and out of the hospital. In 1939, Fitzgerald decided during a Hollywood binge to go and get her and take her to Cuba. They had always liked Cuba.

While there, they went to a cockfight, and he became involved in a fight. They went back to New York, where he was admitted to a hospital for two weeks' treatment and rest.

Zelda came back to Highland Hospital alone.

It was the last time they were to see each other.

Fitzgerald died.

In 1940, Zelda was released from the hospital and returned to her home in Montgomery. She kept some of his things around. It made it easier to believe that he was just out somewhere and would soon be coming back to her.

When Scott Fitzgerald's affairs were settled, it was found that he had managed to set aside something to take care of Zelda for life...

Fifty dollars a month.

In her madness, loneliness and despair, Zelda had become religious. She spent most of her limited funds on religious tracts to send to her friends.

She worried about their souls as she worried about their growing older. By this time, Zelda could see age in her friends, but the mirror had mercifully begun to lie to her.

She was invariably upset when one of her friends became a grandparent.

She was in and out of Highland Hospital many times during the war-plagued early Forties.

She entered it for the last time in November 1947.

Early in 1948 she was given insulin treatments and was moved to the top floor of the hospital for close watching.

The hospital was old. Many a visitor had left it filled with apprehension about what would happen if a fire broke out there.

It happened about midnight on the 10th day of March 1948.

The fire started in a diet kitchen, and it moved fast through the hospital.

There was no sprinkler system to put it out or at least delay its spreading.

There were fire escapes, but they were made of wood, and they burned away almost at once.

Doors were locked throughout the hospital, so getting people out was a problem.

All the windows were barred.

Nine people died in Highland Hospital that night.

All of them were women.

Six were on the top floor.

One was Zelda Fitzgerald.

She was buried in Maryland on St. Patrick's Day. . . next to her husband.

"The most envied couple in America."

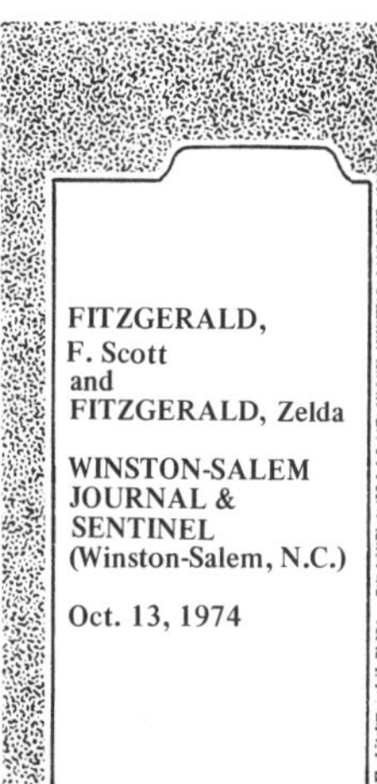

FITZGERALD, F. Scott and FITZGERALD, Zelda

WINSTON-SALEM JOURNAL & SENTINEL (Winston-Salem, N.C.)

Oct. 13, 1974

'Complete' Colin Fletcher—He's a Walker in America

Bulletin staff Photo by William Owens

By JACK BOOTH
Of The Bulletin Staff

WHEN COLIN FLETCHER bums a cigaret, he insists on paying a nickel. It makes him feel less guilty, he says. And when he bums a second and then a third, he doles out yet another 10 cents.

It is that kind of compulsion that probably explains why he would spend six months walking the length of California, or two months threading his way through the Grand Canyon.

When the 52-year-old Fletcher decided to bone up on rattlesnakes, he naturally had to go whole hog, spending $50 for a 1,500-page tome called, "Rattlesnakes: Their Habits, Life Histories and Influence on Mankind."

And when he set out to revise his immensely popular book on hiking, "The Complete Walker," which was published in 1968 by Alfred A. Knopf, he did it right, consuming two years in the process.

Only eight pages, he notes with satisfaction, remained "virgo intacta."

What emerged was "The New Complete Walker," which brings you 117 more pages, 32 new drawings, 21 amended drawings and several new "tidbits of joy."

There is enough detail in this book to satisfy even the most rabid of hikers. A camper will find it useful, for example, to know that three meat bars weighing nine ounces apiece will provide a total of 1,434 calories.

And when walking where water is scarce, you should keep in mind that 20 quarts of water will keep you alive only 4.5 days when the temperature in the shade is 120 F.

Fletcher even includes a hortatory chapter called "Why Walk?" to get the uninitiated into the proper spirit for the "delectable madness" that is walking.

Such thoroughness helped the 1968 edition to sell 150,000 copies, but it also endangered Fletcher's privacy. So now he has a new compulsion: guarding his personal life.

In a recent interview here, he took the fifth even on such innocuous questions as where the hotel was that he once managed in East Africa.

It was too bad, because it would be intriguing to know what inner motivations would lead a man through successive stints as a British Royal Marine commando, a farmer in Kenya, a prospector in Canada and a janitor in California.

Under prodding, the most Fletcher would provide was a brief outline.

A Welshman by birth, he went to the West Buckland public school near Devon, England, and then went straight into the service.

After that he married the first of two wives (he is now single) and managed a hotel in Kenya in a town he grudgingly identified as Kitale.

A year later, he became assistant of a Kenyan farm that had 500 head of cattle and 600 pigs. Next he managed a cattle farm for four years.

Then it was off to Canada, where he continued with writing that he had started in Kenya and took jobs as an assistant geologist and prospector to earn money to live on.

Three years later, he cryptically notes, he headed for New Zealand but ended up in California. There he held "important jobs" like being Santa Claus in department stores and being head janitor at a hospital.

One morning he woke up at 3 A.M. and decided to walk the length of California, an experience that led to a book six years later called, "The Thousand-Mile Summer." Walking the Grand Canyon produced "The Man Who Walked Through Time," and a look at a game reserve in Kenya led to "The Winds of Mara."

It would be nice to know how all this fits together, but Fletcher is adamantly uncooperative. He won't even say where he now lives, of all things.

"You can't tell people where you live when you're a writer," he says, as if the reason is obvious. "My private life and what I want to say about it is my business."

Perhaps he should heed the advice he gives to walkers in his own book. Too much compulsion, he says, can make you a "very tolerably accomplished fuddy-duddy."

FLETCHER, Colin
(1922 -)

PHILADELPHIA BULLETIN
(Philadelphia, Penn.)

Nov. 7, 1974

[See also CA-13/14]

The Land Called... She Answered

By Roy Thompson
Staff Reporter

EDENTON — Bandon is gone, and Nature works tirelessly in her small ways to fill the emptiness left when fire destroyed the grand old plantation house on a golden October afternoon.

Gone, too, is Inglis Fletcher, who heard the Albemarle calling 30 years ago and returned to a home she had never known because she knew the Albemarle was calling its own.

She it was who came to the piney woods along the Chowan River, found Bandon sinking helplessly into decay and, ignoring the well-meant advice of all around her, restored it to its former glory.

It was at Bandon that Mrs. Fletcher wrote most of the historical novels that endowed this charming Colonial town — and all North Carolina — with new pride in our beginnings.

True, she probably made our forefathers grander and nobler than they ever were.

And as Jonathan Daniels said in reviewing one of the novels in what has come to be known as her "Carolina series," her books reflected "less a glory that is gone than a discontent with what is here."

All this can be granted, and yet one must credit the woman with having given us a new awareness of how this state became a member of a new nation of states.

Her writings have given humble North Carolina a transfusion of pride that stands her in good stead, located as she is between the Virginia Cavaliers and the Old Families of Charleston.

Now, as we stand at the threshhold of our Bicentennial, her books are being re-published in paperback.

Old readers are turning to them once more with renewed interest.

Perhaps new readers are being attracted in this, her literary resurrection.

One thing is certain . . .

Mrs. Louise Darby, the librarian here, marveled at the way Mrs. Fletcher's readers still come to Edenton's quiet little place at the meeting of the Albemarle Sound and the Chowan River.

They come on private pilgrimages to see Bandon and, with a bit of luck, catch a glimpse of the writer they feel they know so well.

"They won't believe that she is dead and Bandon is gone," Mrs. Darby said. "They look at me and say, 'I know she can't be dead. I know Bandon can't have burned. I'd have heard about it . . .' "

They come in hope and anticipation.

They leave in leaden sorrow.

Blessed are these pilgrims. Knowing her only through her writing, they may have known her best of all.

★★★

Inglis Fletcher knew her own beginnings, or at least the story of her people back to the west country of England.

She was related to Sir Walter Raleigh on her mother's side.

Her mother's people came out of Virginia about 1684 and settled along the Scuppernong River in what is now Tyrrell County.

Long before she was born, one of the Chapmans left the Albemarle for Illinois. Some said he left because he couldn't get along with Parson Daniel Earle, the fishing parson who bought some promising bottomland more than 200 years ago, made a plantation out of it and called his place "Bandon" for the Irish town he was born in.

Inglis Fletcher, who came to personify the manor lady of the Old South, was born in Illinois in 1888. She was a tomboy in her rambunctious early days, and people called her "Bright Eyes."

Later she reluctantly had to succumb to ladylike conduct, and in her autobiography, "Pay, Pack and Follow," she tells of being coached in fainting by a friend who warned, "Never do it until you have a young man's shoulder to fall on."

She started writing when she was 10 or 11. She made a play out of "Snow White." Disney made more money with his.

She used to tell friends that if there had been an election when she was in school, she'd very likely have been elected "Least likely to succeed."

John George Fletcher, a Spanish - American War veteran and mining engineer, was considered an excellent catch for almost anyone, and Inglis was generally regarded as a poor catcher.

She caught him on the rebound, and when friends asked her how this minor miracle had been accomplished, she answered, "I'm a good letter writer."

Jack Fletcher's work lay in the rough mining camps of our western states and Alaska, and he tried once to leave her in town wnen he headed for the wilderness.

Mrs. Fletcher announced, "I can be just as rugged as a man." And with that, she followed him.

They lived for a time in a recently - vacated chickenhouse.

She carried a gun to protect herself against grizzlies.

She killed a rattlesnake with a shovel. She rode a Concord stage that had a man riding shotgun. They lived in a house haunted by the ghost of a Chinese cook.

One mining company refused to allow wives in camp, so she signed on as cook. This must have been a memorable experience for the luckless miners. Mrs. Fletcher had never learned to cook.

She started writing in the mining camps. She sold stories to magazines. One was "Boys Life." She went to Africa and wrote two books out of the material she brought home. She had a trunkful of material left over, and she always meant to get back to it, but . . .

Most of the time, she just followed Jack Fletcher.

As he approached retirement, she went to work as a writer.

Mrs. Fletcher was a woman entranced by rivers, and she dreamed of writing "the Great American Novel" about a family that came to the New World, settled on a river and eventually, over generations, crossed the continent on the riverways.

Recalling her ancestral home on the Scuppernong, she began to do research on North Carolina, and the digging led her home.

In 1940, "Raleigh's Eden," the first in her Carolina Series, was published, and she found herself spending more and more time in this state.

Two books later, in 1944, she was still writing about North Carolina, so the Fletchers decided to move closer to her sources.

They decided on Edenton, "The little town on Queen Anne's Creek," and they packed in San Francisco and moved east.

Mrs. Jackie Ricks of Edenton knew Mrs. Fletcher, and she said, "She was not a famous person when she first came here."

She was, to the contrary, a writer of books, and chances are she was looked upon with some suspicion, as writers often are.

FLETCHER, (Minna) Inglis (1888 - 1969)

WINSTON–SALEM JOURNAL & SENTINEL (Winston-Salem, N.C.)

Nov. 10, 1974

[See also CA-7/8]

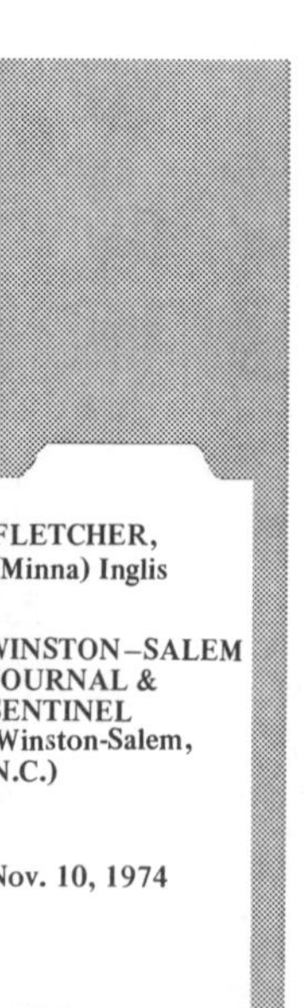
FLETCHER, (Minna) Inglis

WINSTON-SALEM JOURNAL & SENTINEL (Winston-Salem, N.C.)

Nov. 10, 1974

(Continued from preceding page)

For Mrs. Fletcher, the move to Edenton was "A true homecoming . . . I felt that perhaps there was some truth in the belief that the land calls to its own."

If the good people of Edenton had any reservations about the stability of a person who wrote for a living, their suspicions were confirmed by the Fletchers' choice of a home.

Bandon had been empty for 18 years. There were 135 broken windows. Among the things it didn't have: running water, electricity and . . . in places . . . a roof.

There were two "little houses" out back.

Jack Fletcher went to work and got three rooms in shape for people accustomed to living in mining camps, and they moved in.

Some of the plaster on the ceiling was gone, and Mrs. Fletcher lost some sleep while watching rats cross the open spaces over her bed. Her husband finally tacked paper over the holes.

Their nearest neighbor, Mrs. Percy Nixon, recalls that when they moved into Bandon, she "wouldn't have HAD the place."

People in Edenton were telling each other privately that the San Franciscans wouldn't last long.

But the Fletchers had come for Colonial atmosphere, and Bandon had it. What's more, it was a step up from that chickenhouse they had lived in long ago.

Gradually, ever so gradually, Bandon was restored, and Inglis Fletcher could once more devote all her energy to her research and writing.

She looked like the ultimate woman's club president. She wore big, floppy, expensive hats. Her clothes were designed for her with little regard for the style of the moment.

She had the expressive face and hard-working hands of an aging character actress.

Once she became a resident of Bandon, she became a citizen of Chowan County, and, W. P. "Spec" Jones recalled, "Anything that promoted Edenton and Chowan County she was a part of it."

Ask 20 people to talk about the Inglis Fletcher they knew, and you'll hear the word "gracious" used at least 20 times.

And yet the people who knew her best here will admit that they didn't know her very well. They used the word "reticence" in describing her. They referred to her as "a very private person."

About all that remained of the rollicking Inglis of the mining camps was her appetite.

Mrs. Percy Nixon said, "She'd eat anything. You name it. She'd eat it."

With the understanding, of course, that someone else must do the cooking.

People here still marvel at the way the woman worked.

Inglis Fletcher quickly adapted herself to her adopted homeland and successfully blended herself into it until she seemed more native than the natives — in all respects save that of her working habits.

She worked seven hours a day, Monday through Friday.

She wrote in longhand on a yellow pad, and her husband dropped in occasionally to pick up the latest accumulation of words and carry them elsewhere to be edited and typed.

He took care of this. It was slow, laborious work. He was a two-finger typist. He had to be the one. He was the only person who could read her writing.

Jack Fletcher brought coffee when she called for it. He called her when it was time for lunch. He answered the telephone and told people she could not be disturbed.

He lit the afternoon fire at four and informed her that her workday was over. Occasionally he informed her by blowing a hunting horn.

They had tea at 4:30.

Guests were welcome for tea. Or later. Or on Saturday or Sunday.

Not during her working time.

Jack Fletcher was something of a curiosity to the people of Edenton. They weren't accustomed to seeing a man wait on his wife.

But they came to like him. Most of them found Jack Fletcher an easier person to get acquainted with than his wife was.

He just stayed in the background and handled the lights while she was onstage.

Why?

He told the few people with nerve enough to ask:

His wife lived his life for a very long time. Now it was his time to live HERS.

For a time, Jack Fletcher was president of the Husbands of Famous Wives Club in San Francisco. The club emblem looked like a violin, but he explained that it was really a second fiddle.

Looking back on their relationship today, some people in Edenton see Inglis Fletcher as a pioneer in women's lib. She would have been astonished.

Jack Fletcher died, leaving his wife to work alone.

She had a stroke, but she kept on writing.

She had another, but she kept on writing.

The Percy Nixons went to live with her because her family didn't want her living alone.

About noon on Sunday, Oct. 6, 1963, Bandon caught fire, and Mrs. Fletcher, then in her 70s, hobbled out on a cane.

They wanted her to leave, but she said she would stay until it burned down, and she did.

She announced that she would rebuild Bandon, but she never did.

A third stroke left her alive but unable to work.

She lived for a time with her son, Stuart, in Charleston, S. C., but Mrs. Percy Nixon kept hearing that, "She wanted to come back to Edenton bad. She said this was her home."

When she returned to Edenton, it was to a convalescent home. She died there in 1969.

She then followed Jack Fletcher for the last time and was buried beside him in the national cemetery in Wilmington.

Mrs. Percy Nixon was surprised: "I had an idea they'd be buried at Bandon. There is a graveyard . . ."

Bandon and the surrounding land have been bought by a developer from Virginia, and the development has begun.

There seem to be no rules, and most of the homes are mobile, concrete block or cabins. There are probably five tents for every house that cost $20,000.

Near the intersection of Wampanoag and Kickapoo in "Historic Arrowhead Beach" one finds a short flight of stairs that once led into Bandon. Now they stop at an empty place in the piney woods.

Weeds, cacti, briars and small cedars are growing where the old house stood.

There's a bit of smoke - blackened tin from the roof, a few charred bricks.

Spanish moss sways listlessly in a wisp of a breeze.

Across the road is the old kitchen. It has stood there for two centuries and more. Someone has tried to chain it and keep people out, but they have broken down the door, and the place is littered with beer cans.

Mrs. Fletcher wrote long ago:

"A writer is alone so much. I sit in the river room on the second floor of Bandon and look out on the lovely, quiet Chowan River. Sometimes, when I am weary, I think what is the use of working day after day, writing page after page which perhaps no one will ever read . . ."

Bandon . . . Bandon is gone now.

Mrs. Fletcher no longer sits alone to brood in her weariness.

But people have read those pages, and they remember the people that Inglis Fletcher conceived and gave birth to.

Close your eyes at twilight at the corner of Wampanoag and Kickapoo in historic Arrowhead Beach . . .

Listen to the lonely sound of a late-dying leaf as it sighs into the mother earth.

Listen again.

Can you hear them? Those people she created?

Roger Mainwaring and Anne Evans and Michael Cary and Marita and Adam Rutledge and Azizi . . .

They live.

Menace Makes A Good Gothic

Staff photo by Bob East III

By MARGARET HUNTER
Staff Writer

Things can get confused when your son teils people your field is book making.

But a youngster doesn't understand what a novelist does so he says mom "makes books."

Now at 14 Michael Fletcher knows his mother Mary is a writer.

Gothic novels are the Fort Lauderdale widow's specialty. These are tales of young heroines, usually alone in the world and pursued by mystrious terrors in some rambling mansion complete with turrets, parapets, a curse or two, whispering wind and, if possible, fog.

Five of her brooding stories are in publication. The latest, "House Called Whispering Winds," should be out soon and she is working on a seventh novel which takes the heroine from Miami to an estate deep in the bayou regions of Louisiana.

"The basic element is suspense— are they going to kill me or not? In a gothic you have as many near misses as you can. Every chapter should end with some menace to the heroine."

Gothics started in England after the industrial revolution, Mrs. Fletcher said.

"The writers of the day were lampooning the style of those who had the money but not the taste and had built these ruge mansions in gothic-like style only with more gargoyles and turrets and all. The style of the novels stuck."

Before gothic, Mary Fletcher wrote romantic adventures about nurses, one of which is in the public libraries, and before that, romantic short stories.

With her skills of copywriting and display advertising she has held jobs to back up her money from the novels.

And for the past 10 years she has taught creative writing for Broward County schools night school program. More recently she took on daytime classes as well.

Registration begins Jan. 20 for her night class. This year it will be in the Downtown Adult Center, 1441 S. Federal Hwy. She is giving up her Thursday night sessions with the Pompano Beach chess club for this series of classes.

At least one of her students, who will be back in the class this time, has made his own mark with his novel "The Devil's Triangle." Richard Winer plans to start a new book of short stories this time, Mrs. Fletcher said.

"We have a lot of fun but I make them work. They have to make an outline before writing anything. Sometimes people fall in love with their own words and can't be criticized so I never let them read their own manuscripts aloud. And the class is a social thing. There can be a lot of friendship there."

Some of her students don't take too kindly to being told to outline and plot what they are going to write before they actually begin the storytelling, Mrs. Fletcher said, but she insists it pays off.

She spends as long as months working on outlines for her own books. "If you do it right therg's a joy to it, the joy of accomplishment," she said.

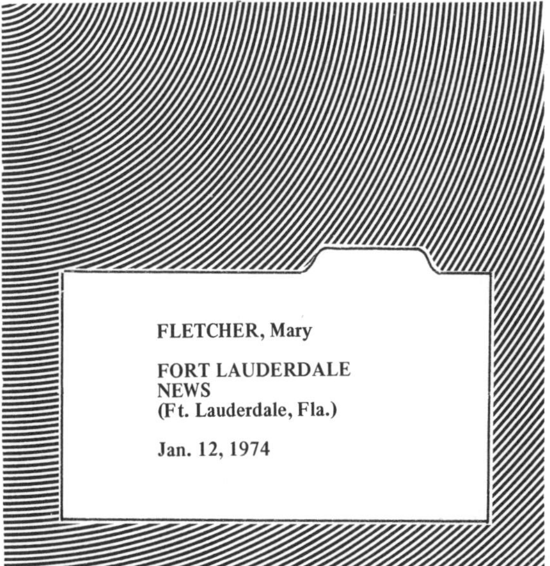

FLETCHER, Mary
FORT LAUDERDALE NEWS
(Ft. Lauderdale, Fla.)
Jan. 12, 1974

There are some hazards in the gothic writing game. Mrs. Fletcher said she will never again visit the "Haunted House," an amusement attraction, the same day she is working on a chase scene for one of her books. "I ran screaming out of there and across the parking lot. It was terrible."

Also, she still finds herelf once in a while explaining what she does for a living, as her son's early interpretation seems to have lived on in the neighborhood. "Just the other day a little girl came up to me and asked where I got the cardboard to make the covers for my books."

Author Criticizes Differences

By Dorothy Sorenson
Bee Home Economist

How do you set up recommended dietary requirements for 200 million people unless you pretend they are all identical? In the opinion of Dr. Carlton Fredericks, "This makes as much sense as a proposal to manufacture false teeth and brassieres in only one size. It would achieve manufacturing economy but would make some awfully uncomfortable people."

Dr. Fredericks, B.A., M.A., PhD., and an author of seven books on the subject of nutrition, is sharply critical of the FDA, medical and dietetics associations in that they do not recognize individual differences in setting up a "standard reference American" for recommended nutritional allowances.

The author's latest book, "Eating Right For You", is devoted to individual differences. "After all," he says, "the medical man insists I don't care if you do have the same symptoms your husband has, don't take the same medicine — you're a different person.' But when it comes to vitamins, minerals, protein or fat, everyone's alike."

"We must come to grips with the realization that human nutritional requirements vary by a factor at least as large as the variance which has been proved in animal requirements."

"There are people who get migraine headaches unless they get five times as much vitamin B-1 as you or I might need — and there are people who bruise easily unless they get hundreds of milligrams of vitamin C a day instead of the 45 that Washington says we need. And there are people who function mentally better when we push down the sugar in the diet which you may tolerate with perfect ease. There is really nothing new about this doctrine — we have just been pretending it doesn't exist in order to arrive at standards."

Dr. Fredericks illustrates his premise with a story about a 15 year old girl named Sara who was treated recently at a neuropsychiatric research institute in New Jersey. She had been diagnosed as a schizophrenic, having all the typical symptoms of distorted perception of space and time. She had total amnesia, three to five convulsions weekly, had menstruated once at the age of 11 and then never again, and from the age of 11 to 15 she had been in psychiatric institutions in which she had been given electroconvulsive therapy, tranquilizers, psycho-energizers and antidepressants because she had made several attempts at suicide.

FREDERICKS, Carlton
(1910? -)

SACRAMENTO BEE
(Sacramento, Calif.)

Apr. 10, 1974

At the New Jersey institute, doctors identified three enzyme disturbances in her brain and gave her 1000 milligrams of vitamin B-6 a day, 8 milligrams of manganese and 200 milligrams of zinc, which constituted 500 times the amount of B-6 the FDA says we need, 8 times as much manganese and about 15 times as much zinc. But — as long as Sara stays on that dosage, she's a normal person — and she's thinking of entering medical school.

Dr. Fredericks has just signed with a publisher to write 20 paper back books on individual subjects of nutrition. He theorizes that many people will pay $1 or $1.50 for a pocket-size book which deals with a particular subject which concerns them, but would not — or could not afford — a book which sells for $7 or $8 just to get one chapter about the subject. For example, there will be a book about nutrition in premenstrual tension, and another about disturbances of the menopause.

Dr. Carlton Fredericks

Dr. Carlton Fredericks, in Sacramento for Weinstock's 100th anniversary celebration, has taught nutrition at City College of New York and Brooklyn College, is an Associate Professor at Fairleigh Dickinson and an adjunct professor in nutrition at New York Institute of Technology. He has many fans and many detractors. But whether or not one agrees with all his premises, there are few who would dispute the need for more nutrition education in our medical schools. At the present time, only 72 per cent of the nation's medical training institutions offer a course in nutrition and, of the 28 per cent who do give some kind of course, the longest is five hours.

Should nutrition really be that low on the medical "totem pole"?

Photos by Margaret M. Grieve

With his wife, Lillian, author John Godey discusses his career aspirations

At long last, writer takes 'Pelham 1,2,3' to riches

By MARK FINSTON

Throw into the stew enormous quantities of perseverance, doggedness, steadfastness, tenacity. Season with generous globs of incredible patience.

Morton Freedgood has been writing books for 40 of his 62 years.

None had made much money, and Freedgood occasionally had to take little odd jobs to support his family, so that he could get to the business of writing another book.

And then, two years ago, Freedgood, writing under the name of John Godey, uncovered the pot of gold for which he had been searching for 40 years. The pot was a novel about a subway hijacking in New York: "The Taking of Pelham One Two Three." The book is now a movie, and has been well received by critics.

* * *

Freedgood no longer has to take odd jobs, like writing press releases for motion picture corporations like United Artists — coincidentally, the company which released the "Pelham" picture.

In person, Freedgood doesn't look particularly dogged. He lives in one of those luxury high-rises in West New York — a sanctuary with a great view of the Hudson, the New York skyline, and, so Freedgood will feel at home after spending two months researching the subways, a bird's eye look at the Weehawken freight yards of the Penn Central.

A sudden bumpy bang reverberates through the apartment, which is on the 17th floor. An earthquake?

"No, just a freight train being made up," sighs his wife, Laura, an artist and a writer of art books ("Great Artists of America and "An Enduring Image" "The railroad doesn't usually start to make them up until midnight, when we're trying to go to sleep."

* * *

The couple moved to New Jersey from New York a year or so ago, when the money from "Pelham" started rolling in at a speed somewhat faster than that of the average subway train.

"I wanted to get out of the city — but I could never afford to before," says Freedgood. "We didn't know what to expect, but we were told that there were, in fact, places in New Jersey to buy Kleenex and cigarettes. It wasn't all wilderness.

"We fell in love with the great view here. I've always been fond of the river."

The Penn Central engine smashes together a few hundred (it seems) more freight cars. Freedgood doesn't even jump.

"I rarely ride the subways anymore," he says. "It's not that I'm afraid they'll be hijacked or anything. It's just that I prefer to walk. My attitude towards them hasn't changed — I still don't like them very much, but they're a good means of transportation."

* * *

Freedgood was born in Brooklyn, and during his childhood lived in the Bronx and Manhattan. His father was an insurance man, and nobody in his family had been a writer, but Freedgood, at age six or seven, decided he wanted to write books. Like many would-be authors he read a great deal (he still does), and became enchanted with the printed word.

He majored in English at CCNY, but never graduated. Instead, he got a job as an office boy at United Artists. He transferred into the publicity department, and wrote canned feature stories about stars and things, resisting all efforts the company made to promote him to higher administrative posts. A promotion would have interfered with his serious writing.

"Those sort of jobs lasted off and on until fairly recently," he says. "They were just to make a little money, and I never enjoyed them. And I fought off 'getting ahead' — savagely."

He wrote four or five "serious" novels. None has ever been published. Then, in 1943, he and his wife went to a writer's colony in New England. Artists go there to concentrate on their work without outside distraction. His wife was on a scholarship, and it cost him only $12 a week.

Freedgood knew he had to go into the Army in a month, which wasn't enough time to write anything serious. So he wrote half a suspense novel — a complete departure for him. Then he went into the Army.

* * *

On retiring from the military, Freedgood read his suspense half-novel over. He submitted a synopsis to Doubleday, which gave him a contract. He finished the book, and the result was, "The Gun and Mr. Smith." The result was also a new name: John Godey.

A pen name was clearly needed. After all, Morton Freedgood was interested in writing serious works. "The Gun and Mr. Smith" was just a temporary, nonserious diversion.

Freedgood thought the book might have possibilities for serialization in one of the woman's magazines. And "Godey's Ladies Book" was a name of one of the old-time, then defunct, woman's magazines. So he became temporarily John Godey.

The books kept coming out under the temporary pen name. The closest Freedgood had to a best seller was in the mid-1960s — a comic suspense novel entitled, "A Thrill a Minute with Jack Albany." The Walt Disney studios adapted it to a movie called, "Never a Dull Moment," with Dick Van Dyke. Freedgood would have been interested in writing the screenplay — he needed the money — but he wasn't asked.

"It was a perfectly terrible movie," he recalls.

He wasn't at all tempted to work on the "Pelham" flick; by this time, he had enough money to move to New Jersey and other pleasures.

Serious writing was being put more and more in the background. Under his real name, Freedgood finally did write a serious work: "The Wall to Wall Trap," a book about the movie business. It didn't do well. And last year, Freedgood wrote a small book of childhood memories: "The Crime of the Century and other Misdemeanors." It also did badly.

He got the idea for "Pelham" when all the stories about airplane hijackings were current. He worked out a sort of plot, and contacted the Transit Authority.

"I didn't tell them exactly what I was going to do," he says. "I told them only I was going to do a novel about a chase in the subways. They cooperated beautifully — they took me into all parts of the system."

(The Transit Authority refused to cooperate at all with the motion picture people since they were wary of the subject matter, felling it might encourage people to hijack subway trains. It was only through the influence of the Lindsay administration the movie was shot at all; John Lindsay was trying to attract movie makers to New York. Neither the book nor the movie has caused a subway hijacking.)

"I suppose that, compared to most people, I am a sort of expert on the subways," says Freedgood. "And I was surprised at the fact that the subway is pretty well run — they do a rather remarkable job."

He is now at work on another suspense novel. He politely declines to reveal the plot outlines, since someone might appropriate them and write it first.

"After being an anonymous writer for so many years, whose books never seemed to be in bookstores, I do enjoy walking in and seeing big piles of 'Pelham,' " says Freedgood. "And I'm enjoying the money.

"Of course, I'm troubled to a degree that I'll never write another hit. But I'm hoping this new one will do as well."

Perseverance, doggedness . . .

* * *

But what about the serious books that still remain Freedgood's prime interest?

"I suppose it's lurking someplace in the backwaters of my mind. Maybe someday I'll sit down and really do what I want. When I mention it, editors and agents all but grow ulcers."

A pause. The freight yard erupts. Freedgood pays no attention.

"If I had three or four spectacular successes, maybe I'd try it. Yes, I do want to do it. I think I will . . ."

And, if the past 62 years is any indication, he probably will. He hasn't yet decided if it will be published under the name of John Godey or Morton Freedgood.

FREEDGOOD, Morton
(pseud. John Godey)
(1912? -)

STAR–LEDGER
(Newark, N.J.)

Nov. 5, 1974

Life's Been Fun Says 74-Year-Old Writer

FRY, Maggie Culver
(1900 -)

TULSA WORLD
(Tulsa, Okla.)

Feb. 2, 1975

World Staff Photo by John Southern

By JUDY WILLIAMS

"Most women my age have a past; I have a future," quipped 74-year-old Maggie Culver Fry of Claremore.

During this time Maggie has had two books of Indian poetry published. Over 500 other poems, stories, plays and articles by Mrs. Fry have appeared in print all over the nation.

"The Umbilical Cord" and "The Witch Deer," Mrs. Fry's books of Indian poetry have each sold well. "The Witch Deer" is in its 3rd printing, having sold several thousand copies.

Mrs. Fry draws upon her one-eighth Cherokee heritage and the Oklahoma wildlife which she loves for much of her inspiration.

She is currently working on a book "Depression Days" which deals with ideas for getting along during hard times.

Much of the material for the book was acquired during the early 30's when Mrs. Fry worked with the Claremore Office of the Oklahoma Emergency Relief Administration.

AS A CASEWORKER, she searched out people with pressing needs, helping them find a way to best meet those needs.

Mrs. Fry never learned to drive but was able to hire a teenage boy for 50 cents a day to drive her throughout her district, which reached from the Sequoyah community five miles north of Claremore across the Verdigris River bottoms to the Keetonville area between Claremore and Owasso.

"We delivered commodities and taught people ways to do without things, Mrs. Fry said. "For instance, I've created a recipe for rabbit chili that is really good. We showed people how to make ice-less ice boxes with an orange crate set in a tub of water and covered with burlap bags. The water rising up through the burlap and evaporating would keep the food inside reasonably cool.

MRS. FRY WAS BORN in Vian, Oklahoma, in 1900. At age 20 she decided she wanted a high school education. "I worked piecemeal on it for 3 years, she said. During this time she met and married Merritt Fry and moved to Claremore.

Undaunted, Mrs. Fry continued her high school work by correspondence from Tahlequah,but was never able to complete it.

The couple recently celebrated their 50th wedding anniversary. They have 2 sons. Bourke and Victor.

During the time her sons were growing up, Maggie often found the only time free for her to study and write was after the rest of the family was in bed. This habit has continued through the years.

People passing the little Cape Cod house nestled in the trees on the top of a hill just south and east of Claremore can see the light burning in Maggie's upstairs study window until early morning.

"A FOND MEMORY for me is the interdenominational Sunday school lesson I gave once a week on radio station KWPR," reminisced Mrs. Fry. The program was aired from 1962 to 1973.

She was editor of the Rogers County Observer, a weekly newspaper, during the 60s but resigned because of ill health. She kept writing a column, "Notes from Mossy Glen" for two or three years, however.

For ten years, from 1950-'60, Mrs. Fry was secretary to then state Sen. Clem McSpadden. She, McSpadden and state Rep. Robert Wadley (now a state senator), and later state Rep. Bill Briscoe commuted each Monday morning to Oklahoma City and returned each Thursday while the legislature was in session.

Her humorous story, "Water Witch Widow," will be included in a "world series of literature" to be released by Harcourt Brace Javonivich, Inc., for use at the high school level.

Mrs. Fry was first runner-up in the 1974 national contest for the five Civilized Tribes for her play "Clouds Over Echota."

In her soft but precise voice, Mrs. Fry related that she began writing when she was ten years old. "I would be picking berries or flowers and would think of little verses and stories to jot down."

HER WIDE CIRCLE of friends includes people from all walks of life, including the late Acee Blue Eagle, nationally-famous Indian artist, who reviewed her first book, "The Witch Deer" for her.

Willard Stone, renowned Indian sculptor and artist, is a personal friend and did the illustrations for her book, "The Umbilical Cord."

Mrs. Fry has five grandchildren whom she enjoys tutoring for speech and reading contests.

"Life has been a lot of fun these 74 years," said Mrs. Fry. "I've always considered myself a free person. I know where I've been, and I know where I am going."

The Other 300 Years

James Mitchell/NEA Grant 1973

by Jerome Tarshis

On May 28, when the National Academy of Television Arts and Sciences announced this year's Emmy awards, one program led all the rest: *The Autobiography of Miss Jane Pittman,* a film made for the CBS television network. It had starred Cicely Tyson, who won an Emmy; the director, the scriptwriter, and the composer of the music also won Emmys. Hardly mentioned in the publicity was Ernest J. Gaines, the author of the novel on which the film was based, and one of San Francisco's best writers.

The Autobiography of Miss Jane Pittman is the story of a 110-year-old black woman, born into slavery in Louisiana, who witnesses the ordinary lives of ordinary black people from immediately before the Emancipation Proclamation, in 1863, to a civil rights demonstration in 1962. According to its introduction, the book has resulted from tape-recorded interviews with Miss Jane. At first she had been unwilling to talk, and her friends ask the interviewer, a young black school teacher, why he needs the material.

"What's wrong with them books you already got?" someone asks.

"Miss Jane is not in them," says the young teacher.

And that, neatly put, is the story of Ernest Gaines and his life as a writer. Gaines has been torn between two worlds. He was born in 1933 on a plantation in Louisiana, not far from Baton Rouge. According to a biographical note in one of his books, he remembers working in the fields at the age of nine, for fifty cents a day.

After the war his mother and stepfather moved to Northern California, and about a year later, when he was fifteen, he followed them. He went to junior high school and high school and junior college in Vallejo, and after two years in the Army, studied writing at San Francisco State College and at Stanford, where he held a Wallace Stegner Creative Writing Fellowship. He has won the Joseph Henry Jackson Literary Prize. In these terms he is a Northern California success story.

And yet, although he has lived here for 25 years, his only subject is black life in the rural South; specifically, in the part of Louisiana where he grew up, and where his brothers and aunts and uncles still live. "That I still write about Louisiana is proof that I have not found complete roots here," he told me, "and yet I go to Louisiana once or twice a year, but I must come back here."

His first novel, *Catherine Carmier,* was about a young black man who returns to his home in Louisiana after having been educated in California. He finds that he can no longer live in the rural South, but also that he cannot feel truly at home in Northern California; it isn't Louisiana, but it isn't the Promised Land, either. The title character is a young woman of mixed blood whose father will not allow her—or himself—to fraternize with either whites or blacks.

GAINES, Ernest J.
(1933 -)

SAN FRANCISCO
(San Francisco, Calif.)

July, 1974

[See also CA-11/12]

Gaines himself is caught in a comparable set of conflicting impulses. I met him at a wine-and-cheese party at a bookstore on Union Street, where a group of nice and literary people had gathered to honor Leon D. Adams, author of *The Wines of America.* Gaines bought a copy of the book, and the author signed it.

I had known and admired his writing for several years, and had been hoping to talk with him, for a book of my own, so I arranged to visit him at his apartment, which is on Divisadero Street, in a largely black neighborhood; he lives a very long distance from Union Street.

As I might have known, Ernest Gaines looks back. He went to predominantly white colleges in the 1950s, when Hemingway and Faulkner were enormously admired in creative writing classes, and he has not been carried away by the furies of the 1960s, in dress or demeanor or prose style. On the walls of his work room are portraits of Faulkner and Hemingway, and moving and even beautiful photographs he has taken himself, of the buildings and the Louisiana countryside he grew up in.

The job he has set himself as a writer is, as I say, precisely to look back. I told him I thought he had written *The Autobiography of Miss Jane Pittman* at least partly so that Miss Jane's experiences, and her perceptions of the truth, would not disappear. "Is that a fair reading of your intention?" I asked.

"I suppose it is," he said. "I wish I didn't have to write it; I wish no one had to write it, because I think telling a story and talking is so much better. It's too bad that we don't have tapes of those older people talking, so we could listen to this without ever having to read it. That *is* one of my aims—for them, in their folk way, to tell what happened.

"Much of our history has not been told; our problems have been told, as if we have no history. So much of our literature deals with the big-city ghettos, and we existed long before we came to the big city. We came to this country as slaves, primarily to till the land.

"Much of this has not been written about sympathetically. Many of your white writers have written about black field workers who were clowns; they had strong backs, and they could pick a lot of cotton, and they could sing and be happy, but they did not have brains.

"Most of your black writers who have left the South have ignored the black peasantry, the people who work the land, as though they want to forget that completely. I think too many of our black intellectuals who have left the South put down those experiences, do not think those experiences are worth writing about. There's too much hurt to go back and do it.

"There *is* hurt, but I think there's much beauty there, much strength there. We've only been living in these ghettos for 75 years or so, but the other 300 years — I think this is worth writing about. I think we've made tremendous sacrifices, we've shown tremendous strength. In the ghetto you see a lot of frustration; you see very little strength.

"The majority of young black writers have concentrated on this one thing, as though there were nothing else to their lives; it gives me the feeling that they are ashamed of things in the past, or that they are ashamed of the people of the past.

"The more popular things you can read about black people today are about black militants, but nothing really true about our lives. The militant thing is true, sure, but there are other things, too; screaming is good, but I don't think it has any lasting force unless one knows himself.

"The books I read, by most of the younger black writers, are almost on the same level as the movies that are coming out, almost on the same level as much of the music that is coming out. Even within the big cities, our experiences are different from these things.

"There are blacks in the city who are not pimps or pushers, who are not in jail and getting beaten up by white cops every day. There are people who work every day, people who don't know what a jail looks like, people who struggle every day, for something.

"Those things are truly worth writing about. What I find in these books is not all that is happening; I think this is as false a view to give as the white writers' interpretation of our lives."

Gaines has been concerned for a long time with finding in books the truth of his own life and his family's life. When he was a lonely fifteen-year-old in Vallejo, his stepfather told him to stay off ➡

(Continued from preceding page)
the streets if he wanted to stay out of trouble, and Gaines took refuge in the public library.

"I'd never read books; I'd never seen so many books. I read and read and read, but I didn't see my people or myself in what I was reading. At that time —'48, '49—you had very few books by black writers in a library like that one in Vallejo. So I read white writers, but they did not write about my people as I knew them.

"I would read about people from the earth, farm people like I was, like my people were. Steinbeck, *The Grapes of Wrath* and *Tortilla Flat.* Willa Cather, who wrote about the Middle West. Chekhov, or Turgenev, anybody who wrote about peasants or outdoor life. So I read and read, and then I thought I could write."

He chuckled. "That's when I tried to write something about what I did not find in the books, about my experiences and the experiences of my people as I knew them. I tried to write before I went into the Army, but I knew I knew very little about writing."

After the Army, he studied writing; to judge from his style, Hemingway and Faulkner must have been as influential as any of the teachers he saw in the classroom. "Hemingway is the great technician, and I think I've been impressed by his lifestyle and of course his style of writing.

"Faulkner, being a Southerner, can help any Southern writer to write. He can make you hear things; he can see things that you might not be able to see, or he can remind you of things. Mississippi borders Louisiana, and much of the way he would say things, his dialogue and the way he would tell a story, I can remember from my part of Louisiana.

"You see, I always knew what I wanted to say; I had to find ways to put it down on paper. I did not have black writers as models when I started out, but after reading the white writers, I could see that even they could show me how to write about my own experiences. Reading *Winesburg, Ohio,* showed me that the place I came from could be made into stories; reading Joyce's *Dubliners* was the same thing. I used this plantation quarter as Joyce used Dublin, or as Sherwood Anderson used Winesburg, Ohio."

Gaines's work room is lined with books. Next to the chair on which I sat were rows of books on Africa, and on black life in America; for a while I asked myself if Gaines could possibly have narrowed his reading so drastically, but then I looked around, and saw that he had arranged his books by nationality or ethnic group. I asked him what he reads that he likes or approves of.

Nodding at the portraits of Hemingway and Faulkner, he said, "Oh, I read the two old men there all the time. I can read Tolstoy anytime; I can read Dostoevski sometimes. I can read Turgenev, whom I love very much. I can read Camus, whom I don't think I understand too well, but I can read him. I can read de Maupassant.

"I can read Joyce; I'd read *Dubliners* before I'd read the novels. 'Ivy Day in the Committee Room' I think is one of the greatest short stories that I've ever read. It's the most universal of his work; it's the kind of thing I'd like to do, the barber shop type of thing: you get together and everybody talks." He told me later that he had originally modeled *Miss Jane* after "Ivy Day in the Committee Room," but later decided that Miss Jane herself, rather than a group of her friends, would have to tell her story.

To retrieve us from Dublin, I asked about novels of rural black life. "Well, the book that I read quite often is Jean Toomer's *Cane,* which I think is a masterpiece, and a lot of it has to do with the rural South. I suppose Georgia is the background there, and mine is Louisiana, and the sugar cane thing is definitely a part of my life, because I came from a sugar cane plantation. So that's the best book on rural life that I can think of, by a black writer."

He also knows Ralph Ellison's *Invisible Man,* and the novels of Richard Wright, and feels that Wright's *Native Son* has had a disproportionately large influence on younger black writers. "So many of our writers have not read any farther back than *Native Son.* Too many of our novels deal only with the great city ghettos; that's all we write about, as if there's nothing else."

GAINES, Ernest J.

SAN FRANCISCO
(San Francisco, Calif.)

July, 1974

In his own writing, Gaines seems divided between his love of old people telling stories and his love of telling history in a more didactic way than the human voice will normally support, and I wondered aloud if he had ever thought of writing history as non-fiction. As it turned out, the idea had been put to him, most recently by three African students visiting the United States who had suggested that he might wish to visit Africa, and write a book of non-fiction based on research. He had rejected the idea; he'd never published anything but fiction, not so much as a book review.

"I suppose I would like to go to Africa in order to move my writing back farther: *Miss Jane* takes place from 1863 to 1962. O.K., so I would like to go back to the 18th century and write up what tribe she could have come from. Or I come from. What actually happened? What about the wars, the tribal fights?

"How did I actually get to the boat? I want to know the exact thing, and so I'd have to go back there to do it, but I would still put it into dramatic form: the short story form, the novel form, the play form, something like that. But to go back there to write a non-fiction book—not now. Maybe when I'm tired of writing fiction, which I hope I never will be, I would try something like that."

I asked him about the book he is working on now. "It's very cynical—not the novel, but some of the characters. The main character is a searcher. He's looking for his son, both physically and philosophically, but the people who surround him are quite cynical. In *The Autobiography of Miss Jane Pittman* you found a hope, I think; although they were getting shot down, there was still much hope.

"Joe Pittman, who must ride the horse, or Ned, who must build schools for young people, or Jimmy, in the demonstration at the end, they all die, but they all keep striving, striving, striving, whereas in the book I'm working on now you find so many of the younger ones who are quite cynical.

"*Miss Jane Pittman* ended before even Jack Kennedy's death; the book I'm working on now is after Martin King's death. It takes place in a small town in Louisiana, and it deals with the attitudes of many of the young people who were sitting-in at lunch counters, and marching, and so on, who have changed so much now, like they don't give a damn, or something else must happen."

Gaines had told me that *Miss Jane* is being taught from Mission High School to Yale, and I asked him about his acceptance by young people. When he gives readings, he told me, more white kids than black kids come up to talk about his work. "In this country there are more white people than black people," I said.

"No, it isn't that," he said. "I can go to universities where there are several hundred black kids and find none of them coming to the reading. I went to the University of North Carolina at Chapel Hill, and this was, I think, in December of 1969. There were two or three hundred black kids on the campus, and Anthony Burgess and I were on the program, and there were no blacks at the program.

"If you were going to write a book, you had to write a *Soul on Ice* or Leroi Jones-type stories to get attention from the black kids on the campus. I don't know whether it was fortunate or unfortunate that my books were beginning to be published at the time when a lot of the militant demonstrations were going on, and I wasn't considered part of that crowd. I wasn't writing in *The Black Scholar,* or *Black World,* or some of the more militant papers, so I was not accepted as that kind of writer."

Looking around me again at the photographs of Louisiana, hearing the police and ambulance sirens from Divisadero Street, remembering the wine-and-cheese party on Union Street where I had met him, I asked to what extent he writes for some real or imagined public, white or black.

"Oh, no, no, no, no, no. I try to write a book that I think is true. I think that I am my own severest critic. My agent, and my editor, those are the people I've listened to. But as for a white public or a black public—I don't care what they think. I care about what they think as far as buying the book is concerned," he chuckled, "but nobody tells me how to write.

"Writing is too goddamned hard for me to think about a soul in the world. I get up in the morning, and when I sit down to work—all my stuff is done longhand—I don't think about a soul, but just try to get those goddamned characters to act right." □

Galella at a New York gallery showing of some of his "takes."

Will Jackie Kennedy Onassis Stop Bothering Ron Galella?

And let him become rich and famous?

GALELLA, Ron

DETROIT FREE PRESS (Detroit, Mich.)

Sept 15, 1974

By CHARLES FLOWERS
Of the Magazine Staff

He calls himself "the world's foremost *paparazzo,*" but Jacqueline Kennedy Onassis has other names for him.

Marlon Brando unhinged his jaw with a right cross in New York's Chinatown last summer, but Ron Galella came up grinning with a new set of six lower teeth and a $250,000 lawsuit against the man who gave us "The Godfather."

Richard Burton threatened to kill him if he didn't go away, but Liz restrained Dick and Burton's chauffeur punched him out instead.

Is this any way to make a living?

Ron Galella says yes. Ron Galella, photographer, supplier to the world's pulp magazines of unguarded photos of Jackie and the stars, says yes, indeed. He takes a lot of pride in his work.

Galella is a man for the '70s. A specialist. Evel Knievel with a camera. He's a 43-year-old Italian bachelor who divides his time between celebrity-hunting, the darkroom, and the hospital. In his best year of photographing Jackie, 1971, he made $40,000. He estimates half of that came from sales of candid photos of the former First Lady.

Maybe the Lions could use him on their suicide squad.

"PRESS LAYS OFF GALELLA, SUGGESTS HE MAY BE 'PEEPING TOM' THOUGH"

Galella was in Detroit last month telling Lou Gordon and Dennis Wholly, J.P. McCarthy, two TV news stations and me how he does it, and perhaps more importantly, why.

Lou Gordon laid off him during his show and then had him come onstage to photograph Connie Stevens paparazzo-style. (Connie and Ron were both guests on Lou's answer to "Masterpiece Theater.")

Dennis Wholey kept him awake.

Over in Windsor, Channel 9 asked him how "Jackie Kennedy" was doing in a short newsfilm they could keep or throw away. Channel 4 used him. And J.P. Mc Carthy sat with him through a half-dozen Marlboros on his WJR radio show, "Focus."

Galella was riding on the crest of a wave during his visit to Detroit, the first leg of national publicity tour. His one-man show of photographs at the Nikon House Gallery in New York had received a favorable review in the New York Times. His first book, "Jacqueline," did not get good reviews, but his advance from Sheed and Ward publishers and serialization in newspapers should help him out handsomely since he will not be photographing Mrs. Onassis anymore.

Oh, didn't you hear? Ron and Jackie are on the outs. After taking some 4,000 pictures that ended up on covers of every magazine from Life to the National Enquirer, Ron is giving up on Jackie. He won his appeal in New York two years ago, got his working distance shortened to 25 feet, but decided even that was too far.

Galella was treated with something bordering on amusement by nearly all the local media. He had ready answers for accusations that he was less than wholesome in his approach to celebrities.

"I'm a romantic," he said. "I idolize celebrities in a way. I don't want to make them look bad. I'm trying to portray them as they are, as real people."

He said he had ethics, that he did not and would not photograph Jackie in the nude because that would be "indecent." He respected her privacy, and the privacy of other celebrities he photographs, but he believes that when they go out in public they are "fair game" for his camera.

"Prince paparazzo," J.P. McCarthy called him, "the man with the galloping Graflex." Then, less humorously, suggested he might be a "Peeping Tom."

Galella answered that he was not a voyeur, that photographing Jackie did not give him any sexual excitement. Brigitte Bardot, yes. But Jackie wasn't his type. But the distinction between what Galella does in the bushes with his Nikon and what a Peeping Tom does in the bushes with his eyes was more eloquently stated the day before by New York Times critic Gene Thornton, reviewing Galella's show:

"Peeping Tom is after the forbidden fruit while Ron Galella is merely making a nuisance of himself in his pursuit of the banal and the commonplace."

Jackie Kennedy Onassis commonplace? Ron Galella would say no.

"THAT FIRST TIME JACKIE SAID 'YOU'VE BEEN HUNTING ME!"

The civil suit and countersuit of Galella vs. Onassis vs. Galella was either a landmark decision on freedom of the press versus the right of public figures to privacy, or else it was the state's answer to a profound failure to communicate. In either case, the trial where Jackie testified packed the New York courtroom for almost a month.

"He lunged at me and he was grunting and he was saying, 'Glad to see me back, Jackie, aren't you baby?'" Mrs. Onassis testified on March 6, 1972. "And then he took his camera strap and he was flicking me on the shoulders. Sometimes he was as close as two feet away. I kept going and I got into the car and I went shopping . . ."

Galella, whose own testimony was contradictory on some points, denies this completely, down to the grunt. "I do not grunt," he says. Still, the picture he took of Jackie during this incident is very close-up.

Galella wants you to believe he was railroaded during his trial, by the high-priced Onassis lawyers, and by the judge, Irving Ben Cooper, a Kennedy appointee.

"This book is my vindication," Galella states vindictively.

Galella looks more like a golfer than a paparazzo on holiday. He stayed at the Shiawassee Hotel on Nine Mile near Southfield, and came down in a beige suit, brown patterned knit shirt open at the neck, flared pants, and a big smile. A hair dryer shared space with his Nikon in his camera bag. He has taste if not breeding, manners if not etiquette.

He has a simple charm. He grew up in the Bronx, the son of an immigrant piano and casket maker. The word "any" is not in his vocabulary. He says, recalling an incident when Aristotle Onassis' bodyguards twisted his camera strap around his neck, "I didn't get

(Continued from preceding page)

no pictures that time." He is a former Air Force photographer, Life photo technician and a '57 graduate of the Art Center College of Design in Los Angeles, an accredited school where Ron earned a four-year Bachelor of Professional Arts degree. His specialty was photojournalism.

The head of the photography department at the Art Center, Charles Potts, remembers Galella as "a very energetic, hard-working boy. You have to have talent to make it here, and he made it. We don't make specialists here, but it was clear Ron was going into editorial work."

From the first, Galella was heavily into freelance paparazzo. (The word, coined by Italian director Federico Fellini means "pesky insect" but Galella defines it to mean photography of people without their knowledge or consent.) He would crash Hollywood premieres to take pictures of movie stars. He had his paparazzo technique pretty well developed when he met up with Jackie Kennedy Onassis for the first time in May, 1967.

They were a perfect match. She was a somebody. He was a nobody. He loved her. She loathed him. They had their first and only real conversation that year. Jackie pinned Ron's shooting arm to the side of his car and said, "You've been hunting me for two months!" Ron, shocked nearly speechless that she had spoken to him, said, "Yes."

At no time after that, Galella maintains, did Jackie ever ask him to stop taking pictures. She was aloof, he says, she would run away, or call her Secret Service agents or, sometimes, smile.

"BRANDO DECKS GALELLA, GALELLA ASKS 'WHY?' NEXT ROUND IN COURT"

Feelings run strong on the ethics of taking pictures of Jackie, who, depending on the feeler, either married or suffered her publicity, and did not ask for or want it. One woman called WJR after Galella's segment to say that he not only should not be on the air, he should be taken out and shot.

Whatever the morality, legality or ethics of taking candid pictures of famous people, Galella has paid a heavy price for it. You can admire his persistence when you see that pair of pink, three-inch scars that wind around his ears to his sideburns — where his jaw was busted by Marlon Brando in New York's Chinatown on June 12, 1973, as Dick Cavett, in sunglasses, looked on. Galella's version of the story reveals his economic philosophy. People are marketable items. Each location photograph is a "take." The more takes the better.

"Brando came to New York to tape the Dick Cavett show," Galella recalls. "I got him at a heliport on the east side coming in. That was my best take. Then he went to the studio and I got him coming in but nothing good. The crowd was too large, so I didn't even try to get him coming out.

After the taping, I followed Brando and Cavett to Chinatown. They got out of a limousine wearing sunglasses and neckerchiefs. I photographed them until Brando stopped to ask directions to a restaurant. I was watching, curiously, not taking any pictures. Brando looked at me and said, 'What else do you want that you don't already have?' I said, 'I would like a few without the glasses," since editors buy pictures more readily if they can see the person. Brando motioned for me to come closer. Brando was standing sideways to me when he hit me with his right hand. He cracked four of my lower teeth. The tips were removed and I had to get root canals for them. I had to get six teeth capped. I'm suing him for compensatory and punitive damages.

"There's laws, but there's no justice. The rich people, the people with power, get what they want. Mister Citizen gets nothing. Sinatra calls the press parasites. Well, who made them the gods that they are? The press!"

"GALELLA SLEEPS ALONE, LIZ TAYLOR WONDERS 'WHY?'"

Oh, such sin, such scandal. Galella dressed as a bandito in Mexico, in sombrero and false mustache, to sneak some pictures of Liz and Dick back when there was a Liz and Dick and

GALELLA, Ron

DETROIT FREE PRESS
(Detroit, Mich.)

Sept. 15, 1974

he got beat up, had the key to his room stolen, and saw 15 rolls of exposed film crushed under the heels of his captors.

The same thing happened when he sneaked onto a movie set in Hollywood to photograph Elvis and they made him sorry. He has photographed a lot of hands of Secret Service agents, bodyguards and others paid to spoil his pictures.

And still he hangs in there.

The paparazzo gave impressions of some of his prey.

Jackie: "Jackie was the ideal subject. Unlike Liz Taylor who doesn't go out, Jackie goes out often, to clubs like "21" and La Cote Basque. She says she's just a housewife and a mother, but she's the most glamorous woman in the world. She doesn't want people to know she's Jackie Kennedy Onassis."

Sinatra: "He'll communicate. When he says 'no pictures' you know you better stop taking pictures or you'll get slugged."

Burton: "He tried to hit me once in front of the Dorchester Hotel in London. Liz held him back. His chauffeur socked me instead."

Sophia: "She's very photogenic. Very warm. And she doesn't mind being photographed, even when she's caught off-guard."

Ari: "Ari is always friendly. Jackie is kind of shy. Ari talks to photographers. Jackie doesn't."

Brando: "Brando does not communicate. He's like Jackie in this regard. He struck me like a snake, without warning."

Elvis: "Elvis Presley is my next big project. He definitely wants publicity on his own terms. He has about 15 bodyguards. He's elusive. You don't see very many candid pictures of him, or especially, of him and his girlfriend."

Over a lunch of Veal Cordon Bleu at Topinka's restaurant on the Boulevard, Galella confided some of his techniques. He studies his prey, he knows their habits. He reads the gossip columns to find out who's in town and what they're doing. He subscribes to Celebrity Service, which tells him a little more about their activities. He talks to fans.

And then he goes gunning.

Galella uses at least one Nikon camera, sometimes two. He shoots black and white with one and color with the other. His favorite lens is an 85mm f:1.8 Nikkor, which gives him good tight shots of two people from a distance, and good close-ups as they come nearer. Contrary to popular opinion, the longest lens he uses is a 500mm with an extender to double the focal length. And, contrary to Jackie's testimony, he likes to work at a distance, unobtrusively.

"The best paparazzo is the invisible one. The best camera is the invisibleone. You have to be a hustler. You have to be ingenious. A Freelancer has to be more aggressive more hungry than a staff photographer because he doesn't have his way paid. He has to meet the demand for the pictures editors and people who read fan magazines want to see. He's competing in a very competitive market."

Galella maintained that the essence of paparazzo-style photography is secrecy.

"I don't ask for pictures because one of two things will usually happen. They'll either make excuses — 'Oh, my hair's not done' — or you'll get a trite expression. Expressions on the human face are much more infinite when the person is caught unawares."

Galella admits that pursuit of his career has left his personal life a shambles. He owns a two-bedroom home in Yonkers, N.Y., but he has never married. He can't even make a date with anyone because he doesn't know if he'll be able to keep it.

"Liz Taylor was in town four days last week. I said I wish she'd get the hell out of town so I can get back to my life. You can't make a date with a girl because Liz Taylor might be going out that night."

It doesn't seem like such a hot life. So why does he keep it up? For the fringe benefits, mainly. He says he gets a lot of "psychic income" out of it.

"Psychic income is the sense of achievement you get out of your work. For instance, in Detroit you got this assembly line. One guy puts on the nuts and another guy puts on the bolts. I buy a new car and it's a piece of crap! And do you know why? Because the guy who makes it is looking at the clock."

The clock is winding down on our visit with the paparazzo. He and his hair dryer have another appointment. He is becoming believable, the little guy in the big world with nothing but his guts and his resourcefulness, the guy so far removed from Her Majesty that she won't even condescend to speak to him. He has landed on Skorpios with a handful of peaches and a camera in a scene out of "Mission Impossible," and he has come out alive. He has taken Brando's best shot and come back for more.

"Look," he says, sipping an iced coffee, "I've got Brando here. I've got Liz Taylor. It's history . . . to get a great shot of Eisenhower, of Robert Kennedy . . . you can't get that anymore. This is me, this is my art."

THE SUNNY TWILIGHT OF PAUL GALLICO

By
MARCELLE BERNSTEIN

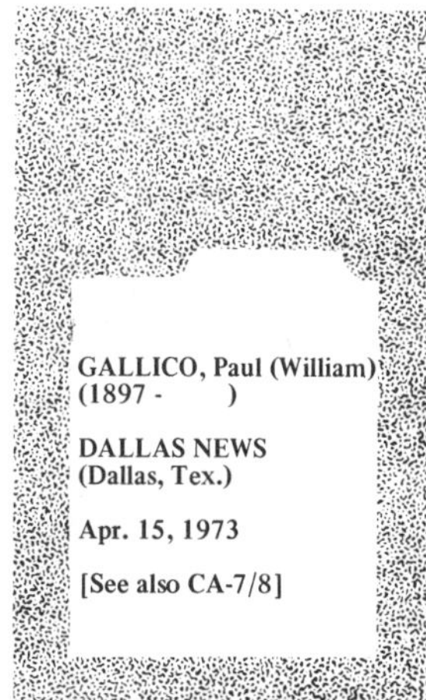
GALLICO, Paul (William) (1897 -)
DALLAS NEWS (Dallas, Tex.)
Apr. 15, 1973
[See also CA-7/8]

In a warm stone courtyard beneath a cream parasol, a table bears a bowl of black cherries, a platter of nectarines, figs laid on vine leaves. A dark-haired woman whose youthful appeal lies in the slight irregularity of her features, the bend of her nose under the straw hat, sips white wine. Beside her, enjoying his after-lunch euphoria, sits Paul Gallico.

He is a big man and his 75 years have not stooped him nor softened the black of his hair. He does not look the kind of writer he is. The face is heavily fleshed, big nosed, Italianate. The mouth is thick, sensual, sardonic. He could be a prosperous businessman, an impresario.

Yet his phenomenal output of books and stories reveal a tenderness verging on the sentimental, a whimsicality which, if handled less skillfully, would be cloying, and a naive quality, an innocence quite astonishing in a man of his age and background.

In his work he does not pretend, or attempt, realism. "We live in a rough, cold world today. But I make a different world when I write: I make it what I think it ought to be." He provides the escape fiction he knows people want, but what matters to him is that the first person to escape is Gallico himself. As he writes he enters another country, another atmosphere, to such an extent that he can hardly bear to pack the book up and send it to the publisher. "I'm very sad for about 10 days, making the transition from all my friends."

So he remains a teller of tales, a dreamer of dreams, a romantic. And for such unfashionable qualities he has always had a vast market, great financial reward and the opportunity to live where and as he wishes, which he utilizes to the utmost with a house in Antibes, an apartment in Monte Carlo and a cottage in London.

But Antibes is his real home, where he and his English wife Virginia have converted two narrow fishermen's houses high on the ramparts of the town over the harbor. In cool, shuttered rooms there are paintings, brass scales full of heather from the Provençal hills, an old rocking horse in weathered wood.

The Gallicos are looked after by Anne and Antoinette, Katherine and Severine. Virginia brings to the house the order of an English country home. There are internal telephones — the extension in the courtyard is hidden in a niche beside a stone unicorn — each with its typed list:

1. Bureau Secretaire
2. Bureau M. Gallico
3. Chambre Madame
4. Grande Cuisine
5. Salon Rose
6. Bibliotheque

The Bureau M. Gallico takes up the top floor, with a wall of window overlooking the bay and the terrace where at nine he breakfasts alone on black coffee and croissants. Against the window is his vast, leather-topped desk, crowded with bric-a-brac. A neatly bound manuscript, a "Don't Forget" notebook with a page of scribble, a pair of binoculars to watch incoming boats, an old flyswat and a Shakespeare Birthday Book. Everywhere in the room the paintings are impressionist, the furniture grey-blue velvet and the lampshades pleated silk.

He contemplates a goldfish called Ivan Awful Jaundice which swims opposite his desk, and says that "there is nothing here that I could not write without." Writing, for him, is like "being at a party and saying, Have you heard the one about?' It's the pleasure of telling a good tale, the logic and neatness of it when you get all the ends to thread up together and it works."

He inherits both his love of storytelling and his long-fingered hands from his musician father. "He was an unexplosive Italian and I adored him." He taught during the day and played in concerts at night. "I can still see him shaving himself with an open razor, very handsome, and saying 'to be continued tomorrow.' He told me about dragons and adventures, and I was brought up on the fairy books of the Brothers Grimm, in a family whose culture was European although they emigrated to the United States two years before I was born."

At 10 years old, left alone in a Brussels hotel, he wrote his first story, about a small boy and an Italian workman. It was the escape from loneliness of an only child to "lie in bed at night and see myself in heroic roles: They kept me busy until I fell asleep."

After studying English at Columbia University, he joined the sports section of the *New York Daily News* and worked there in the '20s and '30s when the heroes of the young were sporting figures and gangsters controlled boxing. Not until he was 36, after 15 years of trying, did he sell a story to a major magazine, the *Saturday Evening Post*. Three years later he moved to a cottage in England to live on the proceeds of a film script and try to turn himself into the writer he wanted to be.

His first book, "The Snow Goose," was to be his tour de force. "After Dunkirk I wanted to write a poem, a song in sympathy." So he created Rhayader, the dark cripple with his bird sanctuary in the marshes, to which a silent girl brings the wounded goose. It was an unashamed tearjerker by a man who says sternly that "emotions are deadly when you're writing. You must never give way to them."

It is his only book to have achieved real critical success. He is no literary lion and all too often critics refer to his charm as "practiced." He does, of course, mind. Although: "I don't think anybody can be more than he is. I can't write like anybody else, and the anybody elses can't write like me." He learned never to envy another writer after bumping into Hemingway at the bar of New York's stylish Stork Club. "My God," said Hemingway, "you're the guy who wrote 'Snow Goose.' I wish I'd written that."

Gallico fingers the flashy golden globe on his desk, an American television film award for "The Snow Goose." "In place of great literary fame, I've got millions of people who care about what I write and who like me. What the hell more do I want?"

Over the years he has achieved a superb professionalism. To feel comfortable he must have a novel "in the works," one "on the runway" and another in the "take-off slot." After two months he has the first draft completed, and by the eighth month the second and final version will be written, "though some go three."

He thoroughly enjoys the whole writing process, even making good badly-written material. He will start work soon after nine, dictating slowly with long pauses to think while his American secretary sits patiently. "I might say a line and then no, hold that, kill it, let's try it this way." He finds this faster than typing himself, which ended 13 years ago when he suffered from pinched nerves resulting from a bent head when typing, which meant ➡

(Continued from preceding page)

wearing what he calls a "portable gallows" for six months.

He delights in the business side: A letter about the planned American musical of "Flowers for Mrs. Harris" to his publishers reads like a publicity handout. He refuses to accept advance payments for a book because "that way I'm in the saddle." He tells how many copies he thinks a book will sell, and claims accuracy.

Everyone, he believes, has a story — "Go and ask your grocer how he got started." He puts his books together like a casserole. "You take something you've learned, something someone has said and everything goes into the pot."

One children's book, "Manx Mouse," came from Princess Grace of Monaco, who promised him a mouse when she started ceramic classes. A year later it arrived with her apologies for its broken tail and rabbity ears. "She didn't know I was writing a book until it was delivered to her bound, illustrated and dedicated."

He puts the mouse carefully back on his study shelf, picks up the phone and dials Virginia's room. "Are you there? No, no, I just wondered where you were — I haven't seen you for a bit." And wanders upstairs for a massage. He has these regularly, and wears a silvered copper bracelet against rheumatism "because, let me tell you, the climate here is punk." An hour later he mixes drinks in the library: A tall gin and tonic for himself, champagne as usual for Virginia.

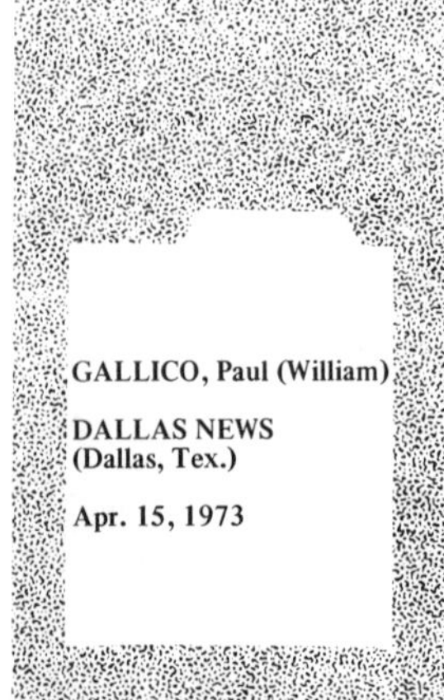

The library is the largest room in the house, dark-paneled, with great round suede chairs, a brilliant fairground painting by an old friend, Dame Laura Knight. And of course there are books, filling every wall, the Koran next to "The Life of the Caterpillar." There are 600 of them. And not one of them is written by him.

"I will not keep my own books in the library. They do not belong in there. I'm not all that modest, and I'm vain, and I prefer not to put myself in a library containing some of the greatest writers in the world. Mine are in my study."

At the moment he is working on an original screenplay, struggling to bend the dialogue into a certain channel. "But the characters won't do it. People are people, and I can't force them to do anything." Names are vital in forming a character, and the blonde heroine of the shipwreck book, "Poseidon Adventure," would not work at all until he re-named her Nonnie. "Then she got up off the floor and began to act like a person. I saw her, I felt her."

Many characters originate from people he knows, and he is always amazed if they do not recognize themselves. Ada 'Arris, the Cockney woman with a passion for geraniums, is really a London charlady called Katie. The tragic Rhayader of "Snow Goose" is Peter Scott — "his lighthouse, his painting, his sailing ability." Both men were once in love with the same girl figure skating champion. "The character came from my admiration, turning him into a heroic figure."

Gallico's female characters are not his strong point, the most vivid being the Marquesa in "Love, Let Me Not Hunger." Bloated, bejeweled and totally bald under her wig, she is, claims Gallico with satisfaction, "My old nannie. I hated and loathed her and I've got her to a T."

He has been married four times. The first marriage lasted 13 years, from the time he was 25, and gave him two sons whom he rarely sees; one is in real estate, the other in the film industry. The other two ended in amicable divorces due, he says, to differing temperaments. "I've never had a divorce which sprang from adultery with another woman."

But now he has "come into port" with the former Baroness Virginia von Falz-Fein, whom he met when living in Lichtenstein. "She not only has looks that appeal to me but she's very bright and full of ideas." Virginia, who does his research, finds that "the marvelous thing about being married to a man 30 years older is that every day you hear him say something about himself you haven't heard before." She brought him the daughter he had always wanted: Ludmilla, an aspiring actress who calls him "Beau" for "Beau-pere." Having a young Virginia and an even younger Ludmilla, Gallico finds that he has "no sense of age, no sense that my machinery is running out. Though of course it is."

Even now he gets pleasure from fencing. Twice a week he dresses in the elaborate white jacket and drives across the harbor to fence with a 36-year-old master built like a wrestler. He invariably wins more than his share of matches, returning home muffled in towels, steaming and beaming. It is for him totally absorbing, "like physical chess." And just occasionally he will swim in the harbor.

He finishes his gin, and dinner is served in the Grande Cuisine. Candles in great pewter stands, roast pigeons and ratatouille. Virginia wears a long dress and talks of London. He wears a T-shirt saying "Frazier the Sensuous Lion" sent him that day by Prince Rainier, and hardly talks at all. At dinner parties, he invariably refuses all conversation with his neighbors until he has eaten and relaxed.

Afterwards he moves back into the courtyard, damp and pungent after its watering, sits in his long chair beneath the purpling ribbons of bougainvillea. He is at home in France now. "We live here," he says, taking Virginia's hand in the darkness, "in the utmost tranquillity and with great delight."

He sips his Perrier. "I've got everything I want. And now I have a sense of impending extinction. How much longer can I wait? I've reached the life expectancy of this generation. I'm prepared for death, hoping I can go as my father did, who went to sleep and didn't wake up." He smiles at Virginia. "I have an adorable GP who was 80 at Christmas. He sits here and says, 'You know, I'm not afraid, I don't mind dying. I just don't like the idea of growing old.' I know exactly what he means — he and I are now vulnerable to all kinds of catastrophes which could turn us into vegetables. A stroke, a heart attack."

He stares at the pale plumbago flowers starring the dark wall. "I am aware, but it doesn't worry me. My natural conviction is that when that happens I am neither going to descend into the nether regions nor be snatched into the higher ones. I shall deeply regret not getting my *Herald Tribune*. I will deeply regret my Ludmilla and my Virginia. But then I shall have nothing left to regret leaving them with."

Gallico crosses his legs, clasps his hands upon his stomach and adds, in his gentle monotone. "And as for the long rest of eternity, I have no quarrel with that."

GANN, Ernest Kellogg (1910-) SEATTLE POST-INTELLIGENCER (Seattle, Wash.) Dec. 23, 1973 [See also CA-4]

P-I photo by Tom Brownell

The Factual Fiction Of Ernest Gann

BY EMMETT WATSON
P-I Columnist

"BAND OF BROTHERS" is a novel about flying. It is not just any novel about flying, not a simple pot-boiler like "Airport," because it was written by Ernest K. Gann, a retired line pilot with a special gift for imparting clarity, meaning and suspense to the difficult business of flying an aircraft. In this respect, Ernie Gann is alone in his field; indeed, he created the dimensions of the field.

Pilots, many of whom do not read much else in the way of books, await each Gann book on flying. Yet "Island in The Sky," "In the Company of Eagles," "The High and the Mighty," and the mother book of them all, "Fate is the Hunter," have transcended the special attention of pilots and attracted enormous numbers of devoted readers. Because he brings to writing a pilot's sense of professionalism, he has turned out an average of two books a year for the last 30-plus years. He writes well about the sea, as in "Song of the Sirens," and about history, as in "The Antagonists."

But "Band of Brothers" is about flying and in some respects, I think, superior to "The High and The Mighty," a best-seller which was made into a highly successful film.

Almost as intriguing as the novel itself is Gann's list of acknowledgements, which fill almost two pages. To give "Band of Brothers" its engaging verissimilitude, Gann traveled to Europe and Asia, interviewing pilots, airline officials, traffic controllers; among those prominently thanked were Jack Leffler, a Seattle-based captain of United Air Lines, and senior test pilot Don Knutson, of Boeing. It was Knutson, in fact, who first checked the manuscript before publication.

Shortly after reading "Band of Brothers," I found Ernie Gann and his wife, Dodie, staying at the Washington Athletic Club. The old pilot had been grounded temporarily by an operation, and was just out of the hospital. He was feeling a bit rocky, but happy, because his publisher, Simon and Schuster, reported that sales of the book were climbing like a Lear jet with a light load.

"A lot of pilots read my stuff," he said, talking about the book's background, "and I knew it had to be absolutely as accurate as I could make it. When I finally finished it, I called Don Knutson and asked him to check the manuscript for errors. When he said I had it down right, I could have jumped with joy. He even agreed with my conclusions."

Like most of Gann's flying stories, "Band of Brothers" is based on an actual happening. The books' genesis was the crash of a Boeing 727 a few years ago at Taipei International Airport, in which an American pilot, employed by a Chinese nationalist airline, hit the ground several miles short of the runway.

Most of the passengers, including the pilots' wife, who had joined her husband for a vacation, were killed. The pilot, a co-pilot and a senior check pilot, riding in the cockpit, survived. But to the astonishment of airline pilots everywhere, the American was jailed, charged with "criminal negligence," and convicted. He was later exonerated and freed, but only after IFALPA, the federation of international pilots, threatened to boycott Taipei International.

To a novelist like Gann, with a feel for intrigue and adventure, this was irresistible. He set about on an exhaustive job of research. He traveled to Taipei and read voluminous official reports of the accident (over the strong objections of Chinese officials), visited the crash site and listened to the flight recordings.

He went to Europe, where he interviewed pilots of Lufthansa, BOAC, Air France and KLM. He journeyed to Denver where he "flew" the actual approach to Taipei International Airport in a United Airlines Boeing 727 simulator. He even looked up the American pilot, now free and living with his three children in the east.

"It was the most painful book I've ever written," Gann says today. "We talked a lot, this pilot and I, but we never actually talked about the details of the accident. It was something too terrible, really, to discuss, but I wanted to get to know him. He turned out to be a fine man, whose life had been scarred by this one tragedy."

"In general the events in this book are fictional. So are the characters." Thus the first two sentences of Gann's acknowledgements. His fictional hero is Captain Lewis Horn, of the equally fictional Trans-Atlantic Airways, "currently qualified on Douglas DC-8, Boeing 720B, Boeing 727. North Atlantic and Caribbean routes. Total flight hours: 11,000-plus."

Horn is astonished and outraged at charges of "criminal negligence" against a highly-regarded, even legendary, figure among pilots of the line. The ill-fated, fictional pilot is Captain Alexander Malloy, held in a Chinese prison, awaiting sentence.

Horn, the stubborn believer that something beyond the control of Captain Malloy had caused the accident, gathered together the "band of brothers."

They were: Capt. William Oliver Chatsworth, of Pilot Imperial Airways (later BOAC); Capt. Jan Anton Van Grootes, command pilot, KLM; Capt. Etienne Diderot, Sabena Airlines, and Capt. Willie Moller, senior pilot Lufthansa Airlines.

How five of these pilots, each of different nationality, different temperaments, all influenced in the past by the legendary Alexander Malloy, set out to exonerate him from charges of "criminal negligence," makes up the suspend in "Band of Brothers."

All, of course, are composites of real pilots, now flying the airways of the world.

"It couldn't be just a group of Americans trying to help a fellow American," Gann said that night in his room at the WAC. "It had to be a representative, international group. I spent weeks in Europe, talking to pilots. What is it like to fly for KLM? For Sabena? How do you get to be a senior pilot for BOAC?

"I wanted to know all these things, and these men were wonderful. Most of them knew me from my previous books, and we sat up nights together, talking, exchanging stories and ideas. It's a little different in each country, on each airline, but when it comes right down to flying, it all goes back to the basics."

Reflecting on his exhaustive research of the original accident, Gann still is convinced "it was a straight railroad job —nothing else. The Chinese simply would not admit that anything they did, or owned, could be at fault."

Gann had another puzzle in putting together "Band of Brothers." He had to take a story, whose genesis was technical, and make it into a swift-moving novel of suspense and Oriental intrigue, "something that would appeal to a wide audience." This he did, I think, by calling on his gift, mentioned earlier, of bringing clarity to th complex business of piloting aircraft.

When we finished talking, he suggested I call Don Knutson, the senior Boeing test pilot, who checked the manuscript. Boeing, of course, sends representatives to assist in any accident involving a Boeing plane—the 727 was pronounced blameless in the original accident, as it is in the book.

"Two of us went over," Knutson said. "Wally Hansen, a technical engineer, and myself. We visited the crash site, listened to the flight recorder and the read-outs, spent about two weeks assisting in the investigation.

"Ernie gave me his manuscript and I sat up all night reading it. He had it all down. There was just one or two suggestions I made, but he had it down right. A fine job."

I asked Knutson if his own conclusion on the real cause of the crash coincided with the one in Gann's book. "Yes," he said, "I think Ernie and I are in agreement on that."

And what are these conclusions? Well, this is a book review—sort of. Read "Band of Brothers," and plan to stay up late. You'll find out

Conversations with John Gardner on writers and writing

photography by HUGH GRANNUM

John Gardner is the author of several novels, including "The Sunlight Dialogues," "Grendel," "Nickel Mountain," and "The Resurrection." He has a new book out called "The King's Indian," which is a collection of several short works.

His books are an unusual combination of lovely writing, fascinating stories, and difficult philosphy. The philosophy has ensured him the sort of favorable critical response accorded writers who are more learned than their reviewers. In his early 40s, Gardner is regarded as being in the first rank of American novelists.

He teaches medieval literature at Southern Illinois University and is presently a visiting professor at Bennington in Vermont. Gardner is the author of several highly respected scholarly works which are never listed under "Other Books by John Gardner" in his novels.

Despite his erudition, Gardner first-hand is scrupulously down-to-earth. His speech is neither colorful nor particularly graceful, and most of what he knows about philosophy he keeps to himself unless you press him to reveal it.

During the following interview he fiddled ceaselessly with a pipe which kept going out. Burnt matches piled up neatly on a tobacco tin beside him. He was born in Batavia, N.Y. and grew up on a farm there. He still has a rural suspicion of sophistication, by which he means decadence, and a directness that perhaps explains the heavy-handed application of uncamouflaged metaphysics in some of his works; that's what he cares about, so that's what he puts in, artifice be damned.

Yet his best-known book, "The Sunlight Dialogues," the story of a battle of wits between an anarchistic Christ figure and a law-and-order police chief in Batavia, was a best seller despite its 673 pages and a style one reviewer called "overwrought." It wouldn't have happened five or ten years ago but, as Gardner says, readers are changing.

Reporter John Askins found Gardner at Marygrove College where he came to give a reading at the request of Dr. Janice Lauer of the English department there. He and Dr. Lauer are friends from the Fall of 1970 when Gardner was a visiting professor at the University of Detroit.

DETROIT: *Is it important to you to get people thinking about philosophical questions?*

GARDNER: I think it's important for people to think philosophically. I think the world is in bad shape, and I think the reason is philosophical. I think people have been believing stupid things for a long time.

For instance, I just read the other day a whiney essay in the *New York Times* literary magazine saying how helpless we are when confronted by our children. That's bad philosophy. We are not helpless. When our children misbehave we can tell them. When our children disappoint us we can show them. Children can be wonderful people. But the sort of general feeling in America is that everything is hopeless. What good philosophy does is fight that, show how bad that bad philosophy is.

DETROIT; *In one of your books,"The Resurrection", you had your protagonist, a philosophy professor, talk about "self-pitying existentialists." Do you share that point of view?*

GARDNER: (Laughs). Well — sometimes. Existentialism, of course, is a very fine thing, but it can be self-pitying. Like, you can choose the best of Jean Paul Sartre and it's very optimistic and brave, very noble. Or you can choose the worst of Jean Paul Sartre and it's stupid.

DETROIT; *Your hero, at any rate, is an appealing man.*

GARDNER: I mean for him to be appealing. I mean all my characters to be appealing. I hate books where there are bad guys.

DETROIT: *But you do need villains, don't you?*

GARDNER; We're all villains. We're all the robbers as well as the cops.

DETROIT: *According to one biographical note, you started writing at an early age*

GARDNER: . . . I was about seven when I started writing poetry. I wrote really good poetry when I was a kid, but when I grew up I didn't write so well. I also wrote novel after novel, thrillers — probably 20 — before I was 15 years old. My cousins all worked on the farm and I used to write a chapter every day and read it to them in the barn at night, and they would all say, 'Ooohh.' Very exciting.

DETROIT: *You're still reading your work aloud today, although to larger audiences. Do you write with that in mind?*

GARDNER: Oh, I think unquestionably I'm writing for oral effect. Often when I write I can't think of a word, but I know the rhythm has to go "ba-da-da," so I just write "Ba-da-da" there and hope that something will come later.

DETROIT: *One reviewer accused you of making up words.*

GARDNER: He's probably right. I have made up words. Like, the Greek word for darkness is 'thestare." It's a really lovely word, but the only way it exists now is in old cemeteries, where you might see on a tombstone the name of some girl who was called Thester. So in one of my books I speak of "thestral" things.

DETROIT: *It has a nice sound.*

GARDNER: Yeah. You don't have to understand words. Language is texture . . .

DETROIT: *I notice "The Sunlight Dialogues" everywhere in paperback. Does that mean you have a larger public than one would expect you to have?*

GARDNER: Oh, yeah. Things are very good for serious writers right now. They're very bad for people who write sort of light, frothy mysteries, love stories, dog stories, things like that. The kind of writers who used to publish in the *Saturday Evening Post* for instance. They can't publish anymore. And the reason is that people like Joyce Carol Oates, who is at the top of the serious market, also writes confession stories, detective stories; you know, everything; whatever there is, she writes. So she pushes these other writers out.

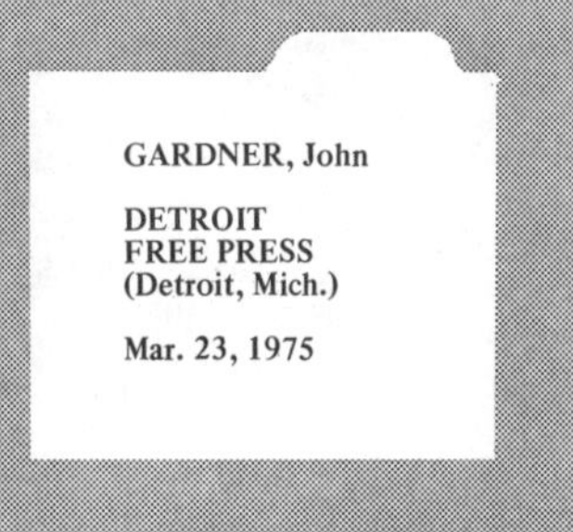

GARDNER, John

DETROIT FREE PRESS (Detroit, Mich.)

Mar. 23, 1975

There are a lot of writers like this. The kind of writer who used to publish only in the *New Yorker* and *Esquire* now publishes everywhere. I don't know what it's the result of, but it's been very bad for those others. Even a guy like Ross McDonald, he's trying to write really serious novels now. I loved his plain old detective stories; I don't like his serious stuff as much. But I understand: his market is being invaded and he's reacting. It used to be when you read science fiction that there was one Isaac Asimov for every 100 dumbbells. Now they're all Asimovs. Which means, of course, that readers have changed too.

DETROIT: *You admire Joyce Carol Oates a great deal as a writer, in addition to being a friend of hers, isn't that right?*

GARDNER: I think she's a wonderful writer, although she's a very different kind than what I am. She has a theory about human beings which I don't share. I really believe there is a human nature, to put it one way. Joyce doesn't, apparently. I believe that a character is a certain kind of

(Continued from preceding page)

thing from one page to another, and I'm going to be able to predict certain kinds of things about that character. Joyce believes that people wander into your life, accidents happen constantly, and there is no sort of "core of being." So her novels are in every case partly a search for a core of being, which turns out to be largely unsuccessful. But we are alike in one thing: Enormous respect for the novel form.

DETROIT: *Is there an overall theme connecting all your somewhat dissimilar books?*

GARDNER: I have a single philosophical question that I'm working on in all the books. I don't repeat myself; once I've worked out one aspect of the question, I don't go back over it. The question is about the nature of human experience in the 20th century and what's wrong and how can it be fixed. There are very precise points where I think we've gone wrong, and I think I could name them in terms of philosophical schools of thought. For instance, I think the 19th century Oxford idealists were beaten by bad arguments and showy, flashy stuff and a really important idea was lost. From there we head into contemporary philosophy, which sometimes is just insane.

DETROIT: *What was the important idea that was lost?*

GARDNER: To simplify it, one could say that it had to do with the question of what makes people happiest. The idea was that man is happiest when he is behaving well. When he's being faithful. When he knows he has certain duties and he performs them. When he has boundaries.

DETROIT: *Where else did we go wrong?*

GARDNER: Well, we keep getting to the edge of very important discoveries and then keep messing them up. One of them that's really important is sexual. In the 20th century we get really healthy about sex, really open about it and valuing it, and then we keep getting mixed up. We go off to the orgy, which is missing the point. Utterly and totally missing the point.

DETROIT: *"Grendel" is charming, but our favorite of your works is your first, "The Resurrection."*

GARDNER: Well, it was the book that I wrote most for myself. In all the others I've been very conscious of an audience. For instance, I now read my stuff to my kids, and if my daughter thinks something is too slow, I change it. But in *The Resurrection* I did everything the way I wanted to do it. As a matter of fact, it did get one good review, from Detroit. Which was one of the reasons I later came here.

DETROIT: *Some writers claim they don't read reviews.*

GARDNER: William Faulkner said, "Any man who tells me he doesn't read his reviews is a liar." And he's right of course. Not only do you read them, you read them three times, to see if it's maybe better than you thought at first. And it's so wonderful when somebody gets it . . .

DETROIT: *Well, if you put things in you know people aren't going to get . . .*

GARDNER: Yeah, but one hopes to write books like the stories of Chaucer, that people will read and re-read again sometimes and keep getting new things from. I want my stuff to be entertaining, to have exciting plots and so forth, and I want them to be as well-built as anybody's. I don't think we have the romantic idea of writers as Shelley or Keats or Byron anymore; we're just workmen. But I want to make really nice houses, things you can live with forever and ever.

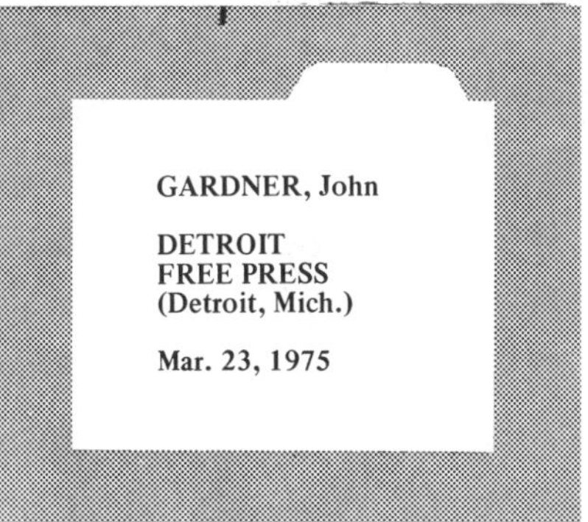
GARDNER, John

DETROIT
FREE PRESS
(Detroit, Mich.)

Mar. 23, 1975

DETROIT: *Some of your work leads us to believe you occasionally have grander ideas. "The Sunlight Dialogues," for instance, sounded in places like the work of someone who was consciously trying to write a Great Novel.*

GARDNER: Mm. Well, you can't do that. Gore Vidal once said very wisely that the reason there are no good novels in America is that everybody wants to write great ones.

DETROIT: *What's your family life like?*

GARDNER: We have a boy 15 and a girl 13, and they're both really incredible people. The boy just a year ago started playing the French horn, which I also play, and he's developed into a really wonderful player, plays six-seven hours a day. My wife, Joan, is a composer, and my daughter has started taking harp lessons. So I spend like all night working on fiction and then I sleep a few hours and then my family sits together and plays music for hours and hours. We also work together a lot. I work with the kids on their schoolwork and their instruments. My daughter and I spend hours and hours going over fiction together, hers and mine. She's written a lot.

DETROIT: *It sounds idyllic. Are their any problems?*

GARDNER: Well, I worry, that things can't possibly continue at this level. But—no. Joan and I spent a lot of years doing work we had to do, that wasn't chosen and wasn't a lot of fun. I, for instance, spent years and years teaching freshman composition. I didn't want to teach freshman composition. Since I've started making money, I do only what I want to do.

We've just bought a house in Vermont, so we'll be living there and in Illinois now. I'm really happy in southern Illinois. I like to ride horses, feed dogs, walk through the woods, look at the rain, all that. But Joan likes to go to symphonies and plays and things. So we sort of do two lives, me for a while and then Joan for a while.

DETROIT: *When you're writing away all alone at night is it the same person as the one who does all those things with his family, or is it another person?*

GARDNER: No, it's the same person. Basically it's a playful person. When we go to the beach, for instance, being the type of people we are, we make not only sand castles but sand people as well, full size people sitting there, made out of sand. One time in Italy we started doing that, and at the end of the day, the Italians being the kind of people they are, the whole beach for a mile was just full of sand people. That's what my life is, just sort of very serious playing. And when I'm writing that's what I'm doing too: trying to make really fine sand people. ■

GARRITY, Joan Theresa
(pseud. "J")

PALM BEACH LIFE
(Palm Beach, Fla.)

Dec., 1973

The Sensuous Woman Talks

Sketch by Authors in the News

By Robert Burdick

Palm Beach is a rotten place to find a man, says the candid and charming author of *The Sensuous Woman*, Joan Theresa Garrity.

She grabbed a chunk of green pepper as she picked over lunch in her cheery green and white Palm Beach condominium apartment.

"Let's face it," she said, munching on the pepper. "If I were in the market for a man, I wouldn't have come to Palm Beach.

But, she allowed, Palm Beach is a great place for writing -- and that's why she was here off and on last summer: writing a book on Florida golf courses.

The switch from sex to golf marks quite a contrast, as do many other things about this woman whose arresting hazel eyes seem to pick up the hue of whatever she's wearing.

The woman whose friends call her Terry has dark hair and an enthusiasm for vitamins. "Oh, I take just about all of them," she said, waving her hands about the apartment that's not far from where her late mother lived.

"Chicago is a much better city for man hunting. There you have oodles of young executives who are marriage minded -- and who are interested in younger women.

"But here, what young men there are often occupy themselves escorting older women -- or are off somewhere looking for younger women.

"Those who aren't can get pretty much of what they want without getting married," she added.

"A young woman's chance of coming here, getting introduced to a rich man and marrying him are pretty slim," she said.

She looked over the lunch table, decided she had eaten all she wanted and walked into the living room, where she draped herself over a chair.

She was ready, she said with her frequent almost-nervous giggle, to talk about whatever subject came up.

And that's where some of the contrasts began to show. In her book, she urges women to learn to enjoy sex, to be unashamed of enjoying it. And, she advises, it's fine to talk about it.

Yet she tried to remain anonymous when she wrote her book.

"I was pretty disturbed when my name became public," she said. "I don't think I would have written it if I had known my name would get out." She wrote the book under the pseudonym "J," the initial of her first name.

Even when one considers her daring break-with-tradition explicit book about sex, she has retained at least one view that any male chauvinist would gleefully label as a traditional one: when asked about her age, she giggled and offered an evasive answer.

"I'm 33." Then she paused briefly. "That's a perfect age. Yes, I'm going to be 33 for 10 years."

But have, perhaps, several of those 10 years already elapsed?

"Oh, I wouldn't say," Ms. Garrity replied coyly. "I'm the one who decides when the 10 years are up. I think a woman should choose her own age. I think she should decide what she wants."

She wasn't as cagey, though, when she discussed the degree of importance of a woman's appearance. In fact, the words on the jacket flap of *The Sensuous Woman* were downright specific as they played down the necessity of physical beauty:

"Even if you're knock-kneed, flat-chested, cross-eyed and balding, you can learn to have a really joyous and fulfilling sex life.

"It happened to the author . . . "

Nonetheless, since the book began advising hundreds of thousands of women that they need not be beautiful to attract (and keep) men, she has dieted and had her teeth straightened.

"If you can afford it, why not?" she asked, smiling through the braces she wore much of the summer.

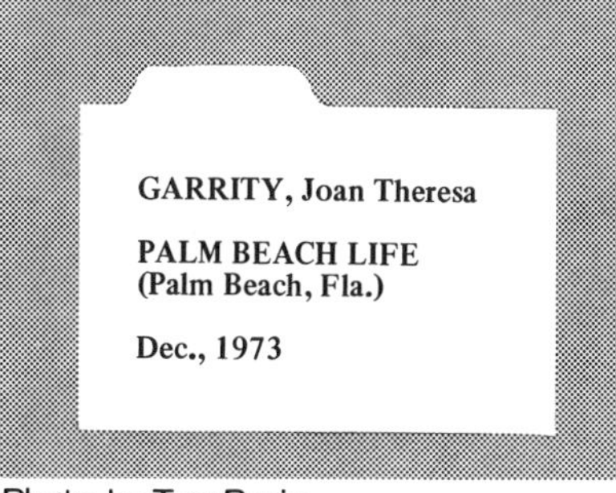

Photo by Tom Purin

(Continued from preceding page)

"I think women should realize they can do these things, that there's nothing wrong with it if they're dissatisfied with the way they look.

"But it's also important to remember that they don't have to have, say, straightened teeth to catch a man."

A listener might get the idea that she's straight out of midwest America, which makes sense. She's from a hamlet outside Kansas City, Mo., and like thousands of other midwesterners, left for a New York acting debut that never came.

But, she said, while trying to make it as an actress she discovered how little she knew about sex when she met some of the young actors.

When she found she didn't know everything she had always wanted to know about sex, she wasn't afraid to ask — or to read.

"That's when I discovered there really wasn't a book for women like me who were interested, but uninformed," she added, giggling again.

So a lengthy amount of research later, she became the anonymous author of *The Sensuous Woman*. She still insists she was shocked and "more than a little frightened" when a weekly newsmagazine found and printed her real name.

Once her identity became known, however, she began a tour of the country, speaking and appearing on radio and television talk shows.

"It was very educational for me," she recalled. "So many people would just come up to me and talk about their sex problems although I was a perfect stranger. I was really flattered — and I felt that my book had done some good.

"Seriously, sex is very important, you know."

But, she added, her eyes twinkling, "it can be fun even when it's not serious."

She believes that sex cannot be truly fulfilling unless accompanied by love — an idea that she could have picked up in the midwest. But, she added quickly, sex can be "fun, satisfying" without love — and should still be morally acceptable.

She also believes that celebrities should venture forth into the public spotlight with opinions related to their specialties if they have something to say about a cause. But Terry Garrity — who offers a big smile when she proclaims she has plenty to say about her specialty, the relationship between men and women — hasn't spoken out on the equal rights amendment (ERA) or the abortion controversy.

"It's partially because I live in a conservative area and it wouldn't be appropriate to say anything right now," she said.

Does she like a conservative area?

"I don't really consider myself a political conservative, but I like Palm Beach," she said. "But not for the reasons you read about.

"The parties aren't for me — and I have been to a few to find out. What I like is the peace and quiet, the chance to walk around without anyone bothering me. It is, like I said, very conducive to writing.

"At parties, many men feel that they have to come up and tell me a dirty joke as a conversation starter," she said. "Well, let me tell you how sick of discussing sex I got after the national tour. It seems like that was all anyone wanted to talk about.

"I was just dying for someone to come up to me and talk about growing marigolds or anything — just so it was something different," she added.

Didn't any men ask her why she — the woman who three years before had advised other women how to find and keep their men coming home every night — doesn't have a man?

"Right now I'm waiting for my own man," she said.

While her knight rears his children from a previous marriage ("It was over long before I met him — I couldn't live with myself if I fooled around with someone else's marriage"), she must remain content as only his fiance, not his wife.

And he must remain anonymous, except to their closest friends. "Oh, I don't want his name to get out. Can you imagine the ribbing he would get? And the calls?

"It's not a difficult decision, really," she said. "Raising children is a great task — but it's not for me as a second mother. I'd have to be in on it from the start."

The Sensuous Woman: Just Putting Around

By KRISTY MONTEE

Staff Writer

There she was bent over the tomatoes at a West Palm Beach supermarket, cropped, brown hair in curlers, no makeup and dressed in Saturday blue jeans.

"Excuse me . . ." the man approached Joan Garrity timidly. ". . . Aren't you the Sensuous Woman?'"

"People expect me to be some brassy, madeup broad or something," Joan laughs loudly. "I'm about as average, woman-next-door as you can get!"

Average is what the author of the infamous best seller "The Sensuous Woman" is now trying desperately to be.

Since her 1970 book catapulted her to dubious fame as an "expert" on female sexuality, she has had more than her share of indecent proposals, crayon-scrawled hate letters, ulcers and wrathful women's libbers.

Fresh out of her braces, ("after 34 years, I've finally gotten rid of my ugly buck teeth") Joan now lives semi-quietly in West Palm Beach with her new husband.

GARRITY, Joan Theresa

FORT LAUDERDALE NEWS
(Ft. Lauderdale, Fla.)

June 17, 1974

And she's gone from writing sex manuals to compiling golf manuals.

Nothing as erotic as "The Sensuous Golfer" or anything. Just a rather unsexy "Golfer's Guide to Florida Courses," the first of many such books she intends to write on the subject.

"People have this strange notion about authors — that they are interested only in what they write about," Joan says. "Just because I wrote one book on sex doesn't mean that's the only thing I know about."

Actually, Joan Garrity is an avid golfer ("I've had a suitcase in one hand and a putter in the other for the past year") and claims her latest book was born from the same needs as her first.

"To write a best seller, you have to fill a void," she says. "You have to ask yourself what information is missing. That's what accounted for the success of 'The Sensuous Woman,' there was simply no good, down-to-earth advise for women who were worried about not being able to achieve orgasm."

Joan candidly admits the "The Sensuous Woman" was based on her own experiences. She knew when she set out on the project there would be problems, but now she says she was not totally prepared for the consequences.

"When you reveal your private life so fully to the public as I did in that book, you have to expect bad things. That's why I chose to write under the pseudonym 'J' and also to protect my family."

Actually, her family took the whole episode with a good sense of humor, she said.

As outspoken as she is on almost anything, Joan refuses to discuss one topic: her husband.

"At the time I wrote the book, we weren't married and he encouraged me to go ahead with it and even helped me on some of the writing. But he drew the line when it came time to promote it in public."

So Joan took to the talk show and newspaper interview circuit herself, ready for the onslaught of curiosity seekers, militant feminists and plain "dirty old men."

Four years later (and 14 million paperback copies of her book in print), Joan Garrity is apt to prelude an interview with "please don't ask me any whipped cream and cherries questions."

"Actually, the boook sold quite well before I even made one appearance in public," she says. "But it was being attacked and I felt obligated to defend it."

Her mail during this time seemed divided into two factions: women wrote to her with more experiences and advice and to tell her they liked the book.

Most of the letters from men accused her of writing a "dirty, erotic book."

"Women tend to see sex differently than men; they are more detailed about it and speak of it in clinical terms," Joan explains. "Men seem to speak of sex in one-line dirty jokes. I think, too, many men resented the book because they took it in the wrong way as something being done TO them.

"I wrote that book because at the time there was a lack of readable information on sex for women," she added. "The sex manuals such as Masters and Johnson were so complex, so pompous. And it's a shame that a country supposedly known for its humor cannot laugh at itself when it comes to sex."

What Joan got out of her experience with "The Sensuous Women" was an ulcer, 40 extra pounds from drinking malts to calm her stomach and a still-pending half a million dollar lawsuit with her publisher Lyle Stuart for back royalties.

And probably a bit of sanity.

"I went into seclusion for a while after that," she said. "I had to pull myself back together."

In addition to the planned series on golf courses (the next one coming out in the fall on the southeast), Joan's revising an old project, children's cookbook and one other book tentatively titled "Love Around the World."

She's spent the last year traveling around the country interviewing couples who have successful marriages of 15 years or more. "There's so much negative about marriage these days I thought I'd found out about how some couples stay happily married."

But no more Sensuous Woman.

"I'm trying to put that behind me now," she says, although strangers looking for free advice still come up to her on the street and start talking about the most intimate aspects of their sex lives.

"I will always still have to remember that the book is still a part of me," she says. "But I'm back to being a normal person now."

"All I really want is a good night's sleep."

Almanac: 'Corny, Not Porny'

BY JUDI MODIE

Seatle's remarkably sunny autumn weather is about to come to an end.

How do we know? Ray Geiger told us so and it's hard not to believe the man whose predictions about annual rainfall and snow storms have become the gospel to more than six million Americans.

Geiger is editor of the Farmers' Almanac 1975, a slim vanilla-colored volume that is not to be confused with the relative newcomer, The Old Farmer's Almanac, now sold on the newsstands.

The Farmer's Almanac, which has been published for 158 consecutive years — 41 of them under the guidance of Geiger — can't be bought anywhere. It's distributed free, compliments of commercial firms such as the Old National Bank of Washington which will offer the complimentary copies of the book to its customers.

Geiger likes to stump the country rubbing elbows with newspersons as he offers his opinions about the weather, other magazines and the general state of the country.

Brilliant blue eyes sparkle as he argues his case on such diverse subjects as the importance of breast cancer checks and why the U.S. Post Office should reinstate the names of towns on postmarks. Geiger is deadly serious about his campaign for the "friendly postmark."

He said, "Postmarks nowadays don't tell you anything. Does OK 740 sound as romantic as Broken Arrow, Oklahoma? No, of course it doesn't. Numbers may be more efficient but they're not very interesting and they're depriving us of an important individualism and wholesomeness we badly need in the world today."

Wholesomeness is a word that creeps often into Geiger's conversation as he talks about his crusade, albeit low-keyed, against tastelessness in the kind of jokes and stories offered to readers today.

He boasts that there is no off-color material in the Farmers' Almanac. "We're anti-pornography at its best. I like to tell folks we're 'corny, not porny.' We don't offer a centerfold but we do give our readers a book of integrity."

Least he sound a little stuffy, rest assured that Geiger is anything but. His eagerness to please is so contagious that it was hard not to giggle.

He tosses out quickies — "Old truck drivers never die, they just can't make the grade" — so fast there's hardly a moment to groan, and bits of advice that he admits aren't always popular.

"The women's liberationists are on my back," he confesses, but pointing out that he is trying to make peace with those who call him a male chauvinist.

"I've printed the feminist party prayer in this year's Almanac, in the interest of fairness to these delightful persons."

He doesn't mention, however, that the prayer is printed on the same page as a suggestion that "If women must insist on having men's privileges, they have to take men's chances."

The Almanac isn't meant to be heavy, however, so Geiger avoids lengthy discussions of such subjects as the women's movement, preferring to save his space for mind games, bright sayings, listing of holidays, planting schedules and general weather predictions.

As strange as it sounds, there even is an informative, did-you-know-this discourse on how cow manure has been converted into a miracle building material in the same half of the book as a description of the metric system and instructions for poaching fish in the dishwasher while doing the dishes. (Sealed in foil, the fish cook perfeectly without mingling with detergent and vice versa).

Some readers keep the Almanac in their kitchens, Geiger says, noting a hole is punched in every edition so it can be hung on a nail or strung to the telephone. Others prefer to stash it in the bathroom.

The Almanac offers something new every year, according to Geiger, but the format stays the same. "People just don't want to see us change. Whatever we're doing, it must be right because our readership keeps on gaining."

—P-I Photo by Tom Barlet

GEIGER, Raymond Aloysius

SEATTLE POST-INTELLIGENCER (Seattle, Wash.) Oct. 27, 1974

Save That Postmark!

By LAURIE LUCAS

"Remember the Friendly Postmark!" has become the battle cry of Ray Geiger, editor of the 1975 Farmers' Almanac.

The 158-year-old legacy of bromidic capsules, weather forecasts, recipes, homespun humor and memorabilia, has been enriched by Geiger's crusade to resurrect the more intimate postal stampings of say, Broken Arrow, Okla., or Oshkosh, Wis., or Syracuse, N.Y.

Affectionately dubbed the purveyor of "cornography," Geiger, now in his 41st year as editor of the almanac, claims the blanket replacement of hometown postmarks with "U.S. Postal Service" is "tearing the heart out of grass roots America."

Pointing an accusing finger at "modern efficiency, that cold pileup of mechanical processes," Geiger included a four-paragraph minifeature lamenting a 1973 U.S. Postal Service decision to eliminate the name of the city or town of origin from postmarks on mailing pieces.

Already, Geiger's efforts to put the pizzazz back in postmarks have come to fruition.

Next week, he will discuss the matter with Postmaster Gen. E. T. Klassen in Washington.

Geiger admits, however, that his present campaign against impersonal postmarks may reflect the zenith of his political traffickings. Although the 1975 Farmer's Almanac keeps abreast with the topical issues of the day, Geiger maintains an unswerving course that eschews both such as "Politicians make strange bedfellows, but they soon get used to the same bunk" — Geiger confessed that hard-core political mouthings have been forsaken since 1824.

However, Geiger noted that the paucity of political statements hasn't deterred notable politicians from dipping into the almanac themselves, to unearth a few political gems.

"Any government big enough to give you everything you want is big enough to take everything you got," was from the almanac for his inaugural address, Geiger contended. "Sen. Muskie," Geiger added, "said he loves my Almanac for its good, clean jokes." Priding himself on "the high moral caliber" Geiger refuses to stoop to even the least off-color or salacious poems or witticisms. "Pornography is so abundant," he sighed, adding that he refrained from including "streaker" jibes because he considers them ribald. Under the heading of "Wife Savers," the Almanac offers some ingenious antidotes to the sugar shortage and ecology crisis. "Don't buy colored paper products," notes one quickie. "Choose white because dyes are pollutants." "No sugar?" queries another little bullet of wisdom. "Use honey in baking cakes and cookies." Furthermore, the Almanac boasts a roster of famous celebrities who have contributed pithy sayings or kernels of truth to the compendium of logic and anecdotes.

"Danny Thomas gave me several Lebanese recipes," recalled Geiger, listing former actress June Lockhart, late, comedian Joe E. Brown, Bishop Fulton Sheen, Norman Vincent Peale and his wife Ann as a few other well-known suppliers.

Devotees of the Farmers' Almanac will have the opportunity to pick up a free copy at any one of nine local offices of Syracuse Savings Bank.

GEIGER, Raymond Aloysius

SYRACUSE POST-STANDARD (Syracuse, N.Y.)

Dec. 5, 1974

Peter Gent and the Football Revolution: Close-up on the Writer of 'North Dallas Forty'

Gent the writer in '74 and the player in '66: "You're taught pure self-interest . . . if the team won and you didn't play well, you lost."

*"The game was finally over. I would no longer fear defeat and failure. I had been trapped on a technicality that explained the ultimate pointlessness of the life I had been living. The game wasn't on the field, it never had been. It was here (in the Dallas Cowboys' front office). I hadn't been beaten and I hadn't quit. I had been disqualified . . . It was over. I didn't have to compete for the right to exist."**

— Peter Gent
"North Dallas Forty"

By CHARLES FLOWERS
Of the Magazine Staff

Peter Gent has found his 40 acres. But they are nowhere near the playing field of the Dallas Cowboys where Gent toiled as a flanker for five seasons. His 40 acres are on a bluff overlooking a lake in Van Buren County, not far from his boyhood home of Bangor, Mich. Pete Gent has

GENT, Peter
DETROIT
FREE PRESS
(Detroit, Mich.)
Nov. 17, 1974

quit the football wars, and Peter Gent has come home.

The story of the kind of life Peter Gent had in Dallas is in his first novel, "North Dallas Forty," ($2, Signet). The novel — all except the shocking ending — is based on Gent's experiences or those of other players on the Cowboys of the late '60s.

They include a crazed, drunken hunting trip with three teammates, pre- and post-game drug and sex rituals, intimidation, sadism and exhibitionism on and off the field, and constant clashes with what Gent describes as a racist, sexist, dictatorial organization of businessmen devoted to winning football games at any cost.

"We were told from all quarters that we were living the American Dream," Gent is saying now from his lakeside home as the September sun invades the dock where his 11-year-old daughter Holly is pulling up a bluegill. "And when they did humiliating, dehumanizing things you told yourself, 'I'm hating it, and going crazy and living in constant fear.' Is that the American Dream?"

Gent is quick to take some of the blame for this deception.

"Nobody made a fool of you but you. Nobody insisted that you believe those things. But what they did insist is that you not call them liars."

The central figure in "North Dallas Forty" is, as Gent was, a flanker from Michigan State who is hanging on despite injuries and considerable rival talent on the same team to his job as a pass catcher. The team in the book looks a lot like the Cowboys of the late '60s — the era when Don Meredith was quarterback and Bob Hayes, Lance Rentzel and Pete Gent were wide receivers. Gent's quarterback hero, Seth Maxwell, bears a strong resemblance to the real-life Meredith, now a TV actor and an NBC-TV football announcer whom Howard Cosell has dubbed "Dandy Don." Like Dandy Don, Swingin' Seth sings snatches of country tunes in the huddle, wears a cowboy hat, is on a first-name basis with his Texas parents, and purely loves to party. Maxwell, like Gent's alter ego in the novel, Phil Elliott, is growing old gracelessly.

"You're the only man I know with a body older than mine," Maxwell said, looking at the large knot sticking out from the side of my ankle, the vestige of a compound fracture and dislocation . . .

I often felt that this brotherhood of mutilation was a very large part of the strange friendship Maxwell and I shared . . . At first the pills were used just to bear the pain of shredded and smashed muscles and ligaments. Then later we combined them with alcohol to shorten the long, anxious return trips to Dallas. We would sit, strapped in our seats, packed in ice or wrapped in elastic, in lengthy discussions of the sounds and feelings of excruciating injuries.

"North Dallas Forty" is a wonderland of pain and pain pills. Everyone from the players to the general manager is high on something from the trainer's medicine chest. Gent's flanker hero seems to like codeine number fours. Pre-game finds the Dallas Cowboys stoned out of their minds on speed listening to an invocation from a tipsy monsignor.

But if the book dotes on injuries and drugs, Gent himself has some fonder memories of his five years with the Cowboys. He equates them with the military experience he never had.

Compressed into 300 pages, Gent's novel could not tell the full story of his pro years. Instead, the focus is on the last eight days of one flanker's football career. Gent's career — which ended when he was traded to the New York Giants and released before the 1969 season — witnessed more obvious changes.

"I came to Dallas in '64 when we were like 4-10 (won-lost), and it was a very warm bunch of goofy guys," Gent remembers. "They did the best they could. Everybody got drunk together, and everybody was concerned about the other guy, how everything was going to work out. Then suddenly, three years later, we're the Eastern Division champions and this whole star syndrome started sifting in. The press started building up certain players and the coaches started building up certain players to the press and suddenly there are stars. Then there's no longer just 40 guys who are at the end of their rope and they're just glad to be close to each other because they know that tomorrow's not gonna come."

Peter Gent (the g is soft) is only 32, but he seems much older. Perhaps that's because he's been so many places in the last 10 years — basketball star and honors college graduate at Michigan State in 1964 . . . that same year signed as a free-agent with the Dallas Cowboys with no college football experience . . . played five years as a wide receiver, and caught 33 passes one year . . . left football in 1969 . . . wrote "North Dallas Forty" until late 1972 . . . moved back to Michigan and began freelance writing early 1973 . . . sold paperback and film rights to first novel, gave up freelance magazine writing all in 1974 — and he hasn't retired, he's just getting started.

Gent has a perplexed look on his flat rugged face, which changes quickly to an insane, engaging laugh. Texas, and the dry, head-scratching humor of that state, has rubbed off on him in many ways. He sounds sometimes like a Texan (although he was reared and schooled in Michigan), and at those times he is indistinguishable from his wife Jodi, who comes from Ft. Worth. Jodi married Pete five years ago when he was suing the Giants for damages to his knee. Their daughter Holly and the two little Maltese dogs scurrying around their feet make them a family.

There is a Texas-sized hospitality to the Gents as they show you around the

(Continued from preceding page)
spread, cursing the absent high-schoolers who left beer cans at the base of their driveway and the equally discourteous snowmobilers who'll be out soon enough roaring over their property; marveling at the birds, the growth among the scrubby jack-pines and the twisted arms and crotchety scrollwork of one giant beech in their backyard. They are all comfortable with each other, and it is not easy to tell who is in charge.

The Gents' home is within eyeshot of two other homes on the lake. But they have a country isolation and a country closeness. Holly runs next door to eat some homemade soup, and comes back to show you her fabulous collection of hippopotami. Jodi is president of the lake association and is also learning photography. Peter plays on a softball team for the bar across the lake, and they just beat the high school teachers for the championship (Gent was the only NFL veteran on the team), and they must just all go over to the bar tonight for supper.

The family is just back home from a coast-to-coast book promotion tour which Holly opted out of early. Jodi is thankful for the experience, but more than glad the whole thing's over. After an interview in Los Angeles, a writer described Mrs. Gent as "washed-out sandy-haired and melancholy." And while she concedes she might not have been in top form, Jodi, who is 28, felt a bit abused.

"Just say that I looked peaked," Jodi says, sitting down and holding her feet in her hands with a grin bouncing beneath her hair. Her small round face shone in the light from the fire she had just built.

But a football game could still be faintly heard that Sunday coming in muffled roars from the bedroom. Gent says he still watches pro football occasionally when Dallas or Washington is playing, but he's no great fan.

"I like to watch to laugh at the announcers," he says. "They're talking about some other game. And the moralizing! People who watch actually do think there are good guys and bad guys, and that if you lose it must be because of some flaw in your character."

It is somewhat amazing from the tone of "North Dallas Forty" that Gent is as closely tied to football as he is. You sense from the total divorce at the end of the book that he is sailing out there somewhere in the cosmos, where football is as alien as forms in a nightmare. Yet he and Jodi drove two hours to East Lansing the day before to sit with the alumni at Michigan State's game with Northwestern.

It is also somewhat ironic that Gent would remember MSU *had* a football team, since he refused to play the sport there despite active recruitment by coach Duffy Daugherty. Gent was voted Most Valuable Player — of the *basketball* team — two of his three seasons, and was selected to the Big Ten second team in his senior year at MSU — and he had football size. He had been an all-state football performer at Bangor High, playing end both ways and offensive halfback.

"I just heard too many bad reports from guys on the football team," says Gent, who may have embarrassed

GENT, Peter

DETROIT
FREE PRESS
(Detroit, Mich.) Nov. 17, 1974

Daughterty and State when he landed a pass receiving job with Dallas. In five seasons there, he would play alongside receivers like Tommy McDonald and Buddy Dial and Frank Clarke and Lance Rentzel and Bob Hayes.

Gent says that Daughterty once offered him a starting position a week before the season was to begin if Gent would come out and play for him. Daughterty was building his powerhouse teams in those years.

"I figured Duffy was either lying to me, or screwing the guy who was playing the position," says Gent, who decided not to go out for football at MSU.

Daughterty answered Gent's charge on the Lou Gordon show in September. He said his '63 Spartan squad was weak at tight end, and that, with hard work, Gent could have made it.

But isn't that what is meant by professional? Isn't that the same philosophy that operates American businesses, schools and homes — someone has the power and everyone dances to his tune, whether it's winning football games or selling insurance policies?

"Yes, but if it's that way in sports, why have sports?" Gent asks. "It doesn't produce anything. It doesn't feed anybody. It doesn't create any real value to the society. Nobody learns any real valuable lessons by it.

"What matters is the total number of points at the end of the game, and how the coach scores your personal performance. There's no feeling there, it's a business. And when they pump that out through the television screen and the sportswriters keep saying that all these guys are making a fortune and boy wouldn't you like your son to grow up and be a pro football star? . . . We have children thinking this way."

But for all his criticisms, Peter Gent is not in the vanguard of the so-called football revolution.

They started coming out of the National Football League several years ago — front-line players who said they were fed up with the way the fall past-time is played and administered. Dave Meggyesy of the St. Louis Cardinals, Johnny Sample and George Sauer of the New York Jets, Chip Oliver of the Oakland Raiders and Bernie Parrish of the Los Angeles Rams were the vanguard. In books like Meggyesy's "Out of Their League" (1970), Oliver's "High for the Game" (1971) and Parrish's "They Call It a Game" (1971), they said that the "sport" had become painful for them, no longer just vicious and brutal on Sundays, which it had always been, but dehumanizing, humiliating. They felt pro football was more of a monopoly staffed by indentured servants than it was an electronic national morality play. Pro football, they said, taught all the wrong values to a nation at a time when it needed straightening out in the worst way.

Meggyesy was the first. In "Out of Their League," he told how he had changed from a $33,000 a year fananti-cal-hitting outside linebacker with the Cardinals to a man who could no longer stomach the system he came to feel pro football stood for. Meggyesy was an articulate sociology graduate from Syracuse University, and his book was a cry for sanity.

"One of the justifications for college football is that it is not only a character-builder, but a body-builder as well," Meggyesy wrote. "This is nonsense . . . young men are having their bodies destroyed, not developed. Few players can escape from college football without some form of permanent disability."

That opinion was echoed by Gary Shaw in "Meat on the Hoof: the Inside Story of Texas Football" (1972). Shaw told how players at the University of Texas, where he was a quarterback, were subjected to senseless crippling drills if the coaches did not believe they could make the top two teams — often because of an injury sustained in trying.

Where does Gent stand in this revolutionary hierarchy? Somewhere between Oliver and Sauer, who returned in different guises to football, and Meggyesy, who is still perhaps the hardest line militant.

And where Meggyesy, who resigned at the peak of his career and wrote the first damning book of pro football, is bitter, Gent is not. Meggyesy, says Gent, expected the world to change after he wrote the book that put "dehumanization" into the vocabulary of American pro football fans. Gent does not, and he wishes Meggysey would write another book about his life since he retired from football. Gent himself only wrote about football because it was a subject he knew, and he wanted to write.

Gent's writing career, which he futhered with a series of articles for Sport magazine after he finished his novel, is now branching out beyond sports. He says he is now working on a screenplay about the life of Pancho Villa with his friend Edwin Shrake, senior editor of Sports Illustrated, and he is waiting for his second novel to come.

Gent's typewriter is out in his front room, and there is a wide variety of books on every subject tucked in among the football pictures in his bookcase. He has a framed poster from the movie "Yellow Submarine" showing the character called Nowhere Man, and tucked into the corner of the frame is a piece of ➡

(Continued from preceding page)

yellow newsprint with this inscription:

"Our earth is degenerate in these latter days. Bribery and corruption are common. Children no longer obey their parents. Every man wants to write a book . . . the end of the world is evidently approaching."

—Inscription on an Assyrian stone slab, 2800 B.C.

The ironic twist in that woeful statement is a key to Gent's personal philosophy: He does not take himself too seriously.

But if coming from college basketball to pro football was an amazing feat, it was at least as amazing a shock for Gent, who for the first time saw how big-time football players are treated.

"I came out of a basketball environment," Gent says, "where athletes were treated like athletes. For years at Dallas I couldn't know anything at all. Nobody knew. Nobody had any idea. Everybody was always bitching about it. Those 3½ hours a week when you played football were such a tiny part of it."

Pain is nothing more than the property perceiving the disintegration of its parts. Teach it the difference between pain and injury. If it is felt by the property it is pain. If it is felt by the corporation it is injury.

Actual, on-the-field football is only a small part of Gent's book. The rest is power play, and the owners have all the horses and all the options. Gent's hero is a hopeless individual, selling his talent and his body — and a little more besides — to a master without a heart.

"Professional football is just a non-regulated monopoly," Gent says, as if making a wager. "Once they own you, they own you. You can't play anywhere else. A lot of players sit around and pretend like they're gonna play out their option (announce retirement from one team to play for another). Well, good luck. They're not gonna sign you. Because if you sign my star, I'll sign yours."

Gent considers himself a spokesman for the average professional football player, the athlete who may make as little as $12,000 per year in an extremely hazardous profession. Gent himself made only $17,000 in his last year with Dallas, and the Cowboys were championship contenders. In a visit to Detroit this fall during the NFL players strike, Gent wore a "No Freedom, No Football" tee shirt. He believes marginal players need all the help they can get.

"In America, nobody identifies with losers. Nobody identifies with all those guys who didn't make it," Gent says, arguing for the guys at the bottom of the NFL's 4.2 year life expectancy.

Who is responsible for this oversight? Gent blames the press, and specifically, the Dallas sportswriters whom he says the owners had in the palms of their hands.

"Most sportswriters up until a couple of years ago were nothing but flacks for professional football. The players would get their lessons from the coach early in

GENT, Peter

DETROIT FREE PRESS (Detroit, Mich.) Nov. 17, 1974

the week about what to say about the opposing team, and the reporters would come in a dutifully write everything down. And if somebody like Duane Thomas (the star halfback who played at Dallas after Gent had left), came along and said that Tom Landry (coach of the Cowboys) was a plastic man and Tex Schramm (general manager of the Cowboys) was a liar, the Dallas writers would leap to the defense of Landry and Schramm."

What, specifically, was wrong with football at Dallas?

"You're taught pure self-interest when they review the films on Monday," Gent begins. "If the team won and you didn't play well, you lost. You could be in big trouble. Or it could work the other way — the team loses and you make eight big plays, you've won. You might be losing playoff money, but you might make it back later."

This lack of what might be called emotional involvement produced a dissention on the team that grew worse as the team grew more successful.

"They (the management) analyze your play very closely and use computers to chart your performance," he continues. "They use terms like 'He is a championship player or 'He is not a championship player.' John Wilbur was playing guard for the Cowboys and one of the coaches analyzed him as 'not of championship caliber.' Wilbur found out about it and started scrambling (looking for another team). He was traded to the Washington Redskins where he started, and got in a few championship games himself, so what does that computer printout prove?"

Playing two men off against one another, a frequent tactic in "North Dallas Forty" to raise tempers for game day, and involving the press to shame players, also bothered Gent.

"Landry had the ability to place the blame for a loss on specific individuals without actually blaming them. He would say 'so-and-so's not doing so well, but we'll work on that next week.' More often than not Meredith was left holding the bag when it was a play Landry had called that had gone awry. The thing I remember most about the '66 championship game with Green Bay (which Dallas lost in the closing moments) was Landry substituting for some guy with one second left after we had run out of time outs and were down on Green Bay's goal line. There was no time to tell the guy the play, and it was his man who hit Meredith and caused the interception."

Were the coach's post-game criticisms racially motivated, as Gent suggests in his book?

"Sometimes. Look at right now. There's Bobby Hayes (a black man), probably the best receiver in pro football, sitting on the bench. They put him there because they don't like his attitude. They did it before by playing Dennis Homan (a white man) instead of Hayes. Homan's not bad, but he's no Bob Hayes. They'll lose three or four in a row and all of a sudden notice an 'improvement' in Hayes."

But what grates on Gent most is the mind control of pro football. His heroes, from the quarterback who calls his own plays to the black wide receiver who doesn't let racism get him down, are triumphant individuals. They defy not only the enemy in the war-zone — where pro football leads all of the major organized sports in the world in casualties per minute — but also the strait-laced cost accountant in the boardroom. Perhaps that is why there is such a thing as pro football, because the players just keep coming.

"No matter how badly I was hurt or no matter how badly I felt, I always got up," Gent remembers of his days as a Cowboy. "And that's the really great thing about competition. You dig down inside yourself and find something you didn't even know was there. But when that just runs away and there's no cooperation and it's cooperation that holds everything together, then it's total madness. Total paranoid madness!

"The thing that was always great about sports for me was that the spirit overrode the facts. You beat a team by one point and you played badly, so what? You won, you can't change it. But all that suddenly changed when we started winning. Winning was what it was all about. And when it becomes winning, it becomes *me* winning."

In 1971, while working as an extra on the film "Kid Blue" in Mexico, Gent concocted a press release that said his role in the film had enlarged and that he was to play a heavy in a role formerly cast for Tab Hunter. Several newspapers picked up the story. Luckily for Gent, the movie starring Dennis Hopper bombed, and Gent's acting reputation has not preceded him. Paramount Pictures which paid $200,000 for the film rights to "North Dallas Forty," wouldn't even let Gent write the screenplay.

The irony in Gent's personal life may be that he took so long to see the physical and psychological destruction football was exacting from him in exchange for $17,000 a year and folk-hero status. But he did finally see, and put it down for others to see. And if he is not Tab Hunter, he is at least not Nowhere Man any longer. It does not seem likely that he will let this Peter Gent slip through his fingers.

EUELL GIBBONS

By Penelope McPhee

If you are what you eat, then author-naturalist-TV personality Euell Gibbons is as varied and delightful as a jaunt in the wilderness followed by a seven-course dinner at Maxim's. For despite the plethora of jokes to the contrary, Gibbons is a gourmet whose tastes include everything from sour grass to Canard a L'Orange. During our interview, for example, we chatted while Gibbons dined on crabmeat crepes and drank milk. (It's an old wive's tale, he claims, that you shouldn't eat fish and drink milk at the same time.)

As the star of TV's "Grapenuts" commercials, Gibbons has been suddenly catapulted to nationwide fame, and he is not above cultivating his image with a bit of judicious showmanship.

Even in the dining room of a plush Miami hotel, he appears in a faded denim suit with a red bandana around his neck. He speaks with the slight southwestern twang that has become familiar on television, and his conversation is generously spiced with down-home humor.

But after a few moments with him, the picture of the country character madly munching his way through the forest rapidly disappears. Because Euell Gibbons is a man of considerable style. With his full head of white hair, his quick wit, and his refreshing combination of simplicity and sophistication, he is reminiscent of no one so much as Mark Twain.

He forages for wild food not out of fanaticism, but out of love, and was eager to take me on a brief sortie in a vacant lot in downtown Miami where we found the makings of a delicious wild brunch.

In addition to his commercials, Gibbons is best-known for his books *Stalking the Wild Asparagus*, *Stalking the Good Life* and *Stalking the Blue-eyed Scallop*.

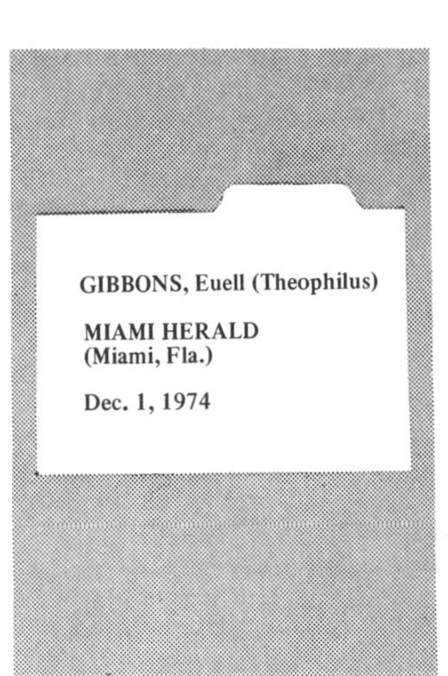
GIBBONS, Euell (Theophilus)

MIAMI HERALD
(Miami, Fla.)

Dec. 1, 1974

Our conversation (with interviewer Penelope McPhee) began over dinner, as Gibbons studied the lengthy menu with the kind of quizzical expression one might expect from a man whose fame rests largely on his taste for "wild hick'ry nuts":

GIBBONS: I'm sure not going to have scallops.

Q. Why is that?

GIBBONS: I'm allergic to them.

Q: Are people disappointed — do they cry fraud — when they learn you eat foods other than wild foods?

GIBBONS: Sometimes — and it's so silly. Recently, a couple in Detroit interviewed me while I was eating breakfast. They made a huge thing of it in their article. "We *caught* him eating bacon and eggs!" All anybody has to do to *catch* me eating bacon and eggs is come around about seven o'clock any morning. I have never at any time claimed that I eat only wild foods. I'm not a nut or a crackpot or a crank or a cultist. (Wife Frieda: "That's *his* opinion.")

Q: How did your interest in wild foods begin?

GIBBONS: Well, it all happened during the Depression, when I found myself in a strange city, flat broke and hungry. I just didn't have the nerve to beg, so I picked out a house, walked up to it and started eating the weeds on the lawn. In a little bit, the lady of the house stuck her head out and said, "Mister, what are you doing out there?" I said, "Lady, I'm so hungry, I have to eat weeds." And she said, "Why, you poor man. Come right around to my back door." So I went around to the back door, and she stuck her head out and said, "We have lots better weeds back here than we have out front. Just help yourself."

(There's a pause, then Gibbons starts to laugh. It's all a joke.)

Now do you *really* want to know what happened? I didn't get started in wild food at all. I was born into it. It started right after the Civil War with my grandmother. Her folks had to live on wild foods for awhile — or at least supplement their diet. They were a bunch of Union people in a great nest of rebels in the Smokey Mountains, and they were really in bad shape right after the war.

My grandmother passed her knowledge of wild foods on to my mother. Then my family lived for a time in New Mexico and my father homesteaded a place up in the Indian country. We lived very, very much in a self-sufficient way, even to the point where we had a little blacksmith shop on the place, and we made our own farming tools. We raised a great deal of our own food. My father taught the Mexicans in town to eat sauerkraut. We used to make barrels of sauerkraut and any time we wanted to go to town we'd hitch up a team of horses to a wagon we'd made out of an automobile and then loadup with sauerkraut, pumpkins and turnips.

My mother loved this sort of thing, and she passed her interest on to me. I can't see why anyone wouldn't find it perfectly fascinating to be able to go out and gather all kinds of good food here, there, and everywhere — and not have to pass the cashier on the way out. This was always fascinating to me.

Q: What made you decide to put your love of wild foods down on paper?

GIBBONS: My first book, *Stalking the Wild Asparagus*, was really an accident. I had always wanted to be a writer. I had written a novel about a poor schoolteacher (Gibbons himself was once a teacher) who buys some land and builds a home in the country and passes himself off as a millionaire by purchasing a dinner jacket from the Salvation Army and giving black-tie dinners at which he serves elaborate and delicious meals prepared from wild foods. My agent said no thanks, but how about writing a straightforward book on wild food?

Q: Are most plants that are poisonous to people also poisonous to animals? Do they use animals as guinea pigs?

GIBBONS: They use guinea pigs as guinea pigs. They also use rabbits and rats. Monkeys would probably be better. If all three eat something and survive, then you can be pretty sure it's OK for man. Then you try it on students somewhere.

Q: A lot of people seem to confuse wild foods with health foods. Are they the same?

GIBBONS: This is an almost invariable confusion. In fact, I think probably Grapenuts was confused about it. That's the reason they got me to make the commercials.

Q: Do Grapenuts have any health value?

GIBBONS: A lot of people don't know that Grapenuts were invented by the grandfather of all the health food freaks, C. W. Post — an absolutely fanatical health food man. He thought he was going to cure the whole world of all its ills. I insisted on going to Battle ➡

(Continued from preceding page)

Creek to see the cereal made before I would take the job on the commercial.

Q: Do Grapenuts really taste like wild hickory nuts?

GIBBONS: I had a letter from a man who said he'd been eating Grapenuts all his life, and it had never occurred to him that they might taste like hickory nuts. So he got some wild hickory nuts and chilled them. And he said, I was right. Since that time he's stopped eating Grapenuts and all he eats are wild hickory nuts! They really are an excellent nut. The fact of the matter is they are a lot better than Grapenuts, but it would take an hour to shell a bowl full.

Q: Are you an avid TV fan yourself? And have you enjoyed working in television?

GIBBONS: No, I almost never watch it. I have too much to do, and too much to read, and too much to see.

You would be surprised to learn that the Federal Trade Commission has forbidden me to mention wild food on TV because they're afraid a child will go out and experiment, and eat something poisonous. This is called "safety through ignorance," which is very, very close to book-burning. I guess we're going to have to take Whittier's poems off the market. Let's take those books out and burn them. Let's take James Whitcomb Riley's books out and burn them. We would have to take Mark Twain's writings out and burn them because they all mention wild food.

Children are killed by the thousands by automobiles. But nobody objects to showing automobiles or encouraging their use. Because being killed by an automobile is a nice, civilized way to die. But you're just as dead as if you'd eaten a poison mushroom. We have a special terror that we reserve in this culture for the undomesticated parts of nature.

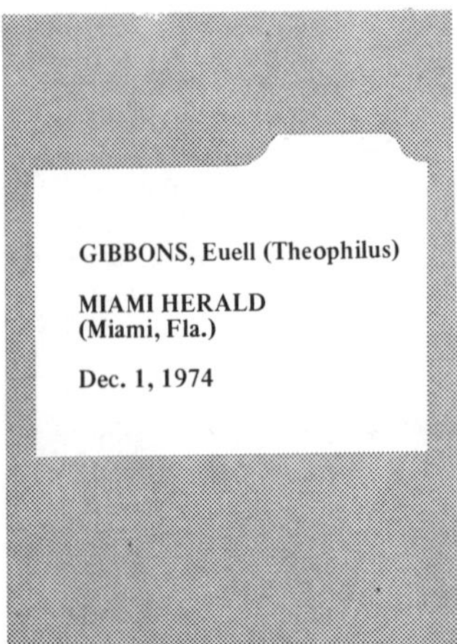
GIBBONS, Euell (Theophilus)

MIAMI HERALD
(Miami, Fla.)

Dec. 1, 1974

Q: If a person tried to live on wild foods exclusively, would that be a healthful diet?

GIBBONS: Well, you'd have to have a very wide variety, with plenty of vitamins and minerals. You'd have to include fish that you catch for protein. A vegetarian can get adequate protein, but he really has to work at it. Whereas, if you're eating meats and milk and eggs and dairy products, you certainly don't have that trouble. You're getting perfect protein. Although someone once said that there's only one kind of person who gets perfect protein for our system, and that's a cannibal.

Q: Is there any truth that there are natural aphrodisiacs? Do raw oysters and certain kinds of mushrooms really make you sexier?

GIBBONS: They all have one thing in common — they don't work.

Q: Given the constant increase in the price of groceries and the predictions of bad crops and famines, could wild foods provide a possible solution?

GIBBONS: It would be a great solution for an individual or a family. But God help us if *everybody* tried it. There simply isn't that much wild food. But, you know, people are always bringing that up. "What would happen if everybody went out and did it?" I usually answer, "What if everybody decided to play golf next Saturday or everybody decided to go fishing?" You just couldn't do it. A professor of economics was asking me the same thing regarding beachcombing. "What would happen," he asked, "if everybody decided to become a beachcomber?" I said, "They would probably get along as well as if everybody decided to become a professional economist."

Q: If you had to survive in South Florida for an indefinite period of time, could you do it and how would you go about it?

GIBBONS: Would you let me take a piece of equipment along?

Q: Like what?

GIBBONS: I'd like to take Julia Morton.

Q: All right. If you and Julia Morton had to survive in South Florida on wild foods, what would you do and where would you go?

GIBBONS: Julia Morton has described about 110 edible plants that are found here in South Florida. Now I'm not that familiar with this flora. But I don't think we'd have much trouble finding enough to survive on in the Keys or the Everglades. If you're talking about an indefinite period, I would certainly resort to fishing, finding bird's eggs, turtle-eating or something of that sort. But if you're only talking about a few days, there would be no problem at all in finding edible plants.

Q: Would it be more difficult or less to survive in Florida as compared with other, more temperate regions of the country?

GIBBONS: It would be more difficult. You simply don't have the wild food plants per acre that you have in Pennsylvania or northern Virginia and Maryland, or even New England. I was out on a vacant lot today, and I had to search like hell to find a single edible plant. *(Mr. Gibbons ate his words the next day when he discovered five or six edible plants in a small vacant lot across the street from his downtown Miami hotel.)*

In most cases I do much better. Like in Indianapolis we found 14 edible plants on a vacant lot. And we found 13 wild edible plants on a median strip in the middle of San Francisco.

I found 16 edible wild plants right in the middle of Chicago in the university district, and I found enough in Central Park in New York to prepare a three-course dinner.

Q: Are you only interested in foraging for wild food or do you also like to cook and develop your own recipes?

GIBBONS: I've done far more research in the kitchen than I have in the field. Many of my recipes have appeared in my books. I like to experiment with combining wild foods. Even as a little boy I used to make my own candy bars by taking wild hackberries and hickory nuts and pounding them together.

Q: Has your TV fame affected your lifestyle in any way?

GIBBONS: Almost not at all — but it has helped me find out some things about myself. For instance, my wife and I both drive Volkswagens, and we learned that we weren't driving Volkswagens because we couldn't afford a Cadillac — we were driving them because we wanted to. You can't really raise your living standards that much. I can only eat so much in a day; I can only wear one suit of clothes at

(Continued from preceding page)

a time; I can only be in one room at a time.

There were some things I thought I wanted, like a boat. Then when I got to thinking about all that darned upkeep, and having to have someone pull it out, and everytime having to go to the same place — well, this all hampered me more than I wanted to be hampered. The same thing was true of a beach house. I have less need for these things today than when I couldn't afford them. You see, I'm perfectly satisfied now. I know I could drive a Cadillac if I wanted to. And so I find I really don't want to.

Q: Have you ever been tempted to pull a Thoreau and go off somewhere to create your own Walden?

GIBBONS: That was an early dream of mine. Even to isolate myself physically on an island. I've done enough of it now to know it wouldn't be my cup of tea for any length of time. I still do it for short periods of time, but I enjoy the best of several worlds. I make no apology for that. I'm simply not a fanatic.

Q: You no longer feel that self-sufficiency is a worthwhile goal?

GIBBONS: I do still have two daydreams about this. I'd like for my son, who is just retiring from the Air Force, to come to Pennsylvania and write a sort of homesteading book about how to make it in the country.

The other dream is Haiti. I have always had a tremendous interest in that island. Haiti is a microcosm of what the world can become. It's overpopulated, and there is no way the land can support the population. It's been farmed out. Children are suffering, and people are starving to death there. I thought one thing I might do is subsidize a young couple to go down there. I would buy the land, and they could hire all the labor they wanted because labor is so terribly cheap there. But the idea would be to limit them, so they could not use anything unless the Haitian could use it too. Then their example would become meaningful. If the Haitian can do it, you can do it. If he has access to something, you have access to it too. This would demonstrate to the Haitians how much could be done with only the resources they have.

Q: It is generally recognized that man is rapidly destroying his environment. Are we too late to halt or repair the damage we've already done?

GIBBONS: No, I think we underestimate nature's powers to recover. But I don't agree with the ecologists who want to set everything aside as preserves, and put a fence around nature. I don't think there's any value in establishing a bunch of little zoos and museums across the country. What we need is everybody living in a more harmonious relationship with nature. You can't love nature and not be willing to get involved with her a bit. And you can't be selective. You have to love all nature because it's all tied together. It's all of one piece. The earthworm, for example, is a beautiful thing with its iridescent skin. And besides that, it is the greatest builder of topsoil we have. A young woman once said to me, "I can love a rose without loving the dunghill from which it grows." I can't. No matter how I look at it, I can't. Because I can't see a rose without thinking of it as a transformed dunghill. And I can't see a dunghill without thinking of it as a potential rose.

Q: What is your prognosis for our environment and what do you suggest we can do to save it?

GIBBONS: I'm sure we're in a transitional period right now: from destroying our environment to cherishing it. The young people coming out of school today are not accepting the attitude and approach to nature that their parents and grandparents had.

In 1888, Thomas Huxley wrote that nature is nothing but a continuous Hobbsian war of each against all. The Darwinists felt we should build a society on ruthless competition, thereby eliminating the unfit — the fittest being the one who is the most vicious, the most combatant, the strongest.

Our own William James in America said that we had to enlist the young in man's eternal war with nature. For centuries, man has believed not only that it was permissible but that it was right that he should engage in the conquest of nature. It was his mission — his manifest destiny. But the young people today don't accept that; they laugh at it.

Q: If survival of the fittest is not the most accurate interpretation of what goes on in nature, what is?

GIBBONS: Many people still hold onto the idea that all nature is divided into adversary groups battling with one another, and that it is the winner of these battles that is the fittest. But this simply isn't true. By that definition, a large predator could never become extinct.

The truth is that survival of the fittest is all right, but that the fittest is the creature which best learns to cooperate with the other life forms about him. I'm not convinced of anything in the world more than I am of the *fact* of evolution. It's the *method* of evolution we have to think about.

In the '50s, Arnold Toynbee wrote a book called *An Historian's Approach to Religion* in which he said that every living thing tries to establish itself as the center of the universe, and in doing so comes into competitive rivalry with every other living thing. That statement is pure bull. It disregards the symbiotic — the cooperative — relationship entirely, which is far more important in nature. In evolution, two creatures move from a parasitic to a symbiotic relationship. It would be contra-survival to go back to a parasitic relationship. A parasite often kills its host and eats itself out of house and home.

My message (my wife says I would sell my soul for a pot of message) is that it is not the competitive relationship which is the guiding force of evolution. It is the cooperative relationship. Why does the persimmon put that beautiful pulp around its seeds? It does it so it can offer a free gift to a passing animal. In accepting that gift, the animals scatter the seed and help to propagate and disseminate the species. This is a direct interchange between the animal and vegetable kingdoms. This is not a symbiotic relationship because the persimmon can get along without me and I can get along without it. But I'm ready to assert with anybody in the world that both our lives are richer because we do have a relationship with one another.

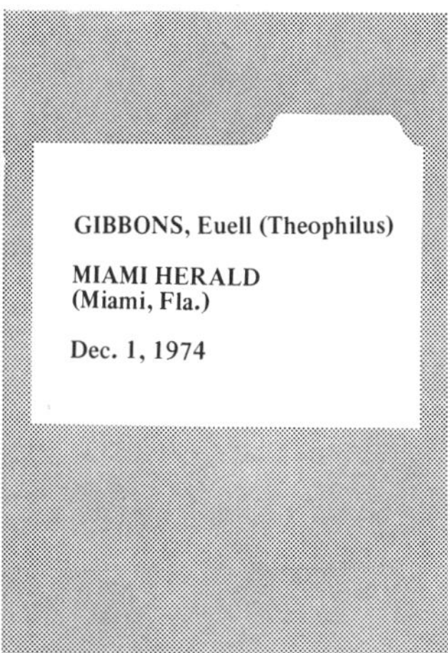
GIBBONS, Euell (Theophilus)

MIAMI HERALD
(Miami, Fla.)

Dec. 1, 1974

Take Pity On This Poor Single Chauvinist

By Judy Flander
Star-News Staff Writer

When George Gilder speaks, the feminists won't listen.

All he's trying to tell them, he says, is that they should realize "the male is different from the female, and the effect of the feminists' efforts is to subvert marriage." Gilder doesn't think it's a good idea for women to make more money than their husbands, and he questions the "equity of a single woman making more than a married man with several children." He's even against the Equal Rights Amendment.

"But I despair of getting the feminists to listen to me," laments Gilder, shaking his head and looking genuinely bewildered. Recently, *Time* magazine called him the "leading male-chauvinist-pig author," and he rather likes the idea. He is, after all, "unalterably opposed to the women's movement."

GILDER MADE his case against feminism last year in "Sexual Suicide." Last week he was back in town to promote "Naked Nomads" (New York Times/Quadrangle, $7.95), in which he outlines the pitiful plight of the single man.

It's just a myth, he says, that the single man leads the kind of life glorified in *Playboy.* According to Gilder, the single man engages in sexual activity only a fifth as frequently as married men and half as frequently as married women. Single men are lonely, he says — so lonely that they have a higher rate of suicide, violence and early death than persons in any other adult category.

"Single men are losers. They cannot commit themselves to anybody," says Gilder, who is 35 and single. He says he's lived with three women in the past 10 years—with a few affairs in between—and he wants to get married. In fact, he was engaged once—to Jane Stanton, a screenwriter, novelist and the last of the women with whom he has lived.

WHAT WENT WRONG? Welll, he says, Ms. Stanton "is very much an individual in her own right, and I don't think she was ready for marriage." Did the women's movement have anything to do with the break-up? "Well, she's anti-feminist, but I think she has been affected by the atmosphere of the times."

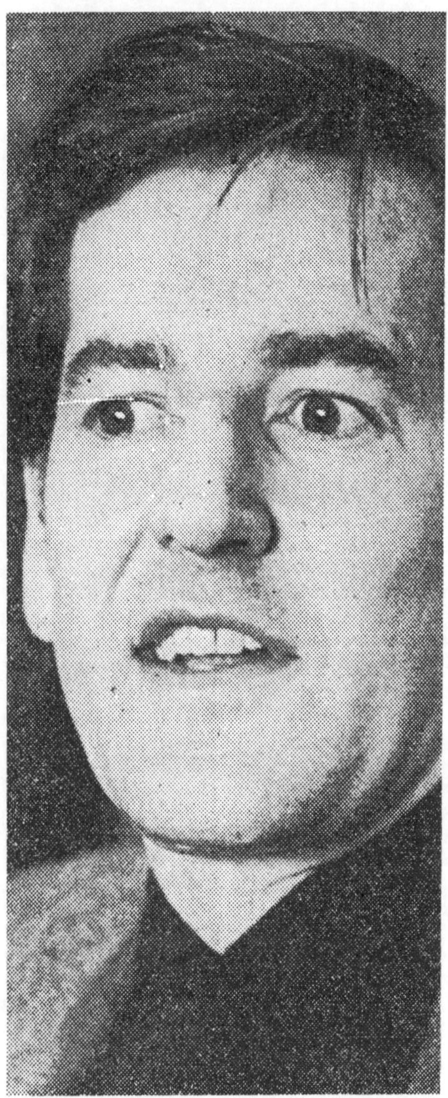

—Star-News Phogographer Rosemary Martufi

He hasn't got anyone else picked out, but he's a man with marriage on his mind. Marriage, he says, is the only recourse in the sad life of the single man. "Marriage is an anchor in one's life, connecting one to other people."

But there must be love, too. "Love is the sentiment of mortality," says Gilder, who believes that most of the married people he knows love each other, "in one way or another."

If marriage is so great, why are there so many divorces? Gilder says one reason is that a lot of married men are seduced by "the myth of the glittering lifestyle of the single man out there." Only when they're out in the cold do they realize how much better they had it in marriage.

SOME MARRIAGES, he believes, are "vulnerable to divorce" because wife and husband isolate themselves from their parents and other relatives and encourage their children to be independent. But husbands, wives and children need to be dependent upon each other, he says. "Society depends on the fabric of interdependence."

In a marriage, the male should be the provider and the woman the nurturer, Gilder says. Unless a man is allowed to assume this role, "he won't feel manly and he won't be able to relate to a woman in a loving and compassionate way."

Gilder says he tried to tell feminist Germaine Greer all about this during a talk show in Toronto recently, but she wouldn't listen, afterwards, though, he took her out for dinner and they talked for four hours and got along very well. ("I paid. I was glad to pay.")

"I liked Germaine Greer a lot," he says. She's intelligent, stimulating, weird, eccentric and fun." He even had a fleeting notion of asking her to go to bed with him. But he didn't. "I couldn't consider her as a sex partner. That's her predicament: She said in her book she only liked to sleep with construction workers."

He doesn't begrudge her that. Nor does he begrudge her the financial success she's had as a writer for magazines (including *Playboy*), which won't review his books.

GLORIA STEINEM may be the only feminist he hasn't met, says Gilder, who was drpped into a nest of feminists recently by the man who interviewed him for *Time.* "He wanted to create a story."

He got one. He took Gilder to a feminists' brunch where, according to the magazine's account, Gilder "was repeatedly invited to leave."

Gilder discounts this version. "At the beginning people told me it was offensive for me to be there," he says, adding wistfully: "But I don't think Barbara Seaman [author of "free and Feminine"] really wanted me to leave."

As much as he'd like to be loved by everybody, including feminists, Gilder isn't about to be an Uncle Tom to the feminists. He thinks anthropologist Lionel Tiger, for one, is "smart and valuable, but he capitulates to the feminists too much. I suppose this reflects an attitude of chivalry. So many men capitulate. They say, 'Gee! No, no! I believe in equal rights and equal pay."

Gilder doesn't agree, and he doesn't mind saying so. Being the leading male chauvinist pig has its benefits—among them notoriety and publicity, Gilder is the first to admit.

But he may be through with women for awhile. His next book will be antidoomsday. "There's this erroneous and widespread notion that the world is coming to an end . . .," he begins.

GILDER, George F.
(1939-)

WASHINGTON STAR-NEWS
(Washington, D.C.)

Dec. 13, 1974 [See also CA-17/18]

Allen Ginsberg spans the years between bohemian and hippie. His poetry is kicking on the campus. And, at 47, he hasn't changed . . . much.

THE HOWL OF ALLEN GINSBERG

By HANS KNIGHT

GINSBERG, Allen

PHILADELPHIA BULLETIN (Philadelphia, Penn.)

May 19, 1974

[See also CA-2]

I had never met Allen Ginsberg before but I had seen news pictures of him.

Usually he was surrounded by long-haired flower power people, leading some protest — against the Vietnam war or for legalization of pot. Often he was the center of "read-ins," "be-ins" and the rest and it was clear that wherever there was an "in" there was room for Allen Ginsberg.

Frequently, too, Ginsberg in the photos was flanked by a couple of policemen grimacing into the camera wide-eyed and open-mouthed, like the wild man the police took him for.

So, as I sat waiting for him in a small office on the Rutgers University (Camden) campus, I found myself tensing somewhat, ready for mutual wariness if not hostility. When collar-and-tied middle class morality meets celebrated street intellect, reportorial cool is not always a reliable defense. After all, was not Ginsberg the author of "Howl," that monumental blank verse scream of protest of the mid-50s, the one that kicked the blinkers from the establishment's face and oozed four-letter words?

Had he not, once, broken bread and taken LSD with the notorious Hell's Angels in Los Angeles, trying to induct them into the Oriental mystique of peacefulness?

And what was one to make of a once nice Jewish boy who got kicked out of Columbia University under a cloud of sexual "immorality" and who, not many years ago, presided over a mass attempt to exorcize the evil spirits from the Pentagon in Washington by sustained chantings of Om? Whose own father had once told him, in loving exasperation, "Allen, you're such an extremist"?

Rutgers had invited him to read during its fifth annual Walt Whitman Day program, to be followed by a pilgrimage a couple of blocks down to the Walt Whitman House. Since Ginsberg had been compared by some to Walt Whitman, the invitation seemed appropriate. Afterwards, the English department could have fun subjecting Ginsberg's lines to scrutiny for weeks. It is becoming a tradition on campuses across the land and has to do with expansion of linguistic consciousness.

He walked in, a medium-sized bear with owlish brown eyes behind round, horn-rimmed glasses. He was high-domed and bald on top, and the side bushes of dark curls flowed into the vast black beard streaked with iron-gray. He was 47 now. He spoke in a mellow baritone, the words formed quite rapidly by full, sensuous lips.

And as we felt each other out, groping around for non-existent mutual acquaintances, I remembered reading that he had once looked out a window into the night, under the influence of peyote, and the shadowy towers of the buildings had reminded him of a Moloch, mindlessly devouring.

I remembered, too, lying in a hospital bed, under pain killing drugs, and gazing in fascinated fear at the tower across the street assuming monster shape, with mouth and fangs, and lumbering closer.

I wanted to tell him, let him know (perhaps in appeasement) that we had something in common, a terror shared and survived, and perchance even benefited from through a fleeting glimpse into what our senses do not normally touch. But of course I didn't. He might

(Continued from preceding page)
have told me, as he once wrote, that LSD and the like could be used as vehicles for sensitizing and educational experiences, and it simply wouldn't have done. I am dead set against drugs except for medicinal purposes.

So, instead, we talked of the protesters. I wondered where they'd all gone.

He smiled with wry indulgence.

They hadn't vanished, he said. "You have some right here in Camden. They are protesting the expansion of Rutgers into the adjoining community, which means tearing down all the buildings where people live. They have been protesting quite vociferously."

I said I meant the larger picture. The demonstrations in the streets, the giant rallies in Washington.

"Well," he said "a lot of the protest has been relatively successful. The Chicago conspirators are now mostly out and into hatha yoga and developing the inner mind.

"Also, there had been a lot of infiltration of the protest movement by the police bureaucracy. It turned out that J. Edgar Hoover had sent out a directive to all the local FBI offices saying to 'identify, infiltrate and disrupt' all movements spreading anti-war propaganda. So there was much disruption of the peace movement, forcing it to decentralize and go into-local areas and local causes—different aspects, like gay liberation or women's liberation, something specific.

"And then there is streaking."

"What is the real meaning," I wanted to know.

"The flag of Adam," he said cryptically. "The flag of naked Adam."

I said some people were laughing it off as a modern version of goldfish swallowing.

Far from it, he insisted. "It is a protestation of nakedness. I see the Russian police bureaucracy denounced it the other day."

What if the streakers had been black?

"They probably would have been shot or lynched . . . The other aspect about demonstrations is that the press has not been very clear about the war. The war is not over. In the last year there have been 800,000 refugees in Vietnam alone.

"Another 60,000 people have been killed in Indochina, according to the Senate Committee on Refugees. So we are not at all out of the war. There has just been a mass hypnosis that has put people to sleep."

Has Watergate diverted the protest movement?

"Yes, it has diverted attention from what is a slow but very ponderous and heavy military takeover in the United States, and an extension of the police bureaucracy to a point where it threatens to put America in the position of Chile or Greece, which I think will happen here."

He sensed my skepticism toward such pessimistic certainty.

"If we get rid of Nixon and get a chump like Ford, it will make it even easier," he continued. "The power of the military is unchanged in America except that it's bigger. It has a hundred billion dollar budget and the power of the police bureaucracy has been aggrandized in the last five years. And now they have nothing to do except go around and infiltrate everybody. They don't have the centralized anti-war groups so they're infiltrating religious cults in California."

"But," I said, "a lot of the young people who were demonstrating in their faded jeans are now wearing collar and tie and worrying about getting jobs ..."

He said he'd thought about that a lot.

"It has to do with the disruption of the anti-war movement by saboteurs paid by the government, from Tommy the Traveler up in Hobart College and the lake area in New York down to the CREEP infiltrators in Miami during the Democratic convention. So protest got kind of dangerous.

GINSBERG, Allen

PHILADELPHIA BULLETIN
(Philadelphia, Penn.)

May 19, 1974

"Secondly, take the series of murders of students right on the campus — Kent State, Jackson State and Berkeley — for which there was no retributive justice and public consideration until the last few days. So there was a three-year hiatus, people committing murder and getting away with it. And there was obstruction of justice. Like John Mitchell refusing to make use of the information given to him in the FBI report on the Kent State killings. So it's getting scary on the campus. The kids know that anybody who wants to organize them is taking his life into his hands and may take someone else's life in his hands, too. And also, he might be working with the campus cop."

But weren't many demonstrators also guilty of violence?

"Yes, there is this final point — the lack of self-awareness on the part of the demonstrators, their lack of control of their own aggression, which made them an easy prey for aggressive cops to come in and whip up hysteria. We had some crazies on the fringes."

The deck, he said, is stacked against peaceful protest as organized by the old Quaker and pacifist organizations.

I reminded him that he came to public fame or notoriety during the beatnik days. How does he see that period, looking back?

"The reason we called ourselves beat was that we thought the battle was over," he said. "But the battle was probably lost in Walt Whitman's day. That's what he thought — that materialism and greed had so taken over the country and driven out all feelings of comradeship that there no longer was the kind of tenderness between the citizens that was necessary for the democracy to function."

Would there be a revival of the beatnik era?

"The nation," he insisted, "is almost inevitably headed toward a situation like Chile or Greece or South Vietnam or South Korea."

Even if President Nixon, whom he regards as the chief culprit, resigns or is impeached?

"In that case, people will feel that they have done something, cleaned up the situation. But actually this will just be an excuse not to recognize the omnipresence of the military-industrial bureaucracy."

I thought back to the age of the beatnik which had come upon the country at the height of the cold war. There was little militant questioning then of traditional values, and student rebellion was something that happened in places like Turkey.

Ginsberg seemed to read my mind.

"There is no going back to that in the political sense," he said, lighting his fourth cigaret in 25 minutes. "There is no backtracking to the kind of hypnosis where everybody thinks this is the best of all possible worlds. There is now too much enlightenment around — possibly," he added sardonically, "the acid infusion, the open mind, our expanded consciousness accomplished a great deal. It's still being used all over, but with more granny wisdom and less noise.

"And there's been the war, and people have seen through that, and there's been Watergate and people have realized that there has been a demythologization of the authority of the Presidency."

Some years ago, I recalled, Ginsberg and his father Louis, a poet in his own right and a Patterson, N.J. school teacher for about half a century, had a falling out over Allen's stand on marijuana.

(Continued from preceding page)

GINSBERG, Allen	PHILADELPHIA BULLETIN
May 19, 1974	(Philadelphia, Penn.)

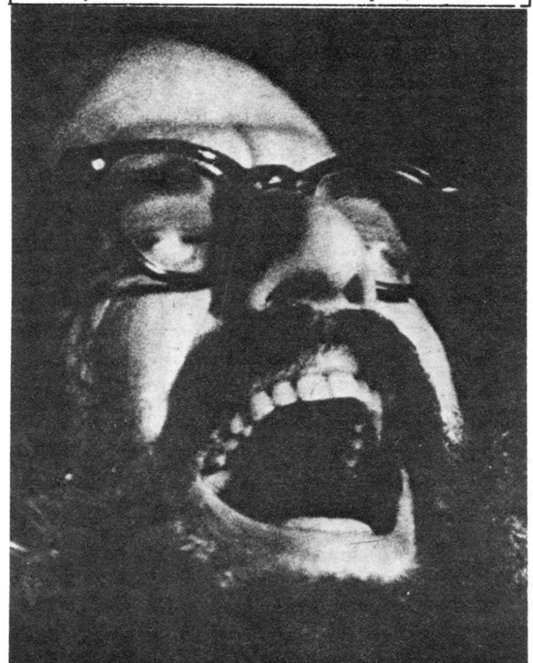

Ginsberg chants along with Indian music at the Asbury Ministry Church on Chestnut.

Ginsberg laughed. "The story was exaggerated in the press," he said. "My father merely told me not to encourage kids to smoke pot because he was afraid they might get caught. My father is for the legalization of pot, but he wants the law changed first before kids try grass. I wouldn't be surprised if my father had puffed a little pot himself."

How, I asked, does he himself stand on hard drugs, remembering he had often shared the limelight with Timothy Leary, considered by many to be the real Pied Piper of drug users in America.

"I'm not in favor of people taking junk or speed," he said. "Or alcohol. And, myself, being a cigaret addict, suffer a great deal from the nicotine pushers — who are mostly Southern military senators, anyway.

"But, I would agree with Leary's recent statement that the street acid being peddled by the police and the Mafia is not as safe as the socialist acid once peddled by our friendly communal acid manufacturers out in San Francisco. So it's not safe to do it on the street."

Well, I persisted, "are you in favor of narcotics?"

"I am in favor of people exploring natural foods, like psilocybin mushrooms and peyote, and seeing those psychedelics as an extension of the diet."

But not heroin?

"I've never been in favor of it," he said sharply. "But the point I've always tried to explain about heroin is that the English system does work relatively well. They've only got about 4,000 addicts and there is a decline in the rate of addiction in England.There, the addict can go to a clinic or a doctor. Here, the medical problem came under the control of the police bureaucracy, the narcotics bureaus, and they were notoriously corrupt.

"So that when Ramsey Clark came in in 1968 as attorney general, he had to indict, transfer or remove something like 49 out of the 80 federal agents in the New York area, and the investigating Knapp Commission said that the entire investigative unit of the New York bureau was involved in peddling or other kinds of corruption.

"So it's foolish to put what should be a medical problem in the hands of the police who have a working relationship with the pushers. As a result of this folly we have, as of a year and a half ago, 300,000 addicts in New York."

Not surprisingly, Ginsberg sees the sexual revolution as one of the bright spots in a rather dark world.

"It's very open and it's one of the hopeful things. Unfortunately the Supreme Court is trying to cut it. Cardinal Spellman once prophesied that the clock would turn back to the days of the liberation of Tropic of Cancer and other books, and Supreme Court decisions have now been repressive under Nixon's regime. They have left it open for any local district attorney to say that community standards are such that you can't have a new work of high class art that involves naked lovemaking. That's already thrown a knife into the filming of Burrough's "Naked Lunch" and Hubert Selby's "Last Exit to Brooklyn." So it's already had an effect on free expression in that area."

But, I said, wouldn't he agree that the establishment is making millions out of the sexual revolution?

"Yes," he said, "but again there's a relationship between cops and organized crime in the porn industry. On Times Square, most of the porn bookshops are syndicate establishments and they're really rough on people. So police have the tendency to bust unprotected porn shops and take payoffs and leave open the syndicate shops."

Where will this lead?

"Because of repressive legislation, really dirty porn will come through, vulgar, ugly, anti-sex porn, manufactured by organized crime for the purpose of just making money — that will flourish. And individual, artistic porn will have a tougher time."

How do people know the difference between good porn and bad porn?

"Well," he said, "the cops should be after busting organized crime, not busting porn. It's as simple as that."

How would Ginsberg like to be remembered?

He hesitated, thoughtfully twisting a strand of his beard.

"Oh," he said slowly, "as someone in the tradition of the oldtime American transcendentalist individualism ... from that old gnostic tradition ... Thoreau, Emerson ... Whitman ... just carrying it on into the 20th Century. For having been fortunate making connections with the Orient and swamis, and finding practical applications for things that were just ideas of the 19th Century."

I mentioned that a few years ago Arthur Koestler had written a scathing book about Asian philosophies, questioning how the West could benefit from civilizations that wallow in misery.

"For one thing," Ginsberg said, "they take their misery a lot better than we do. So we can learn perhaps the virtue of stoicism. For another, they don't threaten to damage the skin of the plant.

"There is not that Faustian pact with the devil of machinery. And a lot of the troubles in India and China were due to mechanical intrusion from the West—like the introduction of opium to China and the cutting down of all the forests of India, making it a wasteland from the 12th century to the 19th. All those lovely teak chests in Great Britain represent forests destroyed in India. . . ."

Students eager to meet Ginsberg began sticking their heads in the door. Ginsberg got up to leave. Suddenly he paused.

There was something he wanted to say. He took a small book from his pocket. He said he wanted to read something that had a bearing on what he felt about America.

"I say all of this tremendous and dominant play of solely materialistic bearings upon current life in the United States, with the results as already seen, accumulating, and reaching far into the future, that they must either be confronted and met by at least an equally subtle and tremendous force infusion for the purposes of spiritualization, for the pure conscience, for genuine esthetics, and for absolute and primal manliness and womanliness — or else our modern civilization, with all its improvements, is in vain, and we are on the road to a destiny, a status, equivalent, in its real world, to that of the fabled damned."

Walt Whitman, he said, wrote that 100 years ago.

"He really had it all down."■

Poet Writes About Love, Talks About Life

—*Journal Photo*

Nikki Giovanni: "I am an individualist."

GIOVANNI, Nikki
(1943 -)

MILWAUKEE JOURNAL
(Milwaukee, Wisc.)

Nov. 20, 1974

[See also CA-29/32]

By Paula Brookmire
of The Journal Staff

She has been called the princess of black poetry — that "brave, quixotic, intoxicating individualist."

But if you expect an ethereal being whose every utterance is poetry, you'll soon come down to earth upon meeting Nikki Giovanni.

You might expect, for example, that a conversation with her would center around the topics of poetry and love and beauty.

What you're more likely to get is a discourse on everything from the election results to the loss of social graces in America (we're "squeakier" because of it, she says).

When interviewed recently in Milwaukee, the poet indicated that she was disappointed in President Ford, against school busing, in favor of quotas, that she thinks the militant teachers' movement has hurt education and that the black movement is nonexistent. The women's movement? Well, she calls some New York City feminists sexual fascists.

Miss Giovanni writes for Encore, a news magazine with the "third world perspective," and covered the recent World Food Conference in Rome for the magazine. She also writes a syndicated national column. In addition, she has written at least seven poetry books, edited an anthology, collaborated on two books of dialog, recorded two albums with a third on the way, and received numerous honors, awards and grants. She lives in New York.

Nikki Giovanni could have been a politician, perhaps, if she weren't so much a poet and chronicler of life.

"People are lonely. They sit in groups but they go home alone. I am a poet, and I try to soothe it."

Reasons for Visit

Officially she was here to help the Delta Sigma Theta black sorority riase money for its toy loan library and scholarship fund.

But she really was here to shed a little of her light and vigor and joy on the almost all-black audience who came to see and hear her at the University of Wisconsin — Milwaukee Union.

From her initial political jabs at Richard Nixon "Who ever heard of phlebitis? — He could have at least caught something we understand, like leukemia" — to her sometimes sentimental, sometimes humorous poetry, Miss Giovanni held the audience.

"I've noticed I'm happier when I make love with you and have enough left over to smile at my doorman."

The audience laughed. She was reading the title poem from her new album, "The Way I Feel," which will be out in January.

She read many of her new verses — some of them love poems, some glimpses into the lives of older women.

No Youth Worshipper

"I'm not a youth worshipper," she had said earlier, in the interview. "What I've been exploring is the older woman because 1) she's fascinating and, 2) if we women live long enough, we will join those ranks."

In "Once a Lady Told Me," an old black woman speaks through Miss Giovanni about enjoying her independent existence in a rambling old house. The children don't come often and when they do, they're always in a rush, she says.

"It's not so very good, you know, but it's my life."

It was not the student activist here that night. It was Nikki Giovanni the mother, the lover, the woman. The only remembrance of her days at Nashville's Fisk University during the '60s was a poem about a black revolutionary she fell in love with while doing her assigned part for the cause: cooking the men's breakfast. The love affair didn't last.

Earlier, when asked about the black movement today, she had answered, "What black movement?"

Not the Same

Although she said some people would disagree with her, she insisted, "There is no black movement as we knew the movement, say, in my college years, 1959-'60 up until around '68."

She blamed the Nixon administration for destroying the movement but added later:

"I am an individualist. And groups are formed and function because of the individual needs. A lot of the needs in the black community at this point are really very personal needs and are not going to be satisfied by group involvement."

Miss Giovanni indicated that she now believed people could get somewhere by working within the system.

"I'm extremely cheered and greatly delighted by electoral politics," she said, especially after this month's election.

Talks on Busing

She had strong opinions on every subject broached, but on education she was especially vehement.

She said the busing situation in Boston was absurd. "To send a kid from Roxbury into South Boston is to send him out of the pot and into the frying pan.

"To integrate for a color reason is really an obscenity, because neither of those schools is up to par."

Miss Giovanni would support school busing only if it bused a child to a better school that was still in his own neighborhood.

"I am a firm believer in the neighborhood school. If that means segregated schools, then I'm willing to accept that.

"This generation of students has been abused by the issue of desegregation. I went to an all-black school and I consider myself an intelligent human being.

"Students today can't read or write. We cannot blame all of that on segregation or integration. Obviously, our teachers are not being equipped to teach."

Stresses Education

Miss Giovanni also said that the more education people had, the better they could express themselves and relieve frustrations.

"As we go forward with all these people who can neither read nor write nor put a logical sentence together, it's going to be a problem because the dumber you are, the more likely you are to violently impose your will."

People succeed in life by one of two ways, she said. Either they are articulate enough to cut down opposition with words or "they are big enough and powerful enough to squash all opposition."

Although Miss Giovanni is a feminist, she did not have kind words for other New York feminists. "They have carried things too far," she said, referring to some of the more radical feminists who have criticized all men.

"They have emerged into sexual fascists."

Aiming at Similarity?

She said she feared that the women's movement was trying to put men and women into a similar mold. "If women merge with men, then they're going to be second class men."

To further explain, she said, "I don't dispute that women have problems. But it's very clear that we are not all the same.

"That should not imply superior and inferior, which is a nasty, narrow, American way of thinking — that either you're like me and therefore we are superior together, or you're unlike me and you are inferior."

To Nikki Giovanni the individualist, it would be better if we worked for individual freedom by learning to take pride in our own being.

"Show me someone not full of herself, and I'll show you an empty person."

Journalist takes post in French cabinet

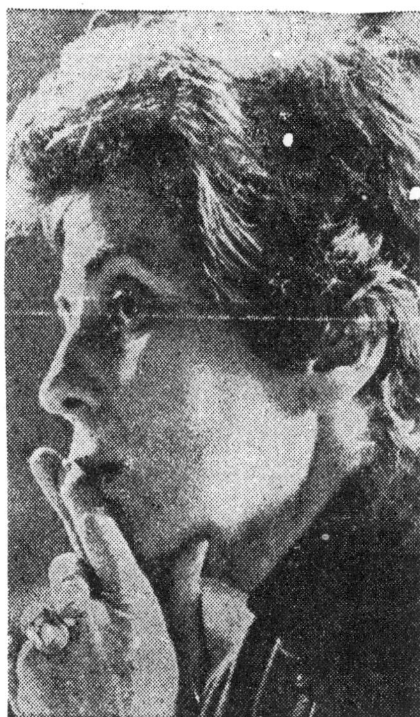

FRANCOISE GIROUD

By ELIZABETH McHARRY

NEW YORK — Francoise Giroud thinks it would be funny "if all of a sudden the primitive woman were to re-emerge, the woman who had to be subjugated, muzzled, humiliated, imprisoned in one way or another so that men could have the strength to do something other than make what is called love and could concentrate on creating civilizations."

It is quite easy to see why she has aroused such great interest in France, and now abroad, since taking over as Secretary of State for the Condition of Women in the French Cabinet of President Valery Giscard d'Estaing, a man she voted against.

Here for a brief visit, racing around with all the unharnessed energy of a hurricane, she urged American women to get on with liberation and stop lagging behind French women, whom she said were freer, if sometimes dirty and unwashed.

Reporters savored her words, even when they were being used to cut off interviews, because she had too many appointments.

Words, one way or another, have been central to Ms. Giroud, now 58, for a long time. She is co-founder of the powerful, independent French newsweekly L'Express (circulation 750,000), in which she formerly voiced her objections to treating women as another category and to the creating of a cabinet post for women as shocking. She called the attitude, "let's be good to the natives."

She also once wrote that in France it is vital for a new administration to make waves in its first three months. In the first three months of Giscard d'Estaing's tenure she says she took her own advice: Announced a series of cabinet-approved edicts to help equalize the status of women in work, education, public life and under the law.

She has a staff of three and no budget and must work for change through other ministries. "Bureaucracy is hard to move, but I am stubborn," she says.

GIROUD, Francoise

OREGONIAN
(Portland, Ore.)

Oct. 30, 1974

There's little need to press the point; she's already proved it.

Ms. Giroud has survived imprisonment by Nazis and persecution by French rightists; the birth of an illegitimate son and his death; divorce, and suicidal depression; there's little doubt she'll survive Giscard d'Estaing.

For women all over the world, perhaps her most single important suggestion is, "Make yourself economically independent; without that I don't even know what the word freedom means."

She believes the women's movement is the most profound revolution that highly developed societies will have to contend with in years to come — it concerns the volatile question of sharing power.

"A fire has been lighted," she says. "It all started with the pill . . . for the first time in history it gave women a choice."

Francoise Giroud was born into the big bourgoise, the fatcat upper middle class of France, was enveloped in luxury, until her father died.

At 15, she dropped out of private school, borrowed 500 francs from an "old homo" uncle, and took a crash course in a business school. Before the year was out she was working as a script girl for Marc Allegret. Soon, she was script writer and assistant director and involved in the making, with Jean Renoir, of "The Grand Illusion."

By the time she was 20, her friends, her speaking acquaintances were celebrities: Fernandel, Andre Gide, Leon Blum, Andre Malraux.

She says she met her white knight (his name is her secret) just days before the Germans marched into Paris and fled to her family's home in the south, in Clermont-Ferrand, pregnant, then, and pleading to doctors in occupied France for an abortion.

She was refused both abortion and rations, including milk rations. Her son survived, only to be killed in a skiing accident in 1972.

After the war was over, she met Helene Lazaroff, wife of a man she came to know in Clermont-Ferrand. It was instant rapport, she says, "coup de foudre." She went to work for Helene's new magazine, Elle, and when Helene took sick she took over, for seven years.

In charge of Elle, she mentioned for the first time two words hitherto taboo: frigid and lover. Also, after a survey, she informed French women they did not wash their teeth and did not wash their garter belts.

She and her best friend, Jean-Jacques Servan-Schreiber, founded L'Express, enticed Francois Mauriac to join them and set up a revolutionary magazine (for France) whose issues were seized a dozen times by the government. Though Servan-Schreiber helped to bring her fame, she says he also brought her pain. When he was drafted into the army and sent to Algeria (to still his editorials), she became suicidal and depressed.

"I teetered and went over the edge," she recalls. "Years went by. I was an endless walking ruin. But I found there is no better method of learning about oneself than psychoanalysis.

"I found intelligence is the art of accomplishment; it does not rule the world. I had always, deep-down, wanted to believe in the supremacy of reason."

Charred ruin though she may be, she gave Giscard d'Estaing a jolt during his presidential campaign last spring. In an effort to shed his patrician image, he played the accordion and posed bare-chested; then, on television, he met up with Francoise Giroud, the journalist, who asked him if he knew the price of a ticket on the Metro. He did not.

He barely won the election, and asked her to join the government. Now she has become his cabinet star, and she is to have a book published soon by Houghton Mifflin of Boston, which promises to bring more worldwide attention. No wonder Giscard d'Estaing encouraged her to visit America.

"There is a casual relationship among strangers in America that doesn't exist anywhere else in the world," she says in her autobiography, "I Give You My Word." It is the essence of democracy.

"There is a strength in the United States that we in Europe constantly tend to underestimate."

She also contends that the position of women in the world is detestable, especially in the United States. In France, there are more women doctors, judges and engineers.

She left New York to fly back to France for an emergency cabinet meeting with these words:

"Fascism's favorite breeding ground is the soil of economic crisis. Fascism is a phenomenon of the masses and the lower middle classes, when political leaders seem incapable of coping, or are simply corrupt.

"And ultimately," she adds, "the more the masses become educated, the more they will demand."

(Also see preceding article)

A Perceptive Frenchwoman Looks Back

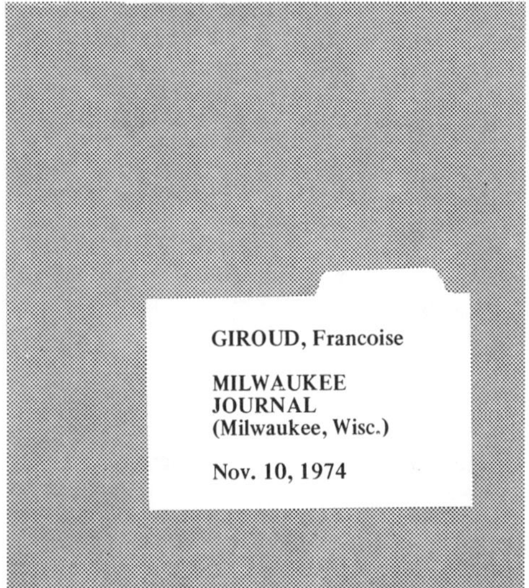

GIROUD, Francoise

MILWAUKEE JOURNAL (Milwaukee, Wisc.)

Nov. 10, 1974

By Marilyn Gardner
of The Journal Staff

Francoise Giroud doesn't consider herself a feminist — in fact, she dislikes many things about the women's movement — but her memoirs present a strong case for what a truly liberated woman can accomplish.

One of Europe's best known journalists, Miss Giroud was recently named France's secretary of state for women.

Her book, "I Give You My Word," was published in France in 1972 and was one of that country's best sellers for many months. For this US edition, published by Houghton Mifflin Co., she has added several new sections of special interest to American readers.

Founded Magazine

After World War II, Miss Giroud joined her friend, Helene Lazareff, in starting Elle (French for she), an innovative, often audacious and highly successful women's magazine.

But, in 1952, "Elle began to pall for me," Miss Giroud writes. "I found myself circumscribed by a number of specifically feminine interests which I didn't scorn — not all of them anyway — but which began to bore me."

Her opportunity came a year later when a longtime friend, Jean - Jacques Servan-Schreiber, asked her to help him begin publishing a news magazine. They enlisted the noted French intellectual and writer, Francois Mauriac, to join them. He accepted their offer and left "the ancient and honorable paper Le Figaro to join forces with two rebels who were putting together a new and virtually unknown magazine."

Their venture proved successful. L'Express is now France's leading and most influential news magazine. Miss Giroud is its editor in chief (now on leave) and led it through sieges of controversy, censorship and suppression by the government because of its opposition to the Algerian war, as well as tough financial times.

Their original goal for the magazine sounds simple but was startling in the highly partisan and politically oriented world of French journalism. "Its original mission was to support and nurture a policy of rebuilding France, a policy backed up by solid information," she writes.

Solid information were the key words in their goal. Existing newspapers and magazines simply didn't provide that, and the French didn't seem to mind.

"It may all boil down to the truth that the French don't like information because it pitilessly reduces their margin of illusions or hopes, because it impinges on their intellectual comfort," Miss Giroud explains.

It's insights such as this — rather than the success story of a woman or a magazine — that make Miss Giroud's book so readable. Her observations about events and people are both simple and perceptive.

Take, as an example, her bitterness at the reluctance of so many Frenchmen to join the resistance movement during France's occupation by the Nazis:

"What it means, if I'm not wrong, is that the majority of Frenchmen were — and still are, although perhaps to a lesser degree — sensualists.

"For example, for a long time, and especially during the war, I was extremely exasperated by the importance the French attached to food. . . . There wasn't 1% of the population that joined the Resistance, but I swear there were 50% who would have risked their necks for a pound or two of butter."

Four or five years later, however, her bitterness faded and she saw virtue in this French penchant for pleasure and beauty:

"If the French remain among the least unhappy people, and most enjoyable to be with — everything being relative — it's partly because, twice a day, they know how to make themselves happy by partaking in a pleasure about which they are meticulous."

Miss Giroud insists she isn't a feminist—"at least not in the general acceptance of the term"—but she agrees that "the place of women in the world—and especially in the United States—is detestable."

She believes that the emergence of the women's movement is a natural phenomenon and is right:

"Habits have deep roots, which endow one class with privileges over another, or one sex over the other, and they go on as though they were quite natural, despite the cultural changes that have occurred. When mores are no longer founded on the law of civilization but on habit, then comes the revolt. This is the situation today with women: Conditions have changed, the old mores are still lingering on and women are rebelling. . . .

"This revolt is part and parcel of the evolution of human affairs and is right. But when it expresses itself as hatred of men, it's stupid. The best way to hurt a man, if you hate him, is to be the object of his desire, not to hustle him into the kitchen to do the dishes. One sometimes has the impression that American women have a kind of dishwashing fixation."

What "bothers and bores" her about the American feminist movement, she writes, "is its 'missionary' aspect. All missionaries are my enemies, even when their cause is good. The world probably needs them, and I respect them for their courage, but only on the condition of not being compelled to endure them, as one endures mass, without having the right to laugh or saying you don't agree with what they preach."

Miss Giroud's book—a combination of life story and political and personal views—grew out of a series of interviews she had with a young French journalist. He tape recorded 30 hours of their conversations, transcribed it into 600 pages and presented them to her. She found them unpublishable.

She rewrote and edited the transcripts and the result is this book.

Although she was born into a wealthy family, Miss Giroud left school at 15 and found a job. Her father had died and her charming but impractical mother squandered the inheritance within a few years.

That first job in a bookshop (she read every book in the store before she left) was the beginning of a series of jobs and enterprises in film making and, after the war, in journalism.

Through her work, she met and became friends with dozens of France's artists, politicians, writers and philosophers. Her book is filled with portraits of them that are often frank and revealing.

She is equally candid about her own sorrows and tragedies. She writes briefly but movingly, for instance, of her first child, born out of wedlock just a few months after Paris was invaded. The boy had rickets, partly because she was in poor health and partly because the government denied her ration tickets for milk because the boy was illegitimate.

"When he was 4, he looked like a child of 2," she writes. "Nothing ever entirely makes up for the misfortunes of those early years. . . One should never be the child of a mother who has had a difficult pregnancy and wept over the birth of her child. Nothing ever makes up for that. Nothing."

In 1972, her son was killed in a skiing accident.

Julian Gloag Feels at Home in America

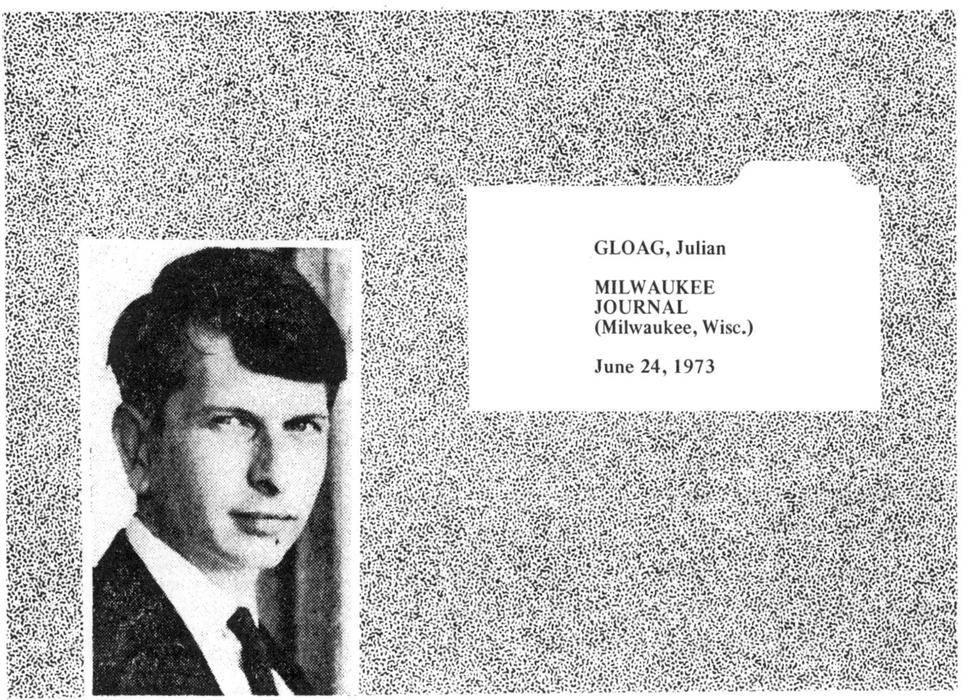
GLOAG, Julian

MILWAUKEE JOURNAL (Milwaukee, Wisc.)

June 24, 1973

By LESLIE CROSS,
Journal Book Editor

JULIAN GLOAG is generally accounted a British writer, but when it comes to living and practicing his trade, he prefers America every time.

Gloag, whose latest novel is reviewed today, first came to America as a lad of 17. He fell in love with it at once. He came back at every opportunity, and now he calculates that he has lived more of his adult life in New York than in London. He gets back to the Home Counties periodically. But he has no desire to stay there.

American periodicals that look to England as a latter day Athens leave him unimpressed. These include some of the most eminent. In his view, that most stratospheric of American critical journals, the New York Review of Books, has been badly taken. For a while, the New York Review imported a large number of its critical articles from the imperial island. But, he thinks, it often chose the wrong writers.

In England, There's a Gap

"These editors," he told me at the offices of Random House, his American publisher, before his latest book appeared, "seemed to feel that British imports carried some sort of intellectual cachet. To me it seems just the opposite.

"Too often, American editors don't know enough about literary politics in England to get the right guy to review books on English writers. They'll get someone like John Hanbury Angus Sparrow, for example, but everyone in England knows that so far as contemporary writing is concerned Warden Sparrow is very retrograde. People familiar with the scene, I think, would agree that the level of criticism is appallingly low in England."

Just the same, Gloag, a brisk, nimble witted man in his early 40s, is fond of British ways.

"English middle class life, which tends to set the tone," he assured me, "is in many ways the most delightful in the world. It is sober, gentle and kindly, very much concerned to spare people's feelings. It's decent.

"But all this is bought at a fearful price. The world is not really kindly and decent and gentle. The result is that a great deal of the real aspects of life is totally ignored. The moral universe as a section of the upper middle class is apt to conceive it is quite different from the structure of the universe as it actually is.

"There is a vast gap between the values a person gives assent to and the way he behaves in his actual life, and a writer can't overlook this."

Although he agrees that American life is sometimes more disorderly than he might like, Gloag thinks Americans are more likely to face unpleasant facts than his countrymen. And, he feels, writers in America enjoy a greater sense of freedom than their counterparts in Britain. For all its commercialism, he is convinced that America is far more hospitable to the life of the mind.

Gloag is a writer by heritage. His father, John, is the author of 65 published books, about a dozen of them novels; most of his books are about architecture and furniture, a field in which he is an international authority. The elder Gloag has also written about social subjects and in 1942 published a book called "The American Nation"; his son helped to revise it for a subsequent edition that appeared in 1954.

"For years," Julian Gloag related, "I tried to persuade him to write a historical novel. Finally he did, and now, at 77, he's doing a second, about the last days of Roman Britain."

He Had a Best Seller on His Hands

Gloag decided to emigrate when he was 28. He had the promise of a job as a glove salesman in Illinois but soon found a place in publishing in New York. His first novel, "Our Mother's House," was published in 1963; unexpectedly it became a best seller, and in 1967 it was turned into a film. His present novel is his fourth.

When I saw him, Gloag was planning to spend a year in France with his Franco-American wife, Danielle Haase-du Bosc, and their 4 year old son. Mrs. Gloag teaches French and humanities at Columbia University and has written scholarly books.

From France, Gloag hoped to get to England about once a month to look in on his parents.

"Mother," he said, "is over 80 and not in good health. Father is still busy writing though."

Who wrote plot?

Murder: a page from his books

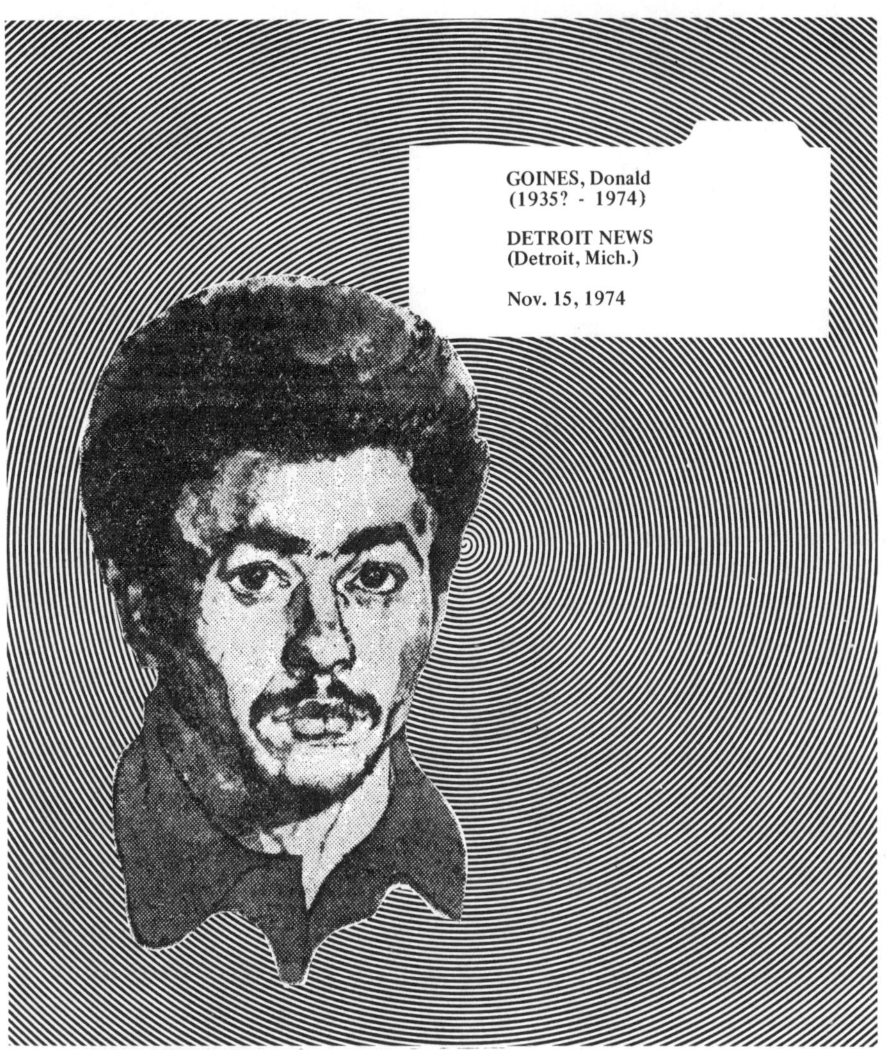

VIOLENT DEATH — This is a portrait of Donald Goines taken from the cover of one of his novels.

By LEONARD YOURIST
News Staff Writer

It was the kind of murder scene described three or four times in any Donald Goines novel.

Pulp novel material perhaps. But nonetheless it reflected the clear, simple image of violence and death as it often occurs in Detroit and other U.S. cities.

The scene was out of Goines' own life and, as it happened, his death.

Highland Park police found Goines — 39-year-old author of street culture novels — and his 28-year-old girl friend, Shirley Sailor, shot to death in their flat Oct. 21. Robbery was the apparent motive.

An anonymous caller told police about the killings, which occurred before Goines' 4-year-old daughter. He was shot three times in the chest, once in the neck and once in the head. Miss Sailor was shot five times in the head.

POLICE SUSPECT Goines was a heroin user and dealer, they said, despite his success as the author of 15 paperback novels.

But Goines' books are specialized: They dwell in that brutal, ruthless, never-turn-your-back world of Detroit dope dealers, junkies, pimps, prostitutes, racketeers and gang wars.

The book titles include "Dopefiend," "Black Gangster," "Whoreson" and "Whiteman's Justice."

His characters, stereotyped and uncomplicated, included people like the vicious, young gangster, Prince, just out of Jackson Prison and planning to have Detroit's dope profits "all wrapped up" within a year. They also featured Porky, the obese dope house operator, who lives life happily abusing addicts.

Highland Park Police Lt. Robert Heine said a quantity of suspected narcotics was missing from the author's flat on Cortland, near Woodward. Also gone were cash from a royalties check and a $400 advance from his Los Angeles publisher for beginning a new book.

TWO DETROIT MEN, both white, were arrested in connection with the murders. But later they were released without being charged.

Goines described himself to his publisher as a former addict and ex-convict.

Charles Anderson, managing editor of Holloway House Publishing Co., described Goines as "energetic and dependable," but "a man always in need of money — even though a lot of money went his way."

Anderson said Goines told him he had his drug habit under control and that his writing had improved.

"When we entered the black experience market in street books three years ago, Donald came to us. We needed black authors," he recalled.

Anderson said Goines was his leading writer in sales and he had a large national following of readers — mostly in urban, heavily black areas of the country.

"He always honored his publishing deadlines and he liked working with other prospective black writers," said Anderson.

"Once Donald told me he wished he had more education because it would make him a better writer. But I told him he already had the kind of education he needed to write," said Anderson, who edited 11 Goines books.

BORN IN DETROIT, he served in the Air Force during the Korean War. He served time in prison for narcotics convictions. He was married and divorced, fathered nine children. And he apparently lived in a tightrope world, balanced between his writing and the street.

"It was incredible when I learned how Donald died," said Anderson. "The man who had created a fictional world of killing and violence came to the same end so many of his characters did."

If Goines' life and world were a tragedy, the tragedy continued beyond his death.

His two sisters and brother were unable to obtain Air Force records confiscated by police investigators at the murder scene. So they had to settle for a routine burial instead of one with full military honors as they had hoped.

And at the funeral ceremony they had put a copy of his newest book, "Inner City Hoodlum," inside the opened casket to be buried with him.

But when the ceremony ended, they discovered the book had been stolen.

Staff photo by Donn Gould

Cartoonist John Goldwater, face to face with his creation, the all-American red-headed kid, Archie.

Kids Learn From Comics

By MARGO HARAKAS
Staff Writer

Twenty-seven years ago, John Goldwater got an idea — to create a comic book character that was the complete antithesis of the high-flying Superman.

He chose for his "hero" a red-haired, freckle-faced All American boy who's only right sometimes, and in trouble almost always. Not bad trouble, mind you, but the normal everyday kinds of peccadilloes that characterize a teenage boy.

Goldwater named his character Archie. And 30 days after the first issue hit the stands, he knew he had a winner.

Now, the perpetually 17-year-old Archie and his galaxy of friends are taking on a new challenge — education. The whole gang, including the unlikely Jughead and Moose, will be teaching math and reading to real-life kids.

"Our intent," says Goldwater, "is to make learning fun."

The format has been proven. For even kids who can't read, "read" comic books. Forty-five million of the Archie gang comic books are sold each year.

Goldwater, vacationing in Boca Raton last week, said he suddenly realized the possibilities of comics as teaching tools about three yars ago when he tried to relate Archie's Spanish lessons to a real news story. (Goldwater claims that most of the plots in the Archie comics are culled from news stories.)

He had read about a Puerto Rican injured in an auto accident, who was unable to make the ambulance driver understand he had a rare blood type.

Goldwater's writers took the story and had Archie happen upon the scene just in time to translate for the injured man. Archie proved the value of his Spanish lessons and became the hero of the day.

Just as Goldwater began seriously thinking about his new project, he saw an article in the Library Journal touting the instructional potential of comics.

Goldwater and his staff began putting together the reading program, asking educators to draw questions from the regular comic book series. Before long, teachers, hearing of the project, came to him asking if a similar approach could be taken to teach math.

Goldwater hired some educators as collaborators for the math series.

"They're all situations the child can relate to," Goldwater said. "They are stories with humor so the kid doesn't feel he's being pushed to learn something."

Jughead, for instance, may drive a jalopy into the local service station. He'll count his money to see how much gas he can afford. And of course, if Jughead can figure it out, the kids conclude anybody can. It's incentive to try. By placing the characters in familiar situations, math becomes more concrete and relevant, said Goldwater.

Each of the remedial kits comes with comic books and question and answer sheets.

The reading course tests comprehension and vocabulary. After reading one of the comic books, students are asked the meaning of certain words and to place events in chronological order.

The programs will be tested in the next few months in New England states. With the median age of the Archie fan from 11.5 years to 12 years, Goldwater explained the materials can be used for grades three through six.

Goldwater sees his newest Archie enterprise in keeping with the status being accorded these little magazines.

"Comics are now being recognized as a true art form of America," said Goldwater.

While this country didn't create the art form (the first comic strip came out in Germany in 1898), no one has taken it quite so far. In recent months, two major art museums mounted exhibitions on comic book art. The small books are being studied and collected in an explosive mania of acquisition.

Goldwater cringes every time someone asks if he has an Archie first edition. "I guess if it were in mint condition, it would be worth maybe $1,000," he says.

But he hasn't got one. The few he had stored in a warehouse disappeared.

Archie was the first comic book character to get away from muscle power. Before Goldwater hit upon the idea of his everyday teenager, he tried duplicating the success of Superman with Steel Sterling, The Shield, The Wizard.

Then he sat down one day to force an original idea to surface. A strong believer in the American virtues of family, country and applie pie, he came up with his normal boy idea. He did a turn-around on the boy-chases-girl cliche, and had two girls, totally different, pursuing Archie.

The two girls, Betty and Veronica, became so identifiable that Glamor magazine once did an article titled, "Are You Betty or Veronica." Betty is the sweet, hometown girl Archie really loves. But Veronica is the wealthy, fascinating tigress. Glamor found that 90 per cent of its female readers would prefer being Veronica.

Over the years, Archie and the spin-off characters and projects have amounted to a $100 million enterprise.

Not one to let his lucrative "pal's" talents atrophy, Goldwater turned Archie loose on TV seven years ago and in short order, the sometimes befuddled hero "became the highest rated show in the history of Saturday morning TV programming,' claims Goldwater.

Out of the Archie cartoon show came an Archie singing group that developed a Midas touch in the recording business. It was The Archies, Goldwater reminds you, who introduced "Sugar, Sugar" and "Jingle, Jangle" both gold hits.

Goldwater credits Archie's lasting success to his believability.

"He's contemporary. He reflects the mores of the times. Kids identify with him. (Even the furnishings in the cartoon panels are copied from Sears-Roebuck and Montgomery Ward catalogs.) He rebels a little now against his parents which he didn't use to do. He's changed with the times. He's involved in peace marches and fighting pollution."

But in the final analysis, Goldwater admits that by some standards, his goody-goody hero may be square. "I think Archie's square. I'm square and I guess he reflects me."

GOLDWATER, John
(? - 1975)

FORT LAUDERDALE NEWS & SUN SENTINEL
(Ft. Lauderdale, Fla.)

Jan. 5, 1975

the two worlds of Gomez-Gil

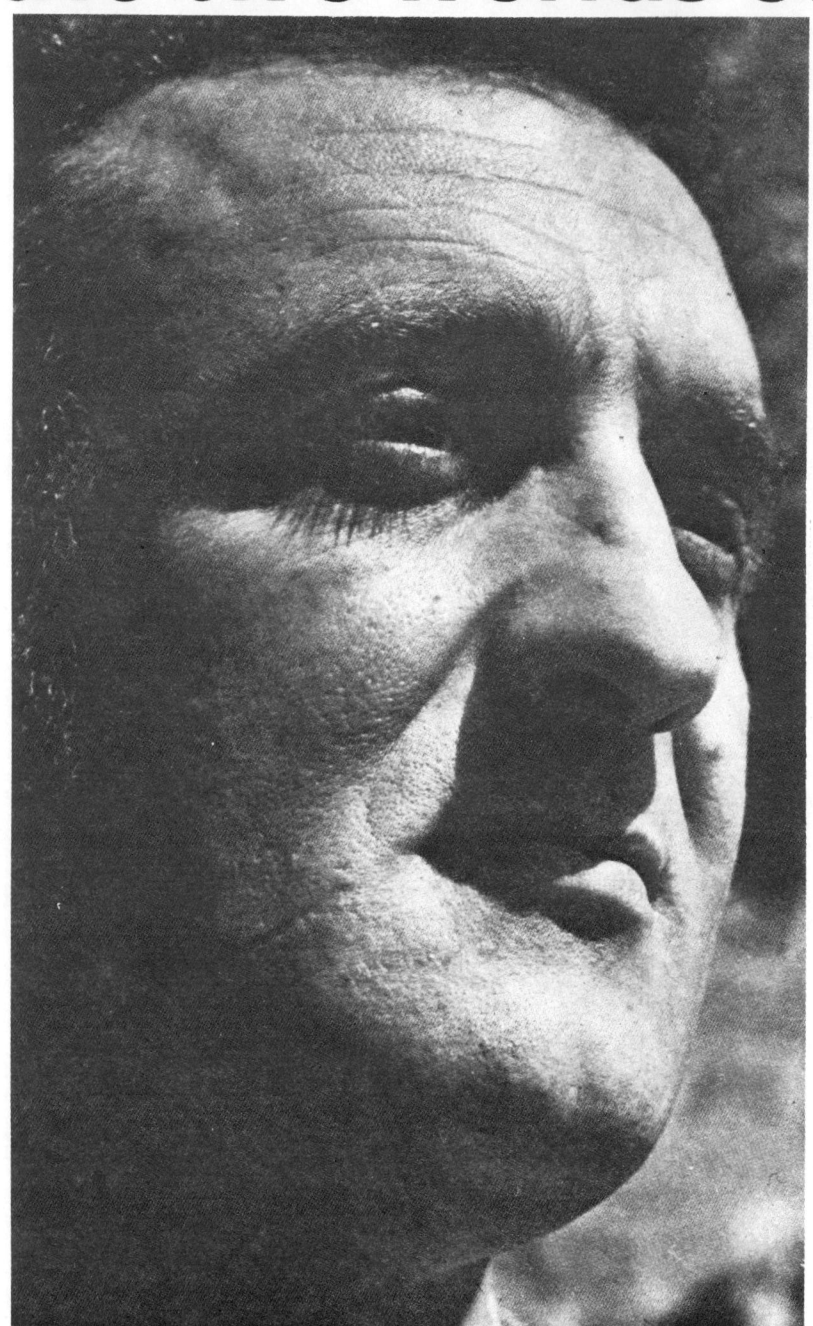

by
MICHAEL PETERSEN
and
JOHN DONOHUE
for The Courant

Alfredo Gomez-Gil is a Spanish poet. Visiting with him in his parlor-comfortable office on the picturesque campus of the Hartford College for Women, that's hard to believe. He dresses like a prosperous European businessman, speaks offhandedly about his friendships with Picasso, de Creeft, and Dali; of parties in Spanish embassies, of the pros and cons of Puerto Rican independence; nevertheless, the message comes through clearly — Alfredo Gomez-Gil is a poet, a poet of the traditional mold. He must write to live.

The poetic world of Gomez-Gil began back in 1940, when at age four he wrote his first poem. Ironically, only last year a student from Spain's University of Barcelona, sent the poet-professor her thesis which included that first effort. He smiles when he tells this story but he refuses to comment further because he believes that no man has the right to evaluate the efforts of a four-year old, even when the four-year-old was him.

Gomez-Gil began his serious writing apprenticeship at the age of eight and in 1962, his first book of poems, Pesada arena (Wet Sand) was published. He remembers the event as being a kind of vanity trip, but admits now that it was a "very, very bad effort." In fact, he destroys every copy he gets his hands on, but he's human enough to admit too that he has kept a copy, one copy, for himself.

Gomez-Gil was born in Alicante on the southeast coast of Spain 35 years ago, a few days after the beginning of the Spanish Civil War. Alicante was a typical, traditional Spanish city then, but today the tourists, mostly European tourists, have taken it over in the summertime.

Among the visitors to Alicante each year is one Spanish poet from Hartford, Professor Gomez-Gil, who keeps an apartment there the year round. Alicante is his roots, his attachment to his native land, a land he loves and cherishes as much as he does the United States, and a land where his mother resides still. Gomez-Gil feels no dichotomy in this dual nations love. He says each visit to Spain "stimulated" him and each time he returns to the U. S. for the fall semester, he is "stimulated" again. He describes the dual existences as "injections of enthusiasm" and senses that they give him the advantage of having two mentalities rather than one. He admits that the differences between Spain and the U. S. are narrowing as the economy there moves swiftly ahead, but still he believes that "the Spanish character, sense of life, feeling of introspection" are almost totally different than those properties in the people of the United States.

GOMEZ–GIL, Alfredo
(1936 -)

HARTFORD COURANT
(Hartford, Conn.)

June 3, 1973

[See also CA-41/44]

To date Professor Gomez-Gil has published 17 books on poetry and essays, with a couple more due out this year. He also wrote a play, Las Camas (The Beds) about life in a U. S. girls college. His play revolves around three girls of different religious and ethnic backgrounds and he wonders now if it might be worth translating into English. But poetry, not the theater and not teaching, is where his heart and head are most of the time.

In Spain as in any other nation, including the

(Continued from preceding page)

United States, a poet's place on the economic ladder is at the lowest rung. "We are a generation of poet-professors. Poets teach because they must earn a living, and because one talent is not divorced entirely from the other," he said.

Jesuit-trained in his early school years, he later went on to earn degrees at the Universities of Granada, Murcia, and Madrid. He was a student-teacher from the University of Madrid when Yale University invited him to join their faculty in 1965-66.

Professor Gomez-Gil followed a long and impressive line of Spanish writers and poets who have made international reputations from other lands. He's quick to point out that six Spanish-lauguage poets have captured the coveted Nobel Prize in literature. They are: Pablo Neruda in 1971; Miguel Angel Asturias in 1967; Juan Ramon Jimenez in 1956; Gabriela Mistral in 1945; Jacinto Benevente in 1922; and Jose Echegaray in 1904.

Spanish poet-professors have been particularly successful in the U. S. as evidenced by Juan Ramon Jimenez at Rio Piedras, Puerto Rico; Luis Cernuda at Middlebury College; Jorge Guillen at Wellesley College; and Pedro Salinas at John Hopkins University. The U. S., for the Spanish poet, seems to happily combine the American view of the future with the Spanish tradition and past. But there is a concession that Professor Gomez-Gil makes which he believes is mostly a psychological one — it's his refusal to become completely fluent in English for fear that it may corrupt his writing. He is, after all, always was, always will be a Spanish poet.

According to Gomez-Gil, Spanish intellectuals who read poetry seem not to be troubled by the "brain drain" of their poets flowing into the U.S. and other countries. They understand it. They wish the expatriots well in nations where they enjoy peace, freedom, and a life with dignity. The freedom part has mostly to do with censorship which has something to do with politics. Everyone knows that poets, for the most part, and good poets particularly, do not thrive under dictatorships. Although Gomez-Gil is published in Spain, one suspects that it is a tenuous acceptance; that on the tip of the poet's tongue are words that would bar his work in Spain.

Gomez-Gil rates the late e.e. cummings and Thomas Merton as his favorite American poets but won't rate living American poets because he knows several. He says there are 23 highly-regarded Spanish poets now living and working in the U. S.

Among his own works, he refuses to name his favorite poem but does say that "China" is one that has won him the most acclaim. The poem, written in 1965, is translated into 7 different languages and is a favorite of his students. His students also favor "Little Black Boy." Gomez-Gil acknowledges that he finds inspiration in writing poems about American children from various ethnic backgrounds. "Children, like poetry, are alive, vital, full of life," he said.

Gomez-Gil's first book in English, "Vibrations of Silence," a selection from his complete works to date is expected to be published and in the bookstores by December.

The poet-professor is close to his Puerto Rican "brothers" in Hartford. He understands their plight and is in sympathy with them, but his activities are kept in low profile on purpose. He considers himself more a cultural activist than a political activist and explains why this way, "I am a guest in this country and it would be wrong for me to voice my political opinions in my host country." Another of his more popular poems in his recitals is "Puerto Ricans."

Last May in Mouguin, Gomez-Gil was a house guest in the home of his late friend, Pablo Picasso. He describes Picasso as "a very special man. A man with different ideas. Emotional. Sincere."

Also numbered among his friends are famed artists Salvadore Dali and Jose de Creeft. He has a couple of Dali's original sketches and also paintings by de Creeft in his Alicante apartment.

If Gomez-Gil found a reason for working in Connecticut at Yale, he found a refuge at the Hartford College for Women. He said, "I have the opportunity to write here," and he means "here" literally, in the office he is speaking in at this interview. It is obviously a haven. One wall is covered with books, another with paintings, prints, posters, broadsides, and other graphic decorations. A third wall holds a window with a view of the green campus and Asylum Avenue off in the distance. The furniture appears to have been chosen for masculine comfort. Nestled as it is, on the campus of the school of some 200 freshmen and sophomore girls, it provides the quiet and solitude a poet needs.

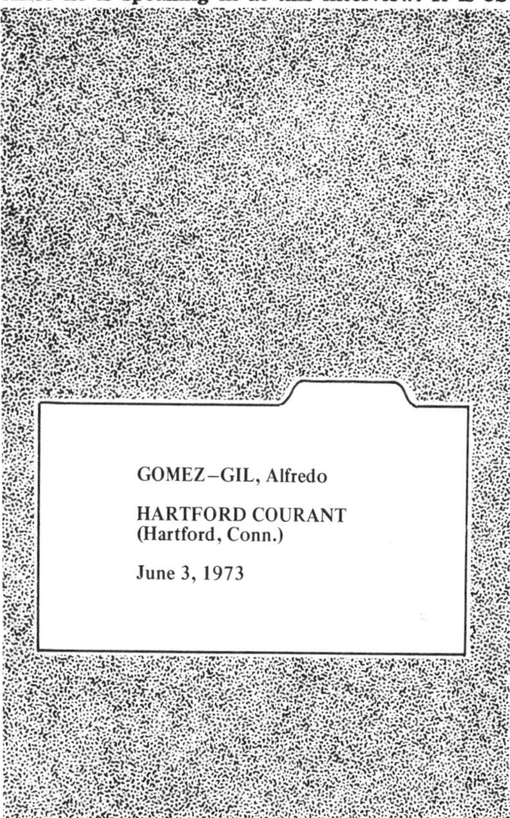

He speaks of working 12 hours a day there, mostly on his poetry. You get the impression that he wouldn't, and couldn't work anywhere else — even though you know he would be writing poetry no matter where he was.

Hartford is not a center of Spanish culture. For Gomez-Gil that is a plus. He said the pressure of social obligations in such a center would cut into his creative writing time. And you know what he means when the conversation turns to the coterie of Spanish intellectuals in America — and throughout the world. They are a closely-knit group, and Hartford's Gomez-Gil, Spanish poet, is very much one of them.

Publisher Kay Graham: the woman

By CHARLOTTE SLATER
News Staff Writer

GRAHAM, Katharine (Meyer)
(1917 -)
DETROIT NEWS
(Detroit, Mich.)
Apr. 9, 1974

PUBLISHER KATHARINE GRAHAM — She'll take on the White House; but a speech to businessmen is "somewhat terrifying." —News Photo by David Kryszak

Katharine Graham, 56, one of the most important women in America, was shaking in her patent leather shoes as she stood before a sea of Detroit Economic Club luncheoners yesterday.

As publisher and chairman of the board of the Washington Post, she was at Cobo Hall to talk about freedom of the press, field a barrage of complicated questions, and be charming.

It was her paper that published the Pentagon Papers. Her paper that first broke the story of the Watergate break-in. It was her paper that survived blasts of vitriol from an angry White House and other more subtle pressures. She was proud of it.

But after the last well-wisher departed, she finally allowed her rush-week smile to collapse into a look of near desperation. "I'm absolutely exhausted," she said. "Such a large group. And all those Fords and Townsends and so on out there in the audience.

"You know, I've only been speaking like this for about two years, and I still find it somewhat terrifying. I'm always afraid I'll go 3,000 miles and then let the team down or something."

That very morning, concerned about the impression she would make, Katharine Graham had read her speech aloud while sitting under the hairdryer in a Detroit beauty salon. Her "audience" had been a woman from the Detroit bureau of Newsweek magazine. (Newsweek is one of the businesses owned by the Washington Post Co., in addition to four television stations and a radio station.)

Mrs. Graham rushed from the Cobo Hall speech to the local offices of Newsweek to make a phone call. She was not only tired. She was worried. The Post was in the last hours of union negotiations with the Newspaper Guild. She came out from the closed-door conversation even more tired.

"It looks like there may be a strike by the time I get back to Washington," she said. "I didn't think it would come to this."

Mrs. Graham, one of just a handful, of female publishers in the country, came to her position with the Post after the death of her husband Philip in 1963. But her association with the paper began long before when her father, the late Eugene Meyer, bought the Post in 1933.

"Father had retired from government service with the Federal Reserve system and had always wanted a paper," said Mrs. Graham. "So he bought the Post — at auction, actually, on the front steps of the paper." Katharine, known to her friends as Kay, married Philip L. Graham, a Harvard Law School product, in 1940. They had four children.

In 1946, Graham became publisher of the Post at his aging father-in-law's request. Upon Graham's death in 1963, Katharine assumed the job.

"My husband and I owned the voting shares of the company. And when he died the other people there (and I myself) preferred that I be involved with the company. There was just an assumption that I would go to work."

Mrs. Graham had worked off and on in various capacities around the paper. But practically speaking, she started from the top.

"Any problems I encountered in the beginning did not stem so much from being a woman. They stemmed from inexperience," she said. "I had the guiding principles from both my father and my husband. I had always listened to them discuss their decisions and problems. But there are certain aspects of management that come only with experience.

"You do have worries and concerns about what the paper is doing and where it's going. But you learn from things that haven't gone as well as you hoped before. The whole management process is something you can't do 100 percent correctly — just the best way you possibly can."

Mrs. Graham's philosophy as both businesswoman and Watergate buster — "Excellence and profitability go hand in hand."

She said the most difficult news-oriented decision she ever made was the decision to publish the Pentagon Papers in the face of a court injunction that had stopped the New York Times that very morning from publishing the same thing.

"The decision had to be made quickly. The story was written and ready to go; it was valid; there had never before been prior restraint of the press. Weighing all factors, it seemed like the right thing to do. And I still feel the same."

The decisions in Mrs. Graham's personal life have been many — not the least of which was to avoid all kinds of "in-between" activities like after-work receptions. "Those things are neither work nor play," she said. "Whatever I do is pretty straight-on. I'm either working or I'm spending time with my family (there are three grandchildren) or just relaxing at a movie."

She doesn't like shopping for clothes, "vacation spots" or staying in hotels. Her favorite activities aside from movies are tennis, swimming and taking long walks at the family farm in Virginia — a week-end and summer retreat.

The farm is a working one and is administered by son Donald who, of the four children, is the only one so far to get into the news business. He works for Newsweek in New York and will eventually associate with the Washington Post.

Daughter Mrs. Elizabeth Weymouth, mother of two, lives in New York and just edited a book about Thomas Jefferson. Son William just graduated from law school at Stanford in California and the youngest, Stephen, is a senior at Harvard.

Mrs. Graham doesn't know how long she'll keep up her hectic business pace (which includes directorships on about 15 various boards in addition to her newspaper and magazine responsibilities). "But at some point, I think it's a good idea to move over and give younger people a chance," she said. "These are very changing times; and experience is only worth so much."

(Also see preceding article)

The Private & Public Wars of Katharine Graham

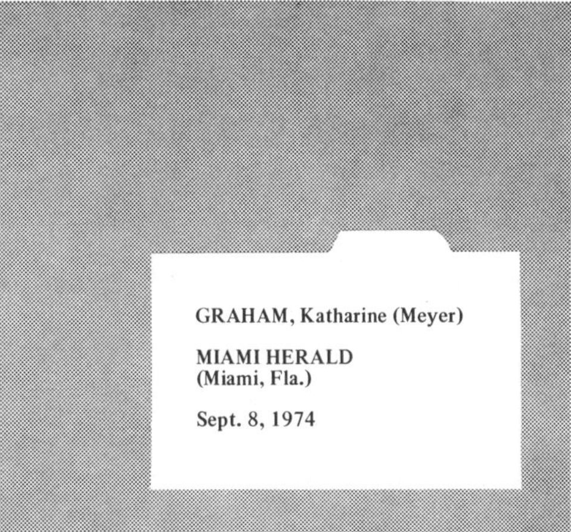

GRAHAM, Katharine (Meyer)

MIAMI HERALD
(Miami, Fla.)

Sept. 8, 1974

By Kandy Stroud

"Moma," as the boys in the *Washington Post* newsroom still call her, has become Katharine the Great.

Katharine Graham is one of the world's most powerful publishers and perhaps the nation's most powerful woman. She is called the Jeanne D'Arc of journalism and the Queen Bee of Washington, and it is she who made the tough decision to have her *Washington Post* print the stories that helped expose Watergate.

With her preeminence, Katharine Graham has changed. Although she protests bitterly what she calls the "opening-flower" theory and calls the idea that she is different "sexist," even her daughter, Elizabeth Weymouth, says her mother has changed "drastically." But the metamorphosis cannot be attributed directly to Watergate.

Forty years ago she was a sickly child afflicted with tuberculosis. She read Proust in bed. A decade ago, she was a withdrawn housewife with four growing children. And she was overshadowed by a workaholic husband, Philip L. Graham, a human dynamo who built the Washington Post Co. into an empire but took his own life in the process.

She was a painfully shy woman eclipsed by an accomplished, domineering mother, Agnew Meyer, who could make her daughter feel insignificant.

"Go away, dear," the mother once said when young Katharine came upon her and Phil Graham conversing in the garden. "We're having an intellectual discussion."

Katharine worked as a reporter for the *San Francisco News* in 1938 and 1939 and the *Post's* circulation and editorial departments from 1939 to 1945. This was hardly enough to give her self-confidence on the day in 1963 when she assumed control of the Post company. The empire now includes not only Washington's leading newspaper but *Newsweek* magazine, a one-third interest in the Los Angeles Times-Washington Post News Service, and radio and TV stations, including Miami's Channel 10 (its call-letters, WPLG, are formed from her late husband's initials). Altogether, her company grosses an annual revenue of more than $178 million.

Even three years ago, when she had run the business eight years, she was just another publisher to her male counterparts. Her friend, columnist Art Buchwald, remembers "she had very few pals" at newspaper conventions. "They sort of ignored her."

Then came the decision to publish the Pentagon papers. At a convention last year, Buchwald continues, "everyone gathered around her, congratulated her. They even wanted to touch her. Sure, she's changed. She had the burden of an entire enterprise on her shoulders. It could have all gone down the drain. She was in a war and she won."

Ms. Graham has also been elevated to super-status by women's groups. "I guess they see a woman in high executive office who has worked her way up, who has made it, even if I got here the way I did," she says, sitting relaxed in her beige-and-white, photo-filled office.

She has dozens of awards. Probably the most meaningful was election as the first woman to the traditionally chauvinist Associated Press board of directors. Last November she was dining at the New York apartment of fellow-publisher Mike Cowles when a call came mid-salad announcing she had been selected by thousands of votes to the position. "I've never seen her so excited," recalls a guest. "There was no veneer of sophistication. She was like a child, clapping her hands. We all rose and toasted her."

Other honors have left her cold. Ms. Graham once expressed her true feelings about collecting gold plaques to a reporter: "I'm sick and tired of all these — awards!"

Thirty-odd people who know her well say that success has brought out the best in Kay Graham. She's more at ease with herself and others, more knowledgeable about the business, more independent. "If there's a major difference in the past two years," says Phil Geyelin, *Post* editorial-page editor, "she's gotten a lot more comfortable about public speaking. She never used to like it at all. But she's accepted her responsibility in the trade to be a public figure.

"She's gotten on top of the business side, too. She's really educated herself. She took a crash course at IBM, she read a lot of books about what it takes to be the head of a large corporation. When she went to Richmond for a wedding recently, she sprinted off between the lunch and the reception to take a look at the Richmond papers' optical scanners."

Reports executive editor — and some say her Rasputin — Ben Bradlee: "She'll go through the plant talking to employes, something that would have made her very uncomfortable two or three years ago."

She's done bold things she might never have had the nerve to do two years ago. Last summer, at a circulation dealer's picnic, she was surprised to be invited to sit with the boys and play poker. "It was very funny," laughs Kay. "They thought they had a pigeon and *I* thought they had a pigeon. I had played poker as a child, but not since. My executives kept saying, 'Don't do it. They play every night on the platform. They're sharks.' But I didn't care. I said, 'So I'll lose. It's fun.' "

Instead, Katharine won a whopping $110 with a full house.

During the *Post* strike in April, Katharine (who has given up her limo and now drives herself because she does not like to be waited on by a chauffeur) could often be seen at 2 or 3 a.m. parking her bottle-green Mercedes in the employes' lot and "hanging out" with the guys on the loading platform, who had been waiting angrily since early evening for their trucks to be loaded with *Posts*.

"Of course I had to," she says. "Those dealers were waiting in the alley all night and they were understandably outraged. I came to listen to their complaints and to tell them what we were trying to do about them in the negotiations. It's just part of the job."

She pitched in to keep the paper going, like every other executive during the walk- ➡

(Continued from preceding page)

out. She played reporter, interviewing Nancy Kissinger and the sister of the Iranian ambassador. She manned the complaint desk. She even took classified ads. One story goes that Katharine was taking dictation by phone from a gentleman who grew more irate as she slowly recorded a technical ad for six Mercedes: "Bear with me," she kept insisting. "I'm new at this."

Finally, when she read back the ad without a flaw, the man was impressed. "You're overqualified," he said. "You must be an executive."

"I didn't say anything," Kay reports. "Then he said, 'You could even be Katharine Graham.' And I said, 'Guess what? I am.'"

A year ago, former Attorney General John Mitchell reacted to a story the *Post* was about to print with the words, "Katie Graham's gonna get her tit caught in a big, fat wringer if that's published." "Katie" showed up in the newsroom brandishing a solid-gold wringer and tit on a gold chain around her neck. When a reporter threatened to tell Maxine Cheshire, Ms. Graham dropped the gold charms back into her blouse. "If you do, you're fired."

"A dentist from California sent the wringer," explains Ms. Graham. He wanted me to have the Wringer-of-the-Year award. "He made it from the gold he used to fill teeth. It had a little handle and little gears that turned just like a washing machine. Buchwald gave me the other thing. I've still got it, but I'm not going to discuss it. I don't wear it anymore."

But friends say she wore the gold charms to her 58th birthday party given by the Osborn Elliotts in New York. They gave Ms. Graham a birthday pie with her face painted on it and a *Newsweek* banner across the pie that read "Too Good to Eat."

"We had to be very careful to cut around the edges and not through the pie," says one of the guests. "No one wanted to put the knife in." How did Kay like the pie? "She adored it. She was very touched by it. There are times that she gushes, but she couldn't say anything," says her hostess, Inge Elliott.

Katharine Graham accepts the theory of change as begrudgingly as she accepts an interview. "I think any more publicity is bad for me, bad for the children and bad for the paper."

Katharine is still tense about questions from other reporters. "First off I haven't changed any way at all," she insists, settling down behind the fortress of her leather-and-chrome desk. "I've worked for 11 years. If I hadn't gained some feeling that I know a little more than I did when I started, I'd have to have rocks in my head. I mean, I should be more secure, and I am because I've been at it for some time. But it's been a gradual process."

Is she more confident, more secure? "Look, I'm not going to go into all that stuff again. It's so counter-productive. These are all rather sexist questions. You ask them because I'm a woman and I don't think it's fair and I don't think you should be a party to it. What business is it of anybody's, anyway? I think it's outrageous. It's time that people started evaluating a job and stopped asking me personal questions.

"I suppose any experience changes you some, but this didn't change me any more than any other experience you undergo. Yes, I suppose my profile is higher, which has both advantages and disadvantages. And perhaps I'm more of a symbol to the women's movement. But that's it."

But Watergate has had its effect. "Obviously I was full of concerns and high emotions and the need to be careful to check out everything. And obviously there was great pleasure and pride in what we had done. It was a very tough and rewarding experience, especially since we were vindicated. But, although it was an extraordinary experience, it happened so gradually. There was no change in my philosophy. It just happened that our reporters got the story and we backed them because we were sure they were right.

"I don't have any new view of the press. It's a very old view — that the First Amendment gets strengthened by exercise and it has just been through an extraordinary exercise. The press role is still the same, to bring information to people — and only that. Our only power is to inform. I don't feel my role is to be a leader or to speak out on issues unrelated to the business. The only public things I take are company-related.

GRAHAM, Katharine (Meyer)

MIAMI HERALD
(Miami, Fla.)

Sept. 8, 1974

"And I don't feel any different about Watergate than any ordinary citizen would. I feel the same dismay. I don't feel any second thoughts about what we did. That would imply we had a choice. But there was no choice. It was just an unfolding story. And I don't feel maybe it would have been better that the country never knew. That would assume ignorance is better than knowledge."

Kay says her relationships with administration friends did not endure stress or change because of Watergate. She never communicated with President Nixon. But Henry Kissinger, before his marriage, was an escort and they kept going to the movies together on Saturday nights.

One difference, say friends, is that it used to be just Kay, Henry and two Secret Servicemen. Gradually the Secret Service contingent expanded until it was Henry, Kay and an entire carload.

She manages to remain very much a mother, talking to her children almost every day. "I'm amazed how often she calls us," says her 29-year-old son Donny, who will eventually control the company. She threw a wedding luncheon at home when her 26-year-old son William married in March. She still taxis to her daughter Lally's apartment when she's in New York for *Newsweek* meetings every other week to have tea with her six- and eight-year-old grandchildren.

She manages to read Solzhenitsyn in her blue-and-white canopied bed in her beige Georgetown mansion. She catches the news at night when there's time and gets to Elizabeth Arden to have her hair done and to Halston to replenish her well-stocked wardrobe. She arranges her schedule to fly to summer weekend seclusion at her new 250-acre farm in Martha's Vineyard to read, walk, talk and dine with close friends. And she gets spring-water solitude at her 350-acre Virginia farm, "Glen Welby," with tennis and superb lunches.

Only rarely, however, does she find time these days to visit Miami, where the Graham family fortunes were founded by her late father-in-law, Ernest Graham, a sugar executive who came to Florida in 1921, and stayed on to raise three sons — Phil; Bob, now a state senator in Tallahassee; and Bill, who looks after the family's local interests, including the New Town of Miami Lakes.

She still gives the best parties in town — sit-down dinners for 40 or 50 on red velvet chairs with gold frames at round tables covered with red-and-green porthault and centered with real red cabbages. "It's the most elegant and interesting table in town," says Sen. Jacob Javits. The dinners are cooked by her Greek chef with the help of three others and range from salmon to lasagna.

Her language is as salty as ever. "Goddam" is an expletive rarely deleted. Once when this reporter wrote about inner strife at the *Post,* Ms. Graham retorted: "That's a lot of crap."

Kay tells it like it is. Not long ago she looked at Barbara Howar and said, "My God, you're getting fat as a pig!" As Ben Bradlee puts it: "I've learned all my bad words from her."

One thing that has not changed is her sense of humor. She loves to laugh, and it's "a hilarious laugh," says managing editor Howard Simon. "She gives a great warwhoop to begin it. Then she doubles over."

Another constant is her self-effacement. Victory has not turned her into a snob. "Maybe an intellectual snob," says Barbara Howar. "She hates boring people. But in no other way." Just a few weeks ago, she was seen helping *Post* writer Sally Quinn clear off the dishes after a Chinese carry-out dinner.

She is humble about her accomplishments. "Have I mastered the job?" asks Katharine the Great, terminating an interview. "No one ever masters a job. I try to do the best I can. You just keep plugging away." T

Grandmotherly Graham Still Wants to Be Noticed

GRAHAM, Sheilah
(Lily Shiel)
(1908? -)

MAIMI HERALD
(Miami, Fla.)

Oct. 29, 1974

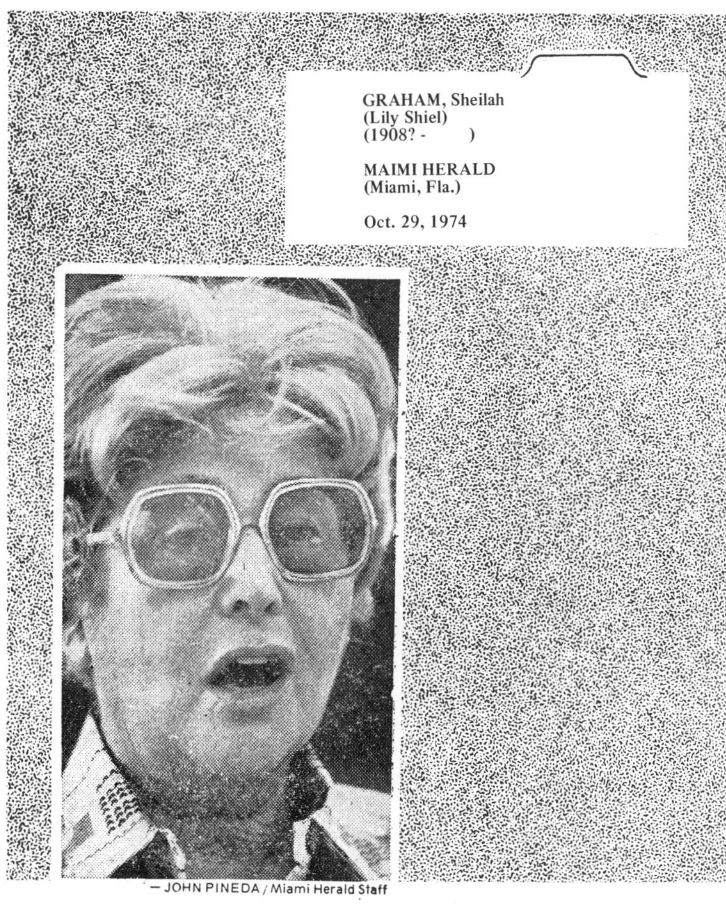

— JOHN PINEDA / Miami Herald Staff

By JANET CHUSMIR
Herald Staff Writer

Once she was both the subject of gossip and a famous Hollywood gossip columnist as well as the glamorous other woman in novelist F. Scott Fitzgerald's life.

But now three-times married and divorced Sheilah Graham is a plump grandmother who wears a print blouse over white pants to hide a thickened waist, and sunglasses to shield the glare — a retina once detached. Now she cautions the photographer about the angle. The double chin.

So that's why the words, even though still English-accented, seem a bit out of place:

"Men have been my problem. They still are. Every time I meet a young man I take stock. I wonder what he would be like as a lover; I wonder how much money he has and what it would be like married to him . . ."

But she knows she'll have to lose weight before she can begin to play the get-a-millionnaire-game.

"I love food. That's one of my passions. But I still say sex is the number one passion. I have marvelous fantasies."

Does she possibly have a motive in saying things like that?

WELL, YES, she concedes. "I've always wanted some attention. I got that from growing up in an orphanage. I wanted to be noticed."

And yes, she does "want to help the interviewer. After all I know what makes a good story."

And so it's not too surprising that when she's talking about her new book, "How To Marry Super Rich" (Grosset & Dunlap $7.95), she gets around to saying she didn't marry rich and she doesn't even have much jewelry to show for a full life. Then, pulling a felt pouch from her pocketbook, she displays an unpretentious watch with diamonds from "a millionnaire who was so stingy he had 'I like you' instead of 'I love you' engraved on the back. And an emerald-studded gold brooch from Howard Hughes "for services rendered" — helping him promote "The Outlaw"; she suspects the late Louella Parsons and Hedda Hopper got better gifts. And a string of cultured pearls from a producer, "who was after my body. He didn't get it."

When the super rich arrive in Palm Beach for the season, she thinks they'll be after her neck. Some of the characters in her book "apparently would rather forget about their past."

Not Sheilah Graham. "I've always wanted the truth."

No, not enough to reveal her age.

She and her subjects don't always agree on what's truth. Cristina Ford, wife of Ford Motor Chairman Henry Ford II, said the chapter about her in "How To Marry Super Rich" is "baloney." While Gregg Dodge Moran, widow of auto heir Horace Dodge Jr., termed her chapter "a fabrication of half truths and outright lies."

She started out as Lily Shiel in London's East End, then moved from the poverty-stricken tenement to an orphanage.

A woman who believes, "You get what you want if you really want it, but you have to be careful what you want," she made up her mind early she wanted money and fame.

SHE BECAME a sort of Ziegfeld girl in London — "The Show Biz Darling" — they called her. Then, at 18 she married a British major 25 years her senior and wrote stories now and then for the Daily Mail.

When she arrived in America she was almost engaged to the very rich Marquess of Donegall. "Best of news, darling," he telegraphed. "Mother approves." His timing wasn't too good. By then she was launched on a writing career and in love with Fitzgerald.

"When Scott Fitzgerald asked me how many lovers I had before him, I said eight. I thought that was a nice round number."

At first, she says, he was shocked. "But he accepted me as I was." And he educated her. And made her Kathleen in his unfinished novel, "The Last Tycoon."

"Beloved Infidel" was her book on the three-year affair with Fitzgerald who died in her arms. Deborah Kerr played her in the movie, "which made me seem as pure as the driven snow." As Sheilah will be the first to tell you, she wasn't. "I was a human being. Sex is a natural thing."

Fitzgerald was an alcoholic; his wife Zelda, was in an asylum. "The two things I was always afraid of were people who got terribly drunk and madness. In this package I had both."

Zelda never knew of their relationship, she says. "We were very careful." Fitzgerald had some guilt, but she had none.

"Why should I? Poor lady, I never saw her. Why should he be celebate when she'd been in an institution since 1930 and I met him in 1937?"

He died poor, but there is "an enormous amount of money now. I see it zinging past my fascinated nose," (to his daughter), she says.

And then Sheilah Graham, who describes herself as a "very private person" who led a public life because that was the best way she knew to make money, confides how she "loathes" interviews. It's only to promote the book.

"My children roar at the stories about me. I'm happiest when I'm with my children. Most of all when I'm with my grandchildren. I like being in a cocoon."

At the end, as she picks up her purse and straightens her blouse, she announces that she always expects "to be murdered in an interview."

Reporters, she explains, think they're more clever than she, so they're jealous that she's done so well.

"I'm always called a bitch."

"It was my honesty in Hollywood and Palm Beach that earned me that reputation.

"You have to decide whether I'm a complete phoney or telling the truth."

Well, which does she think?

"I wish I knew. Sometimes I'm a phoney. Sometimes I'm telling the truth."

But it really doesn't matter. Because as Sheilah Graham puts it, "The worse you are to me, the more it will sell the book."

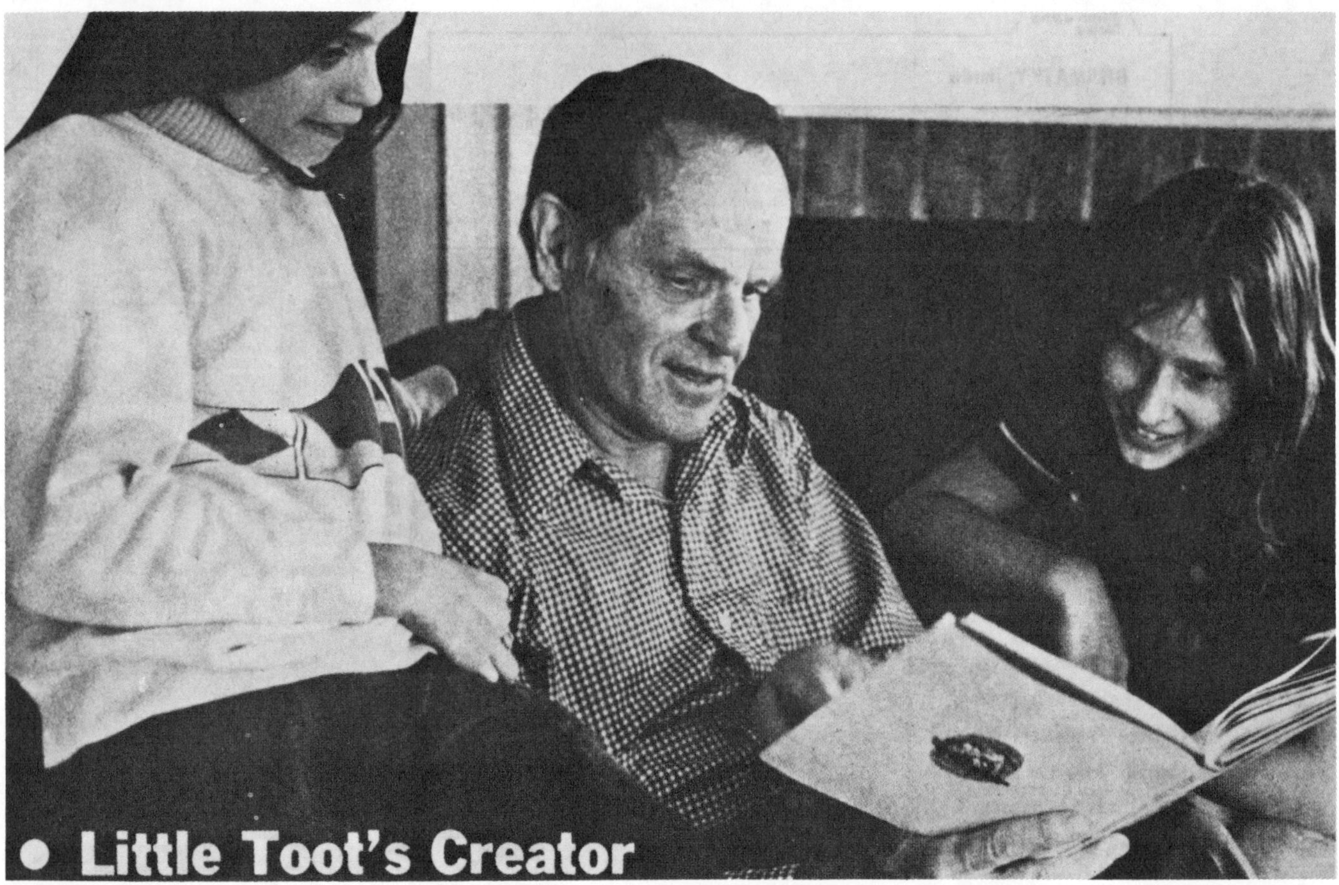

• **Little Toot's Creator**

Little Toot (right) was drawn especially for Sunday, The Hartford Courant magazine, by Hardie Gramatky. Pictured with the author-artist are 11-year-old visitors Jane MacIntyre and Renee Coppotelli, who were happy to see another Gramatky book. The photo is by John Long of The Courant, who did all The Courant camera work for this article.

by EDITH LYNN HORNIK for The Courant

When the Pequot library in Southport was raising money for a new children's wing they invited Hardie Gramatky, author of the *Little Toot* children books, to come and talk. Gramatky answered them, "You know I only give talks for children." The library promptly answered him back. "That's OK. You talked here 25 years ago. These are the same children grown up now."

Hardie Gramatky couldn't deny it for there is hardly a library, a book fair or a children's group in Connecticut where he has not talked since he moved 28 years ago with his wife, the former Dorothea Cooke, from California to Westport.

Gramatky's books for children, especially the *Little Toot* series — the stories about a little tugboat that has adventures all over the world — take him away from Connecticut often on research trips. Gramatky believes firmly that while a story should be imaginative, the geographical and technical background should be authentic. His latest, *Little Toot on the Mississippi,* took him to colorful New Orleans. *Little Toot on the Thames* to England; *Little Toot on the Grand Canal* to Venice; But many of his books — quite unknown to the public — were researched right here in Connecticut.

GRAMATKY, Hardie
(1907 -)

HARTFORD COURANT
(Hartford, Conn.)

Dec. 9, 1973

[See also CA-2]

Homer and the Circus Train, the story of a caboose who sees life and traffic signs backwards due to his position in life, was researched in the New Haven Railroad yard. Gramatky went to the yard not only to study cabooses but he had to make sure that if a caboose could see that he would really see things backwards. *Sparky,* the story of a trolley, is reminiscent of the one that used to run down Main Street in Westport.

Creeper's Jeep (World's Work, London, 1948) was the first book Hardie Gramatky wrote when he moved to Connecticut. His neighbors across the way were onion farmers who told Gramatky the story of how years ago a fire broke out next to their barn. Wanting to save the barn they hitched this huge building onto an ordinary car and pulled it, animals and all to the edge of their property where it sits to this day. In the children's book the story was embellished to include a "lazy" son whose jeep is not acceptable to his old fashioned parents until the jeep proves its worth by pulling the barn to safety during the fire. If one drives to Gramatky's home today one can almost follow the instructions on the first page of *Creeper's Jeep.*

"Five miles from the town (Westport) on road A99 (changed from the Post Road), a side turns off to the Perkin's farm."

The book includes the old Westport fair which used to be known as the "Yankee Doodle Fair" where all the local artists like Gramatky used to give of their time to do for $5 portraits of any individual who wanted to be immortalized. The money went to the local charities.

When Gramatky is not lecturing or researching his books, the actual labor of writing and drawing the illustrations are done in his old Connecticut farm house which sits comfortably on 2 acres of tree-covered fields. On the top floor of this house is an old fashioned bedroom with "running water". It is here that Hardie Gramatky paints and writes.

GRAMATKY, Hardie

HARTFORD COURANT
(Hartford, Conn.)

Dec. 9, 1973

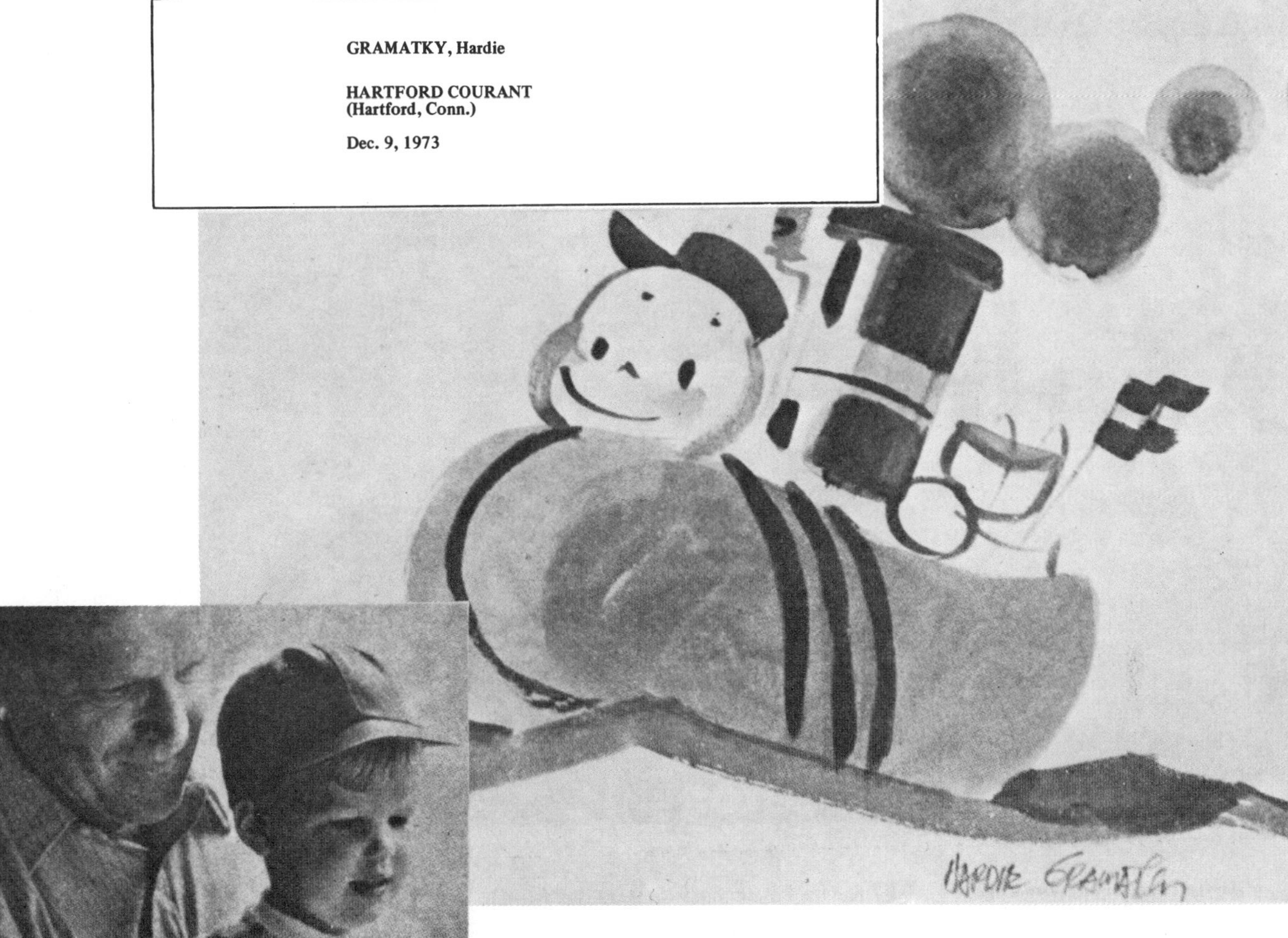

Gramatky and grandson.

(Continued from preceding page)

Hardie Gramatky leaves his bucolic haven often, because he feels it is important for him to keep in touch with the children while he writes. Gramatky, a father and a grandfather himself, tells:

"Children are not only my audience but my best inspiration. When I did my book, *Homer and the Circus*, I couldn't think of a name for the caboose which would appeal to youngsters. As it happened I was talking at a book fair in Hartford sponsored by the Hartford library. One youngster addressed me as 'hey, Homar' and I had the name I was looking for."

Because of that anonymous little boy, the Hartford library is today one of the proud possessors of one of the original illustrations for that book.

Children touch Gramatky to the point where he will change his story to suit them. In *Little Toot on the Grand Canal* the posts where the gondolas are tied up are made of candy canes. Little Toot would like one but no one offers him one. Gramatky was going to let the story end as such. Gramatky was telling this story to a group of children in Connecticut just prior to publication. When these children heard that Little Toot was not going to get the candy cane, they showed such sadness, that Gramatky ran right then and there to the pay phone and told his publisher to stop the presses as another page would have to be added.

When Gramatky first started his career he spent six years as chief animator at Walt Disney studios. He has also done water color illustrations for Fortune magazine as well as for the U.S. Air Force. But when it comes to doing children books, Gramatky has a veritable mission, a mission that has made him primarily an author of children's books: to get children to read. He hopes that through his books children will realize what words can do, and he hopes that the illustrations that go with these words will extend their imagination to the fullest.

Perhaps Gramatky feels this way because he always loved to read as a youngster, and, because it was a teacher in his high school who had the inspiration to launch him on his successful career.

Gramatky, who was born in Texas, lost his father at an early age, and his mother had to struggle to make ends meet. It was this struggle that brought the family to California. Gramatky did not know if there would be enough money for him to finish high school. It was in California that a teacher suggested to him that he show his art work to the Los Angeles Times. The Times promptly hired him to do, on a permanent basis, his Captain Kidd Jr. comic strip and bought some of his cartoons. He now had not only enough to finish high school but enough to go on to college.

Gramatky flies all over the nation to talk to groups of teachers, and to teachers' colleges to convince them of the importance of reaching a child. What good is talent if you cannot read? Gramatky is also consultant to the correspondence school, the Institute of Children Literature in Redding.

When Gramatky talks to pre-readers he "reaches" them by asking them if they like to draw. All children like to draw. Then out come chalk, crayons, paints and he tells the children, "We are all artists together." They now have something in common: a means of communication. Can words and reading be far away? And, when Gramatky is with children, can the inspiration for his next book be far away? □

Edith Lynn Hornik is a freelance writer in Scarsdale, N.Y.

'The Secret Is to Remain A Man Among the Wolves'

By MARCI SHATZMAN

Of The Bulletin Staff

FOR A MAN who has already led four lives, Martin Gray looked remarkably young at 48.

"That's what people tell me." He smiled as he extended his left hand.

"Sorry," he said. "I was in an automobile accident recently and I'm still partially paralyzed on my right side."

He spoke with all the nonchalance of a man mentioning what he just had for lunch. But then Gray already knows death. He has laughed in its face.

The American named Gray was born in Warsaw just in time to learn what Nazi meant first hand. For years he dodged his captors, operating as a smuggler to keep his family alive. And he rode with them on the cattle cars to Treblinka and the gas chambers. But not before seeing his father shot down in the Warsaw ghetto uprising. And not before loosing an eye in a scuffle with a Nazi rifle butt.

Lifetime of Nightmares

For his family Treblinka was the end. But Gray came back, escaping death but not a lifetime of nightmares.

He had worked in the camp loading the bodies of thousands into mass graves. He got out by hiding in a latrine and hopping a train filled with the clothing of the Third Reich's extermination victims.

Gray was then 19. He joined the Russian Army under an alias to fight back at what he calls 'The Butchers.' And surviving the war, he migrated to New York to live with his grandmother, his only relative. By the time he was 35 he had made a fortune importing antiques from Europe. He retired to the south of France with his wife, a beautiful Dutch girl. They had four children.

On Oct. 3, 1970, a forest fire raged through the Gray estate. His entire family perished.

And Gray, saved by his friends from a suicide attempt, was persuaded to write his life story.

"For Those I Loved," has made him a celebrity in Europe where it has sold millions since its publication in 1971. Until recently, all of the proceeds went to the Dina Gray Foundation named for Gray's late wife.

The organization, which has children plant trees to encourage their respect of forests and thus prevent forest fires, is now subsidized by the French government. Gray is trying to spread the idea all over the world.

Martin Gray is tall, well-dressed, and carries himself like a man afraid of nothing and no one.

Over a steak lunch (he abandoned a vegetarian diet because of an ulcer), he talked

Photo by William Owens, of The Bulletin

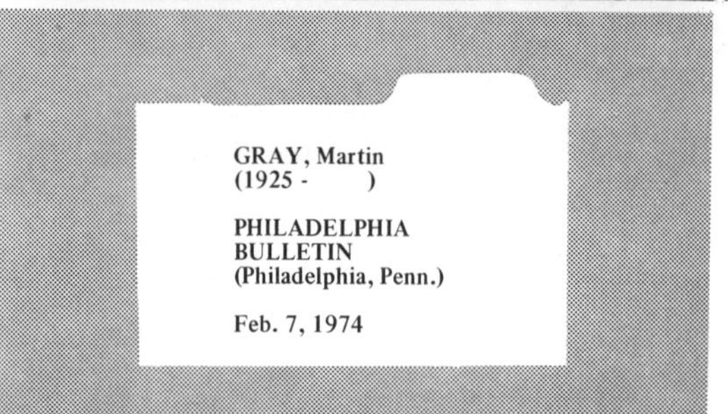

GRAY, Martin
(1925 -)

PHILADELPHIA BULLETIN
(Philadelphia, Penn.)

Feb. 7, 1974

'I Had to Survive'

about his favorite subject—life.

"During the war I knew I had to survive," he said in what is still a strong Polish accent. "It was not so much my life that was precious, but life itself.

"That is what my father told me, and I understood.

"I remember, before my father was shot, he told me, 'Today we must kill. But remember life. Life is precious and you must give it.'

"I think this is the secret," he said softly, looking down at his plate. "I try to live by those words."

"There is some of the beast and some of the man in all of us," he said. "The secret is to remain a man among the wolves."

Gray speaks of his own life in terms of "before my tragedy," and "after my tragedy."

He said the loss of his family three years ago threw him into an emotional abyss.

"It was the second blow, the hardest. It brought everything back—the ghetto, the war, my parents, Treblinka. My children carried the names of my parents and my brothers . . . .

"Afterward I asked myself, what for to live?"

"In a way, the book has helped me to survive those difficult moments," he said. "It was painful. But stones would come out of my heart."

Difficult Moments

Gray said he's glad he was persuaded to write. A European company is now planning to star Malcolm McDowell in the movie version. Gray turned down an offer by Hollywood, fearing the film would be trashy, exploitive.

"I have shown to the world who the six million were," he said. "Not just a statistical number. But people, each one who had a face, a home, a heart and feelings."

"I have been criticized for mentioning the Germans who helped me," he said. "But I cannot condemn a whole nation, a whole race. If we're going to do the same thing, what is the difference between them and us?"

Home Raided

Despite his apparent success and the peace Gray says he has found within himself, tragedy still stalks him.

When a European newspaper ran a photograph of him in the hospital during his recent accident, thieves raided his home. They took everything, including all mementos of his wife and children.

And although he has remarried, a woman half his age, he recently learned she could not have Children. Children have always meant a lot to him.

"There is no greater joy than to guide another's life," he said. "To have children means you will never die, that life will never die."

"We may adopt, I don't know," he said, his voice trailing off.

He stared silently at his scarred hands for a moment. And then he smiled.

His glass eye followed the penetrating look of the one that remained.

"They did nothing to this eye," he said. "It was never attached to the muscle."

Then how does it move, Gray was asked.

His laughter was so infectious, several nearby turned around.

"Because it lives!" he grinned.

Just like the remarkable Martin Gray.

'Butley' To End Season

GRAY, Simon
(1936-)

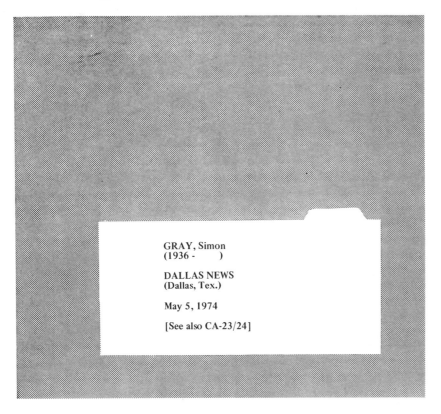

DALLAS NEWS
(Dallas, Tex.)

May 5, 1974

[See also CA-23/24]

By FRANCIS RAFFETTO

Playwright Simon Gray of London is the unusual man who, a teacher, "always assumed I would be a writer" and has never written an unsuccessful play.

"'Butley' (the American Film Theater play-become-movie which ends AFT's first season Monday and Tuesday) has made more money for me than anything I've done," he said in an interview in New York. "I may never make any money again. But I haven't written for the trashbin—everything I've written up to now has been performed."

Gray, a tall fortyish handsome man, said he did once stand in the foyer and try to talk friends and relatives out of seeing a play. He had written it but was not proud of it.

No danger about "Butley's' 'success, however. As a play in London, it was the "best play of the season" in 1971 with actor Alan Bates, the star, winning best actor honors. The next year, Bates repeated his personal success in New York, winning the Antoinette Perry "Tony" Award.

For the AFT movie "Butley," Bates repeats his strong role, as does Richard O'Callaghan as Joey. Fine actress Jessica Tandy was lured back to England from America to play Edna Shaft, a fellow teacher.

FOR GRAY, the teacher-author, who still teaches school by the way, has written about Ben Butley (Bates), a teacher, whose personal life structure seems to collapse during the period of one day.

Butley is a teacher of English in a London university and evidently bent on self destruction. His estranged wife asks for a divorce so she may marry another, his protege and homosexual partner, (O'Callaghan) tires of his cruel wit and incessant badgering and is leaving for another man, and Miss Tandy, the teacher whom he has ridiculed in the past, is having her book published— something that Butley himself never got around to accomplishing.

The play has been termed a tragicomedy, although one is hard put to discover much humour in such an unsavory theme and characters.

AUTHOR GRAY, born in south England in 1936, was educated at Cambridge and now teaches English literature at Queen Mary College, London University.

"If 'Butley' is successful, I hope it is as a liberating experience," he told the writer in New York before the AFT premiere. "You are asked to share a man and his crises Every writer is properly a politician if he can show people that you share someone else's life. If the audience can feel compassion, they may feel differently about the next different person they see on the street."

Directing the AFT's "Butley" is Harold Pinter, the playwright whose own work, "The Homecoming," was an earlier offering this season.

DID PINTER treat Gray's play kindly? Did the movie reflect the play? "Impeccably," answered Gray with enthusiasm.

"Pinter and I worked together on the stage play three years ago. He directed the play, also. He is a totally rational director. Frequently, the roles of author and director seemed to be reversed. I wanted to cut some lines and he objected." Helping the situation was the fact that Gray adapted his own play for the screen.

One of the problems with "Butley" (Gray called it a "weakness" in the play) is, said Gray, "if you have a charismatic actor playing Butley, no one will look at Joey (weak protege of Butley who seeks better romantic pastures)."

"And Richard O'Callaghan's performance as Joey is wonderful. But on film we could control this. We showed them Joey when we wanted to."

One slight difficulty was correcting Miss Tandy's English accent. Her long professional stay in the United States had corrupted her mother tongue. "She had to correct it," stated Gray.

THE ENGLISH playwright views with alarm the Broadway theater situation, with its limited number of theaters compared with London's. "It's appalling," said Gray. "In this state of affairs in New York, you have only hits or disasters and the disasters immediately die. In London, you can have a disaster running for four years."

After "Butley," he doesn't want to write ever for the screen only. "I couldn't bear to have to write in a more marketable scene to please a producer, or suffer with actors who were not permitted by the director to deliver the lines the way I wrote them.

"And I doubt if I would ever find another director as scrupulous as Harold Pinter has been with 'Butley.' This experience has spoiled me for other films."

GRAY THINKS that most plays "are John Wayne and sunsets. And I like them. But as a writer I don't have to write it. Hopefully I will write toward 'Hamlet.'"

"Butley" will play Monday and Tuesday in the following theaters: Casa Linda, Chateau (Irving) Preston Royal, Promenade, Ridgewood and Wynnewood.

Non-writer became man of letters in spite of himself

By Leon Hale

In 1967 the book editor of The Post handed me a sharp-looking volume entitled "Horse Tradin' " and asked if I'd like to review it.

I took it because it was written by a Texan named Ben K. Green. I'd never heard of him but I'll take almost any book written by a Texan and published in New York, so long as it's free. You understand the reviewer gets to keep the book after he reviews it.

This is why newspaper reporters will sometimes have fairly impressive personal libraries, causing visitors to wonder where the money came from to buy all those books. Oh, I don't mean there aren't reporters who'll spead money for books. I've known two or three.

I figured this Ben Green was another of the non-writers who had worried a book out of himself. The initials D.V.M. followed his name. A veterinarian. Some old boy, I guessed, been doctoring horses all his life and getting close to quitting time and he'd felt obliged to satisfy the hankering so many of us have — to write a book about the things we've done and seen and heard.

World's full of books like that. Most are vanity jobs that the writers had to pay to have published. Titles like "My 24 Years of Country Lawyering" and stuff like that. They don't ever sell.

One of the reasons I took the "Horse Tradin' " book, it was published by Alfred A. Knopf and it had a heck of a fine dust jacket design. Had a horse-with-man sketch by Lorence Bjorklund, and a big photo of Ben Green sporting a week's stubble. Not a planned beard. He just hadn't shaved. I figured a guy who wouldn't shave to have a picture taken for the dust jacket on his own book ought to be worth knowing. Might look him up, even if I never read his book.

But Alfred Knopf hasn't got a habit of publishing junk, so I let the horse book lay around where I could admire the jacket for a couple of weeks and finally I got into it.

I didn't quit until I finished. Because it was the freshest breeze that had drifted across the Texas literary scene in a great long while. I breathed it all in and just laughed out loud, I was that rewarded.

And I thought, well, if this horse doctor is a non-writer he's got the best re-write man in New York City, because all those horse-swapping tales come drawling off the pages like they're being spoken by some old trader that lives at — well, at Cumby, Texas, up close to Sulphur Springs in Hopkins County, Ben Green's home town. Writing it and making it talk, that's not easy.

As a sometimes reviewer I've been guilty of getting enthusiastic about a book that nobody else likes or will buy, but everybody loved "Horse Tradin' " and even people who don't know which way is south about horses read it and Ben K. Green's name got spread around the country pretty good. He must have been 55 then, maybe 56.

Then he did another book called "Wild Cow Tales" and blamed if it wasn't better than the first one. I expect by this time those Knopf folks up there in New York had started talking real sweet to old Ben.

The TLE — Texas Literary Establishment (names and organizations on request) — was a trifle slow about accepting Ben Green. Do you expect it was because he didn't shave and all? Seemed sort of rough? Then there were things in Green's background that people talked about, which I bet pleased him because if you're gonna sell books you need to be talked about.

But finally he got all the decorations. Year before last in the Rice Hotel, he was at the head table at the Texas Institute of Letters annual meeting. He stood up in his brown suit and his boots — he still didn't look shaved real good to me but I guess he was — he stood up there surrounded by lacy shirts poking out of tuxedo jackets and he received a special award from the Institute. For his contribution to Texas letters.

By then he was a name. He'd done "The Village Horse Doctor" and he'd done "More Horse Tradin' " and he was a blinking successful writer.

But he never called himself one. Remember one night I was in Austin, at that annual Writers Roundup to-do they have there, to honor just about anybody in the state that manages to finish a book during the year.

So many Texas book writers were present you could have split 'em up and played soccer. They were all parading glumly to the rostrum, to talk about the awful strain of being creative enough to write books.

Then here came old Ben. In that same brown suit, looked to me like. He said he wasn't a writer and he sure was glad because it sounded so blamed hard. (And not a one of the other writers had done as many successful books as Ben Green.) He said he never did write anything, he just talked it. Said he had this sweet-smellin', good-spellin' secretary to take down what he remembered about his horse swapping and ranching and animal doctoring and trail driving, and all he did was just tell the truth and the secretary straighted up the sentences and put in the paragraphs and the periods, so doing a book wasn't anything but a pleasure.

The last time I saw him in Houston I threatened to go up to Cumby to see him, check him out on his home ground. "You come on," he said, "but you better phone first to see if I'm there. The books are selling good and they've got me on the road a lot."

I never did go. I thought about it three or four times and then here the other day I spotted this little two-paragraph AP item in the paper. Ben Green, Texas author, dead of a heart attack at 63.

Whether Green was really a graduate veterinarian or not doesn't make an ounce of difference to me. Whether he told fibs in his books and passed them off as truth, that doesn't matter either. Lot of people accused him of dressing up his game with details that didn't quite happen. I've even accused him myself, in reviews. How could a professional horse swapper stick entirely to fact? Ridiculous.

I am just thankful he passed our way, and did all the talking to that sweet-smellin' secretary. In only eight years, he left four fine books on my desk. They have yielded much pleasure, and taught me things I didn't know.

Anyhow Ben K. Green is gone. I thought maybe you hadn't heard about it.

GREEN, Ben K.
(1911? - 1974)

HOUSTON POST
(Houston, Tex.)

Nov. 3, 1974

Ad Lib

By ROBERT DOWNING,

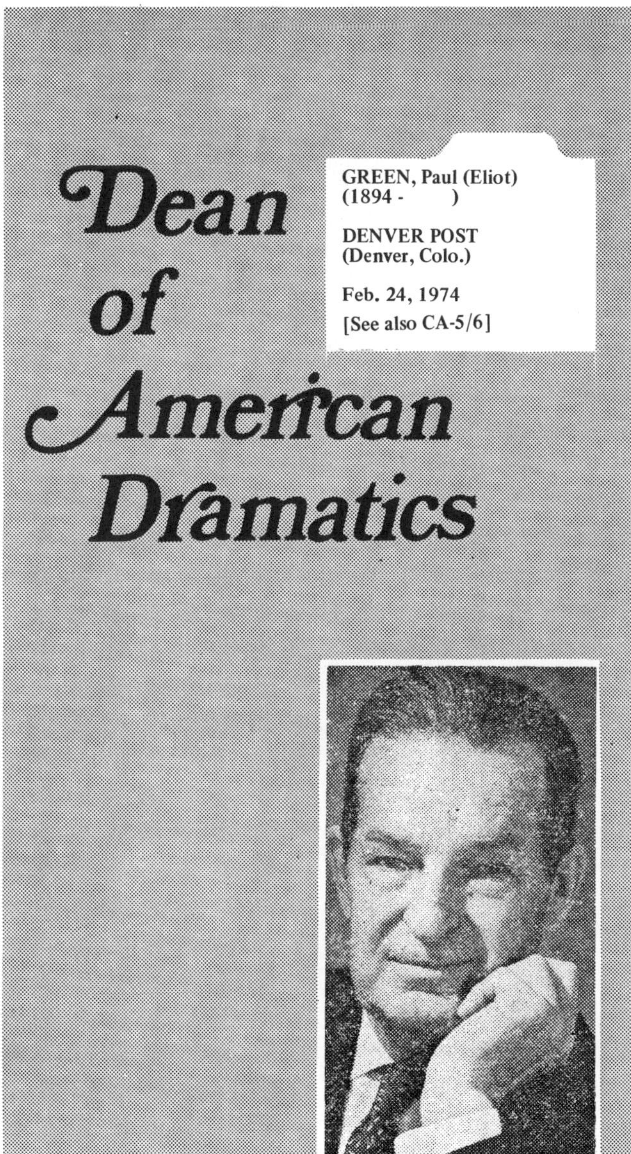

GREEN, Paul (Eliot)
(1894 -)
DENVER POST
(Denver, Colo.)
Feb. 24, 1974
[See also CA-5/6]

PAUL GREEN

CHAPEL HILL, N.C. — Paul Green at 80 is the dean of American dramatics. It's doubtful that Green spends much time contemplating such a distinction. He's too busy being a playwright.

Sitting in his comfortable study in his comfortable white farmhouse near this relaxed and easy-going Southern university town, Green is willing to take a few minutes off from writing his new play to think about the creative life of America.

"The real glory of a nation is in its arts," Green says. It should be noted that this exceptional writer often speaks like a character in one of his many inspirational productions.

GREEN WON the Pulitzer Prize in 1927 for his Broadway hit, "In Abraham's Bosom." Two years earlier he had won the David Belasco cup for his play, "The No 'Count Boy." Green was a folk dramatist then. He still is. "Johnny Johnson" and "The House of Connelly," in spite of being produced in New York, harked back to the Southern land that Green knew and loved—that he still knows and loves.

A number of years ago, Green became interested in writing dramas that could be played out doors—under the stars and close to the land. This has led him, in recent years, to concentrate on such celebrated al fresco productions as "The Lost Colony" (1937), "The Common Glory," "Wilderness Road," "Cross and Sword," "Texas," "Trumpet in the Land" and "Drumbeats in Georgia," among many plays on historical subjects. All his plays are seen annually.

Currently, Green is working on a script for presentation in Louisiana.

"It's called 'The Cavalier,' " the author says, "And it's about early French and Spanish colonies near Saint Denis. You see—there's this free-thinker who falls in love with the Governor's daughter . . ."

GREEN RISES to illustrate a sense from his plot. He is a tall, craggy man. His movements belie his years. He looks like one of the leading characters in one of his own pioneer tales.

It's easy to look at this lively senior citizen and to recall that he was a farm boy in his native North Carolina. Green strides as if there were still fresh-plowed land under his feet. His eyes rest on the middle distance. He sees the dreams many Americans see. The difference is, Green touches the dreams with life.

"You know," he says, "The motion-picture camera is the greatest technical achievement of the age."

If one talks of Green—which means listening to Green talk—one becomes accustomed to following his nonsequiturs. In the long run, these quick changes of thought illuminate a mind filled with darting, useful ideas. There is nothing garrulous about Green. He talks a lot. But he always talks about something. Which makes him different from many men of his age—or, for the fact, much younger.

"You're from Denver," he observes, squinting at the writer. "I was play doctor on a Warner Bros. movie about Haw Tabor and Baby Doe. It was called 'Silver Dollar.' Aline MacMahon played the part of Augusta Tabor. I think it was a good movie."

GREEN WORKED on many films. He wrote dialogue for such stars as Bette Davis, George Arliss, Will Rogers, Lionel Barrymore, Gary Cooper, Clark Gable, Judy Garland and Greer Garson.

"Once I did a script for Sam Goldwyn,'' Green chuckles. "The first scene was in a beautiful cathedral—organ music—the works. There was a funeral going on. "You can't start a picture with a funeral!' Sam yelled at me. So I changed it."

In "Voltaire," the script he wrote for Arliss, Green is pleased to recall that he "snuck" the boy Mozart into the opening scene. "Playing the piano, of course," he grins. "We had all-star casts in those days.!"

Green, the greatest living tourist attraction in the country, like everyone else in tourism, worries about the coming season.

"IT COSTS about $500,000 to mount an outdoor show," he reports. "Here I am, worrying about better technical solutions for some of our theatres, trying to get directors to use light like music to help delineate characters—and what I really have to think about is gasoline for people to get to us. What good is a show without an audience?"

Green admits to memories of a lonely childhood. Often, he says, he was frightened by spectres of God and the devil. In most of his plays, there is a strong streak of fundamentalist religion underlying his writing—although he might refute this strongly. Many have said that if he hadn't become a playwright with a message, he would have made a fine preacher. Green would squirm at such talk.

But he believes in ideals. Especially in democracy. And this theme, too, dominates his work. "The idea is nothing without the idealist," he is said to have said. Then he puts on an expression that would have delighted Osawatomie John Brown, and he intones another thought: "Bring on the jubilation—even if mixed with tears!"

Laughter and tears, faith and character. These are the equal ingredients Paul Green stirs into his dramas of the bright land he sees so clearly and loves so deeply.

Richard Green

RICHARD GREEN

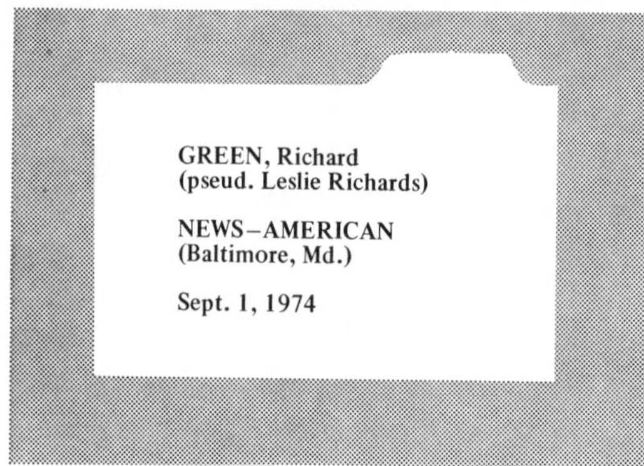

GREEN, Richard
(pseud. Leslie Richards)

NEWS–AMERICAN
(Baltimore, Md.)

Sept. 1, 1974

Isn't Baltimore an unlikely setting for a romantic mystery, a tale of espionage and pursuit?

Richard Green doesn't think so. His soon-to-be published paperback novel is set in an old apartment house which stood near Charles Street and University Parkway, a mansion on the Eastern Shore and a Green Spring Valley horse farm.

Written under the pen name, Leslie Richards, "Pursue the Devil" is Green's first novel. An insurance auditor by day, he was published in a number of "little" magazines during the early 60s, then drifted out of writing until two years ago.

"At that point," he says, "I decided I would try three books, and if none of them sold I would give up."

"Pursue the Devil" is a formula novel, Green admits, insofar as all mystery fiction is formulized. What makes one better than another, he believes, is the characterization.

His favorite character in "Pursue the Devil" is the elderly actress who owns the horse farm. She is patterned after a woman he used to see in the lobby of the Lyric Theater although he never spoke to her or learned her name. The rest of the novel is fictitious except for the apartment building.

"That really did exist," says Green, "but its tenants weren't the wild people in the book." As a matter of fact, he once lived in the building.

Green aimed his novel at the market for original paperbacks as opposed to the one that reprints best-sellers. This decision imposed its own set of limitations. Something had to happen in each chapter, the chapters had to be short and the book had to be of a certain length.

He set a goal of 250 pages and ended up with a total of 236.

After he finished the manuscript, he sent it to an agent in New York, who had promised only to read. She liked it and sent it out to publishers. After several "almost" acceptances (two publishers rejected it only because the action shifted from the mansion in Easton) Manor Books bought "Pursue the Devil" and at the same time suggested that Green write another novel.

His first draft of No. 2 is already out of the typewriter — this one a Gothic story with "Pale Ghost at Grave's End" as its working title.

Is he tempted to pursue writing as a career?

"Success the first time is very satisfying," Green says, "and it does make getting the second book before the publisher somewhat easier, but that doesn't guarantee a thing. Besides, it would be too much of a chore. As it is, writing is relaxing for me, and I like it that way."

Feminist defends right to life

GREER, Germaine

TULSA TRIBUNE (Tulsa, Okla.)

Nov. 13, 1974

By JOY HART
Of The Tribune Women's Staff

GERMAINE GREER, British feminist and advocate of the right to abortion, talked about the right to life in Tulsa Tuesday.

"When we talk about population control, we are, we hope, talking about free choice," she told an audience at the University of Tulsa.

Abortion or birth control or even infanticide are nothing new, she stressed, describing an island in the Pacific where women have aborted themselves for centuries.

When a woman who has decided she has had enough children becomes pregnant, she waits until three months before birth is expected. Then, she lies down on the ground and puts a plank over her belly.

Two women jump on the plank, and the woman aborts.

"A WOMAN living on that small Pacific island knows how many people can live on her island," Miss Greer said. "The woman risks her life so the life of the community will not be demeaned."

That woman, she added, is willing to accept an immense moral responsibility.

But the damage is that the developed countries of the world will become so fearful of overpopulation they will force women to use birth control.

"When people wish to, they will take care of the problem themselves," she insisted. "And they do so."

On a recent trip Miss Greer said she met a woman who lives in a small village in Iran. She is 32 years old; she has been married 18 years; and she has six children.

"Why do you have so many children?" Miss Greer asked.

But as soon as she asked the question, she realized it was wrong. The proper question should have been why do you have so few.

"In many of the countries we are talking about, children are the only joy" she added. "Children are welcome — much more welcome than in ours."

Still, the assumption that life is cheap in some countries, that women in some underdeveloped countries have baby after baby, is wrong, she said.

"We assume these people have no feelings, that they have no organization for controlling their lives."

But they do, Miss Greer insisted. And "we should buttress their ways."

The long term solution is to bring modern medical knowledge to the village, she said. "Go to the midwife, and ask her what she needs to do her job. Treat her as a wise person with some dignity."

ALSO IMPORTANT is giving women status so they will have other ways to be creative and productive besides having children, she noted.

In August, at the United Nations World Population Conference in Bucharest, Miss Greer told a reporter that women were being regarded "as baby factories, the only difference from other factories being that they are being asked to cease production."

To have children or not to have them is a moral choice, Miss Greer told her student audience at TU. And the right to exercise that choice may be in danger.

"We must be vigilant," she said. "We must not allow our actions to be guided by fear."

Dr. Greer, who earned her Ph.D. in Shakespeare at Cambridge University, quoted from that author and a number of other literary sources in her speech. Plato, she said, wrote that moral action is the result of free choice.

For example, she said, recently at Johns Hopkins Hospital in Baltimore, a nurse gave birth to a mongoloid child. The baby also had an intestinal blockage.

"If the child is to live, we must operate," the doctor told the parents.

The parents decided against giving permission for the operation.

The child was put in a crib in a corner of the hospital nursery, where it died 15 days later.

"No crime was committed," Miss Greer said. "The laws had been observed."

But, she added, in the Middle Ages the greatest of the seven sins was apathy, the sin of the small hearted.

"That was the sin committed by almost everyone at Johns Hopkins," she continued.

No one felt an individual responsibility to help the infant. No one, on the other hand, felt enough compassion to end its agony.

"They simply did nothing."

And by doing nothing, they gave up their right to make a moral decision, Miss Greer emphasized.

"Perhaps, morality was once a matter of following rules," she added. "I doubt it. But we can no longer expect our minds to be made up by following rules."

Neither can we impose our moral rules on others, she said.

She recalled a magazine article she read recently which stated many women will have to be forced to accept the goals of the women's movement if the world's population is to be controlled.

"I can think of no distortion more insidious, more hideous," she said. "Women will be 'ripped off' in the name of a new tyranny — population control as the new fascism."

MISS GREER ALWAYS has been a proponent of individual rights. In 1970 she wrote in "The Female Eunuch," "The first exercise of the free woman is to devise her own mode of revolt, a mode which will reflect her own independence and originality."

She was quoted in 1971 as saying, "Bras are a ludicrous invention; but if you make bralessness a rule, you're just subjecting yourself to yet another repression."

At the press conference Tuesday one reporter asked her what are the final goals of the women's movement.

"What makes you think it's my final goal," she replied emphatically. "You think I'm Hitler sitting here.

"Whatever the goals are, they are not mine."

Her own idea? She said she would like for women to be able to find a purpose in their lives — a purpose that is not having children.

The women's movement has made progress, she said.

"There's no question about it. We're moving, but how to quantify it, I don't know.

"I think you can follow it in strange ways in odd places."

For example, she said the media has made changes. "We can't continue to watch 'I Love Lucy' until we die. There must be more to life than old recipes."

Women today, she indicated, expect more.

In her book Miss Greer says any struggle which is not joyous is the wrong struggle. Has her own battle for women's rights been joyous?

"I'm much happier now," she answered. "Most of the time I feel tired, but I sleep well. . . . Very often I feel very angry. That it's happening miles too late."

She feels a sense of purpose, and insists that is happiness. "Some American women smile continuously, but it doesn't mean they're happy."

Griffin ranges from Merton to musicology

Staff Photo by Shirley Williams

GRIFFIN, John Howard (1920-)

COURIER–JOURNAL & TIMES (Louisville, Ken.)

Feb. 11, 1973

[See also CA-2]

By SHIRLEY WILLIAMS
Courier-Journal & Times Book Editor

"I WAS TYPING up in the Hermitage and suddenly on this very, very hot day, July 4th, something hit the roof and startled me. And then a bolt of lightning hit the transformer and came in through the keys of my typewriter and electrocuted me in the sense that it knocked me unconscious. What saved me was that I was in a wheelchair with rubber tires on it or I would have been incinerated."

That is John Howard Griffin describing his accidental near-electrocution in Thomas Merton's old quarters at Gethsemani Abbey, near Bardstown, Ky., while he was working on Merton's official biography there two years ago. Another parallel in the many that connect his life and Merton's.

Thomas Merton (Father M. Louis) died in Thailand in 1968. "When I began work on the Merton biography," Griffin explains, "there was a great deal of speculation that perhaps he hadn't died the way it appeared. He was electrocuted, but the Thai government, because of this kind of thing being shameful, tried to issue it as a heart attack." At the time of the accident, Merton "bellowed in a loud uncontrollable way. The men upstairs came down to see what was wrong, and there was silence. They so respected his privacy that they didn't look into the room. They could probably have saved him at that point if they had." (Merton had gone to Bangkok to study Oriental religions. He was accidentally electrocuted when he touched the exposed cord of an electric fan while staying in a monastery there.)

After Griffin's own accident, he recalls, "The brothers down at the Abbey came up and I had lost my memory and my mind was absolutely scrambled. But the one thing that I could remember was, for a fraction of a second, being utterly astounded by the bellowing that issued forth from me. When I got some memory back my first reaction was 'He (Merton) was electrocuted.'" After Griffin's memory returned, "the Father Abbot came in just beaming with relief and joy and he said 'This is the way you always do things. This was God's way of letting you live the experience of Father Louis's death,' and my first reaction, I blurted out, 'Well, if that's the truth then, by golly, get someone else to write the funeral!'"

A BEST-SELLING AUTHOR, civil-rights activist, photographer, musicologist, farmer and now biographer, John Howard Griffin is truly a man for all seasons. He was in Louisville last month on the Bellarmine College campus, under the sponsorship of the Thomas Merton Studies Center, to lecture on Thomas Merton, racism and creative writing. He also spoke to high-school groups and lectured twice at the Southern Baptist Theological Seminary.

A gentle, compassionate man, soft-spoken, direct and courteous, Griffin has the ability to make each person who talks with him feel he or she has something of importance to say. When he speaks his eyes light up behind the thick lenses he wears (he was blind for 11 years). One quickly becomes unaware that he walks slowly with the aid of a cane and surely tires easily.

Griffin, 52, is best-known, of course, as the author of "Black Like Me," a historic best-seller based on his experiences traveling through the South in 1959 in the guise of a Negro. He had injections to darken his skin and has had endless physical difficulties as a result. The technique used was a new one developed by a Japanese dermatologist, and though his doctors were careful in checking the effect on his blood (he has diabetes) they did not anticipate the other side effects.

Repercussions from "Black Like Me" also have been endless. He has been asked again and again to intercede in racial conflicts and be a spokesman for blacks, to write articles, to lecture. The immediate effect of the publication of the book was threats on his life and those of his family in Texas. Griffin decided to send his family to safety in Mexico but stayed on in Texas himself until the threats had ceased. "They always gave me a date that they were going to get me," Griffin explains. He felt he had to stay until the threats stopped because "every black person was watching." Afterward, he "spent almost all the '60s going into cities where there were problems and trying to set up some kind of communication between white and black leadership."

Griffin is not happy with the movie, starring James Whitmore, that was made from "Black Like Me." "I was very saddened by it," he said. "I didn't want it altered in any way and they introduced new elements—an absolutely revolting section where the man begins having religious doubts." Griffin learned last year that a movie had been made of "Black Like Me" in Russia.

GRIFFIN, a native of Texas, went to France at the age of 15 to attend school. He studied music but eventually turned to medicine. He was in his final year of medical school when World War II began. He lost his sight and suffered some brain damage when he was caught between two bombs that exploded. He had been blind for 11 years when suddenly his sight returned.

The period of blindness turned him into a writer. He began studies on racism and wrote a book in French on "the interpretation of keyboard ornaments in the music of the 17th and 18th centuries." Critic John Mason Brown visited him and suggested that he try writing fiction. "He was a kind of authoritative figure and it never occurred to me not to do what he suggested," Griffin recalls. "This was on Thursday. I called the Lighthouse for the Blind and asked them if anybody over there could teach me to type. I went over on Friday and I learned and I practiced on Saturday and Sunday and on Monday I began my first book. Seven weeks later I had a huge manuscript which was my first novel, 'The Devil Rides Outside.'" It became a best-seller and was banned in Detroit.

"I fluked out, I had bad luck," Griffin smiles. "That first novel created enough critical interest for publishers to start making me terribly flattering lifetime offers. Well, I didn't know how to write, so I began making the mistake of going back and trying to learn and I finally decided that that was suicidal and gave it all up." He feels he has been strongly influenced by Camus' "The Stranger" and by Flaubert's short stories. "I relate very profoundly to Flannery O'Connor and in a less serious way I always had a kind of puppy love for Lillian Smith. I have never done a systematic reading of Faulkner and one of the reasons I haven't is because this is a man whose inner climate is so exciting to my inner climate I just write the most shameful plagiarizations for a few days. I just dimly disguise a figure that I think is startling. I really don't read a great deal in the field where I work. I read a great deal in other fields." He has only read Faulkner in French translations.

ELABORATING on his writing, Griffin explains that "I really haven't the remotest idea by the time I finish a book whether it's for the ash can. Your critical faculties are there and you know if you're putting in clumsy structure or a turgid kind of sentence construction. I have never written a book that ended the way I thought it might. I write very long works and cut them down. I mess with characters until something comes alive, until they get a volition of their own and I don't ever do a great deal until this happens. I always write on a theme, which I say very hesitantly, because I'm not at all sure that's good. I write on the basis of a very firm philosophical structure which I then try to erase all traces of, and I structure it on the two things that I know. I know a little bit about philosophical structure and I know a little bit about musical forms. For example in 'The Street of Seven Angels' (a new novel now with his publishers), which is a great satire on the whole idea of censorship and on true and false concepts of piety and pietousness, the philosophical structure was very clear. But the whole thing had to be classical and so I wrote that entire book—which took me quite a long time to write although its a very, very short work—listening to Mozart.

"My wife has never read a word I have written until it was published. Nobody has ever seen a line I have written until it goes off to the publishers and I send it off with a kind of awful despair. If the publisher writes me back, 'This is good, we are excited over it,' I must admit I feel a terrible release of tensions. But I always avoid the paralysis of waiting for an answer from an editor. I make it an absolute religious principle to begin another book the day I mail a finished manuscript. If it's mailed at noon by two o'clock I'm in another manuscript. So I don't have that awful withdrawal kind of situation.

"In my experience, I don't care how well a thing has gone in first draft, I never trust myself to release any page until it has been in fourth draft. Some of the things that I have published have been in 30th and 40th drafts. On a short novel that I wrote once called 'Nuni' we kept a kind of count—my wife was curious about all the paper I threw away. There were some 20,000 sheets of discards and it ended up being about a 400- or 500-page manuscript."

THE BIOGRAPHY of Thomas Merton which Griffin has been writing is in final draft and is scheduled for publication next fall. "This has been a problem book," Griffin points out, "because one of the things about a man like Father Louis — you get an idea or an episode in his life finished and footnoted and in final shape and somebody digs up some marvelous thing. Research on him is utterly endless and I get these letters that come out of nowhere that are just too good, too much material in them, it's too important not to include." Griffin feels he was chosen as biographer because of "a great similarity in our backgrounds. We had both been in school in France, we both had the same kind of idols, we had both been very close to Jacques Maritain and that whole circle and so there was a kind of parallel in us." They were also both converts to Catholicsm, both writers, both photographers, both humanists, both concerned about racism and censorship, and, like Merton, Griffin has "a deep contempt for the type of mind that requires that everything be consistent."

Instant Intelligentsia

By Diana McLellan
Star-News Staff Writer

We know who we are. We're the ones who slink off to the sidelines when cronies launch fiery debates on books like "Creative Divorce" or "Sexual Suicide." We're the ones who declined to be let in on "The Secret Life of Plants," who didn't go "Upstairs at the White House," who weren't lured into Gertrude Stein's "Charmed Circle."

Does anybody care that we live daily with the disgrace of not having plowed through the best-seller lists?

Somebody does. A new magazine called "Book Digest," due on Washington area stands today, is designed specifically to spare our blushes and give us a peek into what's good and new among the 30,000 or so non-fiction books that pour off the presses each year.

Book Digest is the brainchild of a hyperactive editor - cum - broadcaster - cum - professor - cum - author ("The Doctors" and "The Brainwatchers") named Milton Gross.

GROSS, WHO founded the late lamented "Intellectual Digest" (it died this year, three years after he sold it, because, he says modestly, "It didn't have me") expects "Book Digest" to sell between four and five million copies per monthly issue. His expectations may be fulfilled.

A test issue published in Cleveland last month sold more than 10,000 copies on newsstands alone; and the simultaneous launching of "Book Digest" in Washington, Boston and Detroit today will be followed, next month, by release in New York and Chicago and the month after that by release just about everywhere.

"Book Digest" will contain, each month, either excerpts from or condensations of the "best nonfiction books."

The current 256-page bumper issue, for example, includes parts of "Billie Jean," Ms. King's autobiography; "Thomas Jefferson: An Intimate History," by Fawn Brodie; Jeb Stuart Magruder's "An American Life;" "Khrushchev Remembers;" "Pilgrim at Tinker Creek," by Annie Dillard; James Mellow's "Charmed Circle;" "Creative Divorce;" "Wampeters Foma & Granfalloons" by Kurt Vonnegut Jr.; "Management" by Peter F. Drucker; and "American Masters" and "The Great Escape."

There are also, significantly for its financial health, 21 pages of advertising, "And," says Gross, "41 pages in the next issue."

Gross is 49, but looks much younger. Apparently hard work agrees with him. Singlehandedly he chooses, cuts or condenses or "selects" passages from the books.

"The non-fiction book," he pronounced in quickfire philosophical gulps between mouthfuls of tuna salad at lunch yesterday, "is the repository of Western culture today. The magazine article, which has long been the basic vehicle for ideas in our civilization, is dying in that role. And I say that as one who has written a lot of magazine articles."

In fact he has, for magazines ranging from "Good Housekeeping" to the "New Republic."

HE ALSO SAYS it, presumably, as one whose product will be in direct competition with "Reader's Digest." "Book Digest" is roughly the same size as that multi-million-circulation all-time blockbuster of the mag trade. Its paper is glossier, its graphics are more urbane and its price tag pricier.

Book publishers, says Gross, are not at all reluctant to sell selecting and condensation rights. "They find that sales of the book itself soar after it's been excerpted," he claims. "Consider: there are only about two million basic book buyers, regular book buyers, in the country. What this will do is expose a much wider public to books." He himself "looks over" 200 non-fiction books a month in his quest for contents.

Having picked out a likely seeming selection for a month's issue, he says, "the next step is to lay them all on a couch and go into a trance. I use myself as the universal sample of one. I say, do I really want to read that, and that, and that? And together?"

GROSS, Milton

WASHINGTON STAR–NEWS (Washington, D.C.)

Sept. 10, 1974

Sketch by Authors in the News

If so, the next decision—whether to select passages or condense the whole of a book—is, he says, influenced mainly by the book itself. "In the case of Jeb Stuart Magruder's book, it was obvious that the five chapters about the actual planning of Watergate were the crucial ones."

"Unlike most other intellectuals—and I consider myself an intellectual—I'm not a snob," Gross declares. "These days, if people don't have time to read the whole book, and most people don't, there's nothing at all wrong with the digest form. The authors or publishers have to approve the form. Arthur Schlesinger liked the way his was done. Norman Mailer liked his. Marvin Kalb approved his.

"I cut their work," he says, "as carefully as though I wrote it myself."

The implication is that neither a writer nor a reader could ask for more.

Bill Gunn's Play a 'Mental Trip', No 'Sounder' or 'Jane Pittman'

GUNN, Willaim Harrison (Bill)
(1934 -)
PHILADELPHIA
BULLETIN
(Philadelphia, Penn.)
Dec. 1, 1974
[See also CA-13/14]

Bulletin Staff Photo by Don Pasquarella

By FRED STUART

Special to The Bulletin

NEW YORK — Bill Gunn is a black playwright, director and actor who didn't like "Sounder" or "The Autobiography of Miss Jane Pittman."

Blasphemy? Almost, because of the universal acclaim given the two films (the latter was a prize-winning TV special), perhaps as much for the dignity with which the black experience was portrayed as for their artistic quality.

Nevertheless, Bill Gunn found them pretentious and overdrawn.

Its just what he's trying to avoid in the new "Black Picture Show," which he has written and will direct when Joseph Papp's New York Shakespeare Festival introduces it at Zellerbach Theater, 3680 Walnut st., next week.

After previews this weekend (there's one set for 2 this afternoon), "Black Picture Show" opens officially Tuesday night, running through Dec. 15, nightly (except Mondays) with Saturday and Sunday matinees — prior to opening in New York, at Lincoln Center's Vivian Beaumont Theater.

FOR BILL GUNN, the Philadelphia engagement represents a homecoming. He's a West Philadelphia High School dropout who worked at the University of Pennsylvania as a hospital orderly and library aide before embarking on a theatrical career.

Show business was always part of his life, however. His mother, Louise Alexander Gunn, had her own theatrical group, under the auspices of the Rev. Leon Sullivan's church, and his earliest memories include his mother taking him to plays in Philadelphia theaters.

At 16, after leaving West Philadelphia High, Gunn joined the Navy for two years, then worked at Penn. He realized he had to reach higher or he'd always be low man on the economic totem pole, so he "stole" part of his education by sitting in on classes at the Wharton School of Finance, where he had a library job, while working backstage as a scene painter at Neighborhood Playhouse.

One night, Neighborhood Players needed an extra for "Street Scene," and drafted Bill Gunn. He was hooked.

• • •

"I CAME to New York with 35 dollars and four 25-dollar war bonds, which lasted one week," Gunn recalled the other day. "Through friends, I got a job painting the walls of Katherine Dunham's studios, then a scholarship to study dance. It helped my awkwardness, but I quit after three months — I became too self-conscious looking at myself all day long in the mirror."

Gunn the actor began to click in the '50s — he performed on TV in New York and on the West Coast ("Studio One," "Danger," etc.); on Broadway ("A Winters Tale," "Antony and Cleopatra," "The Immoralist," "Member of the Wedding," "Take a Giant Step"), and in films ("The Sound and the Fury," "The Interns").

But Gunn had more interest in writing and directing than in acting because, he says, "an actor doesn't have the control that a writer and director has."

His first play was produced in 1959 by the Theater Guild — "Marcus in the High Grass," starring David Wayne and Elizabeth Ashley. He won most-promising-playwright accolades with "Celebration," at Mark Taper Forum in Los Angeles, leading to his first screenplay — "The Landlord," based on the novel by fellow-Philadelphian Kristin Hunter.

Another Gunn film is awaiting release. It's "Ganja and Hess," which he directed last year and which he claims has played every museum and film festival, but he's holding back on general release because "the producers want it out as an exploitation film."

• • •

AS FOR FILMS like "Sounder" and "Jane Pittman," Gunn says, "We blacks will grab at anything which gives us dignity."

The leading character in "Black Picture Show" is, Gunn explains, "a black screen writer like myself in his 40s, who's had a series of small breakdowns until one day, he loses his memory. He enters a hospital, and what you see is through his eyes.

"His illegitimate son, whom he accidentally had at 15, comes, as he always does, to help him. Because of their closeness in age, the two are more like brothers.

"But this is not a play about a breakdown. Rather, it's a mental trip. And his last day refers to that moment when he leaves his color and deals with his breakdown and his own fantasies."

Gunn says the play took a month to write, "but it's based on ten years of notes." He wrote it, he said, especially for Joseph Papp, for whom he last worked ten years ago, as an actor.

"I like Joe Papp," Gunn said. "He's passionate about protecting his artists."

Writer deplores Indian plight

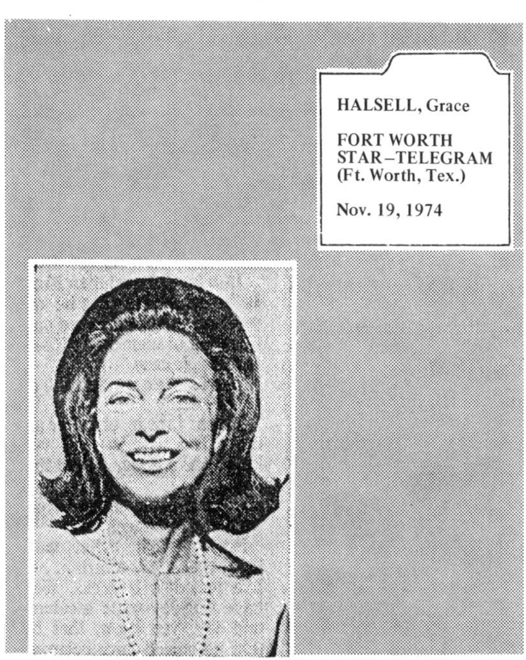

HALSELL, Grace
FORT WORTH STAR-TELEGRAM (Ft. Worth, Tex.)
Nov. 19, 1974

By DAN FRAZIER

HURST — Author Grace Halsell, who has posed successfully as both an American Indian and a black citizen to familiarize herself with the experiences of minority Americans, said Monday blacks fit into the mainstream of American values and ambitions while Indians are definitely of a separate culture.

Speaking at a Tarrant County Junior College Northeast Campus news conference, Miss Halsell told of pigmenting her skin black and living in Harlem and Mississippi. She also spoke of her experiences on a Navajo reservation in Arizona and working as an "Indian" housekeeper for a white California family.

Miss Halsell, a former Star-Telegram reporter and staff writer for former President Johnson, wrote "Soul Sister" (1969) about her life as a black woman and "Bessie Yellowhair" (1973) about her Navajo experiences.

She also is the author of "Black and White Sex," (1970) a book about what she considers the basic problem in racial relationships in this country.

AS A "BLACK" person, Miss Halsell said she got along better in Harlem than in Mississippi, where she worked as a maid for a wealthy white family.

"Harlem was no problem because there was no white influence," Miss Halsell said. "In Harlem, it was live and let live, but in Mississippi I was a second class citizen."

She said blacks share the basic goals of comfort, status and material achievement as whites while the Indian seeks to preserve his racial identity.

"I changed my pigmentation, but I was always me," she said of her experience as a "black" person.

It was more difficult to pose as an Indian, however, Miss Halsell said.

"I had to change myself psychologically among the Indians. The Indian has a whole different set of values. Their emphasis is on being rather than achieving," Miss Halsell said. "Living in harmony with nature, not trying to conquer anything (is the Indian's objective.)"

* * *

SHE SAID she was inspired to share the minority American experience by John Howard Griffin's book "Black Like Me."

Miss Halsell said she also has spent three years living among Latin Americans in Peru.

"There's discrimination wherever you go in the world. This is true in South America, too, but there's no gradation in color," she said.

"I think the Indian has it worst of all. We (white culture) have shoved them back and back and they can no longer live as they did in olden days," the author said. "They are the poorest of the poor. Their plight is by far the worst."

Miss Halsell lived on the Navajo reservation in Arizona, sleeping on the dirt floor of an Indian "hogan" in sheepskins with other members of an Indian family.

She paid her way there by performing menial tasks like sweeping the floor, carrying water, cooking and chopping firewood.

* * *

AFTER ABSORBING the Navajo lifestyle and outlook and assuming the identity of her hostess, "Bessie Yellowhair," she posed as an Indian housekeeper and got a job with a family in California, she said.

She said the most interesting experience in Mississippi happened in the kitchen of the household where she worked when the man of the house attempted to have sexual relations with her.

She said he seemed to regard her as his property and thought himself welcome to her favors.

"This was the worst thing to deal with," Miss Halsell said. "Suppose I had had his child — it would have been my child alone."

It was a 10-minute subway ride through New York City that made her decide to study the lives of minority Americans first-hand, she said.

* * *

"I SUDDENLY wanted to learn what opportunity I would have as a black," she said of the ride which she termed "the most educational experience of my life."

Her study of the Indians was prompted by the reputation her father had as an "Indian fighter," she said.

Asked if she thought she was capitalizing on the plight of other racial groups, Miss Halsell replied she did not think so.

"My search is for understanding," she said. "I feel black. For me it's no pretense. I like to say I'm mixed up."

"To me there's two types of people: Those who are mixed up and know it, and those who are mixed up and don't," she added.

The Lubbock native said she has another book in the works, but declined to discuss it.

Miss Halsell is scheduled to deliver a speech called "The Three Faces of Grace" on TCJC's Northeast Campus at 12:15 p.m. Tuesday in Campus Center Corner.

Writer Impersonates Black and Indian

By MALVINA STEPHENSON

WASHINGTON — A Texas-born writer who previously studied blacks now turns her attention to the plight of the primitive Navajos in Arizona.

Grace Halsell, author of the controversial best-seller "Soul Sister," has entitled her new book "Bessie Yellowhair," the young Indian girl she was permitted to impersonate.

An attractive brunette popular on the lecture circuit, Miss Halsell recently spoke at an editors workshop at Oklahoma State University. Her soft voice and feminine appearance belie her steel will and courage.

In her pursuits as an author, she has driven the desert alone, picking up characters who could provide insight. She herself has hitch-hiked when she felt the circumstances required it.

POSING AS A BLACK maid, her skin darkened by chemicals, she worked in a southern household. Passing for an Indian, she got the same kind of experience with an affluent family in Orange county near the Western White House.

All of this has taken its toll on her health. She presently is recuperating from a bout with hepatitis, contracted from drinking contaminated water on the reservation.

Grace's family has roots both in Texas and Oklahoma. She was in and out of the Sooner State in 1955-56 when she did public relations for the Champlin Oil Co., then headquartered in Fort Worth.

Grace's early interest in Indians was stimulated by the books and stories of her father, one of the most colorful figures of the Old Southwest. When he died at the age of 96 in 1957, the New York Times obituary recalled how he once outfoxed Geronimo and ultimately became friends with Chief Quannah Parker.

Her "Uncle Oscar", who as a boy helped her father escape an Indian ambush, was a pioneer grocer in Oklahoma. He will be remembered as the founder of the Hale-Halsell chain.

For the most of her Indian book, Grace was not disguised. On the Navajo reservation, she identified herself as a writer. She got acquainted with the leaders and then spent some time living in the primitive hogans.

In the opening of an early chapter, she writes, "I know that eventually I will 'pass' out of my whiteness and turn 'Indian,' and on that day the Bureau of Indian Affairs (BIA) will become my Big Brother, or Great White Father.

"The Indians occupy an alien enclave in our midst, and Washington has a special bureau to 'govern' them. No other racial or ethnic group, such as blacks or Chicanos, suffers from this 'alien' status."

With a sympathetic approach, she then proceeds to move and live among the Navajos. She spent much time with the Yellowhair family. Bessie ultimately lent her name and clothes to Grace to work in California.

ONE OF THE MOST INteresting characters with whom she stays is "Aunt Zonie," who raised the Navajo Chief Justice, Virgil L. Kirk. Plucky Aunt Zonie, a widow, lives alone in an isolated dirt-floor hogan, a small round house, built of logs, with mud plaster roof and three small shuttered windows.

HALSELL, Grace

TULSA WORLD (Tulsa, Okla.)

July 29, 1973

With the Yellowhair family, she learned more about the younger generation. Many of them still cling to the old customs and rely on the rituals of the medicine men. It is here she begins to understand the conflicts and differences between the white and Navajo cultures and values.

The family she calls the "Mortons," for whom she works in California, leave a bad impression on author Halsell. The shift from the Navajos to affluent, pressured suburbia was too abrupt.

"How I long to trade my present situation for life back in the hogan," she recalls her feelings at the time.

"I miss people who come into the 'home' as simple as a mud hut may be — and are eager to relax and laugh at the ridiculous, incongruous and even obscene aspects of life. I miss the warmth, spontaneity, joy — that special intimacy of the unpretentious."

She did not return to the Navajos but she ran off from California, long before ending the year her employer tried to require. A wild night of hitchhiking and riding a bus brought her to friends in Los Angeles and finally to her own world of conveniences and sophistication.

Workshops on publishing underscore fresh thrust in art

By BETH FAGAN

of The Oregonian staff

Walter Hamady's workshops on book publishing at Lewis and Clark College, Portland State University and Hillside Center underscored one of the newer thrusts in art activity of this region.

Artist-publisher of The Perishable Press Limited, Mount Horeb, Wis., Hamady is a "pro" in the private press field, and unique in the field, many say.

"I keep hearing that from others," said poet William Stafford. "I don't know of anyone who does it better, and no one who does as much of the job. It's fantastic."

A new Stafford book, "That Other Alone," will soon be the third volume of Stafford poems Hamady has published since 1968.

Since Hamady founded The Perishable Press Limited (named to "describe the human condition") in 1964, it has been devoted to contemporary American poetry and literature.

By the end of this year, he will have published 62 books and 90 broadsides.

Besides Stafford, he has published Howard Nemerov, Robert Creeley, Denise Levertov, Robert Duncan, J. V. Cunningham, George Oppen, Galway Kinnell, Paul Blackburn, Walter Hall, Diane Wakoski, Toby Olson, Kenneth Bernard, George Economou, Loren Eiseley, David Kherdian, W. S. Merwin, John Wieners and Robert vas Dias.

→ Hamady's own poetry, which has been regularly published in New Directions, and poetry by his wife Mary is included.

I don't have an editorial policy," Hamady said, "except that work must be original. If it moves me and makes sense, we publish it."

By "publishing" Hamady means that he and his wife do practically everything in their home workshop, soon to be moved on a 120-acre farm.

Hardcover bindings are sent three craftsmen, including Sandy Cockerell in England.

The Hamadys personally work with writers, collaborating artists (who include Jack Beal, Ellen Lanyon, Bartolomeo dos Santos of The Slade in London, Warrington Colescott), design, handset their type, make their own rag paper and distribute.

It's a highly personal, comparatively small operation, and Hamady has strong feelings about keeping it that way.

"Jeepers, I'm not going to run a factory. If it ever ceased being a pleasure, I'd want out.

"I do this to keep my hands busy and my mind off ugliness in the world."

He has no apprentices, no partners except Mary, "no flunkies," but does teach typography, drawing, lettering and papermaking courses in University of Wisconsin's art department.

"We love privacy," Hamady said. "And I finally learned that selfishness is not a sin—that if I take care of me and keep myself strong I can do things for other people.

"If we do what we like to do—garden, work, publish significant honest work we believe in, then by example we'll help other people to take courage from us—help them see it can be done.

"And we get wonderful letters that are reassuring to us from many people in this country, Mexico and Canada who stumble onto our books."

Hamady said a lot of private presses are springing up, possibly "because there's a lot of activity in good literature, and because big publishers are indifferent about taking on fugitive literature.

"Need for them is probably the same need society has for any loner or researcher who isn't going to pay attention to rules—who is going to be audacious enough to follow the rules of randomness."

He said the upswing of interest in the private press also could be related to young people not wanting to be cowed by the establishment—by today's impersonal, fast, lockstep emphasis on uniformity. "I think there needs to be more individuality."

He said the amount of private press activity sometimes flabbergasts him, as it did at a recent Northern Illinois University gathering.

"There are three wonderful guys there — the president, director of libraries and the director of the University Press who are crazy about private printing.

"They researched and put on an exhibition of private press work from Michigan, Indiana, Illinois, Iowa, Wisconsin and Minnesota—and came up with 125 presses.

"They published a catalog, displayed all these wonderful books, imported the Caxton Club (a bibliophile group) from Chicago by charter and gave a pheasant lunch."

Hamady said everything that's been good in his life has seemed to happen by accident.

After attending Pratt, knocking about the country with his camera and doing some professional photography, he "was turned on to printing and beautiful books" by Harry Duncan at the State University of Iowa.

"He'd moved his Cummington Press from Massachusetts to Iowa City, which was a hotbed of private printing. He and Keith Achepoehl were turning out this beautiful book of short stories by James Agee.

"Duncan was a big gun in the University's school of journalism—he ran the typographic lab."

His next step was Wayne State University, where he took his B.F.A. and began writing verse, which he decided to publish himself his senior year.

Not knowing anything about it, he went to Robert Runser in Detroit, a collector of old presses and type, owner of Rob Run Press and chief of the city's technology library.

He taught Hamady to use a hand press, and gave him coffee cans full of Palatino type which had come with an old press Hamady had gone East to get for him.

Awards received

Graduation from Wayne and publication of his first book in 1964 was followed by an M.F.A. in graphic arts at Cranbrook Academy, where he learned papermaking. There, he published "Six and Six" with Tamarind master lithographer Aris Koutroulis (six poems by Hamady, six prints by Koutroulis).

He then went to the art faculty at Wisconsin, and private publishing in Mount Horeb nearby.

Hamady has continued using Palatino type designed by Hermann Zapf of Germany, "the most significant type designer of this century," and recently has been trying Sabon Antigua designed by Jan Tschichold—"a pioneer in new type faces.

"It's a healthy Roman face, and the first ever designed that's interchangeable in foundry, monotype and linotype."

Hamady has said that a major concern in private printing is contribution to content of work produced. He says artists, as publishers, have odds stacked in their favor.

His drawings and books have been given numerous major exhibitions and received major awards, and his publications were included twice in the American Institute of Garphic Arts 50 Best Books of the Year.

On a Guggenheim Fellowship in 1969-70, he went to the J. Barcham Green Papermill in Maidstone, Kent, England, which was founded in 1810, and is the last mill making handmade paper in the western world.

He's now doing a book on handmade paper, and hopes to do further research in Japan and China.

He and his wife also are researching, testing and writing a cookbook, a "fine Lebanese Druse Mountain Cookery Book."

Wisconsin's Graduate School Research Committee has awarded him a grant for next spring to research the Sequoyah Syllabary. It's an alphabet of 86 characters created by Chief Sequoyah, who was a Cherokee, type is at University of Oklahoma, and Hamady has plans for a book using it.

Perishable Press Limited publications are sold on standing order to individuals, dealers and major university libraries throughout the country.

HAMADY, Walter

OREGONIAN
(Portland, Ore.)

June 3, 1973

Mystery Writer Was Enigmatic Throughout Life

DASHIELL HAMMETT
. . . *Mystery Writer.*

By RICHARD T. HAMMETT

HAMMETT, Samuel D. (pseud. Dashiell Hammett) (1894 - 1961)

NEWS–AMERICAN (Baltimore, Md.)

Aug. 19, 1973

It is not an easy job to write an objective story about a controversial figure, especially when that person is your uncle.

The controversial person was a St. Marys County native called Samuel D. Hammett, best known as Dashiell Hammett. In literary circles he is considered to be the father of the modern hard-nosed detective story. But as a writer, he was a master of the short story almost unsurpassed in American literature.

He came by it honestly. After holding down a variety of jobs he followed up a blind newspaper ad and became a Pinkerton detective, a background he said he used in many of his novels.

He probably was best known for "The Thin Man" which was an instant success when printed during the 1930s and became the basis for a series of movies starring William Powell and Myrna Loy.

Often glossed over is the fact that he created the great "private eye" Sam Spade, the Continental Op, and also authored a plethora of short stories, many of which did not deal with crime.

Dashiell Hammett was born in 1894, the son of a Southern Maryland farmer-politician.

He might still be there had his father not been run out of the county more or less on a rail. A popular but impecunious Democrat, he was persuaded to run for Congress as a Republican in return for Republican financial support. He lost; and eventually was forced to sell his farm and move to Philadelphia and then Baltimore, where Dashiell grew up in the family home at 212 North Stricker Street.

Few remember much of his childhood. My father said he was not a particularly remarkable child except for being quite stubborn at times, a trait U.S. Senate investigators were to discover some years later.

He was a Baltimore Polytechnic dropout prior to World War I in order to go to work to help the family. During that war he enlisted and managed to get as far as Camp Meade as a medical sergeant before being discharged for physical disability (tuberculosis).

While a Pinkerton agent for eight years he investigated the Fatty Arbuckle and Nicky Arnstein cases. He often said his first promotion as a detective came when he captured a man who stole a Ferris wheel. Also while with Pinkerton he was involved in a number of strikebreaking incidents, which may explain his later involvement in labor and leftist causes.

During the thirties and forties he became involved in a number of organizations, some of which were labeled "Communist Fronts." My father feels that the Pinkerton methods of strikebreaking influenced his turn to leftist groups.

During the same period — according to Lillian Hellman — his friend and bed partner for 31 years, he also was the "hottest piece of property" in Hollywood. He wrote the screen play for "The Watch on the Rhine," which was adapted from Miss Hellman's stage production of the same name, as well as many others.

He was being considered to do the screen play for "The Detective Story" which starred Kirk Douglas, when the Joe McCarthy witchhunt of the 1950s hit. He was among the many writers who suddenly became persona non grata in the studios; a name on the "blacklist."

Among his activities allegedly—had been raising bail money for Gerhard Eisler, an American Communist. Eisler promptly jumped bail or fled on a Polish ship to ultimately end up in Moscow.

Hammett was summoned before the McCarthy committee, but stubbornly refused to say where the $80,000 bail money came from. For this he was sentenced to six months in jail for contempt of Congress.

Miss Hellman insists that he was only a trustee of the American Civil Rights Congress and never knew the names of the contributors. Another theory advanced is that he refused to talk to protect a number of "little people" who gave a dollar or two to a cause that rightly or wrongly they believed in at that time.

In any event he spent his six months in jail, and upon release was hauled up before the committee again and again refused to talk.

Sen. John McClellan, D-Ark., said testily, "Mr. Hammett, you certainly don't think much of the power of American public opinion, do you?" The reply was, "Senator, it wasn't American public opinion that put me away for six months, it was your committee and a judge."

The committee gave up.

At the time all this was going on I was in the Navy and much of what I have said was gleaned from conversations with my father and old newspaper files. They jibe.

After his period as the "hottest property in Hollywood" he fell on bad times. He was not only on the then lethal studio blacklist, but either couldn't or wouldn t write. He also had spent large sums in legal fees during his long ordeal. The Internal Revenue Service attached nearly everything he owned for tax claims.

Despite being invalided out of World War I, he managed to get into the Army in World War II. The Army in its wisdom processed him, decided they had a good mind on their hands and sent him to school to be a cryptographer.

Family story has it that after he had learned all about codes the Army finally learned all about him. The story is that someone said, "My God, we may have a Communist on our hands. Send him someplace where he'll never see a code."

Whatever the reason, Hammett wound up in the Aleutians. Miss Hellman described him as saying his greatest contribution to the war effort was assuring young men they would not lose their virility by staying in the womanless Arctic for several years; at the time he was 50.

After the war his health began to fail. He drank heavily for a number of years, then suddenly quit. Miss Hellman thinks he quit because a doctor told him he couldn't, and he was contrary enough to show him.

Unfortunately no one in his immediate family really knew him well after World War I. A very private person, he left Baltimore, seldom to return. However, what he considered his best book, "The Glass Key," had clearly a Baltimore setting.

He had married his Army nurse at Camp Meade and had two daughters.

What little the family knows of him came from letters he sent to his sister, the only person in his family with whom he maintained any contact.

The man was an enigma, even to those who knew him best. In her autobiography, "An Unfinished Woman," Miss Hellman devotes several chapters to him and in effect admits she did not entirely understand him after a 31-year relationship.

On Jan. 10, 1961, Dashiell Hammett died at the age of 67 in New York's Lenox Hill Hospital.

He had lived his life the way he wanted to live it, for his own reasons

No philosophy, but satire lurks inside mythical kingdom of Id

By Beth Slocum
of The Journal Staff

Not every man can say he has gone from the Stone Age to the Middle Ages and lived to tell about it.

But it's a trip cartoonist Johnny Hart makes daily, launching off his drawing board caveman cackles in his "B.C." comic strip and medieval mishaps in "The Wizard of Id," which is carried in The Milwaukee Journal's Green Sheet.

Hart says his career, and life for that matter, started in Endicott, N. Y., where "I haven't yet lived all my life," and where, despite his 42 years as a native, he still doesn't know the names of the streets — he goes by landmarks.

Endicott was where as a high school student he was first inspired to take up cartoons by a local newspaper editorial cartoonist. That source of inspiration is now his partner, doing the drawing for "Wizard" — Brant Parker.

After a brief stint in the Air Force, Hart decided to make a career of cartoons, "because I couldn't do anything else."

Cartoonist Johnny Hart works on "The Wizard of Id" in his studio.

While keeping the family fed with the income derived from magazine cartoons, Hart, whose art education ended in high school, created his first strip, "B.C." It is set in the days when the wheel was the limit of mechanization and anteaters and turtles carry on conversations with the cast of prehistoric characters.

Several rejections

After five syndicates rejected it ("I just kept putting it in another envelope and mailing it to another syndicate and it would periodically turn up at my doorstep several months later with a rejection slip") "B.C." was picked up by the New York Herald Tribune Syndicate in February, 1958. When the Tribune folded, Publishers Hall Syndicate took over distribution.

"'Wizard' got started because I started thinking about the restrictions of 'B.C.' I felt I couldn't get satirical enough as there's no society to work with in 'B.C.' It deals with the basics, man's foibles and follies. So it was an obvious transition for me from caveman to medieval times where there is a set society."

So the wizard, the stunted king, "revolting" peasants and Rodney the chicken hearted knight of the mythical kingdom of Id made their debut Nov. 9, 1964. Now Hart estimates "B.C." and "Wizard's" circulation at between 350 and 400 newspapers each.

Later came the Spook, the hairy dungeon inhabitant. "We were delighted when we came up with him," said Hart. "He's such a wretched character. Then of course, we had to have a turnkey."

And the Wizard's ample wife, Blanche, joined the turnout because, Hart says, the "all-powerful wizard needed someone to keep him in line."

His alter ego

Some of the characters are patterned after real people, two after Hart himself. The stumpy king, who falls victim to short gags, is the 5 foot 7 inch Hart's admitted alter ego.

The perpetually inebriated Bung also vaguely resembles his creator, Hart claims. "I'm prone to take a nip now and then, so my colleagues came up with Bung, the court sot."

Hart says there is no philosophy lurking in his strip. But political satire does creep in.

"The intent of the strip is to be entertaining. To be honest, when we do a gag, it's much more meaningful if it has a message. But the main ingredient in both strips is humor. We try to be funny and if we can say something at the same time, we try to do so whenever possible."

HART, Johnny

MILWAUKEE JOURNAL
(Milwaukee, Wisc.)

Apr. 4, 1973

One issue which crops up occasionally in the strip is the women's liberation movement, in the lonely form of Blanche.

"You must remember we work for humor," explained Hart, "we don't take any sides. The women's movement is personified by Blanche. We put women down sometimes and sometimes we have them put the men down.

"We try to be as nonoffensive as possible. But a lot of times we end up offending everyone."

Get complaints

The syndicate is especially sensitive. One time Hart used the word hell in a strip. A solitary angry letter came in protesting his use of the word and Hart says the syndicate got all upset.

Another incident occurred when he used a Jewish gag. "It was just a silly little gag but it wasn't clear. It was misinterpreted by some as 'mean' or anti-Semitic."

Most of the political commentary comes from one of Hart's assistants, Dick Boland, who contributes ideas for "Wizard."

"Yeah, most of that stuff comes from Boland, who has his nose stuck in the newspaper all the time. I don't read newspapers much, they depress me. Oh, if there's an attack on our town, I'll rise to the occasion, otherwise I stay out of politics pretty much."

Hart's other assistant, Jack Caprio, like himself, is good at "slapstick humor," says Hart. "We enjoy the dumb humor."

Once they crank out the dialog and raw sketches for "Wizard," off each strip goes via mail to Parker in Oakton, Va., for final drawing.

Parker and Hart get together periodically for four or five days, to discuss "Wizard's" direction. Otherwise they do their corresponding by mail and phone.

Does Hart have trouble coming up with fresh ideas for two daily strips?

Ideas flow

"In the early days I'd get to feeling, 'I'm never going to think of a new idea as long as I live.' Now I know that's impossible. Now that I have Jack, we sit down anytime and ideas flow. We end up laughing on the floor, making fools of ourselves," said Hart.

When Hart says anytime he means just that. "It's absolute mayhem every day. I'm a completely unscheduled kind of guy."

And with his output it's no wonder he is becoming a "seven day a week" man.

Besides the two strips, Hart puts out television commercials, decals and posters for NASA, and is in the process of going back and forth to California where he is working on his first half hour "B.C." special for NBC, tentatively scheduled to air around Thanksgiving time.

The father of two teenage daughters, Patti, 17, and Perri, 15, Hart says he has never aimed his humor at any particular audience.

"I always did what I thought was funny. I'm lucky to have fun and make a living doing what I like to do."

Hart's formula for a successful strip?

"I don't think there is one. But for me a good strip has to have appeal and it has to be funny. The drawing has to be adequate and if it can be as funny as the gags and the gags are very funny, then that's the formula for the successful strip."

It's a formula Hart and associates have down pat.

Novelist Shares Tidbits Gleaned From Her Travels

HAWES, Evelyn (Johnson)

SEATTLE POST-INTELLIGENCER (Seattle, Wash.)

July 22, 1974

[See also CA-15/16]

—P-I Photo by Tom Barlet

BY SUSAN PAYNTER

Talking to Evelyn Hawes is like eating at a smorgasbord. You fill your mental plate with a little bit of everything and you may come away with a slight case of indigestion but you're sure it was worth the adventure.

The very human Mrs. Hawes writes very human books about other humans — the kind of books that make people identify and laugh out loud.

The Colville-born writer has just moved back to the Northwest from Buffalo, N.Y., and will be one of an impressive panel accumulated for the July 25 through 27 Pacific Northwest Writers Conference at Pacific Lutheran University.

"Seattle abounds in writing talent and the conference will be a great opportunity for anyone interested in doing a novel to stroll down there and meet those editors.

"I believe in meeting the people wno are going to read your manuscript. When I broke into the publishing business I had to go to New York cold and that's tough."

Mrs. Hawes has written three highly successful novels, "The Happy Land," "A Madras-Type Jacket," and her latest, "Six Nights a Week." The last is based on her personal experience as the wife of a JC Penney executive — the transfers and tribulations of marrying the retail business.

She's taught at the University of Washington and written two textbooks — one a 100-year medical history.

"My novels are lighthearted but that medical text nearly killed me," she said. "I hope I never get involved in something like that again.l I sat up all night for weeks worrying that I'd gotten something wrong.

"But I heard some wonderful stories from the really old people I interviewed for it, some of them 93 and 98 years old. One remembered the first obstetrician who allowed medical students to watch a woman giving birth and how the community became insensed at such an immoral thing."

But Mrs. Hawes likes writing novels and short stories best and bemoans the demise of a short story market. She's written many articles for national magazines and has agents in London and Paris who handle the not-so-lucrative business of translating Americar writings for European readers.

Although the young couple of "Six Nights a Week" are not really Nat and Evelyn Hawes, only the names were changed to protect the innocent. "Fiction has to be true to life. Non-fiction just has to be true to the facts," Mrs Hawes said.

As a Penney manager Nat Hawes was transferred from Seattle to places like Cincinnati, Indiana and Buffalo and Evelyn always went along. But she wasn't led like a lamb, she saw the transfers as opportunities and studied at universities in each new area, even joined the teaching staff of the University of Cincinnati.

"But if I hadn't enjoyed it, if it had been forced on me by Nat, by gosh I probably would have hated him. I would have had 17,500 fits about all the moving around. He really loved the retail business. I never would, but thank goodness some people do.

"I managed to remain pretty independent. But I was lucky because I always worked but didn't have my career outside the home. With the crazy hours of the retail business it would be pretty tough with children if both parents were really involved with something outside."

Mrs. Hawes isn't hawking marriage on street corners but, unlike many current women novelists, she's optimistic about the institution.

"Marriage is a pretty practical, sensible arrangement when you both want children," she said.

"And even if you don't, I think it's a public expression of love and an announcement of your intentions to try for a continuing love. It's not a life sentence.

"It isn't all good. People are different — that's the wonder of it. But if you hang on it's because there's more good than bad.

"It's like the fable of the man who wakes up each morning with the choice — to be happy or not. Everyone has that choice but it's a little easier with help from a partner."

WHAT ONE WOMAN FOUND OUT ABOUT THE PLAYBOY KING

News photos bys HOWARD SHIRKEY

Above is the famed circular bed aboard Hefner's Bunny jet.

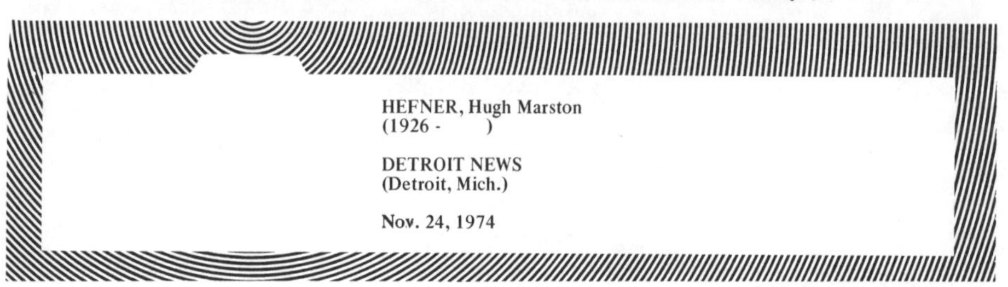

HEFNER, Hugh Marston
(1926 -)

DETROIT NEWS
(Detroit, Mich.)

Nov. 24, 1974

By JOAN WIXEN
Sunday Magazine Contributing Correspondent

A GUY other guys would like to be.

Fame, power, money, and a constant supply of gorgeous young women.

A self-made man worth over $180 million.

He walks with confidence, speaks with ease, knows he has arrived.

Yet, look closely at this middle-aged man in his very mod green velvet suit. Part of him comes across as an adolescent boy who's about to embark on his first relationship with a woman, while the other says . . . I've had it. I've lived, and I know what I'm talking about.

Hugh Hefner, the big boss of the Playboy Empire, is 48 years old, but he tells me he's very young for his age.

"In EVERY way?" I ask, giving him a careful look up and down.

"In EVERY way," he answers, smiling, winking an eye.

"Ahhh come on now," I say to him as we sit across the table from each other on his $5½-million jet black Bunny plane, soaring above the clouds en route to the opening of another Playboy Club. "Don't you think these young girls sometimes use you as a patsy? I mean most of them are young enough to be your daughter."

"You mean, if I weren't as rich and as powerful they wouldn't have any business with me?" he asks.

"Exactly," I say. "Doesn't it bother you that it's because of what you represent rather than what you are that so many of these beautiful young things are making such a fuss over you?"

"What I represent is what I am. You see, it bothers a lot of people because I lead the kind of life they can only dream about, but know they can never have. My life style touches the two great guilts of our society. Sex and material wealth. And naturally there is going to be a lot of resentment.

"People have always been trying to cut me down, but because I believe in what I do, and because I've been able to rid myself of the guilts of my strong Methodist background, I can handle anything that comes along."

"You mean I can ask you any kind of a bitchy question, and it won't bother you?"

"Exactly. I can handle anything you might ask me."

"OK," I SAY, "doesn't it bother you that there are a fair amount of people who think of you as rather an insipid slob?"

"A what?" He looks at me a little bit shocked.

"You heard me," I say with a smile, feeling a little bit funny that I took him at his word. "An insipid slob."

"Well, no one has ever asked me that kind of a question before, but I'll tell you, if some people might think of me that way it is their problem, not mine. You know, it is hard for some people to accept the fact that a person can devote his life to his own personal gratification, and to helping other people find theirs, without being some kind of a nut.

"When I was a kid I used to worry about whether everyone liked me, but as I grew older I realized that your enemies are as important as your friends. Both of them establish what you stand for, and if everyone approves of what you do, you'd be a nobody.

"The people my kind of living threatens most are those who strongly believe in organized religion, those who believe if they work hard and sacrifice they'll go to heaven. But don't you see this is merely a good way to keep the serfs in line? What I try to convey is that we can make our own heaven on earth. We can live and enjoy life to the fullest without being afraid."

"But don't you think you might overdo it a bit? For example, you once said that the most important thing in the world to you is love and having a long-lasting relationship with a woman. And now I hear you've been going with Barbi Benton for about six years.

"Yet, I heard when she's not around you have a slew of others, a second crew and a third crew, and on down the line. Now what is it with you anyway? What are you trying to prove?" ➡

(Continued from preceding page)

"Because there are others in my life doesn't mean I can't have a long-loving relationship with Barbi. I've always had one special woman in my life, and besides, half the things people say about Hefner aren't true. Sure I've had plenty of one-night stands, but believe me I don't have anything to prove anymore other than that a person can survive beautifully if he's willing to let go of his hangups."

"And what are your hangups?"

"You mean what were my hangups? I was born into a very devout religious home where my parents strongly pushed very rigid Puritan ideals. Yet, both my parents were college graduates, and from the time I was a little kid they somehow got it across to me that I should be very skeptical. However, they did such a good job that I also became skeptical of some of the bull they were trying to push down my throat.

"In my home smoking, drinking, gambling, and any off-color conversation was severely frowned upon, and of course sex was never discussed. When I reached my teens my mother gave me a book on sex. Parents can do the right thing and even say the right words, but kids are usually smart enough to conceive what they're really trying to get across.

"And, of course, what I do now is without question a reaction to the frustrations of my childhood. However, I will say this. What my parents did, didn't cripple me. They gave me very strong ideals. And more important, they gave me the strength to go my own way, even if it was contrary to their own beliefs.

"I was closer to my mother as a kid. My father was away a good deal of the time, and I really wasn't too close to him."

"SOME PEOPLE say when there isn't much of a father figure in the home a kid often identifies with his mother. I mean, there's more of a tendency for him to become . . ."

"A homosexual. Well I'm not. I'm quite heterosexually oriented. And my magazine is too."

"I'm not saying it's bad, only that with some men their homosexual feelings threaten them so much they spend their lives constantly trying to prove they're he-men, seeing how many women they can sleep with. Didn't you once say one of the advantages of your work was that it enabled you to accomplish this?"

"Of course. And that's not necessarily a bad thing. And sure I have my degree of sensitivity or feminity or whatever else you may call it, or else certainly I wouldn't be doing the things I am. Maybe that's why I'm so creative."

"You know, you're much more intelligent than I expected you to be. I read you had an IQ of 152, but I felt that was just publicity."

"I was watching you when you first got on the plane," he answered, "when we were all sitting around and laughing and telling jokes and you sat there looking so prim, taking it all in. I was observing you observing us."

"And I was observing you observing me," I said. "I was thinking what kind of a crazy business does this man run here. Doesn't he realize that part of his life is so unreal? Surrounding himself with people who sit and fawn and laugh at his jokes, while he sits like a king with his own special court jesters?"

"I could tell you were giving me the once-over. You looked at me so intensely and I could almost tell what you were thinking, and that is why I told them all to leave.

"But let me tell you this—there is no question I am the king of my own world, but I am very careful about the people I select to work with. And I must be a pretty good judge, because most of the original people who started with me 20 years ago are still with me. I have a sixth sense and I can really tell about people, and I purposely surround myself not only with loyal, intelligent people, but also those who love to have a good time.

"And whether you know it or not, most of these people love me. They really do. And when they were laughing before, they weren't laughing on cue. We're all good friends, and we simply like to be with one another.

"I've always tried to be very skeptical without letting myself become cynical or jaded, without going overboard to become overly suspicious. You see, never in my wildest dreams did I ever envision this incredible success. But now that I have it, I work very hard at keeping my feet on the ground, because I feel the way a person handles his success is a measure of the person, himself.

"I've seen plenty of my buddies spend years and years of struggling to get some place, and finally when they get there they just fall apart. They just can't handle it.

"And believe me I am not being used now. I know exactly what I'm doing. I was brought up in a home that was the center of activity for all my friends, and I have just continued that pattern into my adulthood. I enjoy sharing my good fortune with those I love, and I like to think these people are around me, not because of my money or power, but that it has to do with my leadership and charisma."

"Do you think all these beautiful young girls would be falling all over you if you didn't have all that money?"

"Some would, and some wouldn't, but let me get one thing straight. Being a bunny doesn't necessarily involve going to bed with Hugh Hefner."

"I GUESS what bothers me the most is that you seem to make such a fetish out of going to bed with a woman. I read in some magazine how you have a red carpeted bedroom with a big red circular bed with a big spot light on it. And when a woman enters she hears drums of passion beating on the hi-fi.

"Now I have to admit I'm not your typical bunny type," I continued. "I've had some kids, I've got some wrinkles, and my breasts are only average size. But really, if any man ever walked me into that kind of situation I'm afraid instead of it turning me on, it would have the opposite effect. I'm afraid I'd just stand there and think what kind of a crackpot is this, and I'd burst out laughing in his face."

"First of all, the carpet is not red, it is white. And the bedspread is fur, and there is no spotlight on my round bed. But yes, I guess there are some people who might think it pretty wild.

"As far as preferring younger women, of course I do. They're more sexually attractive. I'm very young for my age, and these women keep me that way.

"But don't you see the way a person views Hefner is a Rorschach Test of himself. Often all he's doing is revealing his own peculiarities. And of course when this happens, it has nothing whatsoever to do with me."

"In other words, how a person views your interpretations of sex is merely a revelation of his own craziness. OK, I'll go along with that. My craziness tells me you make sex a little too artificial, and you dehumanize it."

"What's more important than sex?"

"That's not the point. All I'm saying is it's something that doesn't need so much candy-wrapper selling. It's something natural, and don't you see I'm all for what you're trying to do, but not how you're trying to do it.

"For example, you equate sexiness in a woman with her having big breasts."

"My present girl friend, Barbi, doesn't have big breasts."

"But you carry this theme out in your magazine."

"Bull. Playboy bunnies have always had something more than just good looks. They're attractive in their bodies, and in their minds."

"Ahhh come on . . ."

"No, really. You assume because they're pretty, they're dumb."

"No, I don't assume that. What bothers me is the Playboy philosophy — like women's lib says — you make women into objects. I wonder, do you really like women?"

"I'll tell you honestly the thing that turns me on most in my life, more than power, money, or being a celebrity, is a one-to-one relationship with a woman. It is the most important thing in my life."

"You say this, yet Playboy bunnies don't quite come off as regular women. They just seem to be well-built creatures. I wonder how some men might react if there were magazines devoted to male physical attributes? And we women put you in contests, and we spoke of you as if you were cattle or property, but not quite human beings with the same kind of intelligence and minds as we have."

"For thousands of years women have been the property of men. First they were the property of their fathers, then they became the property of their husbands. I'm not saying it should be that way, only that this is not the invention of Hugh Hefner."

"I HEAR you were married once, for 10 years, to a Millie Williams, and you had two children, a girl, Christie Ann, 21, a Phi Beta Kappa from Brandeis University who just graduated with a degree in English literature, and a son, David, 18, who just entered college. Now, how would you feel about your daughter becoming a bunny?"

"If that was what she wanted, I wouldn't mind at all."

"Would you like to be part of, say, a Jack-Rabbit (male bunny) crew?"

"If in our society men were to wear special sexual uniforms, and I could be a sex object, I'd love it."

"I don't believe it."

"What you don't know is I am a romantic, and because of people like me, and because of what Playboy has done, sex in the United States is better than ever."

"How does your current girl friend go along with your philosophy? Would you go along with her doing the same thing?"

"No, not at all. But then again, maybe someday if I become liberated enough," he smiled, "maybe I would."

"I read you broke off a while back with Barbi, but that you are together again."

"Yes, we broke up for a while because there was another woman in my life who became terribly important to me. But now that is over, and Barbi and I have a better relationship than ever. And it is not just my opinion, it is Barbi's, too. We've both learned not to take each other for granted."

"But I hear she moved out of the West Mansion (Hefner's Los Angeles home). You think she'll ever move back?"

"I wouldn't be at all surprised," he said. "Yes, I think she will."

"You once said marriage was like a jail to you. I would think living in your mansion and in the kind of world you live in might be a jail to some people."

"No doubt I live in a very controlled physical setting. But what you must realize is that something isn't a prison if the person living in it is the one who is in control, the one who has the key."

"Well, what I'm talking about is the way you keep yourself so apart from the world. Whenever you go out, you keep yourself either enclosed in one of your big shiny black limousines or your special private airplane. You never quite go out and touch and smell people and really get a feel for what's around you."

"I don't feel a person is more free ➡

HEFNER, Hugh Marston

DETROIT NEWS
(Detroit, Mich.)

Nov. 24, 1974

(Continued from preceding page)

because he rides a bus. Although there were a few years of my life I definitely was a recluse, I am no longer one now. I'm constantly going around the country.

"And in the Mansion there is a continual influx of people coming in and out from all walks of life."

"I NOTICE you and the people around you speak of 'The Mansion' with a certain kind of reverence, as if it's a world apart from the outside world, as if it's some kind of a Shangri-la.

"I heard the windows are leaded to keep out the daylight. That it has everything from tennis courts and swimming pools to gymnasiums, game rooms, bowling alleys, waterfalls, ponds, and spurting fountains. And I heard there is even a Jacuzzi grotto that goes under the house.

"And I heard you even built your own little mountain to block off the sight of the Los Angeles Country Club a few acres down the hill. And that inside you have every kind of electric gadget conceivable. And that the house staff alone totals over 40 people.

"And when you sleep the whole place becomes quiet, and all activity stops, and only when you wake-up does the activity start and the place becomes alive once again.

"Now, doesn't this give you a rather distorted view of life? Doesn't it sort of make you feel like you're being a little too self-centered? A little too selfish?"

"I feel whatever I have in life I deserve," he said, "and no one knows better than I how hard I have worked for it. It wasn't unusual at all for me in the early years to work for about 35 hours straight without any sleep whatsoever. I remember for a while I almost lived on dexedrene. But gradually I saw what it was doing to me, so I stopped and decided to live a more human life.

"And I feel the way I am living now, what I am doing, isn't just for me. I very much want to give something back to society for my own good fortune, and if people would know some of the things I have done with my money, they might think twice about being so critical of Hugh Hefner."

"Are you refering to your Playboy Foundation?"

"Yes, through the foundation I have donated a great deal of money to the American Civil Liberties Union. I am very much interested in revising some of our drug laws, and getting some better reform laws in our prisons. I bet most people aren't at all aware that we were the major private funder behind the Masters and Johnson program."

"How much did you give them?"

"I'm not sure of my figures, I can only estimate, but I would say possibly we have donated about $75,000 a year for about a period of 10 years."

"How come this never came out? You think Masters and Johnson are a little ashamed of where they got some of their money?"

"No, certainly not. They came to The Mansion and were my guests once, and we're quite good friends."

"A LOT of people criticize you lately because you're spending so much money trying to revise our marijuana laws. They feel with all the earth shaking problems in the world today, like disease and hunger and over-population, you could spend your money on much better things."

"I'm not promoting the use of marijuana. I'm only interested in solving some of society's problems in a rational and serious way. All I want to get across with marijuana is that it's a medical problem, and not a crime.

"You see, I feel some of our laws are so outdated and unrealistic that instead of doing good they rip apart the very thing they're trying to preserve. And don't you see what that does to a society when its laws don't really have any meaning?

"I seriously believe if we didn't make such an issue out of gambling and drinking, and we accepted the drug problem in a realistic way like they do in England, that addicts wouldn't have to go underground and resort to crime, and we'd completely eliminate the Mafia here.

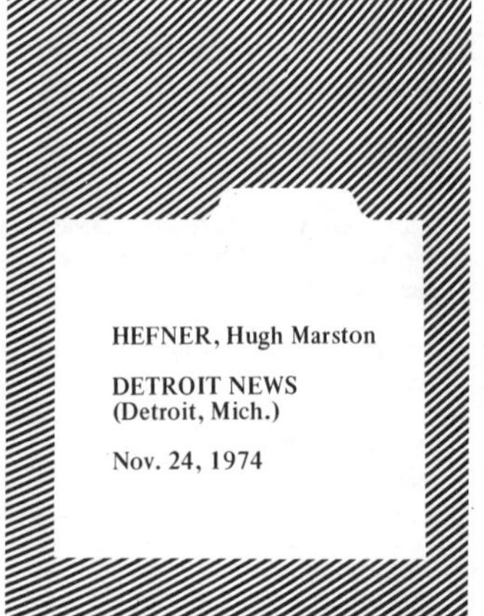

"What people don't understand about Hugh Hefner is he's very much for law and order, but none of this hypocritical crap that seems so prevalent today."

"Why do you keep referring to yourself as Hugh Hefner. I get the impression that part of you is an honest-to-goodness, very feeling human being, while another part of you is standing there very impressed, observing the image your name represents. Am I right?"

"No you are not. I get the impression that you think I am above it all, but I'm not. I use the term Hefner, because I think it is too presumptuous for me to keep using the term I."

"Didn't you start out as a cartoonist who didn't quite make it, so you went to work as a promotion copywriter for Esquire? And then quit because they refused to give you a $5-a-month raise?"

"Yes, they told me I wasn't a good company man, and I guess they were right, unless it is my company I'm working for.

"But cartooning was just a peripheral thing in my life. I was really interested at first in psychology and got my degree in it after 2½ years at the University of Illinois. And from there I did graduate work in sociology at Northwestern."

"I KNOW I've been asking you some pretty rough questions, and you've been nice enough to answer them, but I want you to know that a part of me thinks what you have done was sheer genius, in having almost no money whatsoever and starting up the single most successful magazine of our time."

"It was the right time and the right place, and I happened to have some right ideas."

"Yes, obviously. But please would you be more specific. Why do you think Playboy has over 7½ million circulation? Very few publications in history have ever achieved this kind of circulation."

"Why do you think?"

"Well, I've heard all kinds of explanations. Some people say your main selling point is titillation without threat. That everything in the magazine is beautifully concocted to bolster the illusion of potency without ever putting it to the test."

"Well now," he laughed, giving me a little poke on the chin. "Yes, I guess it would be difficult to put something like that to a test in a magazine. But seriously, what we've always tried to do at Playboy is play it on the level. Whether it's with our subscribers or our advertisers, we've tried not to give anybody any bull.

"Unlike other magazines, Playboy has never bought its readers with cut-rate subscriptions. We feel we have something to offer, good reading and good fun, so we've never had to resort to any gimmicks.

"What we try to do is help people find their identities, and give them a sense of their real self. And, of course, we've always emphasized the play and leisure aspects of life, the part of living that our Puritan ethic makes us shun. A lot of what passes as sophistication in our society doesn't impress me at all.

"We're forever doing studies to find out what readers want, and what their interests are. And believe me it isn't sex alone. We try to have a well-balanced combination of fact and fiction, text and graphics. We know our average reader's age is 29, and we find he is among the highest educated groups of magazine readers in the world."

"THEN HOW COME during the last year circulation went down a couple of hundred thousand?"

"You must have read that in Newsweek. What they didn't say was that because of Playboy's success the market has been expanded and as a result there is an incredibly large group of publications now copying us."

"When you first started out 20 years ago I heard your first issue sold 70,000 copies. Clay Felker, one of the editors of Esquire at that time, who is now the editor of New York magazine, once said a great deal of your success over Esquire was that you simply outdid them on girlie pictures."

"We could have done that with one bosom an issue."

"And now they say Penthouse has outdone you."

"That's accurate, without question. Penthouse is more sexually oriented, but that's all they have. We feel our readers have a mind as well as a body."

"And now they say your new magazine, Oui, is trying to outdo Penthouse."

"That's true too. We realized there is a market for this, and we want to take advantage of it. Oui first came out in October, 1972, and already the circulation is 1,500,000."

"Newsweek also implied you have been very unsuccessful in making some very bad movies, that you've had two magazines that didn't make it, and you made two rotten TV shows. In other words lately, they've implied, you've had one big fiasco after another."

"As far as I'm concerned, that Newsweek story was the most blatant hatchet job I have ever seen. They just took half truths and went on from there. The movies we made both won special awards. 'The Naked Ape' and 'The Crazy World of Julius Vrooder' were beautiful pictures, and although they weren't that financially lucrative, they recieved many favorable reviews. If I was just interested in making money, believe me I would have made something like 'Deep Throat.'

"And what Newsweek didn't say was most of our Playboy clubs have been successful, and the only hotel we've sold was the one in Miami Beach. But all the rest we're keeping and expanding.

"I will admit the TV shows were not as good as they should have been, but we're still learning and we now have about 10 new TV projects in the works.

"But I guess that's what life is all about, going from one thing to another, and learning while you're doing it." And as he said this I could feel the plane was beginning its downward descent.

"The secret is," he said, fastening his seat belt, "is to try to take what I'm doing seriously, but not to take seriously Hugh Hefner, himself."

WHEN WE landed, one of the Bunny stewardesses opened the door and a group of media people descended upon us. And it seemed everyone wanted to take his picture with Bunnies nuzzled up to him on his huge circular fur covered bed in the rear of the plane.

After he got off the plane he was surrounded by still another group of Bunnies, their shapely breasts held high, their hips wiggling back and forth, as they walked with him to his big shiny black limousine.

And suddenly he looked around and saw me once again in the background observing him. And as our eyes met, he winked at me, . . . and I winked back . . . ■

JOSEPH HELLER:

'Catch-22' author takes his time producing another smash novel

Joseph Heller . . . a consummate conversationalist who seemingly has neither the defect of vanity nor its opposite, false modesty

By JACK SCHNEDLER

Tell us, Joe, why do you write so slow?

"Because I can't do it any quicker," says Joseph Heller, in a voice that unmistakably grew up around Coney Island.

"I don't think that slowness in writing is a virtue. I just can't write faster. I'm slow. If I had to write you a business letter complaining that I had been misquoted, I would probably have to do three or four drafts to get it right."

Joseph Heller needed seven years to get his first book just right, but what a book "Catch-22" turned out to be. With more than eight million copies now in print, it is the most celebrated American novel of the 1960s. And Yossarian, the life-loving bombardier of "Catch-22," has become fictional talisman to an entire generation.

* * *

Having made it as a literary saint on his first try, Heller began his second book. In 1962, the year after "Catch-22" appeared, his publisher ran an ad with this optimistic message:

"And the best news of all. Joseph Heller is now working on his second novel, 'Something Happened.' Publication date not set yet, of course — but look for it some time before we get to the moon."

As it happened, the astronauts landed five years ahead of "Something Happened." But now Heller has touched down, after 13 years, and by early critical accounts his second novel is entirely worth the wait. It certainly looks like the novel of 1974.

"From what I've heard, the reviews are going to be almost uniformly favorable," Heller said. "I hope I don't sound too smug, because it's hard for an author to sound otherwise when things are going so well."

Heller is a martini man, and after he toasts our success and we toast his, we begin the questioning in earnest. Our subject turns out to be a consummate conversationalist, who seemingly has neither the defect of vanity nor its opposite, false modesty.

Yes, it's true that he originally thought of having some connections between "Catch-22" and "Something Happened." Bob Slocum, the melancholy middle-aged executive who is the new novel's main character, was to have been in Yossarian's squadron during the war and as Heller at first planned, would occasionally reflect on their military days together.

* * *

"I discarded that idea fairly early," Heller says. "I also had the idea at one point

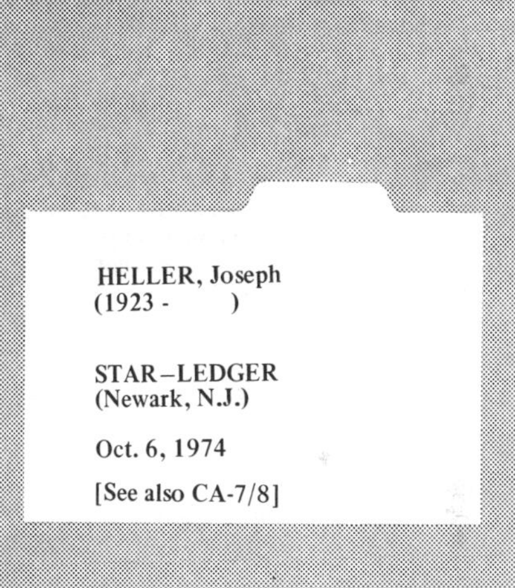

HELLER, Joseph
(1923 -)

STAR–LEDGER
(Newark, N.J.)

Oct. 6, 1974

[See also CA-7/8]

of writing the entire book in children's language, like a Dick and Jane reader. It would have read the way the chapter on Slocum's office now begins: 'In the office in which I work there are five people of whom I am afraid . . .' But I decided it would get pretty tiresome for a whole book."

The vast audience for "Catch-22" has been mainly a young audience, many of whom saw Yossarian's struggles to stay alive as a dry run for the murderous foolishness of Vietnam. Some critics are suggesting that a lot of these "Catch-22" cultists will not appreciate "Something Happened," which is certainly a very different kind of book.

Heller disagrees. "I believe young people will relate to 'Something Happened,'" he says, dipping into a cup of soup. "Many young people today are alienated from the work experience, but they know that they have to work. They know older people like Bob Slocum, and already they're envisioning the same kind of fate for themselves."

Bob Slocum suffers in a corporate world, but Heller believes the same fears and anxieties apply to colleges and universities, where so many young people find themselves these days.

Heller should know. This is his fifth year on the faculty of City College of New York,

(Continued from preceding page)

where he teaches creative writing; he also has ventured forth on the college lecture circuit, doing readings from "Catch-22."

"I enjoy the teaching and the readings very much," Heller says. "One of the favorite questions from the audience after the readings used to be which character from 'Catch-22' I'd identify most closely with Richard Nixon."

* * *

For a while, says Heller, his choice for a Nixon double was Major Major Major, the squadron commander who was always in hiding, from real and imagined troubles. "Then Lt. Scheisskopf seemed just right" (here Heller laughs), "but since Nixon has gone into the hospital, I guess he's most like Chief White Halfoat."

The income from teaching and readings, along with "Catch-22" royalties, has left Heller free in the last few years to concentrate all his writing energies on "Something Happened."

Heller says his income from "Catch-22" was never very great until 1970, the year that the Mike Nichols-directed movie version starring Alan Arkin came out. That year, his royalties added up to $80,000. Now, with "Something Happened" already sold to a paperback publisher and with glowing reviews in the offing, he has hopes of the new novel bringing in something like $500,000 in fairly short order.

Heller does not pretend that money matters are beneath his artistic sensitivities. "I wouldn't ever want to be forced to go back," he says. "Do you know what I mean? No?

"Well, in the early '30s, there were a lot of suicides by people who had seen their income drop in the Depression from, say, $150,000 a year to $40,000. They weren't broke by any means, but they couldn't stand going back to a lesser standard of living. It may have been the humiliation that killed them."

* * *

Heller says he had pretty much the entire story for "Catch-22," and later for the new novel, in mind before he began writing them.

"I don't think I could begin working on a book if I didn't know how I was going to end it," he adds. "It's funny, though — I didn't think either story was going to be long enough for a novel. I thought 'Catch-22' might make 200 pages, and I originally thought 'Something Happened' would be a novelette, maybe 60 or 80 pages."

Many readers have wondered over the years how much of Yossarian's character is based on Heller's own experience, particularly since both were bombardiers. Since "Something Happened" is written in the first person, it raises even more strongly the question of autobiographical content.

"Actually, there is very little of myself in either book," answers Heller. "Of course, the Air Force setting of 'Catch-22' is drawn from my World War II background, and much in 'Something Happened' comes out of my observations.

"But neither novel is autobiographical, certainly not 'Something Happened.' I have always enjoyed my work. I liked writing advertising copy at the time. I even enjoyed my assignment in the war, until the last 15 or 20 missions, when I realized I might be killed.

* * *

"The sensibilities of Yossarian were not my own during the war. I went through that later, and the book is more a reaction to the '50s, to the McCarthy era. In 'Catch-22,' I set down what I felt about a country in turmoil, a turmoil from which we are still suffering. The temporary national unity of World War II had broken down. You'll notice that 'Catch-22' takes place in the final months of the war, when that breakdown has already started."

So, if "Catch-22" is in the third person, why is "Something Happened" written in the first person?

"In 'Catch-22,' the threats to Yossarian are external," Heller replies. "There actually are people out there trying to get him, not so much the Germans any more, but the Cathcarts and Dreedles and Peckems on his own side.

"In 'Something Happened,' all the threats to Bob Slocum are internal. His enemy is his own fear, his own anxiety. The story is his to tell.

"Yossarian, at the end of 'Catch-22,' realizes he can't sell out. So he deserts and has a kind of rebirth through that desertion. He is happy for the first time.

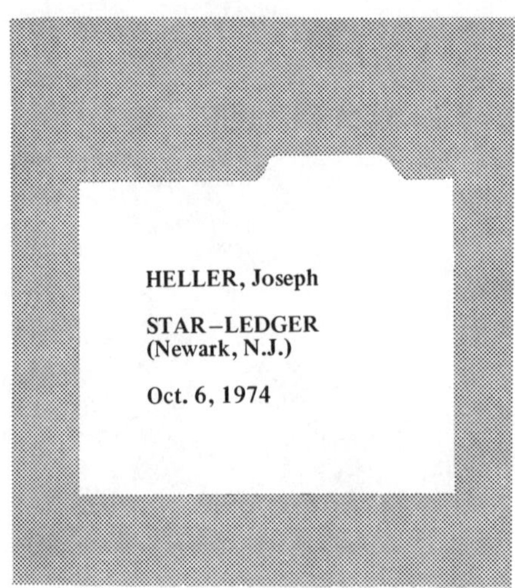
HELLER, Joseph

STAR–LEDGER
(Newark, N.J.)

Oct. 6, 1974

* * *

"Slocum is also brought to the point of decision near the end of his book by the loss of the only thing in life that really mattered to him. He pulls himself together and begins to function in the last section. But this new energy is not going to sustain him long.

"That's why, in the last sentence of the book, he says, 'everyone seems pleased with the way I've taken command.' The word 'seems' is important. Slocum has not escaped his fears."

Part of the reason Heller needed 13 years to finish this novel of middle-aged anxiety is that he took two years off in 1967-68 to write a play, "We Bombed In New Haven." The antiwar drama didn't exactly bomb in New York, but it ran only 12 weeks on Broadway. There's a hint that Heller still carries some pain from the experience, when he says, "An unkind review hurts you. It's a public insult, particularly with a play."

In February, 1969, Heller went back to work on the novel, rewriting his earlier notes. "It was good that I took two years off," he believes. "The texture of the book changed when I resumed. Otherwise it would have been a shorter, less substantial book. It wouldn't have been as good."

Heller guesses he must have rewritten every sentence of 'Something Happened' at least four or five times. "There were days of agony," he says, "when I'd sweat to produce even a couple of handwritten pages on the legal pads I use."

Heller does most of his writing in the mornings, but first he jogs. "I jog three miles a day," he says. "If I tried to jog six miles, I'd drop dead — not from exhaustion, but from boredom. Jogging is the most boring activity I know. So while I'm jogging, I write in my mind."

Heller believes his new novel is better suited for movie adaptation than "Catch-22" (which he had no part in adapting, but still maintains was an excellent film, despite what many critics said).

"In 'Catch-22,' there were a very large number of scenes spelled out in great detail," he explains. "There was little a screenwriter could do beyond selecting and arranging. In 'Something Happened,' scenes are indicated rather than spelled out. The book is in the nature of an illusion, which gives the screenwriter a chance to do the fleshing out."

Meanwhile, what about Joseph Heller's next novel?

"I do want to write another one," he assures us. "But I don't have any specific ideas now."

Right now, Heller points out, he's busy with the triumphant arrival of "Something Happened." But, come winter, he might be concerned about an emotional letdown.

* * *

"If I don't have an idea by January, I could start getting bored," he says, "although I usually handle boredom well. When I'm not writing, I read, and I sleep a lot. I don't really have any recreational activities. I listen to movies, walk the dog, go to the gym. I wish I had an idea now."

There's time for a half-serious question about what Heller thinks happened to Yossarian after "Catch-22" ended ("He's still on the loose. He has not been caught"). And Heller has a bit of advice while he autographs copies of his book for us: "Don't write before you're ready. That's a mistake a lot of people make. I was past 30 before I started "Catch 22."

The inscription on the first page of my copy is worthy of the mind that created Yossarian:

"With good wishes to you — and, of course, to me too. Joseph Heller."

Hellman Talks About Hellman

SARASOTA — Still, I will always remember that when she opened the door of the tree-hidden house she'd rented near the Gulf of Mexico she was worried the "damn cat" would get in. She didn't like it. And it didn't like her.

And I will remember she was much shorter than I expected, maybe five feet two inches, with such a large head and broad shoulders and bust that the slender legs were a surprise as if God had changed his mind partway about the size Lillian Hellman would be.

She was born in New Orleans on June 20, 1905. And then again in the literary sense in 1934, the night they stood and shouted "Author! Author!" when the Broadway curtain fell on her first play "The Children's Hour."

IT WAS WRITTEN, she says, on Key Largo. She and "my closest, my most beloved friend," writer Dashiell Hammett, spent two winters and two springs on Key Largo when only a fishing camp and two houses were there.

Now there are trailer camps and gas stations and restaurants and bars. And lots of other plays, most of them great successes: "The Little Foxes," "Watch on the Rhine," "The Searching Wind," "Another Part of the Forest," "The Autumn Garden," "Toys in the Attic." With them came honor and awards.

In 1969, a memoir, "An Unfinished Woman," won the National Book Award. And now there's "Pentimento," a book of portraits. Because of them, a new generation is getting to know her father's family, the German-Jewish Hellmans, and her mother's, the wealthy, bickering Newhouses — often thinly-disguised characters in her plays.

Not So Easily

HER CHILDHOOD WAS divided between New Orleans and New York, a city she dislikes to this day because it's so big. Her first job was in a publishing house. While she was working there she had an abortion and then married the father, writer Arthur Kober. Then easily divorced him and not so easily spent a good part of 30 years with Hammett, author of "The Maltese Falcon" and "The Thin Man." In fact, he modeled the bright and witty Nora Charles after her. She found out later, the villainesses and the silly girls in his plots, too.

He died in 1961.

She doesn't know why they never married. In the past she's said she supposes she's forgotten many of the bad times and she's talked about the two times they planned to marry and how the first time he disappeared with another lady. And then she's said. "That's not really fair — I was disappearing, too," and she's explained how they believed that alliances could stand up against other people although she had a jealous nature and should have known better.

She's also talked about his heavy drinking.

She stopped hers "because I was going to pieces, because I grew frightened of what would happen to me."

Marriage Was 'Never a Problem'

NOT GETTING MARRIED "never was a problem one way or the other. I got a divorce first; he got a divorce shortly afterwards and I suppose that was the intention. I think it's really quite wise we didn't get married. It's fine, you know, to say that because it lasted in any case. So all one can say when something lasts is it's just as well not to have married. If it hadn't lasted, I suppose my answer would have been the opposite, that if we'd gotten married it would have been better."

Though once she flew across the country to smash the bar in his Hollywood house because a woman answered her phone call in the middle of the night, now she says his "great many ladies" are not the reason. "Those are the reasons that young women tell themselves.

"It's very hard, years afterwards to say with any truth why you did something or why you didn't. I wouldn't like to hear most people telling why they got married."

Nor is she sure that she really regrets never having children. "I'm sorry never to have had children, but whenever I say that to myself I say that's the biggest nonsense ever talked because it's too late now to bother regretting it and if I'd wanted them enough I would have had them, I suppose."

REGRET, ANYWAY, is a waste of time. But, she does regret that she still doesn't own and run the farm in Pleasantville, N.Y. "But it's too late for that because I don't think I'd be capable of doing that and the world has changed so much that I don't think I could do it. I don't think you can find the Farm Labor anymore.

"Yes, that I would have liked to have gone on doing. I was good at farming and I would have liked to have gone on trying it anyway . . ."

There was no choice. It went with everything in the McCarthy era when she was blacklisted for suspected leftist leanings and Hammett went to jail because he wouldn't give the House Un-American Activities Committee a list of names. He wouldn't tell the committee either, that he didn't know the names.

Bitterness, like regret, is a waste of time. "What good does it do?" she asks. But she still feels an overwhelming bitterness about the aimlessness and sort of comedy of it all and how much it affected her and other people. It's one of the reasons she's never been able to write about the McCarthy period.

HELLMAN, Lillian (Florence)
(1905 -)

MIAMI HERALD
(Miami, Fla.)

Mar. 17, 1974 [See also CA-13/14]

SHE DOESN'T single out Joe McCarthy. He couldn't possibly have gotten away with what he did without the time being proper for it "and people aiding him including Mr. Nixon, and Pat McCarran and all the rest. None of it came out of the blue. They came along at a proper time."

She speaks in a low, cigaret-hoarse voice, sometimes interrupted by rasping coughs. A cigaret addict, she wakes up with a "cigaret hangover" each morning and vows to give up the much more than two packs of Marlboros, but then an hour later is lighting up again. She once quit for four days until she decided she didn't want to live her life that way. "It's so disgusting. I'm not undisciplined about other things. To find something that's totally outside of my hands is a shocker to me."

She has emphysema. It has already affected her heart as well as her lungs. It is the escape to warm weather, made with the doctor's warnings to stop smoking ringing in her ears, that takes her South — away from the house in Martha's Vineyard, where she spends most of her time, and the apartment in New York.

Reacting To Age

AS YOU get older, you get frightened of what you can't do physically anymore. She can't handle a boat alone ➡

(Continued from preceding page)
anymore. Her work periods have gone from two a day to one.

She did have an enormous amount of energy and she supposes there's a fair amount left. But to her it's diminished. "I've gotten to sort of come to grips with that, too. Nothing so terrible. It just means watching one's self.

"The one thing I shouldn't be doing I go right on doing. So it gets kind of silly to say I have to go to a climate when I go right on smoking . . . "

HELLMAN, Lillian (Florence)

MIAMI HERALD (Miami, Fla.)

Mar. 17, 1974

SHE ALSO goes right on being hard on herself. She never came to peace with herself. There's no chance of that. "I'm much too critical of myself to ever be at Peace with myself. I could do with a little less of that I must say. That gets to be a bore particularly since it doesn't go very far anymore and I don't correct myself much anymore. But in my kind of nature. I think peace with one's self would be age. I daresay I'll get there. I have no desire to get there."

It's not just her writing. "Nothing on God's earth am I totally pleased with, certainly not myself.

"That would be awful. Imagine being pleased with yourself! My God, that would seem to me death and I don't want to die."

A Discussion On Integrity

A POWER boat pulling a surfer roars by on the bay. Two startled seagulls flee their dock-piling-perch. And Lillian Hellman, admired for her lack of hypocrisy and for her, integrity, deftly fields the question: How did you come out with the integrity you have?

"I don't know that one has the right to think of one's self as having integrity," she says.

"When I was a child my father once said something that I've always remembered and liked. Evidently I used the word honest a great deal and he looked up from a newspaper one morning at breakfast and said, 'I have something to tell you. Honest people don't talk about honesty.'

"I've remembered that. That seemed to me a very profound statement. He said, 'People who don't lie don't say they don't lie. Honest people don't say they're honest.' "

YOU DO something by instinct, she supposes. She never thought of it as integrity or not integrity. It was just what she had to do and she's delighted if other people think it is. She has a theory that whatever is that quality, one doesn't know about it, but probably gets it very, very young. Or the lack of it.

"My father had a kind of integrity, I suppose. My mother did, too. What does the word mean? A difficult quality to put one's hand on, isn't it?"

Then, let's say that she never sold herself.

"I don't know if I did what was right. That I couldn't say. I don't think I ever sold myself. But then I never had any temptation to do it. I suppose it's a matter of temptation. I never wanted money enough to do it, I suppose. It must be awful for people who want something very badly. I don't think I ever wanted anything enough, maybe never needed anything enough. Maybe that's all it is."

Asked to relate that to Watergate, she says, "They wanted everything and nothing else mattered. Nobody else but their own desires mattered. But that's a shabby, shabby crew, isn't it? And they are so pious about it all. I'd much rather have open villains than those pious villains. Every single day there's a pious statement from one of them. One of them's found God or . . . Too bad they didn't find Him earlier.

Lost Interest In Theater

SHE SPENT her life hard at work in a world, the theater, that was not her world, although it has been her life.

Her world, she says, was a strange mixture through the years in the theater of rather simple people — more literary people than theater people.

She lost interest in the theater 11 years ago. "I lost it for a number of good reasons not all of which can be explained," she says. "But the Broadway theater seemed to get to be increasingly a question of money and it occurred to me that I didn't want to live in a world where one was a wild success one minute and a wild failure the next and it seldom depended upon the worth of what one was doing."

But she's rather pleased she did one thing—plays—and turned to another—books. "There's no reason why you should go on doing the same thing all your life. It never occurred to me that would happen. I might go back to the theater. I don't have any rules about it."

SHE FINDS it very hard to write about the living. "You step on toes and you're less free. When I first started 'Pentimento' I had no idea I would do mostly dead people — 80 per cent dead people — and I suppose I did it because it's easier to do it."

It's more than not stepping on toes, it's not causing too much trouble and fights. And it's also "since you see people through your own eyes, how do you know if you're telling the truth? Dead people can't deny it."

But the dead do not always stay buried. Even now, she worries would the dear friend, the heiress of great wealth who was killed by the Nazis because she fought Fascism and helped get people out of Germany have wanted her story told in "Pentimento?"

She strikes a match and lights another cigaret. There is silence as she inhales for awhile.

Has it been a happy life?

She hates words like that. She's scared to death of them. She doesn't know what they mean. "It certainly hasn't been a bad one, though. It's been mostly fun.

"It depends on your nature. Mine has not been a very unhappy nature. It's very often a gloomy one, but not an unhappy one so it would be hard for me to say what was happy and what wasn't happy."

Would it be hard to say what she means by gloomy?

"Well, I get into depressions, but I get out of them very fast."

She takes a few more puffs of the cigaret and goes on to say that she gets great pleasure out of small things and doesn't need large things to cheer her up.

"But I don't know that anybody has a right to look at their life and say it's been happy or unhappy. As you can see, I have a great disbelief in large conceptions about yourself. I always wonder if I'm telling the truth.

"You can stand not knowing the truth about yourself. You'd kill yourself if you did, probably. But it's not knowing the truth about anything else that's so worrisome and as you get older it's more worrisome and you think, 'I must be a fool.' I go around with that so much that . . ."

She never finishes the sentence because it reminds her that Hammett used to have a theory that she made up her mind too fast, that she would come far nearer the truth if she didn't have to make up her mind so fast. "But that was his nature to go slow. My nature is to go fast.

"He understood most people and I don't. He used to say about people, whenever I'd say how wrong I'd been he'd say, 'It's not a question of wrong. You just have to make up your mind for some reason in the first 10 minutes. If you'd go slow and not make up your mind at all and wait to see what happened . . .'

"And then it would occur to me years later that it took too long. It wasn't worth all that trouble." ➡

(Also see preceding article)

Hellman: Doling Out the Tidbits

By Judy Flander
Star-News Staff Writer

The people who came to hear playwright Lillian Hellman speak at the Smithsonian's Baird Auditorium last night were hoping for some more tidbits to add to her two recent autobiographical works, "The Unfinished Woman" and "Pentimento." Those books portrayed many of the well-known people in her life, with tantalizing references to her 30-year-liaison with mystery writer Dashiell Hammett.

She didn't have very much to add. At 67, Lillian Hellman seems world-weary, a bit tired physically (she sat in a chair all evening and chain-smoked), and at first answered eager queries in unsatisfactory monosyllables with a terseness that seemed almost hostile. Later on, as she realized she had an audience of fans who could quote chapter and verse, she softened a little. But not much.

—Star-News Photographer Walter Oates

SHE IS the tough lady who faced up to Sen. Joseph McCarthy's committee on internal security and refused to implicate her friends. The result was a severe setback in her career; but her stand, she says in her writings, was one she never regretted.

She'd like to do something now in the aftermath of Watergate. "If I

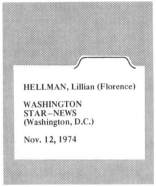

HELLMAN, Lillian (Florence)

WASHINGTON STAR–NEWS (Washington, D.C.)

Nov. 12, 1974

was young I'd really want to renovate this joint (Washington) so it would never happen again. If I was young I would never trust anybody older than I am."

She is amused by the admiration of some young women for her "relationship" to Hammett. "If now it seems strange to people that I lived with someone I didn't marry, I don't take credit for it (being before her time). But I'm delighted they consider me liberated."

THEY NEVER married "because we never thought we'd stay together and when we did stay together, it didn't seem worthwhile. It gets to be if you live with someone long enough, a ceremony seems ridiculous."

She doesn't write for the theater anymore "because I don't think I like it anymore," she says. She "turned away" from the theater because "I didn't want to talk about money anymore. I don't want to depend on two or three people disliking or liking my work."

Is she working on a third memoir? Miss Hellman is again abrupt: "I don't know what I'm doing now and to tell you the truth if I did, I wouldn't tell you."

SHE WOULD only talk in praise of other writers, or not at all. Except for Ernest Hemingway who, she said, "didn't know a thing about women. He did a bad job of portraying women in his books.

"Hammett used to say that Hemingway saw himself as Hercules astride a woman."

A tidbit at last, the audience had its only titillation.

Lillian Hellman Gives Vivid Reading Here

By LESLIE BENNETTS
Of The Bulletin Staff

HELLMAN, Lillian (Florence)

PHILADELPHIA BULLETIN (Philadelphia, Penn.)

Oct. 30, 1974

SHE IS ALMOST 70. She has labeled her own life in the title of her autobiography, "An Unfinished Woman." To anyone but Lillian Hellman herself, such a verdict for such an extraordinary life might seem strange indeed.

She has traveled all around the world for half a century, in guises from journalist to tourist to underground political courier. She has journeyed, seriously ill and half-frozen, the length of Siberia, and worked under siege in Franco-torn Spain.

She has written a handful of the major American plays of this century, turned out screenplays in the money-gilded Hollywood of a bygone and glamorous day, stood up against the witchhunt of McCarthyism in the early 1950s, been a famous and prize-winning literary lady and a contented farmer.

Reads Memoirs

She has counted among her friends innumerable legendary names. Her momoirs are sprinkled with such personalities as Hemingway and Fitzgerald, her beloved friend Dorothy Parker, James Thurber and Tallulah Bankhead. She has married and divorced, but spent 30 years with the love of her life, writer Dashiell Hammett, whom she never married.

Lillian Hellman has led a remarkable life, by anyone's standards.

Last night she came to Bryn Mawr College, mounted the stage, ducked her head shyly and without any preliminaries began to read to a packed audience from her book of memoirs, "Pentimento."

The occasion was because Miss Hellman has been named Bryn Mawr's Lucy Martin Donnelly Fellow in Creative Writing this year; this will be the author's only public appearance during her stay.

She was wearing a flowing floor-length dress of a luscious pink. The lined, craggy face bore a slash of bright lipstick; her hair was immovably set in a sleek blond flip ending in a froth of curls. Dragging deeply on cigaret after cigaret, speaking often with one bobbing from her mouth, she read to a raptly appreciative audience a selection called Julia, the moving recollection of a childhood friend who finally died a hero's death working in the Nazi resistance movement in pre-War Europe.

Lillian Hellman's voice is unexpected. Although she was born in New Orleans and has lived seemingly everywhere, the pronounced accent is not at all Southern, but rather an unidentifiable blend. She reads sloppily, choppily, running her words together in places and turning her own spare and flawless prose into an uneven but engrossing experience. When she got to the hard parts, when Julia was injured and later killed, she had to stop and hold her breath for a moment before she could go on.

Sense of Humor

The rich and varied texture of Miss Hellman's writing is sparked constantly with her own clear-eyed sense of humor.

She is candid and, at least on paper, unselfconscious, whether she is writing about how she got so drunk the night her famous play, "The Children's Hour," premiered that she couldn't remember a thing about it, or in describing to the audience her lifelong inability to cope in times of crisis.

"Decisions, particularly important ones, have always made me sleepy," she explained with the calm resignation of self-acceptance.

She looked very small standing up there, barely as tall as the carved wooden lectern, and dwarfed by the endless folds of opulent apricot-colored velvet drapes rising in back of her. But the auditorium full of middle-aged couples and Bryn Mawr students hung onto every word.

Lillian Hellman is an artist whose finely tuned sensibilities and uncompromising humanity emerge through a beautifully honed craft; in addition, she has led a fascinating life.

The audience at Bryn Mawr last night, watching a small and awkward woman read haltingly from her own written words, was listening to a literary giant. And they knew it.

The Man Who Doesn't Like Secrets: Conversations With Seymour Hersh

A Detroit Interview
By RONE TEMPEST

Seymour Hersh, the nationally-acclaimed reporter who brought you the My Lai massacre and stories of domestic spying by the CIA, is up at the podium in the University of Michigan's Rackham lecture hall, speaking to a highly receptive group of U-M students.

Dressed in a plain gray suit and modest red tie, with his eyeglasses and short brown hair, he could be mistaken himself as the stereotype of an underground CIA operative.

But now he is talking, in that sprinting, aggressive way he has, as though it were high-RPM Italian — irrespressible, critical, crusading language. He is dismissing present and former public officials with caustic, outspoken comments, acting for all the world like some imported "agent provocateur" masquerading as a reporter for the staid old New York Times.

"The best line about Liddy," he says of the unrepentant Watergate burglar, "is that he really does believe it is 1944 and he is in the OSS and he has been captured behind enemy lines."

"I think that Rockefeller," he says in response to a student's question on the vice president's political ambitions, "will stomp all over Gerald Ford."

But he is a reporter for the staid old New York Times.

And for the past seven years, Hersh, 37, has been one of the most prolific and heralded of American journalists. He was in Ann Arbor recently to speak before students in the university's journalism lecture series.

Beginning with the story of the American army massacre of civilians in the tiny

HERSH, Seymour M.
(1936? -)

DETROIT
FREE PRESS
(Detroit, Mich.) Feb. 23, 1975

village of My Lai in 1968, a story refused by several publishers before it was carried by the independent Dispatch News Service, Hersh has compiled an impressive list of breaking stories, any one of which might have made the career of another journalist.

For his efforts he has won practically all of the highest awards in journalism, including the Pulitzer Prize for International Reporting and the George Polk Memorial (2), Sigma Delta Chi, and Worth Bingham awards.

Hersh began his career in 1959 as a copy boy and police reporter for the City News Bureau in his native Chicago after dropping out of the University of Chicago Law School. He obtained his undergraduate degree in history from the same school.

After a few months with the City News Bureau, starting place for many of this country's great reporters, but which he describes now as a "torture chamber," Hersh worked for a year as a United Press International reporter in Pierre, South Dakota.

From 1963 to 1967 he worked as an Associated Press reporter in Chicago and Washington. In Washington he covered the Pentagon, establishing contacts there which would aid him later in the My Lai story.

In 1968 he joined the presidential campaign of Eugene McCarthy, acting for a short time as press secretary.

Disgusted with politics, he quit the McCarthy campaign to write the book "Chemical and Biological Warfare: America's Hidden Arsenal" also in 1968.

The same year, following a tip from a source in the Pentagon, Hersh interviewed individual members of an army unit commanded by Lt. William Calley. Through these interviews he uncovered the brutal My Lai incident, credited by some with changing American attitudes on the war in Vietnam.

The My Lai stories resulted in the arrest and prosecution of Calley and provided material for two more Hersh Books, "My Lai 4: A Report on the Massacre and Its Aftermath," and "Cover-Up: The Army's Secret Investigation of the Massacre of My Lai 4."

Hersh had been turned down for a job at the New York Times in 1967. But in 1972, after he had been awarded the Pulitzer Prize, he reapplied and was hired for the Times Washington Bureau.

Since he joined the Times three years ago, he has produced an incredible string of major stories, including:

- The Nixon administration's secret war in Cambodia;
- The secret, unauthorized B-52 bombing missions over North Vietnam and Air Force Gen. John D. Lavelle's attempt to hide the missions through a double bookkeeping system;
- Secretary of State Henry Kissinger's wiretapping of his top aides;
- The theft of secret documents from Kissinger's office by Pentagon agents;
- The Central Intelligence Agency's secret involvement in the overthrow of Chilean President Salvador Allende, and
- The recent series of stories revealing alleged secret CIA involvement in domestic surveillance in violation of the agency's own charter.

"I hate secrets," Hersh told the students at U-M, "I don't think there should be secrets.

"I'm awfully tired of people in Washington telling me something is secret in the name of national security. I happen to believe that making sure that every car gets 25-miles-to-the-gallon is the most important kind of national security."

In person, Hersh reveals many of the characteristics one would expect in an out- ➡

(Continued from preceding page)

standing investigative reporter. He is extroverted, aggressive, extremely intimidating on the telephone. He is self-confident bordering on self-righteous.

His major criticism of the CIA is that its members are "morally arrogant." If that is true, then they have probably found their match in Hersh, a man who does not hesitate when it comes to taking a stand.

Hersh contends that his personal opinions have nothing to do with his stories. He says that his stories should be judged on their merit as factual news stories. But like many reporters he admits that he usually goes into a story on a hunch or gut feeling and usually has some idea of what his story will be before he begins his research.

And like many great reporters he seems to relish rocking the boat, making waves, disrupting the status quo and all the other old cliches.

"My favorite reaction to one of my stories came in a letter I got after the Calley conviction (Lt. William Calley in the My Lai case)," Hersh tells the U-M students.

"The guy called me a 'sleazy goon'. Sleazy Goon, I liked that. And 'heinous hack' too, I think he called me a heinous hack. That's my favorite."

This gets a grand reaction from the 200 or so U-M students. They are familiar with his work and in their ranks are at least a few who consider Hersh a cultural hero.

Sensing this, Hersh tells them:

"Some of your questions indicate that you think that what I do is heroic or something. It's not heroic. The big question is why more people aren't doing the same thing."

What follows is a rare personal interview Hersh granted to Free Press Staff Writer Rone Tempest near the end of a long day of heavily scheduled activities at U-M January 22.

DETROIT: *The outstanding investigative reporter has become a societal hero and some of the best known, such as Jack Nelson of the Los Angeles Times, Bob Woodward and Carl Bernstein of the Washington Post, and yourself, have become celebrities of sorts. What do you think of this phenomenon of reporter as celebrity?*

HERSH: Oh, I'm very much adverse to it. One of the problems is, of course, I'm saying that as I'm sitting here at the University of Michigan getting ready to make a public speech for money. But basically, with that obvious caveat, I think that reporters are not personalities and shouldn't be. I find it a terrific pain to be constantly asked how I got this story or that story. In fact, since breaking the CIA story exactly one month ago, I haven't done a TV show because I just didn't want to be in the position of people asking 'Oh, what else is going to happen next?' and I'd have to start being coy and cute.

DETROIT: *Do you think the publicity hurts your effectiveness as a reporter?*

HERSH: No, it doesn't hurt your effectiveness. It's just a pain in the neck. If anything, It's probably a plus for your effectiveness. Let's face facts, people like dealing with a celeb. But it's a pain in the neck because you constantly have to go around explaining things (pause) .. but it is nice when you want to cash checks though.

DETROIT: *In a recent magazine profile you were quoted as saying you had a love-hate relationship with the New York Temes, but that its power, or "impact" I believe you said, was your "heroin" which kept you there. Is this a true reflection of your feleings?*

HERSH: There is no question that one of the things that I enjoy very much about daily journalism is the immediacy . . . the impact. In that sense, certainly, it's like heroin. I've never used heroin but I did use that expression.

It's fun to be able to find out something on Monday and write it for Tuesday's paper and have somebody react to it on Tuesday. That's fun and that's what I enjoy about being in the dialy journalism business. I could obviously do a lot of other things and make more money. (Hearsh makes slightly less than $35,000 a year with the Times).

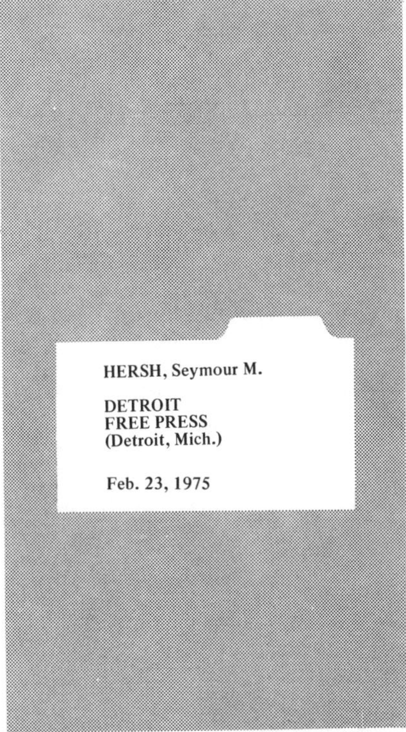
HERSH, Seymour M.

DETROIT
FREE PRESS
(Detroit, Mich.)

Feb. 23, 1975

DETROIT: *Why did you decide to join the staff of the New York Times?*

HERSH: I wanted to join the paper. They didn't come after me, I went to them. The Times is a great institution. It's a great newspaper by the way. I find myself sounding like a company man. I jsut spoke to a group of editors and writers at the Michigan Daily here (The University of Mihcigan student newspaper.) I said, 'look, you know, everybody is so suspicious of institutions like th eTimes these days? The truth is that I have written all kinds of mean, nasty stories for ht eNew York Times over the past 2½ years and I have had no trouble. None.'

They have good editors. The senior editor of the paper is a very, very perceptive guy. But people are very suspicious of the paper. They want to know why the Times is doing these stories on the CIA. The paper isn't doing anything to the CIA. It's news and we are reporting it. Period.

DETROIT: *You followed a fairly traditional path through journalism. . . seven years with the wire services and the City News Bureau in Chicago. Do you consider this time spent in the trenches good background for your career?*

HERSH: Look, I recommend what happened to me in terms of career. I worked in a small town, Pierre, South Dakota, for UPI. I worked for AP in Chicago and Washington. I worked as a copy boy for the City News Bureau, covered some crimes and some murders. I learned the business from the bottom up and I think it had a terrific impact (pause) I think I had a great background.

I spent four years with AP and learned how to write, re-write and edit. I feel that a lot of that stuff was invaluable in the shaping of my career. I don't think I struggled at any point. (pause) I mean, yeah of course I didn't make much money and yeah, sometimes when I was first married my wife worked days and I worked nights and we had all those problems that a lot of newspaper guys have.

There was always a lot of boozing. I remember when we used to finish the shift — I'm 37-years old now and, although I enjoy drinks, I find that if I have too much to drink I don't feel well the next day — but ten years ago we used to close every bar in Chicago we could. A bunch of us. We used to stay in the bars until they closed. Four in the morning sometimes.

DETROIT: *In your career have you had many stories killed (newspaper jargon for refusing to print) for what you felt were political or non-journalistic reasons?*

HERSH: Nope. I've had some disputes. There were a couple of stories the Times didn't run the way I initially wanted them to, but when they did run I could see their point. Here I am sounding like such a good company man again. It makes me nervous.

But you know, the fact of the matter is that if you are a good careful conscientious reporter and write the story clearly and simply and don't try and overwrite it, you won't have any trouble in this business. There are other problems. Journalism has its obvious intellectual limitations.

DETROIT *What about the story that you quit the Associated Press because they cut a story you did on biological and chemical warfare?*

HERSH: That story is simply not completely true. I quit, that's true, but not right away. What actually happened is that the AP butchered a story of mine. They eventually did run a watered down version of it, but they butchered the story and cut it 80 percent. It's true that at that point I decided to leave but I didn't actually leave ➡

(Continued from preceding page)

them until about four or five months later.

DETROIT: *You worked as press secretary for Eugene McCarthy when he ran for President in 1968. Would you do that sort of thing again or do you feel that you are above politics now?*

HERSH: Oh I'm never above politics. I worked for McCarthy because things were so frustrating. I'm not a political person. I don't like politics. I'm suspicious of it. I think it's a lot of crap. I think it's also one of the most poorly reported areas. I mean, when we are all enjoying Hunter Thompson (the Rolling Stone Magazine "gonzo journalist") and still doing straight stuff then there is something wrong. Not that I approve of what Hunter Thompson does, but it shows that there is something wrong with the way we cover politics.

DETROIT: *Do you see any interesting directions that political writing is going now?*

HERSH: Well, it has got to go someplace, but I don't know where.

DETROIT: *Do you have pretty much of a free rein at the Times? Can you go just about any direction you want on a story? Can you decide on your own to go off and dig into, say, multi-national corporations, which you say is your next project?*

HERSH: Yeah, but don't forget that I've demonstrated good judgment and good timing and they have to go along with that. It makes sense for them to go along with that. Another thing is that I work all the time. I work crazy hours. I worked last night for five hours. I was calling people like Howard Hunt (the Watergate burglar and former CIA agent) trying to find two names on a document. And I found them (the two names). I finally got them and one of them may prove very important. I'll go back and look him up. There may be a hell of a story in that. There may be nothing.

DETROIT: *What kinds of things do you see as worthy of investigation on multi-national corporations? What's there that stimulates your interest?*

HERSH: I haven't really thought of anything yet. But I'm looking. I've got the word out.

DETROIT: *But don't you say that you usually have an idea of what you are looking for when you go out on a story?*

HERSH: . . . That's right, I do. Well, I think the multi-nationals are crooks. I think they are crooks and they do funny things with books. I think that they cut corners.

DETROIT: *Do you feel that in this so-called Watergate era, journalism is improving?*

HERSH: Well, I think journalism is changing. I think it's more skeptical. But I think that as an institution journalism still doesn't tackle enough hard questions. We still take too many things for granted. We still don't go beyond the surface on too many stories. We still (pause) . . . here it is January and I still haven't seen enough on Vietnam. We still haven't seen enough on Cambodia. Like I said, I'd like to see more on multi-national corporations. The problem with journalism is that you are always left so unfulfilled. It's one of those things. There are so many of the stories I've worked on which I really don't know the answers — the whole story.

DETROIT: *Like which stories?*

HERSH: . . . for example, who set up the double bookkeeping system for the secret B-52 bombing missions in 1969 and 1970. I don't know why Gen. Lavelle (Gen. John Lavelle, Air Force commander in Vietnam) decided to order those missions. I don't believe he did it on his own, but nevertheless, I don't know why he decided to do those unauthorized raids on North Vietnam.

I doubt also whether we'll ever get the whole story on what the CIA did or didn't do. I can't believe they are dumb enough to not have learned a lesson from Watergate. I have no doubt that there were documents and files (from their alleged domestic intelligence operation) but I assume they are gone.

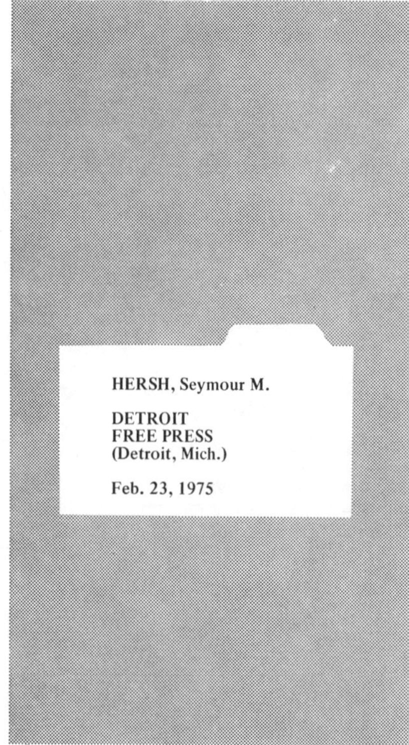
HERSH, Seymour M.

DETROIT
FREE PRESS
(Detroit, Mich.)

Feb. 23, 1975

DETROIT: *If you were running a newspaper and you had a staff of talented reporters, what kinds of things would you have them reporting?*

HERSH: Well, Vietnam. Multi-nationals. I would cover the oil crisis better — things like that. I don't think we should be slaves to public opinion, I think we should set public opinion.

DETROIT: *You have been portrayed often as an anti-establishment reporter and . . .*

HERSH: That's because my stories have been anti-establishment as much as any other reason.

DETROIT: *Do you think it is possible for a reporter to survive in the establishment press and be happy with what he does?*

HERSH: Yeah, as long as you tell the truth. You know I don't find it so remarkable that I flourish at the New York Times. I don't lie and I write good stories and I check them carefully and double check them.

What difference do my personal beliefs make? They are not relevant. I'm anti-establishment in the sense that I don't like people who lie. I'm relieved, like a lot of Americans, that we now have a president who doesn't lie — Gerry Ford. I'm not anti-establishment in that sense. I'm in the mainstream.

DETROIT: *You had trouble getting the My Lai story published, didn't you?*

HERSH: Yeah.

DETROIT: *Why?*

HERSH: Fear. Just fear. People don't want to be ahead. Just fear. I was never afraid of losing the story.

DETROIT: *Do you think that the underground press still has an impact or role to play?*

HERSH: No. No, I'm down on the underground press. There was a time when I was very much excited by it. But they don't seem to be very accurate. There are some terrific underground papers which I enjoy reading, there are some in Boston which I think are very good. But a lot of them have drifted into sex papers—sex nuts.

I think that since a lot of the straight press has become more responsive it has diminished the need for an underground press after the reporting on Vietnam, Watergate and so on. But I still think there is a need for an alternative press. I'd like to see it get better though.

DETROIT: *How do you rate the work of Woodward and Bernstein on the Watergate stuff?*

HERSH: Terrific! Are you kidding? Beautiful stuff. No question but it was eye-opening stuff that showed you could really break out on a story. I'm big fans of theirs.

DETROIT: *What are the stories you've done of which you are most proud?*

HERSH: (without hesitation) I thought the Cambodian stuff was good. I think that I did an awful lot of good reporting on Watergate at a good time when the paper needed good stories on Watergate. General Lavelle's unauthorized bombing of North Vietnam was good. My Lai. The Chile story was good. I liked them all. I can look back on all of them with great satisfaction.

DETROIT: *What do you see yourself doing ten years from now?*

HERSH: I don't want to see myself as a reporter. I don't think I want to be a manager either. Maybe I'll write books. I like the Times, but I don't want to find myself ten years from now chasing stories for the New York Times or for any paper. Among other things it doesn't pay very well.

DETROIT: *What do you enjoy most about your work? Do you like finding two names in a document after five hours work?*

HERSH: I like breaking secrets. I don't believe in secrets.

The Reddening Leaves
of Daniel Whitehead Hicky

By Keith Coulbourn

Photography by Floyd Jillson

HICKY, Daniel Whitehead (1902 -)

ATLANTA JOURNAL & CONSTITUTION (Atlanta, Ga.)

Mar. 11, 1973

If you have any of Daniel Whitehead Hicky's five slim volumes of poetry, hold on to them. They're out of print, hard to find now and valuable, selling for six and eight times their original price.

The first volume, "Bright Harbor," was published by Henry Holt in 1932, the others coming along until the early 1950s. All but one of the books, a group of 13 sonnets about Georgia history, contained 50 to 75 poems, all of which had previously appeared in the very best magazines and newspapers of the time.

"It makes me feel like an idiot to pay so much for my own books, especially when I'd autographed them to other people," Mr. Hicky said, "but it was the only way I could get a copy of some of them."

And the books are worth having, for they mark a most distinguished literary career.

Born in Social Circle, president of the Atlanta Writers' Club in 1926-27, for eight years a columnist of The Atlanta Constitution and winner of the Poetry Society of America's first prize in 1931, Mr. Hicky was, for a time, the toast of the literati.

Now in his late 60s and having retired two years ago after a long civil service career with U.S.D.A. in Washington, he moved back home to Atlanta where he lives a bachelor life in a comfortable old apartment off Peachtree, a modest place with touches of heirloom elegance. He rarely writes poetry now but because of a steady insistence from his readers over the years, he's planning to offer a collection of his best poems for yet another book: "one last farewell," he says of it.

He may call the new book "The Sound of Reddening Leaves," which is from a fragment that came to mind recently and goes like this: "With summer gone, the sound of reddening leaves rides down the listening corridors of the wind. . . ."

And that graceful little snippet is typical of Mr. Hicky's haunting work. It's word play of a masterful type. Illusory. It seems so directly full of imagery, but it's not, of course. Leaves turning red don't make sounds, wind doesn't have listening corridors (whatever that might be). And yet, the feeling of something most vibrantly alive comes through: perhaps that of an aging man, all senses still prickly bright, feeling now an uncanny oneness with approaching death, perhaps the evanescence of all things.

It will be difficult to choose the best 75 or 80 poems from Mr. Hicky's total output of 750 that were published. Traditional lyric poetry, which Mr. Hicky is mostly noted for, wears very well and his poems still have much to say. His most popular works – with readers and editors alike – were always his poems about Georgia, especially those about the coast. As a regional poet, he was considered by at least one critic–Joseph Auslander, poetry consultant to the Library of Congress–as "a fitting successor to Sidney Lanier."

But having been written 40 or 45 years ago, some of Mr. Hicky's poetry does have an old-fashioned ring to it. Which is good, he says. The stuff printed as poetry these days has about as much poetry to it, he says, as beating a tin pan.

Mr. Hicky is a big man with a regal bearing, tall and slightly portly. He stammers sometimes, except when he reads poetry. And he's a veritable lion when he discusses contemporary writing.

"Current poetry has never been at a lower level," he said. "It's impossible to read or to enjoy. There's no sense to it. The editors are simply taken in, don't you know, as they were by Gertrude Stein, who was laughing up her sleeves at them all the time – and she said so."

He got up from a beautiful old gold and red velvet couch in his living room, got one of the popular magazines off a table and opened it to a long, full-page poem. "Read some of that if you can," he said. "It's impossible. It has none of the elements on which poetry has always been based: rhythm, beauty, feeling, color and . . . and . . ."

"Sense?" it was suggested.

"Above all, sense," he said.

He paused for a moment, staring down into the emptiness of that full-page poem. When he sat down again, he was fuming.

"I certainly wouldn't encourage you to get into personalities, sir," it was suggested, "but if you . . ."

"No," he said. "I don't want to say anything about James Dickey (another Atlanta poet). He's the one who has a *two*-page spread in the Atlantic this month, and it's no more poetry than I'm a ballet dancer."

"Did you say 'ballet' or 'belly'?"

"Both," he said with a grin.

With a few exceptions, the magazines and better newspapers stopped printing Mr. Hicky's poems about 20 years ago. Editors told him they were receiving up to 200 poems a day in the mail and so –

The simplest explanation is that the times and tastes had changed. Mr. Hicky continued writing his poems, but less often. He now has about 150 or so that have never been published, but his production is down to a mere trickle: three or four a year.

One of the difficulties, he says, is that he's simply written himself out. When you write 750 or more poems, you've said just about everything you have to say. "If I wrote much more," he said, "I would begin plagiarizing myself."

Even in his earlier poems, the reader may note a certain duplication of effort. The poems are beautiful in that traditional style with rather unfashionably direct things to say. Not that they're really simple, though; much of his poetry has a dazzling complexity on a certain level that still charms anyone who can come to them fresh. And yet without roses and gulls, without dawn, dusk and an emerald this or that, without fingers of wind or wave and the hands of Time, Mr. Hicky would have had to reduce his production by at least a third.

Now that's not as biting a criticism as it might sound. Mr. Hicky wasn't writing his poetry to be read in one big gulp. No poet can stand that. Like anybody else, poets fall into patterns of thought and phrase sometimes, repetitiousness and echoes nearly to the point of self-parody. Indeed, even the best poets are known not for their whole life's production but only for a few poems. And Mr. Hicky, after all, was writing individual poems to appear alone in magazines.

He'll be remembered by a mere handful of poems. They'll include many of those printed in 30 or more anthologies and certainly including "Ivory Towers," "Georgia Summer," "Savannah Waterfront," "I Have a Need of Gulls" and "Never the Nightingale."

Mr. Hicky explains his poetry like this: "I just wrote what came into my heart or mind."

His kind of poetry is called "traditional" to mark it off from what followed. But cultural historians might point out something else that also affected Mr. Hicky's poetry – and life. They might refer such poetry to a phase of a certain rather lovely idea that had come full bloom about that time: aesthetics as a way of life.

It was not, of course, for everyone. Most people, then as now, preferred or saw no further than the private maelstrom of their daily lives. But for a very select few, another whole lifestyle was possible.

Young men, if they came from a good background and got no particular kick out of the battle of wits in the grubby game of sharp deals and profits, young men of that time who felt a larger challenge could, if they dared, dedicate themselves to the arts. (Mr. Hicky, who comes from an illustrious line of Louisianians and whose ancestors include William Whitehead, poet laureate of England, 1757-85, gave up the cottonseed oil business, which his family had been in for many years and which he'd always loathed, as a relative youth; then, over his father's sternest objections, he became a poet.)

This was not of course a formal sort of thing, as education is now, for instance, in which you take a perscribed number of courses and receive a degree of some sort; it depended on a "calling," and thus resembled the religious. The analogy is not far off. The aesthetic priesthood were those like Mr. Hicky who dedicated their lives to it, its trinity the tireless themes of Beauty, Love and Truth, its mode of revelation, Inspiration.

("None of my poems came with difficulty," Mr. Hicky said. "When I wrote one poem, sometimes three or four others would follow rap-

(Continued from preceding page)

idly, in bunches like bananas or like the woman having quintuplets. Then I might go two or three weeks without one. No poem ever took me more than 30 minutes. It's like a cake in the oven; when you pull it out, it's done. And I rarely ever changed any poem. They just pour out like telegrams. I never work over or labor over a poem. They come like a child being born—naturally. And I have never been asked to change 10 lines in all of it. How does it come? Inspiration. I write only from inspiration." He laughed. "If you offered me $1,000 to write a poem today, I couldn't do it to save my life. I cannot contrive a poem.")

The ideals of this tradition lasted well into the 1940s, incidentally, having by then managed to filter down to the masses in a corrupted form via the movies and popular songs. Students of popular culture say that it's all quite gone now, except in parody, in rosy memories and a few usually misunderstood artifacts. It probably burned itself out winning World War II.

NOW the poetry of that time was never really for everybody. Then, as now, few people read poetry. Traditional poetry tended to be ethereal and "aesthetic," a show of sensibilities about the "human condition" that most people didn't have time to bother with. The poetry didn't actually make contact with the daily lives of people, existing rather above the sweat and strain of life. (Carl Sandburg apparently tried to make a connection, but Mr. Hicky says Sandburg didn't write poetry at all except for that little thing about the fog moving in on cat's feet.) If traditional poetry never quite believably was written about real life, it covered with precious sensibility where life *ought* to be lived: in ideals of timeless beauty, for instance, in solitude, and in wonderment at nature.

In 1940, Mr. Hicky was writing some of his best.

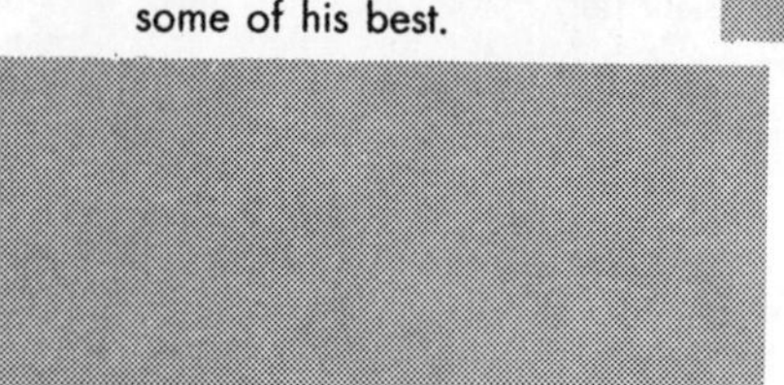

This, for instance, from "Beauty," a sonnet:

Once only shall you meet her face to face
And touch her lips and speak her sacred name:
Beauty is ever elusive, and no trace
Is left of her, like shadow after flame.

And from "Beauty and Beauty Alone," in which, after "the wild tumult of the heart is done/And all our trivial words are less than dust/Each shining victory that our swords have won,/Forgotten . . ." and so on, he says:

Then, only, shall we know no conqueror
Shall capture beauty. Past our little day
A thousand thousand years her hands shall be
Carving the sea's swift patterns, kindling a star,
Shaping a rose to bleed its petals away.
Beauty and beauty alone knows victory.

But then, in "Endings," one of his most beautiful poems, perhaps, some doubts:

I fill my eyes with dawn; I drink it deep,
And day is lost to dusk, and dusk to night;
I watch the moon; it blinds me, and I weep
To see it waning like a weary light.
O earth, O sky, O sea! Tell me these lies:
Beauty lives always—and love never dies!

HICKY, Daniel Whitehead

ATLANTA JOURNAL & CONSTITUTION (Atlanta, Ga.)

Mar. 11, 1973

One might be tempted to call Mr. Hicky a nature poet, and it's true that much of his poetry is about nature; more likely though his concern is with the challenge of putting into words the special aesthetic appreciation of a given moment. The struggle to hold tight to the flying moment—with words—and the awful realization that no word can actually aspire to what the modern crop of critics calls "the facticity of life"—these were often the real subjects of traditional poetry.

"Moment of Yellow Light," for instance, includes this plaintive note:

O autumn day I cry to you:
Must all this splendor pass
Less than a sigh across the hour,
A shadow on the grass—
Will no one come to share this light
Of pear and waning sun?
Autumn, spend gold more miserly
If I must watch alone!

In "Seashore" he writes:

I trace my name into the brightening beach
And laugh, for soon the fingering tide will reach
Inward and bear it outward to be tossed
Like topaz dust that glitters and is lost.

And "The Skier":

How silently, and with a feather's grace
He takes the blinding slopes of glittering ice,
Now swift, now slow, now curving left or right
Over the reaches of a world turned white,
A sweep, a sigh, a surge of ecstasy
Downward, and on, a heart set suddenly free,
Leaping and flowing, patterned like a rhyme,
A bird of air, a moment loosed from Time.

Here, from "We With Our Vanities," is the struggle in its most overt form:

We with our vanities and bright opinions
Our swiftly flashing tongue and quickening eye,
I wonder if we know that we are lesser
Than any shadow we are measured by?

And again from the first three lines of "The Watchers":

"Let us be silent for a little space, Watching the slow stars brighten one by one; There will be time for words when stars are done."

IT would seem, then, that the poems—or many of them—are less about nature than about man's relationship to nature. It's a big problem and led to other solutions later.

But at that time the choice seemed to be whether man was in nature or nature was in man. Both viewpoints are fraught with difficulties, which were being thrashed out in the 1920s. If man is in nature then his ideals and other constructs are real: Beauty, Truth and all the rest, including Time and Memory, all are as real as a duck's quacking. If not, though, if nature is in man, if nature too is but an ideal construct, as strict empiricism held, then man is in some way removed from nature, a solipsist king reigning somewhere between the angels and our animal forebears, or, as some described it, an "amphibian," participating ambiguously in both realms.

The same problem on another level was the conflict between poet and scientist. Poets, trying to maintain their traditional role as custodian of the verities, felt the need at that time to incorporate the methods of science. And science, in its relentless pursuit of basics, had in those days seemingly reduced the world to an incommunicable subjective experience. But how does one write a poem about that? And in a world of ever-changing process, what about things that we cling to in memory? It was rough on poets of that period, torn as they were by two opposing theories. But it produced some of the most admirably tense poems in Mr. Hicky's collection.

Sometimes it took the apparent form of a simple celebration of nature, but usually with a disturbed eye cocked to the proper viewpoint; and sometimes, as in these lines from "For More Than Beauty," it took the form of protest to the poet's monk-like role:

Beauty can fill the sky with light,
But not the empty heart when night
Has strung a million stars above.
She cannot fuel the lamp of love
Nor set it bright upon the sill;
She never has; she never will.
And cold she lies, as cold as stone,
Against his heart who sleeps alone.

It was a very fine style of thought: aesthetic man discovering both himself and the world in the mirror of his reflections. How much it means now, though, one can only speculate. Not many people think that way anymore.

The Royal Oak Teacher Who Writes Poems and Stories Your Children May Be Reading

photo by Steve Thompson

By BARBARA WOOLF
For Detroit Magazine

She lives in a pink-shuttered, white bungalow in Berkley. And from her pink couch emanate such lines as:

"Nobody sees what I can see,

For back of my eyes there is only me."

Simple, childlike thinking that's pretty and ponderable even for a six-year-old.

She is Margaret Hillert, known to the first graders at Royal Oak's Whittier Elementary School as the lady who teaches them reading, writing and arithmetic and known to countless thousands of children in the United States and Canada and even some distant lands as the author of "Farther Than Far" and "I Like to Live in the City" and a series of "Just Beginning to Read Books."

"Farther Than Far" is a 48-page anthology of children's poetry, from which the quoted lines at the beginning of this article were excerpted. The lines are the opening couplet of a poem called "Just Me," which has been adopted as the theme of a new self-concept approach to drug abuse education in LaGrange, Ill. Another poem from the same anthology, a piece called "A Saturday Wind," has been reprinted even more widely and recently was used by the Canadian Broadcasting Corporation on their children's show, "Mr. Dress-Up."

I looked forward to going to Margaret Hillert's house, not only because I wanted to interview her but also because I wanted to see the two cats she wrote so much about. With her, every other word is "cat." I can see why, being a cat lover myself.

As soon as I entered the house, the petite, vivacious poet — clad in a blue zippered shirt, blue wool pants and matching tennis shoes — introduced me to Alexander, the oldest of her cats. You couldn't miss him, really. Alexander, a big orange tiger, was sprawled out in

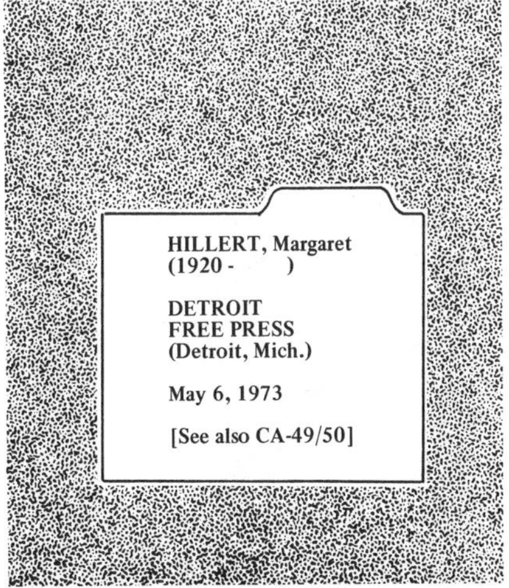

HILLERT, Margaret
(1920-)

DETROIT
FREE PRESS
(Detroit, Mich.)

May 6, 1973

[See also CA-49/50]

regal indolence on a chair in front of a mahogany secretary. He yawned but disdained to merroow a greeting.

Her other cat, Follett, an even larger altered tomcat — named after the company that published "Farther Than Far" — sauntered in shortly after I arrived and, again, introductions were made.

Miss Hillert's house has bookshelves everywhere, on either side of the kitchen door, above the organ and bordering a window to the side of the pink couch.

Poetry has always been part of Margaret Hillert's nature. She told me she had been writing since she was in the third grade but hadn't gotten around to submitting any of her verse for publication until 1961, because it just hadn't occurred to her. "Nobody ever really encouraged me to try to get my stuff published," Miss Hillert recalls.

"But from the time I first saw my name in print, you just couldn't keep me from submitting things."

She writes whenever and wherever she gets "the grain of an idea. If I got an idea, I would start a poem in school. But most of my writing is done when I'm lying on that couch, with my head propped up on the arm."

Since 1961, hundreds of her poems have appeared in a range of publications as diverse as "Humpty Dumpty," the University of Michigan Journal of Nursing and a now-defunct magazine for truck drivers. Several of her poems have appeared in such in-school publications as "My Weekly Reader."

Prior to embarking on a teaching career 24 years ago, Margaret Hillert was a nurse. When she graduated from high school she did not have the money to attend a four-year college right away, so she accepted a scholarship from the University of Michigan's School of Nursing. But she never really wanted to be a nurse; teaching was her ambition. So she worked as a nurse only long enough to pay for education courses, which she took at Wayne State, eventually enabling her to become a certified elementary school teacher.

"People have said to me that it must be easy to write children's poems because I work with kids every day," Margaret relates. "But I really don't take much of my inspiration from my classroom work. Most of what is in 'Farther Than Far' came from my own experiences as a child."

She explains that the lines "Against the old brick building my shadow danced around, but when we turned the corner, it was lying on the ground," from "I Like to Live in the City," also derive from her own childhood. "I was riding my bike one day and I saw where my shadow came across the wall and then fell down."

She wrote "My Teddy Bear," a poem in "Farther Than Far," because "I'm crazy about teddy bears."

It's not unusual for writers to concentrate on particular themes, especially when these thoughts trouble them or have special significance. And, in this vein, Margaret Hillert wrote a poem she called "Encore". . . "I, like a one-songed troubadour, must write the thing I wrote before."

As her credits indicate, Margaret Hillert is by no means exclusively a children's writer. The themes of her poetry range from women's lib to romance to Ellery Queen. ➡

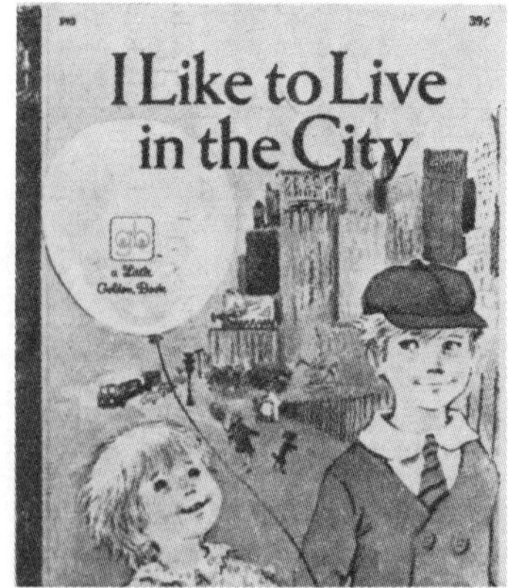

"Balloons . . . I wonder if a bunch of them would float me to the sky," asks poet Margaret Hillert in "I Like to Live in the City."

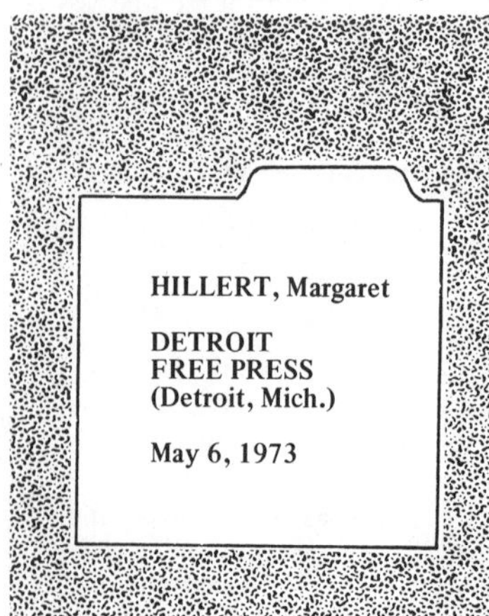

HILLERT, Margaret

DETROIT FREE PRESS (Detroit, Mich.)

May 6, 1973

(Continued from preceding page)

The loss of a limb from her plumb tree — "the once-alive tree whose pink buds matched the roof and shutters of my house" — brought forth "The Amputation," which won her a first prize from the Poetry Society of Michigan.

And it is easy for an adult reader to become thoroughly engrossed in reading "Farther Than Far." The title piece from this anthology has been enterpreted as dealing rather profoundly with infinity, a conception that could prove bewildering and frightening to a small child. But here is how Margaret Hillert treats it:

"I look into the sky and see
The leafy branches of a tree,
And higher still a bird in flight,
And higher still a cloud of white.
Beyond the cloud is lots more sky,
Farther than far, higher than high.
And where it ends, another place
Is filled with space and space and space."

In his guide to teaching poetry in the classroom ("Pass the Poetry, Please"), Lee Bennett Hopkins, poet, author and editorial consultant to "Scholastic Magazine," refers to Margaret Hillert as "one of the best loved children's poets" and says her verses deal with "everything the young child is interested in from the A,B,C's to space and space and space."

Her ordinary, everyday themes, coupled with clever analogies, cover just those topics children are fascinated by: "A jump rope comes in handy for jumping rope, of course. At other times it's dandy for simply playing horse" (from "I Like to Live in the City").

No child grows up without blowing bubbles, and Margaret Hillert's poetry does not miss this integral part of a child's world. She knows how to find just the right word, the right sound to make the poem memorable to a small child:

"Dip your pipe and gently blow.
Watch the tiny bubble grow,
Big and bigger, round and fat,
Rainbow-colored, and then—Splat!"

Asked just why they liked the blowing bubbles poem from "Farther Than Far," two third graders at Oakland Elementary School in Royal Oak responded: "It's true" and "We like rainbow colors."

Margaret Hillert's poems are memorable. They're musical. They're often metaphorical:

"A Saturday wind is a play-with-me wind,
A won't-you-come-out-and-be-gay-with-me wind,
A run-with-me wind,
A fun-with-me wind,
An I'll-chase-you-out-in-the-sun-with-me wind."

"I like the wind and I like the way it's written," said another third grader at Oakland Elementary School.

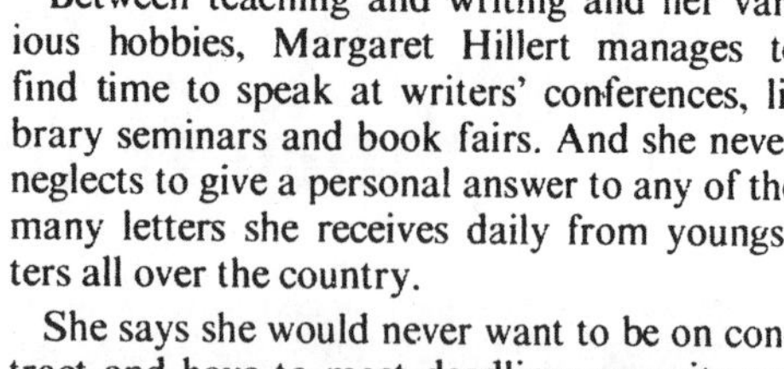

Between teaching and writing and her various hobbies, Margaret Hillert manages to find time to speak at writers' conferences, library seminars and book fairs. And she never neglects to give a personal answer to any of the many letters she receives daily from youngsters all over the country.

She says she would never want to be on contract and have to meet deadlines or write according to the whim of an editor or a publisher. "I don't write poems for anyone," she says. "I write the way I want. It may take me six days or six months."

As her bookshelves might suggest, Margaret is an avid reader. "I'd be lost without a book my paws," she says. But she is not a bookworm. There's a tennis trophy on display in the little house on Phillips Avenue. She's been playing tennis, and quite well, for years. She's also an amateur photographer and used to get up almost before the dawn to practice playing the organ. That's the kind of zeal she has for anything she embarks upon.

Margaret Hillert is the blithe spirit her poems lead you to believe her to be.

She says she used to be "extremely shy," but it's difficult to believe. On a winter walk, she'll tight-rope toe-to-heel along a curb just to see how far she can go before falling off. "I've gotten to the age where I'm completely unabashed, I guess. If I decide to leap from my car and sprint like all-get-out across the street or burst panting through the post office doors, I'll do it. It's not that I'm all that eccentric — I'M HAPPY."

She becomes absolutely ecstatic when she finds her name mentioned alongside those of such writers as Aileen Fisher and Joyce Carol Oates. But, while she's crazy about them as well as W. D. Snodgrass and May Sarton — because "they work kind of traditional but with a novel approach and they're not all that far out that you can't comprehend" — she contends that she wouldn't want a "steady diet of any one writer's things."

This is the teacher I would have liked to have had in my introductory year in school, or maybe all the way through. Who wouldn't.

But for all the children not lucky enough to be in Miss Hillert's class at Whittier, there are her widely used supplementary readers, books like "The Snow Baby," "A House for Little Red," "The Funny Baby" and "The Birthday Car." She's written seven in all, and they've been translated into Danish and Portuguese and distributed abroad.

She's also broken down some of the classic fairy tales — "The Three Little Pigs," "Cinderella," "The Three Billy Goats Gruff," and "Goldilocks and the Three Bears" — into words first graders can read. So if you don't see Miss Hillert at the front of your classroom, kids, take a peek inside the front cover of your book. I'll bet you'll find her name.

The TU Professor Who Puts Six-Gun Heroes In Their Place

By PAT JONES

SINCE the creation of the Dime Novel in the latter part of the last century we have been bludgeoned in story song, and on the screen with six-gun morality.

The upshot, a University of Toledo historian says, is a concept of America's frontier life which is both unearned and untrue.

The American West—its traditions, legends, growing pains, and peculiar problems — has been W. Eugene Hollon's career for almost 40 years, and he is in many ways as much a part of the tradition as the cream-white Stetson he wears on cross-campus walks.

A native Texan, Dr. Hollon is fiercely insistent about the important contributions of the West to American life, as well as angered by some of its more embarrassing characteristics and characters.

This has been apparent in many of his writings, and particularly in his seventh and latest book, "Frontier Violence: Another Look," published this year by the Oxford University Press.

"Frontier Violence" probably is Hollon's most personal book, full of his own love for storytelling, clear expression (an understatement), and unfailing sense of humor.

It is part of a fairly recent trend in western studies to present to the general American reader what scholars such as Mr. Hollon have known for years — that many of the great heroes were not that at all, that "White Man's History" has omitted injustices against the Indian and other minorities, as well as minority contributions to western development.

The Toledo author contends that frontier lawlessness is the result of, rather than the cause of, our violent

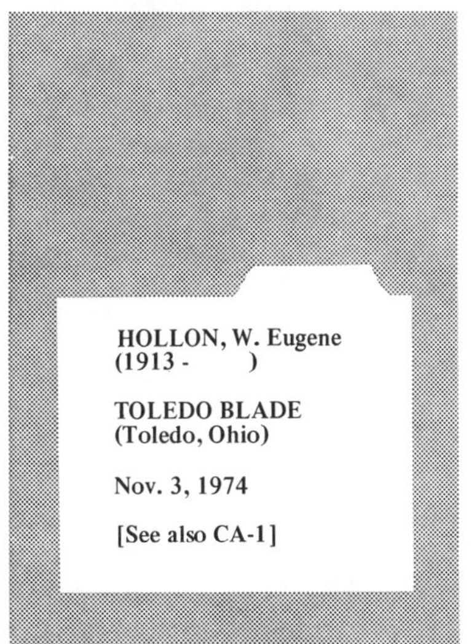

HOLLON, W. Eugene
(1913 -)

TOLEDO BLADE
(Toledo, Ohio)

Nov. 3, 1974

[See also CA-1]

society, though some would use the myths of the West as explanations for violent behavior today.

The frontier, he says, "has lent respectability to certain kinds of violence and provided excuses for various groups — including the government — to parade their barbarities as righteousness. It has served as a reflector of the national psyche and as a never-never land wherein we can play out our fantasies."

The real heroes were the settlers of simple virtues and hard work, whose deeds were the greatest part of the frontier's story. But nice guys, of course, are not the stuff of legends.

This part of our frontier heritage "produced much more of what is good in the American character, than what is bad," the author says.

STUDENTS of western history will recognize many of the incidents and characters recalled in "Frontier Violence" and probably will remember their surprise on learning that heroes fell considerably below either the skills or moral integrity attributed to them.

The Abilene marshal, Wild Bill Hickok, did indeed kill two men in one year in the Texas frontier town, and one of them was his deputy . . . by mistake, we're told. The marshal, "throughout his adult life possessed many of the qualities of a mad dog," Hollon writes.

The book recalls much of the grim truth of frontier justice as well, the realities of greed and grab, the fear and ignorance that produced great cruelties against the Chinese in California and the Chicanos in Texas, and the slaughter of Indians and whites.

In fact, 9 of the book's 10 chapters deal with the violence that Hollon says is such a small portion of the frontier story, and the author recognizes that problem at the outset.

The "Other Side of the Coin," as the final chapter is titled, is a small part of the book, yet weighty enough to cast sufficient doubt on preconceived notions of the violent West.

That chapter, and another, titled "Gun Culture and Cowboy Men-

(Continued from preceding page)

tality," contain many provocative ideas on the impact of frontier lore on the American character.

And many of the observations are pointedly political. Having spent most of his life in Texas and Oklahoma, Hollon was himself part of a small minority surrounded by conservative and ultra-conservative forces in communities and on college campuses.

He did battle with some of those forces as president of the Cleveland County (Okla.) Democrats for Stevenson, and one would have to guess that the odds were not much different from those at the Alamo.

While making some lifelong friends through political activities, Oklahoma Senator Fred Harris among them, Hollon said he is generally "sick of politicians."

And it may be one of life's cruel little ironies that he bears a disturbing resemblance to one of his least favorite politicians, fellow Texan Lynson B. Johnson.

HE describes himself as a "moderate liberal" or possibly a populist. "But people think I'm radical," he says.

That impression is probably true, and not surprising, since Hollon is not among those who save unpopular ideas for the safe surroundings of a classroom. Neighbors, friends, and perhaps even a delivery man or two might find themselves on the listening end of a political argument with him and wonder how it happened.

He is a person pretty clearly devoted to his art — and craft — and it is evident, from the collection of books, memorabilia, and the way he regards his students.

Hollon was influenced by two of the great names in western literature and history, J. Frank Dobie and Walter Prescott Webb.

He "got hooked" as a graduate student in English, and decided, in the mid 1930s, that he belonged in the study of history.

Hollon spent more than 20 years in the University of Oklahoma history department before coming to Toledo. Oklahoma, like Texas, had a prestigious department and one that insisted on a policy of publish or perish, "and maybe both" he says, in an amusing, brief autobiography he prepared when he was fifth president of the Western Historical Association.

He makes no attempts to portray his writing as either intuitive creativity or a happy pastime. It was and is the measure of a successful historian, and therefore necessary, even though departments will profess otherwise.

And because of it, as every one of his graduate students knows, he is the sternest of critics, sending back draft after draft for paring down, honing, and trimming.

THE best teachers he's had, Dr. Hollon says, are good copy editors from publishing houses, who want clear, straightforward writing, not deceptive academese.

As a consequence, he's tough on his students, and toughest on the best ones.

"Your former students are always your best friends," Hollon says. "You work with them so closely, and they appreciate it."

Ever the competitor, he notes that there is no rivalry with a student as there is with colleagues. "But sooner or later you all get mad at each other," he says of departmental relationships.

Hollon will take only a few doctoral students, not out of exclusivity, but because of a long-bred respect for the professor-student relationship.

The tight job market is one reason. "You have an obligation to find them a job," he says, expressing an academic pact that not every professor can or will adhere to with current employment problems in higher education.

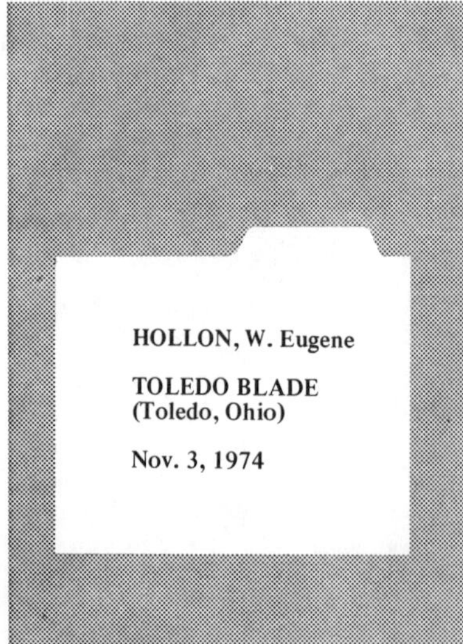
HOLLON, W. Eugene

TOLEDO BLADE
(Toledo, Ohio)

Nov. 3, 1974

"I wouldn't have a job if Dr. Webb hadn't helped," he recalls. "I feel like I'm paying Webb back by passing that on."

And after 30 years of contacts in the profession, he is more capable than most of delivering.

Hollon believes you cannot teach well unless you've written and published, which is what makes him a taskmaster on writing assignments.

"Learning to write is the hardest damn thing in the world," he says. His mentor, Dr. Webb, spent 17 years on his classic, "The Great Plains."

DESPITE his background and research experiences in the early West, Hollon's bigger interest is the 20th-century West and what he calls "the newer states."

The move westward is the greatest migration in the world . . . "5 million people since World War II" he explains.

"That's where the future is," he insists, pointing to what still may be regarded as frontiers in the areas of conservation, urbanization, irrigation, and industrialization.

There's a hint in his voice, that the West can gain from the experiences of the older East, and, hopefully, can be better and wiser for it.

His own study, "The Great American Desert," was one effort to guide that development through scholarly collection of necessary evidence. That book — a nominee for a Pulitzer Prize — he regards as his best, most difficult, and favorite.

It was five years in production, and Hollon drove thousands of miles across the western states to complete research for it.

Accompanied by a graduate student, he visited large cities, remote towns, talked with hundreds of people, and read their newspapers to collect information for the book, published in 1966, a year before he came to Toledo.

It reflects the painstaking research needed to explore the new frontiers of what some still call "cowboy history."

There are, in fact, very few schools east of the Mississippi which offer western history, and only one — Yale — he says, with a strong western history faculty.

Easterners don't have the same regional pride that westerners do, Hollon contends. Regional history courses are a requirement in elementary and secondary schools of the western states and are not regarded as bitter medicine, either, but a means of sectional identity.

"There's still a frontier spirit," the veteran historian says.

Author finds joy in everyday life

—Dallas News: John Rhodes

By KAY CROSBY ELLIS

"If you have to do something anyway, you might as well try to find some joy in it."

That's the philosophy behind "Love and Laughter," the syndicated column by Marjorie Holmes which is carried weekly by The Dallas Morning News.

The column deals with daily occurrences in the life of a wife and mother—from peeling potatoes to caring for a sick child to trying to burp a squirrel—and the author thinks that all such things should be treated with equal and generous doses of those two column titles.

Miss Holmes, who uses her maiden name professionally, was in Dallas Thursday to promote the appearance of one of her two books, "Two from Galilee" in a papeerback edition.

She is widely known for her inspirational books, aimed primarily at women, such as "I've Got To Talk To Somebody, God;" "Who Am I, God?" and "Nobody Else Will Listen," yet she calls "Two From Galilee" her favorite work.

"It means more to me than anything else I have ever written. If I had never written anything else besides this book, I would still feel like I had accomplished something."

The book is the tale of Mary and Josoph, told as a human love story.

"I WANTED the readers to realize that these were two people, not just figures on a Christmas card.

"I wanted to take them out of the art galleries and take away the gold frames and halos which create a barrier for us. I wanted to show them as two people confronted with the great honor but also the great responsibility of serving as the earthly parents of the Christ child."

Miss Holmes says that she was inspired to write the book by the smell of the hay in the manger at a Christmas Eve church service, the presence of her teen-aged daughter beside her and the sudden realization that "Mary was probably no older than my own daughter."

She used what Biblical references to Mary and Joseph were available and constructed her fiction around her study of the social and religious customs of the Jewish people of that period.

The writer adds that she has had numerous requests to do a sequel to the book and has been considering such a project.

Her next book, "As Tall As My Heart," deals with the love of mothers and will be published in time for Mother's Day. Another of her inspirational books is ready for fall publication.

MISS HOLMES is married to Lynn Mighell, a retired executive of an air conditioning firm.

They live in McLean, Va., and are the parents of four grown children, two sons and two daughters, and the grandparents of four girls.

The petite woman, under 5-feet tall, receives many requests for speaking engagements but tries to limit herself to a few major appearances each year.

She also receives voluminous mail, which her husband calls "happy trouble."

"If my readers didn't write it would be too bad, but it is a responsiblility to answer it all, and that's what I do."

THE AUTHOR devotes regular hours to writing in the office in her home, and recalls that as a child she became a "compulsive writer."

She started to sell some poetry as a college student in Iowa and says that she gradually worked her way "up through pulp magazines to general circulation ones."

Her "Love and Laughter" column is published daily in longer form in the Washington Star-News.

She thinks that writing is an excellent professional interest for a woman because it can be done at home and combined with family responsibilities.

However, she adds that too many aspiring writers become discouraged by rejection slips and quit too soon.

"I got discouraged sometimes, but I refused to quit. My perseverance has paid off."

undisciplined sense of gluttony

by Johna Blinn

"COOKING is my passion! I do it instead of boozing or beating children. It relaxes me and gives vent to my frustrations, ego and undisciplined gluttony," confided Barbara Howar. Her dialogue was unorthodox and remarkably candid, typical of the quicksilver mind and blunt outspokenness that has earned her probably more friends than enemies.

A Southern lady, Barbara has been given many labels: "President Johnson's super social hostess" (until he fired her), "intimate of Washington's most powerful cliques," "erstwhile television personality" and "Peck's bad girl." But she defies labeling, although the press has "slotted and pigeoned" her with all those tags. She is brutally honest, funny, and remarkably perceptive, particularly in what she reveals about herself and those who wielded power in the Johnson and Kennedy administrations.

She's also a remarkable cook. "I don't cook by recipes, and while it appears to be more evidence of my unwillingness to obey orders, I find it more fun to fool around with ingredients than to play culinary chemist with the fruits of someone else's imagination. Cooking is an art form, not a scientific exercise and I can never resist making up the rules as I cook."

HOWAR, Barbara (1935? -)

SALT LAKE TRIBUNE (Salt Lake City, Utah)

Apr. 15, 1973

WHEN BARBARA has "the urge, energy and motivation" to get the house cleaned, she invites people, usually eight, to dinner. "I hose off the dirty woodwork and clean out the kitchen. We always eat in the kitchen. I stick everything in the middle of the table and everyone helps himself."

Barbara also loathes the tag, "socialite hostess." "I have this reputation that really kills me. No matter what I've done — and I've done a couple of serious things — I always get called 'a Washington hostess' by the press. They needed to categorize me, so I became the 'socialite hostess.' That was a misnomer to begin with and it galls me because it's an epitaph I'd just as soon forego. I don't want to have spent 38 years here and then have that the only thing somebody could say about me. I'd rather have them say, 'God, she's a horrible witch!' than 'she's a socialite hostess.' I'm sure they say both.

"I don't really like to "entertain" and mostly when I do, it's only a small group of people I like, not people I owe, because I don't go anyplace that means I have to invite people back. I've done that and I don't like it. Besides, I don't have that kind of money."

Advance notices on Barbara's new book, her first, "Laughing All the Way," to be published April 30 by Stein & Day, indicate she'll have no trouble staying off the relief rolls for some time to come. Her Washington memoir is a revealing chronicle of our times starring a cast of two, Washington and Barbara, who have been caught up in and extricated from the web of the power struggle within the LBJ and Kennedy administrations.

We asked about the entertaining during various administrations. Barbara provided an interesting critique and comparison, starting with the Eisenhower days. "I was so young during the Eisenhower administration, I was perfectly happy as long as there was a glass in my hand and I could see across the room. I wasn't really observant enough to know or care who served what or how it was done. I was just excited to be there.

"GRANTED, I've been very hard on the Kennedy administration, but I just felt there was something hypocritical about it. There was this great scream across the nation's press: 'At last the nation's capitol is flooded with individuals, people with an artistic ability to entertain.' But, by and large, there would be one or two pacesetters — the rest would just copy and emulate, so I found no individuality. Again, it was a time with the glass in your hand, staring across the room: a time for seeing and being seen. But I never saw anything unique."

BY JOHN ASKINS
Free Press Staff Writer

She Makes the Drama Unforgettable

Barbara Howar won't tell you who that U.S. senator was she had an affair with, and she kind of wishes people would stop asking. There is more to her book than that, you know.

Actually, what's so special about having an affair with a U.S. senator, particularly when you don't even tell the spicy details? But somehow Barbara makes it seem high adventure. She has that knack.

It's the same with the rest of her book, "Laughing All the Way," her memoirs of Washington in the '60s. Lyndon Johnson held her hand in the dark and she makes it unforgettable drama. It's not exaggeration, just her unshakable conviction that whatever happens to Barbara Howar is by definition terribly important.

She may be right.

There are people who represent an era, and she is one. She seems to have soaked up the light around the Kennedys and the Johnsons and now it glows from her hardy, hungry face. To be around her is to return briefly to those days of gusto just before the world got too complicated to handle.

Her book is not particularly profound, though she may be. It will not topple any regimes. Its most piquant revelation is that Henry Kissinger is apparently only a paper tiger where sex is concerned. Yet "Laughing" is not a nothing book and Barbara is not a nothing writer.

We all read about the Kennedys and their chic and wished we could be a little bit like them. We all read about the Johnsons and wondered at their crude but effective way with power. Barbara felt the same, but she was there and she did something about it. To follow her adventures is to know what it would have been like to be there ourselves.

Not Much Was Plenty

Barbara Howar was an upper-class girl from Raleigh, N.C., who fell in love with Washington when she attended a finishing school there in the early '50s. After her mandatory debut at home she returned, armed with little more than "a vague but cosmetically encouraged resemblance to Grace Kelly and six years at Bootsie MacDonald's school of Tap and Toe." That was sufficient, however.

After a couple of years in a patronage job as a committee secretary, Barbara got bored and decided to marry her persistent millionare suitor, Ed Howar. His money and her own charm got her into the fringes of the Kennedy whirl.

She was with, but not of, Camelot. She says now: "It would have been too demanding to keep abreast of who was in and who was out . . . It was fun merely to watch everyone dashing about frenetically shopping wherever Jackie did; ordering from Ethel's seamstress those sleeveless little gabardine dresses in the right shade of pink at just the right height above the knees."

HOWAR, Barbara

DETROIT FREE PRESS (Detroit, Mich.)

May 6, 1973

She Wasn't Happy

Barbara really hit her stride when Lyndon Johnson took over. It was power she was after, and they had it. She didn't want power for herself, she just wanted to be around it, she says.

She had just turned 30 and she was having her affair with the senator, but that wasn't enough.

She was identified by the media as a delightful part of the Johnson camp, a bright, attractive party-giver who was good for an irreverent quote now and then. She had a lot of enemies but Washington was her oyster.

But she wasn't happy. She was in love with one of the President's advisers and desperate to get out of her marriage to Ed Howar. She told Howar and he told her he would think about it, but what he did, according to her book, was send private detectives with cameras to raid her during a Caribbean tryst with the lover.

The troubles she went through from that point were truly staggering. The threatened scandal caused the Johnsons to drop her and, apparently, started her on the road to maturity.

Today she seems somewhat subdued, wiser, and possibly more genuine. Still you understand, when you meet her, why she appealed to such diverse men as Lyndon Johnson and Henry Kissinger.

I told her I thought she had used the adultress bit to sell books, not because she cared what anyone thought of her. She sort of agreed. "Do you think I would have written this if there had been a market for something else?" she said.

"But I hope it does sell books, for that is why I wrote it," she added with a level stare. That "for" is strictly a North Carolina way of talking, and beneath everything else there is still a lot of small Southern town in her. Small Southern towns are where a lot of legendary politicians and political camp followers come from. And some good writers.

Such origins seem to invest people with a hunger for immortality. Some think they can find it associating with the People Who Matter, and others think they can capture it with words. Barbara has tried the one and now she's into the other.

She wants to write a novel next, about a woman of her generation; the last generation that believed the way to get power was to get involved with powerful men. It ought to be a good book. Believable. As for Barbara herself, she says she's over that.

Pulitzer poet Howard can't escape obscurity

By Allen Wiggins

Richard Howard is a Cleveland native and he is a major force in today's literary landscape, but unless you are seriously interested in poetry yourself, you likely haven't heard of him.

It would probably be fair to say that Howard is the first major serious writer to come out of Cleveland since Hart Crane.

Yet last week, when Howard was one of five persons receiving Cleveland Arts Prizes from the Women's City Club, there was a bare mention of him in the newspapers.

It would seem that the farther we get from the age of the great poetic modernists — Pound, Eliot, Stevens — the more remote become the names of poetry's living practitioners.

Howard is the author of four books of poetry, the third of which, "Untitled Subjects," won the Pulitzer Prize in 1970. He has written a book of criticism of 41 of his contemporary poets, and has just published an anthology of 51 American poets that includes critical comment of his own.

He has translated more than 150 books from the French, including most of the "new wave" novelists and the war memoirs of Charles DeGaulle. He is the poetry editor of a publishing house and of a National literary magazine.

Through the nature of his sympathetic criticism, he has become more or less the proprietor of contemporary poetry.

Richard Howard is a man of a refined gesture, elaborate sympathy and thorny prose. He believes in an elitism of literary interests and writes for that select audience that is prepared to share his tastes. He is, in a word, serious. His work is full of gaiety and play.

It is a style, an approach, a career that sounds solidly Victorian, decorous, genteel, as though it were in another time or another country. Yet Howard is very much a product of Cleveland, and he was at

The Plain Dealer

Richard Howard

Columbia University during the same years that produced Allen Ginsberg and Jack Kerouac.

He was the adopted son of Frank E. Joseph, the corporate lawyer, and his first wife, Emma. The couple was divorced and Howard carries the name of his late mother's second husband.

"Most significantly," he said in an interview recounting his career, "I went to Park School, the old progressive school in Cleveland Heights, where I received a first- class education.

"It was affirmed by the kind of parents I had, and family, who were cultivated people with enormous resource. Not only were they upper middle class and well fixed, but they really believed I should learn things. My mother was a woman of considerable energy and resource who had always believed in a kind of investment of yourself in whatever you wanted to do. You were not to take things lightly.

"I grew up in an enormous house, alone — I was the only child — with a library around me. And I proceeded at a very early age — I was two years and nine months old when my grandmother taught me to read.

"From then on it was learning all the time and that constant commitment to what is usually called culture, but which I don't choose to call that. I call it life itself, the representation of life in the arts.

"My father and my uncle both had a talent for light verse. They used to make up poems at parties. I remember that. Festive occasions required a confirmation of that fact by praise.

"Early on I became aware of the fact that writing could be considered a kind of celebration, that it was to entertain, and amuse and beguile, and that it was part of life. Unfortunately, I think for most of the family it was a diversion and an entertainment rather than something central.

"But my mother, rather against criticism leveled against her by the rest of the family, encouraged me to proceed from the very beginning to be a writer, as I knew I was going to be one from the age of four.

"She didn't think it was necessary for me to, quote, go to work, unquote, and I didn't until I was 24. And then I went to work writing dictionaries, which had considerable to do with what was later to become my career as a translator and you might say as a poet and critic.

"I can remember my mother talking about her brother, who had died at a young age, as having 'nice interests.' And I can remember being appalled at the phrase. It meant he appreciated Sung porcelain, he liked to read books, he went to the orchestra concerts, but somehow those things were things you did to decorate life, to sweeten it, to embellish experience rather than to be experience. And I never felt that way.

"I always mistrusted the notion that one had nice interests because that would somehow suggest that there were other interests which were not nice at all. I learned the truth of that much later and it was indeed the case — they are the interests that run the country."

Park School collapsed at the outbreak of World War II, and Howard went on to Shaker Heights High School. But the experience of Park must have been exceptional. He says he still has contact with a few of his old schoolmates from Park, most notably Anne Hollander, wife of the poet John Hollander and daughter of the late Cleveland pianist Arthur Loesser.

HOWARD, Richard
(1929 -)

PLAIN DEALER
(Cleveland, Ohio)

Mar. 31, 1974

Next came Columbia University for bachelor's and master's degrees, then two years studying in France.

"It was an unhappy time for me," he said. "I was at loose ends, I didn't know what I was going to do, I got jaundice, I was 23 years old, I had no future except that I wanted to be a writer and like all young men I really had no sense of what was to become of me. I felt equipped for nothing at all. I came back to Cleveland."

It was then that Howard went to work for the World Publishing Company, as he says, "writing dictionaries." "I learned a great deal about lexicography and even more what it meant to be serious about one's work. ➡

(Continued from preceding page)
I began seriously writing then."

"Cleveland was not only the place where I spent my childhood but the first place where I did extended writing. The first book of poems was written entirely in 1954 in Cleveland."

Then he went back to New York where in 1957 he had the chance to translate a French book. It was the start of the career that, he says, "put me on the map."

When Howard met the French author he had first translated. "I discovered something about being a translator. I discovered that I knew more about that man's mind than I did about most of my friends because I had worked with his prose. And we became intimates very quickly.

"I would say that the relationship of the translator to the writer is an erotic relationship always, and you learn something about the person that you're working with in an almost plastic, physical way that you can almost never learn about your friends.

"That excited me very much and I realized that there might be a way of making a life that was not 9 to 5 and that was still concerned with the word and with writing."

Translating as many as 15 books a year, and writing on the side, Howard managed to have two books of poetry published, "Quantities" and "The Damages."

"At that point, I began to get uneasy (I was about 34 at the fact that I was translating so much and writing so little."

He applied for a Guggenheim fellowship and got one. And in the next year he realized he wanted to do more than write an occasional poem. "I began to write seriously through the voices, and also seriously writing criticism."

The voices are Howard's trademark as a poet. Starting with that third volume of poetry, which won the Pulitzer, his poems speak as the remarks of other people, most often famous Victorians. He will have a book coming out in the fall, "Two Part Inventions," which will consist of five long poems of imaginary dialogs involving such figures as Oscar Wilde, Walt Whitman and Edith Wharton.

This poetry, the attempt to empathize so thoroughly that the poet allows his own imagination to invent the other man's thought and speak through him, is Howard's alone. It is of a piece with his criticism, which he calls "advocacy, illumination and sympathy," and with his translations.

"The three things I have done are all one thing. They are a way of getting out of the way of voices, letting the voices speak through me and for me, and I have discovered that my own experience can be represented much better than it can be presented."

This sympathy shows again in Howard's newest book, published last month by Viking Press. Called "Preferences," the book is an anthology of contemporary poets that attempts to remove the trench between the difficulty of the modern poetic voice and the voices from the past.

HOWARD, Richard

PLAIN DEALER
(Cleveland, Ohio)

Mar. 31, 1974

Each of the 51 poets is represented by a poem of his own choice as well as a poem from the past that he prefers as sustaining an interesting relation to his own. The choices are brought together, sandwiched by the bread of the poet's image — photographs of the poets by Thomas Victor — and of Howard's commentary on the choices.

It is an attempt to be of help. In a field notorious for its backbiting and treachery, Howard's elaborate generosity to his fellow writers is an exhilaration.

"Years ago, when I first began writing," he said, "I wrote three or four brilliant destructive reviews, and had the usual excitement — the shark tasting blood for the first time — and I met W. H. Auden and he said, 'My dear, this won't do at all.' And I was shocked, because I had thought I had done very nicely.

"He explained to me, very patiently — I think he must have seen something in me besides the ability to slash — that if you're going to write about other writers, the only way to do so is to indicate what's there — what's there to enjoy, to respond to and be illuminated by."

This is Richard Howard on what he does for a living today:

"I continue to write poetry, I write criticism a great deal — in magazines, papers, reviews. I am the editor of a series of books of poems published by Braziller, two books of poems a year, which I choose and write introductions for, and I am the poetry editor of a national magazine, the American Review, which has a very large circulation, and which involves reading about 15,000 poems a month which are submitted — and choosing some 26 poems every three months. Those are my activities pretty much. I travel a lot in Europe and the near East. I'm very fond of the Mediterranean as a center of a sort. I read a lot. I have a dog. Max. I live on 12th Street in Mahattan."

And this, finally, is Richard Howard about the condition of American poetry and why a figure such as himself can seem so remote to so many:

"American poetry at this moment, and in the last 25 years — and I suspect in the next 25 years — is more interesting than it has ever been, except for the great figures of the 19th century. It is very strong right now. I love modern poetry and I can see its relation to the past perfectly.

"It seems to me that painting has sustained a kind of breach — since about 1960 — that is difficult. But poetry and music have maintained, however preposterously, a touch with what has been. And you have to do that.

"I think most of us are taught that the writing we read is not in relation to the writing we write, that there is no way that anything we write has anything to do with what Shelley and Keats, or even Shakespeare and Marlowe wrote.

"It is the trench that is taught, rather than the bridges and planks across it. That is one of the reasons I teach at all myself. I try in all my endeavors to suggest that there is a unity of enterprise, a oneness of the undertaking that, unless it is not only acknowledged but affirmed, will vitiate any enterprise at all.

"One cannot be a modern poet unless one acknowledges the performance of the past. In the same way, one cannot be a teacher, a scholar, a critic of the past unless one acknowledges the primacy of one's own moment.

"You cannot understand the poetry of the past unless you can read the poetry that is being written around you. That is where the mistake lies. Most of the people who teach literature — poetry and prose — at the high school level in America distrust modern poetry, dislike it and are uneasy about it. Therefore they feel called upon to entrench themselves in a certain relation to the past, usually through biography, which destroys in the student any sense that what he is doing or what anyone is doing around him is connected somehow with what has been done.

"It is that notion which seems to be so ruinous and which breeds the nation of 'nice interests,' culture on the one side, everyday life on the other.

"I was fortunate, given every possible advantage by my family. Nonetheless, I made certain choices on my own, one of which was to refuse to acknowledge the trench. I lead one life. There is not something I do for a living and something I do for fun."

Woman novelist binds success to a lot of Romantic notions

Englewood author Susan Howatch shows off several copies of her own book, which have places of honor in her bookcase

Photo by Margaret M. Grieve

By BETTE SPERO

"I'm not a normal housewife," mused author Susan Howatch, in a bit of British understatement.

For Howatch, a native of Surrey, England who now lives in Englewood, is the writer of not one, but two best-selling novels.

Her first major novel, "Penmarric," was also her first best-seller. The second, "Cashelmara," is now following suit, being recently listed among the nation's 10 best-selling, fiction volumes.

Both books were published by Simon and Schuster Inc., New York.

* * *

Though Howatch, a wife and mother, has managed to elude somewhat the normal role of suburban housewife, as an author she manifests another reportedly feminine characteristic. She is a woman of many, many words — as her thick, thick volumes readily attest.

Her novels are in the Romantic-epic genre, one that usually occasions voluminous sagas (according to the dictionary epic ordinarily refers to LONG poems . . .).

"It's a difficult genre in which to write," she noted. "You tend to overwrite. One must edit ruthlessly."

But it's a genre in which she is most comfortable, through she has tried her hand at others (most notably mysteries, of which she has authored six).

"I need the sort of imaginative things that abound in Romantic, epic sagas," Howatch explained. "I find short stories, for instance, too difficult, too specialized."

* * *

Though she writes fiction, it is based on fact. She admits to being an incurable history buff, with one of her passions being the stories of the English kings, particularly the Plantagent line.

"Cashelmara" is based on the English kings, Edward I, II and III but Howatch updated the story from the medieval 12th and 13th centuries to the 19th Century.

In her book the characters are no longer royalty but close to it just the same, being a baronial dynasty that serves in English Parliament and has lands in Ireland.

"It isn't necessary to know the history in order to enjoy the book," she said, "but the great challenge is to fit in the research unobtrusively."

She went to Ireland, where most of the "Cashelmara" story takes place, and did much of her research in the Galway City Library where she found a large store ot books detailing local history.

"The most important part of the story is to get the setting and background right," the author said. "Just being in the place, soaking up the setting, helps."

* * *

It took Howatch about three years to write "Cashelmara," the publication of which is now being launched in Britain and other European countries. "Penmarric," which has been sold to British television for serialization, took her five years to write.

The 33-year-old author said she doesn't really know why she writes (except that she likes it) — but she started doing it at age 12. And by age 16 she was submitting her manuscripts to publishers.

Howatch attended the University of London and originally wanted to be a lawyer. But she came to America in 1964 ("during the age of English secretaries") and soon after became a full-fledged author when she sold a manuscript in 1965 to a paperback house.

* * *

Each year thereafter, through 1970, she sold another manuscript for paperback publishing. All six were written in the mystery, or "romantic suspense" genre.

"I myself, as a reader, like a good story," she said, referring to her affinity for mystery writing. "I always found the easiest stories to read were the 'thrillers'."

"If you're a writer starting out, mysteries are good discipline," she added. "They must have plot."

Soon after arriving in America, Howatch met her husband Joseph, an American, was courted and married, all within a few months. They now have a four-year-old daughter.

The author has since convinced her husband to give up his vocation of working in business and turn to the avocation he shares with his wife, writing. He is now writing his second novel, she said, and also paints and sculpts.

The family that enjoys the arts together, however, doesn't necessarily create them together, noted the author who does her writing in a North Bergen studio.

"At home, we found we kept bumping into each other and stopping to gossip," she said, with a laugh. "It's a good thing to leave the house and close the door on everything when you're ready to write."

* * *

Writing can be exhausting — particularly if you turn out the four or five drafts she does before her final manuscript is ready, Howatch said. But just as enervating for a writer, she noted, can be his relationship with the characters he creates and the stories he crafts about them.

"The people are more real to you than the people you meet every day," she said. "When you deliver the manuscript, you have a sense of bereavement."

But that is only until the next book. And Howatch is already thinking about that.

For her next volume, she would like to write another saga, this one being set between World War I and II in the United States and England.

"The idea is already germinating in my mind," she said.

Success has come early to her in her writing career and, so far, has been sweet.

"I always hoped I would have the success, but I would have written anyway," she commented. "How nice it is, though, to be paid for something you enjoy doing."

"There is a great pressure with the success, the pressure of keeping it up," she added. "But it's a very nice pressure to be under."

HOWATCH, Susan (1940-)

STAR-LEDGER (Newark, N.J.)

June 13, 1974

[See also CA-45/48]

Huie Becomes Hot Property for Filmmakers

By BARBARA THOMAS
Journal Amusements Editor

The balding yet still muscular figure folds himself onto the chair and looks out the glass panel across the front of the house, the same vantage point from which he watched Klansmen burn crosses and neighbors encircle his house in angry caravans.

A white Siamese cat slinks across the room and jumps onto the table, meowing loudly in his face. "I'm one of the last of the autonomous men," he says immodestly. "I've always wanted to be sure in my lifetime I could tell any s.o.b., whether he was standing there with a million dollars or whether he was the President of the United States, to go to hell and I pretty well achieved that position over the last 30 years."

It has been this attitude and his tendency to produce novels that are explosive before their time that has made this southern writer an unpopular figure with many and a praiseworthy rebel to others.

William Bradford Huie has long been considered THE liberal writer in the South. He denies it, would prefer to describe himself as "having perspective,- but members of the Ku Klux Klan and other conservatives have long found him an easy object for their venom.

His novel on racism and fear in the South, "The Klansman," published in 1967, is now being made into a movie in Oraville, Calif., with such notable cast members as as Lee Marvin and Richard Burton whooping it up in the small California logging community. The film could have been made in Alabama but a mutual lack of cooperation between Huie and Gov. George Wallace prompted the author to suggest a search for more fertile fields.

Pushing a two-week deadline on a novel he calls his most ambitious work to date, Huie agreed to spend one hour discussing the film and his other projects. Two-and-a-half hours later Huie, an incorrigible yarn-spinner, ended his nonstop lecture on white liberalism, Alabama politics, the Tennessee Valley Authority, southern writers and filmmaking.

Huie lives alone in a glass-enshrouded ranch style home that was probably once very modern but now seems dated. From his living area, filled with blue sectional furniture (its arms and backs covered with hand towels as protection from the Siamese cats), artificial flower arrangements and plastic doilies covering the hexagonal coffee table, he looks out on the sleepy community of Hartselle, Ala. He grew up in this north Alabama town, met and married his wife, buried her there this year in the family plot where his father also lies.

Except for an occasional golf game, Huie, 63, lives a life of isolation, confronting his typewriter at 5 a.m. seven days a week, racing to meet a self-appointed deadline to finish a trilogy of novels summing up the significant events of the 20th century.

HUIE, William Bradford (1910-)
ATLANTA JOURNAL & CONSTITUTION (Atlanta, Ga.)
Mar. 31, 1974
[See also CA-11/12]

He is garrulous with a vengence and seems unwilling to relinquish his hold on his infrequent visitors.

"I don't associate with many people in Alabama. I don't go to church and I don't belong to anything on earth but Phi Beta Kappa and two country clubs which I gave up after my wife died.

"As for people's attitudes toward me here, all of them I know have been very friendly. There are very few people in this county who read regularly and the number of people here who have read 'The Klansman' is few and the ones who have read it wouldn't object."

Most of Huie's novels center on an individual up against the system. Most are considered ahead of their time in that television and filmmakers are just now getting around to accept them as something other than explosive, "dirty" books.

NBC television recently showed a two-and-a-half hour movie of his novel, "The Execution of Private Slovik," the powerful case history of the first American to be executed for desertion by the U.S. Army since the Civil War.

Several of his other novels, "The Revolt of Mamie Stover." "The Americanization of Emily," and "Mud on the Stars" (renamed "Wild River") also dealt with subjects other authors trying to make a living considered too hot to handle.

Why has he remained in the South in the face of cross-burnings, tirades from politicians, criticism from his neighbors threats to his aged parents?

"For all the things I've said about the South, I'm proud of what is good. It's the demagogues of the South, the hatemongers, I hold in contempt."

Huie seems obsessed with the passing of time and his need to finish his project before his time runs out.

"As you get older in the writing business you get a feeling of urgency. The greatest mistake anyone can make is to assume that he has a lot of time. When you get 60 you know every day has a number on it. Days become precious and the one thing you resent is people wasting your time."

His upcoming trilogy will begin with "Hours of the Night," the story of a man born in 1902 in East Tennessee, a 1922 graduate of Sewanee. It has been called the Forrestal novel since one of its incidents parallels the plight of former Secretary of Defense James Forrestal who became mentally deranged in 1949 after having been privy to the secrets of two presidents and allegedly jumped from the window of Bethesda Naval Hospital.

The second novel, "Battle Without Song," will pick up with the man's son, a graduate of the 1954 class of Sewanee, and will deal with the U.S. involvement in the Korean and Vietnam wars. The third novel will pick up with the third generation of Sewanee men and will cover the events down to 1974, probably ending with Watergate.

When selecting sites for "The Klansman," the film's art editor came with Huie to Winston County in the Bankhead National Forrest.

"We needed a first-rate forestry operation and modern logging equipment. We found some excellent sites but the head of the lumber company wouldn't cooperate. He said they had no black employes. They tried to bring some in about 20 years ago but got burned out and he wasn't willing to chance it again."

There were other available locations but Huie perceived the state wasn't willing to provide the necessary cooperation.

Despite his reputation, Huie says he is actually "very conservative. I've always been a supporter of TVA. That may well be liberal but it might also be called self-serving since I live in the Tennessee Valley. If it's because I'm against the Klan well I come from a family who opposed secession as did all the North Alabama congressional delegates.

"My family was against slavery although we had a few slaves. The old myth of the Civil War has always irritated me, that idea of a united South. The Army of the Confederacy has always struck me as ridiculous—it had the highest desertion rate of any Anglo-Saxon army. The officers were slave holders and nine-tenths of the soldiers were rednecks so, what the hell, they took off.

"My family was against the Klan even when Hugo Black was a member, back in '25 when they wre riding high."

His willingness to speak out against the Klan made him less than popular with some of his neighbors.

"The FBI man in this county used to come by every now and then with a list of the Klan members to tell me which of my neighbors to look out for."

Hunt Spends More Time with His Children

After 21-Year CIA Career

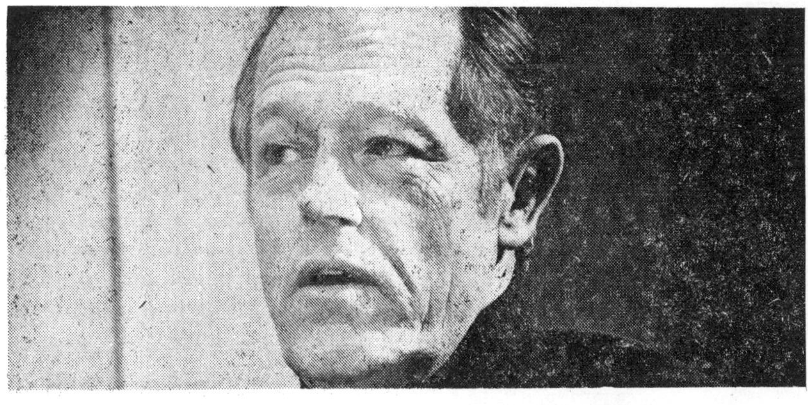

E. HOWARD HUNT—no longer Watergate's super spy; he's a Miami housekeeper.

By DORIS B. WILEY
Of The Bulletin Staff

WASHING an 11-year-old boy's smelly socks and dirty underwear is hardly what you'd expect of a man who has spent a lifetime as a super spy.

But E. Howard Hunt, one of the Watergate Seven, who topped off 21 years as a CIA agent in cities around the world with a disastrous finale as a White House resident snoop described himself yesterday as his son's housekeeper.

Hunt was in Philadelphia to publicize his latest book, "Undercover." In a small room in The Barclay, he talked about his youngest son, David, "who desperately needs me;" his other children, whose alienation from their preoccupied father is now replaced with "closer contact;" his 11 months in 10 different prisons; his health, a non-acid diet to keep his ulcers from "popping"; his "bad Press", and his own disillusionment about "what was going on in the Oval Office — a scramble to see who could put blame somewhere else with no thought given to the men languishing in prison."

What he won't talk about is the Watergate conspiracy trial now going on in Washington.

Testimony Given

Last month, Hunt who pleaded guilty for his Watergate role gave testimony at the current trial, telling the jury a lot of things that he tells about in his book. He's scheduled, he said, to go back as a witness next week.

"I'm under Judge Sirica's gag rule," he explained. Still in general terms, he expressed his disillusion with the people he once worked so closely with.

"I had increasing doubts about their motivations," he said, clamping his teeth hard down on his pipe. "One always likes to think — particularly under hazardous conditions — that one is working for ethical, incorruptible, stand-up types. We were not mercenaries and to read in the transcripts how the selling process was going on, was at the least very disillusioning.

"In the Armed Services you take care of the troops first, before you take care of yourself. In this case the troops weren't taken care of at all, the leaders weren't even trying. It was distasteful and shocking. We trusted our fate to people who didn't understand what was expected of them."

And although he wouldn't comment on Former President Nixon's pardon — "I really shouldn't comment because he is an unindicted co-conspirator" — he has said in his book: "Nixon, the man I had believed in for so many years, turned out to be indecisive, petty and obsessed with self-preservation."

Sustained bitterness, however, doesn't seem to be Howard Hunt's hang-up. The years spent in super-secret missions, talking in codes and symbols, "never giving my right name," wearing disguises, forging documents and making surreptitious entries into guarded premises have molded him into a man who keeps his emotions in check.

Smokes A Pipe

He's been smoking a pipe, he said, since 1938. That was when he gave up cigarets he never inhaled anyway. "I smoked cigarets until the day I was to get married. That morning I coughed so hard, I decided to quit. Cold turkey . . . never smoked a cigaret since."

He seems to accept the future with equal dispatch. "What I do in the future," he said, "depends on what the Court of Appeals does to me."

Hunt was sentenced to 2½ to 8 years and fined $10,000 in January 1973, when he pleaded guilty to burglary, conspiracy and wiretapping. This past January he was freed to await the outcome of the appeal.

Meanwhile "I'm drawn back into living one day at a time," he smiled in a wistful way, the only way he ever seems to smile.

His limit to living one day at a time stretches to at least Thanksgiving Day this year. That's when he hopes to have all his children with him in the home he has established in Miami, Fla.

Of his children, David is his greatest responsibility. "I'm his housekeeper. He has to be gotten off to school. I wash his clothes, dry them and put them in the drawers. I buy the food and prepare it—thank God for frozen pizzas—I make the beds, mop the floors. And I like it very much since it's for my son."

Thanksgiving Reunion

The older children will be coming to the Thanksgiving reunion. Lisa, 24, works for a Washington, D. C. advertising agency; her 23-year-old sister, Kevan, is a senior at Smith College, and St. John, 21, is with a rock group "in Michigan and Wisconsin."

The older children have been pretty much on their own since their mother, Dorothy Hunt, was killed when the United Airlines 553 crashed on a trip to Chicago on Dec. 8, 1972. Even that tragedy was tainted by Watergate when it was found that Mrs. Hunt was carrying $10,000

HUNT, E(verette) Howard, Jr.
(1918 -)

PHILADELPHIA BULLETIN
(Philadelphia, Penn.)

Nov. 14, 1974

[See also CA-45/48]

with her.

Hunt said the $10,000 was part of their savings which they were going to invest in a motel company. But the news stories that followed the crash intimated the money was "hush" money doled out to silence the conspirators.

Hunt said the death of his wife was the most difficult thing he had to face. "I depended tremendously on her, as did the children. She was very strong, capable. Yet in a way I'm glad she has been spared the side effects that have been visited on the children."

Even before Watergate, he acknowledged, his children were "embittered about a lot of things." It wasn't until 1967, he broke his "cover" and told the children he was a CIA agent. "They never understood why I was away."

A career in espionage and family life are incompatible, he found out. "Espionage work is fine when you're young and childless, but it's brutal on children. Cultural rootlessness took its toll. . . always transients in somebody else's country." The Hunts lived in Mexico, Japan, Uruguay and Spain when they weren't in Georgetown or Potomac, Md.

Hunt's writing 53 books in 30 years also deprived his children of his company. "My study was a quiet place where I wasn't distrubed. I was insulated there and I didn't realize that my wife protected my privacy with the caution to the children "Papa's working."

Hunt's "quiet place" now is a retreat to transcendental meditation, a technique he taught himself when he was confined in prison. "I still do it when I can, when I need it, when I've just about run my string. It clears my mind and I focus on the essentials."

'Model' Prison

The ex-spy learned a few other things while he was in prison. "In 10 different penal institutions in 11 months, I've seen a pretty good cross section of penal society," he said.

At Allenwoood, supposedly a "model" prison, he offered to give a short story course, but instead he "shoveled cow manure." It set him to wondering about the "philosophy of incarceration — is its purpose to punish or rehabilitate?"

A prisoner, he said, "can brood about his incarceration and be consumed by it, or he can accept it and construct a livable way of life and exclude bitterness and negative thinking."

He, obviously opted for the latter. His next, 54th book, will be on his experiences in prison, he said.

Kristin Hunter: a Writer and a Fighter

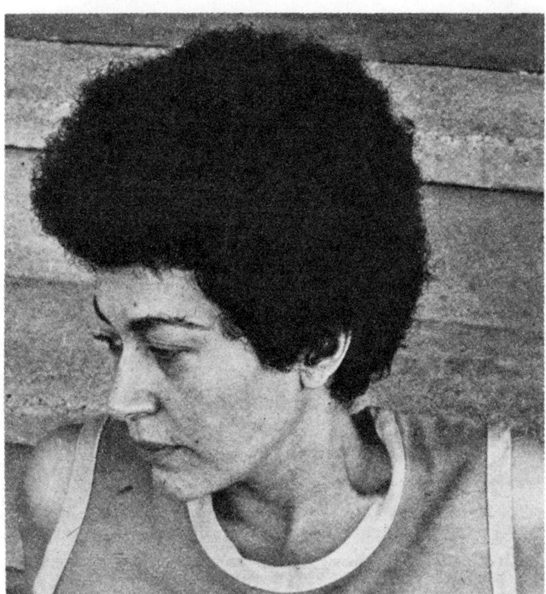
Photo by Margery Smith

BY MARALYN LOIS POLAK

"I simply can't endure anything quietly," says writer Kristin Hunter in her low, tea-party voice. "Sometimes I'm afraid of my own fresh mouth."

Kristin Hunter, the former teenage firebrand columnist for a black Philadelphia newspaper . . . the adult magazine writer whose story on the Cross-Town Expressway ignited a fuse of community indignation that "saved" South Street . . . is now a tall, tan woman near 40 who sees journalism as "a luxury" after writing three novels and selling one, *The Landlord,* to Hollywood.

These days, she teaches creative writing at Penn, which is how we come to be in her office. The most revolutionary thing about her now seems to be a delicately fuzzy head set off by a tangerine blouse, grey vest, and plaid slacks. But she still talks a lot about being angry.

"I was giving a speech before a women's club. No fee—just a meal. The crowning insult was when a lady called me, saying," and she does her best imitation-Social-Register-snob voice, " 'I finally read your novel; I had to get on the reserve list at the Free Library.' " Her voice drips sarcasm. "I got furious. Not only had she asked me to speak for free, but she had the nerve to take my book out of the library instead of buying just one copy to support me. Aaannd," she drawls, "the crowning insult was telling me about it.

"You know, Penn is a rather lonely, faceless place," she tells me, and looks out the window framed by vines quivering in a wind-induced palsy. "I don't see anyone here as far as faculty. I know one or two people to say hello. Actually, I was a student here. I think that's one reason I took this teaching job three years ago. It's about time they remembered me."

But, I remind her, not everyone knows who she is. "You mean, I don't give of myself?" Her voice rises. "I don't have time or energy. Once, almost too many people knew I was here. My address became very public. I was living on Broad Street and when the movie came out, and I didn't feel up to all the appearances and interviews, if I didn't answer the phone, they banged on my door. Or they stood out in the street and screamed my name—I'm not kidding—until I gave in· So in 1970, I moved out of the city. In East Camden, I'm a little less accessible. It's another world across the river, you know, like something created in 1920, covered with glass, and never changed," she says, sipping a can of Fresca.

"Anyhow, I don't like being called a Philadelphia writer and I don't like being called a lady writer. Philadelphia tends to turn even people into institutions. Once you become known as a Philadelphia writer you become a shrine like Independence Square or City Hall and you're not expected to produce anymore. Lady writer suggests something dilettanteish, like embroidery or china painting, not serious pursuits. Male writers manage to pack a lot of disparagement in that term. I've never heard a woman call herself a lady writer."

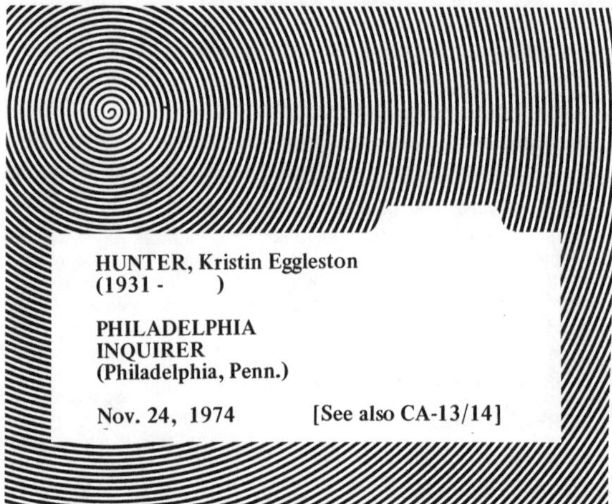
HUNTER, Kristin Eggleston
(1931 -)

PHILADELPHIA
INQUIRER
(Philadelphia, Penn.)

Nov. 24, 1974 [See also CA-13/14]

Has that ever held her back? "No. But once, back in the 50's, I sold a story to a men's magazine, *Rogue*, and they sent me an acceptance letter starting off 'Dear Mr. Hunter' asking me for a photo and background sketch. I decided if they discovered I was a woman, they might not publish the story. That's how it was in those days. So I just never replied."

I am curious about the story. "A movie star, sort of Marilyn Monroe type, had changed her ➡

(Continued from preceding page)

name, personality, identity, accent, hair color so many times at the request of her agent that she finally forgot who she really was . . . And then she started getting homely," Kris Hunter smiles softly.

"Since the bulk of what I've written has been mainly about blacks—or where the two cultures come together — it will not be considered to be 'mainstream.' Whatever that means." Does she have white readers? "Yes. Also white editors and white publishers. But I feel perfectly qualified to write about whites."

Her rather witty 1966 book, *The Landlord,* presented a series of minor comi-tragic skirmishes between black tenants and their well-meaning white playboy landlord. But the movie (starring Beau Bridges in the title role) isn't one of her favorite subjects. She is terse and testy when it is mentioned. "I wrote the novel. They sent me the papers to sign, and that was it. Someone else did the screenplay, probably 50 'Someones.' It's very hard for a thing to keep from getting twisted out of shape. The very reason I'd like to get into screenwriting myself is so if another of my books

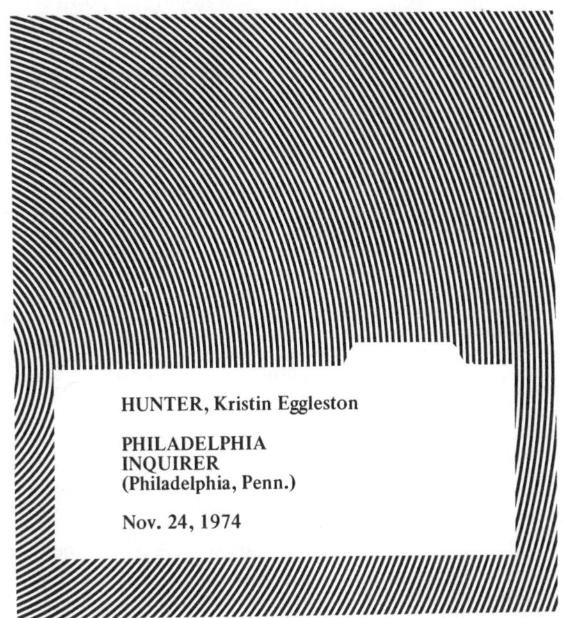
HUNTER, Kristin Eggleston

PHILADELPHIA INQUIRER (Philadelphia, Penn.)

Nov. 24, 1974

hits the screen again I'll have as much control as possible."

She first appeared in print at 14. "I had a youth column for the Philadelphia edition of the *Pittsburgh Courier,* for six years. They gave me a grand $2.50 a week," she recalls. "I covered teenage social life but also could write about anything I felt like. Once I think I advocated violence in a column because an all - white swimclub in Barrington, N. J., had built a wire-fenced pool facing the main street of all-black Lawnside. There it was blazing hot and I said if those insensitive people wouldn't integrate it, blow it up," she declares urbanely. "Of course nothing happened. I would not dare write this sort of thing now."

Of course not. "My mother's side of the family just wouldn't put up with any racist nonsense. They were independent, rebellious. There was a movie theater in Magnolia, N. J., where I grew up, and all the kids went there Saturday afternoons. The theater had a habit of pushing balcony tickets at anyone who was not white. My mother forbade me to go along with this. This left me in a rather lonely position 'cause my black friends wanted to sit together, to be comfortable. But I always demanded a downstairs ticket."

Is she still that much of a fighter? "Yes," she pauses reflectively. "But I do it more with words now." I nod, and she continues. "I was an only child. My parents had middle-class values, you might say. I learned to read when I was 4 and there were always books in the house. My mother was a teacher, my father a principal, and they wanted me to be a teacher. Being around adults a lot I spoke without any trace of slang or dialect. I remember once I bumped into another kid and said pardon me and they laughed saying 'listen to her.' So in school I consciously cultivated a slurred way of speech, and sometimes I went outside and gave away my toys to other children who had less. I guess guilt's built in to my personality, a function of my early privileged status as a child," she admits dryly, shifting in her orange molded plastic chair.

"As a teenager, I admired Isadora Duncan, the dancer, who divided her life between art with a capital A," she singsongs, "and love with a capital L." Has she lived that way? "No. I never lived a crazy life. I was never bohemian. I could never quite make the transition, eating off dirty dishes and all that. I used to agonize over it, but I don't anymore. But I'm not conventional," she insists, then reconsiders. "Alright, I'm conventional to the core.

"I think it's good for a writer to be married. Or to live with someone." I flash to a mental snapshot of my dog and cat. "Because when you get really deeply involved in fiction as I do, you need some contact with real life to bring you out of that, ah, fantasy world which is like some kind of insanity. When I was living alone and working on a book, I'd have to call up someone and say, 'Look, I've been writing all day and I'm a little bit crazy. Please come have dinner with me or go out with me so I can get back down to earth again. It's dangerous living alone doing this," sighs twice-married Kristin Hunter, who declines to discuss her personal life any further.

"Right now, my main priority," she says, her gesture punctuated by a bright round pink plexiglas ring, "is establishing and maintaining the right to set my own priorities. Does that make sense? My main concern is that my life is not determined by others. You see, I have a tendency to be much too nice."

Oh, I say, somewhat surprised.

"Do you really think so?" Kristin Hunter laughs.

I laugh too.

Chet Huntley: He Changed TV News

By Boris Weintraub
Star-News Staff Writer

It is hard, now, to remember what television news was like before Huntley met Brinkley.

Putting it bluntly, television news wasn't much in those days. Television was in its childhood in 1956 — the year the National Broadcasting Company gave Chet Huntley and David Brinkley the job of anchoring its coverage of the political conventions — a potential prodigy with the potential unrealized. It was capable of showing occasional promise, like any bright kid, but more often it was content to take the easy way out, concentrating on the mundane.

NOWHERE WAS this more true than in the news field. The biggest name in television news at the time was the late Edward R. Murrow, but Murrow wasn't a daily personality. The closest to that was John Cameron Swayze, and he wasn't a real newsman at all; he was handed words to memorize, and he said them on the air.

Huntley, who died in his native Montana of cancer yesterday at 62, and Brinkley changed all that. There was a special sort of chemistry between the stern, sober Huntley and the dry, humorous Brinkley that worked, and within a few years, their nightly newscast, expanded from its original 15 minutes to 30, became a necessity in our collective American lives.

Les Crystal, the current executive producer of the NBC Nightly News, was reflecting last night on what Huntley and Brinkley meant a few hours after Brinkley said his last "Good night, Chet" on the show.

"With the popularity and the attention they got, they made TV news important in a way it hadn't been before," Crystal said. "Murrow had established the importance of television news, but Huntley and Brinkley elevat-

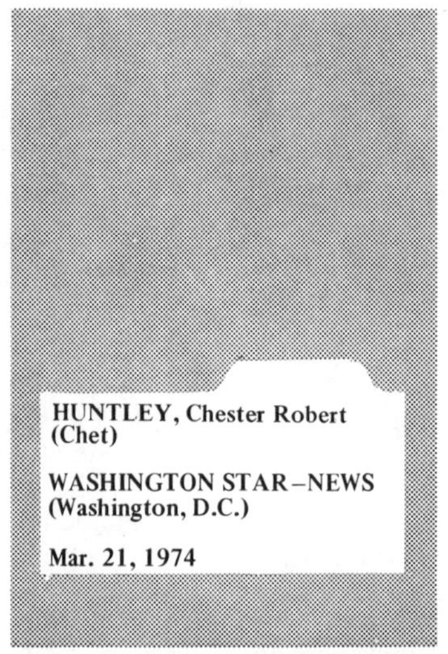
HUNTLEY, Chester Robert (Chet)

WASHINGTON STAR–NEWS (Washington, D.C.)

Mar. 21, 1974

ed the nightly national newscast to its current position as the prime source of daily news for a large part of the American public."

Wallace Westfeldt, who preceded Crystal as the show's executive producer, put it another way.

"EVERYBODY TALKS about Murrow," Westfeldt said. "But when Chet and David came on, the audiences were larger. When you start thinking about who people read and listen to, you might think about Walter Lippmann. But not that many people read Lippmann. Chet and David had more of an impact on the mass audience. They, together, became institutionalized in a way that no one had before."

Part of Huntley's impact came from the way he looked and sounded: he looked and sounded believable. Part of the impact came from the fact that he and Brinkley wrote most of their own copy. They had been reporters throughout their careers; Huntley worked for the Seattle Star while he was attending the University of Washington, and he worked for several radio stations as a newsman before joining CBS in 1939. He remained at CBS until moving to ABC in 1951 and then to NBC in that key year, 1956.

EVEN MORE important, though, was the quality of their writing. As Westfeldt put it, Huntley and Brinkley "were able to talk the language of the people. They didn't talk down to people, but they wrote in a simple language everyone could understand.

"Think of the environment of the nightly TV newscast," Westfeldt went on. "People are home from work, settling down for dinner, the family is getting together; the words must come across in a way that people can understand them right away."

As the institutionalization of the nightly television newscast proceeded, it meant success at NBC and a re-evaluation at CBS, which,, until then, had been the leading news network. Huntley and Brinkley zipped past CBS in the ratings, forcing CBS to upgrade its nightly show by bringing in Walter Cronkite, who became as significant an institution as his competitors.

"What these guys did," Westfeldt said last night, "was to open up the eyes of people who ran television to the fact that TV news was important, and that it was a saleable commodity. They lifted TV news up from snatch-and-read to journalism."

PERHAPS THAT is as fitting an epitaph as any for Chet Huntley. Certainly, it is a remarkable testimony to his standing with the American public that when he retired from NBC in 1970 to his beloved Big Sky country of Montana and then suddenly showed up on television once more doing commercials, people actually complained. We can accept most of our walking institutions doing commercials: Joe Namath, Mark Spitz, et al. But Chet Huntley? Somehow, that seemed wrong.

Chet Huntley meant that much to the American public. ➡

Chet Huntley—the fatherly rebel

(Also see preceding article)

By Bill Barrett

HUNTLEY, Chester Robert (Chet)
CLEVELAND PRESS (Cleveland, Ohio)
Mar. 22, 1974

Chet Huntley had challenged the odds and whipped them all his life, so it was especially shocking to hear of his death the other day.

He had taken on the McCarthy camp and the labor unions and even President Nixon before it was all that fashionable. He survived all the flak until cancer cut him down Wednesday at age 62.

Nobody on or off television looked less likely to attract controversy. Chet Huntley looked like everyone's father ought to look when the rent is due and there's no money left in the sugar bowl — somber, steady, sure to make the safe, dependable move.

But Huntley was a displaced westerner with a go-to-hell spirit of independence that manifested itself in unexpected ways. It was difficult to label this man.

In the early 1950's, when he was still a fairly obscure radio newsman for CBS, he tangled with the mighty forces of Sen. Joseph McCarthy and won a $10,000 slander judgment from a woman who had denounced him as a Communist.

But then years later, when he was a big-name NBC-TV anchorman with David Brinkley, he crossed the picket lines of his striking union, the American Federation of Radio and Television Artists.

"I have been a member of AFTRA since 1939," he told me in a telephone interview. "But from the start I was convinced that newsmen did not belong in the same union with singers and dancers . . ."

Later he made the headlines for saying, in an interview. unkind things about Nixon and even about the astronauts.

He kept doing the unexpected. When everyone expected Brinkley to retire, it was Huntley who made the break. When he went into peaceful retirement back home in Montana in 1970, he got in a battle with conservationists.

And somehow few people really expected him to die of cancer.

His Coworkers Respected Huntley

HUNTLEY, Chester Robert (Chet)
PHILADELPHIA BULLETIN (Philadelphia, Penn.)
Mar. 22, 1974

By Rex Polier

THERE were two things about Chet Huntley's office in Rockefeller Center that told you something about the man.

One was the huge-old-fashioned, rolltop desk at which this symbol of electronic journalism worked. It belonged to his father when the elder Huntley was a telegrapher for the Northern Pacific Railroad. For his son, it was a cherished link with the American past that he loved.

The other: The shelf-lined walls containing hundreds of books. He was usually reading two and three at the same time. He also read newspapers and magazines omnivorously and never missed an edition of the "Today" Show. Huntley valued knowledge for its own sake.

As those who watched Huntley and Brinkley hold the fort at political conventions into the small hours of the morning knew, his encyclopedic mind provided a wealth of information at all times. Huntley scorned having people do research for him, just as he always refused to allow anyone to go to the cafeteria to get him a cup of coffee. "He stood in line like anyone else," an associate at NBC News recalls.

ALTHOUGH he was an integral part of the American Megalopolis for the 14 years he and Brinkley were undisputed kingpins of the network TV news scene, the tall, craggy-faced Montanan never got used to the skyscrapers of New York.

"I don't intend to keel over in these canyons," he said one day to Joe Derby, director of publicity for NBC News, who was also one of his most devoted friends. In NBC News' moving 10-minute segment Wednesday night on his death, Brinkley recalled him expressing similar sentiment during a vacuum in a political convention coverage.

He commanded the respect and affection of his associates at NBC, especially the native New Yorkers like Derby. They recognized him as a Lincolnesque, uncompromising Westerner who knew that he must someday get back to the land. "He was the best of the West's kind of man," Derby noted in a phone conversation yesterday.

DERBY recalled a telephone conversation with Huntley from Montana in February, when his malignancy was becoming known. Joe asked how he might like it handled in the news.

"Tell 'em I've got cancer of the lung," Huntley said. "This G.D. thing is going to win, Joe, but I'm going to give it a fight."

Derby last saw him in person in New York in January. Huntley came back on occasion because he was committed to narrate occasional specials in connection with the American Bicentennial.

"He didn't look well," Derby recalled. "He was sort of pale. But at that time I had no cause to think there was anything seriously wrong with him.

" 'I've got a pain in my back, Joe,' Huntley said. "I think I got it in a skiing accident. I'm going to have to go in and have a checkup.'

"I remembered thinking, 'skiing at 62!,' " Derby recalled.

UNLIKE the late Edward R. Murrow, whose sense of news ran in the direction of ideologies and trends, Huntley favored basic "meat-and-potatoes" reporting and left the job of forecasting and interpreting to others. He studiously avoided anything that could be construed as advocacy journalism.

"Chet used to tell me he didn't really know whether he was a conservative or a liberal, but at times would add: 'Maybe when I get right down to cases, Joe, I'm kind of a conservative. But when it comes to unjust and unfair race relations, I become a screaming liberal.' "

One excerpt on the NBC News obituary was the commentary Huntley delivered, half in sadness, half in outrage, upon news of the assassination of Dr. Martin Luther King.

"He wrote that on a piece of yellow, ruled paper in exactly one minute enroute to the newsroom to go on the air," Derby said. "I can still see him striding down the corridor scribbling away on that piece of paper."

TV has given us a number of spontaneous moments that will live with us. One was the salute given by a frail General Omar Bradley with a trembling hand as the casket of Dwight D. Eisenhower appeared in the church doorway.

The NBC News obituary gave me another. It came at the conclusion of Brinkley's low-keyed but emotional tribute which was sent via satellite from Portland, Ore., prior to air time. Looking much older than he usually does, Brinkley said, with tears:

"So for the last time, good night, Chet."

Clifford Irving: He'd Do It Again

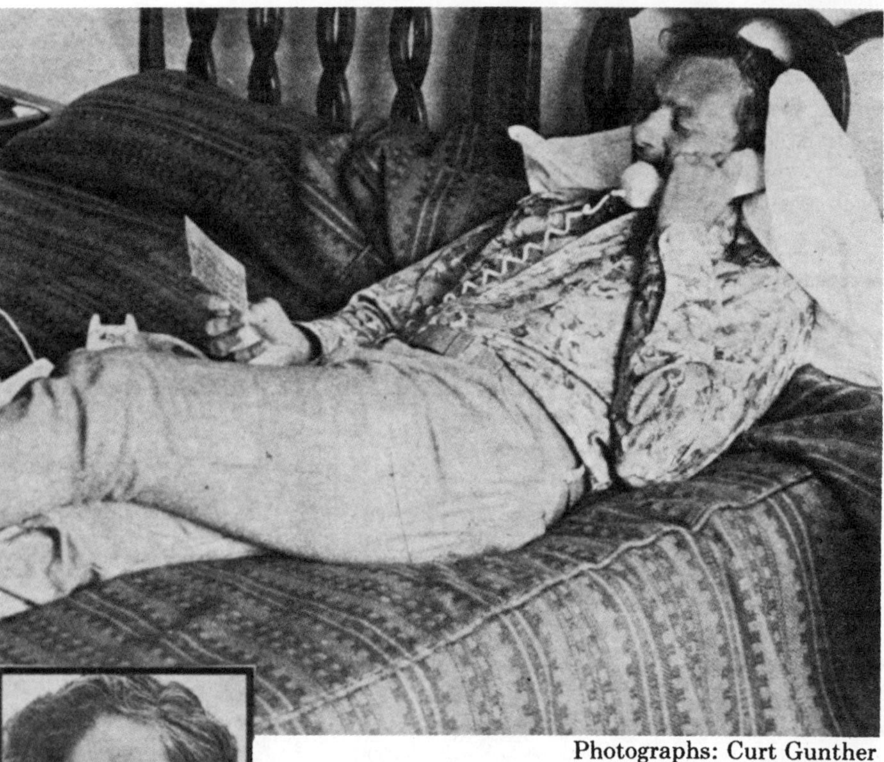

Photographs: Curt Gunther

From a suite in Beverly Hills Hotel, Irving talks with old friends and business acquaintances

IRVING, Clifford (Michael)
(1930-)

MIAMI HERALD
(Miami, Fla.)

Sept. 1, 1974

[See also CA-2]

By Mandy Brown

After 16 months in prison and six weeks in a halfway house, literary hoaxer Clifford Irving is back in business doing what he's best at — writing biographies. But this time, instead of creating fake masterpieces like the Howard Hughes autobiography, Irving is penning legitimate life stories for a fee of $25,000 or higher. He's already at work on the life of Missouri trucking millionaire Cleo Crouch, and is preparing pitches to J. Paul Getty and Richard M. Nixon, among others.

"I plan to function mainly as editor-in-chief of these projects, hiring professional freelancers to do most of the writing," he explains.

At 43, Irving has few assets beyond ambition and good health. The debit side shows a shattered marriage, a criminal record and $1 million owing.

"Before I started this Hughes venture," he says, "I wasn't doing badly as a writer, living on the little island of Ibiza, off the coast of Spain, with my wife, two children, my house and my sailboat. Now, it's all gone. I have to decide where to live and how to live."

Irving was talking in the plush surroundings of the Beverly Hills Hotel where he had a suite, compliments of the television network for whom he was taping an interview. A large portion of his TV appearance was devoted to reminiscences of the Hughes affair, a subject that still makes his face brighten. On the tube he spoke frankly, but off-camera he was even more candid.

"For awhile there, everything was going along perfectly, almost too perfectly. After McGraw-Hill decided they liked the manuscript, they took the ball and ran with it. They were the ones who brought Time-Life into it, and the Book of the Month Club and Dell Publications, who were going to do the paperback. Things were snowballing fast, and it was only a matter of time before the movie rights would be sold."

There are some who say that Irving plagiarized most of his facts about Hughes from a book written by a former aide of the billionaire. The suggestion that his authorship was tainted, even when the book itself was a fake, makes Irving wince.

"What happened," he explains, "is that in the course of researching Hughes' life, we came by pure accident upon the first draft of the autobiography of Noah Dietrich, who was Hughes' right-hand man. It had been done with some reporter — I can't remember his name. And it was tremendously helpful to us in reconstructing the early years of Howard Hughes' life.

(Continued from preceding page)

"But the most important bit of research that I got came as a result of getting access to the private files of Time-Life. I photographed the Hughes material in its entirety and used it to a great extent in the construction of my book. Also included were tapes of conversations between Frank McCullough of *Time* magazine and Hughes. It was from these that I was able to reconstruct the tone of voice that Hughes customarily used when he was talking intimately.

"The people at Time-Life never did put two and two together and figure out that I was using their own files to give them the book which they were buying."

In the course of preparing his book, Irving got to feel that he knew Hughes better than anyone else alive. Success, of course, depended on the eccentric billionaire remaining silent, and Irving was convinced that Hughes would be content to let the matter pass after issuing a few perfunctory denials. But the author recalls, "When Hughes finally repudiated the book the way he did, at that press conference, with all those reporters, I thought, 'How could you *do* that to me, Howard?' "

Although Irving felt shaken up, McGraw-Hill and Time-Life remained undaunted. The hoaxer remembers one editor snapping, " 'Hughes is crazy and this is his way of drumming up publicity. We've known all along he was going to give us trouble at this stage of the game. He's simply changed his mind because there's something in the text that's embarrassing, but we're going ahead with publication, come hell or high water.' I was scared when this happened, but the publisher said, 'Don't worry, kid, we'll take care of this. You stick with us, and we'll be out in print a month or two sooner than scheduled.' "

But when Hughes persisted in his denials, Irving knew the chain of events was out of his control, like "my own Frankenstein monster." The jig was up and the colossal hoax had to be exposed.

This was a far cry from his state of mind in the beginning days when the plot was hatched. "At first it seemed so preposterous, we used to laugh about it," he says. "Dick Suskind said, 'I know it's a wild idea, but why don't we do the book together.'

"I went to my wife and told her, 'Dick and I have this crazy idea, and I want you to talk me out of it.' She replied, 'You've always wanted to do something exciting and far out. I think we should do it.' Suddenly we were a trio involved in a hoax."

If Irving has any remorse about the experience, it's due to what his wife and children had to suffer. His 38-year-old wife Edith spent 14 months in a Swiss jail for her part in the conspiracy, a sentence he feels unfair since she cooperated with the Swiss officials. After her release last spring, she announced

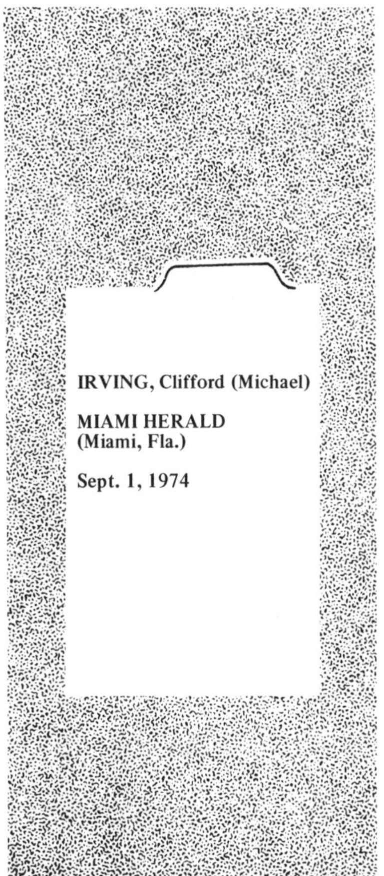
IRVING, Clifford (Michael)

MIAMI HERALD
(Miami, Fla.)

Sept. 1, 1974

she would seek a divorce. Her explanation was that the marriage had been a bad one from the beginning.

"That's not true," says Irving. "We had a good marriage, but the one thing she cannot forgive is my affair with Nina Van Pallandt. It bugged her that the affair had been going on for a long time. No wife likes to see her husband's name linked with some Danish blonde on the front page.

"I suppose I was in love with Nina, and I was very sad and disappointed when she spilled the beans to the press. There was no way we could go on after that. I would never dream of doing that to a friend — let alone to somebody who had the kind of relationship we had. I haven't seen or heard from her since."

Since he got out of jail, Irving has been frequently asked why he didn't serve an extra two years and keep $400,000, instead of returning the money to McGraw-Hill.

"You might say that two years for a half-million dollars is not an awfully long time," he comments, "but I found prison does unpleasant things to you. It's a nasty place, and it can pervert your mind. It slows you down, and I frankly could have done without the whole experience. Like W.C. Fields used to say, 'On the whole, I'd rather have been in Philadelphia.' "

Despite his distaste for prison life, Irving can look back on it with a writer's detachment. "I believe I got at least one good story out of it," he says. "It should make a novel or screenplay. It's not my own. It's based on what happened to another prisoner. It's a love story, but I'd rather not go into it now because I haven't sold it, and it's too easy to swipe."

Irving recalls, "The two things I wanted most when I came out of prison were a beautiful girl and a steak. I couldn't decide which to choose first. As it turned out I took the steak."

He's not unduly worried about his massive debts. "I owe so much I really couldn't give a damn," he notes. "There's no way I could ever pay it back. So I try not to think about it."

Looking back on the Hughes hoax, Irving comments, "I never thought I was getting into a criminal thing. I thought it was a big gag. I never for one moment thought I would be sent to prison. The worst I thought could happen was that I might be severely embarrassed."

Yet when asked whether he'd do it again if given the chance, he doesn't hesitate to answer, "Of course I would — if I could be given a gilt-edged guarantee that I would get away with it." T

Author Remembers Short-Story Days

JACKSON, Margaret Weymouth (1895 -)

INDIANAPOLIS STAR (Indianapolis, Ind.)

Jan. 21, 1973

By SHIRLEY ROGERS

Margaret Weymouth Jackson is a name that, during the 1920s through mid-1950s, was a household phrase synonymous with the good, simple, uncluttered life familiar to a period when the farm was the center of life.

Mrs. Jackson was a writer in the heydays of the magazine short story, before television stole upon the American scene and, with the click of a dial, banished most of America's colorful periodicals to dusty existence on library reference shelves.

HER SHORT stories are well-known by the older generation and still read by schoolchildren, and the author's life, at 78, is far from dusty. She and an older sister, Mrs. Arthur Jones, live at the Altenheim of Indianapolis. Mrs. Jackson likes to recall the days when her typewriter tapped out short stories with regularity, and she and her family enjoyed good cars, good food and an income of $10,000 to $12,000 a year from her creative efforts.

Mrs. Jackson wrote for the Saturday Evening Post and is a member of its elite "50 Club" composed of those authors who had 50 or more stories published in the magazine. Her works are used in English composition classes throughout the country as examples of good short-story writing.

"I wrote idea stories rather than adventure stories," Mrs. Jackson points out. "An idea story is one evolving around the excitement in the mental and spiritual development of the characters and plot, whether it be a change in attainment of one's goals, or a change in one's personality. In an adventure story, the character is involved in physical danger that brings about change."

MRS. JACKSON was born Feb. 11, 1895, at Eureka Springs, Ark. One of seven children, three of whom are still living, she was reared in an environment where writing was the source of the family's "bread and butter." Her father, she recalls, was "always a newspaper editor, working on some metropolitan daily or farm-oriented magazine."

She remembers her childhood as a happy one, because her parents were "strict and loving Presbyterians and my mother wouldn't hesitate to bend you over her knee if she felt you needed it."

Part of her formative years were spent living at Chicago, where her father worked on the Chicago Tribune. It was there that her first real writing success came at the age of 17, as the result of a trip to a Chicago zoo.

"My father wasn't the kind to beat around the bush," Mrs. Jackson says, reminiscing, "and when I came home and began telling what I had seen at the zoo, he cut me off with 'don't talk about it, write about it.' "

"I did and the Tribune bought it."

When Mr. Weymouth moved his family to Spencer, Margaret, then 20, wrote short stories for Farm Life and received $100 a month for her efforts during the next four years.

By the time she began her career writing for the "big-time" periodicals such as the Saturday Evening Post, Cosmopolitan and its sister magazines, she had a wealth of short-story writing experience behind her.

SHE ALSO had married Charles Carter Jackson, an insurance actuary at Chicago and later spent four years living in Manitoba, Canada, where the couple moved to take advantage of the Canadian government's offer of free land to army veterans. Charles was a veteran of Canada's Expeditionary Forces.

While in Manitoba, she bore two daughters. She returned to Spencer shortly thereafter, and lived there 40 years.

When her first short-story for the Saturday Evening Post was published, there was much rejoicing in the Jackson household.

"My husband always encouraged my writing because he thought I had talent," she says, "and I never let it interfere with bringing up my children or running my house.

"My children were proud of me — once a neighbor asked my then small son what was I doing, and he told her, 'she's typewriting on her typewriter.'

"I always worked at home except once when I decided to rent an office. I sat there all day, looking out of the window and wondering what my kids were doing. Finally, I put the typewriter under my arm and went home to see, and I stayed there."

THERE ARE no favorites among the many short stories she has had published, although "The Hero," a tale of a basketball player and his heroics on the court, is her most widely-published and republished story.

"I was always in love with whatever I was working on at the time," she comments, "because I felt it was my best effort."

Mrs. Jackson says a lot of her writing was about "common everyday people and their experiences, people who, after all, weren't really common or ordinary, since everyone has something special and precious about them."

And she wrote a lot about "businessmen."

"America is a place of work and business and I wrote a lot about 'businessmen' — policemen, plumbers, firemen, factory workers, electricians," she says "because we are all businessmen and business is America's preoccupation.

"After I wrote my first draft, I'd go out and see what these jobs really entailed. Then I'd come back home and rewrite it until I knew it was finished, even if I was sick to death of it."

SHE DOESN'T write anymore, mainly because the work is too strenuous and her memory isn't as sharp as it used to be. But also, because the short-story markets of yesteryear are gone.

"When I was writing, I jotted down ideas at the most inopportune times — in church, or at the market on the back of a meat package," she says. "Ideas are fleeting things and it would be difficult for me to write now.

"Then too, I doubt if I could write for today's market. It's too off-beat and off-color. In my day, there was not even the slightest suggestion of smut. You could write a story of a love affair between a married man and another woman, but it had to be pretty high-class stuff. I couldn't give an editor what he wanted today.

"NOT TO mention that the market's gone," she added. "It left with the magazines. To tell the truth, there used to be a lot more room for a young writer out there. Nowadays, though, I don't know where a young writer can go to get experience."

Mrs. Jackson says she has no advice for any writer just starting out.

"I wouldn't have the gall to give another writer advice. Every writer is different, and if he doesn't come up with a new and fresh approach, he's in trouble."

Author is a private person

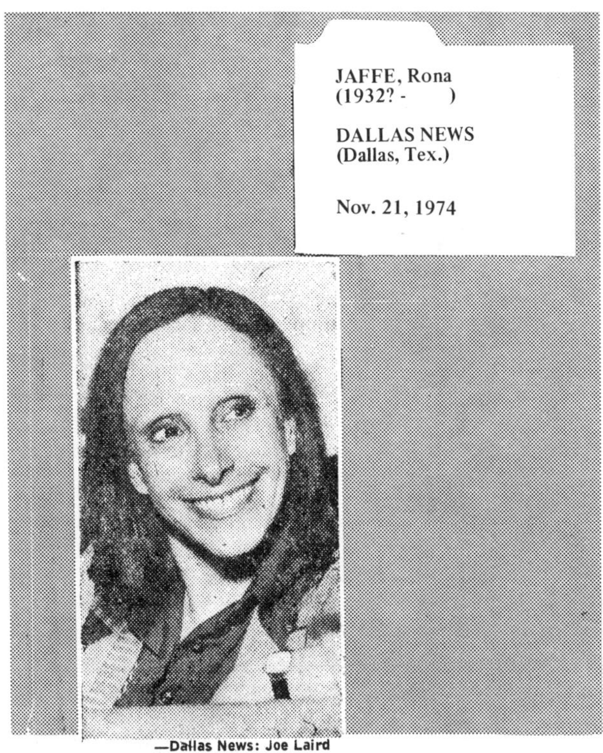
JAFFE, Rona
(1932? -)

DALLAS NEWS
(Dallas, Tex.)

Nov. 21, 1974

—Dallas News: Joe Laird

By JANE ULRICH

She's small and dark—this quiet author who breezed in and out of Dallas in a matter of hours Monday—and as stingy with her feelings in public as she is unstingy with them in print.

It's hard to believe that the Rona Jaffe whose name adorns the covers of eight novels and the Rona Jaffe-private person who breathes and speaks and moves are one and the same.

On tour promoting her latest book, "Family Secrets," a 511-page epic chronicle of three generations in a family, Rona is doing all the typical PR things expected of authors of new books—visiting as many cities as humanly possible in the least amount of days, talking to as many members of the press as may be sandwiched into a tight schedule, smiling for photographers, autographing books in book stores.

Yet she maintains an intriguing distance, always a litle out of reach . . . answering questions without revealing too much self.

WHETHER HURRYING to catch a plane or getting caught up in the red tape checking out of a hotel can sometimes be, she appears to be an almost typical career woman approaching early middle age.

She has known success intimately, without letting it go to her head, and seems to view herself and her work with much less awe than do many who find themselves in the limelight.

That comes from ducking spotlights.

She spends a lot of time in her New York City apartment ("You don't live in a house there unless you're very rich and have guards!"), has never married and doesn't give parties.

"I know a lot of people, but I have a few close friends whom I see often," says the author, who writes on an almost business-hour schedule, working five days a week and attempting to write 10 pages a day.

On her two days off, she accomplishes all the chores that were left undone while she works and thinks about what she's going to write next.

"I'm perfectly happy to stay alone," she admits. "There are lots of things I like to do. I'm also good at doing nothing—that's one of my favorite things."

WHEN SHE'S NOT composing at her electric type writer, she also writes essays, stories and articles for magazines, she reads magazines and other people's novels, "nonfiction about strange and obscure subjects" and has several books at various stages of partly read.

She travels a lot, though mostly for research. "I'd be bored otherwise," she says. "I'm not the type of person who likes sightseeing and shopping."

Rona learned early in her writing career, not too many years after her graduation from Radcliffe and after she had worked a few years for a publishing house, that the party schedule some authors and celebrities keep wasn't for her . . . or she wasn't for it.

"All those fancy parties," she recalled almost wistfully. Yet, she added, she knew she didn't want to grow old in P. J. Clarke's talking about "that novel I wrote 25 years ago."

"That novel," her first, was "The Best of Everything." With it she became a successful author and was introduced to the magical world of movies, a world she doesn't hold much fondness for.

"The Best of Everything," which came out in 1959 with an impressive cast of stars, was many headaches, two years in the making, longer than it took her to write the book.

Since she hasn't had similar bad experiences with television, she'd like to do a movie-of-the-week for TV sometime this year.

JUST AS she travels for research, she also does a lot of things that she hopes will eventually polish her art.

"I've taken acting classes and dancing lessons and all that stuff," she says. It'll all help to teach her to write dialogue for stage and screen, she believes.

Her acting class was the kind where nobody made a fuss over you. It didn't matter who you were.

Rona used things she had already written in class, as did Renee Taylor and Shelley Winters. "Paul Newman wasn't bad," she recalls, "and Marilyn Monroe . . ."

Yet she says she's never wanted to be an actress: "I mean, I'm a writer. Right? That's what I do."

This latest effort she's done, "Family Secrets," is rather an American Forsyte Saga

Replete with a cast of (almost) thousands, it's absorbing and warm and human. Its flow and life may be attributed to all the planning Rona puts into her work.

She planned the whole book in her head, made an extensive list of each generation of the Saffron family (a family tree, of sorts) and minor characters, chose names from "What Shall We Name the Baby" and from a box of soap, researched, plotted her material and worked until she finished.

That's the discipline they tell you about in creative writing classes.

If it's all as calculating as it sounds, it doesn't show. All that shows is the genius of the woman . . . and all the marvelous and meaty things one very quite author tucks away in her head until it's time to put them on paper. ➡

(Also see preceding article)

Rona Jaffe

TELLS 'FAMILY SECRETS'

By JOAN O'SULLIVAN

Rona Jaffe has always been an early-bird. She wrote her first poem at 2, entered college at 16, was a best-seller author while still in her 20s.

When I interviewed her recently, she talked about Radcliffe college days. She was a freshman to remember.

"I had never been out on a date unchaperoned," she said, "and I'd never been kissed. They thought I was hysterically funny."

Miss Jaffe, a college graduate at 19, began writing magazine pieces immediately, supporting herself with an editing job at Fawcett.

Her first novel was born when editor

JAFFE, Rona

LONG ISLAND PRESS
(Jamaica, N.Y.)

Jan. 4, 1975

Jack Goodman of Simon and Schuster read a 75-page novella she'd submitted, and asked her to write a full-length book. Called, "The Best of Everything," it made publishing history, as well as a movie starring Joan Crawford, Hope Lange, Suzy Parker and Robert Evans (then an actor, now a top executive at Paramount).

"That book," she recalled "was about me and my friends, the experiences we had as working girls. I got the idea and then I began talking to career girls in New York and California, getting their life stories. I made up a composite of five girls and wrote the book."

How long did it take? "Five months, five days and 26 years," said Miss Jaffe.

Her new book, "Family Secrets," which is on its way to the best-seller list, is one that's been gestating for 15 years. An American "Forsyte Saga," it tells the absorbing story of three generations of a Jewish immigrant's family. It's the kind of novel you can't put down.

* * *

DESPITE ITS length, the book was written in less than half a year because Miss Jaffe had it plotted out in her head before she started to write.

"I can't stand the thought of looking at a blank page in the typewriter" she confessed. "It's too defeating. Before I start to write, I've thought the book out, I know all the characters, even the minor ones and what's going to happen to them."

"Family Secrets" is a novel with a large cast. Miss Jaffe named each with more care than a mother selecting a name for the new baby.

"The name has to mean something to me and sound right for the character," she said. "After I have the characters in my head, I go through 'What to Name the Baby' and other name books and decide what to call them."

Her own name was decided on with less fanfare. "My mother toyed with calling me Frederica," Miss Jaffe said, raising her eyebrows to indicate this choice would not have been popular with her. "She settled on Rona because she'd gone to Camp Rona as a child and loved the name."

Miss Jaffe, who doesn't cook unless she has to, much prefers stirring plots to pots. She likes to clean, and her neat living room shows it. It's an ecological room with a grass green carpet. The sofa is upholstered in an animal print. Animal paintings and etchings line the walls.

"I like animals . . . but I don't like live ones around the house," said Miss Jaffe.

* * *

PART OF THE fascination of "Family Secrets" is its description of the changing life styles of each generation. The granddaughter, Paris, who is a writer, bears a striking resemblance to Miss Jaffe.

"I knew if I wrote about a writer, people would think it was me," said the author, "so intentionally I made Paris like me.

"Back in the 50s when she and I were in our twenties, we were obsessed with sex and called it love. After a first date, we dreamed about marrying him, and we even named our children."

Miss Jaffe thinks today's young people are far more honest, far more unlikely to make the same mistakes her generation did.

"They've gotten sex out of the way," she said. "So they're free to be friends, free to get to know each other as human beings."

Is marriage dead? The author doesn't think so. "Girls still want to get married," Miss Jaffe observed, "but I hope this generation will choose more intelligently. The girls I grew up with married because he was handsome or had a convertible or was a good catch. It was only afterwards that they discovered they'd married a stranger, someone they knew nothing about and had nothing in common with."

Rona Jaffe

By ELIZABETH BENNETT
Post Reporter

Rona Jaffe, a 40-year-old novelist who never married, just can't figure it out.

"I keep meeting all these unmarried women around the country who always ask me, 'Where are the men?' as if I should know. It's ridiculous. They even ask me that on radio programs (in interviews). Well, how SHOULD I know?"

Jaffe, you may remember, once wrote a book about young career women who went to New York to find "terrific jobs and terrific husbands." It was called "The Best of Everything," became an immediate best-seller for its 26-year-old author, later a movie, and "It was wonderful," recalls Jaffe in a Houston interview.

"All the shouting died down before I could believe it was true," said Jaffe, who since that time has written seven more books and who was in Houston to talk about her latest novel, "Family Secrets" (Simon and Schuster, $9.95).

It's the story of three generations of a Jewish family living in America. Jaffe says she's wanted to write it for 15 years, but didn't feel ready to handle it till now, when, at 40, "you have the understanding and compassion as well as the long, cool look."

EVER SINCE she was a child in Brooklyn, Jaffe wanted to write, she explains.

"So I went to work in a publishing house (in Manhattan) and hoped someday to write a novel. But it never occurred to me I'd spend my life writing them and become a novelist," she adds.

Jaffe was only 19 when she graduated from Radcliffe College and "I'd had all the advantages. My parents were very strict and old-fashioned, but they always gave me lots of books to read and encouraged me in any field I was interested in and encouraged my writing."

Although she was "very sophisticated, tall for my age and looked older" (than she really was), Jaffe had no desire to get married after school, she said. "One thing I had on my side. I was very young and there wasn't this tremendous pressure on me. There WAS terrible pressure to have a boyfriend, though. And if you had broken up with somebody, you had to call all your friends and see if they knew anybody, you know? THAT was bad. People were very lonely and very desperate."

BUT JAFFE was more interested in writing, and after four years at Fawcett Publications, during which time she began to sell some magazine pieces, she submitted a 75-page novella to another publisher, Simon and Schuster. Encouraged by its reception, she began to write "The Best of Everything," which was accepted by S&S on her first 100 pages.

To get her information, recalls Jaffe, "I went around and talked to about 50 girls

JAFFE, Rona

HOUSTON POST
(Houston, Tex.)

Nov. 21, 1974

and heard their stories. It was based on a lot of composites, on friends of mine and on me — I was very uptight in those days."

She wrote the book, says Jaffe, in "five months and five days. I was shocked it went so fast. There was suddenly this incredible fame—and it was almost like it wasn't happening. And I was going all over the country being interviewed and everybody wanted to listen to my opinion and listen to me and I said a lot of snippy things."

But instead of resting on her laurels, Jaffe just kept writing, averaging a book every two years, including one for children ("The Last of the Wizards") and a semi-autobiographical novel called "The Cherry in the Martini."

HER PARENTS didn't like that latter one at all, she re-

(Continued from preceding page)

calls, and "tried to have it banned. Mother didn't like the portrait of her, she thought it made her look bad. And she didn't like the ending—she thought it was dirty. She wanted me to withhold the book and rewrite it. And my father wanted to buy up all the copies and store them somewhere in a warehouse."

The book didn't sell very well, admits Jaffe, who adds, grinning, "I guess, if I'd had a press agent at the time, I could have made hay out of all that scandal."

But she's done all right without a press agent. And today, she doesn't even have a literary agent to peddle her books.

"I had one for years, but he died, and I don't think I need one now. If you love your publishing company and love your editor, they'll take care of you." (And, she might have added, if your books keep selling as well as Jaffe's do.)

BEFORE SHE sits down to write a new novel, said Jaffe, she knows "everything that will happen, the all-over thing, the beginning, middle and end." She works five days a week from about 10 a.m. to 5 p.m., sets herself a goal of 10 typewritten pages a day and does very little rewriting.

She also reads a lot, says Jaffe, "because I like it. In the beginning you read to learn how to write. Now I read for escape—novels, nonfiction, everything."

The last book she read: "Fear of Flying," a novel by Erica Jong that deals with women's liberation, fantasies and a lot of other subjects women are talking about today. Jaffe, who's not the least bit sorry she never married and would "certainly be shocked" if she ever did, is equally interested in women's liberation and all that it entails.

"When you get everybody doing what you've been doing all along," she grins, "it's wonderful."

JAFFE, Rona

HOUSTON POST
(Houston, Tex.)

Nov. 21, 1974

Rona Jaffe makes visit here during book promotion tour

By KAY HOLMQUIST

Generally it takes author Rona Jaffe about a year to write a book, but her latest "Family Secrets," took 15 years from start to finish.

Her newest and longest book also is her favorite, said Miss Jaffe, whose best known book may be the first one she wrote, "The Best of Everything."

"This one is the most ambitious one I've done, because of all the characters," she said last week while she was here on a promotion tour.

"Family Secrets" traces the Saffron family, revealing value systems of different generations through the lives of family members.

"I LOVED having all the characters to work with and would look forward to doing certain parts because I knew what was going to happen," she said.

She calls herself a "very systematic writer" who gets the whole book written in her head before she sits down to a typewriter.

"I work regular business hours five days a week," she said. "I like to do the same as everyone else—it's awful to write during the night and then have no one to talk to about it."

"If I waited for 'inspiration,' I'd get too scared to write at all," she said.

"When I see the pages piling up in the box, then I feel better."

While the idea for the book came to her years ago, it jelled a long time in her mind while she worked out the cast of characters and also gained additional perspective as she grew more mature, she said.

"I wanted to show the way people ignore their parents; the way kids will dump them—that's what we do to old people in our society," she said. "I also wanted to show what parents sometimes do to their kids.

"I wanted to show the falling apart of the American family, and why—but I didn't know why when I started the book," she said.

"I thought if I started from the beginning and followed the family then I would see why it fell apart. The reason I found is that the times and needs are different for each generation.

"TIME WAS when immigrants kept a closeness, even marrying cousins. Immigrants stuck together in a hostile world, but when they Americanized their children, the world wasn't hostile to them—it was their world and they wanted to be a part of it. They were resentful against the older generation, and their parents couldn't understand it."

Miss Jaffe thinks that a facet of the nostalgia phase is the popularity of the family saga.

"People are saying, 'The present is not so great, so let's get into the past,'" she said.

"But for a long time family sagas were books like 'Forever Amber' or 'The Forsyte Saga,' and not American family sagas. About the only historical books we had were westerns, but now the country is old enough for American sagas," she said.

"A friend of mine who lives in San Antonio said that she really identifed with the book," said Miss Jaffe. "She said that old Texas families lived together in enclaves like the Saffrons and that she'd seen families emasculate their young just like their cattle."

She thinks that a family saga about Texans would be fascinating, particularly as it traced the family through the oil boom days to a time of energy shortages and resulting pressures on the family.

When she first looked at the outline of "Family Secrets," Miss Jaffe said that she thought writing the book would be an impossible task.

"I thought it would take an outrageous number of pages and I was terrified," she said.

"Writers have a lot of panic, and so they go through certain rituals," she said. "Some of them can write only in a certain place or sitting in a certain chair.

"I don't do that, but I say to myself that I will write 10 pages a day and out of those I will get 25 usuable pages at the end of the week. That makes it seem possible."

"When I'm writing I'm very much involved with it and I worry about it," she said. "I have a normal life, but I may go off in a trance sometimes because I am thinking all the time about my work."

Miss Jaffe said that she loves her Manhattan home, but she also likes to go out.

"I LIKE TO keep my home just so, with everything in its place, but I'm a terrible cook. It's either eat out or poison myself. But I come from a long line of bad cooks and I don't see why I should worry about changing it."

Although not a "joiner," Miss Jaffe said that the women's movement had "articulated" the feelings of many women.

"When women's lib first came out people said 'Oh, you're not one of those!' but I've always done what I wanted to do for myself—I took all those things for granted. I feel that if I have a relationship with a man then I would do all the housework and my work, too. So my way of making the choice was not to get involved."

JAFFE, Rona

FORT WORTH
STAR-TELEGRAM
(Ft. Worth, Tex.)

Nov. 25, 1974

Gloria Jahoda Doesn't Worry About the Joneses

Democrat Photo by Ray Stanyard

By CINDY MILLER
Democrat Staff Writer

"My father used to say, 'Gloria, you make up your mind too quickly and you're too emotional.' Little did he know that's how I would make my living." Gloria Jahoda laughs big.

Best known for her book, "The Other Florida," Gloria Jahoda has stirred up emotions about the "little towns and dim pinelands" of north Florida.

She writes at home. Inside the Jahoda's tiny home in an unpretentious neighborhood, she begins her day at the piano.

"MUSIC WAS what you did in our family. You didn't consume it, you produced it." Music, art and poetry are part of her Swedish background.

After playing the piano, she writes and then revises. She's now working on a book about Andrew Jackson and the Indians.

The yard at her home on Westridge Drive is overgrown and there's an old boat out front. "It's great," she says. "No one takes care of anything. University kids are on all sides. We park in each other's yards."

Next door is an old van with the bumper sticker, "Jeez if you love honkus." It's that kind of neighborhood.

The Jahodas don't worry about keeping up with the Joneses. "Polished silver intimidates me," she laughs again.

Everything Gloria Jahoda says is punctuated with a large laugh. What she says is not always remarkable, but how and with what passion she speaks her mind is matchless.

GERALD JAHODA, her husband, was responsible for their coming to Tallahassee. Dr. Louis Shores, retired dean of the library school, persuaded him to accept a teaching position in library science at Florida State University.

In 1963, they moved here with many doubts and a shake of idealism, which is described in "The Other Florida."

"Tallahassee's 50,000 people were 170 miles from the nearest big city we knew. Tallahassee was surrounded by swamps, wildlife sanctuaries, and a national forest.

"I was determined ... I was going to read the Tallahassee Democrat as well as the New York Times. I wasn't going to wall myself off from the backwoods and sit in a carpeted living room playing Beethoven and reading Sartre.

"I wasn't going to restrict myself to the academic round. All these people, black and white, would be my friends — somehow. I would try to know them, if they would have me, and to understand them, if I could. If they kept their distance, there was always bird watching."

By the time "The Other Florida" came out in 1967, they were hooked on Tallahassee.

"I am still surprised that after only four years in it I consider it my home town," she wrote. "Perhaps the city's hospitality has been a part of it, perhaps the never - failing eagerness to answer all my questions and to offer alien customs for me to probe. Perhaps, too, I have put down such quick roots because my husband and I found a white house set in pines, firethorns, hollies and evergreen loquat trees."

Now that book, "The Other Florida," turned some folks upside down with emotion. Wakulla County was real upset that she said Crawfordville was not a city. No writers had ever written about north Florida before.

Each town thought the descriptions of the other towns were accurate, but not about their own.

JAHODA,
Gloria (Adelaide Love)
(1926 -)

TALLAHASSEE
DEMOCRAT
(Tallahassee, Fla.)

Mar. 17, 1974

[See also CA-1]

People called up and yelled "Communist" at Gloria Jahoda.

"WE AIN'T the other Florida," said one resident. "We're the real Florida. South Florida is the other Florida."

Walter Cronkite confused the controversy and announced on national television that Gloria Jahoda's life was in danger. Gloria's mother saw the TV show and was "beside herself."

But Gloria laughed her fine, infectious laugh and said, "If they burn a cross in our front yard, it will be great for the sales."

In 1945, Gloria was a student at Northwestern University, and Alan Watts, now famous Zen philosopher, was the campus Episcopal minister. Synchronicity crossed the paths of these two later to - become - famous people.

"Gloria Love had a genius for giving a false impression of total incompetence," writes Alan Watts in his recent book, "In My Own Way." He remembers her as the "zany" student who played the organ for the church.

She remembers him with a beard, dressed in Chinese red robes and smoking a Turkish water pipe — in 1945. He seemed like an interesting person who told people to realize themselves spiritually rather than by making money.

Watts gave Gloria some peculiarly unliberated advice. You've got to play dumb or you'll scare men away. And you must be more submissive. You'll never find a husband if you laugh so much. And you shouldn't write, you should be a concert pianist.

GLORIA LAUGHS. Fortunately, she took absolutely none of his advice.

Married in 1952, her husband appreciates her laughter and her talking. He says he never has to worry about talking, that she takes care of it for him.

Gerald Jahoda was born in Austria, came here in 1942, and is a jazz enthusiast.

The Jahodas live a quiet life of books and music. They enjoy entertaining his library science students. Gloria calls the patio out back their "extravagance" used for dinner parties. She likes to cook, especially with curry. Florida foods and Swedish dishes are her specialty.

She has "passions" for things. First, cats. Working with the humane society, she loves and respects cats. The Jahodas drive their cat all the way to Thomasville to a special veterinarian.

And she has a passion for bad horror movies, the kind you can laugh at — not like the Exorcist.

She attributes her success to "A husband with a job." The money she makes from one book keeps her going onto the next, with little extra.

(Continued from preceding page)

"Stick with it. Develop such a thick skin that nothing matters," she advises young writers.

"ROLL WITH the punches. Just keep believing in yourself."

Her first book was refused by 17 publishers.

Gloria taught anthropology for a few years, then retired in 1957 to write full time. She's rather embarrassed about her first novels.

When asked about her favorite writers, she hesitates. "Music and painting mean more to me than others' writing.

"I'm old - fashioned. My prose is formed on a 19th century model, like Browning."

But she likes Gore Vidal's "Burr," reads some Faulkner, and admires Truman Capote's writing. Her real favorite is Walt Whitman. "People say Walt Whitman's poetry is just a phase you grow out of, but I'm glad not to."

The sensitivity that she shows for the late Jack Kerouac, who is featured in her book "River of the Golden Ibis," is that of one writer for another.

"He would have despised me because of my conventional ways," she says about the beat writer. And yet, maybe he would have seen that bohemianism that lies beneath the surface.

She did manage to capture the vulnerable essence of Jack Kerouac, which so many people miss.

To do so, she tried to talk to his wife. But Mrs. Kerouac thought she might be Jewish and refused.

ASKING FOR gold tequila, which she hoped they wouldn't have, Gloria Jahoda visited the liquor stores near Kerouac's home in St. Petersburg.

In that manner, she was able to ask about the man who started the whole beat generation, the man who ended up with the shaking hands of an alcoholic.

Her sketch of him in the book is sensitive, whereas others, such as "Esquire" magazine, had been so cruel after his death.

She says a writer must deal with feelings, and admits she is not analytical — which gets her in trouble. Some people say she just didn't have the facts straight in "The Other Florida." Others say she grossly exaggerated the ethnic quality of north Florida. But the feelings are real, and she captures them well.

"My mother was a psychic, and I know she was honest. I've had a few experiences. I've seen it working in our own lives."

Not caught in the traditional female role, Gloria Jahoda also lets you know she's no womens libber.

In research, she says it helps to be a woman. "I can find out things no man could."

"I'm not an advocated womans libber, but I would like to see secretaries get out of their ghetto."

Gloria Jahoda, who does not iron sheets or keep up with the Joneses, says "A lot of the fuss about womens liberation is far - fetched." She does believe in job equality.

"CONSCIOUSNESS is at the nearest library," is her retort to women's consciousness raising groups. She can't see joining organizations, like National Organization for Women (NOW).

"ERA (Equal Rights Amendment) is a blow against the family."

"I'm not a very political person, I shoot straight from the hip." And so she does, which upsets plenty of people — like ecologists.

"I think we have gone over-

JAHODA,
Gloria (Adelaide Love)

TALLAHASSEE DEMOCRAT
(Tallahassee, Fla.)

Mar. 17, 1974

board on the ecology kick. People running with their bottles to the supermarket... Well, I don't shoot birds every morning."

She says she does believe in conservation, but thinks the pendulum swung too far.

So much land, she says, has been acquired by the State of Florida, like the Big Cypress and buffer zone, that there won't be any left for the farmers.

A believer in compromise, "I don't want factories coming in here, but some places have to have them."

She does have deep sentiments for her adopted town of Tallahassee and has served as past president of the Tallahassee Historical Society.

Not invited to become a member of the society, she went down and paid the $3 fee anyway. She laughs about the members' puzzlement, and her own surprise on finding out why.

"THIS COMMUNITY is the most marvelous place for an artist to be. Tallahassee really supports its artists."

Concerned with local folk music which may be lost, she praises the Southeastern music archives. She also hopes old people will write down their memories of early times and put them in libraries.

After living on a farm in New Jersey from 1959 to 1963, the Jahodas decided that "A & P has real good food." Strawberries and artichokes were coming out their ears and they decided it was time to get off the farm.

They moved to Florida. In "The Other Florida," she describes the way it seemed to them in 1963:

"Everywhere... there were the pines, their long needles shimmering in a faint wind under the hot subtropical sun. In the country there were empty dirt roads, rutted by mule carts. In the towns, sprawled rows of unpainted shacks without windows. Ancient Negro women sat fanning themselves with palm leaves as they stared drowsily from rickety porches at their zinnias and coral vines and heavy scented honeysuckle bushes.

"MOSS - DRAPED oaks and lacy chinaberry trees shaded sandy door yards. Locusts whined from tall magnolias with the steady pitch of power saws. But mostly there were those pines and the tang of their resiny branches and the dark straightness of their trunks. All of it looked like the south of the novelists and the poets, heavy with antiquity, romance, and misery."

Today Gloria Jahoda is concerned about Americans "getting the vision again."

"With all the discouraging things that have happened to America, we should look at our heritage, and find where we went wrong.

"THIS CYNICISM among the young people is spooky. We must get off the drug kick. If this is all we're going to give our kids. . ."

"It's important that people produce, not just consume — as watching TV or being stoned and listening to music.

"You cannot turn your back on the world. In that way, I'm a puritan. We're here for something. All artists have this in common, that they really live for it."

Most important to Gloria Jahoda are art and love. Instead of a specific religion, she believes in the morality expressed in Nietzsche's "Thus Spake Zarathrusta."

"I do believe there's intelligence behind the universe, but I'm impatient with sects. Morality is the way people treat each other." She's a nominal Episcopalian.

A former teacher of anthropology, she disapproves of applied anthropology that "tries to manage people's lives."

The debate on whether or not anthropology is a science she found tiresome. Her interest was in primitive music, not arrowheads and archaeology.

The Jahodas live quiet lives with books and records, and they like basketball and baseball.

But music is their big love When Gloria Jahoda was a student, she saved all her money to go hear Elena Nikolaidi sing. Now, Tallahassee can boast of having both these talented women.

The Tallahassee Sesquicentennial Concert which will be April 4 is largely a result of Gloria Jahoda's energies. And that handsome baritone Ralph Stange will be sleeping on a cot in the Jahodas' Florida room. Elderly Mrs. Percy Grainger, wife of the late composer, will also be staying with them.

A favorite story of Gloria Jahoda's, which always brings her booming laugh, is about a jazz parade in New Orleans years ago. The Jahodas were proud to be marching in it. And there was Chicken Henry with his trombone.

"Oh, Mr. Henry," said Gloria, "I'm so glad to meet you. I just admire your playing, and I've always wanted to play a trombone."

Chicken Henry looked at her, then looked at his trombone, and said, "Well, sister, you've sure got the mouth and teeth for it."

Yes she does, and she's never afraid to use them. Amen.

'Helping People Adapt to Changes Made'

JANEWAY, Elizabeth (Hall) (1913-)
ATLANTA JOURNAL (Atlanta, Ga.) Nov. 21, 1974
[See also CA-45/48]

Staff Photo—J. C. Lee

By LYNDON MAYES

The Women's Liberation Movement is not trying to change the world.

It is trying to make people adapt to the changes that have already taken place.

Elizabeth Janeway backs this statement up in her book, "Between Myth and Morning; Women Awakening" (William Morrow and Co., $8.95) with the facts that over 34 million women are in the work force, 16 million women are contributing the wages that keep their family above the poverty line and nearly seven million women are supporting their family completely.

"Women's Lib is not trying to get the woman into the work force. She is already there and has been helping to support the family for a long time," Mrs. Janeway said in Atlanta.

"Before the Industrial Revolution the economy was based in the home. The woman helped her husband around the farm or in his business which was either in the home or close to the home.

"She was able to help him because she was either at home with the children or recieved help from the extended family, such as a grandmother, aunt, or older child in caring for the children."

"Women were certainly not equal to the man before the industrial revolution but the work of the woman was more similar to the work of the man than it is today. Her skills were more useful and contributed more to the livelihood of the family."

With the industrial revolution the source of the family income moved from the home to the factory, so did the man and in many cases the woman.

"Few families can live on one income today, so the woman has gone to work to bring in that second income. It's not a question of whether a woman wants to work, many women have to work."

Mrs. Janeway is married to economist Eliot Janeway. They have reared two children, one also an economist, and are now grandparents.

While rearing her children, she pursued a writing career, publishing her first novel in 1943 and five other novels before turning to non-fiction with "Man's World, Woman's Place," published in 1971.

In her latest book, Mrs. Janeway uses her background in history, sociology, anthropology and psychology, to explain how the structure of the family unit has changed since the Industrial Revolution due to technology, social mobility, the flight to the suburbs, the break up of the extended family and the isolation of the nuclear family.

"Many people feel that it is the mother's responsibility to rear the children, prepare them for the outside world and take care of the home. This is almost impossible if the woman is working at the same time.

"In studying this country's past and the different cultures around the world, it's very seldom that a mother will be the only person to care for the children."

Mrs. Janeway tells of a study recently completed at the University of Chicago, where they compared the child rearing techniques in different communities around the world. These communities were in New England, India, East Africa, the Philippines and Mexico.

"The study found that only in New England was the mother taking care of the child completely, spending over 90 per cent of her time with the child.

"In most countries the caring of the child is taken over by another woman, either the grandmother, an aunt, a neighbor or an older sister, allowing the mother to work, at home or away from the home, or have some time to herself."

Mrs. Janeway says that good child care centers in this country could be beneficial to both the child and the parent.

"The child would have the opportunity to associate and interact with children in his own age group, older children, adults other than his parents and retired people (possibly as the grandparent image).

"I think many children are impoverished in not having the larger family and community to relate to as they did in the past.

"A good child care center could give the child the equivelant of this and help him in facing the world.

"Basically you want to rear a child to be a mature adult who can manage the world outside of his own home. It's not completely up to the mother to do this.

"Oftentimes the mother who stays at home and spends most of her time with the children has no idea of the working world."

Mrs. Janeway thinks that a working mother is better because she is more active and involved with the world around her.

"A woman who is in touch with outside events can communicate better with her children as they are growing up. She is more open to change and not frightened of the changes.

"A woman needs a connection with the outside world to help her find her identity and gain self-confidence."

Mrs. Janeway agrees that women have come a long way, but not far enough. She would like to see women getting equal pay but feels that this will not happen until women are given equal opportunity for training in managerial positions.

"Women are not going to get equal opportunities until companies change their attitude that a woman is going to quit work when the children start coming. This calls for child care centers and husbands taking on more responsibilities around the house.

"There is nothing sacred or demeaning about doing housework — it is something that has to be done. Face it, anyone can clean out a bath tub."

One myth that Mrs. Janeway would like to dispel is that women in the work force are taking jobs away from men.

"I get so tired of hearing that line," Mrs. Janeway said with near anger creeping into her otherwise soft voice.

"Women in the work force create more jobs because they are bringing more cash into the economy. The greatest growth factor of the sixties was the increase of working women.

"When a woman's salary is not used to keep the family above the poverty line, it is used for sending the children to college, buying a second car, vacations, or more clothes for the children."

Mrs. Janeway points out other jobs that have been created to help the working woman, such as employes for child care centers and production of convenience foods.

"I don't understand some men when one minute they will say the woman should stay at home because she is inferior and the next minute say that if she does work she will be taking the job away from the man. That's completely illogical. If women are inferior then why should men worry about having to compete with them?"

Mrs. Janeway draws on her knowledge and experiences as a wife, mother and working woman. She discusses the past, present and future of women in society, their psychological make up, their place in the business world and their effect on society and the family unit.

Novelist spins tale about disc industry

—Dallas News: Jack Beers

By JANE ULRICH

Whether it's called "customer relations" or "building good will," it's all the same, says Elaine Jesmer.

It's payola, and that's a loaded term.

Webster's calls it "an undercover or indirect payment for a commercial favor (as to a disc jockey for plugging a song)," and Elaine calls it a way of life in the record industry.

"Number One With a Bullet," though fiction, is the slice-of-life way the author describes what goes on behind the scenes of one of the biggest and most competitive industries around these days.

("Number One" indicates the record's placement on the charts, and a

JESMER, Elaine
(1939-)

DALLAS NEWS
(Dallas, Tex.)

July 10, 1974

[See also CA-49/52]

"bullet" is a black dot indicating that the record's popularity is growing.)

It's a case, she says, of the "big companies exploiting the little people. They say, 'You belong to me; you're a product.'"

SHE BELIEVES that one reason payola thrives in the record industry is the stiff competition.

"There are so many record companies around. They're producing 200 to 250 records a week, and there's only X-amount of air time to play them," she explains.

But the old "wining-and-dining" method of persuasion isn't enough to make a difference any more, says the former press agent.

She told of a man in a large metropolitan city who was paying three promotion men $150 a week to get his record played, and that didn't work.

"The competition is stiff," she says, especially when the big record companies can come up with better bribery: Cocaine ("It's expensive and prestigious"); money ("It's still negotiable"); prostitution, and airline tickets ("They can be exchanged for money, if need be").

BLACK RECORD COMPANIES are just as bad as white ones, she says. "They say, 'We'll do more for you than a white company will.' They'll call you brother and rip you off."

Early rumors about Elaine's novel about an imaginary black record company based in Houston brought some negative response from Motown, perhaps the largest and most successful black recording company.

It's a matter of public record, says Elaine, that Motown thought they were the subject of her book.

"If they're trying so hard to cram their foot into that shoe, maybe it's their size," Elaine says bravely.

SHE'S BURNED her bridges behind her with this book and "has no intention of going back."

"Most of what I say about the practices that go on in the music industry could and do happen. A lot of ex-street hustlers see the big money—(the industry) attracts that kind of street-hardened individual."

Elaine, who has worked in nightclub public relations and for Ray Charles' record company, Tangerine, and for People Records, chose the record industry to work in because she "was the typical nut, right out of school."

The journalism graduate of the University of Chicago found the business "rough and unsophisticated, and exciting, too, in a sense."

She's now in the fourth week of a promotion tour for the book. Possibly the only negative public response she's had was when someone called in a question to her while she was appearing on Atlanta television.

The caller wondered why she picked a black record company as the subject of her book when she wasn't black herself.

"That's something I can't do anything about," she answered.

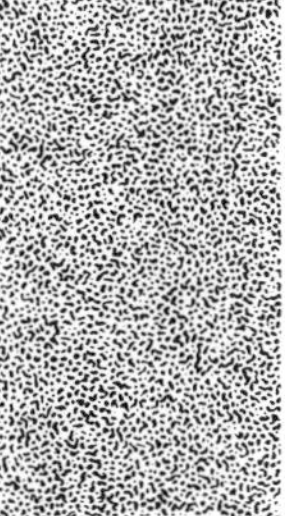

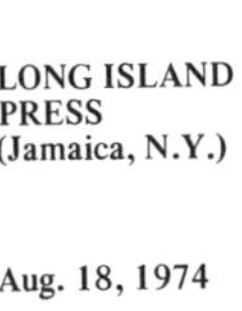

JESMER, Elaine

LONG ISLAND PRESS
(Jamaica, N.Y.)

Aug. 18, 1974

Author has spun controversial tale

By SANDRA GITTENS

"If I could do it all over, I'd do it all over again," laughed Elaine Jesmer, as she began to explain the controversy and reason behind her first novel, "Number One With A Bullet."

An energetic, slim woman of 34, who said she'd just been to about 25 odd cities in a matter of days, Miss Jesmer bounced on her Manhattan hotel bed, smiled and said, "Well, what do you want to know?"

What's the "hangup" behind the book?

It's a fictional piece of writing in which she says she just wanted to tell a story. It's centered around a record company that's owned by a black family . . . it's also filled with sex, violence, and systematic exploitation of major artists.

FOR OPENERS, MISS Jesmer says she's only worked for one record company eight months . . . Ray Charles Records on the Tangerine label.

"Normally I worked clubs, doing public relations work. In connection with the clubs I would be handling the acts that appeared. I kind of got into handling more acts than clubs because the road managers of several acts liked the job I'd done and wanted a service more directed to their client. So I ended up handling Marvin Gaye, Tammy Terrell, Martha and the Vandellas, the Four Tops and the Fifth Dimension . . . mostly for engagements they did in the Los Angeles area."

Pointing out the obvious, that she somehow always worked with black artists, she explained that it was because the clubs she worked for were black-oriented.

Miss Jesmer says there was a definite attempt to suppress the novel. Last October she says she started receiving letters asking to see the manuscript. Her publisher refused.

SHE SAYS THERE was an obvious attempt to suppress it by a record company. "And there was no reason," she says. "My publisher told them it was a novel, but the letters got saltier and saltier. Then, last month, my publisher got a letter saying that they were going to consult their lawyers. They had never read the book, all this time they were asking for the book, so they had never even seen it. It was all on rumor. The same day the letter came, they had a lawyer call my publisher and ask for the manuscript. He told him he could buy it in the store."

Next came a letter from the Justice Department. They wanted to know if she would be interested in contacting them about "anything." "So I had my lawyer call and tell them that it's fictional, and I don't have any facts. I have nothing that would substantiate a legal case for them."

In 1973, the Justice Department began investigaitng reported use of drugs and payola by record companies interested in promoting their own artists. Although no indictments have been returned, grand juries in several states have heard evidence about several alleged payola incidents.

She says what's being done to her is the same thing that happened to the main character in the book . . . the control of output. She doesn't believe anyone has the right.

IF I REALLY had to sum up the book I would say that nobody, no corporation, has the right to tell an artist what to do, no matter how bizarre his product might be. No matter what they think of it in terms of what's current, because art should be free."

Movie rights of the book were sold to Al Ruddy, who also did the "Godfather." Ronie Elder was hired to write the screen play and Paramount was to finance the movie. Elaine says she got the same deal as Mario Puzo.

Later she heard that the movie deal had fallen through. "And that freaked me out!" she says.

"It seems to me that the resentment is due to the hearings, the Justice Department, and the lawyers. Everybody in the business is very jumpy about it. But it's also, I think, the fact that I am a white woman. Not just white, but also a woman. I think that really has an effect." ➡

(Also see preceding article)

Author Claims Motown Squelched Her Movie About Music and the Mob

JESMER, Elaine
DETROIT FREE PRESS
(Detroit, Mich.)
Sept. 22, 1974

BY CHRISTINE BROWN
Free Press Staff Writer

There's a hot movie about the recording industry brewing out in Hollywood these days. But even though most of the people involved think the story idea is a good one, they're all feuding, and the film may never be made.

All the elements for an exciting movie are there: charges that a young author is a raving neurotic, rumors of a secret deal between hostile parties, suggestions that shadowy mob figures and mob money are involved in it all.

BUT THIS is no screenplay. It's part of the complicated, so far abortive attempt to make Elaine Jesmer's "No. 1 with a Bullet" — a novel about the record industry, published in May of this year — into a film. (The "bullet" of the title refers to the large black dot appearing beside a recording title in trade publications to indicate it's climbing in sales.)

The actors in the real life intrigue are Miss Jesmer; Albert S. Ruddy, producer of "The Godfather," who bought the rights to her book; Stanley Polley, a multimillionaire involved in the recording industry, who has agreed to finance the film; and Motown, the former Detroit recording giant, which sees too much of itself in Miss Jesmer's book.

The drama began over a year ago when word got around the recording industry that Miss Jesmer, a 35-year-old ex-Chicagoan who has done publicity and promotion work in Hollywood for about 10 years, was writing a novel based on her experiences.

Rumor said it was going to hurt.

"No. 1 with a Bullet" was coming at a bad time for the industry. Domestic sales of records and tapes had hit $2 billion per year, and too clearly the industry could serve as a gigantic laundry for mob money. Some said it already was.

Clive Davis, the head of CBS's Columbia Records, was fired from his $350,000-per-year job last summer, accused of juggling his expense account to the tune of nearly $100,000.

THE FEDERAL Strike Force Against Organized Crime in Newark, N.J., began looking into these allegations about the record industry:

- Drugs were being supplied by record companies to artists and their managers to win their favor or keep them happy.
- Airline tickets were being bought by record companies and then cashed in by disc jockeys.
- **Payoffs were made to industry tip sheet publishers for favorable mentions of new records.**
- Non-existent limousine services, trucking firms and airline ticket agencies were links for payoffs from record companies to Mafia figures.

This climate made "No. 1 with a Bullet" a hot book even before it was published. And when Berry Gordy Jr., head of Motown, heard about the book's plot, he got even hotter.

Miss Jesmer's book is about a white publicist who falls in love with a black performer. It is set against the background of a black family-owned record company in Detroit which is secretly financed by big money from New York and Chicago, with the implication that the money could be coming from organized crime.

GORDY WAS quoted in several publications as saying Miss Jesmer had been in love with Motown singer Marvin Gaye until Gaye married Gordy's sister. Miss Jesmer said she never met Gaye until after his marriage.

She said, "The book is not about Motown. Someone in Houston asked me if it was about a similar company there. If Motown feels that it is them, then the shoe fits."

Miss Jesmer said Gordy began asking her publisher, Farrar, Straus and Giroux, to see galley proofs of the book.

The publisher got an inquiry from criminal attorney Louis Nizer on behalf of Motown, Miss Jesmer said, but Nizer dropped the matter when he learned the book had already been printed.

Michael Roshkind, vice-chairman of the board of Motown, refused to comment on whether Motown had retained Nizer in the case, but producer Ruddy said it's true.

Roshkind said, "The book is trash, pornographic trash. It's not even interesting."

MISS JESMER sold the film rights to Ruddy after being steered to him by Ed Palmer, an agent, who she said was then hired by Ruddy and refused to do anything else for her.

At this point, the conflicts between Ruddy and Miss Jesmer began, with Motown's name cropping up every so often.

The first dispute between the two centers on the screenplay. Miss Jesmer said Ruddy asked her, "Do you want to do the screenplay?" She said she told him that she did not.

Ruddy said he never offered to let her do it because he wanted to deal with a professional.

Ruddy hired black author Lonie Elder III, who did "Sounder," to turn Miss Jesmer's book into a screenplay.

She charges that the result was a fiasco.

"It was really bad. They took out all the personal relationships. The publicist is killed off at the beginning of the film," she said.

"Ruddy tried to make a black 'Godfather' out of it."

RUDDY SAID he's happy with the screenplay Elder gave him.

"Elaine had a diffuse, vague love story between a black guy and a white girl. She had a very big novel, in terms of length, which had to be reduced to a 120-page screenplay. It deals with power and corruption on a sophisticated level, and I never saw it as a love story," Ruddy said.

Ruddy has a deal with Paramount for several pictures, and at first the company was interested in "No. 1 with a Bullet," but it later backed out.

Miss Jesmer claims the deal fell through for two reasons: The screenplay was bad, and a secret agreement was made by Gordy, Ruddy and Paramount.

She believes that Gordy put pressure on Paramount by threatening to withdraw a three-picture deal Motown had made with the film studio if "No. 1 with a Bullet" ever got beyond the book stage.

She charged that Ruddy has agreed to keep pretending that he'll make the movie but that the film will never be made.

Ruddy said, "This is the absurd ranting of a neurotic. There is no secret deal. Motown needs Paramount more than Paramount needs Motown. Paramount has the right to refuse any film it wants to refuse."

Motown's Roshkind said that the story of a secret deal "is totally false. There's not a shred of truth in it."

Ruddy approached several other studios about financing the film — all had record company subsidiaries — but they showed no interest.

THEN POLLEY, a multimillionaire associated with MGM Records, agreed to finance the film even though he is a stockholder in many corporations dealing with music and the record business.

Miss Jesmer said that a source in what she calls "the syndicate" says Polley has syndicate ties.

"That's ridiculous," Ruddy said. "I never would be associated with anyone in the underworld.

"Elaine sees organized crime mounting a campaign against this film. I'm going to make it. I'll choose a director within six weeks. I'm not in this business to do things imporperly; I'll wait until I can get a top director."

Elaine Jesmer says, "The recording industry is a high-risk cleaning house for mob money. I can't believe what's gone on with this movie deal. It will be my next book. One thing is certain: People will never see this movie."

Michael Roshkind says, "It should be obvious to anyone what they're doing. They're trying to drum up a controversy over the book and the movie to create interest in them. This has been shrouded in lies and press agentry."

JAMES JONES

JONES, James
(1921 -)

MIAMI HERALD
(Miami, Fla.)

Jan. 5, 1975

[See also CA-2]

Interviewed by John Dorschner

After living in Paris for 16 years, author James Jones has come home again. Last fall, settling into a house on Key Biscayne, he began teaching a course in creative writing at Florida International University.

Despite his time abroad, Jones is irrefutably an American writer, still best known for his first novel, *From Here to Eternity,* a panoramic view of wenching, brawling GIs on Hawaii as the Japanese prepared to attack. The novel was a huge best seller, winner of the National Book Award and the basis for an Oscar-winning movie.

Most of his seven novels have been mammoth sagas. His second, the 1,266-page *Some Came Running,* was called by one critic "two pounds, 11 ounces of illicit sexuality and mayhem." Some reviewers have found a certain superficiality and redundancy in his work, while others have praised him for a kind of raw energy and original view of Americans in war and peace.

Born Nov. 6, 1921, in Robinson, Ill., James Jones went through childhood as an indifferent student who liked sports, especially fighting as a lightweight and welterweight in Golden Gloves tournaments.

After high school, imbued with the romanticism and lack of direction of youth, he enlisted in the Army Air Corps. Always a compulsive reader, the young private happened upon a copy of Thomas Wolfe's *Look Homeward, Angel,* and decided to become a writer.

He was in Hawaii when the Japanese attacked Pearl Harbor, which gave him the experiences for *Eternity,* and served as a combat soldier in the bitter hill battles of Guadalcanal, which evolved into *The Thin Red Line,* published in 1962. In one battle, he suffered a head wound and was shipped back to the United States, and these visions of America during wartime are to form the last book in his wartime trilogy, *Whistle,* which he has been writing on and off since 1967. His recent work includes a detective novel, *A Touch of Danger* (1973) and a nonfiction book, *Viet Journal* (1974).

In Miami, he has been teaching one day a week, which he uses as a break from the eight-to-12-hour days he has been putting in on a yet-untitled nonfiction book about World War II, which will combine his words with paintings made in combat.

Each of the three interview sessions was held in the late afternoon, after he emerged groggy from a day in his writing den, where a pool table is stacked with research materials. As a lively household (his wife Gloria and two teenagers, Kaylie and Jamie) swirled around him, he sipped coffee, puffed on cigars and talked about his life and work.

Q: What brought you back to the States? Were you worried that the years in Paris had hurt your American viewpoint?

JONES: I think it probably helped it. I was always like a bird on a branch in Paris. I was never part of it. And I found, increasingly, that I just didn't understand the French mind. It gave me a certain feeling of nostalgia about the United States, being away from it. It made me more American, rather than less. It was something that grew over the years into a very strong force to come back. But more than that, if I had been on the scene, I would have been a lot more critical about America than I was. Living away from it, nostalgia and homesickness had a kind of softening effect, like a filter on a camera.

Q: How do you view America now?

JONES: Ha! I sound like the worst chauvinist of all. I like it enormously. I am very happy to be back. There's no real cultural or spiritual revolution going on anywhere else. Only here.

Q: Simone de Beauvoir complained that you isolated yourself from the French writers in Paris.

JONES: Their writing has become very attenuated and thin-blooded since the days of Zola. Even Camus got caught by it finally. He always thought he was inferior because he wasn't a professional philosopher, but he's more readable and more human because he wasn't. Professional philosophers take human qualities and emotions and intellectualize to the point where they lose all the humanity in them.

Q: That's why you didn't associate with French writers like Sartre?

JONES: I grew up without serious profound training in manners, I guess. I don't go around seeing people that I don't think I'll

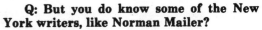

(Continued from preceding page)

enjoy. I probably should have written a letter and gone to pay my respects to De Beauvoir and Sartre and those people. She seemed very irritated that I did not meet them. I *did* meet Camus three or four times, before he was killed. He was a rather pleasant guy. A big woman chaser. Kind of haunted looking. I met him at night, hanging out at bars and dance halls. Gloria and I would just wander around with a few people we'd met, and someone always knew him. A couple of Gloria's friends had been girl friends of his. But I never met Sartre in situations like that, or De Beauvoir.

I wouldn't have wanted to meet them, simply because my approach to writing and observing life is entirely different from theirs. I don't believe a novelist should be *en gage*, as they say. Committed to some political cause. Human themes are going to outlast political themes.

Q: You went to Paris to write a novel on a jazz guitarist?

JONES: Yeah. Django Reinhardt. But that was just one of the reasons. I wanted to live abroad for awhile. We figured to stay for a year or 18 months. Then Gloria became pregnant, and we had to decide to come back or stay there. We flipped a coin. Literally. She wanted to live in Manhattan, and at the time I wanted to live in Sheridan, Wyo. So Paris was sort of a compromise.

Q: Why did you decide to come to Florida?

JONES: I have one or two Western novels that I want to write. Modern books about the West today. In the mid-'50s, I lived all over the West in a house trailer, moving from town to town.

Now, American writers are not really part of the community. You can go to all the PTA meetings you want, but you're still not part of it. That's what gave me the idea of going to a university. I knew Faulkner had gone to Virginia, and different ones have gone to different places. So I started to explore the possibility of going to Fort Collins, Colo., or Missoula. The kind of country I wanted for these novels. Nothing came out of that, but meantime, word got around and several other schools wanted me to come. Stony Brook, Yale. But Florida International, they had a man in Europe at the time, and they sent him to talk to me. I didn't want to live up the East Coast. Being a writer up there is very incestuous. You sort of live off each other, and you start writing novels about writers screwing other writers' wives. Pretty soon, you all sound alike.

Q: Have you avoided the New York literary scene?

JONES: Yes, I pretty much have. And it's probably hurt my sales, as a matter of fact, over the years. But I could never live in New York and work, because they are all so competitive and so full of hate, jealousy and envy that you get involved, in spite of yourself.

Q: But you do know some of the New York writers, like Norman Mailer?

JONES: He and I and Bill Styron ran around together a bit in 1951. I was in New York that summer, and we were all pretty good friends. We used to sit around on street corners, get drunk and talk about art and life and all that.

Q: Mailer's reputation was made by the war, too, wasn't it?

JONES: That's not strictly true. He got a couple of short stories published in the O'Brien Short Story Collections before he ever went off to the war. He himself says that he got in the Army and went off deliberately to write *the* war novel.

Q: Do you have any feelings about Mailer? He's very much in the New York establishment.

JONES: He irritates me a lot. We used to be pretty good friends, Norm and I. But he's the kind of guy who cheats at arm wrestling.

* * *

Q: How do you cheat at arm wrestling?

JONES: If you are lying on the floor, you get your foot against the corner of the wall. Or if you are sitting by a table, you get your other arm under the table. I found this out later. He would probably say that, well, this is legitimate because it's within human action and experience. If you aren't smart enough to understand that and react in your own way, then you are a fool. You can't argue with that philosophically, but it's still a cheap, sneaky thing to do.

And then he carried that over in his writings about his contemporaries. In *Advertisements for Myself* and *Cannibals and Christians*, he has this very appealing way of talking about other writers, looking as if he wants to like them, but he just can't because they don't have his integrity or ability.

Q: Did he mention you in "Advertisements"?

JONES: Yes. I've got a very valuable copy of it. It has the signatures of about 15 writers who he cuts apart. Saul Bellow, William Styron, James Baldwin, and God knows who all. Nelson Aldren. Writers who came through Paris. Jimmy Baldwin and I started it one night in my house when we were drunk, just as a joke.

Q: A few weeks ago, Kurt Vonnegut reviewed Joseph Heller's new book, and he wrote that for a whole generation of Americans, World War II was the most important experience in their lives. Does that apply to you?

JONES: I guess so. When somebody mentions World War II to my son, he asks his mother, "Is that the war Daddy

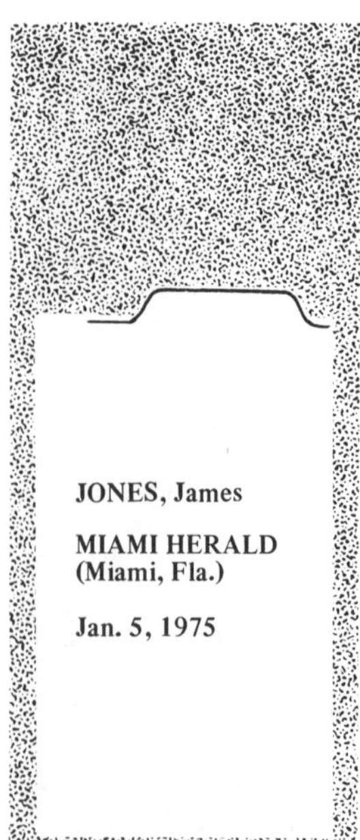
JONES, James

MIAMI HERALD (Miami, Fla.)

Jan. 5, 1975

(Continued from preceding page)

made all the money off of?" I'm certainly associated with World War II. There are a lot of people who aren't writers who this affects also. I have a friend here in Miami who was a bomber pilot in Italy. I was talking to him because I'm doing this book on the war's graphic art, and he said, "Well, that thing is one of the two or three big experiences in my life, maybe the biggest, and it always will be." And he came back home and became an optometrist. He didn't stay with flying. I don't know. It's interesting.

Q: In your writing, you keep returning to the war. It seems to be a powerful theme for you.

JONES: Of course, it is. But I've had a lot of others that interested me, too. In the very beginning, when I first conceived *Eternity,* I had no form for the first novel. I intended to take the characters from pre-Pearl Harbor Hawaii to Guadalcanal and then, corresponding with my own experiences, being shipped back to the U.S. in midwar and what happened then. The coming up against the home-front society, the swinging, high-living, wild-spending, hard-working society. I intended to do all that in one novel. But I wasn't very far into it before I realized I couldn't do it. Not only was the seope too large, but dramatically, I couldn't do it. So at that point, I conceived the idea of doing a trilogy, even before *Eternity* was finished. I still have somewhere old envelopes, yellowed with age, which had the notes in them. Pre-war novel, combat novel, postcombat novel.

Q: There were 11 years between "Eternity" and "Thin Red Line." Why didn't you go ahead with the trilogy right away?

JONES: For one thing, I got off into some kind of mystical bent for awhile. Zen, Confucianism, reincarnation, and I wanted to explore some of that in *Some Came Running.* And I'd been living back home in Illinois a lot. And. . .I don't know exactly. It didn't seem right yet. Partly, I was getting irritated at being classed as a war writer already. "Jones writes well about war, but he can't write about women. He can't write about anything else." That was one of the many reasons that I laid aside the second novel to do this one on the Middle West, with several prominent women characters.

Q: You've put aside the last book in the trilogy several times. Was something going wrong with it?

JONES: I wouldn't have said so then. The first time I stopped was to write *The Merry Month of May,* the book about the Paris revolution. It was the revolution itself which caused me to stop work on *Whistle.* It was too exciting, and I couldn't sit down and work day after day. I'd hear the kids chanting, and see those ballets between the cops and the students going on across the river. While I was exploring all that, I got the idea for the novel. So I just went ahead and wrote it. I figured it'd take a year. It took about two and a half.

Q: Is there something about "Whistle," that it's the last in the series, that makes you reluctant to let go of it?

JONES: No, I can't wait to get it done. I think it's going to be an important work, the three books taken together, in American letters. The first two books are already pretty good.

Q: But you've also done "Touch of Danger," the mystery book, in the meantime. Was there a financial reason for that?

JONES: No. I could use the money. Everybody could nowadays. But it started out as a movie treatment, about a bizarre killing I heard about one summer in Greece. When I got back to Paris, I was working on *Whistle,* and director John Frankenheimer, a friend of mine, lived right down the block. He told me to write a script treatment and we'd make a film out of it. I did, but the initial treatment didn't solve all the problems, and I wanted to do a novel on it, anyway. I wrote it in about a year, or nine months, which was very fast for me. But then Frankenheimer couldn't sell it, partly because at that moment he was not successful and partly because I didn't have any huge film credits in the last few years. But it was fun to write.

I started working on *Whistle* in the mornings and that book in the afternoons. And finally it began to usurp more and more time. Finally, I had to quit *Whistle* and devote all my attention to it.

Q: Is there a love-hate thing with "Whistle"? You said you were bothered by your reputation as a war writer.

JONES: Well, I used to be, more than I am now. I think it's age and the passage of 25 years. It's become such an important book to me. Of course, one always wants every book to be perfect. No book ever is. When it comes to putting words down on paper, you can't recreate the vision you had. But this book is so good that I don't want anything to damage it. I've got two-fifths of it done, and it's damn near perfect, in any real literary sense that you want to name. I don't want to be pressed to finish it. But I'm not running away from it. I've got it all in my head.

It's been a good chance to clarify a lot of my ideas about war. I've been very am-

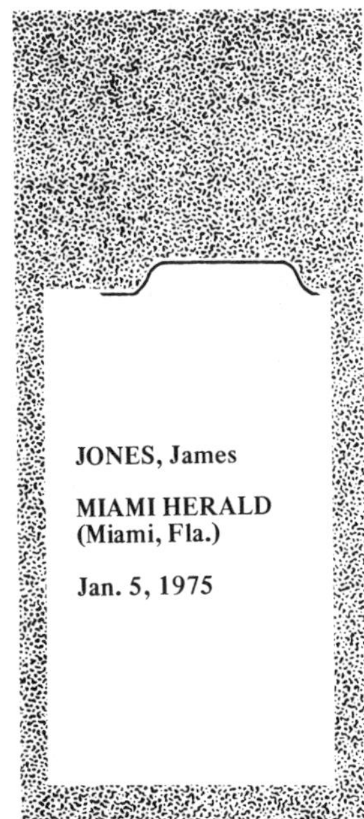
JONES, James

MIAMI HERALD (Miami, Fla.)

Jan. 5, 1975

(Continued from preceding page)

bivalent about war, and the race's addiction to war. I hate it, and at the same time, I agree with what General Lee said: "It is well that war is so terrible lest we come to love it too much." I think almost everybody who ever was in a war had periods when he liked it.

Q: Walker Percy has a line in "The Last Gentleman," about a bored lawyer rushing off to enlist the day after Pearl Harbor: "War is better than Monday morning."

JONES: I think there's a lot of truth in that. A lot of people went off to war very happily, because they were getting away from wives they didn't like and responsibilities that had begun to bug them. Then, when you get into combat, something else happens.

There are moments when you have this sense of power. It's usually when you're winning, but you're in danger, too. The times when you don't give a damn anymore, when you just don't care if you get killed or not. You're released from some reservation. I guess that's what draws men to it.

Q: But you don't think your ambiguity toward war has held up "Whistle"?

JONES: No. In a way, it's been good to have as much time off between books. I don't think I could have written *The Thin Red Line* the way I did, or as well as I did, if I'd written it immediately after *Eternity*. And I don't think I could have written *Whistle* as well, if I'd done it right after *The Thin Red Line*.

Q: In spite of all your other books, most readers still associate you with "Eternity." Does that bother you?

JONES: Yeah. I used to say that damn book has become the bane of my life. I've written at least three novels that are better than that, but everything gets compared to it, adversely, usually, because it was such a huge best seller and such a big film. It's being compared by the notoriety it got, rather than as a work of art.

Q: You said in one of your classes that you had avoided meeting Hemingway.

JONES: Yes. When *Eternity* was in galleys, they sent it to him for comments, like they do with books. There was a lot of excitement about the book, even before publication. Anyway, he sent it back with a letter saying, well, he liked the book, it had certain valuable things in it. and he'd be glad to sit down with the author and show him where he went wrong and how to straighten it out. And I told my editor, "If you do that, you've lost a writer." That's partly vanity, but I think it was justifiable vanity.

I had already begun to hear things about Hemingway which I didn't like. It was about this time when some articles were coming out about him, about his kingship kind of thing down in Cuba. He could be very vindictive to people he didn't like. And he didn't like them if they didn't kowtow to him. So I decided that it was better to avoid meeting him entirely. After *Eternity* came out, I went to New York sometimes for three or four months, working. And, if there was a party he might be at, I'd avoid it. Everybody always tried to put me in the same slot with Hemingway, because I wrote about war, and still do write about war, and the problems of maleness and nonmaleness. But I don't think my approach is the same as his. He's a strange man. I don't want to knock him. He's a fine writer. *The Sun Also Rises* is a classic. His later books went steadily downhill, but he's not alone, it happens to a lot of people.

He worked at his myth as much as he worked at his work. Which gave me the idea that if you can control your personality a certain amount, maybe your work won't become more and more separated from reality as you get older.

Q: Your first editor was Maxwell Perkins, the same man who worked with Fitzgerald, Hemingway and Wolfe?

JONES: I was sort of his last boy, something of which I'm very proud. Perkins died in 1947 and saw only a rudimentary beginning of *Eternity*, the first 200 pages, which he sent back to me with his comments.

Q: In "The Godfather," there's a scene where a horse's head is put in a producer's bed, and that gets an Italian singer a part in a war movie. Many people associate that scene with "From Here to Eternity." Is there any truth in that?

JONES: None at all. Eli Wallach, who is a fine actor and an old friend of mine, accepted the role of Maggio, and then dropped it in order to go to New York to make *Camino Real*, the play. Which, he said subsequently, he regretted like hell. Sinatra had read the book and had associated himself with Maggio. He was in Africa with Ava (Gardner), who was shooting *Mogambo* with Gable and all them. When he heard Eli had turned it down, he flew back to get the role for himself. He went in and talked Harry Cohn into it, if it's possible to talk Harry Cohn into anything. That's how it came about. He got it all on his own hook.

Q: After "Whistle," do you have plans for other books?

JONES: Well, there's a sense of getting older. I've got about three books I want to write before I get the boom lowered on me. After that, I don't care what happens.

Q: Will you be staying in Florida for more than a year?

JONES: I don't really know yet. We'll probably go up to East Hampton for the summer, get a place up there, a small, cheap place. After that, we'll see what happens.

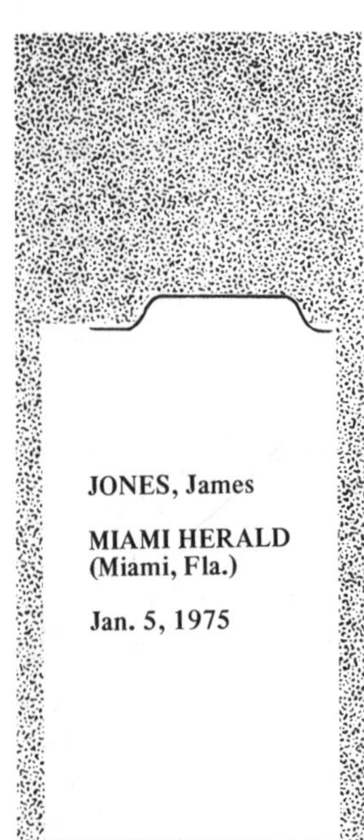

JONES, James

MIAMI HERALD (Miami, Fla.)

Jan. 5, 1975

(Also see preceding article)

James Jones: Coming home

JONES, James

COURIER-JOURNAL & TIMES (Louisville, Ken.)

Sept. 15, 1974

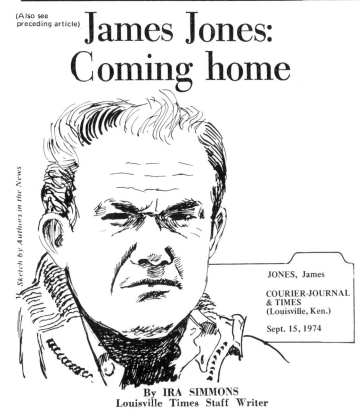

Sketch by Authors in the News

By IRA SIMMONS
Louisville Times Staff Writer

PARIS — The trees along the quay moved gently in the breeze, their leaves flashing in the afternoon sunlight like the trees in a Corot drawing. The Seine sparkled through the line of trees. It flowed slowly by the Ile St. Louis and under the weathered stone bridges toward the spire of Notre Dame.

"Paris isn't as gay as it used to be." James Jones stood by an opened window and stared across the Seine at the Left Bank. "It hasn't been the same since the riots in '68. The police have really clamped down on the Latin Quarter."

Paris isn't as gay as it used to be. Hemingway's Moveable Feast is becoming a cafeteria. The gendarmes are in the Latin Quarter all right — nervous squads of them eying the white-face mimes and the street musicians. But the students also have changed; their blandness is perfectly expressed by the current fad of wearing American university sweatshirts. And while young Parisians walk around with KENTUCKY STATE and WISCONSIN stamped on their chests, a new building boom changes their city permanently for the worse. Construction cranes are everywhere, looming in the distance like the catapults of a barbarous army closing in on the heart of Paris.

FOR JONES Paris was just a place to work on his eighth novel, "Whistle," a book that will complete the war trilogy begun with "From Here to Eternity" and continued with "The Thin Red Line." The book will be finished in the United States because Jones plans to return home for good this fall — a surprising move since the Paris he loves is being spoiled by an encroaching Americanization. But that wasn't the big surprise. Jones is coming home to become writer-in-residence at Florida International University in Miami next month. James Jones, the literary primitive, the terror of overeducated "phony intellectuals," plans to settle down in the groves of Academe.

"I'm really looking forward to it." His voice was husky and surprisingly high. "All that stuff I've said about phonies dominating literature refers to book reviewers, not scholars." He laughed softly, and his head rocked back on the bulging muscles of his thick, weight-lifter's neck. His face — the scowling brows and battering-ram chin — is a caricature of pugnacity.

HE HAD worked on the novel six years. But the idea for the book was born 30 years ago when Jones was a young veteran drifting through a booming post-war America, living in a jeep-pulled trailer and trying to put his experiences into words.

He decided to write three books that detailed what happened before, during and after combat. The pre-combat novel, "From Here to Eternity," won the 1951 National Book Award and made Jones famous. The combat novel appeared 11 years later as "The Thin Red Line." Both were made into successful films. "Whistle" will tell the story of a combat veteran trying to adjust to civilian life.

The novel plays off against the intense friendships that seem to develop only among combat soldiers. "Each character in the novel is haunted by the feeling that he could have done more for his friends," said Jones. "All of them are finally destroyed by that sense of failure."

JONES saw his combat at Guadalcanal. Shrapnel from a mortar blast wounded him in the head and he was evacuated back to the states. He killed his first Japanese soldier with a knife. "Oh hell," he said. "I didn't see that much combat." He smiled faintly. "But what I saw of it was quite enough."

With his literary roots in World War II, Jones has been typed as an old-fashioned *machismo* writer concerned only with a man's alleged need to prove himself on the battlefield and in bed.

But the picture of the Army presented in his books is hardly a romanticized one, and, in fact, Jones has never stopped giving battlefield glory his scowling once-over. "I knew a lot of heroes in the Army," he once said in an interview. "They all had some sexual hang-up."

On a personal level, it's hard to find traces of Jones's overblown reputation as a swaggering brawler. He's polite and thoughtful; his earthy cursing, combined with frequent references to poetry and philosophy, make him sound like a well-read cowboy.

JONES is a fiction chauvinist unimpressed by some of the New Journalism of his contemporaries. "I thought Norman Mailer's stuff about the '72 conventions was embarrassing. It doesn't take any talent to make Nixon look ridiculous. He does it for himself." Other writers, thinks Jones, can splash on the scummy surface of issues that bubble in and out of the public consciousness — bisexuality today; God knows what tomorrow — but Jones scuba-dives below the surface to hunt for the unchanging fears and obsessions. But the best analogy for Jones as a novelist lies in another sport. If the literary-boxing metaphor might be used one last time in this century, Jones is like a guileless slugger who does nothing in the ring but throw leather. Some of his roundhouse punches may miss: he has been accused of lacking style, but he counters by charging that "precious" well-turned phrases often detract from the natural power of a well-constructed sentence. "Just what is it about a sentence that enables it to convey emotion to us?" he asked. "So often it's the timing, you know. Sometimes using a shorter word — removing one syllable from the flow of the sentence — will make all the difference."

Some of Jones's punches may miss, but others land beautifully. His analysis of military society — though made a few wars back — still rings true. The characters of his two best known and received novels are carefully-selected Army types. In "From Here to Eternity" he exposed those characters to the deadening routine and petty brutality of a pre-war garrison. In "The Thin Red Line" he catalogued their reactions to combat. In "Whistle" he will observe their attempts to cope with post-war civilian life. He'll do it for 800 pages or so, all the while trying not to be mannered in his approach or style.

Hemingway was the star of Sribner's when that publishing house brought out "From Here to Eternity." "I was careful to avoid meeting him," said Jones. "He was always bucking for points — you couldn't sit in the same room with him and not hear him tell you how much better he was than you. Hell, I didn't care if he was a great writer and it didn't make any difference to me what Hemingway thought of my work.

"You have to have a huge ego when you first start writing — you've got to be crazy to even try. It's like a ying-yang situation. You need a big ego to get going, but it becomes destructive later. It can destroy your work. It can destroy you."

Jones and his wife Gloria were traveling through Paris 16 years ago when she became pregnant. "We flipped a coin and decided to settle here." Their daughter is now 15. They also have a 14-year-old adopted son.

Jones's presence in Paris has disrupted the legacy left by other American expatriate writers. The Lost Generation of the Twenties was young, poor and struggling. George Plimpton's Paris Review crowd struggled to look hungry in the early Fifties. But Jones has never tried to be anything other than what he is—a best-selling novelist who owns a 17th-century house on the Ile St. Louis and spends $4,000 a year on cigars. He has avoided the Parisian intellectual circles that would have lionized him. The French, after all, have always viewed American culture as a primitive Rousseauan escape from the unrelieved sophistication of their own. They loved Benjamin Franklin when he wore a coonskin cap to a glittering Versailles ball. The Hollywood "B" gangster movie became the model for the New Wave directors, and today Charles Bronson is the most popular actor in France. If James Jones, the Brute of American Letters, had played his cards right, he might have been an existential hero by now.

JONES SAID the years spent in Paris have made him more aware of being an American. "It's helped me realize how different we are as a breed. On trips back to the states, I'm *amazed* by how polite Americans are. If the light changes on you while you're crossing the street, they don't try to run you down with their cars."

He describes himself as "absurdly optimistic" about the future of the United States. "Well, *of course* the United States has problems — problems with pollution and technology and all the rest. We're so much more advanced than other nations. We're operating in situations for which there are no historical precedents. We *have* to make mistakes. . . . We're the head of the comet."

And in Jones's view, it's better to be at the head, in the United States, than in a backwater that receives only the worst features of American culture. But Paris hasn't been completely spoiled. Won't Jones even miss his favorite restaurants?

He dismissed the question with a wave of his cigar. "I could eat hamburgers for the rest of my life." He paused to savor the effect of his answer. "Yeah, as a matter of fact, I want to try some grits as soon as I get to Florida. Haven't had any in a long time."

BUT WHAT about his Cuban cigars? He won't be able to get those in the states. The scowl deepened. There's no way he'll defend the embargo on Cuban cigars as a great piece of statescraft. "That stupid law punishes Americans a lot more than Cubans," he muttered, "but there's a thriving Cuban community in Miami. They make some excellent cigars."

He took a long puff and waited for more irritating questions. He was ready, but there were none. "No, I'm looking forward to seeing Florida again," he said slowly. "I spent a lot of time there back in the Forties when I was living in the trailer and working on 'Eternity.' He grins with an almost boyish enthusiasm. "I'd like to get out west, too. Damn, that was really nice country. I haven't seen Denver since I was bumming around 25 years ago. . . ."

Denver's changed, I told him — growing by hundreds every month; sprawling with plastic and neon; filling the Rockies with its pollution.

"Well . . . " he said finally. "It was a pretty big town even then." He stared at the smoke curling from his cigar. He said he felt tired just thinking about moving to the United States. The collections — his books, swords, paintings and sculptures — will have to be crated up and shipped across the ocean.

There is no time to wonder what will happen when he gets to the states and his expectations meet reality. He has to think about the logistics of the move. And he'll be supervising and giving orders and making sure things are done right.

James Jones is coming home. The country had better shape up.

Mr. Simmons, medical reporter for The Louisville Times, interviewed James Jones earlier this year while traveling in France.

A Nonmilitant Grateful for the 'Strident Women'

—Star-News Staff Photographer Rosemary Martufi

ERICA JONG

By Judy Flander
Star-News Staff Writer

The lines on Erica Jong's brow were deepened by the frustration of having just been on a television talk show with two men whose views of women she considers primitive beyond discussion. "I warned them not to put me on with George Gilder and Dotson Rader, or the whole thing would be a media freak show," she sighed.

Gilder, author of "Sexual Suicide," had, she said, spent the whole time telling her how "those strident women's libbers (of which he assumed she was one) are castrating men," while Rader, also a writer, was blaming Mrs. Jong in particular and women in general for causing wars. "He believes men are killing each other to prove their phallic power to women," said Mrs. Jong incredulously.

Finally, she said, she had blurted out: "Stop horsing around. Don't put me on a pedestal, don't make me the Virgin Mary. Don't put us down." And with that, the TV station's phone switchboard had lit up with calls from irate watchers, shocked by Mrs. Jong's blasphemy and inelegant language. "Who is she?" she heard the studio people muttering as she hurriedly left the building.

ERICA JONG, 31, is a poet who has just published her first novel, "Fear of Flying," which, says novelist John Updike, reviewing it in *The New Yorker,* "feels like a winner. It has class and sass, brightness and bite."

"Fear of Flying" is about marriage and infidelity, a woman's fantasies and sexuality, her search for identity. She says it is "about the conflict of being a woman in a culture that doesn't credit the female experience. We've never been allowed to believe our way of life is a valid way of looking at reality."

On the surface, it seems to be more an autobiography than a novel. Like her heroine, Isadora Wing, Erica Jong is married to a Chinese child psychiatrist, she comes from a "family of yellers," her mother is a frustrated artist, she has had a succession of lovers and psychoanalists; she is blonde and sunny with a turned-up nose, and she has a fear of flying.

"Everyone in the novel is me in some sense," said Mrs. Jong, "but it's fiction." Her parents, she said, are not physically recognizable, and her husband, though physically recognizable, is "not really the husband in the book."

But bits of her family and herself are all in the book, "frozen in moments of time." Mrs. Jong said the book is "the story of a woman bearing witness to her own life, using her own feeling as a key to the world."

WHILE MRS. JONG has "always been a feminist if that means you want to be your own person," she is not in the women's movement. "But I'm grateful for those 'strident women'," she said with a wicked gleam in her eyes. "They're out there doing all those things that make it possible for me to sit in my room and write." During the eight years of her marriage, she said with amusement, she has made some gains. Her husband no longer says he feels like he's being castrated if he clears the table.

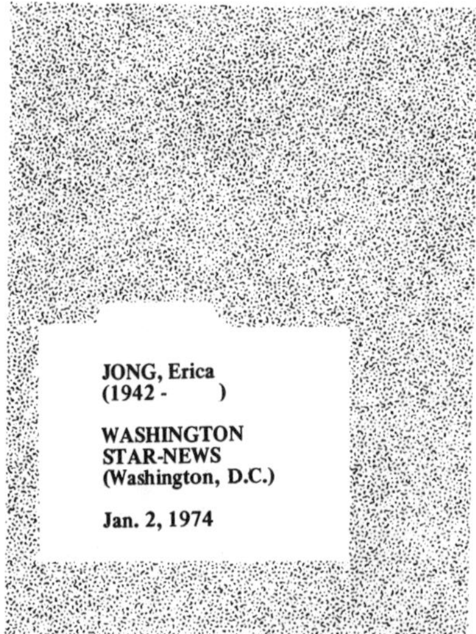

JONG, Erica
(1942-)
WASHINGTON
STAR-NEWS
(Washington, D.C.)
Jan. 2, 1974

"The thing we're all afraid of," she said, "is that our husbands will leave us for some little woman who'll take care of them." She is only half kidding. "The husband of one of my militant feminist friends left her for a housewife in Scarsdale with her own tennis court."

Erica Jones is irreverent, contemporary, and honest. If her book is schocking at all, it may be in its unabashed assertion that women, like men, often have a need for more than one sexual partner.

She says in "Fear of Flying:" "All those happy housewives making breakfasts for husbands and kiddies were dreaming of running off with lovers . . ." Just as Isadora Wing actually does, under the eyes of her husband. She admited that her own husband has told her that if she has any extramarital sex, he'd rather not know about it.

"We all put a heavy trip on ourselves sexually," Mrs. Jong said. Then her face lit up. "One of the things an affair does is make you grateful to go back to your husband and say, 'God! I'm glad I have you.' Most of the men you get you wouldn't want anyway; you'd find them pretty dragging!"

BESIDES, Mrs. Jong believes in marriage. "I like the idea of being married. 'I'm not a loner. Either it is the best way to live or the worst, depending on how it is going at a particular moment.

"The trouble with marriage is that it means so many kinds of renunciation for a woman. There is a mental freedom most women give up along with their names. If we could find mental freedom within marriage, then it would be great. My book is a trumpet for that kind of change."

Mrs. Jong said that she uses her husband's name on her work "because he's such a supporter of my writing and he wanted that symbolism, that representation of himself. It made him happy."

She may have children soon to make him happy, too. Mrs. Jong has "delayed and delayed" having children because she didn't want to be frustrated as a writer and take it out on her children, as her mother has on her three daughters. But now that she is established, she's tempted.

"My husband is 39 and he loves children, and he's getting that 40 panic," she said. She is finding that "as you get older, having no children gets gloomier. When Christmas time comes I find myself borrowing a nephew and worrying about not being connected with life in an essential way."

She said that she keeps telling herself, "Next month, I'll get pregnant."

Mrs. Jong, unlike Isadora, has not lost her fear of flying. "I'm not a member of Cowards' Anonymous," she said. "I'll fly if I have to get somewhere that way. But I get on the plane with my right foot first and I carry with me a little bag of amulets. I have a feelie stone agate that I rub a lot. And a little gold fish with a ruby eye my mother game me. She believes it holds the plane up. And I have a little duck my griend Grace Griffin gave me."

She didn't bring the amulet bag along with her from New York last week. She took the Metroliner instead.

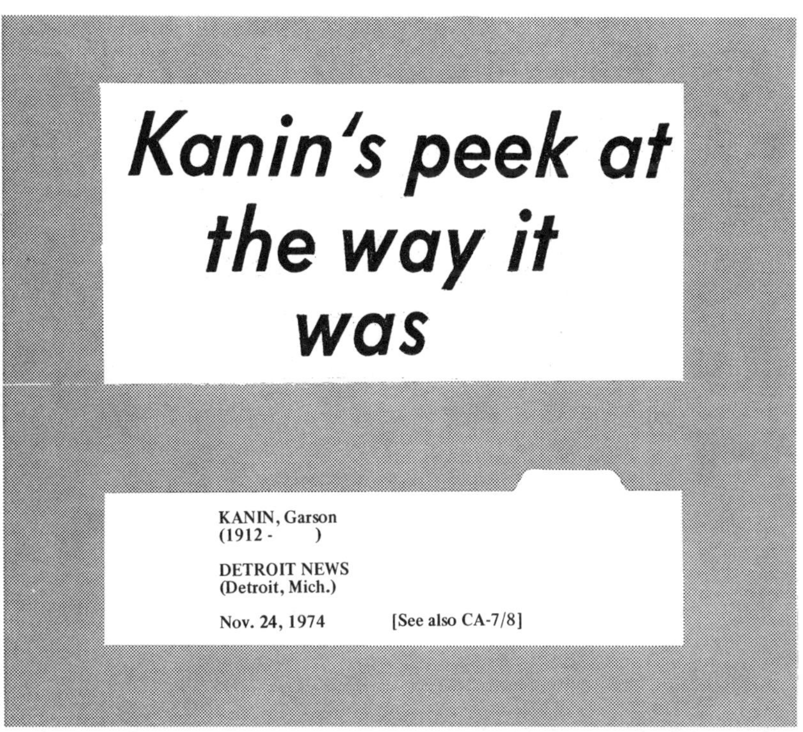

Kanin's peek at the way it was

KANIN, Garson
(1912 -   )

DETROIT NEWS
(Detroit, Mich.)

Nov. 24, 1974   [See also CA-7/8]

By BILL SUDOMIER
News Entertainment Editor

Garson Kanin, the director-playwright-author, stopped in Detroit the other day to push his new book — and catch this title: "Hollywood: Stars and Starlets, Tycoons and Flesh-Peddlers, Moviemakers and Moneymakers, Frauds and Geniuses, Hopefuls and Has-Beens, Great Lovers and Sex Symbols."

Garson Kanin

They'll probably understand at the bookstore if you just ask for Kanin's "Hollywood."

Why was he here promoting it on a rainy day, especially when it's selling well in its third printing? Well, the publisher, Viking Press, is paying — and he says it gives him a chance to escape from the often insular atmosphere of New York City.

"It's stimulating to realize that all of civilization isn't in Shubert Alley or at Hollywood and Vine," Kanin says.

IN ADDITION, Christmas is coming. He figures books make fine gifts, especially his, and book-sellers tell him the book business always goes up in recession-depressions, or whatever you want to call the recent economic unpleasantness.

Yes, but do we really need another book about Hollywood?

Kanin says we do: "Hollywood has shaped our lives, what we eat, wear, how we do our hair, our houses."

Kanin, who was 24 when he went to work for Sam Goldwyn, says his book is more than 393 pages of anecdotes, it's a portrait of a time and place. He says it tells the story of Hollywood, with Goldwyn as the pivotal figure.

"Goldwyn was one of those guys who — once you worked for him — figured you were indentured to him forever. He'd call me up years after (he quit working for him) and tell me to do things and I'd do them. He was a very hypnotic, very powerful man."

AS A DIRECTOR, Kanin says, he never got involved with any of the actresses he worked with. He says more often it was the producer or a friend of the producer. He was, nonetheless, able to observe them closely. Here are his observations of three of them:

•Carole Lombard: "She was the most brilliantly attractive and interesting, tremendously vital. She lived only to 36 but she was very versatile. My observation of her life with Gable was that it was idyllic."

•Greta Garbo: "She was 36 when she made her last picture, 'Two-Faced Woman.' I don't think she was right to stop acting, but MGM was so beastly to her, so rotten, it erased her desire to work. They blamed her for the picture's failure. They didn't send her anything for months. Work is a habit. The more you don't work the easier it is not to work."

Marilyn Monroe: "She was the unluckiest girl I ever knew, in her childhood, in her choice of men. Some women always choose the wrong men. Elizabeth Taylor does that. I was crazy about Marilyn. She wasn't up to doing what they asked of her."

Kanin, a tiny, balding man in perpetual motion, finished his skimmed milk, hopped up to answer the phone. It was his wife, actress-playwright Ruth Gordon, who, at 78, is 16 years his senior, calling from New York to find out how he was doing, how the trip was going, what the weather was like.

"Looks like the rain is stopping," he told her, encouragingly, whispered an endearment and hung up. He snapped shut the bag lying on his hotel room bed, shook hands, and headed out for Cleveland. It was evening, and he had a plane to catch and books to sell before he slept.

Garson Kanin a Man for All Seasonings

By Gerald Kloss
of The Journal Staff

Our first exclusive! Here is Garson Kanin's secret stuffing recipe for a 15 pound Thanksgiving Day turkey. Remember, you read it here first:

6 cups bread crumbs
2 raw eggs
1 cup chicken broth
1 teaspoon sage
1 teaspoon thyme
1 teaspoon rosemary

That's what he plans to put into that festive bird a week from now, and he swears by the recipe, as does his actress wife, Ruth Gordon.

"Hey, I love it!" he said here. "And I love grocery shopping! God, the price of sugar!"

Turkey stuffer, grocery shopper Kanin, who turns 62 Sunday, was in town to plug his latest book, "Hollywood," a 393 page tome of at least that many anecdotes about the good old days of filmdom, involving, as is stated in the longball subtitle, "Stars and Starlets, Tycoons and Flesh-Peddlers, Moviemakers and Moneymakers, Frauds and Geniuses, Hopefuls and Has-Beens, Great Lovers and Sex Symbols."

You can't talk more than a minute to this vibrant man without bumping into such famous Hollywood names as Goldwyn, Barrymore, Garbo, Monroe, Laughton, Bergman, Holliday, Rogers, Wilder, Tracy, Hepburn, Stanwyck, Chaplin . . . the list goes on and on.

Noted Writer

Garson Kanin. Author of one of the century's great stage and screen comedies, "Born Yesterday." Director of more than a dozen Broadway plays, including "The Diary of Anne Frank" and "Funny Girl." Author of five novels, 40 short stories, 10 screen plays and the 1971 best seller, "Tracy and Hepburn: an Intimate Memoir."

When he reaches the punchline of an anecdote, his eyes crinkle up in shared enjoyment. The famous names drop like leaves in autumn, and as colorfully. After a dinner of talk and sauerbraten at John Ernst's, he headed over to WEMP for Ira Fistel's 10 p. m. radio talk show.

Well, the show went on for an hour of chatter on Hollywood, and then Fistel took calls from listeners. Kanin spun out yarn after yarn in response to questions and opinions, and when Fistel indicated that it was about time to close up shop for the night, his guest insisted that they answer a few more calls: "It wouldn't be polite to stop now."

So it went on for another half hour or so. There was the recollection of his conversation with the film pioneer, Carl Laemmle Sr., founder of Universal Pictures in 1912. Laemmle, who once ran a dry goods store in Oshkosh, spoke of how he got into the movie business, shortly after the turn of the century:

A new Enterprise

"Laemmle then had a long dry goods store in Chicago, and a fellow asked him if he could rent the store for $10 to show movies. Laemmle agreed, and the people paid 5 cents admission to see these short clips of people and things moving on the white sheet. Not a real movie, you understand — just the novelty of it all.

"And the man started renting the long store for movie shows every two weeks, and the more people that came, the worse it was for the dry goods, because there were no seats and they leaned on the merchandise.

"So Laemmle rented another long store, an empty one, and put in benches. It became the first Nickelodeon, and Laemmle found he had a good little business.

"But then he had trouble getting enough new material from the moviemakers, so he decided to make his own. That's what led to Universal."

Kanin paused.

"And I remember Laemmle telling me, 'I often wonder how things would have been different if I had turned down that first fellow who wanted to rent the long store.' "

KANIN, Garson

MILWAUKEE JOURNAL
(Milwaukee, Wisc.)

Nov. 22, 1974

Sex and Love—With or Without Marriage

Sketch by Authors in the News

KAPLAN, Helen Singer
(1929 -)

WASHINGTON STAR–NEWS (Washington, D.C.) Sept. 8, 1974

By Judy Flander
Star-News Staff Writer

Dr Helen Singer Kaplan believes in love and marriage. Or love without marriage. But, either way, a loving sexual relationship between a man and a woman "is the most important thing in life."

If this view seems a little old-fashion for a woman who is leader in the new field of psychiatric sex therapy, it's just because Dr. Kaplan approaches sex from a humanistic tradition. She deplores "inhuman, mechanical, commercialized sex." A couple doesn't necessarily have to be in love — although it helps — but Dr. Kaplan believes that "sex is only enjoyable within the context of a human, loving relationship and pleasure is far more important than the actual sex function."

DR. KAPLAN'S philosophy of loving and caring distinguishes her new book, "The New Sex Therapy," (Quadrangle/The New York Times Book Co. $17.50), originally published as a textbook for psychiatrists, psychologists, physicians and med students by Brunner/Mazel.

The book describes Dr. Kaplan's use of many of the "sexual tasks" developed by Masters and Johnson combined with her own psychiatric and psycholotherapeudic techniques she has been developing since 1970 in her sex therapy clinic at the Payne Whitney Clinic of New York Hospital.

The clinic has a staff of 12 and, every year, Dr. Kaplan trains another half-dozen psychiatrists. She also teaches physicians and obstetricians how to diagnose and deal with their patients' sexual problems.

Like Masters and Johnson, Dr. Kaplan prescribes specific sexual exercises (sometimes she calls them tasks; both words were chosen for lack of any other less connotative expression) to help her patients overcome their sexual dysfunctions. But where she differs with them and other sex therapists, is that she also treats her patients psychiatrically.

When a couple comes into her clinic, it is because one of them is having a problem functioning sexually. The woman may be unable to have an orgasm; the husband may suffer from premature ejaculation. Or he may be impotent. Whatever the problem, it naturally affects them both.

Complete case histories — medical, sexual and psychiatric — are taken of the couple and based on this information, the first of the sexual tasks is prescirbed.

"These sexual exercises invoke intense and human reactions; they involve deeply emotional issues," explains Dr. Kaplan. "They are very revealing of psychological factors and enable us to work psychoanalytically with the patients."

ON THE NEXT visit to the clinic, the couple is asked to speak openly about the emotional feelings the sexual task has aroused. Often, they are surprised by hostilities toward one another they never dreamed existed.

"Sometimes," says Dr. Kaplan, "it is simple rage and anger at or fear of the partner which inhibits the sexual response." And, almost always, ignorance and guilt are prime offenders.

The psychiatrist helps the couple discuss these feelings and understand them as well as possible early in the treatment. Then they are sent home with a second sexual task, and the process is repeated.

In several weeks — the treatment is swift — the couple has been given enough insights and psychiatric treatment to overcome the sexual problem. The sexual tasks have provided a casual, methodical process for perfecting their sex life.

"When you combine sexual prescriptions with psychiatry, you've got a very powerful treatment," says Dr. Kaplan.

Why does Dr. Kaplan's ➡

(Continued from preceding page)

psychiatric short-cut work so well? "It is possible to have psychoanalysis for years without specifically mentioning a sexual problem because there's no active intervention by the analyst. But when you confront the patient with sexual situations and combine this with psychoanalysis, there has to be action.

"Masters and Johnson were the great innovators because they dealt with factors we neglected in psychiatry; we dealt with deep factors but we neglected the touching, the actual experience of sex," Dr. Kaplan says. "We only talked about the past. That's a very inefficient method."

Dr. Kaplan and her staff deal "directly with the immediate causes of sexual dysfunction; most often you don't have to go deeper A man may be impotent because he is afraid of impotence. This is a simple, emotional thing to deal with. But a man may be impotent because of problems with his mother, which is a deeper problem. In either case, a very active approach is more rapid than a passive one."

Eight or 10 visits to the clinic may be all it takes to "cure" premature ejaculation" impotency may take 12 to 14 sessions. And simple forms of frigidity are often dealt with in a matter of days.

There are some people who cannot be helped in Dr. Kaplan's clinic. "If a person is in a deep depression, of course we're not going to treat his impotence. He'll be referred for deeper therapy We take people who are not disturbed or whose disturbance has nothing to do with their sexual problems."

DR. KAPLAN doesn't treat people who hate each other, either. She sends them to a marriage counsellor. "If you have perfect mechanical functioning and no human pleasure, it's no good."

Following in the mode of Masters and Johnson, nearly all sex therapists work as male and female teams, but Dr. Kaplan can't see that there are any advantages of two therapists over one, so she does not work with a partner. In her own training program, her students help each other become "sensitized" to the sexual responses of the opposite sex. 'We sit down and talk about it all very explicitly and unemotionally, so we are able to deal with the problems of both genders sensitively."

Dr. Kaplan says, candidly, that she, herself, is very responsive to the sexual response of a man. "Every person who's really together is. If you've made love successfully with a member of the opposite sex, you develop that sensitivity."

She is divorced, but reluctant to admit it partly because she worries about hurting the feelings of her ex-husband. But she's also concerned about her image as a sex therapy counselor. "I don't want people to think I'm just an old spinster who is doing all this sex therapy. I don't want people to think I'm promiscuous or that I approve of mechanical sex. I don't want to be seen as anti-love or anti-marriage."

DR. KAPLAN LIVES in Manhattan with her three children, Jenny,10; Peter,15, and Phillip, 18. And she's engaged to be married. she says, happily.

A small, dark, attractive woman, around 40, whose personality is warm as toast with the crisp crust left on, Dr. Kaplan's manner is one of clinical professionalism. When she talks about sex, she could be talking about somebody's gall bladder.

She states, matter-of-factly that until she came along with her psychiatric approach, "the legitimate psychiatric community was very suspicious of sex therapy; it sounded too gimmicky and rapid."

Now she's been asked by the American Psychiatric Association to organize a session on sex therapy for its next meeting in May 1975. Masters and Johnson are among the experts she has already asked to speak.

Her book has been such a best seller among professionals that it has been put on the popular market despite its steep price.

Dr. Kaplan says she agreed to share the book with a lay audience for whatever educational value it may have. "It won't hurt," she says wryly, but I doubt if it will work because emotional factors have to be dealt with. It will help people gain understanding and provide information, but you can't cut out your own appendix even if you read exactly how to do it."

KAPLAN, Helen Singer

WASHINGTON STAR-NEWS (Washington, D.C.)

Sept. 8, 1974

JUST AS A surgery textbook would describe in detail how to take out an appendix, "The New Sex Therapy" gives directions on how to perform the "sexual tasks" she prescribes in helping patients overcome sexual dysfunctions. There is nothing in the book of prurient interest however; even the seven pen-and-ink sketches by Betty Dodson of couples performing sexual tasks have a romantic, loving tone. (The rest of the sketches look like something out of a biology textbook.)

Dr. Kaplan has received so many requests for more detailed descriptions of the sexual tasks that she is at work on a new textbook for professionals. It will be a spiral manual, containing dozens of drawings so explicit and erotic that it is earmarked for professional use only. Sex therapists may let their patients have a look at certain tasks, however, because it will save long, sometimes embarrassing explanations, Dr. Kaplan says.

She has been developing her psychiatric approach to sex therapy since 1964 when, as chief of psychosomatic medicine in Metropolitan Hospital in Harlem, she discovered a need for sex counseling among her patients. She found that ghetto women, with the least encouragement, wanted to tell her about problems in achieving orgasm. And often, she was able to help by merely providing information and counsel.

Dr. Kaplan is now clinical associate professor of psychiatry and in charge of student teaching at Cornell University of Medicine.

For those seeking sex therapy, Dr. Kaplan strongly advises a couple to go to a group or a person associated with a hospital or a university.

"Then, you're safe; you know they won't just be dispensing straight, mechanical sex therapy." While not all hospitals and universities have this service, many do "and within the next five years, there won't be a single major hospital without it," Dr. Kaplan predicts. And within the next three years, she says, there won't be a med school in the country that won't include human sexuality in the curriculum.

Dr. Kaplan urges too that young people seek help — perhaps just some counseling — if their first attempts at sex are failures. "Prompt treatment can prevent lifelong sexual difficulties."

Honesty Is Author's Policy for Children's Books

By Margo Huston
of The Journal Staff

On Halloween two trick or treaters appeared at the door of Ezra Jack Keats' Manhattan apartment. He gave one boy a nickle, the other a dime.

"Hey man," complained the kid with the nickle, "How come you gave him a dime and me only a nickle?"

In telling the story Wednesday in Milwaukee, while riding back to his hotel after giving a talk at the University of Wisconsin — Milwaukee, Ezra Jack Keats started laughing.

"What could I say? I had to be honest. So I told them, 'I don't know why. I just don't know. That's the way life is.' What was I supposed to do, bite one of the coins in half?"

Illustrator, Writer

Keats, 58, unmarried and one of the top children's books illustrators and writers in the country, spoke Wednesday afternoon and evening at UWM's 10th annual Conference in Early Childhood Education.

He talked about his books, which are akin to his reaction that Halloween: honest.

At a time when four color picture books did not have black children as heroes, Keats gave birth to Peter, a bright, black, fun loving, adventurous kid who lives in an apartment in a city.

For years he had been illustrating children's books and thinking to himself, "If I ever do a book of my own, there'll be a black kid in it."

Snow Storm

A snow storm in 1961 turned his mind back to his childhood and the excitement of waking up and going outside on a snowy day. Using a black child as a model, he made sketches of the boy that was to live as Peter in the minds of city and suburban children and parents around the globe.

"I wanted to make sure I didn't make Peter a white kid colored brown," he explained to his audience which included many black mothers and people who said they thought Keats was black.

"I'm very proud of the fact that people think I'm black," Keats commented in the interview. "Because, if they think I'm black, that substantiates the validity of my books. That means my books are real.

Have to Be Real

"The important thing is that the kids in a book have to be real—regardless of color," he said. "I don't like to emphasize the race thing, because what's really important is the honesty."

He continued: "I think that children look at Peter first of all as a child, who is like themselevs in some ways whether they are boy or girl, black, brown or white, fat or skinny or what."

It is the universality of people that Keats is getting at in his books. Everyone in the world is more similar to each other than different from each other, Keats said.

"The essential thing is that we see each other," he said, defining "see" as perceive, understand, discover.

"If we all could really see each other exactly as the other is, this would be a different world," he said. "But first I think we have to begin to see each other."

Wrote Book

In 1961, he wrote and illustrated "The Snowy Day," which tells about the excitement Keats felt as a boy when he woke up to see snow outside the Brooklyn apartment where he grew up without a single picture book of his own.

"We were too darn poor," he said. "I just never saw a picture book. Really, it wasn't until I was about 35 that I discovered children's books."

In 1962, "The Snowy Day" appeared in the bookstores with all Keats' adventures translated to those of Peter.

In 1963, "The Snowy Day" was awarded the Caldecott Medal as "the most distinguished American picture book for children." Now it and other Keats books are available in paperback at one-fifth the cost of the hard cover.

"The Snowy Day" remains one of Keats' favorites, but, he said, "You always have a special fondness for your newest ones." And he named "Dreams."

Best to Come

A book he is planning, he said, which will deal with the inner feelings of kids, but does not yet have a title or a final format will probably be his best.

"It will be real," he said. "I don't mean photographically real. I mean the inner reality." He illustrated by revolving his fists around each other and adding, "The inner workings."

Bette Peltola, an associate professor in the department of curriculum instruction at UWM who teaches children's literature, escorted Keats around Milwaukee.

"There are only one or two other authors that children turn to as readily as they turn to Ezra," she said. She declined to name the other popular authors, saying they were quite unlike Keats, but she did try to account for Keats' magnetism.

"It's the familiarity of the experiences about which he writes and the excitement of his art," she said.

The afternoon audience appeared to fall in love with Keats at first sight. He has a gentle, soft spoken manner with kids and adults alike. With his long navy pea coat and skipper's hat, he looks somewhat like Captain Kangaroo; without the coat. more like an older version of Mister-Rogers. He respects both of these TV children's heroes.

"You're even nicer than your books," commented one woman.

Other women — many of them black — were quite specific on why they liked Keats.

True to Life

"His books are really true to life. There's no propaganda," said Mrs. Lois Pirtle, 2618 N. 18th St., a practice teacher in elementary education. "And, he shows the black children in a different light than normally seen — in a positive rather than negative light."

Mrs. Lena Talbert, 2833 N. 21st St., a mother of eight who works at the Milwaukee Public Library, said, "I think his books are the greatest. They give black kids a sense of identity and they make them feel important. Everyone needs to feel good about himself."

KEATS, Ezra Jack
(1916 -   )

MILWAUKEE JOURNAL
(Milwaukee, Wisc.)

Mar. 28, 1974

—*Journal Photo*

When asked why his books did not have more little girls, Keats replied, "I write what I know about. I was born a boy. And it was easier for me, being a man, to write about a boy's experiences."

He was asked to depict an independent girl in future books. "I'll try to do that," he said. "But you have to know that when I was a child, girls did not do all the things boys did.

"What's needed in children's books now is the same thing that's been needed all along — honesty," he said.

How can a person who has no children of his own write about children today?

"Well, I'm an ex-kid," he answered. "We all have within us the whole record of our childhood. What I do is address the child within myself. And try to be as square and honest as possible, then hope for the best."

When asked whether he would like to have children of his own, Keats smiled and answered, "Oh, sure." He paused, then added, "But, you know, I feel I have."

George E. Kelly, 87, Noted Playwright, Dies

KELLY, George E.
(1887 - 1974)
PHILADELPHIA BULLETIN (Philadelphia, Penn.) June 19, 1974
[See also CA-49/52]

By HAL MOORE
Of The Bulletin Staff

George E. Kelly, Pulitzer Prize-winning playwright and uncle of Princess Grace of Monaco, died yesterday at Bryn Mawr Hospital. He was 87 and lived in Sun City, Calif., a desert retirement village.

Mr. Kelly was the last surviving member of a generation of 10 brothers and sisters. One brother, John B., built a fortune around the brick business. He was also a sculling champion, and his statue stands on the banks of the Schuylkill near Boat House Row in Fairmount Park.

First Hit Play

Another brother, Walter E. Kelly, became famous in vaudeville and on phonograph records in the early 1920s as "The Virginia Judge."

But it was George Kelly, the playwright, who delighted theater audiences for 50 years with his scathing satire and acid wit. His first play, "The Show-Off," produced in 1924, was an overnight sensation.

It catapulted the young playwright into international fame. Hit followed hit and Hollywood beckoned when the arrival of sound films sent writing offers his way.

Prize-Winning Play

Mr. Kelly won the Pulitzer Prize in 1925 for his play, "Craig's Wife." Its plot revolves around a grasping and unfriendly wife so consumed with fear about her marital happiness that she risks everything for it, and eventually loses the love of her husband and the respect of household servants. She is left alone as the curtain falls.

Its predecessor, "The Show-Off," was set in Philadelphia and concerns a working-class family suddenly beset by a fast-talking, big-scheme boaster named Aubrey Piper, who works for the Pennsylvania Railroad.

Mr. Kelly's other plays included "The Torchbearers"; "Daisy Mayme"; "Behold the Bridegroom"; "Magie the Magnificent"; "Philip Goes Forth"; "Reflected Glory"; "The Deep Mrs. Sykes," and "The Fatal Weakness."

Returned for Visits

Mr. Kelly had made his debut as an actor in 1912 and later written a number of one-act plays before completing his first full-length play.

Mr. Kelly's love for his native Philadelphia brought him back time and again to visit his brothers, sisters and his favorite niece, Grace. When she gave up her career as a motion picture star to marry Prince Rainier of Monaco, he visited her and the royal family on a number of occasions.

Mr. Kelly referred to the theater several years ago as having lost the sparkle and class which had typified it during the period of the 1920s to the 1940s, both here and abroad.

He said he abhorred the trend toward nudity and the use of four-letter words as marking a decline in professionalism among actors and producers alike. "It represents lack of taste and an accent on sensationalism," he grumbled.

Mr. Kelly, a bachelor, is survived by many nieces and nephews.

George Kelly, Playwright Was 87

By FRANK McDEVITT
Inquirer Staff Writer

George E. Kelly, Pulitzer Prize-winning playwright, last surviving member of 10 brothers and sisters of the Philadelphia Kelly family and uncle of Princess Grace of Monaco, died Tuesday in Bryn Mawr Hospital. He was 87 and since 1963 had lived in Sun City, a retirement village near Riverside, Calif.

Mr. Kelly suffered a stroke two weeks ago after coming here to stay with another niece, Mrs. Marion Smith, at her home in the Radwyn Apartments, Bryn Mawr. Mrs. Smith said Wednesday that her uncle came East to look for a new home.

KELLY, George E.
PHILADELPHIA INQUIRER (Philadelphia, Penn.)
June 20, 1974

Mr. Kelly began his theatrical career in 1912 as a vaudeville actor. He then turned to writing plays, some of which he appeared in. His acid comedies and scathing satires delighted the public for more than half-a-century.

He was best known, however, for three of his earliest works, "The Torcrbearers" (1922), "The Showoff" (1924) and "Craig's Wife" (1925) which won the Pulitzer Prize.

His other plays produced on Broadway included "Reflected Glory" (1936), "The Deep Mrs. Sykes" (1945) and "The Fatal Weakness" (1946).

Mr. Kelly received awards from Brandeis University, the Philadelphia Creative Arts Theatre and the Women's Theater Club of New York. He also received an honorary Doctor of Fine Arts degree from La Salle College in 1962.

Mr. Kelly was the son of John H. Kelly and the former Mary Costello. Two of his brothers were John B., the noted oarsman, businessman and father of Princess Grace, and Walter, who was also an actor and became famous as "The Virginia Judge."

Mr. Kelly never married. In addition to Mrs. Smith and Princess Grace he is survived by 17 other nieces and nephews.

A Mass of Christian Burial will be offered at 10 A. M. Friday at St. Bridget's Church, East Falls. Burial will be in Westminster Cemetery, Bala Cynwyd. There will be no viewing.

Mrs. Smith said on Wednesday that Princess Grace might not be at the funeral because of commitments in connection with the observance of Monaco's silver jubilee. The princess is Mr. Kelly's godchild as well as niece, Mrs. Smith added, and was visited by Mr. Kelly "about every other year."

"In fact," Mrs. Smith said," Uncle George planned to visit her this year after he became settled here. He made his first airplane flight, from London to Nice, when he last visited her two years ago."

TALE OF A TYPEWRITER COWBOY

As part of his weekday job, Kelton gets a close-up look at a herd of sheep brought to market at San Angelo's livestock yards.

By CARLTON STOWERS

KELTON, Elmer
(1926-)

DALLAS NEWS
(Dallas, Tex.)

May 12, 1974

[See also CA-21/22]

Rural West Texas, in all honesty, isn't likely to become noted for a great store of literary appreciation. One might even assume with some degree of safety, in fact, that more books have been written *about* this area than have been read by the people who call it home.

Perhaps it is simply that priorities, rather than a lack of zeal, have prevented large numbers of rural folks from keeping abreast of *The New York Times* bestsellers list. After all, there are fences to mend, cows to milk, yarns to swap, six-packs to drink, coyotes to hunt and a myriad of other farm and ranch responsibilities to deal with. Reading time is scarce in a day which begins with the rooster's crow and ends with the 10 p.m. weather report. You're lucky if you can occasionally get to a little Scripture and thumb through a new seed catalog.

Yet from this setting has emerged one of Texas' most prolific and honored novelists. For over 20 years, Elmer Kelton — born on the Five Wells Ranch in Andrews County where his father worked — has been writing a brand of western fiction which has gained him an international reputation.

Nowadays, entertaining a visitor in the recently remodeled den of his comfortable San Angelo home, the 48-year-old novelist hardly resembles a third generation descendent of rugged cowboys, men like the mythical outdoor characters he creates on paper. His hands are those of a city man, years away from hands hardened by ranch chores. Kelton's once lean body has lost the battle to his wife's cooking and the long hours he has spent seated, with only a typewriter, blank paper and private thoughts to provide exercise. His gold-rimmed glasses seem more suited to an educator than to a man with a close kinship to the out-of-doors. Only an abrupt line along his forehead, separating suntan from part of his scalp generally covered outdoors by a straw Stetson, links him to the rangeland which begins a short drive from his home.

Kelton makes no attempt to mask his pride as he ushers you around the spacious den with its rows of bookshelves, massive writing desk and stereo set from which country and western music pours constantly.

"Charlie Flagg helped build this room," he says with a grin. "That crusty old man — hardheaded, old-fashioned and proud — made it possible."

The benefactor he refers to is not flesh and blood. Rather, he is the main character in Kelton's most recent and perhaps most ambitious novel, "The Time It Never Rained," a fictional recounting of the devastating seven year drought that plagued Texas in the '50s. Kelton's treatment of Charlie as a real person is typical of the feeling the author has for characters he creates in his novels.

Since the 1956 publication of his first full-length book, "Hot Iron," the writer has averaged a published novel a year. His output totals 17 original paperbacks published by Ballantine Books (including one due out this year) and two recent hardbacks he wrote for Doubleday publishers. This is an impressive record for a man who readily admits that early in his fiction-writing career the mere thought of trying to write a book-length novel brought on waves of self-doubt.

Today, however, his trophy case includes two Spur Awards (1957 and 1972) from the Western Writers of America for the "Outstanding Western Novel of the Year"; a citation for the "Best Southwest Novel of the Year" (for "The Day the Cowboys Quit," 1972) from the Border Regional Library Association (which includes the El Paso area and adjacent parts of Mexico and New Mexico), and an Award of Merit from the Texas Civil War Centennial Commission in recognition of his 1962 novel, "Bitter Trail," which dealt with Union activities along the Mexican border. He has been feted in his hometown of Crane, Texas, with an Elmer Kelton Day, is a past president of the Western Writers of America and has just been nominated by that organization for the Golden Saddleman Award for his contribution to the field of western writing.

Kelton has come a long way from the time in April, 1948, when *Ranch Romances*, one of the many pulp adventure magazines of an earlier day in fiction history, paid him a penny per word for his first published short story, "There's Always Another Chance" He insists the plot of that maiden effort escapes him today, but he does recall with satisfaction that among the authors whose bylines appeared in that same issue was the late J. Frank Dobie, the lionized man of Texas letters.

Though Kelton is a product of Texas ranchlands where men fought constant battles against drought, feed crop failures, second liens and herd-killing diseases which often ➡

(Continued from preceding page)
struck with deadly swiftness, he points out that he was born too late to see firsthand the real Old West, the pre-1900 era he most often writes about.

"I was fortunate, however, to grow up around cowboys who talked constantly about the old days, the range wars and cattle drives and the struggles of early cowmen who settled West Texas," he says. "Ranch cowboys are great storytellers. They have their own tales to tell, and they also have those handed down by their fathers and grandfathers. I expect in the retelling they are embellished a little, but a germ of truth is still there."

Indeed, as a boy Kelton had to venture no farther than the family supper table to hear many stories of the Old West. For over 30 years his father had worked as a cowboy and later foreman for the McElroy Ranch Company. Only when Elmer reached school age did the Kelton family move from the ranch into the nearby oilpatch town of Crane.

"Mother had been a schoolteacher for years," Kelton notes. "She began teaching me at a very early age. By the time I was five I could read and write some, so when we moved to town they started me out in the third grade."

To the occasional dismay of father Buck Kelton, his son excelled in the classroom and approached miserable failure as a cowhand. "Working with the cowboys, I had two left hands," admits Elmer Kelton. "I can honestly say there was never any phase of the ranching business I came close to mastering."

Though he was a blood member of a family traditionally gifted at working stock, mending fences and shearing sheep, Elmer Kelton seemed beckoned at an early age by other muses. His forte was writing English themes (for which he regularly earned high marks) and short stories (which he carefully hid from the eyes of others). He found his heroes in the books of Will James and Zane Grey and on the silver screen of the Palace Theater in Crane, where the likes of Gary Cooper and Gene Autry fought their battles on horseback on Saturday afternoons and made the West a safer place for us all.

Clearly, Buck Kelton came to realize, his son would never make the grade as a working cowboy. "We were sitting on the porch one evening, and Dad asked me what I wanted to do when I grew up," the younger Kelton recalls. "I was old enough by then to know that he was concerned about my lack of ability as a cowboy, so I felt the time had come to make my position known. I told him I thought I wanted to be a writer.

"I remember he took off his hat and gave me one of those long, disgusted looks of his and then he said, 'That's the trouble with you young kids nowadays. You want to make a living without working for it.' "

With that dubious blessing Kelton, at age 16, took a bus to Austin to study writing at The University of Texas. "My main reason for choosing Texas was so that I could take Mr. Dobie's course in Southwest literature," he explains. "Unfortunately, before managed enough prerequisite subjects to take the course, he had left the university. However, I did take the course later from Dr. Mody Boatright and learned techniques I'm still using today."

World War II interrupted his formal education. While Kelton served in the infantry in Germany he took several correspondence courses from The University of Texas, by then firmly convinced that fame and fortune as a fiction writer awaited only the completion of his college training.

Later stationed in Austria, Kelton met a pretty native named Anna who knew neither English nor anything about life in the parched, breezy flatlands of West Texas. Nonetheless, she and Kelton were married. Today she speaks better English than her husband (Kelton's evaluation) and is an avid fan of her husband's work. They have three children, Gary, 32, who lives in Plainview; Stephen Lee, 22, and 19-year-old Katheryn Ann, both of whom live in San Angelo.

When Kelton and his bride had returned from postwar Europe, they settled in Austin where the young writer completed work on his degree. He also began writing furiously, submitting his western short stories to pulp magazines. The rejection slips mounted; sales never got off the ground. "I know I quit 20 or 30 times," he remembers, "swearing never to write another short story as long as I lived."

Those vows rarely lasted more than a couple of days. "It's like smoking," Kelton says. "You quit, but wind up going back. It was something I couldn't seem to live without."

New hope surfaced when Fanny Ellsworth, editor of *Ranch Romances*, paid Kelton the grand sum of $50 for that 1948 story which turned the young man into a published author. Realistically, though, he knew that he and Anna must have a more dependable income. In time he learned that the San Angelo newspaper was looking for a man with a rural background to write farm and ranch news, so he applied for and landed the job. For the time being, fiction writing would

(Continued from preceding page)
have to get secondary consideration.

Nonetheless, by the early '50s Kelton was enjoying a modest success by writing short stories for *Ranch Romances* and other pulp magazines like *Leading Westerns, Famous Westerns* and *Texas Rangers*. His good fortune was short-lived, though, because in the late 1950s, the pulp short-story magazine market began to issue its death rattle in the wake of competition from television and other leisure pastimes. Kelton's New York agent urged his client to try book-length stories.

"I was firmly convinced there was no way I could do it," Kelton recalls. "I told him I couldn't imagine sustaining a story for 60,000 or 70,000 words. But he kept after me, so I took a novelette I had been working on and expanded it into what became my first book. We called it 'Hot Iron.' "

In precious little time, Kelton had managed to capture the imagination of paperback book readers and of his peers as well. His second novel, "Buffalo Wagons," sold 100,000 copies and earned his first Spur Award. The second award in 1972 was for "The Day the Cowboys Quit." Now, each of his books sells 80,000 to 100,000 copies and some are translated into Italian, Spanish, German and Swedish. Screen adaptations of his stories have appeared on the "Colt .45" and "Maverick" television series.

But despite the rewards, Kelton insists that fiction writing is only part of his career, a satisfying sideline. For unlike many who have gained a foothold in the elusive writing business, Kelton works on his novels only on evenings, weekends and holidays. The rest of his workday, since he graduated from The University of Texas, has been spent as a five-day-a-week newspaperman. For 15 years he held the post of farm and ranch editor of the *San Angelo Standard-Times*, then he left to edit the *Sheep and Goat Raisers Magazine* for a time before becoming associate editor of *West Texas Livestock Weekly*, a newspaper position he has held for five years.

"There was a time when I considered leaving the newspaper business to devote all my efforts to fiction," Kelton says. "But I like the newspaper business. It's a way of life that affords me great personal satisfaction as well as a decent income. When you stop to think about it, I probably reach more people in one issue of a newspaper than with any single book I've ever written. And if I can help a farmer or rancher by advising him of a new trend that might save him some money or make him a little more, or if I can give a youngster some publicity for having raised a prize-winning calf, then I have to feel that I'm doing something worthwhile."

Also, newspapering allows him to keep up with a world he deals with in his fiction writing. The men he interviews for his newspaper column are ones who have stubbornly maintained a strong Western heritage, men who still talk and think as their fathers and grandfathers did.

"A lot of farmers and ranchers around this part of the country know that I write fiction, and they have read some of the things I've done," Kelton says. "Sometimes they compliment me on the dialogue in my books, and to me that is a high compliment, indeed. If it sounds honest to them I can feel reasonably confident that I've done what I set out to do."

While paperback western novels have long been a popular and lucrative segment of the publishing business, both writers and publishers have had to learn to live with the same sort of stigma that literary critics have dealt to "mystery" writers. There are people, particularly in the urbanized East, who seem to pass on all Old West novels as being nothing more than hip-pocket shoot-'em-ups, assuming they are little more than reworded versions of the same stories their fathers and fathers' fathers read years ago. You know the formula: Good Guy gunslinger rides into Dry Gulch, rids it of Bad Guys and rides off into the sunset, more often than not winning the hand of the wealthy rancher's daughter along the way.

KELTON, Elmer

DALLAS NEWS
(Dallas, Tex.)

May 12, 1974

It is an unfair judgment; yet it is one that Kelton and many of his fellow craftsmen have had to accept.

"There is reason to think that attitude is changing somewhat," Kelton says. "In recent years, a few Eastern book reviewers have begun to take a careful look at the western novel, considering the possibility that it just might qualify as literature. Some, fortunately, have tried to search out the merits of this kind of writing, rather than just looking at the cover and assuming that it's another guns-a'blazing book written for someone sitting in a bus station to pass a few idle hours."

Kelton offers no apologies for labeling himself a "regional western writer." For years he has been producing work that goes well beyond the stereotyped western paperback image. His characters do not wear pearl-handled .45s ("Even as a boy I was never really fascinated with guns," he says.) nor do they perform feats that would cause movie heroes Randolph Scott or Johnny Mack Brown to blush. While his novels portray the romance of the Old West, his settings are as authentic as research allows. Kelton has chosen to ignore the myths in favor of a fictionalized treatment of history.

"I read a lot of westerns when I was growing up," he says. "I could see that there were good ones and bad ones. Those which I considered good always had an air of authenticity about them. I suppose many western novels totally lacking in historic truth have sold well, but I have to believe they are the exception rather than the rule."

Kelton studied volume after volume of Texas history before undertaking "Massacre at Goliad," a 1963 novel that is his personal favorite. "I can honestly say that the time I spent researching the book was more than was ever financially justified," he notes. "Still, I was reasonably pleased with the book. And that, I believe, is a major consideration for a writer if he is to survive in the business. We all write to please ourselves first, I think; then we hope our publisher likes it and the public will buy it."

In each of his books, Kelton tries to provide readers with viewpoints of the major characters and at the same time to teach a little history. He favors this approach over the standard one of hero vs. villain, which characterizes so many western novels.

"History books give us carefully documented details of most of the major happenings during the civilizing of this part of the world," Kelton says. "One need only go to a library to read about the wars and historic battles, and the backbreaking tasks that were performed in the settling of this country.

"What you won't find very often, though, is the viewpoints of the people involved — what they were thinking; what their motives were and what their feelings were. With fiction, I have the freedom to assume what they thought — to think for them, so to speak. I'm not saying that what I write should be taken as gospel, but it does provide the reader with a kind of insight that straight history allows no room for. I like to think this style gives my work more depth."

Between bites of enchiladas and refried beans at one of San Angelo's well regarded Mexican restaurants, Kelton talked about his most recent book, "The Time It Never Rained." It is a contemporary western novel dealing with a changing way of ranch life — people forced off their land by drought and economic conditions.

"I first wrote it 10 years ago, or at least a version of it," Kelton says. "It was peddled all over the United States and Canada and never impressed a single publisher. I could never quite put it out of my mind, though. It seemed worthwhile, and I kept going back to it every now and then. Finally, a couple of years ago I rewrote it. It's different now — better, I hope — but the same basic story is there. Ol' Charlie Flagg refusing to accept government help when everybody else was getting it, clinging to the man-earns-his-dollar heritage and confused by those who declare he's dead wrong. He was a good man, a strong man."

Kelton admits there is much of his father in the characterization. "In fact, Dad thinks the whole book is about him, and he liked it."

Buck Kelton, now retired, the man who sold his son's saddle 20 years ago when he became convinced that Elmer would never make it as a cowboy, has reason to be proud.

His 'Sherlock' A Rabbi

BY JENNIE PHIPPS
Sun-Sentinel Writer

Most people admire the genius of Sherlock Holmes from afar. They take a Dr. Watson stance and murmur things like "Why didn't I think of that."

But Harry Kemelman said, "Elementary, my dear," and plunged right into writing detective fiction with a flair. The successful author of a rabbinical detective series which begins with "Friday, the Rabbi Slept Late," will be in Fort Lauderdale tomorrow to promote his latest book, "Tuesday, the Rabbi Saw Red."

The idea for his first story came one day when he was teaching English literature at a college near Boston. He put a sentence on the chalk board, "A nine-mile walk is no joke, especially in the rain." He asked the class to put their imaginations to work and infer as many things as they could from that sentence.

It was one of those dull days when nobody had much to offer and the students just sat there and looked at him. So Kemelman put a few examples on the board himself. "I found I was doing quite well at it. I though this would make a nice story," Kemelman said by telephone from his home in Marblehead, Mass.

When complete, he mailed it off to Ellery Queen Mystery Magazine and it was purchased. In fact, the editor liked it so well, he offered to buy as many more as Kemelman could write in the same vein and pay a little more for each one.

That offer was too good to pass up and the author wrote until he was sick of the format. He compiled the best into a book, "The Nine Mile Walk."

Next he tried a novel about a Jewish community in suburbia. The publisher turned up his nose and suggested facetiously that the only way that book would sell was if it was combined with a little of the detective business.

Kemelman did just that. He went home and wrote all about Rabbi David Small who runs his synagogue with a firm old-fashioned hand and spends his spare hours solving with Talmudic logic the murders that happen in his small community.

The first book, "Friday the Rabbi Slept Late," appeared in 1964 and it was an immediate best seller. It also won him the Mystery Writers of America Edgar Award as the best first mystery novel of the year.

KEMELMAN, Harry
(1908 -)
FORT LAUDERDALE
SUN–SENTINEL
(Ft. Lauderdale, Fla.)
Jan. 20, 1975 [See also CA-11/12]

Part of the reason for its immediate success might have been its clever title. The funny thing, Kemelman said, was people couldn't quite get it right, but they couldn't forget it either. They called bookstores asking for things like "Freddy the Rabbit," and "Run Rabbi, Run."

Two years later when Kemelman produced a second novel, the publisher capitalized on the success of the first one by calling it "Saturday the Rabbi Went Hungry." After that it was an accepted thing. "People began writing in suggesting other topics for Sunday," the author said.

With only Wednesday and Thursday left to write, what is Harry Kemelman going to do? "I don't know," he says, "but it will be logical."

The writer started religious study when he was about 11, but he doesn't even pretend to be a Talmudist. "I never have been or intended to be a rabbi — I'm not over-observant. But I have done a great deal of thinking about it. That is the kind of research that is not common. Most people content themselves with reading other people's thoughts."

Kemelman hasn't taught English literature since his first successful book. It takes him nearly two years of full-time work to pull a plot together, he says. "I start out with a little more than nothing — a very, very hazy idea of what I want to say. I write and revise and then rewrite, one form after another until finally it gets done."

The characters, he claims, are all constructed and not copied from similar people he has known. Names and personalities dredged from imagination are much more workable and less risky. "A person like Rabbi Small wouldn't be tolerated in any synagogue. He's the sort of person every rabbi would like to be, but if he behaved like that, he would lose his job."

Contrived for a purpose or not, most readers are quite convinced. In fact, police departments have been gullible enough to ask Kemelman for a little Small-like logic to help them out of a tight spot. The author just chuckles a little and suggests that they use their own experts.

His own favorite mystery writers are Sir Arthur Conan Doyle, Raymond Chandler and Rex Stout. Unlike many authors, Kemelman does no fact-finding research. "I can always sense a researched fiction and it bothers me. If it isn't something that I know, I won't dare use it."

At 66, Kemelman has a whole new career in front of him, and he is enjoying both the freedom and the responsibilities it brings him. He took up ceramics to get his mind off mystery plots and it was a success for a while, but then he lost interest. "You can make an awful lot of pots in a short time," he said with a chuckle.

He also plays the violin and flute. Every year, he and his wife travel to Israel to visit their son, who is a writer for the Jerusalem Post.

While he was still teaching English, Kemelman wrote a book about the system of liberal arts education in this country. His next project is to get that book re-issued.

The problem, he says, is that we confuse liberal arts and professional study. There is a distinction between what one studies for oneself and what one studies for service to the community. Kemelman offers a Hebrew proverb: "You do not use the Torah as a spade to dig with."

"In America we have confused the two. We have made liberal arts necessary for professional study. Liberal arts schools are crowded by people who don't want to be there and don't belong there."

Staff Photo by Richard Nugent

A Kentucky fellow's city-country conflict

By LANA ELLIS
Courier-Journal & Times Staff Writer

"I WAS BORN in a small town called Casper's Well, a hundred and ten people, fifteen miles or so from Covington, Kentucky. I tried to do in one generation what should have been done in several. I should have gone as far as Louisville maybe. Or Atlanta. Stretching myself but staying in contact with what I was, with where I came from.

"I ran too fast. That's all. My head couldn't hold it, my eyes couldn't handle what I saw, there were critical pieces missing from the mechanism.

"I mean I'm a hick. I need time and space and fresh air. People told me I was something I wasn't and I believed them. Now I'm on the wheel like a sad squirrel and I can't get off." — from "Somebody Else's Wife" by Adam Kennedy. (Simon & Schuster. 349 pp. $7.95.)

IN THIS, his recent novel, Adam Kennedy writes about Chet Rector, "a nice young fellow from Kentucky" who cracks under the strain of the sophisticated New York life and the treacherous friends he encounters.

"It's the conflict between country and city life, he explained during an interview in New York recently. "Rector went into worlds he wasn't ready for. He had some kind of innocence that I believe is associated with country life."

"Almost everything I write is about the Midwest because you have to write about what you know most profoundly. It's the idea of stitching together someone's life."

KENNEDY is from Lafayette, Ind. According to his biography, "he was born in the middle of winter in a farmhouse without central heat or electricity; there was no doctor or midwife present. Two and a half months premature, he weighed less than three pounds at birth. His parents placed him in a peach-box incubator heated by filled fruit jars."

Kennedy not only survived this Lincolnesque beginning, but, after a move to the big city, has also managed to make his mark as an author, actor, painter and screenwriter.

"They paid me the highest compliment in my hometown recently," he says. "'He hasn't changed a bit,' they said. I'm suspicious of artists who reject their backgrounds."

AT 6 feet 3, 190 pounds, Kennedy has an actor's good looks, dresses sedately in a dark blue blazer, blue shirt and gray trousers. Mention a resemblance to actor George Kennedy and he flinches saying, "He's fatter and older than I am."

Kennedy began writing in college, Indiana's DePauw University where he received the President's and Pulliam scholarships. Last May, the school awarded him the honorary degree of doctor of literature.

His first book, "The Killing Season," appeared in 1967. It took a fairly unstereotyped look at the espionage business. "I was tired of the notion that all men who are involved with espionage were tall, lean fellows who slept with three woman every night and drank six martinis," he says.

"I looked at a man involved with an intelligence group, a man in a situation of potential jeopardy, and looked at how this would affect his wife and children."

Producer Joseph E. Levine bought the screen rights, but Kennedy has no knowledge of the story's movie future.

HIS SECOND BOOK was "Barlow's Kingdom," described by him as "doing 'Hamlet' in some other setting. I set it in Montana during the Civil War and retold that story. Some critics got nervous about that." Paramount bought screen rights to "Barlow."

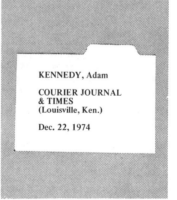

KENNEDY, Adam
COURIER JOURNAL & TIMES (Louisville, Ken.)
Dec. 22, 1974

A good critical and financial success was "Maggie D.", his third book. The book was an interview-novel, a three-day question and answer session involving a woman volunteer and a psychologist-researcher. The woman, known only as Maggie D., told the details of an interesting, though chaotic life. She emerged as one who lived life without regrets, garnering insight, even amusement, from her past. She was liberated without being militant about it.

One question that many critics raised was the accuracy of a man's writing about a woman's innermost thoughts. "I've never thought that women are any more than people," says Kennedy. "This mystique that Freud built up had one question, 'What do women want?'

"Well, I don't think it's that mysterious. Women don't have to be enigmas to be interesting. To me, the whole process of living is self-exploration. It's the only part of humanity we have some control over.

"In every book I write, I find some middle ground between what I want to say about life and myself. Then, I try to make it palatable. I never think about what will sell. My natural instinct is to communicate."

"Somebody Else's Wife" is the examination of three people and their relationships — Rector, the country boy led astray, his first wife, and Helen, the sophisticated woman who proves his undoing.

"Helen had trouble telling the truth," says Kennedy. "In fact, this is a book where nobody tells anybody the truth. But that happens so much of the time. Why? Because when you tell the truth, people think less of you. Your true friends are those who can tell the absolute truth."

Again, the theme of innocence surfaces. "A lot of people would rather be called a bastard than an 'innocent.' But there are those few who would rather have the ability to be hurt than be so covered with scar tissue and not be able to feel. That way you learn. And if you don't learn anything about your relationship with people, you might as well be drunk or dead."

ONLY with the lucrative sale of his books was Kennedy able to quit his job as an actor and devote more time to writing. Prior to that, he had appeared in 12 movies, over 300 television shows and several Broadway shows.

Acting was always steady work. "I took it very seriously because it was very hard work."

For two years, he appeared on the television soap opera, "The Doctors." "I played the boyfriend of a lady doctor. I was Brock Hayden, the richest man in the world. I bought everything for everyone and chased all the girls.

"The viewers liked me so I stayed on the show, but it was hard to figure out what to do with me in that hospital. So I had accidents. Like I got shot in Cuba and my plane crashed in Wyoming. Finally, I was shot to death by a gangster. The producers were mad because I had sold my book and was quitting the show. So they gave me a bloody, grisly death. They had me dying in that hospital for two weeks while my contract expired. Ladies Home Journal did an article about the day Brock Hayden died."

His career as a painter, one pursued now in spare moments, has seen him through one-man shows in Paris, Chicago, Los Angeles and Indianapolis. His proficiency as an abstract artist has been noted in several books by art historians.

IN JANUARY, Kennedy plans to move to California and continue his lucrative job writing screen plays. His first, "The Dove," was produced by Gregory Peck. The movie is the "modern odyssey of a young man who sails 30,000 miles around the world in a 23 foot sloop."

His second screenplay is "Maberly's Kill," a Richard Zanuck-David Brown production that will star Robert Redford.

And, somewhere between the typewriter and the printing presses, is another book, "The Domino Principle." "It's a scary book," says Kennedy. "It's about the power of governments over individuals. It deals dramatically with the question that people have today and that is, 'Why does the public feel or wish certain things and yet see no reflection of them in government decisions?'

"It's a Kafkaesque look at a man who has governmental power and some of the more miserable aspects of his use of the power. We used to say, 'Nobody would do that,' but now we have reached the point where we realize that some men would do almost anything."

The Brief Detroit Sojourn Of Jack Kerouac

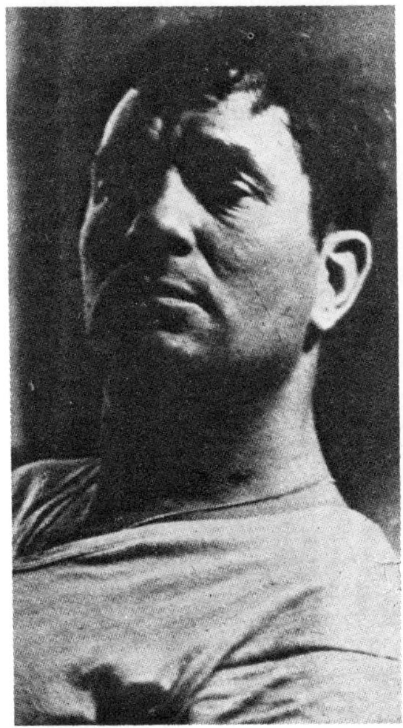

Kerouac in 1966 at Hyannis, Massachusetts, the year before his death.

KEROUAC, Jean-Louis Lebrid de (Jack Kerouac) (1922 - 1969)

DETROIT FREE PRESS (Detroit, Mich.)

Dec. 29, 1974

[See also CA-5/6; CA-25/28]

By HENRY A. KINGSWELL and THOMAS MARTIN
For Detroit Magazine

IN THE Autumn of 1944 Michigan wore a blazer of Indian Summer colors . . . Detroit's "Brown Bomber", Joe Louis, was selling war bonds . . . the Wolverines at Ann Arbor were ranked eighth in the nation, Ohio State number two . . . sugar, pork chops and green Lucky Strikes were being rationed . . . and the Grosse Pointe News society column carried a note that little Edward B. was having a dozen friends over to his mansion to share in his 13th birthday cake.

Another event, not recorded in the Grosse Pointe paper, was the arrival from New York City of local debutante Edith Francis "Frankie" Parker and her man, Jean-Louis Lebris de Kerouac.

On August 22, 1944, at 2:57 p.m., under heavy guard in New York's Municipal Building, the wealthy society girl from one of America's richest suburbs exchanged dimestore rings with the soon-to-be Father of the Beat Generation and Granddad to the Hippies, Jack Kerouac.

Police Detective John J. McKeon signed the marriage certificate. Kerouac was put back in chains and hauled over to the County Jail, until the new Mrs. Kerouac posted bond later that day. That evening, they hopped a train to Detroit. The man, who in later years was to write 18 novels and the beatnik bibles—*On The Road, The Dharma Bums* and *The Subterraneans,* coming to live in Michigan with his college sweetheart.

The newly wed Kerouacs disembarked at the old Michigan Central Depot, pitching battle with the menagerie of cats and dogs they kept on leash, ricochetting like pinballs in the railroad WW II choreography of redcaps, sailors, GI's, WACS and bobbysoxers.

Jack hailed a cab and loaded Frankie's hatboxes, leather baggage and artist's portfolio into the trunk of the sedan and chucked his own seaman's AWOL bag and typewriter into the back seat. Their menagerie of strays from Central Park rode up front with the taxi driver.

Together, the Kerouac caravan headed past Briggs Stadium where Newhauser, Trout, York and Dick Wakefield were chasing the St. Louis Browns for the pennant, turning up East Jefferson . . . Hudson Motor Car Company . . . Michigan Stove . . . United States Rubber . . . Belle Isle, (where Frankie's mother had been trapped in a trolley during the 1943 riots) . . . and across the Detroit City limits onto Lake Shore Drive.

For Frankie it was a homecoming; for "Johnnie" Kerouac it would be a bad time.

"Suddenly, when we crossed over into Grosse Pointe," Kerouac sketched in his notebook, "our '38 DeSoto turned into a chauffeured Packard limousine." Breathless and annoyed, the 22-year-old lad from Lowell, Mass., spied the magnificent homes with their manicured landscapes, the estates of first-generation lumber, banking, law, rail and shipbuilding barons. His black eyes intent behind his fugitive John Garfield cap, as his imaginary Cinderella coach cruised past the yacht marinas, the private clubs, the prep schools and the Gothic mansions owned by millionaire magnates of the chemical and automobile industries.

Jack suddenly rolled down the car window and leaned halfway out the door.

"You're nothing but a bunch of old funeral parlors," he screamed. "A bunch of damn, lousy funeral parlors, filled with dead people."

Kerouac would stick it out in Grosse Pointe only for two months; he was itching to get back on the road.

Back in the Coldwater Flats of bohemian New York, Jack could surround himself in a circle of friends the likes of Ginsberg (America's underground poet-laureate), William Burroughs (described by Norman Mailer as perhaps "The only American writer possessing genius"); Neal Cassady (whom Kerouac made a Saint of Beatitude); and other creative and inspiratianal characters called Corso, Holmes, Huncke, Carr and Crazy Alex.

In Grosse Pointe the social register read Newberry, Moran, Piche, Cadieux, Hecker, Guoin, Stephens, Muir and Pittman. Jack was not impressed.

Frankie Parker's family blood ran into steel yards, shipping cartels and textiles, with thousands of dollars to school and hospital foundations.

"Your mother owns a shoe company," Jack often reminded his spouse. "And my mother works in one."

The contrasts in family backgrounds, lifestyles and values hadn't seemed so important before they were married. But with his wild abandon for life, his unkempt crop of black hair and permanent 5 o'clock stubble of beard, dressed in clean but faded dungarees, old plaid shirts, lumberjack boots and black leather jacket — there were few places in Grosse Pointe where Kerouac could feel comfortable.

Frankie's family belonged to the Detroit Yacht Club. Their idea of fun was a good stiff breeze and a pleasant day's outing sailing up Lake St. Clair with luxurious craft carrying the Wetmores, Lothrups, Millers, Sydneys, Banias, Waremans and Ingersolls.

Jack was a card-carrying member of the Merchant Marine. His idea of seafaring frolic was to pull into the nerest exotic port, brawl, ball, belly-up with brew and crawl back up the ship's rat line in time for morning chow.

As a young man, Kerouac lived for his comrades, the jazz, cheap wine and highs that were so lucidly recorded in his literature. But to be married and living beside the Dodges, Macauleys, Algers, Woodbridges, Duffields, Hudsons, Chapins and Ford was something right out of an early 40's soap opera.

"THERE IS NO TRAGEDY IN GROSSE POINTE,"

Jack Kerouac wrote his own eviction notice even before he moved in. He left it for Frankie in a note the day he left Detroit.

THE Kerouacs moved into a modest yellow-brick flat at 1407 Somerset Ave. in Grosse Pointe Park. Jack shared the bathroom with Frankie, her mother and teenage sister.

"Jack used to sit on the can," Charlotte, Frankie's sister recalls, "reading Shakespeare and the Bible, while us three girls were trying to get into the bathroom. He would sit in there for hours on end, till we would nearly break down the door. I guess it was the only place he could find any peace and quiet."

Years later, Kerouac was to write an entire novel, *Mexico City Blues* sitting on a commode smoking marijuana in the apartment of William Burroughs. In Detroit, the Parker family distinctly remembers, Jack Kerouac smoked Camels.

It was through the Parker's that Jack got a job as a night watchman with Fruehauf Corporation on Charlevoix Ave. on Detroit's eastside. Working the midnight shift, Kerouac would make his rounds as quickly as his 5'9, 165 lb. Muscular body could check the perimeter. Back in the guard shack, Jack would pull out his knapsack of reading and writing materials ➡

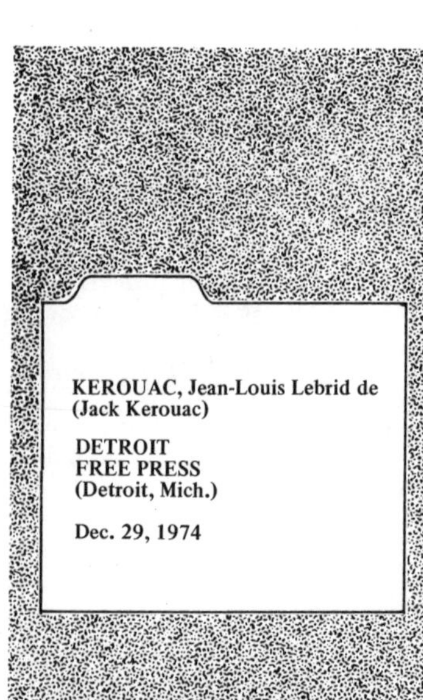

(Continued from preceding page)

and, under a naked lightbulb, practice his life's trade.

"I am an artist," Jack would answer should someone ask him his profession. "Oh, I see," Mrs. Parker is reported to have responded. "But the only writer who makes any money is Pearl Buck."

Jack thought of himself more like a Thomas Wolfe.

"He was a serious young man," says Frankie. "Always running back and forth from the library, loaded down with books. He fantasized a lot, really a night person as far as his working habits. Although he did like to go to the movies and check out the bars every so often."

The Rustic Cabins Saloon, located at Kercheval and Lakepointe, just around the corner from the Kerouacs' flat on Somerset, became Jack's favorite watering hole.

Formerly a speakeasy during the Prohibition Era, the Rustic Cabins during the 40's was a curious potpourri of Pointe freewheelers, Detroit be-boppers and just plain-speaking neighborhood barfolk. Kerouac, no doubt, found the saloon to be a good mix between the small-town corner ale houses of his native Lowell, Mass., and the hip, dark, subterranean dens of his adopted mecca, the Village, in New York.

The Kerouacs came to the Cabins often, sipping brew with Frankie's old high school chums from Grosse Pointe High. Jack liked Ty Tyson's (the Voice of the Tigers) daughter, Jennie, the best. There was also Jean Milner, (from the Milner Hotel family chain); Lee Donley, (Clinton Gables); Millie Fisher and Jane Bebee, among other bright-eyed girls.

Present Rustic Cabins owner, Rudy VerCruysse, was just a kid hanging around the saloon running errands and picking up tips, but remembers Frankie and her friends at the time as "being about as wild and nice a bunch of kids you could find in Grosse Pointe. But Frankie sure did change when she came back from New York. She was a regular fireball,"

Jack described Frankie as being always "alive and pretty . . . with an eageringgrin and laugh; an earerness entire that makes the eyes slit and at the same time makes her cheeks fuller."

It was during their student days at Columbia University when through a mutual artist friend, Henri Cru, Frankie first met Jack.

"He looked like a slob," Frankie remembers, "but he was fastidiously clean. In fact, he always carried a toothbrush."

"We all went over to a deli on 7th Avenue. I ate four hotdogs with sauerkraut piled on top, and Jack was fascinated by my appetite. He had never seen a girl wolf down food so fast, so hungrily. He couldn't keep his eyes off me."

Kerouac was attending Columbia on a football scholarship. He came to New York from Lowell, Massachusetts, a small milltown north of Boston. There he was an outstanding athlete and would-be writer, turning out small and perfunctory pieces of news for local papers and magazines.

He was restless and confused at Columbia. A leg injury ended his football career, and, in essence, his formal academic career. His ambition to become a writer in the Wolfe-Dreiser mold came to the fore and he became a man possessed.

But still, at 21 there was time to be carefree and adventurous. "I ran up to Columbia campus to look up Johnnie (Frankie)," wrote Kerouac in *Vanity of Dulouz.* "Caught up with her at Asbury Park where she was living the summer with her grandmother, she put earrings on my ears and when we went to the sands all afternoon in the crown a bunch of girls said, "What it is it, a gypsy." But this is a gypsy who doesn't eat up others as he goes along."

"I'll get a ship and come back around October and we'll live together in an apartment in New York City, right on the campus with your friend June."

"You're a rat but I love you."

So Kerouac moved into the apartment on 118th Street that Frankie shared with Joan Vollmer, also a Columbia student. Joan Vollmer was later to marry William Burroughs, another Columbian and heir to the business machine company.

Burroughs, whose novels include *Junkie, Queer,* and *The Naked Lunch,* first offered Kerouac hard drugs up in the 118th St. apartment.

"Bill later went the whole route," said Frankie, 'Morphine, heroin, opium. . .but Jack or none of the rest of us back in the 40's fooled around with that stuff.' We did share a marijuana cigaret with jazz musician Lester Young one time heading up to harlem in a cab. But, nobody was into dope back then."

BUT everything else about the lifestyle of the folks living up in room 421 at W. 118th Street was considered radical at Columbia, "Bohemian" to neighbors, and "Ohmygod," to next of kin.

"Nobody was living like we did back in the 40's," Frankie said. "But we weren't like the hippies. Sometimes there would be a dozen people sleeping overnight, but we all had jobs. We all worked, went to school, kept things clean and most of us were into the arts. It wasn't just sex and freeloading."

It was, in fact, Frankie Parker who introduced Jack Kerouac to some of the artists and writers that would influence and change his life so dramatically.

Frankie still maintains occasional correspondence with a few of their old friends and talks about them freely. "I have a lot of respect," she says of Burroughs, "in spite of the strange books he wrote. Burroughs and Jack, I just cannot picture them as they portray themselves in their books. Around me separately or when we were together, which was a lot back then," she continues, "they seemed much different. Maybe I didn't understand their writing."

If it was a case of mutual admiration in the case of Burroughs, her appraisal of Ginsberg was one of contempt. "He was just a hanger on. He was a lot younger than most of us, and I for one didn't want him hanging around my apartment.

"He wasn't serious, Frankie continued. "He was a big hound for attention. Jack wanted to write, Ginsberg wanted publicity." Frankie took out a letter. It was from Jack and dated 1-28-57. In the letter Jack reinforces Frankie's 'hound for attention' opinion of Ginsberg, but does not castigate him as vehemently. "Allen never loses track of me, even when I try to hide. He does me many favors publicizing my name. Well, we're old friends anyway, but I just can't keep up with this 'fame life' he wants so I won't stay long with them in Algiers."

ON August 14, 1943, two friends of Frankie and Jack were involved in an argument which ended in murder.

Lucien Carr, a 19-year-old Columbia student stabbed to death an older man named Dave Kamarer, a teacher and fringe member of the group. Carr fled to the Manhattan apartment where Frankie and Jack were living.

"Lucien came into the apartment and got Jack to Leave with him," Frankie recalls. "I didn't know what ➡

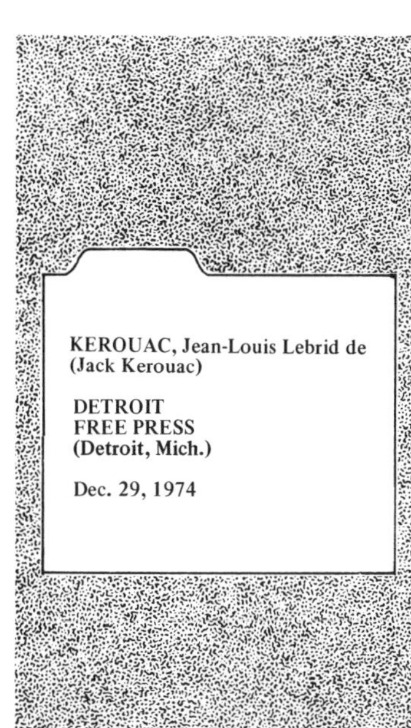
KEROUAC, Jean-Louis Lebrid de (Jack Kerouac)

DETROIT FREE PRESS (Detroit, Mich.)

Dec. 29, 1974

(Continued from preceding page)
was going on. The next day the police came and arrested Jack for being an accessory to a crime and hauled him off to jail."

According to reports in the New York Times, Carr and Kerouac had spent the day of the crime walking around the streets. Kerouac finally convinced Carr to call on William Burroughs for help. Burroughs told Carr to call a lawyer. The following day Jack Kerouac was arrested for helping Carr dispose of the Boy Scout knife used in the murder.

Bond was set at $5,000 but Jack didn't have that kind of money. Frankie did.

Frankie tried to get the money from her late grandfather's estate which was being held up in probate. "The only way I could get any cash was to prove that money was needed for a member of the immediate family," Frankie said.

"We hadn't given marriage a thought up till that moment," Frankie admits. "But, hell, nobody knew how long Jack would have to stay in jail or what would follow."

Frankie Parker and Jack Kerouac were married. Money was secured from the will of Walter Parker and bail was posted to free Jack. Subsequently, Kerouac was found innocent of all charges and Lucien Carr spent two years in prison.

Eight months later the marriage was over. Jack left Frankie with the annulment papers in Grosse Pointe and was on the road. There was sorrow but no hard feelings, Frankie remembers. "Jack called me his life's wife."

The Autumn of 1974, another warm Indian Summer ... Joe Louis watches from closed-circuit ringside as Ali butterflies Forman in Zaire ... U of M and Woody's Buckeyes are going down to the wire for the Roses ... anti-freeze and copper pennies are being hoarded ... and nothing much has changed in the society copy of the Grosse Pointe News.

Frankie Parker, wearing a stylish windbreaker and tailored slacks, her hair fashionably cut, silver framed sunglasses, and as her late ex-husband often said, "A lady endowed with the promise that she will look good all her life" is eating a plate of blintzes with sour cream at Samuels Bros. Delicatessen in Eastern Market.

"You know, I think Jack knew he was going to die. He was calling me almost daily, sending me letters and wiring telegrams asking me to come down to Florida. He was supposed to come up to Michigan to give a lecture at Oakland University, to talk about his books ... But he drank himself to death before he ever made it up here."

The lady from Grosse Pointe pulled out a stack of photos, love letters, poems ... Indeed "Johnnie" kept his "Frankie" well-posted on his adventures. Post cards from Tangier and Paris. Poems written on bar slips from New York and San Francisco. Snapshots of Jack in Greenland and Mexico City. As well as his haunting messages from Florida where "America's fresh breath of pure air" was slowly committing suicide.

From all the clippings, the documents and the recollections, Frankie Parker was putting the mosaic of Jack Kerouac's days in Michigan and life during the years that followed, together.

There was their marriage annulment, granted by the Archdiocese of Detroit, April 5, 1942. And, another, by the State of New York awarding Frankie $1.

"Jack never did pay me that one-dollar," Frankie laughed. "I guess for all practical reasons that we are still legally married."

There was also an old faded pawn ticket among the Kerouac artifacts; Frankie laughed ...

"Oh, yes, I sure remember that time. Jack and his buddy Cassady, that Neal Cassady, the same fellow who drove the bus in Tom Wolfe's *Electric Kool-Aid Acid Test*, well, they came through town. This was during the time that Jack was putting together *On The Road*. They had just crossed the country on another one of Cassady's marathon drives, and wound up in Detroit without any transportation and down to their last buck. Jack gave me a call from the Greyhound station. He and Cassady had spent the entire night stalking up and down Woodward Avenue and finally went to sleep in an all-night theater.

"The boys hitch-hiked out to Grosse Pointe. I couldn't find any money around the house so I picked up a new typewriter that had been a gift to me. So the four of us   Jennie Tyson happened to be over   jumped in my car and we headed down to Lou's Pawn Shop on East Jefferson. I hocked it for $25 and then Jack was almost too embarrassed to take the money. But the guys had to eat. So Jack gave me a little kiss on the cheek and then he and Neal Cassady started thumbing back down Jefferson, on the road to God knows where."

Frankie polished off her plate of thin pancake blintzes, talking in the same run-on fashion in which Jack Kerouac wrote books.

"You know, Jack was a meat and potatoes man until I introduced him to artichokes, and he called before he died and said he was smoking Pall Malls and drinking Ballantine's Scotch   eating nothing   I don't think he really cared anymore. Jack wouldn't like the hippie kids you see around this market, they just aren't coming from the same place that he came from, because Jack might have looked dirty on the outside, but inside he was clean. Now that's what only a woman would know about a man and don't kid yourself, Jack was a real-type man. Nothing like that Ginsberg character. The little creep was at Jack's funeral in Lowell standing by this big flower arrangement of long-stem roses ... And you know what was written across the wreath. It said *"Beat The Heat."*"

Neal Cassady "beat the heat,"' having burned out while chasing a railroad train in Mexico.

Joan Volmer, Frankie's old roommate at Columbia has also beat the heat after husband William Burroughs accidently put a bullet in her skull trying to shoot a glass of gin off her head in Mexico City.

And on October 21, 1969, Frankie Parker's "Johnnie" busted a gut; a "beat the heat" hemorrhage in St. Petersburg, Fla.

The man who wrote that "the only people for me are the mad ones, the ones who are mad to live, mad to talk, mad to be saved ... the ones who never yawn or say a commonplace thing, but burn, burn, burn like fabulous roman candles exploding across the stars ..." left his mark.

Of Detroit, Kerouac has found plenty to be saved, commenting that "if you sifted all Detroit in a wire basket, the beaten solid core of dregs couldn't be better gathered."

Frankie Parker readily admits to not understanding the total Jack Kerouac, although Jack wrote to her saying that she   more than anyone he had ever known   had come closest to knowing him best.

"Jack always said when he left Michigan," Frankie spoke as she climbed into her car to leave Eastern Market, "that he was proud that he had to go his own way. He felt good that he could be a gypsy, and that he didn't want to eat up others as he made his way ... I'm going to miss old Jack." ➡

(Also see preceding article)

Jack Kerouac's Denver Friends Formed Theme for Novel

JACK KEROUAC

KEROUAC,
Jean-Louis Lebrid de
(Jack Kerouac)

DENVER POST
(Denver, Colo.)

Dec. 29, 1974

By IVAN GOLDMAN
Denver Post Staff Writer
(First In A Series)

In 1947, Jack Kerouac, an alternately brooding and enthusiastic author of 25 with movie-star looks and great literary ambitions, hitchhiked to Denver and stayed the summer.

That season of experiences here 27 years ago became the basis of his world-famous novel, "On the Road," and Kerouac's links with Denver, both mystical and corporeal, remained with him until his death in 1969.

Some years ago a book critic observed: "Kerouac is accused of writing about people going nowhere . . . but they were always going to Denver, and that is a definite destination indeed."

Kerouac, amused by the reference, quoted it in a March 1, 1965 letter to Denver architect Edward D. White Jr.

White, who probably was the closest friend Kerouac ever had, was also a part of that mad 1947 summer of long nights, long laughs, reckless drinking, bar fights and subterranean doings.

Kerouac and his friends were, they thought, creating a new romantic blend of adventure and intellectual pursuit. Later, they came to be called the Beat Generation, the young, post-war cult that couldn't, or wouldn't, return to normalcy. Kerouac recorded their lives for all time, when "On the Road" finally was published in 1957.

"God knows," remembered Justin W. Brierly, "they all loved to talk."

Brierly, now assistant to the president at Colorado Women's College, was Neal Cassady's link to the Denver-Kerouac group.

Cassady, who was to become an antiestablishment cult hero to two generations after his depiction as Dean Moriarty in "On the Road," was a freewheeling Denver poolhall hustler and car thief. Brierly, then an English teacher at East High School, met Neal in 1943.

The fast-talking, quick-moving, intense young Cassady had grown up on old Larimer Street with his hard-drinking father. Brierly ushered Cassady over to East, where he enrolled him as a student.

Cassady didn't stay in high school long, but he maintained his ties to Brierly the rest of his life, and it was through Brierly that Kerouac and Cassady came to know each other.

Cassady was to die in 1968, when, in a drug stupor, he fell off a cliff while ambling around the Mexican mountain country.

Neal's was the sort of tragic circumstance that became all too common among the aging, nighttime wanderers who made up the original Kerouac group.

Many of them tiptoed along the edges of madness and destruction, and in their lives the bizarre often became the expected. During World War II, Kerouac was given a psychiatric discharge from the Navy.

"If armies were made up of Kerouacs," Brierly observed, "then there wouldn't be any armies. It's as simple as that."

Kerouac's death in 1969 was due to complications from advanced alcoholism.

Poet Allen Ginsberg, also an integral part of that 1947 summer, was once a patient in a New Jersey mental institution. Upon his release in 1949, the goodhearted Beverly Burford, another member of the original Denver group, was there to greet him.

Now married to Republican State Senator Fay DeBerard of Kremmling, Mrs. DeBerard was named Babe Rawlins in "On the Road." Her double life of subterranean nights and proper, white collar days, she said in a frank interview, had led her into alcoholism, which she conquered in 1959.

But Beverly never blamed her illness on others. She still remembers Jack, Neal, and all the friends of '47 with a warmth that is both benevolent and infectious.

"Those were crazy times," she said. "Jack was a sweet person. And he could be moody, but he had a good sense of humor. He was delightful.

"Neal Cassady was a strange kid all his own. You don't really run into them like that. Because he had a very carefree nature. He wheeled in the real world."

William Burroughs, renowned author of "Naked Lunch" and "Junkie," also moved in and out of the group. He spent much of his adult life as a morphine addict.

In one infamous incident in Mexico, Burroughs imitated William Tell. But instead of putting a bullet through the martini glass on his wife's head, he put it through his wife's head.

After an investigation, criminal charges were not pressed by Mexican authorities. Burroughs was an heir, whose powerful family controlled the cash register and adding machine manufacturing company that bears his name.

But most of the Denver native members of the group generally managed to taste the Beat subculture without allowing it to poison them. Like Beverly DeBerard, they tended to achieve success and quiet contentment.

Her brother, Robert F. Burford, the tough, brawling Ray Rawlins of "On the Road," moved to Paris in 1949, stayed there 13 years, wrote articles and short stories, edited an English language literary journal, but so far, regrettably, hasn't achieved the writing success that many thought would be his due.

He's back in Denver now, 50 years old, living and writing in a small Capitol Hill apartment. Kerouac's early death, he said was a tremendous shock to the pattern of his own life. It prompted him to stand back, look at himself, and move into more meaningful directions.

White, 49, is one of Colorado's most successful architects. He is a partner in the firm that designed the Denver Botanic Gardens.

Ed White was Jack's link to stability. Like Kerouac, he was brilliant and creative, but he managed always to harness his talents without falling into any craters of despair.

Ed was graduated from Columbia University, studied architecture there and at the Sorbonne in Paris. Jack was kicked out of Columbia. Ed served honorably in the Navy. Jack was kicked out of that, too.

Until the end of Kerouac's life, he encouraged Ed White and applauded his successes, never jealous, always concerned.

"I was instrumental in getting Ed White into Columbia," Brierly, now 68, likes to recall. "He was a very bright boy. The reason these people went on to Columbia on scholarships (Brierly's alma mater) was the fact that they were very bright.

"Cassady had an IQ of about 132 (near-genius) and they were all brighter than Cassady."

Said Bob Burford; "Ed had a real staying power for all those guys. All of them, they were living a very fast life. Yet he was very proper. He kept a sense of propriety always."

White, called Tim Gray in "On the Road," has a giant stack of letters from Kerouac that date from 1946 until his friend's death in 1969. In them, Jack poured out his plans, his directions, his innermost feelings. He saw White as a rare human being, someone he could talk to, someone who possessed a unique blend of sensitivity and intelligence.

Also in Denver in the summer of 1947 was Haldon Chase, another Denver native and Columbia student who later went on to become an anthropologist and seagoing adventurer. He lives now in the Big Sur country of California. He was called Chad King in "On the Road."

Frank Jeffries, whose father was a court reporter for The Denver Post, also was a member of that summer group. Jeffries, called Stan Shephard in "On the Road," made the mad trip to Mexico with Cassady and Kerouac near the conclusion of the book. That literary sequence, Bob Burford said, lent more fame to Jeffries than he cared to have.

"Jeffries didn't want to play the role provided for him in "On the Road," Burford said, "so he dropped out of the group. Quit it. Hal Chase did too."

Kerouac returned to Denver many times in his life, always trying to relive the summer of 1947. And in his letters to White, Kerouac, the Massachusets-bred Easterner, constantly suggested that in time he would make Colorado his permanent home. Once, in 1951, a trip to Denver almost repeated his 1947 experience.

In "On the Road," he described his joyous homecoming:

"Tim Gray, Stan, Babe, and I spent an entire week of afternoons in lovely Denver bars where the waitresses wear slacks and cut around with bashful, loving eyes, not hardened waitresses but waitresses that fall in love with the clientele and have explosive affairs and huff and sweat and suffer from one bar to another.

"And we spent the same week in nights at Five Points listening to jazz, drinking booze in crazy Negro saloons and gabbing till five o'clock in the morn in my basement. Noon usually found us reclined in Babe's back yard among the little Denver kids who played cowboys and Indians and dropped on us from cherry trees in bloom.

"I was having a wonderful time and the whole world opened up before me because I had no dreams."

Bob Burford's Summer of '47: A Different Story

(Also see preceding article)

By IVAN GOLDMAN
Denver Post Staff Writer
(Second in a Series)

Ray Rawlins was a tough Denver character described in Jack Kerouac's "On the Road" who knocked out an Argentine tourist in a one-punch, Central City bar fight.

There really was a Ray Rawlins (although that wasn't his real name), and the fight took place in 1947, but Kerouac wasn't certain of the loser's identity, though it seemed to be vaguely South American and aristocratic.

In almost all his books, Kerouac invented names for real characters. Rawlins was his name for Robert F. Burford, an integral member of the Kerouac group that converged on Denver that summer.

Burford, 50, lives in Denver still, in a small apartment on Capitol Hill. He kept his ties to Kerouac and the others down through the years, and spoke to Kerouac on the telephone shortly before the author died in October 1969.

Kerouac had a special liking for Burford. One of seven children, Burford was called the "wild son" by Kerouac, who appreciated his intelligence, manliness and strong penchant for straight talk.

CASSADY A HERO

But while Kerouac admired Burford, and liked to be with him, his feelings for Neal Cassady might best be described as worship.

"They (Kerouac and poet Allen Ginsberg) thought that Cassady represented the midnight cowboy, or something astute," Burford said. "But he was just a delinquent, a bum. And he was very dumb. Really dumb."

Cassady, then only 20 years old, was to be lionized by Kerouac as the famous character Dean Moriarty, star of "On the Road."

"I think Jack and Allen romanticized the West," Burford said, "and they would look at us as though we were very different, because we were from the West."

But the Denver members of the Kerouac group didn't look at Cassady through rose-colored glasses, and rather resented the attention he received from Kerouac and Ginsberg. Burford and his Denver friends didn't see Denver-bred Cassady as a noble savage; they saw him as a savage.

Said Burford: "Neal was a hood, you see."

A CHALLENGE

And so, one night in a Central City bar, with Ginsberg, Kerouac, Cassady and others present, Burford decided to take on Cassady.

"I remember it was a Sunday night," Burford said, "and in those days bars were supposed to close early, but this one didn't. We were upstairs some-place drinking a lot of beer, some big place.

"I started insulting Cassady, and, really, you know, I don't know how the dialogue went, but I was insulting him and he was really, he had no, he didn't have any guts. He was a sneaky, cowardly guy.

"So I lit upon that. I was giving Cassady a really bad time, and the harder I got on Cassady, and I'd really make a point, Cassady would be all frustrated, and he'd have to just sit there.

"Then Ginsberg would get so mad he'd break a beer bottle. He'd start breaking beer bottles every time I insulted Cassady. He broke about six bottles.

"Ginsberg couldn't do anything (he was a thin, owlish youth, no match for the husky Burford), and Cassady wouldn't. So that's how it ended."

It was one of the more graphic scenes during that mad summer of 1947, when so many of the people who later would become known as founders of the Beat movement came here to mingle with Denverites like Burford, his sister, Beverly Burford, Edward White and Justin Brierly.

But Kerouac, who witnessed the entire Cassady-Burford exchange, chose not to record it, in "On the Road" or in any of his other works.

LOOKING BACK

Years later, after the Beat movement waned and author Ken Kesey and others picked up the slack by forming its successor, the hippie culture, people came to see Cassady's non-violence as a precursor to the gentleness of the flower people.

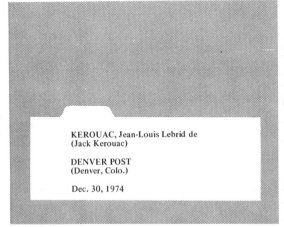

KEROUAC, Jean-Louis Lebrid de
(Jack Kerouac)

DENVER POST
(Denver, Colo.)

Dec. 30, 1974

Cassady, in fact, traveled with Kesey and his Merry Pranksters on their psychedelic bus in the early 1960s. The Pranksters saw Cassady, the fast-talking, devil-may-care driver of "On the Road," as an important link, a sanction from the old Beat movement. They let Cassady drive their bus.

But Burford didn't consider ex-convict Cassady to be a non-violent flower child. He saw him simply as a coward.

"Cassady wasn't gentle at all," Burford said. "He wasn't gentle with anything. He wasn't gentle with cars. He wasn't gentle with people. If he was gentle, it was a lapse."

Cassady died in 1968. Hero to a cult that worshipped youth, fell off a cliff in Mexico on one of his never-ending trips.

Despite Burford's harsh treatment of his friend Cassady, Kerouac still liked Burford, spent much of his 1947 summer with him, and always visited him if Bob was in Denver during Jack's stay.

CLASS FRICTION

But Kerouac tended to think that the dislike Burford and his friends felt for Cassady was really class resentment by middle-class youngsters who couldn't accept a renegade from Larimer Street — then the Skid Row of Denver.

Denver architect Ed White conceded that class warfare may have been part of the refusal to accept Cassady. But as the years went by such social categorizing tended to break down and blur, and Cassady was treated more kindly by the Denver group.

"That was a great summer," Burford said of 1947. "I was impressed by Kerouac, and I felt a real kinship with him. He was very enthusiastic, and he wasn't affected at all. He was honest."

Kerouac's first book wasn't published until 1950, and "On the Road" didn't come out until 1957. When Burford and his friends met Kerouac they saw him as a serious and talented writer, but few guessed he would become famous.

A couple years after his summer with Kerouac, Burford, then 25, took off for Paris, where he spent much of the next 13 years as an expatriate writer. His circle of friends included such famous authors as James Baldwin, Terry Southern, Tennessee Williams, Truman Capote and William Saroyan.

NEVER FAMOUS

But Burford achieved no fame with his works, and it began to appear that his best-known contribution to literature would be not his own writing, but rather the part he played as a character in "On the Road," when he was a tough young intellect seeking adventure with Kerouac.

As years passed, he felt himself sinking along with Kerouac, a friend who achieved fame but not happiness, not contentment.

"I was on the phone with Jack two nights before he died," Burford said.

Burford is now working on a prose trilogy. Referring to his start as a writer, he said: "I'd been recognized as a comer, but then I realized I had nothing I cared to say."

In the summer of 1947, he said, he, an aspiring writer, was much intrigued by the positivism of Ginsberg and Kerouac, two young, unpublished writers from the East Coast who had no doubts about their own talents.

"Allen worked that summer as a night watchman at the May Co.," Burford said. "He had a little flat down on Grant Street.

"I was always very impressed by Ginsberg. He was really a good poet. Right from the start. And I read Jack's journals, and I could see he wasn't playing around either He had a lot of energy, and he was very serious about his writing."

But as the years passed and Kerouac didn't achieve the fame he felt he deserved, he became, Burford remembered, more morose, more apt to be gloomy.

But after the fantastic success of "On the Road," which catapulted Kerouac to immense fame almost overnight, the author, Burford remembered, couldn't handle that either.

"People say that Neal was forced into having to perform," Burford said, "to live up to his Dean Moriarty image. Well Kerouac would have to perform too. Finally, he would have to go off by himself, to figure out what the hell was going on, what was happening to him."

By the time of his death, Kerouac was a recluse and a hopeless alcoholic.

CHANGES OF TIME

As Burford watched Kerouac over the years, he saw him sinking; as he watched Ginsberg, he saw him grow, handle his success with good grace. Cassady, he said, never changed. He was the same "delinquent teen-ager" in his adulthood that he was in his youth.

Cassady, Burford said, rode to Denver in 1966 in a stolen car. "He called me up," Burford said. "He always 'sirred' me after that time in Central City.

"Anyway, he said he had this hot party over on 6th Avenue, and that I should come right over. When I didn't show up, he'd keep calling me during the party, saying it was getting hotter, that I've got to get over there.

"I couldn't believe it. It wasn't even up to his hijinks in 1947, let alone 1966."

Cassady continued to live in the wild, happy atmosphere of 1947 all the rest of his life. But Kerouac never could relive it, though he tried.

"That was just a great summer for Jack," Burford said. "That was a great summer."

(Also see preceding article)

'Doll of the West' Recalls How It Was With Kerouac, Friends

By IVAN GOLDMAN
Denver Post Staff Writer
Third in a series.)

In the Denver chapters of Jack Kerouac's tumultuously successful "On the Road," he described "a beautiful blonde called Babe — a tennis-playing, surf-riding doll of the West."

"Babe," the Babe Rawlins of Kerouac's milestone novel, was Beverly Burford, now Beverly Burford DeBerard, wife of Fay DeBerard of Kremmling, a rancher and Colorado state senator.

Aside from the close circle of friends of the now deceased Kerouac, few people are aware of the incongruous former life of Mrs. DeBerard. But it's a past that, for all its sweet and wild sadness, is a source of pride to her.

Beverly, a Denver-bred, very beautiful young girl with wit and intelligence to match, was used to being pursued by young men.

Headquarters in Denver

When, in 1947, Jack Kerouac, Allen Ginsberg, Neal Cassady and other founders of the new Beat subculture zeroed in on Denver for their headquarters that summer, Beverly Burford was a very integral member of the group.

Later, in the mid 1950s, when the Beat scene moved west to San Francisco, Beverly Burford was there too, working in the city, living in Sausalito, spending her evenings in the bohemian watering places of North Beach.

"Those were the days," she said, "when you wore a hat and gloves to work. That was a crazy existence. I would meet Neal and Jack after work. They would call me, and we'd go to the Place. That was the name of it, in North Beach. There was sawdust on the floor . . . it was crazy. Then I would try to catch the last bus to Sausalito."

Was it a double life?

"No," Beverly laughed. "I've led eight lives. I'm in my ninth now."

Central City Weekends

Back in 1947, the group spent several wild weekends in Central City. One of them was detailed in "On the Road:"

"Babe Rawlins was an enterprising blonde. She knew of an old miner's house at the edge of town where we boys could sleep for the weekend; all we had to do was clean it out."

Everyone from those days remembers the shack well. Bob Burford, Beverly's brother, recalls that one night a bunch of Nevada gamblers, amazed by the size of the partying crowd at the old shack, set up gambling tables inside and apparently made a killing.

At the end of that particular weekend, Kerouac recorded in "On the Road," there was an aura of spent energy.

"As we were going out to the car," the novel said, "Babe slipped and fell flat on her face. Poor girl was overwrought."

But later: "Suddenly we came down from the mountain and overlooked the great sea-plain of Denver; heat rose as from an oven. We began to sing songs."

Fascination for Denver

It was a theme that reappeared repeatedly in the works and letters of Kerouac — his fascination for Denver. But Kerouac, an Easterner by birth, ultimately remained in the East, dreaming of returning to Denver until the very end, when he died a tragic death in 1969 at the age of 47.

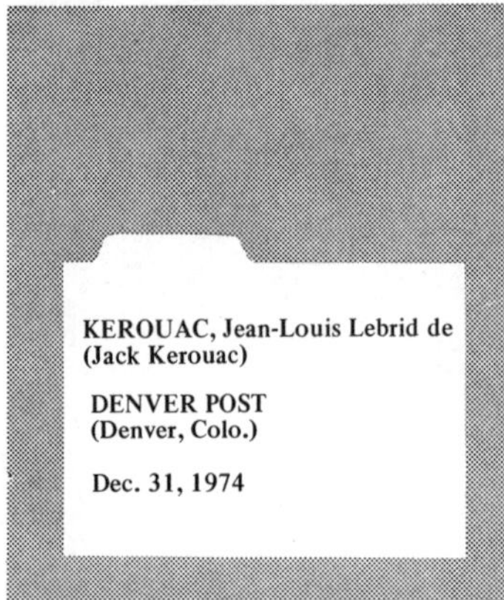

KEROUAC, Jean-Louis Lebrid de
(Jack Kerouac)

DENVER POST
(Denver, Colo.)

Dec. 31, 1974

Kerouac's romantic attachment for the West, in fact, sometimes seemed to go beyond its realities, according to his friends who were themselves Westerners.

When he described Cassady (called Dean Moriatry in "On the Road") he wrote: "My first impression of Dean was of a young Gene Autry — trim, thin-hipped, blue-eyed, with a real Oklahoma accent — a sideburned hero of the snowy West.

Keruouac wrote so much about the West, so much about his sad search for truth by traveling within it, that it's not easy to think of him as an Easterner. But in the few recordings of his recited works, one hears the clipped accent of a Massachusetts man, which he was.

Listen very closely and there is the slight trace of French-Canadian, which were the origins of his family. He didn't learn English until he attended school, and because it was his second language he held a lifelong fascination for the sound of English words.

So the Kerouac who idealized the West idealized as well its men — especially Cassady, and its women — especially Beverly Burford.

In the case of Cassady, most of Kerouac's Denver friends disagreed. Closer to Denverite Neal's origins, they saw him as an untrustworthy bum, a shallow blowhard who had little to contribute to their group.

Still, the lovely Beverly Burford, who seemed able to accept anybody, liked Neal with no qualms. It was a special trait. She was able, without skipping a beat, to be friends with people all over the economic and social spectrum.

"All those guys might not have liked each other," said her brother, Bob, "but they all liked Bev. That was something they could always agree on."

In the spring of 1950, Kerouac returned to Denver to plug his first book, "The Town and the City." There was an autgraph party at the old Windsor Hotel, and all his old Denver friends were invited. Beverly, still enterprising, arranged radio interviews for the young novelist.

"We had a great time," she said. "Jack was a very happy person then. But he would have his moods."

Found Them Again

It was later, after a couple of years in Europe, that Beverly moved to northern California, where she found Neal and Jack again.

"I remember," she said, "Neal's girl, who jumped out a window (and died). And Neal always carried a railroad watch. He was perhaps one of the finest drivers I'd ever ridden with. But he could scare the hell out of you."

"He never used the brakes," added Ed White, another Denver friend of Jack's and Neal's.

"No," agreed Beverly. "And all the time you were with Neal, there was continous talk. And oh, he could con anyone."

When Neal was sent to San Quentin for selling marijuana to a police agent, Beverly was one of the 10 persons allowed to write him.

"One time I came home from work," she said, "and there was a note from Jack. 'I've borrowed your hi-fi. Big party this weekend Mill Valley. I'll see you Friday.' "

Beverly and Jack spent many afternoons together. "Jack was always writing," she said. "He always carried a little spiral notebook.

"But let me say this one thing. I'm an alcoholic (who quit drinking in 1959). At one time I remember Jack and I had only enough money to get a bottle of wine and a bus back to Sausalito, or take a taxi. It was a long walk to the bus station, but we picked that."

Jack and Beverly were sinking into their alcoholism about the same time. But Beverly pulled out, renewed her life. After a previous marriage ended in divorce, she was married to DeBerard.

Ginsberg occasionally visits Beverly and her conservative husband at their ranch, where Ginsberg and Fay like to discuss farming.

Beverly remembers Jack Kerouac as a man who was always searching for something, and could never seem to find it. He studied Buddhism, and often considered returning to his Roman Catholic Church, she said.

"I think he must have realized he wasn't going to last too long," she said. "He was lonely."

(Also see preceding article)

Kerouac's Friend Helped Spark Style of 'On the Road'

By IVAN GOLDMAN
Denver Post Staff Writer

(Last in a series)

Denver architect Edward D. White Jr. has a 1968 postcard from novelist Jack Kerouac that reads simply: "Sir, honored to occupy the globe same time as you."

White, who probably was Kerouac's best friend throughout the troubled writer's adult life, has stacks of such short notes from Jack. The friendship was very important to Kerouac, and he was constant in his efforts to keep it strong.

Much of Kerouac's correspondence to White consisted of long, intense, typewritten letters which reveals the very gentle, brooding essence that was Kerouac. Some of the letters are several thousand words each.

White and Kerouac met at Columbia University in New York in 1946, after White returned from wartime service in the Navy. By that time Kerouac already had been discharged from the Navy on psychiatric grounds and expelled from Columbia.

But he was still living near the campus, tasting the intellectual and subterranean life of New York, making his plans to be a great writer.

White was considering life as an artist then, but later switched to architecture, which he studied at Columbia and the Sorbonne in Paris.

Kerouac's primary reason for choosing Denver as the site of his summer, 1947 headquarters was his friendship with White, Haldon Chase and Neal Cassady. Chase, like White, was a graduate of East High School and a Columbia student. Cassady was also from Denver, a young, ex-convict who had done time at Colorado State Reformatory at Buena Vista for joyriding.

Cassady was to achieve lasting fame for his depiction as Dean Moriarty in "On the Road," as the prototype for the new-breed American hipster.

Allen Ginsberg, then a young, unknown poet from Patterson, N..J, also left New York for Denver that summer in order to be with Cassady and Kerouac. But his important magnet was Cassady.

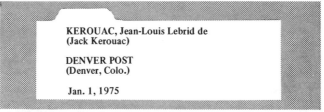

KEROUAC, Jean-Louis Lebrid de
(Jack Kerouac)

DENVER POST
(Denver, Colo.)

Jan. 1, 1975

Ginsberg, who was quite frank about his homosexuality, was immensely attracted to the husky, handsome Cassady, who took bisexuality as a matter of course.

Later on, Ginsberg was to claim that he also had homosexual liaisons with Kerouac. But White is doubtful.

Said White: "The only thing Jack liked better than girls was booze."

Beverly Burford DeBerard, wife of the state senator from Kremmling, and a longtime friend of Kerouac's, said of Jack's alleged homosexual experimentation: "He might have been drunk and tried it. I don't know. But I can't imagine it. He's just not the type."

While Cassady was an inmate at the reformatory, he was allowed, in those days, to correspond with only one person. That person was Justin W Brierly, an older man, now 68, who was then a counselor and English teacher at East High. Brierly now is assistant to the president at Colorado Women's College.

Brierly met Kerouac through Haldon Chase on a trip to New York, and, later, Brierly showed Kerouac some of Cassady's letters and wrote Cassady about the budding young writer Kerouac.

So, after his release from prison, Cassady looked up Kerouac in New York, and thus was formed the famous team of Kerouac and Cassady, now a monumental chapter in American literary history.

Brierly, like White, was a character in Kerouac's "On the Road," and Kerouac's description of him was none too flattering. To this day, Brierly's comments on Kerouac are, in turn, not altogether flattering either.

"'On the Road,'" Brierly said, "was not a first-class literary production, although I know it was one of the cornerstones of a new day.

"You must understand, however, that I was not running around as a member of the Beat Generation. To think so would be absurd."

But Kerouac and Brierly maintained a friendship even after the publication of "On the Road" in 1957. Kerouac solicited the older Brierly for advice, and trusted him on matters of culture. Brierly, for example, was for many years a member of the opera association at Central City.

Brierly, unlike White or Cassady or Kerouac's other friends, wasn't running off to Paris or New York frequently, and so he was the one friend Kerouac could always count on for company when he visited Denver.

When he first met the young Kerouac, Brierly said, he could never have predicted that the fledgling author would drift into hard-core alcoholism.

"In those days," Brierly said, "he wasn't so much an alcoholic as he was a free-for-all adventurer, do you know? He was a typical "On the Road" person, but then such people weren't typical. He certainly was one of the first literary people on the road."

Once, in 1949, Kerouac came west with his mother, with plans to make Denver their permanent home.

"I loaned him a mattress which I secured from an aunt of mine," Brierly said, "and took him out to a house he'd found in west Denver."

"Yes," White recalled, "Jack brought his poor old mother out, and none of us were here. We were all off various places. He found a house somewhere west of Denver, a development house, where there weren't any roads, and it was all muddy. It was doomed to failure, of course. Jack wasn't terribly practical. Neither he nor his mother drove a car.

"Justin gave him advice. He was the only one around." After a couple months, Kerouac and his mother returned to the East Coast to live, and, though all the rest of his life Kerouac continued to talk about returning to Denver to live, he never did. But he did visit here again, several times.

"Kerouac," Brierly said, "continued to call me every month or so, until he got so terribly drunk all the time."

On Cassady, Brierly said: "I didn't, at any time, see the potentialities in Neal that Jack saw in him. Kerouac always saw a great deal more. I think half of Cassady existed in Cassady, and the other half in Kerouac's mind. And I think Cassady spent the rest of his life trying to live up to the image Kerouac created for him.

"As a matter of fact, I got to distrusting Cassady. In later years, when Kerouac was coming through, I asked him not to bring Cassady with him.

(Continued from preceding page)

"You see, Kerouac and Ginsberg are people of really some basic character and caliber. And Cassady lacked it. He didn't have it. He stole from me, he stole from the people in his own group, he stole from Kerouac.

"I don't think I helped Cassady any. But I don't think anything would have helped Cassady, particularly by the time he was 16. He lived on Larimer Street, his father was a drunk, and he didn't know where his family was.

"But Neal was a very good-looking, attractive, young man, with considerable adeptness with cars and things and a real charisma."

Cassady came to visit Brierly in 1967, one year before Neal died. He was in a stolen car, and Brierly let him in for awhile, then told him he had to leave for a previous appointment and ushered him out of the house. But Cassady took it in easy stride.

"No," Brierly said, "Neal wasn't unhappy. He never was particularly unhappy. He was Moriarty. That's who he was attempting to be, and that's who he was. Aren't you more or less what you attempt to be?"

In "On the Road," Kerouac mentioned that Cassady once left him with dysentery in a hospital deep in Mexico, taking the car and deserting his friend.

But Ed White remembers there was more to the story. What Kerouac didn't write was the fact that Cassady also stole Kerouac's money before he left. But Kerouac forgave his friend Neal.

"I got along well with Neal," said White, a good-natured man at ease with almost anybody. "The last time I saw him, it was in 1967, and he came through Denver with about a 20-year-old brunette. I came home and he was upstairs taking a shower in one bathroom and she was taking a shower in the other one.

"I kind of panicked. I didn't know if he was planning to move in for awhile or what. But when he came down all dressed, I gave him a beer, and I think we told him we were going out or something or else we were. I was as bad as Brierly.

"Neal had an old beat-up Pontiac station wagon or something. It was full of, it looked like seabags. It was sort of solid laundry all up and down.

"And he had on one red boot and one tan shoe, I think. He explained that he had a girl friend who got mad at him and threw away his shoes, one of each pair.

"He was very kind, very nice that time. He talked about all these years that had passed. He told me I was a myth or something, and he told me he was a myth. Then he talked about the Kesey thing. (Cassady had been riding around the country with Ken Kesey and his Merry Pranksters, principal founders of the acid-hippie culture.)

KEROUAC,
Jean-Louis Lebrid de
(Jack Kerouac)

DENVER POST
(Denver, Colo.)

Jan. 1, 1975

"This girl he was with was about half his age, and all she could say to him was, 'Oh, you're so wise.' She was a real dumb little chick.

"Then, two months later, Justin sent me a clipping saying Neal had been found dead in Mexico. I sent it on with a note to Jack."

Neal Cassady died the way he had lived, broke, stoned and on the road. Kerouac wanted to believe that the death was a hoax to avoid creditors, that Neal was laughing somewhere about how everyone was fooled.

Jack wrote Ed a letter delineating his doubts. In the letter, dated April 21, 1968, when he conceded that Neal might in fact be dead, he noted there were some people who were "even hinting it was all my fault."

The theory that Kerouac had destroyed his friend Cassady by making him a famous character apparently reached Jack and unsettled him.

White has another letter from Jack, vital to the literary history of the Beat writings, and it's one Kerouac's biographer, Ann Charters, never saw.

"By the way," said the April 29, 1957, letter, "you started whole new movement of American literature (spontaneous prose and poetry) when (in 1951) in that Chinese restaurant on 125th Street one night you told me to start SKETCHING in the streets . . . tell you more later."

Up until then, Kerouac had been struggling to write in classic, traditional ways. His first novel, "The Town and the City," was written in a style similar to Thomas Wolfe's.

It was White who suggested, in a New York restaurant, that Jack had special things to say and so he should say them in a special way, sketch them as one would a painting. It was Kerouac's way ever after.

And the letter to White, thanking him for the suggestion, came on the heels of the instant recognition paid the 1957 publication of "On the Road," which was "sketched."

Jack liked the way his friend Ed handled his own intelligence in such easy fashion, he admired his Denver background, his successes, his more settled home life.

And Jack liked the way Ed tolerated the Kerouac excesses. But as Jack sank into alcoholism, the writer didn't want to talk about it.

"Jack once told me he was an alcoholic," White said, "but he never really talked about it. When he was younger, nobody thought of it. We thought he was just drinking and having a good time."

Kerouac, White remembers, was always searching for a good, permanent relationship with a woman. He was married three times, never happily.

His books conveyed that special sweet sadness of a determined search that never really bears fruit. Ed White never considered himself a part of the Beat Generation, but rather an adjunct to it, a friend from the straight world.

"Beat was a word that we all used when we were younger," White said. "To us, it just meant you were broke, because we were all broke or trying to go to school or something."

And White's respect for Jack remained through to the last. Yet, White, like Bob Burford, another Denver member of the group, considered Cassady a coward.

"But Jack really was non-violent,'' White said. "He wasn't afraid. He just wasn't gentle. And he was very strong, athletic."

Kerouac's travels among the subcultures of America's cities took him among some violent people, but, magically, they seemed to sense his gentleness, and he was rarely bothered.

"I think," White said, "that as Jack's personality began to split further apart, it had a very manic phase to it. He could talk loud and raise hell. This was usually associated with drinking, and he'd become unstrung. But he spent an awful lot of time by himself, too.

"The last time I saw him was at his house on Long Island. I believe it was 1967. And he always used to call, usually about 3 in the morning. Some of them were very interesting conversations, but because I was sleepy I wouldn't remember what he'd said when I got up the next day. I should have taken notes."

In "On the Road," Kerouac described leaving his beloved Denver after the summer of 1947. It was Ed White (named Tim Gray in the novel) who saw him off:

"Tim Gray waved goodby. The bus rolled out of the storied, eager Denver streets. 'By God, I gotta come back and see what else will happen!' I promised."

Kerouac did come back, several times, but he never fully repeated the exuberance and contentment of the summer in Denver when he was 25.

In his letters to White, written from his various reclusive homes on the East Coast, he repeatedly said he eventually would live in Denver. Once he even asked his friend Ed to design a house for him here, which White did. Jack wanted a place in the mountains, difficult to reach.

He liked White's sketch, but wrote back, "Let's get rid of that fireplace and put in a pot-bellied stove," Ed said.

On May 12, 1969, Jack wrote Ed his final letter. It was a short note reading, "Mebbe I go see you in Denver this summer? Hah?"

But Kerouac died Oct. 21, at his house in St. Petersburg, Fla., without again seeing Ed White or Denver

The Retreat of James J. Kilpatrick

By Philip J. Hilts

PHILIP J. HILTS is a Washington, D.C., journalist.

Were you running with us on Carswell? The question was a rite-of-passage at the White House, a loyalty test.

"To have been with him on Haynsworth was easy; Haynsworth was a fine jurist," says James Jackson Kilpatrick. "But I stuck with him on Carswell. That was the litmus test . . . To have been with him on Carswell was to have walked the last mile."

For Kilpatrick that last mile was a little tough, and certainly lonesome. Even conservative Kilpatrick says: "I said at the time that I would hold my nose while I voted for him." Still, he was there with loyalty when they came asking.

Those dues he paid bought him a special seat in the arena: "He is one of the two or three most quoted columnists in the President's news summary," presidential advisor Patrick Buchanan has said. Buchanan's assistant, Mort Allin, adds that Kilpatrick is taken more seriously at the White House than most journalists: "When a guy like Kilpatrick who is generally on your side, takes an opposing position, you're more likely to be concerned. You start thinking, 'We have a problem here.' "

KILPATRICK, James Jackson
(1920 -)

MIAMI HERALD
(Miami, Fla.)

Dec. 2, 1973

[See also CA-1]

Those statements were made, of course, before the Cox firing and the missing-tapes announcement. It was then that Kilpatrick wrote: "The time has come, much as a long-time admirer regrets to say it, to proceed with the impeachment and trial of Richard Nixon." In that November column, he made clear he was *not* predicting that Nixon would be removed from office, but that a Senate trial was necessary to "clear the poisonous air and restore a sense of domestic tranquility."

It is 2:25 p.m., a Thursday. This is taping day for "Kilpo."

He is wearing the image-mandated blue suit and brown wing-tip shoes as he ambles up to the Washington radio station. A gray wreath of tousled hair crowns his red Virginia tan. At age 53, he is often considered the king of conservative spokesmen and earns something in excess of $150,000 a year for it, but he is not pretentious. Just the opposite.

In the studio, he shyly presents a wad of pa-

(Continued from preceding page)

pers to a man reclining, feet up, in a tiny cubicle. "I have three pearls of wisdom here," he says, "would anyone like to string them for me?"

The lounging man smiles. "Ahhh, I don't know. Next door, maybe."

Kilpatrick totes his pearls next door, then shuffles back. "Next door, the cupboard is bare," he says.

The lounging man has pointed him down the hall to the taping rooms, and after an exchange

KILPATRICK, James Jackson

MIAMI HERALD
(Miami, Fla.)

Dec. 2, 1973

about pearls, he is seated at an empty desk in front of a microphone.

He runs through three radio tapings. Two television shows. Three TV commentaries. This is the public Kilpatrick, but it's only part of the output. Some 280 newspapers carry his column three times a week. He raps out a few lecture tours every month, and several magazine articles a year. He's starting his sixth book.

'My heart doesn't go pitty-pat anymore'

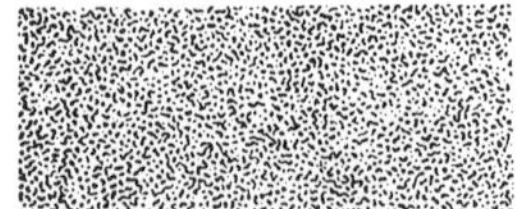

Despite the fact that Kilpatrick's ideas are often laid out in print and on television there is much about him that is puzzling to his colleagues. They see the Kilpatrick image, and hear his political positions, which are not always consistent, and wonder if he isn't just an actor.

For some who know him a little better, Kilpatrick's role-playing for the cameras is written off as part of the strictures of the business. They say that away from the shop, Kilpatrick is a different man. It's not so much that his politics are shallow as he has other, deeper interests.

One acquaintance recounted Kilpatrick's first introduction to Sen. Eugene McCarthy during the New Hampshire primaries. It was over dinner, and it was clearly a situation that could have stirred some fierce political conversation. It didn't.

"It was one of those rare and lovely nights. It was cold as hell outside. We had dinner, and stayed there for hours, drinking Jack Daniels, with our legs over the chairs. We were talking about poetry, 17th- and 18th-century literature, Shakespeare. No politics at all. It was a side of Jack I hadn't seen . . . not the old conservative you see on TV."

James J. Kilpatrick was born in Oklahoma, but it was his trips to visit relatives in New Orleans during his younger years that gave him his sense of being a Southerner. His family was well-off during his younger years, but in 1937 his father's business broke down and young Jack had to work his way through the University of Missouri's school of journalism. He graduated in 1941, and was hired by the *Richmond News Leader* for $35 a week.

Kilpatrick married not long after he joined the *Richmond News Leader.* "We met on Tuesday and I proposed on Friday — it was just one of those things. . ." His wife, Marie Pietri, is a small and slender woman with a large talent for sculpture, whose family is pure Virginia. The Kilpatricks have three boys.

It was clear very early that Kilpatrick was going to be an unusual reporter. "When he arrived, he was rather on the liberal side," says Mike Houston, now a columnist at the *News Leader.* "But he found out we were conservative, and learned quickly which side the bread was buttered on. As a reporter he was one of the most energetic men I have ever seen, he was in there on everything, and he sought out assignments."

He moved up the ladder quickly at the paper, speeded in his rise by the fact that many of the staffers joined the military during the war. (Kilpatrick himself tried several times to enlist, but was rejected because of bronchial asthma.)

He became something of a terror to the bureaucrats and politicians in the local government. "Some people in the state government got up in the mornings with fear, worried that Kilpatrick might call them that day," one former staffer said. "I've heard of times that he marched into a state office and demanded files, saying that he smelled skulduggery."

The editor of the *News Leader* during Kilpatrick's rise was Douglas Southall Freeman, a historian and a figure of some size in Southern journalism. Freeman pegged Kilpatrick early as his successor, and had him moved up to editorial-page writer when he was still in his mid-20s. He became editor in chief at 30 and started a routine of filling something like 43 inches a day.

It was about four years after he began sitting in the editor's chair that he started his biggest editorial campaign. In 1954, the Supreme Court had delivered its views on integration in Brown v. the Board of Education. Things were cool for awhile, until it became clear that the court meant it.

Sen. Harry Byrd, operator of the state's political machinery, began looking for a way to oppose the court and halt integration.

Enter Kilpatrick. Editorially he attacked the "tyranny" of the court and promised a "massive resistance" to integration. Casting about for something more than hot air to stand on, he came across William Olds, a 58-year-old Chesterfield County lawyer, who in looking through Civil War documents had tripped over an obscure doctrine called interposition. Later traced back to John C. Calhoun and others, the doctrine noted that a fundamental flaw in the Constitution was that the Supreme Court had too much power over the states. Unlike the Executive Branch power, it was unchecked. So, went the doctrine, states have a right to hold a Supreme Court decision null and void until the matter can be resolved by constitutional amendment.

The Washington Post reported: "This device for defying the Supreme Court fascinated Kilpatrick, and he went to work on it forthwith . . . The *News Leader* buttressed interposition with interminable research, adorned it with portraits of Jefferson, Madison and Calhoun and broadcast it, both in its regular editions and in folder reprints, far and wide. Interposition became a major Southern issue, and Kilpatrick was its apostle."

Try as he might to stay away from the issue of race, Kilpatrick found himself dipping into it. In his book *The Sovereign States,* which appeared during these years, he came up with such items as: "The Negro race, as a race, has palpably different social, moral and behavioral standards from those which obtain among the white race . . . After years of exposure to the amenities of civilization from which the Negro might profit by example, one out of every five Negroes in the South today is the product of illicit sexual union.

" . . . Such promiscuity must result in wide-

(Continued from preceding page)

spread venereal disease . . . Colored patients account for 90 per cent of all reported syphilis and gonorrhea. The undisciplined passions which find one outlet in sex, find another in crime . . .

"What is it that the court, in effect, has commanded the South to give up? It is no less than this: the basis of the South's society, the vitality of her culture."

(Kilpatrick, asked to comment on the quotation from his book, said that 16 years had passed since he wrote those sentences and that a great many things — especially his own attitudes and prejudices — had changed greatly in the meantime.)

KILPATRICK, James Jackson

MIAMI HERALD
(Miami, Fla.)

Dec. 2, 1973

'Let me sound like an old fogey'

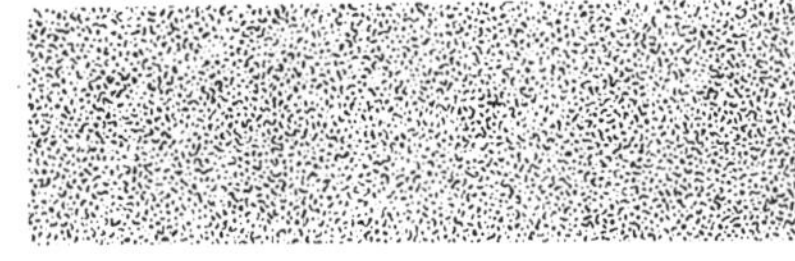

By the time Kilpatrick first began getting feelers to do a national syndicated column in 1964 he called governors by their first names and in his beat-up Stetson hat was a walking landmark of the Richmond landscape. "I was a fairly substantial frog in a small puddle," he says, and was reluctant to accept.

Submerged in local issues for three decades, he had a very heavy schedule without taking on extra work. Also, "he didn't think of himself as a potentially very important syndicated columnist. He was just a provincial editor," says Harry Elmark, head of the Star Syndicate.

Elmark's first offer dropped. But in the summer of 1964, *Newsday* made an offer that Kilpatrick found easy to accept. They guaranteed him a $5,000 minimum per year, and he didn't have to leave Richmond or his job. So, if the column did not go well, he could simply retreat.

Conservatives who were bright and articulate were very difficult to find; the column was an immediate success. By the end of the first year, some 50 papers had picked it up. Harry Elmark and the Star Syndicate were soon back on Kilpatrick's doorstep. They offered something that *Newsday* couldn't match: a Washington audience.

Kilpatrick was 45. The ambition that drove him was still flickering enough to keep him from becoming a Richmond landmark permanently.

In 1966, he moved to Washington to work on the column full-time.

It was perhaps with that decision that the blooming of Kilpo began. In some odd fashion, he became more the Southern country gentleman by coming North. He was not without honor in Richmond country, but in Washington he was standing among taller figures. He set his shoulders back, and shrugged off some of the pettiness of provincial life.

Friends say that the poor-boy complex he carried to Richmond was left there. Now he is more relaxed about money, is more likely to pick up the tab at lunch with friends. His self-assurance has grown: "There was a time when my heart would go pitty-pat at meeting a United States senator," Kilpatrick says. "My heart doesn't go pitty-pat anymore."

For the past few years he has been gradually moving himself out to White Walnut Hill, appearing in the city less and less. In October, he began residing in Scrabble, Va., amid the Blue Ridge Mountains on a full-time basis.

The columns which best show his prose style have been appearing more frequently as he begins to cultivate the country life at White Walnut Hill. He has discovered, he wrote in one column: "It is as important to a country woman to pickle as it is important to a country man to get in the firewood. One measures fulfillments in pints, quarts and split oak logs . . . There is more to think about in August in the country than the abuse of power by the White House. . ."

It is 3:55 p.m. Kilpo is finishing up his Thursday round of tapings. He is standing behind a podium waiting for the TV cameras to start taping. A young black technician walks into the studio. Kilpatrick looks down at his shoes: platforms, high heels, pink and purple. "Wow!" says Kilpo. "Do you wear those things out on the street?"

"Only out to the car and back," says the technician, as he glances at Kilpo's feet. "You still wearing wing tips? You ought to be ashamed."

"Well, I have an image to preserve, you know. I used to wear cowboy boots," he jests.

The red light flickers on the camera. "At the risk of sounding like an old fogey," Kilpatrick intones, "let me sound like an old fogey . . ."

After the taping, Kilpatrick ambles from behind the podium to an adjacent dressing room. The light is dim. He sits down next to a row of makeup mirrors. Soon he is talking about his approach to issues. "You have to see these things through their eyes, just the way they would see them.

"I imagine myself President Nixon. I'm sitting in the office and I look out the window and see all these rosebushes, and gardeners. I would say to Rosemary or Dwight, 'Hey, aren't there an awful lot of gardeners out there? Where did they come from? And who's paying for it?' That's the first question I'd ask, 'Who's paying for it?' "

Kilpo's voice is a little lower now, and he is as much wondering out loud as conversing. "You have to rethink all these things now. I've been writing for years that Nixon is an astute politician. But is he? So many of the things going on are bad political moves. It just never seems to stop now, always more and more.

"The paranoia. The secrecy. The abuse of power! . . . You begin to wonder if the things you've supported all these years aren't rotten all the way down . . ."

He gets up slowly. He will head back to White Walnut Hill and stay until the next taping day.

"An editor of a paper in California read one of my country columns," he says, "and he said, 'Now Kilpatrick is writing about the big stuff, the stuff that's really important.' He's right. The politics come and go, and it will all look different in the history books. But at night when all the lights are out in the country, you can feel that just a few feet away from the house there is another world moving. The animals . . . the fields . . . the stars. That world doesn't change." T

(Also see preceding article)

Leaning Right, But Looking Both Ways

BY MARY HOFFELT

Is commentator and columnist James Kilpatrick the only conservative with a sense of humor?

Kilpatrick answers, "of course not. Bill Buckley has a marvelous sense of humor."

Kilpatrick visited Seattle yesterday to speak at the Bellevue Town Hall Lectures series, presented by the Churchwomen of St. Thomas Episcopal Church, Medina.

In an interview, he discussed the dour reputation of most avowed conservatives: "Taking the conservative stance is saying 'no' more often than not. If you think of the body politic as a machine, the liberals' habit is to accelerate. The conservatives' function is to apply the brakes.

"Certain aspects of the conservative point of view are by nature solemn. But I don't take myself too seriously, said Kilpatrick, who talks as quotably as he writes.

Kilpatrick's been in journalism since he was a 12-year-old copy boy at the Oklahoma City Times. He was editor of the Richmond, Va. News Leader before he moved to Washington, D.C., in 1967 as a political analyst.

His forums now are his syndicated newspaper and TV's column, "Meet the Press" and "60 Minutes," where he contrasts Nicholas Von Hoffman in "Point-Counterpoint." Of the latter he jokes, "It's far better to have the counterpoint side but I usually win more than half the time anyway."

Three months during the year Kilpatrick travels the lecture circuit.

He said the trips give him an accurate feel of the country's pulse and his diagnosis is that a conservative mood prevails.

Despite the recent Republican debacle at the polls, "all the surveys still show a strong conservative sentiment.

"There were no clearcut conservative-liberal issues in the elections. Republicans lost simply because of Watergate and Ford's ill-timed pardon of Nixon."

But retribution for Watergate has been exacted and the voters will put all that behind them, he predicted. And the election won't mean the end conservative strength.

"My gracious me no," he said in a rich Virginia accent, "If the future of the conservatives were dependent on Richard Nixon, the conservatives didn't hava future."

Kilpatrick calls himself a "front office conservative," meaning he's often asked to take a conservative view for the sake of argument. He takes the advocate role because "there is a need to articulate those points of view."

Yet he's honest about it. 'I was once asked to take the side of 'The Conservative's View of Watergate.' And I asked myself 'Just what is a conservative's view of burglary?' "

Nixon once granted Kilpatrick an exclusive interview when the White House was shrouded in silence.

"I'm sure he gave it to me because he though I would be a sympathetic conduit. I think he was disappointed."

Kilpatrick — who stood by Nixon until Aug. 5, "the bitter end," hasn't heard from the former president since he wrote a scathing editorial following that interview.

Kilpatrick receives far more campus speaking invitations than he can accept.

"At the University of Delaware they scheduled 28 speakers. Twenty-seven liberals and me. I was the balance to soothe the board of regents."

Kilpatrick thinks the country's mood is best seen on campuses. "They've quieted down considerably. Just look at the University of Washington. Last time I was here (in 1972) the students met in the quadrangle before my speech. They voted whether to picket the courthouse or interupt my talk. They went to the courthouse.

"Definetely a democratic way to do things," he chuckled.

As a journalist, Kilpatrick believes the transition to "Personality" is difficult.

"I'm embarrassed to have the chairs switched and be interviewed. I try to avoid doing the things I hate when I was asking the questions — like spreadeagling to avoid an answer."

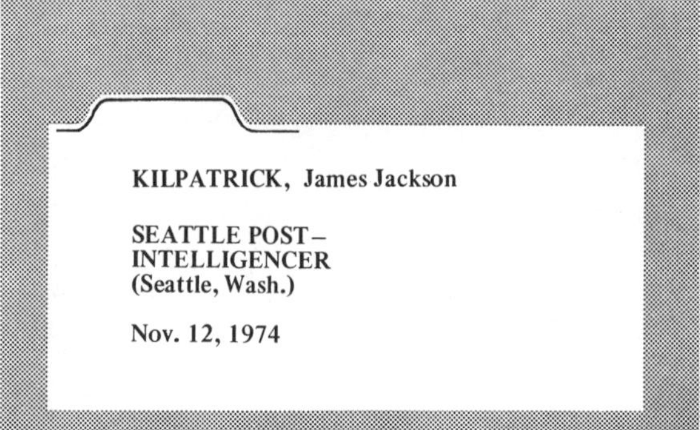

KILPATRICK, James Jackson

SEATTLE POST-INTELLIGENCER (Seattle, Wash.)

Nov. 12, 1974

But he won't debate emotional issues — like abortion, which he supports because "medical and theological evidence has not convinced me that a fetus is a person," although that view runs counter to his conservative philosophy and Catholic religion.

He takes a libertarian tack on such issues, believing "private behavior shouldn't be punished unless it is proved to be socially damaging."

He explains why the view isn't a contradiction to conservatism:

"Most people think of a linear political spectrum from conservative to liberal. Actually political theory is a circle. As you head in opposite directions around the circle, you're bound to occasionally run into the other side."

Good Ol' Florence King

KING, Florence (pseud. Veronica King, Emmett X. Reed, Niko Stavros, Mike Winston, and Cynthia)

SEATTLE POST–INTELLIGENCER (Seattle, Wash.)

May 12, 1974

BY TIM MENEES P-I Staff
-P-I Photo by Tom Barlet

"SHE'S A Yankee," fumed the Tennessee woman in a letter to Harper's magazine. "And all Yankee women are girdle-assed, tight-lipped McGovern Lovers, born in the middle of the week and looking both ways for Sunday!"

"She" is Florence King, now of Seattle and author on subjects from corn to porn. And Ms. King's blast in the magazine's April issue, titled, "The Good Ole Boys," had crimsoned a few necks in Dixie.

She took most of the angry letters in silence, but was moved to write the Knoxville reader from her Queen Anne Hill apartment:

"I'm sorry to report that the Virginia seismograph is now broken beyond repair," she shot back. "When you called me a Yankee, my grandmother started spinning in her grave. I was born on Sunday, in Washington, D.C., product of a long line of Old Dominion residents.

"If you ever call me a Yankee again, I'll whip your tail till your nose bleeds buttermilk and put you in the 'orsepittle."

That sort of gutsy language from author King's typewriter is nothing new. For four years, she cranked out el cheapo pornographic novels, one a month, to the not-so-cheap tune of about $1,600 per book. Thirty-seven volumes in all.

"I was working for American Can in New York," she recalls, "and typing up such things as 'Send Snap-Pak Back and advise that it won't.' One day, I thumbed through a couple of dirty books at a newsstand. I wrote up a 'partial'—three chapters and an outline—of 'Lesbian Sorority' and sent it off. The publisher bought it."

She took the nom de plume Veronica King ("Veronica's my favorite name"), and later wrote as Emmett X. Reed, Niko Stavros, Mike Winston and Cynthia. Occasionally she even used her own.

"Those books weren't all trash," she confides. "They were half-trash. Believe it or not, my publishers wanted good plots and characterization. They even sent back a couple of drafts for revision."

In the early days, she worked over a lot of euphemisms. But as the market began to demand more four-letter words, she complied. Never, she claims, did she inject pain or perversion into her works. Well, almost never.

"I really didn't write consciously for a male audience,' says Ms. King. "I guess I was writing about sex from a woman's point of view." Perhaps. But she did manage to spice up the pages with plenty of buxomy, over-heated beauties trotting around in stiletto heels and dark stockings. Not exactly Woman's Day material.

The blue books, however, were far from an end for the writer. She was out of the business before the picture magazines, movies and Supreme Court all but closed up the paperbacks. It's probably a good thing. Anyone can tire after writing hardcore for 12 straight hours. She did, and took to downing a bottle of whiskey while sniffling alone in her flat to The Rose of Tralee.

Actually, Florence King started out to be a commercial artist. Papa King, a Cockney who met his wife at one of those fancy dress balls in Virginia, was an "early feminist." He encouraged his daughter to draw. "I lost interest in art around puberty," she sighs. "I don't know why."

Then it was French and maybe the Foreign Service. That fell through when she won a scholarship to American University in 1953. American University didn't offer French. So she majored in history, which eventually led her to Ole Miss, True Confessions and The Good Ole Boys.

"When I graduated from American U. in 1957," Ms. King recounts, "I found a job in a reference library . . . you know, one of those glorified file clerk jobs women get." She hated it, and took refuge in a college directory. The page, she claims, fell open to the University of Mississippi, so she applied. She got an $800 grant and was off to Oxford, Miss., for a masters.

"Don't laugh," she cautions. "If you're serious, Ole Miss is a great school. It has a wonderful classics department, for example."

But Florence the Grad Student never wrote her thesis. She started writing true confessions instead.

"I needed the money," she explains. All it took was the prospect of $250 per confession, and Ms. King was down at the drugstore reviewing the pulps. Four hours and 5,000 words of typing, and she had "My God, I'm Too Passionate for my Own Good!" They bought it. And some 100 more.

"Sin, Suffer and Repent," she instructs. "That's the formula for true confessions." But no sex. About the saltiest she got was her stock, "The waters of ecstacy throbbed around us like a magic pool."

It was a writers' market for confession then, and it still is, the author observes.

"The true confessions editors are so nice. They write you letters of advice because they need material." The editors have even accepted for-real true confes- ➡

(Continued from preceding page)

sions. Such as the one, scribbled on notebook paper by a woman in Arkansas. "It was perfect," Ms. King remembers.

Sometimes things went wrong. Like the time in 1959 when she stuffed a scorcher called, "I Was Insatiable" into an envelope and sent it by mistake to the Youth For Christ magazine. But that's bound to happen when you're writing zingers for Dude and Escapade (under men's names) one night and an article for the St. Joseph's Catholic Monthly the next. And teaching 10th grade history during the day.

She hated teaching, too, so she took off to see a friend in North Carolina, and landed a job as assistant woman's editor on the Raleigh News and Observer.

"Brides, obits and t o b a c c o," she grumbles. "That's what southern newspapers hold important. And brides? Whew! One day in June, we ran 40 pictures of brides on two pages.

"And then there are the mothers! They would come in crying about the space we gave their daughters. Southern women can be so domineering in such a sweet way. Vicious."

Ms. King worked for three years at Raleigh, before she got fed up with the news biz. "I wasn't very good with straight news," she admits. "I tended to gild the lily. Besides, I found that presidents of garden clubs had absolutely nothing interesting to say."

Fortunately for her, she later got into magazines. Harpers bought her Good Ole Boy story in January. She has also written a memoir of sorts for Penthouse, called "Confessions of a Lady Pornographer." And the February issue of Playgirl carries a King remembrance of sex past called "Roll Me Over, Lay Me Down," a not-so-nostalgic look at the '50's. And in June, she starts a sex-advice column in Viva. Not to mention two upcoming pieces in Cosmopolitan.

To the northerner, the Good Ole Boy Ms. King conjurs up comes pretty close to Rod Steiger's Sheriff Gillespie from the movie "In the Heat of the Night." He is a beer-bellied, WASP redneck who wears an open white shirt, baggy suntans, garish belt buckle and Marine Corps-issue shoes. His domain is his bar stool and raison d'etre is to worry about the "Negras" and other Good Ole Boys.

They are found, according to the writer, anywhere from the newsroom to the classroom, bound together by a sexual inferiority complex caused by the Yankee victory in the Civil War. They might have become "Superstuds" on the outside but they are shaky on the inside.

Seattle may well have its share of Good Ole Boys, and all males may have a dab of Good Ole Boy in them, Ms. King agrees. But it's different. For one thing, they're not called Good Ole Boys here. "And I can smell a Good Ole Boy a mile away," she boasts.

.. If the Good Ole Boys are as afraid of their Blushing Southern Belles as Ms. King contends, they must be petrified of her. She is, in the vernacular, a liberated woman. She knows what she wants and where she is going, and no man is going to get in her way again.

"I was turned down for the state wire desk in Raleigh," she says. "They wanted a man."

But, she quickly adds, "I've never felt bad about being a woman. Oh some women are as timid as churchmice and are really scared of men. I can't stand people who are afraid. Nor can I worry about tempests in teapots. This 'chairperson' business is driving me crazy. I don't mind being called 'chairman.' After all . . . I know I'm female."

She also knows that her work comes first. She's been here for almost two years and knows hardly a soul. Entertainment has meant ferryboat rides to Winslow and watching Archie Bunker. "He's the only Good Ole Boy I like." But marriage is out. "No time. I don't even have time for an affair. Sex takes time and energy and that means time and energy away from my work. And sex can ruin a beautiful friendship."

Work right now, besides her upcoming Viva missive, includes work on two books. One, "The Male Chauvinist Courtroom," takes a hard look at the fate of several women who have been tried for murder. "I'm finding that if the woman was the 'decent' type, she was treated fairly by the all-male juries. But if there was evidence of extramarital activity . . ."

Also in the running is an epic-length venture about five women, their lives since 1953, and their reckoning with both male and female chauvinism. Ms. King has high hopes for both books. But not so for two suspense novels now circulating among the New York publishing houses. "They're terrible," she confesses. "I just don't have a manipulative mind."

Manipulative? Possibly not. But certainly original. The telephone company found that out.

When she moved here in July, 1972, making good a childhood vow to visit Seattle, Ms. King asked Ma Bell for a red, "trimline" phone. The company's barrage of personal questions ticked her off. And she certainly must have baffled the phone company. She owns no car, has no credit or credit cards, owes not one cent, and is a . . . writer. Hmmm.

She zeroed in on a Bell executive. "I am single," she wrote, "therefore additionally suspect. Plus I am a woman, which makes matters even more tragic. People simply do not believe I can make ends meet, whereas in reality, I have much more money at my disposal than married couples who are often strapped for cash."

She promised to pay her phone bill each month, in person, in cash. In return, she asked the exec to write her a letter of commendation at the end of a year (he did, incidentally).

"P.S.," she snorted, "for your business office records, my blood type is A Positive, and I wear a Number 80 diaphram."

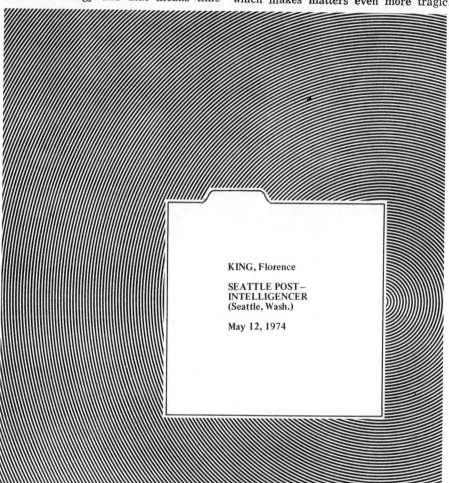

The Kirks in Mecosta Usually Have a Lot of Company

By Bob Burns

OLIVET — Russell Kirk, Ph.D., is proud that he was among the first to boost Gerald R. Ford for president of the United States.

Dr. Kirk, one of the nation's leading conservative intellectuals, wrote to Richard M. Nixon before the 1964 election, telling him the Grand Rapids Republican congressman would be the best man for the job.

Dr. Kirk also said he wrote to Nixon before the 1960 election, recommending Ford as his vice presidential running mate.

These were a few of the things the 56-year-old Kirk, a critic, essayist, historian of ideas, biographer, novelist, syndicated columnist, broadcaster and lecturer, talked about last Wednesday afternoon on the campus of Olivet College.

He also talked about his haunted house in Mecosta, which ironically burned to the ground 12 hours after this interview.

At Olivet, where he gave three series of formal lectures, Dr. Kirk got around to politics by pointing out that he was probably the original "Ford for President" booster.

"I began writing about this to Richard Nixon and others before the Goldwater campaign in 1964," he said. "I told them that Gerald Ford would be the ideal Republican candidate. That didn't come to pass, so I supported Mr. Goldwater.

"I wrote on different occasions to Mr. Nixon, when he was obviously going to be the presidential candidate, saying your vice presidential candidate should be Mr. Ford. He replied that he had the highest opinion of Mr. Ford and he'd take my recommendation into consideration. But, of course, nothing ever came of it, I'm sure later to his sorrow because obviously Henry Cabot Lodge didn't do him any good and Spiro Agnew did him a great deal of mischief.

"So if he would have had Mr. Ford things might have been a lot different for him."

Dr. Kirk believes Ford, who replaced Agnew as vice president in late 1973 and then became President when Nixon resigned six months ago, is in a much more difficult position today than if he had been nominated and elected years ago.

"Ford probably couldn't have won against President Johnson any more than Sen. Goldwater could, but he probably would have made a better showing," Dr. Kirk said.

"But supposing the assassination of President Kennedy hadn't taken place and Gerald Ford had been nominated in 1964. I think Ford probably would have won as thing went then, which was before all the great mass of trouble, problems and burdens descended upon the presidency.

"Now, of course, the circumstances are very difficult indeed and I'll be taking this up soon in debates with Frank Mankiewicz."

Dr. Kirk said President Ford is being increasingly saddled as President Hoover was saddled with the blame for all kinds of policies and problems which are inherited from earlier administrations.

"Whether President Ford can surmount that blame, as Mr. Hoover did not, remains to be seen," Dr. Kirk said. "Nevertheless, despite Mr. Ford's temporary decline in popularity between his taking office and the present, he seems to be regaining strength in public opinion.

"He certainly retains his reputation for probity and honesty and shows a good deal of strength and vigor, remarked upon even by some of the former McGovern supporters.

"Although he faces a hostile Congress, he faces also a confused Congress, as inexperienced as the Congress Franklin Roosevelt brought with him into office in 1933. But unlike that Congress without a strong President to lead them, a strong President confronts them now.

"There is Mr. Ford's chief political opportunity, that he may accomplish something by telling the public — as Harry Truman did successfully — that Congress has caused the trouble and confusion by its inaction and only by restoring some vigor to the presidency of some coherent policy can we make any headway against our present discontents.

"Obviously, President Ford's most immediate problem is the continuing inflation and here he already has had to make large concessions in order to have any prospect of working with Congress at all. But soon there must come a test of strength there. He must exercise the veto, whether successful or not, against the various budgetary proposals and if the vetos are overridden, then he must turn to the public as in somewhat different circumstances Franklin Roosevelt turned to the public.

"Mr. Ford is quite a convincing, obviously honest speaker on television and radio. And while we are not to expect he'll enjoy the same successes that Franklin Roosevelt did with his fireside talks, nevertheless considerable potentialities lie there. And so I still have a great deal of confidence in Gerald Ford and I hope he may be the kind of President which I began to hope some 15 years ago that he might become."

Dr. Kirk said he has known a few presidents — Hoover, Johnson and Nixon. "And I spent a few days in Mr. Ford's company at a conference in Chicago," he said.

"I've known none intimately, but I've done a good deal of meditating on them."

Dr. Kirk said he had an interesting conversation with President Nixon a few days after the Cambodian campaign started.

"On the day all the young demonstrators appeared in Washington 2½ years ago," he said, "Mr. Nixon asked me to the White House to converse with him on general topics and indeed they were general topics. He didn't talk about Cambodia or other immediate tribulations, but rather about the question of whether America was decadent, obviously concerned with his own responsibilities.

"He told me he didn't think the people wanted him to be a moralizer or give them sermons. Nevertheless, he mentioned that he had this responsibility for the future of this country. And so he said, 'Mr. Kirk, do we have any hope?' And he repeated the question. He obviously was terribly depressed by the burdens of the office.

"I said, 'Well, Mr. President, it's all a question of belief. If the majority of the people believe the prophets of doom and say there indeed is no hope, then hope ceases to exist because people will withdraw into their own little corners, refuse to cooperate and things will fall apart. If on the other hand, people don't believe the prophets of doom and say there is hope, then hope exists because they begin to cooperate, to be energetic, to assume responsibilities. So it's a question of belief.' "

Dr. Kirk said Nixon's spirits revived somewhat at his answer and he went on to compare America with the Byzantine Empire, the eastern part of the Roman Empire, continuing after the fall of Rome as its successor until 1453.

"I pointed out that America is young, that we've only had two centuries or 3½ centuries if you count the colonial experience compared to a thousand years of the Byzantine Empire," Dr. Kirk recalled.

"I pointed out that the Byzantine Empire went through a long series of declines, recoveries, declines, recoveries and I told Mr. Nixon that is what probably lies before us. Nobody or no human institution lasts forever, no nation endures always, but we probably still have a long history to go. And we may indeed, even in our present discontent, on the verge of an Augustan Age, a chastened renewal of American vigor."

Then Nixon, Dr. Kirk said, turned to the question of where a president gets his support.

"Nixon said that although people thought he got his support from big business, he ➡

KIRK, Russell (Amos) (1918-)
GRAND RAPIDS PRESS (Grand Rapids, Mich.)
Feb. 16, 1975
[See also CA-1]

(Continued from preceding page)

said that wasn't the case because whenever there was a hard decision to make they were conspicious by their absence," Dr. Kirk said.

"He said he had some friends in the Academy, but not many. And the backing of Main Street. But he was obviously perplexed as to where he should turn. And, of course, he grew much more perplexed and found himself theoretically endowed with more power than anyone in the world, nevertheless helpless even to save himself, let alone others."

Dr. Kirk also recalls a meeting he had with President Johnson.

"I went to see President Johnson in his office to present him a copy of my book about Robert Taft," he said. "He had given one of the funeral eulogies of Sen. Taft and both my wife and I were struck with the fact that he was almost a walking corpse. He was a big, strong man who at this point was heavily made up to preserve color.

"Still, he was physically vigorous, but just beginning to shuffle. And a kind of hollow man, overwhelmed by the office, still a practical politician, still talking while we were there with Sen. Byrd and Sen. Tydings about political deals, but obviously not knowing really where to turn, used to political infighting, wheeling and dealing, but unable to cope with the vast decisions being thrust upon him every five or 10 minutes."

Dr. Kirk said the man who probably has been the most capable president was Herbert Hoover, who was magnificently prepared for the office by experience.

"Hoover was a highly intelligent man, wide fund of knowledge and a hard worker," he said. "But again, he failed largely because of a rather withdrawn and shy personality which prevented him from appealing to the public or indeed making those compromises which he could have made to prevent many of the disasters that fell upon him."

One of the burning questions these days, Dr. Kirk said, is to find the kind of man who possibly can endure these burdens.

"Obviously," he said, "we must stop piling burdens upon the presidency because any person has only 24 hours in a day and no one can stand this strain. But the fact remains that we must find a man with considerable combinations of qualities for the future presidency.

"We'll see how Mr. Ford holds up underneath this. I think he has the stamina and practical experience in the sense of experience within Congress. He may lack imagination as President Hoover tended to lack imagination and as did Presidents Johnson and Nixon. But Nixon tried to attract imaginative people such as Henry Kissinger and Daniel Patrick Moynihan around him.

"But aside from Mr. Ford's situation, what sort of man are we going to find in the future for the presidency? Among the qualities he should have is a high imagination, large practical experience of government, a sense of humor and the command of rhetoric. Among the people in prospect, the one who seems the most possessed of these varied talents is Elliot Richardson, who has been rather pushed aside into the embassy — the Court of St. James — recently."

Dr. Kirk said he thinks Richardson will stay very active in politics and may one day be the Republican nominee. "I feel he could draw a great deal of Democratic support, too," he said.

Dr. Kirk, as a visiting professor here, gave formal lectures on Edmund Burke, T. S. Eliot and the reform of higher education.

"I also am doing a lot of other things at the same time," he said. "It's too bad the day doesn't last a little longer.

KIRK, Russell (Amos)

GRAND RAPIDS PRESS
(Grand Rapids, Mich.)

Feb. 16, 1975

"Let's see — I keep up my nationally syndicated column in newspapers which is distributed by the Los Angeles Times syndicate. I do that twice a week. And I write my monthly page for National Review and a good deal other journalism.

"Here at Olivet I also have given separate guest lectures on Rousseau, one to the University Christian Fellowship on 'Christianity Today,' another one on 'The Teaching of Criticism' and another one on 'Shakespeare's Historical Plays.' "

Dr. Kirk said he'll be at Albion College this coming week for a debate with Frank Mankiewicz, who managed Sen. George McGovern's presidential campaign in 1972.

"We'll debate on the 'State of the Union—Who's to Blame?'," Dr. Kirk said.

As for what's on tap in the next month, Dr. Kirk said he'll journey to St. Mary's College in Los Angeles for a talk on the bicentenary, to the University of the South in Sewanee, Tenn., for another debate with Mankiewicz, to Cornell College in Mt. Vernon, Iowa, for "a talk on something or other," and to Washington, D.C., for a talk to the Intercollegiate Studies Institutes on the moral foundations of America's formative era and to various places in the state for meetings of the Michigan Bicentennial Commission, of which he is a member.

"Oh, yes," he said, "I have to speak soon at Coker College in Hartsville, S.C., and at a meeting of school administrators and teachers at Newburgh, N.Y."

Despite a heavy schedule that often takes him out of the state, Dr. Kirk said he always has been a Michiganian.

"I was born at Plymouth," he said, "almost literally in the Detroit railway yards."

Russ, whose father was a locomotive engineer, attended Plymouth High School and "to my amazement I obtained a scholarship to Michigan State because a scholarship was very rare to those days."

He went on to graduate study for a year at Duke University "because I had nothing else to do during that period of the Roosevelt recession."

After getting his master degree, Kirk came back to Michigan and worked at Greenfield Village and then at the aircraft engineer division of the Ford Rouge plant at the beginning of World War II.

"I went into the Army and served four years there in the chemical warfare service, mostly in the desert and the jungle," he said.

After his discharge, Kirk was offered a post at Michigan State University where he taught the history of civilization "off and on for about four years."

It was about that time he decided to see more of the world, to learn more. "I had read an essay by Sir D'Arcy Thompson in his book, 'Science and the Classics,' " Dr. Kirk said. "It was an essay about St. Andrew's Universitv of Scotland. I was taken by that essay, I applied and spent four years off and on at St. Andrew's and became the only American ever to receive the highest degree of St. Andrew's University, the degree of doctor of letters."

Dr. Kirk, the only American ever to receive this earned degree, said only one other person in the world holds the Saffron Gown from St. Andrew's.

"When I returned from Scotland to Michigan," he said, "I was disgusted with the decline of educational standards generally and resigned at Michigan State in protest against the lowering of standards in 1953. That's when I became a professional writer, more by need than by choice."

Dr. Kirk said he is one of the few surviving serious men of letters who really lives by his trade.

"The Internal Revenue says there are only about 100 people in the whole country who list themselves as writers," he said. "And that includes all kinds of pornographers, so the actual serious writer is a very rare breed nowadays."

Time and Newsweek magazines have described Dr. Kirk as one of America's leading thinkers. He has authored 18 books ➡

(Continued from preceding page)

and several hundred periodical essays, short stories and long reviews.

"My best working hours are from 8 p.m. to 8 a.m.," he said.

Most of his works has been written in his library-study in Mecosta, which is 25 miles west of Central Michigan University. Five years ago he donated more than 4,000 manuscripts and correspondence to the Clarke Historical Library at CMU. And he has donated books to Hillsdale College.

Dr. Kirk's first book, "John Randolph of Roanoke," was published in 1951 and his most recent work is "The Roots of American Order."

There obviously is a market for Dr. Kirk's thoughts, too, for more than one million copies of his books have been sold. His best known book probably has been "The Conservative Mind," which has been translated into several languages since it first went to press in 1953.

"I've written all kinds of things," he said. "I've done books not only on political theory, but on American history and St. Andrew's University as well as a series of ghost stories, a baroque novel and what I call a Gothic novel."

The Gothic novel, "Old House of Fear," was published a decade ago and has outsold all of his serious work put together, he said. said.

"That book revived the Gothic novel in America," he said. "And it's still going great guns."

Dr. Kirk said he has enjoyed writing books on education such as "Academic Freedom" and "The Intemperate Professor and Other Cultural Splenetics." His "Eliot and His Age: T. S. Eliot's Moral Imagination in the 20th Century" has been well received.

He did a book on personal thoughts and experiences called "Confessions of a Bohemian Tory."

"I have a couple of volumes published on literary criticism," he said. "And I contribute to a wide range of magazines, running from the Journal of the History of Ideas to various political science reviews and critical journals like Sewanee Review and Kenyon Review to the Saturday Evening Post and the London Mystery Magazine beside my syndicated newspaper column, 'To the Point.' which is published in more than 100 daily newspapers."

Dr. Kirk was a bachelor for the first 45 years of his life.

Then about 11 years ago he met Annette Yvonne Cecile Courtemanche on a lecture platform in New York.

"She was only 18 or 19 years old," he said, "and a great beauty, whom I described in my National Review page as the conservative beauty. We got to know each other better and we were married in 1965. So Annette transferred from Long Island to Mecosta where she's very happy.

"We have three little daughters, Monica, 7; Cecilia, 6; and Felicia, 4."

Dr. Kirk said his own life is bound up in Mecosta where he has lived ever since he became a man of letters.

"I live there in a house built a century ago by my great-grandfather, Amos Johnson, whose uncle was the great lumber baron of those parts," Dr. Kirk said. "Amos Johnson really founded Mecosta and he later became judge of probate in the county."

The house Dr. Kirk refers to is the one that burned to the ground early Thursday morning, but here are the comments he made about it Wednesday afternoon. "The house my great-grandfather built is notoriously haunted.

"My great-grandfather and his generation were Sweden Borgians and spiritualists," he said. "And those influences seem to linger on. Apparitions are seen from time to time, not so much by members of the family as by guests who we put into the haunted rooms, not for malice but because those are the guests rooms available.

KIRK, Russell (Amos)

GRAND RAPIDS PRESS
(Grand Rapids, Mich.)

Feb. 16, 1975

"The house on what is called Piety Hill has considerable charm and we've added a wing, which is kind of like a tail wagging the dog. It's bigger than the original house, but generally in the same style.

"In the 1870s, my great-grandfather owned a great deal of land around Mecosta, but that all fell away in the Panic of '93 which ruined Mecosta and Mecosta has been ruined ever since. So now I have just about 45 acres on which I planted a great many trees.

"The house is always full of people, not only my three daughters, my wife and myself, but for instance, we now have two students, one from Ohio and one from California who are engaged in private study with me and they will receive college credit for it.

"I have an assistant and there's a girl who is the daughter of friends of mine who is studying to be a nurse. Then we have Clinton Wallace, who is a giant and 58 years old. He's the strongest man I've ever known. He's been a hobo almost all of his life. We picked him up on the road one day and he stayed with us. But he sometimes goes away for excursions on his own and when he returns he makes himself useful by setting the table, shoveling the snow, mowing the lawn and reciting poetry at great length to our three little daughters."

Dr. Kirk said Clinton has memorized poetry in public libraries all of his life and has been a great source of knowledge and wisdom for his daughters.

"Not long ago," Dr. Kirk said, "my oldest daughter Monica asked me how are cirrus clouds formed. I said I knew once, but have forgotten and will look that up.

"She replied, 'I'll ask Clinton. He knows everything.' "

Dr. Kirk said others have joined his menage from time to time. He said his wife is very convivial and a great organizer. "Annette," he said, "is also one of the two most active people on the bicentennial committee in Mecosta County. She's also active on the social services board and is engaged in a work of reform there. So I'd say we have an ideal marriage."

Dr. Kirk, who is the Michigan regent of the American Scottish Foundation, said he and his wife have spent a great deal of their time in Scotland. "I used to go there every year," he said, "and we used to have a 17th century house that I restored. I sold it in recent years, but we still get over there frequently."

Dr. Kirk said he likes to travel when he can. "When I don't have any obligations," he said, "we'll usually go someplace. This June, we plan to go to Madeira, where we haven't been before."

When he's not writing, Dr. Kirk said his favorite diversion is walking.

"I don't do as much walking around Mecosta as I used to because of the growth of lake cottages and what not," he said, "but I love to walk around Scotland. If I have a companion, I like to walk about 40 miles a day.

"I also like conversation as a relaxation and a diversion."

Dr. Kirk said people often ask him "What can you possibly find to do at Mecosta?"

"Of course," he said, "we are incessantly busy with gatherings of friends from Ferris State College on one side and Central Michigan University on the other. And there are all kinds of civic affairs, church affairs and conferences we hold.

"For example, between Christmas and New Year's we had a conference in our house of students and recent graduates who belong to the Intercollegiate Studies Institute, a national organization. About 25 of them stayed in the house and we had four or five days of discussion with myself and Prof. M. E. Bradford of the University of Dallas.

"That sort of thing goes on frequently so our problem is not one of trying to atone for mischief done by idle hands, but where to find enough minutes in the day to fill in all our activities."

Up, down and other misconceptions

By FLETCHER KNEBEL

Not long ago an image surfaced in my memory of a 6-year-old kid in Jackson Heights, N. Y., watching an old steam shovel gouge a pit for building foundations. I recall the boy's feeling of fright and revulsion as the machine clawed at the weedy field where he played with other kids. In the child's eyes, an iron enemy assaulted his turf with evil intent.

That image of myself and my reactions remained buried for more than half a century beneath civilization's topping of rationality, technology and unlimited production. It popped up as I considered the theme of this article: my attitudes have changed enormously in the 40 years since I, an urban, middle-class young man, went forth from Miami University, Oxford, O., with the class of '34. I judge that little of the change can be attributed to the classic gulf between youth and age since many of my current views are shared by the young.

The turbulent sixties, with their cries of revolution and their bitter indictment of the established order, made a profound impression on me. Much as I recoiled from the rhetoric and violence of the New Left, I was forced to re-examine basic assumptions. Yet I failed to sense the extent of my attitude changes until, in these less strident days, I tried to codify hundreds of tumbling impressions and attitudes. Here's the result, subject, as befits our era, to change without notice.

Back then, EXPANSION FOREVER! The America of the first half of my life was one of limitless horizons, soaring expectations, progress, production, prosperity, abundance, expanding forever and ever, amen. Despite its miseries, the Great Depression, which I weathered in college, was seen as but an embarrassing pause in a production miracle which would fetch each American family a spacious home, vacations abroad and two cars in every garage. If the slothful poor of the rest of the world would but follow our example, mass production would surely yield at least a modest cottage with indoor plumbing to every family from the Yangtze to the Amazon.

It was fashionable among young people with intellectual pretensions to scoff at those crafting this forthcoming cornucopia. I joined a handful of would-be cynics in college who reveled in Sinclair Lewis's satire of "Babbitt" and H. L. Mencken's disdain for the "boobs" of the "Bible belt." But I merely parroted. Deep down, I believed. The American Dream soothed all our slumbers. We had but to get on with the job. The JOB. Ah, there lay salvation and riches.

WORLD WAR II confirmed the magnificence of American production. We literally smothered our enemies under an avalanche of arms, all swiftly fabricated, including the manufacture of more than 100,000 warplanes a year at the peak. I came home from the Azores and shed my naval uniform, convinced of American superiority in everything from guns to games. We almost always won the Olympics, didn't we?

But we Americans regarded ourselves as more than assembly-line geniuses and medalist athletes. We had built a spiritual haven, a land of justice for all, refuge for the world's oppressed masses. We saw ourselves as a compassionate people who would share our ideals and some of our bounty with less fortunate humans. As our missionaries once fanned out to bring the blessings of Yankee culture to the savages, so would our Government's foreign aid and our businessmen transform the world in our image. As the power with primary responsibility for mankind, we would chart a course to universal peace, property and social justice.

While I chafed over the mouthings of our more chauvinistic propagandists, I bought the package. A society dominated by the doctrine of material expansion for all is as comforting as it is heady. If there are no limits save individual torpor, then any energetic citizen can attain the bliss of success. So I had a satisfying sense of the fitness and continuity of our way of life. We Americans had the answer.

Now, CONTRACTION. Today I look at the same scene and fear that our vaunted technology and our good American "answer" have become blasphemies against ravaged nature. While medicine cuts the death rate, uncapping a population gush that adds several hundred thousand people a day to the earth's teeming total, the machine and the tarnished miracle of mass production poison the air, land and water. By-products of our automated and swarming civilization read like the protocols of doomsday: cancer in trout, lethal oil spills, vanishing wetlands, whole mountains carved away for iron, copper and other metals devoured by our dishwashers, tractors and air-conditioners, pastures and farmlands paved to superhighways, sludge from dumped refuse threatening to contaminate the shining beaches of Long Island, swiftly dwindling forests and wild life. But why go on? Litanies of ecological atrocities have become commonplace.

My attitude on industrial expansion has changed 180 degrees. Now I believe that in our feverish preoccupation with consumer goods we are looting our only home, EARTH. Now "Small Is Beautiful," to borrow the title of a brilliant book by E. F. Schumacher, a British economist who notes that "infinite growth in a finite environment is an obvious impossibility." Of course, but for five decades of my life, I thought and acted as though it weren't. For years I ignored what my eyes, ears and nose told me on the screeching highways, beside the belching factories and along the fouled rivers and streams.

IF I HAD swung 179 degrees by 1974, two events this Summer completed the reversal. One came in the shape of a 19-mile-long traffic jam on the Garden State Parkway in New Jersey that lasted six hours, snarling 75,000 cars. The ➡

KNEBEL, Fletcher
(1911 -)

AKRON BEACON
JOURNAL
(Akron, Ohio)

Oct. 27, 1974

[See also CA-1]

(Continued from preceding page)

other was a two-part New Yorker article by Noel Mostert who wrote of ocean waters south of the Cape of Good Hope fouled by oil spills from supertankers carrying Arab petroleum to the world's refineries. Monster tankers, ranging from 200,000 to almost 500,000 tons, crack open in wild southern seas, imperiling not only their own crews, but seabirds, fish and other aquatic life in one of the last virgin oceans, breeding place for many species.

I'm indebted to the Whole Earth Catalog for the estimate that 25 tons of irreplaceable ores must be extracted from the ground each year to keep each American going in the style to which he's accustomed.

Occasionally now, I have twinges of panic. My once comfortable civilization seems out of control and headed for catastrophe. And I'm forced to make the link between the oceans' imperiled phytoplankton, conveying o x y g e n we all breathe, and my own lifestyle which depends so heavily on oil. Our Mustang, house furnace and swimming-pool heater feed on it.

Various exhaustible fuels and metals propel my travels and sustain my American consumption habits in a thousand ways. I realize I argue from a privileged position. Money from a number of successful novels provides me a haven from which to decry aspects of a system which made the leisure and rewards possible in the first place. Most workers, depending on weekly pay checks, have no such haven.

While a substantial cut in production might trim my income in a few years, it would mean quick loss of jobs for millions. What I yearn for, and what no national political leader dares advocate, is public policy that charts a slow, equitable transition from unlimited production and consumption to a society of curtailed mass production, high craftsmanship and greatly expanded human services.

In the meantime, I face a moral question: Is it right to partake of this manic consumption which surely must deplete the planet some day? I think not, but I continue to live a style that belies my conviction. I frankly lack the initiative and courage to follow the example of those who live close to the soil, in rhythm with nature and with a minimum of machines and gadgets.

Yet my new attitude persists, nagging me for commitment, and from this basic shift devolves a whole set of auxiliary attitudes. They include:

THE AUTOMOBILE

While I never had the love affair with my car ascribed to so many Americans, I regarded it as a handy convenience for going places with a maximum of ease and freedom. I now view its unrestricted use and multiplication as a national disaster. It kills about 55,000 people annually, injures more than two million people a year, converts hundreds of square miles from green acres to sterile pavement, befouls t h e atmosphere, changes beauty to schlock, drains the cities and makes millions of scattered American households fortresses of isolation. Yet the car has become such a crucial factor in the economy that any proposed shift to mass transport embattles a maze of car-linked lobbies and raises the specter of depression.

WORK

For many years I worked compulsively. I felt virtuous about it, for my society had enshrined w o r k and its purifying benefits since Puritan days. L e i s u r e, play or silent contemplation were suspect. I felt guilty when I wasn't either working or preparing to work and grew irritable when "wasting time," a peculiarly American concept. Today I regard compulsive work as I do any other compulsive act — damaging to the psyche. I view unnecessary work as an abomination and I see no enrichment of personality in those millions of dreary, repetitive jobs on the assembly lines of factory and office dictated by a machine-dominated culture.

Work, as I now see it, falls into two broad slots: the tedious routine chores necessary to survival and the kind of creative endeavor that does nourish the spirit and expand horizons. I believe in performing the first as quickly as possible without any cant about ennoblement. The second, embracing a thousand crafts from carpentry to watchmaking, can be made a vehicle of dignity, joy and pride, but only if society places the needs of the worker above those of the machine. But how can this be done in the age of mass production? You tell me. I'm stating an attitude, not a solution.

NO. 1.

I once took quiet pride in America's seeming superiority in forging the good life. Now I believe that if the whole world followed our example, we would quickly mount an ecological and spiritual fiasco. The last thing Bolivia needs is three million Cadillacs and Ford station wagons racing up and down its mountains, while Africa n e e d s industrial wastes in Lake Victoria, on the pattern of polluted Lake Erie, about as much as it needs the transcendental succor of Disneyland. Now I think that if America would but pause and listen to some of the so-called backward societies, we might gain insights on formulation of a desperately needed new set of values.

COMPETITION

Compete, win, beat out the other guy. So read the counsel of my youth. Pulpit, school and locker room chanted the vast character glories deriving from unfettered struggles to win. I believed. I competed with vigor. Up Knebel. Down you and you and you. I knew elation when I won, misery when I lost. But a funny t h i n g happened on my way through life. I found that, not competition, but cooperation turned me on. I've discovered that the psychic energy generated by group efforts can galvanize and enrich me more than many of my solo stints at the typewriter.

POPULATION

The few savants worrying 40 years ago about the peril of too many human bodies on this small planet did not include me. I assumed that the production of babies in quantity was as much a part of the natural order as the manufacture of refrigerators and radios. I looked with interest and equanimity on those pictures which used to grace the newspapers. Caption: "Mr. and Mrs. Horace Smith celebrate 25th wedding anniversary with their 17 children." When I was a young reporter in Ohio, we had a local judge whose popularity stemmed as much from his prowess in helping to spawn 13 children as from the caliber of his decisions. I did not quarrel with that public assessment.

My attitude changed gradually with the drip of statistics, the sprouting of h u g e highrise apartments and the sprawl of housing developments over meadow and cornfield. Today, with an estimated four billion humans on earth, many of them starving, and predictions of eight billion by early next century, I favor almost every population curb save war and famine.

I'm for birth control devices, vasectomy, abortion and penalty taxes on parents of large families. In an age of dwindling natural resources on a finite earth, I think the champions of reproduction should at least pay something toward the added fuel, water, food and beer cans their offspring will require.

RATIONALITY

American and Western culture, to which I subscribed, extolled the brain beyond all other human wonders. The mind conceived such marvels as science, progress and the indoor flush toilet. Emotions, feeling, intuition and felicities of the body bore the tag: "Use With Caution." Had a cartoonist depicted the prevailing creed of my youth, he would have shown the shaggy head of Albert Einstein above a mechanical body. The prize word was rationality, acclaimed in the West since Rene Descartes said more than three centuries ago: "I think, therefore I am."

I spent more than three adult decades under the spell of undiluted rationality without realizing that Descarte's dictum did not mesh with my own experience, which told me: "I'm aware, therefore I am," the awareness encompassing both thought and sensation.

Back to that steam shovel in Jackson Heights. The 6-year-old's reaction to the earth mover holds more truth for me today than much of what I learned rationally in school, college and 27 years covering Washington as a political reporter. Is this merely the case of a 62-year-old man entering second childhood before the onslaught of senility? I doubt it. For how is the rational to be trusted when today's rational judgment turns out to be tomorrow's absurdity? I think the boy, possessed of scant knowledge, but with a full operational set of those marvelous human senses, was right on.

My change has occurred in the last four or five years as I sampled a smorgasbord of what is loosely called the human potential movement — sensitivity training, encounter g r o u p s, sensory awareness, husband-wife seminars, yoga, meditation and most recently T'ai Chi.

KNEBEL, Fletcher

AKRON BEACON JOURNAL
(Akron, Ohio)

Oct. 27, 1974

(Continued from preceding page)

I have learned enough to understand my ignorance about my own body and to rue those spare hours in a long journalistic career that might have been devoted to self-discovery. Inner space, I find, holds infinite wonders to match those of outer space. The range of my feelings, long suppressed, astounds me and I'm learning to trust those feelings.

I am truly me when I sense the breeze brushing my face, the sun splashing my body or my eyes catching the flutter of a leaf. I do not denigrate the brain. I still marvel at its capacities, but a brain without an aware body belongs only in a medical museum. From this basic shift in viewpoint, a number of altered attitudes flow.

YESTERDAY, TODAY AND TOMORROW

I spent much of my life either anticipating the future or regretting the past. I dwelt restlessly and somewhat apprehensively in the immediate now. These days I confine thoughts of my own future to a modest amount of supposedly prudent planning. When the past intrudes without insight for today, I try to move on. Being aware of myself and my surroundings in the here and now offers an exciting new life. The first precept in "An Eschatological Laundry List" compiled by Shelly Kopp reads: "This is it!" This moment, this instant. Life postponed, I find, is life unlived.

KNEBEL, Fletcher

AKRON BEACON JOURNAL (Akron, Ohio)

Oct. 27, 1974

CONTROL

Self-control, the stiff upper lip, maintaining a pose of imperturbability amid seething emotions, these stood as bywords in my upbringing in the WASP middle class. Later I witnessed my own mother's breakdown, in part resulting from tensions caused by the clash between that code of behavior and her suppressed emotions. Now I believe that self-exposure, a rich emotional life and an awareness of one's own vulnerability offer some keys to health and enjoyment. I thought more, not less, of Sen. Edmund S. Muskie of Maine when he wept publicly in New Hampshire during the 1972 campaign. I believe the person accustomed to open display of emotion is less likely to panic in a crisis than the uptight one who never ventures far from home without a bland, dispassionate mask. To be human is to be vulnerable. The most poignant, beautiful moments of the sexual act occur when the partners cease all efforts of self-control and let emotions sweep them to ecastasy. Which brings up:

SEXUALITY

As a son of a Y.M.C.A. secretary and grandson of pious fundamentalists, I may have undergone more preachments against sex than the average child. Yet clues from society at large told all of us that sex was at best a necessary evil, at worst animalistic rutting that corrupted the soul beyond redemption if practiced for goals other than reproduction. Yet every schoolboy knew that adults had an abiding urge to use their genitals. We lived behind a veil of Victorian hypocrisy from which we peeped longingly at whorehouses, "loose" women and French post cards. At Y.M.C.A. camp, a renowned evangelist warned that masturbation would reduce us all to gibbering idiots. In retrospect, this skein of stupefying nonsense seems beyond all credibility even to one who lived through it. It warped many beyond repair and while I came through only partially damaged, echoes of my boyhood still whisper darkly that illicit sex holds an allure unknown to the legal varieties.

I find today's sexual climate, whatever its surely temporary excesses, far more reasonable and comfortable. I enjoy the erotic. I love the nude female form. I rejoiced in the youthful slogan during the Vietnam nightmare: "Make love, not war." I've lost my taste for dirty jokes. Robust, healthy sex can be radiant, beautiful and powerful and when one views sexuality as an integral part of nature's oneness, life becomes invested with new energy and exhilaration.

AUTHORITY AND CONSENSUS

As a young man I accepted the touted wisdom of authority with but sporadic grumbling and rebellion. Deans, divines, judges, generals and American Presidents had the word. Later, covering Washington, while I saw clay feet and seamy motivations, I for the most part respected authority, gave it obedience and felt guilty when I defied it.

Vietnam changed all that. Initially, I have mindless assent to this extravagant military expendition to the other side of the globe. My wife's opposition was instantaneous and enduring. In discussions I flared angrily like the flagwearers of later years. She had challenged my America, the great and the good. Authority informed us that if the Vietnam domino toppled, then dominoes would crash across Asia and Europe and Communist hordes would threaten the fairest domino of all, the mighty double-six, America. Gradually and painfully I changed, persuaded by my wife and millions of other dissenters from campus to corporate suite. A stench at last filled my nostrils, a stench of bodies blasted by bombers, children broiled in napalm, forests defoliated by chemicals, prisoners dumped from helicopters, civilians riddled in ditches. I saw my country as a swaggering bully engaged in a futile, brutal, immoral enterprise.

And who had triggered America's ugliest epoch but "The Best and the Brightest," to use David Halberstam's apt title, the cream of the American Establishment. They reeked of authority and their blunder had tragic consequences for all of us. Nor was that the end of it.

Men of authority hatched the Bay of Pigs, the invasion of the Dominican Republic, "black" operations of the C. I. A., including such deeds in defense of democracy as murder, bribery, theft and torture and finally Watergate, where the highest authority visited on Americans some of the crimes that had been lavished on foreigners for years under the guise of "national security." I've had a bellyful of unrestrained authority and I trust I'll never again give blind allegiance to anyone solely because of the office held. Many attitude changes devolve from this one. Here is one sample.

JUSTICE

I once believed that the United States system of law and order treated all citizens alike. Disabused of such naivete while covering police and courts as a young newsman in Chattanooga, Toledo and Cleveland, I still believed the law's inequities were more aberrational than endemic. I forgot, of course, that I viewed the police station and courtroom through the eyes of a white, middleclass male who wore a coat and tie and lived at an address deemed "decent." Police outrages against blacks, students, hippies and Chicanos during the rebellious sixties changed my mind. Power and privilege forever tilt the scales of justice in this world and I was a fool to ignore the fact. Perhaps the post-Watergate climate since the fall of Richard Nixon will help balance the scales in America. I hope so, but I wouldn't want to test fate by driving to a sheriff's convention with a "Support Your Local Revolutionaries" bumper sticker.

SAFETY AND TERROR

The first half of my life passed in a comforting aura of safety and familiarity in suburban areas of New York, Chicago, Cleveland and Washington, D. C. In our middleclass neighborhoods murder, arson, assault and robbery seldom struck. The mass killers, wars, plagues and pogroms never threatened American borders. Nature might erupt occasionally, but man-made terror largely spared us. As for my country, it employed implements of war only in defense of liberty.

Then came Hiroshima, shattering my insular, snug feeling forever. On Aug. 6, 1945, with Japan already reeling to defeat under great waves of B-29's, the United States dropped the atomic bomb. In a split second a fireball of incredible intensity vaporized an entire city, killed some 100,000 civilians and condemned others to slow death by radiation. I remember the numbness I felt and the sense of creeping terror when the enormity of instant carnage overwhelmed me a few days later.

Proliferation of man-made terror in the three decades since the unclear weapon made a mockery of human "security" has reached almost incomprehensible lengths, from submarine fleets with pop-up hydrogen missiles capable of erasing civilization overnight to hundreds of nuclear projectiles, some of them hydra-headed MIRV's, poised in the prairies for the ultimate kill. I prefer to ignore the facts during most waking hours, but the terror lurks deep within me, venting occasionally in dreams of holocaustal fury.

I have a hunch that most of us have been psychologically maimed by the Hiroshima mentality which accepts mass incineration as an unavoidable, if unfortunate, aspect of human behavior.

So there, for what they're worth as you mull over your own views, are some of my attitude changes since the days of my youth. I lay no claim to infallible perception. You may conclude that some new attitudes are self-deceptive or unjustified. If you don't agree with me, I'm open to dialog. Just don't shout me down with quotes from high authority, please. (End)

(Also see preceding article)

Truth No Odder Than Fiction For Novelist Fletcher Knebel

Philadelphia Inquirer / ALEXANDER DEANS

By STEVE NEAL
Inquirer Staff Writer

PRINCETON, N. J.—Recent events in Washington may seem strange and unusual to most of us, but not tot the fans of political novelist Fletcher Knebel.

In his book "Night of Camp David," published in 1965, a President resigns with wounded dignity after a delegation of senators, shocked by damaging information about him, demands that he step down.

Sound familiar?

In another Knebel novel, "Vanished," a top Presidential adviser mysteriously disappears, arousing all sorts of speculation and intrigue. It turns out that Steve Geer, the hero of this 1968 book, is secretly negotiating with the Red Chinese.

Remember Henry Kissinger's spurious stomach illness in Pakistan?

Knebel's best known book, written in collaboration with Charles W. Bailey, is "Seven Days in May," a 1962 suspense story about a plot by the military to take over the United States government.

And probably the most frequently used headline in stories recounting Richard M. Nixon's last week in power was "Seven Days in August," an obvious play on the novel's title.

"The title has kind of gone into the American language," Knebel said recently taking off his shoes and settling down on a couch in the den of his cedar-paneled home about a mile south of Princeton University. "It's flattering to see it used so much. It's being used in a much broader context now. You see it used during almost any big government crisis in which the people seem to be the protagonist."

Knebel's almost uncanny way of being ahead of the news and giving his readers an "inside" look at Washington is no coincidence. Before he began writing novels, Knebel was a Washington correspondent, most recently with the now defunct Look magazine. The wall behind his work desk is decorated with photographs of a clean-shaven Knebel talking politics with the likes of Lyndon Johnson and John F. Kennedy; there is also a fan letter from Harry Truman and a number of journalism awards.

One naturally assumes Knebel is hard at work on still another suspenseful Washington yarn, which, if events repeat themselves, will become tomorrow's headlines.

But it's not safe to assume anything these days.

"I'm not touching anything around Washington for three or four years," Knebel says. "The reality is just too overwhelming. What kind of fiction book about politics would anyone buy after Watergate?"

His latest book, "The Bottom Line," to be published next month, deals with the world of big business. "There's a big conglomerate holding its annual meeting in Acapulco. The hierarchy gets to fighting over major issues — ecology versus production, worker democracy, and other issues. There's a lot of international politics in the book. One of the executives, the head of a tennis product subsidiary in Doylestown, is kidnaped by what appear to be Mexican guerillas."

KNEBEL, Fletcher

PHILADELPHIA INQUIRER
(Philadelphia, Penn.)

Aug. 26, 1974

Although Knebel's books have sold more than six million copies in the U. S. alone, that doesn't mean his work is taken seriously by highbrow critics. Indeed, their verdict on Knebel's work is nearly unanimous: His books are potboilers, with about as much literary merit as the script of a television soap opera.

"There are certain deficiencies in my work," Knebel concedes. "Naturally, anybody who makes a living writing would like to be acclaimed. But I know, realistically, that I'm a journalist, not a novelist. I don't think the depth of my insights throws long-term enlightenment on the human condition — which is what a great writer does."

"Now that I've kicked myself around," he says, "I will say that I think I do some things extremely well, like creating suspense. Life is suspenseful. And the only thing a writer can do is make his books more suspenseful. I think I do this really well—and I'm getting better at it.

"Also, I reveal a lot of authentic Washington background that people wouldn't get unless they had worked there in government or as a member of the press. My writing fills in motivations pretty well. Reporters can't deal with this because of libel laws."

Knebel says he got the idea for "Seven Days In May" after a meeting with Curtis LeMay, the superhawkish Air Force general. "It was right after the Bay of Pigs," Knebel recalls. "And it was no secret that LeMay had read Kennedy out for not acting more decisively. Some thought he and others like him would have liked to have overthrown the government."

Twelve years later, Knebel's attitude has changed, primarily because of a long talk with a man he will identify only as "a former chief of naval operations."

"There's really no threat of a military dictatorship, he told me, because all officers going through the military academies are picked politically," Knebel says. "They're very aware that they owe their career to politicians.

"He also told me, 'We don't have to take over because we've got it.' "

Knebel considered doing a book about Lyndon Johnson, "probably the raunchiest President we ever had," but decided writing history served no useful purpose. "By the time I'd finish the book, Johnson would have been out of office 10 years," he says.

Still, Knebel likes talking about Presidents he has known — playing poker with young Richard Nixons, kinny-dipping with Lyndon Johnson in the White House pool, and bantering with John Kennedy, his favorite chief executive.

Knebel's life style has changed a great deal from his days as a Washington correspondent. He's practicing yoga and T'ai Chi and is involved in group therapy "human potential sessions."

"You know," he says, "the interesting thing for me is exploring new things. Books are no longer a big part of my life. I may indeed do other books to help make ends meet, but my mind is going in new directions."

'Indians' Playwright Clarifying History

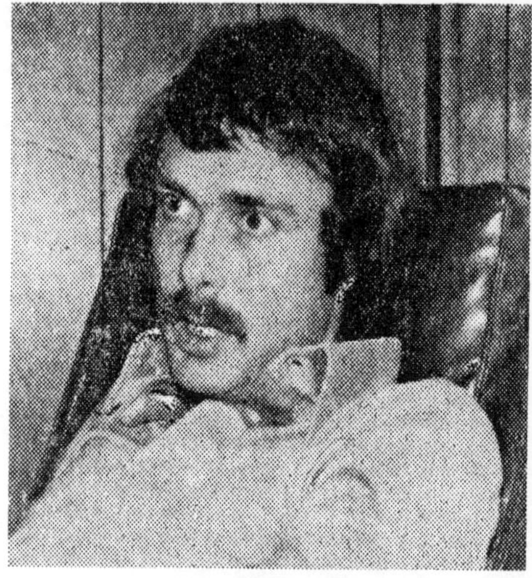

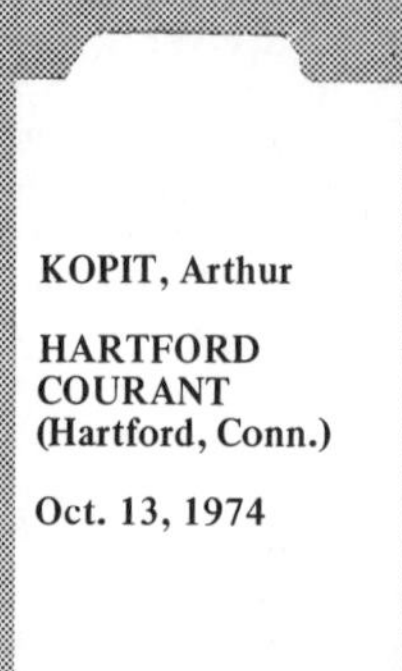

KOPIT, Arthur

HARTFORD COURANT (Hartford, Conn.)

Oct. 13, 1974

By HARRY R. WILSON

Arthur Kopit, whose 1969 drama "Indians," will be staged by the Wesleyan University Theater Department this week, disclaims all but minimal influence on this new production.

The playwright, a confirmed gypsy, has given up his nomadic life this year to teach for the first time as a Fellow at Wesleyan's Center for the Humanities.

"I arrived on campus in September not even knowing "Indians" was going to be produced," Kopit said. "I found out about it through a billboard poster."

Nevertheless, Kopit and director Bill Francisco, who is spending one semester at Wesleyan as an artist-in-residence, have talked extensively about problems of characterization and emphasis. The result will be seen on stage Thursday, Friday and Saturday at 8:30 p.m. in the Theater of the Center for the Arts.

Kopit, a Phi Beta Kappa Harvard graduate, in his mid-thirties, came to Middletown deeply immersed in preparing a six-part cycle of plays entitled "City of Faith." Part I was recently completed after a year of writing and he is presently working on Part III.

In contrast, Kopit spent two months shaping a complete first draft of "Indians" and five days finishing his best-known play, "Oh Dad, Poor Dad, Mama's Hung You in the Closet and I'm Feeling So Bad."

"I've learned to wait for the material to suggest its own form. With 'Indians,' I spent five to six months reading Indian legends and mythologies before I had a sense of the form," he said. Kopit spoke with intensity about his play during an interview in his second-floor office on campus.

The form Kopit finally settled on is episodic and non-linear, a crazy-quilt pattern of scenes and time designed to mirror the characters' own confusion.

"My purpose was not to editorialize on the plight of the Indians," Kopit said. "I wanted to explore the processes of knowledge and understanding that come by experiencing the characters, myths, and events of the period — and share that exploration with my audience."

The play ostensibly zeroes in on the true life of William Cody — better known as Buffalo Bill — and the mythology created to justify the Government's genocidal policies toward the Indians. But Kopit, while admitting to several flaws in the "seams" of the play, feels "Indians" succeeds in trascending topical concerns.

"Yes, the play has specific relevance to Vietnam, among other issues," Kopit conceded. "But I think that, more importantly, it deals with men who believe they have power over events and their need to make heroes to justify the use of that power.

"I really believe that history is not as simple as in the history books. My hope is to allow my audience a chance to discover that, to make clearer that which is confused," the playwright said.

The intervening years between the opening of "Indians" at the Royal Shakespeare Theater in London on July 4, 1968, and the Wesleyan production this week have witnessed a growing sensitivity to Indian and other minority grievances.

To Kopit, this awakened conscience has produced a feeling of guilt in American audiences that allows a too-comfortable condemnation of whites, as in "The Great White Hope."

But Kopit's play, far from giving an audience guilt without pain, refuses to even say that we are all guilty. In the character of Buffalo Bill, Kopit presents a white man who, while caught up in his own myth of manifest destiny, was still regarded by the Indians as a friend.

Buffalo Bill's response — that of hiding his despair and encroaching madness behind the energetic pizzazz of showmanship — represents to Kopit the only viable one available outside of the insufferable paternalism evinced by the United States Government.

The conflicting systems of logic, law, and religion could only result in the Indian and the white man seeing the other in self-referential terms. Without common ground on which to stand, according to Kopit, the two were doomed to conflict, and the less-sophisticated Indians were forced to give way.

That the Indians suffered cruel injustice at the hands of land speculators and government troops Kopit will not deny. But the good guys- versus- bad- guys approach to Wild West history is a denial of the complexity of the forces at work.

Kopit believes his play is an historically accurate depiction of those forces, both as a general outline and also with regard to such specific details as the government-ordered assassination of Sitting Bull or the growing madness of William Cody.

"I'm not interested in having the audience come out of the theater saying, 'Those poor Indians, wasn't it terrible,' " Kopit said. "It really couldn't have happened any differently. My purpose in the play, if there is one, is to say, 'Let's not have this happen again.' "

"Indians" was first staged in London and after constant and major revisions, it arrived in the spring for a short run on the Arena Stage in Washington, D.C. It played more than 100 performances on Broadway the following fall.

Its closing in New York was due more to excessive cost than to lack of favorable critical and public response. It was nominated for a Tony Award and included in the 1969 Burns-Mantle "Best Plays of the Year" volume.

Kopit spent a year writing a screenplay of "Indians" which he has sold, although no movie is planned in the foreseeable future.

Except for an occasional college production, "Indians," is all but behind him, including the initial suspicions of Kopit's intent and sincerity. While acknowledging the validity of recent Indians grievance claims, Kopit maintains that his play should not serve as a vehicle for contemporary protest.

"My play doesn't concern itself with the situation today," he asserted. "I was writing about Indians who have disappeared: those who had the land but were still nomadic and free. Indians who have seen the play agree with that assessment," Kopit said.

Kopit, who shares every playwright's aversion to attending his own plays, will nevertheless be on hand this week for the Wesleyan production.

Jill Krementz: 'Camera Nut'

Jill Krementz at home in the living room of her New York brownstone apartment.

KREMENTZ, Jill (1940-)

DETROIT FREE PRESS (Detroit, Mich.)

Dec. 25, 1974

[See also CA-41/44]

Story and photo by
Ira Rosenberg

It was 10 years ago in the lobby of the New York Herald Tribune I first crossed paths with Jill Krementz.

Ben Price, who was the paper's photo editor, told me one day as I was racing out to cover a report of a shooting uptown: "There's a kid waiting in the lobby. Take her with you; she's a camera nut."

When I got to the lobby the "kid" turned out to be a beautiful young woman with a couple of cameras around her neck. I didn't stop for introductions but headed at full trot for the subway.

We were going down the steps two at a time when I turned to her and told her that if she didn't have a token, I wasn't going to wait for her to buy one. As I dropped mine in the slot and started through, I could feel her in the small space — sharing the turnstile with me.

Jill obviously didn't have a token — she went through with me rather than miss the story. I knew then that she had what it took to be a photographer.

And I was right. In the free lance photo business, Jill dominates the author-personalities field. She's running on a fast track; the competition is tough.

Her pictures of people like Kurt Vonnegut Jr., Tennessee Williams, James Baldwin, Irving Berlin and hundreds of others have been chosen regularly to appear in the New York Times Book Review, Time, Newsweek and Publishers Weekly. Book publishers seek her out to make book jacket pictures. She also is a contributing photographer for People magazine.

After our first meeting, I would find her hanging around the lobby of the Trib, hoping to go out on a news story with a photographer. She would bring in photo stories to sell and also did free lance assignments for the paper.

When she got a full-time job there, she was assigned to me and shared my darkroom. I helped her where I could, and Jill was quick to learn. I remember it took her all of half an hour to learn to make a presentable print.

She was the only woman to work on the Herald Tribune's prize-winning photo staff. A year later, after covering the Harlem riots, she left the paper to free lance in Vietnam. Out of that came her book, "The Face of Vietnam." Those photos are her best work.

In 1969 Jill went South and lived with a black family. She returned to New York with enough photos of the 12-year-old daughter to fill a second book, "Sweet Pea — A Girl Growing Up in the Rural South."

Jill, who is 34, comes from a well-to-do family and was educated at the best schools. She has traveled extensively and to this day will not go on a long flight unless she knows what picture will be shown. She has changed flights many times because she either didn't want to see the movie or didn't care to see it again.

Her work, her social life and her loves keep her on the move.

A year was about the longest she could ever stay in one job; she doesn't want to stagnate.

"Most job challenges can be conquered in about a year, then it's time to find new windmills to knock over," she said.

I accepted an invitation to stay at her place when I visited New York recently, remembering the apartment she used to have on First Avenue. She had asked me to help her turn her kitchen into a darkroom. She had no use for a kitchen then, and it's still true today, because she has difficulty even boiling water.

As we had a nightcap, she promised me a hearty farm breakfast the next morning. That puzzled me until I found out she was taking me around the corner to the Farm Restaurant for breakfast. I'm grateful she didn't try to fry eggs; it would have been a disaster.

Talking over old times, I asked her how much money she had made on the Trib. She couldn't remember, but she did know it was less than the messenger boy was making. Probably about $80 a week.

She does know for sure that last year she grossed $75,000. Now her photographic lab work is done by a custom photo lab. She has a full-time secretary, and the office in her brownstone contains thousands of negatives and prints.

THEY STILL CALL HIM MR. KROCK

KROCK, Arthur
(1887 -)

DETROIT NEWS
(Detroit, Mich.)

Nov. 4, 1973

[See also
CA-33/36]

By ELIZABETH C. MOONEY
Sunday Magazine Special Writer

WASHINGTON

MR. KROCK, as Arthur Krock is known to all but a handful of intimates at the New York Times and the Metropolitan Club, happily admits to a few personal prejudices.

One of his finer moments, he recalls, was when he broke a toe in his haste to get across the room to switch off a TV program featuring Sammy Davis Jr.

There were other things he feels strongly about, and he is not a mincer of words. At 86 he complains that he feels terrible — "there are no compensations for old age," he says, "and few for retirement," but the sentences still come out perfectly parsed and nicely rounded as if they were written in all caps. It is widely agreed that, faced with Mr. Krock's precise delivery, only a fool or a man at the club table with two martinis in him would think of taking issue.

Well, possibly a good-looking woman might. Mr. Krock has the southern leaning for a handsome woman, especially one with brains, and he likes them to talk up.

Mr. Krock, confidant and sometimes scourge of 11 presidents, carries the manner still. The step may be less sure than when he came to Washington as head of the Times Bureau in 1932, but the gimlet eye and the sharp tongue have not faltered an iota. When he steps out of the elevator on the 8th floor of the Railroad Building at 1920 L Street exactly at 11:15 every morning, he proceeds down the corridor to the office he has used since he retired 11 years ago embodying all the dignity and prestige of his earlier days of command. The only difference now is that the newsroom is in the other direction.

Never mind that. Since he stepped down in favor of Scotty Reston, Mr. Krock has written three books, edited a collection of columns, done assorted odd pieces for newspapers and magazines and maintained a voluminous correspondence. When he arrives at the office he has already read the Times and the Washington Post, and before he goes to lunch at the Metropolitan Club at 12:45 he has polished off the Star-News, the Wall Street Journal, the Chicago Tribune and the New York News.

"I read the News because of Suzy (Knickerbocker)," he says. "I know all the people she writes about."

He complains that he sometimes fumbles for a word these days. "The attrition of the human mind is as palpable as the attrition of the body," he says, his eye on his desk. "I was born with a photographic memory and there was a time when I could quote a good deal. Never as much as Alice Longworth, or her brother, Ted, but a good deal. Now I fumble."

If he fumbles, says one of his cronies at the club, it is for somebody's middle name. Like what's the C. for in John C. Calhoun. They say he can quote Shakespeare by the yard, suitable for any occasion.

He is not an optimist. And a lot of things these days incur his wrath, which is more like a carefully contained, coldly distainful distaste for the way the world is going.

"I am very pessimistic about the future of the country," he says, sitting back in his chair and apparently reading the words off his desk, though there is no paper on it. "All our values are disregarded — the old ones of thrift and family responsibility. The courts are lenient, special interest groups are getting handouts from politicians because they think they will get bloc voting, the elderly have a hard time and the young believe they have no obligation."

He picks up a letter from his desk and deliberately slits open the envelope, studies its contents briefly and presses the bell for Miss Waltz, his secretary of 12 years.

"I don't want to pay these cormorants a single penny at the moment," he says, handing her the letter without looking up. She disappears, letter in hand.

"The redistribution of wealth has been a curse," he says, picking up his thoughts as if there had been no interruption. "It's the fault of the liberal Democrats. Including Johnson. They spent the money the government hasn't got. Nixon embraced this philosophy, but he tried to limit it. He tried to get Congress to hold down spending. He's conservative in his welfare appropriations."

ABOVE HIS head hangs a picture of Lyndon B. Johnson shown whispering in the ear of General Eisenhower. It is inscribed to "Arthur Krock, the statesman of the press."

There is a tap on the door and Tom Wicker, assistant editor and columnist for the Times, wanders in paying a call on his old mentor while in town for the day. He sits on the chair opposite the desk, his manner as courteously deferential as if he were a new copy boy come to learn the ropes. He tells Mr. Krock that his son is at Andover this year and that he has a new apartment in New York, but still the South hangs as thickly over the conversation as Wicker's North Carolina accent. They might be two country boys passing the time of day, instead of two of most glittering names in the roster of the country's leading newspaper.

Wicker is writing a new Civil War book and wants to get any material he can from Mr. Krock. Mr. Krock obliges with a story about Stonewall Jackson at Cedar Creek. It's a long story and builds skillfully. Wicker sees parallels with Patton, and it is 15 minutes before he gets up and says good-by.

In the history of the War Between the States there is no differences of ➡

(Continued from preceding page)

opinion between these two southern boys. Nevertheless on some of the events of the last 20 years in American politics, many admit that Mr. Krock is triumphantly and happily at variance with the Times' editorial policy and that of most of the staff.

"The president's confidentiality is absolutely vital to the welfare of the country," he says when Wicker is gone. "Jackson and Jefferson completely defied the Supreme Court at times. Lincoln disregarded the Constitution when he revoked the law of habeas corpus. It was long after he was dead that the court got around to investigating it. I hope Nixon never gives them a smell of those tapes."

He is only warming to his subject. Above him Josephus Daniels, Bernard Baruch and Henry Watterson stare down at him. On his desk there is a bookmark in Dorothy Eden's latest Gothic.

"No," he says flatly, "the Nixon of 1972 will not survive. There will be a Nixon who will be able to survive, but he's wounded by squandering the fruits of victory in an atmosphere of ethical corrruption. Not graft. It wasn't money, it was power they were after."

He doesn't think Nixon knew in detail what was going on.

"He admired the loyalty of his Madison Avenue boys and felt free to indulge in foreign affairs. He failed to keep house. This doesn't mean he will be impeached."

The administration, he feels, is a victim of the new journalism, which permits an anonymous source to put out damaging information. The responsibility of the press is impaired and the grand jury system in ruins, he says mildly, barely opening his mouth to cut these two institutions into ribbons. When he was Washington correspondent for the Times, no such allegations were allowed.

Nobody is more ready to do battle against the new journalism than Mr. Krock, recipient of three Pulitzer prizes. He disapproves, in most cases, of editorializing in reporting and feels that the reporter should keep himself strictly out of the scene. The newsroom now is full of young reporters who, as Tom Wicker says, "feel a revulsion against the dress box mentality," the front seat at the event looking down at the crowd. To the right of the elevator, in Mr. Krock's office, there is no compromise. He believes in the purity of objective reporting and means to go on believing, all flags flying.

He does not give advice.

"Old people who give advice are insufferable," he says, again apparently reading from the varnished surface of the desk.

Mr. Krock was born in Glasgow, Ky., but you don't hear it in his voice. You get it rather like a faint miasma of old world courtesy, with a liberal whiff of tradition and the caste system mixed in — the whole overlaid with a unsurpassed talent for laying any subject open to the bone with a flick of the acid-dipped tongue. He likes a pretty woman, but he likes, as Miss Waltz says, ladies to be ladies. And not at Princeton, one of his alma maters.

"Princeton," he says through lips stiff with disapproval, "should now be called the College of New Jersey. The memory of it is very dear. The fact of it is repugnant. It's a closed chapter in my life since the mixed shacking-up. I gave my papers to Princeton when it was not coeducational. I would now give them to the Library of Congress."

Delivering himself of these senti-

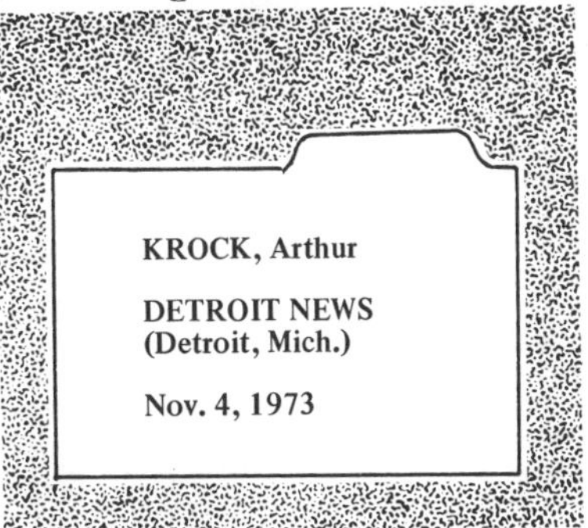

ments seems to improve his health and disposition. When he gets up from the desk for a moment, his step is firmer and his eye brighter.

You wouldn't expect a gentleman of Mr. Krock's regard for words to be soft on television. He is not.

"The tube," he goes on when he sits down again, "is the curse of America. It is the most dangerous invention in the history of man. The public looks at it and thinks when it sees snatches of reports that it knows something about what's going on. The have-nots are encouraged by TV to think they are entitled by birth to what takes hard work and brains to earn. They see a police sergeant living well in some soap opera and they want to know why they can't have the same. The commercials are pernicious and the total irresponsibility dangerous. And of course it's all made possible by the free use of public property — air."

Over on the back of the closed office door is a green and yellow poster proclaiming in large letters, "Every day is a happy birthday."

Mr. Krock glowers at it. He is obviously thinking about a special irritant.

"The liberals in Congress," he says, "are complaining bitterly. And it is they who built up the presidential power by delegating powers and blindly accepting leadership of the kind that led to the Gulf of Tonkin resolution."

He is silent for a moment while he thinks it over.

"But of course they were right," he says and it seems to please him, "because the U.S. cannot be run by committee and is not subject to the judiciary. They make much of Connally's statement that the President is under no obligation to answer the demands of the courts. The uproar makes you believe this is the first time it happened. John Marshall bootlegged into the Constitution the authority of the courts to overturn acts of Congress, and it burst into flower in Roosevelt's court and again in the one headed by Warren."

In 1935 FDR, he says, had a speech ready for radio delivery defying the Supreme Court if it held unconstitutional the 1933 act of Congress which canceled the gold payment clause in private contracts and government bonds. The Court upheld the government case, 5-to-4, but in the minority opinion Justice MacReynolds lamented: "The Constitution is gone."

President Roosevelt didn't get to deliver his speech, Mr. Krock recalls, and he was regretful. In a memo to John P. Kennedy, his SEC Commissioner, the President wrote that "The Nation will never know what a great treat it missed in not hearing the marvelous radio address." In his undelivered speech, the President invoked not the Constitution but the Golden Rule, the Scriptures and "the dictates of common sense" against the adverse decision he expected from the Supreme Court.

Having delivered himself of this obviously important point, Mr. Krock leans back in his chair. It is almost 12:30, the moment when he is ready to go to lunch and join his friends at the special table tacitly reserved by custom at the Metropolitan Club for what is widely known as the club within the club. Unknowing guests who seat themselves at this table have been met with glacial stares and icy silences which usually get the message across. Mr. Krock is a charter member, and the club is the only place where he now dines away from home.

The car is waiting and the elevator door swings wide to admit him, closes behind him, bearing him down to the street below.

In the corridor under the eyes of the pictures of former New York Times greats, Tom Wicker pauses briefly enroute to his typewriter.

"He's the most remarkable human being I have known," he says. "I value him."

Outside the window in the busy traffic of L Street the living legend climbs into his car and is born away, happily anticipating his daily bottle of Tuborg beer. ■

Ernst Krohn Creative At 84

Photo By Richard Benkof

By Virginia Annan Schroeder

Musicologist Ernst Christopher Krohn is brilliant, witty, creative and productive at age 84. He does not complain about his health, and he has plans for indefinite, ceaseless productivity. He doesn't deign to notice his handicap — or to admit his dependency on the electric pacemaker wired into his heart.

"Why do you want to interview *me*?" my former music history teacher asked, genuinely puzzled.

"Because you're a distinguished man," I replied.

He smiled. "No," he said, "I'm an ex-tinguished man." But the twinkle in his eyes proclaimed his triumph over adversity — even in the ultimate.

Clearly he was referring to his physical condition; because spiritually, mentally, and psychologically he is as far from being extinguished as a flaming jet engine.

Ernst C. Krohn at 84 is as busy, or busier, than he was at 48. His latest book, *Music Publishing in St. Louis*, will be on bookstore shelves within a year. He is currently working on a magazine article. He has just published another composition for piano, the most recent of an impressive list. He practices his piano regularly, never deviating from a schedule he fulfills with the regularity and precision of a metronome.

He also keeps up a voluminous correspondence with publishers, other composers, musicologists, and former pupils. And he makes it a point to be "at home" to friends on certain days at certain hours. He has time for everything. He reads; he writes; he composes; and he visits with callers personally or on the phone.

All of this activity and productivity is accomplished in what Ernst describes as a "self-contained" 3-room unit, consisting of studio, bedroom, and bath in the home he shares with his widowed sister and his school-teacher niece.

The studio is a multi-purpose room containing his grand piano, packed bookshelves, his desk and file cabinets — everything crowded but sharply neat and well-organized. The room serves as studio, office, library, reception and sitting-room. In the only available wall-space hang two framed documents: one proclaims Ernst as one of the founders of the Bach Society of St. Louis. The other (his most cherished) is a Citation of Special Merit, awarded him by the Missouri Historical Society (of which he is the only Honorary member), "For Distinguished Research and Publications on the History of Music" — and dated April 23, 1959.

KROHN, Ernst C(hristopher)
(1888 -)

ST. LOUISAN
(St. Louis, Mo.)

June, 1973

[See also CA-37/40]

In organizing these musically dedicated societies — he was also one of the founders of The Musicians' Guild — Ernst created new interest, understanding, and appreciation of music in St. Louis and throughout the State of Missouri. But this was only one facet of his contribution to the culture of his day and time.

For 50 years Ernst C. Krohn taught piano, theory, harmony and music history in his central west-end studio located at Taylor and Olive Streets in St. Louis; for 15 years he lectured at Washington University; and for 10 years (up to 1963) he lectured at St. Louis University. He was considered "THE" Music Department of St. Louis University — and still is — for good reason.

At the suggestion of the Jesuits at the University, he initiated a program that constituted a first in St. Louis — and, in fact, anywhere. He compiled a list of sacred manuscript music from the files of the Vatican. This was accomplished by obtaining microfilmed copies of the Vatican music, which were then Xeroxed for general study and use.

Through this project St. Louis became the only city in the world (other than Rome) to possess the Vatican manuscripts. These copies are now housed in the Pope Pius 12th Library at St. Louis University.

In addition to this vast contribution to mid-western culture, Ernst Krohn sold his private 9,000 volume collection of books on music history and musicology to Washington University — books in all languages that he had meticulously and painstakingly collected for over a half-century.

He has been designated Honorary Curator of the Gaylord Music Library — part of the Music Department of Washington University in St. Louis, a permanent, life-time honorary post.

But these achievements constitute the past, and Ernst is only concerned with the here and now. Before terminating our very productive interview, Ernst handed me a book just off the press — a compilation of his earlier works, with a recently completed new introduction, a supplementary list of Missouri musicologists and composers, together with a bibliography and index completed during the last two years. This monumental 380-page work is entitled *Missouri Music*.

Thus has Ernst C. Krohn contributed — and is contributing — to the cultural riches of the world. He has identified with the past, the present, and the future; and through his unfaltering sense of purpose and direction, he continues to unify scholarship and musical creativity into a comprehensive whole.

Here, indeed, is a man for all seasons, for all people, for all nations — a man with whom others can empathize and identify. A simple man, who has earned his bread (and the respect of his fellows) by means of rigorous self-discipline, dedicated application, and unremitting effort. A man whose philosophy is that to be creative, to be active, and to contribute to his world is the be-all and the end-all — the Alpha and the Omega — of existence. He doesn't falter. He doesn't deign to notice his handicap.

Although the example set by his character in terms of courage, fortitude, and accomplishment is of universal significance, Ernst is his own man, now and always. ✤

Guidebook Through 'Wilderness of Grief'

—P-I Photo by Phil H. Webber

LANDORF, Joyce

SEATTLE POST–INTELLIGENCER (Seattle, Wash.)

Jan. 14, 1975

BY SUSAN PAYNTER

Seventeen years ago Joyce Landorf says she "found God" when she was about to kill herself with a razor blade.

Even though she was a minister's daughter, she says, she was no Christian then. But she is now.

Since she "found God" she's also found a lucrative field, turning out books (seven so far) with a religious theme on everything from suicide to beauty.

The latest, "Mourning Song," is all about death, how to face it in yourself or others.

She said she started gathering material for it seven or eight years ago when she lost three family members, including her baby. In Seattle last week to do a marriage seminar with Dr. James Dobson, the California woman also was promoting her book and talking about death.

"I put off writing the book because I hate the subject so much," she said.

"But I don't get tired of talking about it because so many people need to talk about it. The publishers care about selling a lot of books but, if I've helped just one or two people, that's all I care about."

Mrs. Landorf said her book isn't aimed at religious people. But in it and in her conversation she constantly advises readers to seek "His love," Christian beliefs and Christian strength" when facing death.

She said the book was written because she found no comfort in the usual books on death, filled with cliches and sweet phrases. But her book is filled with Biblical quotations and lines like "Grandpa had caught his flight home and was winging his way upward," or "I was wandering in the wilderness of grief."

She said she thinks everyone, religious or not, gets "instant faith" when facing the idea of dying.

"Even though I had such a strong Christian faith, I was shocked at how shattered I was by death," she said.

"Other people told me that they had no grief, that God took it all away. But I don't believe they were really coping with their bitterness.

"I blamed God and I was angry. Then I felt guilty I couldn't believe that, even with my faith, I was not able to pick up the pieces of my life."

She said she used euphemisms for death: "In the arms of the Lord" etc., because she didn't know who her readers would be and how words would affect them. "Some people prefer 'with the Lord' or 'pass on' while others say 'he's dead' or 'he kicked the bucket'," she said.

"Death already is so cold, so final, it helps to have kind words and things like flowers at the funeral. As a singer, I've attended tons of Christian funerals. They can be everything from just a jar of ahses on the table and somebody saying, 'Well, this is Joe and he's dead,' to something close to a circus."

In her book she tries to help people through what she calls the five stages of death, stages she credits to the research of Dr. Elisabeth Kubler-Ross.

"Not only the dying but those close to them go through the stages," Mrs. Landorf said. "When my mother died, and when I lost my son, I went through them,. and through them all over again.

"First is denial. 'Oh, no. This isn't happening. He can't be dead,' " she said. "This is the stage when you keep the room as it was.

"Second is anger. This includes anger towards God and even anger toward the loved one for leaving you alone. Even atheists feel an anger towards God because he's supposed to hold the strings.

"But for Christians this anger brings on tremendous guilt. You're not supposed to feel it so there's no outlet for your feelings.

"Next comes bargaining for the dying. 'I'll be good, God, if you'll just give me another chance, or if you'll just heal my child.' And in this phase is the element of regret, too. 'I shouldn't have left him alone.'

"Fourth is depression and grief. This is the hardest for those around you to handle. They don't want to talk to you because you may cry. They don't know what to say or say the wrong thing."

She said "the bereaved" don't like to hear that the "lost one's" death probably is for the best.

Last, Mrs. Landorf said, come acceptance and getting used to the "lost one" not being around. But, she said, "the bereaved" often revert back to stage one or two several times. "Grief usually takes two years," she said.

She wishes there were classes for parents of terminally ill children and that "Some day maybe God will open the door for me to do that kind of work."

In the meantime she's turning out another book. In it she's telling men what women want in a man. She said she's basing it on what she wants in a man because, "Evidently what I want is what a lot of people want."

She's calling it "Tough and Tender."

Lasky on the 'real' Hollywood

LASKY, Jesse (Louis), Jr. (1910-)

DETROIT NEWS (Detroit, Mich.)

Feb. 16, 1975

[See also CA-2]

By MOLLY ABRAHAM
News Entertainment Writer

If your father was one of the three pioneers who made the first feature-length film in Hollywood, you cut your teeth on the wooden swords dropped by Cecil B. De Mille's extras, and grew up to be a screenwriter, it seems fairly certain that sooner or later, you are going to write a book about Hollywood.

In the case of Jesse L. Lasky Jr., he resisted until he was in his 60's — and only then at the urging of his wife, sat down and did it. ("Oh, come on, nobody wants to read about the 'real' Hollywood" had been his first reaction.)

"Whatever Happened to Hollywood?", his detail-filled memoir, was delivered to book stores in this country this week. It's a best-seller in England, where it was published last year.

"In England nostalgia is even more welcome than in the United States," Lasky said early this week, sipping a lunchtime old-fashioned in a Detroit restaurant. "Times are terribly difficult there. But I love the British because they are not totally youth-oriented."

LASKY CAN speak with authority about the British, having lived since 1962 in London, where he writes television and movie scripts. But he takes pains to assure his listener that "I did not choose to be an expatriate. Three-and-a-half years overseas with Gen. MacArthur's army (in World War II) is patriotic enough."

A charming, low-key man with a neatly trimmed salt-and-pepper beard, Lasky, who refers to himself as "a sick old man" though neither fact is apparent, speaks with refreshing honesty about himself. "I call this tour 'The Loneliness of the Long-Distance Writer,'" he said, looking small and almost forlorn. "I'm beginning to recycle my shirts. When I get to Chicago I'll have to take a day off to do laundry.

"I won't get back to my wife until March 8. It's our longest separation since we were married some 15 years ago. We are VERY happily married, and we've written some six pictures together. She gets me to the church on time, so to speak, and I'm really lost without her." Mrs. Lasky is the writer, Pat Silver, whom he met while writing the television series "Rescue Eight" in the late '50's.

"I ASKED THEM to please get me some help, someone who could follow my ideas and really work fast. They sent me a beautiful girl who happened to be a damned fine writer. We have been writing happily together ever since. We understand each other's problems."

Lasky is candid and unpretentious in talking about his life in Hollywood. "My father had GREAT ups and downs, and I never enjoyed the benefits of nepotism, though I tried to hard enough, God knows. We weren't generally able to help each other. We'd both be down at the same time, unfortunately."

Lasky, "had a hand in 66 movies," many of them with his father's original partner, De Mille.

"I saw a beautiful movie, 'The Crusades,' in England in the early '30's," said Lasky, who admits a fondness for the epic sort of film De Mille was famous for. "I was working in England at the time on my first screen assignment, working with an English writer on Alfred Hitchcock's 'Secret Agent,' the film that advanced Peter Lorre's career.

"SO I WROTE De Mille a letter and told him how much I admired the film, and asked him to give me a chance to write his next movie. I sent him three published volumes of my poetry. When I eventually got back to Hollywood, I went to see him and told him my dreams and fantasies of medieval battle scenes were bigger than life, just like his pictures, and that I would love to write one of his movies. He said, 'I've got three of the best writers in the business. If you think you can improve on what they've done, take this script and pick any scene you want and rewrite it.'

"Well, I read the script, and my heart sank. It was magnificent, the best screen writing I'd ever read. So instead of rewriting it, I invented a scene, in which a little girl is washed overboard and is saved by pirates because her dog barks.

"De Mille read it and pretended not to like it, and scared hell out of me. Finally, he said, 'You've got a lot to learn, but there's one line in that scene — the line about the barking fish — that's a De Mille line and shows some sense of writing.' He promised to give me a chance.

"Later he sent me a case of champagne, which didn't help me at all. I needed money. So my then-wife and I had champagne and chili. Anyway, he kept his promise, and kept every promise he ever made to me. He was a marvelous friend and boss year after year."

LASKY WORKED for De Mille for some 15 years, on and off. When Lasky came back from service with MacArthur, De Mille asked about the general. "He's not as tough as you, sir," was Lasky's reply.

Of the movies he did with De Mille, Lasky says his favorite is "Samson and Delilah." His most recent film, "An Ace Up My Sleeve," which stars Omar Sharif and Karen Black, is now being shot in the Austrian Alps. He and his wife were hired at the last minute to rewrite the script, when the director didn't like the original version. "We did it in nine days flat, on a German typewriter," he said.

"Of course, I may not even recognize the picture when I see it." If not, it won't be the first time. Screenwriters are quite used to seeing their work changed. He shudders as he thinks of bad films made from his scripts: like "Wizard of Bagdad," "Pirates of Tortugo" and "Seven Women From Hell."

"That one was done on such a low budget they should have changed the name to "Six Women From Hell," he said with a laugh.

"I was never one of the great screenwriters, but I think I've written every type of movie there is. And I've been deeply involved in trying to make life better for screenwriters. There's a great fantasy, just as there is about everything in Hollywood, about the role of the writer. You know, the producer used to be all-powerful. Then it ➡

(Continued from preceding page)

was the star. Now it's the director who is the artistic god of film. He very often writes his own film. Or he refuses to let the actors see the screenplay until they are going into rehearsal."

LASKY GOT UP from the table to go to his next appointment. "Let us be deadly honest, my dear. There have been good books about Hollywood, written by historians, students and ghost writers, but not written by survivors of the old Hollywood because the survivors were not writers. And if they were, they didn't have the advantage of having a father who produced the first feature-length film.

"I had the luck of heritage and have always been a professional writer. I'm my own ghost and that's why I convey a sense of Hollywood from the standpoint of a living experience, without bitterness, and without libraries and old clippings — much of which is fabrication. Mine was done from memory and love, from my own emotional position, which gives me an enormous advantage.

"I have dared add another Hollywood book to the multitudes. I hope to live long enough to write another."

LASKY, Jesse (Louis), Jr.

DETROIT NEWS
(Detroit, Mich.)

Feb. 16, 1975

The Rise and Fall Of Hollywood's Dream Machine ---a Survivor's Tale

BY SUSAN STARK
Free Press Film Critic

Jesse Lasky Jr. Jesse Lasky. Hmm. The name has a familiar ring, but where to place it? And then the little lightbulb goes on, or maybe it doesn't.

Jesse Lasky Jr., son of one of Hollywood's three founding fathers, is pushing 65 these days and, in his little more than six decades, he has seen more changes, experienced more changes, really, than a more commonly born person would be likely to experience in a dozen lifetimes. Lasky was in Detroit recently to talk about all of that and to promote a book he has written.

The senior Lasky, along with his brother-in-law, a man named Goldfish (later changed to Goldwyn), plus their second-choice DeMille (they wanted William and got Cecil B.), are generally credited with producing the first feature film ever.

Lasky tells their story, and the story of the film pioneers who followed them west, in a rip-snortingly anecdotal book called "Whatever Happened To Hollywood?"

When the Depression sapped the senior Lasky's first fortune, Jesse Jr.'s incredibly privileged life-style came to an abrupt end and he turned, for his living, to ghostwriting. He has been writing for a living, sometimes for salaries in the six-figure range and sometimes for three-figures-and-glad-to-get-it, ever since. It would be conservative to say that his style is lively.

OF THAT 1913 triumvirate and their first film project, Lasky writes:

"The three young men, Lasky, Goldfish and DeMille, formed a company capitalized at $20,000 from assorted brothers-in-law. Fifteen of this they promptly squandered on purchasing the screen rights to Edwin Milton Royle's play 'The Squaw Man.'

"Wisdom would seem to have dictated a trip across the Hudson River to Fort Lee, New Jersey, where most sensible two-reel Westerns were then being ground out. But wisdom has never been the better part of showmanship or showmen. They decided on the radical idea of producing their first feature-length Western in the West.

"DeMille led the first film company west by train to Flagstaff, Arizona. Why Flagstaff? It sounded romantic. Since the 'The Squaw Man' involved cowboys and Indians, where better?

"Where better? Anywhere! DeMille and his little film company arrived at Flagstaff to find themselves in the middle of a cattleman-sheepman war. Shooting a film was one thing. Being shot at by drunken wranglers was something else.

"The first telegram back to a worried company president, Lasky Sr., said: 'Flagstaff no good for our purpose. Have proceeded to California. Want authority to rent barn in place called Hollywood for seventy-five dollars a month. Regards to Sam. Cecil."

The rest, as they say, is history, history as seen from the point of view of a boy who watched the "place called Hollywood" become, in less than a decade, the most fabulous dream machine ever known to man.

LASKY, Jesse (Louis), Jr.

DETROIT
FREE PRESS
(Detroit, Mich.)

Feb. 23, 1975

Fifty years later, the dream machine would be dismantled darned near as quickly as it was built. Lasky grew up surrounded by the first flash of glory; his best boyhood buddy was Doug Fairbanks Jr.

Many years later, when the industry (and his father) recovered from the effects of the Depression, the young Lasky worked his way to a top screenwriter's job with C.B. DeMille. Those were the "Samson and Delilah" days, the days of "The Ten Commandments." Then the dream was over, and Lasky, with countless others, once again had to scratch for a living.

"I was terribly conscious of a kind of unreality, a kind of Alice in Wonderland' feeling," Lasky recalled. "Here you were, it was all happening around you and yet it wasn't. I suppose I felt that way even in the early days, even when I was a child, because the ups and downs were so sudden and so dramatic.

"THE SECOND period in my life, the period when I had a certain success as a Hollywood screenwriter, was marvelous because it meant knowing and working with the DeMilles, the John Fords, the L.B. Mayers. And of course, I knew all the great writers, some from childhood, some later on when I began writing myself — Scott Fitzgerald and Dorothy Parker, who were around the house when I was a boy. Later, I had the chance to encourage a Bud Shulberg.

"The war, and my being called off to serve, is what I consider the third period. Out of that experience came a book—a successful book—called 'Spindrift' when it was originally published and then, in the paperback editions, called "Cry the Naked Flesh."

"Now, finally, in the fourth period of my life, or maybe I should call it my fourth life, I live in London, an American writer married to my third wife, a younger American writer who is also my partner. We get an occasional film to write. We just finished a first-draft screenplay in nine days and nine nights for Ivan Passer; my wife's still in Vienna polishing it. But mostly we write for TV, and I do book reviews for the Spectator."

Lasky gave the account of his life rather dispassionately, certainly without a trace of bitterness. He is a small man, recently made consdierably smaller, he said, as the unexpected result of serious and complex internal surgery.

There is absolutely nothing about his appearance of manner that suggests the gross, flashy caricatures of men who built and ruled Hollywood. Quite the contrary. Fine-featured and generally frail-looking, Lasky speaks softly, occasionally even lapsing into an apologetic mood. He made a point of saying that his obviously fake-fur winter coat was fake fur. On the jacket of his book, he is pictured as a youngster with a rather querulous expression on his face, regally robed in real raccoon.

He has hope, not wild hope but the kind of hope that shows when his eyes light up, that "Whatever Happened To Hollywood?" will be successful enough to permit him to write books full-time to support himself and to meet his obligations. With exceptional candor and not a little sadness he admitted to being bankrupt in England, to having been supported by his wife through the writing of the book he is now working to promote. Incredible but true: The source of his misery is and has been alimony agreements made back in the days when he was high on Cecil B. DeMille's payroll.

"IF THIS BOOK is successful" he said, "the publisher wants me to do an informal inside history of the American film. 'Whatever Happened To Hollywood?' is more an inside, informal history of me.

"The book I'm terribly moved by and would love to do, though, is based on a fantastic discovery made after my mother's death three years ago. It would be based on a large collection of letters we found, spanning the years from 1920 to about 1955, all written to me from people like Zanuck, DeMille, from my father and so many others. There's even a letter or two from Thomas Edison."

Lasky brightened visibly as he spoke of the possiblities ahead, and then he leaned forward, to reveal one more possibility so dear to his heart that he barely had the courage to describe it.

"You know, I began life as a poet. At nine, I sold a poem to the New York Herald Tribune for 10 bucks. I would like to end life as a poet. I hope no one else will take this idea if I mention it, but what I have in mind is an epic on John Paul Jones. I wrote a film about John Paul Jones one time and I did a lot of research. There is material on him for an epic with the scope of Benet's 'John Brown's body.' "

If enough people are curious about the old Hollywood and buy Lasky's book, it was facetiously suggested, maybe Lasky would get a charge out of trading in his fake fur for another one of those sumptuous raccoon jobs like the one pictured on the book's jacket.

Lasky didn't miss a beat, didn't even take time to smile at the attempted joke.

"If I ever get any money again," he said, "I know exactly what I'm going to do: Write that book, that poem, the one for which there is only one reader — my wife."

Somehow, the statement and the wealth of feeling behind it seemed like a partial answer, at least, to the question posed by the title of Lasky's book.

Whatever happened to Hollywood?

Lasky contends that the outrageoulsy demanding stars killed the goose that laid the golden egg. Others have different theories. Certainly, this one has some validity: It was not a kingdom to be inherited by poets.

To Victor Lasky, it Was A Ghost's Nightmare

—Star-News Photographer Paul Schmick

By John Fialka
Star-News Staff Writer

It was only Monday, but Victor Lasky was having a terrible week.

First there was the whole fuss about an obscure book he had written about Arthur Goldberg during Goldberg's unsuccessful bid for the New York governorship in 1970. The book has been secretly financed by Laurence Rockefeller. Goldberg was calling it "pornographic."

Then an article in a national news magazine called Lasky a "hatchet man." Finally there was this woman, staring at him from his television set in his comfortable Watergate apartment, charging that he was guilty of "dirty tricks" during the 1972 presidential campaign.

Dirty tricks! The very idea triggered a paroxysm of anger as Lasky struggled into his clothes and ran out, unshaven, into the street to catch a cab.

Soon, there was Victor Lasky, perhaps the most famous member of Washington's sizable but little known stable of ghost writers and "campaign book" journalists, barging right into the studio at Channel 5, demanding an apology right on the air.

But the woman, Bonnie Angelo, Time Magazine's White House correspondent, did not oblige him. Neither did Maury Povich, host of the talk show called "Panorama."

IT WAS a peculiar situation for Lasky, 57, who has "given the needle," as he puts it, to a whole generation of public figures in his books and articles.

Lasky is still fuming about the incident, which happened last week. "I don't want this idiot broad to destroy my reputation," he told a reporter. "She doesn't have the decency to apologize and neither does that idiot station and that idiot program, Panorama."

As for the business about "hatchet man," Lasky insists "I don't know what the hell 'hatchet man' means. You read the papers now and every reporter is a hatchet man. . . . Read Time or Newsweek, they hatchet all over the place. Thjis is the new journalism. I created a new thing, you know."

Lasky's public reputation is that of a conservative columnist writing conservative for the North American Newspaper Alliance. That wasn't what got him into all this trouble and that wasn't the side of Lasky that produced the book "Arthur J. Goldberg: The Old and The New" that may now be a peril to the vice presidential hopes for former New York governor Nelson Rockefeller.

No, it was Lasky's private reputation, that of one of the fastest, toughest campaign book writers in the business, that brought it all on.

A campaign book in a hastily organized fusillade of charges about a political candidate that suddenly appears during the heat of a campaign, usually in paperback, and usually heavily subsidized by the opposition.

Lasky, a former rewriteman for the late New York World-Telegram, can bang one of these out in as little as three weeks. (The rewriteman is the man who puts together fast-breaking news stories on deadline.)

LASKY, Victor
(1918 -)
WASHINGTON STAR-NEWS
(Washington, D.C.)
Oct. 21, 1974
[See also CA-5/6]

HE DID IT during the 1960 presidential campaign with a book entitled "John F. Kennedy: What's Behind the Image." (The foreward of the 300-page book says it was written in "less than two weeks," but Lasky insists it was more like there.)

Among many other assertions, the book charges that John Kennedy "would do anything" to become President. "In short," Lasky concluded near the end, "(John) Kennedy is a ruthless man, who must get what he wants at all costs."

"Ruthless," as he was, John Kennedy came off better in Lasky's book than his brother Robert. ". . . he is more openly ruthless; so much so, in fact, that at the Los Angeles convention, irate Democrats, with whom he had tangled, soon began to refer to him as 'Raul,' after Fidel Castro's brother."

Lasky claims he didn't make a dime out of this book. Rather, he says he donated it to the Nixon campaign effort as "a friend and partisan."

Three years later, Lasky wrote another book about Kennedy, "J.F.K.: The Man and the Myth," which was a lengthier, far more thoroughly researched criticism. It became a best seller and earned Lasky "over 300 grand," according to his estimate.

But even that much money doesn't last forever. And by 1970, when someone suggested that he write a campaign book about former Supreme Court Justice Goldberg for a total of $10,000, Lasky decided he would do it.

Goldberg was running against Gov. Rockefeller. Lasky says the proposal and the money came through Lasky's New York lawyer, John A. Wells. "I had no knowledge of the financing of this operation," Lasky insists, although he says he knew it was going to be used in the campaign.

THE AUTHOR admits to having some misgivings about writing about Goldberg, whom he describes as a "nice guy." The main problem Lasky remembers suggesting to Wells was that Goldberg was not a very colorful character to write about. Wells, he said, still thought the book should be written.

"And I says, aw he's (Goldberg) a bore, but you know you can write a book about anything, even artichokes," recalls Lasky.

Five weeks later, Lasky submitted a manuscript for a paperback that was far more interesting and probably more widely read than any book ever written about artichokes.

The book appears to be aimed at the liberal, heavily Jewish, New York City intellectual community that normally forms a major bastion of power behind any New York democrat in a statewide race.

It shows how, according to Lasky, Goldberg began his successful career as a Chicago labor lawyer by being a "red baiter." After serving in the Armed Forces in World War II as a "labor spy," Goldberg rose high in the ranks of organized labor, eventually became a close friend and secret supporter of Richard Nixon, according to Lasky.

When Kennedy chose Goldberg to be secretary of labor in 1960, Lasky asserts that Goldberg spent much of his time making speeches and giving Kennedy suggestions on irrelevant subjects.

Some of Lasky's sources for the book are not clear. He found a "labor observer" who said "Goldberg never lets himself get cornered where he has nothing to stand on but principal."

Because Goldberg was an ineffective labor administrator, Lasky charges, he was banished to the Supreme Court, where he "was a lackluster jurist," and, according to Lasky, wrote decisions that caused law enforcement to suffer "enormously."

LATER ON, in a chapter called "Goldberg in Arabia," Lasky hints that Goldberg helped the Arabs and hurt the Israeli cause during his stint as ambassador to the United Nations.

Often Lasky's main sources for the book are derogatory items, that may have appeared about Goldberg in the New York Post, The New Republic, or an other liberal-leaning publication.

Lasky is proud of this device, which he calls "cross-quotesmanship." "It's really a beautiful technique. Look, if I quote Barry Goldwater against Jack Kennedy, it doesn't mean a goddamn thing. But when I quote the original liberal sources, Christ it's damning. That's what kills Arthur Goldberg."

For instance, he reprinted one entire New York Post column branding Goldberg a "war criminal" for his failure to stop the spread of the Vietnam War during the Kennedy and Johnson administrations.

"Wow! What a column!" exults the book. "And it shook the hell out of Mr. Justice Goldberg in his posh Park Avenue offices. . . ."

After 192 pages of this, the book concludes with this description of the Democrats' gubernatorial candidate:

"The fact is, of course, that concern for others is not characteristic of a person who, like Mr. Goldberg, has kicked, scratched and thrust his way up the ladder to the positions of prominence which he has held. Such progress is the result of a 'What makes Sammy Run' drive and is the result of continued thought about oneself, one's career and one's record—twenty four hours a day, plus a lot of overtime."

THE AUTHOR has few soft spots for anybody in the book, although he does suggest that the shortcomings of Goldberg and his entourage were making Rockefeller "look more attractive and desirable to more enrolled Democrats."

(Most of the few complementary adjectives in the book are reserved for the author, who is described in a blurb on the back cover as having, "an excellent reputation for a number of hard-hitting books" and being "known for his biting wit and incisive documentary.")

After he handed in the manuscript, Lasky went on a trip to Israel and forgot about the book, which was distributed all over the state before the election. "It was a job. I sent copies of it out as a gag to people. They never read it. Who's interested in Arthur Goldberg," the author explained.

"I'd forgotten about the whole venture until recently when this thing broke wide open," he added, referring to the recent disclosure that the book was funded by the Rockefellers.

And that wasn't the only recent disclosure that has nettled Lasky. Evidence of the financial activities of the Republican Committee to Re-elect the President during the 1972 campaign, disclosed a $20,000 payment to Lasky for unspecified work. During the campaign, Lasky sometimes appeared wearing press credentials.

The payment, Lasky asserts, amounted to fees for ghostwriting speeches for Martha Mitchell, wife of the former attorney general. Lasky produces a small folder of carbon copies of Lions Club speeches and other statements made by Mrs. Mitchell to back up his point.

"I'm not very proud of the fact that I was a ghost-writer for Martha Mitchell," Lasky explains. "I don't want to go down in history for that. As a ghost you normally don't discuss these things. Unfortunately, I'm caught in a crazy position where I have to show you my private business."

Latham Spins Tales

By BEA L. HINES
Herald Staff Writer

As a young girl growing up in Buchannon, W. Va., Jean Lee Latham would sit for hours weaving tales of adventure while her younger brother and his friends sat spellbound.

Today, at 72, she's witty and pert and still weaving tales. And she's loving it more and more each day.

"Writers don't retire," she said. "I never heard of a writer who liked what he was doing retiring. We just dry up and blow away," she said with a hearty laugh.

Ms. Latham, a writer of children's books for more than 20 years said she "just naturally wrote from the time I could spell."

A Late Career

HOWEVER, writing children's books is a Johnny-come-lately profession for her.

Back in West Virginia, the Lathams lived just across from a lovely bit of unpruned forest. The four Latham children spent their younger days romping through the woods and at quieter times, listening to stories made up and told by sister Jean.

By the time she entered college at West Virginia Wesleyan College, she had started to write plays.

After a short career of teaching she entered the field of playwriting professionally and worked for years as a writer for radio shows such as Grand Central Station and First Nighter.

Then came the war, and she went into an entirely different field — training signal corps inspectors.

"Nobody knew I was a writer throughout the war," she said with a chuckle. "The reason I didn't tell anyone was, the only men left in the signal corps were radio hams and it wouldn't have done any good for me to tell them," she said.

Wrote For Television

AFTER THE WAR, she wrote for a while for the Kraft Television Theater.

Later, it was her younger brother, who was at that time working for Look Magazine, who told her of a publishing company that was looking for a book on a certain subject.

The Story of Eli Whitney, a colorful narrative of the famous inventor's life, became the first of many children books written by her.

Since that time, she has won the Newbery Award for outstanding contributions to children's literature and is listed in Who's Who in America.

LATHAM, Jean Lee (1902 -) MIAMI HERALD (Miami, Fla.) July 9, 1974 [See also CA-7/8]

"Writing books for children is very different from writing plays," Ms. Latham said. "Writing plays is like writing a recipe for actors and directors to carry out.

"In books, there's no director or actor. You have to get it all in the book so that the reader carries out all the parts."

She knows when she's done the job, too, because her best critics are her young readers. Even before she sends her manuscript off to the publisher, she calls in one of her young friends to read it for her.

"When I want someone to judge a book I've written, I call in a bright, but lazy 12-year-old boy and ask him to read it and tell me what should come out. If he can't find anything to take out, I know I've made it.

"I never ask a kid what he likes. I just say, 'What should I take out?' "

A Love Of Drama

BECAUSE of her background in plays and radio, Ms. Latham said she is, by nature, a dramatist.

"I look for suspense. Unless you say, 'This thing couldn't have happened in this person's life, but it did,' I won't do it. Every character I've written about, on the surface it seemed whatever he did at the time was impossible. But he did it."

Writing for children has been more fun for her than "you could shake a stick at," she says.

"But if you don't have a feeling for all ages, you can't write for children.

"Once in a while an adult will say, 'I didn't like a scene or character" in one of your books.' "I just say to them, 'I couldn't care less Dear. I didn't write it for you.' "

She respects her young readers and spends years of research on a new book.

"I may have a half million words of research before I start writing," she said.

Most of this research over the past 18 years has been done at the University of Miami Otto G. Richter Library.

"That library has given me a lot of tender loving care," she said.

THAT'S WHY recently, she gave the library a gift — several of her manuscripts and working notes.

"Since a great deal of my writing is based on history and biographies, I depend on the library to have material when I need it. If they don't have it, they will call the Library of Congress or the Library of Collections for me," she said.

A pint-size woman whose big voice, is sprinkled with earthy slangs and warm laughs, Ms. Latham said she is always working on something but she never talks about what she's working on.

"It's like an itch. If you talk about it, then you have to scratch that itch. Once you've scratched it, it's then like warmed over hash."

"Not even my publisher knows what I'm working on at the time," she said.

She enjoys writing for boys most of all. Maybe, she said, it goes back to the early days when she made up stories for her younger brother.

One of the best compliments ever paid her came from a young boy who'd met her at his school after an assembly.

"I sure was disappointed when I saw you," the youngster said to her. "But as soon as you started talking it was alright. You're one of us."

"I get this all the time," she said laughing. "I look ancient to them, but when I get to talking to them, they know I'm with them."

Catching Up With A Childhood Dream

Eugene Lee, son of author Edward Edson Lee, at Hi-Lee Cottage on Lake Ripley

By R. H. Gardner

THE WORD "love" has many connotations apart from romance and sex. This is a love story about a small boy and an aging man. It has no middle, only a beginning and an end, because the boy grew up and the man died.

Among the presents given to me by my mother on my eighth Christmas was a book, which started off:

I got into the bushes quick as scat. Biting hard on my breath, sort of. For right there in front of our eyes was a regular old gee-whacker of a dinosaur. Bigger than the town water tower and the Methodist Church steeple put together. I tell you it was risky for us.

My chum got ready with his trusty bow and arrow.

"Do you think you can hit him in the heart?" I said, excited-like, squinting ahead to where the dinosaur was dragging his slimy body out of the pond.

Scoop Ellery's face was rigid.

"Got to," he said, steady-like. "If I miss, he'll turn on us and kill us both."

"It's a lucky thing for Red and Peg," I said, thinking of my other chums, "that they aren't in it."

"They'll miss us," said Scoop, "if we get killed."

My thoughts took a crazy jump.

"Why not aim for a tickly spot in his ribs," I snickered, pointing to the dinosaur, "and let him giggle himself to death?"

"Sh-h-h-h," cautioned Scoop, putting out a hand. "He's listening. The wind is blowing that way. He smells us."

"What of it?" I grinned. "We don't smell bad."

Such was my introduction to the Jerry Todd series of boys' adventure stories. Not make-believe adventures like the dinosaur game played by Jerry and Scoop here, but real experiences involving cops, robbers, ghosts and similarly stimulating subject matter. For having been made "genuine Juvenile Jupiter Detectives" by an old con artist who sold them membership in a fake detective agency, Jerry, Scoop, Red and Peg spent all their time solving mysteries in their hometown of Tutter, Ill., mystery capital of the world.

One would have to have been a small-town boy himself in those dim, pre-television days to understand the fascination these books held for me and others like me all over the country. It is true that the Bob Dexter and Hardy Boys books also concerned boy detectives, but neither was written with the warmth, color and, above all, humor that made the Jerry Todds and Poppy Otts (a companion series for which Jerry also acted as first person narrator) unique.

To say I loved them would be putting it mildly, but my involvement at first was with the characters only. In my childish ignorance, I had accepted the fiction that Jerry himself was the author. The name, Leo Edwards, on the cover was a meaningless abstraction until a postscript to "Jerry Todd and the Purring Egg," written not by Edwards but by a real boy like myself, changed everything.

To start with (wrote Eddie Blimke) *I heard this story of the "purring" egg before it was put into a book. That is, I was one of a gang of kids to whom the author read the story aloud. My dad has a summer home at Lake Ripley, near Cambridge, Wisconsin, and that is where Edward Edson Lee spends his summers. Mr. Lee is an author. He writes books for boys. This is one of his books, only it has the name of Leo Edwards on the cover. Some authors, you know, have a pen name as they call it, and Leo Edwards is Mr. Lee's pen name.*

LEE, Edward Edson
(pseud. Leo Edwards)
MILWAUKEE JOURNAL
(Milwaukee, Wisc.)
Oct. 13, 1974

(Continued from preceding page)

Well, as you can imagine, we hang around Mr. Lee's cottage quite a lot when we're at the lake. He's jolly and always ready for fun. He likes kids. Whenever he finishes a new book he sends word to us, up and down the lake shore, and that night we crowd around him on his front porch while he reads the book to us. Only it isn't a book then, it's what he calls a manuscript.

Eddie's story concerned an initiation dreamed up by the author and himself in honor of a young summer visitor named Herb Isham. The initiation took place at Hi-Lee Cottage, where the Lees lived, and frankly I found it rather silly. It was the way Eddie wound up his account that impressed me.

I tell you what — if ever you are near Lake Ripley in the summer time drop in and see me for a few minutes. Or, if you prefer, stop in at Hi-Lee Cottage and see Mr. and Mrs. Lee and their boy "Beanie." There's a secret about "Beanie" and Jerry Todd, but I can't put you wise here. I'll whisper the secret to you if you come to see me. A lot of boys come to Lake Ripley to see Mr. Lee. And they all get a warm welcome. I want you to know that.

In J. D. Salinger's "Catcher in the Rye," Holden Caulfield says that, after reading a book he particularly likes, he has a desire to telephone the author. I didn't merely want to call; I wanted to catch the next train to Cambridge. In short, Eddie made me conscious of the author as a real person, who lived in a specific locality and whom I might someday meet. The result was that all the affection I felt for the books became focused on him.

MY AWARENESS of Leo Edwards, as a living reality, as opposed to a name on a dust jacket, was intensified through reading "Our Chatter-Box," a sort of open forum inaugurated with "Poppy Ott and the Tittering Totem," in which the author published and commented on letters sent in by readers. Among the items included were poems, and if a boy was lucky enough to have his poem published, he received an autographed copy of the book in which it appeared. The following — from Charles Hockett, of Worthington, Ohio — appeared in the first chatter-box and set the tone, not to mention the quality, of most that came after:

Our Gang
My name is Jerry Todd,
I live in Illinois,
I have a lot of fun
For I play with the boys.
Scoop Ellery and Red Meyers
Are two of my good friends,
Peg Shaw is the other one.
Why? Well, it all depends.

When I read this composition, which went on in much the same vein for nine stanzas, and realized I could earn a book with Edwards' signature in it simply by writing something like it, I got busy with paper and pencil. The poem I finally came up with was every bit as bad as Charles Hockett's, so I didn't see how I could miss. But a quick scanning of the chatter-box in the next Poppy Ott book showed me I had underestimated my competition. For though it contained no less than seven poems — all terrible — mine was not among them.

Disappointment because my literary efforts had not been fully appreciated did not prevent my taking advantage of an offer made by Edwards in one of the chatter-boxes to send his photograph to any who requested it. My parents

LEE, Edward Edson

MILWAUKEE JOURNAL (Milwaukee, Wisc.)

Oct. 13, 1974

had named me Rufus Hallette after my father and grandfather and, until I changed to "Hal" at the age of 12, insisted on calling me "Rufe." Consequently, the letter I received in reply to my request began:

My dear Rufe:

I am sending you a picture of myself which I hope you will like and I am looking forward to receiving one of you in return.

Hope you will pass Hi-Lee Cottage sometime and stop in and see me. Boys are always welcome and there is always a bunch hanging around. And a good bunch, too, believe me.

Lots of luck and best wishes.

Your pal,
Leo Edwards

Encouraged by all this attention, I decided to try my hand at another poem, which I sent along, together with a snapshot, the next day. But again the Muse let me down. The chatter-box in "Poppy Ott Hits the Trail" had 11 poems, sent in by boys from New York to Texas, but mine was not there. However, under the heading "Pictures," a few pages farther on, I found:

Gee miny crickets gosh! I've got enough pictures here to fill a picture gallery. Pictures of small boys, big boys, long-legged boys, and all kinds of boys. I doubt if I can mention them all in this "Chatter-Box," but I'll do the best I can.

First on the list is the picture of a boy in overalls. This is Rufe Gardner, Mayfield, Ky., with a little black cap on the side of his head and a grin that spreads from ear to ear. Some guy! He's 12 years old, he says. Accompanying Rufe's swell letter is a poem, but it didn't seem quite as good to me as many I have. Here's hopin' I meet you sometimes, Rufe.

After that, I stopped writing to Leo Edwards. It wasn't so much his crummy attitude about my poetry as the fact that, having reached the pinnacle of being mentioned in a chatter-box, I felt there was no percentage in it. I did not, however, stop reading — or, rather, rereading, for at about this point the quality of the books began to deteriorate. The characters lost their charm, and the stories became downright boring. It was as if they had been written by somebody else.

Or was it simply that I was growing up? Girls — who figured only slightly in the books and then more as good "guys" than as females — were beginning to command my attention. So when, in my early teens, we moved from our big house in Mayfield to a relatively small apartment in Nashville, the books, together with other belongings we had no room for, were left behind in my Aunt Mayme's attic. And in the flurry of adolescent preoccupations that followed, I forgot about them.

Aunt Mayme died in 1966 and the following summer her daughter, my Cousin Ann, wrote from Louisville saying she was selling the house and would I please meet her in Mayfield to go through the things in the attic? And there, like a booby trap left for me by my child-self, were the books, with all their memories, waiting. Naturally, I could not resist reading them again, and they aroused more in me than nostalgia.

I had not, I saw, been wrong about Edwards. Unlike the incredible Edward Stratemeyer, who under a number of pseudonyms wrote most of the popular children's series of his day, he had not ground out potboilers with cardboard settings and characters. His Tutter — fictional name for Utica, the tiny Illinois town where he grew up — was three dimensional, rich in atmosphere and geographical detail. And, combined with his ingenious plots and salty, grass root characters, it provided a beguiling picture of small-town America during the early part of the century.

CONGRATULATING myself on the discernment I had displayed as a child, I quickly finished all the books recovered from the attic and began haunting the secondhand stores, hoping to pick up the others. No luck. Nor did the public library offer any help. Not only was Edwards not listed in the card catalog but no mention of him was made in any of the reference books I consulted on American authors, either living or dead. What was the explanation for this oversight? Surely Jerry and Poppy deserved as much immortality as Stratemeyer's Bobbsey Twins and Bunny Brown and Sister Sue. My indignation thus aroused, I decided to put him on record by writing an article about him myself.

My first move was a letter to G. W. Crump, editor of the Cambridge News. Edwards I assumed to be dead, but what about "Beanie"? Did Mr. Crump know of his whereabouts? Weeks passed. Then, arriving at my office one day, I was told I had received a telephone call from a Eugene Lee, of Beloit, who turned out to be "Beanie" himself. An executive with the Beloit Corporation, since retired, he said he still spent part of every year at Hi-Lee Cottage, and Mr. Crump had forwarded my letter to him.

I learned that "Leo," as he calls his father, had died in 1944 at the age of 60. The date surprised me, because the deterioration in quality to which I have alluded began a good 10 years before that, leading

(Continued from preceding page)

me to believe that the books after "Poppy Ott Hits the Trail" had been written by someone else. And the most logical explanation was that Edwards had died.

"No," said Eugene Lee, "he wrote them, but he was in bad shape. Everything sort of fell apart at the end."

Shocked that a man whose attitude, as revealed in his writings, was so unequivocally upbeat should "fall apart at the end," I begged for further information; Mr. Lee promised to write, and also referred me to a St. Louis book collector specializing in Edwards lore. For it appeared I was not the only one who cherished the memory of his father.

"There's a big fan club," I was told. "They have a newspaper and everything."

The idea of a Jerry-Poppy fan club composed of middle aged men intrigued me. I immediately sent off a letter to the St. Louis collector, requesting details. They arrived in the next week's mail.

"I could talk about Leo Edwards for hours," wrote Willis J. Potthoff, a 61 year old engineer with Emerson Electric; and it was obvious from the material he enclosed that he shared this propensity with others. The envelope contained several issues of the "Tutter Bugle," identified as "Voice of the Leo Edwards Juvenile Jupiter Detective Association," the fan club referred to by Mr. Lee.

I have since learned that the "Bugle," started in 1967 by Robert L. Johnson of Bisbee, Ariz., only lasted a couple of years, but at one time its subscribers, reflecting the membership of the club, totaled 100. The first anniversary issue carried the announcement of a projected convention of Edwards fans to be held in his hometown during the coming year (1969). Actually, the meeting took place not at Utica but at Hi-Lee Cottage, and, according to a story in the August-September issue of the Methodist publication Together, it was well attended by a group that included lawyers, teachers, merchants, engineers and bankers, all of whom came to recall what it was like to be a boy "in the days before Hitler, television and affluence came along to change the world of boys as it used to be."

Mr. Potthoff seemed impressed by the fact that I had been mentioned in one of the chatter-boxes and enclosed a Xeroxed copy of a "mention" concerning himself. A few days later Eugene Lee's letter arrived.

I always find this type of letter difficult to write. I do not know exactly where to start, exactly what to say and more important when I've said enough. So I'll make it brief.

Leo died in 1944 at our home in Rockford, Ill. He was just 60 years old, a broken, sick and bitter man. As far as Betty and I were concerned his books died with him and that was that. But it wasn't. As the years have passed by it has all gained a head of steam. Book collectors, a magazine published bi-monthly, the rights sold to a Hollywood group, etc.

Many people come to Hi-Lee Cottage at Lake Ripley. Some come to see where the books were written. Others come to see me, son of the author. These are the ones I have qualms about. They have formed a picture of Leo by reading his books, and they are looking for something they do not find; for while I look much like Leo, I'm not much like him in other ways.

Being the son of a popular author of boys' books has its drawbacks, I gathered during a visit of my own to the Lee cottage a year ago. "This is where they'd land," said my host, leading me down the steep path from the house to the lake. "He'd read the book to them in two installments, half one night and half the next. At the end of the first half he'd treat them to hot dogs, cooked around a fire in the backyard. The next night there'd be ice cream." Somehow, the picture was different from that evoked by Eddie Blimke.

LEE, Edward Edson

MILWAUKEE JOURNAL (Milwaukee, Wisc.) Oct. 13, 1974

As a child, "Beanie," who typed most of his father's manuscripts, had to share him with all the other boys in the area. He still has to do it in a way often at variance with his nature and, at times, a downright nuisance.

For fans, whether they be callow kids or seasoned graybeards, all seem to have one thing in common — the feeling that love gives them proprietary rights. One visitor to the cottage arrived, unheralded, at 3 a.m. with two carloads of friends and relatives. Another, also uninvited, strode in as the Lees were sitting down to dinner and proceeded to join them at the table Autographed books have disappeared from the shelves, such as the two in which Leo acknowledged (the "secret" hinted at so broadly by Eddie) that "Beanie" was the real life model for Jerry Todd.

Despite such invasions of his privacy and violations of his hospitality, Eugene Lee feels a strong sense of responsibility to the hundreds of people who write seeking information about Leo and help in finding his books, out of print since Grosset & Dunlap scrapped the plates during World War II. Only recently he responded to the requests of a 13 year old Shreveport boy and a Virginia housewife (who wanted a Poppy Ott to surprise her husband with on Christmas) with free gifts of books, of which he has a good, if rapidly shrinking, supply.

A far from sentimental man, he still finds it hard to discuss the final years of his father's life, when diminishing sales and the dissolution of his 30 year marriage left him a virtual recluse. Every time I broached the subject, as we sat looking at the lake he told me Leo loved, he shied away from it. I did, however, get certain impressions.

EDWARDS left Utica in 1897 at the age of 13 to take a menial job in a Beloit factory. Later, when he began to write, he drew upon his childhood recollections to create the character and characters of Tutter. Thus, though all the Jerry Todd-Poppy Ott books were written after World War I, they must have reflected a life of a much earlier period. This didn't matter too much when the tempo of life was so slow one could detect only superficial changes between one decade and the next. But, as that tempo quickened with the approach of World War II, the books must have lost their "relevance" to a generation whose eyes were turned not to the pleasantries of the past but to the terrors of the future.

At any rate, Edwards' popularity began to wane. His sales — which, according to his son, never totaled much more than 2,000,000 books — fell off; and his halfhearted attempts to remedy the situation by changing his format and updating his style proved to be disastrous.

Perhaps most disheartening of all, his boys — those loyal legions who every summer crowded his doorstep, warming him with their love; delighting him with their laughter — grew up, married and moved away to adult responsibilities elsewhere. Forgotten (or so it must have seemed), he lived on at Hi-Lee, the memories of happier times insufficient to lift him from the despondency that reached epic proportions with the discovery that he had incurable cancer.

"Sometimes," Eugene Lee told me, "he would lie on a chair in the backyard all afternoon without moving." A dreadful image for one whose childhood was graced by the felicity of his writing.

Eugene and his charming wife Betty were most gracious during my short stay, enduring my persistent questions, stuffing me with delicious fish he (as acknowledged champion of the lake) had caught that same afternoon, and permitting me to spend the night in Leo's room — which, like the rest of the cottage, I found both unpretentious and comfortable.

As I lay there, listening to the midnight voices of boys shouting at one another over the racket of an outboard motor, I wondered if, during those terrible years, Leo had not lain in the same spot and listened to the clamor of similar voices (Jerry, Scoop, Red and Peg?) calling from the past. For I well knew that all the pilgrims to Hi-Lee came in answer to such voices. They heard them when they reread the books, and they hoped to hear them even more distinctly in the house where the books had been written — the piping, proud, pathetic voices that so many years ago had been theirs.

With this in mind, I felt my way through the darkened hall to the bookcase and selected from the two shelves of vellum-encased volumes Gene Lee's own copy of "Jerry Todd and the Talking Frog," the book that, given to me by my mother on my eighth Christmas, had introduced me to hundreds of happy hours. And, returning to Leo's room, I opened it to Chapter 1:

"I got into the bushes quick as scat. . . ."

R. H. Gardner is drama critic for the Baltimore (Md.) Sun. His article first appeared in the Sun's Spectator section.

Law or History, Wake Forest's Lee Sticks to the Facts

Dr. Robert Earl Lee

By Howard Carr
Staff Reporter

Dr. Robert E. Lee rubbed the fingers of his right hand together, trying to get off a bit of printer's ink.

"You get that ink on your fingers and you'll never get it off," he said. "Once you get something printed with your name on it, you're a goner."

As he spoke at his office at the Wake Forest law school, Lee was thumbing through the latest thing to have his name printed on it — a 264-page book on "Blackbear the Pirate: A Reappraisal of His Life and Times." (John F. Blair, Winston-Salem, $8.95).

"I worked on it off and on for about 10 years," the 68-year-old professor of law said. "Writing history nowadays is a lot simpler than it used to be — with the Xerox machine you can stay in your own home most of the time and still do a wonderful job."

Lee painstakingly researched his subject — using both published and unpublished sources — from places as close as the state archives in Raleigh, and as far away as the British Museum in London. The result is a well-documented, interesting account of Edward Teach, a fierce Englishman who fastidiously cultivated his image, not only as a pirate, but also as a womanizer — he was married 14 times — and a drinker — an entry in his shop's log once recorded "Such a day, rum all out: — Our company somewhat sober: — A damned confusion amongst us."

But by 1718 even Blackbeard — his name came from the beard "which a contemporary wrote, "like a frightful meteor, covered his whole face and frightened America more than any comet" — realized that piracy was on its way out, and at the time of his death Teach was in what Lee calls "semi-retirement."

But to the very end, Blackbeard was tough. When he was finally cornered near Ocracoke inlet by an expedition of dubious legality sent by a Virginia governor who was trying to regain his popularity, Teach took five gunshot wounds and 20 sabre cuts before he dropped dead. (His head was then chopped off, and the hard drinker's skull, ironically enough, eventually ended up as a silver-plated punch bowl at the Raleigh Tavern in Williamsburg, Va.)

"History writing can be compared to an iceberg—in the end you can only see about one-tenth of the material you originally had," Lee said. "I don't care for some of these new historians who have people talking back and forth when they really don't know what was said. I only put in what I could verify—I'm a traditionalist in that respect."

Lee's style is also traditional—a New York publishing firm which was interested in the book asked Lee to rewrite parts of it . . . to spice it up a little.

"They wanted it like a movie—an exciting beginning, and then flashbacks to tell about his life," Lee said. "I told them I was too conservative to write a book like that—after studying and writing about the law all my life I'm too old to change the way I write."

LEE, Robert Earl
(1906 -)

WINSTON-SALEM JOURNAL & SENTINEL (Winston-Salem, N.C.) Dec. 15, 1974

The way he has written has been acceptable enough to keep his syndicated legal column, "This Is The Law," going for 21 years. And his style has been good enough for 12 law books, including a three-volume set "North Carolina Family Law", which Pasco Bowman, the dean of the Wake Forest law school, says "is in the office of every family lawyer in this state."

In his own way, "Nig" Lee, as he is known to his friends and students, is as much of a legend in North Carolina law as Blackbeard is in piracy. Born in Kinston, Robert E. (for Earl, not Edward) Lee joined the bar in 1927—one day before his 21st birthday. He was a professor of law at Temple at the age of 22, and after World War II he was chosen to rebuild the Wake Forest law school, which had been merged with Duke's during World War II.

His four years as dean of the school are still known as the Reign of Terror—when students dropped out of school just to escape Lee's merciless questioning, and when ex-GIs looking for a free ride on the GI Bill quickly discovered they had better things do do. An anonymous student's engraved poem on the wall of Lee's office recalls the Reign of Terror in the style of the 23rd Psalm:

"Dr. Lee is my Law professor/ I shall not pass . . . He asketh me technical questions/ He confuseth my mind/ Yea tho I study in Brown until three in the morning/ I shall flunk the finals/ For Lee is against me./ His notes and his lectures they puzzle me/ He contradicteth my answers before me/ In the presence of mine classmates."

Lee may have been a tough teacher, but he was also a good one, and legislators have called on him ever since for advice on pending bills. His best known appearance before the General Assembly came in 1973, when he was asked to speak on the proposed Equal Rights Amendment. With the galleries full of hissing, booing feminists, Lee lambasted the amendment for the chaos he said it would create in North Carolina law. After tracing the rise of women from a "beast of burden" to her present status as a "queen on her throne," Lee concluded his speech with a retort to the galleries: "Just remember this when you go out of this room—all the many legal rights you have now you wouldn't have unless the men had released them to you."

Lee hasn't changed his views on the amendment, but he tries to take a lower profile about it: "My students wouldn't respect me if they thought I were some kind of crusader, and that's the role I was being placed in."

Althought Lee thinks that some of his current students regard him as a "museum piece", most students still seem to appreciate him and his unorthodox approach to teaching — at the beginning of each semester, he sells his students mimeographed "Nig Notes" for his classes, so that he can have more time to lecture on different subjects. His lectures, students say, are among the best in the school, whether he's discussiug his gastronomic theory of law ("Tell me what a judge ate for breakfast and I'll tell you how to handle him") or the legal ramifications of sex, which Lee refers to as "partaking of horizontal refreshment".

One first-year law student said that although he was originally turned off by Lee's old-fashioned manner, he now respects Lee as one of the best teachers he's ever had.

"He's just so bright, but he's not a complete academic like some of those people," the student said. "He always relates the law to what's going on in the real world. He really wakes you up in the morning."

And if Lee is as good a teacher as ever, he is also almost as feared as he used to be.

"The odds of me being called on in class are 143 to one," the student said," but I wouldn't think of going into the Nig's class unprepared, just because of what I've heard about him — even before I came here people were telling me about him."

Lee smiles when he thinks of his reputation. "If they think I'm rough now, they should have seen me during the Reign of Terror. I've mellowed a lot since then" — an opinion which students confirm. Lee shocked some students when he gave out a couple of As during the 1974 summer session, and he has told the first-year students that he and they are members of the same class, referring to the fact that like them, he'll be through with school in 1977, when Wake Forest's mandatory retirement age of 70 finally catches up with him.

"I've loved it here," he said recently. "When I was at Temple, I had to take a train to work every day. Now, I can walk to work. I think I have the finest job in North Carolina."

She Writes About Aliens—Men Included

—Journal Photo

By Paula Brookmire
of The Journal Staff

Ursula K. LeGuin is a successful female writer in a male field: science fiction. In fact, she is probably the most well known woman in the field today.

Yet, by her own admission, she prefers using male main characters and has done so in most of her nine novels and approximately 20 short stories.

Despite her support of the women's movement ("I don't see how you can be an intelligent woman and not be a feminist"), Mrs. LeGuin says, "I have never been able to write a female main character."

She gives various explanations.

Male Viewpoint

For instance, when Mrs. LeGuin was in Milwaukee recently for the annual conference of the Science Fiction Research Association, held at the University of Wisconsin — Milwaukee Union, a woman in one session asked the author:

"Why did you choose technically to use a male viewpoint in the book 'The Left Hand of Darkness'?"

"It was for a very humiliating reason," Mrs. LeGuin replied. "It's because I thought men would loathe the book, would be unsettled and unnerved by it."

Won Awards

"Darkness" is about a world of androgynes, beings who function as both males and females. The book is her best known and it won Mrs. LeGuin the two top science fiction awards, the Nebula and the Hugo, in 1969.

"Since the larger percentage of science fiction readers are male, Mrs. LeGuin continued, "I though it would be easier for them if they had a man — and a rather stupid and slightly bigoted man actually — to work in with and sort of be changed with."

In an interview Mrs. LeGuin explained further why she avoided writing female main characters.

Keeps Distance

"I don't want to write autobiographies," she said. "I want to distance myself from my books.

"That's one of the reasons I write science fiction. I write about aliens. Men are aliens, too. I like the alien point of view."

For the uninitiated, science fiction is the branch of literature and art that speculates on the future or the past, often describing the possible impact of science and technology on society or on individuals.

Much of modern science fiction (usually abbreviated SF) has de-emphasized "hard" science.

Impact of Ideas

It focuses, instead, on social science, speculating on the impact of different ideas and cultures. Mrs. LeGuin's books are generally of this type.

In her latest novel, The Dispossessed" (Harper & Row), she contrasts her ideal anarchistic society with a state run world in which money and status are the ideals — a world much like the US, she said. In her ideal society no one owns anything. Therefore, females can't be viewed as possessions.

Another interesting facet of the society is that people have only one name — and that is handed out by a computer that doesn't distinguish between the sexes.

You can't tell that Takver, Rulag and Odo are female names any more than you can spot Shevek, Palat and Tirin as male names.

With this technique, female pronouns often sneak up on the reader.

For instance, this passage: "The senior physicist at the institute was named Mitis." Most Americans would automatically assume that anyone as intellectual as a physicist must be a man.

But the next line begins, "She was . . ."

In the author's ideal society, also, possessive pronouns are seldom used. Nor are there any husbands or wives— only partners. And it is "the" partner, not "my" partner.

Are Sex Objects

In case the reader doesn't see how that contrasts with the American phrase, "my wife," Mrs. LeGuin pictures women in her fictional American-like world as being treated totally as sex objects. They are not allowed into universities or any intellectual area of life.

If Mrs. LeGuin feels so strongly about discrimination against women, the question comes up again: Why doesn't she use strong, female main characters with whom women can identify?

Her answer is that she is not a "radical" feminist.

She prefers to work on improving her writing rather than to work for the women's movement to the point where she would become known as a feminist writer rather than simply a writer. Some critics—Mrs. LeGuin calls them idiots — even say she writes like a man.

Topics Are Tough

They probably mean that she tackles some pretty tough topics—world politics, theories of time and the universe, basic human motivations—which they usually consider the realm of men.

Asked whether she had ever experienced discrimination as a woman, Mrs. LeGuin said she had found very little in the publishing world—at least "not the kind that would cripple my career."

On the other hand, her original field was French. In the midst of her work for a doctorate, however, she feared that even with a Ph.D., as a woman she would be relegated to teaching freshman French classes.

"So I got out," she said.

When did she start writing? "I think it was when I learned the alphabet," she said. "I always wrote. I didn't WANT to be a writer. I WAS."

Mrs. LeGuin said she was especially lucky to have had such a free childhood.

"I was the youngest (of four children) and was the only girl. And there was no difference in expectations for any of us. Our parents were totally nonsexist."

She is the daughter of a famous anthropologist, the late Alfred L. Kroeber, and author Theodora K. Kroeber.

Her three brothers also have achieved success. One is a psychologist, one a historian and one an English professor.

Happy Marriage

Perhaps because of the stability of her parents' marriage or of her own (at 45, Mrs. LeGuin has been married to the same man for over 20 years), the author often pictures marriage, or what she calls "pair bonding," as an ideal.

"Long term pair bonding—sexuality plus affection that lasts—seems to me one of the most important things human beings can do," she said.

Of course it isn't for everyone, she added.

Has Advice

If there is any advice Mrs. LeGuin would give aspiring women writers, it is this:

"One thing women my age have said to me is that they feel their lives have been so narrow that they didn't think there was anything they could write about.

"All I can say to them is: "'Look at Jane Austen and Charlotte Bronte.' "

Mrs. LeGuin is the author of six SF books and three books that would be classified as fantasy and as directed more for young adults.

Besides her SF awards, she has also won the Boston Globe-Hornbook award, the Newberry Honor Book award and the National Book Award.

The mother of three, Mrs. LeGuin resides in Portland, Ore., with her husband Charles.

Mrs. LeGuin's visit here was sponsored by UWM's Center for 20th Century Studies, host of the science fiction conference.

LeGUIN,
Ursula K(roeber)
(1929-)

MILWAUKEE JOURNAL
(Milwaukee, Wisc.)

July 21, 1974

[See also CA-21/22]

Elmore Leonard (Photo by Sue Marx)

LEONARD, Elmore
(1925 -   )

THE DETROITER
(Detroit, Mich.)

June, 1974

'HEY, DAD... IT'S CLINT EASTWOOD!'

by Gay Rubin

The phone rings. Grouped around the T.V. set are two teenage boys, munching granola, wearing jeans. Father is leaning back in his easy chair, wearing a V-neck sweater, moccasins. It rings again. Silence. The sounds of footsteps echoing on empty pavement. The gloved hand of an unseen villain turning a door knob. A creak. The phone rings again. Nobody wants to answer. More footsteps.

"I'll get it Dad," one boy says.

Dad nods.

Smash. A fist. Glass shattering. A broken window.

"Hey Dad. It's Clint Eastwood."

"Okay, thanks," Dad says. He walks to the phone, his eyes linger on the T.V. screen for a second.

"Clint? Hi Clint. Yes. Fine. Fine, how about yourself?"

This could happen in any living room. A joke. It's the man's accountant calling, and his name is Sam.

Wrong.

Then it is Hollywood. The Dad is a film writer and gets calls from producers, directors, movie stars. He wears antique Indian jewelry and lives a glamorous life, attending famous parties and keeping a gorgeous tan, as he drives along palm-lined avenues in his specially equipped, bronze, super-sports car, or jets to locations around the world.

Wrong. Or half-wrong. The Dad is truly a film writer; he does get calls from movie stars, producers, and directors, and he does travel to locations, but he lives and works in suburban Detroit. His name is Elmore Leonard, and ever since he published his first cowboy story in *Dime Western* (a prestige pulp) in the early '50s, while he was a copy writer at Campbell-Ewald, he has been writing novels and film scripts at a prolific rate. He has quite a list of credits. Among his books are *The Bounty Hunter, The Law at Randado, Escape from 5 Shadows, Stand on the Saber, Hombre, The Big Bounce,* and *The Moonshine War.* His films include: *The Tall T, 3:10 to Yuma, Hombre, The Big Bounce, Valdez is Coming, The Moonshine War,* and *Joe Kidd.*

Now his latest novel is out, *Fifty-two Pick Up,* published by Dial Press. Set in Detroit, it is a suspense novel about a man who owns a plant that manufactures auto parts. He likes his work and his attractive interesting wife, but has been having an affair with a young model, one who poses nude in one of those "adult art studio" places. The affair leads to his being blackmailed and the book takes us from Bloomfield Hills (where he lives) to Fraser (where the plant is) to the inner city (where his girlfriend and her colleagues play and work.) He is a tough, likeable person. We can easily forgive him for his slight transgression and feel along with him, all the horror and frustration he suffers, as he tries to solve his problem and protect his family from his unidentifiable blackmailers who prove themselves to be murderers and rapists, as well.

(Continued from preceding page)

Besides being entertaining reading, there is a bonus for Detroiters. They will wonder if the character is based on anyone they know and should recognize the restaurants, bars, clubs, and streets. It is all familiar terrain.

Leonard explains the beginning of *Fifty-two Pick Up* this way:

"Walter Mirish, the film producer, was in town looking for a plant in which to shoot *Wheels*. I mentioned a scene I had in mind . . . (he described the scene, a pivotal, dramatic point in the book) . . . He liked it. I worked backward from that scene to write *Fifty-two Pick Up*. Someone else bought the film and will be producing it sometime this year."

"I won't be writing the film script. I was taken off," he smiled. "That often happens. And usually it's a good thing. A writer spends so much time on a novel. Writing. Rewriting, that he runs out of gas. He can't see it any other way after awhile. Someone else comes in and has fresh ideas. Then, too, somtimes directors have certain writers they work with."

In front of him on his desk was the first draft of another novel—the written-over, typed-over yellow sheets familiar to all writers. "It's about two men who decide to go into the business they've always wanted: robbery," he smiled. It's clear the movie will be fun and he is having fun writing it.

"I'm putting this aside for a while though," he said. "I'm doing the film script of a novel. He pointed to a larger than usual paperback that had no picture on the unglossy cover. "I didn't write this one," he said. "In fact it isn't out yet, they just put it together like this, a prepublication copy, because they thought it would sell to films. I suppose."

As Leonard taps out the script, Birmingham shoppers pass beneath his windows. They are out to buy a wash-and-wear shirt or to look for suede platform sandals. They would be astonished to know that a movie they will someday watch, perhaps a western set in Arizona, is originating only a few feet from them on Pierce Street.

Leonard works about five hours a day in his cozy, cluttered office. When he needs her, a secretary comes in and types his manuscripts and correspondence. Otherwise, he sits alone at his typewriter, surrounded by books, magazines and movie posters.

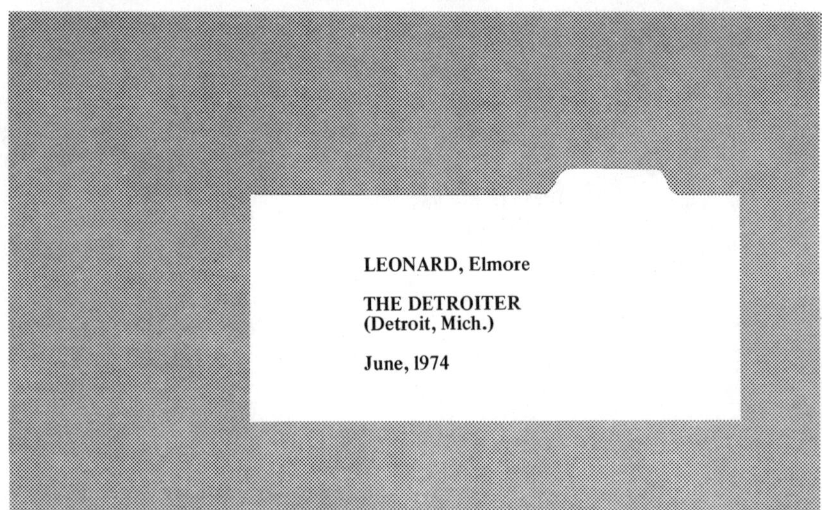

"There's no reason to move to California," he said. "I can work here. If I have to do rewrites or make changes I fly out there. They give me an office. Just recently I spent three weeks working on one film then later went back out and spent another three weeks making more changes."

He does not take his family with him on his work trips. His five children—a married daughter, two boys in college, one son in high school and a daughter in grade school—do help him though. They keep him on his toes.

"Yes. I like my work," he said. "Especially when things are good, but I have to keep going, to stay aware of what's happening. I still have some kids to put through college."

Leonard is very aware of what is happening.

"Right now there is an interest in suspense, mystery, crime and cop stories," he said. "I began writing westerns because there was a market for them. There are so many things to write about. I decided to narrow it. I picked a locale, Arizona. I wanted an Apache flavor. I studied it." He nodded in the direction of a stack of magazines piled on a low table. "I used to read those magazines. I had never actually spent time there, only just passed through.

"Now of course there is an interest in police stories—*The New Centurions, Serpico, The Supercops, The Seven-Ups*. On T.V., Kojak, Ironsides. Police are big now. And crime. *The Godfather, Crazy Joe, Lepke*."

Behind his desk, his manuscripts and folders in front of him, he appears serious, knowledgeable. "I think of writing in a business-like, professional way. My goal is to write as well as I can and make as much money as possible," he said.

Usually he has his idea sold, or almost sold, before he writes the script or novel. Sometimes he is commissioned to work on something or he writes something with a particular actor in mind. (His agent in California handles his movie sales, and his agent in New York takes care of some book sales and reprint rights.)

In the movie business, however, things usually turn out differently than planned. What was supposed to be an artichoke farm will end up being a melon farm, since there are no available artichokes at the time of the shooting and there is a plentiful crop of melons.

"Changes are often made. A director will feel the character should be viewed differently than he was originally written. His motives should be different. This will force other changes in the script. Soon everything is different. Sometimes it's for the best. Sometimes it doesn't work." He shrugged. It doesn't bother him. He is busy thinking of the next project. The next book.

Besides looking forward to seeing the reaction to *Fifty-two Pick Up*, Elmore Leonard looks forward to the release of *Mr. Majestic*, an original film script he wrote that will be produced by Walter Mirish at United Artists. It will star Charles Bronson and will appear at local theaters in June.

"Charles Bronson is No. 1 or 2 as a box office attraction in Europe, especially Italy. He's just starting to catch on here," he said. "Yes. I've met him. We had a meeting in Boston with the producer when he first decided to do it. Since he lives in Vermont, Boston was in the middle."

Fortunately for the city of Detroit, Elmore Leonard stays. And writes. And entertains. □

Lerner Sees Changes Ahead in Family

Max Lerner, author, columnist and social observer

LERNER, Max
(1902 -)

MILWAUKEE JOURNAL
(Milwaukee, Wisc.)

June 27, 1974

[See also CA-13/14]

By Barbara Salsini
of The Journal Staff

Los Angeles, Calif. — What is in the future for the family? Does the family have a future?

Columnist and social observer Max Lèrner believes that it does. But, in his opinion, the family of tomorrow will not necessarily be like today's nuclear family of "papa bear and mama bear and baby bear or maybe two baby bears."

Lerner spoke Wednesday at the American Home Economics Association (AHEA) Convention. He surveyed what he called the pillars of change on which the emerging family might be built.

One is a new political and economic climate that affects women in particular. The American woman has borne a heavy burden in her traditional homemaking role, Lerner said.

To Survive

"The wonder to me is that she has carried it at all as well as she has done and survived it," he said. In order to survive, he said, women have had to make demands, including calls for equality outside the home. He called the home a proving ground for women.

"This thrust for equality . . . could only have come from a woman who has seen what her mother has been able to do in the home and who therefore couldn't tolerate the grotesque inequalities outside of the home.

"I think the successful revolts are never the revolts of the weak," he said. "They are the revolts of unrecognized strength."

Should Broaden

The women's liberation movement will also affect the family of the future, according to the speaker.

He said that the women's movement should broaden its base. So far it has been largely restricted to college educated women who seek fulfilling careers, along with marriage, he said. Noncollege women without high career aspirations still tend toward more traditional goals.

The women's liberation movement has aimed at the fulfillment of women and has not given much thought to family life, Lerner said. He said he saw dangers in alleged tendencies toward man hating or toward "a rejection of the role of mother, which . . would bode very badly for the future of the family."

Lerner talked at length about sexual or erotic liberation. He attributed changes in attitudes toward sex to such pioneers as Freud, Kinsey, Masters and Johnson.

"Historically we may view them as the guilt killers," he said. "One of their historic functions has been to give us some kind of relief from the pervasive sense of guilt which we have had from our puritan values heritage."

Recent studies indicate an increase in sexual activity before marriage. But the studies indicate that there is still an emphasis on love and that, particularly for women, the relationships tend to be with one person.

More Freedom

Some of the emerging forms of family life are moving toward more sexual freedom, Lerner said. But others, notably communal living, do not emphasize sex as much as they stress extended or expanded families.

"My own emphasis for the future of the family is both on sexual expressiveness but also on warmth and concern and a pooling of experience, a pooling of the generations," Lerner said.

Lerner fears that society doesn't have enough concern for children. Children need love that is given with wisdom, he said.

"In our affluent society we think that by giving our children things we have done something — that it's a substitute for giving them ourselves. But it isn't."

He continued, "The family is not going to survive in a meaningful way unless it is a carrier of values. . . . What I mean by values is the questions that we put to life. We've been putting the wrong questions to life and our young people have been rejecting those wrong questions and insisting on asking some of their own."

Right Questions

Asked what the right questions might be, Lerner listed questions about love, relationships and other values. Questions often asked now are "unnourishing questions," and concern money, power, jobs, prestige or security. These are realities in life, Lerner agreed, "but it is one thing to live with them, and it's another thing to make them your life goal."

In an interview after his speech, Lerner said that he was writing a sequel to his book, "America as a Civilization." The new book will look at the America of the last 10 years in terms of life affirmation and life denial, two roles Lerner said were locked together throughout society. One chapter of the book will take up the question, "Is America a Dying Society?"

In Lerner's view, "it ain't necessarily so." In his speech, he had drawn a parallel between America and ancient Rome. In America there is still an emphasis on love and other values that were absent in decaying Rome, he said.

Young People

Lerner likes what he sees in young people today, he said in the interview.

Along with their work and career goals, they show an inner direction and go beyond the world of the senses, indicated by their interest in such things as meditation and extrasensory perception he said.

The current younger generation is not as activist minded as the one of the 60s, Lerner said.

"But when they choose to go to law school, for example, they want to be more than corporation lawyers." Those in medical schools want to be more than Park Ave. doctors, he added.

"You don't have to go out and demonstrate to have social concern," Lerner said of a quality that he has found in the youth of today. A movement away from activism does not mean a movement toward apathy, he said.

—News Photo

Sam Levenson

Levenson: A humorist's life in an 'Era'

By BARBARA HOOVER
News Entertainment Writer

Talking to Sam Levenson is a dish of ice cream. Or maybe a plate of sour-cream blintzes.

At the drop of a "hello," Sam is racing away with the conversation, making further effort on the part of the listener unnecessary and at times impossible.

"Have you read my book yet?" he said, settling down on a couch in The News' offices this week, his slim, still-pretty wife Esther seated quietly next to him, her hands patiently folded.

LEVENSON, Sam(uel)

DETROIT NEWS (Detroit, Mich.)

Nov. 24, 1974

"If you haven't read it, you should. It's a classic. It's a good book; it's for real."

Sam was referring to "In One Era and Out the Other," the humorous, autobiographical opus that was a best-seller in hard-cover and has just come out in paperback.

Now that Sam's no longer a TV regular (he had his own show for a couple of years in the '50's, and later was a perennial game-show panelist), writing and lecturing have become the outlets for his gentle spoofing of marriage, kids, morality and the world in general.

"I work on a library system of 4 by 6 cards. Almost every human experience is worth recording; you become a sort of sociologist. I do institutional performing — colleges, conventions, dinner. I talk about school, church and home. Kids going away to college — the kids from the east go to school in the west, the ones from the north go south . . . A rebellious college kid writes home, 'God is dead, but I'll be home for Passover.'"

WHEN THINGS change, Sam notices. "I remember when public buildings were public. Now every building has somebody who stops you in the lobby — to protect itself from the public. I remember when the public was held in the highest regard. Now it's 'me' that's important; there is no public.

"There's a new slogan for a new era: 'As long as I'm not hurting anybody . . .' But they don't ask if anybody is hurting. Today anything can be made into a public event — sex in the park, for instance. Now the cats and dogs are standing around watching the kids.

"People measure your rights by what they want. When I was bringing up my kids, the kid would say, 'I need this.' I used to ask are they really needs or are they wants?"

Bringing up children wasn't easy even for a philosopher-humorist. "It was a constant battle. Wanna see the scars?" said Sam, laughing and pulling open his suit jacket.

BUT HE SAYS he has pretty much stuck to the values instilled in his boyhood as the 10th child of a poor Jewish family in Brooklyn. "I'm not immune to change, but this is what I am; I'm doing my thing," he said.

"So much of the past is worth preserving. Values like having consideration for others, self-sacrifice when necessary, concern for the welfare of your fellow man. These are limitations on my freedom. I only have the freedom to do what is right; I'm not free to destroy.

"I think the Ten Commandments, the American Constitution and the Bill of Rights are great codes of ethics. They influence my humor. I will not destroy or demean people with a joke. I don't mock deformity. I don't tell fat-lady jokes or bald-head jokes.

"Now you might ask me," said Sam, leaving nothing to chance, "how much of an audience do I have that is still interested in this kind of humor? The answer is that I've been around for 25 years.

"I'm enjoying one of the greatest eras of my life. The affection of people is wonderful. They're happy to see that the values they hold sacred are still publicly held sacred by *somebody.*

"I FIND THE BEST audience is Middle-American women. People make jokes about them, but I find them intelligent, full of character, yearning for truth and knowledge and ashamed of what has happened in our country, and I am one of their hopes."

Sam, a former schoolteacher who'd been appearing here and there as a stand-up comic in the '40's, made his first big nationwide splash on the Ed Sullivan show in June, 1949. He remembers it well:

"It was a frightening new medium. That night I walked out and there were these monstrous cameras and people who looked like men from Mars giving signals. They told me to look at whichever camera had red lights on. I did that and then the lights would go out and I'd think, 'Did I blow a fuse?'

"It was terror. They gave me six minutes and 30 seconds and of course it was a live audience — today they put the laughs in on the tape. I'd tell a joke and it was a dead audience. No laughs. You could hear the air hum.

"Ed Sullivan was standing at one side of the stage staring at me with his arms folded like this," said Sam, leaping up and imitating Sullivan. "The audience kept looking at him, not me, and they'd laugh only if he laughed. But the next day CBS called me and I signed a contract.

"Comedians were the big thing in those days. TV history is divided into Before Berle and After Berle. Berle cleared the streets of America on Tuesday nights. Now the stand-up comics have gone into sketches. Flip Wilson has become an actor and a hoofer. I'm not good at that; I want to talk."

SAM, IN HIS early 60's, seems to have no regrets that that era is over. He says he'd just as soon stay home in the Levensons' big house on the ocean in Queens (N.Y.) writing, and making frequent visits to his three-year-old granddaughter, Georgia. (Levenson has two grown children: Conrad, an architect who is married and the father of Georgia, and Emily, a recent college graduate who writes poetry and is looking for gainful employment.)

"I'm the same idiot as all grandparents," says Sam. "There's no love like that of grandparents for grandchildren. Romeo and Juliet were a couple of bums compared to grandparents and grandchildren. People should be grandparents first, then parents.

"I don't want to travel; I want to write. If they'd (his publisher) just let me write and stay home, but you can't just write a book and send it to a librarian. That would be the end of it. You have to go out and sell it. So it's a choice between death of a writer and death of a salesman."

Old-Timey Kosher Philosophy From Everyone's Uncle Sam

By Diana McLellan
Star-News Staff Writer

Sam Levenson hasn't done badly.

Not for a kid who went to kindergarten in his sister Dora's cut-down bloomers. Not for a kid whose mother used to complain to the butcher, "The liver scraps you threw in for the cat last week weren't fresh.'

"Why, did it make him sick?"

"Sick? He couldn't go to school for three days."

And not for one of nine children in whose family only "Papa" had the right to start a clean towel.

"I still can't use a guest towel," he confided the other day while on a promotional stopover here. "When I visit somebody's bathroom, I look for the old towel behind the door, or use the bottom of the host's bathrobe. That way, my hands and my conscience are both clean."

THE ONETIME teacher, sometime comic and all-time spokesman for better, simpler times, is a funny man, even if he does laugh at his own jokes. ("It's because Papa always told me, Never depend on strangers.")

LEVENSON, Sam(uel)

WASHINGTON STAR-NEWS (Washington, D.C.)

Dec. 16, 1974

His father told him a lot — i.e., "Son, if you ever need a helping hand, look on the end of your arm." And: "If you want your dreams to come true, don't sleep." And: "Next time I take you kids anywhere, I'm going to leave you home."

"Papa," an immigrant Jewish tailor from the Russian city of Vitebsk — also the birthplace of painter Marc Chagall, Levenson notes — was horrified when his son, the promising, young, $2,148-a-year school teacher, decided after 15 years in the classroom to seek his fortune in show business:

"For this you went to college?"

LEVENSON'S 3-year-old son was even sadder: "I don't want anybody to laugh at my daddy." But audiences did. And they still do.

His best-selling and enchanting book, "In One Era and Out the Other," has just gone into paperback. His memories of growing up poor, Jewish and funny in New York tenements have cracked up three generations of television viewers (he got his start with six minutes on an early Ed Sullivan show). His unabashed propaganda for a simpler era with stiffer standards is digested as smilingly by teen-aged kids as it is by their nodding grandparents.

Sam Levenson's hair is now rather gray — after all, he's a grandfather himself — and laugh lines are *engraved* under his eyes. But people in the restaurant here where he was having lunch the other day kept coming up to him — "You 're Sam Levenson, aren't you?" — and people at nearby tables fell silent to listen to the old-timey kosher philosophy at his.

HE TALKED about his parents for a bit: "Mama and Papa didn't marry for happiness' sake," he said. "They married for marriage's sake. My father used to say, 'Love, shmove. I love blintzes, did I marry one?' Love was a word like 'hernia'; you just didn't use it when I was growing up.

"People still marry for better or for worse— but not for long," he said, with his don't-leave-it-to-strangers cackle.

He thinks one of the big problems today is that people think they're entitled to happiness, as though it had a *daily minimum requirement,* like vitamins.

"That's not what the Founding Fathers guaranteed. They talked about the right to pursue happiness. That's completely different. Like my Uncle Benny on the farm says, 'It's not the sugar that makes your tea sweet, it's stirring.' Well, what's wrong with everybody?

"People want their kids to have everything they didn't have. That's terrible. You see kids dragged off to nursery school by their parents, but they'd much rather sit home on the kitchen floor and play with the pots and pans — plank! plonkk! bang! — just like kids always did.

Speaking Of 'Obsession,' Author Levin Spells It Out

By MARGARET JOSTEN
Enquirer Reporter

As he stood behind the podium in his brownish plaid coat and surrealistically-patterned tie, hands flailing the air about him at times to punctuate the more dramatic accusations, Meyer Levin did indeed give the impression he is a man with an obsession.

The obsession in this case dealt with the conspiracy he saw to suppress his own dramatization of "The Diary of Anne Frank" in favor of one that claimed such accolades as the Pulitzer Prize and the Drama Critics Prize.

When Levin discussed his partially autobiographical new book, "The Obsession," at The Enquirer's Book and Author Luncheon in Stouffer's Cincinnati Inn Monday, he insisted that a person with an obsession is not automatically wrong or "out of his skull."

An obsession is something that invades you and you can't voluntarily get rid of it, suggested the prolific writer often dubbed the dean of American Jewish authors.

While the way Levin came into possession of his obsession has been related in nearly every publication touching upon current literature, a repetition perhaps should be presented in the interests of clarity.

Levin had come upon the diary in 1950, following his own exhaustive post-war investigation of the Nazi death camps. He secured from Otto Frank, Anne's father, permission to help arrange for American publication rights.

His adaptation of "The Diary of Anne Frank" became a best seller.

Frank also had given Levin permission to conduct preliminary discussions with potential producers for possible dramatization. Somewhere along the line, however, the prize-winning playwright, Lillian Hellman, felt the Levin dramatization was not the one that should be produced.

As a result, another producer was procured to do a version of the Diary (with Frank's approval) by Frances Goodrich and Albert Hackett, with polishing by Lillian Hellman. It won the Pulitzer Prize, among others.

Levin felt his version had been rejected because it was, as he put it, "too Jewish."

To illustrate for the Stouffer's Inn audience, he told how the original diary had contained this passage, "Who has made us Jews different from all other people?... If we bear all this suffering and if there are still Jews left, when it is over, then Jews, instead of being doomed, will be held up as an example."

The version that was dramatized, Levin said, was changed in this portion of the Diary to read, "We're not the only people that've had to suffer. There have always been people that've had to...sometimes one race... sometimes another."

Levin then told his audience of what he felt was "a hidden censorship" carried out by those, who, in many cases were following the dictates of Stalinism in 1952. .

And he accused Miss Hellman of following the anti-Zionist aspects of the party line to downgrade the Jewish content of the play.

"They got away with it completely," he charged.

The downgrading of the Jewish experience in the Holocaust has been one of the repeated points made by the left wing, he emphasized.

Levin even mentioned that "people don't shrink back in horror" today at hints there could be another Holocaust such as the one that Hitler perpetrated. "Indeed there may be (another Holocaust)," he added.

The author also spoke at length about the way minds are manipulated by "very determined people," by "politicized people."

"If through my obsession I can make people understand what is going on in efforts to control our minds, then it will all have been worth while," he concluded.

The two other speakers at The Enquirer luncheon were much less serious.

Stephen Birmingham, author of "Real Lace: America's Rich Irish," told how he had lambasted the late Joseph Kennedy at some length in his book.

When he sat across the aisle from Mrs. Jacqueline Onassis on an Olympic Airways flight from Paris to New York, he had some fears about her reaction. When she saw him, though, she told him how much she liked his book, "particularly the part about the Kennedys."

AUSTIN WRIGHT, who wrote "First Persons" with a Cincinnati locale, explained what he called the "surrealistic nut" of his book. The main character, Ralph Burr, is an overcivilized man, an intellectual, extremely self-conscious, who realizes he is the protagonist of a novel.

Burr becomes involved in a sudden, violent, seemingly-senseless murder. "He is aware he is in a novel."

Meyer Levin
. . . raps Lillian Hellman

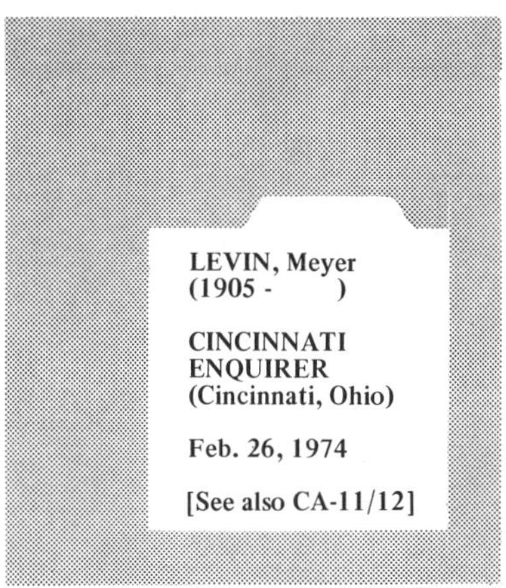

LEVIN, Meyer
(1905 -)

CINCINNATI ENQUIRER
(Cincinnati, Ohio)

Feb. 26, 1974

[See also CA-11/12]

Human Book Machine Grinds 'em Out

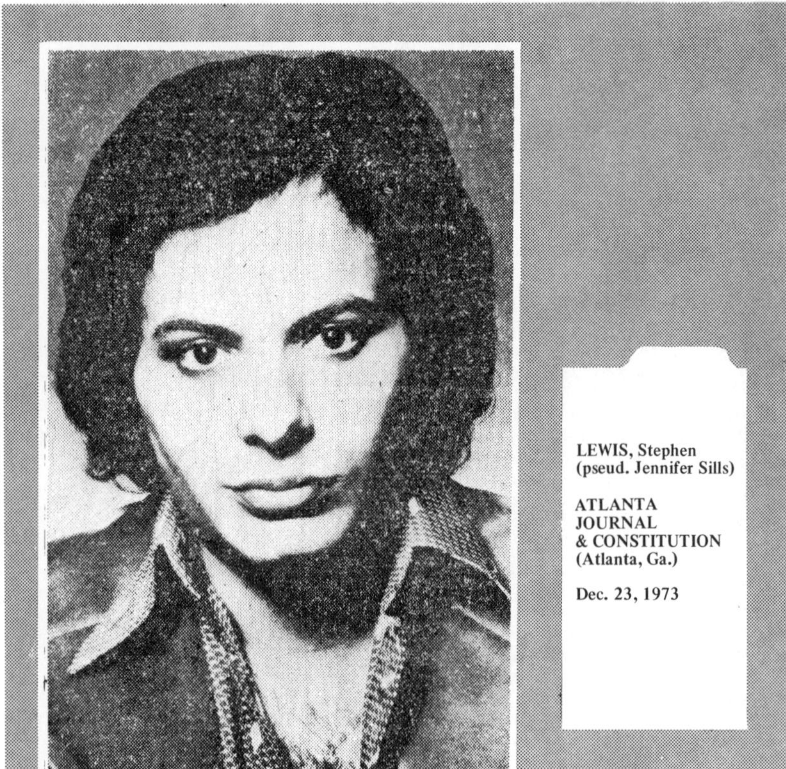

LEWIS, Stephen
(pseud. Jennifer Sills)

ATLANTA
JOURNAL
& CONSTITUTION
(Atlanta, Ga.)

Dec. 23, 1973

HIS CURRENT SPEED: 4 BOOKS A YEAR
Some Call Stephen Lewis, 'Fastest Pen in West'

By EDITH HILLS COOGLER
Atlanta Journal Women's Editor

"I finished high school. I didn't like it, but I finished it."

Here is poor Stephen Lewis today at the age of 26 with only a high school education.

In this college-oriented business world, it's probably already too late for him to soar to top management in a big corporation.

On the other hand, at the rate he's going, he might just *buy* a big corporation — assuming he wants one, that is.

A RECENT magazine article estimated that Lewis would earn at least $250,000 this year.

"Oh, somewhat less than *that,*" his business manager said with becoming modesty.

Lewis has earned it all with his typewriter — not blackmail, books.

He has been called "The fastest pen in the West," but that's not exactly accurate because he lives in Manhattan, and not even on the West Side. More accurately, you could call him "The Book Machine." He is grinding out books as fast as the popeyed public can devour them. And all his books seem to turn into best sellers, not that he has anything really *new* to say about sex.

So far this year — and the year isn't quite over yet — he has written four paperbacks. Four that he remembers, anyway.

VISITING ATLANTA, he explained that growing up in a place named Agawam, Mass., made him somewhat desperate for the big city life, show biz — anything glamorous.

He headed for Manhattan and got a job modeling boys' clothes. He was on a modeling job for a fashion magazine when the editor asked if he'd ever done any writing.

Had he ever done any writing! He was so good at it in high school that his English teacher accused him of plagiarizing everything he wrote. So from modeling, he switched over to fashion writing. "The magazine went out of business, and I began to write a lot of articles about fashionable people. I was fortunate that I really never had much trouble selling these to magazines.

"Then a movie magazine asked if I had ever thought of doing a gossip column. And I said, well, maybe I could do that. And I started a gossip column and it came very naturally. I was 19 then, and I still do the column — I have a couple of people working with me gathering material."

LOOKING FOR MATERIAL for magazine articles, Lewis was prowling around the Broadway area one Sunday night about a year ago. He walked into a massage parlor which offered considerably more than mere massage. "There were about 20 men. And the girls were not tough; they were very pretty. And there I met Jennifer who was very willing to talk to me . . ."

Jennifer, of course, was not her real name, but she was a real girl who came to Lewis' apartment and spent 50 hours talking about her seamy profession while Lewis recorded.

"Then I met an editor from Ace (paperbacks), and she thought it would be a book; she asked how long it would take me to write it because they wanted the book in a hurry."

It took him about a month. "Massage Parlor" by Jennifer Sills was published last February — not the kind of book you'd want to be seen reading, but so far it has sold an astonishing 1.7 million copies.

"One of the women in the massage parlor with Jennifer was a housewife who told her husband she was working as an office temp. and couldn't give her phone number because she was in a different office every day.

"Then the police told me that 10 to 12 per cent of the prostitutes in New York were housewives.

"The original one wouldn't talk to me, but she did introduce me to about 10 others. Some wouldn't talk to me; others weren't good talkers. But primarily, Barbara Lane and her two friends talked to me. For Barbara, I think it was really a form of therapy. Her marriage had broken up, and the husband got custody of the child. Her husband was an old line male chauvinist type, and she just felt out of time and out of place, and she was very afraid of the future. That's why she went into prostitution."

BECAUSE more than one interview was involved, it took Lewis longer to grind out "Housewife Hookers" — all of three months. It has sold a million copies since it came out last May.

In the meantime, he'd been writing book No. 3 in his head. "I'd spent a lot of time in Washington because friends from high school live there, and I'd learned a lot of Washington gossip, so it really all came together nicely. 'The Watergate Girls' was my first novel. It was the book I did the fastest because I'd been thinking about it for a long time and I knew exactly what I wanted to say.

"I wrote it in July in a little less than a month, and it came out in September."

His novel takes a vaguely Jacqueline Susann approach to the problems of some Washington working girls who share an apartment. As you might expect, their problems mainly are men. Sales are fast approaching the million mark.

THE FOURTH BOOK this year is "Sex Among the Singles", published in November. When he toured the country earlier this year, he spent his spare time investigating all aspects of the single life in apartments, in bars, at resorts. "I talked to them in groups and they painted the popularized picture of the singles life — everybody happy together. But when I interviewed them individually, it turned out that they were unhappy, especially the women, because there's so much emphasis on sex.

"They are promiscuous, but don't get any pleasure out of the promiscuity. But what can they do? They come from small towns to New York or Los Angeles, and how can you meet people? You have to go to a singles bar where every man's trying to be the Playboy man, and every girl is wearing three falls and is trying to be the Cosmopolitan girl.

"And all the while, they're looking at the door hoping at that a new king or queen will come in.

"This is something I've learned through talking with them. And the saddest part is that you can't go around making a career out of musical beds and expect to be a satisfied, whole person.

"When I was a kid, kids went together a long time. And I'm sure some of them went to bed, but it was the culmination of something."

THE BOOK is a sad commentary on the loneliness, the reaching out and the emptiness of the lives of the singles he interviewed. Several college professors already have written him asking permission to use it in their courses.

Under terms of his new contract with his publisher, he'll write eight more books on schedule in the next two years.

"My family is very hard working, and I've always liked working hard myself. I like to think of myself as a good business person. I consider writing as a commercial business and I approach it that way."

(Also see preceding article)

The Man Who Turns Headlines into Cash

By William S. Welt

Think of the writer's life and you probably conjure up images of Ernest Hemingway starving in a Paris garret and running with the bulls in Pamplona, or perhaps F. Scott Fitzgerald, running with the rich and drinking too much. Authors, those brilliant, romantic, semi-tragic figures who wring art slowly and painfully from life. It is the childbirth theory of prose production, still dogma among the literati.

Then there's Stephen Lewis, who is 26, and never went to college, and writes as fast as his fingers can find the keys on his IBM Selectric while he watches game shows on television. And who has three and a half million books in print, who had three runaway best-sellers in 1973 and who is getting to be a very rich young man, indeed.

For Ace, a New York paperback house, Lewis has written six books, two of them not yet published. His 1973 output included *Massage Parlor,* which sold 1.5 million copies under the nom de plume of Jennifer Sills; *Housewife Hookers,* by Barbara Lane as exposed by Stephen Lewis, which sold a million copies; and *The Watergate Girls,* Lewis' first novel, which is approaching the million-mark.

Earlier this year, his *Sex Among the Singles* hit the racks. A Hollywood novel, *The Love Merchants,* and an as-yet untitled sequel to *Massage Parlor* will follow shortly.

Stephen Lewis is one of the growing number of American wordsmiths who crank out what the publishing trade calls "paperback originals"—books that are not issued first in hardcover. The subjects are usually related to some item currently in the news, like massage parlors, and the books are written quickly and brought out just as fast, so the newsiness is not lost. "Instant publishing," the industry calls it.

"Literature" is something hardly anyone calls it, but still, it is difficult to ignore an author such as Lewis. Like television, he aims at — and reaches — the masses. And then there is the matter of the $250,000 or so a year he earns, more money than any writer you studied in English Lit 101 ever dreamed of making.

"Those books they write about in *The New York Times* book review section make me laugh," Lewis said as he munched a grilled cheese sandwich in a restaurant during a recent promotional-tour visit.

"The long-lost poems of

LEWIS, Stephen

MIAMI HERALD
(Miami, Fla.)

May 5, 1974

someone or other, or studies of ancient Egyptian art. I'm a great believer in pleasure reading. You shouldn't have to fight to get through a book. Reading should be for entertainment, you know what I mean?"

"You know what I mean" is a phrase Lewis uses often in conversation, but he needn't — there are no ambiguities about either his speech or his writing. His prose is akin stylistically to that of the dime novel and pulp magazine, short sentences composed of easy words, with surface-deep characters and frequent trading upon eroticism.

According to the Association of American Publishers, mass-marketed paperback sales hit $252.8 million in 1972. Figures for 1973 are not yet complete, but the AAP says it is obvious all sales are continuing to grow.

Lewis is a short, frail young man who has the unhealthy pallor of a Northern-states city dweller. This day, his nose is red and runny from a mid-winter cold, and he is dressed expensively in a green checked corduroy suit, high-polished leather boots and a dark brown fur coat.

He is an only child from Agawam, Mass., a small, middle-class suburb of Boston, where his father is vice president of a scrap metal-machinery firm. He hated high school, and as soon as he graduated he took a train to New York, where he got a job modeling boy's clothing for now-defunct *Elegant* magazine.

Lewis began writing articles about clothes and movie stars for *Elegant,* and soon he was writing gossip columns for *Movie World* and *Screen Stars* magazines as well. (He still writes those columns.)

His first book was a hardcover, *The Complete Book of Beauty for the Black Woman,* which he coauthored with Barbara MacNair in 1971.

"It didn't come out until a year after it was done," said Lewis. "I'm very topically minded, and I didn't like the wait. I decided paperbacks were best, you know what I mean?"

He then wrote his first paperback, *Massage: The Loving Touch,* a how-to book that led to *Massage Parlor,* and the contract with Ace.

"He's the fastest pen in the West," said Ace vice president John Waxman. "And I would say that Stephen's literary quality is commensurate with the other authors we publish. We're known as one of the major publishers in the country for science fiction, Gothic and Westerns."

Lewis' editor at Ace is Evelyn Grippo, who says that her star author "is unique, literally, in that he can work on two books at once.

"He writes his books in six to eight weeks, and we can get it on the stands four to six weeks after that, sooner if necessary. Ace Books is famous for instant publishing, literally. We get a book out while an item is still hot in the newspapers."

She doesn't worry about Lewis' spelling or punctuation, or the neatness of his manuscripts, she says. "I'm not the kind of editor who gets hysterical if the commas aren't in the right place. That's the kind of thing I'm getting paid *very handsomely* to take care of."

"I find I work much better on a deadline," says Lewis. "Some days, I work three or four hours, others I may write 18 hours straight. I get excited and don't want to sleep.

"I like to watch TV while I write, game shows, soaps, the news."

He couldn't write without an electric typewriter, he says, because he "loves machines," and would like to live above a factory some day, with a glass floor in his home so he could see the gears burning below. For now, he has an eight-room apartment on New York's fashionable East Side.

His favorite author, he says, is Joyce Carol Oates, "because she writes quickly—and admits it."

Lewis doesn't imagine that his prose will endure the test of time, and he doesn't care. "I'm not really concerned about the future, you know what I mean? I just want to be a part of today. I want to keep on working, seeing America (he visited Europe once and says he didn't like all the old buildings) and having a good time. You can't ask for much more than that."

Ithaca author likes secluded way of life

LIEBERMAN, Robert

SYRACUSE HERALD-AMERICAN (Syracuse, N.Y.)

Jan. 12, 1975

ROBERT LIEBERMAN

By RICHARD G. CASE

Robert Lieberman is a best-selling new novelist who lives on a steep hill he calls a mountain near Brooktondale, southeast of Ithaca.

His book is about a man who also lived on a steep hill he called a mountain in upstate New York.

One morning last week, waiting to be interviewed, Lieberman sat in a walk-in closet of an office of Martha Van Rensselaer Hall, on the Cornell University campus, behind a baby-blue door which carried a picture of a naked soccer team. He's dressed like a woodsman aroused at an early hour to chop fire wood; booted, with purple underwear peaking through a plaid shirt. His long leg was asleep on his desktop.

He was talking on the phone with a secretary of the dean of the State College of Human Ecology about his book, "Paradise Rezoned," a novel of "one man's struggle against a mechanized society."

(Lieberman lost his own struggle with the dean last week; he no longer works for the college.)

"You don't want to read it, it's disgusting," Lieberman said. It's erotic, too, he added, shaking his head. "Well, try the campus bookstore."

Later, as he climbed "Mount Lieberman" on a quiet, snowy ridge seven miles from Cornell, the 34-year-old author explained he has written seven novels and 100 short stories but "Paradise Rezoned" (Berkley Medallion paperback) is his first book.

"Actually, I've been writing for 30 years and never realized it," he said. "I don't know, I guess I was a closet writer. I'd do something and then put it away. I've got no English background. When I started I was illiterate; now I'm semi-literate."

We made the front door of the Lieberman's red leveled house, which is set into a hillside, and the novelist kicked off his boots. "The real reason I started writing," he said with a grin, "is that I couldn't find any good books in the library. Now I think I compare favorably with the classics."

Classic or not, "Paradise Rezoned" seems to be doing well, at least for the publisher. A recent Newsweek article on paperback originals ("Paper Tigers") said Berkley Books had "hit the jackpot in paper with three-month sales approaching 300,000" for the book.

Lieberman is warmed by that, but says he hasn't gotten a cent in royalties yet, beyond a $2,500 advance.

It doesn't seem to bother him that much, though he told me his main concern is to see his work in circulation.

"At first I was upset when I heard this was going to be a paperback," he said. "I thought it was the kiss of death. But if it's selling well, then I'm accomplishing my purpose, which is to be read. I want to be read because I think I have something to say. Money is secondary. If that was my interest I would have stayed in engineering with all of my friends."

He was, he says, "born at an early age in Queens, the son of a Viennese lawyer who wasn't terribly popular with Adolf Hitler." Although his leanings may have been otherwise, he yielded to what he called "family pressure" (his father had three doctorates and two brothers are scientists), and went through Brooklyn Polytech and then came to Ithaca and Cornell with the intention of studying veterinary medicine.

By this time, Mrs. Lieberman, Gunilla, a comely Swede, had set a lunch of wine and toasted tuna on bread in front of a picture window overlooking one of the slopes of the family's 50 acres and a pond which won't hold water. Her husband leaned back in his chair and grunted.

"I should have been a vet. But I got an engineering scholarship and became an engineer."

For a while he danced around the edges of academic respectability, teaching math at Ithaca College and working on his novels, but only "as hunger dictated." When he wasn't teaching at Ithaca or black colleges in the south, Lieberman traveled "wildly — I mean widely" — and worked variously as a deck-hand, photo model, farm laborer, journalist, photographer and water skiing instructor.

Now, back as a free-lance again after a year as Human Ecology's ("whatever that's supposed to mean") "special writer," he intends to rewrite a new novel and work harder on getting "Paradise Rezoned" into form for a film prospect.

Outside, in the cold crispness you usually find in remote places like Mount Lieberman, the author and Gunilla walked back through the woods and talked about the book, which he finished two-and-a-half years ago but couldn't sell until Warner Brothers took what turned out to be an aborted film option on the manuscript.

"I'd call it a highly personal biography," Lieberman explained, jumping a small stream and a swatch of heavy deer tracks. "Some people call it an ecological novel, but it's really not. It's really about people and how Markowitz (Arnold, the main character) relates to his parents and his children. It's the distillation of small insults that man is forced to helplessly and bravely endure."

In "Paradise," Markowitz, an artist, lives with his Swedish wife and two sons (Lieberman's two sons were in school that day) near Whamsattsville in upstate New York on Mount Markowitz, a place "bountiful in wild apples, wild currants and wild thoughts." A local developer tries to build a shopping mall at the base of the aerrie and Markowitz battles the project with the help of a college friend, lawyer Lennie Rosenthal, a character Lieberman considers the book's hero.

Readers familiar with Lieberman and Ithaca may find interesting clues for comparisons in the book but the author of "Paradise" denies his work is a mirror. Rather, he explained as he dipped back toward the house, it is distortion of real places and people to fit his own highly fictional imaginings.

Gould Lincoln Is Dead at 94; Dean of City's Political Writers

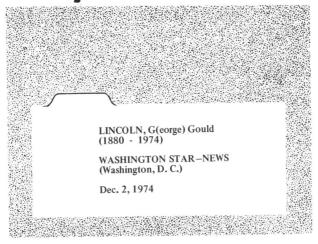

LINCOLN, G(eorge) Gould
(1880 - 1974)

WASHINGTON STAR-NEWS
(Washington, D. C.)

Dec. 2, 1974

G. Gould Lincoln, the dean of Washington political writers who as reporter and columnist had covered every president from Theodore Roosevelt to Gerald R. Ford, died early yesterday at the age of 94. He had been with the Washington Star-News since 1909.

Lincoln had returned to his home in the Kennedy-Warren Apartments, 3133 Connecticut Ave. NW, Nov. 14 following three weeks of hospitalization at the Washington Hospital Center for treatment of a broken hip suffered in a fall. In recent years, until the time of his injury, Lincoln had written a weekly column of political commentary which appeared in the editorial pages of the Star-News.

In a tribute to the veteran newsman, Newbold Noyes, editor of the Star-News, said that "Gould Lincoln was an inspiration to at least three generations of political reporters in this town. All his life, he had going for him the rarest gift that can be bestowed on a journalist — the trust of those he wrote about, all across the political spectrum. He also happened to be a fabulous man."

Lincoln leaves his daughter, Marjorie G. Lincoln, of the Connecticut Ave. address, and a son, Nathan S. Lincoln, of Sayville, Long Island, N.Y.

Funeral services will be held at 2:30 p.m. tomorrow at St. John's Episcopal Church at Lafayette Square. Burial will be in Oak Hill Cemetery.

By David Braaten
Star-News Staff Writer

G. (for George) Gould Lincoln was outstanding among Washington newspapermen not alone for his sheer, incredible longevity — though that would have been enough — but for the stern impartiality with which he covered the fierce partisanship of national politics for over six decades.

He called himself a reporter, and he meant it.

He did not consider himself a Washington columnist, political analyst or confidant of Presidents — though he was in fact all of these — but simply and proudly, a reporter. He saw his role, whether in police court or the White House, as digging for the facts and presenting them without slant to his paper's readers. His lifelong preference for the Republican Party was nosecret to either his sources or his colleagues, but it was to his readers, for he never let it color his reporting of events or his repeatedly accurate forecasts of election results.

If he had a secret of journalistic success, it was probably his preference for personal confrontation with a news source whenever it was humanly possible. He disdained the telephone (a phenomenon that was, after all, only four years his senior) in favor of "legging" his stories literally and talking face to face with politicians, whether Presidents or ward heelers.

THESE ENCOUNTERS invariably provided Lincoln with the expert's candid assessment of a situation, rather than a dubious serving of partisan puffery. Losers as well as winners would look into those alert, penetrating eyes and bare their souls.

"He was," said an editor trying to pinpoint the reason for Lincoln's effectiveness in wringing truth from politicians, "a gentleman. He had this enormous dignity, Lying to Gould would be like, well, lying to a bishop."

It almost seemed as if Lincoln were preordained to cover presidential politics. He was born, on July 26, 1880, a block from the White House, at 1514 H St. NW.

His father, Dr. Nathan Smith Lincoln, was a Union Army surgeon in the Civil War and a personal acquaintance of President Lincoln, with whom he shared ancestral roots in Massachusetts and England. Indeed, Dr. Lincoln once enlisted the President's intervention to get an elderly patient of his released from the old Capital Prison, where he had been confined after receiving a letter from a son in the Confederate Army. Dr. Lincoln went to the White House and told President Lincoln he would vouch for the old gentleman. The result was a letter that became a treasured family souvenir: "Hon. Secretary of Interior, Please, please, see the bearer, Dr. Lincoln, and hear him in regard to a Mr. Chesney. Yours truly, A. Lincoln."

Gould Lincoln's boyhood playground were Lafayette Park and an empty lot at H Street and Vermont Avenue, where he learned to play baseball.

As a small boy, he roller-skated on the broad sidewalk in front of 1600 Pennsylvania Avenue, and he remembered well being taken to the White House lawn for egg-rolling one Easter Monday morning during Grover Cleveland's first term.

LINCOLN RECALLED Cleveland's inaugural parade of 1885 with particular vividness many years later. His father had rented a room on the second floor of an old building on the south side of Pennsylvania Avenue at 15th Street, where the marchers turn right on their way to the White House. Young Gould had a front-row seat, and as the Virginia state militia swung past, led by Gov. William E. Cameron, a crippled Confederate veteran, they celebrated the Democrats' recapture of the White House with "the shrillest, most blood-curdling Rebel yell you could imagine." Said Lincoln in a National Press Club luncheon talk 79 years later: "I can hear it still."

Despite these early exposures to the idea that distinguished neighbors lived just around the corner, Lincoln did not aim for a White House-connected career right from the start. The decision came about quite by happenstance.

He had gone to Sidwell Friends School (where he set a record for the 100-yard dash — 10.2 seconds — that stood from 1898 to 1950) and then to Yale, where he took the usual liberal arts courses, kept his lean, 5-foot 11-inch frame in condi- ➡

(Continued from preceding page)

tion by rowing, and graduated in 1902.

He spent the four months after graduation in the Canadian North Woods on a prospecting expedition sent out by Thomas A. Edison in hopes of finding nickel ore needed by the inventor.

When young Lincoln returned home and began looking for a permanent job, he thought he would probably wind up in either banking or real estate, the city's biggest non-governmental industries.

INSTEAD, he met a friend on the street one day who told him, "They want a young man on the Washington Times," so he went for an interview with the editor, a German nobleman (complete with saber scar on his cheek) named Maximilian Seckendorf. Mr. Lincoln had gone to school with one of Count Seckendorf's daughters, and the editor was cordial enough.

"He looked me over and said, 'It's no job for a gentleman, but if you want it, you can have it.' " Lincoln used to recall in later years, invariably adding: "The gentleman angle did not seem insurmountable. So I went to work for eight dollars a week."

It was early in his apprenticeship, when he and two other neophytes were responsible for covering all the federal agencies in town for a daily column on government employes, that Lincoln made the discovery that was to carry him — literally — to the top of his profession.

"I soon discovered," he said, "that for a reporter, legs are as important as brains — perhaps more so. Legs could keep you going when all else seemed to fail."

Still not committed to a newspaper career, young Lincoln quit after about a year and worked for several months in 1903 and 1904 as an assistant superintendent on a tea plantation in South Carolina. He tore a knee in an accident, though, and hobbled back to Washington and another job on the Times — for $17.50 a week this time.

In the traditional fashion, Lincoln did any and every kind of reporting job, from police court to household hints to Sunday features. His skills were no better and no worse than many cubs of the era: he never did learn to type with more than his two index fingers, his prose style was workmanlike but unexciting, and his spelling was occasionally shaky. ("General Joe Johnston was chided by a friend for spelling the same word twice differently on the same page of a letter," Lincoln recalled once with obvious sympathy, "and the general said with great indignation: I have no respect for a man who cannot spell a word more than one way.' I felt that way myself quite frequently, but fortunately the typesetters have always set me right.")

AT ONE POINT, as a circulation stunt, Lincoln even wrote a serialized mystery novel for the Times. Titled "The Maltese Cross," it included in each chapter a clue to the whereabouts of a $100 money order that had been hidden for a clever Times reader to find. He wrote 65,000 words in a dozen or more weekly installments, and would always remember that he got not a penny extra for his efforts — not even when a Pittsburgh newspaper picked up the novel and ran it in toto. He said the experience had not encouraged him to write any more books.

Lincoln went to the Washington Post in 1906, and there he served a stint as Sunday editor and covered the House of Representatives.

It was in 1907 when Lincoln's remarkable encounter with President Theodore Roosevelt occurred. He had been sent to the White House to ask the President's secretary about a local District matter. There were no guards or Secret Service agents to check his credentials (a good thing as he had none) and he strolled unhindered into the new West Wing of offices. There turned out to be no secretary, either, and the young reporter wandered through the secretary's office, into the Cabinet Room and then the President's office All were empty, and Lincoln pursued his quest toward the White House living quarters when suddenly, glancing down a staircase to the basement, he saw T. R. himself, barrel-chested, clad in a sweater and holding a tennis racket in his hand.

Lincoln, unabashed, got his District story straight from the horse's mouth — a foretaste of the technique he used for the rest of his career.

He joined the staff of the then Evening Star in 1909, and eventually worked his way to the top of his profession, as the premier political reporter in a city where political reporting was always regarded as the best job a newspaperman could have.

AS COLUMNIST Mary McGrory was to note many years later, Lincoln was welcomed "as a brother" by the capital's politicians.

"He had probably never asked a loaded or needling question in his life," Miss McGrory wrote in 1956, when she was covering her first — and Lincoln's tenth — national political convention. "Simply and without malice, he would ask them (politicians), What's going on? They told him."

For years, before the advent of massive polling organizations on the political scene, Lincoln conducted his own personal poll before each national election, and came up with predictions that would make Gallup, Roper or Harris proud. The secret of his success was simple: legwork.

He traveled thousands of miles — when long-distance travel meant trains, not planes — crisscrossing the country to interview his myriad sources, from governors to ward heelers. When he was through, he had an astonishingly accurate picture of the political situation.

As The Star noted with "just pride" in a full-page house ad on Nov. 13, 1938:

"WITHOUT benefit of straw polls or other special devices, The Star supplied its readers with a remarkably correct forecast of the results in last week's election . . . G. Gould Lincoln, chief political writer of The Star, conducted a pre-election survey in 18 important states . . . Just as he has predicted accurately the outcome of every presidential election he has covered, Mr. Lincoln forecast widespread Republican gains in the campaign just ended. In an election-eve summary he gave Gov. Herbert H. Lehman an edge of District Attorney Thomas E. Dewey for the New York governorship, envisioned the defeat of Gov. Frank Murphy in Michigan and sized up other gubernatorial races with typical sagacity. . . ."

Among Republicans making their bigtime debut that year whose victories Lincoln predicted — and whose long political careers he outlasted by many years — were the late Robert A. Taft Sr., who won his first election to the Senate; Leverett Saltonstall, who beat James Michael Curley's re-election bid in Massachusetts, and Harold L. Stassen, who became the "boy wonder" governor of Minnesota.

After covering his first national convention in 1920, Lincoln was named chief political writer of The Star in 1925, and the accumulated legwork of the ensuing years gave him contacts that were unrivaled in the world of politics.

AS MISS McGRORY noted somewhat ruefully in 1956, she assiduously carried to Lincoln all the rumors she dug up at the Democratic convention in Chicago. He smiled graciously.

"It was not long before I realized none of them appeared in his stories, and that I was about as useful as a puppy collecting old bones," she remembered.

"'Mr. Lincoln,' I said, 'you hear rumors; I hear rumors. You hear the right ones.'

" 'Well,' he said, 'the thing is, I have known a lot of people for a long time.'"

Lincoln's personal preference for the Grand Old Party never interfered with the objectivity of his election forecasts. He predicted Franklin Roosevelt's 1932 victory ("It damn near cost me my job," he recalled) and his unprecedented third-term win in 1940.

AND HIS CONTACTS proved the equal of anyone's well into the age of polls and computers. In the close midyear elections of 1954, he made his usual, multi-state first-hand survey and predicted within three the number of Democratic governors, the Democratic margin in the Senate within one seat, and the Democratic majority in the House within a dozen seats.

Although he was the dean of political reporters in town, Lincoln was never above turning his talents to a breaking news story if the occasion arose. The most spectacular example of this occurred on March 1, 1954, when four Puerto Ricans stood up in the gallery of the House of Representatives and opened fire on the lawmakers, wounding five of them.

Lincoln was in the Senate press gallery, covering Earl Warren's confirmation as Chief Justice, when word came over of shooting in the House. Lincoln — being then only 73 years old — immediately set out to leg the story.

The schoolboy sprinter's legs did not fail him. By the time most of his younger colleagues arrived on the scene, they found Lincoln already interviewing doorkeepers and other eyewitnesses.

LINCOLN retired — technically, at least — from The Star after 55 years in 1964. But he could not bear the thought of inaction, and continued to write a weekly column of political commentary for the Saturday editorial pages.

Lincoln never pretended to infallibility, and he was one of many commentators who underestimated the disastrous effects of the Watergate scandals. He persisted in viewing the situation as a partisan Democratic attempt to discredit President Nixon's administration, and felt it would eventually blow over.

When eight of the city's leading journalists were chosen for Medal of Freedom awards in 1970, Lincoln was a natural for the honor. At 89, he was the senior reporter present when President Nixon handed out the awards in the White House East Room.

Lincoln was a member of the National Press Club, the Chevy Chase Club and the Gridiron Club.

His wife, Delia Hazeltine Pynchon Lincoln, died in 1971. They had been married since 1946. Lincoln's first marriage, to Elizabeth Wilder Lincoln, ended in divorce that year.

Lincoln lived in recent years at the Kennedy-Warren Apartments, 3133 Connecticut Ave. NW, with his daughter, Marjorie Gould Lincoln.

LINCOLN, G(eorge) Gould

WASHINGTON
STAR–NEWS
(Washington, D. C.)

Dec. 2, 1974

Walter Lippmann Dies at 85; Journalist, Philosopher

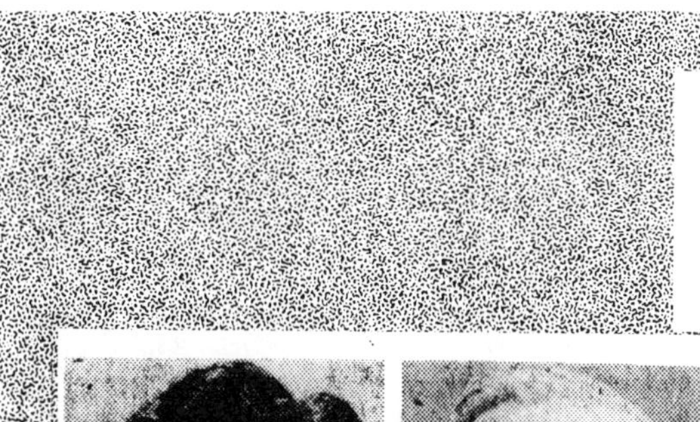

LIPPMANN, Walter
(1889 - 1974)

PHILADELPHIA INQUIRER
(Philadelphia, Penn.)

Dec. 15, 1974

[See also CA-9/10]

Walter Lippmann at peak of career and in 1969

By STEVE NEAL
Inquirer Staff Writer

Walter Lippmann, the brilliant journalist whose flowing, pontifical prose made him America's foremost political philosopher, died Saturday at 85.

Mr. Lippmann, who had been ailing and confined to a wheelchair, died in his Park Avenue, New York, apartment at 7:25 A. M.

For more than 50 years, Mr. Lippmann analyzed world crises with an Olympian detachment that earned him the respect and admiration of presidents, premieirs, and foreign ministers. Nikita S. Khrushchev once praised him as a reporter who wrote honestly and objectively about the Soviet Union.

He was a lean, angular man with a high forehead and big, darting brown eyes. He wrote his columns in longhand while dressed casually in a gray pullover sweater, corduroy slacks, and loafers, frequently coming forth with sapient and profound political judgments. Historian Allan Nevins said Mr. Lippmann was "more conscious than any other newspaperman of the fact that only reasoned argument can overthrow ignorance and prejudice."

Mr. Lippmann's concept of interpretative writing wasn't that of a temporal critic. "The main function of a good column," he said, "is not to say to the reader: 'Now this is what you ought to do.' Rather, I try to say: 'This is what has been developing and this is what it means.' I try to write about something I understand myself. If I can do that, then I expect anyone can understand it."

Reporters, Mr. Lippmann said, had to teach themselves to be not only recorders of events, but also writers of notes and essays in contemporary form. "If we tried to print only the facts of what had happened, who did what and who said what, the news items would be like pieces of a jigsaw puzzle thrown in a heap around the table.

"The way we interpret news is not by fitting the facts to a dogma. It is proposing theories or hypotheses which are then tested by trial and error. If the later news knocks down the earlier story, there are two things to be done. One is to scrap the theory and the interpretation, which is what liberal, honest men do. The other is to dis tort or suppress the unmanageable piece of news."

Mr. Lippmann was born in New York City on Sept. 23, 1889, the only son of wealthy parents. He was an outstanding member of Harvard's remarkable class of 1910 — his classmates included T. S. Eliot, John Reed, and Heywood Broun. Theodore Roosevelt reviewed one of Mr. Lippmann's early books and called him "the most brilliant young man of his age in all the U. S."

Lincoln Steffens, the muckraking journalist, hired Mr. Lippmann, just out of Harvard, as assistant editor of Everybody's Magazine. Mr. Lippmann "caught on right away," Steffens later wrote, investigating corruption in business and politics. Steffens said Mr. Lippmann possessed "the ablest mind that could express itself in writing."

Mr. Lippmann, head of a Socialist club at Harvard, left Steffens' magazine to serve, for a brief time, as an aide to the Socialist mayor of Schenectady, N. Y. During World War I he was an adviser to Woodrow Wilson's top adviser, Col. Edward M. House, and, after the war, helped put together Wilson's "Fourteen Points."

In the meantime, Mr. Lippmann was establishing himself as one of the most authoritative voices of American liberalism first as a founding editor of the New Republic Magazine, then later as the editorial chief of Joseph Pulitzer's New York World. When the World went out of business in 1931, he started writing a column for the New York Herald-Tribune.

It was with the conservative Herald-Tribune that Mr. Lippmann became the most quoted journalist of his time and twice won Pulitzer Prizes. His column, "Today and Tomorrow," which at first was published four times a week and later three times a week, was syndicated in over 250 newspapers in the United States and about 25 foreign countries.

Mr. Lippmann, whose editorials on the World had attacked the Republican administrations of Warren G. Harding, Calvin Coolidge, and Herbert Hoover, disappointed many of his admirers when he moved over to the Tribune. "It was the first time a paper had ever asked someone with opposite views to write for it," he later said.

But his views weren't always that much different from those of Tribune editors. In 1932, for example, he dismissed presidential candidate Franklin D. Roosevelt as "a pleasant man without any important qualifications for the office." And in 1936 he supported Republican Alf Landon over FDR. He preferred Republicans Thomas E Dewey in 1948 and Dwight D. Eisenhower in 1952, only to turn around and strongly back Democrats Adlai E. Stevenson in 1952, John F. Kennedy in 1960, and Lyndon B. Johnson in 1964.

Of his famed putdown of FDR, Mr. Lippmann would admit years later, that, "In hindsight, of course, it was a foolish remark. I didn't believe he had any strong convictions."

Mr. Lippmann, who criticized American Presidents for not recognizing the People's Republic of China, grew disenchanted with President Johnson's military intervention in Southeast Asia. One outspoken critic of Johnson's Vietnam war policies, Sen. Wayne Morse of Oregon, suggested that Mr. Lippmann be considered for secretary of state.

He stopped his newspaper column in May 1967, at a time when Lyndon Johnson was launching a counterattack on an increasingly hostile press, Johnson's administration, Mr. Lippmann said, "was involved in promoting the greatest disaster that happened to this country since the Civil War. It has divided and hurt the country more than anything in a hundred years. History will give it due credit for having passed legislation that was much demanded by the people and was on the whole necessary. But his foreign policy has been a disaster."

Mr. Lippmann's assessment of John Foster Dulles, President Eisenhower's strong-willed secretary of state, was just as harsh. Of Dulles, Mr. Lippmann wrote — "His great handicap, which might be removed by a searching of soul, is that he lays down the moral law without humor and humility as one of the righteous speaking down to the unrighteous."

Charles de Gaulle and Winston Churchill were, in Mr. Lippmann's opinion, the most impressive political leaders of his era. "Nobody that I've known in American history, that I've met, would I put in the same class as de Gaulle and Churchill," he said last year.

Indeed, Mr. Lippmann found Americans painfully inept at diplomacy and regarded U. S. foreign policy, from the days of President Wilson, as a tragic series of errors. Speaking of the polarization of the Cold War years, Mr. Lippmann said, "The world is divided as it has not been since the religious wars of the 17th century and a large part of the globe is in great upheaval the like of which has not been known since the end of the Middle Ages."

(Also see preceding article)

Walter Lippmann, giant of American journalism, dies

Walter Lippmann, a giant of American journalism who twice won the Pulitzer prize, died yesterday after a lengthy illness. He was 85.

Lippmann, a syndicated columnist whose column appeared in The Press and whose influence in American thought was felt for half a century, died at his apartment in Manhattan. He had been hospitalized until recently with a heart condition.

The family said the funeral will be private. Memorial services will be announced.

LIPPMANN, Walter

LONG ISLAND PRESS
(Jamaica, N. Y.)

Dec. 15, 1974

Lippmann's career as a commentator and political philosopher began during World War I when Woodrow Wilson was president, and continued through the administrations of eight succeeding presidents.

He was the author of 25 books and thousands of syndicated newspaper columns which influenced the thinking of leaders in Washington and abroad. He wrote of the tumultuous events of the 20th century not only with unprecedented erudition, but also with an authority and pungency that won him millions of daily newspaper readers.

LIPPMANN'S column — "Today and Tomorrow" — had its inception in 1931 and was published by approximately 250 newspapers in the United States and in 25 foreign countries. He also wrote a column for Newsweek magazine.

A youthful espouser of socialism, Lippmann proved difficult to categorize in the political spectrum as he watched the march of events in Washington and the world for more than 50 years.

He was a confidante of many of the presidents and an exclusive interviewer of such center-of-the-stage international figures as Sir Winston Churchill, Nikita Khrushchev, Charles de Gaulle, Jawaharlal Nehru of India and Gamal Abdel Nasser.

Upon reaching his 70's, Lippmann became acknowledged as "the dean of American newspapermen" and appeared on periodic television programs in which he was interviewed in the style of an elder statesman.

SHORTLY before his 75th birthday in September, 1964, Lippmann received the presidential Medal of Freedom from Presi ent Johnson which read; "Through the profound interpretation of his country and the affairs of the world, he has en larged the horizons of public thinking through the power of measured reason and detached perspective."

In his career, he became known as an independent thinker who would defy labels. One colleague said of him: "He camps neither with the liberals nor the conservatives." Lippmann once gave this credo: "Every truly civilized and enlightened American is conservative and liberal and progressive."

He explained: "This conservative who is a liberal is a progressive because he must work and live, he must govern and debate in the world as it is in his own time and as it is going to become."

Lippmann was born in New York City on Sept. 23, 1889, to a wealthy family of German-Jewish descent. Privately schooled in New York City, he entered Harvard in 1906. He completed his studies there in three years, cum laude, with Phi Beta Kappa honors.

While at Harvard, he served as an as sistant to the noted American philosopher George Santayana in teaching a course in the history of philosophy.

Walter Lippmann–Prophecy's Voice

FOR most of this century so far Walter Lippmann bestrode the world of opinion like a Colossus. Newspaper and magazine editor, finally a columnist

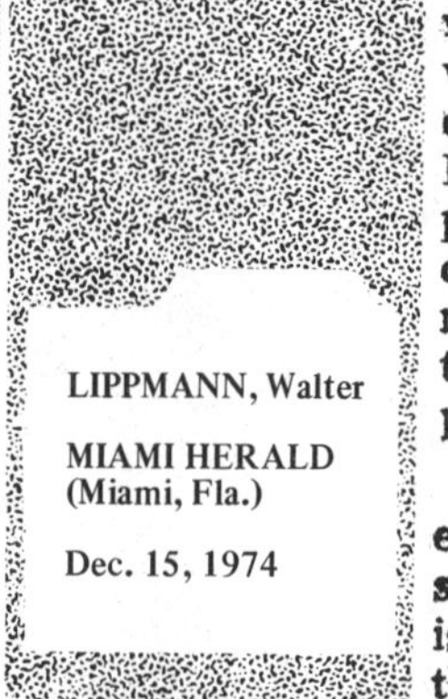

LIPPMANN, Walter

MIAMI HERALD
(Miami, Fla.)

Dec. 15, 1974

whose syndicated words spanned the continent, Mr. Lippmann was a power wherever decisions were made, especially in the field of foreign policy.

He retired several years ago, and so his passing at 85 is less of a shock than his sudden abdication from hundreds of pages such as this one. Presidents and premiers came to him. As much as any writer and perhaps more than all of his contemporaries together he moulded the opinion that made the United States think of itself, and act correspondingly, as a world power.

We remember best some words in "U.S. War Aims" written at the height of what he hoped would be the last World War. A prophetic few of them:

"When we have answered the question of how, as the saying goes, the civilians can win the peace when the soldiers have won the war, we shall have defined our war aims.

". . . The fundamental task of diplomats and public men is to preserve what is being accomplished by war.

". . . First we must make certain that this war cannot be renewed by our present enemies and that our allies will not become our future enemies. Then we can broaden the peace."

No wonder so many read or listened. The wonder is that they did not always heed. Yet in a sense it all came out in the wash: For all the woes of the world, it has yet to suffer War III.

Author Meets His Fans—All Children

LOBEL, Arnold Stark
(1933 -)

MILWAUKEE
JOURNAL
(Milwaukee, Wisc.)

Apr. 25, 1974

[See also CA-4]

Journal Photo

By Bea J. Pepan
of The Journal Staff

It isn't every day a children's author gets to meet his audience. It turned out to be quite an experience for New York writer and illustrator Arnold Lobel who is here during National Library Week.

"It's one thing to write children's books, but it's another to face a roomful of 100 children," he said in an interview.

"I wish I had learned to play the guitar or could tap dance or sing, something to entertain them.

"Since I'm not a Danny Kaye, I wound up reading some of my stories, drawing pictures and showing them slides of some of my illustrations."

Here for three days, Lobel has been talking to youngsters at local libraries. He will conclude his talks tonight at 7:30 p.m. at the Tippecanoe Library.

Marvels at Teachers

"A roomful of children can crush the friendliest of persons. I marvel at how teachers can do it," he said.

The reason his talks went well, he conceded, may be because children relate to his books.

Since he started in 1961, Lobel has written and illustrated 15 books for children and illustrated 40 by other authors. Theoretically he gears his writing to the 4 to 8 year olds, but that's an age span the publisher sets up to assist sales clerks, he pointed out. He has found his books draw an audience of youngsters and grownups.

An artist before he became an author, Lobel is a graduate of Pratt Institute in Brooklyn. He started out as an illustrator for an advertising agency until "the pressures" led him into a quieter field.

Share Studio

Lobel is married to Anita Lobel, who is also a writer and artist of many books for children. The couple do not collaborate on work although they share the same studio in their Brooklyn home. They have two children, Adrianne, 18, and Adam, 15.

His books have been recognized for their humor, whimsy and inventive drawing detail. His most popular characters are Frog and Toad and not surprisingly they have won critical acclaim. In 1971, his "Frog and Toad Are Friends" was named a Caldecott honor book. Its sequel, "Frog and Toad Together," was named a 1973 Newberry honor book.

Writes for Himself

"I write the books for myself," the author said. "I don't think 'children' as I formulate a story. If I did there would be a tendency to be condescending.

"The stories are based on some of my own preoccupations, my childhood experiences. Sometimes they come out of the truth I find in myself."

An admitted daydreamers, Lobel says, "I relate to children, through humor, as most adults do. I couldn't be comfortable doing a book without some element of humor. It cuts down on the sentimentality that somethimes bogs down children's books."

He also seems to be more comfortable writing about animals than human beings, but "animals used as surrogates for human beings."

Hard to Get Started

Lobel feels he was fortunate to get into the children's book field in the '60s when the market began to boom. But it is difficult to make a living at it as a beginner, he said, until one has established a list of books which bring in comfortable royalties.

Has television hurt the reading habits of children?

Lobel said he wasn't qualified to say. He would like to think programs like "Sesame Street" and "Electric Company" encourage reading.

"Unlike TV," he said, "books are something where a child can find a gentleness that he can't find anywhere else. A book is a self-contained, private thing, something on which a child can contemplate."

His books, he said, are meant to be entertaining and to make the child want to read. "Books that deal with social problems are not my metier," he said.

No Vocabulary Limit

His "I want to read" books are an attempt to improve on the old Dick and Jane books, he explained. He tries to keep the text simple without using a limited vocabulary. For example, he's not skittish about using a longer word, like "avalanche," when there is no adequate substitute.

Most of his books have a "they lived happily after" ending. It's the only type of ending that would ring true in the stories he writes, he pointed out. He questions if it would be possible to write a picture book with a sad ending. Would it be more enjoyable for a child to read: "Dog died; all cried; too bad."

Sexism is another thing about which he has no hangups when he writes. He and his wife have always shared in the household chores since both work at home.

Publishers seem more concerned about girl-boy stereotypes in books, he observed. He did a picture story about a squirrel homebody who loved to clean, bake and sew. On the cover he illustrated mama squirrel wielding a broom.

The editors considered this too menial and asked him to change it. He redrew the picture showing the squirrel coming back from a shopping trip with an acorn in a basket.

Whimsically Lobel asks, "Who's going to sweep the floors in the years to come if it's so menial?"

The children's book field is changing in subject matter and approach, Lobel pointed out. "It's part of the natural evolution of our culture." But the best books, he maintains, "have a certain timelessness which cuts through the superficialities of how our life styles change."

How soon should parents start reading stories to their children?

"Never Too Early"

"It's never too early," Lobel said. "At the age of 2 they will be enthralled — even if you read to them from the telephone book."

Being a children's author can be frustrating and rewarding, he said. "It's frustrating because you never get the direct reaction of the child as you would from adults."

Offsetting this somewhat are the letters he gets from children, about 150 a year. He knows most of them are prompted by teachers, but he answers every letter and includes a drawing with his signature.

The greatest reward is seeing the book in published form, he said.

"I can look at it and say it's really mine. I've created the story; drawn the pictures. I can choose the type, pick the paper; I can do everything but the actual printing. That could never happen in an advertising agency where many people are always involved in a single project."

Family 'Trait' Turns Prof Back To Writing

By SYLVIA SACHS
Press Book Editor

If he had been shut up in a room at age 15 or 16 and never had another contact with the outside world, he could have — and would have — written novels, Ernest Lockridge declared.

Lockridge says he began "writing" at 5 when he started imagining characters and plots and telling them to his mother.

Mom Approved

"My mother didn't think I was crazy," Lockridge said. "Writing ran in our family. My great-grandfather was a Hoosier poet. My grandfather wrote historical books, but aspired to be a novelist. My grandmother wrote children's books.

"And during my childhood, until I was 9, my father's typing was always in the background."

Lockridge's father was Ross Lockridge, author of "Raintree County," a best seller in the late 1940s later made into a movie. He committed suicide at the height of the novel's success. Ernest, was then 9.

"I've tried to analyze and figure out why my father did it," Lockridge said. He shook his head. "I don't know — he did it with monoxide; maybe it was a cry for help and he didn't expect it to succeed . . .

"I'm sure he was utterly exhausted. And they say there are two dangers for authors . . . failure and success. Authors become accustomed to failure, but success is equally dangerous."

Because of memories of his father, Lockridge said he tried to stop writing (after having written a "bad" novel at 17.) In college, he decided to be a psychologist, but this resolve didn't last. He was soon back at the typewriter and had a first novel published in 1968 when he was 30.

"I have two brothers and a sister who are all natural writers and are professors of English, but they resisted writing for the same reason I tried to," Lockridge said. "My mother, after 16 years as a widow, married an English professor. I just decided it was my fate and went back to writing."

Loves Teaching

Teaching also came naturally to Lockridge. He is a professor of creative writing at Ohio State University. He loves academic life and enjoys living in Columbus with his wife and family.

He recently published a novel, "Prince Elmo's Fire" (Stein and Day, $8.95), on which he worked six years. He considers it a gut-level book, one that can be praised by academic colleagues while being enjoyed by the woman who cleans his mother-in-law's house.

Lockridge said, "People in the book are loosely based on those I've known, although each was built bit by bit like a Frankenstein until all were really not like anyone else.

"Some of the story line has basis in fact. At age 11, I had a traumatic experience with backwoods people like Elmo's family at the beginning. And there is a movie maker in the book who is based on some of the types I met when my family was on the set of 'Raintree County.'

"But there is no actual reportage in this book. I wanted to write about a person who was very close to some of the basic drives, aspirations and needs people have. I wanted to bring out things we feel and don't like to admit we feel . . . and things we want to do and don't want to admit we want to do. Elmo has no pre-packaged concept of life."

Lockridge has written an elemental novel that has depth and is thought-provoking. His hero, Prince Elmo, is born in a hillbilly shack, has a meteoric success in the art world, goes to college, war and Paris. Eventually, he heads back for his beginnings.

A novelist's son aims for his own style and fame

By LUCINDA INSKEEP
Louisville Times Staff Writer

WHEN Ernest Lockridge was very young, he fell in love with Snow White. So does the hero in his new novel "Prince Elmo's Fire."

And that, Lockridge insists, is the only wholly true story about himself or his family in the book, a lusty portrait of an artist who emerges from the squalor of a backwoods shack in Southern Indiana.

Because his father was the late Ross Lockridge Jr., author of "Raintree County," and because he grew up mostly in Bloomington, Ind., the basis for his imaginary Golden Grove in the novel, the 35-year-old Lockridge is more than a bit defensive of his book's originality.

"'Prince Elmo's Fire' is *not* the 'Son of Raintree County' or 'Raintree County Strikes Again,'" he insisted during a recent interview. "There isn't any resemblance and I'm not trying to emulate my father."

Nonetheless, Lockridge does admit that there are fragments of his past and the people he has known within his novel.

"It is, to a certain degree, remembrances of growing up," he said. "Everything in the novel kind of spins off something I've known. But it is not in any sense autobiographical. Golden Grove is an imaginative rendering of Bloomington and that's where almost three-quarters of the book takes place. I have taken considerable liberties with the geography, however."

LOCKRIDGE, who had just revisited his hometown during part of a promotional tour for the book, laughed about some of the reaction it had received there. "There was speculation as to who was whom in 'Prince Elmo.' But anybody who tries to track down who really is Tarze or Mr. Pickwick is chasing a red herring. When I imagine characters, they come out of everybody. They are from little bits and pieces of people from everywhere. And then, they all come out different."

As for being the son of a famous novelist, Lockridge claims it nearly prevented him from becoming a writer himself.

"Both my brothers and my sister have really tremendous literary gifts and have suppressed them. I did until I was 17. I even went to college (Indiana University) thinking about being a psychologist. But then I decided that if I was born to have any identity, it was as a writer."

He's been writing ever since. First, as an English major at IU ("I wrote five or six novels — none of them any good.") Then while getting his Ph.D. in three years on a Woodrow Wilson Scholarship to Yale and, from 1963 to 1969 as an English teacher at Yale.

"I published a novel in '68 called 'Heartspring.' It sort of vanished into one of those black holes in space," Lockridge laughed. "Then I published a more scholarly book on 'The Great Gatsby' by F. Scott Fitzgerald."

THE FIRST DRAFT of Prince Elmo, all 1,100 pages of it, was written during 1969 and 1970 while the author was on a fellowship to the Center for Advanced study at the University of Illinois.

"I had 10 months to do nothing but write. Then I spent another two years cutting, rewriting and just generally polishing. I overwrite by half — sometimes by 100 per cent," said Lockridge.

"Then when I go back and read what I've done, I think, 'My God, what imbecile wrote that graph?' Almost always the things I go back and think are the most stupid were the ones that I thought 'how beautiful, how brilliant' while I was writing them. I almost never leave a sentence unchanged. I go back and cut and cut. It's like getting rid of unsightly fat, which does account for boiling 1,100 pages of Prince Elmo down to 350."

When he isn't writing, Lockridge said, he is either teaching English and creative writing at Ohio State University (he's been on the faculty since 1971), reading, or "sometimes, just staring at the wall."

Married to the former Rebecca Bryant, his high school sweetheart in Bloomington, and the father of three girls—Laurel, 11; Ellen, 8, and Sara, 5, Lockridge says his only regret is that he doesn't have more time to spend with his daughters.

"I'm not sure I'm a very good father," he admitted. "But I get awfully angry at people who say, 'You've got three daughters, so you must still be trying for a son.'"

THE NOVELIST claims that his two favorite hobbies are cooking and eating. "I've an incredible appetite," he said. "Luckily I burn off most of it. I do most of the cooking at home because I like it. Writing is rough. The rewards are way far away and when you cook they are immediate.

"I never use a recipe—couldn't cook that way. I just make things up. I've only had one failure and that's when I opened a can of corn for a stew and it turned out to be creamed corn. I looked at it and thought, 'Oh hell, why not?' It ruined the stew."

Since moving to Columbus, Lockridge said he has also become a bit of a winemaker, thanks to grapes growing on a lot behind his home.

"Most of them are Concords. But if you do it right, the wine comes out dry, delicious and incredibly powerful."

He is as immodest about his writing ability as he is about his cooking and wine-making talents.

"I think 'Prince Elmo' is a marvelous book," he announced happily. "Which, of course, makes it a lot easier for me to go around being Narcissus. I love to write. When I have a solid block of time, I'll write eight hours a day. Get up early, drink coffee and then start punching the typewriter. I use more of my brain when I'm writing than when I do anything else.

"There are moments in writing when I wish I hadn't been born," Lockridge added. "Times when there's a novel to write and I can't find my first sentence, my first paragraph, my first chapter. But usually, after enough false starts, I feel like a well that can't run dry."

LOCKRIDGE, Ernest (Hugh) (1938 -)
PITTSBURGH PRESS (Pittsburgh, Penn.)
Jan. 20, 1974
[See also CA-25/28]

LOCKRIDGE, Ernest (Hugh)
COURIER JOURNAL & TIMES (Louisville, Ken.)
Dec. 30, 1973

One man's fancy: Pulitzer Prize and Bette Davis

LOGAN, Joshua Lockwood (1908 -)

PLAIN DEALER (Cleveland, Ohio)

Oct. 17, 1974

The Plain Dealer/Richard J. Misch

Director-producer-playwright Joshua Logan.

By Mary Strassmeyer
Society Editor

Pulitzer Prize winner director-producer-playwright Joshua Logan has rubbed shoulders with most of the stars of the movies and the theater since he began his career in the early '30s.

He talked about many of the ones he has known over the years and about himself at a meeting of the Twentieth Century Club yesterday afternoon in Shaker Heights.

Although just as well-known for his films, it is the theater which is his life and to which he constantly returns. Logan's current venture is the musical version of "The Corn Is Green," called "Miss Moffatt."

The musical, starring Bette Davis, opened in Philadelphia a week and a half ago. The reviews, according to Logan, were not kind the morning after opening night.

"Three days later, it was fine," Logan, 66, said. "We worked on it, and we're still working on it. We'll probably be working on it when it gets to the Hanna Theater here in early February for a two-week run."

Logan said the musical was originally chosen as a vehicle for Mary Martin, with whom he had worked so successfully in "Kind Sir" and "South Pacific." He received the Pulitzer prize for his co-authorship (with the late Oscar Hammerstein II) of the latter.

"But Mary Martin's husband, Dick Halliday, died, and she turned down the musical — he was the support of her life.

"She may come back eventually. But she has to be sure of her voice and she has to find a part for a 60-year-old woman, even though she doesn't look her age. She won't be offered many parts like 'Miss Moffatt' because they just aren't around."

Logan said that "Miss Moffatt," which will tour the United States before opening on Broadway next fall, "became a hit the day Bette Davis agreed to do the show."

He advised Twentieth Century Club members that if they had children who wanted to go into the theater to discourage them from it if possible.

"The theater is a profession that is so demanding and so frustrating that young people should try anything else as a career that may satisfy them.

"Yet it is a fabulous world which contains the greatest heights one can reach. Those heights are so heady, you don't need liquor or dope or an anything else."

He said that playwriting cannot be taught. "You've just got to do it," he said. "If you want to be a playwright, write a play. If you want to be an actress, act—or marry somebody with money who'll build you a theater."

Among Logan's great successes over the years are the Broadway musicals, "Annie Get Your Gun" and "Wish You Were Here;" the plays, "Mister Roberts," "On Borrowed Time" and "The Wisteria Trees," and the movies, "Picnic" and "Bus Stop."

He considers "Bus Stop" his own greatest film success and also the greatest film made by its star, Marilyn Monroe.

"She was the last of her breed," Logan said of the late actress. "She was not only beautiful but brilliant and enormously talented. She was the nearest thing to a genius I have ever worked with.

"Everything about her was theatrical. And Hollywood treated her like a dumb blonde. But she wasn't dumb. Uneducated, yes, but never stupid.

"She was called every four-letter woman's name in the book. Her only reaction was to act like an injured animal.

Logan has been a close friend of James Stewart and Henry Fonda since their youth.

Logan is Jane Fonda's "pretend godfather" and has directed the young actress who is Henry Fonda's daughter.

"I'm sure she is sincere about the Indians and all of her other causes," he said, "but I've never heard her discuss them.

Anita Loos

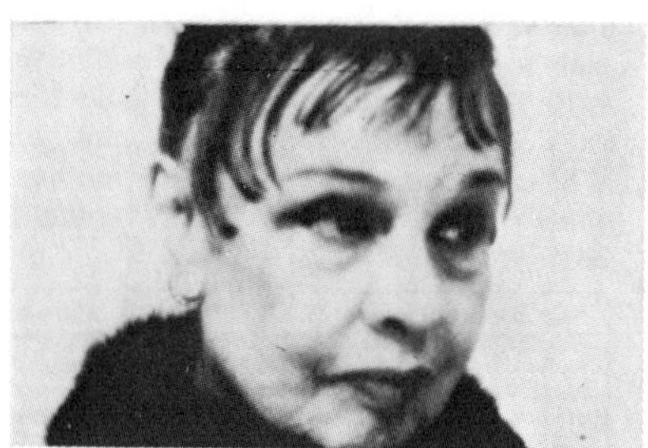

Anita Loos: "As long as those lovely royalty checks keep coming I'll love 'Gentlemen Prefer Blondes'."

BY ROY NEWQUIST

Anita Loos is a doll. She's the size of one, but her wit and energy could never be duplicated by Mattell or the Barbie people. And her magical memoir, **Kiss Hollywood Goodbye** (Viking, $7.95) is much more than a playtime fling. It is one of the most observant and delightful books ever written about Hollywood's late golden years.

I told her how surprised I'd been by her disclosure of Hollywood's intellectual and cultural life of that period.

"Most people are surprised. They think of the old Hollywood as being nothing but glamour and sex and big, wild parties and stars with more money than sense. Oh, there *was* that, and a lot of it was fun.

"But there was more. My dear friend Aldous Huxley lived here, and Mizener, and Artur Rubenstein and Chris Isherwood—oh, so many talented people with great depth. I really doubt if any other place in the world, at any time, had such a concentration of brilliant people. Even a few of the actors were intelligent."

I wondered if she minded being so closely identified, for most of her long lifetime, with "Gentlemen Prefer Blondes."

"Heavens no, not as long as those lovely royalty checks keep coming in. And they *are* lovely. There really hasn't been a year in which it hasn't been produced somewhere in the world as a play or a musical, or reprinted in some part of the world. Right now it's doing beautifully on Broadway as 'Lorelei' and this fall the Book-of-the-Month Club is issuing the novel—the very first time they've ever done a reprint.

"It's grand, of course, having critics regard Lorelei Lee as the all-American heroine, and hearing a few bolder critics calling it The Great American Novel. But ah, those royalty checks. They're this girl's best friend."

I also expressed surprise that "Kiss Hollywood Goodbye" was written totally from memory, not from diaries or notes.

"I've never kept a diary. I started writing when I was very young, writing professionally, and I was not about to put down a word that couldn't be sold." She paused. "Oh, dear, I suppose I could have sold a diary, after all."

How does she compare the film product of her day at MGM with those that are being produced today?

"I really think we turned out a better product. We had great fun writing and producing them; we were never conscious of turning out art, we were more concerned with our films as entertainment. There was none of the self-consciousness or laborious messages or untidy sex that make so many of today's films uncomfortable to sit through.

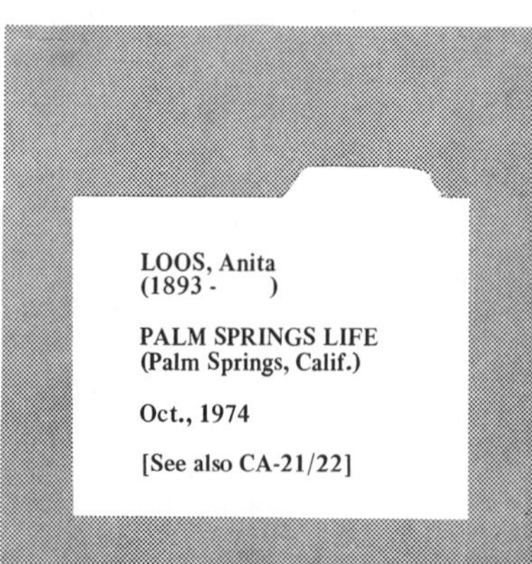

LOOS, Anita
(1893-)

PALM SPRINGS LIFE
(Palm Springs, Calif.)

Oct., 1974

[See also CA-21/22]

"Those of my generation, all that are left, anyway, have been delightfully surprised at discovering that we produced more than entertainment—we *did* create art. In New York, for example, we can hardly get into the theatres they call art houses because lines and lines of kids from 14 to 21 are going to see our films. And loving them."

She shrugged. "But you've got to remember . . . we made them when the world was young, so to speak, before the atom bomb came along to hang over everyone's heads. Life *was* fun, then."

Anita Loos' Favorites... Garbo, Bogart And Tracy

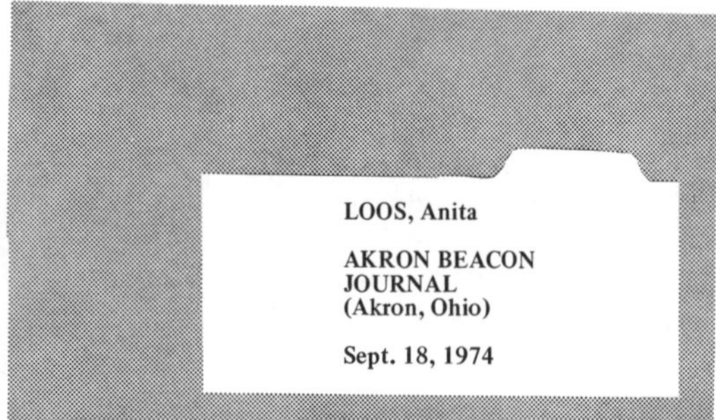

LOOS, Anita

AKRON BEACON JOURNAL
(Akron, Ohio)

Sept. 18, 1974

By SHIRLEY EDER
Knight News Service

HOLLYWOOD — Anita Loos whose new book is titled, "Kiss Hollywood Goodbye," is the only woman in the world who wants to add years to her age.

Anita said her age is now listed as 81. "I know I'm older," she said, "but I don't know how much older because my birth record was burned up in the San Francisco earthquake.

Anita Loos authored the great "Gentlemen Prefer Blondes" and when she was a writer for MGM one of the fabulous films she wrote was "San Francisco," which gave Spencer Tracy his first real starring role.

"I REMEMBER," she said, "being called into a conference with the boss, Louis B. Mayer. Seems he bought a property called 'The Rosary,' which he couldn't peddle to any of the staff writers including F. Scott Fitzgerald. He summoned me into his massive office to try to persuade me to do a screen treatment of 'The Rosary,' which was a silly story even in those days.

"Mr. Mayer had a habit of acting out characters in the stories. I could barely keep a straight face this time when he finally hit the big scene in 'The Rosary.' It was a scene where a little child was saying its prayers for some terrible extremity. Right there before my eyes Louis B. got down on his knees and did the prayer in the voice of a child.

"For those who never saw Louis B. — he was a fat bald-headed little man who was far from pretty. I ran out of the office cause I didn't dare laugh at him in his domain."

WHAT DID Anita Loos think of F. Scott Fitzgerald, with whom she worked and knew well?

"I think Scott was first of all a poet," she said. "I don't think you ought to read him as a novelist. One should pick him up and read two or three chapters at a time. And regard his work as prose poems. He was a stylist and a writer of a particular sort."

Anita has a 16-year-old adopted daughter who recently received a D-minus in school on a paper she had to write on "The Great Gatsby."

"My daughter wrote that the purpose she felt of "The Great Gatsby" was to get into society and that shows how dull a man (Gatsby) he is," she said. "You know, she was right. When I look back on Gatsby, that's exactly what the story's about. And maybe that's why so many people won't sit still for the movie.

"Scott took the dullness of his characters seriously. He let them choose their own importance."

TO MS. LOOS, who knew all the great stars, on and off screen, Greta Garbo was the most exciting actress and Humphrey Bogart and Tracy were her favorite actors.

She sees Garbo from time to time on the streets in New York where they both live. "Sometimes she greets me with a big hello and is very warm," Ms. Loos said. "Other times, she walks by me. But that's Garbo. That's the way she's always been."

LOOS, Mary

NEWS–AMERICAN (Baltimore, Md.)

Nov. 3, 1974

*** Hark, hark the dogs do bark,**
The beggars are coming to town;
Some in rags, some in tags,
And one in a velvet gown.

— Nursery Rhyme

Hark, Hark . . . the 'Beggars' are Here*

By EILEEN BIRO
Staff Reporter

It was only natural that Mary Loos became a writer. She is the granddaughter andniece of writers.

Her uncle, R. Beers Loos did titles for silent pictures and her aunt, Anita Loos, wrote "Gentlemen Prefer Blonds."

Since she grew up in Hollywood society, went to school with Agnes de Mille, dated Charlie Chaplin and rubbed shoulders with filmdom's most glittering stars, it was not surprising that she would combine her experiences to produce a novel about movies.

What was unforseeable was the approach her publisher took with the book.

First novels are difficult to sell and usually received with as much enthusiasm as this year's version of the flu.

But, Mary wrote a winner, and the brass at Bantam Books was quick to recognize it. They gave it the treatment — proclaiming it a super release with a first printing of 575,000 copies and an all-out promotion campaign.

"The Begars Are Coming" couldn't lose. It didn't. It hit the paperback bestseller list immeditely after release last month. Two weeks later, it went into a second printing.

Doubtless, the Loos name carries impact, but, as entertaining reading, so does the book.

"Beggars" is a fast-moving story filled with flamboyant Hollywood characters swept up in a glamorous world. And there is enough sex and romance to provide something for everyone.

Mary describes her novel as "a kind of 'Forsythe Saga' " based on the history of the film industry from 1913 to 1947. She is working on a sequel.

"I figured since I was in part of history and since Hollywood had existed long enough for me to be third generation, it was time to do a kind of saga on it — not just one director, actor or writer but on the whole industry," she says.

"When pictures first began, some kids would get an idea and manage to get some film and find a good looking chick who would wiggle around. They would add a man who looked rough and ready and could get on a horse without falling off, and they made movies.

"Even Chaplin recalls the days when they went into a public park with a stepladder, a bucket of paint and Mable Norman and came out with a movie. Everything was ad lib and youth and ambition. Maybe that's the reason I decided to write 'The Beggars are Coming' as a novel. I wanted to write it as a frontier story."

"I did a little acting, mostly because I wanted to be where the action was," says Loos. "I danced the Indian princess in 'Rosemarie' with Nelson Eddy and Jeanette MacDonald, and I did a small role in Claudette Colbert's 'Cleopatra,' but acting never appealed to me too much. I liked the creative side more."

When television moved to Hollywood, she and Richard Sale, her former husband, were quick to recognize its importance. Together they wrote the series, "The Wackiest Ship in the Army," "Please Don't Eat the Daisies," and "Bewitched." They also produced and wrote "Yancy Derringer."

Her other work includes writing for the annual Academy Awards show and several Variety Club International programs.

As a long-time member of the Hollywood film community, she probably saw more of what goes on behind the scenes than many of the stars. Her book, which follows the lives of three generations of moviemakers, is filled with first hand historical notes and quotes.

Mary Loos' first hand knowledge of her subject couldn't be better. Through her Aunt Anita, she got to know some of the biggest names in Hollywood.

"I met William Randolph Hearst, Marion Davies, Darryl Zanuck, Douglas Fairbanks Sr., Norma Shearer, Garbo and Paulette Goddard. Hollywood was more of a village in those days.

"When my aunt was under contract to MGM I used to go watch — Clark Gable, Spencer Tracy, Robert Taylor, John Garfield . . . " Mary Loos rattles off the names with the same familiarity as someone else might recall school classmates.

Her contact with filmdom was more than social. As a young adult she began to work in bit parts in movies, expressed the desire to produce, and eventually turned to scriptwriting. She collaborated with Sale, on a score of films including "Woman's World," "French Line," and "Gentlemen Marry Brunettes."

The story begins in New York and traces the reasons behind the move of the industry from the east to California. One important element was the pressure the film trust, an all-powerful monopoly of distributors and producers of films, put on independent filmmakers to keep any competition out.

"It was very interesting, the westward movement of the pictures," Loos says. "They were trying to avoid the pressure of the trust which used to come in on independents and break up the cameras and grab the film and try to keep everything under the control of the trust.

"People who migrated out did so in just as woolly times as the covered wagon folk. Around 1917 the trust came under a suit by the U.S. government for monopolistic practices and it was broken. One reason it had to fail was because the companies involved in it didn't realize feature pictures weren't going to come in. They thought of all their pictures in terms of vaudeville timing which is around 12 minutes."

The book includes much more of film history than simply the business side of the industry. The action centers on the lives of several characters, not the least of which is a great Hollywood beauty who rises to stardom and then suffers the inevitable fall.

"I wanted to show what it means to be put on a pedestal so high that no human being could ever really live up to it," says the author, discussing the character."Imagine if you're a sex symbol — any man who wants to have a relationship with you is going to expect you to be the wildest thing in bed that ever was. Any director wants you to be the absolute embodiment of his imagination. Every studio thinks of you as a two, three, four, or five million dollar investment — let her just live up to what we want!

"The star is supposed to do everything in every direction that no individual could fulfill. They work awfully hard when they work. You can't enjoy food too much and you can't go out at night and have an affair of consequence or a drink because it will show on the camera the next day.

"They have to give out publicity and be charming to important people. Look at Elizabeth Taylor. She hasn't had a private moment since she did "National Velvet" and look what happened to Judy Garland.

"Stars walk out on the street and they are sought after, pawed after, pulled after. I know lots of them don't go to a department store because they are so mobbed."

Loos has witnessed such treatment time and again. When she was in Europe with Jane Russell during the filming of "Gentlemen Marry Brunettes," Miss Russell became the target of every fanny pincher and breast grabber on the continent.

And when she attended a convention of Variety Clubs in San Francisco with Cary Grant she was shocked at the women who would "literally look down his tonsils.

"It was embarrassing. Everybody wanted to touch, touch, touch. I've seen celebrities approached by little old ladies who say, 'I know your aunt in Minnesota'; and even if he doesn't have an aunt, he's not going to go into it.

"People ask me, 'How do you like going out with a great star? I say it's uncomfortable."

But the long-time Hollywood observer is quick to add that there's one thing worse than the constant attention for the celebrities she's known. The moment the adulation ends.

"Unless they mature they become a kind of cartoon of what they were when they were younger," she says.

They put on too much makeup, get too girlish or too rugged. The ones who coped with it are pretty strong people — Katharine Hepburn, Ginger Rogers, Anne Baxter, Loretta Young, Claudette Colbert, and Lillian Gish. But for every one who managed well, there are plenty who have suffered."

U.S. Likened to Nazi Germany

Composite Dictator

This is the cover of Stefan Lorant's new book, "Sieg Heil!" a photo-history of Germany from 1861 through World War II. It is a painting by Idabelle Kleinhans after a photomontage by the German political artist John Heartfield which first appeared in a 1932 issue of a Berlin magazine. It is a composite of the three German political leaders who dominated an era. Hitler's face is embellished with a Kaiser Wilhelm II moustache while he wears a uniform reminiscent of Bismarck's.

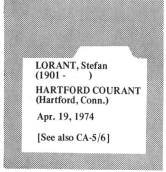

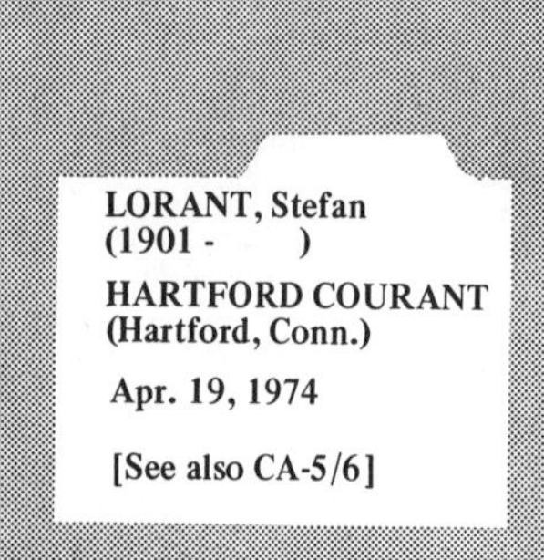
LORANT, Stefan
(1901 -)
HARTFORD COURANT
(Hartford, Conn.)
Apr. 19, 1974
[See also CA-5/6]

STEFAN LORANT

By KEN CRUICKSHANK

"I did the book mostly as a warning—to show how it was. There are so many vague parallels between politics then and today that it's frightening."

The man who lived on the same street as Adolf Hitler in the 1920s, who occasionally shook Hitler's hand and found it "weak and flabby" and who was thrown into a Nazi prison the day Hitler came to power, sat in a straight-backed chair and talked of his new book about the rise of the Nazis.

The book, which author Stefan Lorant calls "an optical symphony, " is a kaleidoscopic, 350-page photo-and-text mantage covering the rise and fall of modern Germany from 1961 to the end of World War II.

It is called "Sieg Heil!"

Lorant wrote, collated and edited the work primarily for the younger generation—a warning of what can happen when politics subverted by power.

Sees Same Problems

He began the book four years ago after seeing many of the same problems he once saw in Germany begin to crop up in America.

"I saw political power being gathered into the hands of industry and the military, I saw high officials cheating, I saw a breaking down of conventions and I saw lawlessness," he said of America in the early 1970s.

"I had seen it all before," he said, adding: "If someone in high office manipulates the institutions of democracy against democracy, we could face collapse."

Lorant is known primarily for his books about Abraham Lincoln. His face lights up when he describes the famous president and he leans forward in his chair, eager to talk.

"I first read a book about Lincoln in a Nazi prison," he said. "Since then, of course, I have studied his whole life. He had everything. He was a humanitarian, he was witty, he was a fine writer and he was a great orator and debater."

Turns to Hitler

But Lorant felt he was in a unique position to chronicle the events leading up to World War II and he turned from the man he admired most in the world to the one he perhaps despised above all others.

Sometimes called the "father of modern photojournalism," Lorant was editor of the Munchner Illustrierte Presse, a magazine in Munich, Germany, at the same time Hitler was the editor of the Illustrierter Beobachter, a competing magazine.

He was still editor of the Presse when Hitler became chancellor of Germany in 1933, and he was one of the first to be jailed by the Nazis.

Released through the intercession of the Hungarian government, Lorant fled Germany for Great Britain, where he published his diary, "I Was Hitler's Prisoner," which sold more than a million copies.

He also created England's Weekly Illustrated (one of the first pictorial magazines), the magazine Lilliput and the pictorial weekly Picture Post.

Lenox, Mass., Resident.

In 1940 he came to America, where he has since written several well-known historical books. He lives in Lenox , Mass.

For "Sieg Heil," which contains more than 700 rare photos, Lorant was able to call on his old journalistic acquaintances from Germany or their relatives for photographic negatives.

Contributors to the book include Hitler's official photographer, Heinrich Hoffman, and Helmuth Kurth, Goering's personal photographer, who had been able to save all his negatives after the war.

"I was looking for a yardstick," Lorant says of the book, "a new kind of book showing a whole era."

He said there are 150,000 words in the volume but that he tried to make them so compatible with the photographs that "you don't know you are reading. I want to carry a message."

Lorant said he has been deeply disturbed at the route America seems to be taking and wanted to warn that "it could happen here."

Watergate, however, has been "a godsend," he said. "It's the greatest thing that could have happened . . . like lancing a boil and all the dirt comes out. The wound has a chance to heal, even though the patient may still be sick."

The words used by the Nixon Administration to berate the press "are exactly the same" as those used by Joseph Goebbels, Hitler's minister of propaganda Lorant said.

"When Nixon accuses the press of vicious reporting, he is saying exactly what Goebbels said to foreign reporters after the 'Night of the Long Knives' (the night Hitler ordered the massacre of many of his old supporters for political reasons)," he said. The adjectives are the same."

"The words 'peace with honor' were first used by Hitler in relation to Poland," said Lorant, "and the phrase 'inoperative statement' is exactly the same in German—and was used by the Nazis."

He hastened to add that all parallels are, of necessity, strained, but that the general trend of America toward power politics had bothered him for some time.

LUBBE, Catherine Case
and
YELTON, Marjorie Ledbetter

DALLAS NEWS (Dallas, Tex.)

Aug. 30, 1974

—Dallas News: Johnny Flynn

Catherine Case Lubbe, right, new chief of the National Federation of State Poetry Societies, with Marjorie Ledbetter Yelton . . . "Poets have a wonderful time. They're not gloomy people, as a whole." Poetry is part of real life.

Poets in the mainstream

By MARY BRINKERHOFF

To some people, poets are refugees fleeing the fearful waves of reality, cop-outs or willing castaways, like the nun in a verse by Gerard Manley Hopkins:

"I have asked to be where no storms come, where the green swell is in the havens dumb, and out of the swing of the sea."

Yet is poetry really a stagnant, shallow backwater, or is it rather the deepest of currents, a medium in which the brave confront their own emotions, and are the scoffers themselves cowards dodging that encounter?

Don't be too sure of your answer until you've sat and talked a while with someone like Dallas' Catherine Case Lubbe, picked for a top national post by fellow poets this summer, or Marjorie Ledbetter Yelton, elected to office with her.

"Many people write poetry and never tell anybody," says Mrs. Lubbe, new president of the National Federation of State Poetry Societies. 'So many people have poetry in their hearts."

KAY LUBBE, whose myriad interests include the collecting of offhand references like "poetic license" and "poetic justice," has no doubts about it: "Poetry is very much a part of real life."

She and Marjorie, new federation secretary, were elected at a June convention on the Dickinson College campus in Carlisle, Pa. Now they're looking forward to the next such gathering in June of 1975 at SMU.

First, though, comes Poetry Day, to be observed on Oct. 15 in Texas and most other states. And in June of 1976, Mrs. Yelton will head for Baltimore, Md., to serve as a chancellor at the World Congress of Poets, a U.S. Bicentennial event.

The two friends have much in common besides fresh mandates for national federation leadership. Each holds an honorary doctorate of humane letters from Pakistan's University of Free Asia. Each is a longtime director of the Poetry Society of Texas.

Together, they have reaped a sheaf of honors ranging from Kay's gold medal at the New York World's Fair to Marjorie's chairmanship of Texas delegates to the World Congress of Poets last November in Taipei, Taiwan.

The new national federation president, an Illinois native, projects a kind of genteel energy. She aspired to an acting career, was educated in drama and speech and later taught these subjects.

She and her husband, John Andrew Lubbe, are parents of two sons and grandparents of 10, at the last count.

Lubbe, a retired federal official, is the Texas society's treasurer emeritus —and a prime example of the "very manly-men" his wife cites as proof that love of poetry doesn't make the lover weak or woolly-headed.

THE LUBBES formerly lived in New Orleans and Colorado Springs. It was in the latter city that Kay, who recalls writing and reading aloud a poem for her grandparents' golden anniversary when she was 12, took to poetry seriously during an enforced rest for the sake of her health.

She has since garnered lots of prizes, offices and acceptances of poems for publication; she has written, edited, lectured, judged, held state and national offices, given programs of poetry (she can never remember her own).

Along with her new national duties, Kay is still engrossed in organizing an irreplaceable literary collection, the treasured legacy of Dallas publishers Whitney and Vaida Stewart Montgomery. She's also the society's representative in charge of its permanent collection at the Dallas Public Library.

The national federation chief has a worthy colleague in Marjorie Yelton, herself a winner of prizes for poems, essays and children's literature, former president of the Southwest Writers.

Marjorie, an executive secretary for 27 years, is the wife of Dallas Symphony Orchestra musician Harold M. Yelton. They have a daughter and four grandchildren.

She endorses such Lubbe views as the importance of fostering poetry activities in the schools (Kay once addressed the national federation on the subject) and the validity of poetry reading as a performing art.

The two illustrate the counsel given Kay by onetime poet laureate Grace Noll Crowell: "If you've got poetry in your heart, stay with it, but do a good job on your boys too."

History of 'Swing Generation'

Bulletin Special Photos by Nancy Doherty

MANCHESTER, William [See also CA-1]
(1922-)

PHILADELPHIA BULLETIN
(Philadelphia, Penn.) Nov. 17, 1974

By NANCY DOHERTY

Special to The Bulletin

THIS MONTH a five-pound book with a golden future was born, destined to draw great critical attention and to wind up under Christmas trees across the land.

"The Glory and the Dream: A Narrative History of America 1932 — 1972," by William Manchester, is a retelling of the last 40 years by a member of the "Swing Generation" which reached awareness during the Depression and has now matured into late middle age. It costs $20 and contains 1,397 pages.

Popular Success

First reactions have been mixed. Historian James MacGregor Burns proclaimed it "a stunning performance," and Publisher's Weekly said it was "brilliant." New York magazine, on the other hand, broke publication date by several weeks to describe the tome as a "hippopotamus" and to say of the author's prose: "The cumulative effect is — well, like being enveloped in a pudding."

Whatever the critics say, the Literary Guild, having paid a record $525,000 to make it their monthly selection, is probably right in predicting it "could easily be the most important new best-seller of the season."

William Manchester has experienced both popular success and critical controversy before. The author of 10 books, most recently "The Arms of Krupp," he is best known for "The Death of a President."

Even those who did not read the book can recall the huge fuss before its publication when Jacqueline Kennedy and Robert F. Kennedy brought suit against Manchester and Harper and Row, publishers, in the winter of 1966-67.

Though Mrs. Kennedy had originally asked Manchester to write this authorized version of the assassination of former President John F. Kennedy, she declared it invaded her privacy and could not be published without her consent. After weeks of uproar, the suit was settled out of court. Inevitably, that spring the book became a best seller not just in the nation but around the world. Three books about the prepublication dispute itself also appeared.

"A great many people tried to use me then. I was exploited and manipulated," William Manchester said to his visitor on a recent afternoon. He was drinking black coffee in his office on the Wesleyan University campus, in Middletown, Conn. enjoying the lull before his publicity tour began. He talked about the major work he took six years to complete, and the trauma surrounding the earlier one.

Labored Long

"I think it would have changed me profoundly if I'd been a younger man. But I knew who I was. My life-style was formed."

The spacious room where he has labored for years suggested that style: The wooden work table with . . . . a cup of freshly sharpened pencils, some family pictures, a coffee maker. No paper strewn about. In a closed bookcase, foreign editions of "The Death of a President." On the walls, pictures, dust jackets, mementoes from his foreign correspondent days, a Purple Heart citation which he got up to straighten while he talked. A couch, shelves of reference works. The den of a very industrious mind.

An electric typewriter sat covered on one shelf. "I can't use it because of the hum. I feel I'm wasting energy," he said, holding up the fountain pen with which he's written his last three books.

Manchester's regimen would stagger many writers, just as the lengthy results overwhelm some readers. "I wrote, as I always do, during a five-hour period each afternoon. Evenings were for research; mornings I edited what I'd written the day before."

Text Was Cut

Ten thousand citations in the chapter notes and a long bibliography testify to endless nights in the library. The text itself was cut extensively by Manchester and his Little, Brown editor to squeeze the 40-year history into one volume. Now the framed dust jacket hung above his work table, the only visible evidence of all that toil in the tidy room.

From 1955 through 1959 William Manchester was editor-in-chief of Wesleyan University Press. Since then he has served as the school's unofficial writer-in-residence.

He and his family of four have lived for years near the campus. They were planning to move in 1966, Manchester said, when news of the Kennedy suit broke. Reporters and television camera crews descended on Middletown, waiting on his doorstep, interviewing his daughter on her way home from second grade, following him to the hospital when he fell ill with pneumonia.

"There was no escape except into the houses of friends. They didn't care about the controversy," Manchester said. Unwilling to break this bond with the community, the Manchesters stayed and built a house instead.

"Eventually I'll put down in writing what happened," he said. His explanation, "in capsule form" was that Mrs. Kennedy brought the suit without reading the book, having been incorrectly informed that he had refused to make personal changes. When she read the book, she dropped the suit.

"I don't mind talking about it," he said, anticipating the upcoming interviews and talk shows. "I do mind someone nudging me and saying 'all that publicity didn't hurt sales of the book any, did it.' "

He took a letter out of his filing cabinet. It was from the Kennedy Memorial Library and stated that as of Jan. 1, 1970, the officials had received $1,057,347 in royalties from Harper and Row.

"I didn't ever want to make money from the tragedy."

This time, of course, there's no tragedy.

Manchester expressed confidence about the book's critical reception, especially from other members of the "Swing Generation."

He dismissed the New York magazine review, pointing out that its author, Eliot Fremont-Smith, was the editor-in-chief at Little, Brown who originally approved the book idea but had since been fired.

Mild Pleasure

Last week someone from Newsweek called and asked how he's managed to analyze the nostalgia market so well. He protested his innocence. "When you're writing you can't be thinking of the market place."

This is a bookish, 52-year-old man who wears suspenders and has pouches of weariness under his eyes; whose manner is courteous but reserved. He was not about to cackle with glee or jump for joy. There was, however, a look of mild pleasure on his composed face as he looked to the future.

Once during the conversation he quoted H. L. Mencken, who said, "Writing does for me what milking does for a cow."

Novelist on the First Try

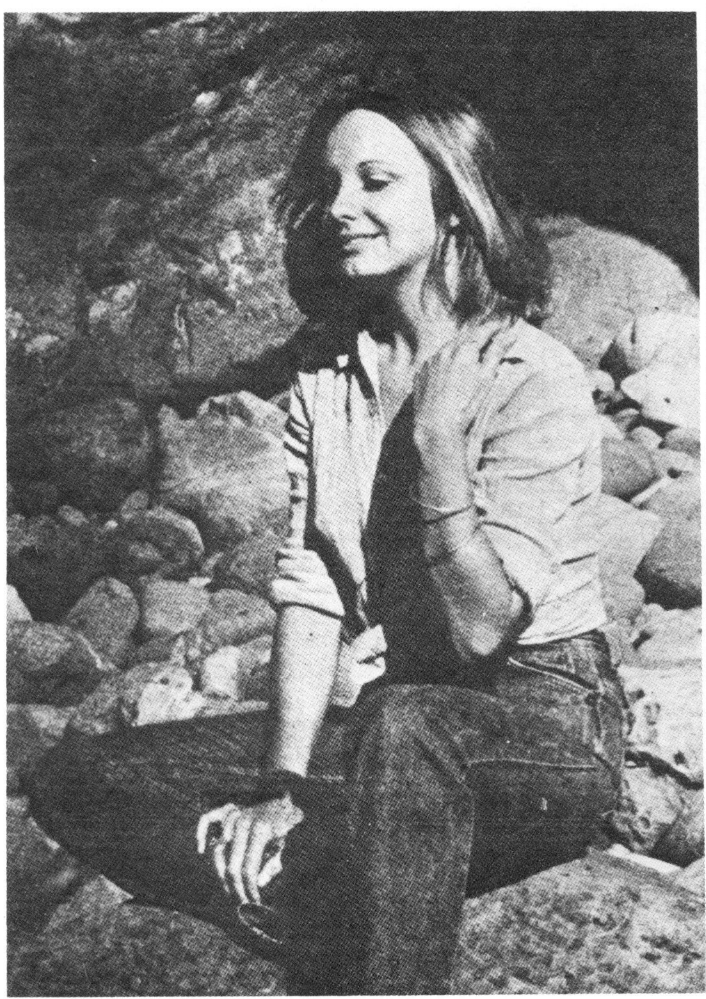

Story and Photographs

By SI DUNN

Scene Staff Writer

The sun had burned away the morning fog. Now the waves rolled tamely onto Laguna Beach, hissed softly and slid back into the Pacific. A few gulls glided overhead, making their cries. Small spider crabs darted from the water and searched for food among the pebbles, shells and rocks dry now at low tide. The sky, cloudless, was one blue, and the sea was another, darker, but sparkling—as far as the eye could see down the coast of Southern California.

Kathryn Marshall sat on a big boulder just above the beach, aware of the sea-sky panorama but more interested in the early afternoon's smaller details: The smell of the wind; the colors of the coastal foliage; the smooth and ragged shapes of the rocks around her. Ten feet below her perch, in tide pools no bigger than her hands, tiny fish flicked about. She saw them waiting impatiently for the sea to rise and set them free again.

There were times in Kathryn Marshall's still-young life—times seemingly yesterday in Arlington, Texas, in Dallas, New York, Austin and other cities—when she felt akin to the insignificant, trapped fish. Caught several times in tide pools of doubt, she had let new identities sweep her away, only to quickly ride them back onto the rocks again.

Seven years ago, at age 16, Kathryn Marshall quit Arlington High School and went to New York to be a ballerina. She had talent, experience and ballet scholarships, but found she couldn't give dancing her whole self. By 17, she was back in Arlington High School. At 18, she majored briefly in drama at Southern Methodist University and formed a few friends who were into drugs. Nineteen, she married, then put on the orange garb of a follower of Hare Krishna and chanted and danced in downtown Dallas. A few months later she was in California and divorced. By 20, however, she was back in Texas, earning a degree in philosophy at The University of Texas at Austin, and winning—because she stood one day in a graveyard at sunset and felt moved to write—a campus short story competition. Soon the story germinated into a novel, and Kathryn Marshall found herself pulled between seeking in Boston a graduate philosophy degree and moving to the West Coast to enroll in the creative writing program at the University of California at Irvine. She chose California and writing, and suddenly, at age 22, her first book, "My Sister Gone," set in East Texas and Dallas, had passed from the approving hands of her classmates and professors into scheduled publication late this spring by prestigious Harper & Row. Kathryn Marshall, still not convinced of her full identity, had become a novelist on the first try, skipping somehow the traditional agonies of art: Struggle, starvation and seemingly never-ending rejection.

MARSHALL, Kathryn

DALLAS NEWS
(Dallas, Tex.)

Dec. 29, 1974

(Continued from preceding page)

She faced the sea now, and the cool, steady wind swirled her short blonde hair into her face, briefly hiding its youth. For a while, she did not push the hair away from her eyes, or say much, for her thoughts had gone deep and part of her mind still was on her second novel, now being written—the hardest one, writers say, since the first novel quite often can be a fluke. Many produce excellent first novels and never are heard from again.

Finally, we talked about her books, about the chaos in her recent past, and about the emerging order in her present. "In a sentence," she said, warming now and grinning unpretentiously, "'My Sister Gone' is about being female and sane in macho territory, namely Texas. The first half is set in East Texas, and the second half of the book is set in Dallas. I try to take advantage of a kind of grotesquery that I find in Dallas: Cowboys who drive Cadillacs, people who make money on the Kennedy assassination, and so forth. There are descriptions of the Hotel Adolphus, the Statler-Hilton, the Sheraton, and one scene takes place in a mansion on Turtle Creek. And to get the feel of the city, I did a lot of scenes with incidental characters who I feel are very much Dallas." The novel's plot concerns two young sisters and the resolution of a deep and disturbing conflict between them.

Kathryn is small and slim and her quiet voice has a full California accent now. "I hated living in Texas," she admitted. "I wanted to live in New York. I wanted to get away. But now that I've gotten away and started writing, I realize that I've got a heritage—a place that I'm from. Texas has character and color and other things that I can put into my writing.

"My second novel," she continued, "is about people who have grown up in semirural parts of Texas. I deal with the problems of them trying to find out who they are in a society that does not seem to encourage people to find out who they are.

"I feel very lucky now," she added. "When I look back over the past few years, I think: 'Well, how much of it really was breaking away and how much of it was just a need to rebel against everything I had grown up with; and in the act of rebelling merely reaffirming where I'm from?'"

I reminded her that novelist Larry McMurtry, an ex-Texan who has published several books set in Texas, once feared being labeled a "minor regional novelist." Did she now feel the same fear? Her reply was quick. "I would not like to be tagged a 'Texas' writer. That's too limiting. I mean, William Faulkner wasn't tagged a 'Mississippi' writer." Suddenly she laughed, embarrassed by the comparison she had set up. "But of course, I'm not William Faulkner . . ."

Those who believe, however, that definite patterns can emerge from the most random of circumstances, would trace Kathryn Marshall's desire to write back to her early childhood in Oxford, Miss.—William Faulkner's town. One day when she was eight, she met the Nobel Prize-winning novelist. "I said, 'Hello, Mr. Faulkner!'" she recalls. "And he just glared at me. That was the start of my literary career. William Faulkner glared at me."

"Faulkner's woods" made the deepest impressions on her. Her father Bill Marshall, now a mathematics professor at The University of Texas at Arlington, sometimes would take Kathryn for walks through the pine forests on some of Faulkner's land. "Something very haunting," an indescribable "mythic sense" felt in those woods stayed with her, and in her first novel, she says, she has tried to transplant some of that mystery to rural East Texas.

MARSHALL, Kathryn

DALLAS NEWS
(Dallas, Tex.)

Dec. 29, 1974

At age nine, Kathryn began keeping a journal of her observations and writing small stories and poems. Two years later, she was reading Faulkner and Friedrich Nietzsche, the German philosopher and poet. She also took ballet lessons and as a teen-ager danced with the Dallas Civic Ballet. She quit New York ballet, she says, partly because "the competition is tough in New York and they just want bodies. They don't want people who think, just people who do."

Cass Canfield Jr., a senior editor at Harper & Row in New York, who discovered "My Sister Gone" at a California writers' conference in 1973, says Ms. Marshall "is a natural writer," adding, "it just comes out of her. And I think she's really quite an extraordinary person. One identifies with the people in her book and one identifies with the places. This is what caught me about it. And even though it's a very strong and, at times, agonizing story, it has a great sense of life to it."

Kathryn Marshall lives in a neat but inexpensive efficiency apartment above a bakery in Corona del Mar, about 40 miles south of Los Angeles. Beneath her balcony is scenic U.S. Highway 1, and the ocean is four blocks away. She gets up every morning soon after dawn, shuts herself in a tiny cubicle between her living room and bathroom, and writes on her next book. Later in the day, she teaches an undergraduate literature course at the nearby Irvine campus and attends classes toward her master's degree in fine arts. She also works part-time as a cocktail waitress. The $3,000 advance royalties she received from Harper & Row when her novel was accepted made few changes in her daily routine. She bought a modest red Maverick sedan, paid some bills and spent most of the balance on food and college tuition. "What happened to me is not supposed to happen," she freely concedes. "I haven't had to go through what most writers go through. It's a writer's dream."

Writers are, by nature, a jealous bunch, jealous of any fellow artist's success. Kathryn's boyfriend, Richard Berg, a 28-year-old Vietnam veteran and writer of short stories, is no exception. He says he frequently compares his writing struggles with her seeming ease of success, and feels an unhideable envy.

One of Kathryn's friends and former classmates, Linda Burnham, now a screenwriter and editor of a university news publication in Irvine, offered a similar view: "We (in the creative writing program) were all incredibly swept away by the first draft and the second draft of the book. And I think we were pretty much intimidated—by Kathryn being admitted to the program practically on wings and then going to the writers' conference and having her manuscript whisked out of her hands by the first guy that laid eyes on it. And then running to New York with it and Harper & Row throwing money at her. We all thought: 'Why not me? Why not me?'"

We were all in Kathryn's car as Linda said this. We were going to the Los Angeles airport. Richard was driving and Kathryn was smiling the smile of someone who isn't quite convinced it's all real and happening to her. She agreed, though, that having her novel accepted has freed her from many of the tide pools of doubt she once knew. "Any kind of confirmation helps. I feel that I'm a writer now, not just for myself, but that I can communicate with other people. There are a lot of things that I'd still like to do, but sometimes you can overextend yourself and wind up with nothing at all."

Does she still wonder who she is and where she's going? Her answer came easily, with no apparent tones of worry: "Oh, I'll probably wonder about that the rest of my life."

Author reaches for ultimate castle

By JANE ULRICH

In a time when despair and chaos and aimlessness are prevalent and optimism and hope and vision are limited, Malachi Martin is a rare species.

Dr. Martin, author of "The New Castle: Reaching for the Ultimate," says this is a good time to be alive, a time for "building a castle of humanness."

The former Jesuit priest, who is religious editor for National Review magazine, was in Dallas recently discussing his latest book and explaining why he feels the stirrings of the spirit, the new vision, the new "castle" are here in America.

AS USUAL, Dr. Martin was brimming with contagious optimism, an unusual trait in a super-scholar, as he told of the "castles" that have come and gone and the challenge of a new vision.

He calls this new vision "the ecology of humanness."

"Not induced by philosophers, theologians, social scientists, novelists, dramatists." his book reads. "But born (as are all life-giving visions) into the consciousness of men and women and itself as yet nameless and faceless; but drawing us on through all our painful fractures and dislocations because, as of old and as it always will be in a human world, our humanness is our sure guarantee of a divine preference."

Malachi Martin's books, as you can see, are not to be read in an hour or two. A reader could feel, with good reason, that an IQ of 180 is a prerequisite for digesting one of his treatises.

Yet the beauty of his writing with its descriptive passages, metaphors and images wears well on a man who exudes love and trust and confidence.

HE HAS the qualifications to be an ivory tower scholar —a Ph.D. three times over, former Jesuit professor at the Pontifical Biblical Institute in Rome, one of the world's foremost experts on the Dead Sea Scrolls, former political analyst in the Vatican and close associate to Pope John XXIII, speaker of a dozen languages.

MARTIN, Malachi

DALLAS NEWS
(Dallas, Tex.)

Oct. 13, 1974

Dallas News: John Rhodes

But he's not even a snob. Animated and lively, the County Kerry-born Irishman is more apt to confront those he meets in a very personal way on a level he says is ABOVE the verbal.

Perhaps that's why he's so easy to talk to and hard to write about. Even the most articulate writer would feel at a loss trying to keep Malachi Martin pinned to a piece of paper by mere words.

He's as dynamic as the spirit he speaks of, popping up in this stream of thought, that pool of ideas, here, there, and back again.

"What is inside you speaks to what is inside me," he told this writer, who hoped she would have the same rapport in "speaking" it to News readers.

WHEN MALACHI came to Dallas in February with a book entitled, "Jesus Now," he said, "I know I'm assisting at the birth of something here in the U.S."

Who could know only a few months later he'd return with yet another book, this one explaining his theory, expanding on it and giving specific examples?

Quite a traveler, he reads every magazine he can get his hands on, looks, listens everywhere he goes—to "catch what's going on here."

"There's a strange identity," he says, "which doesn't depend on color or social card or sex. All that matters is that you're human.

"That inner identity—that's the 'castle.'"

Because the U.S. isn't static ("a fixed system can't hold up politically") and doesn't have just one ideology, one race, one color, one ethnic group, one language —all the things that aren't specially human, that vision is growing here.

'We (here in the U.S.) are the guinea pigs for the rest of the world," he believes. "This goes with the American 'bubble'—just like they used to take our dishwashers and bombers."

ALL THE UNREST, the stirrings, the wanting to-know are just signs that something's happening, Malachi contends.

When movies like "The Exorcist" and books like "Jonathan Livingston Seagull" have such wide appeal, what's underneath it all is akin to what Henri Bergson called "elan vital"—a spirit of energy and life that moves all living things.

It may have been that spirit that brought Malachi from 10 years in the priesthood—"I found I couldn't obey"—to New York with $31 in his pockets, through a variety of jobs (waiter at Schrafft's, taxi driver, public relations, painter, editor-in-chief of the Encyclopaedia Britannica to where he is now.

In Biblical times they probably would have called him a prophet.

It was in a very unexciting New York restaurant—Twin Doughnuts—that Dr. Martin met a man named One-Armed Charlie (the owner) and learned he could communicate with someone who had no education, smelled bad and was different in color and shape.

"He was beautiful." Malachi recalls. "His wisdom was other than learning. It was an abiding thing, a thing of perception . . . it was the power of loving." ➡

(Also see preceding article)

Renegade Jesuit Says a Big Event Is Near

By EILEEN BIRO

Among the ranks of renegade priests, monks and nuns who have opted the secular life there is a wide variety of personalities. Some, as the Berrigans, earned national fame, or infamy, depending on the point of view. Many are concerned, introspective intellectuals. But perhaps none is as original a character as Malachi Martin, a former Jesuit professor at the Pontifical Biblical Institute in Rome and intimate associate of Pope John XXIII.

Martin is a study in contrasts — intellectual-optimist, conservative critic of conservativsm, youth of 50. And unlike many of the seceding clerics, he adheres to the basic principles of Roman Catholicism. At the same time he is vehement in his criticism of the church as an organization, vocal on his opinion of the Pope and pulls no punches when he discusses the state of the church today.

He is also effusive, enthusiastic and something of a wide-eyed optimist, which is in sharp contrast to his scholarly background (he holds three doctorates and is fluent in eight languages.)

But of all Martin's characteristics, the most conspicuous in his optimism.

His latest book, "The New Castle" (Dutton. $7.95. paper $3.95) is a philosophical study in positivism, and if it catches on, the effect could be far-reaching. The Book-of-the-Month and Psychology Today book clubs are offering the volume.

In "The New Castle," Martin sees the current malaise affecting life in the United States — from the Patty Hearst affair to Watergate and the current economic situation — as an indication that something great is about to happen.

"Most people would agree that the waters of panic are up to peoples' chins," says The Irish ex-patriate. "They feel that if there's not going to be inflatión or recession or depression, it's going to be something else — a war or genetic fiddling with us or the races clashing or some calamity.

"I say, 'No, don't be aftraid, there's something lovely and big happening.' "

This "something" is what Martin calls "The Castle" taking the term from historical and literary allusions to a castle as a great, towering, liberating power.

"The image of the castle is a very old one meaning security and height and strength and wealth and happiness and love and compassion and warmth and all those sort of nice things," he says. The concept is primary in his vision of future America.

He bases his his argument — that there is something great on the horizon — on history. "If you examine history from the Jews several thousand years ago to Mao Tse Tung in 1949, you find this funny sort of thing happening. Seven times in history people got together and said, 'Let's make the ideal situation on earth.' The Roman Catholics tried it, the Protestants, the Greeks, the Jews, the Moslems, Mao Tse Tung and a group of men and women in America. This is the only place where it's emerging. This is working. This is beautiful."

For those who might be watching the evening news and wondering what Martin means when he calls the current state of affairs, "beautiful," the ex-cleric has an answer. He attributes the present gloom to our unresolved questions. He maintains the doubts, fears and questions are merely symptoms of changing times. The answers will come of themselves.

"The questions of woman as a second class citizen, sexuality, marriage, love, divorce, the fact that the churches have gone to bits — it's all like somebody blew the cement away from the bricks. But actually we're all making up our own minds (about these questions) and we're doing it slowly, as a body. It's a lovely picture.

MARTIN, Malachi

NEWS–AMERICAN (Baltimore, Md.)

Oct. 20, 1974

"If you go around this country as I do, you find a common element — no matter who people are they find there's an amazing commonality. There is this flow of empathy and sympathy and suddenly people find that somebody they have never talked with has the same sentiments. There is slowly and surely something evolving in the people. I think it's actually Jesus, His spirit, purifying us.

The author of many religious and scholarly books including "Jesus Now," "Three Popes and the Cardinal," "The Encounter," "The Scribal Character of the Dead Sea Scrolls" and "The Pilgrim," left the clergy shortly after the death of Pope John XXIII. Still, he remains a vital voice in the Catholic community. His criticisms of the church are vehement, but he laughs off the possibility of excommunication.

"They (the church) are losing so fast they wouldn't excommunicate anybody nowadays, but actually I'm more conservative in the basic points than most young clergymen I meet," he says. Then, in the same breath he remarks, "Pope Paul is on the way out. He's 78, he's finished. He failed. He set out to retrograde, to hold, and he couldn't.

"That organization (the Catholic Church and other high churches) is going to fade away because it's an organization created by men who were power brokers and still are. They tied it to an economic system and they tied it to political big deals, and now that's all over. It's good that it's happening because dignity, rings, hand kissing and satin slippers and Latin happens to have nothing to do with the spirit whatever."

Since he left the Jesuits, Martin has had a multi-faceted career that only recently culminated in professional authorship exclusively. His rundown of his adventures since coming to America ten years ago reads like a movie script.

"I came to New York and I didn't know what to do," he says. "I had three doctorates and couldn't earn a living so I became a waiter in Schrafft's. The tips were very bad so I found a place called the Twin Donuts owned by a one armed black frcm Alabama. The tips were marvelous.

"I had never worked with may hands, but I loved it. I met every pimp, prostitute, drug pusher, crook and cop on Second Avenue. Then I drove a taxi in the Bronx — illegally. Then I worked as a longshoreman."

It was soon after he took the job on the docks that fate decided Martin had done enough manual labor and threw him together with a public relations specialist who hired him on the spot. From there he went to editing the Encyclopedia Brittanica, then co-founded a company that dealt in antiques for amateur collectors, Collectors Funding, and worked his way up to an annual salary of $800,000 a year.

When an editor told him he would "go to Hell" because he was wasting his education, knowledge and talent, he agreed to devote 10 years to living and working as a professional writer. He has now reached the fifth, and prognosis for the future is good.

In addition to his amazing series of careers, Martin has assisted at 11 exorcisms, became a 24-hour Moslem and visited Mecca, and traveled to China and Cambodia.

The exorcisms made a tremendous impression on him, and he professes to a strong belief in the existence of the Devil, or evil incarnate.

"There are very few possessed people, but . . . evil is something else,," he says. "Of the eleven in which I have participated, nine succeeded."

Matin took a tape recorder to all of the exorcisms in which he assisted, including the two that failed. He plans to publish the transcripts in the near future.

GR Press Photo

MASTERS, William H(owell)
(1915 -)
[See also CA-21/22]
and
JOHNSON, Virginia E.
(1925 -)
[See also CA-21/22]

GRAND RAPIDS PRESS
(Grand Rapids, Mich.)
Nov. 11, 1974

Sex Therapy Hits at Fear, Ignorance

By Jane Haradine

MUSKEGON — Fear and ignorance are the most common causes of sexual difficulties, Masters and Johnson told West Michigan health care professionals here last week.

The famed husband and wife sex research and therapy team from Washington University School of Medicine in St. Louis, Mo., spoke to more than 700 in a two-day symposium sponsored by the Muskegon County Health Department.

William H. Masters, M.D., an obstetrician before devoting fulltime to sex research 20 years ago, said one out of eight couples seen in St. Louis had never been able to have sexual intercourse. One couple waited 23 years before seeking help.

Blaming ignorance for 20 per cent of all sexual dysfunction, Dr. Masters said, "You simply cannot believe the unbelieveable naivete in this age of communication." He told of a couple who came to them because the woman had not become pregnant in six years of marriage. Their problem: They had taken the expression, "sleep together," literally, and had never had intercourse.

Dr. Masters blames "fear" for most impotence. "Whenever a man questions himself once, he is 50 per cent on the way to impotence," he said.

The two stressed that sexual function is "natural," and "one of the best means of communication between a man and a woman." They condemmed sex when it becomes a "performance," saying as soon as one partner becomes a spectator, watching and wondering about his or her ability to respond, there is a decrease in the response.

Virginia E. Johnson, who joined Dr. Masters in the work as a researcher in 1957, and later became his wife, deals with questions about women's response. Her husband answers those about men, a separation they maintain in therapy sessions, although joint sessions also are held.

They treat only couples. They do not insist that a couple be married, but they won't treat a married person with a partner other than the spouse.

Their practice of treating unmarried men, using a woman hired as a "surrogate" partner, was effective, Dr. Masters said, but had to be stopped four years ago after publication of a book on that aspect.

The writer was a man successfully treated for impotence who then ghosted the book for his female partner. Masters and Johnson asked him not to publish the book, because of damage it could do to the program. Dr. Masters said most of the cases described in the book are fictitious. "But to stop the book on that basis, we would have had to reveal the names of the men treated," he said. "And that we couldn't do."

Mrs. Johnson said they had decided even before the book not to offer surrogate partners for women, because "any woman who could learn to respond with a man would have wanted to take him home with her."

Although several women had asked if such help is available, "no woman ever asked us to do it," she said.

The two criticized the popular "how to" books and pornography for the myths and misconceptions they perpetuate.

Dr. Masters traced the history of what he called "great cultural misconceptions" of sexual function. Twenty or 30 years ago, "sex was something a man did to a woman, and most girls, on their wedding night, expected to be done to," he said.

Then, 12 to 15 years ago, this was considered "wrong, and a man was to do it for her, to satisfy the woman. And every man had a tremendous problem. He had to do it for himself and for her, and there was more and more impotence.

"Only in the last three or four years," he said, "have we seen sex as a natural function, with two partners doing 'with' each other, not to, and not for."

Masters and Johnson base treatment on the principle that "any form of sexual expression between consenting adults, in private, is acceptable, as long as one partner is not being exploited."

With that premise, they treat homosexual and lesbian couples who maintain that as their life style. Such treatment, started in 1968, "is the first time this has been done." They plan publication in 1978 of their basic science and clinical treatment data on homosexuality.

Dr. Masters criticized the medical profession for not setting standards for the many sex clinics in the country. "There are 3,500 to 5,000 sex clinics, and not more than 100, and probably not more than 50, are legitimate."

Dr. Masters detailed some sexual complications due to disease. Diabetes in adults can cause temporary impotence, he said. One of the early symptoms of undiagnosed diabetes in adult men is often impotence, and in women, failure to achieve orgasm. Once treated for diabetes, function should return unless fear of performance has caused a barrier, he explained. Then the fear must be treated.

Charging that physicians avoid discussions of sex, Dr. Masters said, "The greatest mistake is to send people home with a medical complication and not tell them ahead of time."

To learn how doctors deal with questions on sex, he interviewed 100 couples after the husband had suffered a heart attack. All were sent home with no advice on resuming sexual activity. Several weeks later, when the couple called the doctor for advice, the response, in 51 cases, was, "Well, O.K., but tell your husband to take it easy."

"That gives you some idea of how little we know about the subject," Dr. Masters said. "Studies are being conducted, but findings are meager."

The normal function of the nerves in sexual activity "is not understood," he said. Funds are needed to set up a laboratory for such research. "Without that, we will never be able to do much for the quadriplegic, the paraplegic, or the person with multiple sclerosis," he said.

Denying sexual expression to the mentally or physically handicapped only adds to the problems, Mrs. Johnson said. She advised "providing some socially acceptable means of expression."

Dr. Masters, saying the issue is "a sore point with me," added, "The concept that (the handicapped) don't have totally involved sexual feelings is an embarrassment to us as professionals. Teaching them to make the best of it turns my stomach."

The two also are concerned with sexual expression for "the aging in nursing homes." Mrs. Johnson said it should be "sustained with grace, dignity and appropriateness."

To discount the myths of sex and the aging, Dr. Masters said a man will experience some changes, such as a slowing of response, just as his abilities in other areas are diminished, but will not lose his ability

Women need not fear menopause or a hysterectomy, Mrs. Johnson said, since sexual response is not limited to the uterus, but is a "total body phenomenon. Nothing need change or it could change for the better."

Contraceptive pills sometimes cause a decreased interest and response in sex for women that is especially prevalent between 18 months and 3 years, Dr. Masters said.

An effective male contraceptive pill is available. "The only difficulty is that every time a man takes a drink he vomits," Dr. Master said.

Masters and Johnson are limiting their lectures to professionals in the field.

They also teach four post-graduate seminars each year in St. Louis. They hope, through their talks, "to increase the comfort factor on sex."

(Also see preceding article)

Masters, Johnson vent anger at sex book boom

MASTERS, William H(owell)

and

JOHNSON, Virginia E.

STAR–LEDGER (Newark, N. J.)

Jan. 22, 1975

By MARK FINSTON

NEW YORK — Masters and Johnson, the sexual scientists, have written two books in scientific language that have turned out, to their surprise, to be best sellers.

Now they have written a third, this one for laymen.

Whether this one, entitled "The Pleasure Bond," and published on Monday, will reach the Top 10 as well remains to be seen.

There is an abundance of sex books, good and bad, on the market today. And this situation is deplored by William H. Masters and Virginia E. Johnson.

* * *

Masters, professor of clinical obstetrics and gynecology at Washington University School of Medicine in St. Louis, and director of the Reproductive Biology Research Foundation in that city, and Johnson, the assistant director of the foundation, and Masters' longtime research colleague (she's also his wife), deplore most of these sex books.

The two sat next to each other on a couch in their palatial suite in the Essex House to talk about their work. Masters, 60, almost as bald as Yul Brynner, is a no-nonsense chap with a piercing gaze, which he frequently reflects toward the ceiling. Johnson, 49, seems softer, smiles more — but is no less sharp and incisive in her answers to questions.

Indeed, at one point, Johnson said whimsically that with so many other sex books on the market, she might have preferred authoring a poem concerning small animals.

The two answer questions almost in a responsive reading technique, never seeming to interrupt each other.

* * *

"Ninety-seven per cent of the sex books on the market have been written by males," says Masters. "They attempt to show how to 'turn the female on,' but they know nothing about it."

"It's very hard to presume that you can convey the concept of personality in 'technique'," says Johnson. "It leaves so much out. It generalizes much too much."

Sitting nearby was magazine editor Robert J. Levin, who translated "The Pleasure Bond" from scientese into English. He proceeded to do it again: "The books imply that if you learn the right buttons to push, you will have this magnificent interaction. That's not the way it works."

So why did the two write "The Pleasure Bond," which is subtitled, "A New Look at Sexuality and Commitment"? (They favor sexuality, maintain it's best with commitment.)

"Research hasn't fulfilled its commitment until it's disseminated," said Johnson, again repeating that their former two books, "Human Sexual Response" in 1966, and "Human Sexual Inadequacy" in 1970, were written primarily for scientists.

Masters feels that one-fifth of those couples with a "sexual dysfunction" (which he estimates as 50 per cent of all marriages) can cure themselves if they have the information to do so.

The rest, presumably, must seek some sort of professional help, like that offered by the Foundation headed by Masters and Johnson, the father of sex clinics, and one of the most expensive: $2,500 for a two-week stay and a five-year followup.

Since the St. Louis operation was founded some 15 years ago, between 4,000 and 5,000 sex clinics have sprung up throughout the country. Like the indiscriminate breeding of sex books, the clinic birth rate troubles the two scientists.

"Not more than 100 are legitimate," said Masters. "By legitimate I mean that the personnel is professional, educated definitively in this field.

"In 1970, at our clinic, 48 per cent of our couples had prior treatment that failed. In the last five years, 85 per cent represent prior psychiatric failure."

Added Johnson: "And those failures are largely coming from treatment centers 'without portfolio.'"

"I think," said Masters, "That most people gather their courage to seek treatment for sexual dysfunction only once. If that's not successful, they feel there's no recourse, and don't try again."

Masters claims the overall failure rate of his clinic is about 20 per cent. This does not mean the "success" rate is 80 per cent; it is much easier, he says, to define failure than success in sexual matters.

About marriage, Masters (he and his wife have each been previously divorced), said, "It's not only here to stay, but it's becoming more and more popular as a procedure."

"We aren't making judgments," said Johnson. "If you're comfortable and can enjoy a relationship outside marriage, be our guest."

* * *

How about the new wave of young couples living together without being formally married?

"There's something even newer," said Johnson. "There's a tendency of people who are living together to suddenly reach for marriage. I don't know why it's happening."

"They're looking for something more to amplify and improve the relationship," said Masters.

Levin said it's harder to break up a live-in love than a marriage: "You don't know where to begin. There's no system, no arbitrator, no rules. Who gets the books?"

Swinging? Group sex?

"The problems is that usually one member of the marriage unit is the encouraging element — rarely will both agree it's a great idea," said Masters. "And sometimes the male finds that when his formerly reluctant wife starts enjoying it — it bothers him."

And if both partners want to indulge?

"Being in favor of it intellectually and being able to cope are too different things," said Johnson.

She added that nobody has followed through with research to find out what has happened to married swingers five years after they started swinging.

Future projects for Masters and Johnson include an update of "Human Sexual Inadequacy" (in 18 months) and a major new work on homosexuality (in three to four years; they have been working on it since 1964.)

They were asked what happens when they go to parties. Dentists are always being asked by strangers about tooth problems. Do Masters and Johnson find themselves continually talking about sex?

"We works seven-day week, and two or three nights a week, and so we don't go out much socially," said Masters. "But when we do, we're rarely asked questions about sex."

Johnson likes to tell this story. The two were attending a conference in Boston. An associate at the conference was asked by a friend, a young pediatrician, where he'd been. The associate replied he had been at a conference with Masters and Johnson.

"Oh, the ice skaters," said the pediatrician.

McCORD, James W(alter), Jr. (1918? -)

PHILADELPHIA BULLETIN (Philadelphia, Penn.)

Oct. 18, 1974

Burglary Brings Fame to McCord

By ALAN RICHMAN

Of The Bulletin Staff

Bulletin Staff Photo by Joseph McLaughlin

AT 7:42 on the night of Oct. 17, one James W. McCord Jr. did willfully enter the meeting of the Newtown Square Rotary Club, place his right hand over his heart and recite the Pledge of allegiance to the flag of the United States of America. So help me God.

Let the record of McCord's appearance last night also state that he arrived in John DuPont's helicopter, which is unusually fine transportation for a convicted burglar out on $100,000 bail.

He wore a neat pin-striped black suit, not unlike the one he had on the night he visited Democratic headquarters without telling any of the Democrats. And he received a warm round of applause, something not often experienced by men who have spent a night locked on murderers row.

"I'm going to be a criminal when I grow up," said one young man in his twenties, as he watched the Rotarians gather in the Newtown Squire Restaurant. "And he was only a second-rate burglar," said another man. "Imagine if he had been top notch."

McCord was more than just another clumsy member of the Watergate Seven. He was chief of security for the Committee to Re-Elect the President. He was one of the first soldiers in Richard Nixon's private army to be taken prisoner. He was the man who broke the code of silence and wrote Judge John Sirica, telling of conspiracy and perjury and cover-up.

For that last action, which he claims was motivated by love for his children, he may be remembered in history as the noblest felon of them all. He has since become a coveted public speaker, although his motives for traveling all over the country in that exhausting capacity are not perfectly clear.

"I'm not a hero," he said during a question-and-answer period. "Since I got involved in this mess, I feel I have an obligation to talk to people, let them hear what I have to say. There's not a town I go into that I'm not asked to speak to the public and I feel I have an obligation to answer questions. I did some things wrong. It's time I did some things right."

Author of Books

Although it was duely noted by the master of ceremonies that McCord is the author of several books and lends his name to "The McCord Newsletter", he did not advertise or try to sell autographed copies at the door. Although he claims to owe more than $60,000 in legal fees, McCord received only traveling expenses for his appearance last night.

"I'm not doing it for my conscience, either," he said. "What happens to me is going to happen in the hereafter. What I say on earth makes no difference."

For 40 minutes, using notes, he delivered a rambling discourse on Watergate. With few exceptions, he said nothing that couldn't be culled out of back issues of Newsweek magazine.

He started with a standard joke ("If you have any trouble hearing in back, raise your hand. I've had trouble with microphones before."), finessed the audience with a few homey references to Pennsylvania (". . . the McCords, from Hershey, fought in the revolution . . .") and then lapsed into bits and pieces of Watergate recollection and opinion.

"I think a great deal of good came out of this," he said. "Most communities I go to now have local grand juries investigating graft and corruption. That would not have taken place.

"Without Watergate we would not have the new campaign reform bill signed by President Ford . . .and then there was Watergate itself. I think the trial will be a deterrent to anything like this happening again."

Praises Committee

He awarded high marks for effectiveness to both the Senate Watergate committee and to the House judiciary committee. The media got passing grades. Low marks for integrity went to both the original Watergate trial prosecutors and to his first lawyer, who he is suing for malpractice.

"That trial was about as corrupt as you can make it," said McCord, who is appealing his conviction. "Two witnesses were perjurers, three others concealed evidence. During the trial I was under constant pressure from phone calls (allegedly initiated by the White House) . . . One day in Boston my lawyer tried to convince me to put up a false defense. I fired him but he asked to be taken back and I turned the other cheek."

McCord called President Ford's pardon of Nixon a "denial of justice" Then he apologized for not being up-to-date. He said he had not had time yesterday to hear the president's testimony before the House judiciary subcommittee on criminal justice.

When informed that President Ford talked about turning the country away from Watergate, McCord shook his head and said, "That sounds like Nixon saying, 'Let's get Watergate behind us.'"

Most disappointing was McCord's unwillingness to discuss Watergate on a personal basis. He seldom talked about himself and he offered only the most superficial opinions of his colleagues. The one exception was when he reminisced about getting caught in The Watergate.

"When they arrested us we were edgy because they were edgy," he said. "They were young, I was dressed about the way I am tonight, and they didn't know who they had caught. They had their fingers on the trigger. We weren't going to give them any trouble. They said later it was the easiest arrest they ever made.

Lavish Accommodations

"After the arrest we were taken down to the precinct, then given lavish accommodations in the D.C. jail. It's called the 100-year old bastille. It was built about 1850. I was, appropriately enough, put in murderers row."

Thus ended the public career of James McCord, former air force officer, former FBI agent, former CIA agent. Why did he do it?

"I did it because I was told the attorney general and H. R. Haldeman authorized it and I knew the attorney general had the authority to justify it," he said.

Why didn't he question it? Few men ever have been able to answer that question in a convincing manner, and McCord is not one of those. But in his case the consequences seem slight. He served his country honorably and obscurely for 25 years and now, along with felony, has come fame.

Writers' Publicity Efforts a Labor of Love

McDONALD, Richard C.
(pseud. Jeff Herrigan)
(1935? -)
and
McDONALD, Paula
(pseud. Jackie Herrigan)
(1939? -)
MILWAUKEE JOURNAL
(Milwaukee, Wisc.)
July 29, 1974

—Journal Photo
Dick McDonald

How do you compete with author Norman Mailer for attention in the media?

Dick McDonald, who operates his own advertising and public relations firm here, thinks he knows.

Last year, McDonald and his wife, Paula, wrote what has since become a rather controversial book under the pseudonyms of Jackie and Jeff Herrigan. It was based on the personal side of marriage and included a frank discussion of marital sex. The book, titled "Loving Free will go into a paperback printing Aug. 12.

But for a time, it appeared that "Loving Free" would face a struggle to get off the ground and onto a bookstore shelf. Norman Mailer was the villain.

Mailer's fictionalized biography of Marilyn Monroe, with a first printing of 285,-000 copies, came off the press just before "Loving Free" was scheduled for publication in May of 1973.

The Monroe biography immediately became a hot topic, a Book of the Month Club selection and the subject of countless literary debates. The publisher, Grosset & Dunlap, all but abandoned promotional plans for "Loving Free" with a first (printing of only 7,500) to concentrate on the Mailer book. They also postponed the publication date of the McDonalds' book six weeks.

Not Enough for Love

This rankled McDonald. "I began raising all kinds of hell," McDonald relates. McDonald could see that without a forceful sales and promotional effort, "Loving Free" would die a-borning.

The first thing he did was suggest that a West Coast public relations firm handle the book and make arrangements for a publicity trip that he and his wife had already agreed to.

For Midwest promotion and for promotion in other regions, McDonald suggested that Grosset & Dunlap hire Boehm & Associates, of Milwaukee. McDonald's own firm — McDonald Davis Weller Inc. — had a working relationship with Boehm— and McDonald felt that Boehm would do a thorough job.

Help Thyself

The publisher agreed. But when it came time to pay the bills, McDonald said he paid $350 to Boehm out of his own pocket for secretarial help and about $400 for phone bills. When Boehm needed an extra hand to help publicize "Loving Free," McDonald said he again dipped into his wallet to pay a five month advance for an agent. The publisher, he said, reimbursed him for the advance.

Was the effort and money worth it? McDonald thinks so. "Loving Free" has sold about 51,000 copies in hard cover, McDonald said.

New Book in Works

Ballantine Books, which is publishing the paperback version, has promised a first printing of 400,000 — roughly eight times the hard cover sale, McDonald said, and much of the controversy that swirled around "Loving Free" has died down.

"The kids didn't catch much hell in school."

Since their identities as authors became public, the McDonalds have appeared at college workshops, spoken before a wide variety of groups and made TV and radio appearances. They are working on a second book, with an outline due Aug. 1.

"Loving Free" is being used as supplementary classroom reading in several colleges, McDonald said. So many letters from readers have arrived asking for help with marriage problems that he has had form letters prepared, advising such people to seek professional help.

McDonald said the portion of the book dealing with marital sex was written to be the last of the book's three sections, but the publisher insisted on moving it to the front. McDonald also felt that the jacket illustration of a nude couple gave people the mistaken impression that here was one more of an endless outpouring of sex manuals.

In later printings, he said, a blue wraparound with quotes from reviews and various authorities partly covers the nudes. And in the paperback edition there is no picture on the cover.

Children Helped, Hurt

On Aug. 12, the McDonalds will leave for a month long promotional tour. Their four children will stay at their northern Wisconsin cottage, with a teacher acting as babysitter. In addition, each child has been given a chance to pick a city he'd like to visit and will fly there to join the parents for a few days during the 23 city tour.

Even when the initial reaction to the book was at its height, the children were not seriously affected, McDonald said.

"People don't choose loneliness in life."

"The kids didn't catch much hell in school. A couple of parents prohibited their children from playing with ours, but they weren't close friends. One teacher told our fifth grader, 'I'm halfway through the book and I want to tell you how proud I am of you and of them.' Two priests told the children they were proud of the family.

"We were scared for the kids, but we found out how supportive people can be. Mostly the reaction the children got from their playmates was along the lines of, 'Wow, your folks wrote a book' or 'Wow, you're famous.

Big World, 1 Response

In traveling around to promote the book, McDonald said, he and his wife have discovered that the reaction of residents of supposedly sophisticated cities is no different than the reaction in Milwaukee.

"The people who live in San Francisco or New York are human boings with the same set of needs. Our basic message in the book is that we believe each person, in the deepest corner of his being, wants more than anything else a deep, trusting, supportive, loving, nourishing relationship with one other human being.'

"People don't choose loneliness in life. What we're trying to say is, let's each search for our own comfort level in life. In love or any close relationship, immorality or hurting doesn't occur.

"If two persons communicate this to each other they can build a couple's comfort level regardless of sex, in-laws, money or whatever."

'Just a Whodunit Writer'

Sketch by Authors in the News

McGEER, Patricia

WASHINGTON
STAR–NEWS
(Washington, D.C.)

Mar. 26, 1973

By RUTH DEAN
Star-News Staff Writer

"Plot too incredible!" commented the publisher when he returned mystery author Patricia McGerr's manuscript in 1955.

Now, dusted off and brought up to date, "Devil With Wings," the story of a flying grandmother hijacked to East Germany, will be published in the fall, the 16th of Miss McGerr's successful string of mystery tales.

"I didn't even use the term 'hijack' in the original; I guess it was 'kidnapped'," the author said, laughing at how the bizarre twist of fate has turned a literary failure into a windfall.

"It's about the world's smallest hijacking," she said. "A woman pilot flying a single engine two-seater plane, is ordered at gunpoint by a stowaway to fly to East Germany."

To update her rusty knowledge of flying, learned at a local field here just before World War II, Miss McGerr took a refresher course in instrument flying, although she doesn't fly any more.

The day after she qualified for her pilot's license, she said, the Japanese bombed Pearl Harbor and all private flying was halted. "I guess it was a relief to my family," she said. "I'd planned to take each one of them up."

Miss McGerr's book titles are matched by her lecture titles. "Murder for Fun and Profit" was the one she chose for a weekend talk.

"It pretty well describes the way I make my living," she said. "I guess I sound like the Mafia. But I do enjoy it."

"But my murderers are not the 'Godfather' type. They're nonviolent. My people get killed, but no one is hurt. Very little blood is shed."

"Poison is the best way. You just leave it in a cup. You don't have to be around when they swallow it. And when you come back there's a nice clean corpse on the floor.

"Another way is to push the victim off a cliff. You never see the body at the bottom. And it saves you describing the murder in all its gory details. I guess I've done away with most of my victims this way."

As she talked, her eyes wandered over to the bookcase in her apartment in upper Northwest Washington and she started ticking off aloud the fates of the unfortunates she's sent to their glory in her books:

"My first book, I strangled her. The next one was poison. Oh, this one, I had a lovely time. I smothered a man with a pillow, poisoned two and pushed another off a cliff.

"Oh, there was bloodshed in this one. He was stabbed. But it was with a knife with a jeweled handle, which made it a really high class murder."

Miss McGerr said she leaves the violence and the macabre to her fellow authors in the Mystery Writers of America, whose motto is "Crime Does Not Pay — Enough."

"I'm just an old-fashioned whodunit writer," she said. "I've always been fascinated with puzzles. You set up the puzzle, then work out the solution."

Miss McGerr began writing in 1946, with "Pick Your Victim," which introduced the plot twist of identifying the murderer and letting the reader find the victim. Another time the murderer and the victim were known but not the detective.

Her most famous character was Selena Mead, who figured in a three-year series of 25 short stories which appeared in the now defunct This Week Magazine. Later, Miss McGerr selected 16 of the stories and revised and combined them into a full-length novel, "Legacy of Danger." She also starred Selena in a 1964 novel, "Is There a Traiter in the House?"

But it doesn't seem likely that Selena will enjoy a literary resurrection.

"To tell the truth, Selena Mead was giving me a terrible inferiority complex," Miss McGerr said. "She was young, rich, brilliant, spoke 16 languages and even understood electrical engineering.

"Every man fell in love with her on sight. Yet she was as pure as the new-driven snow. And her fame grew, as she landed on people's breakfast tables every Sunday in 16 newspapers.

"It got so, that I was introduced at cocktail parties as 'the writer of the Selena Mead stories.' Of course, you know how people expect the author to resemble the heroine they've written about. It does something to your ego when you see their faces fall. I don't have any exceptional qualities, but there was quite a gap between Selena and me."

Tom McHale: "The World's Worst Irishman"

McHALE, Tom

PHILADELPHIA INQUIRER (Philadelphia, Penn.)

Dec. 15, 1974

Photo by James Link

BY MARALYN LOIS POLAK

"I'm the world's worst Irishman. I can't write if I drink. Four or five scotches and I get absolutely lousy, tired, and witless very quickly." Ladies and Gentlemen, it's Tom McHale, "one of this country's more brilliant young writers of serious fiction"—or so they say, safely sipping chablis in his Bellevue suite and trying not to sound witless.

Here he is, clean-cut, athletic Tom McHale—a ringer for Robert Kennedy—who at 32 has made a literary career out of skewering his mother church's supposed crimes against childhood — "hypocrisy, regimentation, and intolerance." The same Tom McHale, late of Temple (pre-med), Penn (creative writing), and the Department of Public Assistance (caseworker), whose first two savagely comic novels, *Principato* and *Farragan's Retreat,* are set on Philadelphia streets teeming with gangsters and superpatriots, boozers and bullies.

Tom McHale, I discover, really reads better than he talks. With his close-cropped brown hair and blue eyes offset by a pigeon-grey turtleneck and tan corduroy slacks, he reminds me of a tweedy book-jacket model. You know, someone rented from the William Morris Agency to prettily pose for photos who—*suprise*—suddenly finds himself stuck with giving an interview; so he does, dutifully but dully.

He's made all the Right Moves for a writer. Paris and Spain bankrolled by a "doting old aunt." The University of Iowa's 'literary finishing school' on Philip Roth's say-so. Rustic New England retreats, a National Book Award nomination, and this year, a Guggenheim Fellowship which feeds him so he only has to teach one day a week in Boston.

"I wrote," he underscores the word with a bite of shrimp "in the beginning to exorcise certain personal demons. Now I write because I don't know what else to do. "Besides," he grins, "I have mortgages, places in Boston and Vermont. I guess it's true though that you are a born writer in the sense that you wouldn't do anything else. And except for violent physical things like building walls and repairing cars, there's not really anything else I want to do."

Three years ago, Tom McHale was compared to heavies like Philip Roth and Joseph Heller. Has he borne out that promise? "No," he laughs, balancing his glass on his knee. "I was bemused when they said that. Did I find it burdensome to live up to? No, because there's nothing I *have* to live up to, no sense in me that I must be at a certain place at a certain time doing a certain thing."

Right now, McHale faces a dilemma. "When my earlier books used an Irish Catholic Philadelphia family framework, critics suggested, 'Maybe he's purged his venom and can move on to something new.' I think I have used them up, and I'm either mellowing or taking another look at the whole tradition. But when I did move on to something ➡

(Continued from preceding page)

else in my third book, *Alinsky's Diamond,* they were disappointed, saying it was unfamiliar terrain, that I should stick to what I know.

"Now I'm kinda superstitious about using the word Philadelphia. I'm thinking of sticking it in for luck in every book. It's curious," he crunches a cracker, "but Philadelphia wasn't mentioned anywhere in *Alinsky,* about an international diamond intrigue. I wonder if I had given them something just a little bit familiar, the book might have succeeded better," he speculates.

"I always start with a bizarre idea and a very simple plot, and I expect to finish it in five months and walk away with another check. But then I get terribly bogged down and uncertain about what I'm doing, and my characters begin to grow on me. I drink loads of coffee and usually lose 20 pounds at a shot when I'm writing.

"I think it's fair to say, though, a lot of writers won't admit it," he looks up at the crystal chandelier, "that you're fulfilling your own fantasies through your characters, that you're always the protagonist in a faceted way. I write about men seeking balance, stability, amid the madness that often surrounds them."

Someone said facetiously, I tell him, that the Irish either fight or write. "I fight too," he laughs, flexing a skinned finger. "I got a new car, a Citroen, and it's my think-tank. I like to take long 50-mile drives and think about my writing, especially if I come to a snag at the typewriter. The only problem is, since I've gotten this car, I've noticed it antagonizes certain people who might be easily threatened by an expensive French sportscar.

"I was coming back home to Boston the other week and a guy in a new Mercedes convertible was right on my back, flashing his lights, beeping, tailgating me for miles. I tried to let him pass but he wouldn't. When we stopped at a toll booth, I got out of the car, boiling mad, and went back to see what was happening. This real greaser, a middle-aged guy with a silly cap, gets out of the other car.

"I nailed him right there and broke my hand. Glass hands," he says ruefully. "I knocked him into his car and the girl he was with—I guess he had been trying to impress her—started screaming." Who was McHale trying to impress? "No one. I was just trying to get home," he says levelling. "I can't remember the last time I was in a fight."

Of course it all goes back to his youth. "Now I better watch what I say," he grins, shifting in his chair. "I grew up in a small Pennsylvania town near Scranton named Avoca—2,000 people. My father worked in the post-office. I went to parochial schools and a Jesuit high school. Everybody in town seemed Catholic, pro-Joe McCarthy, and very patriotic. I can't remember the things that made my stomach grind. I'm trying to cloud the issue but everything is a blur.

"We almost lived in a theocracy. I can't tell you how many funerals and viewings I've been to in my life. Grotesque. We learned by rote and no one was tempted to think. Of course I became well-disciplined, and that's helped me as a writer," he concedes. "But I felt the regimentation was kind of absurd and began to be interested in ideas that weren't looked on favorably in school. I began to read ravenously—James Joyce, Balzac, Tolstoy.

"I never knew an un-Catholic until as a teenager I worked summers as a waiter in the Poconos at a Jewish resort called Tamamint. I learned who Lenny Bruce was," he laughs, munching on a shrimp. "What a great thing to learn at a time like that. Obviously I was attracted to him because he was irreverent. It never dawned on me that he was Jewish. When I met Jews, I didn't know they were Jews and I certainly never knew blacks til I came to Philadelphia to attend Temple. It's incredible."

He abandoned his childhood dreams of becoming a doctor after getting a biochemistry degree from Temple in '63. "It annoyed me that I was doing it for money and security. I realized I just wanted to bum around for awhile, not take a job or go to grad school, just get the hell out of the states. I had introduced two Israelis to each other, and went over for their wedding. I ended up staying a year and a half, living and working on a kib-

McHALE, Tom

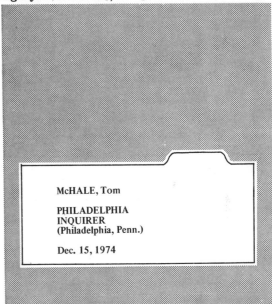

PHILADELPHIA INQUIRER (Philadelphia, Penn.)

Dec. 15, 1974

butz. There were," he jokes, "no Irish Catholics around. I was suddenly safe among all those Jews."

Is he bitter? Does he feel maimed or scarred? "No, I'm actually very happy about what happened. If I hadn't gone through that childhood that messed me up, I'd be terribly afraid that I'd wake up at 40 and do myself in out of absolute despair and disillusionment. But having experienced that anguish at an earlier age has helped considerably because I'm able to set out and define my goals and where I want to go and not be the victim of an inertia, a predictability." He gets up, picks up his bags. I'm afraid he'll leave me in mid-sentence.

Who's the strangest person he's ever met? I ask Tom McHale on a whim, trying to catch his attention, before he leaves for the airport limousine waiting downstairs.

He muses for a minute, then answers, "Me." □

McKuen Getting Back at Critics

McKUEN, Rod
(1938-)
DALLAS NEWS
(Dallas, Tex.)

Sept. 1, 1974
[See also CA-41/44]

By MARYLN SCHWARTZ

The critics have been known to be snide about poet Rod McKuen.

They accuse him of being "commercial" because he's written 1,500 songs and put out a calender that features a "month of Sundays."

But McKuen insists he's not commercial—just creative.

His latest creative endeavor is something that might be called get the critics.

"It started," he explained here, "when I tentively named a book I had not written yet. I called it 'I Started Out By Not Loving Anyone.' The only reason I gave it a title was because the man who I was writing it for kept bugging me to do it."

"When I had given him the title, he had a book cover jacket made up and sent it to book review critics explaining the book was being written and would be available soon."

McKuen was amazed to find that two of the critics panned the book just by looking at the jacket and another gave it a rave review.

It confirmed what he had always suspected about critics. Then he started plotting.

He says he then invented a poet and wrote a book of poems under a pseudonym. "I did the poems entirely from captions from Time and Newsweek Magazines and from the Beverly Hills telephone directory yellow pages."

He says the book has already won two major book awards and has been nominated for a third. The poet has gotten so popular, McKuen explains he's going to have to "kill him off" because too many people are asking for interviews and of course we can't produce him.

One critic even wrote, "after the pap of Rod McKuen, a poet like this is a refreshing breath of fresh air."

"I'm writing a book about all this and wil expose the whole thing in the book. I think it will prove my point. But I won't reveal the name of the poet and ruin the surprise in my book."

He says he's also pointing out in his book what he calls "the family tree" of bok review critics.

"I started paying close attention to who did book reviews. I discovered that one writer would write a review of another writer's book and in a month or so the reviewer had his own book reviewed by the writer who he had previously reviewed. It goes on and on and on like that. It's amazing. I will have this well documented in the book"

McKuen was in Dallas to promote the publication of his first paperback, "Seasons in the Sun."

He's not too worried about what the critics say about this one—it's already sold 3 ½ million copies.

McKuen Working Just For the Pleasure of It

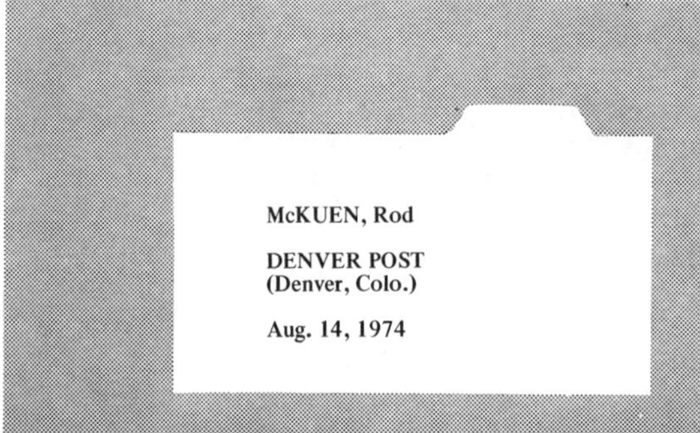

McKUEN, Rod

DENVER POST
(Denver, Colo.)

Aug. 14, 1974

By ARLYNN NELLHAUS
Denver Post Staff Writer

Other people grew up knowning that some times you stop working and take a rest. But not Rod McKuen.

On his own since he was 11, he has worked so hard and productively to support himself, now he works for the sheer pleasure of it. What's more, his favorite people are those who work hard.

His songs, poems and classical compositions keep rolling out of his pen. He is working on a U.S. Bicentennial commission for a two-hour ballet score utilizing chorus, narrator and full symphony orchestra.

'OLD BOOT'

On Sept. 1, his cartoon strip, "Old Boot," the adventures of an Old English Sheep Dog, will be syndicated in 100 newspapers.

He is writing albums for Diana Ross, Andy Williams and Marlene Dietrich (whom he calls "terrific—she's a workhorse"). This will be Dietrich's first new album in some 20 years.

He manages a business empire of four record labels, three book-publishing divisions, two music-publishing companies, a mail-order department and Rod McKuen Casuals, a clothing outfit.

To be doing all this, you'd think he would be a cross between a tightly wound watch spring and Sammy Glick. But no.

At rehearsal Tuesday afternoon before his opening that evening at the Warehouse Restaurant, where he will appear through Sunday, McKuen was relaxed, occasionally humorous and as direct as his famous poems.

He took obvious joy in being able to announce that he is singing more than ever. He lost his voice completely several years ago during a stint as a rock singer.

What he finally regained is hoarse, but now his range has increased to three octaves. He is pleased that he now can tackle "An Impossible Dream."

Also, he said his Warehouse show is more upbeat than anything he has done before. Included will be eight new songs of his.

Also programmed is a French children's song his 15-year-old son sang when he was little. The boy lives in France. His mother and father never married, thus repeating McKuen's own history of being born out of wedlock.

'A WONDERFUL MAN'

"I don't think people should get married just because a child is on the way," the thin, bearded McKuen said. "But I didn't want being born out of wedlock to be a hangup for my son. His mother is married now to a wonderful man, and I visit them often."

McKuen was wearing his usual garb — blue jeans, a white shirt, with the Rod McKuen Casuals insignia on it (a pair of sneakers over the pocket), and of course, a pair of sneakers.

Between sips of coffee, he would rehearse a ballad, come off stage and talk with a visitor, rehearse some more, discuss plans for his week's activities in and around Denver, rehearse and talk with the guest some more, and while he sang he held a red dog someone had brought into the night club. It was all casual and relatively unstructured.

Of his many business concerns, he commented, "I never meant to be conglomerate, but my interests are varied. When anyone suggests I cut back on some of my activity, it would be like cutting off my arm.

"I want to work. Without working, you go bananas," he said.

'11 CATS AND FOUR DOGS'

He works out of his 46-year-old Spanish-style Beverly Hills mansion, rather than at his office, because "I don't like to go the office," he explained. "I'd rather be at home with my 11 cats and four dogs."

But much of the money that his conglomerate takes in, goes back to the public. McKuen's foundations give money to schools where veterinary medicine and animal husbandry are taught, to the American Cancer Society and other recipients, which he refused to name because "I don't want to look like a professional donor."

"Life has been very good to me," he said. "One should give back what one has gotten. I sometimes feel I have a gigantic debt to pay back."

McKuen believes the reason he has been so well received by the public is "because I've been honest. I've had little formal education, and I taught myself to write music.

"I didn't know there were defenses you could throw up to keep yourself hidden. I just wrote straight ahead. By the time I learned about those defenses, I was too old to do otherwise."

At 41, McKuen is the best-selling poet in history. He has sold more than 10 million books of poems.

His next venture will be prose. He plans to spend four months next year "writing a book about the 'rear-end' of America — about those little towns no one ever sees.

"I want to find out what people there really think about. I have a feeling we're not as bad off as a nation as it's sometimes thought. As a writer, you have to put down your impressions — it's an obligation to yourself."

➡

(Also see preceding article)

McKuen: Clean Shorts, Hard Work

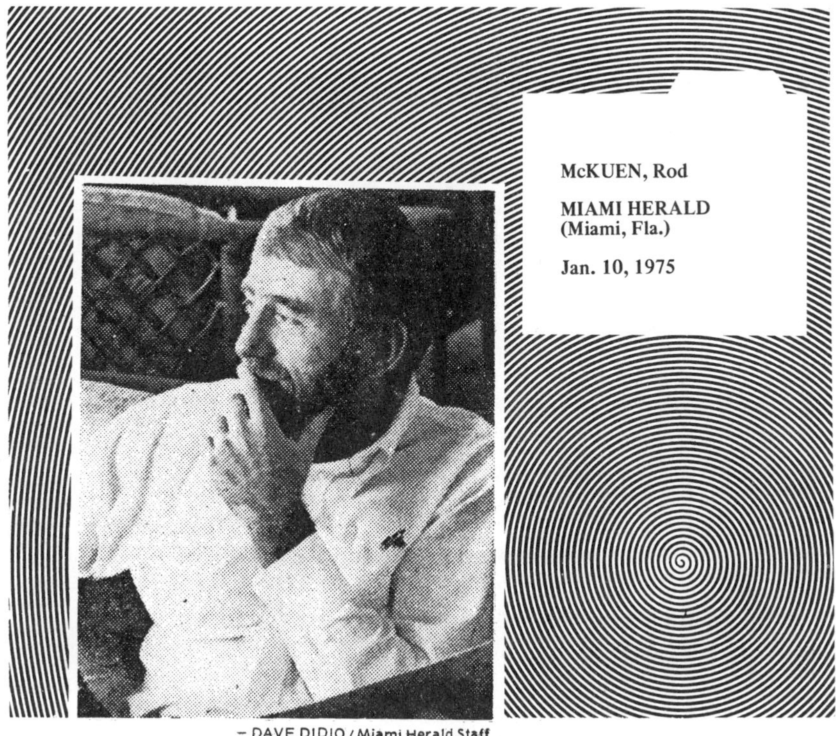

McKUEN, Rod
MIAMI HERALD
(Miami, Fla.)
Jan. 10, 1975

– DAVE DIDIO / Miami Herald Staff

By BILL HUTCHINSON
Herald Staff Writer

Occasionally, Rod McKuen will pick up one of his books, or a record of his songs, or a magazine article about himself and feel both a mild shock and a vague sort of detachment from this person who has become the best-selling poet of this century and perhaps, according to The New York Times, of all time.

"It is a constant surprise," he says, as such success would be to anyone who has achieved so far beyond what might have been predicted for an illegitimate child born in a Salvation Army hospital, a boy who started work at 11 to support his foster family, a young man without a high school education who odd-jobbed around the country because he figured that "if I just kept working everything would work out okay and I'd find out what I should be doing."

HE DISCOVERED a gift for words and for what he calls "one to one communication" more or less by accident 20 years ago.

A decade after that, he'd begun to develop more than a cultist following. Gradually, with the phenomenal sales of volumes like "Stanyan Street and Other Sorrows" and "Listen to the Warm" he received both material affirmation of his ability and the kind of criticism that often falls to people whose words are too accessible and whose success is too great.

"I THINK I'm a great poet," he says. "I'm writing because I have something to say and people are responding to it and what better measure is there? Those writers who say they're only writing for themselves . . . well it's true if what they write ends up in filing cabinet, but most everyone needs an audience.

"The people who find it easy to criticize my work more often than not haven't even read it. That's snobbery. It's become fashionable to dismiss me, and I would be dishonest if I said it didn't bother me."

But McKuen will not brood. He once went through an Esquire magazine profile of himself and Erich Segal, to whom he has often been compared (the reason he wouldn't read "Love Story"), and underlined the factual inaccuracies, but he rarely wastes time on such things.

"THERE IS always time to do whatever you want to do, for good or for bad. Fortunately, I like to work. Work is fun, and if it's not then you're doing the wrong thing. I don't understand those people who don't like their work because I can't imagine what they're doing to fill up their lives.

"I'm working harder now than I ever have. It's the old syndrome, like when you're a little boy and your mother sends you out to the store for a loaf of bread and tells you to put on clean shorts in case you're hit by a truck. She doesn't want you to end up in the hospital wearing dirty shorts. It's the same with me. If I'm hit by a truck I want the last thing I've written to be the best thing I've ever done. The only danger in success, at least for me, is not that you'll slack off but that you'll start giving people what they want instead of what you have to offer."

WITH TIME OUT for concert appearances such as tonight's performance at the Dade County Auditorium, occasional night club engagements and work on the music — both classical and pop — that has won him an Academy Award nomination, a Grammy Award and several European citations, McKuen is in the midst of researching his first straight-prose book.

"This country has been very good to me and I want to give it something back. I wanted to write a positive book about America, a book that would relate what people are really talking about and what they think about the country. If the things I discovered had been completely negative, I wouldn't have done the book. But the overwhelming majority of the people in this country like what they're doing, like their lives and are reasonably satisfied."

McKUEN HAS spent most of the past year working at odd jobs in American cities, including a week's stint as a Miami garbageman last summer, "listening to people talk under very plain circumstances where they don't know who I am. (McKuen will be returning to Miami for an additional four days' work as a garbageman sometime in February because "I didn't get enough information last time.") I don't want to talk about the book because, well, it's more fun writing it than talking about it and I don't want to blow (my energies) but it's a straight report on what people are thinking and feeling.

"It's funny, the people knew a year ago that we were in the midst of a recession, something the government just started to admit a few weeks ago. Now they know we're in a depression, so you can expect the government to confirm that too in time. But they're optimistic, though almost to a man they mistrust the politicians."

Students Listen to Her Wisdom

MEAD, Margaret
(1901 -)

WINSTON–SALEM JOURNAL
(Winston-Salem, N.C.)

Sept. 21, 1974

[See also CA-3]

By Janice Gaston
Staff Reporter

An overflowing crowd of Salem College students sat enthralled yesterday at the feet of a dumpy little gray-haired woman who outlined for them their responsibilities as future citizens of the world.

The crowd, swelled by an influx of Wake Forest University students, faculty members and townspeople, was listening to Dr. Margaret Mead.

Dr. Mead, known as an anthropologist, author and psychologist, is a 73-year-old woman who except for her extensive knowledge has no place in the generation gap.

She told them with wit and humor that "Never before has the human race been responsible for the human race."

She explained it this way: "In the mid-40's, the world became one. We knew who was here. We invented a bomb that would blow us all up." And, she went on to say, "we came up with things that could destroy the whole world."

Now the world faces the dangers of a technology that "has just been rollicking ahead with no assessment and no care," she said.

"We know we've got to stop using fossil fuel energy that gets used up and use energy that doesn't get used up," referring to wind and solar energy.

"We're very fortunate that a more human life, a more humane life will be produced by better use of energy," she said.

"If we keep on the way we're going, the chances of having a world in 25 years are very poor."

She advised the students to decide what they wanted to do, then to find an occupation that will be meaningful. She told them that they would get a lot of bad advice along the way, because "we're always preparing students for today, not tomorrow."

These students will have an opportunity in the next 25 years that the human race has never had, she said. In the past, man worried about his own terrain his land, his community, his country.

But the chief thing to worry about now is "not the frontier of our own community . . . but the air." This is where the majority of dangers are coming from, "and you can't draw lines in the air," she said.

"For the first time since man settled down . . . our own interests and the interests of our neighbors are one. Every step we take to protect our own country, our own children, the things we love, will protect the world," she said. And everything we do to endanger these things will also endanger the world, she added.

As a preface to her look at the future, Dr. Mead gave the students a look at how things were in the 1950's, when apathy was all the rage. "It was very hard for anybody to do very much," she said. "People couldn't imagine a world that would be different enough to have a different kind of station wagon."

Everybody rushed through college and rushed to get married, have children and settle down. "The one thing people wanted was a home where they could lock the door . . . a place in the suburbs, entirely surrounded by strangers and a great distance from their mother-in-law."

It was a time when a woman wasn't anything unless she was married, a time when a man's ultimate threat to a woman was, "If you don't marry me, I'll marry somebody else."

From this plowed the unrest of the 60's, a generation of students that did not go back to the suburbs, but who "went to Washington and voted to stop the SST; who went to law school and invented advocacy groups to protect people; and who went to the schools, with the result that high school students now have teachers who are on their side of the generation gap, Mrs. Mead felt.

The students of the 1970's are not going back to the apathy of the 1950's, she said, although the mass has decided that they have.

"I get far more serious questions from students this year than in the last 10 years."

Author Says It's Still Marriage

MEAD, Margaret

WINSTON–SALEM JOURNAL
(Winston-Salem, N.C.)

Sept. 21, 1974

by JANICE GASTON

Those who attended a news conference with Dr. Margaret Mead, and those who stayed for a question and answer period following her talk yesterday at Salem College, got the full impact of her wit as she gave her pointed opinions on a variety of issues.

—On marriage and living together: The big debate over marriage versus living together is "an infernal amount of nonsense," Dr. Mead said. When people live together publicly . . . they may not call it marriage — they can call it climbing trees — but it's marriage.

"We have a very narrow notion of what is legal, Christian marriage that we have imposed on the rest of the world."

—On the women's movement: The women's movement is going on all over the world, not just because of the Americans," she said. The emergence of public health facilities has assured women that the children they bear are going to live, and the world population explosion has relieved the women of the need to have so many children, she said.

This has liberated women from continued parenthood until they die. "And every time you liberate a woman, you liberate a man," she said. When husbands had to work all their lives to feed the children that their wives produced year after year, "they never had time to be people."

—On aging. "Everything that we know at the present time, and it isn't much, points to the fact that if people continue the same pattern of life, that they age more gracefully."

An abrupt break in that pattern makes it harder. "It's beginning to look as if one of the ways we're destroying people is retirement," she said.

Men die earlier than women because their lives are wrecked when, after leaving their careers, "they have no pattern of life to follow."

Career women have usually also had responsibilities at home, so that "they still have a pattern of life that is familiar.

—On the Equal Rights Amendment: She was against it at first she said, calling it a piece of nonsense. But now she is in favor it, "because of the people who are against it. There have been a number of lies about it — almost as much as against sex education and marijuana."

—On single sex colleges: "I'm greatly in favor, if they're like the ones we had in the 1920's, with a woman president; eminent women on the faculty; and men on the faculty a decent rarity."

In more recent years, the trend was for faculties to be predominantly male. "Higher education became more and more one-sided," Dr. Mead said.

"But there is still one advantage in single sex colleges. You can be as bright as you want to be without hurting your matrimonial prospects."

Meet Mark Medoff, a writer in a hurry

Mark Medoff is an American who zig-zagged his way across the country and wound up . . . well, he still figures he has a long way to go.

A boy in southern Illinois. A college kid in Miami. A grad student in California. A teacher in New Mexico.

The cashmere-sweatered comfort of the sleepy 1950's. The rougher-textured denim of the turbulent 1960's, with a pause that failed to refresh — a camouflage-fatigued coming of age in 'Nam.

Medoff wore the fabrics — the fabrics of American life in two of its 20 decades — and he watched and he waited and then he wrote.

He wrote well enough to win the Outer Critic's Circle Award for 1973-1974 as "the best new American playwright of the season." And his play — "When You Comin' Back, Red Ryder?" — won the Obie Award as the best play of 1974.

Mark Medoff is 34 now . . . and counting.

LET'S CORNER him in the Music Hall, where his play is in rehearsal for its Detroit opening Monday night.

We find him preoccupied — new cast members, the set unfinished — at first. Then he warms up.

"No," he says, "I don't want to be 'another Arthur Miller.' I want to be the first Mark Medoff. I want to write as much as I can, as long as I can. I want to be immortal, all writers do, but my prime concern is pouring out the ideas welling up in me as intelligently as possible."

A pause. He glances around, his brown eyes flicking over the set — a greasy spoon ("rancheros huevos: $1.95") on a highway in southern New Mexico.

While he's checking details — there're a couple nails sticking out of the wood in that booth, Mark — let's oversimplify the plot: A disillusioned young man in a field jacket and jeans — maybe he's an ex-Vietnam officer — wanders into the eat-and-get-gas joint, dragging a teenaged female dropout behind him. His VW bus, full of dope, conked out. While he's there, waiting for a part, he declares a verbal war on everyone in the diner, putting down people like a Viet Cong grenade. Finally, he pulls a gun.

"BUT TEDDY (that's the lead character) cannot or will not kill anyone," says Medoff, who's back with us.

"Teddy's become purposely aimless, about to leap into the brink. I can see some of myself in Teddy and much more in Richard (the other pivotal character in the play, the husband of a violin player — the man Teddy harasses the most in the play).

"Richard is us, in that he is a stereotype husband who is forced to react with gratuitous bravado."

The play — which has been called everything from "slick and shallow" to something that "will rate an asterisk in the annals of playgoing" — will open at 8:30 Monday and run through next Saturday, with two matinees, at 2 p.m. Wednesday and Saturday.

Let's get back to Medoff for a moment before he starts rehearsal. He's pretty busy, since he plays Teddy and also directs.

MEDOFF SAYS he got the idea for the play when he stopped at a Toddle House (he says he had to change the restaurant to a greasy spoon because the Toddle House was spotless) and watched as two hippie-types, a fat girl and a slim guy, wandered in.

"They had an elusive kind of love," Medoff says. "The boy was tearing her to shreds, and she was just feeding him. I knew they were in a play. I just had to write it."

Medoff did, down in Las Cruces, N.M., where he lives with his wife, Stephanie, 28, and his daughter, Debra, 6, from whom he says, "I learn a lot." Then he took it to New York, got it produced, and even stepped into the lead part at the last minute.

His second play, "The Wager," which is about four grad students who make a bet about a professor's wife, took over after "Red Ryder" closed in August.

The third play?

"I can see ahead four or five plays," Medoff says.

Which isn't going to leave much time for the six-foot, 165-pound "first Mark Medoff" to do much more than become immortal.

By BILL SUDOMIER
News Entertainment Editor

—News Photo by Herman Allen

MEDOFF, Mark (1940? -)
DETROIT NEWS (Detroit, Mich.)
Dec. 1, 1974

A Hot Young Playwright Brings His Genius to Detroit

BY LAWRENCE DeVINE
Free Press Drama Critic

Where, wail the doom-sayers, do you find the hot young American playwrights? This year's stage meteor is usually found in, of all places, Las Cruces, N.M. But this week playwright-actor Mark Medoff is in Detroit prepping his prize-winning stage surprise, "When You Comin' Back, Red Ryder?" for its Monday opening at the Music Hall center.

Medoff's Off-Broadway hit may come as a surprise to many Detroit theatergoers, since the show was booked only a month ago. And word of even the best of Off-Broadway sometimes filters slowly out past the Hudson. But, at hand is the first of two straight Medoff plays that hit New York fans like a fistful of metal shavings in the space of only 13 months.

The week-long run of "Red Ryder" will be the Music Hall audience's first look at Medoff's work. It will also be their first look at the tall, 34-year-old Medoff himself. His leading-man good looks will stand in him good stead, since he is taking over the leading role in his own play here.

Bristling with intellectual alacrity, the darkly handsome Medoff says his "Red Ryder" is his gut reaction to what he calls "the lunatic Pablum" of the 1960s. "It came from all the frustration born in those of us with some intelligence versus the sheer lunacy of the '60s," he said, propping his feet up on a dusty rehearsal-hall desk.

"Growing up in the '50s, we all had our myths — Red Ryder, the Lone Ranger, all the ball players had crew cuts. Then, in the aftermath of Vietnam, we went into a decline of myths to believe in. What have we left? It's essential we create belief; if it's enlightened belief, so much the better."

Briefly, "Red Ryder" is the story of a violent young nomad who invades a small-town New Mexico diner, alternately terrorizing a handful of patrons and shattering their illusions about themselves. It opened in New York last year and won three Obie Awards, including one for Medoff as best playwright. His "The Wager" opened last month in New York, called "a dandy new comedy" by New York Times critic Clive Barnes. Both plays were recognized as dealing with an exceptionally bright young man driven into perverse violence by the shocks of an erratic, troubled American society.

With the success of his first two major plays, Medoff has an envied streak going, coming as close together as they do. And, perhaps whimsically, coming also from an author who lately has been a university professor in the New Mexico outpost of Las Cruces.

"WHEN I FIRST got there, I drove in from California with my old black VW and a girl I didn't like very much. I didn't know what I was doing there. Cows, manure and me, this Jewish kid from Miami Beach."

Whatever one's idea of a successful, dissident Off-Broadway playwright is, chances are the gracious and articulate Florida-bred New Mexico college professor is not it. Medoff was raised as a young Jewish prince in Miami Beach, where his physician father is medical director of a hospital and his mother is head of psychological testing at Barry College in Miami Shores. He graduated from the sunny University of Miami, and later went west to immerse himself in writing studies at Stanford.

There was born his recent hit "The Wager," a bitter-funny play about California grad students. He was hired out of Stanford for the first teaching post he sought, at New Mexico State University. In the ranch-country academe, Medoff wrote "When You Comin' Back, Red Ryder?"

It was inspired, he said, by an early-morning stop he and his wife made at a Toddle House in Albuquerque. "I knew it was a play — this fat counter girl and her boyfriend, a real 1950s greaser coming in after his shift. My wife Stephanie wrote down some of their dialogue on a Sunday page out of Parade magazine. Later, I got the idea about someone coming in there and doing terrible things to people who are comfortably inured to any outside turbulence."

"The lead character, Teddy, holds them hostage. The very theme of holding hostages is such an American thing—all those Western movies, it's almost generic to our forms of entertainment. Someone hijacks a plane with people on it, holds up a subway train, grabbing off a woman, it's one of our fantasies.

"The situation forces people to examine their own motives. In the play, a man thinks Teddy's going to rape his wife, so should he step in and say, 'You'll have to shoot me first?' In a situation like that, he gets shot and THEN gets his wife raped. That guy's a moron. But what would you or I do?"

Posing hard questions is Medoff's styling in his plays. Lately, acting in his plays also is up to him. During "Red Ryder's" first road production last summer in Chicago, one-time child evangelist Marjoe had been signed to play Teddy. Four days before opening Marjoe proved to have "a bad back," a gentle producer's public solution to the wrong actor in the right play. Medoff himself stepped in. With two day's rehearsals, he went on to win Chicago's local Jefferson Award as the season's best actor.

In Detroit, the versatile Medoff also is directing his play. He said he is not sure he has all the answers to "Red Ryder" himself. Charming, but still restless, he said: "I hope now that Nixon was the final exclamation point at the end of an incredible sentence of an era. I don't know the answers. I think it's my job to raise the questions. We will insist on finding something to believe in."

MEDOFF, Mark
DETROIT FREE PRESS (Detroit, Mich.)
Nov. 29, 1974

Michener to Critics: 'Someone Reads Me'

(Also see preceding article)

ART COLLECTORS Mari and Jim Michener stand in front of favorite personal collection of abstracts, painted by author Michener.

By D D EISENBERG

Of The Bulletin Staff

THE DINING room of the Barclay was closed for the afternoon so that some of Philadelphia's most "beautiful people" would not be disturbed during the shooting of one of those chichi commercials.

Pulitzer Prize-winning novelist James Michener was obviously not on the B.P. list. When the 67-year-old author walked into the restaurant from his upstairs suite to be photographed by the Bulletin, he was promptly shoved out of the room.

It was only after the head waiter was informed that the intruder was none other than James A. Michener that he was allowed back inside.

"Oh my goodness," said the waiter as he threw his hands in the air, "if only I had known who you were. I'm Hungarian and I read your book 'The Bridge at Andau.' I wish I had the book here for you to autograph. If only I had known . . . "

If only he had known.

Not a Bit Offended

Michener scratched his freckled forehead, which was beginning to turn a soft coral. He wasn't the least bit offended. The bespectacled gentleman with receding hairline, who prefers white-shirt-stodgy to flash, could easily be mistaken for an insurance salesman, accountant or maybe even a school principal.

But what's so bad about anonymity when you are a millionaire? Michener's first book, "Tales of the South Pacific," was written under a pseudonym, won a Pulitzer, was made into a successful musical. Although he was already 40 when he wrote the book, he's still reaping benefits.

He has managed to churn out bestsellers like "The Source," "Hawaii," "Caravans" and "Sayonara" — 20 books in all, seven of which have been made into movies.

Michener arrived in Philadelphia last week from his comfortable Bucks County home for

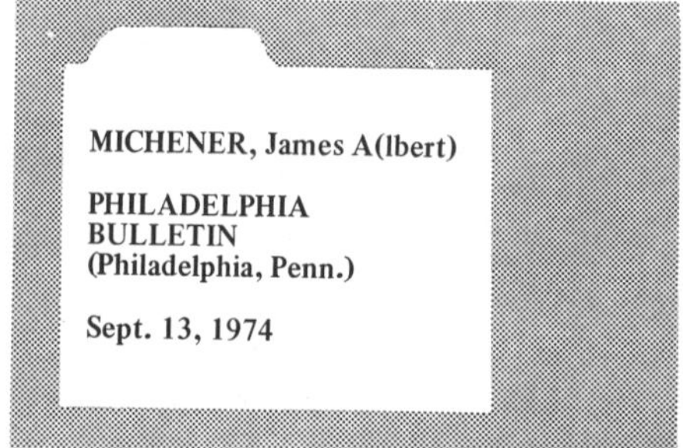

MICHENER, James A(lbert)

PHILADELPHIA BULLETIN (Philadelphia, Penn.)

Sept. 13, 1974

two celebrations. One was to participate in the reconvening of the First Continental Congress and the other was to help promote his latest literary undertaking, "Centennial" (Random House, $10.95).

"I'm not into this promotion thing. The publishers love to have authors tour the country talking up the book but I really hate it," said Michener.

The book takes place in a town called Centennial located on the South-Platte River in north - central Colorado (known as the Centennial state because it joined the Union in 1876).

The 909-page meganovel with its 14 chapters and 70 "chief" characters (counting humans only) spans 160 million years beginning with prehistoric times and ending with present day 1973. The book, everything you wanted to know about America but were afraid to ask, took Michener four years to write.

The Real Motive

"I've been wanting to write a novel about the North American West, particularly Colorado, since 1936 when I moved there to accept a teaching position. The job paid more than the $2,100-a-year salary I was making teaching high school in Pensylvania," he said.

It wasn't until 1970 when Michener started seriously planning to write the novel. The real motive for the undertaking, he says, actually was his disillusionment when plans for a significant national celebration of America's 200th anniversary in 1976 were "thrown in the mud and jumped on by politicians."

Michener was one of several "bright and dedicated Americans" named to a committee back in 1969 by President Lyndon Johnson to draft an overall plan to mark the nation's birthday. The plan fizzled.

"Dissident members of the group who wanted us to celebrate by having 'some Harvard students dress in red uniforms and march up Bunker Hill,' leaked the splendid plans to ill intentioned legislators who ridiculed every intellectual proposal, scuttled every promising possibility, and reduced the whole to one half-baked fair in the city of Philadelphia, where the leadership of the city couldn't even agree upon a site or what should go on it if one were found," writes Michener in a separate 57-page synopsis of "Centennial."

When plans began to disintegrate and the "grand design was dead," Michener then decided it would be "up to each citizen in our country to assume responsibility for his or her own celebration."

Thus, we have, for better or for worse, the by-product, "Centennial."

Some literary critics who have panned Michener's previous monumental heavyweights as pompous and pretentious have already unloaded some sarcastic, devastating digs. But when the intelligentsia look on his novels as low-brow, Michener remains unmoved.

"This is what I do," he said. "This is my view of storytelling. The critics are justified but I'm not sure relevant. If you look at the enormous distribution figures, you know that SOMEONE is enjoying my books."

How can anyone argue with that logic? So far, 300,000 copies have been printed and the official publication date is not until Sept. 18. Bookstore ➡

(Continued from preceding page)
shelves are beginning to sag with the lavish displays. And "Centennial" is sitting high on the list of several major book club selections.

Paperback rights have been sold to Fawcett for $1 million.

MICHENER, James A(lbert)

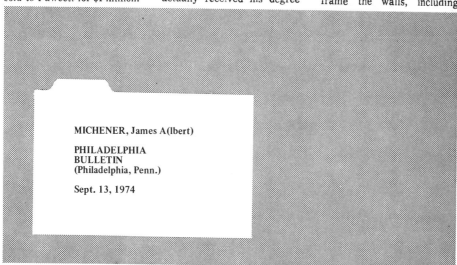

PHILADELPHIA BULLETIN (Philadelphia, Penn.)

Sept. 13, 1974

Michener still seems infatuated with his own success as a free lancer. "Some writers couldn't take the insecurity and uncertainty that goes with the job. My great success and happiness stems from the fact that I'm terribly individualistic. I do it my way and I'm able to get away with it."

A Mixed Breed

He claims his reading audience is a mixed breed. "There are those who like to read bulk, and apparently mine. And there are those who are fed up with the brief episodes of television. I get a stack of mail from all over the world and more times than not the readers complain that the novel was too short.

"Often purists don't like my work. They say my writing is too tempestuous and chaotic, not in the tradition of the short, well-crafted novel. I try to write one of those a year. Really I like something more wild with a much bigger canvas."

Michener admits he has always been stubborn, aloof and at times a drifter. "I was always a diffident, free-spirited, don't-give-a-damn sort of guy. I've never had any ambition to be anyone. In fact friends used to assume I would be a professional bum," said Michener.

He was born in New York in 1907, was orphaned and soon adopted by Quaker parents from Doylestown where he lived most of his childhood. Before he was 20 he had a dozen odd jobs and had traveled 45 states. A graduate of Swarthmore College, he was expelled twice before he actually received his degree and his Phi Beta Kappa key. "I was in all the big movements, especially the one to get fraternities off campus," he recalled.

Michener still manages to have his own way. He and Mari, his wife of 19 years, live in a secluded home perched on top of a hill in Bucks County where the nearest grocery store is 15 miles way.

'It's awfully good living here," said Michener in a recent interview at his home. "I bought the land fairly cheap years ago. When you stand on the hill in front of the house you can see for 10 miles."

Michener says he planted many of the trees on his 75 acres of land. He even has his own private forest consisting of two or three miles of trails where the former high school basketball star runs daily to keep in shape.

Everyone's Home

The atmosphere at the Michener home is informal and almost folksy. Although they have no children their home is everyone's home. Neighbors drop in and out all day — like Mary, a friend from up the road who stopped by briefly last Sunday to drop off a dozen tomatoes.

Mrs. Michener, the former Mari Yoriko Sabusawa, just shook her head and smiled. "It's always like this. We always seem to be on the run. I haven't unpacked my suitcase from our recent trip to Hawaii for the American Bar Association convention.

The living room is simply furnished. Temple masks surround the fireplace and some of their favorite paintings frame the walls, including some unsigned abstracts done by Michener himself. The rest of their art collection, some 500 20th Century paintings assessed at $1.2 million are now part of a permanent exhibit at the University of Texas.

Michener's office is organized and functional. The desk, a door shellacked and stacked on top of custom-built drawers, is stuffed with library books, a dictating machine, a world globe and the typewriter where Michener pounds out those 500,000-word novels with his two index fingers.

The bookshelves are lined with books, both classic and contemporary, classical records, a can of tennis balls, dog itch spray and a few other unrelated odds and ends.

"We live very simply," said Mrs. Michener as she finished the house tour. Although the house is markedly comfortable, it is anything but showy.

Both seem to love the spontaneity of their lifestyles, but they also appreciate the permanence of a home base.

"You have to be flexible and capable of adjusting to different situations when you are married to a writer," said Mrs. Michener. "When Mich is working on a novel and we move to another city for his research, I become his social and corresponding secretary. When we moved to Colorado in October 1972 for his research on this new book, I went ahead to find us a place to live.

"We had two prerequisites — the apartment or home must be within walking distance of the Colorado Historical Society and the Denver Public Library."

Where They Met

Mrs. Michener felt very much at home in Colorado. She was born in Colorado but is of Japanese descent. She met her husband during a Chicago luncheon sponsored by Life magazine.

"I was in the field of sociology and race relations at the time" said Mrs. Michener, who graduated from Antioch College. "Mich had written a story on Japanese war brides and was being honored that day. We attended a Christmas party together continued to correspond and were married in 1955."

Mrs. Michener does not seem to suffer from the "wife of" syndrome. She has managed to stay active in the community, serving as Democratic state committeewoman in her district, developing a highly respected profile of her own.

And when it comes to politics, she is very opinionated. On matters such as President Ford's full pardon to Richard Nixon, they are divided. Michener agrees with his wife that the pardon was premature. But he also feels that Mr. Nixon and all the Watergate participants should be granted amnesty, as long as there is some bill of particulars so that the historical record will be straight.

"I think we should just wipe the slate clean, admit that we made grave mistakes concerning the war, Watergate and Kent State and start all over again."

After Michener finished stating his opinion, admitting that perhaps some of his thoughts were influenced by his Quaker conservatism, he looked through his thick glasses toward his wife and waited for the explosion.

"Full pardon?" shouted Mari Michener. Oh, cookie, how can you say that? You don't really believe that we should let all those crooks free?"

It was just the beginning of what was to become a spicy Sunday morning political chat at the Micheners.

(Also see preceding article)

Michener: Surprised At Success

By BILL HUTCHINSON
Herald Staff Writer

James A. Michener reads sports paperbacks and calls his wife 'Cookie' and greets strangers with the affable ease of a successful salesman.

At 67, he is one of the most widely read authors in the world, but his manner and appearance are less those of An Artist than, as he says, of "the mild-mannered banker type, the guy who heads the grocery store down the street."

"I do wear dark suits, and I am low-key," he admits. "I get along well with most people. I am very cautious by nature, conscious of the fact that everything I say will be weighed on the scale of almost unbelievable success. I dampen and dilute myself all the time. I don't know why, but I am very apprehensive about any kind of flamboyance."

There are those who have suggested that Michener writes like he looks — capable but a little plodding, altogether ordinary. He is, they say, a writer whose limited quotient of real creativity was exhausted by the early works, "Tales of the South Pacific," which won him the Pulitzer Prize, and "The Bridges at Toko-Ri." The 22 books he has produced since, from "Hawaii" to "The Source" to the current "Centennial," have left critics sputtering over their length more than their literary merit.

In town this week to promote his new novel and accept an award from the American Association of State Colleges and Universities convention, Michener passes off such analysis.

"FOR THE most part, critics have been extremely fair to me. I have said often that I am not a writer in the same sense that somebody like Gore Vidal or William Faulkner are writers, and it is possible that my novels aren't novels at all but panoramas or mosaics. But what I have always wanted to do, overwhelmingly, is to communicate on my own terms. It's easy for me to accept the jibes of some university professor, because I may know a little bit better than he what it is I'm up to.

"No one who does not have a career like mine can visualize what it's like. On Tuesday, as a concession to a personal friend, I agreed to a little autograph party in Alabama, something that wouldn't happen in 100 years. Now you don't think of Southern Alabama as a big book-buying center, and I expected to see 10 or 15 people on hand, most of them thinking that I'd written "The Naked and the Dead" or "From Here to Eternity."

"The lines, my God, they were a block and a half long . . . hundreds of people who'd come from six or seven counties, other states. Many had half-a-dozen of my books with them to be signed.

"It was a staggering experience. To think that you can absorb the time and attention of so many people. We live at a time when people do not read, and I am very worried about what this may mean to all of us, to the society, but I don't think there will be an end to the basic human enjoyment of what I call a long reading experience, and that's what I set out to provide."

MICHENER'S exhaustively researched and meticulously detailed novels run 700, 800 and, in the case of "Centennial," 900 pages, the product of as many as six drafts written on a tightly disciplined schedule — 7:30 'till noon, seven days a week — for as long as two years. Dental appointments are the only variations he will permit in the writing routine.

"I've never felt that I could allow myself to slack-up, never thought, 'Well Michener, you're home free, relax.' I'm not that sort of person. Discipline is so much what separates the writer from the talented might-have-been, and once you have found the most productive system, you must stay with it."

Many of his contemporaries, he points out, have developed reputations on the strength of their private excesses while holding their public output to a minimum. "In a sense, I'm sorry I haven't been able to give up the routine and fall into that maelstrom. I think on the whole that I've been more Spartan than I needed to be. I suppose there was always an element of social fear that kept me from it."

Michener was a foundling who "never learned who my parents were, lived in the poorhouse and had a hell of a youth until I was 14 or 15 and discovered athletics, fell into the All-America pattern.

"I STILL have a profound touch of bitterness about my past that I cannot dispell. That keeps you in control . . . the fierce desire to achieve beyond what it appeared you'd ever be capable of. British novelist George Gissing wrote that poor boys spend the first 30 years of their lives battling for what more favored boys have from birth, and that is certainly true in my case.

"I read with great interest all the recent research into the relationship between inheritance and environment — I call it nature versus nurture — because I'd always assumed that I was 80 per cent the product of my environment, good schools and so forth, and only 20 per cent the product of genetic factors. Now I've been forced to readjust my thinking. I guess I wouldn't be so different from what I am if I had been born into more privileged surroundings.

"But if I had been more physically comfortable as a child, I think I may have turned out like the Southern writers. I would have been a word-monger . . . not in a negative sense, but like Faulkner or Carson McCullers. I think that the great stylists of language are produced from patrician backgrounds, and I admire them greatly.

"There are basically two kinds of writing — the Flaubert approach, work like Updike and Bellow produce today, and the Zola approach, the category in which I, like Dickens and Sinclair Lewis and Tolstoy, belong. The great books come out of the first category, but the best books in the second category don't need any apologies."

MICHENER says if he had been more physically comfortable as a child, '. . . I think I may have turned out like the Southern writers. I would have been a word-monger . . . not in a negative sense, but like Faulkner or Carson McCullers . . .'

MICHENER,
James A(lbert)

MIAMI HERALD
(Miami, Fla.)

Nov. 15, 1974

JAMES MICHENER

MICHENER,
James A(lbert)

PALM SPRINGS LIFE
(Palm Springs, Calif.)

Oct., 1974

BY ROY NEWQUIST

Centennial, by James Michener (Random House, $10) is more than a novel. For almost 1,000 pages we are totally absorbed in the story of Colorado and a mythical town called Centennial which sits on the Platte River. We move from the far reaches of prehistory to the present year, our interest steadily peaking as the author details the past two centuries.

It is impossible to name a better novel written by an American. (At the moment, still under its spell, I can't even think of a better novel, period.) Each of the dozens of major characters, whether Indian, French, German, Mexican or latter-day American, leaves such a distinct impression we don't think of Michener's creation as fiction. In impact, and in total accomplishment, it tops "Hawaii" and "The Source."

If you read no other book this season read "Centennial." As I said, it's more than a novel; it is a beautiful and moving experience.

I asked Michener how he felt now that the book was on the market and the reviews had started coming in.

"Words like 'depleted' and 'exhausted' come first. I spent almost four years on the book; it's by far the most ambitious thing I've ever done. At the moment, in fact, I haven't even got another major project in mind—'Centennial' took a lot out of me.

"I also feel elated. The first reactions, from readers and reviewers, are encouraging. I don't mean in simple terms of praise, either, because a writer can be praised for the wrong reasons, and then he's not apt to regard his book as a success. Success, to me, is when a book is praised or appraised for the right reasons, and people seem to be grasping what I tried to do in this book, and that makes me feel wonderful."

What did he try to do?

"Well, I tried to relate the American experience as it hasn't been done before, using original themes, not those that have been worked over. Our history is rich—rich with accomplishment and destructiveness, with vision and shortsightedness, with altruism and greed. There's nothing noble about our treatment of the Indians and other minorities, nothing courageous about our slaughter of the buffalo, and nothing commendable about the way in which we progressively contaminate our air, land and water.

"But on the other hand there are so many splendid things we've done in creating a great nation, and we're old enough, now, as a nation, to take real pride in our heritage. Ecologically speaking we're at a point when we really have to determine whether or not our nation will endure.

"I wanted 'Centennial' to be a strong American book. A reaffirmation, so to speak, that follows the disillusionments of Watergate. The spirit that built this country hasn't gone under, in spite of the bad things that have happened during these past years. And I'm elated, as I said, to find people reviving that spirit by reading the book. This is much more important to me than any degree of popular success or any financial profits could ever be."

James Michener, looking younger than he did fifteen years ago when we first met, has every right to be elated. 'Centennial' is a triumph at every level.

By JAY CARR
News Drama and Music Critic

Arthur Miller sheds light on 'Salesman'

Arthur Miller just wound up a two-week stay in Ann Arbor where, among other activities, he discussed his plays informally with students and other interested parties in the University of Michigan's Trueblood Theatre. One recent afternoon he sat on stage, lanky and relaxed, wearing a tobacco-colored corduroy suit, a red and blue-striped shirt that looked lavender at a distance, and a benign smile.

He discussed his first two playwriting successes, "All My Sons" of 1947, and "Death of a Salesman" of 1949. Both plays deal with men who destroyed their souls and their children because they lived by wrong values. Joe Keller's aviator son died knowing that his father made money selling badly made airplane engines. Willy Loman turned himself hollow because he wanted to be liked.

BOTH PLAYS are morality plays, and Miller discussed aspects of both, as well as his oft-remarked-upon affinity with Ibsen. He also offered some illuminating comments on how his plays got written. His remarks, spoken in deep, measured tones colored by a Brooklyn twang, shed some invaluable light on his work. Some just made plain good sense. Here, without further ado, is a sampling of Miller's comments:

"From the time I first read Ibsen I always felt that his methodology — using antecedent material, using the past — pays off in the present. The story of any play is how the birds come home to roost. Ibsen's way of using the past I found terrifically moving. There is that similarity in 'All My Sons,' a sense, also in Ibsen; of a disastrous mystery which I always felt came from northern Europe. That play was written in 1947. From 1936 to 1947 I must have written 12 or so full-length plays and a number of short ones, none of which were in this style. I was nearing 30 and I said, 'Well, I'll see if I can make myself clear . . .' "

Q: I wonder if a figure as idealistic as Chris (Keller's son) would be possible in the 1970's?

A: "I don't write the same now, but Chris was always a minority. Even in 1947 he was a minority. By the way, I wrote that play during the war. An idealist is never realistic. Anybody who rose today and issued a moral condemnation would be unusual. He (an idealist) is around here somewhere. His time will come again. The whole thing horrifies Chris because they weren't better than they are.

"They got from their upbringing a certain idealism. It was that idealism that killed them. By the way, there was no telling at the time how much longer that war was going to go on. Now a number of letters arrived to the newspapers saying that inspection procedures would catch the bad (airplane) parts. . . . But a Senate committee found that some executives got together with certain Army guys and snipped off the red tags and put acceptance tags on 70 or 80 of the red-tagged engines. Thirty engines failed and the planes crashed. When I am accused of melodrama my own feeling was that I hadn't been tough enough.

"The play's mistake was in being timely with a limited point of view. True, it's dated in that anything that's 30 years old is dated. But the fundamental conflict in that play is forever. If you had Nixon in front of you saying, 'What could I do? I had all these clowns around me,' there is something in you that says, 'You should have been better. You're the leader.' You may not say it, but you feel it.

"The rationalizations of a Joe Keller are the rationalizations of a whole class of people. We continue to dispute this to preserve the human race, so that we don't murder each other without remorse. What are we complaining about? It is that no one will take any responsibility."

Q: Is the play about the disintegration of Joe Keller's power?

A: "It's about the surrounding social milieu in which the power is exercised and what it amounts to. The stripping away of the justifications — that's fundamentally what the play's about."

Q: To what extent do you sympathize with Joe Keller?

A: "Very much. I say very much because I do the same thing all the time. He's recognizable. He's the bedrock of our country. He's out there selling stuff and distributing it. I recognize him. He hasn't gone away. Continuity is what he wants through his son. Once you take that away there is very little left . . . It was that his pretensions had been collapsed. That can be quite a wound. He's not a cynic."

Q: Is 'Death of a Salesman' about just another middle-class European family where the second son doesn't exist?

A: "I don't know how to answer you. The second son thinks he is a character. It never entered my mind. When you create these plays you usually don't know how they're going to end."

Q: I knew he was going to die . . .

A: "If the forces are vital that you set in motion they determine their own arc. A character is part of a complex of forces . . . you can take a family like this and write innumerable plays about them . . . I have a preconception about what it is in them that preoccupies me."

Q: Did Willy Loman ever come to an understanding of his situation equal to your own?

A: "On one level, no. I haven't killed myself . . . but there is a kind of visceral comprehension of where he's at. It doesn't come from a shallow understanding. He is at the lip of the grave because he sees the utter desolation . . . He does, somewhere in him, understand . . . There is a kind of understanding in suicide. It's a profound act. A person may have come upon a profound glimpse of the void. To me he's a tragic figure . . . I probably couldn't write if I didn't leave my persona. It's not me. I know more than he knows. He's possibly more vivid than I am. This is like two mirrors talking to each other!"

Q: Did Willy Loman know he failed?

A: "Yeah. He would say he blew it. It would be mixed up with the idea of bad breaks. He got on the wrong escalator. It was going down, not up. But it was moving."

Q: How do you manipulate . . . ?

A: "I believe in mimicry. I do accents well. It's musical, for the ear. That's why dramatic dialog and dialog in books are not the same. To me life is bizarre. You can stand on 44th Street and Broadway and in 20 minutes you will see more absurdity than you will see in the whole history of theater. The question for me is, how does one arrive at some form. . ."

Q: Do you hope to have the audience identify with your characters?

A: "I don't view man as an intellectual apparatus. It is of no interest to demonstrate on a stage something that people agree is a bad thing to happen. The alternative is to hook them as I have been hooked, on the pathos, to carry them into my world . . . There is a wisdom to be wished for. That's the only therapy. They never understand that unless they feel the suffering.

"You don't move unless you're worried. We have racism. One race isn't moved by the sufferings of the other race. The theater to me is a place of feeling, not what critics make of it. They can't feel, so they think. Art is a felt knowledge. I'm trying to reproduce on stage . . . a felt condition."

Q: How much of your writing is based on philosophical ideas and how much on characters?

A: "I don't know because with me it all goes together. Something happens which mystifies me and makes me want to know more about them. I fill in what I don't know. I'm not sure that the theater cures people. I'm not sure if it's important politically. What you can do is lay open the fundamental wages of sin — to use the Bible — to say, 'Now this is what you're really up to, people. Now if you want to do anything . . .' Hopefully you educate. If you can nail down the truth . . . 'Know the truth and it will make you free' . . . Man wants to isolate what he feels is destructive."

Q: Do you think writing is a responsibility or an occupation?

A: "I can't separate them. I just want to create something beautiful on stage and have it go like hell. It has a shape and the rest is just what I say afterward.

"As for Willy, I'm not blaming this man — I sound like one of the characters. I'm not in the blame business. I'm criticizing these values in society which drive people crazy . . . values that destroy their souls and their children."

Q: Is writing a cure for the writer?

A: "It's a cure for the feeling of total uselessness. The language is the most important thing, the sheer use of language . . ."

Q: How much of Willy Loman do you feel in yourself?

A: "I feel a lot. I couldn't write if I didn't feel."

—News Photo by Philip K. Webb

Arthur Miller

MILLER, Arthur
(1915 -)

DETROIT NEWS
(Detroit, Mich.)

Nov. 25, 1973

[See also CA-2]

No More Wine and Roses for JP Miller

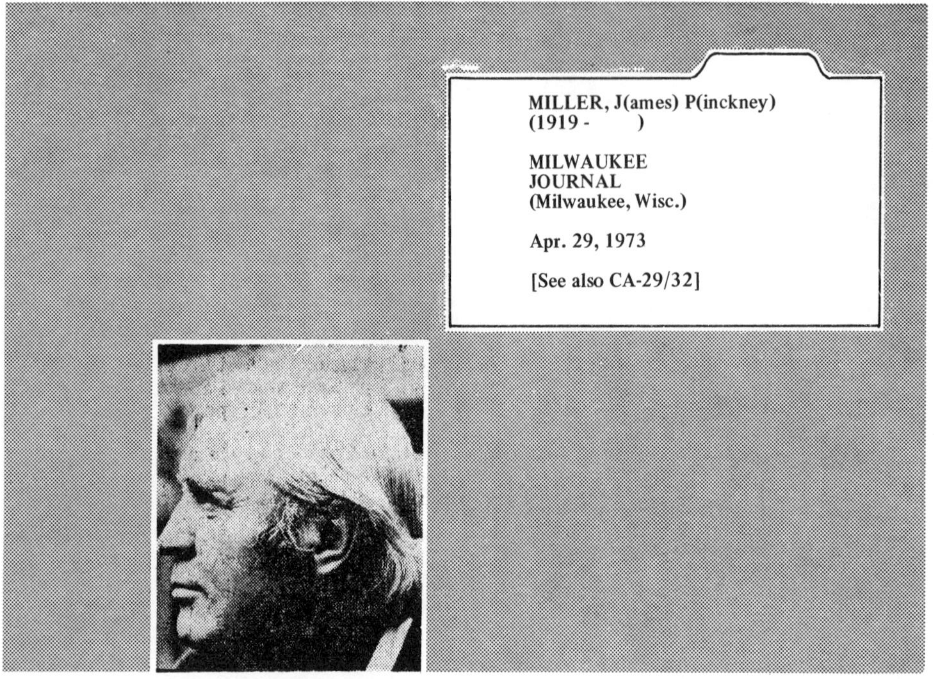
MILLER, J(ames) P(inckney) (1919-)

MILWAUKEE JOURNAL (Milwaukee, Wisc.)

Apr. 29, 1973

[See also CA-29/32]

Miller would rather write books.

By LESLIE CROSS, Journal Book Editor

THE movie, as a rule, follows the book. With JP Miller (who doesn't use periods with the initials that stand for James Pinckney), it was the other way around.

"The Days of Wine and Roses," his best known title, started as a television play. Then it became a movie — a spectacularly successful one. Then Miller turned it into a book.

But Miller doesn't intend to let that happen again. Having spent most of his writing years on film and TV scripts, he is now a confirmed book man. Four years ago, Dial published what he considers his first real novel, "The Race for Home." The other day it issued a second one, "Liv." It is about a woman psychologist who tries to brainwash a dangerous habitual criminal into wholesome innocence, and was reviewed on this page last Sunday.

The Fresh Air Agrees With Him

Miller talked about his changed life when I saw him at his publisher's office before his new book came off the press. It seemed to be agreeing with him. He is a big, robust man in his early 50s, a Texan by birth, and looks like a former prize fighter, which he once was. He lives in the country near Hope, Pa., and gets plenty of fresh air and exercise.

"When you write a book," he said, "it's yours. A script writer is a second banana to some director. You don't know what's going to happen to your story. I've been lucky in casting and so on, but after a while the situation just didn't appeal to me."

Just the same, Miller has kept his left hand in films and TV. A few months after his first "real" novel appeared, the Columbia Broadcasting System aired an original Miller script about drug addiction in ordinary families, "The People Next Door," as its premiere offering on the CBS Playhouse.

Miller got into television by what he calls accident. After he got out of the Navy he went to the Yale Drama School. He wrote plays that he hoped would end up on Broadway; they were apt, he told me, to be seven hour spectacles that would have to run three nights.

Television was in its early days, and one afternoon he met a friend in Actors' Equity. The new medium was using up scripts rapidly, he learned. He submitted a play for a detective series, then discovered the Philco Playhouse. He wrote a script called "Hide and Seek." Betty Fields and Mildred Dunnock appeared in it. Hecht and Lanchester bought a later play, "The Rabbit Trap," for the movies, and he went to Hollywood for a couple of years.

"It victimized me," Miller reported regretfully. "I'm a natural born hedonist, and here I was inundated with big houses, swimming pools, starlets, 12 year old scotch. It wasn't worth it."

An Old Friend Saw the Light

Back in television, he wrote "The Days of Wine and Roses," which he in turn adapted as a film. Starring Lee Remick and Jack Lemmon, this heart wrenching saga of love and alcoholism turned in a dazzling performance at box offices across the country. Some 10 years after its release, the movie shows up from time to time on late late television shows.

"I get letters about it all the time," Miller told me. "About three years ago an old, old friend saw it and got in touch with me. She wrote that she had become an alcoholic. She was sitting up one night boozing when the picture came on. At the end she was bawling. She called up Alcoholics Anonymous right away. That was about 2 in the morning."

"I hope she's done all right. I was a big boozer myself at one time and went to a lot of AA meetings. That's what got me interested in the theme. I knew this was something that could happen to anybody."

Miller's present novel has a timely connection with agitation for prison reform. But the book wasn't planned that way, he assured me.

The idea came to him shortly after the Korean War, when he read about American prisoners who had been brainwashed by the Communists. He asked some psychiatrists and prison officials whether similar methods might be used to rehabilitate convicts. They conceded that the techniques might have a measure of success but predicted that they wouldn't get far, the prison bureaucracy being what it was.

Anyway, Miller's heroine, Liv, tries them on her special convict. However her story may do as a book, it has obvious movie possibilities. So Miller may find himself writing another screen play after all.

By CANDICE RUSSELL
Herald Entertainment Writer

Actually, Jason Miller considers himself an actor first and foremost.

This may seem peculiar coming from the man whose "That Championship Season" swept New York in the spring of 1972, becoming the undaunted victor in a spate of theatrical seasons that were imitative or nostalgic or dull. (Besides the Pulitzer Prize, the play won the New York Drama Critics' Circle Award and the Antoinette Perry Award two years ago.)

"Writing is a more private satisfaction," Miller says. "Acting is more public. When both are going badly, I wish I were somewhere else. Writing doesn't come easily for me. I don't begin until I have a good character. Then the story takes care of itself."

When his vigorous drama came to the Coconut Grove Playhouse for a two-week run recently (it closes tonight), it was preceded by a reputation for excellence and controversy. Its sensitive playwright need hardly have worried.

YET AT THE after-curtain party on opening night, Miller looks haunted, as if the crowd has booed and hissed his acclaimed drama. This brooding conveys his concern for the show two years after its off-Broadway premiere, its triumphant move to Broadway several months later, and its reception that night, tumultuous by Grove audience standards, measured by five curtain calls.

Of slight build, Miller is fiercely alert, somber, quickwitted, responsive. There simmers in him a rapacious energy centered now on the play. A bejewelled theater patron asks him about the inspiration for "That Championship Season" and the words come quickly: "It was a blend of imagination, compilation of real people and fiction. A woman was the inspiration for James (the martyr figure in the play)."

"It's funny; people have commented on how the play reminds them of their friends, but never of themselves. Apart from some negative reaction, by and large, a number of people realize that it was not just an attack on the American dream, or winning and losing. It was about friendship as well, and the loss of innocence. I thought this cast had a sense of that loss of a kind of faith in each other that was shattering; they conveyed this better than the original cast."

A circle of followers leans on every

He Sold Blood on the Bowery Before Selling a Play on B'Way

Jason Miller

MILLER, Jason (1938? -)
MIAMI HERALD (Miami, Fla.)
Jan. 27, 1974

word as he comments on the brouhaha at the Parker Playhouse in Fort Lauderdale which helped delay the play's entree into this area by nearly a year. "If there is an enclave of people who think it's not for them then why put it on? Why go through the hassle?"

Shortly before the seering drama premiered in Joseph Papp's off-Broadway Public Theater in May, 1972, Miller was collecting unemployment, out of work again as an actor. His "overnight success" actually took years of dedication and endurance, yet somehow he anticipated his play's triumph.

He met and married a fellow thespian, a beautiful girl named Linda who is Jackie Gleason's daughter. They went around the country, acting wherever they could and, over the years, produced three children. Besides directing off-Broadway, "I tried writing poems and short stories, but they were bad. I worked in resident theater, dinner-theater and off-Broadway. I had no acting training, thank God. In New York I think the best thing you can do is just to act, to do it."

In 1969 he wrote three one-act plays under the umbrella title "Lou Gehrig Didn't Die of Cancer" that were produced on off-Broadway. "Nobody Hears a Broken Drum," his first full-length play written one year later, was given a student production at Notre Dame. When moved to an out-of-the-way New York theater, it died after a two-week run and split reviews. While performing in a dinner-theater production of "The Odd Couple" in Fort Worth, Tex., he wrote the third and final draft of "That Championship Season." His famous father-in-law never interfered.

"He did a very good thing. He never tempted me by opening any doors, which would have been debilitating, and I respect him for that. He gave me his own kind of encouragement. Otherwise, I probably wouldn't have written 'That Championship Season.'"

Coincident with the blockbuster success of his drama was director William Friedkin's casting him in the film "The Exorcist." As Father Karras, a priest asked to exorcise an evil spirit from a young girl, he has a key role in one of the most troubling, popular films of this or any other year.

IF PAPP had turned it down, he would have been crazy," Miller laughs. "No, I would have gotten someone else to put it on." He continues matter-of-factly: "I'd checked the show on Broadway and off, and it was the best play of that year. Then it started to grow as A. J. (Antoon, the director) did his magic and the actors did theirs. It was produced well and directed well. There was no interference from Papp. It had to make it.

"Absolutely, luck has a lot to do with it, too. It's a miracle if it happens right, because it NEVER happens right. Most plays come out stillborn. There have been other times in other plays when I'd watch the stagehands like scavengers auction off the furniture in the set."

The day after the Grove opening, sitting in the sun over brunch at a quasi-health food restaurant, the upbeat, more accessible side of Miller surfaces in his discussion of the imminent film version of his prize-winning play. "I want to keep it away from an allstar cast. Warner Brothers wanted Robert Redford and Paul Newman. Luckily I was able to get the rights away from them."

Optioned to Playboy Films, which will produce it in conjunction with 20th Century-Fox, the drama will have a screenplay by Miller. "We'll shoot this summer in Pennsylvania. I'm going to try to bring in the town, the look and feel of it, because the people are so tied to the earth and landscape. The land is tipped and crazy from being strip-mined so close to the surface. The emptiness of the towns thematically goes to where the five guys are at."

UNIVERSAL in application, autobiographical in origin, the play concerns regular Joes who believe in the work ethic and competition with winning as life's most important goal. Born in Long Island City, N.Y., Miller grew up in Scranton, Pa. An only child in a prolific Irish Catholic community, he was something of an oddity. "A strict upbringing allows you to rebel against it. The rules were fun to break." His first touch with show business was an appearance in a school play "Man Without a Country," at age 10.

Miller was educated by nuns until senior high school, after which he attended the Jesuit college: "I couldn't play quarterback for Notre Dame so I became an actor-playwright for the University of Scranton." Less conventional experiences followed.

"When you're 18, 19, 20, New York is the capital of your fantasyland. I'd sell blood for $10 on the Bowery and go to the Seeder Bar where Ferlinghetti and Ginsberg used to hang out, at the height of the beatnik movement.

"I suppose because I'd read **On the Road** by Jack Kerouac, wanderlust got in me in '62 and '63, after college. I wanted to do Shakespeare, so I went to Washington to act with a touring Shakespeare company, in combination with graduate school. I couldn't handle the academics because I didn't go to classes. The dean once asked me, 'Why don't you join the Army?' Last year I was named alumnus of the year."

Set for summer release is a film he finished for director Robert Mulligan called "Nickel Ride," in which he plays the lead.

Though concerned as an actor about keeping in touch with himself and his own feelings, he's not keen on psychiatry. "Shrinks are the high priests of the technological age," he says. "I tried psychoanalysis for 20 minutes; that's all I needed. Confession is more therapeutic; it gives you a buoyancy and it's certainly as good as psychiatry. I believe in religion but I have problems with the institution, with the bureaucracy of religion. Yet where would culture be without the Catholic church? Look at all the cathedrals, the architecture, the paintings."

Miller doesn't believe that success has changed his lifestyle, though he and his family have two homes now, in New York and Saddle River, N.J. "I just want to maintain a low profile and keep moving," he says with a laugh, a rakish playful air peeking through his seriousness. "You can get off on the business of being a celebrity for about a week. I like to come here and just hang out."

Already he's learning that the dream doesn't quite measure up to reality. Informed while filming "The Exorcist" that he'd won the Pulitzer Prize, Miller immediately started thinking of his acceptance speech. The comedown came two weeks later, when he was sitting at home. Laughingly he recalls, "I figured I'd get to meet all the great writers, everybody sits around and gets drunk, you have a great time. Instead, the mailman comes with a big brown envelope, containing a certificate that says you've won, and a check for $1,000. It was nothing, man."

The boyish Miller grin, however, says that it was something indeed.

(Also see preceding article)

A champion for all seasons

By Tonny Mastroianni

Devilishly strange as it may seem there is a connection between "The Exorcist" and the recent Play House production of "Look Back in Anger."

Few may remember, but Jason Miller, Father Karras of "The Exorcist," was on a list of tentative guest actors at the Play House last season. That was pre-"Exorcist."

" 'Look Back in Anger' was a play I definitely wanted to do and that's why I was willing to go out to the Play House," Miller recalled in a phone interview

"But then the filming of 'Exorcist' took longer than anyone expected and it screwed it all up."

Anyway, that's how "Look Back in Anger" got into the Play House schedule. But it was neither the play nor the movie that was the reason for the interview, but "That Championship Season" which comes to the Hanna Monday evening and which Miller wrote. That too was pre-"Exorcist"

He won a Pulitzer Prize for it. Now he is an Oscar nominee for his movie work which makes him the first man who could win both awards.

No matter how things work out the versatile actor-writer intends to pursue both careers.

"The two careers feed off each other," he explained. "When I wrote 'Season' I was acting in a dinner theater evenings and writing in the afternoon. While I'm acting I learn about the problems of writing for the stage and when I write I'm aware of acting problems.

"Most good actors have a literary sense. Eventually,

MILLER, Jason

CLEVELAND PRESS
(Cleveland, Ohio)

Mar. 15, 1974

I'd like to direct, and that calls for a higher awareness."

Miller says he has no intention of acting in "That Championship Season" or anything he has written.

"At this point it would be too discomfiting to me," he explained. "I'd be a writer acting in front of actors. The rest of the company would be actors acting in front of the writer. I can imagine too many problems. I don't know; maybe they're not there."

Miller is in Los Angeles working on the screenplay of "That Championship Season." He has just finished another movie, "The Nickel Ride."

"I play a small time hustler and gambler, definitely not anything like another priest," he said.

He said he also is working on another play, one about three priests on a vacation.

Miller is a Roman Catholic, was educated by the Jesuits at the University of Scranton (Pa.) and studied at Catholic University.

He has acted with the Champlain, Cincinnati and New York Shakespeare Festivals; appeared as Edmund in "A Long Day's Journey Into Night" with Helen Hayes, and in "Juno and the Paycock" with Geraldine Fitzgerald. His other plays are "The Circus Lady" (three one-act plays) and "Nobody Hears a Broken Drum."

"The Exorcist" has added to his fame, cut down on his privacy.

"I'm keeping as low a profile as I can," he said. "It becomes detrimental to working, even out here. I have to get out of this hotel and find a quiet place. I'm not big on parties and crowds.

The movie and the nomination have also caused a larger number of interviews than a playwright normally endures and he indicates that there has been a goodly amount of misinformation printed about him.

There was a report that William Blatty, "Exorcist" author - producer, was involved in his next play; that women pursue him as a result of the priest-actor combination.

"I read about myself and I get discouraged," he said. "I always end up sounding like an idiot. No, I'm not working with Blatty on anything. Women? I scoff at those reports.

"I also avoid possible situations. There may have been one or two times that women showed interest. I think a priest is innately attractive to women because of his inaccessibility.

"Some people I meet think I'm a priest. A number of priests — regardless of what they think of the movie — have been very complimentary about the role. They feel that for the first time a priest has been presented as a human being.

"They're especially complimentary about the priest's relationship with his mother, which apparently is something most priest go through.

"People ask if I believe in the devil. Of course, I do. But when someone comes up to me and starts telling me about a brother with the problem of demonic possession, I run the other way."

"That Championship Season," which also won a Tony Award and a New York Drama Critics Award, concerns the 20th reunion of a high school champion basketball team.

"It's about value systems, the struggle under it all, the illusion of winning and even in the long run about the illusion of defeat," Miller said.

"The business of winning at all costs is still with us. People read Watergate into it, but the play was written before Watergate."

Miller is high on the touring company of his play, a rather muscular, shouting, locker-room dialog sort of work. He is especially high on Forrest Tucker as the coach.

"Everyone has this television image of him but he's good, he's stretching his chords like they've never been stretched before."

But prize-winning play or not Miller's life is inexorably affected by "The Exorcist." He will be at the Oscar ceremonies Apr. 2. Moviemakers continue to send him scripts which he continues to reject.

"Surprisingly they're not about priests," he says. "But they're bad, all bad. I'll just keep writing."

Author Does Own Thing

By HELEN PARMLEY
Religion Editor of The News

The first time Keith Miller gave his Christian testimony in public, he was seated on a platform between evangelist Billy Graham and evangelical industrialist R. G. Le Tourneau.

"I felt like a stripper with a different kind of figure," said Miller in an interview.

An author and Episcopal layman, Miller is ont a conventional evangelist. He hit the best-selling list with his first book. "A Taste of New Wine." His most recently published work, "The Becomers," is a best-selling primer on what a person should expect when he "becomes" a Christian.

("A becomer," writes the author, "is a Christian who is in the process of seeing who he is and what he can be . . . with God's help. It is a scary, but exciting adventure.")

MILLER WAS in Dallas recently to speak to a seminar for single adults at Park Cities Baptist Church. With little of the ecclesiastical jargon many have grown to expect from an evangelical Christian, he converses about his faith in much the same way a businessman describes his product.

A charming man with a quick wit, Miller said the "God thing" came into his life after a series of events had left him in a state of helplessness.

Like his father, Miller was in the oil exploration business in Texas. But several deaths in his family drove him to think about God, and he enrolled in seminary for the next two years.

"More and more," he recalled, "I felt the seminary was dealing in abstractions rather than with questions people were asking (the subject for his next book), so I quit."

NOT A quitter by nature or heritage, he was overcome with guilt. He got into his car and drove until it ran out of gas.

"There seemed to be no hope for the future," he reflected. "Until that moment, I thought two martinis and a good night's sleep could solve any problem.

"I thought about God and I prayed, 'If there is anything in my life you want, take it.' I would like to say that Jesus Christ suddenly appeared on my hood, but that is not the way it happens.

"After that night, however, I began to feel it was okay to be me, that I no longer had to try to be something I was not."

GRADUALLY, and not without mistakes, he said, he stopped hiding his real feelings from himself and others.

"I realized how self-centered my life had been," he said, "with no room in it for God. I also realized I am not responsible for everyone. I believe there is a God who is aware of people and their problems.

"A neurotic Christian thinks he has to solve these problems. I feel free to do my own thing, to learn to live creatively and to help others . . . listen to them and communicate real feelings and faith."

Miller, who lives with his wife and daughters in Port Aransas, at first was embarrassed to talk about his conversion. But soon he found himself not only learning to pray and reading the Scritures, but also relating in a more personal, vulnerable way to other Chrstians.

"JESUS talked to people in their language," he said, "and they felt at home with him. People are beginning to feel at home with some Christians today, in some churches too."

Miller believes in the charismatic gifts of the Holy Spirit, but does not practice glossilalia (speaking in tongues).

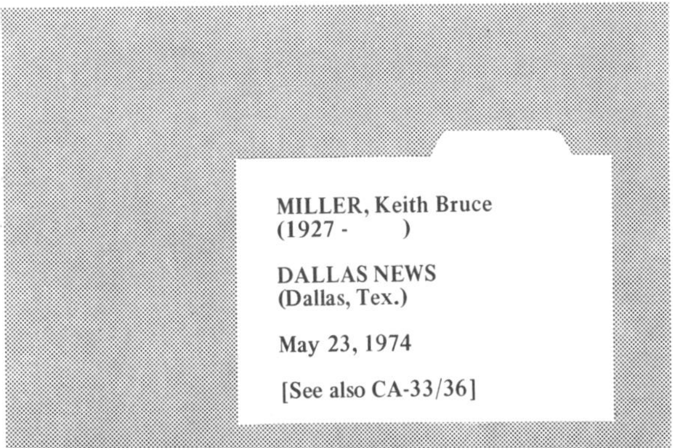
MILLER, Keith Bruce
(1927 -)

DALLAS NEWS
(Dallas, Tex.)

May 23, 1974

[See also CA-33/36]

Keith Miller . . . "People are beginning to feel at home with some Christians today."

"Maybe that too is a gift of the Holy Spirit," he said. "It is a wonderful thing if it frees people to talk to God. After all, I didn't believe in conversion until I was converted.

"I would speak in Mandarin Chinese if God wants me to."

Harry Truman Forced Miller Into Best Seller

Sketch by Authors in the News

By LESLIE BENNETTS
Of The Bulletin Staff

"What I really had in mind was doing a long dull book that nobody would read," says Merle Miller cheerfully, contemplating a copy of his sure-fire new bestseller, "Plain Speaking."

"But I decided I'm too old and tired." Looking neither, he waves a hand at his book, an "oral biography" of the late President Harry S. Truman from interviews Miller taped in 1961 and 1962. A proposed television special never came to pass, but the book finally did.

"Some people say it's not scholarly,

MILLER, Merle
(1919-)
PHILADELPHIA BULLETIN
(Philadelphia, Penn.)
Feb. 1, 1974 [See also CA-9/10]

but for chrissakes, I'm not a scholar! Anyway, anecdote can be history. Maybe the best kind of history."

He grins. "I always planned to do the definitive biography, but I was feeling my mortality. These days I read the Times' obituary page every morning to see if I'm on it." Miller's age hovers capriciously in the early 50s, "depending on where I choose, between 1920 and 1925, as the starting point," he explains.

These days, whatever his age, life for Merle Miller is rather pleasant. The book's candid and revealing comments about the most important political figures of Truman's lifetime has attracted a great deal of attention, which Miller is thoroughly relishing.

Live on Royalties

He announces gleefully that he hasn't worked a day since September, and at the moment all he is planning is to live on his royalties.

"I am enjoying the fact that for the first time, I don't have to write a piece for the New York Times Magazine," he says.

"I used to make a living writing television scripts, but I don't do it any more, mainly because I haven't been asked."

Although he has written eight novels and "Plain Speaking" is his fifth work of nonfiction, Miller confesses that what he really wants to do now is "to write another novel which nobody would read or buy. I think my last novel sold three copies. It certainly made me realize nobody wants to read about queers." He chortles, but without rancor. Whether he's discussing his own fiascos or anybody else's, Merle Miller seems to have a fine time just being Merle Miller.

That last novel was the author's first about homosexuality, but whatever its reception, a great number of people were interested in reading his memorable personal confession of homosexuality. A New York Times Magazine article which appeared in 1971, it created quite a literary and social uproar. "That was free," Miller explains. "They didn't have to fork over $4.95."

The immediate repercussions of that article included a flood of mail from strangers as well as famous but still-secret homosexuals, and the fact that Miller's mother, who still lives in his native Iowa, disinherited him.

'Take You Back'

She has since relented. "She reinherited me after a year and a half," he reports. "One day I answered the phone and it was her. She said, 'Is my son there.' Then she announced, 'We have decided to take you back,' meaning she decided and my father said yeah. Actually, we had not been in much contact long before that. Since I was about 6 months old." The diabolical cackle peals again, but it is not unkind.

At least the Truman book is creating a different kind of furor. Miller says a dear female friend of his recently exclaimed, "Oh, Merle, how wonderful — now everybody's forgotten you're queer."

"I think, in attitudes toward homosexuality, there is a definite generational difference," he muses. "My generation still doesn't want to know about it. They say, why tell me? The only reason one talks about it is so you won't have to talk about it, you know? I don't think it's very important, but other people do."

In the Times article, Miller admitted that, given the choice, he would rather have been straight — but today he says he's gone beyond that. "It seems to me that people in Gay Lib are perfectly right in saying that's a cop-out. It's saying I wouldn't like to be me, and I can't say that any more. I'm as happy to be me as anyone is to be himself or herself. I'm still not completely liberated, though. I would like not to care what anyone thinks of me, but I care more than enough.

Won't Change?

"Now I'm looking forward to having money, which I've never had, and I expect it's going to be just glorious — but it's not going to change anything. I've spent my life with people whose names are household words, who have had much more money or been more famous than I — and I haven't seen that they've been any happier or more relaxed, or felt more at ease in the world. I guess I would like to love myself more, but I've discovered I really don't do that any better in a Mexican resort, because what I can't leave behind is myself. Sometimes I'd like to say, Hey, Merle, stay home, but you never can."

In any case, Miller says he's very happy with the domestic side of his life. For the last 10 years he has lived in Brewster, N.Y., with another writer, David Elliott, whom he describes as a brilliant novelist. "We're both impossible and totally neurotic, but although it's impossible to live with someone, it's truly impossible to live alone."

There are also a Lhasa Apso and a sort-of Pomeranian, not to mention the surrounding chipmunks and pine trees. "I have loving companions, two-legged and four-legged, and I cook and I listen to music, and I'm happy with that part of my life. One need hardly say that one would prefer to have been William Shakespeare, but I have realized that that isn't going to happen. So — with my talents and energies diminishing by the second — I'll go on with this. At this point I'm perfectly willing to settle for the way it is.

"I've never felt really at ease at any given moment in my life, but I suspect if you do feel at ease you just aren't thinking. You certainly haven't read the day's newspaper, anyway!

"What does one want out of life? To get through till next Tuesday, perhaps. I guess the reason I get up in the morning is because it's interesting." He grins, and winks, and bustles away.

KATE MILLETT

—P-I Photos by Cary Tolman

BY SUSAN PAYNTER

Feminist author Kate Millett is a quiet revolutionary with no room for compromise — even for the women's movement.

In Seattle to keynote the International Women's Day Celebration Friday and Saturday at the University of Washington, the author of best selling "Sexual Politics" is celebrating more than a movement for women's rights.

She sees the struggle as part of a total revolution of all oppressed people. Her concepts may go a step farther than some of her sisters would like.

"National Leader" in the women's liberation movement is a label that's stuck with her since "Sexual Politics" won her a Ph.D. at Columbia University and the wrath of much of the nation.

But Millett eludes labels. Author, Teacher, Artist, Bisexual, Lesbian — although all apply, she defies pigeonholing. Even Leader doesn't fit.

She said, "The Media has created its own 'stars' within the movement and it has isolated women from each other. There shouldn't be any 'stars.' Everyone is a leader."

Within the revolution, Millett sees gay liberation as women's rights' closest ally. "Because they're both fighting against a patriarchal society and the stereotyping of sex roles."

She's aware the alliance may not win friends and influence people for the movement but expediency isn't her aim. "If your goal is just to change some damn mealymouth law, then you've got a problem. But this is an entire social revolution. It's not going to affect just laws but the entire social structure."

Persistent legal change is necessary, Millett admits, and she's glad groups like National Organization for Women (NOW) are doing it. She wants states to "hurry up" and ratify the Equal Rights Amendment.

But her approach is more philosophical than practical. "I'm a radical, not a public-relations expert for the movement," she said.

"To deny your lesbian sisters their part is immoral. Gay women always have been at the vanguard of the movement. I couldn't deny them anyway because I'm gay and I can't deny myself.

"It's eminently valid to get rid of sex roles and, if we permit ourselves to be peeled off from the rest of the movement, we're at a point of impotence."

She thinks the press has played the name-calling game, using charges of homosexuality to discredit the movement. "After publication of my book, they put my picture on the cover of Time Magazine, without my permission, and made me a 'star.'

"I'd been telling the media all along I was gay but they'd never print it. Then, in a later edition, Time said I'd 'admitted' being bisexual as if to say, 'You people had better take a closer look at this movement and see who's running it.' I was gay and I was proud of it. I didn't need a magazine to say I'm a coward."

Millett's used to adverse reaction. After the publication of "Sexual Politics" she said, "I'm going to get killed for this book. But the reaction was much worse when I 'came out' as being gay."

Now she's just completed a new book, still unnamed, as a journal of her life in the revolution and as a lesbian. "I'm really going to get killed for this one," she said.

Millett's concept of the women's rights revolution

MILLETT, Kate

SEATTLE POST-INTELLIGENCER (Seattle, Wash.)

Mar. 4, 1973

confirms what some people fear most — that total involvement in the movement means bisexuality. Is bisexuality the next step?

"Yes, it can be," Millet said. "In the process of building the movement, we should be falling in love with each other. Right now we're the most interesting people to be with. The men are catching up, but slowly.

"What are they doing to liberate themselves? Are they holding their own conscienceness-raising sessions? What are they doing to help pass the ERA? They're always telling us how important we are to them. This is their chance to prove it."

Millett is anything but a man-hater. She's married to artist Fumio Yoshimira and has loved him for 10 years. But the legal marriage was a formality to satisfy immigration laws. They consider themselves friends, not spouses.

She said, "I believe everyone is really bisexual but there's always been a class of people you're not supposed to fall in love with. For awhile it was people of a certain race, now it's people of a certain sex. When men get their heads together, we'll get back together.

The author isn't advocating homosexuality for everyone. "I'm not telling anyone how to live or trying to say some happy housewife should run out and do it. After all, what if she liked it?"

She said she is advocating free choice without public censure.

But overall social, not just sexual, change is Millett's concern and she uses her teaching, writing and speaking talents to make her contribution, preferring to leave TV appearances to the more quotable movement leader, Flo Kennedy, "the mother of us all."

When she does make personal-appearance tours, she gives away the paycheck. The money from her Seattle visit will go to a New York artist friend who is going blind.

"But I don't think sponsors like the Abortion Action Coalition hosting this visit should pay their name speaker. They should go to the University and say 'We want $500 for our program,' whoever is speaking.

"People should be just as willing to hear what Mary Smith has to say but they won't pay her. Of course, some speakers do need the money just for subsistence. For now I'm still living on the royalties from my book." She also teaches at Sacramento State College.

When the money runs out Millett may have her new book to pay her way — "If I can get it published!"

A Man Who Captures Detroit--- And Life

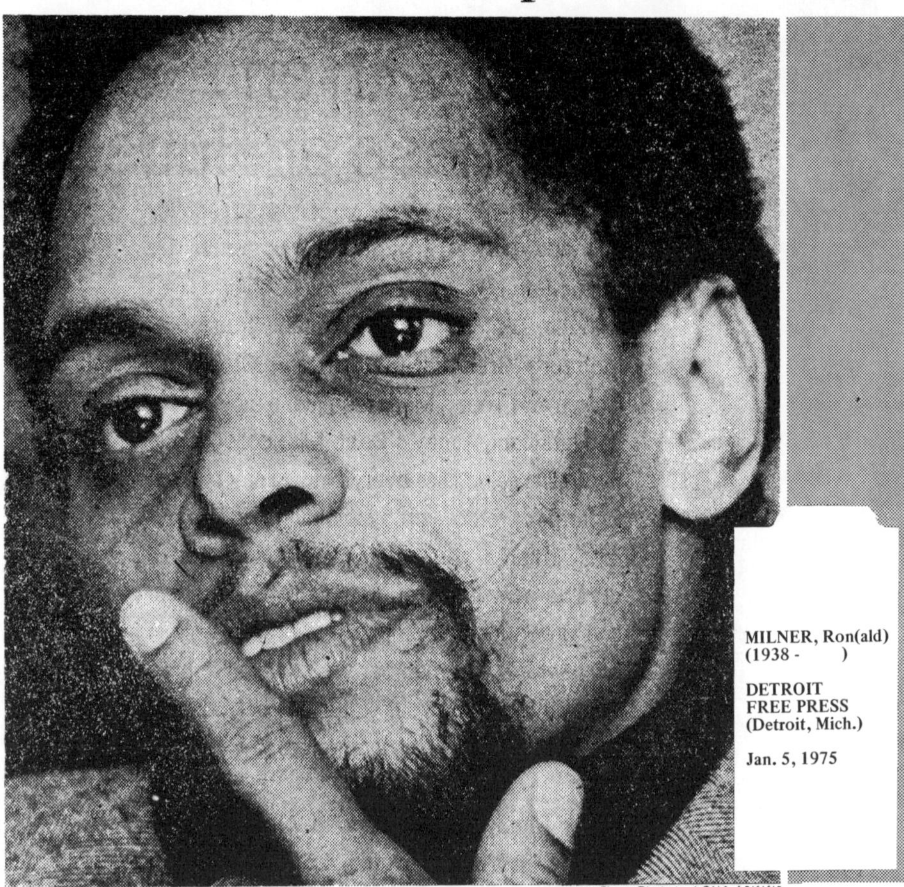

Free Press Photo by LONA ASKINS

MILNER, Ron(ald) (1938-)

DETROIT FREE PRESS (Detroit, Mich.)

Jan. 5, 1975

BY BETTY DeRAMUS
Free Press Staff Writer

Most serious writers and musicians in Detroit gradually drift away, lured by the sharp scent of success that hovers like smoke over the shining cities on the east and west coasts.

Detroit playwright Ron Milner is different.

Milner, 36, whose play "What the Wine-Sellers Buy" is at the Music Hall Center in downtown Detroit, says proudly that he's "hooked on the city."

He says it with joy.

And he says it with some pain, too.

Milner grew up in Detroit's old Hastings Street area, a hodgepodge of shops and smelly bars and painted ladies screaming "turn the corner, baby" at cruising cars.

It was a Detroit where a young boy could grow up in the streets and either sample all of its pleasures or never know that they were there.

It was a Detroit where old women rocking on porches kept the peace and tried to keep the innocent pure.

It was a community.

"To me, Hastings Street was like an open air market where people talked to each other across the street," he says. "You could grow up and never know what was going on.

"It might take you years to find out what was happening . . . "

But if Milner was later to find cities like New York cold and "inhumane" when compared to the Detroit of his youth, he now worries that his favorite city is growing crass, too.

When he returned to the city five years ago, after an absence of five years, he says he found it greatly changed:

"Nobody has time to talk to anybody, it's grab, grab, me first . . . our whole sense of values is just a hustle about money.

"At the same time, our (black) consciousness was rising in the '60s, the other thing was rising too, that whole hustler philosophy of anything for money. We forgot about that black germ growing.

"The murder rate (and other problems) is happening because that other value is starting to grow . . . in that one film 'Superfly' (the story of a cocaine dealer) the Afro hair style was replaced by slick hair . . ."

Milner's works — particularly "What the Wine-Sellers Buy" — reflect his concern for the declining quality of life in Detroit.

The play tells the story of 17-year-old Steve Carlton, a bright, high school basketball star who falls under the spell of the pimp, Rico, who tries to convince him to turn his girlfriend, Mae, into a prostitute.

Essentially, "Wine-Sellers" is a morality play in which Rico and a church deacon war for the soul of Steve. As in all morality plays, good and the power of love triumphs.

But what makes "Wine Sellers" different is that the villain, Rico, is no cardboard figure who is easily knocked down. He is, in fact, so persuasive and logical that he seduces audiences as well as Steve. And he is sometimes strongly defended by people who see the play.

Milner thinks this is because Rico is really the typical American businessman, and, as such, an American folk hero.

"The people who pollute the air and water for profit have no right to point fingers at Rico," Milner says. "When he talks about everything for profit, trading everything for money, he's talking about society.

"What he says about society is correct, but he is wrong in what he decides to trade. If you trade life, what do you buy?"

He is puffing on a pipe, a small, reflective man with piercing hazel eyes, whose own life has involved some hard choices.

"I was raised by Ricos," he says, admitting that he, like Steve, was once tempted to try the hustler's life.

His family was not "poor poor," just average for the time and the place: "We were sometimes broke, but it seemed like there was always someone in the family who saved the boat if it was starting to sink."

He flirted with trouble, but never fell over the edge, talking his way out of whatever scrapes he got into. He played basketball at Northeastern High. And he wrote.

After graduating from high school, Milner briefly attended Highland Park Junior College and Detroit Institute of Technology and worked as a messenger, stock clerk, hotel busboy, hospital porter.

"I've taught at college more than I've attended," he laughs. "In class, they always talked about what other people had written, Henry James, Ernest Hemingway . . . I could do that at home."

In 1962, when he was 24, Milner got a $2,500 fellowship from the John Hay Whitney Foundation which enabled him to support his family while he completed a novel.

Since then, Milner's plays "Who's Got His Own" and "The Warning—a Theme for Linda" have been staged both in this country and in Europe. And "What the Wine Sellers Buy" became the first black play ever staged by producer Joe Papp at the New York Lincoln Center's Vivian Beaumont Theater.

Despite several years spent in New York and as writer in residence at Lincoln University, Milner's roots have remained in Detroit, where he lives on the west side.

Milner is not a man who needs to be in the center of the creative swirl of a city like New York in order to write. He thinks spending too much time talking to other writers can make a man forget that art springs directly from life and from the streets.

At a ritzy party several weeks ago, Milner didn't really get into the swing of things until the party thinned out and he got a chance to shoot some pool.

And while striding through downtown Detroit one recent morning, he got the biggest chuckle out of seeing two small boys walking a huge pair of St. Bernard dogs.

"There's no telling how or where they got those dogs," he grinned.

He was one of the original founders in 1964, of Detroit's Concept East Theater, a center for black theater and the arts.

And he believes that as a black playwright he has a responsibility to try to change the way blacks in Detroit and elsewhere view themselves.

"It (art) should be functional . . . should be a direct tool for illuminating the past, future, present . . . to work on the damaged psyche black people have had for years.

"(Art) has to educate as well as entertain. When people call me a preacher I consider it a compliment . . . when you get an emotional response it's easier to involve the mind . . ."

His basic message is not angry, though he has been accused of writing at "fever-pitch" and piling on too many layers of emotion.

His message, says Milner, is the message of the old-time revival preachers who make tears roll and stomachs jump when they talk about salvation. His message is that love — not money or power over others—heals.

"In the '60s, we forgot to deal with little basic things. Some people really thought money was power and it never became clear what it (the civil rights movement) was all about.

"People went around saying so and so 'sold out' when it was there all the time.

"I thought that what we were fighting for was . . . to have some space to love in."

(Also see preceding article)

Black theater in transition, playwright says

MILNER, Ron(ald)

DETROIT NEWS (Detroit, Mich.)

Oct. 20, 1974

By BILL GRAY
News Entertainment Writer

Black theater, says playwright Ron Milner, is in a period of transition — from reacting to asserting and from trying to appease a white audience to dealing directly with blacks.

Detroiter Milner, 36, is back home this week preparing his all-local cast for a showcasing of his newest work, "What the Wine Sellers Buy" Nov. 21 at the Art Institute. A recipient of Rockefeller and John Hay Whitney fellowships, he's best known for "Who's Got His Own" and "The Warning — a Theme for Linda" which have been staged both in this country and in Europe.

"THERE USED to be a lot of screaming and hate," he says of black theater which surfaced as a major theatrical form in the late 1960's. "It was reacting to white racism and the themes were defiant directives at the white community."

But today, Milner insists, the shouting is over. "We're at the end of a catharsis," he says, "We're no longer dealing with 'I am somebody' but more of who that 'somebody' really is.

"In talking now to our own people black playwrights now center on things like love stories and parental relationships. There's a broader balance, a freer atmosphere which is good because you can't constantly create out of defiance."

Also, Milner says, black theater is moving away from needing a general audience for commercial support. "We've established black theater and have developed our own audience. Seven years ago in New York the black playwright was in the position of having to write for white producers, white directors and white audiences. So whatever you had to say was done that way for the broadest kind of acceptance."

MILNER USES two early works — "Purlie" and "Raisin in the Sun" as examples. "They were originally intended as black plays but were changed so that the final result was commercial theater. I call that 'Negro Theater.' It's based on reaching the broadest audience, especially whites because that's the biggest audience.

"But today, real black theater is less concerned with appeasing whites as it is having something to give to blacks.

"At one time black actors couldn't even deliver lines in the black speech rhythm because they'd been trained to speak to white audiences. Schools trained them that way. But now the black playwrights are saying, 'Speak like your mother and father. Keep your inflections.'"

MILNER SAYS black theater today is neither preaching separation or integration but an awareness of black problems and philosophies., "We have problems inside that we have to deal with."

Milner describes his latest work as "a black morality play. "It's about a 17-year-old black man in Detroit and it centers on the variety of choices he has to make in a ghetto setting. The conflict for this young man is deciding between the hustling type philosophy of the streets and the philosophy of his family."

It isn't any less intense, he says, than the works of Melvin Van Peebles in the late '60's. "But the voice of black theater is lowered into a more natural tone and I think that's much more effective and much more revolutionary because you can't move the body without the head."

Ron Milner's Upbeat View of the Ghetto

By David Richards
Star-News drama critic

At 36, playwright Ron Milner is considered to be one of the more positive voices writing today for the black theater. "What the Wine Sellers Buy," his drama about the pressures and seductions of ghetto life in Detroit, his hometown, opens a four-week run Tuesday at the National Theater. Widely discussed when it was staged in New York last year at Joseph Papp's Vivian Beaumont Theater, "Wine Sellers" relates the story of a 17-year-old high school student who rejects the temptation to become a pimp, even though his family is desperate for money.

Milner, a slight, agile man who also runs the Spirit of Shango, a community based theater in Detroit, recently talked with Star-News drama critic David Richards about the motivations behind his play and the state of black theater in general.

● *Is "What the Wine Sellers Buy" an autobiographical play?*

A similar incident happened to me when I was young. But I think I would have just passed over it, except that I saw the same thing happening to other

MILNER, Ron(ald) WASHINGTON STAR-NEWS (Washington, D.C.) Jan. 5, 1975

guys as well — young guys who were clear-headed and intelligent, and able to achieve, suddenly using all their energies to turn over dope. They'd bought a system of values that says anything you do to get a car or money or clothes is all right.

(Continued from preceding page)

When you live in a city that has the highest murder rate in the world, you begin to ask yourself why. You trace it back to the same type of incident again and again: Someone embracing the street. It's always been my belief that you can't say the ghetto is hip, because it is very dangerous. Youcan love it and learn from it, as long as you can perceive the good AND the bad of it.

I've actually seen a 10-year-old boy sniffing salt — not cocaine; he didn't have any concept of what cocaine was — but salt, because he wanted to look like Superfly. You see enough cases of this and it suddenly becomes important enough to write about. The big thing I ask in the play is, what do you care more about: People or things? How much of yourself are you willing to sell?

● *In your play, though, the hero resists the temptation to sell his soul. This ending was regarded not only as unusual, but actually surprising, by a lot of people. Why?*

A lot of people were disappointed by it, too. You know the idea that you can't have a drama, especially a black drama, unless it ends in some kind of tragedy. This is related to the Western concept of drama as despair — what O'Neill called "impending doom."

It's hard for me sto say I've written a happy ending when the kid is still faced with the same temptations. He's merely said no in one instance. But I think there has to be some kind of belief that you can do something about your life — and not just suffer what's imposed upon you. For a long time, black writers dwelled on our negative history. They could never see any real victory. For them, the only victory lay in the ability to endure defeat. I was consciously trying to break that.

I function a great deal on what I intuitively feel are the needs of the time. And the needs of the time are for the positive. I don't think black people, people in a crisis, can afford a theater that is merely artifact or entertainment. It has to have a functional effect. Like the African artist: He carves a stool you can sit on, or a spoon you can use.

● *You don't believe in the theater for its own sake?*

Theater for theater's sake is incest. It gets thinner and thinner each time and drifts off into abstraction. But when it's directly involved in life, even when it's badly done, it can cause people to argue, discuss, grow, or at least clarify where they stand. It's true, the aesthetic side can do something for you spiritually. But you can't let that prevent you from communicating on a basic level.

MILNER, Ron(ald)

WASHINGTON STAR–NEWS (Washington, D.C.)

Jan. 5, 1975

● *Several critics referred to "Wine Sellers" as a morality play. Do you object to that description?*

To me, it is directly, obviously and consciously a morality play. The only thing that bothered me was the way the term was used — as a put-down. What kind of a person would consider a morality play unreal at the same time Watergate was going on? By and large, the critics are white, 50 and suburban, and they feel they've had their morality plays. I happen to think they're wrong. I also know that the young, black audience I'm writing for needs this morality play.

● *You mentioned Superfly. Was that a direct influence on your writing the play?*

I could have written it five years earlier or five years later; it was always stting there in the backlog of my memories and ideas. Superfly gave me a sense of urgency to get it out. But the hustler has been in the ghetto all along. A big mistake that many black writers made was thinking that because they had escaped his kind of philosophy, the problem had actually gone away.We all jumped directly into the political arena. And one day, we looked up and the character was still there, magnified 20 times on the movie screen and doing his thing on a grander level than ever before. I believe the artist and the people walk side by side — maybe the artist is one-half step ahead sometimes, and sometimes it's the people who are leading. But this is an instance in which the black writer was out of touch with the people. We should have dealt with this problem of values years ago.

● *Much of the black theater of the 1960s was a vilification of whitey and his values. Is this still an important strain?*

Well, it's still there, but much more in the background. In the 1960s, even though we were developing a black audience, there was a strong consciousness of the white audience. We felt we had to strike out at it, explain ourselves to it, relate to it somehow, even though there may not have been any actual whites in the theater some nights. I think we've cut down on that negative white influence, worked out our own aesthetic, and developed our own criteria. Now our plays are aimed at a totally black audience, which makes for a completely different tone and effect. You have to have something to say to your brothers or else shut up. What shape are we in? Where do we go from here? It's like the difference between the way you talk to your family when you're alone, and the way you talk when there are other people in the room.

● *Did you always want to be a writer?*

Every neighborhood has a dude who tells stories, makes up the characters, and does all the sound efects as he goes along. I was doing that when I was five or six. I never thought of it as writing until I got to high school, although that's what it was.

I grew up on Hastings Street, which was pretty infamous and supposedly criminal. I guess it was. But it had other sides, too. The more I read in high school, the more I realized that some tremendous, phenomenal things were happening around me. What happened in a Faulkner novel happened four times a day on Hastings Street. I thought why should these crazy people Faulkner writes about seem more important than my mother or my father or the dude down the street. Only because they had someone to write about them. So I became a writer. Ultimately, I got a John Hay Whitney Fellowship and a Rockefeller Fellowship for a novel I was doing, "Life With Father Brown." I met Langston Hughes and we became friends. That's when things really began to get clear in my mind.

● *Is there any special reason why you've chosen to live in Detroit?*

People always ask me why I've continued to live in Detroit. I've had chances to move on.But it seemed to me they were saying, "you're something, but the rest of the people there are nothing." How can something come from nothing? I'm an extension of the place and people I come from. So I've never wanted to leave. The neighborhood grows with you if you grow, and it doesn't grow if you don't grow. But basically, it's always with you, wherever you go.

'Old Wit' Still Shines For Ex-Newspaperman

—Press Photo by Albert M. Herrmann Jr.
KASPAR MONAHAN
Relives the 'good old days.'

By ANN BUTLER

It was a cold gray winter day. Kaspar Monahan was wearing a huge black overcoat and his woolen "Mother MacCree" cap with the ear flaps down, when he shuffled into The Press newsroom.

The former newspaperman looked rather rumpled, reluctant — and rascally.

The twinkle of the rogue is in the eyes — smoke-blue, the kind of eyes a poker player ought to have. The hair is snow white, the face softly featured. And the mind is as clicking quick-witted, as razor sharp as ever.

"I think this is all very foolish, but what the hell?" mumbled Kap, who obviously would have preferred doing the interviewing.

After all, he claims he's "interviewed everybody except God."

Among the biggies were Herbert Hoover ("no more personality than a dead codfish"), Adm. Richard E. Byrd ("a very handsome modest young man"), and Beatles John Lennon and Paul McCartney ("Liverpool boys — they were all right, (except they started the plague called rock 'n' roll").

During his 36-year tenure as Press drama editor before he retired in 1968, he interviewed and became friends with the show biz greats.

And the man could write. Recognized as one of the nation's finest critics, Kap Monahan had a style so original, a way of describing things so accurately you always knew exactly what he was getting at. More than that, he had a heart of gold that somehow flowed right into the prose.

It's enough to make the gonzo-novice exclaim: "I wish I could write like that," Indeed the man they used to call a "walking cocktail mixer," this tall Irishman, so gruff and yet so gentle, seems to embody newspapering in the '20s.

"Naw, I don't write anymore," says Kap, who will admit only to having "reached three score and ten."

For the past 10 years, Kap has been married to the former Lois M. Naylor, who was supervisor of The Press Classified Ad Department for over 40 years before her retirement in 1968. They live on a Mercer County farm near Slippery Rock. "But I'm not a gentleman famer," Kap is quick to note.

MONAHAN, Kaspar

PITTSBURGH PRESS (Pittsburgh, Penn.)

Jan. 13, 1975

The couple enjoys traveling, and they have been to Ireland, Belgium, Mexico and Canada. In 1973, they journeyed through the jungles of Guatemala, exploring the Mayan civilization, in a battered old Volkswagen.

The son of Irish immigrants, Kap was born in Kentucky and raised in Colorado. His father died when he was two months old. He is proud to say he hails from a railroading family, and that he himself worked in the round house, laying track, and driving spikes — in order to pay his own way.

He was educated at the University of Colorado and worked on several Colorado newspapers, including one in Pueblo, where Damon Runyon once toiled, before Kap joined the UPI in Denver for starvation wages $17 a week."

"We covered everything and we stole a lot — from Kansas City to the West Coast and from Canada to Mexico.

"It was only two of us—the manager and me. Very primitive. You'd be sitting in one of these cubicles, sweating, and you'd have to pace yourself because you'd be reading the news out over a telephone to seven or eight newspapers at once.

"I was lucky being in Denver for interviews. Everybody had to pass through Denver in those days."

In 1927, Kap interviewed Charles Lindbergh after he had flown across the Atlantic, from New York to Paris in 36 hours.

"Lindy was an extraordinarily handsome man," Kap says. "I damn near lost a pair of pants, because the women souvenir hunters were grabbing at everything."

Lindbergh answered all questions except the last. When Monahan asked him, "Why didn't you fly back?" he just glared.

In 1928, Kap traveled to Hollywood, where he met "the whole gang — John Gilbert and Greta Garbo, stars of silent film . . . and blundered in on Clara Bow, the 'It Girl,' when she didn't have a stitch on."

He was wearing a straw hat and the rest of the cast was in armor when he butted in on the filming of "When Knighthood Was in Flower." The director yelled at him, but Kap contends it would have been the best scene in the movie.

Kap joined The Press as drama editor in 1931. "I did everything. It's not like today—they just go to the shows." Kap told one story about a Press old-timer who loved gin so much that when he dropped his bottle in the men's lounge, he knelt down and wept.

"People used to sing around the office—especially around the holidays," he added. In fact, Kap does a little hum-te-dum number himself. Every time there was a lapse in the conversation, he'd commence to hum-te-dum-dum-dum.

He even sang a soft tuneful rendition of "Over There," explaining that George M. Cohan was inspired to write the song after hearing the sound of the engine exhaust from the steamers that would carry the WWI troops overseas.

"George told me he was so excited he wrote down the words on the back of an envelope. He was always one for flag-waving. Back then, wars were romantic."

Kap adopted his personal philosophy from Harold Lloyd, "one of the finest men I ever met. I went to his mansion after he retired to interview him. And just like you're asking me, I asked him his credo for daily living.

"He told me: 'It's not original, but I've always gotten along with people, because I like people. It's the old golden rule. That, and I've always been willing to meet the other fellow more than half way.' "

He says his best interview was with Ralph Fleagle, a notorious bank robber, who disappeared to a hideout in Kansas, was later caught, jailed, sentenced and hanged.

"A no-good dog, but fascinating," says Kap, who interviewed Fleagle in his jail cell. "He was 5-feet-3, 52 years old, with eyes like a lynx that would glitter and gleam. He told me, 'This shirt is too tight. I feel a tightness around my throat.' And then he'd throw his head back and bellow. His sense of humor was rather twisted.

"He had killed the president of the bank and the president's son. He told me, 'I had to kill the man. He was honest. Never trust an honest man.'

"My mother used to get so indignant about me writing up bad people. But I'd rather talk to someone who had done something wrong or was fleeing .... You write what the people want to read.

"Things have changed for the better," he added. "We had nothing — one man typing on a little typewriter. But I thought it was the greatest job on earth.

"I was lucky to be a newspaperman.

"There's too much violence today — but then there was always violence," Kap reflected. "Medical science has improved. People were dying of everything, when I was a boy."

Journalists rarely live to enjoy old age. How did Kap manage to hang on for so long?

"Keep healthy and don't worry," he advised. "Watch your food, as you grow older. Eat something raw everyday — raw celery, raw fruit . . . raw whisky.

"I love whisky," he admitted, then stopped short. "My wife Lois told me, 'Don't go telling her all your bad habits." Lois is the one you ought to be writing about. She never did a bad deed in her life.

"Who wants to read about an old man?" he grumphed. Brightening, he added: "Always remember this, there's nothing worse than an old man — unless it's an old woman."

What's it like, Kap — growing old?

"I don't mind it," he replied. "I've had a good time. That's why I don't want to go to Florida. I like the change in weather. And I don't want to be with old people. I can't imagine sitting there, surrounded by old people."

As Press photographer Al Herrmann focused his camera for a shot of the rougish countenance, Kap reckoned: "If I frown, I look like a mean old man. If I smile, I look like an idiot."

Then the veteran newsman turned to the novice, and he warned he: "Now don't you make me out to be a pious old curmudgeon."

Take it easy, Kap. How can you call a man "pious" after he tells you that his life credo has become: "I've learned how to grow old disgracefully."

Photo by Sarah Lansdell

A Southern writer at home

By SARAH LANSDELL
Courier-Journal & Times Staff Writer

CRAWFORD, Ga. — "Anyone in Crawford can tell you where I live," Marion Montgomery said on the phone, "but it will help you to find it if you know it's a big white house with white columns facing the railroad track."

It sounded like a proper setting for Montgomery's kind of Georgia-born writer still resident in the South. He's descended from the literary brahmins who settled in the English faculty at the University of Georgia 30-odd years ago, bringing with them the life style or aspired-to life style of the Agrarians, those poets and writers of the Thirties who advocated a return (some said flight) to an agrarian life and mutually supportive culture and agriculture.

Montgomery is 49 and has been at the university since 1947. He reckons the time from the year he enrolled as a student. He has left his teaching post there only for two years at the University of Iowa's Creative Writing Workshop. And, of course, for some six months each year that he tries to devote almost entirely to writing, becoming a sort of writer-in-residence.

MONTGOMERY fits rather well the pattern of the early Georgia brahmins who founded the quarterly, The Georgia Review, in 1946. His education is classical. There is no hint of sociology in his directions. His own version of Yoknapatawpha County is better defined than that of most writers of today and he lives the life of the mind (Montgomery might prefer "soul"), concerned with the struggle between good and evil. Like Flannery O'Connor, of whom he has often written, he believes that evil really exists. Have no doubts; he means original sin.

On a summer morning the Montgomery front porch is cooled by a breeze from the south. Birds sing madly. In Montgomery's talk of home and town is a tinge of protest against being thought simply a Thinker. He is a member of the Crawford Volunteer Fire Department, rabbit-hunts in fall with one neighbor, fishes in summer with another, and has roots in the county from which he has drawn a lot of atmosphere for his new novel, "Fugitive" (reviewed on the opposite page).

Still, one is never sure what synthesis is going on in his mind. Oglethorpe County and Crawford, 14 miles from the University of Georgia in Athens, are constantly being translated into fiction. Crawford, with a population of 350 to 400, was named for William H. Crawford, secretary of war under Madison and secretary of the treasury under Monroe. Montgomery's three acres on the town's edge have a few apple trees and strawberries, two rows of beans for Yeats and a muscadine vine. Not a farm, but then the Agrarians always advocated more sweat over art than over the soil.

THE HOUSE is not pretentious. It is cloaked by large oaks and like Montgomery himself is hospitable enough but not broadly extrovert. It is sparely furnished. Part of the pattern of the Southern brahmin is that he wins considerable critical acclaim but little financial success.

Montgomery lives there with his wife, Dorothy, their son Marion, 16, and daughters Heli, 14, and Ellyn, 11. Two older daughters, Priscilla and Deana, live elsewhere. Several pets include a cat called Sophonsiba for a character in Faulkner's "Go Down, Moses," and Uncle Hal, a beagle, who makes his debut as a literary character in "Fugitive," appearing more or less as himself.

Teen-ager Marion has been reading "Fugitive," Montgomery said, and is now "wrestling with the problem of how history gets translated into fiction." He is fascinated by the way things he knows have been used in strange and different ways. "Is Hal really Hal, you see, or not? The really important thing, though, is the nature of the translation."

Montgomery has a typewriter in the family menage, just in case, but for really high-powered work he has his "office" a short walk away. It's a former doctor's office above a sundries store and though it's at one of Crawford's main intersections it's quiet. It opens with the tug of a key in the lock. There is no doorknob. "And once I'm inside, I'm safe."

THIS SUMMER Montgomery is continuing his critical commentary on the work of novelist and short-story writer Flannery O'Connor, who lived at Milledgeville, Ga., 60 miles from Crawford and who died ten years ago at the age of 39. At mid-morning Marion bicycled to the Post Office with his father's latest O'Connor-related magazine article (or candidate for same), an aside, Montgomery said, written in a fit of enthusiasm, "because I've been reading Solzhenitsyn's new book and I saw Walter Cronkite interview him.

"I began to notice similarities in Solzhenitsyn's burning intensity and Flannery O'Connor's, and it set me reflecting why so many Southern writers are fascinated by the Russian writers. They both have a concern for evil. They believe evil exists. They don't shy away from it. And what you don't find pointed out in most treatments of Solzhenitsyn, now that he has become so popular, is that he made a very painful progress out of communism to the Church, and two or three years ago made his first Communion. Why wouldn't Walter Cronkite ask him that? It's a curious omission."

The Montgomerys are Episcopalians. Montgomery says "Anglo-Catholics," and it is clear he takes the "Catholic" quite seriously. He switched from the Baptist Church about 25 years ago.

In his "aside" he drew parallels between Solzhenitsyn and O'Connor's comments on critics "who refused to go beneath the surface of her work to see that what she is dealing with is evil, the problem of evil."

WRITING on Flannery O'Connor is an "old malady." Montgomery has published about 15 pieces on her "and I thought I was just about finished. Then I got an invitation to speak on her work this summer and the malady set in." He began to write an hour's speech and it became 50 pages and then 75. "My son is worried how I'm going to condense that into an hour. We've decided to record it on 33 and run it on 78."

Montgomery is not overly defensive, but he has some of the ambivalence of writers who live in the South — pride in being Southern and resistance against being thought "regional" just because their characters have Southern accents.

He shares with O'Connor, he feels, the interest in transforming the local into the universal. "Her early critics saw her either as a horrifying cartoonist or as a writer of local color. What has fascinated me is that in her character of Haze Motes in "Wise Blood," she seems to be writing a portrait of a Nietzchean character, and demonstrating that Nietzsche's direction just won't work. She says somewhere that she's interested in dealing with that country held largely by the Devil. It sounds Southern because she happens to be Southern. But it isn't really the South. I contend that in Haze Motes, who seems to be a Southern grotesque, she is really doing a marvelous portrait of the Western intellectual."

MONTGOMERY is the author of four novels, almost 70 articles and essays, three collections of poems and three long poems, 26 stories, and books of criticism dealing with Ezra Pound, T. S. Eliot, Dante and Wordsworth. About 200 of his poems have appeared in some 100 periodicals.

His first novel, "The Wandering of Desire," prompted Flannery O'Connor's often-quoted statement: "The Southern writer can outwrite anybody in the country because he has the Bible and a little history" . . . but she had added, "but Mr. Montgomery has more of both than most and a splendid gift besides."

A 1964 novel, "Darrell," set "approximately" at Athens "is a sort of love story without sex. That's a hard thing to try. It's a little difficult to find villains in it, for instance. I was interested in showing an attempted struggle to escape evil, so you don't have villains as such. I think the same thing is true of "Fugitive." You have many errors, but not deliberate and vicious evil. It makes for an extremely difficult thing to write. There is an advantage to villainy as far as spectacle — the goings-on — is concerned."

It took a while to find a publisher for "Fugitive." One sent it back saying, "We are looking for a Southern novel, but this isn't it" — possibly because of what one of the reviewers, a New Englander, pointed out: "It could have been a New England small town instead of a Georgia one."

The word "fugitive" means a great many things in the book, he said. One thing it does is to tie the central character to his source, which is Nashville, Tenn., and specifically Vanderbilt University where the "fugitive" Agrarians grew up.

MONTGOMERY corresponded "along the way" with poet John Crowe Ransom, one of the early Agrarians, and through this correspondence Ransom is a contributor to "Fugitive."

"I had written him in the mid-Sixties asking about his feelings on the Agrarian position he held in the Thirties. He wrote back a warm letter. Obviously he hadn't surrendered any of those feelings, and I used a section of the letter as a part of the text. I have him, the literal poet and critic John Crowe Ransom, writing a letter to a fictional character in a novel. I hope he was amused by this." Ransom died a few weeks ago.

Before the publication of "Fugitive," Montgomery's score was ten books published, seven unpublished. Now it's 11 to six, and another unpublished one is certain to be along soon. Montgomery has vowed to spend more time in his office. "Sort of my first obligation."

MONTGOMERY, Marion H., Jr.
(1925 -)

COURIER-JOURNAL & TIMES
(Louisville, Ken.)

Sept. 1, 1974

[See also CA-2]

Author Believes What She Writes

By BILL HUTCHINSON
Herald Staff Writer

Ruth Montgomery, after five books one of the country's most prominent and widely read reporters on psychic matters, is A Believer.

But she understands why many people — including highly skeptical members of her own family — cannot accept her best-selling contentions that reincarnation and extrasensory perception are as real as the political matters in which she specialized for 25 years as a newspaper woman.

"WE THINK we know everything. Of course it's hard to admit that there are things we might not be able to even begin to understand. I wouldn't have believed most of this either at one time. In fact, I wouldn't have given the psychic a second thought.

"In 1958, when I was a columnist covering politics and all that, I did a series just as a change of pace on the experiences of a reporter going through seances, going to mind-readers and fortune tellers. I found a great deal of fraud, of course, but I also dealt with some people who seemed to know what they were doing, which surprised me a little."

"Then, a couple of years later, I met Arthur Ford (the late psychic whose spirit guided Mrs. Montgomery, she says, to write "A World Beyond"). I knew him through the research I'd done for the series, so when he came to Washington I arranged an interview. He went into a trance for me, and he saw the darndest things — communicated with relatives of mine, told me things about myself that he couldn't have known.

"IN THE middle of the trance, he mentioned a man's name that I'd never heard. He said the man wanted to talk with me about something to do with the Congo. I brushed him off, because I thought it was far more interesting to talk to my dead relatives and besides I'd never heard the name."

After the interview, Mrs. Montgomery was told to ask her husband about the mysterious man with a message from the Congo. She did, and with some surprise he explained that the man had been an uncle, a missionary in the Congo who had died when Mr. Montgomery was two years old.

MONTGOMERY, Ruth Shick

MIAMI HERALD (Miami, Fla.)

Mar. 30, 1973

[See also CA-4]

Arthur Ford's trance was Mrs. Montgomery's first major experience with the psychic and, like a child who has tasted ice cream for the first time, she couldn't get enough of it. Gradually, she reduced her journalistic commitments to the point at which she is now writing and lecturing exclusively on psychic phenomena.

"Every time I finish a book, I tell myself 'That's it, no more.' But then, some new door will open and I'll become fascinated with some new area and I end up writing 'just ONE more.' I don't know where it will end.

"My mother and brother cringe when I come out with a new book. They're, you know, Midwestern Methodists, and they say 'Oh Ruth, do you have to? People are going to think you're some sort of screwball.' My mother keeps telling me what a shame it was that I'd gotten so far in my profession and then ended up doing this."

OF COURSE, "doing this" has made Mrs. Montgomery a great deal of money and has given her a comfortable life in Cuernavaca, Mexico, that is free of the daily pressures that characterized her career as a nationally syndicated columnist.

"I don't need the money," Mrs. Montgomery insists. "My husband and I have plenty of money. I made a great deal of money as a columnist. I certainly don't have to do this. It's absolute sincerity on my part."

Despite her apparently genuine acceptance of psychic phenomena, Mrs. Montgomery regards each newly "opening door" with the same skepticism that typified her approach to political goings-on on her previous career.

SHE APPROACHED reincarnation with strong feelings that it was "absolutely ridiculous." Her research for "A World Beyond" introduced her to her two previous lives (as a Tibetan mystic and a sister of Lazarus) and left her convinced that people are all just recycled versions of their ancestors.

The subject of her most recent book, "Born to Heal," published last month, is a California-based "healer" who is reputed to have effected thousands of miraculous cures with a variation on the Biblical "laying on of hands" technique.

Not a faith-healer, Mr. A., as Mrs. Montgomery refers to him in the book, contends that man's physical well-being is controlled by the balance of internal energies that make up his "magnetic field."

Some people have a surplus of these energies and have learned to convey them in a curative capacity to others whose energies have been jolted by emotional or physical shock out of natural balance.

"THIS SOUNDED pretty preposterous to me," recalls Mrs. Montgomery. "I was introduced to him by friends in Washington several years ago, and I just assumed that all the things I'd heard of him doing were not really possible.

"I said, 'All right, if you're so good, cure my bursitis.' At that time, my right arm was pretty nearly locked to my side and I knew he wouldn't be able to do a thing about it.

"He said, 'Give me your left thumb,' and I did, and he held onto it for a few minutes and then let go. An hour or so later, he told me to lift my right arm above my head. I laughed at him.

"I said that I could barely move it. But I lifted it, somehow I managed to lift it and swing it around my head. I haven't had any serious trouble with it since."

MRS. MONTGOMERY interviewed nearly 100 of Mr. A's patients for the current book. The diseases he has cured range from cancer to asthma, she says. "I have absolutely no question that he has healing powers.

"I checked the medical records of these people before their treatment with Mr. A and interviewed them after treatment — in some cases, several years afterward. His results are incredible, but I have seen proof of his abilities.

"I have two personal physicians, and I asked them both about Mr. A. One said that it was ridiculous, that no man had such powers. The other, though, told me that this is an area about which many doctors have a totally open mind.

"I think that's true of a lot more people today. More of us are willing to accept that the fact that we cannot explain something does not mean that it doesn't exist."

In the Miami area to promote her new book, Mrs. Montgomery will speak at an open meeting of the Palm Beach Roundtable, at 4 p.m. Sunday at the Breakers Hotel.

The Problems of the Happy Author

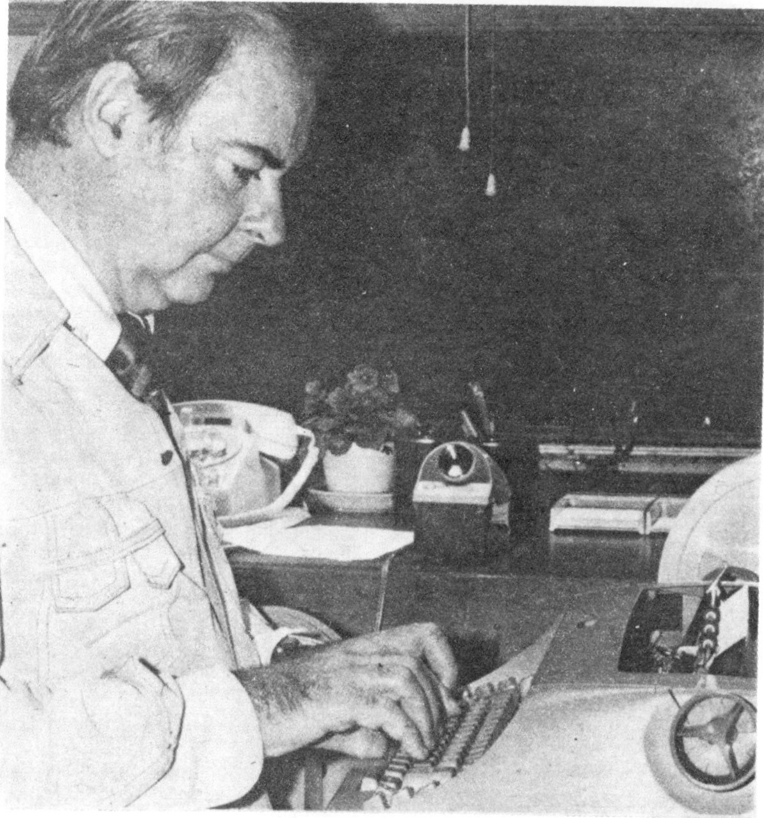

At his Westport home Moore begins writing at 6 a.m. and usually works 10 or 11 hours around a three-hour lunch break. His wife, the former Mary Olga Troshkin, is an actress and singer.

by WILLIAM WOLF
for The Courant

Since 1961, Westport author Robin Moore has averaged better than a book a year, four of them — "The Green Berets," "The French Connection," "The Khaki Mafia" and "The Happy Hooker" — super-bestsellers, with combined sales of more than 14 million copies. Yet Moore, who has sometimes risked his life to get the facts for his books, said he's now engaged in a mortal struggle to save his writing career.

"The trouble began when I wrote 'The Green Berets' and John Wayne made the movie based on the book," Moore said. "The New York literary Establishment decided that I was a hawk like Wayne, that I favored the Vietnam War.

"From then on, they made me the victim of a conspiracy of silence, refusing to review my subsequent books, often refusing even to mention their publication dates. Not even Jacqueline Susann gets such treatment."

The 48-year-old Moore, who looks taller than his medium height when he's sitting down, was sipping coffee in Sardi's, where he feels at home surrounded by theater and movie people. "I know I must sound like some kind of nut to say these things," he continues, "but I have a friend who holds a top job with a major literary magazine and he gave me the word: 'Robin, you've got the blackball. I know it's unfair, but there's nothing I can do about it.'

"The funny thing is, I never approved of the Vietnam War. Doesn't anybody remember that the Pentagon condemned 'The Green Berets' when it came out as undermining the war effort? The 'Brass' thought the existence of the Green Beret fighting force should have remained secret."

To offset his handicap, Moore has been his own press agent, traveling from city to city, appearing on radio and TV talk shows and at bookstores for autographing sessions. "Sometimes I've had to take extreme measures," he said. "For example, 'Court Martial,' which told about the Green Beret group on trial for executing a Vietnamese they believed to be a double agent, was selling badly. Getting the book mentioned in book reviews seemed hopeless, so I decided to try for front page headlines instead.

"I went to a friend of mine, Robert Marasco, the former Green Beret who actually killed the Vietcong agent, and I asked him to confess his deed. Since he'd been acquitted, I knew he would be protected from double jeopardy. Marasco was beginning a career in politics, but he decided to confess the murder anyhow. We made the front pages, all right. 'Court Martial' sales zoomed, but poor Marasco's political career got nipped in the bud."

A more recent book whose sales Moore would like to hype is 'Phase of Darkness,' about the uprising in Uganda. Some people, including the publisher Joseph Okpaku of The Third Press, believe it contains Moore's finest writing to date. "I turned 'Phase of Darkness' over to The Third Press because it's a new publishing house, a black minority operation that deserves a break," Moore said. "I figured somebody with a sales track record like mine could help them a lot. So I let them publish my book without even asking for an advance payment. Do you think we could get any kind of notice from the literary-in-groupies? 'Dogs of War,' Frederick Forsyth's book on African turmoil came out about the same time as mine, and got reviewed all to hell."

Moore talks softly but rapidly spins an account of a colorful life that seems at odds with his surface calm. In addition to being a ready man at the typewriter, he does nearly all of his own leg work, often digging into places where a guy could get hurt. He spends anywhere from a year to two years preparing for a book.

Some of his most dangerous research was for "The French Connection." He spent nearly

MOORE, Robert L(owell), Jr.
(pseud. Robin Moore)
(1925 -)

HARTFORD COURANT Sept. 15, 1974
(Hartford, Conn.)

[See also CA-15/16]

two years cruising New York with the narcotics detail, becoming intimate with Eddie "Popeye" Egan, the model for his hero. "I got a tip that a lot of heroin was going to disappear from the New York Police Department. Sometimes possessing information of that sort could be dangerous. Then came a mysterious phone call, advising me to leave town for awhile. So it seemed the right moment to take a research trip to the Middle East which I'd been planning anyway, for my novel 'Dubai.' "

After "The French Connection" came out, a couple of underworld characters described in the book were being prosecuted, and their attorney, Henry Lowenberg, obtained postponements claiming he'd come down with sudden heart seizures. Moore told reporters that Lowenberg was faking the illness to delay the trial, whereupon Lowenberg sued Moore for libel.

"Then before trial," the author said, "my attorney and I got together with Lowenberg,

(Continued from preceding page)

and he said to me, 'Mr. Moore, I loved your book. Ever since I read it, it was my dream that someday you might write my life story. If you agree to it, I'll drop my lawsuit.'

"How could I refuse? Moore notes. "Here was perhaps the underworld's number one mouthpiece. If the book didn't sell a single copy, his contacts and information alone were worth my time and effort.

"Needless to say, it came out in 1971 with the title, 'Until Proven Guilty,' and it was a success. It has a sad aftermath. Two days after I'd put a freshly printed copy into his hands, Henry Lowenberg died. I never knew he'd been suffering from lung cancer."

Aided by invaluable Lowenberg contacts, Moore was able to write "The Fifth Estate" about the tie-up of the underworld with big business. Moore observes that he got a few more threatening phone calls to get out of town. "Only by this time, the underworld knew me well enough, so that when they called they didn't have to conceal their identity. Also, when they threatened me, they did it jokingly - but the threat was still there. So I answered this guy, 'Go out of town? Where? The South Pole wouldn't even be safe.' The hood answered, 'You might go to the South Pole. The boss doesn't like penguins.' Then he broke up over his own joke. Apparently the boss enjoyed his joke, too. I never did hear from them again." Since then, Moore has intrepidly come out with another underworld novel, "The Family Man," co-authored with Milt Machlin. "It's about a Mafia hit man who campaigns for the governorship of New York," he said. "Though it's really based on a composite prototype, most New Yorkers will recognize the main character."

On his trip to Dubai to get away from the heat in New York, Moore took along his wife, the former Mary Olga Troshkin, an actress-singer. "I was proud of the way she handled herself during some tough moments in Dubai," he recalled.

"It seems we got caught in the middle of a tribal confrontation when shooting broke out. She's not the worrying type — not even when I have to leave her at home."

Moore insists his wife's insouciance wasn't even ruffled during his collaboration with Xaviera (pronounced zahv-yair-ah) Hollander on "The Happy Hooker" — even though the ex-madam once insisted to a reporter that she couldn't trust a man she hadn't slept with. As the author remembers, the collaboration came about quite by accident. He had been using the apartment of a friend whose name, also Moore, was listed in Xavier's little black book. When she happened to call, he was so intrigued by the sound of her voice and her sexy sales pitch that he decided to pay her a visit. "Nobody ever worked a phone the way she did. Just hearing her was enough to get you interested," Moore said.

A collaboration grew out of that meeting, and Moore then brought in electronics expert Teddy Ratnoff to wire Xaviera's apartment. While Xaviera and her girls played, Ratnoff's tape machines also played, recording all the sounds and conversations picked up by the planted bugs. The result was more than enough to put into the best-selling book Moore and Xaviera did together, assisted by Australian journalist Yvonne Dunleavy.

The result was also more than enough to put an end to Xaviera's lucrative New York business. As it turned out, Teddy Ratnoff was actually an undercover agent for the Knapp Commission which was investigating corruption in the New York Police Department. The tapes were full of incriminating evidence of police shakedowns and Xaviera's bribe payments. Unfortunately for Xaviera, her share of the royalties from seven million paperback copies sold was tied up by the Internal Revenue Service. Because of this, she attempted to write three other books abroad under her own name, but sales hardly matched those of "Happy Hooker."

According to Moore, "The Green Berets" remains the most difficult of his writings to research. "Part of the reason it was so hard was the fact that I didn't have to much money at the time," he said. "I had alimony payments of 250 dollars a month to keep up, with no advance from the publisher to help me out. While 'The Green Berets' was my fourth book, I didn't yet qualify for an advance."

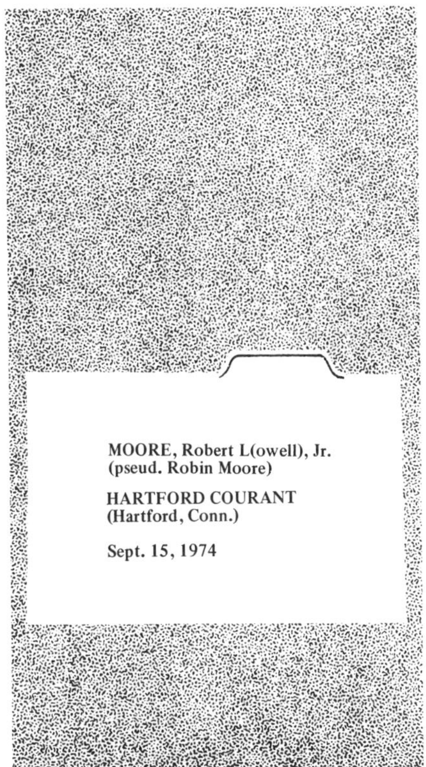

To prepare for "The Green Berets," Moore took Stateside training with the Special Forces, and then joined them in the front lines in Vietnam. "By the time we got around to making the movie, I was still in pretty good shape, good enough to go along with the cast during the filming," he said. "Old John Wayne — he must have been over 60 at the time — did pretty well, considering his age and the fact he had only one lung left since his cancer operation. He kept his trusty oxygen machine right beside him, because he'd get out of breath a lot.

"One thing I'd have to say for him — being the drinking man that he is, he was the model of self-discipline. Didn't take a drink in all the weeks we were together."

The route Moore traveled to becoming a best-selling writer is as colorful as the fictional paths of some of his characters. After serving in the Army Air Corps in World War II, he went to Harvard where he majored in English. He was never successful in his creative writing courses, and although he spent a summer in Europe as a foreign correspondent for the Boston Globe, his professor still took a dim view of his future as a writer. After graduating, Robin broke into the mushrooming TV field in New York, working as a video pitchman. He also had chances to write and produce. But his father, Robert Lowell Moore Sr., co-founder of the Sheraton Hotel Corporation, talked him into joining the family business. The youngster eventually became vice president in charge of advertising and public relations. Meanwhile, he burned the midnight oil working on his first novel, based on his television experiences. Titled "Pitchman," it was published in 1956.

After his book came out, Robin was sent to Jamica to help open a new Sheraton hotel. He fell in love with the island, bought property there and built a bar and restaurant he named Teahouse of the Blue Lagoon. He also started an air charter service in Jamaica.

Robin likes to recall the days when Errol Flynn, another Jamaica enthusiast, had a house next door and they lived it up together. "We were great friends. I used to go over to see him when he was still in bed in the morning, and he'd give his girlfriend a pat on the rump and tell her to jump out of bed and fix us drinks. She'd complain she had no clothes on, but Errol would say, 'So what?' and then she'd do as she was told. Errol was fantastic."

While Moore was handling the hotel on Jamaica, the then Vice President, Lyndon B. Johnson, stayed there wnile attending the island's independence ceremonies. Robin's second novel, "The Devil to Pay," with Jack Youngblood, a notorious gun runner and adventurer, had come out. It was about supplying arms to help Castro take over Cuba. Moore had copies of "The Devil to Pay" placed in all 40 rooms occupied by the Veep's entourage, a maneuver that eventually paid off when Moore decided to do "The Green Berets." Vice President Johnson's military aide liked the book so much that he interceded with the Special Forces to let Robin train at a guerrilla warfare camp in the U.S. By now, Moore felt confident enough to sever his ties with Sheraton and begin a full-time writing career.

Despite his four bestsellers, three of which were made into movies, Moore insists he still has to work hard for a living. Income from investments is hardly enough to sustain a lifestyle that includes a home in Westport and an apartment in Manhattan, besides his Jamaica residence.

When he isn't abroad to research a book, Moore begins his working day at six a.m. He uses the method of his idol, Ernest Hemingway, writing while standing up. "Hemingway, you may recall, wrote longhand," he said. "I find it easier to type standing up. My head remains clearer for a longer time." He usually quits around noon and resumes work about three p.m. this time on another book that needs to be finished or on a magazine article or story, writing until about eight o'clock. His afternoon output is accomplished in the sitting position. "It is never as demanding," he said.

Moore, who says he likes meeting people too much to call himself a work-aholic, admits his fascination with all kinds of undercover activity, be it sexual, military or criminal. "I draw the line, though, at the petty, backbiting character assassination I've been subjected to by the New York literary Establishment. This group is no larger than 50 people — awfully small to have so much power. They regard themselves as outspoken liberals, when actually their motivation is as self-serving as the bunch who made Watergate a household word."

(Also see preceding article)

WHAT MAKES ROBIN RUN?

Photograph by Frank Moore

BY WILLIAM WEIR

"He's always been a non-conformist," Frank said as he eased the Pontiac away from the toll gate. "But he's a warm, outgoing, generous person who'll do anything for you."

Frank Moore, general manager of radio station WELI in New Haven and avid amateur photographer, was talking about his cousin, best-selling author Robin Moore.

"There are two ways the son of a very successful business man can go," Frank said. "He can coast or be an achiever. But Robin could never live as an ordinary business executive." The car swished another mile or so over the rain-drenched turnpike as we headed toward Westport to keep an appointment with Robin Moore. Frank continued: "Robin likes to work hard. He wants to do what he feels like doing, go where he feels like going.

Vincent, Robin Moore's Jamaican man-of-all-tasks, answered the door of the sprawling Westport ranch house. Moore, in the living room, waved energetically without slowing a heated telephone conversation that included references to movie rights, *The French Connection* and astronomical sums of money. His wife, Mary Olga, came over to offer drinks and introduce us to a second couple, Al and Paddy Dempsey. Al Dempsey, former airline pilot, former *Time* reporter and former television executive, said he was working on a book with Robin.

"We were staying with Al and Paddy at their place near Dublin when we were in Ireland," Mary Olga said. "Then they came back with us."

Did they visit Northern Ireland?

"No, Robin talked about taking a trip to Belfast, but he had too much work to do," Mary Olga said.

"We did talk with the IRA, though," Al Dempsey said. "We had the head of the local Sinn Fein Party over. We talked a lot, but when we were finished, I didn't know any more about why they were fighting than I did before. They're weird people, and they have a weird cause."

"I didn't understand why they were fighting before I went over, but I do now," said Robin Moore, who had finished his phone conversation and come over. "It's very much like the situation you had in the black colonial nations. The Catholics feel they're being oppressed by the Protestants. And they are. A Protestant minority controls all the wealth, all the business of any importance. But what's happening in Ireland now is just more of what's been happening all over the world."

After showing off "the monster," an enormous Xerox machine that can swallow a 400-page manuscript in one gulp and zip out any number of collated copies, Robin Moore demonstrated his electric tape typewriter. The machine cuts a tape as he types. After correcting a draft, the tape does 99 per cent of the work involved in producing a clean copy.

The tape he used for the demonstration was from *The Treasure Hunters*, a novel he is now completing. He was working on the novel while visiting Al Dempsey, but it's not the book he and Dempsey are working on together.

"Al has a couple of projects. One is a series—something like *The Executioners* or the Matt Helm series. It's about the top guy in a worldwide security agency who travels from country to country. The other is a longer story set in one of the emerging nations in Africa.

"A couple of years ago, a friend and I started a business to help writers put their books into publishable form. We do a lot of the work publishers used to do but don't do any more. Publishing's gotten too complicated. We combine the work of an editor with that of an agent. I really started the business so I could have something when I retire, but it's coming along now. We should have six books out next year."

Al Dempsey, Moore explained, is "an old pal" who knew him a dozen or more years ago when Moore owned a charter plane service in Jamaica. (That enterprise brought Moore into contact with a gunrunner named Jack Youngblood, who had worked both for and against Fidel Castro. The book that resulted from their partnership, *The Devil to Pay*, led to a second book on ir-

MOORE, Robert L(owell), Jr.
(pseud. Robin Moore)

CONNECTICUT
(Stratford, Conn.)

July/Aug., 1973

(Continued from preceding page)

regular warfare, *The Green Berets*. And that made Robin Moore a best-selling author.)

Not all the books Moore's publishing service packages come from old pals.

"The two best-selling commodities in publishing today are sex and the Mafia," Moore said. "A little while ago, I got a call from the wife of one of the hoods I wrote about in *The French Connection*. She claims to have slept with every big mafioso from Dancing Joe Columbo down. She said she wanted to do a book about sex and the Mafia. So we assigned a writer to work with her."

Another in his stable of authors is a prostitute who served only top-ranking athletes. Among other things, she claims one pro football team hired her to weaken stars of an opposing team.

The unquestioned star of Moore's team is Xaviera Hollander, the New York madam listed as the author of *The Happy Hooker*.

"She had paid $10,000 for a book with the names of the best johns in New York. One of them was an R. Moore. She was verifying the list by phone, and she called me by mistake. I talked with her for a while and decided she had a hell of a story to tell. She agreed to do the book. She's made four times as much money vertically as she did horizontally.

"I arranged with the Knapp Commission to have her house bugged. They authorized it, but I put in the bugs. Then we got Philips (Patrolman William Philips, who became a key witness) and had him bugged, and he led to the lieutenant, and so on. This was after we were well along with the book."

So, soon after the Commission hearings began and the beautiful Miss Hollander appeared on TV screens, *The Happy Hooker* hit the book stores. It sold five million.

Inevitably, mention of bugging led to Watergate.

"The Nixon people didn't handle that right," Moore said. "They denied it and tried to lie out of it. They should have admitted it and then used the Big Lie. If you're going to lie, you should do it right. They should have said, 'Sure, we were in there, and we found a serious threat to national security,' and then made up the details.

"I used that technique once. I was on a talk show, telling how I'd gone on missions with the Special Forces troops as part of the research for *The Green Berets*. Somebody asked, 'Did you shoot any Communists?' and I said, 'Yes.' The next day, every paper in the country had headlines reading, 'Author Robin Moore admits executing Communist Prisoner.' I didn't waste time denying the story or correcting the papers. I said, 'Sure. I shot him right in the chest with an AR-15 and blew him apart.' I threw in all kinds of gory details—I can't remember them all now—and the next day everybody forgot about it."

Frank Moore suggested to Robin that Mary Olga join him in some pictures. "Mary Olga's going to appear in the movie version of *The Happy Hooker*," Frank said as Robin went out to find his wife. "She gets to sing. She has a trained voice.

"Robin is successful because he does three things well. He can sell, write and direct," Frank said. "He

MOORE, Robert L(owell), Jr.
(pseud. Robin Moore)

CONNECTICUT
(Stratford, Conn.)

July/Aug., 1973

did a lot of selling during the short time he was in the hotel business. He sold when he was in television before that, and he did a little directing, too. He got into television in the late forties, right after he graduated from Harvard. He'd joined the Army Air Forces during World War II and was a tail gunner at 17, so I guess it would have been about 1949 that he got into television. He was writing even then. He went on writing when he was with his father's hotel chain. He was working for them when he published his first novel, *The Pitchman*. It was about television."

The host and hostess returned. While Frank was arranging his lights, Robin explained that he owned all movie and other rights to *The Happy Hooker*. "If I don't direct, they don't produce the movie—unless they pay me a hell of a lot of money.

"I directed one other movie. It's one you've never heard of—called *Hot Pants Holiday*. Distributed by Joe Levine. I got the idea from a friend of my second wife. It's about a wife who decides that her husband is dull, so she flies off to the West Indies and has an affair with a black man. Joe Levine gave it the title. I objected. I said, 'This is a sensitive story about . . .' and he said, 'It's a story about some broad who gets bored and goes off to screw . . .' And, he was right.

"It got an X rating when it came out three years ago. Now it has a GP rating. The movie hasn't been changed. The standards have."

Frank was setting up a series of pictures in the living room when another couple arrived, Paul and Beezee (Bertha) deFur of Wilton and Jamaica. DeFur was the television producer who gave Robin Moore his first job. The Moores, deFurs and Dempseys, all broadcasters or former broadcasters, began reminiscing about the early days of television.

Meanwhile, Vincent had set the table for Robin and Mary Olga and all of their guests.

"I think we've been invited to supper," Frank whispered.

Until his guests were served, Robin just looked at the martini he'd been nursing, with rather infrequent freshenings, all afternoon. Then he, too, took some roast beef, corn on the cob and new potatoes. Paul deFur, a natural raconteur, dominated the conversation.

"There were only seven stations in the NBC television network when Robin and I were together," he said. "I'd always thought he was just a kid who needed a job when I hired him. A rather strange kid, but not all that unusual. Then one day, he said, 'Paul, I'd like to take you to lunch.' He seemed set on the idea, so I decided to humor him. I expected a hot dog at Nedick's—I didn't pay him all that much, you see. But he said, 'Let's go this way,' and he took me through an alley and around a couple of corners, and we came to this hotel. The doorman saw him and saluted, then practically got down and kissed his foot. I thought that they really make visitors feel welcome here, but I didn't think much more about it. After we'd finished the meal, I said, 'This is a pretty nice place.' And he said, 'Yes, this is my favorite of all the places we have.' That was the first hint I had that he wasn't just some kid who needed a job."

The meal over, Robin Moore and Paul deFur retired to Moore's office for a private conversation. Frank Moore and Al Dempsey shot skittles, an English game played on a miniature pool table with holes drilled into the middle of the felt. Paddy Dempsey watched. After several games. Paul deFur reappeared.

"I've been talking to Robin like an uncle," he said. "He's been driving himself too hard for the last four or five days. He's asleep now. He really needs it."

The Pontiac climbed the ramp to the turnpike. The rain was still falling, the road still glisteningly wet.

"He's really a great guy," Frank Moore said of his cousin.

The Total Woman and How She Grew

By PAT ROBERTS
Herald Staff Writer

She has been called another Ann Landers. An old-fashioned girl. The antithesis to Woman's Lib. The Total Woman.

Marabel Morgan was just a Miami housewife two years ago when she shipped off her hand-written manuscript to a publisher of religious books. Her message: Accept, admire, appreciate and, above all, ADAPT to your husband. Even if he's a slob. Even if you hate him.

The Miami housewife has become a celebrity. "The Total Woman" has sold nearly 200,000 copies and is in its eleventh printing. More than 6,000 women across the country have taken Total Woman courses — four sessions of do-it-yourself marriage improvement taught by Mrs. Morgan and her former students.

WOMAN'S LIB groups picket her courses. She appears on national television talk shows and feminist hurl accusations like "You're a nothing! You've lost your whole identity!"

She gets about 10 interview and speaking requests, and 50 to 100 fan letters a day. Women write to say she saved their marriages. Men send flowers and call to ask, "How can I give my wife a copy of 'The Total Woman' tactfully — so it doesn't get thrown at me?"

"All this acclaim is not customary," says her husband, Charles, an attorney. "She's still a housewife and mother. We still try to keep a normal life."

YET IN a sense, he is the man who made "all this acclaim" come about. Five years ago he came home to find his wife had made dinner plans that conflicted with his own. He laid down the law.

"From now on when I plan for us to go somewhere, I will tell you 20 minutes ahead of time. You'll have time to get ready, and we'll do without all this arguing!" he said.

Marabel cried a while, then dried her eyes and started reading. She read the Bible, Shakespeare, Ann Landers, Dr. David Reuben and many others. She did not read Germaine Greer, Betty Friedan or Gloria Steinem.

SHE READ a scripture stating, "You wives must submit to your husband's leadership in the same way you submit to the Lord."

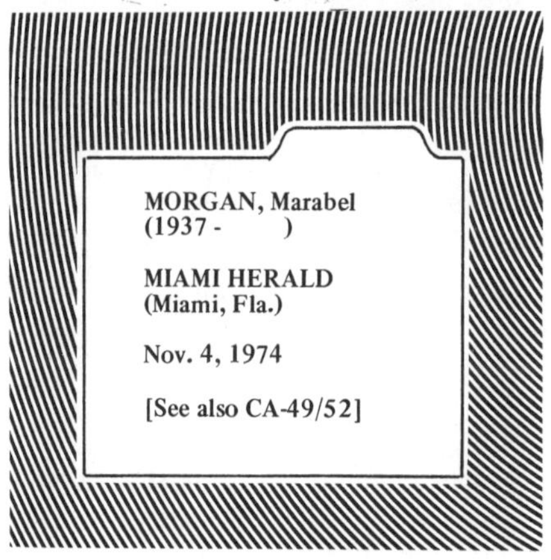

MORGAN, Marabel
(1937-)

MIAMI HERALD
(Miami, Fla.)

Nov. 4, 1974

[See also CA-49/52]

She read that the Queen of Denmark had been submissive to her husband even though he was only a Prince.

She read that Mrs. Albert Einstein had answered "Oh, my no," when asked if she understood her husband's theory of relativity. "I just know how he likes his tea."

MARABEL Morgan started saying "yes" to Charles, and then added what she terms "a little sizzle." One evening Morgan came home to find her dressed in pink baby-doll pajamas and white boots. He dropped his briefcase and chased her around the dining room table, she says. The Total Woman was born.

Charles Morgan makes the family decisions. He is, as she puts it, "president of the marriage corporation," while she is "executive vice president."

Mrs. Morgan is, however, president of the second family business, Total Woman, Inc. She signs the checks, but says she doesn't know how much money has come in from the enterprise. "Charlie handles the finances."

"MONEY is frankly the least of it," says Morgan, an attorney in the firm of Peters, Maxey, Short and Morgan. "We've never advertised. And we're no longer accepting new teachers."

Reading the book, one would have the impression that Morgan is a hulking, supermasculine, super chauvinistic Joe Namath or Norman Mailer type.

Actually Charles Morgan is a conservatively-dressed, briefcase-carrying lawyer in horn-rimmed glasses who finds it "very gratifying" that his model marriage is helping other couples solve their problems. Lately, he does a lot of babysitting while his wife travels around the country.

To get an interview with Mrs. Morgan, one must ask her husband. "I just LOVE to be interviewed," she said. "But I will just let Charlie make the decision. I have to practice what I'm preaching."

MORGAN said "yes" and contributed a bundle of Xeroxed news clippings to the cause, including a column from Viva magazine that listed Marabel Morgan under the heading "People You Should Forget."

There was a Newsweek article and a column of reader responses. One called the Total Woman a "plastic wind-up toy." Another said she "obviously feels her husband is too insecure to accept criticism, so impotent that he needs constant sexual stimulation and too selfish to take care of anyone's needs but his own."

A third letter asked why "all these cute little womanly women who believe woman's place is in the kitchen or in the bedroom are in the studio banging out best sellers or riding the lecture circuit telling off those feminist freaks."

"IF I'M married to a wind-up toy, that's the first I've known about it," Morgan said. Then he read aloud a letter from a California woman who said she had been saved from divorce, that she had been a "very blinded wife, mother and incomplete woman" before reading "The Total Woman." Now her husband was taking her to Hawaii and they were "on our way to the most beautiful life we ever knew could exist."

"That's just beautiful," Morgan said when he finished. "We've got thousands like that."

★ ★ ★

At 10 a.m. Mrs. Morgan appeared at the door of her home in Bay Point. Stylish dress. Heels. Stockings. Make-up. (The Total ➡

(Continued from preceding page)

Woman is, according to the book, always well-groomed — no frumpy robes and curlers).

"Do you mind if I tease my hair a bit?" she asked and stood in front of a mirror a moment, putting the final touches on her short curled blond hair.

"I'M A working woman now. I really have to scramble to be organized and get everything done and still keep my life serene," she said. "I realize it could all get out of hand. I want to keep my priorities in order."

She listed her priorities: (1) God, (2) her husband (3) her two daughters and (4) "those people out there."

In the book, she advises housewives to write a daily list of priorities. Getting the evening dinner ready should be first, with the table set by 9 a.m.

HER TABLE was bare. "I haven't set the table yet, but the fruit salad is made, the hamburger is in the skillet, and the bread is ready to go," she said.

She talked a bit about the 85 Total Woman courses now being taught in the U.S. and Canada. The wives of the Green Bay Packers and the Jacksonville Sharks are becoming Total Women.

Now she gets letters from the Minnesota Vikings and the Dallas Cowboys saying it's not fair — after all, the year the Miami Dolphins' wives became Total Women the Dolphins won the Super Bowl. The month after Joe Frazier's wife became a Total Woman he won a big boxing match.

IT ALL proves, Mrs. Morgan said, that if a wife makes her husband happy at home, he's going to do a better job out in the world.

"I'm not anti-women's lib. I'm not anti-anything. I'm just pro-happiness in marriage," she said.

"I think men and women are equal, but different in function. For instance, men don't have the babies. That's my point."

SHE LEANED forward and confided, "I realize that as a single girl you must think 'this woman is a ninny, a slave.' But I don't advocate slavery. I'm not a ninny. If you can't adapt to a man, I advise you not to marry — it won't last. He'll find some gal who knows how to adapt."

Can't a man adapt? "He'd be Casper Milquetoast in the first degree," she answered. "Any woman with anything going for her would just realize how sick that was."

Mrs. Morgan grew up in Ohio, left home at 18, worked her way through Ohio State University where she was a beauty queen, saved money for a trip to Europe, then worked seven years as a beautician before marrying Charles Morgan 10 years ago. She is now 37 and he is 35.

"AS FAR as being out in the world, I saw that it's not exciting and glamorous. It was just work. Any job is just a job," she said.

Marriage is not necessarily glamorous either, she found. "I was a typical woman's libber. I'd called my own shots for 27 years. I wasn't ABOUT to go some man's way. I opposed Charlie in every subject. I tried to make him over. It didn't work. Our marriage was not sweet and happy.

"I thought marriage would be a snap. I had no idea what was required. It was work, work, work, my work multiplied by four. Moonlight and roses turn to daylight and dishes."

> *"I thought marriage would be a snap. I had no idea what was required. It was work, work, work ... Moonlight and roses turn to daylight and dishes.'*
>
> *— Marabel Morgan*

MORGAN, Marabel

MIAMI HERALD (Miami, Fla.)

Nov. 4, 1974

GLORIA Steinem might have thrown the dishes through the window, hired a babysitter, and headed for the nearest employment agency under the same circumstances.

But Marabel Morgan chose to organize her work as a business executive would — leaving enough time to have a bubble bath each day at 4:30 p.m. and be ready to greet her returning husband like she'd greet a date — candlelight dinners, perfume, cuddling on the sofa. She decided that that's what a man wants when he marries a woman — a date for life.

She had once taught a Miami Bible College course in "Christian beauty and ethics," which included lessons in good grooming, etiquette and how to win a husband.

NOW she turned her discoveries into a "Total Woman" course for her friends, charging them $15 each for four two-hour sessions, enough, she reasoned, so she could hire a babysitter and get herself a new outfit to wear to each class.

Soon there was so much demand for the course she started writing a book. She couldn't type, so she scrawled it in longhand, doing most of the work in her bedroom "in five-second segments — I was always getting interrupted by Charlie and the children."

"The Total Woman" was published in October, 1973.

★ ★ ★

"A MARRIAGE is a partnership like any business. It's a question of who makes the decisions," says Charles Morgan. "When there's a conflict, it's easy to cop out and say 'You do your thing and I'll do mine.' The point is, only one person can make the decisions."

Does that one person always have to be the man? "I'm not personally the kind to be dominated or controlled by my wife," Morgan replied.

Did he have any advice on how to be The Total Man?

"I don't think a man would take advice like that from another man," he said. "I just couldn't imagine going down the street to buy a Total Man book. The title even sounds sort of silly, doesn't it?"

Kuralt & Moyers

By Frank Chesley

Bill Moyers and Charles Kuralt, two of the more perceptive observers of the American parade, flashed through town recently, leaving a scattering of observations in their jet stream. If nothing else, they showed that today's observer of Americana had better have an understanding wife, a familiarity with airline schedules and an immunity to jet lag.

Both were in for speeches, Kuralt taking time out from an "On the Road" assignment in Iowa; Moyers squeezing in a day between Denver and Yakima.

Kuralt's seven years of slice-of-American-life reports for CBS News have become a television institution, with KING's Al Wallace among the best of local newsmen around the country practicing this specialized trade.

Moyers, of course, has squeezed a lot of doing into his 40 years: press secretary to President Johnson, publisher ("Newsday"), author ("Listening to America"), award-winning television journalist ("Bill Moyers' Journal").

The inevitable mood-of-the-country question brought cautious, if hopeful, responses.

"I don't claim to know the mood of the country," said the generally self-effacing Kuralt. "It's unpredictable and varied. But I've reluctantly come to trust (pollsters) Gallup and Harris. . .There's a lot to be confident and reassured about. I've never heard calamity from the people. They seem to have a mystical confidence in themselves."

In some contrast to old-shoe Kuralt, Moyers sees "a mood of acquiescence, uncertainty, disenchantment, which defies articulation. We've spent 200 years getting through adolescence, but no one has told us how to live in a society beyond adolescence . . . The distribution of affluence," he said, is giving way to the distribution of scarcity . . . An Arab sheik can have more influence on your lifestyle than the President of the United States."

And there were contrasting views of the country's campuses.

CHARLES KURALT

MOYERS, William Don (Bill) (1934-)
and
KURALT, Charles (1934-)

SEATTLE POST-INTELLIGENCER (Seattle, Wash.)

Oct. 29, 1974

BILL MOYERS

Kuralt said collegiate response to his "On the Road" pieces has been unusually complimentary. "They see them as the way America ought to be; used to be. An idealized expression of America."

Moyers sees a quiet on the campus. "All of the many concerns the students were pressing for in 1968, '69, '70 have been fulfilled.

"The war has been ended, LBJ was shoved from power, Richard Nixon is gone . . . and things that seemed radical are now accepted."

Of the media, Kuralt said, "It's shameful that there's no primetime news or documentaries. In times like these, it's wrong—irresponsible—not even to have a half-hour devoted to the real problems of our times."

Not surprisingly, Moyers had kind words for public television, calling its potential "larger than any of us can imagine . . . We need a medium in this country which is not always trying to hustle the ends of human life."

He said the past few years have created a greater respect for journalism. "You can no longer get away with mistakes and prejudices or excesses that you might have gotten away with before TV came along. As long as TV acts as a corrector of print and print acts as a challenger of TV, I think the public interest is going to be served. There's not enough of that yet."

Moyers, incidentally, quit his weekly series abruptly last May, saying, "I have said about all I have to say for now in current affairs . . ."

But he said in Tacoma that he was dickering with public television for an on-the-road series on international politics, "to keep the conversation about the world going . . . People are less intensely preoccupied with themselves elsewhere. The rest of the world is more interrelated."

Moyers also is continuing to do occasional specials for PBS.

Bill Moyers Knew He Must Opt For Public Television

By REX POLIER
Bulletin Television Critic

One morning last Spring, Bill Moyers, who was Lyndon B. Johnson's confidant and press secretary, and afterwards, head of the Peace Corps, newspaper publisher, magazine columnist and public TV figure, awoke in a San Antonio motel and, for a while, couldn't figure out where he was.

Since the 40-year-old, ordained Southern Baptist minister doesn't drink excessively, his predicament was not due to alcohol. The calm, conservative, thoughtful Texan, however, knew what was wrong:

"Moyers," he remembers telling himself, "you have been on the road too long. It is time to knock it off."

He immediately abandoned plans to continue his successful Bill Moyers' Journal, which had been on national public TV for three years and won critical plaudits for its scope and professionalism. It also had a lot to do with Moyers hopping from motel to motel searching for new material to keep his series fresh.

Moyers, a brilliant, capable journalist and administrator, who is never without job offers, elected to remain at home in his suburban New York home with his wife and three children. He continued to write a column for Newsweek and a few other things while he thought of the future.

NBC wanted him to replace Frank McGee as Today Show host. But Moyers refused to do the commercials the job demanded. Besides, he doesn't feel that commercial TV can offer him the freedom and independence that public TV can. Basically, Moyers is a writer, teacher, poet and philosopher who values media as a means of turning minds on rather than entertaining them. In the end he knew he must opt for public TV.

The result is a 20-week, hour-long series, Bill Moyers' Foreign Report, which will premiere on Saturday, 8 P.M., Channel 12. (The station carries it on a delayed basis from the Public Broadcasting System). It features a potpourri of reports, most of them to be done in Europe and England, designed to making U.S. citizens realize their interdependency upon the rest of the world now more than ever before. Included will be interviews with Europe's top statesmen, top newsmen, economists, historians and others. There will be press roundups showing the U.S. how the rest of the world views it. Every so often, Moyers will originate a live, forum-type discussion of issues in the U.S.

MOYERS, William Don (Bill)

PHILADELPHIA BULLETIN (Philadelphia, Penn.)

Jan. 12, 1975

He could have selected any number of lucrative opportunities in commercial TV or commercial publishing which would only have required that he report for work. But so dedicated is Moyers toward his ideals that he went out and personally raised the more than one million dollars in funding from various private and public sources to underwrite the Journal. His compensation is considerably more modest than hadhe reached for the Dollar Sign.

"I've got nothing against making money," the slim Moyers remarked one day last week at his favorite Italian restaurant a short distance from studios of WNET-TV, New York City, which produces the Journal and where he has his modest offices.

"No, nothing wrong with making it, but too many fellows spend their tme making it the wrong way . . . they give their lives over to it. I wouldn't want to be poor — I've been there. The only recommendation I have for poverty is the getting out of it. The only other word for poverty is 'boredom'.

"I've had the best assignments of all . . . the White House, Newsday, the Peace Corps and Public TV and the rewards have been eminently satisfactory to me. I have always had a tremendous curiosity and the places where you feed it is in government, politics, and journalism. One lives with an overriding feeling of insecurity. In the end your only salvation is to produce. You live by producing."

Moyers, who was conservatively dressed in a low profile gray business suit with conservative tie, was asked if he hasn't succumbed to the urge experienced by over 40 males to go "mod" in an effort to appear youthful.

"The only flamboyant piece of clothing I own is a beautiful white Stetson that was given to me by a rancher out in Colorado last summer to replace my old worn-out one," the commentator said with a slight smile. "I have to tell you that I wear that Stetson proudly when I wear it around home. I have got deep feelings for Texas and I don't go around publicly proclaiming them."

But then he returned to his commitment to public TV:

"The compensation for me in public TV is freedom. I don't report to anyone except the audience. That freedom valve is greater than security. I spoke my mind on Watergate and impeachment. This is important in TV because I think people want to judge their own opinion by the insight and judgement of other people. I get mail from people who state their opinion and then ask what I think of it. People want to test their convictions against those of professionals in news."

Muggeridge On Critics, Christianity

Malcolm Muggeridge, the editor, writer and critic, was interviewed for the Star-News in London by Tom Ascik.

Question: *After decades of social commentary and literary criticism, why are you now turning to the autobiography to reflect your views?*

Muggeridge: Because, in the end, if you want to write about life, the only data you have is your own life. In other words, I could have written a novel and it would have been essentially the same book. But that seemed like a cumbersome thing to do. And so, I thought that I would put down my own life. Take someone like Tolstoi who wrote the greatest novels ever. They're all about his own life. You can identify every character. Serious writers use the data of their own experience of living.

Question: *Do you think that all the characters of Shakespeare are contained within his own personality?*

Answer: I do, absolutely. I think that they could even be identified. There was an American scholar whose work fascinated me when I was young and interested in Shakespeare. He managed to identify, by going through all the records, people like Shallow and Falstaff. I'm quite sure that Shakespeare drew on his own experience because there is nothing else to draw on. It is one of the great fallacies of the Twentieth Century to think that people look on life scientifically. We think that people are ever thinking, writing, reacting about what goes on outside themselves, when, in fact, they are thinking and reacting about what goes on inside themselves. There is a line of Blake's that I am always quoting because it is so true, "They ever must believe a lie,/Who see with, not through, the eye." It's quite true. An artist sees through the eye.

Question: *How would you characterize your place among those who write today?*

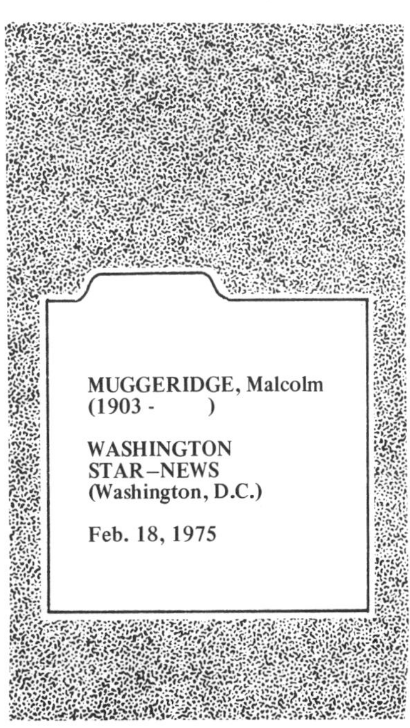

Answer: That's difficult to say really. I think that the whole business of literary criticism is a kind of invented subject. Obviously writers influence each other. But the idea that you have Romantic writers, and then you react against them, and so on, is all English literature rot really. I can't characterize myself. I've spent most of my life as a journalist. A journalist surveys the public scene. He has to report it or comment on it or attempt to make sense of it. That's what most of my life has been spent doing. It's a *voyeur* life really. You observe the public scene without being yourself involved. Take a writer like Norman Mailer for instance. What is the difference between his writing and his fiction? They're both attempts to make sense of life as he knows it.

Question: *How did you move from strict journalism into advocacy journalism and your writings about Christianity?*

Answer: Well, I wouldn't say that it was a sort of dramatic choice. The experience of being a Christian is part of one's experience of living in the world, observing the world and trying to understand it. There was never a sort of moment when I said that I was going to stop being a journalist and start being a Christian. The two things are closely related. At whatever level you write or think or speak you are trying to make sense of life. You may try to make sense of it by simply reporting it, simply giving a picture of it, or you may try to make sense of it by drawing certain moral or philosophic conclusions from it. Or you may try to make sense of it in relation to a religious faith, in the case of Western man, Christianity.

Question: *I gather from your writings that you are not interested in philosphy.*

Answer: I am completely uninterested in it because I don't believe that anyone could ever arrive at a serious conclusion about life through thinking. Nor do I think that you could arrive at a serious conclusion about life through experiment. In other words, I would say that the religious impulse at its most primitive takes you nearer to the significance of life than the intellectual impulse at its most involved. I would say that a savage kneeling down before a stone is nearer to the truth than Einstein.

Question: *Do you think that the intellect functions only in a scientific way?*

Answer: No, I don't, not at all. There are many ways in which the intellect can operate. You have someone like Pascal, a great scientist, who decided that science was inadequate. He said that science was a cul-de-sac, a lie, and that only faith is true illumination. He forswore science although he was a master of it.

Question: *You reviewed Solzhenitsyn's Gulag Archipelago. What do you think is his purpose in writing?*

Answer: Solzhenitsyn has emerged from the most oppressive dictatorship the world has ever known, a dictatorship dedicated to extirpating Christianity. And yet, out of that emerges the most brilliant, perceptive Christian of this century. The question is how did he know about Christianity? The answer is that he knew about it because of Tolstoi. Tol-

(Continued from preceding page)

stoi's was the only truly Christian literature, the only Christian propaganda, which was not suppressed. All others were. Dostoievsky was suppressed. Now he has recently been allowed. But Tolstoi not. And yet, if you had been in a position to nominate somebody to keep Christianity alive in the hearts of the Russian people, you couldn't have hit on a better man. His exposition of the New Testament is luminous. His short stories are parables of perfection. He is the perfect man to keep Christianity alive in an atheistic state. A man like Solzhenitsyn is only the tip of a very big iceberg. In fact the Christian ideology is very widespread in Russian society. And the reason is obvious. If you have a completely oppressive tyranny, ultimately the only alternative is Christianity.

Take Solzhenitsyn himself. He doesn't oppose the Soviet regime in the name of liberalism. He opposes it in the name of Christ. If you were to say to Solzhenitsyn, "I suppose what you want is one man-one vote," he would fall off his chair laughing. Take the letter that Solzhenitsyn wrote to Brezhnev and company before they deported him. It's absolutely fascinating. He says there that he thinks that in many ways the Russians have to go on with the dictatorship. The spirit that he evokes as an answer to materialistic Marxism is transcendental Christianity. He says that what is wrong with Russia is not that Stalin was a tyrant or that you, its present leaders, are a collection of buffoons. What's wrong with it is Marxism.

Q. *Let's talk about education. You say that Solzhenitsyn received his inspiration from Tolstoi, but only through an ideological error of the Soviet regime. Who will be the source of inspiration for our young men? Tolstoi died in 1910 but already his writings do not seem "relevant" according to our modern educational doctrine.*

A. In my opinion public education today is the greatest enemy that human enlightenment has ever had. Public education, supported by the media and by the scientific-humanistic consensus on which our society is based, represent the greatest menace to the free human spirit that has ever existed. Western civilization is not going to be destroyed by bombs; it is not going to be destroyed even by the Communists; it is going to be destroyed by its own educational system. That's my opinion — answering your question emphatically.

Generally, people think that I'm trying to be funny when I say that. They say, "That's a poor joke," or, "You're just being a humbug." I don't agree. It is my considered opinion, and I worry incessantly about my grandchildren: whether there is any possible alternative to them being put through this process which I really regard as diabloical.

Q. *What is the falsehood of public education?*

A. It's based on all the great fallacies of our times. It's based on the

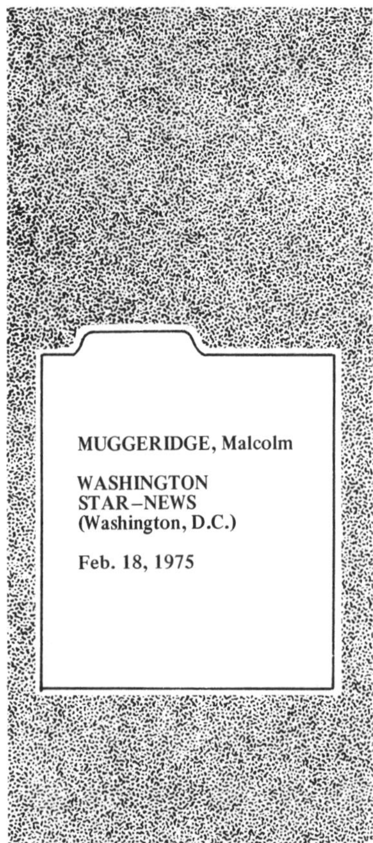
MUGGERIDGE, Malcolm

WASHINGTON STAR-NEWS (Washington, D.C.)

Feb. 18, 1975

idea of progress which is a completely absurd notion. It's based on the idea that through information and facts you can make people rational and enlightened. It's based on the completely fallacious idea of equality, as distinguished from brotherhood. It's based on materialist values which, I think, must always destroy man.

Q. *What is the fallacy of the idea of equality?*

A. If you say that all men are brothers because they all belong to a family whose father is God, that is true. The idea of equality, on the other hand, this so-called "self-evident proposition," which is not evident to me in the least, is completely phony and much different. The idea of equality produces inequality in practice. The idea of brotherhood, which is incapable of being anything but noble and true, has produced the only true unity of man that has ever existed. In other times when both a king and a peasant acknowledged on their knees together that they were the unworthy children of a loving God, that was a real bond. Such a bond was infinitely more significant than the king giving the peasant the right to vote, which is the most appalling thing that you can give to anybody.

Q. *Is contemporary education ensuring that we will never again have any great leaders?*

A. As Western Civilization nears its end, which I am quite sure it is, what happens is that there is a death wish, and part of that death wish is to destroy the possibilities for survival. One of those possibilities is producing some sort of disinterested, enlightened leadership. Similarly, the possibilities for the practice of the moral virtues, which are essential in a decent civilization, are being destroyed.

Q. *How did Christian values and democratic-socialist values come to be regarded as identical?*

A. Through the sentimentalization of Christianity, and from the turning away from Christianity's spiritual values in favor of sentimental-humanist values. If you translate Christian faith into terms purely of what are called "good words," whether arranged privately or through government agencies, then you completely destroy it. The one absolutely certain way of destroying Christianity is to say that when Jesus said his kingdom was not of this world what he meant was that it was of this world.

Q. *One gets the impression from your writings that you think that all men of action today are ridiculous. Has there ever been a man of action who was not a ridiculous figure?*

A. Not all men of action have been ridiculous. But, to me, there has never been a man of action who could measure up to the humblest mystic. I think that whatever wisdom is available to man comes not through men of action, but from mystics and clowns. These are the real sources of wisdom. Of course we must have a Caesar. Some Caesars are better than others. But, on the whole, the affairs of Caesar are not as estimable or as interesting as the affairs of God.

Q. *But how are the affairs of God proclaimed to us? Aren't they sometimes proclaimed through action?*

A. Sometimes. But not through men who seek power. And the worst seekers of power are the ideologues, men who seek power on behalf of an idea. This is another point that Solzhenitsyn constantly makes. He says that the awful thing about Marxism is its seeking of power on behalf of an idea. That is the most diabolical kind of all.

NEWMAN FOR ALL SEASONS

NEWMAN, Edwin S.
(1919-)

MILWAUKEE JOURNAL
(Milwaukee, Wisc.)

June 30, 1974

By MICHAEL H. DREW
of The Journal

NEW YORK

YOU WOULDN'T expect Ed Newman, who has made a career out of being unflappable in public, to sound very excited discussing his chances of becoming "Today Show" co-host. And you'd be right.

"I have no idea if I'm a candidate. I decided that I wouldn't even think about it unless they offered it to me," he said. "They're supposed to make an announcement in August.

"Off the record — oh, I deplore talking off the record in my new book, so ON the record — since it's taking so long, I suppose the decision is being made at the top of the company."

The network has been trying out replacements for the late Frank McGee — Tom Brokaw, ex-Milwaukeean Tom Snyder and Garrick Utley, for three. Newman got his hearing in May. That was about as necessary as auditioning Artur Rubenstein as accompanist at a voice recital.

Over the last 13 years, easy Ed has done four to six weeks annually on "Today."

"I did more," Newman said in his small office in NBC's news department here, "when Hugh Downs was host, with his propensity for driving, and riding horseback, into walls."

The wryness was pure Newman. It's appreciated most when it springs out full blown, before millions of viewers, in one of the hot seats the network regularly assigns him, on "instant specials."

But today he was leaning back in his office chair, thumbing through wire service copy as he prepared for 11:55 network radio news, another of his regular assignments. The answers come slowly, framed precisely, after consideration. Which is just what you'd expect from the author of "Strictly Speaking — Will America Be the Death of English?" his new book on language due out in fall.

"It's intended to be funny," Newman added helpfully. "There are chapters on various languages — Washington, sportswriting, food and travel, business, British, etc. The message is that if we all speak and write more specifically we'll be less likely to fall for foolish ideas."

That precision has marked his career, which began when he graduated from the University of Wisconsin, with a political science degree, in 1940. He returns to the state regularly for speaking engagements. The next ones are to the Wisconsin Broadcasters Association in Oshkosh July 19 and in Madison Sept. 20, for the dedication of the Vilas Communications Hall.

New Yorker Newman attended Wisconsin, from 1936 to '40, because his brother, newspaperman Morton Newman, went there first. After graduating, Ed did graduate work at Louisiana State University, served as a Navy officer in World War II, worked for the United Press and CBS and joined NBC in London in 1949. He became bureau chief there in 1956, worked in the network's Rome and Paris bureaus and has covered many major national stories — conventions, elections, assassinations.

Besides his newscasts and documentaries, Newman does regular radio features and conducts a weekly "Speaking Freely" interview for three NBC stations. The network donates the hour chats with leading newsmakers to 65 PBS stations, including Milwaukee's Channel 10, which carries it at 3 p.m. Saturdays. One of particular local interest, with bandleader Woody Herman, a Milwaukee native, is scheduled July 13.

But Newman's chief value is as the calm presence in instant specials during, or just after, major breaking stories. It's surely not Arrow Collar looks or pear-shaped tones that have earned him those assignments.

At 55, he's getting a bit jowly and his widow's peak is losing a battle with an encroaching forehead. Newman's strangulated baritone comes out as if it's doing pushups with his tonsils. It's coolness, perception and wit that distinguishes Ed Newman.

How did he go about becoming what somebody once described as "NBC's Instant Renaissance Man"?

"Well, the reading I do is connected with my work. I do very little for pleasure. For my 'Speaking Freely' interviews, I have to read the subject's books first — it's a matter of conscience. We've done 200 interviews in seven years — they're neither edited nor interrupted and communicate subtleties and nuances. It's a valuable program.

"I also read The New York Times, Time, the New Yorker, New York Magazine and bits and pieces of Newsweek, Business Week and Psychology Today."

Until a couple of years ago, Newman reviewed New York theater and was considered one of the best of the Broadway critics. Why did he give it up?

"Some very good people spend their lives doing reviewing but I'd had enough. It added hours to my working life and I didn't see it as a fruitful way to spend that time. You find that 75% of what you see isn't worth seeing. And when you're out 70 to 90 nights a year, a lot of reading doesn't get done. I see very little theater now."

Has Spiro Agnew's demise muted the criticism of the TV networks?

"Yes, that and Watergate, and it's unfortunate. During my talks, I find a great many questions, still, on how we function. People have a right to be concerned. We've never been sufficiently appraised."

Could the networks be serving us better?

"It's not my job to evaluate how they allocate their time. I don't find sponsors or meet budgets.

Would he like to be anchor man?

"Since it's the leading news job, it probably sounds churlish of me to say 'no.' But I'm lucky. I have great latitude, I like to travel and anchor men are confined. In recent months I've been in Russia, Switzerland, Poland and Paris."

When he's home, Newman and wife Rigel live in an E. 46th St. apartment, within walking distance of NBC. They have a grown daughter. Newman plays tennis in the summer and enjoys listening to classical music. Also, he said, "I have an interest in food and wine. But I don't get hysterical about it."

How about people who criticize "instant analysis" after network speeches?

"I regard it as the same kind of reporting done on newspapers all over the country, or like play reviewing. There's no reason for the president to be exempt from the news process.

"Ad libbing is easy sometimes. But when Bobby Kennedy's funeral train took eight hours instead of four to get to Washington, it was exhausting. I was on the air three days, the network couldn't supply help and I ran out of things to say.

"On State of the Union messages and others, you get just seconds to collect your thoughts. That's difficult, and also the most fun. When things go wrong, your job is most interesting. No one goes into this business looking for tranquility."

Maybe not. And no one yet has ever caught Ed Newman looking frazzled.

This Ney sayer has a special gripe

By RAY DE CRANE
Business Editor

Richard Ney, the maverick investment counsellor who shook the investment community with his book, "The Wall Street Jungle" four years ago, has done it again.

This time his "Wall Street Gang" (Praeger Publishers, $8.95) has been on the best seller list consistently since its June 5 publication date.

"I thought "Jungle" would bring a tide of reform," Ney said in an interview here.

"When it failed to do that I wrote "Gang" to show the public how they could beat the specialist at his own game."

The movie actor-turned investment counsellor (he starred with Greer Garson in Mrs. Minever a generation ago) singles out the stock market specialist as the villain who "rigs" the stock market in both of his books.

The specialist is supposed to buy when most investors are selling and to sell when most are buying. His function is to stabilize the market.

But since the specialist is also a dealer for his own account, this presents what Ney calls "a conflict of interest which would tempt a saint."

Never one to hesitate prophesying stock market turns, Ney said the Dow Jones industrial average is headed below the 800-mark after which it will then rally sharply.

"During the rally the specialists will have time to clear their shelves of all their accumulated stocks. After they have done this they will halt the rally, start selling stock short and the ensuing dive should take the average down to around the 700 mark."

"The New York Stock Exchange is like a dark alley," said Ney. "More muggings occur on the floor of the stock exchange in one day than on the streets of the country in one year."

The Wall Street foe cautions: "Never buy stock on the basis of a good earnings announcement, a broker's recommendation or a research analysis. Rather, buy off the information on the ticker tape."

NEY, Richard
(1917? -)

CLEVELAND PRESS
(Cleveland, Ohio)

June 25, 1974

The author feels that a close study of the tape will reveal what the specialist is doing. Instead of trying to beat the specialist, he suggests joining him. "Buy when the specialist buys; sell when the specialist sells."

To understand the specialists' practices, says Ney, "the investor must learn to think of specialists as merchants who want to sell an inventory of stock at retail prices. When they clear their shelves of their inventory they will seek to employ their profits to buy more merchandise at wholesale price levels."

Study the volume of trading in a given stock, Ney advises.

"Volume is like a guillotine," he said. "When the volume of trading goes up in a rising market, look out. The specialist is raising the guillotine in preparation for letting it drop."

Ney said the ticker tape in his own investment counselling office is programmed to give him the action on only 40 stocks, including all of the 30 Dow Jones industrials.

Official averages mean little to him, he said. He is interested only in the action, with emphasis on the volume and direction, of his key stocks.

"I only buy and sell at the opening prices," he said. "At the opening the specialist is pretty well forced to abide by his on-balance buy and sell orders.

"For the rest of the day, he said, the specialist is permitted to alter the price almost at will to serve his own ends.

Ney said that because of his order book which records the prices at which investors want to buy and sell, and at specificed prices, the specialist acts from the best of "inside" information.

"Everything I learned about economics in college cost me money in the stock market," Ney said. "If I had been an 'A' student I probably would have gone bankrupt.

"It was not until I understood the movements of the specialist and learned how to make my bets along with him that I started to make money in the market," he said.

Las Vegas-East: Manipulator's Game?

By WILLIAM H. WYLIE, Press Business Editor

Richard Ney is better known to moviegoers and watchers of the late TV show than to investors. But this may change.

The actor who played Greer Garson's son in "Mrs. Miniver" and the role of Clarence in "Life With Father" has found a new and possibly more exciting part—that of the Wall Street critic.

A man of great charm and articulation, the actor-turned-investment counselor hits hard at "The Wall St. Gang"—a catchy phrase that serves as the title of his new book published by Praeger of New York.

During an interview, Ney touched on some of his philosophy about the money game and how he believes the cards are stacked against the average investor seeking a fortune in stocks by using conventional methods.

He offered this analogy: "The only difference between Las Vegas-West and Las Vegas-East is that is Las Vegas-West the dealers aren't allowed to place bets but in Las Vegas-East they are."

When Ney refers to Las Vegas-East, he means the New York Stock Exchange, of course, and the "dealers" are the specialists who make markets in large blocks of stock. He contends the specialists use their customer's money to manipulate stock prices for the benefit of themselves and other "insiders"—scoring well in good or bad markets.

He writes in his book, "As merchants, specialists will expect to sell at retail what they have bought at wholesale. The longer specialists remain in business, the more money they will accumulate to buy stock at wholesale, which they then want to sell at retail."

As an investment counselor, Ney claims he has found a way to beat the system. (If you can't lick 'em, join 'em.) He says he has the ability to "read" the "insiders' moves" and contends that if investors follow the lead of the manipuators they can be winners, too.

Complicated systems of charting the market and other techniques used to detect the specialists' strategy are discussed in "The Wall Street Gang," Ney's second book about the money market since he abandoned Hollywood for greener pastures in 1961. His first effort, "The Wall Street Jungle," also was an attack on the investment establishment.

He shrugs off some of the time-honored indicators of whether a stock is a good investment or not. "The price-earnings ratio is absolutely absurd," he remarked.

"Also, every time there is a favorable earnings projection, brokers get on the phone to their customers urging them to buy," Ney continued.

He argues that neither the price-earnings ratio nor bright profit forecasts have anything to do with whether a stock will rise or fall.

Big block transactions and knowing how to understand them are much more enlightening, he said.

Ney advises buying only stocks on the Dow Jones list, contending this is where the big money is made in the market.

Also, if a broker gives an investor a bum steer, he ought to sue, Ney argues. "Even sue the stock exchange," he added.

He talks of Wall Street being tightly controlled by the so-called establishment and notes that President Nixon was a Wall Street lawyer, Maurice Stans, the former commerce secretary, a "notorious stock broker," and so on.

Ney is equally hard on the communications media, suggesting "they" are in league with the Wall Street manipulators. He claims newspapers dispense the Wall Street line and complains coverage of his pronouncements is banned by such publications as the Chandler papers in Los Angeles, Hearst in San Francisco and the New York Times.

Where is the market going? Are stocks finally headed for an upswing? Not at all, said the investment counselor who claims he has correctly predicted every market turn since 1961.

"The Dow will plunge below 800," Ney predicted, well under the 843 at which it opened Monday.

NEY, Richard

PITTSBURGH PRESS
(Pittsburgh, Penn.)

June 19, 1974

Peeking into the Very Private World Of Joyce Carol Oates

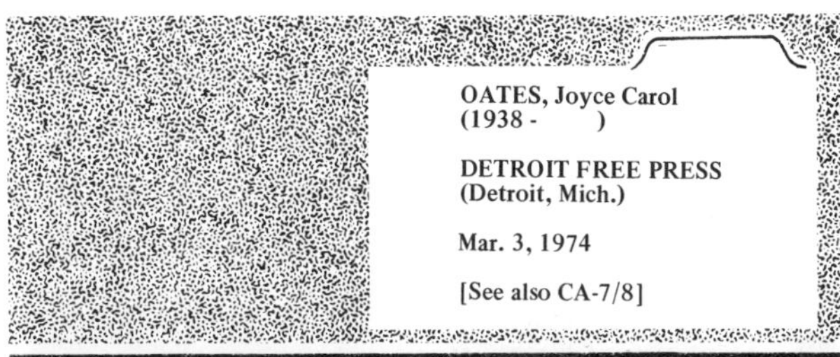
OATES, Joyce Carol
(1938-)

DETROIT FREE PRESS
(Detroit, Mich.)

Mar. 3, 1974

[See also CA-7/8]

"So much of real life is a disappointment. That's why we have art . . ." —*Joyce Carol Oates.*

UNIVERSITY OF WINDSOR
WINDSOR 11, ONTARIO
TELEPHONE: AREA CODE 519
253-4232
DEPARTMENT OF ENGLISH

January 18, 1974

Dear Ms. DeRamus:

I appreciate your interest in me, and I'm pleased that you liked the novel—what "the novel" needs these days is a touch of romance!—among other things—but I tend not to want much publicity, especially of a local nature. The subsequent nuisance of people—and cranks—makes any public notice a double-edged event, and I really prefef a very quiet, retiring life.

If you'd like to interview a fascinating person, contact John Gardner, novelist, Route 1, Boskydell Rd., Carbondale, Illinois. He's very successful and very talented and would give you a marvelous interview (and his house is extraordinary—including a 3-storey book tower with observatory on top.) You could write a much more lively story about him.

All best wishes, and I hope you understand my point of view—

Sincerely,
Joyce Carol Oates

◆◆◆◆◆◆◆◆◆◆◆◆◆◆

Dear Ms. Oates:

Indeed, I do understand. But my editors are hungry tigers, snapping at my wrists. They say they want you. A hint of bones, an outline of flesh, maybe even a trace of the spirit.

You have protected yourself well from "the nuisance of people;" you have built a high fence.

The telephone in your one-story house on Riverside Drive in East Windsor has been disconnected. You are no longer active in NOW (National Organization for Women) or any of the other groups that used to steal your precious time and take you away from yourself. You don't even throw those intimate little parties for twenty you used to give so well, doing all the cooking yourself.

You and your husband now live the "very quiet, retiring life": just one car, a Mercedes-Benz, the teaching you both love at the University of Windsor, and your work, always your work. You write like someone trying to get high on words, churning out novels, short stories, plays, poems, criticism, in the automatic way Detroit's assembly line workers slam together cars.

Detroit. That fascinates you. Even though you spent only five years here — from 1962 to 1967 at the University of Detroit — this is your town.

You wrote about Detroit in "them", tracing the lives of generations of lower-class whites. You wrote about Jules, the spirit of Detroit, a man redeemed, brought to life, by a murder he commits at the height of the Detroit riot.

(Continued from preceding page)

You write of people who are half-asleep. Passive people stirred only in the flesh. People who fall through brutal shock after shock, like sand through a sieve, before they finally learn to wrest control of their lives, to decide what they will do. Is that you?

"She's extremely shy or has been," says Pat Burnett, a friend. "When I painted her, she would almost go into a trance. She writes whole pages in her mind and hardly retypes.

"Since she took a year's sabbatical in England (in 1972), it has changed her whole perspective. She has much more faith in the world, a positive, optimistic outlook she had not held quite as much before.

"She came back and simplified her life: social activities steal so much time from you . . . but she's a good friend to her friends; I come from her feeling well-nourished."

Joyce Carol Oates. Born 1938 on an acre of farm land outside Lockport, N.Y., near the Erie Canal. Daughter of tool and die designer Frederic Oates, and his wife, Caroline. A quiet girl who used to sit in her room, reading. A girl educated in a one-room school house, and surrounded by flat, dull farmland lacking any "touch of romance." When young Joyce began writing stories, she added mountains and secret pathways to her world.

She wrote by hand until the age of 12 when she discovered the typewriter. At 15, she submitted her first work for publication — a 250-page novel about a dope addict redeemed by the gift of a black stallion. A New York publisher rejected it as too depressing for other 15-year-olds.

Later, she was to tell a magazine reviewer who asked her about those early days that "a great deal frightened me."

Something frightened her. And her face was always to wear the startled look of a victim, begging for her life. It is the face of a mystic, a deliberate dreamer, who has sometimes preferred art to life, form to chaos, and who has felt and been keenly moved by the menace of urban living.

She told the reviewer: "So much of real life is a disappointment. That's why we have art . . . Art does the same things dreams do. We have a hunger for dreams and art fulfills that hunger."

But in an article in the Writer, she admitted that the words, themselves, — their beauty, their precision — didn't really matter; it was the energy, the seething violence, they represented that was important.

"It isn't 'words' or 'style' that make a scene," wrote Ms. Oates, "but the content behind the words, and the increase of tension as characters come into conflict with one another . . . if violence erupts in fiction, it should be the outcome of tension; it should not come first, nor should it be accidental.

". . . Don't labor over little cameo works in which every word is to be perfect," she admonishes writers.

Joyce Oates earned a New York State Regents scholarship in 1956, which allowed her to enter Syracuse University. She plunged into a study of literature, turning out a novel a semester.

Later, came a masters degree at the University of Wisconsin and marriage to Raymond Smith, a tall, quiet scholar who was working on a PhD. They spent a year in Beaumont, Texas, where Smith taught and Joyce didn't. Then Detroit, where they both taught.

OATES, Joyce Carol

DETROIT
FREE PRESS
(Detroit, Mich.)

Mar. 3, 1974

"She was impressive, she had incredible recommendations," remembers Clyde Craine, the professor of English at the University of Detroit who hired Ms. Oates.

". . . We had no idea we were hiring a genius . . . She and her husband wrote to separate places under two different names . . . I didn't know I was looking at a husband and wife . . . but all we had was an instructor's slot, and her husband had a Ph.D.

"I told her I would like to see her . . . for an interview . . . I told him I was afraid I couldn't afford him."

Wayne State hired Smith, U-D took Ms. Oates. In Detroit, she made friends with other writers and artists and college people. She is still intensely loyal to these Detroit friends — and they to her. The picture they paint of her is not the somber, aloof picture some writers have painted.

"She has a marvelous sense of humor," says writer Marge Levin, "a great gift of mimicry. She doesn't like large crowds when she relaxes, but she's very interested in people. She observes people and can imitate them sometimes.

"She's fun to be with, not one of these heavy people at all . . . but she's a very private person."

Marge Levin is one of the many persons whose own writing has been stimulated by Joyce.

"She always tells me, 'Why don't you write a novel?' She can't understand how people can't do it. She said it's very easy, you just write out the plot in one paragraph and write every day."

Her days in Detroit did more for Joyce Oates than bring her together with new people — it gave her a tradition to write from, the so-called American Gothic tradition of exaggerated horror and gloom and mysterious and violent incidents. Only she did not view her writing as an exaggeration of the reality of Detroit.

"Things like that happen every day in Detroit," she told a Newsweek reviewer.

Since "them", which won the National Book Award in 1970, Joyce Carol Oates has written another powerful book set in Detroit, "Do With Me What You Will". It is the absorbing tale of a dreamy, passive woman married to a cold, insensitive lawyer who learns the primal power of fierce emotion and love when his wife leaves him for another man. The book, published on Oct. 12, 1973, has been on the Chicago Tribune best seller list and the New York Doubleday bookshop best seller list.

And "the words" continue pouring out. An Oates work, "Miracle Play", was recently produced off-Broadway by the Phoenix theater. Short stories pop from her electric typewriter like 30-second toast.

A filmscript entitled "Dawn" has been sold to Paul Newman and Joanne Woodward and the teaching goes on, too.

It all has to do with Women's Liberation in a way. With deciding whether one will cook, clean and have babies or devote a life to art. For Joyce Carol Oates, the fact of being a woman is secondary to being a spirit, a self a personality, encased in flesh.

"One has the time to contemplate an ego — to achieve a personality," she wrote in Atlantic, "only when he or she is liberated from the tyranny of physical burdens, whether they are external in the form of housework to be done eternally, or a commuting distance to be traveled, or whether they are internal, the processes of a body unaltered by technology and human choice.

"Throughout human history women have been machines for the production of babies. It was not possible for them to live imaginative, intellectual, fully human lives at all, if indeed they survived.

"The only reality is personality. Not sex."

Yes, Ms. Oates, I do indeed understand.

Very Sincerely

Betty De Ramus

Betty DeRamus

20 Years Later, O'Neill Revival Under Way

O'NEILL, Eugene Gladstone
(1888 - 1953)

MIAMI HERALD
(Miami, Fla.)

Mar. 24, 1974

O'Neill with his second wife Agnes Boulton and their son Shane.

By CANDICE RUSSELL
Herald Entertainment Writer

Celebrated, misunderstood and damned in his lifetime, Eugene Gladstone O'Neill died quietly, almost unnoticed, in November 1953. Many theatrical people were ignorant of his passing (New York being in the throes of a newspaper strike) and those friends who sought to attend the funeral were barred by his widow, the strongwilled Carlotta Monterey O'Neill.

An invalid whose hands shook badly, O'Neill had trouble thinking clearly toward the end of his life. A doctor in attendance described him then as "burned out, like a dried up cinder." The creative embers had cooled several years before, along with his reputation as America's foremost playwright.

It was an odd ending for a dramatist whose plays were widely produced and popular for most of his lifetime, a man who sought early in his career "to be an artist or nothing," who accepted three Pulitzer Prizes (a fourth was awarded posthumously) and a Nobel Prize for literature in 1936. Odd indeed that a man like this should die with his reputation in question.

"THERE WAS very little retrospective appreciation of him at the time," says Barbara Gelb, co-author with her husband Arthur of the mammoth, newly-revised biography **O'Neill.** "He was regarded, unjustly so, as a forgotten man, a playwright who had not made it."

Three years after his death, in the 1956-57 Broadway season, interest in the enigmatic playwright revived with productions of "The Iceman Cometh," "New Girl in Town" (a musical version of "Anna Christie"), "A Moon for the Misbegotten" and "Long Day's Journey Into Night."

Though critical fashion in the intervening years toyed with O'Neill's memory, his pre-eminence among American playwrights seems, at last, indisputable. The retrospective appreciation that he failed to receive at his death is exploding today.

The Gelb book is part of it, as is the second biographical tome by Louis Sheaffer, **O'Neill: Son and Artist.** "A Moon for the Misbegotten" with Jason Robards and Colleen Dewhurst is Broadway's most resounding success, following on the heels of James Earl Jones in "The Iceman Cometh" and the recent Chicago revival of "Hughie" with Ben Gazzara.

FOR HIS first season of the American Film Theater, Ely Landau chose "The Iceman Cometh" as one of eight specially subscribed movies. Regional theater companies grapple with O'Neill's complex characters and tackle the six-hour-long "Mourning Becomes Electra" as often as the more accessible plays.

Even television has gotten into the act. Last year, ABC presented a 2½-hour version of "Long Day's Journey Into Night" with Laurence Olivier from Britain's National Theater. This spring, public television will present "A Touch of the Poet", pairing Robards and Dewhurst again, along with Fritz Weaver.

With Broadway recently soggy from nostalgia, aberration and Pinteresque sophistication, the plays of O'Neill seem like fine, aged whisky by comparison. "He is just considered THE playwright this country has produced," says John Frankenheimer, director of the AFT's "Iceman" by telephone from Marseilles, where he has been shooting "99 and 44-100% Dead." "Oh, there are Miller, Williams and Inge, but history has not judged them. Also, there is a dearth of new writers, a condition which prompts producers to revive O'Neill."

"In the case of our O'Neill hit, it was a great shock to everyone," says Colleen Dewhurst. She also appeared in "More Stately Mansions," "Desire Under the Elms," and "Mourning Becomes Electra." "For years we had been thinking that the fabulous invalid was dead, that no one would pay to see serious theater.

"I THINK audiences now are able to face the emotional reality he brings to light. We're so bored with this kind of plastic world, the pseudo-analysis of everyone and everything in books that tell us how to react and why. We've become human robots without true spontaneous feeling, drives or passions.

"O'Neill insists on stripping off the layers and masks, so that we react fully to each other, even though it is agonizing. Each person in the audience for 'A Moon for the Misbegotten' takes it into his own experience and seems to go through his own catharsis."

"I guess he dramatized all the feelings that we all have," Jason Robards told a New York interviewer. "We don't play them out to that extent. But all those little seeds, he was able to dramatize and bust out of the proscenium arch and out to the people. You can feel it in this play."

O'Neill found tragedy in the mundane; the loser was an infinitely more fascinating subject for him than the winner. One of the rare heroic figures he wrote about was Kublai, the Great Khan, the aging ruler-seer of a vast Oriental kingdom in "Marco Millions." Fated to be forever mystified at life's trickery (his only grandchild, a young princess, dies of a broken heart over an insensitive fool), he is sublimely resigned and ennobled by the tragedy.

More commonly found in his plays is the doomed, God-forsaken figure smitten by self and circumstance. As O'Neill himself explained: "To me, the tragic alone has that significant beauty which is truth. It is the meaning of life — and the hope. The noblest is eternally most tragic.

"The people who succeed and do not push to a greater failure are the spiritual middle-classers. Their stopping at success is the proof of their compromising insignificance . . . Only through the unattainable does man achieve a hope worth living and dying for — and so attain himself."

THE FAILURE of cantankerous Cabot in "Desire Under the Elms" to be rid of a haunting loneliness; the failure of Yank in "The Hairy Ape" to come to terms with the society girl or anyone who represents the oppressive upper class that keeps his kind in line; the failure of black Jim Harris in "All God's Chillun Got Wings" to break loose from his crazed but beloved white wife; the failure of Josie to admit the goodness in herself in "A Moon for the Misbegotten" — these represent victories of sorts, as interpreted by O'Neill. For the playwright, it was enough that his characters had striven for the impossible.

(Continued from preceding page)

Though not a religious man himself, O'Neill expressed in his plays a need for faith in a faithless world — not the faith of dogma and creed, but the faith of hopeful vision. His plays reflect a sympathy for the underdog ("The Hairy Ape," "The Iceman Cometh.")

Not one to shrink at the wretched side of life — which he'd experienced first-hand — he pictured it truthfully dealing with such then-controversial subjects as infidelity ("Strange Interlude," 1926-27), the ethical question of abortion ("Abortion," 1913-1914), drug addiction ("Long Day's Journey Into Night," 1940-41), and mixed marriage ("All God's Chillun Got Wings," 1923).

His subject matter put him ahead of his time, as in "The Emperor Jones," (1920), called the first modern play to present the black man as a tragic hero. His body of short sea plays, peppered with what must then have been bold language, are hardly less unrelenting in their depiction of people and places as he saw them.

HE DRAMATIZED society in upheaval and pictured the class struggle, without permanently adhering to any political point-of-view. Presaging a now-chic ethic, he was against materialism, particularly in the later plays.

"A whole new generation is now aware of him," Mrs. Gelb says. "The country is aware of the values he championed. He has such wide appeal because his themes are eternal, global, elementary, about love, compassion, guilt. He writes of elementary passions, between man and woman, parent and child, in a way that is human and understandable."

The mirror his art held up to life gave an often uncomfortable reflection of his own private emotions. Again and again, he tackled the feelings he had about himself and his family in the plays, as if cleansing the demons of his spirit through the written word. He may have felt a whimsical condescension toward critics ("I like to read what the reviewers find in my plays — things I never knew I had put there"), but the autobiographical strains ferreted out by them were not to be dismissed.

IF THE findings of biographer Sheaffer are correct, O'Neill's one-act play "Exorcism" (1919) was based on his suicide attempt at 24. His third wife Carlotta was thought by some to be the model for "Strange Interlude" (1926-27) and "Mourning Becomes Electra" (1929-31). The uneasy relationship he had with his second wife Agnes was spelled out in "Welded" (1922-23).

The maddening ambivalence he felt toward his parents was repeatedly given voice in his dramas. Chained to them emotionally, as Sheaffer puts it, he remained to the end of his days more a son than a husband or father, longing for protection and an all-consuming love.

He played out these feelings in the autobiographical "Long Day's Journey Into Night." Written, he said, with "deep pity and forgiveness for all the haunted Tyrones" (the barely fictionalized O'Neills), he entrusted the manuscript to Carlotta with the stipulation that it not be published until 25 years after his death. He never wanted it performed. But it was hailed a masterpiece three years after his passing, when the Broadway production prompted a re-evaluation of his career. And it won him a fourth Pulitzer Prize.

The target of O'Neill's sorrow, confusion and resentment, the mother in the play is a drug addict. As a teenager, O'Neill learned that he'd been the inadvertent cause of his mother's addiction to morphine. Given the drug to allay the pain of childbirth, she had never rid herself of its soporific charms. Blaming himself for her destruction, yet harboring a hatred for this irresponsible woman, the playwright couldn't properly resolve his feelings.

ALSO PICTURED as O'Neill knew him, his vainglorious actor father is seen as a cruel skinflint who'd put his own welfare before the health of an ailing son. Yet there emerges O'Neill's affection for this parent who, like his alcoholic brother Jamie and his tormented mother, was merely a victim of his own pathetic impulses.

He may have captured the public imagination now because of his willingness to bare his soul's darkest secrets. "O'Neill dealt with truth and the inner self in ways that were very empathetic to his own life," says AFT producer Landau." I don't believe anyone else has interpolated personal experience into drama in such a fashion."

The seeds for a brooding romantic personality and a love of theater were sown by intense, expressive parents to whom he was born in 1888. Sixty-five turbulent years followed in which the young man savored racy Prohibition days, the succor of alcohol and a wanderlust that took him to three continents and gold-prospecting in Spanish Honduras. Seaman, actor, O'Neill was these things before deciding to write plays.

He became an unreliable husband to three wives and the half-hearted father to as many children (he abandoned his first wife and child). Attractive, magnetic when he wanted to be, he saw himself as the pawn of forces beyond his control; what he was sure of was that writing came first.

O'NEILL, Eugene Gladstone

MIAMI HERALD
(Miami, Fla.)

Mar. 24, 1974

"Beyond the Horizon," a realistic rural drama, won him his first Pulitzer Prize in 1920, followed two years later by a second for "Anna Christie," the seaside tale of a young prostitute's redemptive romance. He indulged in an inventive urge experimenting with masks in "The Great God Brown" (1925) and novelistic techniques in the five-hour-long "Strange Interlude." The latter play, the story of a New England woman's search for romantic fulfillment, won him a third Pulitzer. A busy decade for O'Neill: Between 1920 and 1931, he penned 21 plays.

BUT THEN his reclusive nature, as much as his recurring ill health and a foredoomed multi-play Cycle, accounted for O'Neill's work being bypassed in the ensuing decade. There was no new play of his for the 1934-35 theater season and there wouldn't be one for more than 10 years. Demoralized by the events of World War II, he would allow the turmoil to interfere with his writing.

Secretly he longed to forget Broadway, to have his plays merely published instead of produced. He rarely attended the theater, believing that his mind's eye could put on a better show than any cast on a stage.

Shunning the spotlight, he hid himself away with Carlotta in 1935 to proceed with a series of 11 plays concerning a family's development over 150 years. The never-completed cycle gave way to more urgent projects when O'Neill embarked upon "The Iceman Cometh" in 1939 and the torturous task of "Long Day's Journey Into Night" in 1940.

The occasion of his winning the Nobel Prize for literature in 1936 prompted his detractors to assail him in print. "At worst he has written some of the most pretentiously bad plays of our time," wrote the Saturday Review of Literature's Bernard De Voto. He went on to say, "Whatever his international importance, he can hardly be called an artist of the first rank; he is hardly even one of the first-rate figures of his own generation in America."

THOUGH THERE were O'Neill revivals (the tender nostalgic 1932 comedy "Ah, Wilderness!" received good notices) and plans for other projects in the succeeding years, it was not until the 1946 Theater Guild production of his new work, "The Iceman Cometh," that attention was again paid to the playwright. He emerged from seclusion to greet the flurry of popularity.

But the infatuation ebbed with the play's mixed reception. The critics tempered their praise with complaints that it was repetitious and over long. An anonymous Time magazine writer opined, "O'Neill does not seem to be a man of great, searching or original intelligence."

O'Neill's was a cry out of tune with the times. "People wanted escape after the war," Mrs. Gelb says. "It was a bleak, despairing period but O'Neill would not compromise or pander. The people were not ready for it. Also the production was not terribly good and so it was used as an excuse to discredit him."

This inhospitable atmosphere for his ideas, coupled with his waning creative energy, stilled the playwright's pen. In 1951-1952, Broadway presented two O'Neill staples, "Desire Under the Elms" and "Anna Christie," but both lasted for less than 50 performances.

As Sheaffer puts it, "Rather than signaling a new generation's interest in O'Neill, the productions suggested that theater-goers had relegated him to the past, that they considered him at best to be of historic importance, not of permanent value and interest."

His hypochondria was replaced by real ailments. Gradually, he was dying of palsy, Parkinson's disease and a rare disease of the cerebellum. He had written 70 plays, destroyed 10 and wouldn't live to see the production of six.

PERHAPS O'NEILL'S current popularity is attributable to his unfalsified view of life at a time when knowing the brutal truth is fashionable. He dissected man's fate in forthright, plainspoken language that communicated anguish and joy more substantially than any other playwright. It is eaay to identify with the pain he illuminates, the fractured desires, the goals always tantalizingly beyond reach.

"The country is going through a period of self-analysis", says Theodore Mann, artistic director of Circle in the Square and director of Broadway's "The Iceman Cometh." "O'Neill plays look at the American character and personality, and the country as well, much more severely than the works of other playwrights. His plays are not fabricated or illusionary or elusive, but concrete and specific. They provide that greater understanding which people are looking for."

"The theater to me IS life," O'Neill wrote, "the substance and interpretation of life . . . (And) life is struggle, often, if not usually, unsuccessful struggle; for most of us have something within us which prevents us from accomplishing what we dream and desire."

In an era rampant with sham and suspicion, it is simply that his plays make sense now; they are meaningful, lasting, and above all, true. Moreover, they speak to the times. O'Neill removes the sanctity of pretense while reinforcing the belief in dreams. He tampers with our illusions about ourselves while boosting our illusions about what life can be. His frank, edifying vision reinforces the poignancy of being alive.

About 1942, in refusing to release one of his scripts to a persistent Broadway producer, O'Neill wrote, "There will again be an audience able to feel the inner meaning of plays dealing with the everlasting mystery and irony and tragedy of men's lives and dreams . . ."

That time, it has become apparent, is now.

Gears Meshed, O'Neills Shift Into Second Book

GEORGE O'NEILL
. . . "it's hard to get a little time apart"

By PAT RAVENSCRAFT
Beacon Journal Staff Writer

When George and Nena O'-Neill came to town this week, his light blue ascot was the only theatrical hallmark of the New York City pair who made themselves and their marriage famous two years ago by publishing the best-seller "Open Marriage."

Other than that, the loving anthropologists might have been a suburban couple browsing through the glassware in a local discount house. Or chewing tuna sandwiches at the neighborhood park.

In town to promote their new book, "Shifting Gears," which tells how to find security in a changing world, the O'Neills finished each other's paragraphs without malice and joked about the technical difficulties which had delayed for an hour taping an interview for educational TV station 45 at Akron University. The problem, it seemed, was that Nena's mike didn't work.

"THAT'S OK," she told her husband. "I'll use yours."

Ironically, it would not have been enough. The couple who in their first book decried the "couple front," or expected joint appearances by husband and wife, now can satisfy no one unless they interview jointly — both talking and responding to each other in glib, talk show dialog.

"It's hard to get a little time apart," George complains. "What a couple front. We get tired of responding to each other."

His wife of 29 years, who moments before had been trimming one of his unruly locks with the scissors she keeps in her purse, broke in teasingly. "Can't you shut up? We're on the air."

THEIR FOCUS these days is no longer limited to marriage relationships. Instead, after interviewing people around the country about their problems, they've decided that individual adjustment is a prerequisite to ideal marriage adjustment. And individual adjustment, to beg the obvious, depends on shifting gears.

By that, the O'Neills mean deciding what one really wants to do at a given time in life, then exerting control over life by doing it without worrying what others will think. Shifting could involve changing careers or abandoning in mid-life goals that are no longer satisfying.

Admittedly, deciding what one really wants is a difficult first step, but one George O'Neill offers a simple solution for. (The simple, common sense approach to problem-solving is, after all, why their books sell, the O'-Neills say).

"The best thing," he suggests, "is to make a list. Put down every time in the last three months when you said yes but really wanted to say no. Or said no but really wanted to say yes. Then decide what is the worst and the best thing that could have happened if you had decided the other way."

He gave an example: "There's still the young woman who'll turn down a Friday afternoon phone call for a date that night because she doesn't want it to look like she doesn't have anything planned. If she wants to go, she should say yes and have a good time."

O'NEILL, WHO himself changed from an engineering career to anthropology, blasts also what they call "the maturity myth," which holds that by age 40 or 45 a person should have established his career, family and in essence "have it made."

NENA O'NEILL
. . . "nothing is wasted"

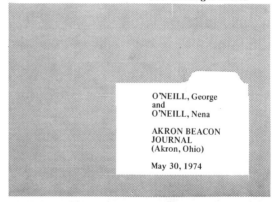

O'NEILL, George
and
O'NEILL, Nena

AKRON BEACON JOURNAL
(Akron, Ohio)

May 30, 1974

According to Nena O'Neill, the person who lives under the maturity myth "either makes it,is disappointed, and wonders 'Is that all there is?' or doesn't make it and feels like a failure."

"Nothing is wasted," believes the Akron native who spent her first college days attending evenings at Akron U. "I've done everything — statistical typing, nurse's aide work. In all of it, there's been something I could use later."

What confuses people these days, the O'Neills say, is the variety of lifestyles they learn about in the media. They compare the varied choice, which they call "the option glut" to a cafeteria, where some people want everything and eat too much while others can't decide on anything at all. In this respect, they see potential dangers in popular current movements like transcendental meditation, health food, youga, women's liberation.

"There is nothing wrong with yoga or women's lib for example," Nena O'Neill explained, "unless you throw yourself into it so you lose all balance and it runs you.

"Women's lib can give you a balanced view, to correct your life if it's not the way you want it. Instead, some in the movement become bitter about their past lives and the time they think they've wasted. Yoga can bring peace into your life."

Happy Hooligan and Frederick Burr WHO?

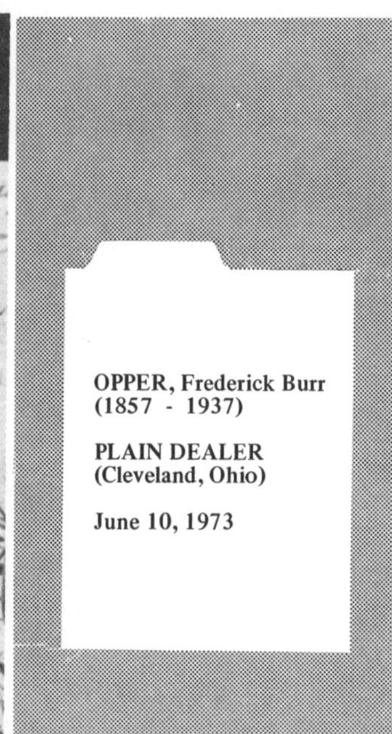

OPPER, Frederick Burr
(1857 - 1937)

PLAIN DEALER
(Cleveland, Ohio)

June 10, 1973

At his 77th birthday party, given by fellow cartoonists in 1934, Opper recreated Happy Hooligan

By Dwight Boyer

●One hundred years ago, just about this time of year, Frederick Burr Opper shook the dust of Madison's Main Street from his feet, climbed aboard an eastbound Lake Shore & Michigan Southern train and was seen only once again in the village of his birth. And that's probably why, although Madison has historical markers at the corporation limits proudly denoting the Lake County community as his birthplace, an inquiry as to the identity of the honored one there today gets a pretty much standard reply ... "Frederick Burr WHO?"

The tow-headed lad born to Lewis and Aurelia Burr Opper was apparently afflicted with an early but understandable distaste for hen house and barn chores and spent as much time as possible on the usual boyhood distractions such as gathering nuts in the fall, ice skating on Ford's mill pond in winter, skinny-dipping in the Grand River in the summer, occasionally hiking five miles to swim in Lake Erie. Higher education held no lure for him either so he quit school at 14 and got himself a job in the general store. This he found extremely frustrating and soon "accepted a position," as mothers were fond of saying, at the village newspaper, where he found the tasks of sweeping up, cleaning the press and setting type equally repugnant.

Hence the decision to depart, at the tender and impressionable age of 16, for the opportunities and rewards Horatio Alger and others were insisting lay in New York for all those pure of heart, honest, industrious and thrifty ... opportunities and rewards rarely encountered in little Madison. This was good thinking and understandable since the peak traffic period on the main thoroughfare was usually at eventide as children drove the cows home to be milked. And a mischievous dog, nipping at the heels of the beasts and spooking a couple of them, was about the most newsworthy item to be expected on any particular day.

Apparently unbeknownst to his youthful associates, Opper even then had dreams of becoming a famous cartoonist, as evinced by his scrawling of funny pictures on boxes and bags at the general store and on the walls at the newspaper. A realist despite his modest exposure to worldly affairs, he was obviously aware that spawning a career in this field in Madison was as unlikely as being appointed First Sea Lord of the British navy. Besides, country folks had a thing about young men yearning for artistic endeavor instead of honest toil in the fields and were prone to look upon them in a manner such as to cause great pain and mortification to their parents. Wise beyond his years, young Opper quickly shed the country bumpkin role, adjusting to the metropolitan atmosphere of New York with remarkable ease.

Opper's first job in the big city was lettering window signs for a department store. But the desired messages sought by management were also uncompromising, permitting no outlet for the inventive and creative instincts which burned to be released. So, in his spare time he produced a series of drawings depicting various characters in humorous or ironic situations, creations which he sold with little trouble to Wild Oats, one of the early comic papers. This led to a three-year stint with Frank Leslie's Weekly before embarking on an 18-year career on the rollicking staff of Puck, a prestige magazine heavy on humor. He quit Puck to accept a lucrative offer from the Hearst organization in 1899. William Randolph Hearst was inordinately pleased when Opper made his debut in his New York Journal.

By this time Hearst had successfully brought the Spanish-American War to an end and was again devoting his time to circulation battles with the other titans of the printed page in New York, notably the Herald and Joseph Pulitzer's World. ➡

(Continued from preceding page)

Early in the new century Opper was producing three Sunday comic strips and knocking out some devastating political cartoons, the latter, of course, voicing Hearst's policies and viewpoints. Comics and political cartoons were always signed simply "F. Opper."

The comic strips for which Opper gained fame were Happy Hooligan, And Her Name Was Maud, and Alphonse and Gaston. The first became a classic, the latter made excessive courtesy forever ludicrous.

Happy Hooligan and his family members, male or female, wore tin cans for hats, had round heads, button noses, impossibly long upper lips on mouths that appeared to be immediately above their necks. Happy Hooligan had big feet and a patch on each knee of his trousers. He was less than bright but infinitely more kindhearted than the other inhabitants of the cruel world. Everything he touched turned into disaster. And where the characters of other comic strips were often outrageously extroverted, Happy Hooligan was the eternal butt, rejected by nice people, arrested by the police, scorned and maltreated by animals, jostled and beaten by passers-by.

And the incidents that gave rise to the mayhem were never his fault. They began, usually, when he tried to do someone a good turn. He was the scapegoat, the dumb cluck, the man to whom all readers were superior except in good nature.

Maud, of And Her Name Was Maud, was an endless variation of an old and explosive theme . . . never let a mule turn his, or maybe her, back to you. Maud was an amiable-looking beast surrounded eternally by men named Si and Ezra, men who resembled, some said, Opper's neighbors back in Madison. The plot varied only in nonessentials. The last panel of each strip was, of course, Maud's revenge, a triumphant, double-barreled blast of the hind legs, propelling the innocent victim clear out of the panel.

Alphonse and Gaston, like Happy, became national celebrities and, ultimately, symbols, their names standing for the finest qualities. Their unbounded politesse carried them into spectacular difficulties which ordinary mortals, rude and aggressive, were spared. As they bowed and scraped, nature took its course and the simple became catastrophic.

Opper used his three strips as the occasion and his mood demanded. Some Sundays all three would appear, but often he would run only one. Maud was the first of the Opper strips to disappear from the scene. It was the thinking in the comic world that the growth of the newspaper syndicates increased rural readership tremendously. And the farmers, seeing themselves in the world of Maud, often as stupid louts, eventually rebelled at being the butt of Maud's jolting kicks. Alphonse and Gaston had a longer life, but Happy Hooligan ran for over 25 years. Cartoons of the day, including Opper's, had none of the sublety of today's strips, relying mainly on the obvious and a slapstick formula.

Very prolific, Opper also illustrated the works of famous authors including Mark Twain, Bill Nye and Finley Peter Dunne, whose Mr. Dooley stories achieved some sort of immortality.

In the field of political cartoons, and he somehow found time to accommodate Hearst, Opper was in a class by himself. The one-time Madison farm boy had the power to make political figures writhe or dance in anger and frustration or leap for joy,depending upon which side of any political fence they and Hearst happened to be sharing at the moment. Hearst, an avowed enemy of all the so-called trusts, including the steel, shipping, starch and school book trusts, apparently gave Opper free reign, and among his frequent targets were the Ohioans, Sen. Marcus Hanna and President McKinley. He often depicted McKinley as a White House puppet, with Hanna pulling the strings. Sometimes, too, Hanna was drawn as McKinley's nursemaid. On the other hand, President Theodore Roosevelt took delight in Opper's humorous depiction of his African safaris, frequently complimenting the artist. And like the early comic strips, the political cartoons had none of the sophistication or sublety of today and were often savagely direct, the kind that would send Spiro T. Agnew drumming his heels in petulant frustration.

OPPER, Frederick Burr

PLAIN DEALER
(Cleveland, Ohio)

June 10, 1973

Newspaper publishers and editors of the day made little effort to balance the news. They hit hard and often and fair play was seldom a consideration in their editorial credos.

Some years before his association with Hearst, Opper married Nellie Barnett and the couple had two children, Lawrence and Sophia. For most of his productive years the artist lived in their rural New Rochelle home. But when he was in the big city, he moved in exalted circles and was a member of the New York Athletic Club and the Player's Club. The famous and near-famous, none of whom had ever heard of Madison, O., sought him out.

There is only one documented record of Opper returning to Madison and that was in 1910, when he was already an established celebrity. It was apparently a spontaneous junket, and the doughty artist arrived by train unannounced but with three trunks and assorted baggage, expecting to check in at the local hotel for a three-week period of renewing old acquaintances. But the hotel had burned down, the boyhood friends were long gone and the reigning citizens were profoundly unimpressed with his fame and Broadway wardrobe. Completely disillusioned, he stayed briefly with relatives before fleeing to New York, never again to return.

Opper's amazing versatility and productivity continued until 1932 when failing eyesight forced his retirement. He died in 1937, still considered the dean of American comic artists.

Recognition of his accomplishments where he would most have appreciated it, in Madison, came long after Opper and the beloved Happy Hooligan had passed away, along with the generations they entertained and amused. Forty-odd years after the chagrined artist shook the dust of Main Street from his shoes for the second time, the state put up the signs at the corporation limits, paying homage to a hometown boy and reminding motorists of a once-famous artist and comic character, Happy Hooligan. There were brief ceremonies which belatedly rekindled a modicum of pride.

Frederick Burr Opper would probably have cherished every moment of it.

Remembering That Age

ORGEL, Doris
(1929-)

HARTFORD COURANT
(Hartford, Conn.)
June 3, 1973

[See also CA-45/48]

Sketch by Authors in the News

By Monica M.Carroll

"A writer between books is in a state of courtship," says Doris Orgel, children's book author. Ideas for stories can be found anywhere, but she frequently draws on the daily events of her reading audience between the ages of nine and 12 for her books.

Her most available source may be her three children and their activities, but her best source is the memory of her own childhood. Born in Vienna and raised in Yugoslavia and England, she came to the United States in 1940. But whatever the location, she remembers that children at that certain age, nine to 12, have their problems. "Their main preoccupation is the daily events in their lives, and though they are limited in what they can do to affect their surroundings, they are not limited in their fantasies."

While her recent books deal with reality in a child's life, Mrs. Orgel introduces only the fantasy that a child would in real situations. The very real, cruel teasing of a chubby girl in "Next Door to Xanadu" is offset by her escape into an imaginary friendship with a girl who lives next door. When a real girl does move in, the fantasies are transformed into ordinary make-believe play that two good friends share.

Mrs. Orgel's current project is a book about the difficulties one sixth grade has in establishing a student council in the face of adult opposition. Tentatively entitled "The President Is Throwing Meatballs," it also points up the self-consciousness and pre-adolescent teasing that get in the way of boys and girls working effectively at that age.

The problem of being treated like a child when one doesn't always "feel" like a child involves the 12-year-old girl of "The Mulberry Music." Even when Libby is mature enough to babysit her kindergarten-aged brother, her parents do not entrust her with the knowledge that her beloved grandmother, who often wears a mulberry sweatsuit, is dying. Libby must "assert" herself in her parents' eyes to prove that if children are "treated in a more adult way, they do respond," according to Mrs. Orgel. Libby alone must come to terms with her grandmother's death.

Handling the death of a main character, Mrs. Orgel deals realistically with the conflicts that arise in that age group without writing down to her readers. They're over the fairy tales of childhood and looking for something they can relate to right now. Mrs. Orgel also makes a point of using "real" names like Santaniello and Gleisheimer. She notices that the letters she receives corroborate these identification factors.

While readers' letters are "like icing on the cake" to her, Mrs. Orgel has found that a book "is all over and done with" once it's published. The only one "alive" for her is the one she's working on at any particular moment. But that, too, has its drawbacks. Great ideas for new stories come to her "often at night or in the bathtub" and only delay her current project. "A terrific idea is a copout," she says. "It may make you abandon what you're working on and rush headlong into something new."

Even while delaying projects, Mrs. Orgel has published 26 books since quitting the magazine and book publishing career that followed her graduation from Barnard College in 1950. A Phi Beta Kappa, she began by translating and adapting old German fairy tales for her American readers. The fairy tales and picture books grew up with her children, the oldest of whom, Paul, is now attending Oberlin College. Laura is a sophomore at Staples High School in Westport, and her 13-year-old Jeremy is busy as an ornithologist right now.

Mrs. Orgel enjoys reviewing children's books for The New York Times and attends the Bank Street Workshop to "get out and meet" her fellow children's authors.

Doris Orgel remembers a promise to herself when around seven or eight years old that she would "never . . . forget, no matter how old I got, exactly how I felt about things as a child . . . Making that promise was a lot easier than keeping it. But I do try to, with everything I write."

'We Don't Know Each Other'

BY DOROTHY WEDDELL
Free Press Real Estate Writer

Author and social critic Vance Packard, who two years ago called Detroit "one of the least appealing cities in North America," came to town this week as the first speaker in a guest lecture series at Lawrence Institute of Technology.

Well, not quite to Detroit. Lawrence Tech is in Southfield, and Packard is staying at a motel in the Metropolitan Airport complex.

But he agreed to talk with a reporter Thursday morning about what he sees as the problems with today's urban society. And the man who has picked at the hangnail of more than one American city is still a no-holds-barred observer.

The author of such best-sellers as "The Hidden Persuaders," "The Status Seekers," "Sexual Wilderness," "Naked Society," and, most recently, "Nation of Strangers" tilts at both cities and suburbs with equal vigor.

"One of the biggest problems with society as we live it today is that, by and large, we don't know each other. At one time, everybody in town knew who was a bum or a cheat or a liar. But today we're anonymous," he said.

Packard's last book dwelt on the gypsy-like mobility of Americans, how they're always moving from place to place without stopping long enough to put down roots.

"Usually, skilled working class people are the most stable in our society. But that doesn't hold true in Detroit because many of your working class are basically in love with Appalachia," he explained.

Packard bases this observation on conversations he's had with people down South.

"Folks talk about both Detroit and Cleveland as their working bases, but Detroit most of all. And on Sundays, the highways in Kentucky are packed, almost murderously, with cars bearing Michigan license plates and drivers tearing along to get back in time to report for their shifts at the factory."

The author — who used to give as many as 60 lectures a year but now limits his speaking enegagements to no more than 10 a year — doesn't use such terms as low or middle or high income groups. He speaks of working class and managerial class. And he assesses the community contributions of the managerial class with an edged tongue, too.

Free Press Photos by STEVE THOMPSON

PACKARD, Vance (Oakley)
(1914 -)

DETROIT
FREE PRESS
(Detroit, Mich.) Sept. 27, 1974 [See also CA-11/12]

"Managerial types are even more mobile. In your beautiful suburb of Birmingham, for example, people are in, then out, with the average stay three years," he said.

"The corporations who employ these wage earners pressure them into participation in community affairs. But it's a pseudo-citizenship. A role playing. They act as though they're involved, but they're not really."

Isn't any city doing anything right?

His not surprising answer: Toronto.

"Ten years ago I thought Toronto was a dull place. But today it's exciting. It has glorified its waterfront. Romanticized its ethnic mixture. It's clean and it's safe."

"And I think Detroit has started lots of exciting things since the riots. You're finally looking at your waterfront as an asset. Detroit isn't the only American city that had an ugly waterfront. Chicago and San Antonio are probably the only cities that have done otherwise."

Don't forget, said Packard, that we Americans have traditionally regarded a body of water as a nuisance that simply had to be gotten across. It didn't occur to us that it was scenic.

Asked his opinion of the contributions of American architects and planners, Packard took another swipe.

"I think they've been very negligent. Much too mechanistic and utilitarian. Bloodless and inhumane. I remember once being out at your Cranbrook Institute. Everybody was tremendously excited about a project that a student was working on. You know what it was? A mechanical metal tree that revolved and tinkled and who knows what else. It gave me the creeps."

Packard wouldn't talk about the book he's working on now.

"I'm sworn to secrecy by the publisher who hopes to bring it out next year. But the subject will have a broad range and take a look at how various sciences have changed our lives. One of those sciences will be psychology."

Before he leaves town, Packard will meet with a psychiatrist who is associated with University of Michigan.

Packard's lecture at Lawrence Tech was the first of a series, co-sponsored by the Lathing and Plastering Institute, that will feature such speakers as New York Times architecture critic Ada Louise Huxtable and builder-developer William Levitt.

Padilla, Once Poet of Hour, Forgotten in Havana

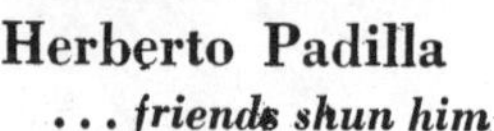

Herberto Padilla
. . . friends shun him

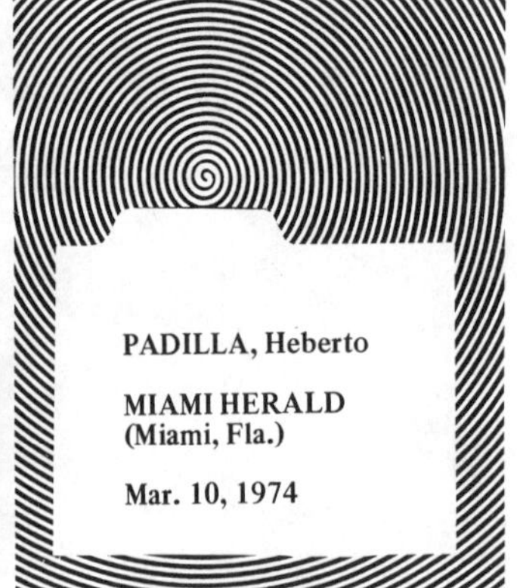

By FRANK SOLER
Herald Latin America Staff

Once he was the stalwart of Cuba's intellectual set. He wrote poignant poetry. He penned meaningful words. He won impressive awards. And for a time he rubbed elbows with the revolutionary elite.

But Heberto Padilla's name has succumbed to the relentless passage of time and — very especially — to the political whimsies of the Fidel Castro regime.

THE WRITER'S name no longer makes the headlines, as it once did. Not inside Cuba. Not outside the island. Nowhere.

Once he shook the literary world much like Alexander Solzhenitsyn is doing today, being jailed for writing critically of his homeland's government; now Padilla toils as just another faceless worker of the state.

Once, like Solzhenitsyn, he was the cause celebre that rallied a veritable who's who of leftist intellectualdom; the Jean Paul Sartres, the Simone de Beauvoirs, the Alberto Moravias, the Julio Cortazars and the Pier Paolo Passolinis all flocked to his defense.

Today Padilla is a literary non-entity, languishing in solitary non-fame.

The erstwhile poet extraordinaire and enfant terrible of post-Batista Cuban literature now earns a meager living by translating books from French and German into Spanish for the University of Havana.

OLD FRIENDS shun the modest Havana apartment where he lives with his wife, Belkis Cuza Male, also an award-winning writer.

The man who not long ago knew international adulation and acclaim today lives the life of a virtual recluse, a pariah whose solace is found in his one-year-old son and amidst his dog-eared books.

It was not always so.

For in the early days of heady revolutionary ardor, Padilla knew success.

He visualized great literary achievements under Castroism's tutelage; he foresaw new opportunities for budding writers and intellectuals; he anticipated an era of enlightenment where the individual Cuban might be allowed to express himself as he never had done before.

But by 1965, Padilla's exasperation with the government's ideological regimentation began undercutting his glory days.

In 1968 Padilla rose to the zenith of his career by winning the national poetry prize of the Union of Cuban Artists and Writers (UCAE) for his book "Outside The Game."

Ironically, it was this, perhaps his biggest triumph, that paved the way for his eventual disgrace and arrest.

The UCAE jury felt Padilla deserved the award. The government disagreed strongly, branding the book 'revolutionarily unfit."

"Outside The Game" won the award anyway. And the manuscript eventually was published — albeit with a lengthy precede warning that it was full of "skepticism, ambiguities, critical philosophy and anti-historicism."

INSTEAD OF abating with his literary victory, the attacks against Padilla took on a harsher tone; they were spearheaded by the armed forces which, in their official publication, Verde Olivo, claimed that the poet's "frankly counterrevolutionary" writings were aiding the CIA

Padilla became a marked man. So much so that by 1970 Cuban intellectuals muttered amongst themselves of the possibility of a Stalinist-like repression by the regime.

Their fears materialized on the night of March 20, 1971, when a score of government security agents fanned out throughout Havana and arrested several top intellectuals; among them was Padilla.

Most of those arrested recanted within hours; but they kept Padilla for 36 days as a prisoner of the state.

Finally, he emerged from jail, pale and haggard, ready to "confess," in a 4,000-word statement, that his writings indeed had slandered the Cuban revolution. A book he had been writing, "Heroes Graze in my Garden," was torn up.

Padilla's "self-confession" triggered an international outcry, even from intellectuals who previously had had nothing but praise for the regime.

The criticism infuriated Castro, who accused the foreign intellectuals of betraying the Cuban revolution; he described them as "disrespectful pseudo-leftists" who wanted to win "laurels in Paris and London instead of being in the front lines of combat."

Part of Padilla's self-confession included a denunciation of the intellectuals. "Everytime you have an opportunity, you launch your poisonous darts against Cuba," he said.

THE POET then dropped from public view.

He surfaced some weeks later as a citrus farmer in a government agricultural project outside the town of Cumanayagua, in Las Villas province.

There he and his wife lived in a modest two-bedroom home with a small living room, the principal feature of which is a vintage television set made in the United States.

It was only after expurgating his anti-revolutionary thoughts-sins for months on end that the government permitted him to return to Havana.

He is there today, in his apartment, leafing through some of the volumes in his extensive library, unaware still of the shock waves he once stirred.

Gloom spurs Peale revival

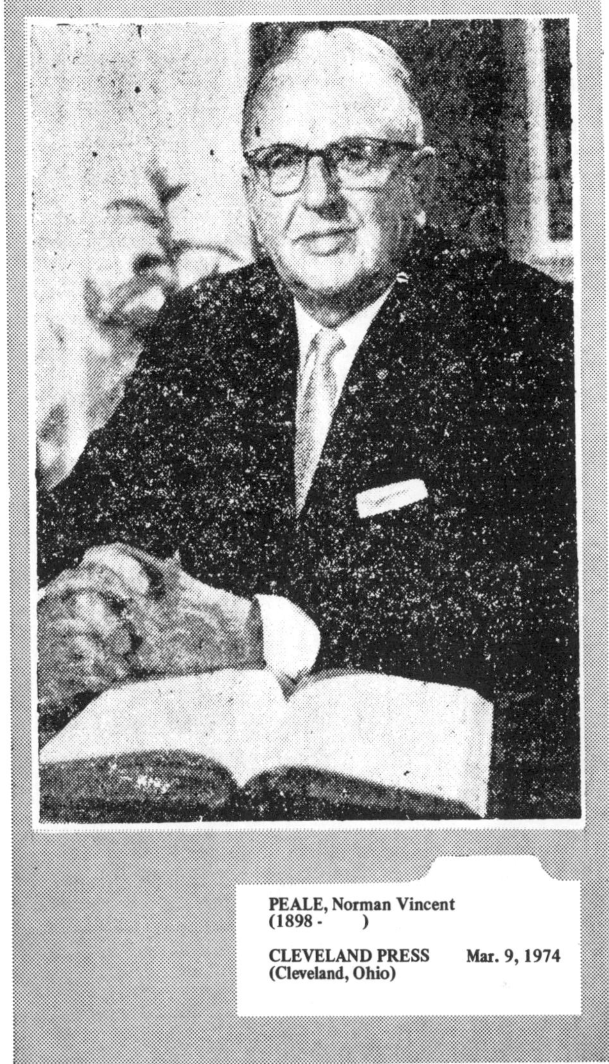

PEALE, Norman Vincent (1898-)
CLEVELAND PRESS (Cleveland, Ohio) Mar. 9, 1974

By GEORGE R. PLAGENZ, Religion Editor

Few television performers make it back to prime-time TV when they are in their 70s. Norman Vincent Peale has. He will be 76 in May.

His 10 p.m. Sunday program on Channel 61 here is attracting more viewers than the Sunday night movies, part of whose time-slot he took over in January.

"Our ratings are definitely up since Dr. Peale came on," says a Channel 61 spokesman.

Peale, the clergyman whose book "The Power of Positive Thinking," rose to the top of the best-seller lists in 1952 and stayed there for two years, is heard also on 39 other TV stations in the U.S.

The sponsors, Guideposts magazine, say Peale will be on 50 major stations by spring. This is his first television venture in 20 years.

Some TV critics — who normally rate even the best religious programs on a par with "Ozzie's Girls" are joining in the praise of the Peale revival.

"Dr. Norman Vincent Peale came on like gangbusters last night," wrote the TV writer of the Philadelphia Evening Bulletin, Rex Polier.

"I was merely dial-switching after watching my favorite program, 'Upstairs, Downstairs,' " said Polier, "when I came upon Dr. Peale. The sheer forcefulness, humor and vitality of the man was such that I stopped dial-twisting and watched — spellbound."

What held the TV critic "spellbound" was the same thing that gripped Peale fans 20 years ago. The times now, Polier believes, are ripe for the old Peale message of positive thinking.

"When everybody is on the verge of saying, 'What's the use?' Peale's simple, powerful little pep talks are immediately useful," Polier says.

He says Americans "in this most confusing moment in our history need to be told all over again that they CAN overcome their problems and that they CAN realize their dreams."

Polier found Peale as convincing as "listening to Vince Lombardi before a football game."

(Continued from preceding page)

There may be other reasons too for Peale's sudden reappearance center stage on the American religious scene.

"With all the outer supports crumbling — government and, the rest — we've been thrown back again on our own individual resources," says a Peale listener in Bay Village.

"We were carried along effortlessly for so many years on the tide of affluence and well-being that we lost the knack of self-reliance and how to depend on our inner selves."

Dr. Peale, this listener believes, "can not only pick up our flagging spirits. He can teach us the technique for taking hold of our lives."

Others cite Peale's continuing belief in America at a time when faith in this country is at one of its lowest points in history as another reason for his appeal to depressed Americans in 1974.

"People want to go on believing in this country," says a clergyman here. "Peale tells them they still can. He talks of 'the things that made America great — faith, discipline, love of country' in a way that can reawaken the banked fires of patriotism in a lot of people."

In a story in Reader's Digest on the returning POW's — the magazine's philosophy and Peale's are alike at practically all points — Peale wrote movingly of a "black sergeant weeping on the shoulder of a white Marine captain as a band played 'America the Beautiful.' "

He recalled a Fourth of July in his home town of Brownsville, O. — "flags snapping, trombones blaring, red-white-and-blue bunting on the speakers' platform, the gleeful stutter of firecrackers, the hot sunshine, the gentle sky, and over everything a wonderful, soaring sense of pride and patriotism and belonging."

To still others, Peale is a bit of nostalgia which takes them back to "the happy days" of the '50's.

"Who else from that period in our lives is still around to remind us of those better times?" somebody asks.

Peale himself claims his message is no different today from what it has always been.

"My principal emphasis has always been on God," he says. "Positive thinking is the way we bring God into our everyday life. That has always been my message."

The minister of Marble Collegiate Church in New York City since 1932, Peale preaches every Sunday to overflow congregations of 2500. He still lectures extensively — principally to businessmen's groups.

His monthly inspirational magazine, Guideposts, has risen to 21st in readership among all U.S. magazines. Circulation is 2½ million.

He has just published another book, "You Can If You Think You Can" — his first book in the positive-thinking field since 1967.

Peale himself is an example of many of the old-fashioned traits he extols. It was perseverance, for example, which made him a best-selling author.

His first books, written before World War II, were not successful. "The Art of Living" was written in the popular anecdotal and inspirational manner of the later Peale books. But instead of being a program for the mastery of life, it counseled escape.

"The world is too much for us," Peale lamented. "Many yearn for a little cottage by the sea, for old grape arbors and green meadows with golden cowslips." Religion, said Peale, is that cottage and that meadow.

His second book, "You Can Win," still suggested that people should react to the harshness of the world with flight rather than competitive fight. But the theme that would establish Peale as the foremost expounder of the doctrine of positive thinking was becoming apparent.

If, said Peale in the book, you "saturate your subconscious mind with good, clean and noble thoughts, by and by your subconscious will send up good and clean and noble thoughts to rule you."

Peale's first best-seller, "A Guide to Confident Living," was published in 1948. In 1952 came "The Power of Positive Thinking."

Religion was no longer "the cottage and the meadow." It was now a power that could make a man a winner against all odds. It could turn business failure into success and sickness into health.

"The ideas or thoughts which finally determine our actions and character are not those we receive and examine in our conscious mind," said Peale. "They are the thoughts we send into the subconscious" (which Peale later identified with the soul).

A man, in the last analysis, said Peale, "is what he has been predominantly sending into his controlling thought center" — or the subconscious.

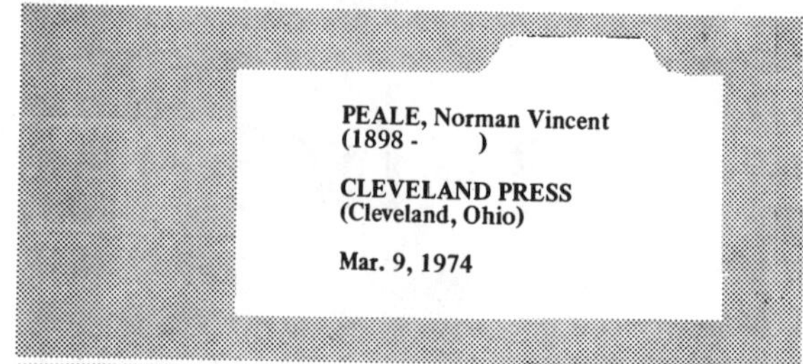
PEALE, Norman Vincent
(1898-)

CLEVELAND PRESS
(Cleveland, Ohio)

Mar. 9, 1974

The technique Peale recommended was to repeat "health-producing, life-changing, power-creating thought conditioners."

"Savor the meaning of each 'spirit lifter,' " he counseled. "and feel it drive deep within your nature."

These spirit lifters were to be repeated before sleep with the words, "The spirit lifter lies embedded in my mind. It is now sending off through my thoughts its healing, refreshing effects."

The power at work here, said Peale, was divine.

"In the subconscious," he wrote, "God presides with his illimitable power. If you are allowing yourself to be defeated, practice thinking positively and focus your thoughts on God. This inward power is so tremendous that under stress and in crises, people can perform the most incredible feats."

As a critic remarked, "Peale had re-discovered the power of suggestion over the human mind. 'The Power of Positive Thinking,' catching its audiences full in the throes of post-Korean, McCarthyite anxiety, running up a sale of two million copies in the Eisenhower years, simply wove status and success into a smooth identification with the mind-cure techniques, thus becoming the Bible of American auto-hypnotism."

Catching his audiences now in the throes of Water gate, energy-crisis anxiety, is Norman Vincent Peale ascending to another plateau of popularity?

S. J. Perelman Is Back on Broadway

Bulletin Staff Photos by Frederick A. Meyer

By **WILLIAM T. KEOUGH**

Of The Bulletin Staff

AS THE CURTAIN rises on the Manhattan digs of humorist-playwright-raconteur S. J. Perelman, we find the great man ensconced on a sofa, cigaret in hand, deftly fielding queries from a mild-mannered Bulletin reporter.

The place is tastefully decorated in early steamer trunk. Two large trunks are, in fact, parked behind the sofa where they serve as end tables, but obviously are ready for a quick getaway at the drop of an expense voucher.

Perelman has squeezed this interview in between rehearsals for a revival of his 1962 play, "The Beauty Part," which just began a four-week run for subscribers at the American Place Theater in New York.

"What do you do when you're not writing?" the reporter asks.

"Chase women," says Perelman.

He waxes chauvinistic for a few moments, discussing the relative merits of Penthouse and Playboy magazines. "The gals are just as pretty as ever," he opines, "although I still think a bit of concealment is a good deal more attractive than complete revelation. I suppose it's all very healthy to let it all hang out, but I still think a flash of undergarments is necessary to give it spice."

At the somewhat ripe age of 70, Perelman has settled for the nonce in a hotel overlooking Gramercy Park. "It's as good a place as any as some sort of base," he says.

From there he can keep in touch with his book publisher, the producers reviving his play and the New Yorker magazine, which "has about six of my pieces backed up on their bank; I guess they'll get around to running them someday."

91-Acre Farm

Four years ago, after his wife died, Perelman sold his 91-acre farm in Erwinna, Bucks County, where he had lived about 37 years, and moved to England. "I've had all of the rural splendor that I can use," he said, "and each time I get to New York it seems more pestilential than before."

In 1971 he took an 80-day trip around the world to mark the 100th anniversary of Jules Verne's fantasy about Phileas Fogg. This inspired several pieces for the New Yorker that will be part of a book coming out next spring called "Vinegar Puss."

Perelman won an Academy Award in 1957 for the screenplay he wrote for Mike Todd's epic film, "Around the World in Eighty Days." Actress Hermione Gingold read his acceptance speech, in which he said he thought he could benefit more from a good night's sleep than from attending the ceremony to accept the "bourgeois bauble" in person.

He abandoned his self-imposed exile to England in 1972 and returned to New York, saying he found "there's too much gentility in London — too much couth."

PERELMAN, S(idney) J(oseph)
(1904 -)

PHILADELPHIA
BULLETIN
(Philadelphia, Penn.)

Oct. 27, 1974

"The rye bread in London is below par — it has no caraway seeds on it," he explains. "And the corned beef, which they call salt beef, is sub-standard. And they've never heard of bagels, which I consider a flaw in the English character."

Using excellent hindsight, Perelman now admits to a touch of myopic planning when he sold off all his Bucks County land.

"I'm sorry I didn't save a couple of shabby acres out of the spread to build a quiet hideaway," he says. "The Delaware Valley is really one of the loveliest sections in the world, and I really get very homesick for Bucks County. The one drawback was that in the summer the heat was as oppressive as it is in Bangkok.

(Continued from preceding page)

"I do get back once in a while — to Bucks, that is, not Bangkok. As a pledge, I left a 1949 MG — which I had bought in Siam strangely enough — in a farmer's barn in Erwinna. I occasionally go back to see if the pistons are still rusted up so no one can steal it."

Magazine Pieces

Shortly after his return to New York in 1972 he took off again for the Far East to write a series of magazine pieces.

"I'd always wanted to see the Seychelles," he says. "That's a group of islands in the Indian Ocean, about 1,000 miles off the coast of East Africa. They're supposed to have the most beautiful women, and legend has it that all the cables in the world cross there.

"Late at night, so they say, radio operators on all the ships at sea exchange dirty stories and the cable office in the Seychelles is supposed to have the greatest collection of raunchy humor in the world."

"But how were the women?" the reporter asks. "And were the jokes any good?"

"The women have very large posteriors and they're kind of idiotic," Perelman replies. 'Bad musical comedy types, I'd say. I was disappointed in the jokes too. I think you could do better in a Philadelphia barbershop or in Captain Billy's Whizz-Bang."

The conversation turns to Perelman's health, which he says is holding up admirably. "I can still sit in a bar for eight hours," he says, "although I'm not a notable barfly or drinker. I can't pride myself for that.

"I know a lot of writers have been heavy drinkers, though. Especially if they came from newspapers, Heywood Broun Sr. used to put away a few and Ben Hecht had some fabulous drinking stories. Then too, I guess there's a drinking tradition in literary circles that you can trace back to Ben Jonson and those people who seemed to spend all their time in the Mermaid Tavern.

"Most of them died in their 30s too — writers like Christopher Marlowe. They all led dodgy lives. Newspaper men still drink, don't they?

"When I was in London I did some pieces for the Sunday Times. As soon as they were done with work the entire staff would move from the city room to the bar across the street. Is it like that on the Philadelphia newspapers?"

Very Sober Lot

Perelman is assured that Philadelphia journalists are by and large a very sober lot.

"Ben Hecht used to tell a marvelous story about a time when he was on a Chicago paper, about 1911 or '12," Perelman says. "The windows were covered with dust, so they set up a stage and a window cleaner got up there with a bucket and a sponge.

"Out the window the cleaner could see the rear of another office building and there, before his eyes, was a boss quite romantically involved with a secretary.

"The window cleaner called down to the staff and they all got on the platform and started looking out the window, which caused the boards to bow a couple or feet in the middle. Ben Hecht looked out and saw the name on the office where the boss and the secretary were.

"Hecht looked it up in the book and called the number. They could see the boss interrupt his romance to answer the phone. Then Hecht, in a low, lububrious voice said, "This is God. Aren't you ashamed of yourself?"

Perelman says he'll be 71 on his birthday, which falls on Feb. 1. "That makes me an Aquarius, although I'm not sure what that means," he says.

Memorable Birthdays

Asked if any of his birthdays have been very memorable, Perelman says:

"I remember the glorious occasion when I became 57. Much to our surprise, my wife and I received a large expensive box from Pittsburgh. It was from the Heinz Soup Co., which is famous for its 57 varieties.

"But they only sent me 39 varieties — not 57.

"Apparently this is an automatic thing that Heinz does when anyone of any prominence becomes 57. They send him 39 cans of soup. I don't know that this crank fact has ever been published before. It certainly surprised me."

Perelman says he has supported himself as a freelance writer since 1925, including stints writing the Marx Brothers films "Monkey Business" in 1930 and 'Horsefeathers" in 1932.

"I was really spaced out when I saw Groucho in 'Animal Crackers' on Broadway in 1930, so I sent a card backstage telling him how much I enjoyed it," he says. "He suggested I write a thing for radio for the Marx Brothers and he teamed me with Will Johnstone, who was on the 'New York World.'

"We evolved the idea of the Marx Brothers as stowaways in four barrels and took it to them. To our vast surprise, they said, 'This isn't a radio program. This is our next movie.' The next thing I knew I was on the Chief to Hollywood."

'Reading Trash'

Perelman says when he was growing up in Providence, R.I., "I used to take out seven books at a time from the library and sit in the kitchen, with my feet in the oven, eating cookies and reading trash.

"I think trash is a very important part of youth reading," he says. "It acts like a mulch and helps fertilize the brain and allows creative ideas to germinate and grow. A writer has to be a reader. And now a pompous remark:

"I don't think the present writers read enough. I'm a great believer in tradition. None of us springs full blown from the head of Zeus. We're all part of the flow of a river of life. If you know the past you can fit in and flow along with the river.

"Frankly I think some of the modern writers and painters have divorced themselves not only from the past but from reality, they're so far out. I think the drug culture did this with its writing."

Regarding his own writing, he says, "I'm what they call a bleeder in the trade. I don't have any real facility and I have to work it out slowly. I really envy the people who can write rapidly because I frequently wonder whether it's worth the trouble agonizing over it."

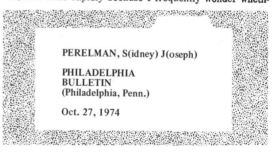

PERELMAN, S(idney) J(oseph)

PHILADELPHIA BULLETIN (Philadelphia, Penn.)

Oct. 27, 1974

Turning to more pretentious subjects, the reporter asks Perelman for his views on the question, "Whither mankind?"

"Well, we're all headed for extermination," he says. "It's only a question of when. And I have profound faith in mankind's ability to destroy himself and the earth.

"We've made great strides in that direction, and with the assistance of whizzes like Richard Nixon we're gonna get there pretty fast."

As a parting shot, the reporter asks, "Do you have any advice for the current generation?"

"Just, 'Duck, for the night is coming.' "

The reporter ducks and exits stage left.

Fifty Years Of Mysteries

by TIM DUMONT
Staff Writer

A paperback publisher touts him as "the most dazzling mystery writer since Rex Stout.' Author-editor Ellery Queen calls him "a pro among pros." Judson P. Philips of North Canaan has been around long enough to earn those accolades. He's been pounding out detective stories for 50 years and, at 70, still maintains his yearly output of four novels.

His dedication to the genre was rewarded last spring when the Mystery Writers of America — a professional society he helped found — presented him its Grand Master Award for outstanding accomplishment in the field. The trophy is a small bust of Edgar Allan Poe, the same statuette used for the annual "Edgar" award for the best mystery novel.

Fans are more likely to recognize Philips by his pen-name, Hugh Pentecost. Three quarters of his work is done under it, but he retains the Philips byline because "if I were to do them all under the same name, they would begin to tread on each other's toes." He has produced about 100 novels and countless short stories.

An indefatigable producer, Philips juggles a variety of side enterprises when not turning out fiction.

He contributes a political column and book reviews to the Lakeville Journal and does a weekly half-hour talk show on radio station WTOR in Torrington. There, he expounds his "somewhat liberal" political views and plugs Sharon Playhouse, which he founded, and other theatrical ventures.

In 1949 he became co-owner and editor of the Harlem Valley Times, a weekly newspaper in Amenia, N.Y. He sold his interest after seven or eight years when he became too busy to stay involved.

His first fiction sale was to Argosy Magazine 50 years ago, when he was a junior English major at Columbia University and was inspired to a writing career by the late poet Mark Van Doren, his faculty adviser.

"I never had any job in my life (except summer work) that didn't have to do with writing," he said with satisfaction.

His first professional job was reporting high school sports for the New York Tribune. His love of athletics had led him to stints on Columbia's football and baseball teams, where he was in the same lineup as baseball great Lou Gehrig.

"All this time I was writing fiction," he recalls, adding he was drawn to mysteries by their drama. "I wanted to be an actor ... When I was about 18, I got to make some silent movies."

He also selected the mystery field because there was a market for it, one which has been kind to him while he has watched less adaptable practitioners wither on the vine.

"I've tried to write stories that fit into tne current climate," he said, and this forces him to amend his style constantly. He balances this with a lifelong quest for literary economy that has led to spare, straightforward prose and a uniform book length of about 185 pages.

"I think he's one of the best consistent mystery writers," said Mrs. Margaret Norton, his friend and mystery editor at Dodd, Mead and Co. "He never repeats himself."

Philips' five decades of pleasing readers and appeasing editors has led him down many streets. He started with the "pulps," where he turned out 80,000 words a month during their heyday in the 20s and 30s. He turned to radio scripts when the pulp market tapered off and graduated to the "slicks" — Saturday Evening Post, Collier's, etc. — where he flourished until Hollywood beckoned in 1929.

He collaborated on the first "talkie" script for John Barrymore, something called "General Crack."

"After awhile I decided I didn't want to work in Hollywood," he said. "There were too many fingers in every pie."

PHILIPS, Judson Pentecost
(pseud. Hugh Pentecost)
(1903 -)

HARTFORD COURANT
(Hartford, Conn.)

June 30, 1974

He returned to the big magazines and did so well financially that he founded Sharon Playhouse in 1951 and bankrolled it during its fledgling years. He headed the professional theater until 1972 and remains one of its governing body.

It was there he met Norma Burton, an actress who became his wife in 1951. They have a son, Daniel, and he also has three children by an earlier marriage.

While the theater was in its infancy, Philips also turned to television writing, where he scripted about 18 episodes of "The Web." He lost his program clearance when the advertising agency for the cigarette sponsor objected to his pruning an overlong scene by having a dying villain smoke a short cigarette. He recalls with amusement that the sponsoring cigarette was one of the nation's first long varieties.

He also wrote for some early TV greats: "Studio One," "The U.S. Steel Hour" and "Robert Montgomery Presents." By coincidence, the now-retired Montgomery is his neighbor on a farm in Canaan Valley.

With his Hollywood experiences still caught in his craw, Philips decided to fade from the scene when production gravitated to the West Coast in the mid-50s.

He admits television was a great way to make money, but adds there was "no way to have any fun at it" because there was so much interference with the writing process.

His magazine writing hit a crisis in 1957 when Collier's and American magazines both folded within months. This cost him $40,000 to $50,000 income per year.

As his income became ever more dependent on book-length material, Philips defied a trend toward series characters. "I didn't have any 'Sherlock Holmes.' I thought as a writer it limited me," he said. Nevertheless, he succumbed to the urgings of his book publishers about 10 years ago.

"God help me, they were right. The paperbacks, which hadn't wanted to play ball with me, suddenly began to," he said. Today, his paperback reprints are regular attractions on the racks.

Appearing under both pen-names, his continuing characters are Pierre Chambrun, suave manager of a chic New York hotel; Peter Styles, Newsweek-style reporter; John Jericho, artist-crusader; and his newest, Julian Quist, a public relations genius.

The three Quist hardcover editions will make the transition to pocket book format this year when Philips produces an original fourth title for Award Books. The package will include a printing of 200,000 copies per volume.

"Paperback people today don't like to publish isolated books," he concedes.

He also maintains the "Whodunit" is dead. Nowadays, the reader knows the villain's identity 80 per cent of the time. The emphasis instead is on conflict, stratagems and detail, he explains.

He expects to maintain his schedule "as long as God is willing" and, in fact, will accelerate it this year. The new Quist book will mean an output of five novels instead of four, and Philips has been working about a year on a partly autobiographical novel "about guilt." A sporadic and difficult labor, it is about half done and he expects it to be a departure from his usual form.

He also has two books under option for films: one to an Italian production company, another to a TV movie producer.

Although he bemoans the decline of the hardcover book trade, he consoles himself with the knowledge that two of his last three titles also have appeared in Cosmopolitan Magazine digest versions.

"That ought to prove to you that you're up to date," his publishers reassure him. □

By George, He'll Try Anything

For the past several seasons, George Plimpton has intended to play hockey with the Boston Bruins. But something or other has always gotten in his way.

This fall he was in Zaire covering the Ali-Foreman fight for Sports Illustrated and hobnobbing with his old boxing opponent, Archie Moore.

So he'll try for next year, Plimpton assured about 200 Marquette Universtiy students Monday night during a talk at the Union Ballroom.

"I expect to play goal," he said. "It's the only position I could possibly play because I can barely skate."

Being unable to play well has never kept Plimpton, 46, out of professional sports. He played last string quarterback with the Detroit Lions in 1963, losing 35 yards in four plays; subbed two minutes for John Havlicek of the Boston Celtics and never touched the basketball, and played in the professional golfers' tour with an 18 handicap.

PLIMPTON, George (Ames) (1927 -)

MILWAUKEE JOURNAL (Milwaukee, Wisc.)

Nov. 12, 1974

[See also CA-21/22]

Way of Life

"Trafficking in someone else's profession," as he puts it, has been Plimpton's way of life ever since he was a student trying out for a slot on his college humor magazine, the Harvard Lampoon. As an initiation stunt, he entered the Boston Marathon two blocks from the finish line, and lost.

Plimpton, who is the editor of a small, New York based literary publication called Paris Review, has written books about his experiences. The most famous was the 1966 best seller, "Paper Lion," about his football efforts.

His most recent book, "One for the Record," is an account of Henry Aaron's pursuit of the home run record. He wrote it in two weeks, expanding on an article he had written for Sports Illustrated.

Latest Venture

In addition to playing hockey, Plimpton hopes to play chess with Bobby Fischer and sing with the Metropolitan Opera sometime soon.

His most recent venture into new territory will be visible in the January issue of Playboy magazine. He photographed the centerfold.

His resourcefulness came in handy Monday night. Plimpton, the perpetual overreacher, failed to get off the plane in Milwaukee and continued on to Madison. As soon as he realized his error he rented a car and drove back here.

Plimpton 'Just An Author'

By CAL REYNARD
Star Staff Writer

George Plimpton doesn't want to be known as an athlete. He figures his role in sports is that of the spectator, but he wants to get closer to the game than the stands.

Plimpton has authored several books as a participant in sports activities, but contends he is nothing more than an author.

"I don't worry about a failure," he said, "because my function as a participant is not to be a great athlete. I'm not all that far removed from the average person in the stands that hasn't played since his school days.

"What I'm doing is telling what it would be like if he experienced the same thing I experienced."

Plimpton has raced along the dirt roads of Baja California, fought with former world champion Archie Moore, tried baseball and twice tried his hand at professional football.

"Paper Lion" was the book that won him thhe most fame, but he says a new book about his experience as quarterback of the Baltimore Colts, "Mad Ducks and Bears," is more interesting.

What Plimpton wants to uncover are the non-statistical emotions and facts in sports.

"The tennis story in there," he said, pointing to a local newspaper, "is mostly statistical which is what people want to know. They want to know who won.

"It's a different type of reporting. It's factual reporting where as the type of stuff I would do if I was on the tour would be perhaps to find out what that headline means to the player, whether he saw it this morning, what did he think about, did he say 'well, I'll go out and show those bastards, whoever wrote that article, that headline, I'll show them.' "

"For me, it's (sports) a terribly foreign world," he said. "I know about tennis, but I don't know about something like football. I've got to do a thing on hockey and I'm going to do one on ghosts."

Plimpton says his ventures as a participant have been "discomforting" experiences. He points to his participation in the American Airlines Tennis Games' pro-celebrity-executive doubles as an example.

"I played with somebody today that couldn't hit the ball at all," Plimpton said. "I've never seen anybody go through that much anguish. Humiliation is almost inevitable.

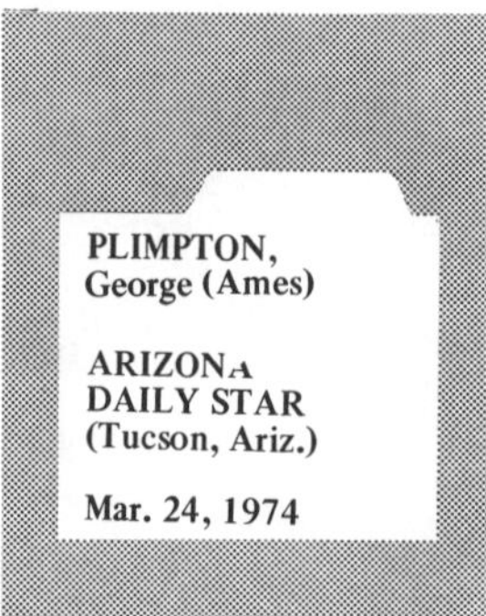

PLIMPTON, George (Ames)

ARIZONA DAILY STAR (Tucson, Ariz.)

Mar. 24, 1974

"Everyone says what fun it must be to play with the Baltimore Colts or the Yankees. What's fun is the opportunities and the friendships you make and getting to know about the sport.

"The actual participation is almost inevitably going to be keenly disappointing."

Plimpton found the experience with the Colts "vicious."

"The 'Paper Lion' thing wasn't vicious, but 'Mad Duck and Bears' is vicious. I played there in a game against another team," he said.

"I remember on the first play, I got knocked down by a man named Mitchell. He's a big defensive end. He just saw me standing there and he went (Plimpton swings his arm through the air). I picked up 15 yards on a roughing the passer penalty.

"I made seven yards on a quarterback sneak and that was a tremendous surprise. Nobody could really believe that I was going to do a quarterback sneak.

"It was the most frightening seven yards I've ever done. The emotions that run through your mind in a situation like that are what are my assignments, what am I supposed to do."

Plimpton, who was 47 last week, says he never worried about getting hurt.

"It never occured to me, until there was an injury. It's like going to war and thinking you're never going to get hit, not that that's any reason for doing it."

Chaim Potok: Man With Two Countries

POTOK, Chaim (1929-) [See also CA-19/20]
PHILADELPHIA BULLETIN (Philadelphia, Penn.)
May 16, 1974

By NANCY GREENBERG
Of The Bulletin Staff

NOVELIST Chaim Potok was back in his center city Philadelphia office this week, weary but seemingly unable to relax, reading manuscripts.

His office—Dr. Potok is editor of the Jewish Publication Society of America — seemed appropriate enough for the bearded Jewish scholar who has written sensitive and acclaimed novels ("The Chosen," "The Promise" and "My Name is Asher Lev") about Orthodox youths finding their way in contemporary American society.

It was floor-to-ceiling books. Ancient and contemporary, Hebrew and English, Eastern and Western. And what weren't yet books were big, bulky manuscripts, overflowing Dr. Potok's desk.

But for a man in his element, Dr. Potok appeared somewhat ill at ease. He had returned from Israel for a week, where he, his wife and three children have lived since leaving their Wynnefield home last July, for the sole purpose of wading through the piles of manuscripts.

Writing a Novel

"I'm in the middle of writing a novel," he said, "and when I'm in the middle of writing I do nothing else. I turn down engagements, lectures, everything.

"But I have a responsibility to this job, this office. Leaving was wrenching. You can say it was devastating . . . devastating, devastating."

His words surprise because he is a precise man who normally does not repeat words even twice. He eyes the piles in front of him.

"I'm not only a writer, a novelist doing my thing — there is responsibility to one's people. There is commitment."

Like the proverbial Jewish father committed also to his children's education, Potok sees the move to Israel primarily as an enriching one for his son, 5-year-old Akiva, and 8- and 12-year-old daughters, Naama and Rena.

"We're struggling," he said, "to experiment — to set up a life style in both worlds. I have a profound commitment to the Anglo-Saxon culture, to the English modes of expression—to Shakespeare—but I worry too about this experiment of ours—this going back and forth—you may end up diluting both cultures."

Going Back and Forth

For the protagonists in Potok's novels, going back and forth is a problem which round trip air fare is unable to solve. Asher Lev, for instance, is a painter forced to alienate himself from the Orthodox community which cannot accept his artistic gifts.

The author himself comes from a similar community in the Bronx which responded to his talent with some measure of hostility.

"Growing up I felt like an alien," he smiled, "but I was never sure what I was alienated from—I know I felt terrible that I couldn't speak English with a marvelous, flowing Connecticut accent."

Today the man could pass for a native of Massachusetts if he wanted to—in political morality, if not voice.

America, the Bastion

"I wouldn't call my home America as much as Western Civilization," he said, "but you can't lose sight of the fact that America is the bastion of that civilization. What bothers me about Watergate is not this charade of shabby gangsterism per se—it is how it is affecting the progress of Western Civilization. God, you are affecting the morality of a generation of kids. The president of the bastion of Western Civilization is a gangster—and the children know it."

Asked how he felt taking his children to a country where there was a war, Potok said there was no time for misgivings.

"They went to the bomb shelter and I went to synagog. It turned out that from my military experience in Korea, I was the highest ranking officer in my apartment building. I was supposed to give orders — I had trained with tank divisions in the U. S. and had some feeling for 2,000 tanks heading towards Jerusalem. The enormity of that possibility—tanks in Jerusalem — left no time for misgivings.

"The losses were tremendous — the country was in a first-class depression. So many times I listened to fathers say Kaddish (the prayer for the dead) for their sons. How many times can you listen to fathers say Kaddish . . . It is very depressing."

Returning to Israel

Potok is returning to Israel next week, where his family has decided to stay another year. They will be in Philadelphia for part of the summer.

"My kids are very American and very Israeli," said their father. "I guess in a practical way, loyalties come down to which Army do you want to serve in. I'll let my son make his own decision . . ."

Suddenly, Potok jumped up from his chair and said, "Here, let me show you something dear to me."

He held up a shiny release from the Jewish Publication Society — the Book of Jeremiah just published with woodcuts made by a Greek artist living in Jerusalem.

"Here—it can be done—the fusing of two cultures, it can be done," he pointed to the contemporary looking edition and spoke with a satisfaction that was at best, bittersweet.

Inner Conflicts, Writing Topics of Chaim Potok

By MILLIE BALL

Even the vastness of a partially filled hotel ballroom cannot chill the warmth exuded by Chaim Potok.

Intensely personal in his novels, the author of "The Chosen," "The Promise," and "My Name is Asher Lev" is also quietly honest in his speech.

At the Fairmont Roosevelt Hotel Potok invited a group of strangers to become friends as he talked of his inner conflicts which have helped him to write some of the most moving fiction of the past decade.

"I've spent my life attempting to fuse two conflicting commitments," the bearded author, who is also a Jewish rabbi told the Second Pan American Reunion of Adolescent Psychiatric Societies.

"Insofar as my religious tradition is concerned, the whole enterprise of writing fiction is not anything to look on with any degree of seriousness," he said.

Potok admitted that even his mother doesn't fully understand what he is trying to do with his life.

POTOK, Chaim
TIMES-PICAYUNE (New Orleans, La.)
Feb. 25, 1973

FASCINATED BY WRITING

His fascination with the written word began when he was about 15 years old and read his first serious piece of adult fiction, Evelyn Waugh's "Brideshead Revisited."

At that time his whole world consisted of his Jewish school and family and an occasional radio show.

But when he started reading the novel about a Catholic British family, he found that "the space-time slice of that book became more real than my world."

From that time he had a committment — to learning how to create worlds on paper. But that commitment conflicted with his Jewish heritage and commitment to learn about the Talmud and to become a rabbi.

His teachers and friends were amazed and angered.

His Talmud teacher was particularly concerned.

"He was amazed because I was taking time out from the study of the Talmud to read fiction and to write, and he was angry because of my sense of preoccupation with writing fiction," said the author-rabbi. "He let me know in no uncertain terms that this was a threat to the sanctity and wholeness of the tradition he represented. He was quite right."

During the following years Potok found himself in the midst of a hated culture conflict.

"I found myself juggling two antithetical conflicting commitments, which is no pleasant thing to do," he said. "A commitment means investing all of your energy into reaching a goal, and you cannot make that kind of investment in two directions at the same time.

"You either fuse them, drop one, or end up being creative in neither.

Potok chose to fuse.

If mental anguish was inflicted during the fusing years, Potok said it was done so out of the need for honesty. "When you have a collision of loves, there's bound to be pain," he said.

His books, which are said to be at least partially autobiographical, reveal feelings of isolation and attempts to understand their heritage by Jewish boys and men.

Potok, who is a resident of Wynnefield, Pa., said he tries to write about small particular worlds so he can open them up to people who are not parts of these worlds.

"In the particular is contained the universal," he said. "When you write about one person or set of people, if you dig deeply enough, you will ultimately uncover basic humanity."

As he came to understand the world of a British Catholic, he hopes nuns will understand the pain of a Rev. Saunders in "The Chosen."

Though the path to his dual careers has been tedious and painful, Potok said he has no regrets.

"It's no small thing to feel yourself fulfilled as a rabbi, writer, and teacher," he said.

Writers' Best Friend Puts Up Quill

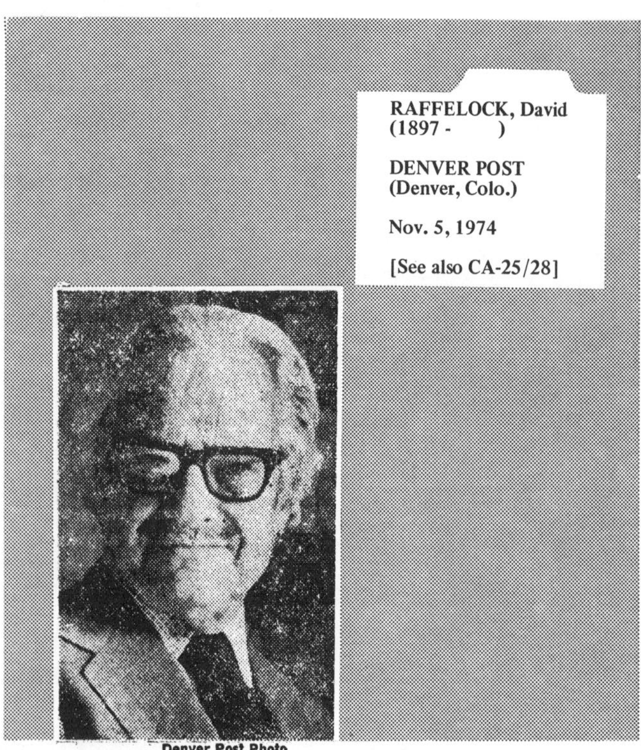
RAFFELOCK, David (1897-)

DENVER POST (Denver, Colo.)

Nov. 5, 1974

[See also CA-25/28]

Denver Post Photo

DAVID RAFFELOCK

By HELEN M. CASS
Denver Post Staff Writer

David Raffelock has signed "30," or at least "29," to his long literary career.

He has retired as director of the National Writers Club, which he founded in 1937, but will remain with the nonprofit organization on a consulting basis until the first of the year, and then as an adviser.

Raffelock, a noted author, critic, lecturer and pioneer in many literary fields, said "when you reach three score, ten" it is time to pursue other interests. He will now turn his talents to photography and study of pre-Columbian civilization and will take his wife, Esse, on a cruise.

During a writing career spanning more than 50 years, Raffelock has devoted his time to helping hundreds of free-lance writers, has made information about authorship available without charge to hundreds of schools and universities, has kept his finger on the pulse of markets. He also has written several books for writers, including "Writing for the Markets," published by Funk & Wagnalls in 1970.

A native of Topeka, Kan., Raffelock's decision to write was reached at an early age. While at Columbia University he sold children's articles and later short stories, and finally gave up a good job with a New York advertising agency to make his way to Denver.

That was the turning point in his career. He established a home-study course for free-lance writers, now the oldest. In 1937, deciding to devote his life to part-time writers, he founded the National Writers Club. The course is now a part of the organization. As he became involved with helping others, he became less interested in his own writing. Years of dedication to the field kept him from becoming a prolific writer.

Membership in the club fluctuates, but Raffelock estimates that more than 5,000 writers have joined during the past 37 years. Membership now includes about 1,500 from all over the United States and five continents.

There have been many changes in the writing market during Raffelock's career. A major one has been effected by the disappearance of the 1930s and '40s' pulps, which once provided a remunerative and prolific market.

"The market for short fiction now is restricted — television has been a factor in this," he said. "Big-paying magazines are now either nonexistent or restricted. Playboy is the best-paying magazine today, but it is not an easy market."

New women's magazines such as Playgirl, New Lady, Ms. and others put the older magazines in the shade, he believes. They deal much more frankly with subjects and are willing to discuss anything.

Certain publications, such as religious, juvenile, sports and outdoor, as well as how-to magazines, are dependent upon free-lance articles. Trade journals offer an extensive field, but often lack appeal of part-time writers because they pay little but demand perceptive writing and time-consuming interviews.

"To sell a novel today is a difficult achievement," Raffelock said. "The cost of publishing is so high, most publishers are unwilling to take a chance on a new writer. Most of the prestigious publishers have smaller lists of books."

Short fiction has changed, too, according to the author Twenty years ago a definite formula was used: Get the central character in a deep hole, throw rocks at him and finally get him out. The story also came to a definite climax. This formula still is used by some religious magazines as well as old, established magazines like McCalls and Ladies Home Journal.

Today's short stories are open-ended. There is no plot as such, there are high and low points, but "it never comes to a definitive end and the problem present at the beginning usually is still there at the end," Raffelock said. He believes there is a slight trend today to return to the old, but trends usually are subtle and gradual

Exposing phony literary agents has been one of his major efforts and "one of the most exciting" aspects of his work during his lectures, which have taken him from coast to coast.

At least two of these unscrupulous agents who preyed on writers were jailed, mainly because of Raffelock's efforts.

During his long years as a critic of part-time writers, Ruffelock has learned to temper honesty with graciousness, to give encouragement where warranted.

He recalled early in his career, sending back a song with the comment that it had no possibility of ever being published. A short time later a letter came back. "I'm a 93-year-old man," the letter said, "and I've worked on that song for years and now I'm disappointed."

'MORE CONTACT'

Another time Raffslock advised a student in Chicago who wrote trite things to "get out and have more contact with the life about you." Later, a letter came from the man's wife complaining he had started "running around with other women."

Although the Denver man's dedication has been to the club he founded, he has a long list of other achievements to his credit.

He is a former editor of The Author and Journalist, and published and edited The Echo, a magazine of comment on the arts which ceased in 1929, after four years of publication, longest record in the area for this type of magazine.

Raffelock founded the Writers Colony in 1926, and arranged the first exhibit of modern art by Denver painters in 1928. He staged the first national writers' convention in Denver, which brought together editors of leading magazines and publishing houses and also pioneered a book-jacket competition in which most important publishers participated.

PLANT HUSTLERS

RAPP, Joel
and
RAPP, Lynn

MIAMI HERALD
(Miami, Fla.) Oct. 13, 1974

— ALBERT COYA / Miami Herald Staff

By FELICE DICKSON
Herald Farm and Garden Editor

Exploitation is a dirty word and, connected with plants, it can get even dirtier.

The current plant boom all over the country is prompting every avaricious soul who can tell a leaf from a rock to cash in on the craze. They are writing books — or, rather, rewriting old books — whose accuracy barely extends beyond the title page.

They are selling as plants cuttings that scarcely know what life is all about.

And, with innocence and half-answers they are turning off a lot of new plant growers who blame themselves for the downfall of those $10 hanging baskets that used to sell for a playful two-fifty.

STILL, they are in the minority. As every veteran gardener will tell you, plants have an integrity that's catching and most commercial plant people have come down with it.

For awhile, the P. T. Barnum of plant promotion was Jerry Baker, a Troy, Michigan, garden writer with a scruffy lawn who dubbed himself "America's Master Gardener" and has been propagating fact and plenty of fancy as fast as you can root aralias in water — in hard and softbound books, on TV and radio talk shows and through commercial endorsements. He's the talk-to-your-plants popularizer that a legion of philodendrons can blame for bending their arborescent ears.

Now Baker's being put in the shade, promotion-wise, by a couple that makes him look like a shrinking violet but are heliconia-bent on being the ones to make growing the national sport.

IN MIAMI last week on a break-neck tour to push theri second book, "Grow With Your Plants The Mother Earth Hassle-Free Way," Lynn and Joel Rapp are just the Geminis the plant kingdom needs to promote the living stomatas out of it. (One of the chapters in the book is a "hortoscope" that matches up astrologically-right plants to people signs.)

Joel was a comedy-and-otherwise TV script writer who threw in the towel when they wanted him to walk Ironsides down the wedding aisle. He does the actual writing of the books which are one laugh after another, not overburdened with carpring horticultural details.

"Nobody wants Latin," he said confidently. "And everything basic was in our first book. Who cares about details? In 14 seconds you can tell someone how to care for a lawn. So we thought we'd make this the Jonathan Livingston Seagull of plant books."

INITIALLY, they wondered just how they'd go about that. Their first book had sold over a half million copies at $3.95 each. It was excerpted by Family Circle magazine and reprint rights were sold to a British publisher. Bantam wanted the paperback business.

Lynn, a radio show producer and TV production aide dropout who had "gone as far as I could as a woman," said they were worried about blowing it with number two.

"With the first book you've got nothing to lose. But when we were asked to write a second, we were afraid."

"SIMON AND Schuster offered us a $50,000 advance for our second," Joel reminisced. "And we went to New York. But they were New Yorkers. They didn't smile. Now everyone doesn't love you in Los Angeles but once in a while someone will smile. So when we told Jeremy — that's Jeremy Tarcher, our publisher in L. A. — that we turned down the $50,000, he said we were crazy. But we knew he would tell us what to write, at least."

J. P. Tarcher, Inc. is no Doubleday but it is a pop-culture hotbed, responsible for making almost-authors out of Dinah Shore, Totie Fields, Phyllis Diller and Johnny Carson with little books of recipes and gags in large type.

IT WAS a natural choice for the Rapps, who had a respectable number of celebrity friends when they first thought up the idea of a fun-chic plant boutique ("We were the first to create one and call it that as far as we know, unless there was one in Holland or some place," said Joel.) After they built it into a 10,-000-square-foot wonderland for plant freaks, they attracted all manner of star types. Even jockeys — "not Willy Shoemakers," Joel hastened to explain, "but all the next level. It was weird to see jockies in our plant school courses."

(Continued from preceding page)

Lucille Ball would call for a fern at amusing times like 7 a.m. Ruth Buzzi ("She has too-perfect plants," said Lynn) would buy, buy, buy — and hang around to give other customers advice on their plants. John Huston took bromeliads back to Ireland. Julie Andrews ordered plants as Christmas gifts by proxy. Sally Struthers, Jack Lemon, Mike Douglas, Lily Tomlin — all succumbed to the Rapps' showmanship with green things. Even the lead singer for a rock group called something like "Three Dog Night," whose manager told him he wasn't spending enough money.

"PLANTS ARE a good investment today," said Joel, "if you buy right. "About the most expensive we sold was a 15-foot dracaena for $300. The same plant today might go for $600."

Before Mother Earth — the store after which their books are titled — shrank to "a little doll house" of 1,000 square feet, its present size, the Rapps tried to propagate their upper-crust approach to plant sales. They installed a Mother Earth department in Orbach's, a quality department store, but couldn't get experienced plant people to maintain it.

"We had to close in three months," said Lynn. "We realize now that you just can't mass merchandise plants."

SO THEY branched out into other areas.

"We fantasized a whole plant trip," Lynn said. "Like a five-year plan — the books, the interviews, products we'd put out, a television show. We're just about ready to start manufacturing Mother Earth's Indoor Plant Care Products. Actually, Johnson's is making them but we are supervising them closely. They're going to be as natural as possible."

But the store started to suffer. Absentee ownership, they found, didn't work with their kind of shop. And it was getting a little sticky to explain to old friends-customers why a plant they bought at the store four years ago now costs triple the amount.

"We just couldn't justify the plant increases without a long spiel," said Joel.

THEN THERE was the almost over-night flowering of dozens of competitors — "at least 500 new plant boutiques in L.A. now," said Lynn. "When we came back from one promotion trip for our first book we found four new boutiques right in our store's neighborhood."

They couldn't sell the shop because they needed the active Mother Earth identification for their other projects, but they were able to reduce the sales force — the ex-Playboy bunny, the "gay boys," dancers and the Mark Spitz look-alike who thought working in the shop was an amusing way to make money — and to hand the management over to Lynn's sister.

Joel, a football fan, said the high point of the boutique experience was an episode with the owner of the L. A. Rams who needed a fast gift for his wife. Rapp put together a football field of plants in gargantuan basket using about 47 pots of artillery plant as the field and spelling out something in chrysanthemums between not-so-miniature goal posts. The floral tribute earned him two season passes with undercover parking "right alongside all those Rolls Royces"-a $400 thank-you.

NOW THEY get a kick out of being recognized from the cover photographs of them together, smiling blissfully out of thickets of plants. "Most people say, 'Are you the plant people? My philodendron ...'

"With our new book," said Lynn, "we were trying to find some selling point and decided it was what your plants can do for you. When we get some land we can do a book on growing vegetables — that would be a natural extension of our other books."

The Rapps currently have "about 400" plants in their Los Angeles apartment — "maybe that's why we like L. A.," said Lynn. "We seldom look outside the apartment. Maybe it is smoggy."

JOEL MAINTAINED that the plant boom is not a fad.

"Huge ads are running in The L.A. Times with a $14,000 sofa next to a $20 pot of creeping-charley. THe interest is growing, and has been for the four years we've been into it. Plants create a relationship, a responsibility that people today want to feel toward something living."

Added Lynn, "But plants can be pretty boring. That's why people read us who aren't even interested in them. It's our approach — humorous. The wife of a photographer we know left a copy of our book in the bathroom and now he has his own plants — and he couldn't have cared less before."

PRODUCER Bob Banner who succeeded in making Peggy Fleming almost interesting, among many other accomplishments, has asked them to talk about turning their plant boutiquing into a TV situation comedy. They think about it in between interviews in Atlanta, Baltimore, Washington, D. C., Hartford, Boston, Toronto, Chicago, Cincinnati, Indianapolis, Milwaukee, and a few other places.

"The interest is this big," said Joel. "The publisher foots the bill for everything, including $65 hotel rooms."

"It's fate," said Lynn. "The two of us are very strong, and talking to different people keeps our energy up and the plants were there, waiting for us."

Plant Fever is sweeping the land.

— Illustrations by Marvin Rubin from GROW WITH YOUR PLANTS THE MOTHER EARTH HASSLE-FREE WAY

Born to be eaten.

RAPP, Joel
and
RAPP, Lynn

MIAMI HERALD
(Miami, Fla.)

Oct. 13, 1974

Dan Rather's Career Crisis

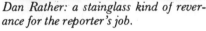

Dan Rather: a stainglass kind of reverance for the reporter's job.

By HUGH McCANN
Free Press Staff Writer

For 10 DAYS in August Dan Rather, the White House correspondent for CBS television news, the 43-year-old Texan who personifies authority and self-confidence for millions of viewers, hid his personal misery.

He had survived toe-to-toe verbal jousts with former-president Nixon. He had endured the censure of White House strongmen Ehrlichman and Haldeman. and he had withstood the complaints of dozens of stations affiliated with CBS that he was badgering the president

All this he had weathered. But now, it seemed, the network that had stood by him through it all was capitulating to the accumulated pressure; shunting him off the White House beat after ten years and into some "safe" assignment.

As one of television's highest-paid newsmen, (more than $100,000 a year,) and with a few months to go before his contract with CBS was to expire, what should he do?

Rather was in Detroit October 28 as a guest on the Phil Donahue Show, which was being telecast that week from the Detroit Institute of Arts. He talked about his new book, "The Palace Guard," about men who surrounded President Nixon and their motives; and he candidly discussed the career crisis in his life.

"The White House job is a terrific job," he says unreservedly.

From that it must follow that Rather was disturbed when, at an August 15 luncheon with CBS executives, he was asked if he would like to do something different.

If they were bowing to the pressures, thought Rather, then he wanted no part of the deal — no matter what new job they might have in mind for him. He would simply walk away and find a new line of work.

"I went home," he recalls, "and said to my wife: 'Hey, this is what they're proposing. What do you think? Is it a move to pressure me out? Or does it appear to be what they say it is — a golden opportunity?"

At CBS News headquarters in New York the executives were sternly close-mouthed. But inevitably a rumor leaked out: A major shake-up in the network's news coverage — with the Washington Bureau and Dan Rather in the eye of the storm.

If it was true, thought Rather, it was a devastating vote of no confidence — especially after all he and CBS had been through together.

There was the time at the Republican rally in Houston when he had risen to ask the president a question — amid a burst of applause. "Are you running for something," President Nixon had inquired quizzically. To which Rather, master of the ad lib, responded: "No, Mr. President. Are you?" And there was the time when Haldeman had censured him for posing as an expert on the White House while, claimed the president's strongman, Rather didn't have the vaguest notion how it operated.

Both he and CBS, he'd always thought, had come through the flak he'd drawn with renewed mutual confidence. They believed in him, they had faith in him, he'd always thought — until the August luncheon. And for the following ten days he was miserable with doubt.

DAN IRVIN RATHER believes that "you appear to be on television what you are." And to millions of Republicans he seemed anti-Nixon. He told his viewers one evening that a Nixon visit to Macon, Ga., for example, looked like "a carefully arranged campaign trip." And shortly after the president had appealed for a national speed limit of 55 miles an hour, Rather had noted that Nixon's motorcade had been traveling at speeds of up to 60 miles an hour.

To Nixonites this was cheap shot reporting; to Rather it was performance of his job which, he says, "is to tell the people what goes on in the White House. It's not to lead the cheers, and it's not to be hostile."

There is more to Rather than television's epidermal image; there's a third dimension so palpable in the person. Despite his exposure, he still regards himself as simply a broker of information — no more, no less. There is, too, an elusive quality; perhaps it's a combination of civility and grace, a choirboy sincerity, a stainglass kind of reverence for the reporter's job.

"The mark of a professional," he says, "is his ability to (be objective) over a broad spectrum of work in the same way that a professional boxer is trained not to show when he's hurt.

"A reporter can take an awful lot from people and put himself away and say: 'Look, as well as I possibly can, as humanly possible as it is, he can say to you: I'm trying to be an honest broker of information . . . And my own feelings aside, there is the truth as best as I can get it, as much of it as I can get.

"No reporter worthy of the name approaches the job in any other way. And no reporter would last who wasn't able to do that week in and week out, knowing full well — humbled by his knowledge — that he can't be perfect . . .

"I can't remember a time when I didn't want to be a reporter." Yet having said that, he can't explain why. There was no hero, no specific incident — only a home chronically littered with newspapers. His father, a pipelayer in the gas and oil fields around Houston, read voraciously. The Houston Chronicle and the Houston Post couldn't sate his appetite for news on politics and world affairs. He imported papers from out of state, and although not a Christian Scientist, the Monitor was one of the staples.

Rather remembers the walls of his home reverberating with the voices of the radio pundits of the day — H. V. Kaltenborn, Gabriel Heater, Edward R. Murrow. He was about eight years old when he started going along to precinct meetings with his father, whom he remembers as being politically unpredictable, sometimes voting Republican, sometimes Democratic.

Rather was passionately fond of sports. On the mile walk to elementary school in the morning and the mile back he used to do play-by-play broadcasts of the football and basketball games going on inside his head.

And yet, he says, it was newspaper reporting he yearned to do; not radio, not television.

One suspects Rather may be a solitary man whose deep convictions don't easily lend themselves to crowds; not the kind to reveal himself ➡

(Continued from preceding page)

readily for fear — perhaps — that he be judged quaint. His dress, fashionably understated, provides the only material clues: dark-blue suit, light-blue shirt, striped tie reminiscent of the stockbroker; black shoes as plain and unembellished as those once popular among seminarians; black hair flecked with grey and barbered in a style that concedes but does not capitulate to the vogue.

And the voice: Clipped and affirmative, with the Texas version of the vowels making Dimocrats of Democrats, for example. Too subtle to sound provincial; just enough to be distinctive.

Politically, his friends say, he's hard to plumb. For all his seeming aggression toward Richard Nixon in his reportage, he admits "great empathy" for the former president; but given the choice to make, he points out, "Richard Nixon is not the important thing. The important thing is the country, the Republic, what we are about as a people."

A close personal friend, Gary Gates, the co-author of "The Palace Guard," has discerned "a strain of Southern populism in him. He doesn't care for elitism. He has always felt very strongly — like so many Southerners who have gone to Washington — that one of the things he found most offensive was the cynicism, the dishonesty, in dealing with people . . .

"The Texas thing is quite important to him. He doesn't like to get too far away from those roots. His family — his wife Jean, his 16-year-old daughter Robin and his 14-year-old son Dan — go out to Texas twice a year on vacation. That's important to the man."

"I'm not an advocate of the so-called new journalism," he says solemnly. "I'm a journalist of the old school which says: The first thing you do is get it right. Be fair. And try your best to get it fast . . .

"In general I subscribe to the theory that it's scary — and it should be scary — to write a news story. And it's particularly scary to sit down and write a news story about anything as important as the presidency of the United States.

"I've never walked through those (White House) gates a day but I didn't say to myself: This is not just another beat; this is not just another assignment . . . This is a public trust, and you'd better do your best to be worthy of that . . ."

RATHER LEFT KHOU-TV in Houston, where he was news, special-events director, and joined CBS in 1961 as chief of its Southwest Bureau in Dallas. His coverage of the Kennedy assassination in 1963 and his strong, Celtic looks inherited from his father's Welsh forbears attracted front-office attention. The following year he was assigned to the White House beat.

With the exception of 21 months during which he reported from London and Saigon, he stayed on the White House beat. In 1970 he began pulling extra duty as anchorman on "CBS Sunday News," special reporter on examinations of the Watergate Affair and the shooting of Governor Wallace in the 1972-73 season, and since July 1973 he's been anchoring "CBS Sunday News."

Off camera, says a CBS bureau manager who has worked with Rather frequently, "he's probably one of the nicest non-superstar types around. He's a guy who, when he anchors a broadcast, will send off cables to the Paris or Saigon bureaus, telling them what a nice job they did."

"When he comes into the studio he doesn't say: I want a desk. I want a phone. I want a secretary. He says: What desk do you want me to work at? He's always courteous. He treats the secretaries just like he treats an executive producer. He's very sensitive to people."

The nature of television is such that it makes personalities of its reporters — whether they want it or not. Rather is an established personality and wears it well, but he doesn't want to become a celebrity.

For a newsman, says Rather, this could be a "real danger. Number One is you get full of yourself. I think, as Adlai Stevenson said, that stuff's all right if you don't inhale. Traveling around in Rolls Royce automobiles and walking into rooms where people applaud you, whisked in and out. You know, big deal! You forget what you're about — if what you're about is being a reporter."

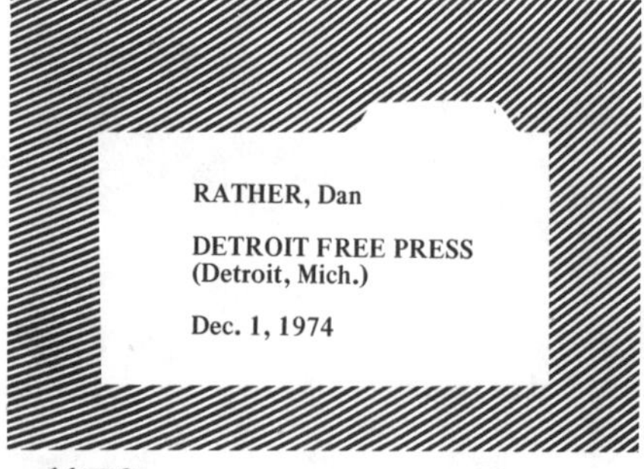
RATHER, Dan

DETROIT FREE PRESS
(Detroit, Mich.)

Dec. 1, 1974

"I'M NOT GOING to say Dan was a good student," says his journalism professor at Sam Houston State College, Hugh Cunningham. "He didn't have time to be a good student" because he was working so many part-time jobs. "He was an interested student. Cunningham also did sports publicity for the college, and he first met Rather, who was at school on a modest football scholarship, during try-outs.

His first impression of the dark-haired young freshman was that "he wasn't very big. He wasn't very good, and he stood along the sidelines mostly.

"He wanted to know who I was, what I was doing. And he expressed a great interest in sports writing.

"That's what hit me about him: I'd tried out for football when I went to college, and I was no good for the same reason. I told him: 'I'm attracted by what I think may be your better-than-average mind. Instead of playing football, why don't you write about it?' "

When the football scolarship didn't work out and Rather was running low on funds, he decided to work a year in the oilfields. Cunningham wouldn't hear of it.

Cunningham scratched around his contacts and got him part-time work stringing for various wire services and local newspapers so he could stay in school. In return he wanted the best out of his protege.

"He demanded the highest standards of excellence," said Rather. "He'd say: 'You're in a backwoods teachers college. You're not going to make it unless you made of yourself something really extraordinary . . ."

He was a nagging dissatisfied critic of Rather's reporting. "He was very heavy with the Elmer Davis philosophy: Don't let 'em scare you. He'd say: You know, Dan, you go down to the police chief and you let him scare you, cow you. You're not worth a damn as a reporter if you let that happen . . ."

HE DIDN'T LET Haldeman and Ehrlichman scare him at the White House. "These people," he explains, operated on the premise that "if they push you hard enough and long enough, they'll get rid of you. And they could do one of two things: Either they could get you run off — by getting fired; or they could get you to sit down and shut up. Now once you had made it clear that neither one of those things was going to happen, then on a limited basis you could do business with them."

But suddenly in mid-August, a week after President Nixon had resigned Aug. 8, Rather was struck with the demoralizing suspicion that the CBS executives with whom he was lunching didn't want him doing business with the White House any longer. For all his civility and Southern courteousness, he was capable of righteous anger.

"What Texas gave me," he says, "is a feeling of independence. The people I grew up with were never impressed by anyone or anything.

"These were people who had to deal with the realities of life. They were not born to privilege or place: If you make it, if you survive it, you're not better than anyone else — but not less than anyone else.

"I have a sense of that."

And it was that sense that guided him through his 10 days when he tried to make up his own mind if CBS was subtly trying to elevate him or eliminate him.

In his new job as anchorman for "CBS Reports," he is the first reporter to hold the job permanently since the highly esteemed Edward R. Murrow, whom Rather regards as one of the top reporters of his day.

His first responsibility in his new slot was anchoring an hour-long documentary look at Cuba and Castro, which was aired October 22. He found it "one of the most fascinating assignments" he ever had, he says.

But whether the fascination will persist is a question only time and he can answer. He still maintains that the White House is a beat nonpareil.

Dan Rather comes across as loyal to CBS. One can't quite shake the feeling that it is this loyalty that tipped the scales in favor of him remaining with the network. "I thought about it," he says. "I tried to do some reporting of my own" . . . He says he convinced himself that CBS was not trying to get rid of him because of pressures from the White House and some CBS affiliates." If I thought that were the case, I would not be here.

"But what they offered me, what I'm now doing," he adds, "may be (better than the White House beat) and that is the chance to do what I think I do best, and that is . . . reporting in depth."

Wilson Rawls found his rainbow's end

(Tribune Staff Photos by Lynn R. Johnson)

By Harold Schindler
Tribune Staff Writer

"I never wanted wealth or fame — I just wanted to tell stories; to write them down. As far back as I can remember that's all I've ever wanted to do. But this compulsion to write almost ruined my life. I spent 40 years trying and it made me a loner, cost me my friends. I never had a pal or a buddy . . . ever."

Woodrow Wilson Rawls, now a successful author, agonizes still over those childhood years in northeastern Oklahoma where the lack of a formal education dogged him as fiercely as the hunting hounds he knows so well.

Seamed and Seasoned

Tall, angular, his features seamed and seasoned by the out-of-doors, Rawls ("call me Woody") speaks slowly and in measured sentences. He seems uncomfortable around people, especially strangers, and his eyes break away after a few moments to search for a window, a cloud, a tree . . .

But not so with children. Rawls thrives on telling youngsters how it was as a boy back home hunting raccoons in his native Ozarks; and the thrill of hearing his hounds "bugling treed." Even the rowdiest of 9-year-olds fall under the spell of this gifted story-teller, himself a child of the Cherokee nation, who grew up "just about as wild as the gray squirrels in the sycamore trees and as free as the hawks in those Ozark skies."

A Sore Thumb

Woody Rawls at 61 can now contemplate with some amusement a sore thumb, blistered while autographing stacks of "Where the Red Fern Grows," his marvelously popular novel (an autobiography, really) that captured the imagination of school children the world over.

Discovered in 1960 as a three-part serial in the Saturday Evening Post, Rawls' story of a boy and two redbone hunting dogs was expanded and published in hardcovers by Doubleday & Co., whose editors recognized its potential as a book but insisted on a change of title.

A Change in Title

"They didn't like the Post's title, 'Hounds of Youth'," Rawls remembers, "and I wasn't too fond of 'Where The Red Fern Grows.' It sounded like a manual on gardening."

Fourteen years and 87,500 copies later, he is willing to bow to Doubleday's judgment. And for Rawls that is no small concession; he treats his novel as he would his flesh and blood. It is to him a dream come true . . .

"We almost lost this book," he says. (The "we" is not editorial, he means it to encompass his readers.) "Doubleday was ready to remainder it once."

Literary Euthanasia

(Mention of "remaindering" is poisonous to authors, who consider it a form of literary euthanasia. It involves elimination of inventories, based on sales figures, with losses absorbed by profitable books.)

"'Red Fern' didn't sell a dozen copies for the first seven years," Rawls says in gentle exaggeration. "Then a miracle came along to save us." It took the shape of an invitation by Dr. Elliot Landau of the University of Utah to speak at a summer teachers' workshop on children's books.

"They liked what I said about 'Red Fern' and told their pupils about it that fall. That was the spark and the book has been selling ever since."

2,000 Classrooms

Rawls estimates he has visited more than 2,000 classrooms across the country to carry the message of "Red Fern" and to impress on his young audiences the importance of staying in school and learning to read, to write and to think.

He tells them of his love for dogs and the outdoors. Of how he used to tell stories to his blue tick hound.

"My first writing was done in a very crude way. Using my finger as a pencil, I scrawled sentences on practically everything that had a smooth surface; in the dust of country roads and the white sand along the river."

Discovers Libraries

After moving from the hills to the town of Tahlequah, he managed "a little more schooling" and there discovered libraries. "I didn't just read those books, I memorized them."

Woody attended Central High School in Muskogee, Okla., before being forced by the Depression to leave home in search of work. "Wherever I could earn a dollar, that's where I went. I sent my mother half of everything I earned, and tried like hell to live on the other half."

He shipped out with an oil company to the jungles of Old Mexico; followed the trails to Yucatan and into South America. A job on the Alcan Highway took him to Alaska and later to five dam construction projects across the United States.

Boxcar Paper

When writing paper wasn't available or he couldn't afford to buy it, Rawls used brown packing paper from boxcars and cut it into pages. The writing went on. "I wrote hundreds of thousands of words in the smoky glow of a hobo campfire, in cheap hotel rooms and riding in Greyhound buses.

"Why I didn't try to publish something, I don't know. I was sure it was pure trash and no one would waste time printing junk like that. I also knew my grammar was poor and my vocabulary was zero."

A Toolshed Trunk

Yet he kept it all. When the manuscripts became too much to carry conveniently, he stored them in a trunk in his father's toolshed. (By now Rawls' parents had moved to Albuquerque, N.M.)

In the 1950s Rawls was working for a lumber company in British Columbia when a friend told him of a little town in the Snake River Valley of Idaho that was booming with atomic construction . . . and the fishing was said to be great. "I couldn't think of anything better," he said. The next day he was off to Idaho Falls.

A Budget Analyst

There he met Sophie Spyjiziniski, the future Mrs. Woodrow Wilson Rawls. She was a budget analyst for the Atomic Energy Commission. Two years later they were married.

But before they could live happily ever after, winter came and there was precious little work for carpenters. In the months during their courtship, Woody had made a clean break with his ambitions to be a writer.

"For a while I was happier than I had ever been in my life. I decided to forget all about writing and let it remain a secret forever."

In the Incinerator

Just before the wedding he went home to New Mexico to get his personal belongings and there, on a steaming August day in 1958, opened his trunk of manuscripts and carried them to the incinerator.

"I burned them. The first story was 'The Secret of the Red Fern,' next was 'The Locks of Hell,' then 'The Story of Dottie,' 'Wheels of Destiny,' and 'Kitty of the Bad Lands' — five complete novels destroyed because I was ashamed to send them to a publisher."

Shares Secret

In Idaho Falls, without work, a wife to support and his patience wearing thin, he told Sophie the truth: of the stories, his ambitions and the burned manuscripts.

"She just sat there, spellbound. My wife is a very intelligent woman. She didn't laugh at me."

When he was through talking, he waited for her response. "I think that's wonderful," she said. "I've never heard anything like it. The first thing in the morning we'll go down and get a typewriter."

But Woody couldn't type. "I have to have pencils and paper, and erasers and a lot of them."

For the next three weeks he rewrote "The Secret of the Red Fern" from memory. Thirty-five thousand words without punctuation of any kind. When it was done he let his wife see it for the first time and left the house.

Hours later he telephoned. "Well? . . ."

"Woody, this is marvelous. Come home and work on it some more and we'll send it to a publisher," said his wife and editor-to-be. ("Red Fern" was on its way to becoming 'Hounds of Youth' in the Saturday Evening Post.)

Now for Second Book

Now that "Red Fern" has come full circle, even to being adapted for motion pictures, Rawls is ready to send Doubleday his second book.

"For a long time I've wanted to write a story that was full of humor," he said. "Summer of the Monkeys" is it. In this book Rawls tells of a boy and a blue tick hound and the wreck of a circus train.

Unlike the autobiographical "Red Fern," this story is wholly fictional and relates the misadventures of a boy who searches for a pack of monkeys freed in the train accident and living in the Ozark countryside. The boy spends a summer trying to recapture them for the circus reward money.

"Summer of the Monkeys" is written and in final draft. Mrs. Rawls, by the way, does the punctuation and typing from Woody's pencil manuscripts. Once it goes into print, Woodrow Wilson Rawls will start recollecting the third of his burned novels.

"I'm going to publish them all yet," he insists. There are at least 85,000 youngsters who are betting he will.

A SHOT OF WRY

BY WOODY KLEIN

Harry Reasoner, who is seen nightly by millions of Americans on the ABC Evening News, appears to be a stolid, low-key anchorman whose commentaries reveal a dry, affable wit. He is, in fact, the same modest man in person as he is on the television screen.

"I would be uncomfortable any other way," he tells a visitor in the living room of his large, comfortable home in Westport. "It would be impossible for me to put on an on-air or an off-air personality. There are people who do this. They have a certain on-air style. I don't."

Reasoner's "style," as he describes it in his typical self-effacing way, "is to read the news without stumbling too much. I would hate to be tagged permanently with either 'dry' or 'wry.' From the time I started in journalism, I've always felt that humor or irony in the news is as much a legitimate part of it as a war on Congress is. As long as it arises out of the news, I think wit is fine, but comedy is not," he says in his characteristic tight-mouthed manner.

"I refuse to be bored myself. When I find things to prevent the viewer from being bored, I try to pass them along. And there is a lot of it in the world. This is not a conscious attempt on my part, but I refuse to be stuffy. I hate pompous reporters just as I hate activist reporters," he continues in that mellow, resonant voice which is one of his trademarks.

Smith & Reasoner. News with a view.

REASONER, Harry

CONNECTICUT
(Stratford, Conn.)

July/Aug., 1974

With co-anchorman Howard K. Smith, Reasoner and Smith have become a well-known television team since they first combined talents in December, 1970. Reasoner had previously been with CBS News since 1956—in Washington as White House correspondent and in New York, reporting mostly on politics.

Why did he leave CBS after 14 years? "Well, Walter (Cronkite) gave no indication of wanting to retire. He refused to get hit by a truck. And furthermore, there was no commitment that I would get his job if he did retire. And it seemed that if I was ever going to be an anchorman—at the time I was 47—that was the time to do it. It's what I had always wanted in television."

The man who has since attracted nationwide attention is known for his droll treatment of every day news. For his unusual style and his insight, he has won a host of awards during his career. The ideas for his distinctive commentaries include stores, hotels, automobiles, women, movie actors and actresses, politics, the energy crisis—even one on his own 25th wedding anniversary on September 7, 1971. There is virtually no subject that he has not touched upon—a good deal of it based on his own personal observations.

All of which draws a large number of letters, including a predictable amount of both right and left wing mail. "Without realizing it, I guess I'm always trying to stick something away in my head to talk about. Howard and I do serious commentaries, but I think people get fed up with analysis. They know all that. They can't do anything about it. So we talk about other things. The biggest response I ever had was a commentary on panty-hose for men. It gave the initial feeling that people like triviality. But I don't think of it as trivia. They really can't do anything about the United Nations or the Middle East or the energy crisis, but they can do something about their own underwear so they're glad to hear about it."

When Reasoner signed on with ABC four years ago for a reported $200,000 a year over a five-year period, ABC was clearly running a distant third in viewing evening news. The figures at the time were approximately 30 per cent for NBC, 30 per cent for CBS, and only 15 per cent for ABC. Now, according to the latest ratings, NBC and CBS are in the area of 26 to 27 per cent, while ABC has attracted about 24 per cent of the viewers.

Does Reasoner see a time when ABC will take the lead? "Our research department likes to say there is virtual parity. That means you're still third, but it's close. You run into a plateau problem that is hard to lick. ABC was the third network organized. The process of growth is slow, but I think we have a good chance for being second. And we're first in what is an important group of advertisers, that is, the 18- to 49-year-old group."

Does this mean ABC is attracting a younger audience? "Yes," Reasoner replies, unsmiling, "but I'm always asking our researchers that if the statistics are so good and we have mostly young people, how come every other commercial seems to be for something to hold your false teeth in."

Reasoner and his wife, Kay, and their family (they now have seven children, a boy 26, a boy 12, and five girls in between) have lived in Weston and Westport since 1956—longer than in any other place since they have been married. "We like Connecticut," he says. "So while I think of myself as a midwesterner (he was born in Iowa on April 17, 1923), actually I am more Connecticut than midwest. I consider myself a Nutmegger. I've seen a fair amount of the state—enough of it so that if I should decide to go into politics, this would be the state."

Is he thinking of politics in the near future? "Everybody toys with the idea," he replies openly, particularly if your profession and life in general have been good to you. You get the feeling that maybe you should do something for your country. Then you have to make the egotistical jump that maybe you could do it. I have not made that jump. Also, I don't know if I have the temperament to be a public animal. I can drift around Westport with my daughter on a Saturday looking like a candidate for urban renewal myself and that's all right. But if you were the governor you couldn't do that. I don't know if I could live 24 hours a day with a public image."

TV viewers also get a look at Harry Reasoner on his Saturday night "Reasoner Report" program—a show which has been described in The New York Times as "an important image-maker." The Reasoner style is by now familiar to most viewers and the "Report" gives it a very effective showcase. As The Times puts it: "As usual, Mr. Reasoner is low-keyed, unflappable and fond of gently humorous observations. Just below the gentleness, the insights can be razor-sharp." Jack Gould of The Times once described Reasoner as a man with a "beguilingly light touch."

"As a boy," Reasoner recalls, "I read books the way some people take dope." But his tastes were nonetheless no more precocious than any of his peers. He conveys the clear impression of being down to earth. He is. "I liked the first two books of Tarzan very much. I still do. It's a really creative description of something no one has ever seen—how you would learn you're a man, if nobody told you, how your thinking would develop. I also liked Kathleen Norris, the Tom Swift books, Robin Hood ... I've really read very few classics. Most aren't very readable. I prefer to devour great quantities of cheap paperbacks."

Reasoner actually became a writer in his late teens. "My fiction," he recalls, "tended to be third or fourth-rate Irwin Shaw," he says flatly. Obviously, he has been more successful as a newsman. After working as drama critic for The Minneapolis Tribune during and after his college years at Stanford University and the University of Minnesota, he served in the Army ("I never heard a shot fired in anger until I was in Saigon in 1967"). He married the former Kathleen Carroll and broke into broadcasting in 1950, as a news writer for a CBS radio affiliate in Minneapolis. In 1956, he came to New York.

The friendly, familiar face of Harry Reasoner, which people have come to know well as part of America's current television news world, is also a man, one senses, who is more serious than most people realize. In private, perhaps even sad at times.

This may be because he has known personal tragedy in his life. Although he enjoyed a happy childhood in Iowa, his adolescence was traumatic. Both of his parents were school teachers during the depression, but his father left Iowa for financial reasons to found a business in Minneapolis. Harry remained behind with his mother for three years. Then he moved to Minneapolis to an apartment house district in a big city. He didn't adjust very well. A year later his mother died. He was 12 years old. Then, a few years later, his father died.

Like all of his stories, on or off the air, Harry Reasoner tells you about his life without much sign of emotion. It is purely factual. Terse. Always the reporter. Reasoner is quoted in *TV Guide* as saying: "A basic philosophy of life came out of that period. I felt like an outsider. There's a tendency among such people to join up with other outsiders. The basic decision I made was *not* to seek that kind of ➡

(Continued from preceding page)

comfort. *Not* to indulge the emotions that bugged me. *Not* to be a rebel out of personal pique."

Perhaps Harry Reasoner's outstanding charm is that he does not pretend to be anything he is not. His name stems from his father's Pennsylvania Dutch family. ("Since I've been on the air," he says, "I've gotten a lot of letters which indicate the name may be Huguenot. I just don't know. My paternal grandparents were born in the U.S., but my maternal grandfather was a Scottish Presbyterian missionary to Canada.") Reasoner is, above all, a man who does not seem to have been affected one iota by success.

Asked if he writes his own material, he replies in typical fashion: "Walter Cronkite always says, 'I write as much as I can.' I always say, 'I write as little as I have to.' I don't think it's anything to make a fetish of. Except for my commentary, I am a reader of news. I pay more attention than most people to the quality of writing of the newscast. I think it's very important. I work closely with the writers. I respect them and they respect me. But I believe *they* should do the writing, not me."

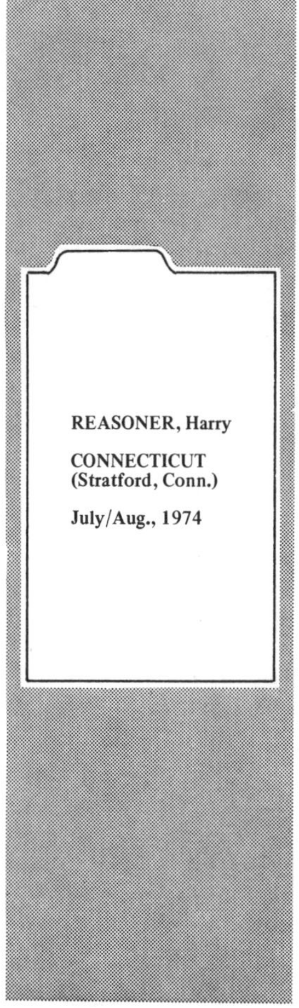

REASONER, Harry

CONNECTICUT
(Stratford, Conn.)

July/Aug., 1974

His commentaries, although occupying only a few minutes of air time, do not always come easily. "You can get an idea driving into town (he reads the morning newspaper while a driver drives him into New York at about 9:30 every day), you can turn it over in your head if you like it, you can sit down and write it in five minutes. But if you haven't got the idea by the time you reach the office, you can sit there and scratch your back and drink coffee and look at the ceiling for four hours and nothing will happen. It's impossible to say how long it takes, on the average."

As for his personal views, he says that "as a reporter I give up my rights to dogmatism and I approach all issues with an open mind. There's always the temptation to lead people with your own views, but this is dangerous for journalism. I try not to do it. I try not to insert my personal political views. If I did it, I'd lose my credibility on all other subjects. Everybody likes to get out once in a while and play reporter to keep the franchise. I greatly enjoyed the years I spent as a traveling reporter for CBS. It was one of the most satisfying things I did when I was fairly junior, and later on with *Sixty Minutes*. But except for four or five times a year that I get out from my Saturday broadcasts, those days are gone. And it's just as well. Reporting is a young man's game.

"One of my most challenging and exciting experiences was the good old days of the civil rights revolution in the South. I spent enough time in places like Little Rock and Montgomery so that I felt I understood both sides of the story. There are always two sides, of course. And I tried to contribute to better understanding in this area. Since then, the busiest time I had was the three years on CBS' *Sixty Minutes* when either Mike Wallace or I went to the scene of almost every news story in the world with the time and the facilities to do something about them. That was challenging—to get something different than you would get on a daily news show."

In more recent years, he says, his most memorable assignment was covering President Nixon's visit to Red China. "It was both fascinating and wearisome," he says succinctly. "I think the circumstances were not really to any American's credit. It happens that China was afraid of Russia and Russia was afraid of China, so each one was willing to turn to the United States. Still, Nixon is probably the only man who could have done it, considering his old anti-Communist attitude. I don't think even President Eisenhower could have done it. If Mr. Kennedy or Mr. Johnson had proposed it, they would have been accused of treason."

What does he think of Richard Nixon and the entire Watergate scandal? "I have only seen the President on occasion. I don't know him very well at all. I try to be careful about personal views of the President —any President—because I don't think journalists should think of themselves as being that important. But I'll answer the question. Mr. Nixon is, of course, the supreme pragmatist. He can switch on China politics, on price controls overnight without bothering his conscience. The thing I've noticed about him over the years is that he wants to give the impression of complete coolness when it is just not so. I think he boils a lot of the time underneath. I think we've seen that, understandably, due to the strain he's been under. As for Watergate, I think it's still very much a significant and major issue. I have the feeling that some people are sick of it, but, on the other hand, I don't see how we can play it down. I would hope for a reasonably speedy windup, but now that it's in the hands of so many lawyers, I don't think that's likely."

What does he think of the Nixon Administration's attack on the news media? "Well, I wasn't on the 'enemies list,' " Reasoner replies with a smile.

In a more serious vein, Reasoner says he is not surprised by the Administration's attacks on the press. "All administrations are basically anti-press," he explains. "There's a built-in antagonism between reporters and government at any level. Different administrations go at it in different ways. Eisenhower ignored the press and got along just fine with them. Kennedy charmed them and used them. Johnson twisted their arms. Nixon and his people were never comfortable with the press, perhaps because it grows out of his earlier experiences. But the attitude of government that they want to do good things and the press is nipping at their heels is not new. Insofar as government's criticism is directed at our faults, criticism is good. It makes us stronger. In this case, I am sorry that the question of government and the press got blurred by government's own problems. Commentary labeled as commentary can not be objected to. What I think they object to is bias in the news. As for those officials who would curb the networks, I would say this: In the first place I don't think we're biased. As far as stricter controls, I think the idea is ridiculous. I don't think we have a perfect record, but I would say it is outrageous that we have any controls at all on radio and television. I don't think the Federal Communications Commission would have anything to do with broadcast journalism. I think we should be on the same footing as newspapers—completely free."

How does he feel about America—looking back to the 1960s and forward in the 1970s? "The story of the 60s," he replies grimly, "was the great collapse of trust in traditional values. I describe it as probably the longest period of national introspection that any country has ever gone through. It began roughly after the Kennedy assassination, continued through our involvement in Vietnam and we came into the 70s almost as if we had a hangover. What got ripped up in the process was the supreme confidence this country had in itself—dating back to the end of World War II.

"You keep thinking there is going to be a period of time when things will calm down, but things always come up. Journalism should be able to foresee things better than we have. But we don't. I'm not profoundly optimistic but on the other hand I don't see any reason why we can't improve as a nation. One of the reasons I'm not worried is because I was never an optimist. I don't expect that much of humanity. But America is coming up to 200 years old and not many democratic countries make that. Most fail. It's happened to every democracy in the history of the world except Great Britain and us. The question is: Do we find some new means of reorganizing ourselves and develop a new vitality for the next 100 years or do we go into a state of decline? We presumably know more about how to analyze ourselves and how to analyze social and economic forces than did Rome. Perhaps we can do better."

When he's not busy with his time-consuming profession, Harry Reasoner rarely watches television. Instead, he likes to swim, play tennis, listen to "country" music and entertain friends at home. "I don't like big parties," he says. "We see mostly close friends, on weekends. In the wintertime we try to get away to the Caribbean. I try to live as normal a life as possible, even with the schedule I have in television."

Who is his most severe critic?

"My wife," he says, breaking out into a broad smile for the first time. "She watches me on the evening news. And she watches Walter. And when I get home at 8:30 she tells me what I did wrong that night. She's a great help to me."

Does he ever see himself on TV? "Unavoidably, when we're editing, I do."

His opinion of himself? "I wonder how I ever made it," he replies with characteristic Harry Reasoner understatement. □

Here's a new book you can Reed

REED, Rex
(1940 -)

CLEVELAND PRESS
(Cleveland, Ohio)

June 14, 1974

REPORTER MEETS REPORTER—Rex Reed tells Press reporter Barbara Chudzik about his book, "People Are Crazy Here."
(Press photo by Bernie Noble)

By Barbara Chudzik

Rex Reed has been called the hatchet man of show business journalists for his scathing movie reviews and brutally honest profiles of famous folks which appear in Showtime.

But catch him away from his typewriter and he is a soft-spoken, mild-mannered Southeran gentleman who would never strike terror in anyone's heart.

Reed was in town the other day to promote his new book "People Are Crazy Here." As we sat in a downtown restaurant, he ate Southern fried chicken and french fries with his fingers and told me what it's like to be Rex Reed.

"I am in an enviable position as a writer because I have total autonomy. Occasionally I accept magazine assignments, but usually I write only what I want to write," he said.

"I'd never waste my time writing about Julie Andrews because I could care less about Julie Andrews," he said. "Sometimes I'm desperate for a column so I have to interview anyone who's in town, but usually I can pick and choose my subjects."

Reed researches his subjects in the New York Public Library, sometimes uses a tape recorder to get the revealing quotes which have made him famous, but prefers to take notes by hand and "just print conversation."

"My biggest problem in life is that I'm so totally disorganized. I'm descipilined in many ways but not in my work habits," he said. "I never work ahead of schedule so I'm always up all night before deadlines."

"I'm one of the all-time great procrastinators. I will do anything to keep from writing — make 40 phone calls, water my plants, watch television. I hate the actual sitting down to write so I usually end up doing my columns at 3 a.m. when the phone has stopped ringing," he said.

Reed added that when the phone does ring he answers it himself "because I can't stand not knowing who's there." He has no secretary, maid or cook. "What I need is a slave."

Reed said his book was in its second printing even before publication date last Friday. It is a collection of 40 interviews which Reed describes as his most controversial, lively, interesting and well-written. Many have appeared in Showtime.

Among the stars Reed has interviewed and disliked are Barbra Streisand ("She kept me waiting five hours, then said 'You have 20 minutes what do you want to know?'"), Ava Gardner ("She would'nt let me take notes so I kept running to the bathroom to jot down what she'd said") and Lana Turner ("She was too drunk to answer any questions").

Notorious for printing everything he hears and sees in an interview, Reed said he isn't sure why people open up to him.

"When I started writing people told me everything because they thought I was too young to be smart and I would never remember what they said. Then as my reputation grew, people began to respect me," he said. "Now people know I tell the truth so they come to me with stories."

"These days people don't get as angry about my personal profiles as they do about my reviews," he said. "Show people are so insecure they can't take professional criticism."

Reed, who made his movie debut in the box-office flop "Myra Breckenridge," recently completed a new mini movie, "Illusions," with James Coco, Katharine Ross, Zero Mostel and Marcel Marceau. It is about swinging singles and loneliness, and is one of four short stories tied together in one movie.

A bachelor, Reed, 33, lives in the Dakota, a New York apartment which has been declared a historic landmark. He is a cook who loves to prepare Louisiana creole dishes, beef with onion gravy and lemon icebox pie.

In his spare time, he likes to go to Nantucket, read and sleep.

"Most people spend their vacations on some backbreaking adventure," he said. "For me doing absolutely nothing is the greatest way to spend spare time."

James Reston: Just Another Puzzled Man

JAMES RESTON AND HIS WIFE, SALLY

By MADELEINE BLAIS

MARTHA'S VINEYARD, Mass. — It was quite possibly the lovliest day of the year on this island community off Cape Cod, but like a lot of Americans, James (Scotty) Reston sat in a darkened room and watched television.

Reston, vice-president of the New York Times and the most influential of its Washington columnists, had returned here from a European vacation, spent a morning playing tennis with Walter Cronkite and now, with his wife, Sally, sat glued to the tube.

Much of Scotty's television viewing this year was of Watergate which he sees "as a kind of national education course on democracy.

"The questions that have been raised are more important than who goes to jail," he said. "It's not merely a matter of a good show; the net effect should be a body of legislation which will tidy up this mess, make it impossible for it to happen again. In the end, there will be guidelines on who among the White House staff should be confirmed by the Senate, on who should have access to TV."

IT IS RARE FOR Reston to sound off so, because he would listen quietly and ask questions. He habitually down plays his role as one of the foremost political commentators of our time.

"I am just," he says, "a puzzled man making notes, drawing sketches in the sand which the sea will wash away." He cheerfully credits Walter Lippman with the line.

Scotty and Sally Reston maintain an extra home here and for five years they have been to the Vineyard even in the off months to lend a supervisory hand to their pet project — the Vineyard Gazette newspaper. When the Gazette was put on sale in 1967, its editor, Henry Bettle Hough, approached the Restons (he considers them "brimful of newspaper know-how") and asked them to buy it. They did.

"HE WANTED IT to go to a newspaper family," explains Reston. "Sally and I knew we wanted to take an increasing amount of time off from the Washington whirl, to stop throwing presidents and continents around and do something simple, together."

"And of course the children are all grown now," says the woman Reston refers to as "My girl, Sally." There are three sons, one a reporter at the Los Angeles Times, another a professor at the University of North Carolina and an embattled pro-amnesty activist, and a third at the University of Virginia law school.

The Restons are wearing twin outfits — Mao jackets hand-tailored in China.

"You can't get anything like this here. They're 100 pct. cotton and loaded with pockets," observes Sally, who at 60 is three years her husband's junior and still an exceptionally pretty woman with a forthright face framed by brown curls.

THE PHONE rings and Sally says it's Harrison Salisbury, a Times colleague. "He must be back from somewhere important," ventures Reston as his stocky, slow-moving frame ambles toward the phone.

"Oh, yes, I had a great vacation," Reston says into the phone. "I spent a week in the heart of France fishing. I only made one catch, so I figure with the devaluation of the dollar, that put me out $285."

The banter lowers to a guarded mumble as the two Times executives get into something a bit heavier. The conversation eventually concludes and Reston turns from Times talk about his other paper, the Gazette.

"The paper has total absorption of the island homes," says Reston, "but it's a publication with limited advertising possibilities."

His wife translates: "The paper makes friends, not money."

Like the Times, it is, according to Reston, "a newspaper of record, sometimes devoting thousands of words to a single town meeting." It never endorses political candidates.

The biggest difference is that inaccuracy is a personalized problem and you're liable to get a punch in the nose if you misquote someone," he says.

IF YOU ASK THE RESTONS what first attracted them to the Vineyard, they are at a loss for words. "The beauty and quiet, I guess," Sally replies haltingly. "Maybe it's the melody of the place," her husband injects.

Later, at dinner, the newsman in Reston surfaces again.

"Quick! A pencil!" he demands, having surveyed the menu and noting that steak au poivre is going for $12. He says he is plotting a column on rising prices.

When it's time to order, the table is evenly divided between meat and fish, but Reston rejects rose as the wine choice: "It's too Republican, too safe, neutral, in-between." Red wine is served.

THE CONVERSATION TURNS to his marriage and Reston is hard put to reveal the secret of his successful union.

"I guess we just did things different in my day," says Reston. "Why, when Sally and I were young, sometimes we'd just spend long hours reading to each other. It was a way, really, of making love."

Somehow, the talk sifts to Watergate and the wives of the central figures. Reston says:

"You have to wonder whether the wives of Nixon and Ehrlichman and Haldeman and Magruder ever turned to their husbands and demanded, 'What is the truth?' Women have always been, to some extent, the keepers of moral standards in the family.

"One of my favorite definitions of civic duty comes from J. B. Priestly, who said, 'We should behave toward our country as women have toward the men they love. A loving wife will do anything for her husband except to stop criticizing and trying to improve him. That is the right attitude for a citizen. We should cast the same affectionate, but sharp, side-glances at our country. We should love it, but also insist on telling it all its faults.' End of quote."

HIS VOICE TRAILS and he upbraids himself: "This is a little ghoulish. You see, I think Watergate has already raised the broader philosophical question of the division of power in this country. Impeachment would have the effect of riveting our attention on the man, not the problem. As it is, the problem is partly solved.

"Now, instead of a strong Nixon with Ehrlichman and Haldeman and their system of doing things in the White House, we already have a weaker president."

And that's something that seems to give Scotty Reston a great deal of comfort.

RESTON, James Barrett (Scotty) (1909 -)

AKRON BEACON JOURNAL (Akron, Ohio)

Nov. 4, 1973

Does a Third Sex Book Spell 'Sexploitation'?

By JACK BOOTH

Of The Bulletin Staff

REUBEN, David
(1933 -)

PHILADELPHIA BULLETIN
(Philadelphia, Penn.) May 1, 1974

[See also CA-41/44]

Bulletin Staff Photo by Dom Ligato

HE MAY look bland, but Dr David Reuben is a skillful man who knows how to handle success.

HIS BOOKS have sold more than 18 million copies throughout the world, but somehow Dr. David Reuben just doesn't look the part of the man who made sex a safe subject for the dinner table.

Syndicated columnist Margo probably said it best after she interviewed him in 1971.

"Dr. Reuben," she wrote, "is slight, short, wears brown frame glasses and has a rather high voice. He looks like all the boys I ever knew who had trouble getting a date."

The frame glasses are black now, but little else has changed about the famous author of "Everything You Always Wanted to Know About Sex — But Were Afraid to Ask."

He still looks like a diminutive traveling salesman, particularly in the oddly cut suit with cloth-covered buttons that he wore in an interview yesterday at the Holiday Inn, 4th and Arch sts.

Figure of Authority?

With his nervous little laugh and hyperactive movements, he was hardly a figure of authority.

But it would be a mistake to underestimate the shrewd intelligence of a man who skipped three grades in grammar school and graduated from medical school at 23.

The same man was treating movie stars in a successful psychiatric practice in California long before his first book became the number one best-seller in 1969.

He skillfully followed that book with another number one best-seller in 1971 entitled, "Any Woman Can!"

And now his third book, "How to Get More Out of Sex — Than You Ever Thought You Could," already has sold 60,000 copies since its publication four weeks ago.

In the new book, the 40-year-old doctor carefully retains the question-and-answer format and sophomoric humor that have made his books palatable to millions of Americans.

Crossed the Border

And in interviews like yesterday's, he carefully defuses charges that, with three sex books under his name now, he has crossed the border into sexploitation.

"I got 60,000 letters from the first book and the second," he said, "and so many of them said, 'Well gee, now I know all these things about sex and it's all very interesting, but how do I use them to get more out of sex?' "

That answer, incorporating as it does the title of his new book, is typical of the self-promotion Dr. Reuben injects into his answers.

Fair Amount of Ego

It's a self-promotion that, despite his seemingly bland appearance, stems from a fair amount of ego.

He was familiar with the quote from Margo, for example, and he knew just how to reply.

"I don't really look on my life as a popularity contest," he said. "I don't feel the need to answer to people like Margo."

Then, grinning impishly, he added: "Did you know that Margo is Ann Landers' daughter?"

The ego was even more obvious in his surprisingly defensive reaction to the observation that the sports jacket he wears in a photo on the cover of his new book looks like it dates back to around 1966.

"That picture was taken like in 1970," he faltered, "and that was one of two sports jackets I owned. The other one was a light one and the photographer said to wear this one."

No Career Problems

But if the doctor has problems with his image, the same cannot be said of his career.

Born in Chicago in mid-Depression to an immigrant Hungarian lawyer, he finished high school at 15 and enrolled at the University of Chicago.

After graduating from the University of Illinois Medical School, he spent three years at Cook County Hospital in Chicago and then two more in the Air Force before marrying in 1961 and setting up a clinic in La Presa, Calif., near San Diego.

He now has a home in San Diego and one near Fort Myers, Fla.

Success, Dr. Reuben insists, has changed his life only in that he now spends only about 25 percent of his time on his practice. Another 30 percent goes to writing, and the rest goes to studying and reading.

"My life hasn't changed much," he said, "because I made a conscious decision that it wasn't going to change.

"Before my books I treated so-called celebrities and I saw the disturbances it introduced into their lives and how it really worked against them, and I decided it wasn't going to happen to me. So I'm not a celebrity or anything like that."

Critics of His Book

Some critics have said his new book, "How to Get More Out of Sex," details so many problems that can arise that it might actually make people worry even more.

It goes into great length, for example, about all the potentially disastrous side effects of various birth control methods, leaving the reader with the impression that the only truly safe method is to seal off the woman's fallopian tubes.

Enough stress is placed on the mental causes of male impotence that most sufferers will probably despair of never finding a solution.

And so many other potential problems are detailed that even well-adjusted readers may feel queasy after finishing the book.

Dr. Reuben's answer is that preparing for the worst is a highly necessary thing.

"This is the problem with sex," he said. "Everything can be fine today but tonight, tomorrow or next week you can yourself have a sex problem or your wife or your children or your parents can have one."

Richler:

Movie initiation of a Canadian author finding honor in his own land

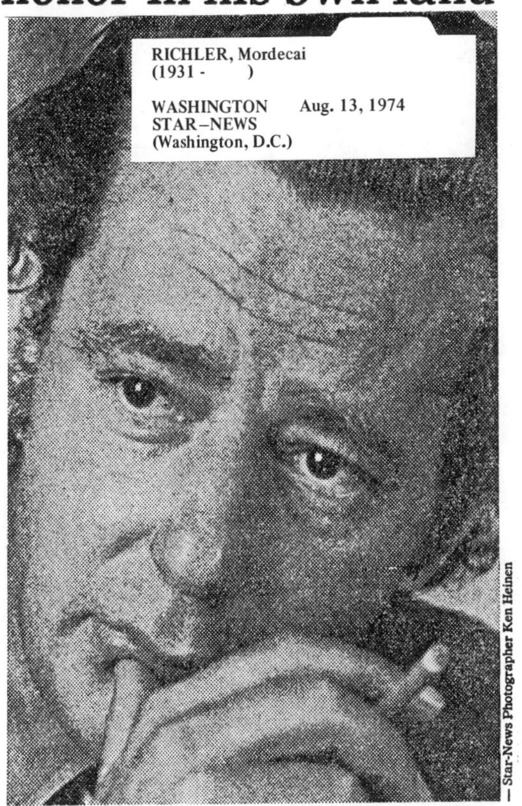

RICHLER, Mordecai
(1931 -)
WASHINGTON Aug. 13, 1974
STAR-NEWS
(Washington, D.C.)

— Star-News Photographer Ken Heinen

By Donia Mills
Star-News Staff Writer

"This is all a bit ironic," the Canadian novelist Mordecai Richler said with a benign smile, spreading his arms to embrace the hotel suite, press agent, reporter, photographer angling for a close-up, and breakfast waiting under a white linen cover on the sideboard. "To find myself associated with a big-time film this way, when my reputation has been strictly quiet and literary up to now.

"I'm having a great time, of course, but I keep reminding myself I'm still just a writer — in the long run, what this all means is that my books will reach a wider audience."

THE MOVIE Richler is traveling all over the country to promote, at Paramount's expense, is "The Apprenticeship of Duddy Kravitz," which he adapted from his own semi-autobiographical novel. The book, he says, "sank without a trace" when it first appeared, in 1959, though today it has become a sort of coming-of-age classic, and is taught in Canadian schools the way "Catcher in the Rye" and "A Separate Peace" are in this country.

Directed by a longtime friend, Ted Kotcheff, Duddy on film has a similar rags-to-riches history.

"Kotcheff and I shared a flat in London when we were both in 'Canadian expatriate status,' doing the best-paying work abroad we could get, which usually meant film and TV drudge work on other people's stories. Ten years ago we used to sit around and drink and dream about making a movie of 'Duddy Kravitz,' but I had really given up hope. Kotcheff was the one who pursued it.

"The major studios just weren't interested. 'A movie about a young kid struggling to get ahead in the Jewish ghetto of Montreal in the 1940s?' they'd say. 'Are you kidding?' "

THE PICTURE was finally financed by the Canadian Film Development Council. Initially budgeted at $600,000, it was ultimately brought in for the relatively modest cost of $930,000, plus a few ulcers and a lot of gray hairs.

Happily, like so many of Duddy's wild-eyed gambles, the movie about his frenetic adventures paid off handsomely. Paramount president Frank Yablans loved it, picked it up for international distribution with a blockbuster promotional campaign and, after only 13 weeks in release, "The Apprenticeship of Duddy Kravitz" is already the highest-grossing film in Canadian movie history — and an important breakthrough for the native industry.

"The last thing Canadians will do, usually, is go to see a Canadian movie," Richler said, explaining why it was absolutely necessary for the producers to make 'Duddy Kravitz' an "international movie for an international audience" if they ever hoped to earn back their investment.

Unsatisfied with the young Canadian actors available for the crucial lead role, Kotcheff flew to Hollywood last summer and tested 20 American actors. He found his ideal Duddy in Richard Dreyfuss star of the then-unreleased "American Graffiti", who heads the cast of primarily American and British character actors they'd already signed.

"EVERYONE in the cast was enthusiastic about the film — they had to be, they were working for so little money. Denholm Elliott playing the hilariously besotted film director Duddy teams up with to make wedding and bar-mitzvah movies) flew over from England, tourist class, and stayed in a tiny hotel. In the end, I think not having great sums of money helped us out — it got everyone in the penny-pinching mood of the story."

"Duddy Kravitz" was filmed largely on location in a three-block roped-off area of the same old St. Urbain Street neighborhood where Richler was born in 1931, the son of a struggling junk dealer.

Ours was definitely a working-class household. We never had much money — but somehow we didn't feel it. There was a rich street life, a lot of communty spirit."

ASPIRING TO a literary career, and feeling that Canadian standards were "picayune and parochial," he left Montreal after high school and settled in France. There, along with such author-companions as Terry Southern and Herb Gold, he pursued the kind of "moveable-feast" life glamorized by his literary idols, Hemingway and Fitzgerald.

"Believe it or not, it was possible to live in Paris in those days for $100 a month. A lot of guys were there on the GI Bill, and somebody was always getting a check. There were a lot of 'little magazines' to write for. You never made plans — you walked down to the local cafe to meet your friends, and the evening just happened."

His first novels, written during this time, were heavily derivative — of "Hemingway, Sartre, Malraux" — and not very good, Richler says. "I took myself and my art far too seriously back then. I guess 'Duddy Kravitz' was the first time I really came up with an original work drawn from my own real experiences."

AFTER LIVING and writing abroad for 20 years, the author said, he felt it was "time to come home" because his life had become parochial.

"Everyone I knew was in the arts, and I was closing myself off into a very dry and sheltered existence. I just don't have the kind of imagination to propel myself from one novel to the next without refueling with new and different experiences."

Richler now takes on a lot of free-lance journalism assignments, like covering the witches' convention in St. Paul for the July issue of *Playboy*. "Imagine what material I was exposed to there — all those witches from all over the country meeting in St. Paul for a convention!"

Today he lives with his wife and five children in Montreal — ironically, in the posh Westmount area of hillside homes that represented an indomitable gentil stronghold to Duddy and his friends.

"Westmount isn't really a dream come true for me or anything," he shrugged. "I never had any real desire to live there — it just wasn't in my frame of reference. Most of that boorish anti-Semitism is gone now — the restricted clubs and neighborhoods — along with the 'second-class-citzen' attitude of the English-speaking toward the French Canadians. Montreal used to be one sprawling succession of ghettos — WASP, Jewish, French — but now there's much more integration. It's a beautiful city, with a distinctive charm all its own — if Toronto is the New York of Canada, Montreal is its San Francisco."

THEN, in the very next breath, he's badmouthing his countrymen again; its easy to see why he rubs Canadian nationalists the wrong way.

"I've never felt there's any stigma attached to Canadian work per se — but a lot of artists there with chips on their shoulders will assume that if it's Canadian, it's not going to sell. Canadians seem to prefer failure to success — failure is somehow more reassuring. Just wait — if Duddy Kravitz continues to do business, particularly in the United States, the Canadian critics will start doing 'reexaminations' and get all huffy because there are no Canadian actors in it."

It's safe to say, however, that there is nothing the Candian critics can say at this point to harm Mordecai Richler, who appears to have nowhere to go but up. He expects spring publication of a children's book he's been promising his kids he'd do for years — "Jacob Two-Two Meets the Hooded Fang" — and he's in the early stages of another serious novel.

MOREOVER, he and Kotcheff are collaborating on a movie version of "Cocksure," a "scatological satire of Canadian mores" he wrote in 1967 to the chagrin of a lot of Canadians. And producer-director Alan Pakula is expected to direct a screen version of his 1971 novel, "St. Urbain's Horseman," an even more autobiographical story based on one of the minor characters who appeared briefly in "Duddy Kravitz" — Duddy's writer-schoolmate Hersh.

"I would love too write a whole body of literature about these St. Urbain characters." he said. "Would I write about Duddy Kravitz and what he's become 20 years later in his life? I've thought about it, but I don't know. I'm not sure there's enough there to tell without becoming repetitious — and, of course, I don't want to start trading on Duddy's success that way. It's a very delicate question." ➡

(Also see preceding article)

Mordecai Richler: Humane Vision, Healthy Distrust

By JONATHAN YARDLEY

Herald Book Editor

Fame, or at least a small measure of it, is at last coming to Mordecai Richler.

Mordecai Who?

That is exactly the question the proprietor of my friendly neighborhood bookstore asked when a customer wandered in the other day to ask if he "had any books by Mordecai Richler." Not merely did he have none of Richler's books, he had never heard of him.

UNTIL QUITE recently, mention of Richler's name met a similar response almost everywhere; two decades after the publication of his first novel, he remained a virtual unknown. Now, however, one of his novels has been made into a successful movie, with the result that attention is finally being paid to the author himself.

The film is "The Apprenticeship of Duddy Kravitz." It has enjoyed a highly profitable New York run, and recently opened in a number of Miami neigborhood theaters. Though the merits of the movie are open to debate — it is a fine entertainment, but not much more — the production will be more than welcome if it leads readers to Richler's fiction and essays.

That is because Richler is, and has been for some time, one of the finest writers around. His novels have elicited wide critical admiration for their wit, rich characterization, elegant prose and thematic consistency. His essays are equally admirable, for the same reasons as well as for their telling commentary on a broad variety of contemporary pomposities.

The trouble is, Richler exists in a peculiar literary limbo: He is a Canadian. As he has pointed out in some of his essays, his fellow countrymen either take their native writers too seriously (especially, it seems, the bad ones) or not seriously at all. Readers in other countries, the United States in particular, seem persuaded that nothing of value can issue from a nation that appears condemned to occupy a perpetual (and distant) second place on the North American continent.

For Richler, the consequence has been that, favorable reviews notwithstanding, sales have been low and popular following minimal. Much the same fate has befallen other Canadian writers of comparable talents, among them Morley Callaghan, Northrop Frye, Margaret Atwood, Richard B. Wright and Robertson Davies.

In the past couple of months, however, things have begun to turn around for Richler in the United States — where, like it or not, literary reputations and royalties are in large measure determined. The film version of "Duddy" is doing well, and a Ballantine Books paperback edition of the novel ($1.50) is getting prominent display on bookracks.

The man behind this ripple of literary interest was born 42 years ago in Montreal. Richler's family was both Jewish and poor, so it lived in the Jewish quarter of that city centered around St. Urbain Street. Richler attended public schools in the neighborhood and, for two years, Sir George Williams College.

THEN HE got restless and decided to strike out on his own. As he recalled in a recent article, "In 1951, I had left Canada, a cocky 19-year-old, foolishly convinced that merely by quitting the country, I could put my picayune past behind me. Unpublished, but hopeful, I sailed for England, fabled England, all my possessions fitting neatly into one cabin trunk and, in my breast pocket, a letter from the managing editor of the now defunct Montreal Herald, saying I had been loyal, industrious and (the clincher, this) a sober employe."

Richler remained in London for 20 years, supporting himself with writing of various kinds and writing his own books as well. The first, a novel called **The Acrobats**, was published when he was 22. Among the generally favorable reviews it received, a particularly perceptive one appeared in the British magazine, The Spectator. It said in part:

"Mr. Richler is of the generation which has missed the opportunity of taking a physical part in the good-evil struggle. There have been for him no easy externalizations of his own problems, no Smash the Hun, no Save the World from the Red Tide. But all around him wash the ripples of these simple causes, echoes of clean, harsh storms far out at sea whose origins he can only wonder about . . . This isn't a brilliant answer. Because for Mr. Richler's generation there isn't one. But the failure to find an answer is what **The Acrobats** is about."

The Apprenticeship of Duddy Kravitz appeared five years later, and in dealing with the adventures of a young Montreal Jew on the way up it established that, though Richler himself might be in England, his preoccupation remained Canada. Though an engaging movie has been made from it (with a script by Richler), it is far from his best work. There are many fine passages in it, but it wavers uncertainly between toughmindedness and sentimentality, finally opting for the latter.

The novel does, however, set the stage for Richler's finest work to date — St. Urbain's Horseman, published in 1971. This is the novel in which Richler's manifold talents all come together, the novel to which readers interested in making Richler's acquaintance are best advised to turn.

St. Urbain's Horseman is vastly more complex, intricate, ambitious and successful than **Duddy Kravitz**. It is about Jake Hersh, a boyhood friend of Duddy's in Montreal, who is living in London and finding himself, at the age of 37, creeping inexorably toward middle age. It is a novel about that time of life when people realize that they are not fated to do all the great things they once dreamed of, when the fabrics of their lives suddenly seem less secure, when the knowledge of death becomes immediate and personal.

It is also a novel about the theme that The Spectator's reviewer recognized in **The Acrobat**:

"Young too late, old too soon was, as Jake had come to understand it, the plaintive story of his . . . generation. Conceived in the Depression, but never to taste its bitterness firsthand, they had actually contrived to sail through the Spanish Civil War, World War II, the holocaust, Hiroshima, the Israeli War of Independence, McCarthyism, Korea and, latterly, Vietnam and the drug culture, with impunity. Always the wrong age. Ever observers, never participants. The whirlwind elsewhere."

This sense of being unengaged leads Hersh into a number of feckless attempts to involve himself in the world's business, but eventually it leads him further — to an understanding of the unique position his generation occupies:

"WHEN IT wasn't the children's safety, death, or the Germans' second coming that plagued him, it was the fact that he felt his generation was unjustly squeezed between two raging and carnivorous ones. The old establishment and the young hipsters . . . Unwillingly, without justice, they had been cast in Kerensky's role. Neither as obscene as the Czar, nor as bloodthirsty as Lenin. Even as Jews, they did not fit a mythology. Not having gone like sheep to the slaughterhouse, but also too fastidious to punish Arab villages with napalm. What Jake stood for would not fire the countryside: decency, tolerance, honor. With E.M. Forster, he wearily offered two cheers for democracy. After George Orwell, he was for a closer look at anyone's panacea.

"Jake was a liberal."

The passage is quintessential Richler, and as much as anything he has written it demonstrates why he deserves to be widely read. Both his fiction and his essays are dominated by a civilized, humane vision, a healthy distrust of rhetoric and bombast, a wry, humorous acceptance of life's imperfections. Touches of those qualities shine through in the film version of "Duddy," but to find them in abundance one must go to Richler's books. The trip is well worth making.

'Show Me Quality'

Photo by Joseph Tritsch, of The Bulletin

By NESSA FORMAN
Bulletin Art Editor

The first day of class he stands high on the platform in the dimmed room. Just before the first slide appears, he says:

"My name is Robb. You can see me, but I can't see you. If you see me on campus, say 'Hello.' I'm the man with the cane."

With that, art history professor David M. Robb transports the classroom at the University of Pennsylvania to the Middle Ages.

And with that Dr. Robb also draws a sharp line between the students and the professor.

It's a position from which he—as a superior teacher and a scholar — does not waver. If some view his approach as gruff or old-fashioned, he ignores it.

Man With a Mission

He, as described by one of his colleagues at Penn, is a man with a mission in art history. That mission has two broad goals: to present the material honestly and to tell the student why he should consider it important.

For some reason, Dr. Robb has put teaching first. Art history for him is a serious discipline. It's not so much art appreciation or the ability to turn a pretty corner in conversation as it is an intensive study of the objects of the past. It is the glue of culture that shows where we have come from.

Students who have shuddered at his stern, strict and autocratic method — often calling it his fear approach — have come to learn that Dr. Robb has no time for fools. His unspoken view: "Show me quality. Grasp the material, put it together. If you make a statement, back it up with facts. Slipshod ideas and unproven intuition have no place here."

But underneath Dr. Robb's curmudgeoned facade lies a complex humanistic man, with an eye for good wine and food, an ear for a ribald story, a tongue for a witty remark.

He is a man who deeply cares.

On Wednesday, April 11, the Philadelphia Art Alliance will publish Dr. Robb's manuscript on the "Art of the Illuminated Manuscript." An accompanying exhibit will also open to the public.

Like his earlier books, "Art in the Western World" and "The Harper History of Painting," this one represents a high point in art history in America.

ROBB, David Metheny
(1903 -)

PHILADELPHIA
BULLETIN
(Philadelphia, Penn.)

Apr. 8, 1973

This will be one of the first, and probably the best, of the books on manuscripts in English.

It is a book intended for the scholar and student but written in eloquent and flowering prose for the interested. Dr. Robb's genius in this book, as in his teaching approach, lies in his gift of clearly synthesizing and analyzing the objects in stylistic and icongraphic terms and relating them to history of books, ideas and art.

Dr. Robb was born in China of missionary parents in 1903. It was no accident that the Occidental and not the inscrutable Oriental mind appealed to him, although it was an accident that he was drawn to art history. He went to Oberlin in 1922 to become a musicologist, although he now describes his base-baritone voice as sounding like that of Oliver the dragon. One chance art history course, and he was sold.

From there he went to Princeton where he received his Ph.D.

He came to Penn's fledgling art history program in 1939. Then, art history was under the wing of fine arts, and Dr. Robb taught just about every course except the medieval, at first. After 1955, he added his special medieval courses.

It has been said that Penn's art history department—now ranked in the top ten of U. S. universities —is Dr. Robb. It was mainly he who seized the opportunity, in 1959, to take it out of the fine arts department and make it its own discipline.

If Dr. Robb is the first to pay tribute to his mentors—Clarence Ward, C. R. Morey and Erwin Panofsky — he himself has influenced practically everyone who came out of Penn's program.

'Is That All?'

His former students, who teach and head art programs across the country, are the first to applaud the man who made them sweat bullets. His curt "Is that all, Mr. So and So?" could send a student back to the books for weeks. In the end, it was the student's gain.

Not just a Robb student, but anyone who ever took the basic survey course at Penn will always remember Dr. Robb's emotion-packed lecture on Leonardo. In that one hour, his distant, monotone became vulnerable.

Dr. Robb leads up to his last Leonardo slide by explaining the Renaissance master's tragic inability to complete his works.

Then he shows "The Last Supper," saying that Leonardo had decided to portray the moment when Christ says "One of You Shall Betray Me." The apostles pull back saying, "Lord, is it I?"

Dr. Robb says: "Only One could give the answer. He could, but he would not."

Exit Dr. Robb with tears.

From the students: A standing ovation.

William Robson: Still Living For Radio

By Boris Weintraub
Star-News Staff Writer

A hand-lettered sign hangs over William N. Robson's cluttered desk in his tiny basement office in the Broadcast Support Division of the Voice of America. It reads:

"Documentary: the creative treatment of actuality."

ON SUNDAY night between 7 and midnight, WAMU-FM will pay tribute to William N. Robson's 40 years of creating broadcast documentaries by playing a number of his landmark radio programs, interspersed with live comments by Robson.

A good documentary could be made of Robson's life itself—five Peabody awards, his five nominations for the annual award of the TV-Radio Writers, his outstanding programs, such as a remarkable half-hour on the 1943 Detroit race riot which Time Magazine called "one of the most eloquent programs in radio history."

And it would also include the low points, such as his being listed in the infamous "Red Channels" during the McCarthy era, which led to his being fired by CBS's "vice president in charge of treason," as Robson calls it.

ROBSON got into radio by accident. His first job was with Paramount Pictures in the early days of sound motion pictures, but the Depression hit even Hollywood.

"I heard they were looking for a writer at KHJ in Los Angeles, so I had lunch with the man," he recalled. "That was on the day that President Roosevelt closed the banks; I had 35 cents in my pocket. But I got the job."

His first radio creation was a series called "Conquerors of the Sky," dramatizations of stories about World War I flyers. His second was a pioneer effort, "Calling All Cars," the first radio series based on actual police cases.

"It predated 'Gangbusters,' and we outdrew 'Amos 'n' Andy' and 'Myrt and Marg' on the coast," Robson recalled.

IN 1936, Robson moved to Chicago to produce a variety show called "Sears, Then and Now," then went to New York a year later as a director. Soon he became director of the Columbia Workshop, which experimented in the broadcast medium. (One of his later Columbia Workshop shows, from 1946, will be heard on WAMU Sunday night; Igor Stravinsky's "Ebony Concerto," played by Woody Herman's orchestra, conducted by Stravinsky and introduced by a young Chet Huntley.)

Robson returned to Hollywood in 1939 to direct the original "Big Town," with Edward G. Robinson playing the role of Steve Wilson, crusading editor of the *Illustrated Press.* He also did "Hollywood Playhouse" with Charles Boyer and an Old Gold show with Don Ameche; for a while, he directed all three at the same time.

When World War II broke out, he returned east as "a 50-cent-a-year man" turning out documentaries for the Office of Emergency Management in Washington while continuing to work for CBS. During the war, he began his series, "The Man Behind the Gun," telling the story of America's Armed Forces. It won his first Peabody.

THE SECOND came for the show on the Detroit riots; it was called "Open Letter on Race Hatred."

"I was a friend of Walter White, who was then executive secretary of the NAACP," Robson recalled. "They wanted a show on the riot, so we did it."

Though the show, which also will be heard Sunday night, sounds a little over-dramatic today, it crackles with reality, and it was unique at the time in presenting the black side of the troubles. It ends with a five-minute speech urging Negro progress and rights by Wendell Willkie.

—Star-News Photographer Joseph Silverman

After the war, Robson worked on a number of programs, and was just getting into television when disaster, in the form of the little book entitled "Red Channels," struck.

"I was one of the honored 100," Robson said. "I hadn't done anything, but that didn't matter; once you were accused that was it; you couldn't be unaccused." He lost his CBS job.

HE BECAME a "writer in exile" in Paris. He turned out a few Hollywood free-lance offers for those who didn't worry about the blacklist. Mostly, he waited for times to change.

"The day after the vice president in charge of treason at CBS resigned, I was re-employed," he said. "But that hit me at the peak time of my career; I should have been going into TV, the whole bit."

He resumed his career in Hollywood, but then radio was drying up; he saw the future when CBS moved the "Suspense" show, on which he was working, from Hollywood to New York to save $80 a week.

IN 1962, his old friend Edward R. Murrow became director of the United States Information Agency, and Robson sent him a congratulatory letter. In return, Murrow offered him a job at the Voice of America.

"Since this was the only place radio was being done, and since I loved Ed Murrow like a brother, I took it," he said. "I've been here 12 years; it's the longest I've ever worked in one place."

He has never regretted his involvement in radio.

"I don't like to write for television. I don't even like to look at it."

ROBSON, William N.

WASHINGTON STAR–NEWS (Washington, D.C.)

Apr. 18, 1974

Novelist pans riches with fantasy, adventure

—Treganza Photo

ROGERS, Rosemany (pseud. Marina Mayson) (1932-) [See also CA-49/52]
FORT WORTH STAR-TELEGRAM Dec. 31, 1974 (Ft. Worth, Tex.)

By TOM E. HUFF

Who is Rosemary Rogers?

A year ago she was a completely unknown divorcee living in California, working as a secretary and struggling to make a living for herself and her four children, two of them in college. Today she is the best-selling novelist in America, with two phenomenally successful novels breaking all existing records in publishing history.

Avon books brought out "Sweet Savage Love" as a paperback original in January, 1974. First novels generally don't sell well. They usually sink into rapid oblivion. "Sweet Savage Love" was on national best-seller lists within a week of publication and is now in its seventh printing with over a million copies sold.

Sages in the publishing industry considered this a freak success and doubted it could be matched with a second novel. Lightning never strikes twice in the same place, they observed, predicting modest sales and listing writers who, after a successful first, bombed disastrously with second books. "The Wildest Heart" appeared in October and, in less than six weeks, sold some 782,000 copies, with orders still pouring in and publishers rushing to the presses for yet more printings.

* * *

IT WILL EASILY have passed the million mark by the first of 1975, surpassing even the incredible success of "Sweet Savage Love."

"I feel exactly like Cinderella," Ms. Rogers confided in a recent interview. "I just can't believe it. It's like having all my dreams come true."

Attractive, vivacious and personable, Ms. Rogers speaks in a lilting, melodious voice with an accent difficult to pin down. Perhaps this is because her ancestry is a wildly assorted mixture of French, English, Dutch, Irish and Italian. Born and raised in Ceylon, Ms. Rogers attended St. John's school in Panadura and the University of Ceylon. After a stint working on the Ceylon Daily News, she traveled extensively before coming to this country in 1962. Now an American citizen, Ms. Rogers resides in Fairfield, Calif., and staunchly declares her feelings about it.

"I love America," she states in that mellifluous voice. "I've traveled all over, and there's no place else I'd rather live — no place at all."

Phenomenal literary success is a distinctly American institution, and Rosemary Rogers follows in the footsteps of Kathleen Winsor, Grace Metalious and, more recently, Jacqueline Susann, each of whom provided fiction that filled readers' needs at the time they appeared.

* * *

MS. WINSOR offered flamboyant costume romance for readers distressed by the grim realities of war, Grace Metalious suggested that sex existed during the strait-laced 50s and, in an era of conflict, computers and credit cards, Ms. Susann gave readers a glimpse of glamorous people living glamorous lives.

Perhaps Kathleen Winsor is her closest antecedent, for, like Amber, Ms. Rogers' heroines are beautiful, passionate, sumptously gowned and invariably surrounded by handsome, dashing, magnetic men. Greatly expanded daydreams played against colorful and exotic backgrounds, the novels are filled with adventure, excitement and, always, wildly tempestuous romance.

"Sweet Savage Love" takes Virginia Brandon from the ballrooms of Paris to colorful old New Orleans to the glamorous and intrigue-filled Mexico of Carlotta and Maximillian. In "The Wildest Heart" Lady Rowena Dangerfield is pursued by a prince in India, raped by her aristocratic stepfather in London and captured by Apaches in New Mexico.

Impeccably researched, written with great aplomb, both books provide vicarious experience for women whose lives are slightly less exciting. Women in the business world today are subjected to the same problems and pressures as men, and they require an outlet for their fantasies, as do housewives whose days are a constant round of supermarkets, washing machines and dentist appointments for the children.

* * *

"THE MOVIES no longer supply that outlet," Ms. Rogers states. "All those wonderful films that used to satisfy us are a thing of the past. Nor does television provide an outlet—at least not for women. Men have their football games to watch, but there's very little for women. We have to turn to novels in order to find temporary escape."

Ms. Rogers confesses that she reads constantly and is weary of the "life-is-grim, life-is-harsh" school of fiction.

"Life is hard, yes—how well I know," she remarks, "but all of us have a need for fantasy. When I started 'Sweet Savage Love' I set out to write the kind of book I would like to read myself."

Like so many writers, Ms. Rogers began to write as soon as she could hold a pencil, filling innumerable notebooks with neatly printed stories at an age when most little girls were content to dress up like Mommy and push dolls around in a perambulator. Writing has always been a compulsion for her, and she continued to write throughout her childhood, during her teens and on into young womanhood. She always intended to become a novelist and never gave up that dream, even though marriage and the responsibility of four children made it seem increasingly remote.

"During all those years when I was feeding and diapering the babies I would fantasize in order to keep myself sane," she confesses.

* * *

"I JUST KNEW it was something I had to do — writing I mean — and I had to believe that someday it would all be possible."

Ms. Rogers works every day, striving to complete at least 10 pages. A night person, she finds she works best from 10:30 at night 'til 5 in the morning.

"It's so quiet and peaceful then," she says rather pensively, "and all the problems of the day are behind me."

When the words don't come easily, when she is unable to get them down on paper, she frequently takes long walks, thinking about the scene in progress. She sees her novels in cinematic terms, "like mind movies," she declares, adding that she often dreams about her characters and gets a number of ideas that way.

"The characters are so alive, the things they do so very real," she states. "It's . . .," she paused, reflecting. "It's almost as though they haunt me, and the only way I can exorcise them is by getting it all down on paper."

Ms. Rogers feels a particular kinship with Texas, shyly confessing that one of her "favorite boyfriends" was a Texan, a tall, lanky gentleman who spoke with a "delicious accent" and, years ago, stirred her imagination with tall tales of derring-do about his native state.

* * *

THIS EARLY interest has been augmented over the years by continuous reading about the state, its history and the rugged, colorful individuals who gave it such a special flavor. A large section of her third novel, "Dark Fires," which Avon will bring out next July, is set in Texas.

"I've given the place a fictional name," she claims, "but actually it's set around your Caddo Lake, such a fascinating area."

Amazingly enough, despite almost two million books sold during the past eleven months, despite trying to do 10 pages a day and maintaining a large and active household, this remarkable mother of four still holds down a full-time secretarial job. She may feel like Cinderella, but, like Cinderella, she has her eye on the clock and isn't altogether sure it won't all evaporate at the stroke of midnight.

"It's all so wonderful," she confides in her quiet, musical voice. "It's wonderful to think people are actually reading my books and enjoying them, but — well, my secretarial job is real and substantial, something I can depend on."

Come July, when "Dark Fires" appears, Ms. Rogers is likely to break even more records, and as hundreds of thousands of her books continue to sell like the proverbial hotcakes, perhaps she'll even give up her job and devote full time to writing.

Elliott's FDR and Eleanor

ROOSEVELT, Elliott (1910-)

WASHINGTON STAR–NEWS (Washington, D.C.)

Apr. 20, 1973

By DIANA McLELLAN
Star-News Staff Writer
—Star-News photographer Brig Cabe

At 62, Elliott Roosevelt flashes a many-toothed Roosevelt grin, wears his hair smoothed back from his leathery brown face in a low-profile, just-graying Roosevelt pompadour over lightly freckled ears. He sits with the stolid, gentlemanly sprawl of a large man accustomed to settling down to long hours of boring noblesse-oblige conversation.

And he tries very hard not to talk about his parents' sex life.

A DIFFICULT subject to avoid, since the printing of choice portions of his soon-to-be-published book, "The Roosevelts of Hyde Park: An Untold Story," in the Ladies' Home Journal.

The four other children of Franklin Delano and Eleanor Roosevelt have all indignantly disassociated themselves from his book, which follows the family — a little too closely for their taste — from 1916 up until the early days in the White House.

That doesn't bother Elliott a bit.

"Nobody," he points out, "asked my opinion of 'Eleanor and Franklin'" That book, published in late 1971, first officially told the story of the former President's 30-year relationship with Lucy Mercer Rutherford, and was "family-authorized."

"It certainly wasn't authorized by me," sniffs the middle of the five scions.

In his book, he goes even further: He pinpoints the date Eleanor discovered irrefutable proof of her husband's relationship with her beautiful social secretary; he reveals her subsequent concession to the family that she would live as his public partner but not as his wife, rather than getting a divorce; and he reveals what the Ladies' Home Journal calls "the long-hidden love story" of FDR's other long-term attachment — his aide Missy LeHand.

"It's very frustrating when people keep coming back to the sex part of the book all the time, because that is actually just a small part of it," says the author. "But it's the part that seemed to make headlines."

"AMONG THE family, there was never any effort at all to dissemble about Missy's role. The children all accepted her completely, and mother did too. She was in the position of an intimate member of the family."

In fact, to the family at the time, the closeness of FDR and Missy was acceptable enough to figure in household arrangements. With FDR's election to governor, the family's move into the Executive Mansion in Albany saw Elanor in self-imposed exile in a back bedroom, and Missy's and FDR's rooms joined by a small, glass-paned door.

Elliott, hunched cheerfully over coffee at the Georgetown Inn the other day, along with his co-author James Brough, is an easy-going, shamblingly large figure with the disconcerting air of a man dressed in somebody else's clothes. He obviously belongs in shapeless tweeds, but was attired instead in a Navy blue double-knit suit with silver buttons, a navy blue shirt, a shiny navy blue tie, and a apair of shoes as brown and solid and simple as flower-pots — doubtless old and English, like the ones he remembers his father wearing in his ebullient, pre-polio days.

The picture that emerges of Eleanor Roosevelt from his book is of a chilly, introverted woman; withdrawing haughtily to the sidelines of family fun, secretive, and miserably self-conscious until wheedled into public life by Roosevlet's political mentor, Louis Howe.

"YES, THERE'S quite a difference between my picture of my mother and the one you read in 'Eleanor and Franklin.' That one had a completely inaccurate depiction of my parents, as they were during these early years.

"It painted Father as a crippled, weak person completely dominated by his wife and mother. That just wasn't true. During this period I'm writing about, mostly up until around 1932, my mother was just as I've shown her."

"Remember, she made a complete metamorphosis during her life. The younger children don't remember Father as he was during the early years — he was a very dominant figure indeed. It took a long time for her to evolve from a shy, chronic introvert into 'The First Lady of the Western World,' as somebody called her."

"SHE COULD only build her own character later, when Father ceased to be the middle of the limelight. She really didn't become fully herself until she became a widow."

Her son is convinced that Eleanor Roosevelt regretted her proud decision to stop living as Franklin's wife.

"I think there were times when she would have liked to change everything back. I think she had second thought about her role. But by that time, it was so well-cast that it would have been impossible to change it."

It was after his father's death that Elliott became closest to his mother.

"My closest period with my father was during World War II; between 1946 and 1950. Mother was completely a public figure; I was her agent, and produced her television and radio . . ."

He credits Mrs. Roosevelt's emergence as a public figure almost entirely to the patient, decades-long coaching by Louis Howe, a man to whom he ascribes a far bigger role in the careers of both Roosevelts than any earlier biographer has done.

"Probably the most important person of all the people who played any role at all in shaping Father's destiny," he says decidedly. "He and Father plotted and planned Father's presidency from 1910 on. He was the one who knew that the polio didn't mean an end to their plans."

HIS FATHER'S contraction of polio, the Campobello doctor's tragic mis-diagnosis and the resultant disastrous and painful hours of massage treatment he prescribed figure in the book. "I don't think Louis ever forgave himself for all the massage that he and Mother carried out on Father. It was completely the wrong thing to do. The doctor just knew how to send the bill.

"In the light of what we know today, we realize that we children all had polio too — very slight cases, with headaches and stiff necks. But of course in those days we had no idea that that was what it was."

The polio, he believes, left fewer effects on the family than the presidency.

"Having a President for a father," he opined, giving the grin and spreading his freckled hands on the table, "severely hampers the normal development of children. It's harder on a boy than a girl. And it's particularly hard on a grown man. Especially if you're exposed to the business contacts who have an axe to grind and are interested in reaching the head of state."

Does the son of a head of state feel debilitated afterward?

"Well, it certainly had a bad effect on Randolph Churchill," he says with a guffaw. "I couldn't stand him when I met him. Actually, I remember, I dropped him from a plane in World War II, when I was doing photo reconnaissance. . . ." He and Brough, his co-writer, both chortle at the joke that could have been made but wasn't.

ELLIOTT Roosevelt may have been affected by his father's position, but he's never been a shrinking violet.

He's had five dramatic marriages and four moderately juicy divorces. He raised a few brows at the outbreak of World War II when he was commissioned a captain in the Army Air Corps Reserve (critics said he should have been drafted).

There was a brouhaha later when a couple of airmen were bumped from a cross-country plane ride to accommodate Blaze, his 135-pound bull mastiff.

But he chalked up a distinguished service career, and ended the war larded with medals, including that of a Commander of the Order of the British Empire, the Croix de Guerre and Legion of Honor or in the rank of Chevalier from France.

In 1948, he was the leader of the draft-Eisenhower movement. He's been in advertising, in cattle, in journalism, in radio, took a brief foray into politics in the '60s: first, as Democratic committeeman from Florida, and then as mayor of Miami Beach.

To the last post, he was adoringly voted in by senior citizens living on the fruits of his father's social security plan.

He believes, though, that other, younger Roosevelts will follow in his father's footsteps. "Among 30-odd grandchildren, I should think there'd be another Roosevelt with political ambitions emerging. I think social consciousness comes every other generation. My son David was a delegate to the last Democratic convention. . . ."

His own awareness of politics grew as a small boy in Washington where his father first came as Under Secretary of the Navy. He first lived here on N Street, in one of those tree-shaded, gas-lit row houses in the 1700 block; later, on R, at 2131.

HE REMEMBERS a childhood crowded with social duties: "We were all forced to go to the old British Embassy for dancing classes. No, I'm not a good dancer, never have been. I dance as little as possible now. Detest formal social life."

He and his fifth wife Patricia live as informally as they can — "But it's hard, in Portugal, it's a very formal country" — outside Lisbon, on a quinta.

"I'm even learning Portuguese."

His last language course, he remembers, was "a crash course in Russian I took at Columbia University right after the war, when LOOK Magazine sent me to interview Stalin. I wasn't fluent, but I could understand it. And Stalin could understand English. But we operated entirely through an interpreter.

"It was really quite funny, both of us pretending not to understand what the other one was saying. . . ."

WHATEVER morsels he digs up from memory about the years following those he describes in "The Roosevelts of Hyde Park," he'll find it hard to top some of his recent reminiscences.

Could there be one left to top what happened when Joseph Kennedy, then Ambassador to the Court of St. James, responded to a criticism of his friendship with Gloria Swanson by suggesting that FDR give up his relationship with Missy LeHand?

Instead of sending a ranking cabinet member to meet the returning Ambassador at Washington airport, he sent — "all smiles" — Missy LeHand.

Institutions

'Shock Treatment Is an Abuse of Medicine'

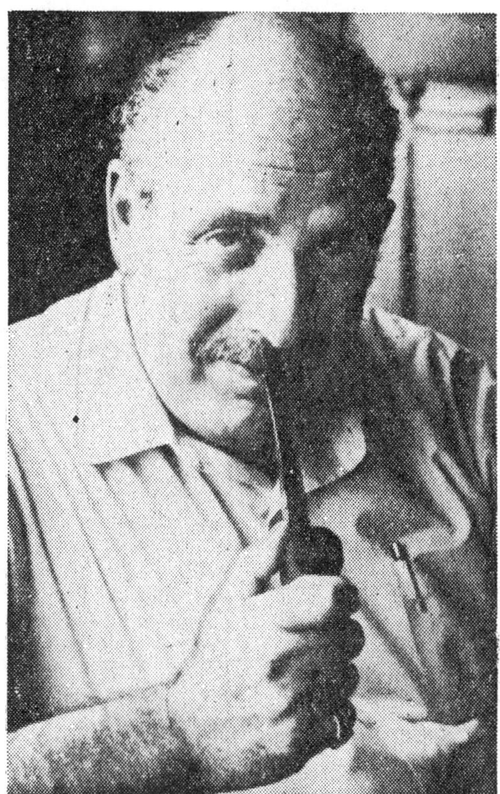

Dr. Theodore Rubin

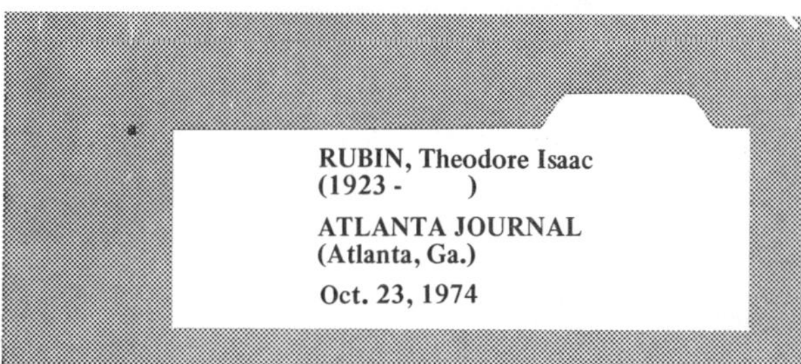

RUBIN, Theodore Isaac
(1923 -)
ATLANTA JOURNAL
(Atlanta, Ga.)
Oct. 23, 1974

By JEAN TYSON

Things haven't changed all that much in mental institutions from what they were 20 years ago, perhaps longer. But what has happened the last 20 years is what Theodore Rubin, M.D., is most familiar with because that is how long he has been in the psychoanalysis field.

Dr. Rubin, before he went into private practice, and became president of the American Institution of Psychoanalysis, worked in two large state mental hospitals — one in Southern California, the other in New York State.

"I was one doctor with 700 patients to take care of," Dr. Rubin said. "It was impossible to see all of them. How demoralizing this is for both doctor and patient. What goes on in these institutions is an over use of shock treatment. I don't think much of the use of shock treatment. To me, this represents one of the greatest abuses of medicine. Shock treatment has its uses, but it is over used.

"In 20 years, I have recommended shock treatment only once, and this was because it was the only way to save the man's life. So this tells you what I think about the practice of using shock treatment."

Dr. Rubin said there is a need for more in the way of training psychoanalysts, more needed in the availability of treatment and more clinics.

"The institutions I have seen are mostly populated by poor people. I don't think they are any sicker than rich people. They just don't have the availability of treatment. What we need is more money for training and clinics.

"We have a non-profit clinic, and the waiting list is a mile long. Without the money, we can't train adequate personnel and staff these places properly. If we had more clinics and better trained personnel, our state hospitals would be pretty much empty."

Dr. Rubin has written his 15th book. The latest one is "Shrink" (Popular Library, 1.50) and it tells what is going on in the larger mental institutions.

"The book tells about psychiatry itself and what it is like to live in a mental institution as a doctor, a doctor's family and a patient. It describes many incidences that happen in these institutions.

"The book begins with a patient biting off a psychiatrist's finger. This psychiatrist had the habit of pointing his finger at people when he talked."

Dr. Rubin, who is also a columnist for a women's magazine, said that the biggest problem people write him about is emotional depression.

"This comes through in their letters. But everybody is depressed at one time or another. And at least once or twice in a lifetime, every individual goes through deep depressions. I think they need treatment — psychoanalysis, not shock treatment."

He said that people today are terrified and that they have become conditioned to violence.

"I think we have become addicted to violent news. We adapt so rapidly today. We aren't shocked at the things we ought to be. We have become complacent, and we accept victimization.

"One of my friends made a study of the victims of crimes. Like a woman who has been raped for example. Initially she gets sympathy, then in a short time she gets indifference, then this turns to rejection because the feeling is she is contagious. This is a sad commentary.

"A vast population of people are enraged and frustrated. When you have a close proximity of the extreme have nots and the extreme haves living one street apart, it is testing human conditions. You can't expect not to have difficulties when this happens.

"We will be better off when we have a more equalized society even if some have to give up part of what they have. This is inevitable.

"I think this country is going through a struggle which is growing pains. I don't think you can grow up or be sure without growing pains. I don't think this country is going to come apart.

"It is a great experience we are going through — to bring all these people together to live under one culture. It can't be done overnight. It is going to take time, struggle and pain. Right now we are in the painful period and we must not be indifferent toward the things that are horrendous and cruel wherever they show themselves."

Dr. Rubin said he wanted to be a doctor since he was a child. When he as an undergraduate at the Univeristy of Rochester he saw a state mental institution for the first time.

"I realized that many doctors function as amateur psychiatrists, so I figured why not be a professional. I realized this was one of the few specialties where you treated the whole person. This was one of the things that really got to me.

"I think a lot of people go into this field as a way of resolving their own problems. I like to believe we are tuned into the fact we have problems and want to do something about them.

"Also I have always had a curiosity about what makes people tick. I felt from the beginning this is the area where people need help more than any other. It is gratifying to see somebody begin to get over depression, and begin to get well. It isn't always easy and not always possible, but when you can get somebody well, it is a tremendous feeling."

(Also see preceding article)

The Shrink Says That Psychiatrists Are the Bad Guys

By NANCY GREENBERG
Of The Bulletin Staff

THEODORE ISAAC RUBIN, the psychoanalyst with a column in the Ladies' Home Journal, figures that most Americans have either schizoid or moderately manic-depressive personalities, and that one person out of 10,000 will go through life without a trauma "of cataclysmic proportions."

That takes care of the patient population.

The author of "David and Lisa" and "Dr. Rubin, Please Make Me Happy" just came out with his 15th book, "Shrink!" an incredibly detailed account of his psychiatric residency, considering it occurred 25 years ago. In it, he goes to town on the psychiatrist population.

"I couldn't in good conscience send anyone to a psychiatrist," he said in Philadelphia this week traveling on a publicity tour against his will, he says, to please Popular Library which is experimenting with issuing a Rubin book for the first time in paperback.

For after becoming a psychiatrist Rubin went to a psychoanalytic institute — he is the president of the American Institute for Psychoanalysis — and came to the irrevocable conclusion that the psychoanalysts were the good guys and all the others were the bad guys.

(Psychoanalysis is the therapy designed to unravel the unconscious processes — like the Oedipus complex — which are part of the Freudian concept of the psyche. Classical psychoanalysis involves free association from the couch, although today many psychoanalysts, including Rubin, use analytic techniques in a less formalized encounter.)

A Horrible Crowd

Rubin writes of about three dozen psychiatrists and psychiatric residents, all renamed to match their ethnic backgrounds, and, in truth, it's a pretty horrible crowd.

There are the "shockiatrists," the sadists, the just plain insensitives. At one point when a patient almost bites off one of the therapist's fingers, you feel yourself cheering and wondering why more patients don't resort to this technique.

The rest of Rubin's classmates are simply uptight, compared to the author who is frequently critiqued by superiors as "rebellious towards authority" (and, implicitly, proud of it).

Rubin writes that his adviser "told me that it's important to have some kind of food available for oral satisfaction. This is especially true for patients (catatonics included) who are regressed to the oral stage. Can't he just say that it makes things friendlier to have some warm drinks available? The Freudian hogwash gets to be too much! . . ."

You find yourself cheering for the old Rubin and wondering how come he now must divide the world up into cowboys and Indians.

The Family Sweetheart

"Most psychiatrists don't see depression as the healthy thing I do," he tells you. "The depression is like a temper tantrum. It shows some real yearnings bursting through.

"There was a young man living at home with his parents who, at the age of 27 was considered by everyone, including himself, to be the family sweetheart. Suddenly he went into a severe depression with ruminating thoughts and had to be hospitalized.

"The regular psychiatrists all wanted to get him back to his sweetheart state. However, I saw the depression as the best thing to happen to him. The wild thoughts he was having were just to keep him from feeling his rage, his sexual feelings and especially the anger against his parents.

"During therapy when he would say, 'Oh, I had a bad thought — I thought of my parents dying,' I would tell him to get out of my office — that I had no time for patients who wanted to be saints. He had to learn to accept his 'bad' feelings and not apologize for them.

"When he would say, 'Gee, I saw a girl I'd like to sleep with,' and I saw a guy who wanted to be a real person and I would treat him with utmost warmth."

Shock Treatments

Then Rubin points out that your average psychiatrist would have given the lad electric shock treatments.

"In this culture," the analyst goes on, "we express our feelings by way of Poughkeepsie. A mother promises to take her son to the circus and when the time comes she doesn't feel like it. Instead of saying so — after all, she has the right to dislike the circus — she says to the kid, 'Honey, you really look too sick to go.' . . . The way people talk, it's a miracle anyone's normal."

Asked who was normal, Rubin gave his one in 10,000 statistic, adding that psychoanalysis is the only way he really know of to normalize the other 9,999.

"I've heard in Japan," he adds thoughtfully, "that they give disturbed people paper and tell them to just write everything they can think of. That's not so different from free association so there might be something to it."

Rubin notes that one of the many crazy things about our society is the demand to stay young.

"This is against nature," he states flatly. "Can you imagine a cultural value against nature? It's like telling a 6-year-old there's something wrong with him if he grows a few inches. Anyway, how many beautiful people are there?"

Wrong With Society

The other thing wrong with our society, he observes, is that everything has to be "great."

"What's this great?" he begins. "Happiness is not a peak experience. Real highs, in fact, are a precursor to real lows. One of my greatest objections to Nixon wasn't Watergate. It was the fact that he always said we had to be a great country."

"That," he concludes, "is malarkey" — a word we haven't heard in a while and a refreshing change from great words and psychoanalytic concepts.

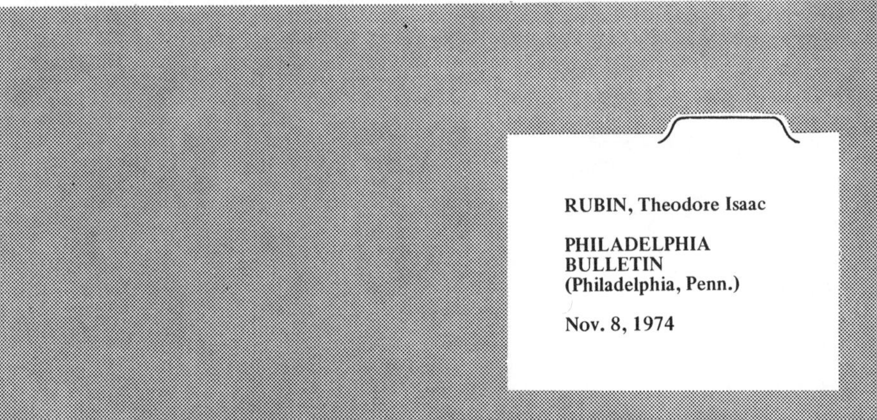
RUBIN, Theodore Isaac

PHILADELPHIA BULLETIN
(Philadelphia, Penn.)

Nov. 8, 1974

Adela has opinions, definitely

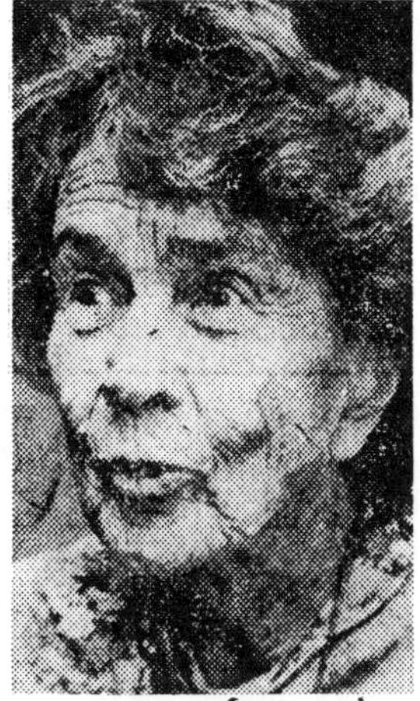

ST. JOHNS, Adela Rogers (1894 -)

CLEVELAND PRESS (Cleveland, Ohio)

Oct. 23, 1974

By RUSTY BROWN

Venerable newshen Adela Rogers St. Johns stood in a blue dressing gown at the window of her hotel room and looked down at the people waiting to glimpse President Ford on his arrival in Cleveland last night.

She said, with a harrumph, "That's not much of a crowd. Not like the excitement of the old days. Not like when Bobby Kennedy came to California.

"People are apathetic now, and I don't think Ford can bring them out of it."

Still as full of opinions as during 50 years of newspaper reporting, the 80-year-old columnist-author dropped the following:

About recent coverage of breast surgery:

"I am strenuously opposed. Is there nothing left that is private? Why shouldn't a woman want to conceal it?"

Her choice for President: Sen. Henry Jackson. "But, then again, I'm such a baseball fan, I might push for Reggie Jackson (of the Oakland A's).

About Ted Kennedy: "The sooner he retires, the better."

Spry and happy to be her age ("I consider 80 remarkable."), Adela likes to reminisce about the "greats" she chronicled.

She knew Richard Nixon when he was seven and eight years old, helping his father deliver groceries from the family store.

"And I was one of the first democrats to campaign for Nixon for the Senate. I thought it was so great that a grocery boy could run for Congress."

Adela St. Johns came to Cleveland to speak at the Town Hall lecture series today. She has a new book out, "Some Are Born Great" (Doubleday $7.95), about women she considers extraordinary. She talked about them.

She would like to see a women's Hall of Fame, and her first choice is Anne Morrow Lindbergh.

"I regard her book, 'Gift from the Sea,' the best written, most illumined and illustrious book of our century. It is a gift to every woman in the world."

Despite her praise of women, she does not consider herself a women's libber at all.

"The famed Frenchman deTocqueville wrote more **than 100 years ago that America owed its strength to the superiority of its women.**

"Now why do women want to come down to be the equal of men?"

Adela a pro at having the last word

By Joyce Haber

Last year, I was one of the guests on a Merv Griffin show. The late, lovely Jackie Susann was plugging her latest, now last, best-selling novel, "Once Is Not Enough." Washington's feminine variable, Barbara Howar, was plugging her book, "Laughing All the Way." I was plugging nothing although, along with Merv and Jackie, I was trying to quell Barbara's gratuitous attack on the U.S. press.

As on other talk shows she seemed determined to use Watergate for all it was worth to promote her memoirs of life in the capital—although her book had nothing to do with Watergate.

Suddenly Merv introduced his next guest, a spunky, many-sided lady, then 79, who had shot to national fame a decade before as Griffin's unofficial great-grandmother.

Adela Rogers St. Johns, whose talk is as concise as her build, took on Barbara. "If the press is 'bought,' as you say, then why did Bernstein, Woodward and the Washington Post reveal Watergate? Young lady, I was tracking down stories before you were even conceived." It takes one who isn't to know one. Mrs. St. Johns was the instant star of the show, the only authentic antique in a curiosity shop.

"When I worked for Mr. Hearst," she declared, "we couldn't even belong to a club or a church. We couldn't take presents. He even paid for my clothes when I went on interviews."

I remarked that, in my 19 years of reporting, the same rules have applied. Adela fixed me with her eyes and smiled approval. "Hedda and Louella," she said, "used to take diamond bracelets from someone and then next day report the thing the donor didn't want them to." Off camera, the assistant director was signaling Merv to wind up the show.

"No one has ever offered me a diamond bracelet," I said. "They will, my dear, they will," replied Mrs. St. Johns. To audience applause and laughter, Adela had the last word.

For more than 60 years in journalism, writing, teaching, delivering sermons and lecturing, this remarkable intelligent woman who recently turned 80 has had the last word.

As the first woman sports writer, she was there the day Babe Ruth, "punted it over the fence." She attended the Hauptmann kid-

ST. JOHNS, Adela Rogers

PLAIN DEALER (Cleveland, Ohio)

Oct. 25, 1974

naping trial. She watched Anne Morrow Lindbergh as she waited to take the witness stand. Her ninth book, "Some Are Born Great," was published by Doubleday recently.

As I turned into the driveway of the unpretentious six-room beach house on the Pacific Coast Highway above the Malibu Colony, a sprightly Mrs. St. Johns came out to greet me. She wore a blue pants suit that accented the azure eyes and the tanned,

(Continued from preceding page)

gnarled face. Red beads and a Maltese cross pendant in gold were the only accessories for the lady who used to dress for interviews in Hattie Carnegie and send the bills to W. R. Hearst.

Mrs. St. Johns has been married three times, a fact little known and less reported, because she prefers to talk only about her first husband, Ike St. Johns. She was fond of him, but their marriage broke up, she admits, "because I had no interest in it."

When I asked her about her second husband, she said: "Oh, I've forgotten his name and so has everyone else. I think every woman's entitled to a middle husband she can forget." Her last husband was Patrick O'Toole, who is in the aviation business.

Mrs. St. Johns is the daughter of the late, great lawyer Earl Rogers who, among other things, sharpened the courtroom cross-examination technique and once defended Clarence Darrow on a bribery charge. Adela, an only child, started following her father to court when she was 8. There she observed policemen, gangsters and legal procedures. A Hollywood High School flunk-out (she failed at math) in 1910, she received an honorary alumnus award from that school in '51. In 1913, Adela began as a cub reporter for Hearst on the San Francisco Examiner at a salary of $7 a week. Later, she became the highest-paid newspaperwoman of her day.

She was also writing hundreds of short stories and novelettes: "I brought up my family on short stories," Adela said while preparing a fresh pot of coffee. "When I was really broke, I'd write for a studio."

With her keen reporter's sense, Adela isn't easily fooled by ego. She tells of writing an interview with Clara Bow at the "It" girl's peak. "She told me this terrible story about her mother and father. I printed it because she'd told it to me. She never spoke to me again. But she wasn't mad about that, as she pretended to be. She was mad because I hinted that her hair wasn't red, that she dyed it." Any experienced reporter knows that most interview subjects aren't offended if what they say is offensive, but rather by something so sensitive they refuse to mention it.

As reporter-cum-gossipist, she covered Liza Minnelli's ballet recital, at the age of 8, at Hollywood's Buckley School. A series covered "Bette Davis' Darkest Hour," describing the death of Bette's husband, Arthur Farnsworth, after a fall on Hollywood Blvd. The cause of death was determined to be a wound from a blunt instrument.

Adela followed the long questioning period that ended with Miss Davis' vindication.

One of Adela's funniest anecdotes concerns her days as a sports writer. "Damon Runyon, Westbrook Pegler, Granny Rice and I — all of us didn't think Ring Lardner would get his story in because he was so tight. So each of us wrote an extra piece on a baseball game and signed it 'Ring Lardner.' The editor called us and said 'I have seven stories by Ring Lardner. You can stop writing now.' "

Mrs. St. Johns, who calls herself "a lifelong Roosevelt Democrat" (she covered the White House under FDR for three years), had supported Nixon against Helen Gahagan Douglas for the Senate in 1950. ("He shouldn't have made the Senate, but we had to beat her because she was left wing.") In 1952, it was Adela who wrote Nixon's famous "Checkers" speech. "His other speeches have been so bland, I've offered to write every one of his other speeches.

"Nixon was always bad with the press. Roosevelt had great class. He not only handled them, he used them. FDR would send for reporters and pick their brains. He'd ask one to stay after conferences, sometimes me, and tell stories about Eleanor. He adored Eleanor. He had mistresses, but let's face facts. If more people would face facts, there'd be fewer broken marriages.

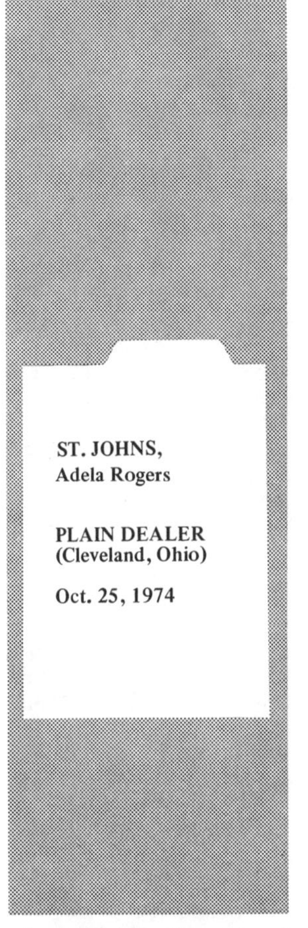
ST. JOHNS,
Adela Rogers

PLAIN DEALER
(Cleveland, Ohio)

Oct. 25, 1974

"After he was elected to the Senate, Hedda and I went up to Nixon's room at the Ambassador. As we approached the door, we heard him say 'My God, don't let Hedda Hopper in here.' Well, the guy was naked. But instead of picking up a towel and saying 'Hedda, come in at your own risk,' as Kennedy would have, he gave the impression he scorned Hedda. This man came out of a small town, Whittier, and out of the Quaker church.

"I've often thought with Nixon that if he'd made the football team, his life would have been different. This man had greatness thrust upon him. Helen Douglas, who we had to beat, and two assassinations. He couldn't have beaten either of the Kennedys, honey."

Almost five years ago, Nixon gave Adela the highest civilian award the President can confer: the Medal of Freedom.

She recalled, "He gave it to me with the words 'For 50 years of devotion to the ideal that a democracy cannot survive without a free press." And Mrs. St. Johns' voice was sad.

"Why keep the tapes around?" she asks perplexedly. "It's like you left the corpse in the bull ring." Then she added lightly, "I've been reading Agatha Christie again. You know in April, '72, I told Nixon: 'Get all the networks cleared and tell them everything you know about Watergate. Say, "The Bay of Pigs is my fault," and you'll be right up there with Kennedy.' "

This legendary lady of both Hollywoods says "I'm sorry, I can't see when they compare Robert Redford to Clark Gable.

Gable was the best friend, the straightest guy, I ever knew. I miss him, terribly. He made Carole (Lombard) stop talking dirty, you know? He told her, and I was there: 'If anyone's going to talk dirty in this house, it will be me.' After she died, he gave me all of Carole's spiritual books. She had a wonderful collection. I wish we could have a Gable again."

For Lee Salk, His Children Come First

SALK, Lee
(1926 -)

MILWAUKEE JOURNAL (Milwaukee, Wisc.) Feb. 20, 1975

—Journal Photo
Lee Salk

By Margo Huston
of The Journal Staff

Last night Pia Salk's dad was not out in the audience watching his daughter perform in a sports program at her school.

Her father, Lee Salk, author of books and columns advising others on how to be good parents, was in Milwaukee on business. He arrived Tuesday evening and planned to return to New York City Thursday, after conducting two days of workshops on humanism in hospital care at Family Hospital here.

In an interview Wednesday, Salk was asked how well his own expert advice worked in his own real life. He is married, the father of two — Pia, 7, and Eric, 13 — and works as director of pediatric psychology at The New York Hospital — Cornell Medical Center. He lives in Manhattan and his children go to the United Nations International School, also in the city.

To answer the question, Salk offered an anecdote: He said his plane for Milwaukee was scheduled to leave New York City at 3:40 p.m. Tuesday, but son Eric was scheduled to appear in a play at school between 1 and 2 p.m. that same day.

"I had many pressing things to do, but top among them for me was seeing my son's play," he said.

How was it?

"Excellent," Salk said, his eyes full of enthusiasm. The play was Noel Coward's "Hands Across the Sea" and Salk said he arrived early enough to have lunch with Pia, who then accompanied him to Eric's play.

'They Come First'

"I wanted to see the play. That is very important for children, but it's even more important to make them feel that they come first in my life."

He paused, then articulated the lesson from his anecdote: "Even busy fathers can do these kinds of things for their children."

Another anecdote: Salk said that on his first night in Milwaukee he phoned the children and Pia told him she would be appearing in the sports night at her school.

"I said, 'Pia, I'm terribly sorry that I'll have to miss it.' " Then Salk laughed out loud as he recalled how Pia responded by saying she would ask her teacher to schedule her gym class to put on another demonstration — some day when her father could attend.

Rearrange World

The lesson of that anecdote: "To her, it's important enough to rearrange the world a little bit so our relationship won't have to suffer."

In his new book, "Preparing for Parenthood" (David McKay), Salk talks about how important it is for an infant and young child to spend time during the day with one parent or the other.

With business trips such as the one to Milwaukee, is it possible for him to be around his children as much as he recommends?

"I don't take business trips like this very often," Salk replied. "Oftentimes, I arrange my trips so that my children can come with me."

Not as Eager

And your wife?

"Let's just say there are some things that the children like to do that the mother is not that eager to do," Salk replied, giving skiing as a for instance.

He said that when he went to Twin Falls, Idaho, on business, he arranged his schedule so that he could take his children skiing at Sun Valley. When he went to Washington, D. C. on business, he took his children to tour the historical sights and to have dinner with his friends, Sen. and Mrs. George McGovern. When business took him near Detroit, he took the children to an automobile museum there.

As a parent-child expert, could not such chumminess between the children and one of the parents cause the other parent to feel left out?

Salk, a short, balding, graying, controlled man of 48, pursed his lips then said, "Right now is not a good time for me to be talking about my wife." he declined to elaborate on the subject.

Salk then went on to say many of the things he has been saying since the publication of his first two books — "How to Raise a Human Being" (1969) and "What Every Child Would Like His Parents to Know" (1972).

Cookbook Approach

The cookbook approach to child rearing doesn't work, he said. Guiding principles are needed, not specific dos and don'ts. Nonetheless, he said, pacifiers are no good, nor is letting a baby cry it out.

Salk described himself as a feminist, said he had long been involved in the women's movement and believed, "The father is every bit as important as the mother."

Getting to Parents

As a psychologist treating persons with emotional illness, Salk said, "I kept getting the recurring thought that I wished I could have gotten to the parents of the person."

Now, he said, he is scouting around for businesses or industries to start pilot projects in which parents would be paid for eight hours when they worked six hours and spent the other two hours taking care of their babies.

The Schickels Keep Up the Good Work

SCHICKEL, Richard (Warren)
(1933 -)
[See also CA-3]
and
SCHICKEL, Julia Whedon
(pseud. Julia Whedon)
(1936 -)
[See also CA-49/52]

MILWAUKEE JOURNAL
(Milwaukee, Wisc.)

Mar. 3, 1974

By **LESLIE CROSS,**
Journal Book Editor

WHEN I last saw the Richard Schickels, the hour was late. Their daughters, Erika and Jessica, had been put to bed — or at least out of earshot. And so the Schickels had leisure to talk — about Wisconsin, California, films and books, the New York writing scene, the problems of authors today.

Julia's first novel, "Girl of the Golden West," had been out for some months. Dick had wrapped up his seventh book for publication. Charterhouse Books has just published it, under the title "His Picture in the Papers: An Inquiry on Celebrity in America Based on the Life of Douglas Fairbanks Sr.," and it was reviewed in The Journal last Sunday.

Julia and Dick Schickel are members of a diminishing breed, full time free lance writers. Like most notable exemplars of their trade, they live in New York. When I visited them, they occupied an apartment on E. 88th St., near Central Park. They have since moved to their own house on E. 95th St., fairly close by; here—for the time being, anyway — they have room for the profusion of reference materials indispensable in their profession.

A Writer Does Well to Branch Out

Dick, who was born in Milwaukee 41 years ago, moved to New York a few years after he took a bachelor's degree in sociology at the University of Wisconsin-Madison in 1955. He took some graduate work but decided he'd rather write than teach or otherwise sociologize.

After editorial stints at Sports Illustrated, Look and Show magazines, he made the plunge into full time writing. The publication of his first book, "The World of Carnegie Hall," in 1960 gave him enough money to start out on his own. Since then he has written, besides his books, innumerable articles for a variety of magazines, both popular and intellectual. He was a film critic for Life and after its demise has contributed film criticism to its sister periodical, Time. Lately, with the shrinking of the magazine market, he has been directing and producing television shows.

"When I came to New York," Dick said, "there was a market for what used to be called free lance writers. That's been drying up. All the big magazines are gone. Since I moved here, four major places where a writer might sell pieces for big money have folded up. Today a writer has to develop a capacity to do work in television or something like that."

Julia's problems have been similar. After she and Dick were married in 1961, she sold short stories to several large magazines. Now the market for short fiction is very small.

"I could spend half a year writing a short story that would satisfy me," said Julia. "A novel isn't that much harder to write, and you have something more substantial."

Movie Fans With a Difference

The Schickels share a strong interest in films. For Julia—who writes under her original name, Julia Whedon — it was almost a birthright. Her father was a screen writer in Hollywood, and she spent much of her girlhood in its environs. Four of Dick's books have had to do with movies and movie people. Julia, who came east and went to Sarah Lawrence College, returned to California in memory for her first book. Her second novel will be about basketball.

"Why?" I asked her.

"For one thing," she said, "I'm wild about sports. Then I'm interested in the kind of celebrity that overtakes athletes, as so many other people."

The nature of modern celebrity and how it is manufactured have been a recurrent theme in Dick's books and articles. His latest book began as an article for American Heritage. After the article was published, he had a 22 page letter from Douglas Fairbanks Jr. and he found himself, after some digging, with enough material for a book.

He is committed to do a book on Harold Lloyd, the great comedian of the silent pictures. He is halfway through a large scale biography of D.W. Griffiths, the legendary director who was perhaps the greatest figure in the early history of the movies. The Griffiths project is a difficult one (the edges of fact and myth have been much blurred over the years) and he doesn't expect to complete it soon. After his Griffiths book appears, he doesn't intend to write any more books about films.

Dick's career as a television writer and producer began a few years ago with a series called "The Film Generation," created for educational broadcast. He contributed sections on movies to subsequent series on life in the 1930s and '40s, "You Must Remember This." Then, a little over a year ago, he started work on his own series, "Men Who Made the Movies." It dealt with eight major directors and ran as a Public Broadcasting Service presentation from last fall until about a month ago.

"Actually," said Dick, "you can spend a year on something like this — about as long as it would take you to write a book. It's fun — but also hysterical sometimes.

He hopes to turn the interviews from which the program was distilled into a book — while the Griffiths endeavor waits.

His latest television enterprise is an NBC documentary on Arnold Hammer, the oil magnate whose picturesque exploits have encompassed America, Russia, Europe and much of the rest of the world. It will be aired April 3.

A Younger Schickel May Join the Team

Another writing Schickel may be on the way up. Erika, who is 10, has been committing stories to paper for several years. Her mother's book moved her to begin a novel which she called "Boy of the Silver East."

"Her books," said Julia, "are very raunchy. They're full of wild women and gambling and things like that."

Thus far, Jessica, who is 6, doesn't seem to have been bitten. But, with Schickels, who can tell?

Phyllis Schlafly's Woman Power Beating Down ERA

SCHLAFLY, Phyllis
(1924 -)
TIMES–PICAYUNE
(New Orleans, La.)
Apr. 13, 1973
[See also CA-25/28]

By MARY KIMBROUGH
(Times-Picayune National Service)

ST. LOUIS—During World War II, Phyllis Schlafly worked a 48-hour swing shift in a defense plant test-firing ammunition for American troops. She has been shooting it out ever since.

Those who have felt the barb in the thick of the battle respect her sharp eye and her trigger finger.

Her targets for many years have been communism and America's defense policies.

Now is added a third: the Equal Rights Amendment for women (ERA).

Phyllis Schlafly is national chairman of Stop ERA, a suddenly sprung-up organization dedicated to the sole purpose of preventing the amendment's ratification. Many standing on the sidelines in the wordy warfare, predict she may be just the one to deal the death blow.

ALREADY, the wife of Alton, Ill., attorney J. Frederic (Ted) Schlafly Jr. and mother of six has addressed 10 state legislatures in opposition to the amendment. Seven of those, including Missouri, have voted it down or shelved it for the present, a fact for which officers of Stop ERA take considerable credit. (As of now, 30 states have ratified it; a total of 38 is required).

Mrs. Schlafly is a socially prominent matron who would rather go to a legislative battle than a tea. She's a Phi Beta Kappa who puts her brain power to work digging up facts to fight with. She has the political philosophy of a Barry Goldwater and the savvy of a Harry Truman. She taught each of her children to read because she didn't like the way the schools were doing it. She's a sure-fisted infighter who will take on a ward heeler or the White House.

Even those on the other side of the hot-tempered controversy, those millions of vocal ERA proponents who disagree fiercely with her, respect her battling spirit.

Of all the large Schlafly family, none, aside from her husband, is closer to her in political philosophy than her sister-in-law, Eleanor Schlafly. Miss Schlafly is director of the Cardinal Mindszenty Foundation, an avowed anti-Communist organization. Phyllis has served as the foundation's research director and recently she and Eleanor went together to Vienna for first-hand research into the imprisonment of Cardinal Mindszenty. Out of that came Mrs. Schlafly's latest book, "Mindszenty the Man," with Dr. Joseph Vecasy.

She is as forthright in her position as are ERA advocates, even though each side is convinced the other is, at best, fuzzy-brained and, at worst, a traitor to her sex.

SHE FINDS IT logical to assert (over the indignant rebuttal of her opponents) that "the laws of every one of our 50 states now guarantee the right to be a woman—protected and provided for in her career as a woman, wife and mother.

"The proposed Equal Rights Amendment will wipe out all our laws which—through rights, benefits and exemptions—guarantee this right to be a woman.

ERA will replace these present laws with a doctrinaire equality under which women must be treated exactly the same as men . . .

"The laws of every one of our 50 states now require the husband to support his wife and children—and to provide a home for them to live in. In other words, the law protects a woman's right to be a full-time wife and mother, her right not to take a job outside the home, her right to care for her own baby in her own home while being financially supported by her husband.

"If the Equal Rights Amendment is passed, every wife and mother will lose her right to be supported by her husband unless she has pre-school children, and she even loses the right to be supported by her husband while she has pre-school children if child care centers are available. No more radical piece of legislation could have been devised to force women outside of the home."

Mrs. Schlafly has reared six children, run for Congress twice, written six books, served as president of the Illinois Federation of Republican Women, as state central committeewoman, as state convention keynoter and national convention delegate.

She has given innumerable speeches, testified before the Senate Foreign Relations Committee against the U.S.-Soviet test ban treaty and organized a Midwest regional seminar on the techniques of communism.

She writes, edits and circulates a monthly "Phyllis Schlafly Reports" and for some years was news director for a series of interviews with scholars and scientists in America and England aired on TV and radio. (They were taped in her own home and her eldest son, John, served as engineer).

WHEN AND HOW did it all start, this crusading zeal which has thrust her into the thick of battles most women (and most men, for that matter) would gladly leave alone? What drives her into the buzz saw?

She really doesn't know, any more than most people would know why they prefer peppermint to pistachio. In grade school, as she recalls, she wasn't even much of a rebel, just a rule-abiding student.

But by the time she got to college (she once said she chose political science because the class met at the attractive hour of 10 a.m.), she began to hunger to put her burgeoning political theories into political action.

In her first congressional race in 1952, in which she unsuccessfully challenged the veteran Democrat C. Melvin Price after an impressive primary victory, she told reporters:

"As a housewife, I'm concerned about the fact that we have the highest prices and highest taxes in our country's history, caused by wasteful government spending."

Her research gradually transformed her into one of America's most vocal and vehement critics of national defense policies. Her first book, "A Choice Not an Echo," is credited by many observers with influencing the nomination of Barry Goldwater for the presidency. Later books, three of them written with Adm. Chester Ward (U.S.N. Ret.), discussed nuclear strategy and weaponry, predicted Soviet superiority over the United States in nuclear weapons and warned of the dangers of a policy of freezing U.S. production which, she charges, made her grim forecast come true.

AND SO Phyllis Schlafly, the Midwestern housewife, has become spokesman for a large percentage which she says are not represented by ERA proponents, although she does go on record in agreement with "another type of women supporting the Equal Rights Amendment from the most sincere motives—many of them have felt the keen edge of discrimination in their employment."

In fact, she says, she could conscientiously support the ERA had the Hayden modification remained in it. (This modification stated, "The provisions of this article shall not be conferred by law upon persons of the female sex ")

"Without the Hayden modification, the Equal Rights Amendment won't give you anything—but it will take away fundamental rights and benefits from the rest of women. You have every right to lobby for the extension of your rights—but not at the expense of the rights of other women."

Schlesinger: A New Phase Of Life

By CHRISTOPHER SHARP
Knight News Service

NEW YORK — Arthur Schlesinger Jr. has come full cycle.

Like Henry Kissinger, his old colleague, he armed himself for public service at Harvard's history department. He shared with Kissinger the conviction that a sense of history is the difference between competent and incompetent politics.

BUT THE former special assistant to President Kennedy and court philosopher of Camelot (he is now called King Arthur, but he more closely resembles Merlin) says he is through with government service. As a professor of the humanities at City University, he has recycled himself to his scholastic roots.

And he is clearly enjoying a phase of life that comes to few 56-year-olds. His 1-year-old son, Robert, and his young, vivacious wife, Alexandra, have restored a youthful vigor to the Pulitzer Prize winner.

"We have never had grandchildren," says the father of six, playing with his sixth. "So Alexandra and I collaborated to manufacture our own."

LITTLE ROBERT is the beneficiary of a rare treat: He has the luxury of a full-time mother. Although Alexandra is taking history courses, she has little interest in competing with Arthur as a political activist.

They met when she was a student at Radcliffe, but, according to Arthur, "We became aware of each other only a few years ago, at a cocktail party." They have been married for over two years, and they've lived in their East Side townhouse since September.

Throughout the Schlesinger household, there is an a emphasis on style. A sense of style is a quality that Schlesinger says is distinctly missing at the White House. He cites the people President Nixon surrounds himself with as an example of a styleless executive branch.

"JOHN KENNEDY PROVED his manhood in the Pacific. He didn't have to prove it as a commander-in-chief. Nixon spent the war in office. Now he has a great psychic need for a rigorously controlled environment."

Schlesinger's voice is resigned when he talks about the Kennedy and Nixon administrations. He does not seem to comprehend some subjects. One concerns his old colleague, Kissinger.

"Henry Kissinger," he says, "has learned about the advantages of double talk."

SCHLESINGER'S LATEST book, "The Imperial Presidency," examines the historic precedents that have left the presidency in its controversial state. He looks upon presidential decisions as dependent on eventual public approval, a pattern that did not backfire until the 1960s. As a precedent for the U. S. entry into the Vietnam war, he cites the deployment of American troops to the north Atlantic before Congress approved the action.

Reading the book makes one realize why Schlesinger is called King Arthur. His stylistic superiority over contemporary historians leaves him in a class by himself, almost in regal solitude.

Most recently, he has drawn upon psychology for some of his conclusions. He sees the roots of many of the nation's problems in the roots of Richard Nixon.

"HE DOESN'T have his bearings He doesn't know what's appropriate. I don't think he is making policy decisions anymore. He is reading a speech written for him on the energy crisis; he's sleeping while decisions are being made on nuclear alerts . . ."

SCHLESINGER, Arthur (Meier), Jr. (1917 -)
AKRON BEACON JOURNAL (Akron, Ohio)
Dec. 30, 1973
[See also CA-4]

Then Schlesinger perks up a bit. "This may be a change for the better. Most of the policies he made by himself were terrible."

SCHLESINER is convinced the present form of government in the U. S. is the best possible for the country.

"It's been said that the British would have removed their government a long time ago if it suffered from Watergate-type scandals. But when was the last time a prime minister was retired for reasons of scandal?

"Our government at least suits our history and genius. The parliamentary system requires a discipline that wouldn't suit our loose coalitions.

"Despite what is being said, it's actually been a hell of a long time since the British underwent an emergency change of government."

MORE THAN anything else, Schlesinger wants to dispel political myths. One that particularly irks him concerns the role of the so-called "egg head" in government. He worries about the apparent distrust of the Ivy League community by the Nixon administration.

"Much rests on a president's security. President Truman had less education than any president of this century, yet he was quite comfortable in the company of scholars. Nixon doesn't want to be challenged. He wants to be reassured. This results in his closest advisers being Ron Ziegler and General Haig."

Nixon's lack of intellectual security, says Schlesinger, has resulted in a need for the President to test himself publicly.

THERE IS another myth Schlesinger would like to destroy.

"Camelot is a lot of nonsense. It was something that was never heard of until after the murder of President Kennedy. President Kennedy would laugh at the idea of Camelot of if he were alive today."

Schlesinger's oldest friend among the Kennedy's was Joe Jr., a classmate at Harvard. "He was the closest to Ted in temperament — very outgoing, gregarious. John and Robert were the introverted ones."

DESPITE Schlesinger's attacks on the abuse of presidential power, the last thing he wants to see is a weakening of the presidency.

"I still favor presidential discretion on troop deployment. I think the President should be responsible for balancing the budget. The worst thing that can result through the present administration is a weakening of responsibilities, due to massive irresponsibility."

It isn't only this country that is lacking in leadership, according to Schlesinger. "The world is suffering from a tremendous defici in leadership."

But he thinks both Congress and the presidency will regain their power. "There have been strong and weak periods of executive and Congressional power before. My father had established the idea that history evolves through cycles.

He is positive of one thing. He has no intention of going back to government service — even if Edward Kennedy were to become president.

"I think I have already served under the most exhilarating circumstances possible."

Sybil's 16 Lives Changed Life for Best Selling Author

SCHREIBER, Flora Rheta

MILWAUKEE JOURNAL (Milwaukee, Wisc.)

Oct. 1, 1974

Flora Rheta Schreiber, author of the best selling nonfiction novel, "Sybil."

By Constance Daniell
of The Journal Staff

She's a journalist turned novelist whose first book, "Sybil," hit the best seller list four days after publication in May, 1973. It's been there ever since.

She's a full professor of English and speech at New York's John Jay College of Criminal Justice; a prolific writer on everything from science to politics, and a member of the writing faculty of the New School for Social Research.

Flora Rheta Schreiber is all of the above and more, and as you might suspect, an extremely busy woman.

She was in Milwaukee Monday to promote the paperback edition of "Sybil," also a best seller since its publication in May of this year, and to make her 91st — she counted — appearance on a television or radio show since she wrote the book.

"Original Ham"

"I essentially think of myself as a writer," she said, "but I'm beginning to feel more like a performer. I guess I love it," she added. "I trained to be a dramatic actress and you might say I'm the original ham."

In the political field Prof. Schreiber has written 29 magazine and newspaper articles on Lyndon Johnson alone, including a retrospective memoir on the late president's funeral for the New York Times.

Wrote on Nixon

She also came to know former President Nixon's mother well while writing a piece called, "My Son, Richard Nixon," by Hannah Milhous Nixon "as told to Flora Schreiber."

During the latter assignment she gained what she called an "interesting perspective on Nixon through the eyes of his mother and study of his childhood. I know the child very well and as Wordsworth said, 'The child is father of the man.' In this case that is true indeed.

"I said it long ago and it's been said many times since. Nixon is basically a self-defeating person even though he tried so to succeed. There was an Achilles heel there.

"He didn't have to get into the Watergate business, and even when he was in it he could have destroyed the tapes but he didn't. It was a triumph of self-defeat. That's a simplistic appraisal but basically it's true."

Prof. Schreiber established and maintains close ties with the woman, now 51, whose story she tells in "Sybil." Their first meeting in 1962 was arranged by Dr. Cornelia B. Wilbur, Sybil's psychoanalyst. Prof. Schreiber had been psychiatry editor of "Science Digest," and had written psychiatric articles for magazines. Dr. Wilbur thought she might be interested in writing about Sybil.

Cases of multiple identity have been documented in psychiatric annals, but Sybil's was unique. Her analysis covered 11 years, included 2,345 office sessions and revealed an astonishing total of 16 different "selves" in her life.

Until well into analysis, Sybil was unaware of her other personalities. She knew only that she had "lost" periods, when she couldn't remember what she had done.

She was a third grader and 9 years old when her grandmother, the only person who had given her love and understanding, died. Two years later Sybil "came back," surprised to find herself in fifth grade. She had no memory of the intervening two years and, afraid to tell anyone what had happened, she was unable to explain satisfactorily why she could not do the multiplication tables.

Happy or Not?

The book has a happy ending in the sense that Sybil finally becomes one person, Prof. Schreiber said. That happened nine years ago.

"She lost time but she also lost something else — the best years of her life," Prof. Schreiber observed. "Those years were not returned to her and in that sense it is an unhappy ending.

"In the first year or two after the cure, she was a person who had more serenity than anyone I have ever known. 'To wake up in the morning and know you have a whole day you can count on! You cannot know what it means,' she used to say to me. Now she has had whole days for nine years and that total euphoria she sensed at the beginning has left her."

Prof. Schreiber spent more than seven years researching Sybil's case. The actual writing, which did not begin until after the cure had been effected, took one and one-half years.

Lived in State

The research took the author to a tiny town in southwestern Wisconsin, where Sybil spent her childhood. Using names that Sybil had given her, and posing as the writer of a series on life in small town America, Prof. Schreiber called Sybil's former friends and acquaintances.

"I would introduce myself, explain my ostensible reason for being in town and say Sybil asked me to say hello," the author recalled. "It was surprising how much information they gave me."

The reason for the subterfuge was to protect Sybil's identity and Prof. Schreiber is delighted that now, 18 months after initial publication of the book, her identity has not been revealed.

Share Profits

Today Sybil is an assistant professor of art in a New England college. Prof. Schreiber is sharing the royalties from the book, which has been published in 14 different countries, with Sybil and her analyst, Dr. Wilbur. They will also share in profits from the movie rights, which were sold to a film producing company in Burbank, Calif.

Sybil can use the money, Prof. Schreiber reported. When she could no longer afford the analysis, she was treated without charge by Dr. Wilbur, now a professor of psychiatry at the University of Kentucky. Sybil began repaying the doctor as soon as she obtained a job following her cure.

Little in Common

"Sybil is a fantastically intelligent human being," Prof. Schreiber said. "The whole business of multiple personalities is a defensive maneuver growing out of the subconscious and it probably took a hell of a lot of intelligence to construct these other lives even on a subconscious level. Someone less intelligent would either have died or ran away."

The only disturbing aspect of the book's success for Prof. Schreiber is that "people who do not understand the role of the biographer" frequently think that she herself is the book's subject.

"The only thing we have in common in the family syndrome is that we are both only children," Prof. Schreiber said. "I had the most marvelous parents who really made a career of parenthood. She had the worst parents imaginable.

"She was raised in a strict fundamentalist religion. I was raised an agnostic.

"Her father was a builder. Mine was a librarian at the New York Public Library, a Phi Beta Kappa, a Pulitzer Prize winner.

"The philosophy of child raising in the two families was diametrically opposite. Sybil lived in a little concentration camp; I lived in a paradise of permissiveness."

Planning Next

Writing the book was a Herculean task, the author related. "It was very difficult writing. I came to feel I had lost the one personality I had and was living Sybil's life instead of mine. I became depleted."

When the book was finished, Prof. Schreiber said categorically that she would never write another. "Now," she said, smiling, "I can tell you just as categorically there will be another. I want to write again. I am tuning up the orchestra trying to find what the next book will be."

Rod Serling disappointed with radio drama

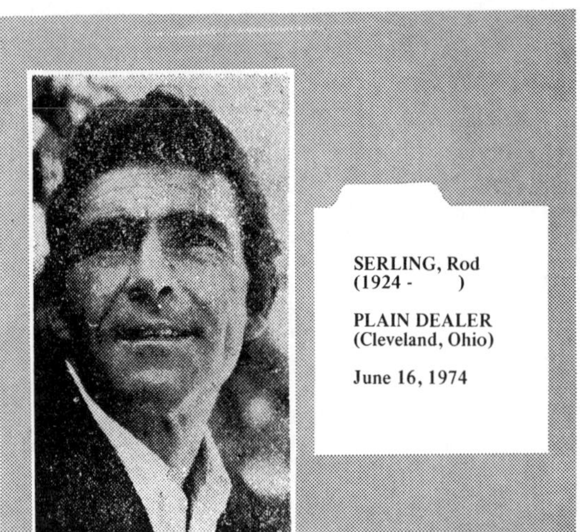
SERLING, Rod
(1924 -)

PLAIN DEALER
(Cleveland, Ohio)

June 16, 1974

Rod Serling

By Raymond P. Hart

Rod Serling, master writer of the mysterious and macabre, is playing a game of suspense with the good earth.

And unlike his nail-biting tales, he has no control of how things are going to turn out.

He is, you see, garden farming on the family place two miles east of the New York village of Interlaken, near Ithaca.

Trying to fool Mother Nature into giving him a good crop, teaching creative writing and film criticism at Ithaca College and narrating television and radio commercials are taking up most of the time and talents of one of the most creative and popular suspense writers of our time.

On the side, he serves as host of "Zero Hour," a weekday radio mystery series beamed by the Mutual Broadcasting System and aired, since its inception last Feb. 4, on WSUM in Parma at 5:15 p.m. and, since April 29, also on WJW at 8 p.m.

Serling's feelings about the recent upsurge in radio drama—not his success, or lack of it, in growing vegetables—prompted a call to his rural home.

It soon became apparent that he is disappointed with radio drama and television.

First, Serling made it clear that he merely serves as host of "Zero Hour," having nothing to do with the writing or producing of the 25-minute dramas.

"I've caught the show about three times," he said, "and one was passable and two I would have flunked off the air.

"What they're trying to do—and they may succeed—is a show that is contemporary. But it sounds campy.

"The same thing applies to 'The CBS Radio Mystery Theater' (aired Monday through Saturday at 11:07 p.m. and Sunday at 7:07 p.m. on WERE).

"It has to be relevant stuff ... 1974. Short of that, why not resurrect old 'Shadow' recordings? So far, I have yet to see either show relate to our time, either in story or techinque," Serling said.

Why doesn't Serling, who has been writing since 1946 and has a bachelor of arts degree in literature and languages from Antioch College in Yellow Springs, O., and served "apprenticeships" at several Ohio radio and television stations, apply his talents to the writing of radio drama?

"I find I get more satisfaction seeing something grow out of the earth than seeing it come out of actors' mouths—unless it's six ears of corn, which you sometimes get anyhow," he said.

"I'm too accustomed to showing my people where they are (on television). The only guy who really could write proper radio drama now would be Norman Corwin (veteran at the trade)."

Serling thinks that "if they're selling us nostalgia, they've succeeded. It's thoroughly reminiscent of radio 25-30 years ago.

"I'm not bad rapping it. It's just not what I expected," he said.

"I realize the economics of the situation. But I don't want to spend my time writing what would hopefully be provocative drama—and get a check that would buy me a carton of cigarettes."

Serling believes that radio drama "is a little kinky ... a look what we're doing, ma," kind of thing. It's mostly sound effects tied together by a thin thread of story.

"Radio drama currently has the value of an antique."

Won't it change for the better?

"I don't know," Serling said. "I have no idea.

"I'm frequently wrong, anyhow. I thought Nixon would be out (of office) by now. And I thought Sonny Liston would be (heavyweight boxing) champion for 20 years."

Switching mediums, Serling said, "Television serves a purpose—if you can assume its purpose is to titillate people.

"During the last year, I saw maybe six memorable shows out of a couple hundred."

Serling, 49, believes that "most of the older guys (writers) have been passed over—those who were unique for television.

"It's not a question of the rats deserting the ship, but the ship deserting the rats—as far as taking anthology dramas off television.

"I don't say that plaintively. The medium treated us fairly for a long time. Television made it for us."

Serling does write an occassional television special and feature film—"If they allow me to."

Meaning?

"If I have an idea they think is purchasable."

He has penned a one-hour television pilot, a four-part TV special and a (movie house) screen play in the last three months.

What about writing for television on a regular basis again if radio drama turns Serling off?

"I don't think I could hack it being in a room with a network vice president telling me what I should write," he said. "I don't want to be in that profession again. I was there for 20 years."

Then what direction will his writing take in the future?

"I don't know and don't much care," Serling said. "I'll worry about my profession in the fall. I write only what I want to write."

A prolific writer, Serling has turned out 3 TV series, countless other shows for the tube, 3 made-for-TV films, 10 movie house flicks and 7 books. He has never written radio drama, except as a summer replacement at WLW in Cincinnati.

Summing up his feelings about radio and television, Serling said, "I feel the same way about radio as I do television as an art form. It doesn't rise to the occassion like it should ... although television occassionally has.

"Radio today is more of a display case than an art form."

Serling could switch to just writing movie house films.

"Yes. But first, I have to keep the raccoons from eating my corn."

Serling, who was graduated from Antioch in 1950, recalled his Ohio days.

"I worked at radio stations in Springfield, Marion, Columbus and Cincinnati," the native of Syracuse, N. Y., said.

While at WLW (radio and television) in Cincy, he met the late Jim Runyon, who was toiling in the Queen City before climbing the ladder to Cleveland's electronic mediums.

"I knew Runyon more socially than professionally," Serling said.

Serling attended many Ohio State football games and commented on Woody Hayes, the Buckeyes' coach who recently suffered a mild heart attack. "He's indestructible."

Serling remembered not leaving the OSU stands at halftime to get a hot dog "so I wouldn't miss the band."

He met his wife-to-be, Miss Carol Kramer, at Antioch and they were married in Columbus, in his sophomore year.

"We'll observe our 26th wedding anniversary on July 31," Serling said.

Yesterday, the Serlings saw their daughter, Jodi, 22, married to Steve Croyle in Ithaca.

"It will be just the immediate families in attendance," he said beforehand. "Like 1,500 couples."

The Serlings, who have another daughter, Anne, 19, spend six months on "the farm" and the rest of the year in Pacific Palisades, Calif.

Now, it will be back to grooming his couple of acres (out of 14 on the property) of vegetables.

"We haven't had any rain, but the corn looks good," Serling said.

Now, if Serling only would change "crops" and write radio drama and do a lot more TV suspensers ... and forget that darn garden.

Besides, of all people, doesn't Serling know it's not nice to fool Mother Nature?

The Poor Little Rich Boy

By KANDY STROUD
Knight News Service

WASHINGTON — Eric Sevareid, 61, trim and white-haired, sits in his cluttered CBS office, surrounded by photographs of himself and past presidents, chain-smokes . . . and ponders.

He reflects his own tightly disciplined, church-going background and a boyhood that was marked by a poverty of material things, a richness of culture and a reverence for learning.

BROUGHT UP in Velva, N. D., a town of 850 on the Mouse River, Sevareid recalls he was "pretty damn broke most of the time," but he also remembers his heroes:

"My father was a farm boy who wanted to be only a businessman, yet he learned Greek, Latin, philosophy and theology. It may have been a small town, but it was full of men of exceptional quality."

Those men included a family doctor who "played many musical instruments and composed symphonic music, as well as keeping us all alive," and the editor of a weekly newspaper, a man who had no children but who "adopted" the young Sevareid and fostered in him a strong desire to learn and to write.

"I never wanted to be a fireman or a cowboy," says Sevareid. "I knew from the start I wanted to be a reporter."

NOW HE IS one of the deans of American television, a man with a six-figure salary, two homes and the fame of instant recognition, but he remembers the old lessons and applies them to today's headlines.

"I think Nixon and the men around him were totally uneducated men," he says. "They were skilled lawyers, great at the nuts and bolts, the mechanics of the law, the pragmatic aspects, but they didn't understand the Constitution. They didn't comprehend that every single paragraph was based upon centuries of human suffering.

"In some of Nixon's speeches, can you find a sense that he was steeped in history, or the great religions of the world, or in the great philosophers, as men like Adlai Stevenson and John Kennedy were? And that's the education that counts.

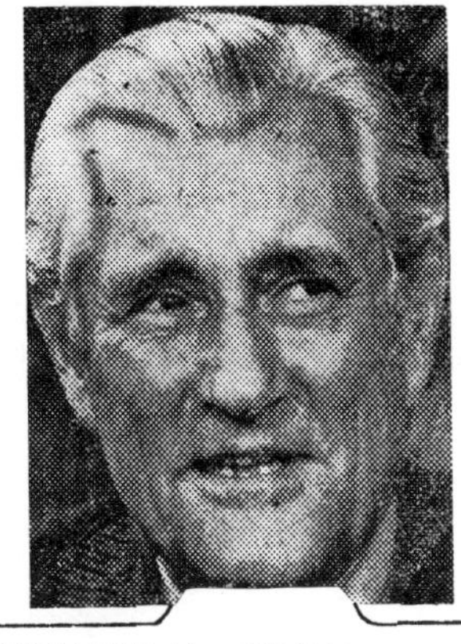

SEVAREID, (Arnold) Eric (1912-)
AKRON BEACON JOURNAL (Akron, Ohio) June 30, 1974

Sevareid says there have been several efforts to muffle him.

"I've been attacked publicly by Spiro Agnew and privately by Patrick Buchanan and others. Bill Safire (a former Nixon speechwriter, now a New York Times columnist) said Nixon sent word around the White House that no one was to talk to me. They had a regular system. They'd call me up to chew me out and also feed rebuttals to their favorite columnist. They'd rebut with intimidation and harassment. You'd think it was all they had to think about. They were always on the defensive . . . paranoid.

"AT FIRST it didn't bother me, but then I found for the first time in my life that I was having to defend not my function but my honesty. I've resented that very much. I think as a whole we've won the day. The American people know that the press has been 90 pct. right on this thing. These people in the White House have destroyed themselves. They will go, but the press will still be here."

"I've been in this business 40 years. I remember the real yellow press — the bad tabloids, the radio screamers like Walter Winchell who used to tout his favorite stocks on the air. That would never be allowed to happen today. The press is much better educated, much more responsible. Bias is not the basic internal enemy of the press, as the White House charges. It is haste. And in broadcasting, it is not only haste that is our enemy, but a compression of material."

TAKE HIS own job as an example.

"It's easier in a way than beating the bushes. And I get to sit on my rear a lot more. Yet it's much harder than people think. The average newspaper columnist has trouble banging out three columns a week. I have to go on the air four or five nights. They get 800 to 1,000 words; I only have 400. How do you document anything?"

What does he think of so-called instant analysis following presidential press conferences?

"I don't like it at all. I've tried hard to get it off the air. I don't think you can do it without having an advance script. No one is that smart. You find yourself unable to remember things the President has said, salient points. We don't perform as well as if we were prepared. I'm not so worried about doing an injustice to the President as doing an injustice to ourselves."

Surrounded by copies of the Wall Street Journal, the New York Times, the Washington Post and the Washington Star News, with a large television set at one side, Sevareid feels Americans are too barraged with news.

"People are fascinated by it, but they get drugged on it. Besides, reality is more bizarre than fiction now and we are assaulted by it every day. How can the human mind and heart absorb all the world's problems every day, or even react to them? That is why people withdraw and concentrate on their own problems. It is not apathy. It's news pollution."

SEVAREID IS up by 6 a. m., wading through five or six newspapers plus the morning news shows. He often lunches with sources at the Metropolitan Club and spends more time reading such esoterica as seminar reports from the Brookings Institution or the National Academy of Sciences. He takes home a briefcase filled with work.

"It's the life of a perpetual graduate student," he says. "There's not enough time to get it all done."

One reason there isn't is a 9-year-old daughter, a child by Sevareid's second wife, who separated from him last year and moved to Europe. Sevareid now finds his leisure time occupied by the sort of trivia many wives handle: cleaning, laundry, etc.

"I find I'm thinking of things other than my work. It's dangerous and I can't afford to, but what do you do?"

He says he has finally learned sympathy for a housewife's daily travail: "Getting ground down into a routine ... not getting any intellectual excitement . . . and when the kids get bigger, she rebels."

HE DOUBTS he'd ever marry again, asking, "Who'd want a 61-year-old man with a bad back and arthritis?"

Yet he copes, and although he is one of the most familiar personalities on TV, he says it is "agony" facing a camera: "I know I've been in the business all my life, but I hate the damn lights and camera."

He also hates the loss of his anonymity. Women clutch his arm on street corners and ask about Watergate; strangers approach him in restaurants. "Some people thrive on that," he says, "but I'm not very gracious about it. I'm almost rude.

"I hope I have not come to believe my own publicity. I often think I'm just plain lucky to have a good job. And I get such diverse mail that I'm not even sure what my image is. I think I know my own shortcomings. I'm not your All-American freckle-faced boy next door. I'm not even a performer type. I can't cajole people or talk to people. I m just an ordinary writer who reads what he writes."

Shaara: A Writer's Battles

By CINDY MILLER
Democrat Staff Writer

Michael Shaara, author of a triumphant new book about the battle at Gettysburgh, has fought the battles of life.

His heart stopped beating for 55 minutes after a heart attack in 1966. There's only one person in medical history whose heart had stopped longer and lived.

Riding on a Vespa motorcycle in Florence, Italy, in 1972, he swerved to miss a car. Shaara hit his head on concrete curbing and was semi - conscious for a month. He woke unable to talk.

Meanwhile, in 1974, Michael Shaara finds himself on the very edge of a sweet success for his book, "The Killer Angels." After a visit to Gettysburg in 1964, the Tallahassee - based author felt moved to write about the battle.

Comparing his compelling drive to Stephen Crane's, author of "Red Badge of Courage," Shaara says, "In order to live an experience, you have to write it."

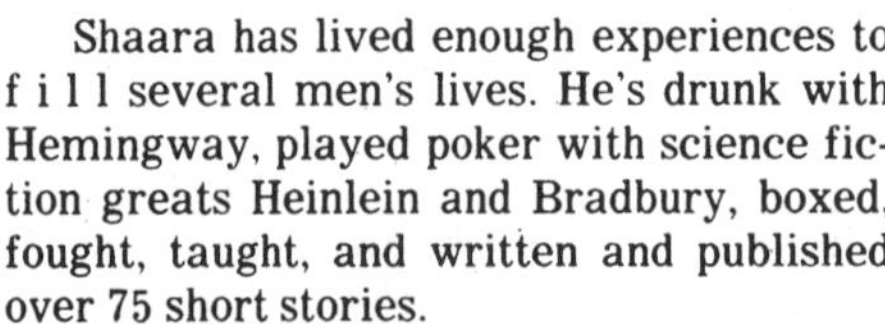

Democrat Photo by Sage Thigpen

SHAARA, Michael

TALLAHASSEE DEMOCRAT (Tallahassee, Fla.)

Sept. 15, 1974

Shaara has lived enough experiences to fill several men's lives. He's drunk with Hemingway, played poker with science fiction greats Heinlein and Bradbury, boxed, fought, taught, and written and published over 75 short stories.

Living the ups and downs of a writer's lonely life, he's soberly joyful about recognition for his new book.

He is proud of "Killer Angels," grateful for readers' praises, almost incredulous that Book of the Month Club has chosen it as **the** book of the month, although he hasn't been notified which month.

Michael Shaara has a special quality about him, a reflective quality. Something profound seems to be lurking behind what he does not say.

Friends say he's a genius: others say he's a man alone. With a shock of dark hair and a broken nose, and a way of leaning into conversations, Shaara is no aloof intellectual in an ivory tower.

This man who talks with gestures and looks like your neighborhood workman, is also a prince! Shaara found his noble ancestry when he stumbled across a marble bust --- a mirror image of himself --- at Villa Sciarra in Rome.

His mother's famous Southern ancestry, dating back to Thomas Jefferson, was early knowledge. But he knew his father only as an Italian immigrant, a northerner whose liberal life revolved around unions.

The son of a Southern woman and a Yankee man, Shaara felt the split personality of the two cultures of America.

Growing up in both Jersey City and Waco, Tex., "in the days when they were two different worlds," Shaara says he has spent much of his life trying to see what America is.

"You see, I've lived half and half, two different worlds. Both worlds are gone today. The loss of the South is like a fantasy that's disappeared."

While his mother taught him the gentlemanly manners of the South, he also learned the street ways of Jersey City.

In high school, Shaara graduated with more awards than any student before him. He had varsity letters for basketball and baseball and track. He was president of his class, yearbook editor and president of the choir.

HIS ACTIVE, INTENSE LIFE continued at Rutgers. He wrote and published science fiction short stories, fought in 18, and won 17 professional boxing matches, and met and married his college sweetheart Helen.

In the army, he was a paratrooper in the 82nd Airborne Division. Then he was a policeman in St. Petersburg. In 1957, he came to Tallahassee to study music.

The Florida State University English Department faculty must have seen some of his short stories (published in Playboy, the now defunct Saturday Evening Post, Redbook, etc.), because in 1961 they asked Shaara to teach a class on short story writing.

At first, he couldn't imagine himself being a teacher, but he gave it a try. By 1967, he was elected by the students to receive the Coyle Moore Award as outstanding teacher at Florida State.

His rapport with students was known all over campus. They could talk to him. He would understand. He was hip to what was going on.

Shaara says receiving the Moore Award was "the biggest moment of my life." He adds, "I worked at teaching very hard. There were students with talent and no desire; desire and no talent; and a little of each. It's a challenge to find what you can do for each of them."

Pushing ahead with his writing, Shaara authored "The Broken Place," published in 1968. That was the same year he had the heart attack from so many pressures, and it took six months to recover.

IN THE "BROKEN PLACE," the main character McClain, like Shaara, feels, "What matters is that a man has to be of use, a man has to try to do something. A man is built for use, his hands, his brain, his feeling, and you can feel the pressure all the time. I should be somewhere doing something that matters and that I was made to do ... I want to believe."

One critic calls him "a born writer." But, as his family knows, that does not make one's life easy.

Helen, his wife of 24 years, says understandingly, "He lives through a lot of tensions and disappointments. He does a great deal of analyzing.

"It's difficult for him to small talk, for him to sit down and talk about the weatther. So he doesn't have much of a social life. In any gathering, he ends up lecturing."

The Shaaras have two children. Jeff is grown and married and lives in Tampa. Lila, their 15 - year - old daughter,, is a source of great joy. She's a voracious reader, likes music, and "is into plants and herbs."

(Continued from preceding page)

Overgrown with Tallahassee's foliage, the Shaara home is off Thomasville Highway. They've lived there 10 years.

Van Gogh prints, Italian memorabilia, books, and classical music fill the home. This is Michael Shaara's office since he left the university.

After his motorcycle accident, he was unable to continue teaching. He says he has lost his memory and his vocabulary. Those losses take their toll on a writer.

A believer in writing in "instinctive times," Shaara follows no routine. He's a late movie fan and also likes early rising.

The only time Shaara hesitates for an answer is when asked if he sees an overall plan to his life, a direction. The question seems to nag at him.

"The best thing I've learned," he finally says, "is that you yourself are the judge of whether or not you've done your best."

He adds, "When I finished this book, I was so tired. They talk about post partum depressions that happen to writers.

"But I can say, that I have done the best I can do."

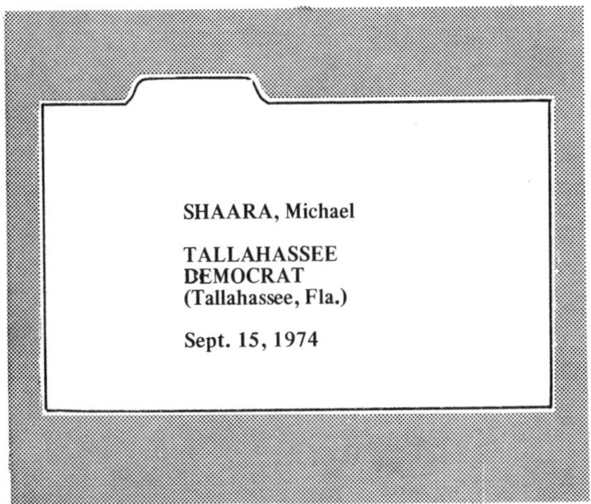

SHAARA, Michael

TALLAHASSEE DEMOCRAT (Tallahassee, Fla.)

Sept. 15, 1974

Now in his mid - 40s, , he wonders what he will do with his life. He's frustrated with the effects of that accident, like problems with articulation.

Always an active man and a believer in an active life, he now has to sit and wait. His wife says, "He's done so much throughout his life, that it makes it harder now."

Helen, who has worked with the Division of Family Services for 18 years, says, "Life is very rough on him. It's easier on me --- I can get away to work and not think about worries."

The Shaaras are a close-knit family. The first thing Shaara shows to a visitor? Photographs of Lila's birthday. Helen believes her husband is a genius and lives his frustrations with him, daughter Lila turns her dad onto Bob Dylan; Shaara dedicated "The Killer Angels" to Lila.

Catherine Setzer, a former graduate student in Shaara's class, has lived with the family since 1970. She came just to babysit, but stayed on to become a great admirer and friend.

THE JOY THAT CAME from writing "Killer Angels" was all - involving for Shaara. Into his research, he seemed to pour his whole life — to live it and breathe it.

To him, Gettysburg was overwhelming ... the feeling of the past, of being on sacred ground, where men like General Robert E. Lee, his distant ancestor, fought.

That day in 1964, Shaara climbed to the top of a cupola to look over the battlefield.

"When you get deeply involved with Gettsburg, it becomes real. It's like 'In Cold Blood,' you're telling a story that really happened."

Shaara had always been intrigued by the words of Winston Churchill, who wrote that the American Civil War "was the noblest and least avoidable of all great mass conflicts of which until then there was record."

He wanted to know why Churchill wrote that, and since he felt himself a man in the middle of two cultures, Shaara was even more interested.

Shaara empathized with figures in that battle. "I found out that Lee was feeling the effects of a recent heart attack. I know how that feels."

There's Joshua Chamberlain, a colonel in the Union army, who had been a professor of rhetoric at Bowdoin University. Through this figure, with whom Shaara easily identifies, came the title of the book.

When Chamberlain had recited a line from Hamlet to his father, "What a piece of work is man ... in action how like an angel!", His father replied, "Well, boy , if he's an angel, he's sure a murderin' angel." As during the years when Shaara taught a Shakespeare class at FSU, he is always aware he is telling about 'real people.'

Shaara sees the Civil War as a conflict between the idealistic individualism of the North and the aristocratic, tradition - bound ways of the South.

"The North was fighting for being treated as an individual, the South was fighting for the family. In the South, they were unified — all Protestants and English. But the North was totally a mixture.

"I'M GETTING TO AN IDEAL I would like to see some of the gentlemanly ideas retained and the individuality."

Shaara fondly recalls the gentlemanly lessons his mother taught him at the same time he was learning to be tough in Jersey City.

"My mother said, 'Never try to insult someone unless you mean it. But say it loudly and clearly if you mean it, and live by the word you say.'"

To Shaara, this book is about America. "When you wander around in this country among Dutch, Greek, German, Italian, what is American?"

Paperback rights for the book should pay him three or four times his yearly salary from FSU. After two years on disability retirement, that will be welcomed. There's also talk that Warner Brothers might make a movie of the book.

The fruits of success are sweet. Next month, Shaara will televise a show in St. Petersburg with Haslam's Bookstore.

"When I was a cop walking the beat in St. Petersburg, I used to walk by Haslam's and think, 'Gee, I'd like to have a book in that store."

On the subject of perfect men

By SHELBY HODGE
Post Reporter

Since the publication of her book "Some Men Are More Perfect Than Others," Merle Shain has been on the receiving end of a multitude of kindnesses—roses stuck anonymously in her door, violets delivered to her home, phone calls from across the country and stacks of mail detailing the lives of readers.

What has generated the personal response to her book on loving, a book that began as a feature article for the Toronto Globe? Perhaps it is the sensitivity of the vignettes recorded in each chapter. The openness with which Shain expresses herself and her feelings. Or simply the subject matter approached from the " let's understand each other" viewpoint.

When Shain undertook the newspaper assignment of writing about the makings of a first class man, she had definite feelings about where men and women were going. Although she was in sympathy with the feminist movement, Shain said that things on the whole were getting better for women but "personal relationships on an individual man and an individual woman basis were getting worse. Transition was frightening men."

Men were confused as to what strength really was. Whether it was understanding or beating the woman about the head. Men were blaming women, women were blaming men, she said.

"They had been manipulating and bullying each other for so long that it was time to be very honest very quickly," Shain said.

She spent an entire summer working on the article. A good bit of that time was spent wringing her hands. She worried that if she wrote in the "detached oberserver's way it would be an attack to the head. But nobody would be terribly moved."

In deciding to keep her writing open, Shain feared that she was running the risk of being "snickered" at. And she describes in her book the thin line between being honest, writing from her experiences, and being indiscreet. The brief lines devoted to that subject belie her preoccupation with becoming a "stripper" of sorts. A preoccupation which explains why it took three months to write a single article.

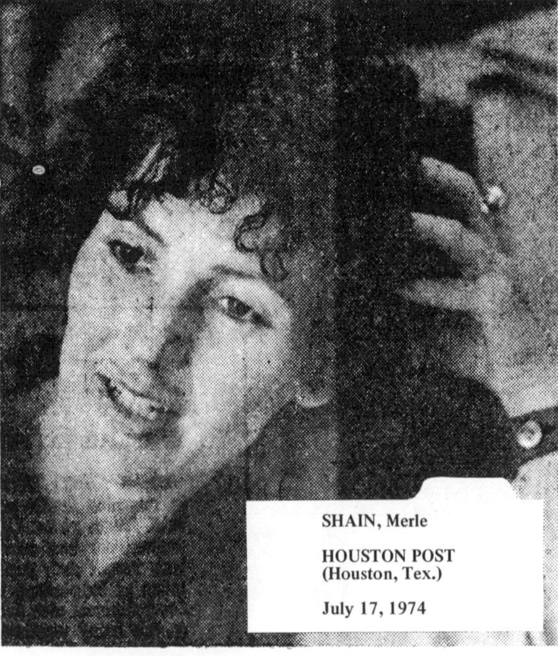

SHAIN, Merle

HOUSTON POST
(Houston, Tex.)

July 17, 1974

Nevertheless, her article hit home with the gist being, "A lot of things you guys do we really love, but there are other things you do we wish you'd stop doing," as she explained it.

Following the publication of the article, Shain was bombarded with fan mail and phone calls from publishers wanting her to do a book. In fact, she says the practical reason for her writing the book is that publishers forced her into it.

Shain spent another nine months working on the manuscript. Much of her experience as a married woman, mother and divorced woman went into the book. A book that covers such topics as romantic love, love and making love, married women and other men, married men and other women, being true and when a marriage ends.

A book that includes, "We are all very frightened of love's power to create and destroy but if there were men who were capable of valuing the best that women have in them, women would always be glad to love them."

Shain said that after completing the book she imagined it would be a book given to men by women. And indeed it has been. She has gotten letters from men who have received copies of her book from both their wives and their lovers. But in turn men have been reading the book and giving it to their wives or girlfriends.

"Some Men Are More Perfect Than Others" (Bantam Books, paperback $1.50) is Shain's first book but not her last. Before undertaking another book, however, Shain is working on a movie "about feeling, loving, all the awful things done in the name of love. " It is a movie about a young, divorced woman with a child —the mirror image of the author.

Before her stint as a feature writer, Shain was an associate editor of Chatelaine, Canada's women's magazine. And she worked on the staff of Prime Minister Pierre Trudeau during his first election campaign.

Author Writes About Life, Loving

BY JANET GRIMLEY

Merle Shain had written volumes of newspaper and magazine articles about other people's thoughts but panicked at the idea of writing about her own.

But, after the panic subsided, the Toronto woman wrote a magazine article, then a book about loving and being loved. Her book, "Some Men Are More Perfect Than Others," has been a big seller since publication a year ago.

Since Bantam Books released the paperback Ms. Shain has flown around the United States — including Seattle — and Canada to talk about her toughts of love.

The book is not a how-to manual nor a dry research project. It's light, gentle reading that often makes a reader comment, "That's happened to me, too."

Putting personal feelings into a book was not easy for Ms. Shain. She said, "I really suffered, trying to put my feelings into words. But, after the magazine article, it seemed like the whole world was calling me to talk about the book."

The magazine article grew into a handbound book and then a paperback. "When I was approached to write the book I told them I had said it all in 2,000 words and couldn't possibly write any more. But I did."

Her research was life itself. She drew from her own experiences and those of friends. When she needed a real story to illustrate a point, she picked one from her background of living and loving.

"In Toronto people come up to me and say, 'How did you know that such-and-such happened to me?' Of course, I didn't know. It's just that many people have similar experiences. I guess that is why so many people identify with the book."

SHAIN, Merle

SEATTLE POST–INTELLIGENCER
(Seattle, Wash.)

Sept. 19, 1974

Many quotes sum up feelings succinctly. For example:

— "Loving can cost a lot but not loving always costs more . . ."

— "Marriage is supposed to do everything, like Duz, which is more than half its problem.

— "Marriage is considered to give women an identity but sometimes it costs them one instead."

—"Women want to be valued for what they are instead of what they do."

Ms. Shain said she was amazed at the thousands of letters she's received since the book appeared and the copies sent to her to be autographed. "And passages are underlined and pages are marked. Several caution me not to remove bookmarks because they mark a favorite comment."

Ms. Shain considers herself a feminist but is disturbed by those who consider women's liberation only as working outside the home.

"Liberation is being able to do what you want to do. If you want to work, fine, but if you want to stay home, that's right, too."

Her book was geared to women who grew up in the '50s as she did, she explained. They were told to get married, then be sex objects, adoring wives and loving mothers. If a woman wanted a career of her own she was put down. She was supposed to help her husband be a success. "In the '60s I was a terrible thing because I wanted to work. Now I'm a success story in the '70s.

"Things are changing today but many people from that era aren't equipped emotionally to handle the changes. I'm trying to show them they can have a good life in ways not learned in the '50s. I've also found that people not from my age group identfy with the book, too."

She has no plans for another book but is working on a movie script. "The idea is involved. Just say it's a sad-funny movie about real people."

Bruce Shanks Retires as News Editorial Cartoonist And Pokes Fun at Himself in Farewell Sketch

Bruce Shanks has packed his old drawing board and has taken it with him to his retirement home in Boca Raton, on the east coast of Florida.

Migration of the drawing board to Florida is not necessarily bad news for the thousands of admiring fans who look each day for the Shanks editorial page cartoon in The News.

News readers will still enjoy occasional Shanks cartoons with their distinctive humor and illuminating insight into the news.

Bruce closed his desk in The News office after 41 years as a staff artist and cartoonist and 23 years as the editorial page cartoonist.

He left behind one final cartoon, appearing on today's Editorial Page, which, characteristically, pokes fun at himself. His familiar "Average Guy" is asking the retreating cartoonist: "Smater, Shanks, run out of ideas?"

* * *

THE VALEDICTORY cartoon typifies the impression held by many of Mr. Shanks' fellow News staffers and close friends — the impression of an easygoing man who enjoys light conversation and practical jokes.

People who worked closely with Mr. Shanks knew better. They know him as a painstaking craftsman — a perfectionist who drew and re-drew rough drafts and pondered carefully what he considers one of a cartoon's most important components, its title.

A frequent question from visitors to his working area was whether Mr. Shanks ever "ran dry" of ideas. He grinned and asked the visitor to open a desk drawer.

It always held a stack of rough sketches of potential cartoons.

Mr. Shanks never had a formal art education and he came into the newspaper business in the transitional years of the late '20s.

Born in Buffalo of Scottish descent, Bruce McKinley Shanks received his schooling at School 38 and the old School of Practice at the former Buffalo Normal School, now Grover Cleveland High School.

* * *

AT LAFAYETTE High School, he began showing his interest in cartooning, as he now recalls, "to the annoyance of some teachers." But Miss Elizabeth Weiffenbach, head of Lafayette's Art Department then, became his first fan and encouraged him in his sketching.

He went to work in 1927 as a copy boy for the former Buffalo Express, then located at Washington and Exchange Sts., only one block north of the present News office.

Even as a copy boy, he began drawing cartoons and, to his surprise, the Express ran some of them. He later joined the former Buffalo Times as a regular cartoonist.

He found his permanent newspaper home at The News in 1933.

For many years, his drawing board was occupied with the routine chores of retouching photographs, as well as drawing sketches to illustrate feature stories.

He still remembers the roar that emanated from a usually mild-mannered news editor when he drew a necktie on the photo of a news figure who was known as "Tieless Joe."

Some of his early years were devoted to a form of journalistic art that is only now coming back into prominence.

HE DID courtroom sketches of jurors, witnesses, attorneys and defendants.

He also remembers a trip in sub-freezing temperatures in the Adirondacks to cover an early airliner crash with Charles A. Michie, then aviation writer for The News, and Walter Bingham, early News photographer.

Once he began specializing in the editorial page cartoon in 1951, Mr. Shanks won an international reputation. His cartoons were reprinted in newspapers throughout the world.

And he often got requests for original cartoons from notables — even those who were the subjects of uncomplimentary cartoons.

When a big news story broke, Mr. Shanks often would come to the office at 6:30 AM and within an hour would have a cartoon ready for approval by the editorial page editor. He thinks some of his best work was done under the pressure of an impending deadline.

And, he adds, some of his worst ideas came to him while he was away from the office. They often didn't seem as brilliant when he sat down to work in the morning.

* * *

HE CONSIDERS his greatest helper to have been Alfred H. Kirchhofer, retired editor of The News. He recalls Mr. Kirchhofer's "suggestions, patience and kindliness" and he remembers his pleasure when the editor would pick the top cartoon of a stack of 10 "roughs" that he submitted each day.

His many honors were capped in 1958 by the Pulitzer Prize for a cartoon, "The Thinker" showing a working man pondering the then-current abuses among top leaders of some unions.

A favorite cartoon was one picked for a top award of the National Safety Council. It was a holiday season cartoon showing a car crushed against a tree and titled, "Life of the Party."

BRUCE SHANKS
41 Years at The News

SHANKS, Bruce

BUFFALO NEWS
(Buffalo, N.Y.)

Apr. 22, 1974

Earlier this year, he received his 12th award from the Freedoms Foundation. He received 11 Page One awards in the annual competition of the Buffalo Newspaper Guild.

* * *

OTHER AWARDS included the Christopher's Medal, the Patriots' Award for a cartoon on the fight against communism, the Grenville Clark Award for a cartoon on behalf of the World Court and three State Cancer Society awards.

Booklets of his cartoons, published by The News, were best sellers in area book stores.

Mr. Shanks also answered many personal appeals for specially-drawn cartoons. These included cartoons drawn for News retirees and for any fellow staffer who was seriously ill.

His favorite hobbies are closely related to his job. He enjoys work in watercolors, oils and ceramics. Another hobby, sculpturing, spilled over into his work a few years ago when The News ran pictures of caricaturing busts of national leaders.

He and his wife, the former Louise Van Vleck, have lived in recent years in the Westbrook Apartments. Mrs. Shanks enjoys painting with oils.

Mr. Shanks first grew to like Florida during World War II as an Air Force Intelligence staff sergeant, stationed in Orlando, Fla.

* * *

IN A BUSINESS that often rubs nerves to the raw, Mr. Shanks never lost his composure and was universally liked by his co-workers. He never took himself too seriously or lost his ability to poke fun at himself, even after he achieved celebrity status.

Some of his most memorable escapades involved memos he shot off to staff members on the managing editor's memo pads. He usually was able to intercept the indignant worker before he got to the editor's office.

Talking to co-workers in recent weeks about his imminent move to Florida, Mr. Shanks has been musing about his fondness for water skiing.

"But," he has added, "I'm having a little trouble with equipment now. I want to master the one-ski style."

As usual the reaction has been, "Does he really mean it?"

However, after the jokes fade into the past, Mr. Shanks will be remembered by News workers and readers as a craftsman who never spared himself at work.

His work showed it. And, hopefully, that work is a long way from being finished.

Shame of a Nation

Empty Bowl

Government of the People . .

'Wonder Who Won?'

IRWIN SHAW

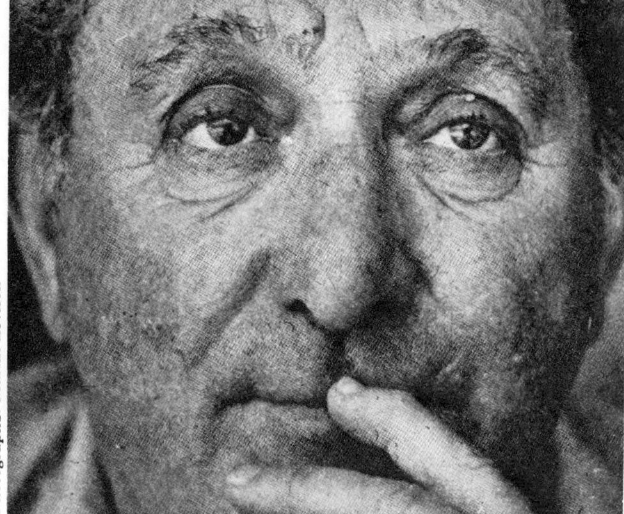
Photographs: Marlin Levison

SHAW, Irwin
(1913-)

MIAMI HERALD
(Miami, Fla.)

Dec. 15, 1974

[See also CA-15/16]

Like the epic novels he writes, the life of Irwin Shaw is a saga from American history: the poor Jewish boy from Brooklyn who escapes, by talent and hard work, to a life of luxury in France and Switzerland.

Most readers know him today for his novels. His first was *The Young Lions,* a 1948 book that showed World War II from both the German and the American viewpoints. His latest is *Evening in Byzantium,* a 1973 best seller about a once-famous Hollywood producer who worries about his drinking, a failed marriage and a lack of purpose.

Critics have admired Shaw mostly for his early short stories, many of which appear in anthologies. One of these, a haunting tale of the aging football hero, *The Eighty-Yard Run,* was reprinted in *Esquire's* 40th Anniversary Issue.

His novels have received mixed reviews, drawing praise for his craftsmanship and readability, while being assailed for superficial, overworked themes. One critic called his 1970 book, *Rich Man, Poor Man,* "exciting reading. It's a book you can't put down. Once you do, it wouldn't occur to you to pick it up again."

Born in the Bronx, on Feb. 27, 1913, he moved to Brooklyn's Brighton Beach when he was seven, fishing and canoeing in an area which is now a slum. He attended Brooklyn College and played blocking quarterback (in those single-wing days) on "one of the worst football teams that has ever been fielded by any college."

His writing success came quickly. After a short stint doing soap operas for radio, he had his first play on Broadway when he was 23, and was published in *The New Yorker* when he was 25.

He temporarily abandoned his writing career after Pearl Harbor, and went off to war as an enlisted man, covering the campaigns in North Africa and Europe for various publications.

When the war was over, he returned to Hollywood for a brief — and frustrating — bout as a screenwriter before moving to Paris for good in 1951. He was divorced in 1970, after a long marriage which produced one son. His mother lives on Miami Beach.

These days, at age 61, he alternates between his home in the small town of Klosters, Switzerland (where he loves to ski), and an apartment in Paris.

Recently, he finished a draft of his latest novel and was relaxing in London when he decided on a whim to fly to Miami and visit friends.

Staying in the Key Biscayne house of author James Jones (a friend from the Paris days), he sat still for two tape-recorded sessions with *Tropic* writer John Dorschner. The first was on a cool morning, as Shaw sipped a beer beside the swimming pool. The second was the following afternoon. Both times, Shaw talked about the changes, in himself and in society, that he has chronicled in 40 years of professional writing.

Q: In much of your work, there's a theme of the American-Dream-Gone-Sour. After all your success, do you still feel that way?

SHAW: Yes. Even with everything there is in America, people aren't as happy as they think they should be.

I think life is too tragic to admit the purely euphoric notion which the American Dream represents. I mean, look at Nixon now. There's the American Dream come to complete fruition. The poor kid who becomes President of the United States. You would think the euphoria would be absolute. But he didn't believe it, and he had to do things that no sane man would do. That's because he never could have enough. He got 49 states, and he wanted 50.

It's that constant search for the impossible that is damaging to the American psyche. There's the story of the famous railroad man, I forget his name. He lost $6 million and had $4 million left — and he committed suicide.

Q: But you have been close to the Hollywood crowd, to the celebrities. Don't you yourself have a certain fascination with the dream?

SHAW: Yes — and I've been lucky. We were very poor during the Depression, and I wrote my way out of it. That part of the dream was possible for me. But that doesn't keep me from using my eyes and my critical intelligence on what it means: not wanting too much. For example, if I wanted to be the richest writer in the world, I could have just stayed in Hollywood. That wasn't what I was after.

Q: You wrote the screenplay for "The Young Lions"?

SHAW: I wrote a screenplay, which they threw out. They got somebody else to do it, because they wanted to change the essential meaning of the book.

Q: They tailored it for the stars?

SHAW: They tailored it to Marlon Brando, and they tailored it to the temper of the times. Dulles was secretary of state then. The idea was, "Let's not be beastly to the Germans." Marlon went along with that. The scheme I had was that the German soldier started out with ideals, and inch by inch he became more and more brutalized by the events of the war. Until, at the end, he's just a beast. But Brando didn't want to do that. So he went through the war innocently and in the end was shocked by what he saw. He gave a great performance. Unless you had written the book, you would have liked the movie very much.

Q: What about your other movie scripts?

SHAW: The only one I was really happy with was the one I produced myself. *(In The French Style,* starring Jean Seberg, 1963). Because people change and change and change your scripts. It's out of your hands. There's one man I admire very much: Paddy Chayefsky. Did you see *Hospital?* He wrote it, and he produced it. And it came out very well indeed. He did the same thing with *Marty.* He can slug it through with businessmen, with the director, and I admire him for it, but I haven't got the patience.

Q: So you dislike Hollywood?

SHAW: I'll make a terrible confession. I loved living by the Pacific Ocean. I'd go out there, even when I had nothing to do with the movies. I finished *Young Lions* out there. I had a house on the beach, my idea of heaven. A friend of mine had a beautiful cottage back in a canyon. We rode along the beach. I was only 34 years old then, and I loved to play tennis, and ski, and go horseback riding. It was a great place to work. Remote. Nobody could even get you on the phone. And then when you wanted, there were charming, funny people — and wonder-

(Continued from preceding page)

fully intelligent people. Thomas Mann was there then, and Aldous Huxley. Christopher Isherwood. And that's just for openers. Orson Welles was there, John Huston, Walter Huston, Billy Wilder, Fritz Lang. All these people from Europe. And one beautiful woman after another. It was an exciting, intellectual time. Now, I imagine it's not like that anymore. I haven't been back there for so long that I don't know.

Q: In "Evening in Byzantium," the protagonist is recently divorced, a faded Hollywood producer who wanders around Cannes looking for meaning and romance. How close is he to being Irwin Shaw?

SHAW: He's not close at all. He reflects my ideas, but I've been a producer only once. I have no daughters. I'm not a ladies' man, in the term that he's a ladies' man. He is younger than I was. I used incidents of people I knew, all mixed up.

Q: Do you write your novels with the idea of selling them to the movies?

SHAW: I never do that. It's hard enough just doing the best novel I can. The only financial success that anybody's had with a movie from a book of mine came with *The Young Lions*. Then they bought another novel, *Lucy Crown*, and they never made it.

Q: Is it too personal to ask how much they paid for "Lucy Crown"?

SHAW: Yes. I won't tell you, but it was a lot. I got very little for *The Young Lions*, because when it first came out, it was considered too controversial for the movies. By the time they got around to making it (in 1958), it was no longer a best seller. They gave me a grudging amount. Another novel, *Rich Man, Poor Man*, was bought for television by Universal, and theoretically they are making four two-hour movies out of it. That's been a project long in the making, and I don't know how they're doing on it.

SHAW, Irwin

MIAMI HERALD
(Miami, Fla.)

Dec. 15, 1974

Q: Why did you move to Europe?

SHAW: I entered Paris on the Day of Liberation, with the first Americans in the 12th Regiment of the Fourth Division. It was the first time I'd seen the city. It looked so glorious that I decided I wanted to come back and live there. And I did.

I must say, I had been fired by the stories of Fitzgerald, Hemingway, Malcolm Cowley, in the '20s. I went there in '49, but I found out my wife was pregnant, and so we came back to the States. Then, when my son was a year old, we went to Paris. We were only going to stay for the summer, but I found myself enjoying it very much. I got out of the life I had been leading too intensely in the United States, in the theater, in the movies, in the magazine world. Paris gave me new outlooks. And my writing has resulted from that. That is, I wrote so much on European themes — Americans in Europe, actually.

Q: But you stick to American characters..

SHAW: Oh, purely American. I would hesitate to write anything major, a big book, solely about Europeans. I don't get out of touch with America. There are so many Americans who come there that Europe is like the 51st state. You carry a country around in your head. You don't have to stand at 33rd Street and Broadway.

Q: You associate with the movie crowd in Europe, too?

SHAW: Yes, but mostly with the young *Paris Review* kids — George Plimpton, Philip Roth, Bill Styron. I had a house down on the Basque coast for the summers, and they would come down there and visit for a month or two. But I like the movie people too. They're interesting. A lot of them are real artists. Remember my first success came in the theater, so that's a natural connection.

Q: But you left Broadway after writing a bitter attack on the critics. Has your opinion mellowed over the years?

SHAW: Well, I've survived it. I have written 15 plays, 13 of which flopped. In the theater, I thought they were going to destroy me. But they didn't. So now I can say, "OK, screw you." All those critics, the ones who castigated me, are dead now, or retired, and I've quit the theater. They made it impossible for me to continue, which may have been the luckiest thing that ever happened to me.

Q: So you're sensitive to reviews?

SHAW: I like to get good reviews, and I hate to get bad reviews. I'll brood for a couple of hours after a bad review, go have a couple drinks, play some tennis or ski and then say, "To hell with 'em."

What are you going to do? By and large, I've been lucky because even when I've got very bad reviews, I've gotten balancing reviews from other people of equal weight. And also, all but one of my seven novels have been very popular successes. Which has a lot to do with the way you ➡

(Continued from preceding page)
react to a book. Because for a book to last, it has to have a popular success. Otherwise, people forget it. It's awful, but it's true.

Q: In some reviews of your latest, "Evening in Byzantium," the critics said they admired the craftsmanship, but thought the theme was old-fashioned.

SHAW: That was not true, naturally. As soon as you write about Hollywood, that's what they say. Most reviews were fairly good. In fact, they were the best reviews I've had in a long time. A lot of reviewers today object to what they consider professionalism. They feel that somehow it's not true if it's artfully done. They like confessional novels, where the man lays bare his soul. That's one way of writing, but that's not my style.

Starting with the first minute I got my first paycheck, my object was to be an absolute pro. What does that mean? A man who does hard things and makes them look easy. Who doesn't get rattled, who knows what to do, when to do it, who takes his time.

Q: Is that the way you approached your early short stories, the ones that are now used as models in creative-writing classes?

SHAW: The funny thing is that when I wrote them, they were considered almost avant-garde. Formless. At that time, the endings seemed inconclusive. Now, they seem as conclusive as can be, because that's the way the short story has developed.

Q: What do you think of some of the modern short-story writers, like Donald Barthelme?

SHAW: I like his stuff very much. He's got a brilliant sense of improvisation, and I think he's a very good writer, although I don't see what he's getting at.

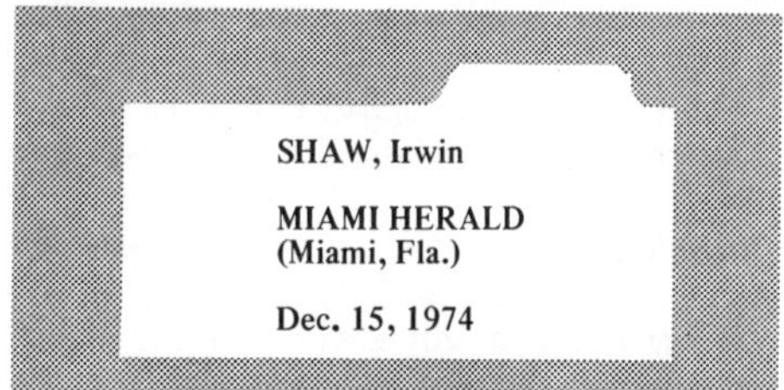
SHAW, Irwin

MIAMI HERALD
(Miami, Fla.)

Dec. 15, 1974

Q: What about the new movies?

SHAW: The business now seems to be in the hands of the young hot directors. I was a judge at the film festival in Cannes this year. I saw two brilliant American pictures there. One was *Conversation* with Gene Hackman. The other was *Sugarland Express*. They were made by kids.

Q: How do you view that?

SHAW: I'm all for it. The older guys can still make pictures they want. For example, Billy Wilder, who's made about 100 pictures, can walk into any studio and say, "I want to make this picture." And they'll give him the talent and money to do it.

Some of the old guys, who were good in their time, have had flops and they can't get a job. I won't mention names. There's a natural erosion process in any field. The kids have to come up. And, because of the changes in our society, they can be a lot more blunt and honest than the old fellas, who had to suggest or hint at everything to get around the moral code.

Q: Do you try to keep up with the times in your own writing?

SHAW: No. I just write the way I want to write. As the mood seizes me.

Q: When you're writing in Switzerland, do you live like a hermit?

SHAW: No! Would that were true! Klosters started out as a tiny place. Then skiing became more and more popular. It attracted Hollywood people, and some French movie people who like to ski. So now the town has quadrupled in numbers. But I manage to make myself a hermit when I work. I've got a little room, with no telephone. I can work and not be disturbed, then go skiing and have someone over for dinner. A lot of interesting people come through there. Writers, movie people, businessmen, CIA agents.

Q: Who would you list in your coterie of writers?

SHAW: I know just about everyone. I associate mostly with James Jones, Bill Styron. Peter Viertel lives close by in Klosters. He's the husband of Deborah Kerr. He wrote a very good book about the movies called *White Hunter, Black Heart*. And when I was on Long Island this summer, everybody was there, of course. Joe Heller, Kurt Vonnegut, George Plimpton, Willie Morris, Bob Alan Aurthur.

Q: So you haven't isolated yourself from the New York literary establishment?

SHAW: No, I haven't, although I'm not in the establishment that much. I go in and out. I don't make it my whole life.

Q: Do you have enough money now so you could quit writing?

SHAW: I did, but I lost it. With the divorce, the market and inflation. I have to keep working, but I don't mind that. I get nervous if I'm away from the typewriter for too long. That's why I came to Miami. I finished this book, and I wanted to put it aside for at least a month before I even re-read it. I'll start working on it again next week.

Novelist, Playwright, King: Robert Shaw's Not Bored

Robert Shaw as himself and Henry VIII

BY BETH GILLIN POMBEIRO
Knight Newspaper Writer

NEW YORK — Untold millions have walked right past Robert Shaw without pausing to think, for even a fraction of a second, "Where have I seen him before?"

Not that he blends easily into the faceless mob—you'd hardly take him for a bus driver or a checkout clerk, this English actor who's played kings, hirelings and Gen. Custer with equal success.

It's just that he throws himself so completely into his various roles that his off-stage and-screen recognition factor is practically nil.

"IT'S FREEZING, oh God, it's freezing," were his first dramatic words as, blowing into cupped hands, he loped into a Chelsea pub called The Angry Squire on a frigid February afternoon.

His garish plaid slacks were tucked into high boots; his hooded fur parka covered a tweedy Norfolk jacket that in turn hid a bulky Navy blue sweater. He looked like an eccentric naturalist fresh from a tramp on the moors.

"I know I'm supposed to be on the wagon, but I've got to have a drink," he said, heading for the bar.

His hair! Its length, surely no more than 1-16th of an inch all over, would put early H.R. Haldeman's to shame. But instead of standing on end like the bristles of a toothbrush, it is plastered forward, near-black, smooth and shiny, so that his head looks not unlike a hairy 8-ball.

Could this be the muscular, menacing blond Russian agent whom Lotte Lenya belted in the diaphram in "From Russia with Love"?

The stocky Irish crook with the black mustache whom Paul Newman and Robert Redford outconned in "The Sting"?

The red-bearded Henry VIII who leered hotly at Ann Boleyn (Vanessa Redgrave) in what is surely the sexiest 50-second out-of-bed lust scene in movie history in "A Man For All Seasons"?

The very same.

He shrugs good-naturedly but with a trace of defiance, his sapphire-blue eyes glinting or twinkling—it is hard to tell which. "I'm recognized in two places, London and New York, and nowhere else. It's a question of what you want to do. The way to perpetuate that other kind of movie star career is to play yourself all the time, like John Wayne for instance.

"But that has to do with money and a certain kind of American success, and there's no interest in it. It is totally and unutterably boring."

THIS IS apparently a touchy subject with Shaw, for after he orders a steak and kidney pie, well browned and very done, he allows that he's been a very busy actor for 25 years.

"I have nine children to support, you know," he says proudly. He reflects upon "all the commercial actors who only last 10 years."

Recently, he's been doing quite well indeed, going directly from "The Sting" into "The Taking of Pelham One Two Three." One long weekend after wrapping up that film he began rehearsals for "The Dance of Death."

When he isn't acting, he writes: screenplays, like "Figures in a Landscape," in which he starred; plays, like "Cato Street," which ran last season in London's Young Vic, and five novels, the most famous being "The Man in the Glass Booth." (It is also the most controversial. It begins: "Jesus," said the dead man, "the Pope has forgiven the Jews.")

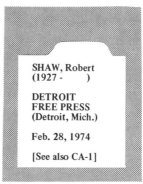

SHAW, Robert
(1927 -)

DETROIT
FREE PRESS
(Detroit, Mich.)

Feb. 28, 1974

[See also CA-1]

Shaw has that type of stolid, self-assured masculinity that makes strong women faint, and a rough-hewn raffish charm that could lure birds from trees — and actresses from their husbands' beds.

He created quite a scandal in 1963, when both his wife and actress Mary Ure, then the wife of playwright John Osborne (Britain's original Angry Young Man) were pregnant with Shaw's children.

"I have two kids three weeks apart," he confesses, not at all penitently. (He and Mary are now married.)

In "The Dance of Death" Shaw plays one point of a love triangle, an Army officer whose wife is being pursued by a quarantine officer and former lover. Like all August Strindberg's works, this one is largely autobiographical.

"In real life," said Shaw, "Strindberg loved a major's wife. The major would have been quite happy with a menage a trois, but Strindberg couldn't stand the idea, and he ran away from her."

SHAW HIMSELF once noted: "Jealousy, that's what binds a marriage together."

"Did I?" he says, raising his eyebrows. "Hmmmmm. Yes, I believe it, in certain marriages. Yes, of course it does. Yes, it does, doesn't it? That's quite good, and I'm not at all ashamed of it."

Shaw currently is working on a sixth novel, "Flesh and Blood," about an old people's home in New York. "President Nixon is dead, New York has a woman mayor, and a piece of Manhattan falls off and floats out to sea," he synopsizes.

"Writing is very difficult at the moment, but for some reason, acting is very interesting. I used to find it boring. I don't know what it is."

He grins. "Perhaps I'm on the verge of doing it well."

When the tab arrives, Shaw digs into a parka pocket and extracts eight crisp $100 bills, while his luncheon companions flutter and warn of incipient muggings. He says Mary's always telling him the same thing.

He may be easygoing about trifles like cash, but Shaw says he does tend to worry about his performances. "Less than most, though," he adds. "I do worry, but not in a neurotic way, and I worry in terms of those I think are intelligent, my friends rather than the critics. I worry for myself.

"There's a line from the play that I like very much. It goes, 'I can cancel out and pass on.' Yes, hmmmmm. I can cancel out and pass on. That kind of sums it all up, doesn't it?"

Do-It-Yourself Publishing

— BOB EAST / Miami Herald Staff

EXUBERANT Louise Mattlage, author of 'Faith Dancing,' lets herself go whenever the spirit moves her.

ROY Sheldon's friends said 'you ought to write a book' . . . and so he did.

By BILL HUTCHINSON
Herald Staff Writer

There was for each of them a moment's sense of elation that could not be shared with wives, husbands or friends.

Unless you've actually published a book, seen your name on the dustjacket and read the little back-cover biography that transforms the mundane details of your life into the exciting stuff of a Hollywood publicity release . . . well, only someone who has had the experience could possibly understand.

"IT'S LIKE having a baby," speculates Miamian Roy Sheldon, who last year gave birth to a slim volume called "Know the Ins and Outs of Condominium Buying."

No, says Leah Udell, a Miami Beach widow who has produced both children and a published collection of her poems. "It's better."

It can also be quite a bit more expensive. Sheldon and Mrs. Udell paid roughly $2,000 apiece to have their books printed by subsidy publishers, companies that promise editing services, distribution, some advertising and promotion and a great deal of ego-massage

SHELDON, Roy
and
UDELL, Leah
and
MATTLAGE, Louise
and
PEARSON, J. Michael
and
GOODMAN, Robert

MIAMI HERALD
(Miami, Fla.)

Feb. 9, 1975

for fees that range from $750 — what Key Biscayne resident Louise Mattlage paid for her "Faith Dancing" — to over $15,000 — Michael Pearson's cost on the first 5,000 copies of "American Cut Glass for the Discriminating Collector."

Negative Reputation

CALLED THE "vanity press," a term that people who have published with them do not much care for, such companies have a largely negative reputation within commercial publishing circles. Newspaper book editors usually know at least one elderly widow who has signed away her last pension check in some vague hope of making a quick and enormous fortune on her subsidy-published collection of children's stories or memories of a Nantucket girlhood or essays on the meaning of life.

SUBSIDY publishing is an unquestionably big business, producing — according to some estimates — as many titles each year as the commercial publishing industry. Though several major commercial publishers are reported to have made subsidy arrangements with some authors and most large printing companies will accept book-printing (though often not binding) contracts from individuals anxious to publish their own work, most of the country's subsidy publishing is done by a handful of specialty outfits dominated by Vantage Press Inc. and Exposition Press Inc., both in New York.

Writers are drawn to vanity press operations mostly by advertisements in literary journals, writers' handbook-type publications and newspapers. The larger companies send field representatives to major cities several times a year in search of manuscripts. Speed of publication is their most heavily promoted selling point.

SHELDON, Roy
and
UDELL, Leah
and
MATTLAGE, Louise
and
PEARSON, J. Michael
and
GOODMAN, Robert

MIAMI HERALD
(Miami, Fla.)

Feb. 9, 1975

— ALBERT COYA / Miami Herald Staff

LEAH UDELL isn't likely to recoup her investment in publishing her book, 'Today I Laugh,' but it doesn't bother her. She's content knowing that people like her work.

(Continued from preceding page)

An unpublished writer, even one with a passable or better manuscript, is often discouraged by the months likely to be consumed by literary-agent referrals, publishing house readings, revisions and the actual printing of his book. He is usually in a hurry to see the book in print, especially so if the material in it has a time element.

Roy Sheldon contacted a few commercial publishers with his condominium-buying manual, but worried that by the time he received a favorable response the laws dealt with in the manuscript would have changed. He went to a subsidy publisher that assured him the book could be produced in 90 days.

Can't Expect To Make a Living

"YOU CAN'T go at this sort of thing expecting to make any money," warns Roy Sheldon. "If you can break even on your initial investment, you're lucky. I'm maybe $500 to $800 away from breaking even, which is pretty good, but it doesn't matter to me one way or the other. I wrote the book because I had something I wanted to say."

Louise Mattlage, a woman of uncontainable exuberance, a dancer who, according to her dustjacket biography, "dances impromptu when the spirit moves her," felt the same way about both of her subsidy-published books.

" 'Dances of Faith' (published in the mid-60s) was my Jesus-y book. I did it because I was offended that children didn't have any religion in their educational experience and I thought that the book could be used in the classroom to familiarize children with the spiritual in a way that wouldn't bother anyone."

Mrs. Mattlage published a second book, a collection of abstract photographs and spiritual excerpts from a variety of religious sources, called "Faith dancing," last year.

"I CONTACTED a few commercial publishers and they seemed to be interested in the book, but everybody told me it would be two years or four years before it was published and I'm not that young. I couldn't wait. It looks like I may break even on this one, which is nice, but the important thing is that I have reached people. If it's only one person, it's all worth it."

Mrs. Mattlage was 11 when she decided she wanted to "spend my life communicating the spiritual nature of man through the dance." Her Boston family did not approve. Her friends did not understand. Her classmates at Boston University wondered idly if she might be mad.

"The young people today are marvelous in that they have come around to accept that people are different. My generation didn't understand. They didn't know how to respond to me because I wasn't like them. Gradually, a person has to come to the point when they realize that the inner person is what is important and if the inner person has some thing to offer it doesn't really matter how people react to what they see."

Her books, says Mrs. Mattlage, are a kind of physical testament to the work she has been doing for more years than she will admit ("Just say I'm a grandmother"). She sells copies at her recitals, frequently gives an inscribed copy to someone who has grasped the message she has tried to communicate, as her scrapbooks indicate, in India, Hawaii, Greece, the Caribbean and throughout the United States.

"I DON'T really think of myself as a writer but as a communicator who is willing to try any medium of self-expression."

Leah Udell thinks of herself as a writer, a good one, but until she went ahead and published "Today I Laugh" in 1973, she never thought that anyone would be interested in reading the verse she'd been writing off and on since the death of her husband 15 years earlier.

"I never thought I was good enough. Now that I know that people enjoy my work, I feel certain of my abilities. It is very gratifying. I feel that whatever I do is good enough, and that's that."

Mrs. Udell, 78, has been able to write very little within the past year. Illness has occupied most of her time, though she discovered during a recent stay in the hospital that "I am still moved to write when something really strikes me. I have enough material almost for another book, and I hope I will be able to get to it before too long."

Roughly half of her 500 copies of "Today I Laugh" have been sold or given away, and Mrs. Udell has accepted that she is not likely to recoup her investment.

"Oh, I don't care. You know, when you're young your eyes accomplish a lot of things that your hands don't. You're always looking around for things you'd like to do. As you get older, you realize that you'd better do some of it. I used to spend a lot of my time playing cards, but I can't do that anymore. It only passes the time and when you're my age tomorrow becomes today before you know it. The book proves that I've made some use of yesterday that I can enjoy today and for the rest of my life."

Until she began to write poetry, Mrs. Udell had undertaken nothing more ambitious than an occasional 20-page letter to a brother in the North. She never particularly wanted to be a writer, a trait she seems to share with other subsidy-published authors, who are moved to the typewriter or the yellow legal pad less by any desire to Create than by a simple need to, as Roy Sheldon explains it, "get something off my chest that other people might be interested in reading."

Sheldon, too, trained for his current craft by writing long letters, often to himself and usually after midnight.

"I'm one of those strange people who does his best thinking between 11:30 and three in the morning. I'll sit up all night writing a letter about the ➡

— ROY BARTLEY / Miami Herald Staff

DOROTHY and J. Michael Pearson look over the books he's written on American cut glass. On the table are examples of the fine cut glass Mrs. Pearson has collected over the years.

SHELDON, Roy
and
UDELL, Leah
and
MATTLAGE, Louise
and
PEARSON, J. Michael
and
GOODMAN, Robert

MIAMI HERALD
(Miami, Fla.)

Feb. 9, 1975

FORMER sheriff in a New England resort town, Robert Goodman has published two books. His first, 'From the Files of a Town Cop,' didn't sell well, he laments.

(Continued from preceding page)

economy or something that's bothering me and then I'll just throw it away because I'll feel better."

A RETIRED dress manufacturer, Sheldon decided to write his "Know the Ins and Outs of Condominium Buying" after Northern friends asked about his experiences in trying to find a South Florida retirement home. "They kept telling me I ought to write a book, so I did."

"You ought to write a book" is an almost irresistible phrase to anyone who believes he might possibly do so, and after years of hearing it from friends and cocktail-party acquaintances who were fascinated by his past as a sheriff in a New England resort town, Robert Goodman sat down in the study of his Fort Lauderdale house and produced "From the Files of a Town Cop" in three months of 12-hour days.

Goodman sent his manuscript to several commercial publishers and although "the reports were not absolutely negative, they wanted more length and some editorial changes that I didn't want to make. I didn't want to put in the time and energy, frankly. I'm stubborn and I figured I'd said what I wanted to say the way I wanted to say it."

So, he contacted a subsidy publisher, paid $3,500 for 3,000 copies of the diary-form reminiscence of rape and incest and petty burglaries, and waited for all the people who urged him to write the book to go out and buy it.

"TOWN COP" did not sell very well, which Goodman blames primarily on the lack of promotional effort on the part of his publisher. But, he says, "Some people told me that the reason the book didn't sell was that it didn't have enough sex in it. So I thought, all right, I'll write a sexy book and see what happens."

"Anytime Bedtime" was written in three months and published in 1973 by a different subsidy publisher. The story of an ambitious waitress that Goodman had employed in his New Hampshire ski lodge (purchased after he left the town's police department), the novel is under consideration by at least one movie producer, he says.

"Luckily, I never expected to make any money out of the books themselves. I believed, and still do, that 'Town Cop' would make a great TV series — people are tired of murder and big-city crime — and that 'Anytime Bedtime' will become a movie. I don't know when, but I have confidence that it will happen."

Until either of the books progresses according to his plans, Goodman does not intend to continue work on the 700-page novel he completed in four months last year. It must be cut, he admits, and there are probably some grammatical changes that should be made, but "I just don't have the ambition. If something happens with the other books, maybe I will. I just haven't felt like writing.

"I like to write, but I don't think I'm a good writer. I think I'm a good story teller. I like a book that just progresses, something that writes itself and doesn't have to be thought out at every step. That's a book that makes the best reading. As long as you can enjoy doing it and there's a possibility that it'll make the movies or TV, the sales don't matter so much."

THOUGH MOST of them deny any financial motivation, a few subsidy-published authors will admit that their books were more than labors of love. Educators caught in the "publish or perish" squeeze but unable to interest a commercial publisher in their texts sometimes seek out the vanity press for reasons of job security. A retired Miami physician who spent 30 years trying to convince a skeptical public that processed foods are a more certain threat to life than automobile accidents finally paid to have a 500-page diatribe published. "So what if nobody reads it? I got it all out of my own system," he says.

J. Michael Pearson, a retired attorney now living on Miami Beach, wrote his "American Cut Glass for the Discriminating Collector" and "A Study of American Cut Glass Collections" for money. And, somewhat uniquely, he has made quite a bit of it. The two books have grossed roughly $100,000, and a third now in progress will be "even bigger" when it is available sometime in 1976 for between $65 and $75 a copy.

Pearson, by his own admission, is more a businessman than a writer. His wife Dorothy (who is given a credit on both books) had been an antique collector and dealer specializing in American cut glass when, in the early 1960s, Pearson decided that a need existed for a comprehensive volume in the field. He learned that a commercial publisher planned a similar book, but that publication was still many months away. Only a subsidy publisher, he reasoned, could manage to get his book produced ahead of the competitor.

The first 2,500 copies of "American Cut Glass" sold out within 18 months. A second printing of the same size sold out within another year, and Pearson decided that he was ready to become his own publisher. A third printing of 5,000 "American Cut Glass" and 5,000 copies of his second book were printed by a Miami firm and distributed exclusively by the Pearsons, many of them to the contacts Mrs. Pearson has developed as a collector.

"There is a lot of money to be made with a solid, well-researched book in a field that no one else has covered," says Pearson.

"It's a lot of work. I've re-written things eight or nine times and spent months researching a single fact or authenticating a single piece of glass. It sound like a lot of money, $100,000, and it is, but you have to consider the expenses and the hours you've put in. Then it doesn't look so impressive.

"But there is nothing so satisfying as just picking up a book that has your name on it. It is," he agrees with Roy Sheldon and Mrs. Udell, "just like having a baby. You forget about the money, you forget about the work. It's like a secret thrill nobody else understands."

How can Sidney Sheldon write so easily?

By MARK FINSTON

"Most writers would like to kill me," admits writer Sidney Sheldon, with just the proper mixture of humility and glee. He mentions such writers as Irving Wallace and Harold Robbins as wanting to kill him.

Well, we all know writers — like everyone else — are sometimes petty, but Wallace and Robbins are more famous than Sheldon.

After talking to Sheldon for a couple of hours, this writer decided he wanted to kill Sheldon too. And it had nothing to do with a famousness quotient.

Nor with the awards Sheldon has won, honors received, etc. His current novel, "The Other Side of Midnight," published by Morrow, is on the top 10 list all over the country. He has won an Academy Award, a Tony Award, two Screen Writers Guild Trophies and an Edgar for the best mystery story some years back.

I resent him none of these. Nor do Irving Wallace or Harold Robbins.

In addition, Sheldon created "The Patty Duke Show" for TV and wrote 60 scripts; he created, produced and wrote all the scripts for "I Dream of Jeannie."

* * *

Nobody wants to kill him for that. If a guy wants to be a millionaire, that's his business. Even snobs don't resent it too much; churning around in TV leaves a guy independent enough to write worthwhile books, which "The Other Side of Midnight" generally is.

The problem with the 57-year-old Sheldon is his work habits. He writes at incredible speed. No painstaking hours hunched over a typewriter, no wastebasket-full of crumpled pages from yellow legal-sized pads.

He simply sits down and dictates: "I make enough money to afford a secretary." Get this: He dictates 40 to 50 pages a day without sweat or trouble.

He makes one of the world's hardest and loneliest jobs look easy. He can work at once on all sorts of different writing projects.

* * *

And he has turned out a prodigious quantity of work as a result: 250 TV scripts, 25 movies, six Broadway plays (he won the Tony for "Redhead"), one play in London, two novels, song lyrics . . .

"Yes, most writers would like to kill me," he repeats, with more emphasis on the humility, less on the glee.

"Most writers hate to write. They like having written, but they hate the act of writing. So my work habits drive everyone crazy. They want to know how I do it. But there's no way actually to explain how I do it. You kind of relax into it and let the ideas come to you."

Sheldon has always been energetic, a kind of scribe's version of a three-minute miler.

He was born in Chicago; his father was a salesman of everything. He spent six months at Northwestern, but it was the Depression, and had to drop out to work full-time hanging hats and coats at hotels.

But other people's hats and coats were not the career Sheldon had in mind.

"I always read a great deal," he recalls. "And I wanted to be known. No one in my family had ever gone past the sixth grade. My reading made everybody nervous — I didn't go out and get into something healthy, like fist fights."

At age 11, he sold a poem to "Wee Wisdom Magazine." He wrote a song, "My Silent Self," at age 17. Horace Heidt, one of those legendary Big Bands, was interested, but nothing ever came of it.

He came to New York, worked as a theater usher and barker, and migrated to Hollywood, having failed to race down Tin Pan Alley as a songwriter.

* * *

He heard about "readers" in the Hollywood studios. These are faceless humans who read through potential properties, and write synopses so that higher-ups can make higher-up decisions. He called the story editors at every studio, and one said there was a thick novel — Sheldon can't remember its name — which had to be read and synopsized by 6 p.m. that day.

"I said, 'Sure, of course,'" recalls Sheldon. "It was noon when I picked up that thick book."

Already his work habits were firming. As he scanned the book, he dictated the synopsis to a friend who could type. He got the assignment in by 6 p.m., and received $3.

He worked at Universal and Fox as a reader, working on screenplays with buddy Ben Roberts (now producer of "Mannix") at night. The two once wrote — and sold — two stories in 24 hours.

"The way to be a successful writer is to write," says Sheldon.

That Academy Award came from the story and screenplay for "The Bachelor and the Bobby Soxer," which starred Cary Grant, Myrna Loy and Shirley Temple. The Screen Writers Guild trophies were for "Easter Parade" and "Annie Get Your Gun."

Sheldon is married to actress Jorja Curtright.

"We buy houses and she decorates them," he says. "We've been in 22 apartments or houses since we've been married." They now own only three houses: In Bel Air, Beverly Hills and Palm Springs.

Their daughter, Mary, 18, once sold a poem at age nine, or two years before her father sold HIS first. Mary goes to Oxford Preparatory School in England, and according to her father is a fine writer, with a better memory than he has. She is also a homegrown critic.

"She starts out by saying that a particular work I wrote is very good," chuckles Sheldon. "Then she gently tells me what she thinks can be changed or improved. My wife does it to me too. I don't resent it. I've been around a while."

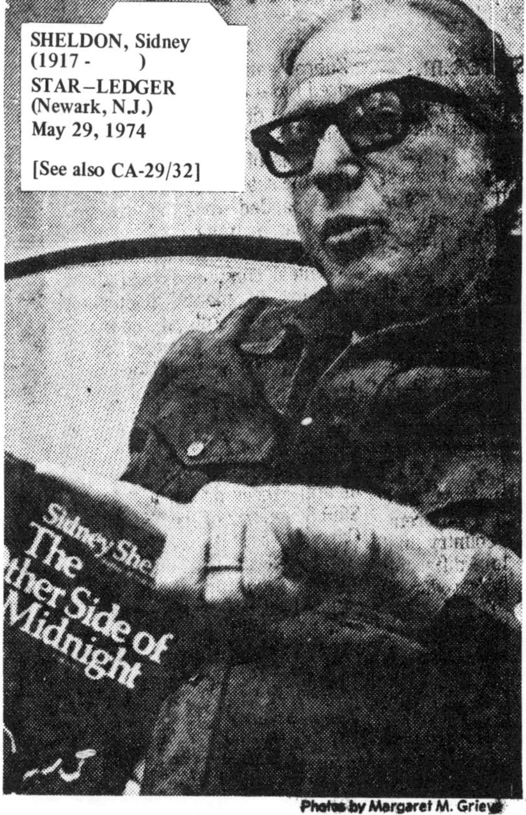

Photos by Margaret M. Griev

Three years ago, Sheldon sold out his ownership of "I Dream of Jeannie" for $1 million; he still gets residuals from his Writer's Guild contract, receiving a check for $10,000 or $15,000 every three months or so. He has been asked again to get involved in TV.

"I'm very attracted by the idea, but no," he says. "The novel is a more satisfying form. I do it alone — right to the printed page without anyone's interfering. And I think the intelligence of the people who read books is higher than the intelligence of the people who watch television.

"So if I got involved in TV again, it would be seven days a week, and I couldn't write the next two novels I want to write. You have to make choices."

* * *

It is suggested that maybe Sheldon has outgrown the Tube.

"Oh, no," he says. "If someone brought me an exciting project, I wouldn't look down my nose at it. I'm a storyteller. I'll tell a story in any medium. I can do a dozen projects at once."

It's just a statement, no bragging. I ponder suggesting that maybe Sheldon could take a week: Get a year's supply of TV scripts finished on Monday and Tuesday; settle the novel Wednesday through Friday, and still have a weekend to travel or something.

I don't say it. Sidney Sheldon's a nice guy, despite his peculiar work habits that drive crazy Irving Wallace, Harold Robbins and me.

Aristotle Onassis eyed as film star

By Donna Chernin

Movie lovers of the world: How does the prospect of Robert Redford, Candace Bergen and Catherine Deneuve starring together in a film excite you?

Add to this the slight possibility of Aristotle Onassis appearing in a feature role, and even movie cynics would have to admit that this would be a remarkable cast.

Author Sidney Sheldon, on a recent visit to Cleveland, explained that he is, in fact, trying to negotiate with just these personalities to star in the film version of his recent best-selling novel "The Other Side of Midnight."

While Sheldon admits that the likelihood of getting tycoon Onassis to agree to make his movie debut is remote, he is optimistic about securing the other stars.

After finishing the screenplay, he hopes to begin shooting the film at the end of the year, with Paramount Pictures producing.

Although "The Other Side of Midnight" is only Sheldon's second novel, the prolific writer has six Broadway plays, 25 motion pictures and over 200 television scripts to his credit.

Sheldon received an Academy Award for his screenplay of "The Bachelor and the Bobby Soxer," and he also won the Screen Writers Guild trophy for his screenplays of "Easter Parade" and "Annie Get Your Gun."

In addition, he was the recipient of Broadway's Tony Award for "Redhead," which starred Gwen Verdon. For television, he created both the successful "Patty Duke Show" and "I Dream of Jeannie" shows, writing most of the scripts.

Now he is elated to have discovered the medium of the novel.

"In writing for films and Broadway, I find a special form of excitement in each," Sheldon explained, "but only in a novel does the author get that one-to-one relationship with the audience.

"It's not that I crave the public notoriety, but it's the great personal satisfaction of being told by a reader, 'I loved your book. I couldn't put it down.' "

Truer words could not have been spoken about Sheldon's "The Other Side of Midnight," a taut tale of suspense, romance and revenge, that I myself simply could not put down.

Set in the decades of the '30s and '40s against the backdrop of some of the world's most glamorous locales, the novel explores the consuming love of two very different women for one man and of yet another man who is able to bring them to ruin.

"It's rumored that Onassis is angered by the depiction of the Greek tycoon in the novel, the powerful character who spells doom for the three others," Sheldon said.

"Onassis apparently feels that I've modeled the person of Constantin Demiris too closely after him."

Of all four central characters in the novel, Sheldon's favorite is the personality of Constantin. He is the most complex and exciting, waiting 10 to 15 years to weave a web of revenge. When he finally destroys those people who have wronged him, they don't even know what has happened to them.

"It would be wonderful if I could get either Redford or Paul Newman for the role of Larry Douglas, the handsome, vibrant war hero with whom both women are in love," Sheldon continued.

"Douglas must be portrayed as a man too shallow to love deeply, a ruthless and utterly amoral character. He is a person who is so weak that he would kill his wife, a man who takes his pleasure as it comes to him and then instantly forgets it.

"Douglas's charm pulls the women into his grasp and that same charm destroys all those who come into his power. It's amazing, but three women have already said to me, 'I was married to Larry.'

"I don't interpret the character of the glamorous actress Noelle, hopefully to be played by Catherine Deneuve, as being evil," Sheldon continued. "I believe that she did what she did out of the love and passion she felt for Larry Douglas."

Sheldon feels that the other side of the coin of love is hate and revenge. This accounts for the title of his novel, "The Other Side of Midnight."

Sheldon works backward and forward on his novels, never knowing how a story will end until the last page is completed.

"I began 'The Other Side of Midnight' with only the simple idea of a man who conspired to kill his wife because she wouldn't give him a divorce," he said.

The intricacies of the finished novel are amazing, with two surprise twists that will shock the most avid mystery readers.

Besides working on the film script of "The Other Side of Midnight," Sheldon recently completed an original screenplay entitled "Caper" about two con men. His suspense drama "Gomes" is currently on the London stage, and there are plans to produce it on Broadway.

Sheldon considers his wife, Jorja, and his 18-year-old daughter, Mary, as his severest critics. Yet not even they are allowed to see any of his creations until the story is completely finished.

When asked what the newest novel he is working on is about, Sheldon answered, "It's about 450 pages."

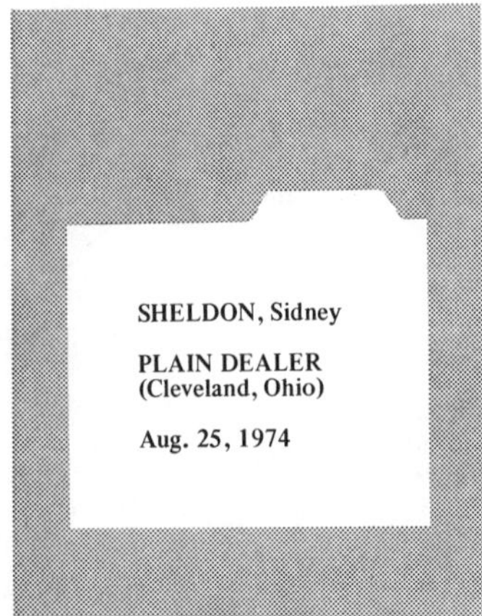
SHELDON, Sidney

PLAIN DEALER
(Cleveland, Ohio)

Aug. 25, 1974

Artichoke Plots From Bellingham

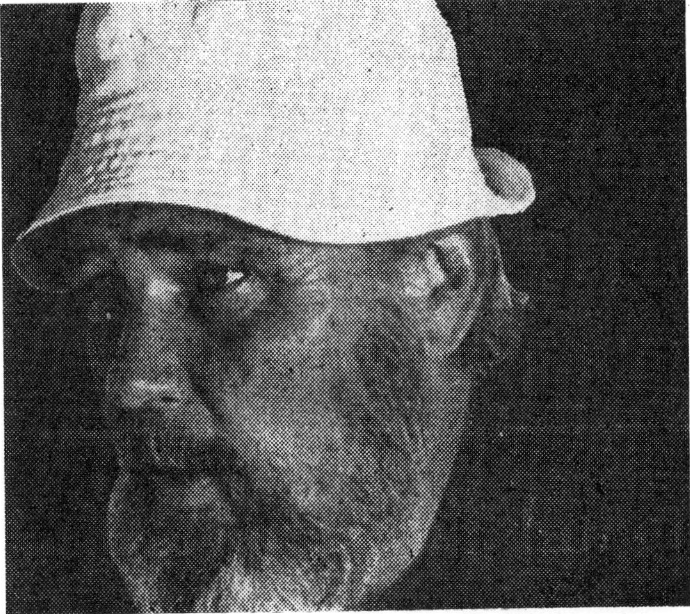

SHELDON, Walter J. (pseud. Shelly Walters) (1917-)

SEATTLE POST-INTELLIGENCER (Seattle, Wash.)

Oct. 13, 1974

[See also CA-25/28]

BY JIM SCHWARTZ
Special to the P-I

WITH HIS gray-tinged beard and explosive, wheezy laugh, Walter J. Sheldon is hardly the writer you'd pick to pen suspenseful tales of heroines trappped in eerie gothic settings.

Move over Bronte sisters. Sheldon, who writes under the name of Shelly Walters, wrote some 20 books and more than 200 magazine articles before he got turned onto modern gothics two years ago.

The result is "The Dunes," a tale of mystery and horror set in a decaying mansion — the type you'd see if you roamed the beaches in Delaware. Which is exactly where Sheldon went to research the setting for his book, due out soon by publisher David McKay.

Sheldon, who moved to Bellingham from Tokyo last year, already has sold the movie option for his 100,000-word thriller and is busily researching other gothics to be set in the dank, gorge-cut forests of Mt. Baker National Forest and the wave-lashed San Juan Islands.

The 57-year-old retired government employe sees no problem writing mysteries from the feminine point of view.

"I pack a lot of emotionalism into my plots," he explained.

Asked how he can verbally react to the heroine's fright in a creepy mansion, Sheldon took another drag on his Silvathin and shot back, "Hell, I jump at strange sounds as fast as any woman. I don't think there's any real difference between a man and woman's reaction in those situations."

Sheldon writes what he terms artichoke plots, rather than asparagus plots.

"Asparagus plots are linear, with the story blossoming at the end," he explained. "Mine peel off layer by layer like an artichoke."

His serious free-lance career began in the mid-1940-s. As an Army man in China, he tired of reading trite aviation stories and tried his hand at a few yarns for "Wings" magazine. Before the war he had written some stores for a collection called "10 Detective Aces" and had been published in several "little religious magazines."

Soon he was writing regularly for the aviation pulps, then the westerns, then the love magazines and science fiction books.

"They all folded," Sheldon said, laughing, "at least most of them did."

In 1952, his first full-length book, "The Troubling of a Star," the story of the Korean air war, brought him financial success. Five non-fiction books followed, including the widely acclaimed "Honorable Conquerors" (Macmillan, 1965) about the occupation of Japan by U.S. forces, and "Hell or High Water" (Macmillan, 1968), which described Gen. MacArthur's invasion of Inchon, Korea.

Sheldon also wrote a series of Far East thrillers — the "Red Flower Kill," "Blue Kimono Kill" and "Yellow Music Kill"—during the late 1960s.

By then, he was retired from his civilian job with the Army and was looking to fatten his lean government pension with free-lance writing.

"My agent (Scott Meredith in New York) said I should look into modern gothics. Said they were selling like hot cakes," Sheldon explained.

"Hell, I told him I hadn't even read any gothic novels, but I told Scott I'd page through the five books he sent."

Sheldon read about 15 before tackling "The Dunes." Now he even enjoys reading gothics.

"It's a mistake to think in male-female terms—the women's lib gals will be glad to hear that," he said.

Though his Japanese wife Yuki has trouble reading his books in English, she keeps him abreast of the latest women's fashions. Sheldon's editor at McKay's, Pat Johnson, tipped him that modern girls are more apt to use facial blushers than old-fashioned pancake.

"I think gothics are popular again because of the resurgent interest in the mystic and occult," Sheldon said, pulling thoughtfully on his cigarette. "Science and engineering haven't made a very good world and people are looking for magic.

"There's also the unisex trend," he continued. "The sexes are increasingly able to adopt each others' outlook."

Above Sheldon's desk, near the photo of his look-alike grandfather in a merchant marine uniform, is a small card defining the five M's he works into every gothic — mansion, menace, mystery, money and mate. He meticulously "interrogates" each character in his novels and tramps through much of the country that forms their settings.

Then he writes a 20,000 to 30,000 word outline for his agent. Sheldon also forces himself to write at least 10 pages of copy during his daily 5 a.m. to noon stint at the typewriter.

Often he exceeds that self-imposed minimum. Seldom does he make final drafts before the novels reach the revision stage at the publisher's.

"For some reason, my books always depart from the outline around pages 70 or 80 and start writing themselves," Sheldon said.

Impatient with overnight poets and undisciplined, would-be novelists, Sheldon tells beginners to concentrate on writing clearly before they launch professional careers.

"I tell them to learn to write a grammatical English sentence. And they should practice writing clean copy the first time. Dammit, to a pro, time is money."

For pro Shelly Walters, that next chunk of green might emerge from "Castle Dark" and "Phantom Isle," two gothics that Sheldon is betting will have both sexes cringing at things that go bump in the night.

Houston author has storybook working conditions

—Post photo

By Leon Hale

Some of us imagine that an author, the same as a TV personality or a big film star, lives a fish-bowl life. I expect we get that notion from the few really visible book writers this world has had — guys like Hemingway who drew crowds every time they went out into daylight.

Houston author William R. Shelton grins at the notion that he might draw admirers just be walking down a street. He has written six books and a great raft of national magazine articles. But he can go into a Houston book store where his own works are sold and graze around all afternoon and nobody will come up and ask, "Aren't you William Shelton, the writer?"

It's pretty remarkable how much writing success a person can achieve and remain obscure locally. Houston has dozens of citizens — I don't know how many — entitled to call themselves professional writers but I can't think of one who has achieved greater status than Shelton.

Yet until a about a year ago I didn't even know he lived in Houston. And hadn't met him until a few days ago. I went to see him after I read his latest book, a novel called "Stowaway to the Moon."

Shelton lives with his wife and two stepdaughters on Legend Lane, in the Memorial Area. They have pretty much the kind of attractive home you'd naturally expect to see on the bank of a little creek in that woodsy section.

That's where Shelton does his writing. He's got the kind of setup people imagine all writers have, but few do. He rebuilt his garage and made an office out of it. There's a door that locks out the world, and a sign telling the world to knock because work is going on inside.

I guess Shelton could survive in that office for a week. He's got what he calls a thinkroom, with a red overhead light and a comfortable bed. There's also a little refrigerator stocked with ham and cheese and strawberry jam and nuts and fruit and a big jug of red wine. A desk and tables and stacks of yellow legal pads. A typewriter, I guess, but I don't remember it. Shelton writes long-hand, on those legal pads.

He even looks like an author. Almost nobody who writes looks like an author anymore but Shelton does. He has a beard. Yes, and smokes a pipe. And wears the heavy-rimmed specs.

He's a stocky, strong-looking, and before he speaks you're certain he's going to boom at you. But the voice is quiet, almost gentle, smooth, scholarly. This is a man truly educated, by both books and experience. Sometimes I have trouble talking easily with educated people but not with Shelton. The only thing, I hesitate to quote him directly, afraid I'll mess up his beautifully correct grammar. He spoke of airplanes, wars, books, writing, movies, space ships, animals, plants, oceans — all in a reflective, confident fashion, as if he'd thought out everything in advance and knew what he was going to say. I wish I could talk like that.

SHELTON, William R(oy)
(1919-)

HOUSTON POST
(Houston, Tex.)

Oct. 20, 1974 [See also CA-5/6]

Shelton is 55. He came to Houston with the space program because he is basically a science writer. Here are his books: "Countdown," "Flights of the Astronauts," "American Space Exploration: The First Decade," "Soviet Space Exploration: The First Decade," "Man's Conquest of Space," and now the novel, "Stowaway to the Moon."

He's been in the magazines that most free lance writers just dream about. Saturday Evening Post. Life. Atlantic. Fortune. Reader's Digest. Saturday Review.

He's been a bomber pilot in combat, a bureau chief (at Miami) for Time and Life, an English prof (in Florida at Rollins College), a movie director and producer (mainly educational films).

His first novel has turned out to be the biggest thing that ever happened to him, from a money standpoint. "Stowaway to the Moon" has just been filmed, and will be televised Jan. 19 as a CBS two-hour special.

When I first saw the "Stowaway" book I decided not to like it in advance. It's about a schoolboy who slips onto a space ship and goes as a stowaway on a moon mission. That sounded pretty Walt Disney to me.

But Shelton brings it off, I think mainly because he knows so blamed much about space travel, and so has made the story believable. He even thinks it's possible that a stowaway could get on board a space ship. He got the idea for the novel from Banana Creek at Cape Canaveral, when he noticed how close that stream comes to the launch area. That's how the boy, in the story, got to the rocket. By boat.

Readers and critics have found a great range of symbolism in the "Stowaway." To me the main accomplishment of the story is that it gives us more than just a hint of the real personal thrill that astronauts must experience, of the incredible beauty they see.

As Shelton says, astronauts on space missions have so much to do, they don't have time to be good reporters even if they had the capability. So here's a stowaway, an intelligent boy small enough to hide in a space ship's garbage compartment.

He's idealistic and hasn't any worries about saying what he thinks and he's totally lacking in the cynicism and skepticism that's affected the world and he brings back from the moon something no astronaut ever has. This may even be a very important story one of these days when it gets old enough, and it was written out there on Legend Land, in the woods of Harris County.

Which reminds me. All my life, as a writer of sentences, I've personally dreamed about a special place to work. I wanted to live in a house with woods and a creek in the back, and I wanted a narrow little bridge leading away from the house, and it would cross the creek, and a path would disappear into the trees, and at the end of it there would be this rustic office, a quiet place to think about and to write beautiful things.

Well, Shelton has got this. He outgrew the little office at the end of the the bridge and had to move into the renovated garage but he still goes out there, when he needs to. I don't know if I can ever forgive him, for having the bridge and that path disappearing, into the woods.

Speaking of People

STAFF PHOTOS BY PAM SPAULDING

By JOAN KAY
Courier-Journal Staff Writer

The escapades of June and Ken Shore and their five children could provide a lot of material for her writing.

Such as the time they were stranded for a week on a cloverleaf in Florida when their traveling vehicle, a red school bus, broke down.

But, as she said, "If you're too close to it, you can't write about it. If it's too fraught, you don't get enough objectivity."

However, the family's style of celebrating Christmas does get a true-to-life portrayal in one of her most recent works, a book for juveniles, called, "What's the Matter With Wakefield?"

Last fall the book won the $5,000 1973 Abingdon Award for a book for children, and Abingdon Press of Nashville will publish it April 8.

Her book was selected as the best book of fiction for ages 9 through 12 in depicting the story of a child in a family with a working mother who successfully copes with both family responsibilities and a career.

The hero, Wakefield, is in charge of his class' funds, and he is supposed to buy an aquarium. Instead he buys a long-coveted fly rod. The plot hinges largely on how he keeps the secret from his family and manages to recoup the money.

Wakefield "is 9, almost 10," said the author. "That 'almost 10' is very important. He tells the truth 90 per cent of the time.

"I hope there are some believable characters." There is a bully, for instance, and "we don't have to love and understand the bully. He remains a bully all the way through," she said with zest.

The Shores' 17-year-old son is named Stephen Wakefield, but "the book is not biographical except in the sense of the problems children go through. It is a picture of our kind of Christmas.

"Sometimes we get so creative around here I long for a commercial Christmas." The house gets covered with materials for and the finished products of handmade Christmas cards, trim and papier-mache figures.

"Wakefield" has been picked up by the Junior Literary Guild, a division of the Literary Guild, and Mrs. Shore is "pleased about that."

She also likes the cover designed by illustrator David K. Stone, who has designed the commemorative stamp for the 200th anniversary of the founding of Ft. Harrod.

The drawing on the cover "looks like the characters I had in mind. The little girl at the top looks like the smarmy type who always reminds the teacher to collect the book reports."

Though the Abingdon contest did have some restriction on the choice of subject matter, in general, she said, "there's a lot of freedom in writing for children. Whereas if you write for adults, you almost have to tailor it to the market or to what the publishers think the market is.

Occult is popular

"The things selling now are anything about the occult, very violent books. Sex always sells well. It's very difficult to write a novel of modest suspense."

Mrs. Shore's agent has told her, "Don't write about little old ladies. Little old ladies are out, and Gothic novels are in."

SHORE, June Lewis

COURIER–JOURNAL & TIMES (Louisville, Ken.)

Feb. 3, 1974

She hopes to finish up a Gothic mystery this month, and a suspense novel, now circulating to publishers, concerns a little old lady in Victoria, British Columbia, where the Shores lived for five years.

The book was finished a year ago, but "publishers move very slowly, I found out." Good Housekeeping purchased one novel and didn't publish it for two years. The editors also changed the plot, the ending and the title to "Search for a Little Girl." It was also bought for publication in a magazine in Denmark.

Mrs. Shore, a native of Louisville and daughter of Mr. and Mrs. Rue Lewis of Jeffersontown, was graduated from Jeffersontown High School and received a bachelor's degree in 1952 from Western Kentucky University, where she majored in art and English.

She taught art and English in Battle Creek, Mich., and in several Jefferson County Schools.

Shore, a native of Owensboro, attended Western, was graduated from Lake Forest (Ill.) College and received a master's degree from the Kent School of Social Work at the University of Louisville.

They met at Western but "didn't date much," she said, "till he moved to Lake Forest and I to Battle Creek to teach — 250 miles apart."

They were married in 1953 and lived in Victoria while he was director of a home for emotionally disturbed children. They moved back to Kentucky in 1962, and he is with River Region Services as director of mental health centers in Area B, which comprises eastern Jefferson County, Oldham, Trimble and Henry counties.

"So his training in mental health may equip him to be the husband of a writer," she said, teasingly.

The Shores' children, in addition to Stephen, are Melissa, 11, Alison, 12, Becky, 14, and Susan, 16. Cumulatively they play about 10 instruments. One used to play bagpipes, said Mrs. Shore, but she gave it up.

"If you don't know bagpipes, it's worse than beginning violin. Now they also play stereo, which has only one volume — loud!"

Shore is president of the Mansfield Players, an amateur theater group in Jeffersontown, and last month the children were involved in various ways in an all-youth produced musical revue.

In 1971 Stephen won third award in junior article and fourth award in junior poetry in Scholastic magazine's national competition, "the first time anyone in Jefferson County had won two prizes," said Mrs. Shore.

She began writing about 10 years ago "when there was a spate of novels without any plot. I like a story with a beginning, middle and end," and she contended she could do as well as the writers who were being published. "The family challenged me," and she began to write, starting out with shorter pieces.

She enjoys writing short humorous pieces the most. One in the North American Review, called "Reflections on an Image," dealt with the housewife, "whom everyone thought was dull. I said it was very exciting with Mr. Clean popping in" and other events in that vein.

With five children "I'm at the mercy of the school system," so she usually begins writing when they leave for school and stops at 3 p.m.

"My husband does my spelling — I don't spell," and since "he doesn't cipher, I do the trigonometry homework and the income tax reports."

Mrs. Shore reads voraciously, with Carson McCullers, Eudora Welty and other Southern novelists her favorites. "If I get trapped, I have to read my husband's dull journals and the kids' books."

She designed the Shores' house in Jeffersontown, and an architect did the plans. She also invented a toy, only to find it had already been marketed.

It was a variation of a hoop and a stick, which she had her father create into a reality. "I was thinking one day how colorful children's books are today, and how dull our children's books were — there was only that picture at the top of a boy rolling a hoop."

All the toy companies rejected her idea, and finally one sent her a catalog, showing that a hoop had been on the market 20 years ago.

With a big family "I almost have to" bake a lot, and one year Mrs. Shore entered the Kentucky State Fair baking contest and won third place in a cookie category and second in coffee cake.

On trips in the red school bus "we've met a lot of interesting people when we've broken down." Once the family, plus a St. Bernard, Samson, spent the week between Christmas and New Year's in the parking lot of a gas station on a cloverleaf near Ocala, Fla., waiting for a replacement part for the bus.

Endured a cold wave

"They had a cold wave in Florida that year — it was warmer in Louisville," and running out of bottled gas, the family managed to hook up the bus to electricity in the gas station.

"The only thing we could think of for the kids to do was pick up discarded bottles along the highway," but at the end of their enforced stay, no one would redeem them. "So we brought $9.32 worth of bottles all the way back to Louisville."

On a trip last summer to Nova Scotia, without son and dog, Mrs. Shore left the family asleep one morning while she went out to find some breakfast.

"I had on a sporty caftan," and two policemen arrested her, thinking she was wandering around in a nightgown. Her husband managed to rescue her from the situation, and "later I sent the police department pictures of caftans from a magazine.

"It was so funny because I don't tear tags off of mattresses or open asparagus cans at the wrong end — I'm so law-abiding."

Prof-Poet Shuford Retiring

SHUFORD, Cecil Eugene (1907-) STAR-TELEGRAM (Ft. Worth, Tex.) Mar. 17, 1974 [See also CA-13/14]

"There is an angel in each man's life he dare not touch."
—"Bitter Creek Newcomb" by Gene (C. E.) Shuford

By RAYMOND TEAGUE

DENTON—There's still an untouched and perhaps untouchable angel or two in C. E. Shuford's life, although he seems to have met and charmed them all by now.

His personal angels, maybe drawing back in shock at times but more often nodding in pleased unison, have watched over Shuford's simultaneous rise in two spheres:

—Journalism education: Shuford created the journalism department at North Texas State University in 1946 and for 28 years has been the department's only chairman. The NTSU journalism building is filled with awards won by student publications, and the nation's newspapers are stocked with Shuford graduates.

—Poetry: Shuford is a nationally known poet whose works have been selected, collected and honored. He has won 46 annual Poetry Society of Texas awards and two annual Poetry Society of America prizes.

NOW THE venerated prof-poet, whose gentle manner still is edged with the sternness that molds tight verse and dominates classrooms, is entering a new sphere — retirement.

Shuford, 67, will conclude 45 years of teaching when he retires as NTSU journalism department chairman and professor at the end of the first summer term.

Looking back on his careers recently in his typically newspaper - magazine cluttered, memento-filled small office in NTSU's journalism building, Shuford discovered a web of associations and similarities between his seemingly incompatible passions for journalism and poetry.

"The first poem I ever published I wrote in high school (in his hometown Fayetteville, Ark.), and it was put in the high school paper. It was a journalistic publication of poetry."

His first long poem was published on the front page of the Fayetteville Democrat (now Northwest Arkansas Times), where he worked as a reporter while attending the University of Arkansas. The Whitmanesque poem, called "Mountain City," developed out of research he was doing for a story on Fayetteville's centennial celebration.

SHUFORD EARNED his master's degree from Northwestern University in 1929 with a thesis on H.L. Mencken, and then went to the MacDowell Writers and Artists Colony, where he studied with such literary notables as Thornton Wilder and Edward Arlington Robinson.

In 1933 Shuford sold nine of his 50 free verse "Spoon River"-type poems on bandits and gunmen titled "Flowering Noose" to Scribner's for $100. It was his first publication in a national magazine and a real coup in those hard-time days.

"I was able to write them because it was in the middle of the Depression. I was home and out of a job. So I started digging through outlaw history and then reading biographies of bad men."

Scribner's bought another of Shuford's poems, a long free verse about the national election, in 1936 and illustrated it in color.

"That poem was related to a news event and shows the timeliness of what I was trying to do. So I have been at times a journalistic poet."

Shuford said he was the "journalistic poet" also in his two poems which won Poetry Society of America awards. "Sonata for the Time After Sunday," about the suicide of Ernest Hemingway, won in 1963 as best entry in free form. "The Death in Our Family," about the assassination of President John F. Kennedy, won in 1966 as best original unpublished poem in free form.

WITH BACKGROUND in reporting and literary writing, as well as teaching experience at Alabama Polytechnic Institute, the University of Arkansas and Trinity University (where he also handled public relations), Shuford arrived in Denton in 1937 to direct publicity for what was then North Texas State Teachers College.

He was publicity director for the school for five years and taught journalism (and one English course the first semester there) before joining the Army Air Force in 1942 (where he also was an instructor).

"I came back in the fall of 1945 and the college announced a journalism major in August 1946. We converted an English major, and that's when the department started. And I've been here ever since."

More than 600 graduates have gone through NTSU's journalism program, now recognized as one of the finest in the Southwest.

Among Shuford's ex-students, who include executives, editors and writers in many areas of journalism, is Bill Moyers, who was press secretary to President Johnson.

"The biggest challenge has been to turn out graduates who, hold professional jobs successfully and who justify their training. Everything else is window dressing. We are proud of our publication record, but the publications are used as training devices.

"The journalism graduate has been through boot camp. He has an advantage over other journalists because he knows what he is trying to do, if not doing it perfectly yet."

IF JOURNALISM school is boot camp, Shuford may be a dual-natured Army officer, cursed by some and admired by others.

The two nicknames students have given Shuford over the years reflect the ambivalence. "They called me Colonel when I first came, but I don't know why. Maybe I looked like a colonel. They later called me Papa."

Certainly Papa fits the calm, white-haired man better now. But there are former (and probably some current) students who mostly good-naturedly recount tales of a none-too-gentle Colonel.

"Some say I'm a hard taskmaster. But I've never had students resent what I've done in the classroom, and I've done some dramatic things to show them right or wrong."

A Shuford graduate who is now managing editor of a Southwest Texas newspaper tells of drinking through the night and writing an assignment at 3 a.m. for Shuford's class in editorial writing the next day.

He was pretty proud of the editorial, and at first thought Shuford concurred. "I want to put this editorial on the bulletin board," he recalled Shuford telling the class, "as an example of how not to write an editorial."

MRS. JUNETTA DAVIS, a former NTSU journalism instructor, tells of misspelling a name in the NTSU student newspaper when she was a student. Shuford jumped up on a horseshoe copy table in the newspaper office, stamped his foot and screamed, she said.

Mrs. Davis said the incident made an impression, but that Shuford doesn't remember it.

Another former Shuford student, Mike Cochran, Associated Press correspondent for Fort Worth, said he nearly quit school after one of Shuford's tantrums.

Cochran recalled, "We had to write a brite (a short, humorous story) and Pappy read mine, wadded it up, walked over to the wastebasket and threw it in and said it was one of the worst damned things he'd ever read."

"I sometimes think the students make these stories up," Shuford said.

"I don't go after them, but whatever faults I can find. I do say this is a good story or this is beautifully done. I try to give them a sense of integrity and responsibility. What else can you do?"

ONE STUDENT, James Bowman, who now handles public relations for Texas A&I University in Kingsville, wrote a 241-page master's degree thesis entitled "Papa Shuford."

In Bowman's thesis, former student newspaper editor Jack Maguire said that Shuford seemed absent-minded, a "Mr. Chips" prototype and was popular with students.

Of the thesis, Shuford said, "It made me feel overblown, like an old buffalo about to be shot, stuffed and mounted." But he's obviously proud of it.

Staff members of the student newspaper, then the Campus Chat and now the North Texas Daily, many years ago at a Christmas party gave Shuford a whip, which he occasionally takes from its place over a picture of several former students in his office and pops in class. A nameplate on his desk reads "C. E. Shuford Chief Whipcracker."

Roy Busby, assistant to NTSU President C. C. Nolen and an ex-student of Shuford's, called Shuford "the Vince Lombardi of collegiate journalism education."

Another former student, Reg Westmoreland, director of NTSU journalism graduate studies and designate chairman of the journalism department, said students have developed a very close relationship toward Shuford because the department was small for so many years.

"I am concerned about keeping up the quality of the department, plus the close personal relationship of faculty to students" in the fast-growing department.

Westmoreland said Shuford always has been a stickler for details. "He has really been known for making people watch the little points of the language and writing. Even today he makes red marks on all the errors in the (Daily) papers and goes over them with students."

SOMEHOW, IN the midst of administrative and teaching duties, Shuford has found time to write poems, under the name Gene Shuford.

Shuford has authored more than 70 poems and articles in magazines and other publications.

He is the author of "The Red Bull and Other Poems," which won the 1964 South and West book-brochure publication award. A 1972 NTSU Press publication of Shuford's "Selected Poems 1933-1971" won the "best book of poems written by a Texas author in 1972" Texas Institute of Letters, Voertman Award.

Shuford is listed in "Who's Who in America," was 1964 Arkansas Poet of the Present and has won numerous awards for journalism education.

"There is a lot of satisfaction out of the process of writing. People are frustrated if they don't do something creative," Shuford said.

"I don't have the extended concentration for the longer forms of creative writing. With this kind of job my writing has had to be hit and miss, and writing poetry can be hit and miss."

Shuford said his poetry develops in different ways. "It comes out of your basic emotions and moods. It has to gestate and develop, then surface eventually."

A LONGTIME friend of Shuford's, Dr. Arthur M. Sampley, former poet laureate of Texas and retired NTSU English professor, speaks highly of Shuford's poetry.

"He is nationally known as a poet and deservedly so," Dr. Sampley said. "I think of him as not under the influence of any particular writer but under the Whitman tradition, and also as a poet of the Southwest."

Material for much of Shuford's poetry has come from travels over the country with his family.

Shuford's wife Catherine is head of the English department at Denton High School.

The couple's three children have continued the journalism-literature tradition. Their oldest son, Tom, is a journalism professor and student newspaper sponsor at Tarleton State College ("almost the same job I had when I came here," Shuford said). Another son, Dan, is a Yale graduate. Their daughter, Mrs. Betty Grace Crow, is a teaching fellow in English at the University of Maryland.

WHAT DOES retirement mean to Shuford?

"First, de-compression.

"I won't make predictions. I want to go on enjoying life."

He said he'd like to read, perhaps write some more poems, maybe even a short story.

Who knows what new angel may be in reach.

Special Photo

SHULMAN, Morton
(1925 -)
ATLANTA JOURNAL & CONSTITUTION (Atlanta, Ga.) Sept. 16, 1973
[See also CA-23/24]

He Made a Million on Stocks—So Can You, He Writes

By EDITH HILLS COOGLER
Atlanta Journal Women's Editor

Closeted with Morton Shulman, Canadian internist, the patient almost forgets to describe the *mysterious ailment.*

The temptation is to ask one, or all, of these questions:

"Look, I've got $1,000, what's a good stock to invest in?"

"What were you legislators thinking of when . . . ?"

"What's it like to be a best-selling author?"

"Can I make a million dollars as you did?"

SHULMAN, the composite man, is somewhat more than the mind-on-the-street can grasp all at once. Visiting Atlanta, he tried to explain rationally how he happened to turn out this way. The occasion was publication of his new book "Anyone Can *Still* Make a Million." (Stein and Day, $6.95.)

His careers in medicine and the stock market all started about 20 years ago when he was an intern. "I got married, and her cousin advised us to take our $400 and invest it. We lost nearly all of it in penny stocks . . ."

His book points out, "The dream of every stock-market gambler is . . . to invest $1,000 and see it turn into $500,000." Even now, years afterward, he is somewhat less than enthusiastic about penny stocks.

But in 1952, he treated his loss like a challenge, "I started again, and it was a new issue market. And I made mistakes, but it didn't cost me money. In six months I made $25,000.

THAT WAS EXCITING. Before long, I *could* have quit medicine, but I love medicine; it is my way of life. I am still practicing in Toronto every morning, and I am still into the stock market, but that is just a hobby."

However, thanks to his hobby, he estimates that he's worth about $1.8 million today.

In the '60s, as a doctor he was appointed a coroner, "And they built a fireproof hospital using shoddy materials. There was a fire and some people were burned to death, and I was in charge of the inquest.

"The government was behind the building of the hospital, and the attorney general fired me so that the inquiry could be run by their own man.

"I WAS FURIOUS when they fired me. It was a conservative government, and I ran against them on the opposite ticket and whipped them. After all, who's against a doctor? And aside from that, there was a lot of public excitement over the hospital, and the public knew my role in it. I had it made.

"I became a member of the legislature in '67, and I still am. I didn't know anything about politics, but I'm learning. I still practice medicine every morning, and in the afternoons (except in summer) I'm in the legislature in Canada.

"It doesn't take more than a half-hour a day to keep up with the stock market, to read the New York Times and the Wall Street Journal just so I'll know what's happening and phone my broker in the morning.

"MY FIRST investment was in a new copper mine at $10 a share, and it immediately went up to $14 a share. And we didn't put any money into it, but just sold it immediately. My broker sent me 400 bucks, and I said, this is great!

"In a rising market, you can buy a quarter of a million worth of government bonds and hang onto them about three or four minutes, and there's a $2.50 markup — as soon as you get the confirmation, you phone the broker and say, sell them.

"In the beginning, I was making only a few hundred dollars at a time, but later, the best I ever did was $22,000 on one government issue in five minutes — it was just incredible; the world had gone wild.

"I'm still playing the market, but in a different way today — food commodities — I must change with the times. I've made most of my money in the past six months in barley. I've invested in corn, cattle, anything.

"I went in heavy when the Americans announced the sale of everything to Russia. The only good thing about the American government is that it allows people like me to make fortunes — even some people like *you.* There are a lot of new millionaires in the U.S., just from reading the newspapers.

"AS SOON AS the government attempts to put on price controls, you start getting a black market, a lesson in history which your government didn't bother to learn. Price controls make the commodities disappear, that's why there's a cattle and beef shortage right now and a black market in meat, and new millionaires. And no signs of understanding even yet in Washington; they're still making no attempt to balance the market.

"In the next year, prices in the U.S. are going to rise 10 to 15 per cent, which is rampant inflation, which means you can't put money in the bank or buy government bonds. Your money won't be safe. The paper is there, but your buying power is gone.

"You have to buy something to protect you against inflation. Municipal bonds? No! Mortgages? No! Brokers have spent many years doing the same thing, but the secret of investing is to adjust to the changing times.

"I HAD an aptitude for investing in the first place, but anybody can learn.

"If you want to make a million in a short period of time, buy convertible bonds in an industry with wealth in the ground. Or there are commodities, or the money market — buying foreign currency, selling the U.S. short.

"If you'd bought wines and cognacs from the top French chateaux, you'd have made at least 100 per cent profit in the last 10 years."

In his book he points out that recent, plentiful vintages are still an excellent investment offering rapid, large profits. But you wonder how many people are going to buy your fine wines if the nation tilts into a depression.

"But if you have a depression, the bottom will drop out of *everything.*

"I ALSO RECOMMEND buying antiques, but antiques are for people with extra money because they're not liquid. Still, you get pleasure out of owning them in the meantime. You don't get pleasure out of owning a stock certificate."

He offers one example of art appreciation — appreciation in every sense of the word — in the book. In 1956 he bought a small Renoir painting for $15,000. He and his family loved it so much that they didn't think of it as an investment. Through the years he turned down increasingly high offers.

Since publication of the book, he sold it. "Yes, just three weeks ago two Japanese dealers came wanting to buy it. I thought it was worth between $35,000 and $50,000. But they offered me $80,000 for my Renoir, and off they went with it — you see, as long as the dollar devalues, the antiques have to keep going up."

BUT HE WOULDN'T buy Impressionist artists today because prices have gone too high. Instead, he recommends American and Canadian primitive art. It's still available at reasonable prices and he feels certain that it will increase in value.

His new book is a complete revision and up-dating of his 1967 best seller "Anyone Can Make a Million" — as he says, your thinking must change with the changing times, and he passes along the uncanny knowledge that has made him so terribly-terribly rich today.

Here is a man who clearly revels in the joys of earning it and spending it. He said, "We live high on two acres in the center of Toronto. We've got two swimming pools, one inside, one out. We've got all the automatic and electronic gadgets — the garage doors that open as you approach. We've been the whole route. We travel a lot. China. A boat down the Amazon. And after my tour is over, North Africa.

"I'm driving an Excaliber. It's the ultimate in an automobile. Made in Wisconsin, it's an exact copy of a '29 Mercedes convertible. (In Canada it costs $22,000.) This car is really an experience, when I drive past, all the beautiful young ladies say, 'Take me!'"

But the stock market still is *only* his hobby. He Really loves medicine. He said, "My son who's only 18, had $500 last July 1. He's been investing, and last night he had over $22,000. I'm getting a little nervous. I want him to be a doctor."

John Shuttleworth

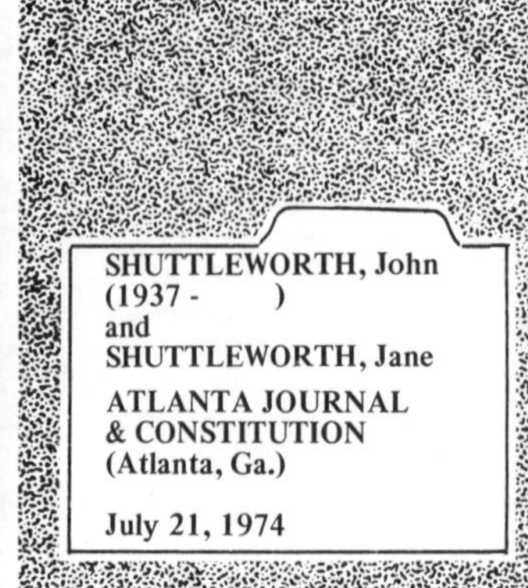

SHUTTLEWORTH, John (1937-)
and
SHUTTLEWORTH, Jane

ATLANTA JOURNAL & CONSTITUTION (Atlanta, Ga.)

July 21, 1974

Mother Is a One-Man Show

By Henry Woodhead

Photography by William Wages

LEON decides that he will not work any more today. He will sit at the picnic table and drink home-made wine with ice cubes and talk to his visitors. He savors the thought of his decision, lets it loll on the mind like wine on the tongue. During his years in the machine shop in Detroit, such a decision was prohibited. But the dues have been paid, and now Leon Blythe is one of Mother's children.

About a year ago Leon answered this ad in a magazine called the Mother Earth News:

"We're looking for a family to share our organic homestead in the southern Apalachians. We have plenty of room, clean air, good water and fertile soil. The land is low priced and we'll provide some of the tools to work it. Jobs are available nearby, and we have a typesetting business (thanks to Mother) which is beginning to show a profit. We'll share that, too. While we're always open to social experimentation, we also value our privacy and wish to maintain a traditional family structure. Please write for details.

Bob and Ina
Lenoir, N.C.

Leon now lives on the land, 35 acres owned jointly by him and the writer of the ad, Bob Holland, an ex-school teacher. Together they own a pick-up, a 1951 Ford tractor, and a tiller. Each supports his family by reading meters for the local electric company part-time. Bob's wife Ina earned about $9,000 from a typesetting operation last year. Each man is building a new house for his family. They have chickens, pigs, gardens, a new orchard and grape vines. They are deep into life-styles which have come to be called alternative. As they make their way down this particular path, they often refer to the guidebook for alternative life-styles, the Mother Earth News, or as they call it, "Mother."

From Mother come a lot of good things for people like the Hollands and the Blythes. Mother, for example, brought them together. From Mother came the idea for the successful, in-home typesetting business. Articles in Mother helped teach them how to raise hogs, to garden organically, to keep goats. "If you're moving to the country," Leon said sipping his wine, "you have to have Mother."

"The business was the main thing we've gotten from Mother, but there's been so much other stuff, too: new ideas about forest management, about building farm buildings," Bob Holland said. "And you learn a lot from the letters to the editor. New recipes, how to make a baby carrier, for instance. And then there's the articles on alternative energy sources. Solar heating, and windmills. We're thinking of building two of those.

"There's really no better magazine for our kind of life-style."

THE letters section of the Mother Earth News—entitled "Dear Mother,"—is often a liturgy of gratitude from readers who scrutinize the magazine with the intensity of a fundamentalist Baptist reading the Old Testament. Thanks to Mother, a typical letter might say, I'm no longer a frustrated high-paid executive. I'm a happy homesteader. Or, thanks to Mother I've found my life's companion. Or even, thanks to Mother I've decided not to commit suicide.

"We get thousands of these letters every month. Great testimonials pouring in. People love what we're doing, and that's nice. But we're more self-serving than that," said John Shuttleworth, a 36-year-old ex-farm boy and public relations man. "We're just trying to get the numbers on our side so that more than half of the population believes in the gentler way of living and the more ecologically sound way of living. There's no great vision involved. We're just little people in way over our heads on a job a lot bigger than we are."

One thing you should keep in mind, Shuttleworth says. He and his wife Jane started out only to print a newsletter. This was four years ago. They worked on the kitchen table of a tiny house in Madison, Ohio. They had $1,500 in savings and when that ran out they borrowed $1,500 more from a shyster loan company. Twice in the first few months Shuttleworth wrote and had printed a letter saying, in effect, "We tried, we're sorry, but it's all over." Twice his wife Jane told him to wait a couple of days before mailing the death notice.

And now the chatty, reassuring, down-to-earth, muslin-simple prose of Mother circulates to 200,000 people. But the magazine itself is just one extremity of Mother's healthy anatomy. There is Mother's Bookshelf, a mail-order operation handling some ➡

(Continued from preceding page)

500 titles. There is Mother's General Store, in downtown Hendersonville, N.C., and Mother's General Store catalogue. There are the syndicated newspaper and radio columns—the newspaper column, Mother Earth News, appears in the Dixie Living section of the Sunday Journal and Constitution. And two paperback books: the Mother Earth News Almanac and the Handbook of Homemade Power, both published by Bantam.

And looming over it all, John Shuttleworth's dream: a 500-acre research center in North Carolina, nestled in an isolated mountain cove, where the sun heats the houses and the cars run on gas extracted from manure, where the power comes from windmills or waterwheels and the crops are organic. It would be a model for a depleted planet. And then Mother will build another research center in Costa Rica, and a third in the Pacific Northwest, and yet another in New Zealand.

"I'm tired," Shuttleworth said. "I can't keep up with it. I've aged 20 years in the last four. I've been putting in 18-hour days, seven days a week, with little breaks in the routine like working all day, all night, all day, all night, and into the third day to get an issue out."

Here is John Shuttleworth, hollow-eyed, gray-skinned, bearded with a stubble, exhausted, overworked, apprehensive about the fate of the planet—the same man who publishes a magazine which helps the "little people" lead peaceful, quiet, satisfying and creative lives. The irony is not lost on Shuttleworth, but never mind. There is work to be done yet. "I give the planet 15 years," Shuttleworth says, using one of his frequent apocalyptic references. "Unless we get the larger percentage of the planet's population realizing that solar energy is where it's at, cutting consumption and cutting population, forget it.

"Forget grandchildren. If there are grandchildren, they'll curse our generation.

"There's a photograph of the planet, out there in space, in this black void, a lush, beautiful blue and green and white planet, the white clouds and the blue and green oceans, and it just makes you want to cry when you see that thing and realize that we're screwing it up completely.

"So I'm on a desperate quest now . . ."

The various enterprises of Mother are housed in part of a defunct dress factory called the old Ruth Originals building, just outside Hendersonville. The functions are partitioned off with bookshelves of a design Shuttleworth says he invented when he was seven years old. His 60-odd employes, excepting a handful of editorial staff, do factory-like work. Their machines are file cabinets, computer cards, electric typewriters, wrapping and tying and coding and mailing devices, and, in its own air-conditioned sanctuary, the big computer, which keeps track of Mother's children. Faces, on one recent day, tended to be businesslike and edging toward grim. Efficiency is required to save the planet. Shuttleworth has no use for smarmy idealists who exist on vaporous dreams, many of whom have shown up at Mother's to help save the planet.

"People who love Mother and just can't wait to be a part of this thing are the least likely to work out here, these great idealists who think they can stay grassed out of their minds all day and play the guitar and somehow this groovy magazine gets put together. They think this is some kind of never-never land, and when you ask them to work, they don't like it," Shuttleworth said.

ON Bee Mountain, about an hour's drive from the Mother complex, Leon Blyth, late of a Detroit suburb, has been fooling with his pig pen, but now he sips his wine at the picnic table beside the equipment shed. The stone foundation for his new house, which he is building with help from his 16-year-old son, has risen to three feet. The topmost layer is still drying in wooden frames, a building technique Leon learned from a book called "Living the Good Life." Later he and Bob will check out the cornfield on the far hill, and the young grape plants below, and finally, the garden in the valley. But Leon now talks of the machine shop. His wife Gail is gathering the eggs.

"There was a time I enjoyed going to work. Ask Gail. I did time studies and flow charts and all that, and I could see what I did, that I was accomplishing something. Then the shop just got too big," Leon said. "I became the middleman."

Once management told Leon he had to tell the men never to sit down. This was a new rule. He felt stupid and guilty enforcing such an arbitrary rule, because he believed that a man who had completed his job was entitled to sit down. He used to buy Rolaids in economy-sized bottles. He had the shop nurse order Maalox for him. He was working 67 hours a week. Then he read Bob's ad in the Mother Earth News.

"I wasn't able to quit work, of course, but I did it any way. My father worked all his life for the government as an immigration officer. He had fine retirement benefits. He retired at age 65 and died at age 65½ on his way to Florida."

After Leon came to North Carolina with his wife and four children, settled into his temporary house trailer and built a plywood shed for the two oldest boys, he received a visit from an old Detroit friend. The friend was so shocked at Leon's new life-style that he stayed only six hours. "It blew his mind. He has his own shop, he's on his second wife, his oldest son is into dope real bad. He was so upset that I wasn't working my tail off like he does."

AT the Mother factory in Hendersonville, three fluorescent light fixtures have fallen from the rafters in the shipping department. No one is hurt. Shuttleworth investigates. Then the president of Bantam is on the line. Jane Shuttleworth, a diminutive, taciturn woman, summons her husband to the phone.

"I got a bone to pick with Bantam," Shuttleworth says. "They're trying to screw us out of some royalties right now. It's the usual thing when you're small and they're big."

The Shuttleworths moved Mother from the dim and putrid banks of Lake Erie to the clean mountain air of North Carolina last year after

SHUTTLEWORTH, John
and
SHUTTLEWORTH, Jane

ATLANTA JOURNAL
& CONSTITUTION
(Atlanta, Ga.)

July 21, 1974

investigating a number of potential sites for the prospective research center. Despite offerings of land in New York and Florida, they chose North Carolina for its diversity of flora and fauna, for its lack of cloud cover that would inhibit solar energy experimentation.

Although the couple owns Mother, which last year did some $2 million worth of business, and although some of their employes are making $20,000, the Shuttleworths say they have taken a $208-per-week salary for themselves. "We're a couple of the least-paid people around here now. But we don't spend much money. Hell, we work all the time. On an hourly basis I guess I'm making about a buck-58 an hour.

"We still don't have enough money to buy a nice place for ourselves. We rent a big old Southern mansion, fantastic place, for $125 a month, but we're glorified house-sitters. We rent it from some wealthy people in Georgia who use it only one month out of the year. This means that for July we live in a motel room."

MOTHER seems to be self-perpetuating. The money generated by the ➡

(Continued from preceding page)

magazine sales and the syndicated columns and the books and mail-order hardware is plowed into research into alternative energy sources, and from this research comes material which shows up as stories in the Mother Earth News. The focus of Mother's research currently is the Shuttlebug, a car in three models, one of which is powered with methane gas, another with electricity, and the third with gasoline burned at the rate of some 50 miles per gallon.

"Jane and I started out to do something in our spare time, and you see what it turned out to be," Shuttleworth said. "Like the car alone could be a multi-million dollar business. We started to publish a newsletter, and we fell off the edge of the earth. We are alone in the field. People are hungry for this kind of information and we're the focal point."

Shuttleworth dropped out of Ball State College in Indiana as a sophomore, and spent the next 12 years as a "high-class bum," rambling over the United States and Mexico and Canada, living in 80 places and going through 157 jobs, and winding up in a public relations job with an aircraft company "telling too many lies for them . . ."

"The country was in turmoil at the time," he said. "There was Nixon and Agnew on the one hand, really polarizing the country, and there was Jerry Rubin and Abbie Hoffman on the other, polarizing the country. Both groups were really dumb. Everybody had a little piece of the truth, and what we tried to do was put those pieces together. We did something right along the way. We hit the market at just the right time."

In Shuttleworth's office file cabinets are some 2,000 unpublished manuscripts, bought and unbought. More pour in every day. Shuttleworth does extensive rewriting of every article destined to appear in the magazine, having hired and fired a succession of "$30,000-a-year editors" who didn't measure up to his standards. "I'm the guy with the magic words," he says. He writes the syndicated columns, and he writes the books, and recently he was trying to decide whether to sign a contract for a syndicated television show. He flies all over the country to conferences on alternative energy, showing off the Shuttlebug. Mother, it would appear, is a one-man show.

"BE sure and ask Shuttleworth what the hell's happening with the magazine. Ask him about that piece on ham radios. There aren't six people in this country who give a damn about keeping in touch over ham radios. That piece was way out in left field," Leon said. He and Bob Holland, who have read every issue of Mother, from one to 27, think they have detected a subtle turn in the content of the magazine from the practical to the esoteric, and this bothers them. The article on ham radios, they feel, is a good example of this turn.

Mother is not often criticized, and Shuttleworth bristles slightly. "I have to expand people's horizons a little bit. I see some awful bad times coming. I mean super bad, worse than I ever want to think about. On a global scale, depressions, food shortages, just complete anarchy and chaos. And I'm working right now to get people's eyes on what can be done, how you can keep some links with the kind of people you want to keep links with.

"I mean, let's face it. How many times can you tell people how to milk goats? We got to move on to other things."

The Mother's General Store, situated in downtown Hendersonville, has just had its grand opening, and the tourists are buying its wares: Safari water bags, Aladdin kerosene lanterns, Sudbury Soil Test Kits, Dixie Brand Pine Tar, boot jacks, snowshoes, Stetson hats, Big Stinky fly traps, hay hooks, recycled paper stationery. In the back of the retail store, the catalogue mail-order department is humming. But not enough for Shuttleworth. He dispenses some harsh words to the department manager, something about people just standing around. And later, he comments: "The people over at the magazine are just working their tails off, and down here at the store we're running an old folks home . . ."

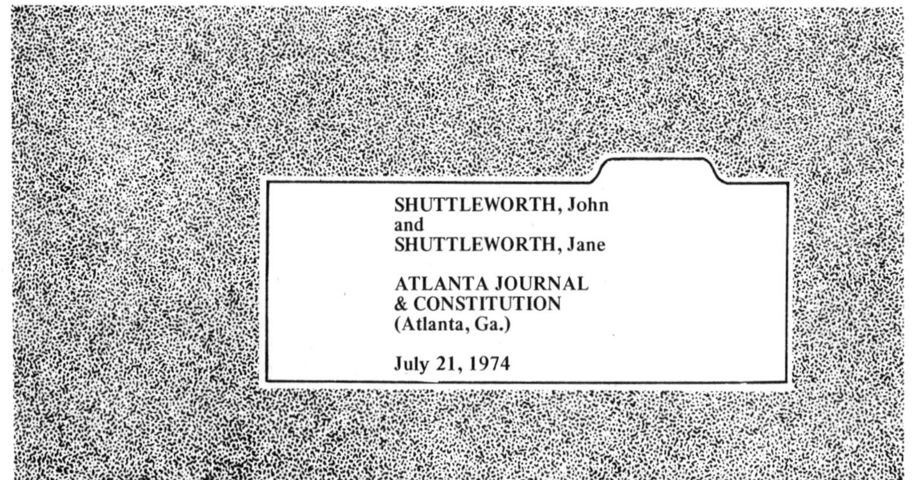
SHUTTLEWORTH, John
and
SHUTTLEWORTH, Jane

ATLANTA JOURNAL
& CONSTITUTION
(Atlanta, Ga.)

July 21, 1974

ON Bee Mountain, the sun is slipping behind the tree line above the cornfield on the cleared ridge, and the locusts in the woods are quieting down for the night. On the lawn outside Bob's cabin the picnic table is set for supper. There will be a roast from the freezer full of beef, homemade bread, bowls of carrots and mashed potatoes and peas from the garden. The new litter of Dalmatian pups play on the grass, white and black against the green. The rooster pecks at the ground around them.

There is no talk about the fate of the planet. Bob and Leon, instead, discuss whether the locusts finally were dying out and whether they really would come back in seven years, and the damage they had done to the orchard, and whether to buy a milk cow and if so what kind. In this decision, they would consult the Mother Earth News article on milk cows. Leon is puffing his pipe. He looks exactly like a man who made a narrow escape from a machine shop.

In Hendersonville, the Mother Earth factory hums on, and John Shuttleworth is missing the sunset.

"I'll be as honest with you as I can," Shuttleworth says. "Jane and I have been really dumb. We've sacrificed our personal health. I get to the point where I make myself physically sick. I ache all over, like I have a bad cold. We're not out for a power base for ourselves. We've done it because somebody had to do it. One of these days I'm going to surprise everybody by saying to hell with it and walking out and leaving it to the people here.

"Sometimes," Shuttleworth adds, apropos of nothing, "I view myself as an insane old man leading a bunch of squabbling children around . . ." □

The Loneliness of the Long Distance Writer

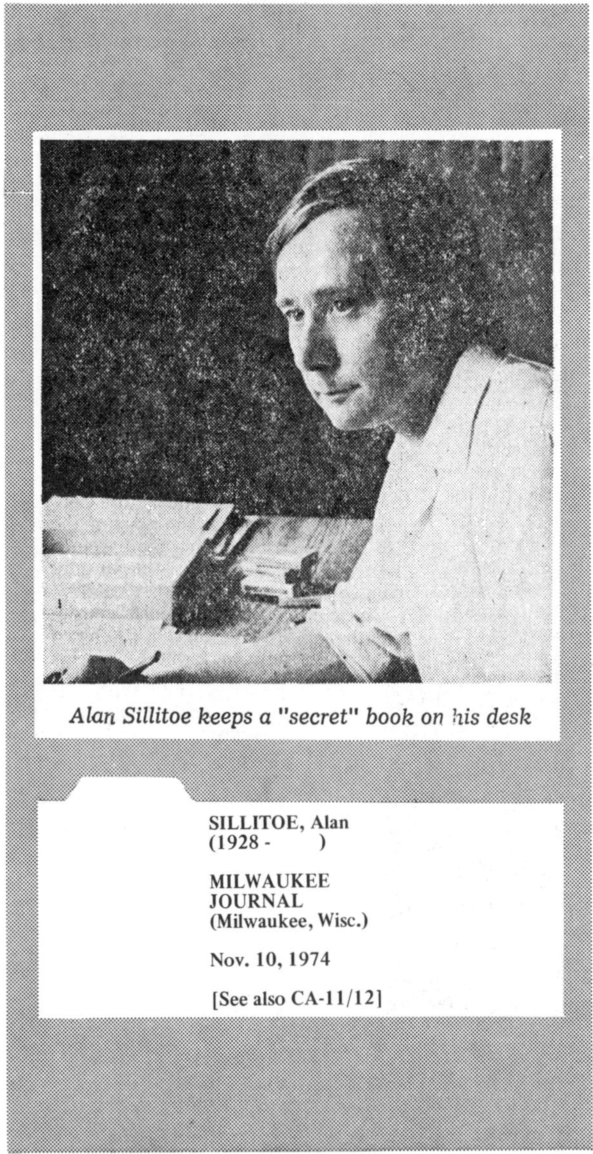

Alan Sillitoe keeps a "secret" book on his desk

SILLITOE, Alan
(1928 -)

MILWAUKEE
JOURNAL
(Milwaukee, Wisc.)

Nov. 10, 1974

[See also CA-11/12]

By LESLIE CROSS,
Journal Book Editor

ALAN SILLITOE, who considers himself something of an American in spirit, got his first look at the country the other day.

The author of "Saturday Night and Sunday Morning" came to give two lectures at the University of Nebraska and let the students there know what a British author looks like and how he works. Before taking off for Lincoln after his arrival in New York, he stopped at Scribners, which had just published the American edition of his latest book, a collection of nine stories called "Men, Women and Children."

"I think you'll find Nebraska quite different from New York," I told him at his publisher's office.

"I expect to," said Sillitoe, a slender, wiry looking man of 46. "New York, though, is very interesting. I've seen Manhattan, and the Brooklyn Bridge at dusk. I'll be in America three weeks in all."

One of his lectures in Nebraska, he said, would deal with his most famous novel and "how a boy with no education came to write it." The book, turned into a much noticed movie, is about a young English factory worker and his struggle to find personal dignity in a world of unrewarding toil, pubs and bleak sex.

It was a world that Sillitoe knew well. Nevertheless, as he pointed out when I saw him, it took a long time before he could write about it. The son of a tannery laborer, he went to work in a bicycle factory at 14. He was called into service with the Royal Air Force as World War II ended and was sent to Malaya as a wireless operator. The military doctors found he had tuberculosis. Discharged with a tiny pension, he determined to learn how to write.

Road Back Home Was a Long One

He lived cheaply in France and later in Majorca. "Everything I wrote came back," he said. His wife, a Nottingham schoolteacher who was born in the Bronx, kept him at it. In Majorca he met Robert Graves, the poet and mythologist. "Why don't you write about Nottingham?" Graves asked. The result was "Saturday Night and Sunday Morning."

"I was 20 when I first tried to write, and it took 10 years before I learned how to do it," Sillitoe recalled.

Besides having an American wife, Sillitoe had a measure of guidance from work that he read in American magazines. "I lost contact with British magazines," he said. "The English language publications I was apt to see in a place like Majorca were American."

In them he read some of Hemingway's later stories and sketches, and the work of writers like Truman Capote, Gore Vidal and Norman Mailer who were just coming into eminence. He found them congenial to what he was trying to do. "I saw that fiction could be much more vigorous than it had been."

So he wrote stories in a new vein, most of them about working class life. "Working people comprise 75% of the population in a country like England," he explained, "yet, with a few exceptions, writers paid little attention to the great fund of human experience represented in their lives."

These stories, too, came back. A year after his first novel was published, he gathered some of them into a book whose success almost equaled that of the novel — "The Loneliness of the Long Distance Runner." The title story also became a major film.

Some Advice for the Young

Now the Sillitoes are living in a cottage in Kent, at a convenient distance from London. Mrs. Sillitoe is the author of four books of poetry and a collection of stories published under her maiden name, Ruth Esther Fainlight. The Sillitoes have two children — a daughter, 13, and a son, 12.

What advice might Sillitoe have for a young man or woman determined to write? His students in Nebraska would be sure to ask him that, I reminded him.

Sillitoe thought for just a moment.

"First," he said methodically, "a writer has to be very well educated — whether he educates himself or goes to school. He should know a language other than his own, so that his own will become comprehensible to him.

"Second, he must try to read every book of note in every literature, so that he will know what's been done before.

"Third, he ought to spend two or three years outside his own country.

"Fourth, he should write as much as he can and never be discouraged."

After a pause, Sillitoe added:

"I'd say this as a little postscriptum: He must strive to find his own voice and write about what he knows."

It might also be said that he has a little personal secret. He keeps a Bible on his desk. When he feels that he is faltering, he refreshes himself with its plain language and the grandeur of its themes.

"I read it as literature," he said. "I take care never to preach in my work."

Getting Sick? Emotions May Be 1st Clue

By Barbara Salsini
of The Journal Staff

When someone has a fever, it's a sign that an illness may be on the way. Pain is another signal that something is wrong with one's body, and strange lumps or bleeding can be ominous warnings of physical disorder.

But by the time these symptoms appear, the disease is probably present also, maintains Dr. Samuel Silverman, author of a new book on what he considers the emotional indicators of physical illness.

Silverman was interviewed this week while in Milwaukee to promote the book, "How Will You Feel Tomorrow? New Ways to Predict Illness" (Stein and Day).

Psychiatry Professor

The author of two other books about psychological factors in disease, Silverman is an associate professor of psychiatry at Harvard Medical School and is affiliated with the Boston Psychoanalytic Institute and Massachusetts General Hospital.

Silverman explained that his book did not describe the causes of physical illness or claim that emotions were the major causes of bodily sickness.

Instead, he said, it is an "attempt to familiarize people with certain warning signals that come from their emotional state which then suggest the possibility of some form of body disorder."

The presence of just one of these signals does not mean there will be an illness, Silverman said. But the possibility of physical sickness becomes greater if a group of the signals are present. He emphasized that he was "talking exclusively about physical illness."

30 Year Practice

Silverman based his theory on 30 years of medical practice. During consultations, he observed that not only did patients have emotional reactions to illness but they had undergone emotional troubles before becoming physically ill. He decided to collect data on his psychiatric patients who were in good bodily health to see if he could predict illness from their emotional signals.

His studies indicated that many patients exhibited clusters of emotional signals before any physical symptoms were evident. From these signals, he was able to forecast illnesses, he said.

—Journal Photo
Dr. Samuel Silverman, psychiatrist-writer.

SILVERMAN, Samuel
MILWAUKEE JOURNAL (Milwaukee, Wisc.)
Jan. 18, 1974

"When I had the feeling that something serious was pending, I told my patient, 'Get checked over right away,' " he added.

"Dew Line"

The psychiatrist refers to the emotional signals he has defined as a "DEW Line (Distant Early Warnings) of possible physical illness."

High on the list of emotional signals is stress. Not all stress is bad and some forms, such as exercise, social exchange and mental stimulation, are healthy, Silverman said.

Besides obvious stresses like a death in the family or an accident, there are more subtle stresses, according to Silverman. One of these is the "anniversary reaction."

Significant Dates

He explained: "I'm referring here to dates of, let's say, weddings, divorces, deaths, birthdays, even the beginning of a certain kind of work, the beginning of school or examination time in school. All these days may have had an unpleasant emotional significance for the person involved."

When the anniversary of the event rolls around, the individual concerned may not even be aware of it but may feel ill.

Another form of stress is success. "Some people carry a burden of guilt and can't stand success. They feel they don't deserve it," Silverman said. When people show no reaction to a dramatic stress, it indicates that the "stress has gone underground," Silverman said.

Good Clue

"That's an important clue that the person involved has not adequately coped with the stress and discharged the tensions it produces. . . . That's the kind of situtation to make us alert to the possibility or likelihood of physical illness."

Silverman believes that it is often possible to predict target areas in which illness will strike. Heredity and the way one has reacted in the past can be indicators of future sickness, he said.

Someone with a pattern of heart irregularity under stress "could begin to think the heart is a target organ," he observed. He also spoke of "somatic identification" in which one person identifies with another to the extent of showing signs of a common ailment.

Repressed thoughts and feelings sometimes surface in disguised form in dreams, Silverman said. Physical symptoms of illness may be at such a low level that they are not noticed during waking hours. But these signals may "make their way into our dreams," he said.

Emotional indicators are also helpful in predicting the outcome of an illness, according to Silverman. Recovery may be slow for apathetic and depressed patients or for those who regard their illness as punishment, derive benefits from being sick or deny their illness.

"Every illness has an emotional component before it starts, and of course, after it has developed," Silverman said.

He believes that emotional as well as physical health should be checked during physical examinations. Emotional tensions can be eased in a number of ways, ranging from relaxation and exercise to professional help, he said.

SIMON, Neil
(1927 -)

STAR-LEDGER
(Newark, N.J.)

Oct. 23, 1974

Photos by Dwight J. Johnson

'Doc' Simon pays theater call with remedies for jittery show

By MARK FINSTON

NEW YORK — Neil Simon, Broadway's most successful playwright, walks through the stage door of the Eugene O'Neill Theater on West 49th Street, where the first rehearsal of his new show, "God's Favorite," is about to begin.

"Hi, Doc," says some stage official.

"Hi, Doc," calls another.

Prior to the time Simon arrived, several people had been discussing how Simon got the nickname "Doc." There were a number of versions, but nobody was really sure.

"My brother gave it to me when I was two years old," says the 47-year-old Simon, a faint note of anguish in his voice. "He was seven years older. I used to play with a stethoscope. I've been trying to get rid of it all these years. Neil is my name.

"When I open a new play, everyone asks me if I want them to call me Neil or Doc. I say Neil. The next day, everyone says, 'Hi, Doc.' "

His wife, actress Marsha Mason, calls him Neil. His brother, Danny, a writer and director, still calls him Doc.

This will be Simon's 14th Broadway show. Many of them have taken place in the Eugene O'Neill Theater. This isn't surprising. Simon owns the theater.

"I really never wanted to own a theater, but it was a business proposition," He says. "Still, in a way it may be helpful. It says to me, 'Write a play. You have to fill your theater this year.' "

Simon has no plans to rename the theater the Neil Simon Playhouse or the Doc Simon Theater or anything like that. Eugene O'Neill is good enough for him.

Simon gives the appearance of being a quiet, meek man. He is balding and looks faintly owlish in his round glasses, and he talks in a shy tone.

And though the show has three well-known stars — Vincent Gardinia (who won a Tony for his performance in Simon's "The Prisoner of Second Avenue"), Charles Nelson Reilly and Maria Karnilova — it is meek, shy Neil Simon who causes the most commotion. It's Neil Simon this, Doc Simon that, get Doc a cup of black coffee, impress Doc.

Simon sits and sips his black coffee. He is amused, but unimpressed, at least with all the efforts to impress him.

"I'm very nervous," says Simon, as he sits in the darkened, empty orchestra and watches the actors and directors and technicians cavort on the stage. "To me the first day of rehearsal is almost like opening night. All the other days of rehearsal are too. Thank goodness I have eight weeks to fix it."

The play will open in New Haven on Nov. 16. It will preview on Broadway starting Dec. 3, and will premiere Dec. 11.

Others are nervous too.

"I'm frightened, very scared," says Vincent Gardinia. "This is the first time you meet the entire cast — and you're reading for Neil Simon. You want to make a good impression. It's like going through a terrible illness."

"You always feel nervous — it's like the first day of everything," says Charles Nelson Reilly. "So I tend to push, overdo my voice. I do that to show people they hired the right actor, eat your heart out Spencer Tracy. Then when I get home, I can't talk. It goes away in a couple of days."

Simon's nervousness won't go away in a couple of days. He's a big rewrite man. Originally, he wrote "God's Favorite" three years ago. It seemed wrong. He did it again a year later. It still wasn't right.

"This summer, it finally made itself clear to me," he says. "It was before neither fish nor fowl." A pause. "I think it's fish now."

The rewriting will continue.

"Most playwrights don't rewrite a lot," says Simon. "Maybe they can get it right the first time, I can't. Right now the script is like a blueprint to me. I rewrite it every day. We had a reading last week, and just since then I've rewritten 15 or 20 per cent of it. By the time it opens, it'll be 35 per cent changed."

Simon is asked what the play is about. He smiles shyly.

"I don't like to talk about what the play is about. If I could say it in two or three sentences, I would have said it — and I wouldn't have written a play. Besides, the critics will tell me what it's about. I'll wait for them. I'm amazed to find out how many diversified opinions there are."

Though he has been productive and busy, Simon, for the past few years, says he has been in a "blue funk" so far as playwriting is concerned, a funk that's lasted till recently.

"I'm treating this one as though it's my first play on Broadway — and it works," he says.

"I don't know why it got harder for me after 'Plaza Suite.' I suppose it's like the Miami Dolphins. After two Super Bowls, they let down a little. But I'm really up for this game. I think one reason might be that Broadway is much more vital this year than it has been in the last few years."

Simon often interjects his conversation with sporting images. He's a tennis player, and enjoys all sports, except boxing.

"Sports are the only kind of drama you rarely know what the ending will be. Except the Jets, I guess."

When his 17-year-old daughter graduates from high school in June (he also has an 11-year-old daughter), he'll move from New York, his birthplace and long-time home, to southern California.

"I was able to write movies in New York, so I ought to be able to write plays in California. I'm moving for health reasons, and the sun. I'd rather live in a warmer climate. I get terrible colds, terrible sinuses. Watch: I'll move out there, and it'll turn cold."

He has written the movie script for his Broadway smash, "Sunshine Boys," and is working on an original screenplay to star his wife. (Simon's first wife died.) He has no desire to write a novel ("It would take forever. I've learned my craft in the theater. Besides, you have to be a genius to write a novel. Anyway, I love live audiences. If I could read my novel out loud to an audience, maybe . . ."

He might like to write a mystery, though. He has never written one.

Simon strolls onto the stage. Reilly is trying to put everyone at ease by joking about his wig: "There's only one guy who can fix my hair, and he's in California. So if it comes off, what're we going to do? It's from three Sicilian women . . ."

Neil Simon smiles. He turns to someone close by, says quietly, "All these revivals are such hits these days, next year I'm going to write a revival. An original revival."

A defense of America finds a respon-sive chord

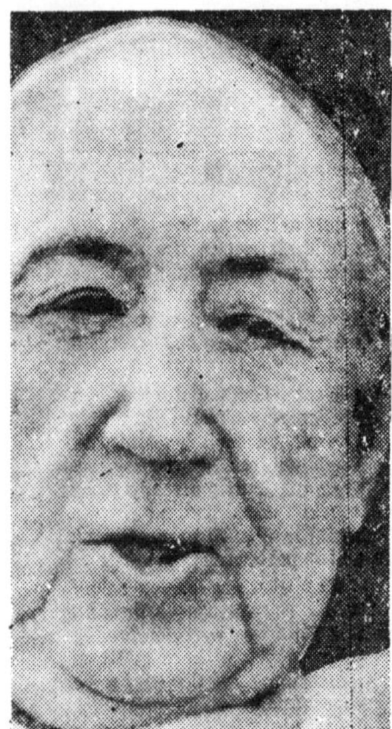

SINCLAIR, Gordon (1900-)

DETROIT NEWS (Detroit, Mich.)

Jan. 6, 1974

By PETER WARD
News Special Writer

TORONTO—The favorite journalistic sport in the later half of 1973 seemed to be taking a kick at the United States.

As if that were not enough, Europeans mounted renewed attacks on the dollar, South Americans and Asians intensified their imperialist charges and the Arabs — joined by Canada — turned the screws for price and supply on oil.

Belted from all sides by foreigners, shattered by Watergate and presidential uncertainties from within, it is not surprising that the United States reacted collectively with enthusiasm when someone outside the country finally said something nice.

The "someone" was a onetime Toronto Cabbagetown kid, Gordon Sinclair — Canada's original rags-to-riches journalistic success story — whose writing and broadcasting over more than half a century have taken him from the streets to a millionaire status.

Gordon Sinclair praised the United States and slammed her critics in a four-minute Toronto broadcast on June 5, 1973.

IN DECEMBER his broadcast was made into several records and before the end of the month over a million copies had been sold.

There are three versions of the Sinclair broadcast, which is called simply "The Americans," and sales are booming for all three.

One is by Sinclair himself, backed by the music to the "Battle Hymn of the Republic"; one is an "unauthorized version" by Windsor broadcaster Byron MacGregor, backed by a group from the Detroit Symphony Orchestra, and the other is one of the last records made by western singer Tex Ritter before his death last week.

Ritter cleared his recording with Sinclair before making it.

Sinclair has been the star newscaster-radio columnist for CFRB — Canada's largest private radio station — for more than three decades.

Born in 1900, Sinclair bounced from one respectable job to another: he was fired from a bank for insubordination and sacked as a department store cashier.

After joining the famous kilted 48th Highlanders Regiment too late to see action in World War I, Sinclair went back to civilian attire but still had trouble with conventional employment.

When he was 22, he landed a job with the Toronto Star at about the time Ernest Hemingway was working for the paper.

Sinclair worked at various newspaper assignments — from police beat to politics to women's editor — and eventually the Star gave Sinclair an unprecedented plum; they sent him to travel the world as a wandering reporter with no specific assignments.

By the time he came back Sinclair was an institution in Toronto and he added broadcasting to his repertoire. An instinct for the outlandish and a shrewd investment mind combined to pyramid the Sinclair fortunes.

At 74, Sinclair is still one of the best television interviewers in Canada and no subject goes through his probing without facing the question: "How much do you make?" He is Canada's most vocal opponent of fluoride additives to municipal water supplies. "Rat poison," he calls it.

Sinclair and his wife, Gladys, have become institutions throughout Canada.

HE APPEARS WEEKLY on a Canadian national panel TV show, "Front Page Challenge," and daily on CFRB with his noon newscast and an opinion piece, "Let's Be Personal."

It was the four-minute "Let's Be Personal" program which produced the Sinclair record which is now sweeping America.

On June 5, Sinclair watched the morning television news which showed disastrous floods in the Mississippi Valley. He heard also that the American Red Cross had already overspent the year's disaster budget.

It bothered him that the United States, beset by trouble from without and from within, was now suffering natural disasters while the rest of the world did nothing about it.

He sat down at the typewriter and knocked out his editorial, "The Americans," in 18 minutes, cataloging the number of times Americans have helped others and wondering why nobody ever helped Americans. He broadcast the item at 11:45 a.m. that day and promptly forgot it.

CFRB reports that it was a listener in Buffalo who first wrote about the Sinclair editorial, requesting a reprint. There were small sparks of interest from other U.S. centers during late summer and early fall. Then it was recorded.

Sinclair's record was released in the United States Dec. 21. Avco of New York, the distributors, report that in the first 10 days, half a million were sold. The other two versions, by Ritter and Windsor's MacGregor, started earlier and hence have so far sold more copies.

U.S. INFORMATION SERVICES, the Washington agency, has sent copies of the script and the record to all of its overseas stations in more than 100 countries. The result has been a deluge of letters on Sinclair's desk in Toronto, including one from John Wayne, who told Sinclair it was time somebody spoke for the United States.

Sinclair, who has assigned all his personal royalties from the record to the American Red Cross, is bemused by the whole affair. He says he doesn't want anything for doing something he believes in, and he claims the four-minute radio script has become so popular "because it hit a lot of Americans just when they needed a lift."

'The Americans'

Here is an edited version of Gordon Sinclair's recorded editorial, "The Americans." However, it should be noted that the statements pertaining to foreign debts to the United States are not accurate. It also should be noted that probably the first incident of foreign help being given to this country occurred during the Revolutionary War, and that as recently as 1972 the Japanese sent aid to unemployed workers in Seattle when that city was hit by an aircraft industry slump. Despite these inaccuracies and omissions, it is a fact that the editorial has struck a responsive chord in the United States:

"This Canadian thinks it's time to speak up for the Americans — the most generous and possibly the least appreciated people in all the earth.

"As long as 60 years ago, when I first started to read newspapers, I read of floods on the Yellow River. Who rushed in men and money to help? The Americans did.

"TODAY THE RICH bottom land of the Mississippi is under water and no foreign land has sent a dollar to help.

"Germany, Japan and to a lesser extent, Britain and Italy, were lifted out of the debris of war by the Americans who poured in billions of dollars and forgave millions in debts.

"None of those countries today is paying even the interest on its remaining debts to the United States.

"When distant cities are hit by earthquake, it is the United States that is there to help.

"So far this spring, 59 American communities have been flattened by tornadoes. Nobody helped.

"The Marshall Plan, the Truman policy, all pumped billions upon billions into discouraged countries. Now newspapers in those countries are writing about decadent, warmongering Americans.

"I'd like to see just one of those countries ... build its own airplane. Come on. Let's hear it.

"Does any other country in the world have an airplane to equal the Boeing jumbo jet, the Lockheed Tri-Star or the Douglas DC 10?

"Why does no other land on the earth even consider putting a man or a woman on the moon?

"You talk about Japanese technocracy and you get radios. You talk about German technocracy and you get automobiles. You talk about American technocracy and you will find men on the moon — not once, but several times.

"You talk about scandals and Americans put theirs right in the store window for everyone to look at.

"Even the draft dodgers are not pursued and hounded. They are here on our streets...getting American dollars from ma and pa back home to spend here.

"When the Americans get out of this bind — and they will — who can blame them if they said, 'The hell with the rest of the world. Let someone else buy the Israel bonds. Let someone else build and repair foreign lands.

"I can name 5,000 times when the Americans raced to the help of other people in trouble.

"Can you name me even one time when someone else raced to the Americans in trouble?

"I don't think there was outside help even during the San Francisco earthquake.

"OUR NEIGHBORS have faced it alone. And I'm damned tired of hearing them kicked around.

"They'll come out of this thing with their flag high. And when they do they are entitled to thumb their nose over the lands that are gloating over their present troubles.

"And finally, the American Red Cross was told at its 48th annual meeting in New Orleans that it was broke.

"This year's disasters have taken its toll and nobody — but nobody — has helped."

Singer Writes to Please Himself

By JANET CHUSMIR

Herald Staff Writer

SINGER, Isaac Bashevis
(1904 -)

MIAMI HERALD
(Miami, Fla.)

Mar. 3, 1974

[See also CA-1]

It's a long way from a Polish shtetl to a Miami Beach high-rise, but Isaac Bashevis Singer, who grew up in one and now lives part-time in the other, says the sun is the same and the people are the same . . .

. . . "Although one human being is not like another, just like the fingerprint of one is not like another . . .

. . . **"AND PEOPLE** these days don't have faith like the people of the shtetl. And they're not satisfied as they were. In the shtetl when they got a pice of bread or an onion, they were satisfied."

A piece of bread. An onion. Maybe that's partly why at 69, after a long and distinguished career as a novelist and short story writer, Isaac Bashevis Singer, just back from a lecture tour, is astonished and pleased to find that the American Journal Book Club made his latest book, "A Crown of Feathers," its main selection, that the New Yorker Magaine, to which he's a regular contributor, has a story in the issue that just arrived, and that the New York Daily News Sunday magazine has a several-page layout of his favorite spots in New York, the city he's called home since 1935.

These things, the most recent in a series of accolades and accomplishments, are quite astonishing to Singer who thinks every human being is in a way a pessimist and every human being is also basically modest so he feels he doesn't deserve it — "the gifts of grace."

"I HOPE I'm telling the truth about everyone," he quickly adds, knowing quite well that there are some who, no matter what they get, find it too little.

For Isaac Bashevis Singer, the son and grandson of rabbis, it isn't too little. It isn't even too late. Although, when you consider a lot of other American writers, it has taken a long time.

He started writing professionally as a journalist for the Yiddish press in Poland after graduation from the rabbinical seminary in Warsaw. The rabbinste, he'd decided, wasn't for him.

AFTER HE came to the U.S., he worked for the Jewish Daily Forward where his stories were first published in Yiddish, as they are even now. In the beginning, he wrote in Hebrew, but he later switched. Now he does a rough translation into English; others, more comfortable with the language, polish it up.

Always, he has a real topic or a theme; always, a real passion to write the story; always, the conviction — or at least the illusion, he says — that he is the only one who can write this particular story.

"Being convinced that I'm the only one for me is not so difficult because I write about Polish Jews," he says. Needless to say not many American writers do the same.

Until he was 45, he wasn't known at all except by a group of Yiddish readers who were getting older and older and leaving few children who knew the language.

Then the translations began. Now included among his literary awards are the Louis Lamed Prize and grants from the American Academy and the National Institute of Arts and Letters. His work has appeared in Commentary, Midstream, Mademoiselle, Esquire, Partisan Review, and, of course, the New Yorker.

Among his books are "Satan in Goray," "Gimpel the Fool," "The Family Moskat," "The Magician of Lublin," "The Spinoza of Market Street," "Short Friday," "The Slave," "In My Father's Court," "The Seance," "The Manor" and its sequel, "The Estate," "Enemies: A Love Story" and the newest, "A Crown of Feathers." There are others especially for children.

HE HAS NO regrets that fame came late. "It is healthy for a writer not to become too famous when he's young," he says. "It's done a lot of damage to American writers. When you're famous when you're young, you don't learn you're not God's gift to humanity."

It has done damage, he says, to even such great writers as Lord Byron. "Not to his work, but to his person." Fame and a million dollars when you're young make you conceited, you think you can't make a mistake. "You see a man like (J.D.) Salinger, famous when he was young, is silent many years."

There is nothing harsh to his tone. He sounds as he looks — like a frail, kind, and scholarly zedye (grandfather) with warmth and wit who long ago came to know and accept that every man is flesh and blood and you can expect little from him. Why even when he tries to do good sometimes, it comes out wrong.

AS HE speaks a plane with a banner advertising "The Devil and Miss Jones" interrupts the blue sky behind him that melts into the ocean at the apartment's back door. The movie is playing at a theater to the north of him. "The Exorcist" is to the south.

The strange thing is his first book, "Satan in Goray," was about exorcism. He was always fascinated by the metaphysical, by the supernatural, by the dybbuks. When he began writing in the U.S., the editor at the Jewish Forward said, "Whoever is going to read such stuff about devils? Who believes it?" Write about David Dubinsky, about tailors in New York, about strikes, he said.

He wrote about devils. "You know, writers are very stubborn people."

HE FINDS it natural that others have jumped on the bandwagon. They think if there's redemption, maybe it's in this. Neither psychology nor sociology nor even the exact sciences have given them the answers they seek.

"The belief that a few rocks they'll bring down from the moon will reveal forever the secret of creation is very naive. They'll reveal as much as rocks here."

He's sure they'll turn away from the occult. It is as much the nature of people to jump off bandwagons as on. Besides, after awhile they'll be disap- ➡

(Continued from preceding page)
pointed in it. "Some of the writers are liars," he explains.

HE MADE up his mind when he was a child — the day he collected neighbors' contributions to his rabbi father — that he'd never do anything for money that goes against the grain. So he never writes for money. Others when they start to write think of the movie rights and wonder, "Who will play the heroes?" And so they write young heroes. Singer's are often old.

He also wanders in and out of some of the stories. He may put words in his characters' mouths he doesn't believe, but in or out of print, never his own.

And so, it doesn't matter whether he says it in a story, like Hanka, which appeared in a recent New Yorker, or he says it directly to your face. "If the existence of God, the soul, the hereafter, special providence and everything that has to do with metaphysics were scientifically proven, man would lose the highest gift bestowed upon him — free choice."

"HAVE YOU had personal experiences of that sort? Have you ever seen a spirit?" a character in the story asks.

"All my experiences have been ambiguous. None of them could serve for evidence. Just the same, my belief in spirits becomes ever stronger."

He sees a grain of truth. "From a grain of truth you can make mountains. If we would know one grain of sand thoroughly, its history and how it came, we'd know the universe."

EVERY ONE of us, he says, has it in us to a degree — telepathy, clairvoyance, premonitions. Some have it more. Some less. "There's not a single love affair between man and woman when there's not elements of telepathy. They know each others' thoughts."

Just as he knows that when people give up the metaphysical, they'll go elsewhere in the search for redemption.

Redemption is a need in human beings, he says. "Even though he does a lot, every human being feels he's a failure. The fact we are born and die and are forgotten is in the mind of every human being.

Is Isaac Bashevis Singer a failure?

"WE'RE ALL failures," he answers. "The human race is a failure if it can have, after all, in this century a Hitler, a Stalin." They were not alone. Millions put them in power.

"And, the very fact people in New York are afraid to go out at night — like the caveman was afraid of the tiger and wolf — shows in a moral way we've made no progress whatsoever."

He's optimistic as far as the universe is concerned. God conceived it and he's sure the Almighty knows what He's doing. But man doesn't. "We haven't accomplished a thing in a moral way. Man is still wolf to another man." When there's **the slightest revolution or social disturbance, he says, "man becomes brute."**

HE IS, he readily admits, a pessimist. Yet within him there is hope. "There is hope in everyone, no matter how pessimistic we are.

"If humanity would keep the Ten Commandments, life on earth would be, if not a paradise, half a paradise. It is in our hands. We haven't made up our minds to do it.

"One day when I'm in an optimistic mood I think humanity will make up its mind to keep the Ten Commandments." If not, he's convinced we will perish.

IN THE meantime, he believes that the best thing you can do is run away from evil, not fight it. "Those who decide to fight evil often fall into evil themselves." There are plenty of examples. Communism for one. It spawned Stalin, he points out.

He gives his readers stories not messages. He believes in social justice but he doesn't preach it. There are enough preachers, enough messages. Our problem isn't a lack of messages but rather that we refuse to fulfill them and practice them.

SINGER, Isaac Bashevis

MIAMI HERALD
(Miami, Fla.)

Mar. 3, 1974

He is a man who doesn't go against the world. He "smuggles" himself through the world as if he's in the jungle sneaking by the animals who are out to destroy him.

HIS IS THE old Jewish attitude, not the modern one. Old Judaism was not out to change things, only to keep its own laws. Old Judaism kept to itself in the ghetto. If there was great trouble in one country, it went to another.

New Judaism fights for change, and fights for Israel where Singer's only child, a son who is also named Israel, and his three grandchildren live.

After 2,000 years of trouble, "Jews made up their minds they have to be like other nations. Whether Israel will be a moral success — it may be a secular success — only God knows.

"IF THE diaspora was no good, if Israel is no good, where should we go?" he asks.

The waves splash against the sand and for a few moments that is the only sound. He fingers his glasses and sips the ginger ale his wife, Alma, served.

They were married on Valentine's Day in 1940. It has lasted he says, "because I'm an old-fashioned man. To me, marriage is still something . . ."

It has lasted, she interrupts to say, because "I'm a patient woman."

He laughs. The patient woman is married to a religious man. He may not observe all the rituals, but he prays to God whenever he's in trouble. "Since I'm always in trouble, I pray a lot. If I don't have trouble, I make trouble like losing my plane ticket."

He also believes in guilt. "Although Freud thinks it is a very bad thing, it is a good thing. If Hitler had gone to an analyst, he would have told him, 'Don't feel guilty, Adolph.'

"IF MAN doesn't feel guilt, he is sick."

He would have liked to have lived a life without hurting any human being or animal. He should have become a vegetarian before 12 years ago, he says. He also regrets that he may have insulted some or hurt some in his stories and reviews.

All of living is a sin, he says. "We all step on the graves of other people. We all enjoy ourselves while others are dying . . ."

IF DESPITE his sins he ever gets to paradise, he'd like to have lunch every day with his readers, because "Every human being is a treasure. Every human being is a potential story teller."

He would like to see more story **telling in modern literature. It is too filled with psychology. "If I want psychology, I can read Freud."**

And, if you want insights into human nature, you can read Isaac Bashevis Singer, although he'd tell you, "I only make you believe for a moment that I understand, which is enough, which is all a writer has to do."

But then, as he wrote in his last book . . . "if there is such a thing as truth it is as intricate and hidden as a crown of feathers."

CAFE
SPEAK TO ME, PET, IT IS OUR WEDDIN' ANNIVERSARY

Andy Capp

His Creator Intended To Loaf Too

By JAKE PENLAND
Tempo Staff Report

There are bunches of people in many countries who rate a five-foot, four-inch, 46-year-old, pot-bellied, wife-harassing loafer — the funniest man ever invented.

That man would be Andy Capp and he was invented — by a Britisher, Reggie Smythe. Andy is the sassy star of the comic strip read in some 33 countries and 13 languages. He is the brain child of a fellow from the northeast of Britain who dropped out of school at the age of 14.

Reggie Smythe's father was a boat builder who spent a lot of time on the charity rolls. Reggie intended to do likewise, including the charity bit, but instead he joined the army, spent ten years in the Middle East and North Africa, then became a postal clerk.

He got into cartooning by accident. Although, as he recalls, "I could hardly draw," he had had a few art lessons in school and he agreed to do a poster for a show. It was good enough to bring compliments, and Smythe was sufficiently encouraged to start drawing free-lance cartoons for Britain's largest daily newspaper, The London Daily Mirror.

The Mirror was seeking to boost its circulation to the north with a new comic strip. Smythe, a product of that grimy part of the island, was the logical choice.

He drew on his experiences as a youth in the north of England as well as on his encounters with types he met in the army to develop the character, Andy. "I had to draw the people I knew," he says, "and most of the humor is theirs — in the homes and in the pubs."

Andy Capp is a composite of the men and Andy's long-suffering wife, Flo, he admits, is Reggie Smythe's mother. "She's just like my mother," he says. "You know, with her big bust and big backside."

SMYTHE, Reginald
(1918? -   )

THE STATE
(Columbia, S.C.)

Sept. 9, 1973

The Daily Mirror hoped with the comic strip to woo readers in the north, but to their delight the comic strip became a hit all over England.

Smythe was earning 35 pounds a week, the strip was doing nicely, and then came the big break. Robert Hall, president of the Hall Syndicate of New York, saw the comic strip while on a vacation and found himself getting a daily hearty laugh from the antics of Mr. Capp.

Upon his return to New York, Hall contacted the London Daily Mirror Syndicate and arranged to have the strip sold to newspapers in this country.

"I owe everything to Bob Hall," Smythe told a reporter in London in 1970. "They think more of Andy in the United States than they do here. Now I'm getting 1,000 pounds a week, and I do no more work than I did before."

This essentially British cartoon character was an immediate hit in the United States. The syndicate sold the strip to 90 papers in a month. Andy's appeal was to then become almost worldwide.

Wherever the strip was sold, readers adopted Andy as one of their own. Said an editor of Istanbul's Hareket Gazetesi:

"Andy is as much Turkish as he is English, and he is probably Greek, Italian and Polish too. Our readers got addicted to him in a week. As one of them put it, he is what every man wants to be in his spare time."

As one writer noted, "Andy Capp is a paradox. He's a cocky little British Limey and he's a bully. He has never worked a day in his life and he never intends to. He can be sarcastic, but he never really hurts anyone. Somehow or other he emerges as a lovable little guy to daily newspaper readers. . ."

Andy is no help around the house. "I thought I asked yer to notice when the pan boiled over," says Flo. "I did," replies Andy. "It was a quarter past 11."

The creater of the comic strip says that "Andy is Flo's 'handicap,' but all around the world where Andy appears it's thought that Andy is the most popular name in England." He explains that the cockneys drop the H in handicap, and that leaves you ANDY CAPP.

A reporter who interviewed Reggie Smythe about his creation wanted to know what Andy was like as a boy. Said Smythe:

"Just like any other lad, y'know, high-spirited, adventurous — when he was 16 his parents ran away from home."

How did he meet his long-suffering wife, Florrie?

"Passing a local pub one day, she tripped over him. She picked him up and hasn't been able to put him down since."

Has Andy ever had a job?

"No. And it isn't easy. It's awful not to be able to come out on strike like other men. The thing that decided him against having a job is the insecurity. When you have a job you never know when you may lose it. But when you don't have one you know exactly where you stand."

Solzhenitsyn Threatens Soviet's Very Foundation

SOLZHENITSYN,
Aleksandr I(sayevich)
(1918 -)

MIAMI HERALD
(Miami, Fla.)

Jan. 20, 1974

[See also CA-25/28]

By FOY D. KOHLER

If Stalin had not died in 1953, the genius of Russia's greatest living writer, Aleksandr Isaevich Solzhenitsyn, might long since have been buried in the wilds of Siberia without ever flowering.

If Khrushchev had not found it politically expedient himself to denounce Stalin and to authorize the publication in the Soviet Union of "One Day in the Life of Ivan Denisovich," the Soviet people would still have had no firsthand acquaintance with Solzhenitsyn's works.

If the Soviet secret police, the KGB, had not driven Solzhenitsyn's friend to suicide in extracting from her a hidden copy of his major expose of the Soviet police and prison system, even the West would not soon be reading this new work.

If Solzhenitsyn were not now a world famous author and recipient of the Nobel Prize for Literature, he would certainly feel the unrestrained wrath of the Kremlin rulers and be heard of no more. This could still happen, of course, but would present many problems to the Soviet leadership

ACCORDING to advance reports, the new book, "Gulag Archipelago" is a factual documentary — "an experiment in literary investigation" — which Solzhenitsyn accumulated over the years with the help of over 200 fellow victims of the Soviet system of terror. It examines in great detail, through innumerable case histories, the operations of the Soviet apparatus of repression established by Lenin after the Bolshevik take-over in 1917, built up by Stalin, briefly relaxed under Khrushchev and now, according to the author, again operating with renewed vigor under Brezhnev.

The full 260,000-word manuscript of "Gulag Archipelago," which apparently reached the West some time ago, was published in the original Russian on Dec. 28, 1973 by the so-called YMCA Press in Paris, a small publishing house supported by Russian emigres. Harper & Row will publish an English translation in the United States in April, and translations in other major languages will appear shortly in Western Europe.

Solzhenitsyn has made it clear that he had intended to withhold this explosive work for an indefinite period for fear of compromising still living individuals identified therein. However, in August 1973, after a week of brutal interrogation, the KGB succeeded in extracting a hidden copy from Solzhenitsyn's friend, Mrs. Elizaveta Voronyanskaya, who had typed the original manuscript. Mrs. Voronyanskaya committed suicide. In the circumstances, the best way to provide some further protection to the persons named in the manuscript was wide publicity and Solzhenitsyn authorized publication.

IN A SENSE, Solzhenitsyn's new book will reveal little new to those who lived in the Soviet Union in Stalin's day or who follow Soviet affairs closely. Western scholars have researched and published studies on the subject, based principally on accounts of victims who escaped to the outside world. However, Solzhenitsyn has deliberately chosen — even fought — to remain in his homeland. In this atmosphere and with firsthand access to unique sources, he has probed both more broadly and more profoundly.

Even in the relatively short advance excerpts which have been published in the American press, I find the case histories of two friends of mine — one an employe in the American Embassy with dual American and Russian nationality and the other a Soviet artist and state employe authorized to associate with foreigners — both of whom disappeared without a trace in 1948, during Stalin's purges.

Inquiries as to their fate at the time were rudely rejected by the Soviet authorities as being none of our business. Like Solzhenitsyn himself, both reappeared after the limited amnesty following Stalin's death, older than their years and suffering from the physical results of the brutalities inflicted upon them.

Nor will there be any great surprises for anyone familiar with Khrushchev's "Secret Speech," denouncing Stalin's crimes at a closed session of the 20th Congress of the Communist Party of the Soviet Union in February 1956. However, Khrushchev fumed at Stalin and wept for his fallen Communist Party comrades; Solzhenitsyn fumes at the system and weeps for an enslaved and maltreated people.

ALEKSANDR Solzhenitsyn was born on Dec. 11, 1918, son of an officer in the Czar's army who had died a few months earlier. He was a brilliant student, particularly in mathematics and science. Despite his so-called bourgeois origins, he became an active and devoted member of the Komsomol, the young Communist organization, and a firm believer in the Soviet system.

Gradually, however, the purges of the 1930's began to shake his faith, at least in Stalin's leadership, and his skepticism was intensified by the indecision and chaos which, in the first days of World War II, brought Russia to the brink of defeat. By that time, Solzhenitsyn was in the Red Army, first as a private, then a captain and made the mistake of hinting at some of his critical views of the "Big Shot" in correspondence with a like-minded school friend serving on another front.

This indiscretion did not escape the fine sieve of the secret police. Consequently, the next eight years of Solzhenitsyn's life were passed in a series of interrogation sites, ordinary and specialized prisons, labor camps and isolated places of exile which he has described partially in previously published works and examines in depth in "Gulag Archipelago."

In these grim surroundings he came in contact with hundreds of other victims — former political personalities,

The world has been awed by Aleksandr Solzhenitsyn's audacious defiance of Soviet authorities in authorizing publication in the West of his newest book, "Gulag Archipelago, 1918-1956." The Herald asked Foy D. Kohler, professor in the Center for Advanced International Studies at the University of Miami, and one-time (1962-1966) ambassador to the Soviet Union, to comment.

KOHLER

(Continued from preceding page)
errant intellectuals, religious leaders and members of Soviet minorities. These associations furthered his disenchantment, not just with Stalin but with the Soviet system as such.

I WAS BACK in Moscow as ambassador when the November 1962 issue of the literary monthly, Novy Mir, came out with Solzhenitsyn's "One Day in the Life of Ivan Denisovich," describing in graphic and grisly detail the life of a political prisoner in a hard labor concentration camp in Siberia. The editor let it be known that Khrushchev had personally approved this publication and it was enthusiastically received by the Soviet public and press. However, it soon became clear that Khrushchev had not fully consulted his party associates and that the story had come as a bombshell to them. They apparently persuaded him to back down. In the ensuing months, he undertook a sort of half-hearted crackdown on the intellectuals and nothing else by Solzhenitsyn was published during the remainder of Khrushchev's tenure.

Khrushchev's successors took a harder line in attempting to control the continuing intellectual ferment. In December 1965, the KGB arrested two Soviet writers, Andrei Sinyavsky and Yuri Daniel, for sending manuscripts surreptitiously out of the country for publication. After a farcical trial, they were sentenced in February 1966 respectively to seven and five years of hard labor.

However, the Khrushchev era had removed some of the fear prevailing in Stalin's day and this trial provoked not only a stream of protest abroad but new mainfestations of dissidence at home.

Solzhenitsyn joined in the movement. In May 1967, he addressed a letter to the Soviet Writers' Union, calling on the union actively to seek the abolition of the repressive official censorship. When the manuscripts of his two new novels, "The First Circle" and "Cancer Ward," reached the West and were published in 1968, he again addressed the union. He denied that he had authorized their publication abroad, but at the same time protested the refusal of the Soviet authorities to allow their publication in the Soviet Union without the complete rewrite from an "ideological point of view" which the censorship had demanded.

IT SHOULD be noted that at this time the Soviet leaders were worried not only about intellectual dissidence at home but by the even greater and potentially contagious ferment in Czechoslovakia which had led them to take the drastic and politically expensive step of invading that country and suppressing "Dubcek liberalism" there in August 1968.

In 1969, the authorities stimulated Solzhenitsyn's expulsion from the Writers' Union and he has been subjected to official condemnation and increasing harassment in the ensuing years, being denied permission to live with his wife and children in Moscow, having his friends interrogated and harassed by the KGB, not daring to go to Stockholm to receive the Nobel Prize for Literature awarded to him in October 1970 for fear of having his citizenship canceled while he was out of the country.

Despite the wealth he has accumulated abroad, his ouster from the Writers' Union has meant the end of his ruble earnings at home and he has even had to find shelter in the country house of his friend, the great Russian cellist Rostropovitch.

NOTWITHSTANDING his problems, Solzhenitsyn has neither compromised his dignity and ideals, nor ceased his activities. In August 1971, his book "August 1914" was published abroad — the first volume of a planned epic study of World War I and the revolutionary era in Russia which Solzhenitsyn apparently hoped would be his major life work, comparable to Tolstoy's treatment of the Napoleonic era in "War and Peace." His eloquent protests to the Writers' Union have circulated in the underground "samizdat" (self-publishing) channels in the Soviet Union, and have found their way to the West.

So too have his appeals on behalf of other victims of the current purge against nonconformist intellectuals, his protest to the Russian Orthodox Patriarch against the church's role as a tool of the state, and his condemnation of "the demeaning compulsory internal passport system in which a place of residence may not be chosen by an individual but is chosen for him by the authorities . . . (a system which) does not exist even in the colonial countries of the world today."

SINCE 1970, Solzhenitsyn has from time to time joined his efforts with those of the famous Soviet physicist, so-called father of the Soviet H-Bomb, Andrei D. Sakharov, who long ago became disillusioned with the regime's policies and organized a "Committee for Human Rights in the USSR." However, in the past few years, the supporters of these two leaders have been largely cut way away or have been too terrified to stick to their guns, so that the two intellectual giants today stand practically alone as representatives of the yearnings of the Soviet people for a freer life and for human dignity.

The main feature of the current suppression campaign has been another publicized court process. Arrested in June, 1972, the historian Peotr Yakir and the economist Victor Krasin were finally tried and received light sentences in September 1973. KGB interrogation methods had paid off during the long months between the arrest and the trial. The underground newsletter "Chronicle of Current Events" which they had edited and which had circulated for five years

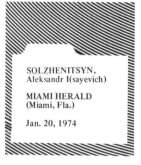

SOLZHENITSYN,
Aleksandr I(sayevich)

MIAMI HERALD
(Miami, Fla.)

Jan. 20, 1974

disappeared in November 1972. The accused apparently fingered some of their associates, who have disappeared from view, and in a staged press conference after the trial, they "confessed" that they had been working for an anti-Soviet organization abroad.

The effect of these public "confessions" was attenuated in the West by the recollection that Yakir had told Western correspondents before his arrest that: "If they beat me I will say anything. I know that from my former experiences in the camps. But you will know that it will not be the real me speaking." In April 1973, the man responsible for the successful crackdown, Chairman of the KGB, Yuri V. Andropov, was elevated to the top ruling circle as a full member of the Politburo of the Communist Party of the Soviet Union, the first Soviet secret police chief to be accorded this top status since the infamous Beria was liquidated in 1953.

UNTIL A YEAR ago, the Soviet government depended on secret police methods, the discipline of the Writers' Union, the official censorship and the like to enforce its monopoly of the written word. Early in 1973, it moved to establish a new legal basis for its control by adhering to the International Copyright Convention and establishing an "All-Union Copyright Agency" with the exclusive authority to transfer to foreign publishers any rights to the work of Soviet writers.

Although there may be some technical question as to timing, Solzhenitsyn's decision to authorize publication of "Gulag Archipelago" in the West stands in violation of at least the intent of the new law, and in clear violation of a host of other laws and decrees regulating the conduct of Soviet citizens. Worse than that in a social order based on the concept of man as servant of the state, rather than the state as servant of man, Solzhenitsyn's actions threaten the basic foundation of the Soviet establishment.

Such a situation would certainly never have been allowed to develop in Stalin's day, and even now any lesser figure would already have been taken in hand.

HOWEVER, Moscow has for some years been preoccupied and continues to be preoccupied with its conflict with Peking. Highly allergic to the idea of a struggle on two fronts at once, the Soviet leadership has sought to stabilize its relations with the West. This it has tried to do in the form of its normalization treaties with West Germany, through the convocation of a so-called "Conference on Security and Cooperation in Europe" (CSCE), and by improvement of bilateral relations with Western countries, especially the other "super-power," the United States.

Plagued by economic deficiencies and management problems, the Soviet leaders have also sought access to Western trade and economic cooperation and to Western science and technology. But these Western democracies are sensitive to the state of human rights in the Soviet empire and have repeatedly raised a hue and cry about Soviet persecution of individuals and suppression of human rights. Particularly in connection with CSCE, the West has made a great point of seeking a freer flow of people and ideas between East and West, as the price of confirming Soviet World War II gains in Europe and agreeing to increased cooperation in other fields.

THIS HAS given Moscow a considerable problem since Soviet policy has been precisely to tighten the screws at home while promoting "detente" — which it calls "peaceful coexistence" — abroad. Drastic and dramatic action against such figures as Solzhenitsyn and Sakharov would thus risk bringing Soviet foreign policy goals into jeopardy.

At least for the present, this is perhaps the best protection that Solzhenitsyn could have for his defiance. However, the very subject matter of "Gulag Archipelago," of which the Soviet people will learn through foreign radio broadcasts and by word-of-mouth, should provide some additional protection. There is hardly a Soviet family which did not suffer from Stalin's long reign of terror and the abiding fear of a return to his extremist methods would be stirred up by repression of Solzhenitsyn.

Promptly after the Paris publication of "Gulag Archipelago," the official Soviet news agency TASS, on Jan. 2, 1974, issued a statement condemning Solzhenitsyn as a tool of reactionary foreign circles "trying to poison the atmosphere of detente, to sow mistrust in relations between peoples, and to blacken the Soviet Union, its people and its policy."

A FURTHER TASS commentary the following day labeled Solzhenitsyn a "renegade" with a "a really fierce hatred of his country." Both of these documents were for foreign consumption and did not appear in the Soviet domestic press. On Jan. 9, a commentator on Soviet domestic TV attacked Solzhenitsyn as a "turncoat and internal emigrant" and warned his viewers against listening to foreign radio broadcasts about this new "evil smelling" book which "deviled and muddied" Soviet life.

The Party daily, Pravda, and other journals have reprinted foreign Communist comment critical of Solzhenitsyn. No Soviet source, however, has discussed the actual content of "Gulag Archipelago."

Character assassination and police harassment will surely continue but the Kremlin must weigh its actions very carefully in dealing more forcefully with Solzhenitsyn.

(Also see preceding article)

Solzhenitsyn's ex-wife labels work 'artistic research'

SOLZHENITSYN, Aleksandr I(sayevich) and RESHETOVSKAYA, Natalya A.
OREGONIAN (Portland, Ore.)
June 30, 1974

By NOVOSTI PRESS AGENCY

The following article was submitted to The Oregonian by the Information Department of the Soviet Embassy. Novosti Press Agency is "a non-governmental news agency sponsored by the Soviet Journalists Union, the Soviet Writers Union, the Union of Soviet Societies of Friendship and Cultural Relations with Foreign Countries and the Society for the Dissemination of Political and Scientific Knowledge."

The article was elicited in response to a report from the New York Times telling of a manuscript attributed to Natalya A. Reshetovskaya, ex-wife of Alexander Solzhenitsyn, purportedly revealing the true story behind "The Gulag Archipelago."

A review of "The Gulag Archipelago" by Associate Editor Malcolm Bauer appears on page 15 of the Sunday Day Section.

"MY DEAREST of all! Even if we are to live as absolute strangers you should know that you are dearer to me than all, all others . . .

". . . And, in any case, I did not save your life, but you saved mine, and even more than my life . . ."

Solzhenitsyn once wrote these words to Natalya Reshetovskaya, who lived with him for more than a quarter of a century, as his faithful friend, wife, secretary and who was his moral support in moments of trouble. It was to her that he told his innermost secrets.

Reshetovskaya lives today in Ryazan, an ancient Russian city on the Oka River. She has a documentary on her life, which she dedicated to the women of her generation.

Novosti Press Agency correspondent Boris Antonov visited Reshetovskaya.

RESHETOVSKAYA: "Solzhenitsyn and I met in 1936. Both of us were first-year students at Rostov State University, he attended the Faculty of Physics and Mathematics, and I studied at the Faculty of Chemistry. In 1940 we were married.

"In 1970 we celebrated our thirtieth wedding anniversary and on March 13, 1973, we were divorced. In articles which appeared in connection with his (divorce) in foreign newspapers, attempts were made to sympathize with me, a lot was written about the material side of the question. But for me, our divorce was a moral problem. I am well off. I have a good profession — I am a chemical scientist. Twenty-five years ago I did my thesis and earned the degree of Candidate of Science (Chemistry). For twenty years I lectured to students at the Ryazan Agricultural Institute. My earnings were quite enough for both of us."

Is your book dedicated to Solzhenitsyn?

RESHETOVSKAYA: "This book deals with my life. It covers a long time span, actually the first book (maybe there will be another) is from 1936 to 1964, almost 28 years. I wanted to present my life with Solzhenitsyn as accurately as possible, or rather, reproduce it as accurately as possible. I don't want any legends to confuse the story of our life together.

"My old habit of keeping a diary has helped me be as factual and honest as possible, and I inherited the habit of keeping all my mother's letters. I have letters from my father to my mother, written before the revolution; letters from Solzhenitsyn to me; letters written during the war; altogether 248 letters, 220 of which have been preserved. We numbered our correspondence. Here are my own letters to him at the front. They are nearly all intact since I brought them back myself when I visited him at the front. These photographs taken at the front, in the Byelorussian forests, in the spring of 1944 will be included in my book.

"I was Solzhenitsyn's secretary. I read and registered, sorted and classified all incoming letters, all documents and materials. Everything was pasted together, everything was filed. We both took photographs and I kept a photo-diary.

"He always approved of my looking after his affairs and keeping diaries. In the end, when I decided to write a book, he would read my notes. Sometimes he would laugh: 'Oh, and I had forgotten all about that.' Sometimes he prompted me: 'Here, I'll add something for you.' So my 'creative work' was fully approved in the beginning, and I continued it, my basic principle being the desire for maximum accuracy."

And have you read the Gulag Archipelago?

RESHETOVSKAYA: "I am familiar with the Archipelago since I typed it myself. I participated in all of Solzhenitsyn's work.

"In the West attempts were sometimes made to present the Archipelago as veracity of the highest degree. Such unconditional recognition of everything that Solzhenitsyn says is proof of an absolutely uncritical attitude toward him. I know well that Solzhenitsyn's personal impressions about people, events and the like were his main criterion of truth. He unconditionally accepted information which required careful verification and specification as truth. It is known (and this refers to any country) that if you listen to the stories of people who have been in prison, you get the impression that only innocent people languish behind bars. Not many convicts like to tell the truth about what they were sentenced for. A man will invent a 'fairy tale' and tell it to others. Solzhenitsyn sometimes accepted such stories as truth. He formed certain ideas from them, rejecting everything that did not fit in with it.

"To a considerable extent this material is camp folklore. But in the West this folklore was declared to be a genuine reflection of history. That flattered the author. After all, he did not accidentally subtitle his work 'An Experiment in Artistic Research.' It is an experiment, an attempt. And not historical, not scientific research."

Did you know Nikolai Vitkevich, Solzhenitsyn's old friend, who is mentioned in the Archipelago?

RESHETOVSKAYA: "Me? Good God! I knew Nikolai before I knew Solzhenitsyn. We shared the same desk for five years in Rostov University, studying chemistry. Here is a photograph from our student days — here am I, here is Vitkevich, this is Solzhenitsyn, this is Kirill Simonyan and his wife Lida Ezherets.

"During the war, Vitkevich and I corresponded. Look here, these are his letters to me from the front. In the sixties Vitkevich lived and worked in Ryazan, he used to visit us."

Do you believe Vitkevich?

RESHETOVSKAYA: "I have no grounds not to believe him; I cannot disbelieve him. He is an exceptionally honest man. Open, outspoken, simply not capable of telling lies. He is even somewhat antagonistic, due to his habit of telling the turth to one's face."

Do you mention Vitkevich in your book?

RESHETOVSKAYA: "Of course I do, where I write about our student years, about the war and the front."

Vitkevich wrote a letter to Novosti Press Agency, accusing Solzhenitsyn, and then made a statement over TV. I quote his words:

"According to the law, when I was being rehabilitated I was shown the papers of my trial," Vitkevich said. "That was the most terrible day of my life. I saw the minutes of Solzhenitsyn's interrogations. From them it appeared that beginning with 1940 I had systematically conducted anti-Soviet propaganda, attempted to set up an illegal subversive organization, drawn up plans for forcibly changing the policy ➡

(Continued from preceding page)

of the party and the state, slandered (even 'maliciously,' that is what Solzhenitsyn wrote) Stalin, etc. I did not believe my eyes. But I knew the signature well. Nor did the handwriting leave any doubts, in which Solzhenitsyn himself had made additions and corrections to the minutes, signing in the margin each time.

SOLZHENITSYN, Aleksandr I(sayevich)
and
RESHETOVSKAYA, Natalya A.

OREGONIAN June 30, 1974
(Portland, Ore.)

"Having thus proved the 'sincerity' of his confessions, Solzhenitsyn was recommended for mercy. I was given two years more, although I was accused of a lesser crime."

RESHETOVSKAYA: "Yes, I know about this statement by Nikolai Vitkevich. What Koka said explained many things to me, which formerly had seemed strange. Solzhenitsyn, a highly intolerant, rigidly exacting man, who constantly insists upon sacrifices from others, yet does not forgive them the slightest mistakes, in the Archipelago suddenly asks for mercy for those who were not sufficiently brave, who were weak at the interrogation. And this is asked by a man who himself does not forgive others anything, who demands s a c r i f i c e s from others, who flings stones at each and all."

Solzhenitsyn: Man and Myth

SOLZHENITSYN, Aleksandr I(sayevich)

MIAMI HERALD
(Miami, Fla.)

June 23, 1974 [See also CA-25/28]

By JONATHAN YARDLEY
Herald Book Editor

Solzhenitsyn Now
. . . he is in exile

It is time to come to grips with Aleksandr I. Solzhenitsyn. For more than a decade the Russian author has been the uncomplaining beneficiary of a mythology and hagiography unmatched, perhaps, by that accorded any other serious artist of his time. Now, with the publication in the United States this month of three of his books, the process of sanctification may well be completed — which means that now is a propitious moment for looking at Solzhenitsyn and his work with clinical dispassion, for attempting to separate the man from the myth.

The myth is utterly enormous. Since the publication 12 years ago of his first novel, **One Day in the Life of Ivan Denisovich,** Solzhenitsyn has become a hero in almost every country except his own — and even there he has a wide underground following. His books have sold millions of copies. His picture appears on magazine covers the world over. Presidents and prime ministers quote him and praise him. Critics rank him with Tolstoy and Dostoyevsky. Young people — and millions of their elders as well — revere him as the most prominent living symbol of artistic freedom and resistance to oppressive authority.

OURS IS the age of the superstar, and Solzhenitsyn is the undisputed superstar of that world where politics and letters intermingle. There is, in fact, good reason for him to be so widely and deeply admired. At the age of 55, he has done much:

- Three of his novels — **Ivan Denisovich, The First Circle** and **The Cancer Ward** — are among the most important works of fiction of the postwar era.
- His survival of the Russian prison camps, "eternal exile" in his native country and a near-fatal siege of cancer is a model of personal courage and endurance which all must respect.
- His fidelity to his literary and political convictions despite merciless official harassment is an inspiration to all artists and political dissidents.
- His outspoken criticism of Soviet governments, both past and present, has awakened millions in Russia and abroad to the outrages perpetrated in the name of Marxist ideology.

ALL THAT is true, and for all that Solzhenitsyn deserves praise, admiration and respect. But there is more to him than that, and it too must be taken into account:

- The claims of his Western admirers notwithstanding, he is neither a "liberal" nor a "democrat." He may be anti-Marxist, but he is also a fierce Russian nationalist who is contemptuous of the Western democracies and sympathetic to authoritarian rule.
- His writing, in particular his nonfiction, is marred by melodrama and exaggeration. He is blatantly conscious of his literary reputation, pitting himself against Tolstoy, Dostoyevsky and Chekhov much as Norman Mailer publicly goes "into the ring" against Tolstoy and Hemingway.
- He is adroit at self-promotion, and has skillfully used the Western press both to enhance his "image" and to advance his own purposes. There is no evidence that he is offended or embarrassed by those who would portray him as the Joan of Arc of the Russian intelligentsia.

TO SAY all of this is not to say that a man almost universally regarded as "good" is in point of fact "bad." It is to say that Aleksandr Solzhenitsyn is a considerably more complex man, artist and politician than his

(Continued from preceding page)

public image suggests. That contention is vigorously supported by the three books that have descended upon American readers this month. They are:

The Gulag Archipelago (Harper and Row. $12.50 hardcover, $1.95 paperback). This 660-page volume, subtitled "An Experiment in Literary Investigation," contains the first two parts of a seven-part account of Russian repression under Lenin and Stalin — a repression that, Solzhenitsyn says, claimed 66 million Russian lives. It has been translated, with apparent fidelity to Solzhenitsyn's style, by Thomas P. Whitney.

Letter to the Soviet Leaders (Harper and Row. $3.50 hardcover). This is the text of a 15,000-word letter Solzhenitsyn sent to the Kremlin on Sept. 5, 1973. He decided to make it public after being expelled from Russia last February.

Solzhenitsyn: A Pictorial Autobiography (Farrar, Straus and Giroux. $8.95 hardcover, $2.95 paperback). First published in 1971 by The Nobel Foundation, this collection of photographs is accompanied by quotations from the author's books, lectures, occasional writings and interviews.

The last is certainly the least important of the three. In fact, its only justification appears to be to cash in on the cult that has arisen around Solzhenitsyn. The older photographs have clear historical interest, but the more recent ones are familiar to any reader of newspapers and magazines; most of them show the author in the solemn, beard-ringed pose that the world now knows so well.

(In a brief but penetrating article in the current issue of The Columbia Journalism Review, entitled "The Selling of Solzhenitsyn," the Sovietologist Jeri Laber quotes a 1972 New York Times interviewer as commenting: '"When he posed for pictures with his family, Mr. Solzhenitsyn was all smiles. But posing alone, he was somber and refused to be coaxed into a grin. 'This is a time to be serious,' he explained, evidently thinking) of his world image."

THE BOOK, which one must assume has Solzhenitsyn's approval since there is no indication to the contrary, is prefaced by a comment from the German novelist Heinrich Boll:

"What surprises me most in Solzhenitsyn is the calm that he emanates — he who has been threatened and fought over more than any other man on earth. Nothing, it seems, can destroy his serenity, neither the terrible insults to which he has been exposed in his own country nor the banishment — the 'one-way ticket' — which he has been offered and which he has refused. At the same time, Solzhenitsyn's calm is not at all that of a gilded Olympian monument but that of a living man, concerned and involved with the course of human events."

That is strong stuff — the material of hagiography. It ought to bring a blush to Solzhenitsyn's cheeks; apparently it does not.

SOLZHENITSYN, Aleksandr I(sayevich) (1918-)
MIAMI HERALD (Miami, Fla.) June 23, 1974

Letter to the Soviet Leaders is another matter. It was widely published and discussed upon its release last winter, so readers doubtless are aware that it is a powerful call to the Soviet hierarchy for an end to ideological haranguing, for a national policy that places the interests of the Russian people ahead of international aggrandizement, and for a sensible development policy that uses the environment without exploitation. Few passages in any of Solzhenitsyn's work are more damning than his outcry against the possibility of ideological war with China.

"And what do you think will happen? That when war breaks out, both belligerents will simply fly the purity of their ideology on their flags? And that sixty million of our fellow countrymen will allow themselves to be killed because the sacred truth is written on page 533 of Lenin and not on page 335 as our adversary claims? Surely only the very, very first of them will die for that . . .

"Give them their ideology! Let the Chinese leaders glory in it for a while. And for that matter, let them shoulder the whole sackful of unfulfillable international obligations, let them grunt and heave and instruct humanity, and foot all the bills for their absurd economics (a million a day just to Cuba), and let them support terrorists and guerrillas in the Southern Hemisphere too, if they like."

THAT IS wise counsel, delivered with great passion. But there are other aspects of the **Letter** that have received less attention. Solzhenitsyn dismisses the Western powers as "weak and effete" (yes, "effete"), and claims that "the United States has a weak and undeveloped national consciousness." He sneers at "that turbulent 'democracy run riot' in which once every four years the politicians, and indeed the entire country, nearly kill themselves over an electoral campaign, trying to gratify the masses (and this is something which not only internal groups but also foreign governments have repeatedly played on); in which a judge, flouting his obligatory independence in order to pander to the passions of society, acquits a man who steals and publishes Defense Department secrets." Small wonder that William F. Buckley Jr. so ardently admires Solzhenitsyn's **Letter.**

The **Letter** reveals Solzhenitsyn as an elitist: "Yes, of course: freedom is moral. But only if it keeps within *certain* bounds, beyond which it degenerates into complacency and licentiousness." It also reveals him (as do many passages in **Gulag**) as a not-very-thinly disguised Tsarist, one who looks back with no little affection on an "authoritarian order (which) possessed a strong moral foundation, embryonic and rudimentary though it was — not the ideology of universal violence, but Christian Orthodoxy." Or, as he says later, "It is not authoritarianism itself that is intolerable, but the ideological lies that are daily foisted upon us."

Those ideas are fundamental to Solzhenitsyn's philosophy, and no one should dispute that he is entitled to them. The difficulty is that, in the general excitement over his political and artistic boldness and his vigorous embrace of Russian Christian Orthodoxy, these ideas have been clouded over. They simply do not sit well with Solzhenitsyn's "image" as a symbol of freedom, so they have been conveniently ignored. This is not Solzhenitsyn's fault, but that of his idolators; presumably, as a serious artist and Russian patriot, Solzhenitsyn would wish to be judged on the whole body of his thought, not merely those aspects of it that happen to suit the convenience of his admirers.

AND THEN there is **The Gulag Archipelago.** Its monumental importance is beyond argument. According to Sovietologists, it adds little crucial new information to our knowledge of the Lenin-Stalin holocaust, the ghastly essence of which historians have discovered in recent years. But it puts an intimate human dimension on "the other holocaust" that no other document can rival. It is the result not merely of Solzhenitsyn's own prison-camp experiences, but of intensive research and "reports, memoirs and letters by 227 witnesses." It is the report of a writer obsessed with his obligation to history and to his fellow countrymen.

The title is explained by Thomas P. Whitney: "The image evoked by this title is that of one far-flung 'country' with millions of 'natives,' consisting of an archipelago of islands, some as tiny as a detention cell in a railroad station and others as vast as a large Western European country, contained within another country — the USSR. This archipelago is made up of the enormous network of penal institutions and all the rest of the web of machinery for police oppression and terror imposed throughout the author's period of reference on all Soviet life. Gulag is the acronym for the Chief Administration of Corrective Labor Camps which supervised the larger part of this system."

The years covered begin in 1917 almost immediately after the Revolution and end in the middle 50s with the ascension of Khrushchev — Solzhenitzyn makes clear, as does his own life, that per-

(Continued from preceding page)
secution and oppression are scarcely things of the past in the Soviet Union. The portrait Solzhenitsyn paints — in detail so fine and careful that it is excruciating — is of a nation in the grip of insanity. At the beginning of the third chapter of the first book, there is an utterly chilling passage:

"If the intellectuals in the plays of Chekhov who spent all their time guessing what would happen in twenty, thirty or forty years had been told that in forty years interrogation by torture would be practiced in Russia; that prisoners would have their skulls squeezed within iron rings; that a human being would be lowered into an acid bath; that they would be trussed up naked to be bitten by ants and bedbugs; that a ramrod heated over a primus stove would be thrust up their anal canal (the 'secret brand'); that a man's genitals would be slowly crushed beneath he toe of a jackboot; and that, in the luckiest possible circumstances, prisoners would be tortured by being kept from sleeping for a week, by thirst, and by being beaten to a bloody pulp, not one of Chekhov's plays would have gotten to its end because all the heroes would have gone off to insane asylums."

THERE ARE many themes in **The Gulag Archipelago,** but that perhaps is the crucial one: the appalling contrast between the civility of Chekhov's Russia and the insanity of Stalin's Russia. Throughout the whole length of the book, the reader can feel Solzhenitsyn struggling for an answer to the question that torments him: How could his Russia, his beloved "Motherland," have done this?

Implicit in that question is the acknowledgment that all Russians — that all people — have within them the capacity to do unspeakable evil. It is an acknowledgment that Solzhenitsyn somewhat trickily escapes: "But no; that's not the way it is! To do evil a human being must first of all believe that what he's doing is good, or else that it's a well-considered act in conformity with natural law. Fortunately, it is in the nature of the human being to seek a justification for his actions . . . Ideology — that is what gives evildoing its long-sought justification and gives the evildoers the necessary steadfastness and determination."

THAT IS rather a chicken-and-egg argument. What comes first, the ideology or the evil? Is the evil lurking inside man, awaiting an ideology to spring it loose? Or does the ideology arise and awaken an evil previously unsuspected? Solzhenitsyn evidently argues the latter, because his overriding purpose in **The Gulag Archipelago** is to place the blame for the holocaust squarely at the feet of Marxism, the "discredited and bankrupt doctrine" which he so tellingly attacks in the **Letter.**

Perhaps, in fact, Marxism is the villain. But there is a complex philosophical question here — a conundrum, really — that Solzhenitsyn gets around in slippery fashion. To blame evil on ideology, or to say that ideology gives men the excuse they seek to do the evil they wish, is too pat. For a Hitler or a Stalin, a Goebbels or a Molotov, the argument may work; it can be contended that these, and others like them, were demented men who used ideology as springboard to the evil that was their real purpose.

SOLZHENITSYN,
Aleksandr I(sayevich)

MIAMI HERALD
(Miami, Fla.)

June 23, 1974

But what does one say about evil that is unwittingly committed in the name of good purposes? To take a contemporary case in point, what about the American role in Vietnam? A good argument can be made that the United States committed considerable evil against the people of that country. Yet neither a Lyndon Johnson nor a William Calley is an "evil" man , and the "freedom" for which Vietnam fought was not a handle the United States grabbed in order to flush the evil out of its system. The roots of evil are complex, and often cannot be traced at all. Solzhenitsyn's reasoning, however well intended, is too slick.

BE THAT as it may, his portrayal of Russia under Lenin and Stalin is devastating. He describes, in deeply personal terms, the splintering trauma of arrest: "Arrest! Need it be said that it is a breaking point in your life, a bolt of lightning which has scored a direct hit on you? That it is an unassimilable spiritual earthquake not every person can cope with, as a result of which people often slip into insanity? . . . That's what arrest is: it's a blinding flash and a blow which shifts the present instantly into the past and the impossible into omnipotent actuality."

He describes the elaborate legal traps devised by the regime to round up political dissidents, suspected dissidents, eccentrics — anyone who for whatever bizarre reason it felt posed a threat. He describes the tortures of the interrogation, the great public trials and the private hearings that always reached the same result, the crowded, fetid prison trains, the transit camps. And in the end of the second book he anticipates the agonies he will document in the third:

"We have reviewed and considered all the methods of delivering prisoners, and we have found that they are all . . . worse. We have examined the transit prisons, but we have not found any that were good. And even the last human hope that there is something better ahead, that it will be better in camp, is a false hope.

"In camp it will be . . . worse."

What Solzhenitsyn has done in bringing together this mass of detail cannot be underestimated; he has drawn up the most sweeping indictment yet delivered against the rulers of the Soviet Union and their henchmen — an indictment that surely must give pause to the leaders of other nations as they move toward "detente," or "peaceful coexistence," with the heirs to this awful legacy.

Yet **The Gulag Archipelago** is far more persuasive as an indictment than as a work of literature — which is no small irony when one considers Solzhenitsyn's literary standing. It is loosely organized and, as was suggested above, at times loosely reasoned. Solzhenitsyn is not content to let the horrible details of his story speak for themselves, but frequently insists on trumping them up with contrived melodrama and heavy-handed sarcasm. His wit can be mordant, but it also can be inappropriate. He uses both italics and exclamation points to excess.

The Gulag Archipelago may well be a "great book," in the sense that it doubtless with change many lives, alter many preconceptions, and perhaps someday even may help change an entire nation. But it is not great literature, and anyone who claims as much for it is letting political enthusiasms override basic literary considerations.

All of which leads us back to the question of Aleksandr I. Solzhenitsyn. He says that **Gulag** is not intended to be a "political expose;" neither is this intended to be an "expose" of Aleksandr Solzhenitsyn. There are no grounds upon which to vilify him, no grounds upon which to deny his high position in the world of letters, no grounds on which to question the hold he has upon the contemporary imagination. His reputation is secure, as it should be.

But Solzhenitsyn is neither a superman nor a saint, and the problem is that he is too often represented as either or both. It does not seem to be enough for us — particularly those of us in the media who have celebrated him so lavishly — that he is a genuine hero; we seem intent upon making him into the hero that he is not. We deny his blemishes in order to fawn over his virtues — and in so doing not merely delude ourselves but do a disservice to his real accomplishments.

It is not a matter of demeaning Solzhenitsyn; it is a matter of keeping him in perspective. Jeri Laber, in The Columbia Journalism Review, has done so:

"Solzhenitsyn is alive and well among us. That he is not the 'liberal' we would like him to be should not really matter. We can admire him for his courage and for the cause which he has made his own without necessarily embracing his entire worldview. Perhaps now we can set about learning what we can from his extraordinary life."

Baby MD is desexing famed book

SPOCK, Benjamin H.
(1903 -)

LONG ISLAND PRESS
(Jamaica, N.Y.)

Aug. 19, 1974

[See also CA-21/22]

By KAY BARTLETT

Dr. Benjamin Spock, pediatrician, presidential candidate and peace protestor, muses on a theoretical problem that a Spock baby may have in raising his or her children.

"I can see a 10-year-old coming to the mother or father and announcing he or she wanted to try sex or drugs or something. And the bewildered parent countering with, 'Well, I wish you'd wait until you were 15 like I did."

Dr. Spock laughs his almost booming laugh as he hypothesizes. He's not really serious It's just interesting. He's really more interested these days in promoting his brand of "democratic socialism" and bursting the rumor that he changed his mind about how to bring up baby.

The author of "Baby and Child Care" is 71 years old now . . . still a strident 6-foot-4, still riding his five-speed bicycle in Central Park every day, still his own best public relations man. He's working on the fourth version of the famous book . . . first published in 1946 . . . that has sold 26 million copies and been translated into 32 languages, including Urdu, Bahasa and Tamil.

"I'm in the middle of desexing it," says Spock, who described himself as a former male chauvinist. "We were all sexists. Gloria Steinem once told me Freud and I were responsible for all sorts of sexist attitudes. I was delighted to have been put in the company of Freud, but that was just the general attitude then."

IN THE NEW VERSION, which he hopes to have out in about a year, baby will be referred to as he or she . . . instead of just he. It will not always be mother doing this or that. It will be the parent. Spock, the adored baby doctor whose book is as warm and friendly as he is, turned many mothers against him when he protested against the Vietnam War in the late 1960s and ran as a presidential candidate in 1972 on the People's party ticket.

"When I used to be recognized on the streets on in airports, I would always smile and nod. And then after this, when I'd be recognized, I would sometimes see a dark cloud of anger sweep over the person's face," Spock says.

He also says his political activism has caused him and his wife, Jane, to get a whole new set of friends. His old establishment friends found themselves no longer compatible with the man who marched beside hippies in the 1960s, was convicted of conspiracy in 1968 and sentenced to two years in jail, later overturned by a higher court, and preached there was no difference between the Republican and the Democratic parties so the only hope was a third party.

Spock spends six months of the year sailing . . . either on the 35-foot ketch he keeps in the Virgin Islands or on the smaller 23-footer he keeps anchored off the coast of Maine. He's trying to get his legal address changed to the Virgin Islands but he says the IRS is not crazy about the idea.

The rest of the time he lives in a Manhattan apartment on the chic East Side. He still lectures six to eight times a month, down from six times a week during his notoriety. "Undergraduates were very interested then in a man indicted by the federal government. I guess I'm old hat now."

He speaks on politics, baby care, education and recently was asked to speak on human sexuality. "That surprised me since I am a known conservative in that area. What was even more surprising was that the students were enthusiastic about what I said."

Spock was the first lecturer, followed by Bob Guccione, publisher of Penthouse magazine, Christine Jorgensen and Dr. Joyce Brothers. "Only undergraduates would consider that a balanced panel on sexuality," Spock laughs.

Spock donates his honorariums to the People's party. He also finds time to write a monthly column for Redbook magazine, and to collect $60,000 a year in royalties from his famous baby book.

WHAT INFLUENCE has this man had on the generation he helped bring up,—the generation that burned draft cards, took over administration buildings at the universities, replaced "neat" and "cool" with a more shrill and graphic vocabulary, marched on the Pentagon, crusaded for Eugene McCarthy, stumped for George McGovern, fled to Canada and Sweden to avoid the draft and generally defied authority?

"I think I played some part in making parents trust their children more than parents in previous generations did. But actually, the underpinnings of 'Baby and Child Care' are Freudian and Deweyian psychology. Freud said love is much more important than punishment and Dewey said children are wild to learn if you just give them the proper materials. I was really picking up and advocating the concepts of Freud and Dewey."

The conservatively dressed doctor also maintains that the permissivist label was never pinned on him until after he entered the mudslinging world of politics.

SPOCK'S POLITICS have gone full circle, starting with the father who looked like and admired Calvin Coolidge and instilled in his son the virtues of the Republican party and the establishment. He was a New Deal Democrat for most of his adult life, campaigned for Lyndon B. Johnson in 1964 and then, as he puts it, "Johnson knocked the blinders off."

"I did enough campaigning that he called me up to thank me two days after the election," Spock recalls. "He said, 'Dr. Spock, I hope I prove worthy of your trust.' And I, having no idea he was completely unworthy of our trust, at least as far as Southeast Asia was concerned, said I was sure he would be. Three months later he suddenly did the exact opposite of what he said he would do. The second jolt came when he tried to throw me in jail for telling the truth to the American people."

Spock figures his legal defense cost him $80,000 . . . $60,000 of which was raised by friends.

The white-haired doctor attributes the success of "Baby and Child Care" to a number of factors.

"First of all, it was cheap. It was 25 cents when it first came out and now it's 95 cents. That's still pretty good for 650 pages. And it's a mine of information. It contained both the psychological and the physical. Previous pediatricians' books were just rules of thumb. Like, if a baby sucks his thumb, put some nasty stuff on it." Spock was one of the first doctors to intern in both psychiatry and pediatrics. His book was friendly and not dictatorial.

In fact, it starts out in boldface: "You know more than you think you do." In the 1957 edition, Spock says he put more emphasis on the child's desire for leadership from the parents, and in the 1968 version he added more on adolescence.

* * *

SPOCK BELIEVES the most fundamental thing that has happened to young people is that they no longer are intimidated by authority. And he thinks that's good.

Spock's eldest son, Michael, is 41, the father of three and the director of the Children's Museum in Boston. His other child, John, is 30, an architect by training but now involved in counseling in Los Angeles. He is not married.

* * *

SPOCK AND a grandson had long discussions on pornography. The youngster thinks anything goes. The doctor is conservative. Spock recently volunteered to pick up his grandson at camp. The youngster asked if "Ben," as he calls his grandfather, would make a speech. Sure, said Dr. Spock.

And then the teenager added: "But don't make it on pornography. That wouldn't go over so good."

Spock's mother, who lived until she was 93, brought Ben up in a very stict manner. "I was the most intimidated child you've ever seen. I was scared of dogs, policemen, I was such a goody-goody all my life. Even now when I see a policeman I wonder what I did wrong,"

His mother was ill in 1968 when she was told her son had been arrested. The response, from the mother who trusted her son, was simply: "Well, I'm sure it's for a good cause."

(Also see preceding article)

A New Spock? The Doctor Says No

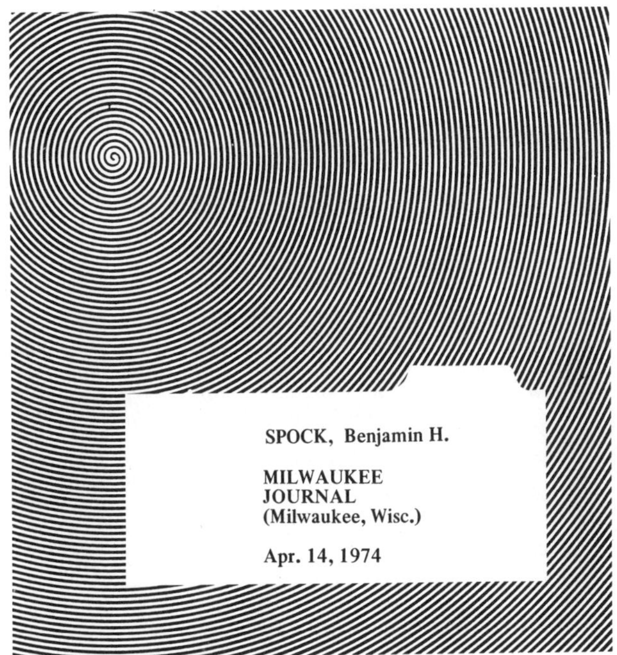
SPOCK, Benjamin H.

MILWAUKEE JOURNAL (Milwaukee, Wisc.)

Apr. 14, 1974

By Lois Blinkhorn
of The Journal Staff

Dr. Benjamin Spock, it seems, has fallen upon hard times.

The celebrated pediatrician, whose classic book "Baby and Child Care" has seen thousands of children through croup, toilet training and teething, is now blamed for nearly all that is young and disagreeable. And that includes everything from the drug culture to the runny nosed kid down the street who doesn't say please and thank you.

Even the doctor himself has joined his critics, if one is to believe recent wire news reporting that Spock, writing in Redbook magazine, admits he must share the blame for the brattiness of some of today's children.

A Turnabout?

Has the good doctor done a turnabout? Does he look upon what he has wrought and find that the product is bratty, un-co-operative and unpleasant? Has he changed his philosophy on bringing up children? And was that philosophy as permissive as his critics charge?

Spock answered some of those questions in a telephone interview last week as he discussed the Redbook article along with his new book, "Raising Children in a Difficult Time" (W. W. Norton & Company, Inc.). The book will be published next week.

No, he hasn't recanted his philosophy of child rearing and, yes, his Redbook column was misinterpreted, declared the feisty pediatrician.

"In the first place, I made the mistake of using the word 'bratty' in the article. Then the editors titled it 'How Not to Bring Up a Bratty Child.' That one word released a lot of hostilities," said Spock. "There are lots of people who like to think I'm wrong." Why?

"Because of my involvement in the antiwar movement, of course," he replied.

But back to that Redbook article. What did he say to get everyone so excited?

Can't Be Firm

He started out with the statement that the inability to be firm is the most common problem of parents. One basic reason is that — consciously or otherwise — they don't want to stir up the same kinds of arguments and conflicts they remember from their own childhood which left them feeling tense and guilty, Spock wrote.

No fireworks there.

Then he enumerated some other factors: a greater awareness of psychological responsibility (we don't blame everything on a "bad seed" or evil companions or maybe the devil himself, as earlier generations could); an increasingly mobile society, which means grandparents are often not available for advice and support, and even "an unconscious, vicarious enjoyment at seeing their children misbehave in a way the parents were never allowed to do."

But the statement that put Spock on the front pages was this: "In the 20th century parents have been persuaded that the only people who know for sure how children should be managed are the child psychiatrists, psychologists, teachers, social workers and pediatricians like myself.

"We didn't realize, until it was too late, how our know-it-all attitude was undermining the self-assurance of parents."

Spock considers this a subordinate factor that got blown all out of proportion by the press.

What does he think of the young people whose upbringing he has influenced? (That influence is hard to deny considering the fact that "Child and Baby Care" has sold over 22 million copies since its first printing in 1946.)

They Can See

"They're marvelous!" boomed the doctor. "The great majority of young people are wonderfully clear eyed in seeing what's going on."

What they see going on is obviously the same thing Spock sees and doesn't hesitate to speak about: war, racial injustice and the environment.

"I think it's marvelous that they refuse to be intimidated by authority," said Spock of the younger generation.

"When I was a first year medical student I was terrified of the lowliest instructor. But in my last year of teaching before retirement from Western Reserve University Medical School, I discovered how much things had changed.

Student Complaint

"Here I was, a full professor with years of experience, and my students had the nerve to send a delegation to me complaining of my course!"

They had no particular sense of guilt or fear. That absence of guilt and fear the doctor finds healthy and remarkable.

The only subject, evidently, on which young people and the doctor are not sympatico is sex.

"You know, I have very old fashioned ideas about sex. I think there should be strong laws on pornography and they should be strictly enforced. Those things are simply not good for children," said Spock.

When the subject comes up at college and universities, where Spock does most of his speaking, "they are usually enraged at my opinion," he said with a chuckle.

But he holds to the Freudian theory that civilization is created by the partial suppression of sexuality and agression.

He recalled a recent appearance at Washington University in St. Louis where he was scheduled to speak along with the editor of Penthouse and Viva, Christine Jorgensen and Joyce Brothers. ➡

(Continued from preceding page)

"A lineup like that shows the kind of imagination those kids have!" Spock said with a laugh.

Bad Start?

In his new book, Spock says that early dating and sexual experimentation may get sex off to a bad start. He likes the idea of group dates for 15, 16 and 17 year olds and has nothing good to say for the mother who feels a trip to the gynecologist for the pill is a prerequisite to college registration.

On the other hand, young people in their 20s who are serious about each other and live together openly, represent a "promising trend," according to Spock, giving them an opportunity to find out whether they are compatible and lessening the possibility that physical sexual attraction is the main thing drawing them together.

A close comparison of "Raising Children in a Difficult Time" (the very title has got to strike a responsive chord in the heart of every parent alive) with "Baby and Child Care" reveals that Spock's approach has not changed basically over the years.

Readers who think "Spock" and "permissiveness" are nearly synonymous will be surprised to find that the two books are strikingly similar in the area of discipline and firmness.

"The way we avoid irritation. . . whether we realize . it or not, is by keeping our children under reasonable control and by being extra firm or sufficiently disapproving when things first threaten to go wrong. Such firmness is one aspect of parental love. Firmness, by keeping children on the right track, keeps them lovable. And they love us for keeping them out of trouble," wrote Spock in his first baby book.

25 Years Later

A quarter of a century later he wrote, "I want to give my usual plug and express my own preference for firm leadership, whether it's obvious or subtle. This makes for a better behaved child and a more peaceful family life as well as for a happier child."

That theme of firmness threads its way through the original baby book, aimed at supporting new parents through the hurdles of infant feeding, dietary problems, sibling rivalry, discipline, growth and development and childhood diseases from birth through puberty.

In his new book, drawn largely from his regular Redbook column material, Spock goes beyond "Baby and Child Care" to talk about child-parent conflicts complicated by new circumstances: increased violence drug use, affluence, the feminist movement, the breakdown of marriage and institutional religion.

Feminism Topic

Of all these, one senses that the most difficult for Spock to rethink is the knotty problem of feminism and its implications in child care.

A young child, Spock writes, is by her very nature meant to be intimately dependent on her parents, acquiring security and character through them, particularly her mother.

(Describing the child in the feminine gender is a departure for Spock. When interviewed, he said he was currently at work taking all the male chauvanism out of "Baby and Child Care.")

If her mother is gone most of the time, the infant or young child will grow part of her roots into the substitute who cares for her. Spock believes that in cases where a child's dependence has been repeatedly established and then broken, she may react eventually by refusing to develop love or trust in any more people.

Anti-Day Care

He will undoubtedly draw fire from the feminists for his views on day care centers, but the doctor is not deterred. He sees them as a poor substitute for parenting a child under 3 years of age.

A career in the home, he suggests, combined with community activities or arts and crafts, may be just as productive for society and as fulfilling for women as an outside career — at least until the youngest child is 6, 7 or 8 years old.

What if both parents want careers? The doctor has no solutions to that one. He can only hope that soon the social climate will make it possible for men to share a larger part of the homemaking responsibility.

And how about raising little girls exactly as we do boys, Dr. Spock?

Sexual identity is important, he insists, and it comes mainly through a good identification with the parent of the same sex.

A good deal of soul searching, he says, has convinced him that traditional clothing and playthings and household jobs are not important.

The important thing is the chance for a boy to pattern after a father who is confident in his masculinity and for a girl to identify with a mother who enjoys her role, whatever it may be in her particular society or community.

Preparing girls for careers is another dilemma for Spock.

"If we bring up all girls assuming they will have careers like their brothers, will they have a decreased enthusiasm for bearing and rearing children of their own? And will we be instilling in them the same compulsive drive for success that creates ulcers in men and that keeps so many fathers from giving enough time to their families?"

Less Enthusiasm?

Spock has no answer to that question.

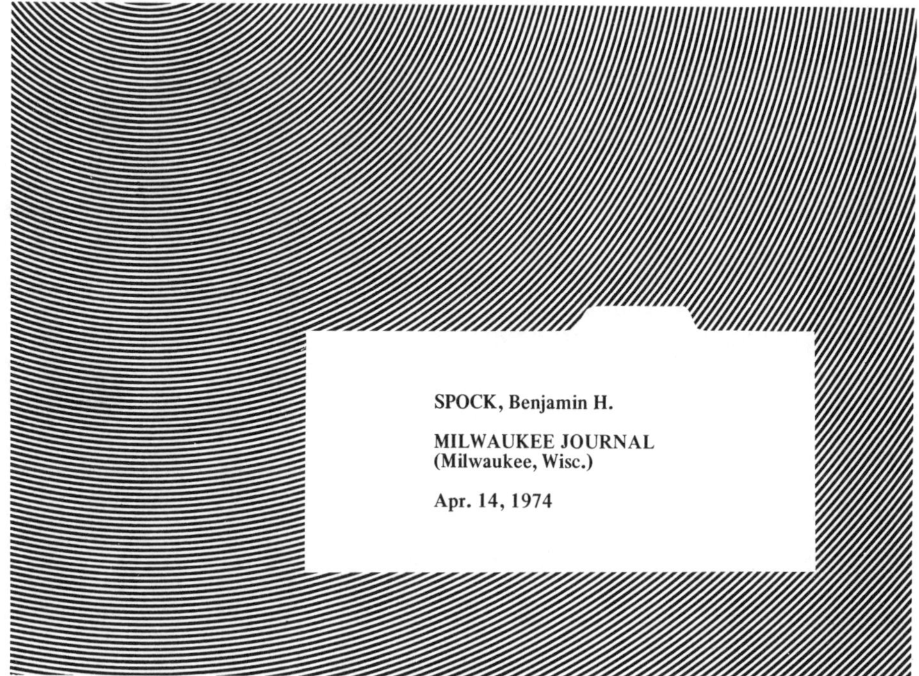

It's clear he thinks we have overemphasized certain aspects of what he calls the American credo: "Competition, materialism, each man out for himself, and success measured in dollars and cents."

His is an idealistic, humanistic philosophy and, ultimately, a hopeful one.

"The main factor that makes children's characters turn out sound is their deep desire to grow up to be like the parents they admire and love," says Spock. "Most of that work is done by the children themselves."

Artist's Legacy: Eye Disease

By ENA NAUNTON
Herald Staff Writer

Albert Staehle is not the first artist to die poor.

But, with the scattering of his ashes last summer over a lake in Bavaria, the man whose artistry touched the hearts of millions of Americans was gone from a life that ended in apparent poverty in Miami.

Gone, too, was the home that Staehle lost several years ago in the sudden, crippling financial demands of a "balloon" mortgage. And also lost was the comfortable income from national weekly magazines, some now as dead as their once popular cover artist.

ALBERT STAEHLE, creator of Smokey the Bear for the U.S. Forest Service, and Butch, the lovable cocker spaniel who brought a smile to the face of wartime America in the 1940s, also originated ideas that blossomed into national advertising gimmicks for major milk, soap and oil companies. He was honored three times with the Kerwin Fulton medal for The Advancement of Art in Outdoor Advertising.

Yet he left only two legacies in the seedy, North Miami house where he spent his last few years:

A bureau full of drawings, clippings and magazine covers.

And a disease of the eyes, called congenital macular dystrophy, that he carried unknowingly in his genes and passed on to three of his four young daughters. The three are now legally blind.

"If we had known, we would never have had four children," said Marjory Houston Staehle, the artist's third wife, who accepts cheerfully her present straightened circumstances and the fact that her predecessors possibly shared more of the comforts and fewer of the woes of her husband's professional career.

"He got $12,000 for this one poster," she said, waving a sample. "But he was married to a Ziegfeld girl at the time. He did rather well financially, but I wasn't married to him then."

SHE WAS not even born when Staehle won a contest, in 1918, to design a milk-promotion poster. It was the forerunner for the Borden Company of its later developed trademark, Elsie the Cow. Much later, he drew the original art for an Esso Oil billboard called "All Spots Checked." On it was a leopard, whose facial expression bears a marked resemblance to the later famous "Tiger in the Tank" promotion. And Staehle also drew the swan for the soap of the same name.

What Marjory and Albert Staehle had that his other marriages did not was children. Her husband, who was 21 years her senior, became a father for the first time when he was 56. He was ecstatic. There was still enough money coming in then for him to rush out and buy "exotic things" like strained papaya to put in the baby's formula.

TO THE END, he adored his daughters and they returned that affection. Selene, the youngest and now only 10, was shopping with her father when he collapsed with the stroke that proved fatal last April 5.

Selene was a baby when her parents, who had moved to Miami in 1958, decided there was something seriously wrong with her eldest sister's eyes. Anna Marie, who had not walked until she was nearly two, was about eight when an eye specialist detected that she had a congenital problem she had begun to cover up by pretending to see the things she knew she could identify.

EXAMINATION of all the children, including the baby, Selene, showed that Anna Marie, now 18, Marjory, 11, and Selene all were affected by macular dystrophy. Somehow, the congenital disease had bypassed one of the sisters, Linda, 16, whose sight is excellent.

With special schooling at the state-funded St. Augustine School for the Deaf and Blind, the three sisters have learned to handle their handicaps, especially Anna Marie, whose control of everyday activities is such that sometimes even her teachers at Miami-Dade Community College do not realize she is almost blind.

"I can see close up," she said. "But far away, not so well."

STAEHLE, Albert
(1899 - 1974)

MIAMI HERALD
(Miami, Fla.)

Nov. 19, 1974

BECAUSE she is legally blind, Anna Marie could draw the $75 a month Social Security she applied for after her father's death for the rest of her life. But she is determined to become a lawyer. She entered Miami-Dade a month after her 17th birthday. Although she is color blind, she can see sufficiently, with strong magnifying equipment, to differentiate between fingerprints in criminology classes, she said.

The other two affected sisters have differing degrees of blindness. Marjory has the best sight of the three girls. She would like to work with animals and, until recently, when she returned to school in St. Augustine, she was able to exercise horses occasionally at a stable in Carol City.

Selene, who has spent half her 10 years in the school at St. Augustine, is still too young to voice future ambitions.

THE ONE sister with normal sight, Linda, is in senior high school and wants to be a dancer. She has studied ballet since she was three.

As their father's health and career began to fail, their mother went back to school herself to prepare for her own career, perhaps as a teacher.

A professional photographer, she had tried to run a studio with her husband — "He did a few portraits and things, but towards the end he didn't do too much," she said. Running the studio single-handed became too much and so she became a full-time student and a part-time teacher at Miami-Dade Community College and Florida Atlantic University.

HAVING laboriously earned first an Associate of Arts degree from Miami-Dade, then a B.A. and a recently completed M.A. from Florida Atlantic, Mrs. Staehle will be qualified to teach through junior college, she said.

She has been teaching part time and is also a counselor for the Miami-Dade outreach program in the Martin Luther King Educational Development Center, at NW 14th Ave. and 62nd St.

Last spring, when her husband died, she was going through his desk and found a hand-written note, which had been notarized, asking that he be cremated and his ashes scattered over the Bavarian Lake at Starnberg, near Munich, his birthplace. Staehle's sister, a retired school teacher, who went to Europe in May on vacation, took the ashes and fulfilled his wish.

IT WAS the last journey for the man who had art in his blood. His father was studying art in Munich when he met Staehle's mother, whose father was court painter to the former royal house of Bavaria. The senior Staehle returned to America and became a newspaper cartoonist and illustrator in Philadelphia.

As for Albert, his wife said "He always felt it was a puppy that gave him his start."

Commissioned by the Saturday Evening Post to create the kind of dog cover picture that would boost newsstand sales, Staehle discovered Butch the cocker spaniel in a pet shop. He took him home to live with him for the next 17 years. From the first drawing, showing Butch tearing up a book of wartime meat rationing coupons, the puppy was an American favorite. Letters — and even substitute meat coupons — poured in. (A later picture, showing Butch running through the house, trailing a streamer of toilet paper, got an equally delighted reader response, and a few parcels of replacements for the paper.)

BUTCH became so famous that he once traveled with his master, to Germany, to pose for figurines made by the Hummelwerk company.

Now it is all over, except in one place, the Museum of Science, where a small exhibit of Staehle's work is on display now through Jan. 5.

On a recent sunny morning, volunteer guides at the museum rushed groups of schoolchildren past the exhibit. In hot pursuit of the official stuffed-animal nature tour, the guides ignored two of the best known animals of all time.

Even the children would know the one in the Forest Ranger's hat.

'Missionary' Mark Starr still working on causes at 80

Mark Starr tells his wife, Helen, of his plans to attend a conference in Germany on Esperanto.

Who's Who doesn't take note of Mark Starr's agility on a bicycle.

STARR, Mark (1894 -)

LONG ISLAND PRESS (Jamaica, N.Y.)

Apr. 28, 1974

By ANN McCALLUM

"My mother always said I was a missionary."

Mark Starr the one-time Queens Liberal party chairman, who was 80 years old yesterday, has spent his life championing causes. He has won some, and others, if not quite lost, were at least less than successful.

Starr's causes have earned him a place in "Who's Who" for the last 40 years. The veteran trade unionist is listed as an author, and one-thrid of the entry is devoted to the titles of his books and pamphlets on labor and economics.

The rest leads the reader from Starr's youth in the Welsh coal mines and the British Socialist movement to his career in the International Ladies Garment Workers' union, the American Federation of Teachers and the United Nations labor and education agencies.

The thread that connects the various portions of his life is teaching, especially of the international second language, Esperanto, which he learned during "a short period" in an English prison as a pacifist in World War I.

* * *

ESPERANTO took him to Russia in 1926, during the general strike in England. As a member of a workers' delegation to a conference on the language, he found the early Stalin era bloody and rife with suspicion.

The stalinists had built up their secret service to keep the White Russians from coming back, and in the light of later events, Starr was to concur that "the means create the ends."

"The way you do a thing determines how you will carry on," he said.

"Curiosity", sparked by the awe in Europe at Henry Ford's paying workers $5 per day, caused Starr to volunteer to come to the United States in 1928 to teach at Brookwood Labor College, a union-sponsored institute in Katonah, N.Y.

He struck a deal with labor leader A. J Muste, later to become a fervent pacifist, to teach British labor history in exchange for being allowed to sit in on classes.

It was at Brookwood that he met his wife, the former Helen Norton, the daughter of a railroad worker from Kansas and a teacher of journalism at the school. They have one daughter.

* * *

PROSPERITY in the United States gave way to depression in 1929, and Starr "found it was harder to be poor in the United States than any other country" because of the lack of social-welfare programs.

Brookwood ran into financial difficulties, too, and Starr became the educational director of the International Ladies Garment Workers Union, a post he held from 1931 to 1961.

During that time, because he was the only man on whom the leaders both of the American Federation of Labor and the Congress of Labor Organizations could agree, he was often labor's representative on government committees.

He was to spend World War II touring Army camps for the Office of War Information, and to arrive in Japan in 1946 with Gen. Douglas MacArthur, after having been part of the group that helped found the United Nations Economic and Social Commission in 1945.

Starr's disappointments have vied with his successes, but seldom overwhelmed them.

In pursuit of a government career, he has faltered here and in his native England. While still a British citizen, he stood for election to Parliament as a Labor candidate from Wimbledom in 1924.

AFter WWII, he was the Norman Thomas of the Queens Liberal party, running unsuccessfully for the city council, the Assembly and Congress in a half-dozen elections between 1943 and 1962.

* * *

BETWEEN ELECTIONS he travelled widely for one or another of his causes, usually as a lecturer on trade unionism or Esperanto in such places as Singapore and Tanganyika.

But his most celebrated political tangle, one he seems to take a rather mellowed view of now, occured in 1943, when he was the only candidate to survive the examinations and qualify for the post of director of adult education for New York City schools.

The Board of Education twice split over his appointment, because he was what the board president labelled a "labor protagonist."

Starr and his wife still smile over that phrase, and both translate it to mean that Starr espoused birth control education for the working class.

But that's a generation ago, and Starr's only regret is the 21-year evolution of a system of sex education.

* * *

HIS VIEWS on many things have mellowed, to judge by his latest book, "The Amercian Labor Movement," a volume of the Oxford series on contemporary life. In it he stresses the "social responsibilities" of union as well as employers.

His birthday yesterday found him deep in preparation for trips to Esperanto conferences on the West Coast and in Germany this summer.

Obviously, though 20 years into official retirement at his Sunnyside home, Starr has not given up, even on those causes the world considers half-lost.

And therein, he says, lies his formula for a vigorous old age: "Learn to do something, do it well, do it when you're old — that's my advice to other octogenarians."

Biography of a literary friend

STEGNER, Wallace Earle (1909 -) and DeVOTO, Bernard Augustine (1897 - 1955)
COURIER–JOURNAL & TIMES (Louisville, Ken.)
July 28, 1974

Staff Photo by Shirley Williams

"MARK TWAIN was a professional writer, which may be described as a body that will go on moving a pen even with its heart cut out. So was Bernard DeVoto."

That's the way another writer, Wallace Stegner, described the subject of his biography in his latest book, "The Uneasy Chair" (464 pp. Doubleday. $12.50).

Recently, in the pleasant living room of his rambling hilltop house in Los Altos Hills, Calif., Stegner talked freely about his long acquaintance with DeVoto and his decision to write the biography after time had tempered controversial events (DeVoto died in 1955).

STEGNER'S LIFE has paralleled that of his old friend DeVoto in many ways. Both lived in Utah in their youth, but had very different reactions to the Mormon influence there. Both were friends of and influenced by Robert Frost, though DeVoto's later years were marred by the loss of his reverence for Frost. Both wrote history and novels. Stegner's novels were far more successful than DeVoto's, and he won the Pulitzer Prize for fiction in 1972 for "Angle of Repose." But DeVoto won the Pulitzer in history in 1948 for "Across the Wide Missouri."

They both wrote a great deal of short fiction. Stegner's short stories are widely anthologized; DeVoto wrote for the slick magazines throughout his life to keep the pot boiling, usually under pen names (John August, Fairley Blake, Richard Dye, Frank Gilbert, Cady Hewes). Both taught writing at the Bread Loaf Writer's Conference. DeVoto wrote The Easy Chair for Harper's for over 20 years. One might say that Stegner's "easy chair" was the Stanford University Writing Program, which he directed for over 20 years.

IN 1935 DeVOTO "signed up to conduct the oldest feature in American journalism, begun in 1850," Harper's Easy Chair, from which he pontificated until his death. He had a brief stint as managing editor of the Saturday Review of Literature, several years of teaching at Bread Loaf. A life-long ambition, never realized, was to gain a faculty position at Harvard. In 1944 (six years after he left Saturday Review) he suffered a public rift with Sinclair Lewis via the pages of Saturday Review, in which Lewis referred to him as "a fool and a tedious and egotistical fool, as a liar and a pompous and boresor liar." A private rift with Robert Frost occurred in 1937, after a display of incredible pettiness on Frost's part at Bread Loaf.

His life was further colored with fights with Clara Clemons Gabrilowitsch in his attempts to publish some of her father's (Mark Twain's) more controversial writings. A failed novelist, a successful historian and essayist, an espouser of many causes, DeVoto was an insecure man "always urgently in need of friends, companions and the comforts of. acceptance." He relied heavily on psychoanalysis and work to make life bearable.

STEGNER brings him stunningly to life. The novelist's training gives the biographer an unerring ear for the right phrase: "to ask impartiality of Bernard DeVoto was like asking docility of a wolverine. . . . He had no gift for living small or living dull."

He was uneasy about painting an unvarnished portrait of DeVoto because of his wife Avis, but found that "she can take it. She's actually pretty hard-boiled and tough. She was a little shaken at first because I think it just brought too many things back, but by the time she read through the first draft and then the finished draft she was all hardened and toughened. She's been completely supportive.

"Some people objected that I missed his personal life with Avis and so on. I very carefully left out his personal life, his family life, most of it (except when the maid comes up with a positive Wasserman). That didn't seem to me to be anybody's business. That wasn't the kind of biography I wanted to write. What I was really trying to write, you know, was a picture of somebody who was crosswise to and in opposition to an awful lot of what went on in his time. And yet who, if you looked at him closely, was a kind of capsule of his time, if only because of his oppositions. And all of the literary history of that time has been written by people essentially from the fashionable, literary, leftist, aesthetic, Marxist kind of pattern that Benny was at odds with. And as a result nobody ever put Benny into the history of his time. In the Thirties for a while he was a kind of literary dictator of the Middle, working on Saturday Review, writing The Easy Chair. But the Middle didn't come out of those times very well represented.

THE FIRST CONTACT between the two men was auspicious for Stegner. "He (DeVoto) was on the board of judges that gave my first little book, "Remembering Laughter," the Little, Brown Novelette Prize in 1930. I was 27 or 28 then, and in the middle of the Depression the $2,500 prize was a fantastic amount of money. It was the equivalent of $20,000 now. So all of a sudden we were liberated in odd ways. I wrote to DeVoto full of gratitude and thanks and sophomoric requests for advice and he wrote me back a very generous letter and then I met him the following winter."

During Stegner's first summer at Bread Loaf, in 1937, he reencountered DeVoto and met Robert Frost. That was the summer of the Frost-DeVoto rift. "I was so green I didn't know what was going on," Stegner recalled wryly. "It was kind of a funny business. You think of it as a quarrel but it wasn't actually. It was just a kind of falling out.

"Frost was, I think in many ways, the only authentically great man I ever knew. And you don't want to knock him down. But you have to say also that he was a mean old man and on occasion he was malicious. He liked to crack jokes that drew blood. And this was not what a sensitive and ardent son needed. All of Frost's children suffered from that too. One of them went crazy, one of them died young, one of them committed suicide."

STEGNER spent five years writing the DeVoto biography. He was also responsible, in 1955, for Stanford University's acquiring DeVoto's library and papers, which eventually made research for his book much easier.

WHEN STEGNER was directing the writing program at Stanford, several Kentucky writers passed through his portals, including Wendell Berry, Ed McClanahan and Gurney Norman. "They were all good kids, too," Stegner recalled. "We got very fond of Kentucky. If we could have just kept Kentucky feeding into California we'd have been very happy."

He retired early from Stanford three years ago, feeling the generation gap.

"The age gap gets wider and wider and makes an inevitable kind of difference. The difference between me as an individual and the student as an individual was greater in 1970 than it was in 1945."

Stegner is now at work on a new novel which "revives old Joe Alston of 'All the Little Live Things.' That's what it starts to do, whether it finishes doing that or not. Anyway, I'm using him as a narrator and it seems so far to work. And it lets me play around.

"One thing I found out while I was writing 'Angle of Repose' was that you can handle more than one layer of time very much better in a first-person narrator than you can in any other way. Or I can. And I wanted some more split time in this. A kind of summer in Denmark 20 years ago sandwiched into the present in California. So it's half Danish and half California and maybe all dull. You can't really tell. I wish I could."

our foibles in simple lines

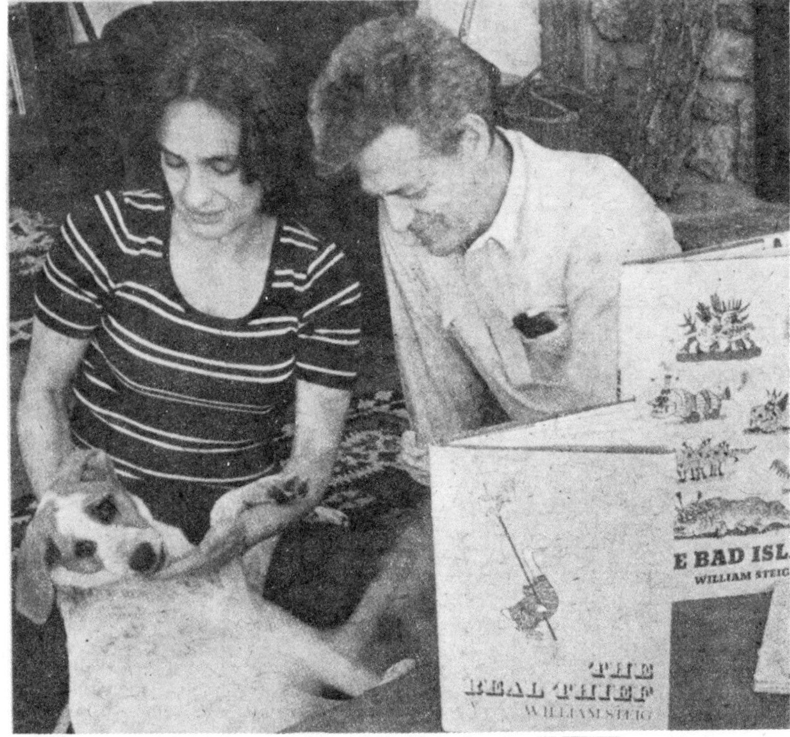

Jeanne and William Steig with their dog Pearl. On the table is a collection of children's books which were written and illustrated by Steig.

by ALISON WYRLEY BIRCH for The Courant

The drawing is simple — not more than a dozen or so briliantly placed black lines. It shows a little man crunched into a small, open upended box. His knees are drawn up, his arms are folded on his lap and his face is sagging with downward lines of dejection. Under the cartoon is the caption: "People are no damn good."

With a minimum of ink and invective William Steig created a clasic that has stayed in print for 25 years. It appeared first in 1942 in a book by Steig called "The Lonely Ones." His title too caught on and started a rash of books by others titled like "The Brave Ones" and so on.

Bill Steig started out as a cartoonist working on a free lance basis for LIFE, JUDGE and THE NEW YORKER. Now he only does NEW YORKER cartoons. The bulk of his working time is spent in writing and illustrating books for children. Bill and Jeanne Steig live in Kent Hollow with a very small puppy named Pearl who "does absolutely nothing that is constructive." said her master.

Bill and Jeanne met at a mascarade put on to celebrate the end of winter. "We were both recovering from broken hearts" said Steig. Before Kent they lived in Sherman and Sharon and before that in Manhattan.

The Steigs love Kent. "We fell in love with the fire department." Steig said. "Our roof caught on fire and the postman came with a lot of other people to help fight it. It was a festive fire. We're crazy about country people. The most interesting people in the world live in the country!" The house that they bought in Kent Hollow had come complete with a fire alarm system. "We never took it serously." Steig said "Then a spark from the fire place caught the roof ablaze and the alarm system went into action. At first we couldn't figure out what it was."

Bill Steig's career in art was preordained. Art runs in his family. His father and mother, three brothers and his brother's children all followed careers in art, as well as his own daughter. He used to copy his brother's cartoons, Steig said, then when he was in high school he did his own cartoons for the school newspaper. Later he studied art at the National Academy in New York City.

"I had a choice; go to art school or go to work. "I didn't want to go to work so I went to art school."

The Wall Street crash wiped his father out financially so Steig no longer had a choice and he began doing cartoons professionally. "Magazines kept coming up and disappearing at that time," said Steig. "JUDGE went bankrupt owing me about $20. That was good money in those days!"

The Steigs love Kent for reasons other than just its fire department and its country people. It's convenient enough to the city for artists and writers who must have contact with publishers. However, working out of Kent is harder, said Steig, than working in the midst of the pandemonium of pressure and panic called New York.

"I used to hole up in the city and not answer the door bell. "Here people think free lancing isn't work and it's open house all day long.

"We're night people. People call us at seven or eight in the morning and that's the middle of the night to us."

Unlike many another cartoonists or humorists, Bill Steig has no interest in topical or political affairs. "I don't know what's going on in the world," he said, "I only know it's bad. Cartoonists criticize from two points of view. "Some will criticize like for not knowing ettiquette. "In my cartoons, for instance I tend to criticize people for caring too much about what they are."

STEIG, William (1907 -)

HARTFORD COURANT (Hartford, Conn.)

Sept. 8, 1974

Illustration by William Steig.

(Continued from preceding page)

"Bill has a certain comical way of looking at people's foibles and hang ups," said his wife. "He's not a gagist. He's a literary cartoonist."

"Of course all art is social commentary automatically but it doesn't do much to change the world," added Steig. "There are lots of media for social reform. Art is only good for people who don't need it. Not even dynamite will change an idiot's point of view. What we need is world-wide mass psychiatry."

Whatever the message is, however, Steig cartoons point out unequivocally and comically the lovable and not-so-lovable weaknesses in man.

STEIG, William

HARTFORD COURANT (Hartford, Conn.)

Sept. 8, 1974

Steig became a children's writer and illustrator by accident. Someone asked him to do a book and he did it. "Writing is a pleasure," he said. "It's a nice change from drawing. Doing the illustrations is harder than writing the book. I can write a book in a few days but it takes me a month to illustrate it."

He said he loves to draw but hates to illustrate — even his own books. It doesn't pay to illustrate other people's books, said Steig. He used to worry about running out of ideas — the classic phobia of all creative persons — but this no longer concerns him.

"I constantly loosen up new areas in myself," he said. "It just flows out. I used to panic that I'd never think of another joke. I've done so much by now I feel I have my whole vocabulary on tap where drawing is concerned. I could work endlessly."

He paused. Then:

"I've been laid up with the flu for three weeks, so now I can't wait to get back to work."

Steig says that he is not disciplined and that he might work 12 hours one day and two the next. He doesn't get an idea until he starts to work— it never hits him unawares. All his books are about animals — anthropomorphic, or talking, creatures that sometimes get him in trouble. In one book he directed his anthropomorphic protagonist into a police station where policemen force were depicted as pleasant looking pigs. "That was written and illustrated before the thing started about police being called pigs," Steig said. "It passed over my head and over the editor's too. The police are after me about it! And there have been editorials about it. But I was innocent. I couldn't be less political! Besides who would want to bother kids like that!"

Bill Steig, whose audience is composed of the 5 to 12-year olds, has many fans among the younger set. Children write to him a lot. "I get marvelous letters from them," he said. "I think sometimes a teacher can't think of anything else to do so she'll say 'Why don't we all write a letter to Mr. So-and-So who wrote the book we just read.' One youngster wrote recently: 'My dog just died her name was Lucky.'"

In April Steig got a phone call from a whole classroom full of kids. One eight-year-old asked him: "Do you write any true books?" "No, only lies," Steig told him.

Steig has the magical capacity for thinking from a child's point of view. In one of his colorful, charmingly illustrated books a young kid donkey named Sylvester finds a magic pebble. He discovers it is magic when he makes the rain stop just by wishing it to. Then he meets a lion and in order to protect himself he turns into a rock. The pebble falls to the ground during this magic feat and he can't wish himself back to being a donkey when the lion has left, much as he would like to.

His parents are terribly upset when he doesn't come home. Eventually they picnic near the rock in an effort to salve their sadness, and they see the pebble and think how much Sylvester would have liked it. The pebbles magic goes to work and the rock turns back into Sylvester and there is great rejoicing.

Before he began writing for children, Steig did some advertising work but disliked it so much it made him physically sick, he recalled. He also used to do sculptures in wood. Nelson Rockefeller has several of these and one of Steig's wood sculptures is in Franklin Delano Roosevelt's home at Hyde Park. He was a champion water polo player years back and recently a new talent surfaced when Steig was caught and captured by the Watergate hearings. He couldn't stop watching the hearings but he needed something to do with his hands, so he created a magestic and colorful panel in needlepoint.

Among his many contributions to new trends in art, Steig is responsible also for originating the idea of the humorous, contemporary greeting card.

"Greeting cards used to be all sweetness and love," he said. "I started doing the complete reverse — almost a hate card — and it caught on."

Bill Steig's children's books have brought him several awards including the Caldecotte Medal and the Christopher Medal. He's been nominated for the National Book Award three times. □

Alison Wyrley Birch is a free-lance writer in Kent.

Sol Stein—publisher-author with best-sellers in both fields

STEIN, Sol
(1926 -)
HOUSTON POST
(Houston, Tex.)
Apr. 19, 1974
[See also CA-49/52]

By ELIZABETH BENNETT
Post Reporter

New York publisher and novelist Sol Stein has more than a little confidence in his new book, "Living Room."

He's convinced that nobody who starts his novel can put it down—and he's probably right.

"If you read the first scene and don't feel compelled to go on," he said in a Houston interview, "don't take it back to the book store. Send it to me—my address is in the book—and I'll personally refund your money."

Few authors, and even fewer publishers, have ever made such an offer. But few authors or publishers have had the success rate of a Sol Stein either, an extraordinary man who has managed to combine both careers and come up with best-sellers in each.

As president of Stein and Day Publishing Co. in New York, he has overseen the creation of such money-makers as Washington society girl Barbara Howar's "Laughing All The Way" and Elia Kazan's "The Arrangement," the biggest seller of any hardcover novel published in the 60's.

AS AN author in his own right, he has had plays produced on and off Broadway and written poetry, articles and reviews for everything from Commentary to The New Republic.

As a novelist, his very first book, "The Husband," sold nearly 400,000 copies and was translated into seven languages. His second, "The Magician," with some half a million copies in print in the U.S. alone, was a Book-of-the-Month Club selection. And his third novel, "Living Room," about a 28-year-old brash, opinionated, successful advertising woman, has been chosen by the Literary Guild, another book club.

And if super-salesman Sol Stein has his way—as he usually does—his newest book will probably also be a best-seller.

It's the highly readable story of a totally liberated woman named Shirley Hartman who operates in a man's world and conquers it. Written simply and graphically, the book is getting good reviews all over the country, including the following comment from Caroline Bird, author of "Born Female": "Shirley Hartman is my sort of heroine—she probably will be 1974 woman-of-the-year."

PART OF the attraction of Stein's book is his deep understanding of the subject. He's married to a liberated woman, for one thing, his publishing partner Patricia Day. And he works with a lot of other successful, independent women, including six of the nine editors at Stein and Day.

"I've been surrounded by successful women all my life," explains Stein, who is 47. "My mother was a very early success—a school superintendent at age 22. And I had two female bosses when I was in my 20s — and that helped too, I suppose. It's (being a liberated man) a matter of exposure."

But women who finally become equals of men in business, "who finally get there," said Stein, often find that "it's a hell of a way to live. They've found what I've found. And they want to reform it."

He wanted to reform his world, too, said Stein, after he found himself hating the sterile New York office and dreading the commuting time spent every day to and from his home in Scarborough.

"SO WE moved the whole company out to Westchester, out of the city and closer to where we all lived. Every editor has an office with a fireplace—and every office is decorated like a living room.

"You live in an office. Why should it be a monastic cubicle? Why can't a living room at work be as nice as your living room at home?

"And now," adds Stein, "I have a two-minute commute to work if I drive slowly. Pat and I now save 20 hours a week commuting time. That's half of a working life."

He also has more time now for his novels which he devotes two hours every morning to from seven to nine. Except Saturday. "And that's a new thing for me, to have a day off. And I'm taking more and more time with each book now. This one took two years and I did four drafts. And I try to write about four pages a day."

Why do Stein's novels, plus the books his firm publishes, sell so well? What's the real secret of making a best-seller?

"OVER 90 per cent of the job is making people aware of the book," he believes. And that's not easy to do: Some 38,000 new hard-cover books are published each year. But he's promoting his book the way "it should be promoted," he thinks: By doing newspaper, radio and TV interviews in most major cities across the U.S.

Another secret of making a best-seller "is coming out with a book before it's time," and that's what Stein thinks he's done with each of his three novels.

"The Husband" was about divorce and came out before people were openly talking about divorce. 'The Magician' was about extortion rackets in high schools which have proved to actually exist since the book was published."

And "Living Room," he thinks, paints a picture of what more and more women will become as they become more liberated. The main character, he grins, is "Sol Stein in drag plus lots of women I've met thrown in."

BUT PERHAPS none of his novels and none of the best-sellers published by his firm have had the impact of the book he's working on now, not as writer but as publisher. The title: "My Story." The author: Marilyn Monroe.

The manuscript was uncovered, said Stein, by a friend and business partner of Marilyn's. It will be published, after months and months of negotiation, in May. He also predicts "a big brouhaha. People are going to be saying, is it a hoax? Who really wrote it?"

They're also going to be buying copies like mad, no doubt, and once again, Sol Stein will have a runaway best-seller on his hands.

GR Press Photo by HENRY ZEMAN

Author Tells How He Handled Bette's 'Filmography

By David Nicolette

Bette Davis has made 84 films.

She denies being difficult in any of them, unless fighting for honesty and high standards in her profession as an actress is being difficult.

The fact concerning the number of films she's made is easy to verify. There they are, listed in chronological order, complete with title, studio, cast and opening date.

Her defense of her standards — and the matter of irritation over being called Bett rather than Bette (Betty) — comes a little slower in the new biography by Whitney Stine titled "Mother Goddam."

Almost everything about the book raises questions, the kind of questions you'd like to ask the author.

Because he was in town recently to visit friends and makes it a point to pay attention to the business of selling the book ($12.95), Stine made himself available.

"The title always is asked about," said Stine. "I took it from a Time magazine story about her (Bette Davis). It is the main character in the play "The Shanghai Gesture" and she really wanted to play that. When it was made into a film in 1941, Ona Munson got the part and the name was changed to Mother Gin Sling."

Odd part of the title is that Stine picked it before ever meeting Miss Davis. The character in "Shanghai Gesture," a powerful operator of a brothel, seemed to have all the qualities that Miss Davis could play so well — and one she would like to have played but, now, never will.

"When I finally met Miss Davis she said, 'I have often called myself this to my children."

Miss Davis had other things to say about Stine's work, but mostly as asides, not corrections or additions or any such tampering with the writing.

"I asked her to add her comments," he recalled.

"She said, 'Oh, I don't know whether I can.' "

Finally convinced that she should try, Miss Davis took the original script and as she read marked places with a number as she wrote out comments on the back of the manuscript.

"I swear, we hardly changed a word," said Stine. "Greatest trouble we had was deciding how to get them into the book. Italics wouldn't work, a different typeface looked terrible and boldface was hard to read."

It was finally settled that the actress ' comments would be printed in red, though that did boost the cost of printing.

So, Stine has the unusual distinction of having written a biography of a celebrity without direct contact with the person until after the book was written, but collaborating latter with inserted comments.

"I think it worked out fine," he said.

The reader will find it unusually interesting. The comments are sometimes commonplace, but often an insight into the star. They also immediately answer any doubts about the authenticity of the author's material. After all, the main character is right there commenting.

Stine has made no attempt to reflect the private life of the great screen star. She did that herself in the autobiography "The Lonely Life," to which he sometimes refers. Instead, he traces the film career, picture by picture, date by date, a style which in the telling sounds rather tedious, but in the reading is intriguing, particularly to a Bette Davis fan.

The book is certainly a necessary addition to any library, with its 374 pages loaded with interesting facts, a "filmography" for reference to the star's films and a carefully arranged 12-page index for easy search of individuals, books and other things mentioned.

As to leisure reading, it certainly is a book you can put down, because the details get a little confusing unless you pay attention. Even so, Stine's style doesn't completely eliminate a touch of suspense, a thread of continuity and rousing of curiosity. Main complaint is that vital situations in Miss Davis' life are sometimes mentioned but never really clarified.

Examples are some of the battles with studio heads, her first divorce and some of the more personal matters involving her family. But personal life is not the aim of the book and the tracing of that professional career is certainly complete, right through 1973, in which Miss Davis, despite her candidly admitted 66 years, was almost as busy as in the peak of her career back in the late 1930s and 1940s.

Stine had plenty of background for his work.

His research really started when he was eight years old, more than 36 years ago, while he was recuperating from a combination of German measles, mumps and some other childhood illness.

"I guess I was really a pest and one day one of my sisters handed me a paste pot and dumped a bunch of movie magazines and scrap book pages on the bed and said, "Here, get busy.' "

He filled the pages with pictures and stories and somehow kept it up through the years, after finding that the star who appeared most in that early scrapbook was Bette Davis.

"The scrapbook weighs about 200 pounds," he says with a rueful look.

Meantime, he always knew he would someday write about his favorite movie performer, so talked with those who knew her whenever he had an opportunity.

Stine's interest in films started in Garber, Okla., where he was born and remained until he was about 14, when his family moved to Wichita, Kan.

"There isn't a whole lot to do in Garber, so I saw a lot of movies."

He later went to live with relatives in California, served briefly in the Army after World War II, where he learned to cook, and made his living as a chef nights while writing daytimes.

"I did that for 10 years, until my first book was published in around 1958."

Don't look for the book, he says. He wrote under the names of Jonathan Ward and Garen McLeish for paperback publication. Ultimately, he published "Lover Under Glass," "Fury," "Bed and Board" and "Cruise for Love."

"They're really pretty bad, but I learned to write a simple sentence."

His writing attracted "ghost" work and he figures he's done 30 books for other people, some of them widely known figures of the movie industry. He will not reveal, or even hint, who they are. That's the ghost writer's code.

He figures "Mother Goddam" is his best work and is pleased to report it is in its third printing, with $36,500 worth sold. Paperbacks are coming out in June and a publisher in England has bought the rights.

Editors cut about 100,000 words from his original draft and Miss Davis added around 25,000 with her comments.

He's most pleased that Miss Davis approved his work the first time it was placed in her hands.

"I was really very fortunate," he said. "I just wrote the thing, never having even met her, and just sent it out to her for approval. Well, she gets hundreds of scripts to read and had been on a trip and those things piled up. Luckily, one of her secretaries took note of it, read it, and called her the very next day and said, 'Bette, this one you have to read.' "

A meeting was arranged soon after.

"I was very nervous, but she was gracious and said immediately she liked it and would approve its being published."

That's all he needed. The person he had admired so many years turned out to be his greatest booster.

STINE, Whitney (pseud. Jonathan Ward and Garen McLeish)

GRAND RAPIDS PRESS (Grand Rapids, Mich.)

Nov. 17, 1974

Author's 'Recipe'

Add Talent To Volumes Of Reading, Writing

STOLZ, Mary (Slattery)
(1920 -)

HARTFORD COURANT
(Hartford, Conn.)

June 2, 1974

[See also CA-5/6]

By LINDA GIUCA
Courant Women's Reporter

To young people everywhere, Mary Stolz is a familiar name. She is associated with growing up, a friend who understands growing pains.

Her books, which have been translated into more than 20 languages, are sensitive and perceptive. Whether writing for children or teenagers, Ms. Stolz strives to make a definite point.

Values, morals and truths are dealt with in a clear, flowing style. Her own personality—her wit, vibrancy and outspokenness—shines throught the pages. "There is more to life than dates and the telephone," the author remarked. "Social conditions and family relations are important."

Many of her stories deal with young love, independence and maturity. "By the Highway Home," published in 1971, describes a family's attempt to cope with the untimely death of a son in Vietnam. A vacation in Florida inspired the 1973 book, "Lands End." She is intensely aware of the world around her and uses "a lot of what I see."

Mary Stolz will speak June 3 at the Children's Book Festival, co-sponsored by The Courant in conjunction with the Capitol Region Library Council.

What will she say to a group of fourth and fifth graders? Ms. Stolz has prepared herself for an inevitable question. "Many students ask me for my special 'recipe.' They think I'm chintzy when I don't hand one out," she confessed.

"But, there isn't a magic formula to becoming a successful writer. The only advice I give is 'read, read, read!' I don't know a writer who doesn't read."

She herself is a voracious reader, especially of poetry. Mary Stolz recalled reading constantly during her childhood and expressed a desire then to become a writer. The budding young author found it "fascinating to put my own words together on paper."

Some of her favorites are Emily Dickinson ("she is very good especially on death and rebirth"), Lauren Iseley ("he's a science writer but very close to poetry"), Jane Austen and Colette, to name a few.

Her list of preferred authors was mostly women which brought an "I wonder what that means?" expression to her face. "Women authors are as good if not superior to the men," she said with conviction.

Living in a New Canaan townhouse with her husband, Dr. Thomas Jaleski, the tall, gracious woman leads a busy and interesting life. An assortment of sons, nephews and nieces have provided endless inspiration and experiences for her books.

An excellent cook, the author is as comfortable in her kitchen as at her typewriter. She has recently begun to bake her own bread and loves the feeling of "kneading the dough, watching it rise and smelling freshly baked bread."

Even though Ms. Stolz has written more than 35 books, she "still loves writing chapter 1, page 1." Her first book, "To Tell Your Love," was published in 1950 and is the story of "a 17 year old who is jilted."

"If I had ever known the chances of getting a first book printed," she claimed, "I never would have sent it in (to the publishers)." Ms. Stolz chose Harper and Brothers publishing house "because my family subscribed to Harper's magazine and I thought it was a good magazine."

"I have a great editor, Ursula Nordstrom at Harper's, who keeps me on the track," she continued enthusiastically. "I don't feel that my every word is chipped in marble — and I sometimes tend to wander off. A good editor is a good part of any book."

Her opinions and beliefs are firmly and sincerely stated. Sometimes, Ms. Stolz finds, it is difficult to keep her political beliefs out of a book.

As a mother who didn't allow television or comic books for growing youngsters, the author feels "television has much to do with the fact that today's children don't read."

On the topic of the educational magazines and books available for youngsters today, she thinks they have their place. But, the "romantic" states firmly, "children should read fairy tales and nursery rhymes. "Little Women" is a wonderful book—do you think young girls still read it?"

The Stolz name will be added to more children's books, but the successful author doubts that she will pen more books for high school students.

"I don't understand the drug culture of today," she said thoughtfully. "You can't write about what you don't know." High school students are more sophisticated in today's society, feels Ms. Stolz, while young children still seem to grow according to certain patterns and stages.

Ms. Stolz's latest tale for youngsters is in the April issue of a delightful new magazine for children, "Cricket." She contributed a short story called "Chino's Tale" which teaches a very important lesson.

As for herself, the author abides by her own adage, "read a lot, write a lot." She is thankful for a year at Katharine Gibbs where she learned to type—that also is advice to hopeful writers. "Can you imagine Jane Austen writing in longhand," Ms. Stolz asked in total amazement, "or Tolstoy writing out War and Peace'?"

The Agony Of Irving Stone

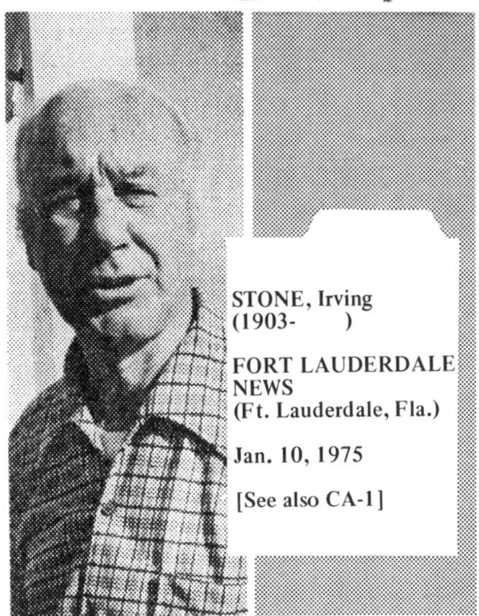
STONE, Irving (1903-)

FORT LAUDERDALE NEWS (Ft. Lauderdale, Fla.)

Jan. 10, 1975

[See also CA-1]

Staff photo by Ursula Seemann

By SUSAN FORREST
Staff Writer

Irving Stone can let go again. Another thick novel is finished and he can lapse into another lifestyle.

Yesterday morning after he finished breakfast, he slushed a good three ounces of yellow Old Grandad over ice and added a splash of water.

"I never drink, smoke or get involved in business when I am writing," said the 71-year-old novelist and biographer who is famous for "The Agony and the Ecstasy," (about Michelangelo), "Clarence Darrow for the Defense," "The Immortal Wife" (about Jessie Benton Fremont), "Lust For Life" (about Vincent Van Gogh) and 21 others.

Now that the prolific Los Angeles writer has finished another book, he's not sticking to the strict guides he uses when he writes his lengthy novels in pen and ink.

"I feel all written out — as if all the writing was drained out of me. The last book had over 700 pages and I wrote seven or eight drafts."

"The Greek Treasure" is complete and will be published soon. It is about Heinrich Schiemann, German archeologist who excavated Troy, Mycenae and Tiryns. He is known as the modern discoverer of prehistoric Greece.

Stone broke his writing regimen in Fort Lauderdale yesterday as he prepared to sail on the Royal Viking Sea on a three-month cruise around the world.

His approximately $20,000 cabin for himself and his wife was paid by the ship company, and he will lecture on board.

Perhaps Stone relaxes so fervently because his four-year periods of work that go into each novel are so intense.

"I live with the character. I must. And I have to feel myself inside the character's skin, head, mind and brain. I live where he lived, eat what he ate, go among his people. During this time I don't do anything else. There is no other way to write a biographical novel."

For the last novel, he lived a year in Athens and eight months in a town near Troy. His wife studied Greek before they traveled, while Stone read letters, journals, books, "everything I could get my hands on."

After such a voyage into another's being, how does he feel?

"I suffer when they suffer. I am exhausted. Yet, this way I am able to become the universal man. I have been inside so many men and so many women and have lived their lives. I have lived with them in almost every country and at many times in history. I can feel as they felt."

The inside of others minds can be a terrifying place. And Stone did become terrified as he researched "The Passions of the Mind," a biographical novel of Sigmund Freud.

"When Freud began to do self-analysis, he went through a six-month period of such intense hell that he couldn't read, write, sleep or make love.

"Then, I began to research that period, and bango! It happened to me. I couldn't write or read. I kicked the dog and beat my wife. I had to work this through in my own life before I could continue with the book."

Not all of Stone's writing experiences are so violent. This was the most frightening one, he said. But he agonizes before he actually, as he says, "becomes the other person."

He experienced more agony trying to become a female character for his first of four books about women—"The Immortal Wife."

"I told my wife there was no way for me to become a woman. But she said that men and women are of the same species, and that I should try. Otherwise, I would never be happy.

"The first chapter I wrote carefully. And when my wife read it, she said that under such circumstances, a woman would think like this. But after I wrote the second chapter quickly, she returned holding it at arm's length like it was a smelly fish."

When the manuscripts are sent to the publisher and Stone crawls from the character's skin, what is left?

"I feel Irving Stone is a struggle. Struggle, oh yes, it is the essence of life."

Another part of the author is troubled.

"I find a certain sense of chaos among authors and other people. We don't know where we're going. We don't know how we're going to overcome the overwhelming social and political problems."

Helplessness is another part of the man who has been able to support himself practically all his life writing books.

His wife of 40 years is his editor, business manager, critic and helper. She organizes dinners for 20 about once a week, and Stone said she almost singlehandedly reared the children, 26 and 30. He keeps less than $50 in his pocket, and doesn't know about the rest of the family finances. "The only time my wife can't stand me is when I'm not writing."

Mrs. Stone was not to join the ship until later in the cruise and he appeared disorganized. He wore houndstooth pants, plaid shirt and seersucker pinstripe jacket.

"There was no one to unpack my bags, and I haven't packed for myself in 40 years. When the maid came in, I asked her to find the pants that go with this jacket."

Stone said he always writes about charaacters he admires, and could never write about Hitler, Stalin or Mussolini.

"I have to love a man or woman—to admire them greatly or what they have acomplished."

He grew up reading Jack London, Tolstoy and Dostoyevsky, and compares his work with that of the Russian novelists. He says the greatest contemporary writer is Kurt Vonnegut Jr.

"I told a group of students that I thought there was no second choice to Vonnegut. And I have never seen such a reaction. Some cried, some stood up and applauded. They thought I was going to say Sinclair Lewis or Harold Robbins."

Stone's next project after the cruise is a secret. But his research on that secret involves a trip to London to get copies of 1,700 letters he has located. When he has time, he plans to write another chapter for "They Also Ran" about Adlai E. Stevenson.

"My publisher keeps asking me to write my autobiography. But I'd rather write about all these other people. I don't have that kind of ego."

Unjoining a Family

SULLIVAN, Judy
(1936 -)

WINSTON–SALEM
JOURNAL & SENTINEL
(Winston-Salem, N.C.)

July 14, 1974

By Janice Gaston
Staff Reporter

During the years Judy Sullivan was growing up in Hamilton, Tex., the 1940s and early '50s, it was almost unthinkable for a girl to have ambitions to be anything other than a wife and mother.

So she followed the pattern that had been laid out for her, marrying in a storybook wedding at the age of 18 and producing a daughter, Kathleen, several years later. She got her education piecemeal, while she worked to help put her husband through graduate school, looked after the house and cared for her child.

"We all did what we were expected to do, what society had said we ought," she said. "We all did that for a long time.

"Then I stopped."

Her book is about her progression from a passive, dutiful housewife to a radical feminist, and her painful decision to leave her husband and daughter to find a life for herself in New York.

The book is written in first person and appears to be the offshoot of the journals Mrs. Sullivan kept during her marriage.

It begins with a description of her parents' wedding, the joining of two fine old families with a tradition that was to dictate Mrs. Sullivan's future from birth until her re-birth, at the age of 33, when she "became more the person I should have been all along."

After a childhood in which she "learned the complex and elaborate rituals and postures of young southern ladies," she fell in love with a man who had been raised in the same mold.

She was only 18 when he asked her to marry him, and, although she felt she was too young, "I figured I'd never do any better than John, no matter how long I waited. I admired and loved him deeply . . ."

He had a lot of self-confidence and would take far better care of her than her parents had done, she said, and she was ready to give her life over to him.

But in the years that followed she found that, more than anything, she wanted her life back.

Several years after she was married, when her daughter Kathleen was small, she came down with a case of what she called "the running blues," the loss of control suffered by housewives who are trapped — "and bored, bored, bored."

A psychiatrist made her see that her main problem was the burden of guilt she carried for wanting more than a home and family.

While her husband was working his way up to becoming a college professor, Mrs. Sullivan shoved her academic ambitions in the background. It took her six years to get her undergraduate degree and four more to get her master's.

She worked at a series of somewhat unsatisfying teaching jobs, winding up teaching art history at Emporia State University, where she fervently resented the fact that she was underpaid and not taken seriously by her male colleagues.

She wasn't taken terribly seriously by her husband, either. He made all the decisions—when they would move on to a new town, where they would live.

He even bought a house — a huge one that they couldn't really afford — without consulting her. She liked it, but she never felt that it was hers.

"From the day we moved in, I had a fantasy that I didn't really live there, that someday I'd see the true owner come floating down the stairs. And it would be Myrna Loy."

It was after a mind-stretching summer in Baton Rouge, La., where Mrs. Sullivan attended a series of workshops on teaching black studies, that she came to the realization that "life in Emporia was not nearly enough."

One night, after a faculty party she had hated, her husband announced that he was thinking about moving to Taos, N. M., for a year, so that he could write, or taking a new job as a college dean.

Again, he was making decisions about her life.

This time, she said "no." She told him she wanted to get a Ph.D. from Columbia University and to write a book on black art. And she was going to New York — alone — to do it.

"I'm taking over my life and this is the direction I'm going," she said.

Then she prepared to join the ranks of the runaway wives — but with a few differences. She announced her decision nine months ahead of time, giving her family plenty of time to get used to the idea. When she went, they knew exactly where she was going.

It was her final act of rebellion, the explosive reaction to a lifetime of suppressed rebellion.

It is a moving story — one told with a lot of wit and humor, underlined with pain. It is the story of a woman too weak to break the mold she was born into until it had hardened and she had gotten deeply involved in the lives of others, her husband and daughter.

"It would be lovely if it had been free," she said, "but the price was steep. It would have been lovelier still had none of this been necessary."

It's Back to the Bank For Jackie Susann

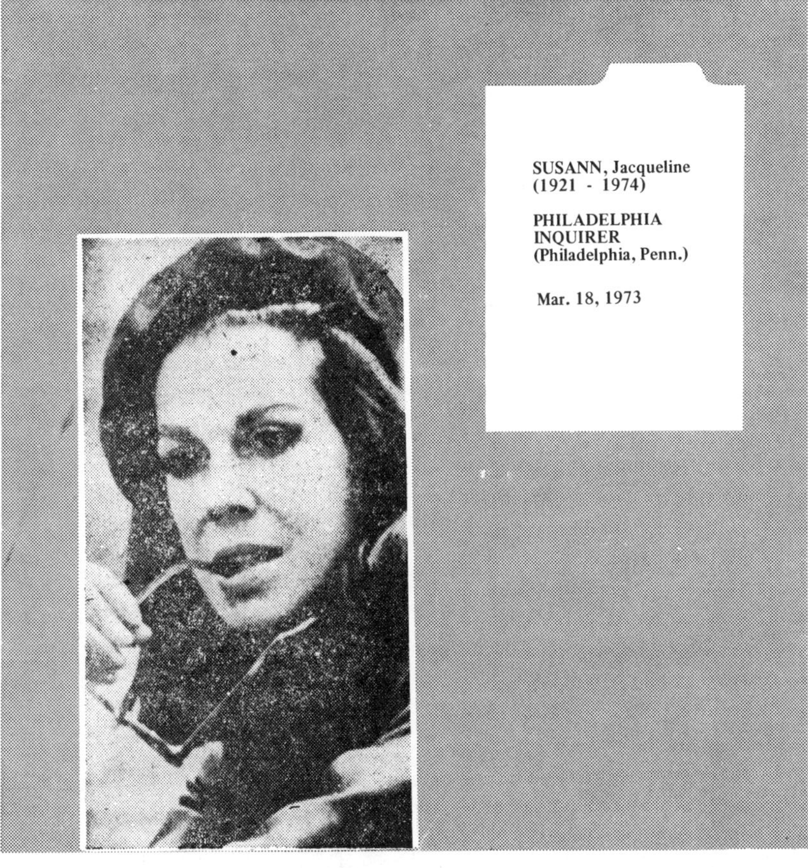

SUSANN, Jacqueline
(1921 - 1974)

PHILADELPHIA
INQUIRER
(Philadelphia, Penn.)

Mar. 18, 1973

JACQUELINE SUSANN

Her friends call her Jackie. Her enemies call her lots of other things. Jacqueline Susann used to worry about it. When Truman Capote called her a "truck driver in drag" on the Johnny Carson Show, she threatened him with a law suit. But now she has mellowed toward her critics. She knows that writers are the bitchiest people in the world, and since she has sold more books than any female writer in history, she is going to turn some people green with jealousy and that's all there is to it. Looking about as much like a truck driver as Raquel Welch, now she just laughs at her assailants. Especially Truman Capote. "Poor thing. You realize, don't you, that he has never written a full-length novel in his life. There has to be something wrong with a man who, in 'In Cold Blood,' had more empathy for the two killers than he had for the murdered Clutter family because of his way of thinking the Clutters were middle-class."

SO JACQUELINE SUSANN is crying all the way to the bank, and after this week she'll be making several more trips. This week is D-Day in the publishing world because it marks the publication of Jacqueline Susann's newest novel, "Once Is Not Enough," and there is no reason to suspect history won't repeat itself. "Valley Of The Dolls" sold 25 million copies and stayed on the best-seller list for 65 weeks. "The Lovze Machine," on the list for 37 weeks, sold 10 million and is still climbing. The new one is expected to break all previous records. Forty-eight hours after her photo appeared on the cover of the Feb. 5 Publishers Weekly, 56,000 orders had been taken. The book isn't even in the stores yet and it already has a guaranteed first printing of 150,000 copies. So say anything you like about Jacqueline Susann, but spell the name right.

I'll tell you something. I've read "Once Is Not Enough" and all I can say is fasten your seat belts. Not only is it the best book Jacqueline Susann has ever written, it's like a pot of fudge. You can't put it down. It has warmth, humor, wit, sharply-defined characters, complex relationships, startling plot twists, a hypnotic story, and enough thinly-disguised public figures to keep cocktail parties guessing and every movie star in Hollywood fighting duels to get into the movie version.

I LIKE Jacqueline Susann, too. She's generous and kind and candid and enormously intelligent. The door opens to her lemony chiffon penthouse 25 floors above Central Park and the first thing I see is a giant pop-art book cover that says "Once Is Not Enough" in bright red neon lights. All the salesmen for her new book chipped in and bought it. She's talking to Doris Day on the phone about animal shelters, so I settle down with a Dr. Pepper in a Tiffany glass served on napkins advertising "The Love Machine." Then she flows in like somebody in a Noel Coward play, and we're off.

"Don't say I'm 'a fortyish novelist,' for God's sake. Just say I was born in November, 1963 because that's when my first book 'Every Night, Josephine' came out. It was about my poodle, who was a bigger celebrity than I am, and it's still my favorite of all my books. It took nine years to get 240 good pages and it sold 35,000 copies. The new book took 3½ years to write, and I edited it in five days. I'm a natural-born editor. "I write by myself and nobody sees it until I'm ready. Then I sit down and tell Irving 'Welcome to the Monday night fights!' and he reads it. If he objects to something, we talk about it, but I don't always change it. He hated the name Neely O'Hara in 'Valley of the Dolls' and it stayed in. But Irving is the only o ne who reads it before the final draft."

Besides being a great businessman, her husband Irving Mansfield is also the best press agent an author could have. Each of Jackie's books is treated like a production and together they have revolutionized the promotion and publicity of publishing. She married him when he made $250 a week producing Fred Allen's radio show and they've been a team ever since. Now he has edged out of a successful career as a TV producer and devotes full time to Jackie. Together, they've made millions, but Jackie insists she does not write for money. "All I care about is my husband, my friends, and my work — in that order."

"THERE ARE no simple folks in my books because I don't know any simple folks. I write about people I know. This book is about spiritual and mental incest. It's about a girl who loved her father but only saw the glamorous side of his life — the black limousine, the corner suite at the Plaza, dinner at "21." Then after a motorcycle accident that keeps her in a hospital for three years, she returns to New York all grown up to discover the whole world has changed. It is not a frivolous book. I did tremendous research."

She begins a book with yellow scratch paper in her typewriter, sitting on an orange leather chair covered with a white towel because the upholstery makes her fanny perspire. Then she types on the back of press releases. ("The only thing I'm chintzy about is paper.") Thousands of pages come out of her typewriter without the aid of a secretary. Every word of her books is typed with two fingers. She corrects the yellow pages by hand. Then as the book progresses, it travels through drafts on blue, pink, and finally white paper. Then Irving reads it and Jackie Xeroxes it herself fof the publisher.

THIS BOOK has taken a lot out of her. She worked night and day for 3½ years to meet her deadline, and has been ill ever since with eye infections, double pneumonia and bronchial asthma. But she did it all without a cigarette. "I stopped smoking in January, 1968 and I've had a cough ever since," she laughs. "I'm always making bargains with God. I gave up drinking for Lent. One year I gave up hash brown potatoes for 12 months. I promised God if I made the best-seller list on 'Valley' I'd give up smoking. Then I got so nervous going on talk shows I had a cigarette in both hands. So then I promised I'd give God a month for every week I stayed on the list. Well, who would have thought I'd be on it for 65 weeks? I was picking up butts out of other people's ashtrays. It was disgusting. Then Irving had a polyp removed from his intestines and I promised God if it wasn't malignant I'd give up smoking for good. I finally made it."

Jackie's father, Robert Susann, was a portrait-painter who lamented the fact that he had no sons to carry the family name. Her new novel about incest has a dedication: "To Robert Susann, who would understand." Raised eyebrows? "I loved him. He taught me a lot about people and everything he taught me has stayed in my mind. It comes out in my books like litmus paper. There's a sculpture of him that dominates my living room and I often talk to him. I say: Don't go away, I'm getting a drink, be right back.' I guess I wanted to make it as an actress to on Studio One. Then one day George Abbott turned me down for a part and I said 'I hope he dies, I hope he gets leprosy!' silly kid stuff like that. And Eddie Cantor said, 'Kid, if you'd just take that energy and turn it into being a success, George Abbott will say, 'I could have had her and I blew it!' That's always been my philosophy, and now the Susann name is still alive through my writing." ➡

(Also see preceding article)

Jacqueline Susann, 53, Dies; Author of 'Valley of The Dolls'

JACQUELINE SUSANN

SUSANN, Jacqueline

PHILADELPHIA INQUIRER (Philadelphia, Penn.)

Sept. 23, 1974

By LARRY SWINDELL
Inquirer Book Editor

Jacqueline Susann, a Philadelphia girl who succeeded modestly as an actress before attaining sensational fame as a best-selling novelist, is dead at age 53.

Miss Susann died Saturday night at New York's Doctors Hospital, a victim of cancer.

Her recurrent attacks of pneumonia had been widely reported but the seriousness of her illness was not generally known.

Her death was immediately mourned in the world of show business and publishing, and among her many friends in the Philadelphia area.

Identified most often with the novel "Valley of the Dolls" and the more recent "'Once Is Not Enough," Jacqueline Susann was born and raised in Philadelphia, and was the daughter of the late Robert Susann, a portrait painter held in high esteem nationally.

Last November, when she was a guest at an Inquirer Book and Author Luncheon, she recalled that as a little girl she was the unofficial mascot of the Penn and Pencil Club, the Philadelphia newsmen's social organization in which her father held membership.

A graduate of West Philadelphia High School, she lived at the Garden Court Apartments at Pine and 47th sts. before going to New York in 1940 to try her luck on the Broadway stage..

She once said "I've always had brass, or whatever it is that makes people push themselves. When you're starting out, that's more important than talent. So I never had difficulty getting established as an actress. Fame kept eluding me, but I was never out of work."

Gregarious, witty and vivacious, she seemed predestined for Manhattan's cafe society. In 1944 she married radio producer Irving Mansfield, later a TV and movie executive, and believed to be the catalyst for Miss Susann's spectacular writing career. The Mansfields were one of the most devoted and popular couples in the show business environment.

Her first Broadway appearance was in 'Banjo Eyes," an Eddie Cantor starring vehicle; and her first serious role was in Lillian Hellman's "Watch on the Rhine." She alternated light and heavy acting stints and appeared in a score of plays on Broadway and the road.

In the 1950s she entered television acting in such dramatic shows as Studio One and Playhouse 90. She also became a frequent panelist on TV game, shows and sometimes was an interview hostess.

She became an author in 1963 with a small nonfiction book, "Every Night, Josephine" which remained her own favorite work. She described it as "the story of Irving, me, and 'Josephine, the poodle who owned us." It was republished this year by William Morrow & Co.

"Valley of the Dolls" catapulted her to world fame in 1966. So extraordinary was its commercial success that the Guinness Book of World Records cites it as the fiction sales champion with 17 million copies.

"The Love Machine" was published in 1969 and also topped the fiction sales charts, as did "Once Is Not Enough," which was published in the spring of 1973. All the Susann novels reflect the glamorous world of show business, with its wheeling and dealing and the tempestuous private lives of its luminaries.

She said she was never bothered by negative reviews of her books unless they became personal attacks rather than literary ones. She once said "I have no literary pretense whatever. I tell stories that I think the girls will enjoy reading under the hair drier."

Nevertheless, critics generally were kinder to "Once Is Not Enough" than to her earlier novels. The Mansfields became involved in the recently completed film version of "Once Is Not Enough" and Miss Susann acknowledged that she had not been happy with the movie renditions of either "Valley of the Dolls" or "The Love Machine." She hoped this time to be associated with "a really good picture."

The Mansfields had commuted between New York and Hollywood for most of the last year, which may have taxed Miss Susann physically. A family spokesman indicated that her losing struggle against cancer actually began a dozen years ago, before her late-blooming fame as novelist. Once a heavy smoker, she contracted emphysema and stopped smoking entirely but was teasily felled by simple colds.

Miss Susann is survived by her husband; their son, Guy Mansfield; and her mother, Mrs. Rose Susann of 1320 Somerville ave., Philadelphia.

Preparations for a private funeral early this week are incomplete. Until the private ceremony, Miss Susann's body will repose at the Frank E. Campbell Funeral Chapel at Madison avenue and 81st st. in Manhattan.

Jacqueline Susann Dies of Cancer at 53

Jacqueline Susann, the Philadelphia-born writer whose novels reflecting the seamier side of modern society are among the biggest sellers in publishing history, died Saturday night in New York City. She was 53.

Miss Susann, daughter of a prominent Philadelphia portrait painter, died in Doctors Hospital of cancer after a 12-year battle against the disease.

Her ailment had been a carefully kept family secret and the dark-haired Miss Susann never gave an indication that she was dangerously ill.

SUSANN, Jacqueline

PHILADELPHIA BULLETIN (Philadelphia, Penn.)

Sept. 23, 1974

'Valley of the Dolls'

Miss Susann's first novel, "Valley of the Dolls," about sex and drugs among Hollywood's rich and famous, has sold a record-breaking 17 million copies, 7 million in this country and 10 million abroad. It was published in 1966.

Favorite Book

Her second novel, "The Love Machine," published three years later, became an immediate best-seller and held that position for five months.

When her third and last novel, "Once Is Not Enough," was published in March 1973, it, too, rocketed to the top of the best seller list and established Miss Susann as the first author in history to have three consecutive number one best-sellers on the New York Times list.

Family friends said her favorite book was a work of Josephine," about her husband and their pet poodle, Josephine.

The book is estimated to have sold more than 2 million copies. Bantam Books, her publisher, said it was one of the first three American books to be ordered by the Peoples Republic of China last September.

Bantam Books president Oscar Dyspel said Miss Susann's books grossed "well beyond $60 million." He said more than 50 million copies have been sold worldwide and they have been translated into 18 languages.

The film version of "Once Is Not Enough" was scheduled for release next spring.

Miss Susann was the daughter of Robert Susan, portrait painter who died in 1957.

Early Ambition

His daughter, who added an extra "n" to her name, was graduated from West Philadelphia High School. Her early ambition was to be an actress.

Her public career began in April 1936 when she was declared the "prettiest girl in Philadelphia" by Earl Carroll in a beauty contest in the old Earle Theater.

She won parts in 21 plays in New York and on the road, including "Banjo Eyes" with Eddie Cantor, "Jackpot," and the road versons of "The Animal Kingdom" and "Watch on the Rhine."

Returns to Stage

She returned to the sage in 1970 to appear in an off-Broadway production of "The Mad Woman of Chaillot." She also made appearances on the "Mannix" TV series.

Miss Susann had an unusual writing method. She would first select a theme, main characters and an ending, then develop other characters and incidents as she wrote.

A blackboard stood in her den studio in Manhattan and was used to chart the evolution of her characters. She would write four or five drafts, each on a different color of paper — first on yellow, then on pink, followed by blue and finally white.

Miss Susann's private life was far removed from those of the characters she created in her fiction. She was married to one man, movie producer Irving Mansfield, for 30 years, and when not out promoting her books, lived the quiet life of a New York matron.

Besides her husband, Miss Susann is survived by her son, Guy, and mother, Mrs. Rose Susan, of Philadelphia.

Funeral services will be private.

Author finishes diary of Khrushchev here

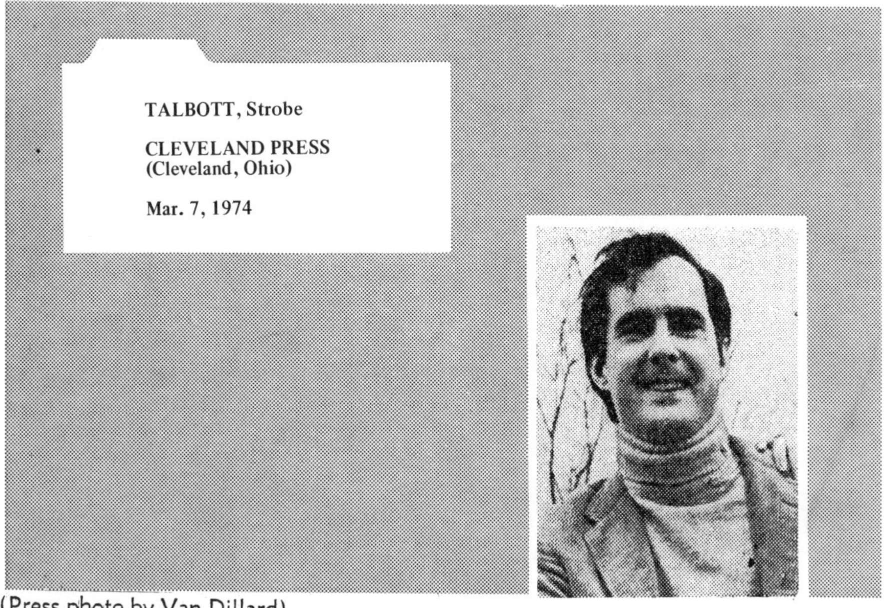

(Press photo by Van Dillard)

By PETER ALMOND

For the past nine months a 27-year-old Clevelander has been working in total secrecy in Hunting Valley on a translation of the memoirs of Nikita Khrushchev, the former Soviet premier.

Entitled "Khrushchev Remembers: The Last Testament," the translation is by Strobe Talbott, a former Press intern.

The book is of major international importance and concentrates on Khrushchev's recollection of his leadership of the Soviet Union from 1954 to 1964.

Today, publishers Little, Brown and Co. of Boston announced that Talbott's edited translation is complete and the book will be published in June.

It's the second half of some 180 tapes and other documents by Khrushchev, who died in 1971. The first half Talbott also translated and it was published in 1970. It aroused considerable controversy and its authenticity was doubted by the Kremlin, Khrushchev's wife and Svetlana Peters, Stalin's daughter.

Today at the home of his parents at 37070 Shaker Blvd., Hunting Valley, Strobe Talbott talked about his new work and the authenticity of the material he worked on.

"We have known all along the tapes were authentic and we are glad we are now in the position of being able to persuade some of those who doubted the first book that the tapes are authentic," he said.

Talbott said all the tapes and Russian transcripts have now been acquired by Columbia University and can be examined by anyone. The documents include reports of an independent voice-printing company.

He added that Edward Crankshaw, the British journalist who has written a biography of Khrushchev, also believes in its authenticity. Crankshaw has written an introduction to the new book.

Talbott was naturally reluctant to discuss some of the more interesting details of the new book, since it has not yet been published.

But he did say it reveals a lot of new and different information about the Kremlin's view of the U2 spy plane incident of 1962, the Cuban missile crisis, the Berlin crisis and Khrushchev's own version of the shoe-banging incident at the United Nations in 1960.

"Khruschev explains exactly how Gary Powers' U2 plane was shot down over the Soviet Union in 1962," he said. "And he explains the direct connection between that incident and the collapse of the Big Four summit meeting in Paris shortly afterwards.

"The first book covered a lot of ground, including the Cuban missile crisis, but this new book contains a lot of additional material.

"One thing I think Americans will be interested in is Khrushchev's puritanism. He displays plenty of indignation about Indonesian President Sukarno's sex life," added Talbott.

I think Americans perhaps have viewed Khrushchev as more of a buffoon with a wild temper and more of an ideological enemy than he was in real life," said Talbott.

"This book will go a long way toward correcting that impression.

"The value of this second book, I think, is that it gives us an idea of the mentality of the Soviet leadership."

The job of translation has taken a lot of intense concentration for Talbott, who explained it was largely for this reason and for secrecy that he came to Cleveland with his wife Brooke Shearer to work on the project.

He said he worked from a direct Russian transcript of Khrushchev's tapes, which were dictations directly off the top of his head.

"Much of it was rambling and sometimes confusing, so I had to do quite a bit of editing to make it into a readable book. Some of the dates he refers to are faulty and should be checked against other sources.

"But although he was in his late 70's I was amazed at how he remembered events of 50 and 60 years ago. He was by no means senile."

Although he is only 27 Talbott is no beginner at scholarly subjects or understanding the Russian mind.

After attending University School in Shaker Heights, he went to Hotchkiss prep school in Connecticut where he was first introduced to Russian. He then went to Yale University where he majored in Russian. It was while he was there in 1967 that he worked as an intern at The Press.

After Yale he continued his Russian studies at Oxford University, England, where he was a Rhodes scholar. He has worked as a reporter for Time and Life magazines in London, Moscow and Belgrade, Yugoslavia.

His wife is a freelance writer.

By KAY HOLMES
Sunday Magazine Contributing Correspondent

NEW YORK CITY

FOR THE past two years Gay Talese has been leading the fantasy life of many an American male.

He has pored over pornographic publications, surfeited himself on blue movies, gone to peep-shows by day and orgies by night.

He has managed not one but two massage parlors in New York, spent six months in a California nudist-sex commune, and he still has another year to go.

Hugh Heffner is probably jealous. But Gay Talese is no flimsy-carbon-copied Playboy. He is a 14-year happily married man, with two young daughters and a very understanding wife.

What's his secret? He is writing a book on the American Sexual Revolution and he never does anything by halves. He seizes gargantuan subjects and then totally immerses himself in them. As much as possible, he lives the lives of his characters.

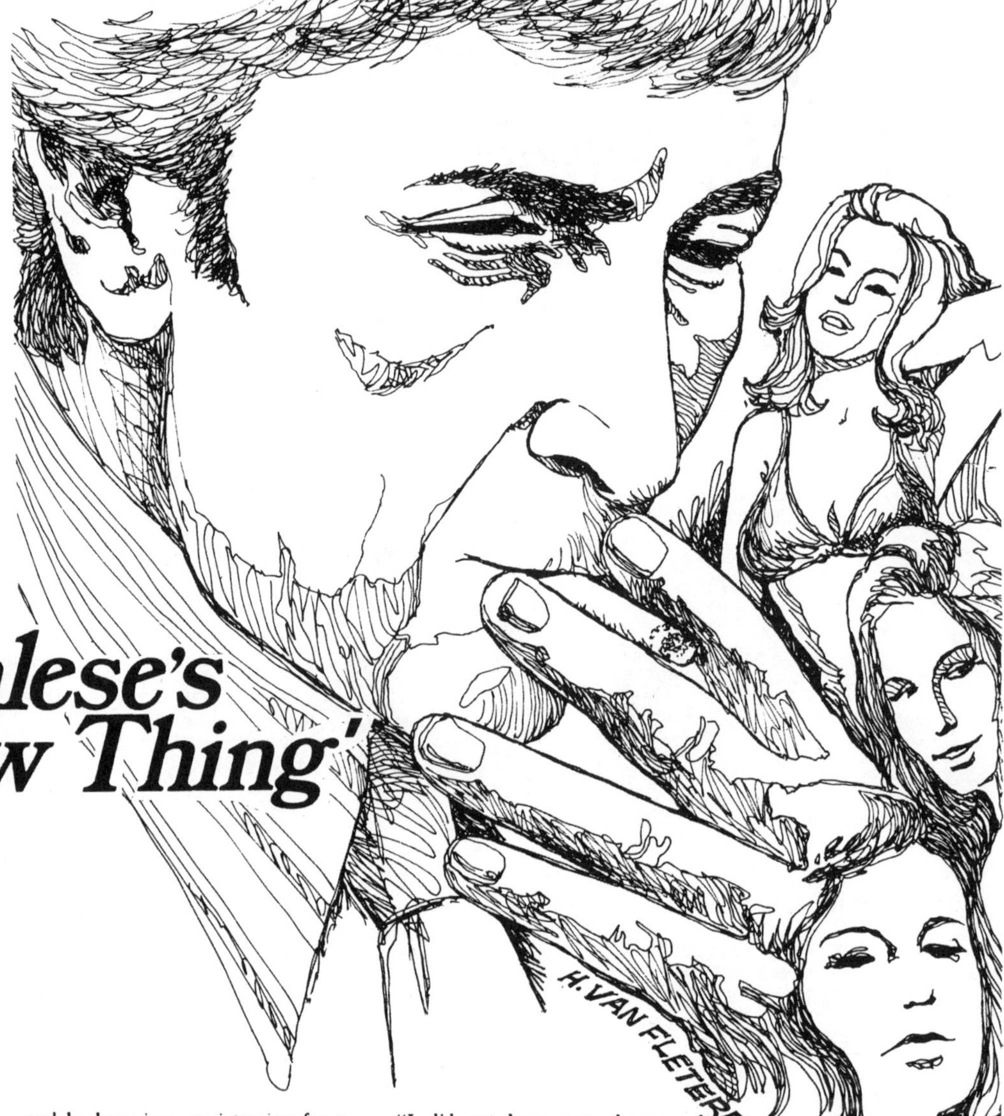

Gay Talese's 'New Thing'

For his best-seller, "The Kingdom and the Power," on the New York Times, he interviewed hundreds of Timesmen, past and present, talked with the paper's owners and executives, and devoured personal files, letters and memos which would choke an army of termites.

He took six years to write "Honor Thy Father," another best-seller, about a Mafia family, and during his research he lived with the Bonanno family, sharing their frustrations and fears, their exaltations and excesses. He even got Bill Bonanno to talk about his sexual relationship with his wife — which leads back to the subject at hand.

After two mammoth best-sellers, Gay Talese had to find an even greater challenge as a chronicler of today. Sex has never been more with us, and it is a subject of immense appeal.

When I arrived at the barred doorway of his elegant, eastside brownstone, Talese was on the phone. Some well-placed young man from Mississippi wanted to do a book on Martha Mitchell and could Talese suggest an agent? He listened with interest and courtesy and 20 minutes later the young man was talking to Talese's agent.

Gay Talese is very approachable. And he works at it. As a Timesman of 10 years, a contributor to Esquire and Harper's, and now a writer of nonfiction novels, he believes journalists must be available.

Otherwise, how can they criticize public figures who fence questions, give severe no-comments or simply disappear when the heat's on?

His number is in the phone book — and he has given an interview for a high school newspaper in Queens.

One plus for availability. Several more for being kind, sincere, straightforward and charming in a European way. He is an intriguing blend of the casual and the formal — the kind of person you seem to know quickly, but later you discover you've just begun to penetrate the recesses of his mind.

TALESE is lean, 41, and beginning to gray. He has impeccable taste, a Cardin wardrobe and no false modesty. He likes to reread his books, and he says he can write as well as any novelist today — only he doesn't want to write fiction. He believes "reporting is an art form."

To gain a bit of perspective, we talked about his two best-sellers. He is tremendously proud of "The Kingdom and the Power," his delightful, gossipy, human interest packed history of the Times.

From its inception, it was a monumental undertaking. He was writing for a very tough audience — the 5,000 people who work on the Times and have very firm ideas about what it was and is.

"I did not have any charges of inaccuracy in that book — and that's what I'm proud of." Pause. "I have never had a libel suit or defamation of character action brought against me."

In the book he observed that if drink was the vice of the Herald Tribune, then sex was the vice of the Times. Such insights did not endear him to the establishment

But Talese says: "It wouldn't have been a very good book if it had the unified approval or praise from the many members of the hierarchy of the Times.

"I don't believe I lost a friend because of it. A.M. Rosenthal, the managing editor, was closest to me on the Times. He didn't find it easy reading, particularly the part about himself, but it never meant that he became angry with me."

Similarly, not all of the Mafia liked Talese's chronicle of a Mafia family, "Honor Thy Father." Even its chief character, Bill Bonanno, had to reread it four times before he gave his verdict. (He read the book in jail, while serving four years for a white-collar,

TALESE, Gay

DETROIT NEWS
(Detroit, Mich.)

Dec. 9, 1973

[See also CA-4]

(Continued from preceding page)

credit card crime.)

After it was published, Talese expected a subpena from some federal court, but none came. Perhaps because he'd said repeatedly and publicly that all he knew about the Mafia was in that book. "I'm not going to my grave with any great untold stories."

He couldn't resist the irony of observing how honest Bill Bonanno was: "If he were the reporter and I the subject I don't know if I would have been as candid and open. He really wanted to talk about himself for the first time, and deeply—and he did."

BACK TO the subject at hand — the sexual revolution. Talese's interest in it started with a sign, "LIVE NUDE MODELS," which he spotted one night while walking home with his wife, Nan. He felt compelled to see for himself. Nan demurred and walked home alone.

He began thinking of other signs of sexual ferment. Characteristically , he

plunged headlong into the subject. He managed two massage parlors — one just around the corner from Random House, where Nan Talese works as a senior editor.

While Nan stayed home and helped their daughters, Pamela,, 9, and Catherine, 6, with their homework, he chatted with nude girls at the poolside of a health club.

While Nan preferred the warmth and privacy of the home hearth, he spent six months in a nudist-sex commune in California.

Despite the Taleses' contrasting life styles, he says firmly: "I am a very happily married man. I have a wonderful relationship on every level with Nan and the children. Our marriage has succeeded because we've been able to be one another's friend. There isn't anything we will not talk about."

He says this with studied precision, as if he were speaking a foreign language — and perhaps to some people he is. He shrugs and says others may doubt it, but there it is. He told Nan from the beginning that if he was forced to choose between the book and her, he would give up the book. But Nan never precipitated such a showdown.

"Our marriage might not work for a man who wants his meals at 6 o'clock sharp — Nan has a very fulfilling career and she won't be home until 9 tonight. There are no enticing smells coming out of the kitchen; we seldom use it. But it works for me."

He admits that whereas previous books drew them together — Nan would come home and read and comment on what he'd written during the day — the sexual revolution holds little interest for her. It is potentially divisive because it isn't shared.

"We don't live an alternative life style. We are very much within the system. Her style and my style are not the same. She is a very private person — public sexuality is totally antipathetic to her. I respect her wishes and she respects mine."

She did agree to go to a nudist camp in New Jersey, because she made a distinction between open sex and open nudity. Talese was proud of his wife, but he kept peering at her as if he expected her to dissolve.

TALESE, Gay

DETROIT NEWS
(Detroit, Mich.)

Dec. 9, 1973

USUALLY, Talese has no trouble getting people to tell all. For a start he doesn't use a tape-recorder, which he believes hinders direct communication and really is an intrusion. He seldom takes notes except of dates and addresses and spends many hours just getting to know his subject.

Take the man from Detroit who is one of the main characters in his unwritten book. Talese met him at the sex commune in California, where the man and his 28-year-old wife were exploring alternative life styles. Both had been married before and found traditional marriage lacking.

"He's a 40-year-old college professor, an ex-Marine who thought of going into the Church. At an age beyond which most people think of dropping out, at 33, he became a dropout. I found him one of the most intelligent people I have met. Since I am writing nonfiction and it is important that people I write about be communicative and perceptive, he is a very good character in the book.

"You have to get close to people so they are willing to confide in you. You have to convince them that you understand. When I am researching a book, I am totally absorbed in it. I live the life style of the characters as much as possible."

Talese ceases to be an interloping reporter — he becomes a friend. And perhaps it is sometimes even hard for him to remember who is the chronicler and who is the man. He is a chameleon.

As a child he never could blend into his environment. Born Gaetano Talese, he grew up an Italian Catholic in an Irish Catholic school in a Methodist town, Ocean City, N.J. He was a natural outsider. And his tailor father didn't help. He loved elegance and made Talese be different at an age when he wanted to be the same.

He was a consistent under-achiever in school. He scraped through parochial school because his father owned a dry-cleaning business and as long as Joe Talese's son was passed from grade to grade, there was no charge for cleaning the priest's dirty linen.

His high school principal said he wasn't college material, and he was turned down by 16 colleges before the University of Alabama accepted him.

After blue law Ocean City, Talese found the South sensuous and liberating. He studied and liked journalism. In 1953 his degree earned him a job as copyboy at the Times.

By 1957 he was earning bylines in the Times, and that's when he met Nan. They were married two years later when Talese was covering the making of "La Dolce Vita" for the Times in Rome.

TALESE says he is a person "more bemused by life" than he appears to be. He is basically serious and has a deep commitment to his family and friends. "It is very important to be available when they need help and to help those who cannot reciprocate, at least today and possibly ever."

He eschews any philosophical ramblings.

The closest he came was: "Hardly a day goes by when I don't wish things were different about myself. If I lapse into a fantasy about being somebody else, I quickly recognize it as being based on a series of false assumptions about their happiness. They don't have everything any more than I do.

"Anyway, my goal is not happiness. I don't want to be unhappy and I'm not."

Right now his goal is to write the first paragraph of his book. He is a painstaking writer — the sort who rewrites sentences 12 or 15 times. It is a tortuous task; each word has to be the RIGHT one.

His methods have brought him recognition in the past — but he needs to be reassured. Most of all, he wants to be respected by the people he respects "for being a hell of a good reporter and for writing well. I never won a prize. Never ever. But then, I don't think that winning prizes now will make a bit of difference."

A crack appears, marring the luscious good life of Gay Talese. His goal is not happiness — it is recognition. He's earned laurels in abundance, but recently he's been catching thorns. Thorns from people who think the sexual revolution is passe or that his lengthy research is a con job.

When this kind of talk starts, the jaw hardens, the eyes turn icy and the voice dangerously smooth. He could leap at your throat. Ever since he started researching the sexual revolution, Talese has taken the offensive. He's been criticizing, justifying, and proselytizing. He has enjoyed the action and adversity.

But this night he is tired — tired of talking, of explaining, of redefining and reaching out. And a lingering sadness sits between us.

As I move to go, I reconsider. I turn and ask him to autograph two books he'd given me.

The lethargy leaves him, he smiles benignly and signs with a flourish. Graciousness itself. That moment is perfect — he is a serious writer being taken seriously. ■

He Fears Being Typed A Pornography Freak

TASCA, Jules
PHILADELPHIA BULLETIN (Philadelphia, Penn.)
June 23, 1974

Bulletin Staff Photo by Vincent Gonzales

By JOE ADCOCK
Of The Bulletin Staff

PHILADELPHIA playwright Jules Tasca fears being typed as a pornography freak. His comedy about pornography and censorship, "The Mind with the Dirty Man," has had some notable theatrical successes in Los Angeles and Chicago, but he claims no special expertise as an erotic impresario.

"Just because I've written about pornography doesn't mean I'm addicted to it," he said. "When I went out to Los Angeles the producers put me up in a place on Sunset Strip, where all the pornographic movies and shows are. I guess they thought I'd really appreciate that.

"There was a place next door that had what they called live sex shows. Friday nights were amateur night. Imagine that. Couples would come in and compete, I guess. I'd be afraid to go into a place like that. You might go to the john and be declared the winner. Or, worse, the loser.

"When they wanted to do another play of mine in L.A., "Tadpole," about baseball, I wrote to them, 'Please don't put me up out by Dodger Stadium.'

"I've only seen one pornographic movie in my whole life. That was years ago. It was called 'Couples.' I think I'd read something by Ernie Schier in The Bulletin saying it was a cut above your standard show becaue it had some semblance of a story.

"Maybe it was a cut above. But it was still awful. Who needs that stuff? What I'm concerned about is censorship."

• • •

"THE MIND with a Dirty Man" will have its Philadelphia-area premier this week, opening tomorrow at the Bucks County Playhouse in New Hope.

Tasca's play concerns a young man who makes pornographic movies. He buys a theater in a small town to show his work. His father happens to be a member of the town's censorship board. To further complicate things, the son is enamored of his leading lady, a Linda Lovelace type.

"Okay, it's a situation comedy, like on TV," Tasca said. "It's meant to entertain. If people start thinking about it later, and decide that censorship is really kind of silly, so much the better. But there's no sense in satirizing an attitude if you turn off the types that may hold it.

"Acting superior to your audience is no good. The Greeks, Shakespeare, Moliere — they were all very popular entertainment in their own times."

• • •

TASCA IS from South Philadelphia, near 22d and McKean sts. He now teaches drama at Gwynedd-Mercy College and lives in Norristown.

He did theater graduate work at Villanova University at the same time David Rabe, author of "Sticks and Bones" and "The Basic Training of Pavlo Hummel," was studying there.

"David and I have similar concerns," Tasca said. "We both have reservations about middle class attitudes and behavior: you know, him calling the couple in 'Sticks and Bones' Ozzie and Harriet and all.

"But David goes about his satire so harshly, so darkly. I'm not trying to compare myself to him. But I can't help mentioning that difference.

"I'm influenced by George S. Kaufman. (Kaufman wrote many popular plays, including "June Moon," "You Can't Take It With You" and "Dinner at Eight.") I wrote my thesis about him. I'm listed in the sources of the new biography about him—beside Thurber and Steinbeck! Wow!"

• • •

TASCA is 35. He and his wife have three young children. He feels an often-voiced distress about the state of the American theater.

"I write plays because that's what I like to do," he said. "But what a profession! I was talking to an editor at Samuel French. (French is a publisher of plays.) He said people were calling in from dinner theaters and summer stock places asking, 'What's new? What's hot?' And he told them, 'Nothing.'

"It used to be the little theaters fed on last year's Broadway hits. But 'Irene?' 'Grease?' 'No, No, Nanette?' That's what Broadway's doing. It's not new and it's not hot.

"Young people don't go to the theater. The audience is 40 and over. What young person is going to pay $6 for a theater ticket?

• • •

"THE COSTS of production are killing off anything fresh. No one wants to take a chance. New York is not a place where you can try and fail and try again, the way it was for Kaufman 40 years ago.

"I saw this year's list of new works by Drama Guild members. Most of them were novels! Even established playwrights don't bother writing plays.

"Thank God for the regional theaters like the Mark Taper Forum in Los Angeles. My agent sent 'Dirty Man' out to them. They gave it a small, experimental production three years ago. The audience liked it. So they did a full scale show last year as part of their regular season.

"But I live in Philadelphia. Why doesn't Philadelphia have a regional theater?"

How Jerry terHorst Could Make That Decision To Leave the White House

News Photos by GARY PORTE

terHORST, Jerald Franklin

DETROIT NEWS (Detroit, Mich.) Oct. 13, 1974

By AL STARK
Sunday Magazine Writer

JERRY TERHORST, the man who quit as President Ford's press secretary because he could not accept the pardon of Richard Nixon, was driving home out the George Washington Parkway toward Alexandria, Va., when he took his pipe out of his mouth and said:

"I just remembered something I wanted to tell you about my mother.

"My mother used to recite this little ditty to me and the other children," terHorst said. "I think it probably is more melodious in Dutch, which is the language she used when she taught it to us, but it is pretty good, too, in English. I've recited it to each of my kids, too. It goes:

"'Dare to be a Daniel — Dare to stand alone — Dare to have a purpose firm — Dare to make it known.'"

TerHorst laughed, then said:

"My wife, Louise, had called my parents and her parents and our children as soon as I had made the decision to resign, because we wanted them to know first and we didn't want them, particularly the children, caught off guard by newsmen.

"But I didn't talk to my mother until after it was done, and the first thing she said to me was, 'I see you haven't forgotten Daniel.'"

TERHORST has returned to The Detroit News to write a national political column that is being distributed to many of the nation's leading newspapers by Universal Press Syndicate, and to that new venture he brings a suddenly national reputation as the man who could say no when his conscience demanded.

At 52 he finds himself a pundit and as such plans to make his column ring a bell when a bell needs ringing.

On the George Washington Parkway a day or so after his resignation, another driver, a stranger who apparently recognized terHorst by his pipe, beeped his horn and gave the thumbs-up sign. He is not alone; terHorst has been flooded with mail and telegrams from citizens all over the country, almost all of it congratulating him.

One woman wired: "My protest will reach only the White House; yours reaches the nation."

TerHorst also brings to the new column almost 17 years experience as a Washington correspondent.

And he brings with him tne convictions that spring from a deeply religious upbringing and a continuing religious life.

His parents, John and Maud terHorst, immigrated to the United States separately from Holland as teen-agers, met and married in Grand Rapids, and raised their three children in the strict Calvinist atmosphere of the Christian Reformed Church.

It was a home where grace was said after every meal, as well as before, and a home where, should one person be breakfasting alone and saying his grace privately, everyone else in the room would stop and stand still until the private prayer was finished.

It was a home where certain rules were set and everyone took responsiblity for meeting the rules. Moral convictions were dearly held.

TerHorst, the oldest child, went to a church school for nine grades; he says the church was not only the religious center for the family but the social and cultural center as well.

His father, an elder and a deacon, "lived for two things, his family and his church." TerHorst, who changed years ago to the Presbyterian Church, also Calvinist, is an elder today at the Old Presbyterian Meeting House in Alexandria, Va.

"Religious people believe a certain way where forgiveness is concerned," terHorst said. "They believe that act of true contrition has to precede forgiveness. If you do something wrong and if you make that act of true contrition, then maybe you are entitled to an act of forgiveness.

"But not without contrition.

"I simply was morally offended by the pardon of Richard Nixon, and I knew I couldn't stay.

"When I think of the damage done to this country in his name, when I think of how this country and this government stood still for so long while we agonized over him and his Watergate problem when there was so much else to do...

"And not a word of penitence from him, not a bit. What has he said? That he is sorry he didn't act more quickly when he found out about Watergate.

"That simply isn't penitence in my mind, nor is it contrition.

"I could never face my kids if I went along with this kind of thing," he said. "How can you convince kids that the system works, or that there is justice, or that our system is the best system in the world and should be kept when acts like this go on?

"No, each of us has to stand up somewhere for what we believe.

"Me? I might be very naive in this sophisticated day and age, but if I am it is me."

AFTER GRADE SCHOOL, terHorst's family moved to a farm about 20 miles from Grand Rapids, and after a year of high school terHorst decided he'd be a farmer.

He quit school, rented a neighboring spread and, he says, was something of a success at the soil.

"I did pretty well. I made enough. to buy a Model A and I had a little money in my pocket." He also was a success in 4-H, particularly in contests where youngsters judged livestock.

He also had a regular visitor, his high school principal.

"He would drive by all the time, and if he saw me out in the field plowing with the horses he'd park the car and come over and talk. Talk about me coming back to school.

"Finally I realized that a farm is fine to come back to. But I was renting. ➡

(Continued from preceding page)

The place wasn't really mine. And I went back to school.

"After high school, I won an agricultural scholarship to Michigan State College at East Lansing. It was known then mainly for agriculture. Cow College.

"I got a job there at a radio station as a continuity writer. I would write the things that student announcers would say between recordings of classical music. It paid $8 a week, and I learned a lot about classical music."

A friend suggested Jerry join him on the staff of the campus paper, the State News, and by the end of his freshman year he was night city editor. "I found I really liked that nonsense," he says.

He also by then had met his wife, Louise. She also was on the newspaper staff. She smoked the same brand of cigarets he did, Lucky Strikes, and they got to know each other, he says, because he was always running out of smokes and bumming from her.

TerHorst enlisted in the Marines while World War II was on and was sent to officers candidate school at the University of Michigan. He and Louise were married at the Marine base at Quantico, Va., on Jan. 20, 1945, the day FDR was inaugurated for his fourth and last term. He was commissioned in March and served out the war as executive officer, Marine detachment, aboard the carrier, the USS Intrepid.

After the service, the terHorsts went back to Grand Rapids. TerHorst took a job as a reporter on the Grand Rapids Press and got his degree from U. of M. via correspondence. Louise was a reporter for the Press' twin paper, now closed, the Grand Rapids Herald.

TerHorst's long association and friendship with Gerald R. Ford in Grand Rapids as politician and reporter is well known. As terHorst recounts in his book about Ford, soon to be published, he met Ford when Ford ran first for Congress 25 years ago. And their paths kept crossing.

After Marine duty in the Korean War, terHorst joined The News and, in 1957, was sent to Washington, where Ford was slowly making his way up the ranks of Congress. Ford rose to be minority leader in the House and terHorst to chief of his paper's Washington bureau.

When Ford became president it was terHorst he chose to restore credibility and something less than outright acrimony in the White House press room.

TerHorst, feeling all the excitement and emotion that went along with a drastic change in government and his own new role in a time when the nation cried for healing, signed on.

THEN IT ALL burst. On Saturday, Sept. 7, terHorst (who had expected to be an advisor to his old friend, President Ford, as well as an answer man), was "stunned" to learn the President was going to pardon Richard Nixon, before indictment and before trial.

TerHorst recalls:

"I wondered very briefly that afternoon whether there wasn't some way I could serve my conscience and still stay on at the White House. But that period of consideration was very short. I knew I couldn't."

Then, with all the professionalism that is familiar to those who know him, he set up the White House forum in which the announcement he so strongly disagreed with would be made.

He got home about 9 p.m.

"A friend of one of my daughters was there," he said. "He's a fine young photographer, and he had taken pictures of each of the family. He was there so we could look through them and choose the ones we wanted.

"That took until 11 or so.

"Then, while Martha, who is a high school senior, was upstairs getting ready for bed, and Peggy, who was home from college in Richmond, was busy somewhere, Louise and I talked.

Now, he says, "the discussion of my decision to resign wasn't very long and it wasn't traumatic, either. But it included the President's reasoning about the pardon.

"I told Louise how I felt, and she asked one question, 'If you feel that way, COULD you stay?' I said, no, and that was that.

"We called the girls down then and told them and, after a minute, they understood and accepted it, too. They, of course, had been quite excited about my taking the job — the limousine that picked me up in the morning and brought me home, the White House dinners, all of that.

"But I told them my reasons for resigning, and they understood."

TerHorst then wrote his letter of resignation.

It took some time, of course, because this was an old friend he was leaving.

Another factor, one guesses, is that terHorst looked forward to the White House job — he is a very thoughtful man, and he had substantive ideas about making more of the press secretary's job than simply an answer man or no-comment man. Also, the lure of the White House — to be near the center of things around the most powerful man in the world, the President — is very strong. History shows that can create very deep loyalties.

As he recounted to a highly interested press, this struggle with the letter lasted until early morning. By then it was time for the limousine to arrive to transport him to the White House. Louise, meanwhile, had called their daughter, Karen, 26, in Atlanta, where she teaches and does graduate work, and their son, Peter, 19, who was at the University of Virginia.

He had hoped his resignation would not create an undue stir. Of course, it did.

He laughs about the constantly ringing phone at his home the night the resignation became known and says, "My family would all make good press secretaries. You should have seen Martha in action. And Louise."

More than that, Louise and Martha (and one presumes the children away from home) seem to wear terHorst's decision with the same quiet sureness that he does. They are people who seem to have a very real style and no airs. No one seems down or emotionally wiped out. Their conviction of right done seems very solid.

On the way to dinner four or five days after terHorst resigned, Louise was telling how she tried and tried to explain things to a friend who couldn't figure out why Jerry couldn't have found some way to stay on at the White House.

Martha, in the back seat, said very quietly, "Because you have to live with yourself."

ONE OF THE MARKS of terHorst's professionalism all his years as a Washington reporter is that people who read him regularly could never say

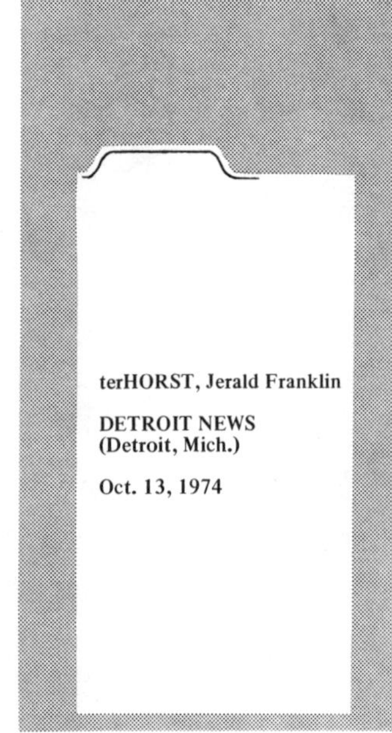

with any conviction what his own politics were. He firmly believes a political reporter must be nonpartisan to be fair.

He covered and presented the news, keeping his own opinions to himself, in journalism's once-traditional way.

His new column gives him new freedom to express opinions.

"A lot more of who I am shows now," he said. "And the column, I hope, will benefit from my experience."

A lot of who he is shows, too, in the now-scrapped plans he had for the press secretary's office and his continuing affection for President Ford.

TerHorst said, "I wanted to eventually turn the press secretary into a true spokesman for the President, and I thought I would have a great opportunity to do that because of my long association with him.

"I wanted to do more with the job than answer phone calls from reporters or tell them no comment or ignore their calls. I wanted to do more than that kind of reaction work, where everything is in reaction to a reporter's call.

"For instance, I wanted to sit down with the experts in various fields and with the President and look ahead. Take the arms limitations talks. Where should the U.S. be six months from now? What is apt to happen between now and then? If this happens, what moves do we make? If something else happens, where do we go?

"A long-range, more reflective look at things — not just the question and answer thing. A press secretary who was a real spokesman for the President could sit down with reporters, out of the heat of a moment of crisis, and explain what the long-range situation was.

"I think that would be beneficial to everyone, and I wanted to get at it as soon as things had settled down. Now, I hope some other press secretary will try it."

It is obvious, talking to terHorst, that he thought the combination of President Ford's candor and their long friendship produced exactly the kind of rapport in which the spokesman concept could flourish.

TerHorst talks with affection of that candor, on the occasions when he has seen it. The announcement that the President had changed his mind about running in 1976 is an example.

Nelson Rockefeller, the vice-president designate, had told reporters that he expected Mr. Ford to run in 1976 — a statement contrary to everything the President had said. TerHorst knew he could expect a rash of questions, and he caught up with the President near the Rose Garden to ask him about it.

TerHorst said, "He looked at me and said, 'Well, the truth is that I probably will run. Circumstances have changed, and I have changed my mind.'

"Just like that," terHorst said. "No hemming or hawing. No dodging. I asked if I could put his new position out, and he said, 'Sure. It's true.' That openness is a wonderful thing to work with.

"The same thing with the pardon. Another president might have sent the pardon to Nixon surreptitiously, telling him that here it is and it will be announced when you need it, when you are indicted or convicted.

"But that isn't President Ford's way. He did it — he issued the pardon — and he said he did it. No hiding. He stood up and owned up and that's the way he is.

"No, we are not enemies. I still have respect for him. As I said when I quit, he did what he did out of conscience and I acted out of conscience, too. I respect him for following his conscience and I hope he regards me the same way."

Certainly Mr. Ford hasn't forgotten terHorst, or the reasons he chose him in the first place.

The phone rang in terHorst's office and it was one of the men assisting William Scranton in his search for people to fill important spots in the Ford administration.

Although terHorst had just left Mr. Ford's White House in protest, that same White House had suggested to the head-hunters that the man whose brain they ought to pick about the press operation was terHorst, resigned or not.

TerHorst said he'd be happy to share his ideas.

Studs Terkel Believes in Work So He Writes About Workers

TERKEL, Studs (Louis) (1912-)

PHILADELPHIA BULLETIN (Philadelphia, Penn.)

Apr. 17, 1974

By LEWIS BEALE

Special to The Bulletin

"I BELIEVE IN WORK, not the work ethic," says Studs Terkel, as he lounges on the bed at The Barclay sipping Scotch "mainly because the work ethic has with it the implication 'one must or else.' Work is actually part of a man's being. Something inside a man compels him to create; that, to me, is work."

Terkel should know of what he speaks, for his latest book, "Working," is a fascinating, disturbing compilation of over 130 interviews with common (and some not so common) working people, ranging from elevator attendants to corporation presidents. Already a smash bestseller, "Working" explores just what it is that people do, and exactly how they feel about what they do.

"I celebrate the non-celebrated," says Terkel, as he paces the room with long strides. "I've found that average people want to talk about themselves, their hopes, dreams, aspirations, provided they sense that you're interested in what they're saying. In fact, this book is not just about work, it's about the human comedy as well, the human condition."

New Scholarly Endeavor

WHAT TERKEL IS involved in is, in fact, a rather new scholarly endeavor known as oral history. Simply put, oral history involves a researcher, writer, or what-have-you going out into the streets, farms and factories armed only with a tape recorder, for the purpose of recording the 'average' man's reactions to the events of today or yesterday.

"After all," asks Terkel rhetorically, "who has been writing history? For that matter, who, in times past, could write? Most of our history has come from official documents and the memoirs of kings and foreign ministers and the like. But no one ever bothered to ask the common soldier how he felt about the Battle of Hastings, and I think that that's a real tragedy. But then the tape recorder came along, and changed everything.

"I really don't have any set rule for how I talk to people," says Terkel. "A lot has to do with the person, the time, the place. I'll talk in a bar over beers, at home, in the street; wherever the person feels most comfortable. Improvisation, in fact, is part of my work.

'Interesting' Criterion

"SOME OF THE PEOPLE in the book I already knew, and some were recommended to me by friends and acquaintances. My only criterion was that the person be interesting, and have something to say. But that's not much, for I feel that everyone has something interesting to say."

Not the least of whom is Terkel himself, a graduate of the University of Chicago Law School who has worked for the Depression-era WPA writers project, acted as a gangster on radio serials, hosted a jazz radio show and written two outstanding books of oral history ("Hard Times" and "Division Street, America"). Currently, he handles a very free-form talk show broadcast over a Chicago radio station.

"We're at a crossroads today," he says. "There just doesn't seem to be any particular vision at the moment. We seem to be going two ways. There's this incredible horror of discontent, which you see a great deal of in the book, coupled with an openness of discussion. The problem is, though. that the discussion isn't deep enough, it's on a very banal level. I mean, Hannah Arendt talked about the banality of evil, but I think that banality is an evil in itself.

"I think that the machine has something to do with all this, because it's made so many people machines. The thing is that the machine can liberate man. After all, work should be part of man's creativity, not something that's a chore. There'll always be some type of work that's rather demeaning, but it doesn't necessarily have to demean the person who's doing it.

"For instance, one of the happiest people in the book is a man who's a parking lot attendant. Every time he gets behind the wheel of a car, he feels that he has some kind of power, some sense that he's controlling his own destiny. There's no reason why every worker in America shouldn't be able to feel that way, but obviously that's not the case.

"That's one of the reasons why I'm particularly gratified at the success of the book, because it lets the common man speak, and it brings out a lot of discontent with things the way they are. And there's certainly nothing wrong with some healthy criticism."

Terkel pauses to ruminate over the last thought, and then, suddenly, an almost childish grin spreads over his face. "Ya know," he says, with a soft chuckle, "I'm chronicling the lives of non-celebrated people, of people who need to be heard and recognized, and strangely enough, me, the man who's editing the tapes, becomes the celebrity. Now that, to me, well, I find that funny."

(Also see preceding article)

Working Man

No Tape Gap for Studs Terkel

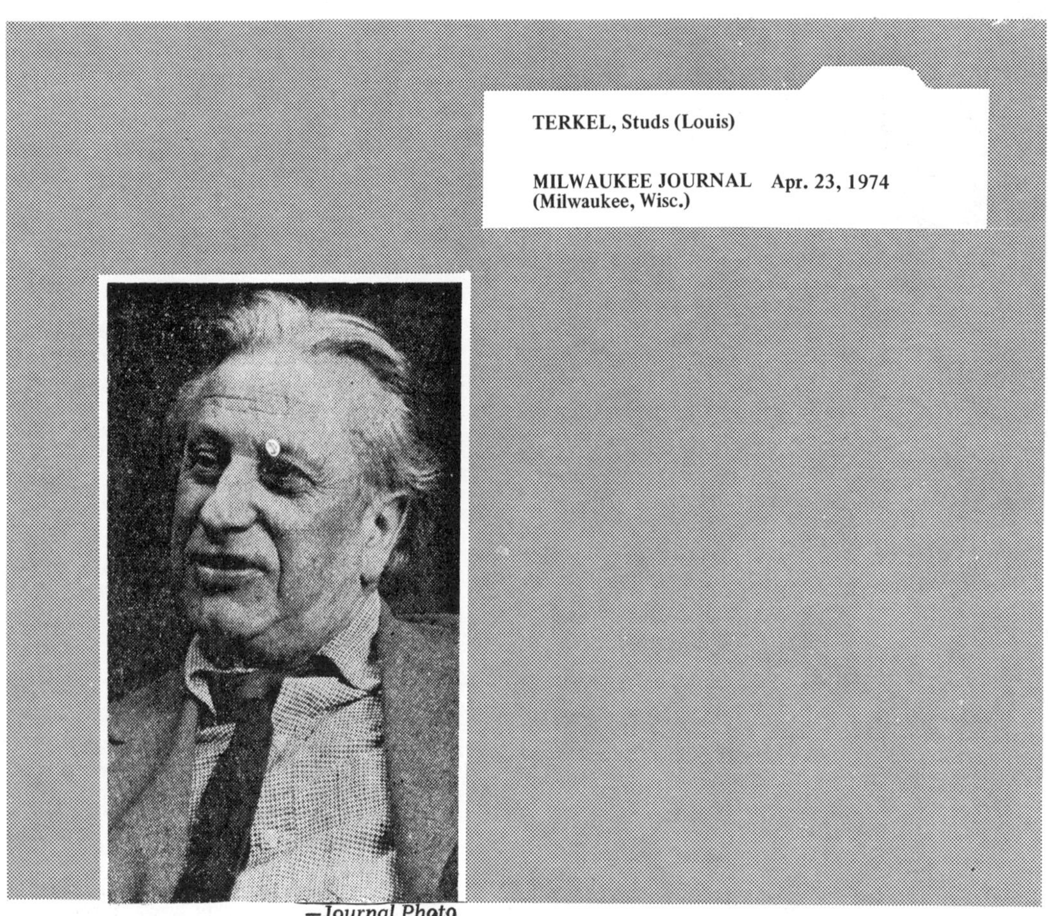

—Journal Photo

By Gerald Kloss
of The Journal Staff

Studs Terkel is a short, ruddy faced, 61 year old Chicago author with thinning silver hair. He speaks swiftly and with facial animation — a man accustomed to interviewing and being interviewed.

He was in town Monday to promote his latest book, "Working," made up of 133 tape recorded interviews he held with working people of all trades over the last three years, from gravediggers to supermarket checkers to streetwalkers to factory owners.

The 589 page volume is the Book-of-the-Month Club selection for May, and has been praised by the eminent critic and philosopher, Lewis Mumford, as a "powerful, original, indescribable and incredible book," created by "an interviewer of genius." In a conference room at the Boston Store, Studs Terkel lighted up a long cigar and spoke about his own work:

Well, about the name Studs. I just sort of adopted it in the mid-1930s, when I played gangster parts in radio soap operas, and have kept it ever since. Never had a legal change of name. My given name was Louis.

In my interviews for this book, I used the same brand of tape recorder that was involved in the 18½ minute gap on the White House tapes. Of the thousands of hours of tapes I recorded, I never accidentally erased a minute, even though I'm not mechanically minded. In fact, sometimes I punch the wrong thing, and the person I'm interviewing corrects me.

The idea for the book came from my brilliant editor at Pantheon Books, Andre Schiffrin, who also got me to do my two other interview books, "Division Street: America," about contemporary life in the big city, and "Hard Times," about life in the Great Depression of the 1930s. I made maybe 200 interviews and used 133.

In a typical interview, I might have recorded 10 times as much as I used in the book. It's like gold mining. You have to go through so much material to find the gold. Then it has to be refined, and then minted.

The interviewing technique was informal, starting out with casual conversation. Then the person would open up, about what bugged him on the job, or what feelings of pride or lack of pride he had in it. Astonishing things came out, and sometimes the person, listening to the playback, would shake his head in wonderment at what he had said.

That's a thing I've never found in interviewing celebrities — a feeling of astonishment. They've been interviewed so many times themselves that they flow the practiced words right past you. All through the gathering of material for "Working," by the way, I had a daily radio show in Chicago.

I have my own pride in this, that when I interview an author about his new book, I always read the book from cover to cover, taking notes, before talking to him. Which means I'm sometimes up till 3 or 4 in the morning, finishing the book. You'd be amazed how many TV and radio interviewers do their homework by scanning the book jacket.

No, a lot of the names in "Working" are not real, for obvious reasons. They'd get fired if their identity were known, and the whole book wouldn't be worth it to me to have one person fired, even if he hated the job.

As for myself, I enjoy working. I can't imagine myself stretching out on a beach for a week and doing nothing. I enjoy good food, but it's no big thing with me. A sandwich will do if I'm in a hurry.

Sure, I'm happy that "Working" is a Book-of-the-Month choice, which means it'll be a top seller. But more than that I prize the opinion of someone like Lewis Mumford. That's where my pride is. That's what it's about, for me.

The Voice From Everywhere

By FRANKLYNN PETERSON

"When I did my first news broadcast, Walter Cronkite was 9 years old. In fact, half of those active on the air today weren't even born when I broke into broadcasting." So says Lowell Thomas, 82, who's logged more network air time than anyone in the history of radio and is still on the job after 44 years before the mike. His career has been studded with such pioneering feats as the first to broadcast from a ship, from an airplane, from a coal mine and from a submarine.

Thomas, whose name became synonymous with news commentator, was even paid tribute by Mutt and Jeff creator Bud Fisher in a 1945 comic panel which punned about an aristocratic young potato who wanted to marry Lowell Thomas. "But you can't marry Lowell Thomas," said the mother Tater. "No," said the father Tater, "he's just a common-tator."

Thomas' comments on the news are usually colored by his view that life itself is a lot of fun. "I try to make news somewhat entertaining," he explains. "It seems to me that the day-by-day exploits and adventures of mankind are fantastic, fabulous. Why shouldn't they be entertaining? And why shouldn't you tell them in a way that brings it out in that fashion? I've always tried to do that."

Adds Thomas, "I give listeners a glimpse of what's happening in some far-off part of the world. But if it's a big story, my listeners have to go to a newspaper to get the whole story. Same is true of television."

In order to satisfy his own appetite for a fun-filled life, and thereby enjoyable newscasts, Lowell Thomas has practically become another satellite of the earth. He's journeyed to both poles and almost everywhere between. Back in 1917, he helped make famous an unknown, young Oxford-educated archaeologist living with Bedouins — Lawrence of Arabia. At the time, Lawrence was wearing a golden sword, leading Arab raids against the Turkish army. The time was World War I, and Lowell Thomas "scooped" everybody else with his story. He followed up his reports about Lawrence with a worldwide tour and a book.

For an encore, Thomas crossed through the Khyber Pass and into the then forbidden land of Afghanistan. Most often, in those days before and during the Roaring Twenties, Thomas was accompanied by his wife Frances and by movie cameraman Harry A. Chase, who filmed the exotic lands they visited for early Lowell Thomas adventure and travel films.

During the 1930s Thomas visited Central America, Tibet, Australia, Alaska, all the while producing films, as well as broadcasting newsy tidbits to spellbound millions of folks back home.

In 1937, this human communications satellite hopped a steamship for England to cover the coronation of King George VI. En route he gave his nightly newscasts while aboard ship. In 1939, he launched NBC's experimental TV news program.

When World War II came to the airwaves, Thomas broadcast directly from Manila, Guam, Cairo, Okinawa, Iwo Jima, Paris, Rome. He used a specially outfitted truck as his mobile broadcast studio. On April 24, 1945, he flew over besieged Berlin in a P-51 Mustang so he could report first hand about the European theater's last battles.

In 1949, Lowell Thomas and son Lowell Jr. climbed over the Himalayan Mountains into forbidden Tibet. The aura of Lhasa, the country's capital, a real-life Shangri-La, was captured on film, ➡

THOMAS, Lowell (Jackson) (1892-)

DALLAS NEWS (Dallas, Tex.)

Sept. 1, 1974

[See also CA-45/48]

(Continued from preceding page)

in books Thomas wrote and in his daily newscasts.

Lowell Thomas' Himalayan trip lost its enchantment with the personal news that a horse backed him over a mountain ravine. His leg broken in eight places, hundreds of miles from the nearest doctor, he was carried on horseback 200 miles over rocky trails and through narrow passes, suffering intense pain all the way.

Within months after his harrowing Himalayan misadventure, the peripatetic newscaster was back on the mountain slopes again. An ardent skier, Thomas literally follows the snow, often to Alaska where Lowell Jr. is a state senator.

Despite his reputation as a galavanting adventurer, Thomas comments, "I have no great aversion to the word 'adventure.' Yet, if you go on an expedition which is well planned, you should have no hair-raising adventures." Day-to-day life is an adventure all by itself, he insists.

"I consider giving birth one of life's greatest adventures. A clergyman saving a soul, if he can, is another of life's great adventures. Surgeons, schoolteachers, they're all adventurers.

"Home is one of the most dangerous places to be," Thomas says. "The hazards there are so much greater than on a ski slope." Which may be why he's such a hale-and-hearty looking 82-year-old — he spends little time at home.

Home is Quaker Hill, a sumptuous estate in ritzy Dutchess County, a two-hour drive north of New York City. His income reportedly hit the quarter million mark very early in his career, enabling him to buy Quaker Hill after World War I. But he still looks for things to improve on it as he rides around the grounds, sometimes in a golf cart and often on his old one-speed, thick-tired bicycle.

Lowell Jackson Thomas entered the world in Darke County, Ohio, but his father, a doctor, soon set up practice in the Cripple Creek mining camps of Colorado. Young Thomas grew up peddling papers in saloons, packed a pistol, and remembers walking to Sunday school by way of the town's red-light district, hand in hand with a young lady who later became speakeasy queen Texas Guinan.

High school for Thomas was back in Ohio, but college included stops at Valparaiso in Indiana for a B.S. and M.A., the University of Denver for another B.S. and another M.A., Kent College of Law in Chicago, and finally Princeton, where he studied constitutional law.

Between studying for degrees, Lowell Thomas worked as a gold miner, a reporter for the Cripple Creek *Times* and the Chicago *Journal*, as well as a professor of public speaking. Already, Lowell Thomas liked to speak almost as much as he liked to travel.

He soon took to the lecture platform and found that audiences in the millions, literally, would pay to see his mixture of movies, slides, music and commentary. India, Lawrence of Arabia — the subjects didn't matter. "So long as my show was exciting, the audience was absorbed," Thomas recalls.

To this day, he says, "There are three words missing from my vocabulary: 'Lecture,' 'travelogue' and 'documentary.' If you use any of them, you chop off a substantial portion of your audience because they don't want to be bored by you." And that's about as universal a word or two of wisdom as you're likely to get out of Lowell Thomas' modest lips.

He seldom admits to having anything more highfalutin than a hunch. And when asked for those ephemeral words of wisdom we expect 82-year-old celebrities to have, inevitably he says gruffly, "I haven't any." But Lowell Thomas can spin a lot of enjoyable yarns which end up as the next best thing to infinite wisdom.

"I've seen lots of news stories coming and going. Watergate, for instance, is nothing new. I've seen the Teapot Dome, the Five Percenters, the vicuna coats . . .

"I don't even know how much of a crisis Watergate is. I'm not enough of a prophet to predict what the outcome will be. But here's an interesting sidelight told to me by Lord Beaverbrook when Lady Astor was after him to stop publication of a book, quite unflattering to Lawrence of Arabia: " 'Number one, just keep in mind that the man who made the attack will probably be the one to suffer the most. Number two, no truly great man in the history of the world has ever escaped vitriolic attack whether Christ or Caesar.'

"I've known President Nixon a long time and have never seen a sordid side to him," Thomas says. "But then I haven't been opposing him in political combat.

"The Nixons have visited us here, which is true of other presidents. Mr. Roosevelt (Franklin, not Teddy) was an extraordinary individual. Yet there were literally millions of people who wouldn't mention his name. They called him 'that man.'

"Mr. Hoover used to come and stay with us after he left the White House. He once told me that he had to invite 44 important Americans before he could form a cabinet. Really few really great men really wanted a cabinet post. First of all, he'd say to himself that whatever the height is in his profession, he's there, there's no place for him to go. If he goes to Washington, all he can do is get in trouble. And that's one reason why it's so difficult to get good people in the cabinet."

Then Thomas complains, "But we're just chatting about nothing!" He's been chatting about such nothings for 44 years on the air. And he's been turning such chatty nothings into books since the 1920s. Even Lowell Thomas can't remember how many books, but the figure is close to 50.

In his Quaker Hill offices, Thomas has two books in the works. He's written about 2,000 pages over the past two years on a book of reminiscences and says, "We're only up to 1938 so far." One feature of the book will be a collection of cartoons about the genuine voice of America, Lowell Thomas.

The other Thomas book in the making is a biography about Jimmy Doolittle, a project he started in 1928 and is only now getting around to finishing. "This country needs some real heroes right now," says Thomas. "The astronauts would be great hero material except there are too many of them. How many can you remember by name? There was John Glenn who was the first one and then what's-his-name who walked on the moon first. And all those other guys."

You can get an idea of the kinds of heroes Thomas has in mind by the subject of some of his books: Charles Lindbergh, "Count Luckner, The Sea Devil," General Smedley Butler, Rudyard Kipling and "Burma Jack."

But a neighbor of the Thomas family comes close to hero status in his eyes, Norman Vincent Peale. "I admire him enormously because of his positive outlook," says Thomas. "We're on this planet, we don't know where we came from or where we're going. So why shouldn't we have a positive outlook while we're here? People should be doing something which interests them."

It's pretty obvious that Thomas is plenty positive about the life he's still enjoying to its fullest at 82. Every evening — Monday through Friday — he winds up his 5-minute, CBS radio newscasts with the same sign-off he's used for 44 years: "So long until tomorrow."

THOMAS,
Lowell (Jackson)

DALLAS NEWS
(Dallas, Tex.)

Sept. 1, 1974

'The President was tainted and corrupted by Haldeman'

By PHILIP NOBILE

RALPH DE TOLEDANO wrote two Nixon biographies and had been an intimate friend for over 20 years before H. R. Haldeman put the hex on him in 1970.

According to de Toledano, Haldeman heard that he was trying to warn the President against him. (Maybe this explains why de Toledano blames Haldeman more than Nixon for Watergate.)

In any case, de Toledano's observations are fascinating, even though they are heavily weighted toward the right.

TOLEDANO, Ralph de (1916-)

DETROIT NEWS (Detroit, Mich.)

Nov. 10, 1974

[See also CA-11/12]

* * *

QUESTION: As friend and biographer of Richard Nixon, did you ever think him capable of such duplicity as he admitted?

DE TOLEDANO: Anybody's capable of anything. It's standard behavior for presidents to try to protect their administrations. The Watergate coverup was actually a minor offense. Nixon's "crime" was in letting friends go out on the limb for him when he wasn't 100 percent clean.

Millions of Americans believed Richard Nixon until the bitter end. But you knew the man intimately and shouldn't have been fooled.

Nixon's character changed markedly when he became President. The Nixon I knew pre-1969 and Nixon post-1969 were completely different persons. He isolated himself in the White House and lost touch with reality in a sense. Maybe what was latent in his character then surfaced. But I don't know. I'm not a psychiatrist.

How do you explain the hold Haldeman and Ehrlichman had on the President? To say the least, these are extremely limited figures.

Perhaps great men reach a point where they need the company of sycophants. Truman had his cronies. Douglas MacArthur surrounded himself with the biggest bunch of intellectually dishonest creeps I've ever seen.

Were Haldeman and Ehrlichman "sinister influences?"

The President was tainted and corrupted by Haldeman. I don't know much about Ehrlichman. But Watergate would never have happened if Haldeman had been a decent guy.

He was in on everything. On a number of occasions he deliberately violated presidential orders. He probably thought he was doing the right thing, but he didn't know what the right thing was.

Richard Nixon sounded so unpresidential on his tapes. Do you suppose he was really comfortable in the White House?

He hasn't been truly comfortable since he was a little boy. He never got over his miserable childhood and was always compensating for it.

Nixon was also unhappy in politics. He is the most introverted man I've met in public life. And an introverted politician is a contradiction in terms. Nobody, not even Bebe Rebozo, ever got close to him. I don't imagine he's let his hair down to anyone in his entire life.

There is the argument that Richard Nixon didn't do anything his predecessors hadn't done before him. Only he got caught. Could Presidents Johnson, Kennedy and Eisenhower have survived impeachment investigations?

I doubt it. For example, LBJ was involved in the Billy Sol Estes and Bobby Baker coverups. He abused his office by lining his pockets with millions of dollars from his TV monopoly in Austin.

Washington is full of substantiated stories abour JFK's sex life. After all, adultery is a crime in every state.

And how about Eisenhower's little deal on his war memoirs, "Crusade in Europe?" Instead of having the book's royalties taxed as income, the way any writer is taxed, he made a lot more money by taking his earnings as capital gains.

I have tremendous admiration for Harry Truman, although he covered up for Alger Hiss when he realized Hiss was guilty.

The point is that the press didn't dig into or blow up these matters like they did with Watergate.

Therefore, on a moral scale, Nixon is less guilty than his predecessors?

Than some, yes.

And the press did him in? Did the Washington Post reporters, Woodward and Bernstein, break into Watergate, too?

Look, the coverage on Watergate was not just a case of reporters' digging up stories. The whole thing was carefully orchestrated. The Woodward and Bernstein book tips their hand — they admited to holding up stories until the stories could be used more effectively.

Can you give me an instance of where the press was wrong on Watergate?

Not at the moment, no. But my memory, not my argument, is at fault.

Why hasn't Nixon made some sort of confession? Could he still believe he is innocent of all charges?

I have it on very good authority that after Harry Truman dismissed the Hiss case as a "red herring," he turned to an aide and said: "Sure Alger Hiss is guilty. But they're not after him, they're after me."

I wouldn't be surprised if Nixon feels the same way about Watergate, that the press has been after him since 1948 and simply used Watergate as an excuse. So why should he give them the satisfaction by an admission of guilt?

You are one of the hardcore Nixon supporters who, according to conventional wisdom, would have torn the country apart if he had not been granted pardon. Exactly how would you have reacted if your former leader were not on trial?

I'd have been very sad.

But isn't it manifestly unjust to prosecute people for following Nixon's orders and not prosecute Nixon himself at the same time.

First, Haldeman, Ehrlichman, Mitchell and the rest of the defendants in the coverup trial must prove they were following orders. But I don't believe they were. These guys were self-starters.

However, if Haldeman and the others were acting on the orders of the President, then you have the Nuremburg situation. Under these circumstances, perhaps suspended sentences is the best course.

Tolkien, master of fantasy

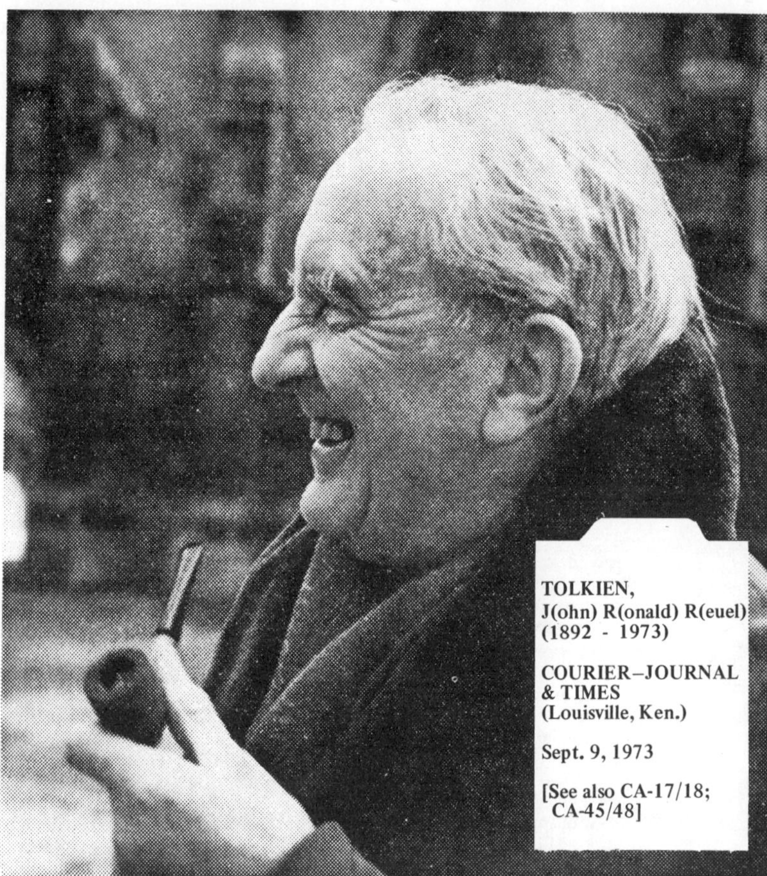

TOLKIEN,
J(ohn) R(onald) R(euel)
(1892 - 1973)
COURIER–JOURNAL & TIMES
(Louisville, Ken.)
Sept. 9, 1973
[See also CA-17/18; CA-45/48]

By ADELE VINCENT

IT'S DIFFICULT to believe that J.R.R. Tolkien actually died last weekend, at the grand old age of 81. Like his books, he was ageless, timeless; he should have been immortal.

My memory of him goes back to the mid-1950s when "The Lord of the Rings" was first published. At the time I was a student at Oxford University where Tolkien was Merton Professor of English Language and Literature, but at that point I hadn't heard of him except as a name that appeared on lecture lists. Somehow, in my childhood, I had escaped reading "The Hobbit", the early fairy tale which had originally been written as a story for children but which turned out to be the prologue for the great trilogy of the Rings.

But many of my fellow students, especially those who, like me, were English majors, had read "The Hobbit" and from them I caught Tolkien fever. I found a copy of the book, read it and was stricken for life.

After that it was just a question of persuading my family that hardback copies of the newly published, three volume, "The Lord of the Rings" were just what I needed for my next birthday present, and then finding time to read close to 1200 pages. Once you have been swept up into that strange, magical world of Middle-earth, with its elves and dwarves and orcs and the friendly little Hobbits, it's hard to get back to everyday reality.

YET, ENTHRALLED though we all were with the adventures of Frodo and Samwise, of Gandalf the Grey and Aragorn, and with their perilous journey to the land of Mordor, an even greater thrill was to meet their creator himself.

I heard him give a series of lectures on "Sir Gawayne and the Green Knight", a 14th century Arthurian romance written in a Middle English dialect that is largely incomprehensible to anyone who hasn't studied the origins of the English language.

The style of this long poem is the alliterative verse form characteristic of early English poetry, and the highlight of each lecture was when Tolkien would move away from his lectern and pace back and forth at the front of the room, his black academic gown billowing round his shoulders, as he recited whole sections of the poem. One sonorous line would follow rapidly after another, now rippling like a running stream, now roaring like a raging torrent. He always spoke quickly, as if there was so much to say that he couldn't get the words out fast enough. When he was explaining a passage it was something of a strain to follow him, but when he was reciting, it was enough just to sit back and let the sound float over your ears.

He was a robust-looking man, with a kindly face, just what one would expect of the man who created the Hobbits. He wore dull, academic tweeds rather than the brightly colored clothes that the Hobbits favored and he was quite a bit taller than they were, for even in ancient days they were said to be no more than four feet tall. Yet we Hobbit-lovers were continually surprised to see that he wore shoes, instead of having the tough-soled, hairy feet of the little people. Like the Hobbits he smoked a pipe and like them, too, he wore life lightly, enjoying a jest, scorning pedantry.

MUCH OF THE CULT that has subsequently grown up around the Tolkien books has centered on their possible "inner meaning." Is "The Lord of the Rings" an allegory, an attempt to dramatize the primordial clash of Good and Evil, or even to clothe in a fantasy of the past the great conflicts of our time?

Tolkien himself always rejected any such interpretation and to anyone who ever listened to him it was clear that, above all, he was fascinated not so much with ideas themselves but with the tools men devised to express them. It was language that inspired him, the forms and sounds of words and their power on the ear.

The mythology of Middle-earth, which fills both "The Hobbit" and the trilogy, grew out of his invention of the Elvish language. This was such a complete language, with a script and pronunciation so detailed, that it's hard to believe that it didn't ever exist, alongside Anglo-Saxon and Old Norse and Gothic. And the books themselves cry out to be read aloud, as they apparently were to family and friends during the long years of their gestation.

It's because of the essentially oral nature of the Middle-earth mythology that Tolkien always resisted attempts to represent his legend visually. At the height of the Tolkien cult, for instance, stores carried many posters supposedly portraying characters and scenes from the books, yet the author himself sanctioned only a couple of them, ones where no faces were shown, where nothing could detract from the pictures that the reader—or listener—could have formed in his own imagination from Tolkien's words.

Tolkien's voice is now silent, but there may be one more work still to come. Among the many papers he left behind there is believed to be the much-revised text of a book called "The Silmarillon."

Tolkien was always reluctant to publish, preferring to re-write and re-write. But even if there is no complete new novel, the old ones will more than suffice. Tolkien may have been mortal, but Middle-earth is indeed ageless.

Home with the Author-Eater

By

Midge Grossman

Calvin Trillin is sugar and spice and everything nice to the women who surround him! He's husband to Alice, and father to Sara, age two and a half, and to Abigail, five years old. He's not just the connoisseur of the BBQ rib, the sometimes lowly hamburger, and the ambrosial bowl of chili.

The Trillins live in Greenwich Village, New York City, on Grove Street. Calvin met Alice at a what-you-think-of-as-a-typical New York party; though she's not the usual what-you-think-of-as-the-usual New York type, but more like the girl you'd most want to meet in the fresh-as-air commercials. She is as natural and pretty as a summer bloom without any artificialities.

Alice, according to "Bud," is great on leftovers, which he thinks, "is the real test of a good cook!" though she does put him on a strict salad diet when she feels that all of his "constant struggle, researching to get something decent to eat, country-wise USA" catches up with him. He is nix on diets, feels that it is better if you are weight watching to eat all you want of one item at a time. Once he attended a dieticians' convention which was a disaster because he followed their suggestion of a menu confined to brussel sprouts and carrot juice!

The Trillins find that entertaining no more than eight people at home in their apartment is the most pleasurable and the easiest. "They are all sit-down dinners, rarely are they two or three course affairs, and our schoolgirl helps out," Alice said. Usually Italian fare is served, surrounded as they are in their neighborhood by an Italian melting pot. EVERYTHING can be brought in FRESH, whether it be cheese in a basket, ricotta made daily, or pastas. One of their favorites is Contagine, an Italian sausage lentil soup; and Alice makes her own breads. Her favorite is Nova Scotia brown bread, a recipe she learned from their summers in the Maritime province.

Bud's office is in their apartment, but if family-living gets to be too distracting, he does have a desk at *The*

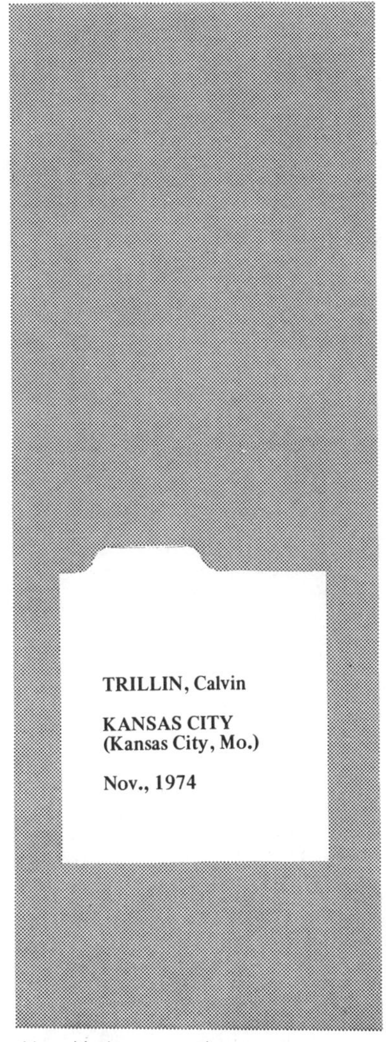

TRILLIN, Calvin
KANSAS CITY
(Kansas City, Mo.)
Nov., 1974

New Yorker magazine.

Memories of the Midwest are all very, very good for Calvin Trillin. After graduation from Southwest High School, where he said, he "had no special talents in written projects," he attended Yale, majoring in English, but now wishes he could have had more exposure to history. His comment on the new KCI made reference to the fact that the airport to Hertz is now farther than the old airport was to downtown Kansas City.

As a champion of Kansas City food, Trillin loves telling an anecdote about receiving a somewhat flattened but still recognizable hamburger from Winsteads, IN THE MAIL. It had evidently been purchased here and flown to NYC by two priests who well knew his liking for same. They had inserted the hamburger into a formal wedding-sized invitational envelope and mailed it to him locally! How truly frustrating — and inedible!

For Sara and Abigail (to be six in October), visiting with their grandmother and family here several times a year is made all the more exciting by stopping at the Chocolate Soup. This children's shop, owned by the Jim Levitts (Ms. Jim does all the designing) is on Gregory Boulevard and is managed by Ms. Georgia Van Cleave. She said, "the girls make great models; some kids hate to try on clothes, but they can't wait to and enjoy it tremendously." She went on to say, "They are really lovely people, and it is always a pleasure when they come back."

Trillin published his first book in 1964, and it was dedicated "To my parents." Titled *An Education in Georgia,* it was about the integration of Charlayne Hunte and Hamilton Holmes, of which chapters 1-12 appeared originally in somewhat different form in *The New Yorker* magazine.

His better known *Barnett Frummer is an Unbloomed Flower and Other Adventures of Barnett Frummer, Rosalie Mondle, Roland Magruder, and Their Friends* was published in 1969. These were stories that had originally appeared in *The New Yorker,* and "were written for Alice."

American Fried, his most recent novel, states: "there is still great food in the USA, and this is...(Trillin's) quest to get his hands on as much of it as possible." He is the kind of eater that people in some parts of the country call a Big Hungry Boy. Trillin says, "When I hear someone dismiss a quiche Lorraine as 'not a true quiche Lorraine' I always want to shout, but did you like it? Did it make you happy? Did you clean your plate?" This volume is dedicated "to Alice and Sara and Abigail, who when she was four, polished off a particularly satisfying dish of chocolate ice cream saying, 'my tongue is smiling.'"

Aren't you?

Full-Time Writing Makes Tryon Yawn

TOM TRYON: Next, a love story?

By LARRY SWINDELL
Knight News Service

During his tenure as a celluloid cardinal or a moon pilot space-walking in harm's way, Tom Tryon had a reputation for intensity. Being a successful author apparently is more relaxing, or perhaps more fatiguing.

He's an amiable, quiescent interviewee, slouching drowsily while being asked yet again if he's really through with the movies.

"As an actor, yes. Because I never had this compulsive thing about being an actor. It just happened."

YOU CAN see why. Swarthily handsome at 47 and reaching a good lean altitude even when he droops, Tryon looks like someone who simply belongs in pictures. No doubt a similar thought obsessed Gertrude Lawrence when she discovered young Tryon, just out of Yale, and nudged him toward the theater.

"I've always written — I enjoy it. I spend all my time writing, morning to night."

Tryon's new novel is "Harvest Home," and likely to adorn the charts for months to come.

TWO YEARS ago his ghoulish first novel, "The Other," was a surprise best-seller; this time the surprise would be if "Harvest Home" were anything else.

It is, one might say predictably, another bizarre American gothic, perhaps less metaphysical than "The Other" but no less macabre. The girls especially will holler for more.

Yet Tryon (as an author he's billed Thomas) gives caution that he is not a formulated writer, nor will be one. If "Harvest Home" echoes an old theme, there'll be new melodies in more books. Many books. He writes fast.

"This one ('Harvest Home') is not really the second book," he yawns. "I wrote three books between 'The Other' and 'Harvest' and the manuscripts are all under my bed. Eventually all will be published. But Bob Gottlieb, my editor, decided that 'Harvest' was the right one to follow 'The Other'. The fact that it's also a spook story is mainly coincidental. The next book will be very different. No ghosts. Actually a tender love story."

IN THE BOOK business Tryon may attain the superstar status that eluded him in films, but Hollywood isn't exactly a thing of the past. "This year I'll realize a long-held ambition to direct a picture. It's not an adaptation of a novel, but an original screenplay —my own. So if I fail, I can't blame the writer. Or vice versa."

So don't blame anyone, Tom. Just reach under the bed for your bail bond.

Tryon an Author, Not Ex-Actor

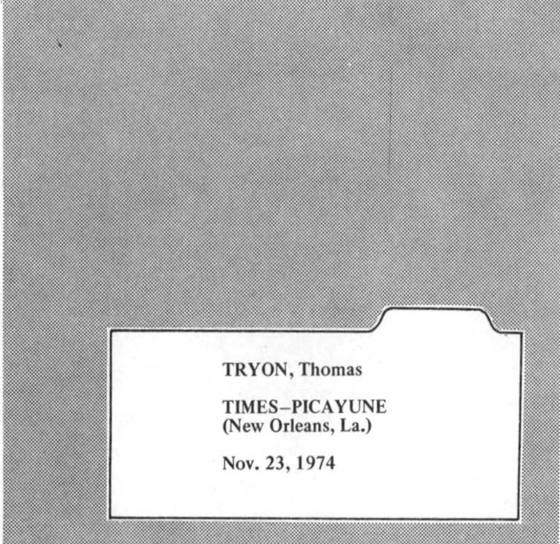

By FRANK GAGNARD

Tom Tryon was nice about it, but really, he'd rather be somewhere else. Meaning not in this particular section of The Times-Picayune, with its movie ads and what.

Tom Tryon, the "former movie star"...Tom Tryon, the (even worse label) "ex-actor"...between sips of Blue Nun wine in his Maison de Ville room the other night, Tryon recited a personal lexicon of dirty words. They keep cropping up in interviews and book reviews, and Tryon has had enough of it.

For one thing, he hasn't made a movie since 1969, a little-known "bomb" called "Color Me Dead" filmed in Australia. Furthermore, Tom Tryon, star of the highly publicized bomb "The Cardinal," is now Thomas Tryon, author of the best-sellers "The Other" and "Harvest Home," and of "Lady" published on Wednesday.

"It is very difficult for people to allow me to be a writer," Tryon said, "because they have slotted me as an actor. I think people will be fair to me because I have proved myself. My track record is such that they should allow me to do what I want to do."

Ring down the curtain, bring on the galley proofs. There's no business like book business. But Tryon, stung by labels and perhaps a snippy review or two, gives the impression that he's capable of complaining all the way to the bank.

Smarting, perhaps, but victorious. "I've become very wealthy in the last few years, and I don't have to do anything I don't want to do."

Mostly, he indicated, he's working, and enjoying. Here for a recent autographing session for "Lady" at the D. H. Holmes book department, he luxuriated in the comfort of the distinctive, regional swag-drag decor of his hotel room. And in the visual appeal of New Orleans, which, he said, satisfied the Gothic in his nature.

"I've been working on a project for three years," he said, "with the locale originally in Connecticut. Then I moved to New York, and it became New York. But in the back of my head was, 'Someday, you're going to move the location to New Orleans, I know you are.' I've already done so in the time I've been here."

However this property comes out, it won't be out for a while. Tryon considers it a sure-fire investment, is under no pressure to cash in—"That's in the money-in-the-bank vault."

He added, "The two things I'm working on now are so contemporary that I want to do them now."

* * *

Tryon, now in his late 40s, is tall, ruggedly handsome and still leading-man material. When asked if he was definitely through with acting he nodded but then said, "You've read 'Lady'?," and he quoted the book, "'Never is a long, long time'."

Some other subjects and Thomas Tryon responses follow:

Stereotyping — "In 'Lady' I am trying to get away from the thriller category. I wanted to try something different without going totally out of my territory, my proven ground, so to speak. I wanted to try to make strides in another direction.

"I think the danger in writing or in being considered a 'best-selling author' is that you can as easily get typed in that as in acting. I waged a long battle in Hollywood for 15 years or something to avoid getting typed as an actor. By the same token, I don't want to be typed as a writer of thrillers."

On the other hand, "Anything I write is going to have Gothic overtones because I have kind of Gothic overtones."

* * *

Reading habits — "I don't read thrillers, mysteries, detective stories, or, what do you call it, sci-fi."

A possible screenplay: "I would like to do a good old-fashioned melodrama with some class. Not a Hammer Studios movie, nor Roger Corman, but something a cut above and a bit beyond."

The novel "The Other" — "I hadn't been long into it when I realized I had something." Not necessarily a best-seller or eventually a movie, but "I knew if I finished the book that I had something, that it would be published, that it would make some kind of a mark.

"I did know that something had happened . . . The book was an act of faith, it really was."

The movie "The Other"—"No, not really satisfied with it, though I wrote the screenplay and was executive producer. But when we shot it and put it together it ran three hours. We made radical cuts and it was a bad mistake. But I learned an enormous amount from that picture and I don't regret it."

Regrets are for losers. Author Thomas Tryon is a winner.

Divorcee Writes Handbook to Help Other Divorcees

By JOHN DORSCHNER
Herald Staff Writer

When Helen Tumpson moved to Miami in October 1970, she was feeling down.

Her marriage of 20 years was finished. Her five children had all left home. She was 43 and starting life again, alone.

"I was depressed, sinking more and more into a morass of self-pity," she remembers. She rented an apartment, found a job with Third Century, U.S.A. — and then wondered what to do with her lonely nights.

THE ANSWER was a book. "I started to write it to help myself," she says. "When you're used to having someone to be with, even if it's only to argue, it's hard to adjust to loneliness. So I started working on the book."

The book that finally emerged is "The Sensuous Divorcee," published in April (Dell Publishing Co. paperback, $1.25), with the cover duplicating other books in the "Sensuous" series right down to the typeface for the title.

But unlike others for the genre, "The Sensuous Divorcee" is not a first-person confessional and handles such everyday matters as how to get a job "You can fudge a little" on listing past work experience and dieting ("You mustn't gain an ounce") along with the compulsory sex material.

"The experiences in the book are all true," she says, but not all are autobiographical — some of them happened to friends, or people she talked to.

"The title of the book sells many copies. I just hope that when they open the book and find it only slightly risque that they won't be disappointed," said Mrs. Tumpson recently after returning to Miami from a publicity swing of 25 radio shows, 10 TV shows and seven newspaper interviews in nine cities.

"For me, though, it's a very sexy book. When writing some parts of it, I blushed." She showed the book to her children, and asked if she should use an initial. "They told me, 'No, it's great. Put your name on it. Right on!' "

NOR, SHE says, has she received

—Miami Herald / JOE ELBERT

TUMPSON, Helen

MIAMI HERALD
(Miami, Fla.)

June 16, 1974

much negative reaction around Miami, where she is known as the project director of Third Century, U.S.A., an organization started by the Greater Miami Chamber of Commerce to promote the bicentennial celebration.

"Everybody sort of teases me about it," says the lithe 47-year-old, "but I haven't gotten any flack at all."

Though she mentions vibrators and swingers' clubs, the basic message of her book is conservative. "It's usually the people who have been married at least 10-15 years who suffer the most dreadful loss," she says.

"Men usually, but not always, are able to cope with the sex part. Women encounter the new sexual arena and often they go in for sexual anarchy. They don't know how to say no and they don't know why they say yes. It takes about a year to get your balance back and realize that sex without love is basically empty."

IN THE BOOK, she says she opposes three things that many divorcees get into: (1) Going out with married men "trouble arises"); (2) "overexposure in bars — if you become too familiar a face, you acquire a reputation of some sort, either that you do a lot or that you don't, and neither is good;" and (3) promiscuity ("A sense of inadequacy comes from it").

She also suggests something that many professional therapists frown on as being too traumatic a change after the trauma of divorce: Moving to a new town.

"Your married friends slip away and you can't take any steps in the sexual arena without someone looking over your shoulder."

ONE OF the cities that she advises the new divorcee to stay away from is, paradoxically, Miami.

"It's a great city, but they're so many single women here. My advice to the newly divorced is to stay away from any resort area as a place to live.

"The men are spoiled. They don't have the same attitude as men from a small town, and they have all the women they possibly want, a feast of women."

Why, then, did she choose Miami after her divorce? "I didn't know then anything about where the men were. But I love Miami — it's the place where I feel most at home. If I had read this book, probably I would have thought Miami too tough a market to handle. Maybe ignorance is bliss."

Mrs. Tumpson is on leave from the Third Century, U.S.A. project, and is planning a publicity tour through the Midwest and East before returning to work in July.

She's also planning a new book, based on the question divorcees have most often asked her: "Where Women Can Meet Men — 150 Possibilities."

The Ik Gave Him a Jolt

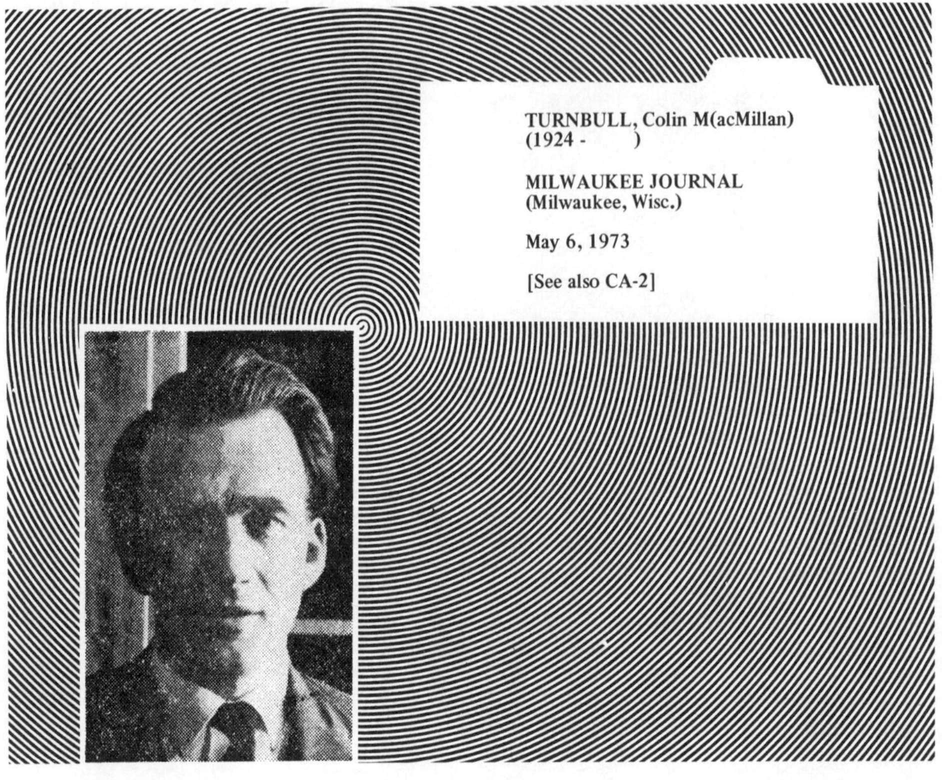
TURNBULL, Colin M(acMillan)
(1924-)

MILWAUKEE JOURNAL
(Milwaukee, Wisc.)

May 6, 1973

[See also CA-2]

By LESLIE CROSS
Journal Book Editor

ANTHROPOLGIST, come home!

Colin M. Turnbull, who has spent a lot of time with primitive tribes, thinks the return is overdue. His last trip, to the Ik of East Africa, shook him up a bit. He decided, after two years with this uncommonly repulsive people, that the human race isn't very human after all.

As readers of his much discussed book, "The Mountain People," have learned, the Ik are the reverse of the "noble savage" of optimistic philosophy and legend. They are, on the whole, consistently cruel, deceitful, vengeful and selfish. They happily abandon their children almost as soon as they can walk, and laughingly put out their old and crippled to die.

Could that happen here? Turnbull is convinced that it could, and has set forth some of the reasons in his book.

In a chat at his publisher's office, he enlarged on them.

"I've been forced to conclude," he said, "that the supposedly human qualities that we prize so highly — like love, generosity and consideration for others — are not basic aspects of human nature. These may be social qualities; they are not biological."

The Terrible Tribesmen Aren't Unique

Displaced to barren uplands from the hunting grounds of their ancestors, the Ik have had to settle for a dog eat dog existence in order to survive. "The real tragedy is that the system works," Turnbull observed.

Now he sees similar forces grinding away on his doorstep. Leaving his respectable Chelsea neighborhood in New York, he finds himself stepping over sprawling drunks. He learns that a neighbor has been mugged or shot. He has found, like most New Yorkers, that it is best not to get involved in these things.

"I have to seal off whole portions of my mind," he said, "just for personal survival. I'd have a nervous breakdown if I didn't.

And he feels that in this area of modern experience, fellow anthropologists could help. They can find out just how the workings of our society are breaking down families and other social groupings and are reducing their members to a crude level of every man for himself.

Just the same, Turnbull doesn't think he's the man for the job. He is a naturalized American, but he has been out of the country longer than he has been in it, and he is not satisfied that he knows it sufficiently.

Actually, he is fond of his adopted country, and he doesn't see catastrophe as an immediate prospect. Besides his New York apartment, from which he drives to his office at Hofstra University on Long Island when he is not off to remote regions, he has a house in rural Virginia. Here, he reported with approval, there is community feeling in the old sense.

A Trip to India Changed Him

Turnbull, a youthful looking man of 48 who was born just outside London, drew his first breath of non-Western air in India. He went there on a fellowship to Banaras Hindi University, and the experience changed his life. He wasn't an anthropologist then; "I was trying to be a philosopher, and just before that, I gave up trying to be a musician," he said. Back at Oxford, he took his doctorate in his new discipline.

Field trips to Africa followed. The outcome was two books that have had considerable scientific notice, "The Forest People" and "The Lonely African." His decision to studv the Ik of Uganda and its northern borders grew out of his extensive work among the forest people, the Mbuti Pygmies of the Congo.

Though he doesn't think that goodness is an innate trait of man, he doesn't dismiss the human race out of hand.

"Goodness," he said, "is something we have to work at. The potentialities are there. Basically, I believe, the race is rather gentle. Our tooth structure shows that originally we were not a carnivorous species. Violence comes out of the kinds of systems we live in. We have the choice of changing them."

And anthropology, he believes, is not a one way investigation.

"When I was studying these various people," said Turnbull, "I discovered that they were studying me, too. One of them told me, "You Europeans smile with your teeth.' How true that is! Often we do smile with our teeth, without feeling the emotion that the smile is intended to convey. When an African smiles, he's apt to smile with his heart and eyes and his whole being."

It's a Big Year For Tacoma's William O. Turner

TURNER, William O(liver)
(1914 -   )
SEATTLE POST–INTELLIGENCER
(Seattle, Wash.)
Mar. 10, 1974
[See also
CA-1/4]

William O. Turner

BY ARCHIE SATTERFIELD
Editor ARTS Magazine

Illustration by Stu Moldrem

THE RECENT federal court decision in favor of the Nisqually Indians' fishing rights gave one white man, Bill Turner, the right to assume an I-told-you-so air.

The Tacoma author (byline William O. Turner) just completed a novel called "Medicine Creek," due out this summer by Doubleday, that tells the story of the treaty signed beneath the old tree beside Interstate 5 on Nisqually Flats.

"The treaty was a joke," Turner says, "but one that was immediately ratified by Congress. And Stevens (Isaac I., the territorial governor of Washington in the 1850s) knew it was a joke."

But, Turner continues, the Nisqually tribe is a small one and has been ignored by national historians, such as Dee Brown in "Bury My Heart at Wounded Knee." The situation could change with Turner's novel, which tells the story of Chief Leschi, who was betrayed by a member of his own tribe and hanged for a crime he did not commit.

Turner is having a big year. His last novel, "Call The Beast Thy Brother, was published around Christmas and received good reviews in the East. Later this spring his western novel, "Mayberly's Kill," will be made into a movie starring Robert Redford.

"It was my first movie sale," Turner says, "although options were bought on other novels, then dropped.The appeal of 'Mayberly's Kill,' I think, is that it has a strong woman character, who was emphasized in the movie script, and a bandit who dresses like a woman."

"Call The Beast Thy Brother" and "Medicine Creek" are what Turner calls his most ambitious books, and both are historical in subject matter. "Call The Beast . . ." begins at Fort Nisqually and winds up in the Queen Charlotte Islands. It was complimented by several critics for characterizing the Indians as people first, and members of a race other than white, second.

But one of the most interesting characters was the super-religious missionary, Alexander Cargo, who first loses his wife, then is kidnaped, loses his religion and shifts from Christianity into mysticism and self-mutilation.

Almost casually, Turner comments that the novel was cut by 25 per cent. He mentions it offhandedly, like he does most things important to him and his personal feelings are couched in the normal conversational tone.

A few years ago a friend wrote that Turner has the personality of a good poker player. "He is the kind of player you cannot analyze . . . Just when you think you've got him figured he does something unpredictable. He's silent, easy-going and way ahead of you."

He is a "55-year-old liar" about his age and a life-long bachelor.

"It's an advantage," he said. "On the other hand, Bill Gulick (the Walla Walla author of several books) said the greatest asset a writer can have is a wife who will go to work while he works on a major book."

Turner, like most writers, is an avid reader. He reads philosophy, all the classical philosophers from Plato to Kirkegaard — his favorite — and Sarte.

"Every couple of years I reread 'Huckleberry Finn.' Mark Twain was the father of American literature. You can trace Salinger, H. L. Davis and Hemingway back to him.

"There's one chapter in 'Huckleberry Finn,' when he's on the raft, that reads exactly like Hemingway."

Of Northwest writers, Turner believes there is only one great writer so far: H. L. Davis, who wrote "Honey in the Horn," "Team Bells Woke Me," "Winds of Morning," "Kettle of Fire" and several other books.

Next on his list is Ernest Haycox, the Portland western writer whose books frequently are reprinted in paperback.

"Haycox had a unique style, and Hemingway gave a list of what he liked to read, then added that he read the Saturday Evening Post when there as a Haycox story in it."

He regrets that Northwest writers don't get together more often to talk about markets, trends and whatever comes to mind. But, he says, too many are jealous of each other and they try to establish territories and keep the others out.

American literature, he believes, is at a low ebb, and there is no writer of the stature of Hemingway, Faulkner, Sinclair Lewis around now.

"Norman Mailer writes like an angel, but he's too screwed up.

"The writer who can combine 'fine writing' with a good blend of plot and characterization is too rare, but that is what it takes for great literature. But of them all, a great style of writing is the most important."

Turner dismisses the theory that the Northwest has produced little literature because its history is too tame.

"The Southwest has a great history, and who has it produced? Writers like to head down there to live because of the climate, but there's no great Southwest literature yet."

"Call The Beast Thy Brother" was Turner's 21st book since the early 1950s when his first novel, "The Proud Diggers," was published. Most of the books have been westerns, sometimes taking less than two months to complete.

"The western market is awfully easy to get stuck with. They are formula books, but if you're writing a formula story, it should be a good formula story."

A Puyallup Valley native, Turner worked in the Midwest and East in newspapers, advertising agencies and edited a magazine in Iowa for short time. Eventually, he returned to Tacoma where he keeps two typewriters in his apartment-without-a-view ("I'd look at the ships rather than write"). One typewriter is used for manuscripts, the other for letters and "whatever."

Turner's books have had a good market in Germany, Norway, Italy, Spain, The Netherlands and Denmark.

With two difficult books to write behind him, Turner now is back to work on other projects. He has a western and a mystery in outline form.

He admits it is a lonely life, but one he obviously enjoys. And, for those who plan to start writing westerns to make a living while devoting most of their time to writing serious fiction, Turner has a warning: "They're all hard for me to write."

She's All Bronx And A Millionaire

UHNAK, Dorothy

AKRON BEACON JOURNAL (Akron, Ohio)

Apr. 29, 1973

By JUDY BACHRACH
Knight Newspaper Writer

NEW YORK — Some time within the last few months, Dorothy Uhnak became a millionaire. It was an uneasy transition, since Mrs. Uhnak's life up till that point had been devoted to three things: her writing, her family, and the New York City police force.

Before she resigned a few years back, Mrs. Uhnak's specialty was nabbing muggers and rapists and the dirty old men in the subway who expose themselves.

Dorothy Uhnak's novel, "Law and Order," contains 512 pages detailing the intense corruption that infests New York's Finest; but in a peculiar way, it is also the story of what drives them collectively to the brink of outrage.

SAYS MRS. UHNAK, "I lived since 1953 in an exclusive man's world. I know how they talk. Whenever I'd walk into a room where a bunch of cops were talking—well, they'd stop the vulgarities immediately." She chuckles. "Kind of endearing, isn't it? Because there I was fighting off rapists and muggers—and yet I had to be protected from a dirty word."

She bobs her head over the paradox. At 42, Dorothy Uhnak has prematurely white hair and an owlish face just this side of pretty. When she talks (which she does incessantly) her entire body swings into motion. She is half Irish, half Jewish, all Bronx, and she uses the crisp inflections of the gym teacher:

"You can't imagine what being a woman on the transit police force was like. Chauvanism. Completely. The only thing they couldn't do was pay me less than a man. However, when I was on the job, I was not permitted to take promotional exams. I mean they just sat there and said, in effect, 'How stupid! You're a lucky person to be here in the first place.' The other women were reconciled. But I never was. I did get promoted to detective—three times. But that's another story altogether."

AT 24, SHE got her first big break. If you can call being attacked by a rapist-mugger a big break.

The entire transit force was aching to get a hulking 6-footer who was attacking women in the subway. One night Mrs. Uhnak caught sight of a man who fit the description exactly. There was only one problem. She wasn't working with her regular partner.

And that, apparently, is a tremendous problem, because when you're in the force you develop a rapport of silences and signals with your partner that no one else can quite match. Dorothy Uhnak found a hand around her neck and a gun pointed at her forehead and a partner out of sight and out of reach.

"So I hit the rapist on the wrist with the heel of my hand. And his gun went flying up the staircase. And I lunged for him, and then it occurred to me: 'There's nobody here helping me.' So I let out a yell and my partner comes down with his gun."

For that she got a medal and her detective classification.

IN 1956, Mrs. Uhnak became pregnant. Under normal circumstances, this wouldn't be very remarkable. But in her case it was. First: "Because well, I knew I had to get pregnant then or I might never be able to. Well, because my insides were all messed up. See, I chased this one pervert through the subway and he threw me down the escalator stairs and I was just covered with blood."

And secondly because:

"Do you know what the force did?" Mrs. Uhnak leans forward conspiratorially. "They took away my detective classification when I took a leave for pregnancy. And by that time I had been promoted twice. And you wanna know something? They didn't tell me I'd be demoted. Just got a letter after the fact, 'You are now a policewoman.' "

She came back though. After the birth of her daughter, she returned to the transit force as a special assistant to Tom O'Rourke, the chief of the department.

WITHIN THE context of "Law and Order," corruption is a fact of life as natural as drawing breath. On the very last page of her book, the hero turns to his son and says, "God knows how it starts or how far it goes before it has no way of stopping. It's life, kid. Maybe, I'm a corrupt man, maybe not. Maybe there are circumstances none of us really know how to cope with . . ."

In extra-literary confines, the author explains it this way: "When you're on the force, you get very defensive. You feel that no one from the outside can with any validity make any judgment. Oh, when I was 21, I thought, 'Justice will be done. I will go into court and the bad man will be punished by the judge.' But it's baloney. I would go into court and all of a sudden everybody's having at me. I'm being made into a vampish woman who causes men to go insane."

By 1967, she quit the force. There were a lot of reasons. Partly because she was a woman and therefore exempt from egalitarian promotion standards; partly because she couldn't stand the new chief; partly because she had an ulcer. But mostly, one suspects, it was because Dorothy Uhnak was always something of an outsider on the force, because there's always something peculiar about a woman who speaks her mind. Writing is a natural outlet.

SHE BEGAN her latest novel in 1969. There had been others, but they were always slighted by the critics. This one she researched for months on end.

"Oh God, it was a murderous book to write. I became my characters. So when something really devastating happened to them, it happened to me. I rode every wave of emotion."

By the book's end, she was physically exhausted. Simon & Schuster ran a first printing of 100,000 copies and paid her "an enormous sum." For the first time in the interview, Dorothy Uhnak flushed crimson.

"It's still embarrassing me. Paramount paid me $350,000 to turn it into a motion picture. Pocketbook books paid me a quarter of a million bucks. And the Literary Guild bought it for $85,000. You just can't imagine what it's like after earning $12,000 a year."

WHAT MRS. UHNAK turned out — aside from a moneymaker — is the most totally masculine book ever written by a woman. It isn't only the dialog that is male; the descriptions are, too. And while her men are alive and vital; her female characters are stick figures; either docile police wives or bitchy career girls.

So why, Dorothy, why didn't you create a female character who's well — say, like you?

It's very simple," smiles Mrs. Uhnak, "I don't know many women like me."

Novelist Uris' Muse Is Peace

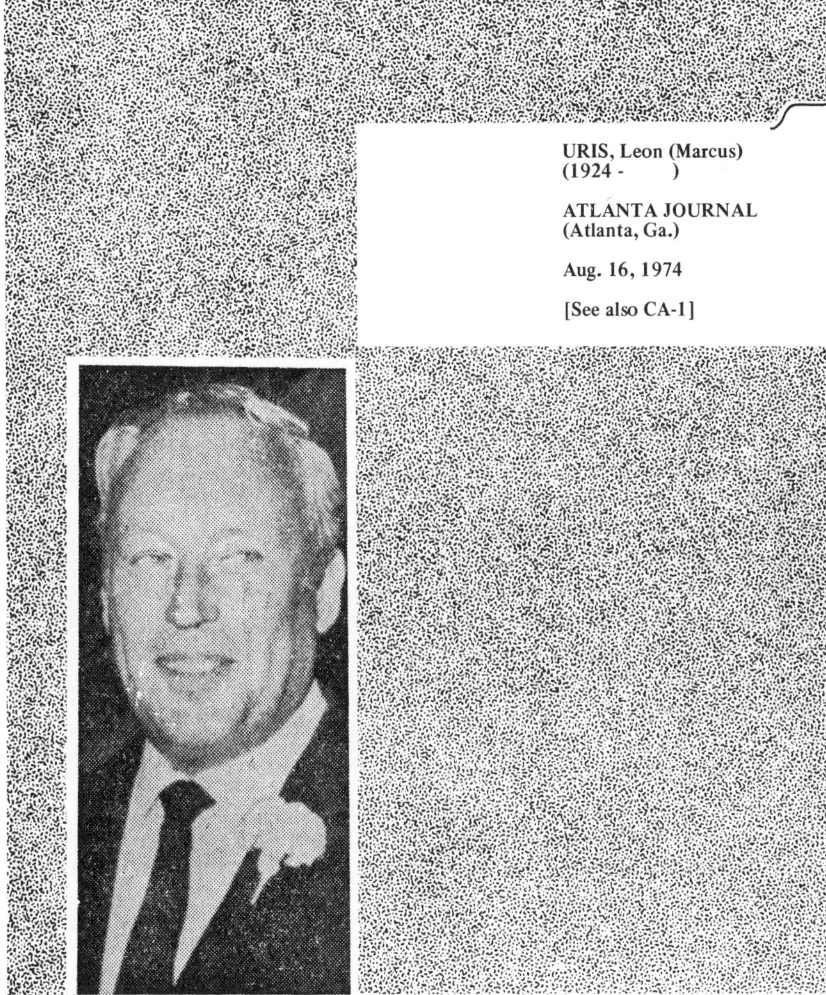
URIS, Leon (Marcus)
(1924 -)

ATLANTA JOURNAL
(Atlanta, Ga.)

Aug. 16, 1974

[See also CA-1]

By BARBARA THOMAS
Journal Amusements Editor

For the first time in his life, novelist Leon Uris says he's found complete peace and it's showing in his work.

Credit this, he says, to his 27-year-old wife, Jill, a professional photographer he married four years ago, six months after the suicide of his second wife.

They met in Aspen, Colo., when he bought a camera for his son and needed some instruction on how to work it. She went to his house with a girlfriend and the romance that has changed the life of the famous novelist began.

Uris is in town to judge a competition for the Atlanta International Film Festival. Why is he a judge? he was asked. "Why not," he smiled," I'm a screenwriter and a playwright. Beside I have a good friend here I wanted to see."

At 50, Uris is tanned, grey-haired and radiates a vitality a 25-year-old would envy. He appears confident, assertive, and, indeed, happy. He and his wife have a set of books out now on Ireland—his is called "Trinity," a look at the Ulster conflict set in the Victorian era, and hers is a photographic study called, "Ireland, the Terrible Beauty."

He's wearing a brown shirt open at the neck, showing off a gold shamrock engraved with the names of his novels, a 50th birthday gift from a friend.

His wife gave him a stained glass window bearing the name of his books, also as a birthday gift.

When he met Jill things were going badly, he says. He had been through a "very ugly" divorce from his first wife, whom he divorced after 22 years and three children, his second wife's suicide came six months after their wedding. A play of his closed very quickly on Broadway, and his now third wife went through brain surgery following a bad accident. "I think I deserve a little peace now."

Uris has had little luck with the transformation of his works to the screen. "Battle Cry" was the closest "because I did the screenplay. I was fired from both 'Angry Hills' and 'Topaz.' I was told I didn't understand the characters in 'Angry Hills.' I just don't accept the writers' position in the hierarchy."

He credits some of his success at writing to his facility at self-discipline. He lives in Aspen, skis in the winter and plays tennis on summer mornings, never going to his office to write until late in the afternoon. "I'm a twilight writer—very unusual since most writers get up early and begin their meditative period. I sleep late and never get going until around three in the afternoon."

It is dangerous, he said, for writers to go "on inspiration. It will destroy you. It's like fighting three hot rounds in a 15 round fight. Before you know it you're back on your heels. When things start pouring out of you like that you know you're going to pay for it later."

How does he see himself as a writer? He says that's an unfair question since he should be the last to judge himself: "Naturally I have one opinion of myself and it's very high."

However, he added, critics see him as a populist writer, short on skill and long on chutzpah.

His writing skill has blossomed in his latest novel on Ireland, a growth he noticed beginning with his novel "Topaz."

"Writing a novel gives me brief flashes of extreme pleasure and long hours of torment. I was in Ireland for a year on this last book and we had some fun together but being in Ireland was no fun."

Of his seven novels, "Mila 18" is his favorite because, he says, it was written with no commercial motive. "It was the first novel I've gone into without some sort of prejudgment on the impact it would make. I shouldn't have written it after 'Exodus' because it follows the same theme. I was so taken by what happened in the Warsaw ghetto that I felt I had to write about it. I had no other purposes. I didn't know whether it would sell two copies or two million. Fortunately it sold two million."

He doesn't try to aim his books at a particular audience, since he does have a large following. "This is one of the things that burns the critics—two things they can't stand are a successful novelist and a person in love and I'm both of those things."

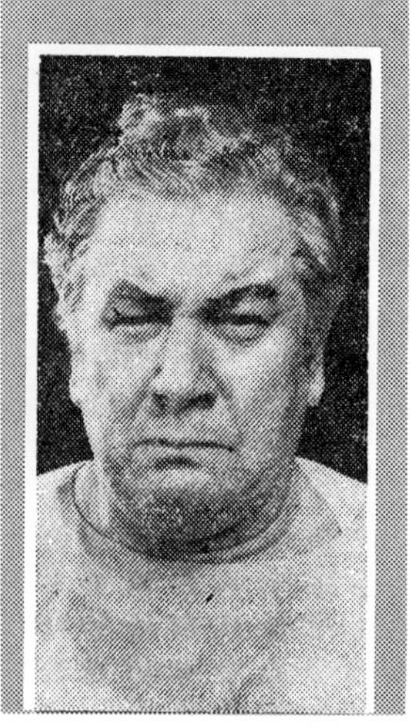

Peter Ustinov: Novelist, Mimic, Playwright, Actor, Director, Singer

By AL HAAS
Inquirer Staff Writer

NEW HAVEN

The curtain has just descended on a matinee performance of the comedy, "Who's Who in Hell." The audience, dominated by women of pre-prohibition vintage, is receding toward the doors of New Haven's Shubert Theatre. Boris Vassilievitch Krivelov, the assassinated Russian premier, makes his way from the stage to a microscopic dressing room.

Inside this virtual phone booth, the large man shucks the hospital gown with the large red bloodstain on the front and once again becomes mild-mannered Peter Ustinov, actor and playwright.

Ustinov is indeed a playwright and actor. The list of awards won by his scripts and performances over the past two decades is substantial enough to make its mere recitation almost idolatrous.

In addition, he has functioned as a director, producer, novelist, BBC political commentator, mimic, raconteur extraordinaire and Unicef ambassador of good will. He's also made some delightful records, like the one devoted to his imitation of a Grand Prix race car in action.

At the moment, however, this talented 53-year-old man is really none of the above. He is essentially a physician attending an afflicted play — his own — and he is using his role in it as an audience stethoscope to pinpoint its disease.

This is not to say Ustinov's 17th play is seriously ill.

It is, in fact, as robust as it is imaginative. (It is about a U. S. president and Soviet premier who meet up, in a waiting room between heaven and hell with the American kid who died in the process of assassinating them during their joint visit to Disneyland.) It is also frequently funny and provocative as it comments on politicians — and the rest of the species.

But it does have its ailments, ailments which Ustinov hopes to cure by its Nov. 18 arrival in Philadelphia, the play's last try-out stop before it opens on Broadway.

"Who's Who in Hell" seems to suffer principally from excess verbiage. It's lingual obesity manifests itself most obviously in the second act, when a series of attenuated monologues do to dramatic movement what 90-second stoplights do to traffic flow.

"I'm trying to come up with something more liquid, with less set pieces," Ustinov observes, leaning back in his dressing room chair and lighting a cigar worthy of W. C. Fields.

"The first act is pretty watertight, I'm trying to get the rest of it into that tradition. That's what I'm really trying to do."

"I have a feeling I've hammered certain nails too hard," he adds. "I probably could be more subtle." (Audiences are becoming quicker and quicker because of television, Ustinov feels. As a consequence, he doesn't think they require the emphasis and explanation they needed even ten years ago.)

Ustinov isn't exactly ecstatic about messing with something that took him three years to write. But it is as necessary as it is unpleasant and lonely. (Ustinov communes only with himself when revising, depending solely on "the things I feel on stage." He knows "the committee" can ruin a play if you let it.)

The gravity of the revision discussion leaves Ustinov impatient for a laugh. He apparently can't repress his sense of humor very long. Shifting into a commendable W. C. Fields imitation, he waves his cigar at a departing colleague and says, "Yes, indeed, Senator, good caucusing with you."

Waxing equally Fieldsian a bit later, he tells another associate: "You will find me at the New Haven Club."

Ustinov gets a twinkle in his eye when asked to elaborate on a cryptic note in the biography supplied by the show's publicist. It seems that in 1936, while a 15-year-old student at Westminster, Ustinov wrote a satirical piece about a classmate which was published anonymously in the London Evening Standard.

The classmate, it turns out, was the son of Joachim von Ribbentrop, the German ambassador to Great Britain who would subsequently become the Nazi foreign minister.

"He had entered three watercolors in the school art competition," Ustinov recalls, smiling at the half-forgotten inspiration for his journalistic debut. "They featured a wealth of helmets and such and he had entitled them 'Armed Strength.' "

The sport with the son of a man of Ribbentrop's stature was quite upsetting to the school brass, Ustinov recalls, and they were very anxious to find out who had written it. Knowing Ustinov's father was a London newspaperman, they prevailed upon Peter to go down to Fleet Street and trace this article to its villainous source.

"After two weeks of fruitless search, I had to admit to them I couldn't," Ustinov notes gravely.

The man's humor runs through other reminiscences. His parents didn't have a car when he was a kid, so he pretended he was one.

"There was a pang of regret when I finally bought a car — I could no longer be one."

An astute as well as a humorous political observer, Ustinov makes a point in the play and our conversation about the obligatory religious veneer of U. S. presidents: "After Nixon's operation, Ford's immediate reaction was to say, 'Mrs. Ford and I are praying for him.' "

U. S.-Soviet coexistence is another play theme that seeps into the interview.

"A country the size of this one and the Soviet are virtually ungovernable . . . I think that's why the U. S. and Russia have so much in common"

Whatever the reason the two superpowers have been putting their heads together of late, Ustinov is quite sure it has left smaller states quite uncomfortable. Quoth Unicef ambassasor Ustinov:

"The vice president of Bulgaria told me: 'We have no objection to the U. S. and Russia talking. But if the subject happens to be us, we would very much like to know what they are saying.' "

Ustinov has a way of inobstrusively slipping these sorts of little nuggets in your pocket. Consider these:

- On how he got the role of Premier Krivelov: "I never played a Russian before, so I thought I'd ask myself."
- On the relationship between the film role one is playing and the treatment one receives in contract negotiations and studio commissaries: "Never sign a contract while playing a weak, wizened bank clerk . . . Similarly, an emperor gets immediate seating in the commissary."
- On why his several antique cars don't constitute a collection: "They don't run well enough to get together."
- On the faint line between acceptable conduct and corruption: "If you give a maitre d' a tip before you eat, that's corruption. If you give him a tip after you eat, that's compensation for services rendered. Then again, if you plan to come back again, and give him the tip because you want him to remember your face, that's corruption."
- On his comedies: "They're really serious plays in which your laughter is solicited."

With the close of the interview, Ustinov announces that he's going to go back to his hotel room, order a beer, and work on the revisions suggested by the last performance. We leave the darkened theater and walk down an alley past a large municipal parking garage whose landscaping suggests esthetic pretention.

"They always build these things next to something like this," he laments, motioning toward the adjacent glass-paved vacant lot. "It looks like the border between Serbia and Montenegro in 1912."

With that, this large man moves off into the New Haven night, in the direction of a hotel room-sized community he calls "ulcerville."

USTINOV, Peter (Alexander)
(1921 -)

PHILADELPHIA INQUIRER (Philadelphia, Penn.)
Nov. 17, 1974
[See also CA-13/14]

Cornelius Vanderbilt, Jr.
. . . shunned society life

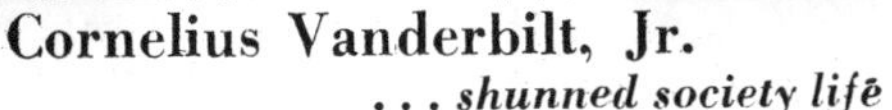

Cornelius Vanderbilt Jr., Author, World Traveler

VANDERBILT, Cornelius, Jr.
(1898 - 1974)
MIAMI HERALD
(Miami, Fla.)

July 8, 1974

[See also CA-9/10]

Cornelius Vanderbilt Jr., great-great-grandson of the founder of the Vanderbilt fortunes who broke with the world of tycoons and kings of his youth to become a globe trotting journalist, died Sunday. He was 76.

By CATHY GROSSMAN

Herald Staff Writer

A winter resident of Miami Beach for several years, he moved his permanent home here in 1969. He died at his home, 5013 Delaware Avenue, following a lingering illness.

His legacy to Miami, his wife, Mary Lou Garner Bristol Vanderbilt, said could be found in the public library.

FROM THE age of 21, when he turned his back on his Fifth Avenue youth to become a $25-a-week reporter for the old New York Herald, Vanderbilt was a writer, a chronicler of historic sidelights, author of several books.

Vanderbilt in his memoirs recalled 15 interviews with Stalin, a dozen with Mussolini, making the first report of the Reichstag fire and dining with Bedouins on fried desert worms.

His most popular books, Mrs. Vanderbilt said Sunday, were those about his family and society — the very people who disowned him and crossed his name out of the Social Register when he turned to writing.

He was born in April 1898, to Cornelius Vanderbilt, whose fortune was based on ferry boats, railroads and industry, and Grace Wilson, queen of New York society and a founder of the famous 400 Families — society's definition of "Society."

THERE WAS a house on Fifth Avenue with 70 rooms, 33 baths and 35 servants, another palatial villa in Newport, R.I., and a steam-driven ocean-going yacht with silk-walled staterooms in his youth.

There were summers playing tennis with the kings of Sweden, Norway and Denmark in Copenhagen, and nights playing charades with the King of Greece in his Athens palace.

But Vanderbilt decided that life among "the best people" would be "staid, placid and probably insufferable."

At the age of 21 he chose to ignore the advice of J.P. Morgan, the financier, that "a journalist usually winds up a chronic drunkard or remaining a journalist. I do know now which is worse," to begin his writing career.

From January 12, 1925, until June 16, 1926, he published the Illustrated Daily Tab in Miami before the publication folded. He went on to roam the world as a news and later travel columnist and lecturer.

His memoirs for a magazine, like his fifth book, "Man of the World," recite moments such as walking in on Stalin to find him reading the Bible.

Mahatma Ghandi asked him if he was "a gentleman, a gangster or a cowboy."

Al Capone told him, "I may have made a dishonest dollar or two in my time, but think of all the dough you millionaires have taken from poor people . . ."

Mussolini, as well as Morgan, gave Vanderbilt advice.

HE RODE out with the Italian leader on an inspection tour of factories and troops once, riding in Il Duce's open sports car at 90 miles an hour, the car preceded for miles by the sound of its high-pitched siren.

"I saw a boy trying to beat our car across the road. The car didn't waver, but I felt it go up and down as it passed over some object. I turned around and saw people gathering in the middle of the street around a limp figure," Vanderbilt recalled.

"Mussolini put a hand on my knee and said, 'Never look back, Mr. Vanderbilt. Never look back.' "

VANDERBILT did look back on his own life, though, and wrote possibly his best-read book, "Queen of the Golden Age," the story of his mother.

Grace Graham Wilson's father, Richard, had been a cotton broker, commissary general of the Confederate Army, and a friend of Mark Twain (who dangled young Vanderbilt on his knee and told him cat stories).

Ambitious and charming all her life, she gave a formal dinner in the wake of a hurricane once and entertained on a budget of $250,000 a year in Newport, New York and London.

The Irreverent Gospel Of Gore Vidal

Who else would expound the virtues of bisexuality, write an etiquette book on how to attend an orgy, give inside gossip on the Kennedys and Roosevelts — and still be a fellow from the "Social Register"?

By Susan Barnes

Photograph: David Bailey

SUSAN BARNES was born in Baltimore and now lives in London with her husband, Anthony Crosland, a Labor member of Parliament.

VIDAL, Gore
(1925 -)

MIAMI HERALD
(Miami, Fla.)

Nov. 25, 1973

[See also CA-7/8]

"As a matter of fact," said Gore Vidal when I arrived at his Italian villa to commence work, "I'm not sure if I want to go ahead with this interview."

"Why on earth not?" I asked, reflecting on the endless international telephone calls and travel arrangements and homework that had led up to this meeting.

" Because of last night," Vidal replied. "Is your husband always like that?"

The previous evening this husband (holidaying in Italy) and I had been to dine *chez* Vidal before I started work. Now I have never pretended to myself that I'm married to the most equable of diners-out. But how had even he on this occasion given quite such deep offense?

By failing to recognize that our fellow guests were the famous Paul Newman and Joanne Woodward?

By shining in debate with Vidal on the relative merits of Joseph Conrad and Evelyn Waugh as novelists — a debate whose ground he had, I suspect, carefully chosen?

Which of these no doubt irritating responses had so markedly offended Vidal's vanity?

Vidal — writer, playwright, television star, polemicist, international socialite, general mischief-maker — is usually thought of as the urbane sophisticate. Long ago, I gather, he cast himself in the role of the Renaissance man of letters — rational, controlled, omniscient, to whom *nihil humani* is *alienum*. In real life, however, he can react to things like a schoolboy. But being a highly intelligent man capable of self-analysis, he knows *why* he reacts in certain ways.

Certainly different facets of Vidal's life do get muddled together in people's minds. He has taken courageous stands on homosexuality in a country where its practice is still publicly disowned. He was an outspoken preacher of bisexuality long before the current cult began. He is a defender of Women's Lib, seeing Henry Miller and Norman Mailer as logical literary precursors of Charles Manson. "The Miller-Mailer-Manson man (or M-3 for short) has been conditioned to think of women as, at best, breeders of sons; at worst, objects to be poked, humiliated, killed."

But these advanced and heretical views have been confused with a quite separate thesis that he propounds: that the carnal pleasures of the body are irreconcilable with the so-called soul. Lust and compassion do not mix. "I can understand companionship. I can understand bought sex in the afternoon. I cannot understand the love affair." For awhile he thought highly of the orgy as a method of erasing all sentiment from the sex act, and wrote an essay giving the rules of what you should do at one — a mixture of Petronius and a Victorian book of etiquette.

His radical mores in no way inhibit him in his role of a conventional socialite who knows everybody and lets you know it. "He mocks his world," says his friend Anais Nin in her notorious journals, "but draws strength from being in the *Social Register.*"

His gleefully malicious dissection of politicians has the love-hate quality of the man who perhaps himself wished to be one. His friend Stephen Spender observes that: "Even when Gore is describing with genius every detail of Governor Reagan's face, comparing it with the work of a skillful embalmer, you sense that he is admiring the show. You feel his cynicism is irrelevant: you feel Gore ➡

(Continued from preceding page)
wouldn't mind being governor of California." But it's only the radical cynicism that's been noted by the new left intelligentsia for whom Vidal has lately become a prophet.

Yet he applies his scalpel equally cheerfully to the young. *Myra Breckinridge* is laced with biting sarcasm about the generation brought up on the mass media. "Like. Like. Like! The babble of this subculture is drowning me!"

Physically, Vidal looks the stereotype upper-class American male — fit (he takes a lot of trouble to keep so), good-looking and casually well-groomed. "He loves being able to come in a room," says Stephen Spender, "looking like a most respectable young man and then expressing the most unrespectable views. He loves to startle. He's a fun character.

"And he's a man who's come to terms with himself. He's almost scientific about his life — how much money he wants, what kind of sex he wants and so on. He separates himself into compartments. I'm sure this is self-protective: he's not a deeply cold-blooded person. He likes to think of himself as Flaubert, projecting the whole of his sex into male prostitutes. He keeps his emotions for his friends."

In his work, Vidal is professional and disciplined. With a new editor or producer, he starts off by putting on an act. But once he's finished his repertoire, he gets down to concentrated work. Hillard Elkins produced Vidal's play *An Evening with Richard Nixon.* The two men disliked each other initially, largely because of Vidal's displeasure that his close friend Claire Bloom should want to marry Elkins. Vidal had put up with 10 years of her first husband, Rod Steiger. He didn't want to put up with a second, who in this case was "just a little businessman."

But, says Elkins — a striking man who when we met was wearing a flowing white kaftan and chain and was addressed by an assistant as "Jesus" — he and Vidal turned around and ended in liking each other, which is always particularly pleasing. "I don't think he's as narcissistic as he claims to be. I just don't buy it. In true work situations he'll occasionally remember it and do something to demonstrate it. But in our 10- or 11-hour sessions, we were work oriented, not ego oriented."

But the narcissism is essential to the public *persona* which Vidal himself has so lovingly created and nurtured: *The Gifted Bitch.* A born actor, he delights in projecting this image. The price he pays is that he has not been taken seriously as a polemicist.

If Vidal is now obsessive about Watergate, it's hardly surprising. That's the way things are done in Washington, D.C., he repeatedly said in his books and plays. And no one believed him: "It's just Gore doing his thing." Is he bitter at finding himself as Cassandra? "It's not my *style* to be bitter," he replies. The actor and the man are inseparable.

With his reputation for destructive bitchery, it comes at first as a surprise that he enjoys close friendships which endure down the years, through bad times as well as good.

Most of his friendships are with women, all of whom insist that once you get through the outer crust, he is kind and solid. Claire Bloom says that when she's been deeply hurt, she has sought his company. "I wanted to be near someone who would understand how I felt without my talking about it.

"I've never seen the cynical side of him that comes out in public. I've never heard him say anything personally hurtful about any of his friends. Gore makes a great division here. I love gossip about my friends. He loves gossip about public people." Vidal says this is an exaggeration. "It was I who wrote: 'Whenever a friend succeeds, a little something in me dies.' "

In male company, Vidal is often uneasy because he's so competitive. He likes to watch his adversaries squirm. His pleasure in waspish debate depends on his winning the argument — and being seen to do so. I came to think that this is where his vanity is greatest.

VIDAL, Gore

MIAMI HERALD
(Miami, Fla.)

Nov. 25, 1973

Gore Vidal was born 47 years ago in the squarest of all possible settings — West Point, N.Y. — where his father, a distinguished athlete, was an Army officer. "I was delivered by a future surgeon general of the Army who became Eisenhower's physician in the White House, most famous for saying, 'Mamie, it's just gas' when Eisenhower suffered his first heart attack. He also made a mess of my navel."

Vidal's father, handsome and charming and always adored by his son, later left the Army and became a member of Roosevelt's Cabinet, moving along the way into the extremely comfortable Washington home of his father-in-law, Senator Gore of Oklahoma.

The senator's many distinctions included facing a rape charge and surviving it politically — and in 1911 — a fact to which Vidal refers when he speaks contemptuously of British ministers resigning because of their sexual peccadilloes.

"In the United States, politicians don't resign over this kind of thing. The Kennedys and the movie world were inextricably bound together — and still are with the surviving Kennedy. Everyone knew that one of Marilyn Monroe's last telephone calls was to Bobby — though poor Norman Mailer is now being accused by the Kennedys and their outriders of having made up the whole incident in his book about Marilyn.

"When I was a child in Washington, everyone knew that Lucy Mercer was President Roosevelt's mistress. *I* knew that Princess Martha, the crown princess of Norway, also was. True, Roosevelt was an old man by then, so whether it was sexual at that point, who would know — or care. But he was besotted with her, and she moved into the White House — to the consternation of Missy LeHand, his secretary and — well, morganatic wife, according to Elliott Roosevelt's new book. He presented Norway with a submarine chaser. Someone said at the time: 'How like Roosevelt. Anybody else would have given her a diamond ring. He gave her a submarine chaser.' "

When Gore Vidal was 10, his parents were divorced. "My mother married Auchincloss and I moved into Merrywood (Mr. Auchincloss' lavish home on the Potomac). He was a very rich man."

Vidal is reticent about his mother in his public comments, but his feelings about her are vividly described in *The Journals of Anais Nin,* the writer he lived with when he was 20. "Psychologically he knows the meaning of his mother abandoning him when he was 10, to remarry and have other children. . . But he does not know why he cannot love . . ."

If Miss Nin's psychological analyses are sometimes simplistic, there is no doubt that the young Vidal was so badly bruised that he determined to avoid any future emotional involvement in which he might get hurt again.

He was sent away to boarding schools and holiday camps, changed his Christian names (Eugene Luther) to Gore and on graduating from Exeter enlisted in the Army. "I was thrilled to be paid money while being no more uncomfortable than I'd been for years. In the Army it was the middle-class boys whose ➡

(Continued from preceding page)
mothers had always made their beds who whined. We'd been brought up like little Spartans, to help create the American Empire. Sound familiar?"

He had an undistinguished yet painful war in the Aleutians, plagued by premature arthritis brought on by the cold. Long stretches in the hospital gave him the time to write his first book, a war novel called *Williwaw,* which was published and acclaimed when he was only 20. He and Truman Capote, who published his first work the same year, have — naturally — been archenemies since they were jointly celebrated as The Boy Wonder.

Vidal was instantly taken up by An Older Woman cum Writer cum Priestess of Love, Anais Nin, who apparently introduced him to the pleasures of bisexuality.

Meanwhile, Vidal's mother divorced Mr. Auchincloss. They'd had a daughter, Nina, the half-sister whom Vidal loves dearly. "She's the only member of the family whom I see. She has the burden of being enormously intelligent, which no other member of the family is." The family now came to include Jacqueline Onassis, and her sister Princess Lee Radziwill, who were in their teens when *their* mother, Mrs. Bouvier, became Mr. Auchincloss' next wife. It was their turn now to move into Merrywood, later to be good-humoredly described by John Kennedy as "that den of little foxes."

This period is clearly alluded to in Vidal's novel *Two Sisters,* a study in mirrors of vanity, bisexuality and incest. Vidal writes of his half-sister, Nina, to whom he dedicates the book: "As if being my sister was not sufficient burden, she is also stepsister to the two most successful adventuresses of our time.

"They were pubescent when they moved in, and Nina was a little girl. They'd been brought up to be adventuresses. Their father had it in mind for them — Black Jack Bouvier, dark, handsome, alcoholic."

Although the joint stepfather Mr. Auchincloss was rich, he wasn't keen on passing his money along to his various stepchildren. "The American magnate says: 'I'll give you everything until you've finished your education and training. Then you must live on what you make.' There might be a little trust fund, but nothing of consequence. I've never had a penny from my family apart from a $20,000 trust fund, which means about $2,500 a year. The Bouvier girls got nothing at all. So they had to marry well."

In 1948, two years after Vidal's first novel had made him the critics' darling, they cast him down from the heights to which they'd raised him. His third novel was a rather plodding book about homosexuality called *The City and the Pillar.* But it was the first book of its kind: where Capote had made homosexuality decadent, Vidal made it normal.

VIDAL, Gore
MIAMI HERALD
(Miami, Fla.)
Nov. 25, 1973

"It is inhumane to attack Capote," says Vidal. "You are attacking an elf. Over the years he has taken no position on sex. Or on anything except capital punishment, which rather thrills him.

"But I'm a polemicist. I was also touching on that raw nerve in the United States — the sexuality of men. For the tough war novelist to treat homosexuality as something ordinary made people — to use the current phrase — blow their minds." *The New York Times* refused to advertise the book. Vidal's subsequent novels were brushed aside by reviewers.

While he exaggerates his poverty during these years, which was not as great as most of us have known, his income was inadequate for his chosen style of life, and he was reduced to writing detective stories under the name 'Edgar Box.'

Like many writers — and other people — he seems to cherish his grudges, like a schoolboy writing down the names of people who hurt him so that he can get back at them some day. Without doubt he delights in feuds. "I *like* Norman Mailer personally, that patron saint of bad journalists. It's his views I can't stand."

For awhile Vidal lived in Guatemala — a country at once beautiful and cheap. But in 1950 the Establishment part of his nature asserted itself, and he bought a grand house on the Hudson River. To pay for it, he embarked on his Five-Year Plan — hiring himself out to Hollywood and television for money, and writing essays as a relief valve. By 1960 he'd worked his passage back to fame and riches. He had his own television show. Two plays were Broadway successes. It was time now for Vidal the Politician to step forth on the stage.

He ran for Congress as a Democratic-Liberal, and though he didn't win, he ran a good race and was proud of it. And, oh happy day, his stepsister's husband became President of the United States. For two years Vidal was an intimate of the White House. Escorting Mrs. Rose Kennedy to the opera, Vidal — enormously attractive in white tie and tails — looked the part of an extra. Who would have guessed that he would become the first of the insiders to debunk the Kennedy legend, frolicking through that family's enormous reputation with unrelenting glee? Was he smitten with them at the outset because of what was in it for him?

He concedes an element of that, but can't resist adding: "Though you must remember that I was brought up in the shadow of the White House. We were never very impressed by those people. 'The passing parade,' we called them. But I was charmed by Jack, as indeed I was until the end. I was pleased that Jackie came back into my life."

In his own way, Gore Vidal retains a considerable admiration for his stepsister. "Jackie is subtle, shrewd, I think the word is 'cultivated' — in a decent way. She's always wanted money more than power. Most people are the reverse.

"Her sister Lee's first husband was Michael Canfield (once private secretary to the American ambassador in London). The English assimilated him and adored him. I don't think Lee has — how shall I say? won the hearts of England. In the immortal phrase of Judy Montagu about another American lady who crossed the ocean and failed to make it: 'Not enough jokes.'

"But Jackie has always had what Tiny Truman would call 'star quality.' Whatever she does — whether she has jokes or no jokes — she will always get good publicity. She wanted to be a movie star without actually having to make the movies — every woman's dream: the full attention without the work and pitfalls. As recently as '58 when I was with MGM, she was talking rather wistfully about whether Jack would let her make a movie.

"My sister Nina is puritanical and hardworking and tortured. Jackie once said: 'Nina, why are you wasting yourself?' Nina was driving herself intellectually, in every other way. Jackie said, quite sensibly: 'This isn't important.' Nina said, equally sensibly: 'It's important to me. And what's important to *you,* I'd like to know?' Jackie replied: 'Being attractive to men.' It's really quite odd, because it's not sexual at all. It was to create an *aura.*"

When did Vidal's disillusionment with John Kennedy set in?

"I *always* enjoyed his company," says Vidal. "At the outset I thought that someone as intelligent as Jack, as knowledgeable of the world of politics, with all his irony, would make a marvelous President. I was wrong. I guess there were indications that he was a little light-minded for ➡

(Continued from preceding page)

such a great task, but by God we'd been through Eisenhower and Truman, so I wasn't too disturbed until the Bay of Pigs. Even then I found myself chattering on television in his defense. Then I began to think: 'I've never been very strongly against Communism. I do not believe in interference in small countries.'

"Jack really *liked* war — all that mucking about in the jungle. In three years as President, what did he accomplish? He begins with an invasion of Cuba and ends with starting the war in Vietnam, our Syracusan catastrophe. Domestically the black issue was the last thing he was interested in — like Johnson having to deal with foreign affairs. Johnson," Vidal adds in his digressive way, "though he was a crook — took money and made a great fortune — *did* get domestic legislation through Congress that Kennedy, who was such a crybaby, said he could never do.

"Yet I'd rather spend an hour with Jack than anyone I can think of; he was really droll. But he was limited by the family that produced him. Certainly I don't think he had

VIDAL, Gore
MIAMI HERALD
(Miami, Fla.)
Nov. 25, 1973

a commitment to much of anything except getting elected. But on almost every important issue he gave at least one *very important speech* that made perfect sense. Then, of course, nothing further happened."

By 1962, Vidal's period of intimacy in the White House began to draw to a close. Bobby Kennedy found it difficult to be in the same room with him. The feeling was mutual.

"It was chemical," says Vidal. "Put us in the same room and I'd want to kick him." He nearly did so at a White House party when Bobby took umbrage at Vidal's putting his arm around the First Lady. "The final break came over the piece that I wrote in *Esquire* in 1963. (Dismissing Bobby-the-civil-rights-crusader as calculated image, Vidal depicted the man as an instinctively anti-liberal authoritarian, closer in outlook to Barry Goldwater than to John Kennedy.) I felt it was time that Bobby's character was drawn large for the electorate. That was the end of my relations with the Kennedys."

Even with his stepsister? "I've not seen the woman since. She adored Bobby. I think she probably liked him better than Jack — I mean this with no innuendo. Bobby was genuinely good with women. My sister Nina always felt she could go to Bobby when she was having a difficult time. He had that nice side to him. Jack only liked women for sex."

"Gore," says Stephen Spender, "genuinely sees through all that life, so he was not too disappointed when he was rejected. It's perfectly consistent to want to be part of a way of life, but to regard yourself as superior to it if it rejects you."

In 1964 Vidal decided not to stand again for Congress. "I wanted to be noticed and *right*. By 1964 I realized I would have more notice and independence on television and in my writing than if I was in Congress. As the late John Kennedy said: 'The House of Representatives is a can of worms.' "

And by then, for the first time in 10 years, Vidal was working on a novel — *Julian*. He gave up his television program, moved to Rome and finished the book. In America it was a best seller. Since then he has written three more best sellers: *Washington, D.C.; Myra Breckinridge; Two Sisters*. Just published is a historical novel, *Burr*, which throws a very different light on America's revered founders.

Vidal and his companion, Howard Austen, remain based in Rome. The house on the Hudson has been sold, the spendid villa in Ravello acquired. Vidal does the writing, Howard does everything else. I had been told that Howard likes to project the image that his main role is to arrange orgies for Vidal and his friends. But the only side of Howard that I observed was an engaging, ageless man (in fact he's 43) who is obviously highly competent: he runs the two households, directs the farming at Ravello, acts as personal secretary and general factotum. If ever a person deserves to be named in a will, I reckon it is Howard.

Presumably their relationship fortifies Vidal's running feud with psychiatrists and churchmen, between whom he sees little to choose. "Jewish psychiatrists are fundamentalists who should have been rabbis. They present their Mosaic taboos in the guise of science. The Jewish code was monstrous. The Christian one is equally monstrous. The Jews thought women were s--- and passed this on to the Christians. And they also passed on the rabbinical concept that there is something wicked about the homosexual act. We all know what the Founding Father thought of Sodom.

"All I have ever argued is that the heterosexual and the homosexual act should have absolute parity. Instead we are taught all this nonsense by Dr. David Reuben: if you're a homosexualist, you're immature; if you're promiscuous, you're not capable of a sustained emotional relationship. Oh, dear."

Vidal and Howard have lived together for 23 years. "It's never had anything to do with the romanticism that goes into male-female and certain kinds of homosexual relationships. The affection we have for each other is that of friends: we put up with each other's limitations. It might look like a marriage from the outside, but it isn't from the inside. None of the assumptions are there. Each marriage I know of *starts* on the assumption of sexual exclusivity.

"I've never had any sexual jealousy in my life. I've never cared for anybody? That's the obvious assumption for people to make. But I *think* they're wrong."

He remains utterly mystified as to why the Western world tries to combine lust and compassion. "The two are separate and most people know it. But they won't face up to it. Instead they put themselves through all this misery about love."

He breaks off into a brutal mimicry of a married couple called Marvin and Marian who year after year strive earnestly to attain together what Vidal calls "The Big O." "Of course," he adds, "homosexuals also have emotional hangups — though that usually comes to an abrupt end when the boy asks for more money.

"I seem to have missed the romantic programming that everyone else got. I never had any confusion between the needs of the body and the needs of the soul. They can coincide briefly, but then only because of a misunderstanding — each person thinking the other is different from what he is. In time, my point of view will prevail."

Supposing, I said, you had some human beings who apart from romanticism might intellectually choose to combine body and soul in order to heighten a relationship. "Then they're putting all their eggs in one basket," he replies. He would never let himself in for the extreme pain that attends one partner in such an intertwined relationship.

Of Vidal's 13 novels, only three are directly autobiographical. But his essays — which perhaps are his most acute and searing and hilarious work — are becoming ever closer to portraits of the author.

"I'm being pressed by my editor," Vidal says, "to be garrulous — like Montaigne: 'I woke up this morning and I urinated and passed a stone,' after which he turns to morality. I'm doing it with some reluctance. But I realize the essay form requires certain personal reference. If it gets people to read the serious part, I'll endure the humiliation of being thought garrulous, and er, vain." [T]

Living together should bring out best in both partners

—Star-Telegram Photo

VISCOTT, David S(teven)
(1938 -)

FORT WORTH
STAR–TELEGRAM
(Ft. Worth, Tex.)

Dec. 17, 1974

[See also CA-29/32]

The breaking up of families is the most bitter problem many people have to face, in the opinion of young, poetic psychiatrist Dr. David Viscott, author of "How To Live With Another Person."

His new book has to do with the rights of both partners to a marriage, the rights of kids in relationship to parents — and the rights of parents.

Most books on family problems are "more sensational than helpful, and more obfuscatory than clear," Dr. Viscott found. He decided to put "in the most useful way possible" his own discoveries in the truths that "may help people make a good relationship."

HE WROTE THE book in 16 days — "but this is characteristic of the way I work," he adds. "The point of a relationship is to allow the people involved to share the experience of becoming their best selves."

Married, with three young children, the author has been a resident in psychiatry at University Hospital in Boston and chief resident in its psychiatric clinic. A former member of the faculty of Boston University Medical School, he is a fellow of the Law-Medicine Institute and a member of the American Psychiatric Association.

His new book has become an alternate selection of the Book of the Month Club.

His theory of people living together is forthright: "Each must continue to grow into the best person possible. Everyone retains his rights and options that he would have outside the relationship. The only thing he or she gives up is the most precious gift — life. To yield any corner of our world and call it compromise is cowardice at not being able to face ourselves: this can undermine the relationship.

* * *

"WORSE, YOU SET the other person up as a roadblock. You have to be aware that you are responsible for your own life; nobody else is.

"We should not need other people in order to be ourselves: it leaves the other person obligated to fill the holes in our being."

Psychiatric insight, he believes, is the next central market in the book world: "People feel that society is crumbling, and they need to be strong within themselves."

Nowadays, Dr. Viscott spends most of his time writing.

"Facing my own limitations, I have embarked on a life of freedom from office hours and appointments. But you can never stop constantly partaking in what everyone else is up to."

He has foud it "easy to judge the world when you use your own experiences and how other people alter or affect them.

"Because you are your own barometer, you no longer apologize for shortcomings.

"But first, you have to accept your limitations. Besides, other people can see through them."

* * *

FOR RELAXATION, Dr. Viscott has invented a card game called "Sensitivity." He writes music and lyrics, and has done movie adaptations. He skis and plays the piano.

"The Making of a Psychiatrist" and "How to Live With Another Person" are two of a projected series of four books. The next will have a title like "Creating a World of Your Own" and will deal with his favorite theme of developing one's "best self." The fourth is tentatively titled "How to Live With Your Family."

"The best therapy takes place between people who care about each other," he says.

"Everything I have achieved has been done simply by facing the truth," he says. His theories on this subject were published in March issue of "Today's Health" and picked up by "Catholic Digest," and will be a Reader's Digest reprint. They have appeared in American Woman magazine and various newspapers.

" 'I can remember saying to my wife, 'That's a good article, but I could have made it better,' " he says, It tells how to make magic out of bad moods: "I think I know the process I am involved in," he adds.

* * *

ON THE WHOLE, Dr. Viscott has adjusted to success. "Sometimes I have difficulty in realzing it is me," he says. "Usually I am isolated from family and friends: I spend a lot of time by myself.

"I don't take myself too serious: I'm not really an author, I'm just on very good terms with a dictaphone. A life force lives inside each person and seeks expression. Each person must find what he is designed for and then let the life force flow. That's not terribly complicated, and it makes good sense. It is a lonely force, and sometimes frightening. Everyone is inclined to run away from it the first time. The worst therapy makes this most difficult, and the best allows it to happen. Both are painful, and many persons get involved in a process that is meaningless. People have spent years on the couch doing little more than make excuses for themselves.

"It's fascinating. The reason some people do not like people is that they can't stand themselves."

Psychiatrist loves stage

By LUCILLE DeVIEW
News Staff Writer

Dr. David S. Viscott is a psychiatrist turned show biz personality.

His own wonder at such a transformation was the subject for his talk yesterday at Detroit Town Hall.

A slightly rolly-polly man with a wide, I'm-a-bad-boy-but-I-love-it grin, he sat on a stool, hunched toward the audience, and told what a laugh it was to find himself occupying Jane Powell's dressing room.

His unkind remarks about Miss Powell ("she's a messy lady") shocked more than one listener because Dr. Viscott has always presented himself in his writings (he does that, too) as a very sensitive, caring, feeling individual.

AMONG THE BOOKS he's written are: "The Making of a Psychiatrist" (Arbor House); "The Dorchester Boy" (Arbor House); and an upcoming one

VISCOTT, David S(teven)

DETROIT NEWS
(Detroit, Mich.)

Jan. 23, 1975

called "How to Live with Another Person."

He was the originator and manufacturer of sensitivity greeting cards ("The real you is so much more."), sensitivity games, sweatshirts and dog-tag jewelry.

Certainly he is very charmed with his new role on stage.

"How could this strange thing happen to a nice Jewish boy?" he asked and then explained:

"I GOT STARTED on the wrong track. When I was born, my father, the pharmacist, said, 'My doctor was born today.'"

He did grow up to be a doctor but found it a bore. And found the world of medicine as disillusioning as he was later to find psychiatry.

"I keep expecting people to be better than they are," he explained. "Med school was run by people who invented little nitches for themselves and created esoteric garbage."

As a med student, he said, he was expected to be interested in "money and broads." Instead, he was interested in cancer research which "got me nowhere."

AS A YOUNG intern, he did one stint in psychiatry. It was a turning point.

"Everybody knows psychiatry is a lot of nonsense," he said. "You couldn't believe how strange the shrinks were who taught at that med school. They were unapproachable."

For himself, he said, the first time he felt like "a healer" was when he listened to a patient confined to a hospital for electric shock treatment.

"She was a nice lady, like one of my mother's friends," Dr. Viscott said. "I spent the week talking with her. She didn't need electric shock. She needed someone to talk with her."

OFTEN HE FOUND himself telling patients "what my mother used to tell me — and it worked."

Things given out of love work, he said. Things not given out of love won't work "because the patient knows you are faking it."

Dr. Viscott always had a love of the arts. As a boy, he played clarinet and spent long hours listening to classical music. He wrote. And while in med school, he was asked to work with a student theater group.

Later, in private practice, he had many patients who were in the creative arts. He said he often thought: I should be doing what they are doing.

He published some poetry and began his now full-time work of writing books.

Author Says He'll Find Proof of Ancient Astronauts

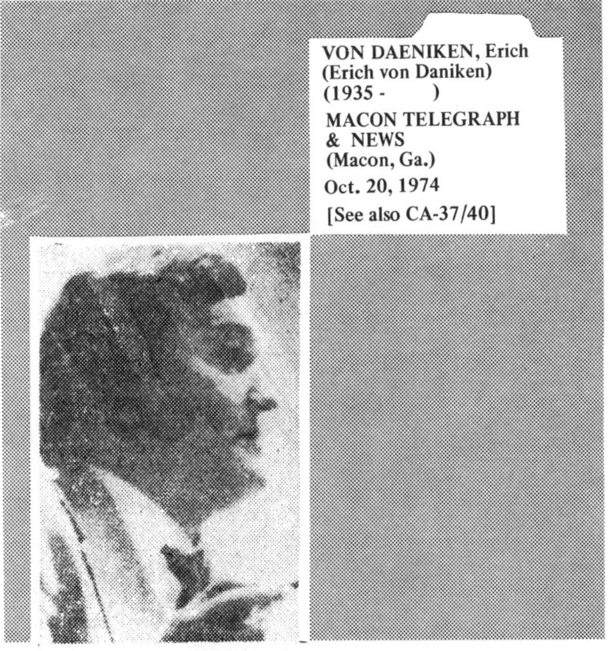
VON DAENIKEN, Erich
(Erich von Daniken)
(1935 -)
MACON TELEGRAPH & NEWS
(Macon, Ga.)
Oct. 20, 1974
[See also CA-37/40]

ERICH von DAENIKEN

By MADELEINE HIRSIGER
News Staff Writer

There's a silent underground movement spreading across the world.

"This may be the largest silent movement ever," explained Erich von Daeniken about his theory that ancient astronauts may have visited the earth.

"I mean how else do you explain that 28 million people have bought my books all over the world and that since I first published 'Chariots of the Gods?' in 1968 many others have begun writing about this theory. In all about 100 million books dealing with this subject have been sold."

The Swiss author credits religious conflicts with his interest in the subject. "I was in a very strict Catholic boys college in Switzerland. I couldn't take it any longer and started asking myself why Jesus was going to punish, why Jesus was going to return to save the world and so on. I then began reading many, many books about other religions and mythologies and there I found a similarity I was astounded at."

MANY OF his first findings were based on the prophet Ezekiel and his vision of four cherubims and four wheels. "NASA in Huntsville reconstructed what Ezekiel could have seen. They drew a replica of the spaceship he describes when he said 'A whirlwind came out of the north, a great cloud, and a fire infolding itself, and a brightness was about it, and out of the midst thereof came the likeness of four living creatures.'

He described how every one had four wings and that their feet were straight feet and the sole of their feet was like the sole of a calf's foot."

According to NASA, said Von Daeniken, the four creatures had four wings because it was a spaceship which had four helicopters with four blades each. "You have to remember that what Ezekiel saw hadn't been seen by anyone. He had to use words known to him to describe the apparition. Then his story was handed down through many generations and you know how people like to brag and add things."

It took Von Daeniken 13 years to complete his first book, published in German in 1968. Although it was a No. 1 bestseller in Europe it made no impact in America until NBC television telecast "In Search of Ancient Astronauts" based on "Chariots of the Gods?"

Two more books followed and he has just released a fourth in Europe called "Apparitions," now being translated into the English language.

Von Daeniken, who last year spent 301 days on the road researching and appearing at lectures, said during his visit to Milledgeville on his present lecture tour in the United States, to last through December, that it will be his last for some time.

"I don't mind it when people criticize me. In fact, I get stacks of clippings at my office in Zurich every day and I look through them and find both criticism and encouragement. Let them criticize and shout as much as they want. I have a goal which I'm working towards."

His goal, he said, is to search for proof. "I will find it. Next year I will start out with my Land Rover and travel to collect more proof. You won't be hearing anything from me for several years."

It won't be the first time the author has traveled to some far away place to see for himself what people have written to him about. His only regret is that he cannot freely travel to Red China and Tibet.

"THERE ARE skrolls and round stone plates, like records, in China and Tibet that describe in detail how space crafts landed on earth thousands of years ago but the government won't allow anyone to research them yet," he said.

Among the mail he receives each day he finds more and more letters from scientists offering advice and proof of findings. "I have never said my thoughts are facts although many critics claim I've said that. I speculate as do all others who write about findings. Today," he said, "we have optical indications that are hard facts."

His "evidence" has been collected mainly in the Near East and South America, "but evidence can be found everywhere. Primitive drawings and sculptures resembling each other can be found here in America as well as in Africa or the East."

His hypothesis, he says, is open to debate, of course. "I have a lot of imagination but I find it sick when critics attack me for distorting the truth. You can imagine that especially Christian people find it hard to believe that what I'm finding could be true. On the other hand, I have professors in India, where my books have been translated into four different dialects, offering me help and guidance."

Von Daeniken, although he only spends a short time each year at his home near Zurich, speaks fondly of his wife and 11-year-old daughter. "My wife doesn't like my style of life. She doesn't like to travel. So she stays at home, works in the house and the garden and cooks and takes care of the two dogs.

"She has to make sure my daughter gets up each morning to go to school," he said and was astonished at a question about Women's Liberation. "My wife likes what she's doing and she doesn't mind my being away."

He had, however, never imagined his success when he finally found a publisher interested in his first book. "I never though," he said shaking his head, "that I'd be speaking to universities all over the world."

(Also see preceding article)

'Gold of the Gods'? There's Gold in Books for Its Author

By GERALD KLOSS
of The Journal Staff

ERICH VON DANIKEN is a compact, 39 year old Swiss who believes, with verbose sincerity, that astronauts landed on Earth in prehistoric times because of some cataclysmic war in another galaxy and inspired such mighty feats as the building of the Egyptian pyramids, landing strips in Peru and a vast system of underground tunnels in Ecuador.

The difference between him and the guy at the next barstool is that von Daniken has sold some 28 million copies of books, in 34 languages, explaining how it all happened. He was in Milwaukee the other day to promote the soft cover Bantam edition of "The Gold of the Gods," a sequel to his other best sellers, "Chariots of the Gods?" and "Gods From Outer Space."

Someone Must Be Joking

He sat down and started humming the opening bars of Scott Joplin's "The Entertainer."

"Are you aware," he was asked, "that that tune was inscribed on the walls of a cave in Juneau County, Wisconsin, probably left by some ancient astronaut?"

"You are kitting!" he said (he has a quaint Swiss-German accent). "On ze other handt, you hef so many unexplained mysteries here in America. What about the Thunderbird cult in your Pacific Northwest? The great bird, six canoes long, glittering like metal? What is zat but a space ship, dimly recalled?"

(We'll drop the German accent, if you don't mind.)

"About that interview in the August issue of Playboy, Erich. Any comment?"

He shook his head and sucked on his Pipstar pipe, a Swiss model of straight stem and a bowl that extends horizontally, with an aluminum screen over the end.

"It was, um, dishonest," he said. "For example, in the introduction is quoted three brief remarks about me from newspapers and magazines. Why were they selected, and not the nice things that were said?"

"Oh, you mean the quote from the Miami News, describing you as 'the Clifford Irving of the Cosmos?' That was pretty funny."

"Yeah, that was one of them. But I have bales and bales of clippings that say otherwise."

"According to Playboy and Newsweek, Erich, the guy

Erich von Daniken in Milwaukee (Journal Photo)

VON DAENIKEN, Erich (Erich von Daniken)
MILWAUKEE JOURNAL (Milwaukee, Wisc.)
Nov. 3, 1974

who discovered that vast system of astronaut tunnels in Ecuador said that you never got to see them yourself, although you describe them vividly in 'Gold of the Gods.' How about that?"

"He is, of course, a liar," said von Daniken. "He did not, I admit, let me into the main entrance, but he did through a side entrance. I was there. I have pictures. I have slides."

"Something has puzzled me, Erich? Why did you add the question mark to the title of your first book, 'Chariot of the Gods?'"

"Funny!" he said. "I don't know, myself. I write in German, and the original title, roughly translated, was 'Souvenirs of the Future.' The English publishers changed it to the other title. Why the question mark? Maybe because the book posed 238 questions, unanswerable except through my theories."

Those Tunnels in Ecuador

He leaned forward and grasped his hands.

"Look, I will tell you something," he said. "I cannot believe that **all** of my theories are correct. My first book was a mind opener — one to pose questions of things that have not been challenged. Many scientists think I am wrong.

"Here is a picture of a large, sculptured slab in Mexico. Look at that central figure of a man. He has, to me, an oxygen mask on his face, and he is controlling some instrument in front of him. Behind him you see these waves, which I take to be the exhaust of his space ship.

Going Around in a Circle

"Ah, but what do the archeologists say? I talk to one of them, who says, 'But that, my dear young man, is the stylized beard of the Mexican Weather God. So-and-so wrote about it six years ago.'

"So I go to see So-and-So. And he says, 'Well, of course, young man, that's the flowing beard of the Weather King. Prof. X. defined it 20 years ago.' So I go to Prof. X., and he says,, 'Young man, don't you know that that is the beard of the Weather King? I learned that from . . .'

"One scholar would refer me to another in an endless circle. Really, they were taking each other's words in faith, and wrapping it in the cloak of science."

He leaned back and sighed.

"Yesterday, Pittsburgh," he muttered. "Tomorrow, Cincinnati. Then Florida and Boston. Ah, well. But life goes on."

And as he left, he hummed the theme from "The Entertainer."

He might just explore that cave in Juneau County after all.

'Earth Has Been Visited'

VON DAENIKEN, Erich (Erich von Daniken)
CINCINNATI ENQUIRER (Cincinnati, Ohio)
Nov. 3, 1974

By OWEN FINDSEN
Enquirer Book Editor

"I am sure the theory is right. We have been visited from outer space, there is no doubt about that. There are too many indications. I know too much about the subject to doubt it. And those visitors even have created our intelligence. We Homo Sapiens Sapiens are the product of an artificial mutation. There is no missing link.

"Now if I were an astronaut in the same situation I would have the wish to deposit a definite proof, something for later generations which says 'Listen, I have been here."

If all that sounds like something out of Erich von Daniken, it is. The world's leading authority on ancient astronauts was in Cincinnati last week promoting one or more of his books in which he claims God was an astronaut. By coincidence, his film version of *"Chariots Of The Gods?"* is also in town, at a number of theaters.

THE BOOKS are *"Chariots Of The Gods?," "Gods From Outer Space," "The Gold Of The Gods,"* and *"In Search Of Ancient Gods."* All but the last are Bantam paperbacks, and the other is a Putnam edition of photographic evidence, at $8.95. There are dozens of paperbacks by other authors, all exploiting von Daniken's theory. "These books are full of photographs that I took, but they never mention my name. Okay, they support the theory."

Von Daniken has been studying ancient cultures since high school, 22 years ago. Before devoting full time to "the theory" he was a hotel manager in Switzerland. The tourist season was only four months long, which gave him eight months to study ancient cultures. His first articles appeared in his native Germany in 1954 and his work has been available in English for 10 years. But it was two years ago, when a television showing of a portion of the movie of *"Chariots Of The Gods"* was broadcast, that von Daniken became a household word.

"THEY CALL me a crackpot. I have read all the books. I know all the official explanations. I have visited all of the ancient sites that I write about. I do not put everything in my books, only those things that fit my theory." He feels that archeologists are "like concrete," gathering their facts from each other's writings, rather than making their own conclusions.

"They are doing yesterday's thinking. I try to see with tomorrow's eyes."

He admits that he has written his books "in an explosive and provocative way" to create controversy, but he often finds that he is challenged in an unfair manner. "Crash my facts," he pleads, "but do not say that I said things that I did not say." He has recently been victimized by a Playboy magazine interview in which he was quoted out of context and presented as a compulsive liar. The lying charge came out of the testimony of a psychologist who testified against him in a tax fraud case. Von Daniken was acquitted and the testimony was proven false, but the article skipped these facts.

WHATEVER, the example proves a point. Presently the von Daniken theory is widely seen as a hoax, by people who read an article that did not give the facts. When we do not have all the information we are bound to make false conclusions.

And concerning the pyramids of Egypt, the Mayan temples, even Ohio's Serpent Mound, we do not have all the facts. Von Daniken's theory is at least as sincere as the official conclusions of archaeology. Were they built by the hand of man? Or were they built with the advice and assistance of visitors from another planet who put them there so that they would raise questions in the minds of a generation that understands space travel?

VON DANIKEN feels that his view is soon to be accepted. Just before our interview he received a copy of a paper written by a biologist at Heidelberg University who believes that he has found designs in 20,000 year old cave paintings that are genetic models of the mutation that astronauts produced in pre-historic creatures to create man in their own image.

There will be no more books for some time. Von Daniken has wearied of trying to spread his gospel. He will disappear from public view, he says, and concentrate on tracking down his evidence, in search of the ultimate message which, he is sure, is hidden somewhere on this planet.

Vonnegut arrives to fight Strongsville ban on books

By JIM DUDAS

Author Kurt Vonnegut testified in Federal Court today in defense of two of his books that have been banned by the Strongsville School Board for classroom use.

"I would like to hope that I have good morals," said the tall, droopy-mustached father of six.

"I consider writing an act of good citizenship."

Vonnegut was brought here by the American Civil Liberties Union, which filed the court action protesting the ban on Vonnegut's "God Bless You, Mr. Rosewater" and "Cat's Cradle" and on a book by Joseph Heller, "Catch 22."

Questioned by ACLU attorney Michael Honohan about his background, Vonnegut said he has written 12 books which have sold about eight million paperback copies and one million in hardback.

He said they have been translated into about every language "except Chinese."

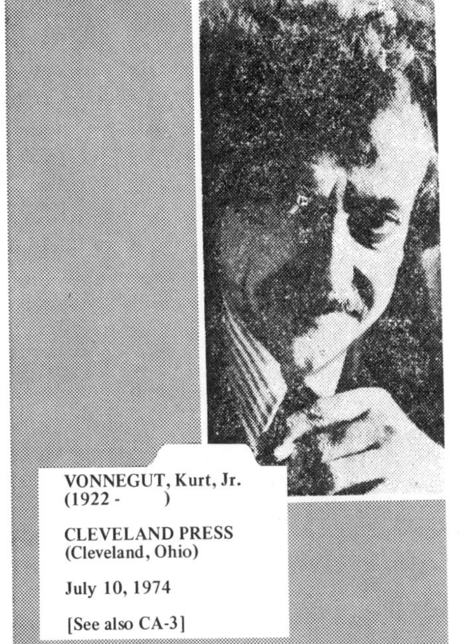

VONNEGUT, Kurt, Jr. (1922-)

CLEVELAND PRESS (Cleveland, Ohio)

July 10, 1974

[See also CA-3]

Vonnegut, 52, has been a professor at the University of Iowa and at Harvard. He has held a Guggenheim Fellowship and he is a distinguished professor of literature at the City College of New York.

Of his "Rosewater" work, Vonnegut told the court:

"It is about persons in hopeless situations that can be comforted by ideas alone."

As for his "Cat's Cradle," he said: "A skeptical book. The character in the book abhors the damage that has been done to the American dream."

Honohan asked the tan-suited Vonnegut weather he considered his books suitable for high school students.

"I think my books are easy to teach and learn and would be suitable for high school.

"From the many letters I get from high school students who ask help for term papers, I assume that many high school students read my books."

Outside the courtroom, newsmen asked the author why he thinks his books were banned.

"Maybe they think my books are why people smoke dope and get pregnant," he replied.

Vonnegut, who was a college lecturer for five years, said he sympathized with aspiring writers today because many of the magazines for which he wrote as a young man have perished.

"Some of my students were so good they didn't need any more training and yet there is nowhere for them to take their writing," he said.

The Strongsville case opened yesterday before Federal Judge Robert Krupansky.

The ban followed a resolution by the board in 1972. In November that year the ACLU filed acomplaint on behalf of five students or former students.

In stating reasons for banning the books, one of the board members said there were too many referrals to sex and dishonesty of the characters in Heller's work.

Like Heller's book, Vonnegut's work takes a sarcastic look at society and many of its institutions.

Vonnegut's books were called "trashy" and "stupid" by Strongsville School Board member Ellen Wong.

God bless you, Mr. Vonnegut

By Jim Dudas

It is nearly midnight when Kurt Vonnegut Jr., in all his disheveled glory, shuffles into the lobby of the Hollenden House.

He looks like he has been hiding in a storm sewer during a downpour, drying his suit and hair in a wind tunnel.

Lighting the ever-present Pall Mall cigaret he apologizes for being late.

"I'm a little fogged in," he says through the Pall Mall smoke. He means he has been drinking.

And so he talks about his occupation. "Writing used to be a discipline for me. Now it's a habit."

He talks about aspiring writers. "They don't have as much opportunity as they did when there were all those slick magazines. Writing is becoming a gentleman's occupation again.

He isn't really late for anything because he wasn't expecting an interview. But nice guy that he is, he many times apologizes for things that aren't his fault.

"If you want to talk," he says, "let's go someplace where we can have a drink."

"Only those with money can afford to take the time to learn the craft because the poor ones can't support themselves in the meantime."

He talks about his future. "I wouldn't mind sitting down and having nothing happen; of not being able to write. It would sort of amuse me in a way.

"I've done so much more than I thought I would be able to do. I wouldn't be any more ashamed of not being able to write than I would be of growing old."

Vonnegut, 52, quit a job in public relations at General Electric in New York 23 years ago. Today he is one of the most popular authors in the country, especially among high school and college readers.

His books have sold more than nine million copies and have been translated into nearly every language. He has also written a play which flopped.

"I left public relations because it was dishonest," he says. But he hastens to add that working at GE allowed him to learn a lot of science which ultimately winds up in his works.

He cites "ice nine" the ultimate destructive chemi-

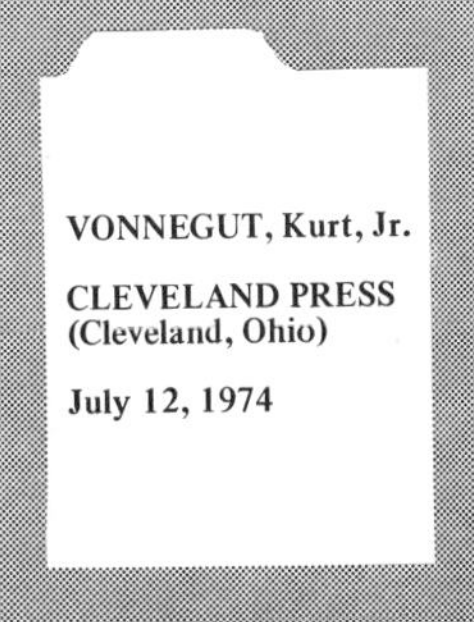

VONNEGUT, Kurt, Jr.

CLEVELAND PRESS (Cleveland, Ohio)

July 12, 1974

cal referred to in his book "Cat's Cradle." The idea came from a visit by H. G. Wells to GE laboratories.

"To entertain Wells, scientist made up the idea and how ice nine would work to destroy the world. Wells wasn't impressed with the story and after he and scientist died I used the idea."

Eliot Rosewater, the main character in "God Bless You, Mr. Rosewater," is fashioned after an accountant Vonnegut knows on Cape Cod.

Like Rosewater, the accountant is devoted to helping those less fortunate than himself.

"But he doesn't have as much money as Rosewater," Vonnegut says.

In his home in New York City, Vonnegut writes every day from 8 a.m. until noon.

"I write a lot of letters to the editors, answer my mail and sometimes work on a book. I don't work very hard."

If he were a young man today. Vonnegut said he would like to work for the New York Times.

"There are so many superb writers around without anyone to buy their work that free-lancing is much more risky than it was when I started," he says. "Watergate has shown that reporting can be respectable."

Although he has been a professor at Iowa University and Harvard University and is distinguished professor of literature at the City College of New York he is not particularly fond of writing courses.

"I taught because I needed the money. English departments don't produce writers. You find more writers in med school and law school because they haven't been misinformed by writing instructors.

"College professors say, 'my boy, this is very good writing, but let me show you how James Joyce would do it.' We don't need another Joyce or another Hemingway for that matter."

Then Vonnegut gets very quiet. Looking through the bottom of the glass that had once held gin and tonic, he politely announces he must get some rest and he shuffles off to his room.

By ROGER EBERT

It is a little awesome to listen to Irving Wallace talk about the sales figures of his novels. He has sold something like 92 million copies of them, in 31 languages, and, as his daughter once pointed out, "There's the Bible and then there's daddy."

Now he has just published a new novel called "The Fan Club," and it promises to be his biggest seller of all: Not least because of the coincidence that its plot resembles in some ways the Patricia Hearst kidnaping.

Wallace has been promoting the book in a national tour, and I asked him if the books he toured for did any better than the ones he did not. National promotional tours are part of the routine for best-selling authors like Jacqueline Susann, but Wallace avoided them for years.

"Let me tell you a story about tours," he said. "The first book I went out and toured for was "The Seven Minutes.' It had a trade sale (that's hard covers in bookstores) that was about the same as for 'The Man' — about 125,000 copies. And I hadn't done a thing to promote 'The Man.

"So I decided the whole business of touring was a waste of time. But then we got the figures from the Literary Guild, which selected "The Seven Minutes, as what they call a special selection. That means it doesn't come to you automatically; you have to order it. If they sent out books with my content automatically, they'd freak out a lot of their members.

* * *

"So, anyway, the guild figures come in and they've sold 435,000 copies of the book! And then there was the paperback. It took a book of mine like "The Chapman Report" six or seven years to sell 3,000,000 copies, which is considered a big-league sales figure. 'The Seven Minutes' sold two and a half million in 10 months! Apparently I have a larger number of loyal readers who are going to buy my books anyway, and then the publicity reaches lots of others."

He is sitting in his hotel suite, puffing on an omnipresent pipe and discussing these extraordinary figures with every appearance of outward calm. He has been a professional writer for so long, has written so many millions of words and sold them for so much, that millions of sales no longer astonish him.

And yet there is a new book out, "Irving Wallace: A Writer's Profile" by John Leverance (The Popular Press, Bowling Green) that examines his professional career even down to reproducing a chart of his production in 1941. That year, he recorded, he wrote 41 pieces, sold 33 of them (mostly to Liberty and Coronet magazines) and earned $5,398.

He had been a free-lance writer for several years, and a screenplay writer for 10 years (at various times at all the major studios) before "The Chapman Report," in 1959 finally brought him big money. He is now, with Susann and Harold Robbins, one of the three superstars of best-sellers.

* * *

"The Fan Club" is quintessential Irving Wallace. A schizo who is obsessed by his love for a Hollywood sex goddess recruits three other men, and together they kidnap the actress and imprison her in an isolated cabin.

After she is raped, she realizes that only she can save herself, and she uses all of her skills as a manipulator of men to bring about a rescue. Her final stroke of genius is to convince the men to ask for ransom for her. Before they do, there was no evidence that she had even been kidnapped, and thus no official police interest in her case.

"The book was off the press when the Hearst kidnaping happened," Wallace said. "The timing was incredible."

He says he remembers precisely where the idea for "The Fan Club" came from — "and that's unusual, because most of the time an idea will germinate over a period of months and years and you won't know quite where it came from.

"But with this one, the inspiration came exactly five years ago last month, while I was on a train from Boston to New York. I was all alone in the club car, and then we stopped at this junction and some railroad men got aboard. There was a newspaper, and they saw a headline about Burton buying Taylor the world's biggest diamond.

* * *

"That started them talking about Elizabeth Taylor, and one guy said he'd trade his house, his wife, his car, everything, for one night with her. The others said that guys like themselves would never have a chance at a woman like Taylor.

"I'd heard that kind of talk all my life. I didn't make a note about it in my journal as a possible story idea; I thought I'd forgotten it. Then, a few days later in Los Angeles, I heard an item on the radio about Taylor flying in for the Oscars. That somehow started me thinking about an evening I'd spent at a party for Marilyn Monroe, and about another party where Lana Turner was my dinner partner — and how she'd talked about men she'd known, and how she'd handled them.

"The moment I got home, I sat down at the typewriter and typed out a one-page outline of 'The Fan Club.' I had four different endings on that one page, and I didn't know if any of them would work, but I knew I had a story. I've known a lot of these women, the so-called sex symbols, and what they're like, and how they think, and I thought it would be fascinating to create a character who tried to save her own life through manipulating the fantasies that her kidnapers had about her."

How are sales going?

"Good. This book seems to have created a bigger split between the review and the readers than any other book I've done. But I try to write a novel you can't put down. Every time I see a lot of bad reviews, I think, oh, boy! They're gonna block me from the public. But the book has been out three weeks and it's already in the top 10.

And the Literary Guild hasn't even been heard from yet.

IRVING WALLACE:

Fans are grabbing his latest book by the thousands

(Also see preceding article)

A Storyteller With the Midas Touch: Irving Wallace – 'The' Writer

By SUSAN JENKS
Of The Bulletin Staff

While thousands of would-be novelists bite the literary dust each year ("slush pile" casualties of the publishing biz), somehow Irving Wallace manages to stay at the top, one of the 10 most widely-read authors in the world—a consummate storyteller with the Midas touch.

Just a Wallace "idea" is enough to send his publishers scurrying for another contract, or movie moguls into frantic bidding over film rights. Sight unseen they buy his material, knowing that all nine of Wallace's novels and four of his non-fiction books have been best-sellers, snapped up by an eager, adoring public.

An 'Ordinary Homebody'

The object of all this feverish adulation is surprisingly unaffected, an "ordinary homebody" as he was once described, who has been married to the same woman 33 years and eyes his success with a cool, objective eye.

"I'm very conscious of the trappings of success," he admits, flashing a warm, broad grin. "Many people who are successful get very arrogant because suddenly they get so much attention . . . so much fawning.

"What helped me is it took so many years to get there . . . to be successful. Now I can get outside myself to see me in this whole mobile world of celebrities and parties. What nonsense it is . . . we're just people."

In his conservative dress and manner, Wallace does exude a "just people" look. A shortish man, with silvery-gray hair worn casually to his collar, he seems more like an energetic professor than one of the world's leading popular novelists.

Latest Fictional Effort

This week Wallace was in Philadelphia on a rare promotional tour of his latest fictional effort, "The Fan Club" (Simon and Schuster), a sex-spiked tale of four nonentities who kidnap America's most coveted screen star. (Columbia Pictures has already bought the picture rights).

Many of his critics contend that it is his titillating approach to similar subjects that has won him so massive a readership over the years. But Wallace, sensitive to the phenomenal abuse that has come with phenomenal success, refuses to be so easily categorized.

"Sex has nothing to do with literature," he insists, patiently puffing on his pipe. "What they're saying is Irving Wallace caters to the public because that's what sells . . . that he's creating formulas for best sellers . . . But they don't know a damn thing about the creative process.

Nobody Knows What Sells

"There are 12,000 novels that come out every year. Why don't all the books that carry sex sell? The reason is nobody really knows what sells books—though I have my suspicions.

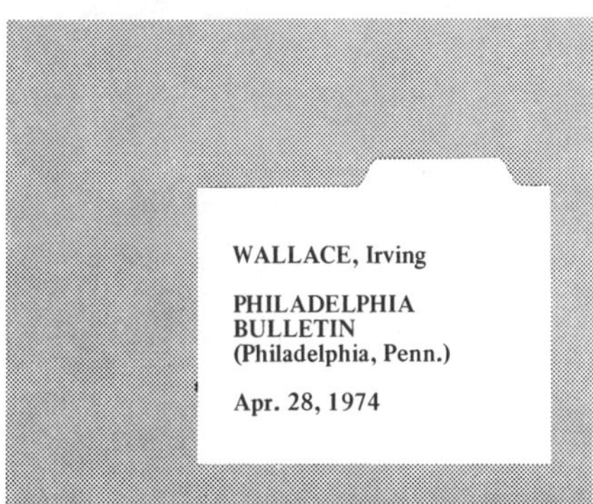
WALLACE, Irving

PHILADELPHIA BULLETIN
(Philadelphia, Penn.)

Apr. 28, 1974

"People just don't get enough story in novels. When a story comes, one where they are excited about flipping each page, it adds to their lives, enriches it. If sex is in it, that's fine. If religion and peace of mind are in it, that's fine."

Wallace, who sees himself as a "sociological novelist" rather than a highly-stylized writer, is convinced that most literary criticism has little to do with the quality of the book being reviewed.

"It has to do with the motivations of the novelist," he contends, "or what the reviewer THINKS are the motivations of the novelist. And yet writing is not made up of just style . . . it's made up of unique characters, intricate plots, so many other things. What's to be said about millions of people who like books that relate to their lives

"As Mark Twain said, 'The only critic I respect is the public'."

Highly Disciplined Writer

A highly disciplined writer, Wallace, who lives near Los Angeles, spends roughly 12 to 14 hours every day writing in the solitude of his study. Because he is superstitious, all 16 of his publications to date have been typed on the typewriter his parents gave him when he was a teen-ager, and every book begins with the word "the" in the title.

"The first four times it was an accident," he says of his title peculiarity, "but then I wrote 'The Chapman Report' (1960) and the book was such a big hit—my first such hit—that I've had 'the' in every one since."

His superstitious nature also gets the better of him when he's about to fly somewhere — a way of traveling he shunned completely until two years ago. Nowadays, he always wears the same pair of knit trousers on every flight, just as a precautionary measure.

"I'm very creative about my superstitions, though I do follow some of the old standbys like knocking on wood," admits Wallace. "I do, however, walk under ladders and I love black cats."

Something of Himself

While Wallace has used very little superstition in the characters of his novels, he does put something of himself or his Kenosha, Wis., background in each of his books. Often his protagonists smoke pipes or at least make passing reference to Wisconsin whenever possible.

But more than any other quality, Wallace prides himself on the "Everyman" in his work, always set against a backdrop of factual information. Creating "faction," (mixing "fact" with "fiction") as this distinctly Wallace technique is called, involves not only painstaking research of people, but also of whatever theme happens to catch his fancy at the time.

"Why should popular culture be disdained?" he asks rhetorically. "So many writers are scared to write because you can't be another Flaubert. They don't realize their stories have validity for our time . . . Flaubert didn't know how psyches would be affected by television, feminism or landing on the moon.

"There is only one 'you', even though the idea may be the same as someone else's . . . but writers have to have the kind of ego that people want to hear what you have to say."

Being a Cop Is 'Where It's At' For Author Joe Wambaugh

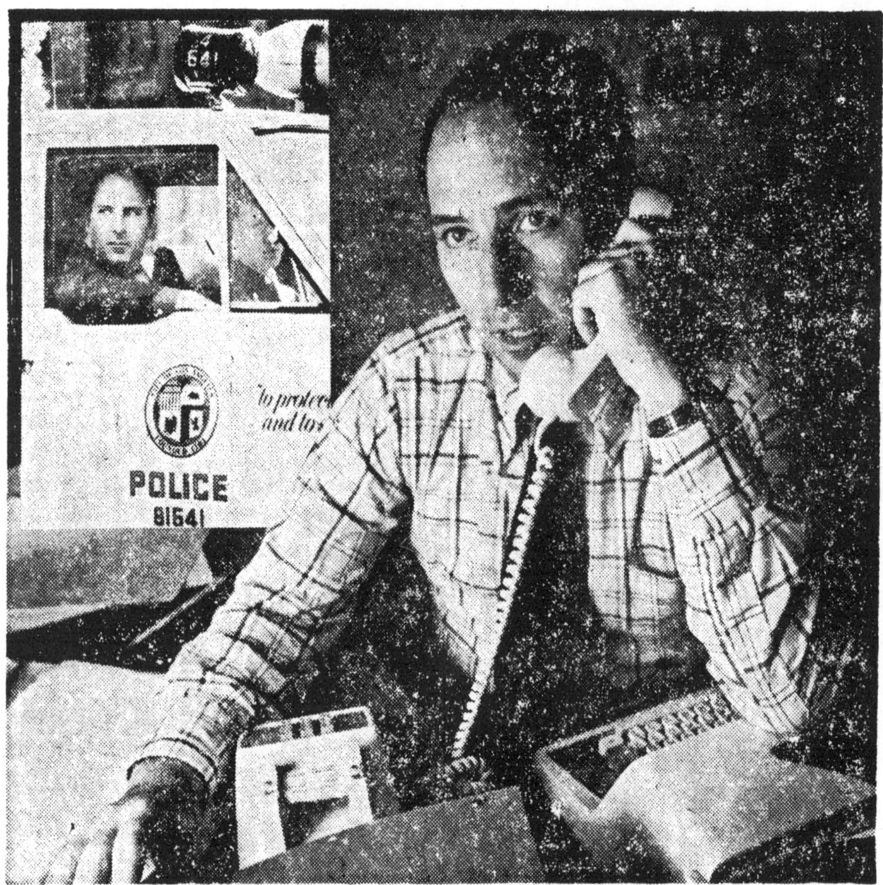

When he's off duty, Detective Joseph Wambaugh writes novels and also finds time for TV scripts about policemen and their battle against crime. On duty (inset), Wambaugh works as a plainclothes cop. Police work is a family tradition. His father was police chief in East Pittsburgh, Pa.

By JERRY LeBLANC

Q. Will you state your name please.

A. Joseph Wambaugh, detective, robbery division.

Q. You carry a gun and a badge in your job, is that right?

A. I carry a gun. I'm carrying a gun right now. And a badge. I work an eight-hour shift out of Hollenbeck Station in Los Angeles.

Q. Are you also the millionaire author of "The New Centurions," "The Blue Knight," "The Onion Field" and the TV series "Police Story"—the Joseph Wambaugh who drives to work in a Cadillac from a suburban mansion? Does this sound right to you?

A. That's me all right. I'm a cop—and a cop-writer!

(Wambaugh, green-eyed, with short-cut, receding dark hair, leaned forward, his arms folded, his lips firm. There was little humor in his face and when he glanced around the neighborhood cafe where he was lunching, he seemed to be looking for faces on a wanted poster. His beat is a tough, barrio-type area and by training and instinct, he's suspicious most of the time.)

Q. Your latest book—it says here Truman Capote helped you with it—tells how two small-time punks took two cops for a ride, killed one and left the other, er, emotionally slaughtered while justice dallied and fumbled for years. The book doesn't give one a very hopeful feeling about justice, does it?

WAMBAUGH, Joseph
(1937-)

HARTFORD COURANT
(Hartford, Conn.)

Dec. 16, 1973

[See also CA-7/8]

A. No, I guess it doesn't.

Q. Do you feel like that?

A. Yeah, I guess I do.

Q. Isn't it hard to work as a cop when you feel like this?

A. You get resigned to it. Take the analogy of the Jews in Israel. They live resigned to their fate. Tragedy and misery forever more.

Q. Then why do you do it—you could retire and live like a playboy.

A. For me being a cop is 'where it's at.' It's what I want.

(Under questioning, Wambaugh turns stubbornly brief. 

(Continued from preceding page)

Questioning people is his game and he bristles at having the tables turned. But when he chooses the topic, he becomes emotional and outspoken.)

Q. You sound like an angry man. What makes you angry?

A. I'll tell you what makes me angry. These simplistic minds that they put on federal commissions that keep coming up with answers to the crime problem. Like the one I just read about, says prisons don't rehabilitate so we should close the prisons, let all the non-violent cons out. Everyone seems to have answers except the police.

Let me tell you, I work mostly with poor people who can't afford to be burgled, and yet I have maybe a hundred people a month who get ripped off of everything they have of value. No insurance, and they can't afford to buy a new television. I think these people would regard a burglar as a danger to the community even if he isn't a dangerous type like Charlie Manson or Richard Speck in Chicago.

Lot of Misery

A burglar isn't usually a violent criminal but they victimize countless people who can't afford it. One lousy little hype (addict) burglar can commit 30 or 40 jobs a month and that causes an awful lot of misery in my community. If you're making eight grand a year and save six months to buy a ten-speed bike for your kid, then some addict burglar steals it and sells it down the street for twenty bucks so he can get a pop, I think the s.o.b. is dangerous. He's victimizing my people.

Q. What about rehabilitation?

A. You can't rehabilitate a guy who's been a hype for 20 years, and he's shooting four or five bags a day. With a habit like that he'd steal from his own mother every chance he'd get. I want those guys kept away from my people. Jesus, protect the people for a change. We can't even send a paroled addict back if his arms are full of needle marks. Have to catch him in the act. No matter that he's obviously got a hundred dollar a day habit and no job. On my beat almost all adult burglaries are done by heroin addicts. Do away with prisons? Hah

Q. What would you do?

A. I'll give you an idea. If we are prepared morally, if we are prepared to supply them with heroin, all they want—and I don't mean methadone or some substitute, because what they want is 'H' and I don't mean enough to make them nod. I mean all they want, and what they want is enough to kill themselves—if we'll supply them with all the heroin they want in federally sponsored clinics, for now, forever more, then I say let them out of prison. Within a year, half the hypes in the city would have killed themselves. What I'm saying is silly because no medical doctor would do it. It would be euthanasia.

More Comfort

I'll tell you one thing they could do, instead of phasing out prisons, they should make them more comfortable. I'm for all the prison liberties, letters, visits, everything they want. I'm for conjugal visits. I want the prisons to be comfortable.

But I want these types to be there. I think you'd find these fellows, a lot of them, wouldn't be in any hurry to get out if the prisons were more comfortable. Sure, it'd be expensive, but what's the cost in human misery alone, not alone the dollars and cents when they let them out and they commit 200 burglaries a year or 80 robberies?

I'm not optimistic. There's no answer. But all these commissioners have got an answer. I'll tell them all you've got is a holding action, and that's what the police job is.

Q. Is police work any good? Is it as bad as justice?

A. Police work isn't as good as televison or novels, but is it any good? Well, I think anything works better than justice does. I don't see that we're all that successful. It's pretty much a piecemeal job. Most of the time you have to admit that you're going to be doing your job after the fact, after the robbery, rape, theft.

Generally 90 per cent of your success, such as it is, is because somebody talks to you. You're only as good as the information you get from citizens. Without that information you're out of business. All the other things, computers and technology are just so much window dressing.

Q. You're painting a pretty dreary picture of police work. If it's so bad, not to mention the danger, why do it when you don't have to?

A. The physical dangers are overrated. I've only fired my service revolver once in 13 years on the force, and that was during the Watts riots. I don't think I hit anybody. We were shooting at shadows in panic. I was just trying to stay through it alive. But emotionally, police work is the most draining job there is — the constant frustration.

In the Vietnam protests we were sent on the barricades to catch hell, standing there as targets, the visible representatives of Washington. It should have been the Marines. We're not equipped to engage in guerrilla warfare, then suffer the pangs of city police a week later.

Vice is a dangerous job, a dirty job. You're taking a risk for very little, putting your life on the line for things punishable by a fifty-dollar fine.

Q. Crime and police work nevertheless fascinate you. All you write about is crime. Does it bother you that the two killers, Jimmy Lee Smith and Gregory Powell whom you wrote about in "The Onion Field" are basking in a kind of celebrity status in prison while there's one policeman dead and another discharged in a kind of trauma?

A. Smith wrote me a letter the other day. Said the book still frightens him but he doesn't know why. Must be some things that touch nerve endings. I called him a coward and a sniveler, and I think he knows it's true. I'm glad they didn't get executed. I don't want any harm to come to them.

Whenever they need anything, all they have to do is write to me and they'll get it. And I'll do that the rest of their lives. It's my responsibility now. I've changed their lives. They're different people in prison because of what I've written.

Q. Did you make them heroes?

A. Yes, yes. I made Jimmy Smith a folk hero in prison. All his buddies have read the book. They tell him they're going to get the Shaft character to play his part in the film that'll be made from the book. Well, I don't begrudge them their moment — one of the brightest moments of their dull little lives — because they've both had dreadful lives, mostly in prison. Smith is ecstatic. I'm the best friend he's ever had. Powell, I don't get along with as well. He's more cunning, twisted.

Q. What do your fellow officers think about the book?

A. Police Chief (Edward) Davis told me he liked it. Had lunch with him the other day. But I'll tell you, on the firing range recently a young patrolman stopped me and told me he learned more about police work from my book than he had in all his experience on the force. It was a good feeling. It was enough reward for writing it.

Wambaugh talked a little about the rewards of being a writer. Yes, he's living a lot better. "I'm sure my wife would tell you being a writer's wife is better than being a policeman's wife," but living a double life has presented problems.

The detective, whose history dates back to the time his father was chief of police in the town where he was born, East Pittsburgh, Pa., respects the demands of his workaday life despite being pursued by directors, agents and others in the celebrity writer world.

"There's one hard and fast rule: they're not allowed to call me, to bug me in my other life; that's my other world. They can't call me at the police station. I don't have any private secretary. I work in a squad room with a bunch of other detectives and they get pretty annoyed with taking personal calls for me. Even my publicity agent has to call my wife, and I call her to pick up messages."

Officer Wambaugh looked at his watch and fidgeted. It was getting time for him to report back for duty in that squad room, but he answered one more telling question about his two boys, age nine and eleven.

Q. How do the kids feel about you're being an author? I mean, which is worse, your being a writer or a cop?

A. Being a writer is worse to them. The kids are getting sick of people asking questions about their dad's television show and the books. I think the notoriety bothers them. I think they're probably prouder that people say to them, "Your father is a policeman.'

WAMBAUGH, Joseph

HARTFORD COURANT
(Hartford, Conn.)

Dec. 16, 1973

(Also see preceding article)

'Police Story' Author Strives for Realism

WAMBAUGH, Joseph

ATLANTA JOURNAL
(Atlanta, Ga.)

Dec. 28, 1974

By BOB GOODMAN
Journal Television-Radio Editor

"It was gratifying to see the acceptance by the press and public for 'Police Story.' I wanted to show policemen as they really are and police work as it really is."

So spoke Joe Wambaugh not long ago in describing his reaction to the overwhelming success of the NBC series which is now in its second year. And his desire to "tell it like it is" has obviously been achieved — those in the know say that the series is the most realistic of its sort ever produced.

As you probably know by now, Wambaugh is the creator and consultant of the series. It came about after the smashing success of a couple of books he authored: "The New Centurions" and "The Blue Knight." Both were best-sellers for months, as was his later book, "The Onion Field."

"Centurions" was made into a feature film — George C. Scott starred — which did well at the box office, while the second was an NBC mini-series which starred William Holden. "Onion Field" will soon be coming out in motion-picture form, as well.

"Centurions" was written in Wambaugh's spare time while he was a detective sergeant at the Hollenbeck Precinct of the Los Angeles Police Department. He served 14 years with the LAPD until he resigned earlier this year.

I spent some time in an interview session with Wambaugh not long ago, and here's what he had to say:

Q. First of all, you told me a year or so ago that you had no intention of leaving the LAPD. What made you change your mind?

A. After 14 years on the force I suddenly found that the job I loved so much was no longer enjoyable. I never thought that would happen. The other cops were starting to treat me differently — sort of like a star — and I couldn't bear being different. So, on March 1 I left the force.

Q. You've made a big point of keeping the series as realistic as possible. Are you satisfied with the treatment it is getting from the network, insofar as "censorship" is concerned?

A. If "Police Story" is not realistic and up-to-date, it's nothing and it won't last. We're succeeding only because of our realistic stories. I constantly have battles with the network to preserve and protect the authenticity. The ratings and reviews have have been very good thus far, but when the stories leave realism all this will end — and I'll bail out. You'll see my parachute. It's not easy to convince the network that cops are humans, just like everyone else. They sometimes kill their wives and they sometimes kill themselves. They do the same things — both good and bad — that everyone else does. And this is exactly what I want to portray in the series.

Q. I know that George Kennedy will be playing the chief role of Bumper Morgan in "Blue Knight," soon to be made into a television series, and we all know that William Holden was Morgan in the NBC miniseries. What did you think of Holden's work, first of all, and, secondly, was he considered for the role in the upcoming series?

A. I liked Bill Holden in the show. I think that he is a marvelous actor. But the Bumper Morgan I created for the book is not like the Bumper Morgan portrayed by Holden in the shows. Morgan, as I created him, is a huge man, just like Kennedy. Holden played the part marvelously, but he just doesn't fit the physical characteristics of Bumper Morgan.

Q. How much control do you have over each episode of "Police Story"?

A. Technically, I have my say with each script. But I don't go onto the set where the episodes are being filmed. A real policeman is on hand, however, for technical advice, and he calls them to task if performers stray from realism. And, of course, if he can't straighten them out, I get a phone call and do my part to put them back on the right road.

Q. What sort of response have you gotten from other police officers?

A. Cops the country over are saying the same things: "We love it; it's the most realistic police show we've ever seen." And let me tell you this: If these cops didn't think the show was realistic, I wouldn't be associated with it any longer. I would get out.

Q. Did you go to the network with the original idea for the series, or did the network come to you?

A. I didn't go to them, but my producer, David Gerber, did. It's not up to me to get a show on TV. I'm just sort of a glorified story editor. David takes care of all this. I just write nasty letters to him whenever things don't go to suit me. Seriously, David is a brilliant man and I am absolutely delighted to be associated with him. He does all the work.

Q. With a second series scheduled for sometime in the future, has the thought ever occurred to you that you might have bitten off more than you can chew — at least chew comfortably?

A. Not really. I feel that I'm primarily a writer of books now. I do think, however, that I can handle both "Police Story" and "Blue Knight" and still write books. At least, I hope I can. We'll soon find out.

Q. Do you ever go back and visit your old precinct house and chat with some of the people you worked with for so many years?

A. No. In fact, I have not set foot inside a police station since that first day of March when I walked out for the last time. I miss a lot of the people, certainly, but I simply couldn't stand the emotional impact of going back to those surroundings. I loved the work and I always expected to stay on until I retired. But when I made the decision to leave I left. And I don't plan to go back.

Q. What sort of future plans do you have?

A. More of the same. I intend to keep on writing books and I'll continue to keep the series as realistic as possible. I'm almost ready to start another police novel, too, but it won't be nearly as heavy as my first three were. There's a lighter side to police work, and that's what I'll be trying to tell.

Wambaugh Disliked Role of 'Celebrity Cop'

By ROBERT L. ROSE

joe Wambaugh loved being on the police force. He loved it so much he quit. But the love is still there so much so that he drives around the block to avoid a police station.

"I tell my wife when the dreams stop then maybe I'll be over it. But I still have these crazy dreams, full of symbolism. I'm not dressed in a suit and tie. I have a uniform on and a big badge and a gun. I wish they'd stop."

Wambaugh quit the Los Angeles force six months ago after deciding that his success as a best-selling writer — three hits out of three tries — made it impossible for him to be a success as a policeman.

"After 14 years it just became impossible for me.

"So one day, when a lot of things happened, I very emotionally asked my boss, the captain, if I could have a quick vacation, an emergency

WAMBAUGH, Joseph

NEWS-AMERICAN
(Baltimore, Md.)

Sept. 25, 1974

leave. He said, 'Are you ill?' and I said, 'No, but I will be,' and he gave it to me and I left and knew I'd never go back to a police station for the rest of my life.

Wambaugh's bestsellers include two novels, "The New Centurions" and "The Blue Knight," as well as "The Onion Field," a factual account of a notorious kidnap-murder case. He is also the creator-adviser of the NBC-TV anthology "Police Story," and has announced that "the Blue Knight" will become a weekly series, starring George Kennedy.

We talked at Perino's, perhaps Los Angeles' most expensive restaurant, a place of sad-happy memories for Wambaugh.

"This is the second time I've been here. The first time I was with my wife and a lawyer friend in 1971 just after 'The New Centurions' was published. We decided to celebrate. I made everybody order a different entree. I was paying for it. I insisted on sampling each entree, everyone's appetizer, and I ordered a different dessert for each one and tasted some of everything.

"Well, here I was a cop accustomed to eating burritos in East L.A. I had never tasted this kind of rich food. Ten minutes after dinner we were making casual conversation, I broke out in a cold sweat, started getting dizzy, my shirt collar got tighter, I got up and so help me God I threw up $75 worth of food in Perino's rest room. It's a true story."

But back to why he quit the cops:

"Other police started treating me like a celebrity. A guy who had traded insults with me for 14 years suddenly started treating me with a little deference. That I couldn't bear. The insults I welcomed.

"Even the crooks treated me different. Instead of answering my questions about a burglary, they'd ask me, 'Is William Holden really a nice guy?' or 'What's George C. Scott really like?' Or 'Do you need a heavy in your next movie?'

"I don't know what the final straw was, but it just became impossible for me to function as a policeman."

Wambaugh says he wins a few and loses a few in his job as production consultant on police story. Mainly he threatens to quit if they get too far off base and into fantasyland.

But it's a tough fight in two particular area. Story ideas and language.

"I do my best to preserve the integrity, the nitty gritty of the show. If Police story is not realistic, up-to-fate realistic, then it's nothing and it's got to go.

Wambaugh talked about casting. William Holden did the Bumper Morgan part in the four-part NBC mini-series of Blue Knight, but Wambaugh is happier to see George Kennedy now in it.

"I love Bill Holden in that role, but the character I created is really George Kennedy, a man 275 pounds who's funny, witty.

"Bumper Morgan likes eating and women, in that order. I saw Kennedy one night at the Director's Guild. He could barely get in his chair, he's that wide. He'll be perfect, I think. He's Bumper Morgan."

Wambaugh likes off-beat castin too. He'd like to use his friend, Dave Toma, the New York cop they made a series about, and Bill Bonnano, the son of Joe Bananas, the Mafia chieftain.

"Only I'd use Dave as a crook and Bill as a cop. Bill Bonnano is tall, handsome, clean cut, articulate. He looks like a cop and Dave Toma looks like a crook."

Columbia made a movie out of Wambaugh's first book, "The New Centurions," and it bought the rights to his "The Onion Field," for upwards of $350,000. But they are having script problems, mainly because Wambaugh insists they stay faithful to the people and the words they said.

'I Walk With Truth, Not Away From It . . .

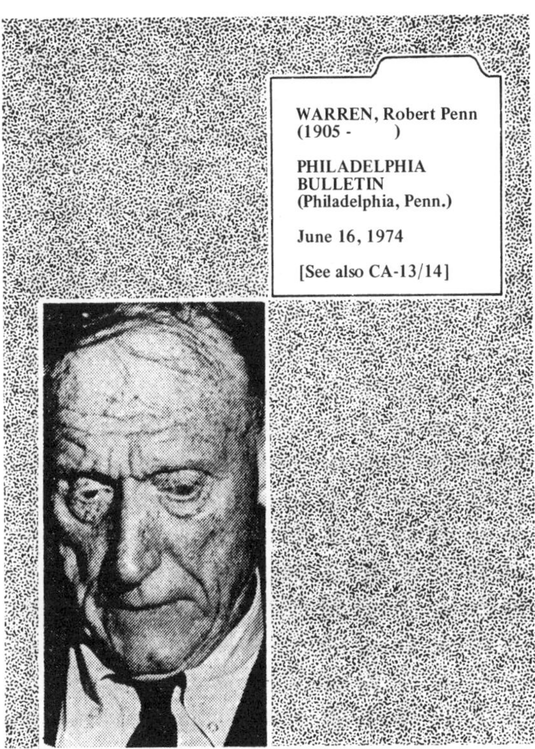

WARREN, Robert Penn (1905-)

PHILADELPHIA BULLETIN (Philadelphia, Penn.)

June 16, 1974

[See also CA-13/14]

Robert Penn Warren
. . . dramatic "reinterpretation"

By RAYMOND C. BRECHT
Of The Bulletin Staff

SITTING IN his study in Fairfield, Conn., Robert Penn Warren said he'd like to be in Philadelphia this Tuesday night, but he can't come.

That's the night Trinity Square Repertory Co. opens its presentation of the poet-novelist - critic - dramatist's book-length poem, "Brother to Dragons," as dramatized by the author and directed by Adrian Hall. It will be at the Walnut Street Theater through June 30.

To Warren, this production is a "reinterpretation" that he finds "provocative and stimulating."

Mild and modest words, these, for a historical piece that searches out the truth in singing language but in terms of brutal murder and emotional shock.

Warren, the only writer to be awarded the Pulitzer Prize in both poetry and fiction, published "Brother to Dragons" in 1953.

• • •

ITS SOARING eloquence and stark realism tell a tale that begins in December of 1811 in the smokehouse of a plantation in the wilderness of Western Kentucky. There Lilburn Lewis, with the help of his brother Isham, butchered a black slave. Lilburn and Isham Lewis were nephews of Thomas Jefferson.

Although the crime was a matter of public record, Jefferson, as far as biography and research show, never commented on it, never mentioned it in his writings or even acknowledged it.

It is in this tragic tension that Warren made his poem search for truth; a recognition of that traitor in our blood which makes us brother to dragons. ("I am a brother to dragons," is from the Book of Job, 30:29).

IN 1967, Warren said in a telephone interview, the poem was done in dramatic form in Seattle. Then there was a New York production — first in the East. In the 1968-69 season, it was produced under Adrian Hall's direction by Trinity Square, at Providence, R.I. The version opening at the Walnut Tuesday evening, to run through June 30, opened Oct. 24, 1973, in Provincetown.

"Adrian (Hall) brought an entirely different production," Warren said. "I greatly admire this. He did a reinterpretation that I find very provocative and stimulating.

"I find his production enormously fruitful for me. It opens my mind to other possibilities of the play itself."

Warren said he has seen the play three or four times. "I think there are more things I could do with it," he said, disclosing that he is still revising, even after its winning a Pulitzer, before publishing it as a play!

• • •

IN ANSWER to a question about the work being a "search for truth," Warren said, "This particular piece of work was an attempt to show Jefferson — this man of high motivation, high ideals — caught in a complicated bind. That is a truth that will never die."

How do we face it? is what the play and the poem are asking.

It is not a racial play, nor a play about social injustice or inequality. It is a play about facing one's self, in terror or in agony, but finally accepting the truth — a glimmer of hope for us all.

Playgoers will find in the production at the Walnut a joining of the very real and historic with the imagery of poetry — symbolisms calling on the imagination, even the subconscious.

In his preface to the poem, as published by Random House in 1963, Warren said:

"I have tried to make my poem make, in a thematic way, historical sense along with whatever other kind of sense it may be happy enough to make. Historical sense and poetic sense should not, in the end, be contradictory, for if poetry is the little myth we make, history is the big myth we live, and in our living, constantly remake."

Author Relaxes Techniques

By June Rice

NORWICH – "Writing is a way of life - be open, be aware!" Robert Penn Warren, one of America's foremost literary figures advised prospective writers at Mohegan Community College

The winner of two Pulitzer prizes earlier this week shared insight gained during his literary career of more than half a century. He was born in 1905, and is the only american to win Pulitzer Prizes in both fiction and poetry, for "All the King's Men" and "Promises."

WARREN, Robert Penn

HARTFORD COURANT (Hartford, Conn.)

Sept. 29, 1974

A new book of poetry is scheduled to be released Oct. 7. Waren dislikes format and ritual. His face crinkles around intense blue eyes, and his sentences are slurred in a soft Kentucky drawl. When he smiles it's like sun spreading on a pale granite shelf.

He believes writers tend to lead "double lives" and have a great need for solitude as well as family life. "Interruptions are fine, he says "They make you appreciate the other life." But, he adds, "If I don't have my solitude I'm pretty miserable to live with."

Warren finds that chopping wood, jogging or swimming are excellent respites and often free the mind Swimming is like being in a very busy womb ... ..Your mind is working, groping around," he said.

Once, Warren said, he made the mistake of "planning" a book, but was stymied, completely paralized" He said he had to discard the outline and begin a fresh. "I knew too much of everything about the book," he said.

Story ideas spring from incidents gleaned from history or heard in conversation; he said. The idea evokes feeling and "sticks like a cockleburr to my spiritual clothes." He begins to ponder it, asking at great length, "what does that mean to me?"

Slowly, the answers come, Warren said. Sometimes I meditate on it for years, but at a certain point it is moving toward a rounded thing and taking shape - although still uninterpreted."

Waren feels strongly that "the writing business and the reading business can't be separated. I write, thank God, he says.

His poems have a "germ of action behind them, a dramatic, circumstantial germ, Warren said.

"I begin with a rhythm, a phrase that catches," he said. A picnic in the woods once gave him the first two lines of a poem, but the rest didn't come for several weeks, the author related.

"Several years ago I wrote novels on a typewriter." he said. I never wrote poetry that way. I walk it, carry it around and mumble it."

He has been a writer since the age of 18, but has never felt "placebound." Although living in Fairfield, Warren cannot visualize writing a novel not set in the South. "At a very early stage you develop images that stay with you," he explained.

After 30 books of fiction, non-fiction, poetry and two major plays, the author finds it hard to pin down a favorite, but admits, "there are two or three I like best."

"All the King's Men" is among them. "What a book means to me now gets mixed up with an objective judgement ... It's hard, very hard to sort these things out ," he said.

His word to aspiring writers is that "writing is not a profession like dentistry ... It is a way of life, a state of mind. It is very important a serious writer develop a relationship between living a life and writing it there is no formula. Some people keep a stack of notes. I can't live that way. I say to be open to possibility..Be aware!"

The Writing of 'Jane'—One Constant Giggle

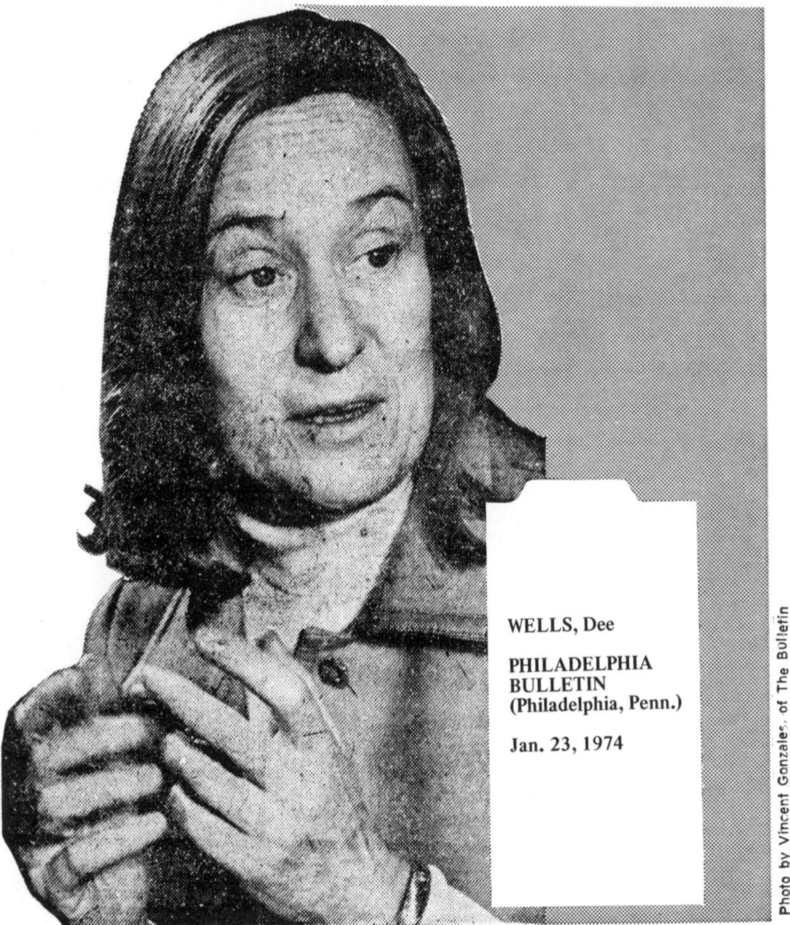
WELLS, Dee

PHILADELPHIA BULLETIN (Philadelphia, Penn.)

Jan. 23, 1974

Photo by Vincent Gonzales, of The Bulletin

By SUSAN JENKS
Of The Bulletin Staff

COMPARED to the rigid discipline of journalism, Dee Wells finds novel writing a little like having a "bowl of jelly inside," which can go anyway you want it to — before reaching an appropriate ending.

And yet despite this fluidity, she contends, taking the literary leap into noveldom for the first time is a lot easier than one might suspect. After all, writing "Jane" was "just giggle, giggle the whole time."

When she wasn't giggling her way throuh her novel debut, Miss Wells apparently spent most of her time listening to storytelling tips from friends or struggling to make Jane's situation believable, without resorting to all those "lovely, literary-type sentences" most novelists use.

"Books just don't talk the way people talk . . . the very ordinary way people talk," she insists, vigorously. "So I tried to write one that does."

Already picked by the Literary Guild as its featured alternative for March, and considered a hot enough literary property for movie production very soon, "Jane" is the story of a 34-year-old American woman living in London, who has not one, but three lovers that drop by her apartment on different days of any given week. (The book is published by Viking Press.)

Included in Jane's "menage" for four, so to speak, is Anthony, a starchy though impoverished British lord; a youthful burglar named Tom, who is at the other end of the English social scale; and Franklin, a magnetic black attorney whose American upbringing has been far less tumultuous than Jane's own.

The inevitable complications arise when Jane becomes pregnant and neither she, nor her trio of weekday paramours, knows whose baby it might be.

Within this framework, Miss Wells is able to take potshots at not only traditional sexual attitudes about women, but also at those pontificating "bores," who through heredity, constitute Britain's so-called upper-class.

"Their arrogance and their self-satisfaction is enormous," she suggests with the certainty of someone who has lived and worked in England for the past 20 years. "It's a thin layer of English society that has changed very little . . . that has no wish to change."

Making literary hay of this sentiment, Miss Wells allows Jane to speak for herself when she lashes out at Anthony's mother and friends at the aptly-named estate, "Cravenbourne." Of course, their reaction is comically predictable: "They all looked like startled fawn and very silently your name (and in this case, the very gauche Jane's) is crossed off still another list."

Interwoven with this class attack, which Miss Wells describes as her "subtle sledge-hammer approach," is an attack on that romantic conditioning women receive — particularly American women — on love.

"I don't care how emancipated women are . . . underneath it all, that same romantic creature is lurking . . . the idea of one true love," she says. "As Jane herself expresses it, 'I don't want to get married, but I wouldn't mind being married.'

"Her expectations are terribly high and Jane's just old enough to get under the wire as a romantic."

Before writing her novel, Miss Wells, who also happens to be an American living in London, wrote for the New York Times, Punch, the Manchester Guardian, the London Sunday Express and numerous other journalistic publications. But aside from a similarity of occupation and place, there is apparently little about "Jane," which is autobiographical.

"I put her in a newsroom because that's what I know best," explains Miss Wells. "The rest of her is purely my projection of what she would be like."

Brutally honest — amost irreverent — about the success of this venture, Miss Wells concedes, that "Jane" does indeed have its share of literary loopholes.

Franklin's rapid personality change towards the end of the book, for instance, is "bothersome" and unconvincing. But pleading a kind of literary Fifth Amendment, she laughs, "there was only a week left to finish the book and I had to end it somehow."

Tom's dramatic entry into Jane's life, on the other-hand, Miss Wells defends, as culturally plausible. Call it deus ex machina or an exaggerated sense of poetic license, he literally falls into Jane's life through the skylight of her London flat on a "cold, rainy night."

What is worse, his sudden appearance arouses no fear or suspicion on Jane's part — only her best maternal instinct come rushing to the fore.

"If you were living in Greenwich Village in New York, you'd be awake at every noise," argues Miss Wells. "But in London, something like this just isn't all that scary.

"Incredible as it may seem, I know a wealthy British couple who caught a young kid burglarizing their apartment . . . sat him down and offered him some tea. To this day, they're the only real friends he has."

If this distinctly British "stiff upper lip" is just too foreign for the American mind, it doesn't phase the unflappable Miss Wells.

In what may seem more to the point, she adds, "It had to be a happenstance kind of thing. How else could someone like Jane meet a boy like this."

Elie Wiesel

By David Richards
Star-News Staff Writer

There was something ineffably sad about Elie Wiesel that day. Something about the hollowed cheeks, the thinly drawn mouth, the velvet eyes of a deer that stares down its executioner less in rage than sheer injured puzzlement.

The voice for a generation of homeless Jews — those who escaped the horrors of Buchenwald and Auschwitz, as well as those who didn't — Wiesel was in town for a final rehearsal of his first, last and only play, "The Madness of God," which opens tomorrow night at Arena Stage. Was that why he appeared to be elsewhere, shielded by his own inner visions from the lunch-time throng about him?

The ecstatic of religions, the solitude of the victim, the utter incommunicability of experience, the hell of the German holocaust, the guilt of the survivor — these have long been themes in Wiesel's 14 books. They weave their way darkly through his play. They are, one gathers, the preoccupations of his daily life.

WHEN HE talked, it was with a heavy French accent — since World War II, French has been his adopted tongue — although somewhere in the furry consonants, there were echoes of Hungary, his birthplace. "I love the theater too much to enrich it with plays that are not absolutely good," he was saying. "I do not see myself as a playwright. My play may be good, but then that is an accident. My role is that of a witness."

"The Madness of God" was written in 1966, after Wiesel visited Russia and observed what was to him the incredible: Russian Jews demonstrating for their human rights. "I did not believe that those young men and women could have such courage. I had to go back a second time to see if it was true. And I left with a tremendous amount of guilt. They were alone and they did not not know it. Maybe we cannot help them, I thought, but there is one thing we *must* do. We must let them know they are not alone. This play is my way of paying homage."

Weisel's drama centers on a Russian rabbi, prodded by a mad beadle to speak up years later about the fate of the Jews in their small town during the war. "The rabbi breaks silence for once in his life, talks of his ordeal, the destruction and solitude he has known. This is the gesture that is to justify his existence," Weisel explained. Or did the rabbi just want to speak up? By shrouding his play in a kind of poetic mysticism, Wiesel leaves the question dangling.

"Madmen have always occupied me," he continued. "But not killing madmen — mystical madmen intoxicated by God. Rather than provoke solitude, they try to combat it. They are very beautiful madmen."

A REBELLIOUS strand of his thinning black hair fell over his face, bisecting it and rejuvenating him by a decade. Wiesel pushed it back in place, regaining the 10 years with a single gesture.

"As a Jewish child in Europe," he said, "I had two very close friends. We wanted to live so intensely that we would bring the Messiah. You must understand what the mystical theory proclaims: God is in exile, but every individual, if he strives hard enough, can redeem mankind and even God himself. The three of us were going to bring the Messiah, as simple as that.

—Star-News Photographer Joseph Silverman

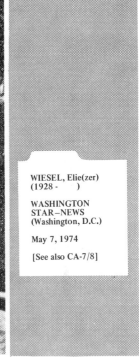

WIESEL, Elie(zer)
(1928 -   )

WASHINGTON
STAR–NEWS
(Washington, D.C.)

May 7, 1974

[See also CA-7/8]

"After a couple of months, one of my friends went mad. And then a second. They wouldn't speak, couldn't speak. An eminent Swedish pyschiatrist diagnosed it as aphasia. But I understand now; they were just terribly, terribly sad that they couldn't bring the Messiah. I'm convinced I would have gone mad, too, if the Germans hadn't come into our little town."

The Germans came in 1944. "There is no little town now," Wiesel said. He and his family were deported to concentration camps, a nightmare he chronicled starkly in his first book, "Night." Miraculously, Wiesel and two sisters survived. The others didn't.

"AFTER THE WAR," he said, "I had a true existential choice: ta become an anarchist, on the theory that soxiety was not worth the effort, or to make a leap of faith and confidence, although I had every reason to hate the world. I spend a year of silence in Paris, and I decided what I wanted to do — still want to do — is understand what happened.

"I know people who spent five and six years in prison camp. What did they learn? The Germans taught them that only strength survives, that morality doesn't count. Why shouldn't those people who escaped, bitter and familyless, have destroyed the world in their turn? We had a right to accuse the whole world. But a peculiar thing happens. Instead of accusing others, we accuse ourselves. Why me and not another? I once made a survey of the 400 child survivors of Buchenwald. Most of them became normal people, chose philanthropic careers in the best sense of the word. That must mean something."

As journalist, novelist, and professor, Wiesel has devoted his life to recontructing a faith, mortally shaken by the war. It is a rootless, largely subdued existence. With his wife, Marion, who translates his works into English, he currently lives in New York.

"I CAN'T SAY taday that I could be attached to any place, though," he confessed. "Or anything. I can't own anything in gold. It's like I'm allergic to it. One night the German officers in camp ordered all valuables to be thrown in a pile. I saw a mountain of wedding rings and watches and jewelry. And it hit me. For this, my mother and father struggled all their lives. I don't even have a bank account.

"I work four hours a day on my books. I sleep four hours. I don't need any more. And I have a little boy, which is good, because it keeps me at home. I believe in small miracles — a good friendship, a good concert, a good surprise. Maybe a few people will be changed by my writings. I don't know. A gesture is never lost, although it may not attain its ultimate goal.

"I have always been very serious. As a boy, when I went out with a girl, I would talk to her about Kant and generally never see her again. But the truth was so important to me. In America there days, it's hard to believe in anything. Something is happening. I don't know what."

Elie Wiesel furrowed his brow, ran a ringless finger over his chin, looked off into space, and was quiet.

'Foxfire' Founder Says Culture Preservation Begins at Home

WIGGINTON, Eliot

MIAMI HERALD
(Miami, Fla.)

Apr. 21, 1974

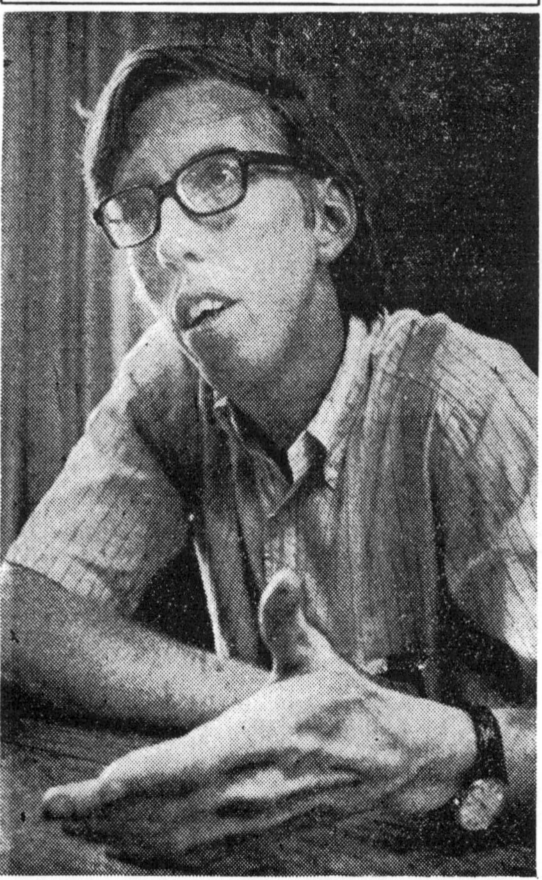

—Miami Herald / JOHN COPELAND

Eliot Wigginton on the Road
. . . lectern fire set him thinking

By BILL McGOUN
Broward News Editor

Once upon a time, eight years ago, an idealistic young teacher in the mountains of Northeast Georgia wanted his students to spend their time learning rather than setting fire to his lectern.

He decided the best way was to get them to do the teaching, to observe and record the culture about them before those who remember the old days of highland isolation pass away.

The result was "Foxfire", a magazine with subscribers in all 50 states and a dozen foreign nations. Also two books, with a third in the works.

TODAY, Eliot Wigginton is older but still idealistic. He's as low key as Rabun gap and erudite in a mod manner.

Last week he was almost 800 miles from Rabun Gap, in a second-floor office overlooking Andrews Avenue and the newly vacant lots that will become downtown Fort Lauderdale's new shopping mall.

Wigginton is a somewhat reluctant missionary. He believes that the impetus for cultural studies must come from within the community, not from "outsiders" such as himself. The message he had for Broward school officials, who plan to start a program similar to his this fall, is that the best way to follow "Foxfire" is not to follow it.

WIGGINTON was fresh out of Cornell, a university he attended solely "because my father went there", when he began teaching ninth- and tenth-graders at Rabun Gap-Nacoochee School. After six weeks most noteworthy for the lectern fire — which was set during class — he decided that the students weren't interested in what he was teaching.

He recalled his own lower education in Athens, Ga., as a time of "monumentally boring texts and lectures, all forgotten; punishments and regulations and slights that only filled a reservoir of bitterness; and the three blessed teachers who let me make things, helped me make them, and praised the results."

The idea he came up with was for his students to go into the community and talk with old-timers about how life used to be in the Southern Highlands before roads and radios ended the region's isolation — an era in which the motto was "make it yourself, or do without". The stories would be compiled into a magazine.

IT WORKED so well that the magazine became a regular thing. The youngsters wrote and illustrated stories about log-cabin construction, quilting, soapmaking, butter churning, hog slaughtering and old-time burials.

They recorded the how of woolen clothing, starting with tips on raising sheep. They perpetualized the colorful reminiscences of mountain people such as aged Aunt Arie, who still raises her own vegetables and lives in a log cabin without running water.

How does all this relate to an urban area such as Broward? What advice does Wigginton have for the teachers and students at Fort Lauderdale and Stranahan high schools who next year will participate in a similar program?

THE KEY is to let the character of the area determine the program, he says. Since urban areas such as Broward have no distinctive single culture, the students should concentrate on the types of people that are here and tell the readers that "here's a melting pot."

At the moment, there are only two "Foxfire"-type programs in urban areas, one in New York City and one in Washington, D.C. Wigginton considers the former locale particularly rich in material:

"New York City has 10 million stories per square block . . . What about the little guy who drives a subway? What's going on in that dude's head?"

Wigginton is particularly intrigued by one facet of the Broward program, the availability here of many persons who remember the county's pioneer days at the turn of the century.

His visit to Broward last week ended on a hectic note. He almost missed his plane to Denver — he was going on to Laramie, Wyo., to explain his program there — because the two Rabun students who were traveling with him were so interested in the beach that they were late returning downtown for their ride to the airport.

He didn't seem to mind. At least they weren't burning his lectern.

Her Writing Career Runs At Ovals

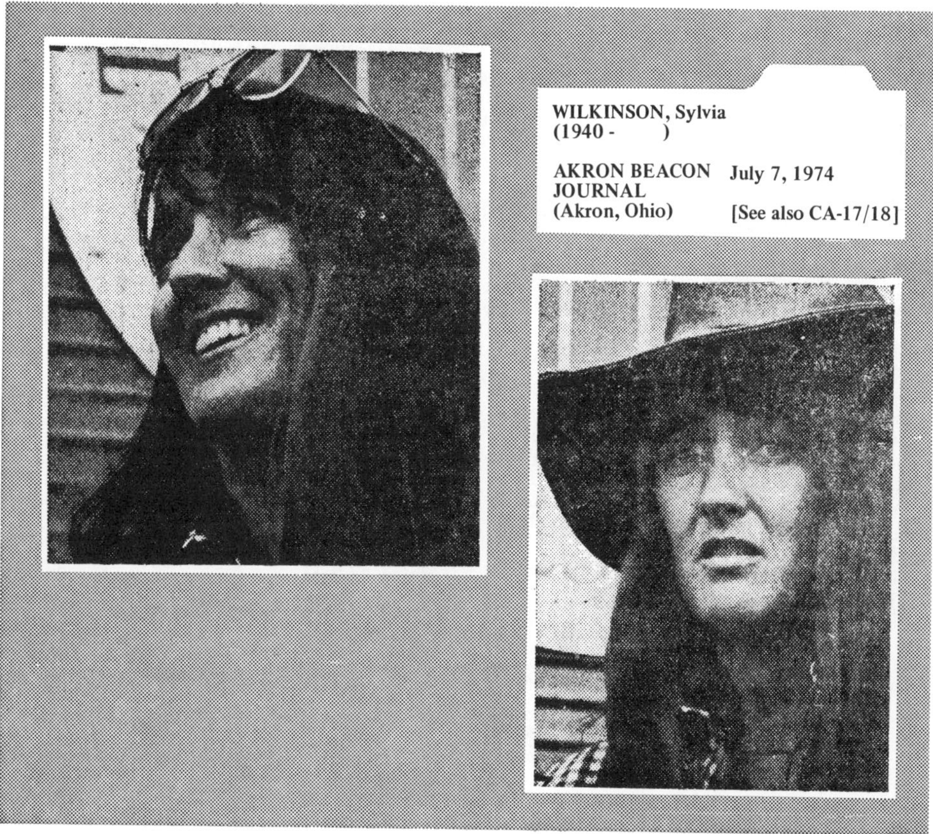

WILKINSON, Sylvia (1940-)

AKRON BEACON JOURNAL (Akron, Ohio) July 7, 1974 [See also CA-17/18]

By FRAN ARMAN
Beacon Journal Staff Writer

From a souffle to scrambled eggs. That's how authoress Sylvia Wilkinson described the difference between her serious writing and her ghosting for a boys' series.

Her "scrambled-egg" efforts concern ghosting for a new adventure-mystery collection of stories for boys. The series, built around auto racing, is slated for release next Jan. 1.

The author of record is the same man who has written a long-running boys' mystery series, but she is not allowed to mention his name or the series. Contractual agreements with her publisher also prevent her from identifying her ghosted series and taking credit for it.

IN HER "gourmet" efforts, she has authored three novels, one education book and a non-fiction book on auto racing.

In fact, auto racing brought her to the Akron area last week, keeping a time chart for one of the teams at the Mid Ohio Sports Car Course.

Wearing jeans, a blue and white checked blouse and a floppy denim hat, the petite Ms. Wilkinson sat cross-legged on a grassy spot near the track. Often interrupting herself to talk about a race driver that was in view, she told how she cared little about her ghost-writing efforts.

"It's money," she said. "The income is iffy in writing. Survival is impossible with book royalties — I only get 3 to 5 cents per copy and it takes two to three years to realize any profit. I have to have many side things to earn a living so I can write."

MS. WILKINSON handles the adventure half of the series receiving a plot outline for the book from her boss. She then writes the 18-chapter book, making sure each chapter is the same length.

"It's all very mechanical," she said. "I use my writing ability with a personal detatchment, just as a musician can play the correct notes without much feeling."

Ms. Wilkinson said she can finish a book in approximately 36 days: drafting a chapter a day, and doing any rewriting the next.

She was chosen for ghost writing on the basis of her knowledge of the auto racing world.

"RACING has been with me since I was a little kid," said the blue-eyed North Carolina native. "When I received my degree from grad school, my present to myself was a sports car."

Along with many magazine articles on racing, Ms. Wilkinson's latest book — "The Stainless Steel Carrot" — is the story of the one and one half years she spent with an auto racing team.

"The final race is just the tip of an iceberg," she said. " 'Carrot' features the guys who make the cars.

"I used to help with the car preparation, so I would walk around taking notes, overhearing conversations," she said in her Southern drawl.

Ms. Wilkinson started writing her first novel, "Moss on the North Side," when she was 12. Eleven drafts and 13 years later, the book was completed.

"THERE IS a 10-year lag on my writing," she said munching on a piece of grass. "In my mid-20s when I was a teacher, I could write about my childhood, but not about teaching. Time is a selection process."

Now in her mid-30s, she is working on her fourth novel about a young teacher in Appalachia.

In addition to her writing, Ms. Wilkinson teaches creative writing for the one-month Winter term at Sweet Briar College in Virginia.

"Sweet Briar is an all-girls college and they try to hire professional women since it is encouraging for the girls to see a woman who's made it," she said.

She also lectures at universities around the country from January to May. The rest of the year, she is free to work on her books.

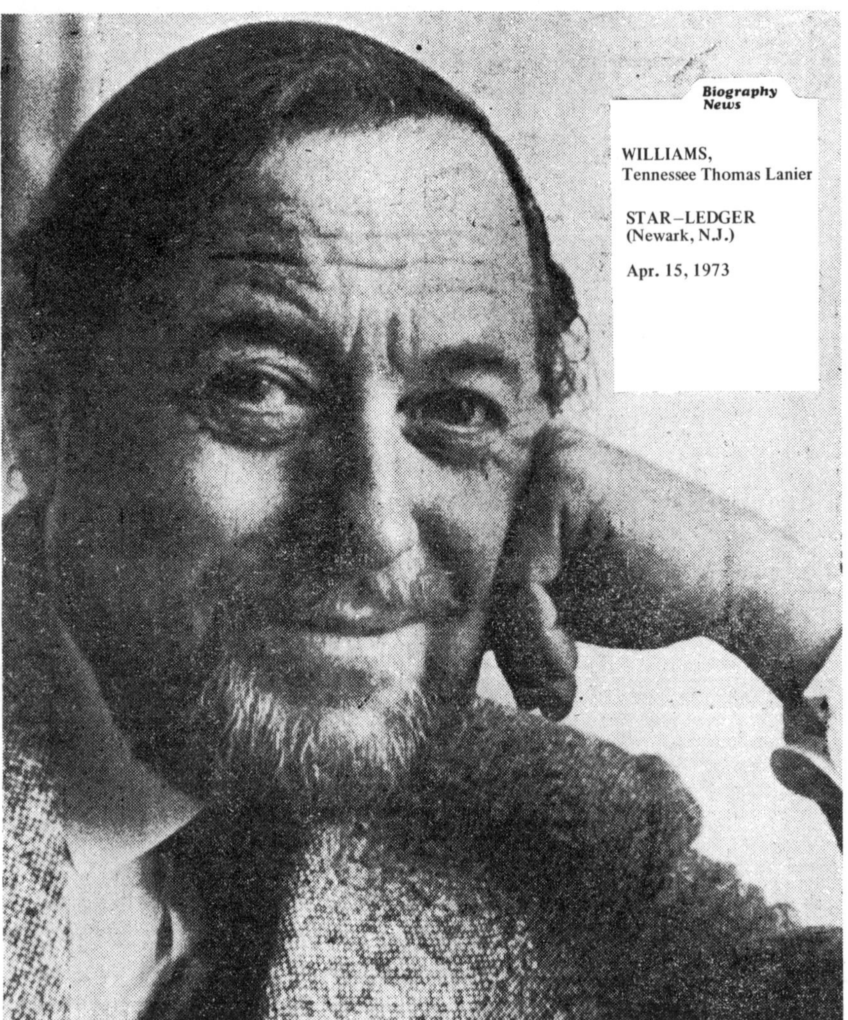

TENNESSEE WILLIAMS:

After a bad time, he has finally got his stuff together

By DAN SULLIVAN

NEW YORK — "I'm a peculiar blend of the pragmatist and the romanticist and the crocodile. The monster. And then I gotta be all those heroines. And all those heavies."

Big easy laugh. Tennessee Williams is having a quiet Sunday lunch at the Algonquin (minute steak, just one vodka martini) and he is nothing like a crocodile. A possum, maybe — lazy on the surface, sly underneath. But mostly just a man who, after a bad time, has finally got his stuff together.

"Comparatively." The lightly self-mocking tone says: don't expect too much. At 62 a man doesn't have the energy he had at 36, which was Williams' age when he wrote "Streetcar Named Desire." But a man of that age can still have some good work in him if his devils leave him alone, and Williams thinks he has finally got his devils back in the corner where they belong.

* * *

"I was as spaced-out as any hippie in the 1960s," he says. "I even went to the loony bin for awhile (Barnes Hospital, St. Louis). But all that is over for me now. Because physically I can't take it and because I realized it's a dead end.

"I believe in commitment now, to whatever it is you love, whether it's writing or your social feelings or whatever. Especially at my age, when you've got just so much energy. You've got to channel it very carefully."

For instance: Before the Broadway opening of Williams' new play, "Out Cry," he caught a plane to Key West, where he loafed and swam in his pool and "got a whole new rhythm of life going." Eventually someone called him with the good or bad news from New York. He didn't anticipate it would be good. (It wasn't).

"Out Cry" is about madness and "people who have not had that experience just — don't — dig it." Well, he settled for "perceptive" reviews, instead of raves. And when the production failed, he's been around long enough to know that there will be other productions, sooner or later.

* * *

"I don't want to sweat any more," is the way he puts it. So when the 25th anniversary production of "Streetcar" opened on the West Coast he didn't hang around rehearsals tinkering with the text. Well . . . maybe just a few cuts. Possibly a few words to the actors.

"I've talked with Johnny Voight. I don't think he's playing Stanley like Brando, which is the mistake most of them make. I think it's a Stanley that's very expressive of Johnny Voight. I'm happy that Faye Dunaway has a great deal of humor, because I think that's what keeps the part of Blanche from aging now. She's funny when she wants to be and funny when she doesn't want to be."

Williams chuckles affectionately, as if Blanche were some scampy relative. They've been together a long time. Of all the actresses who have played her, does he have a favorite?

"It's always the original one that's a little closer to you, you know? Jessica Tandy was the original one. I thought she had just the right delicacy. Uta Hagen was powerful, but a little like a valkyrie. Vivien Leigh was fabulous. Of course she had precisely the same problem as Blanche. Constantly on that terrible margin of fantasy."

* * *

Williams has had some tough years, but his sense of humor hasn't deserted him: In some way he's been amused by it all. The talk turns to religion, and he advises you that his famous conversion to Roman Catholicism a few years ago came "at my brother's instigation when I was stoned." The laugh forgives himself, his brother and the church. "I haven't kept up with it."

"Do you keep the Ten Commandments?"

"I've forgotten what they are. Let's see. I don't steal. I don't kill. (I do have a mean tongue, though.) I don't bear false witness. I bear excessively true witness for most people."

Adultery?

"Heavens, yes. I don't regard that as a sin at all, do you? That commandment was just a bit of Old Testament pomposity."

Does he at 62 have a lot more to say as a writer?

"I doubt it," he answers evenly. "But if I continue to live, you know, in a way that's stimulating, if I continue to stay in touch — who knows? I never run out of things to say, actually Getting the energy to say them is the problem.

"If I work in the theater at all in the next few years, I think it'll be in the English theater. I think there's more of an audience in London for my kind of theater just now than there is in America."

So Tennessee Williams' future probably will be plays, even if he does go off to raise goats in Italy. There will be revisions of past plays that didn't make it — he is reworking "The Milk Train Doesn't Stop Here Any More" for Angela Lansbury and Michael York — and there will be new plays. It is suggested that homosexuality might be a good subject for one of them. Williams rejects the suggestion. It has been an appropriate way of life for him, he says, but it's too limiting as a theme for a full-length play. The world is men and women.

* * *

As a young writer he said that he feared "the catastrophe of success." Has fame been so bad?

"No, because I've mostly lived in places where it didn't intrude too much on my life. Had I stayed in New York, I would have found it burdensome. I was crossing a street just yesterday and I heard two ladies say, 'Yes, that's him, and he doesn't look at all like himself anymore.' Hah! I was very angry about something and musta looked like hell. Been a long time since I looked like anything else."

The interviewer told him he looked pretty good.

"You flatter me, suh. Let's say I've got it together. Comparatively. They are doing a film on my life in Toronto. They are under the impression I'll be dead soon, so they're doing these elegiac things. I don't think they realize the longevity with which my family is gifted. Or afflicted, I don't know which. If I continue to live, it can only by an anticlimax. But I intend to live a very different life."

Here's to that.

(Also see preceding article)

TENNESSEE WILLIAMS

Photograph: Michael Lloyd Carlebach

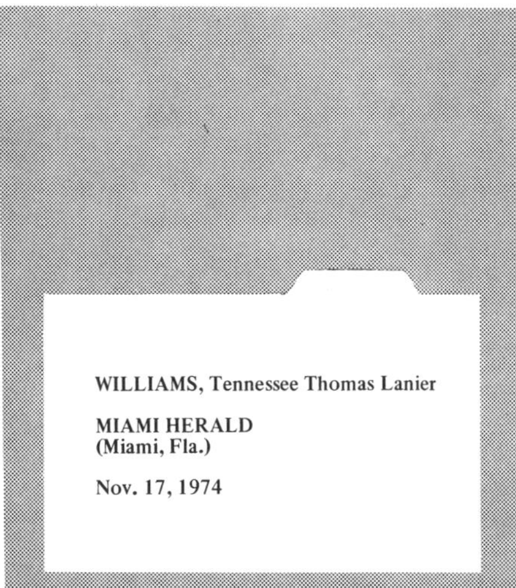

WILLIAMS, Tennessee Thomas Lanier

MIAMI HERALD
(Miami, Fla.)

Nov. 17, 1974

Perhaps the most frequently heard observation about Tennessee Williams is that he is America's greatest living playwright. The evaluation rests on his succession of brilliant plays in the 1940s and '50s in which he dealt in a lyrical style with such themes as loneliness, illusions, virility, sex and death.

The man who was born Thomas Lanier Williams in Columbus, Miss., 63 years ago, and has been a resident of Key West for many years, first burst upon the public consciousness with *The Glass Menagerie* in 1944. In the years that followed, he won acclaim and awards for such plays as *A Streetcar Named Desire* and *Cat on a Hot Tin Roof*, both of which won the Pulitzer Prize.

In the '60s, however, Williams seemed unable to write anything but critical failures, and it was widely assumed that his career as an important playwright was over. During this period, Williams underwent a long bout with alcohol and pills, which resulted in his involuntary commitment to a mental institution in 1969. Among his plays since then are *Small Craft Warnings* and the two-character *Out Cry*.

Q. You've just rewritten the third act of "Cat on a Hot Tin Roof." Why have you gone back to revise this and other plays?

WILLIAMS: Because you always want to leave them behind you in the best possible shape. Plays are never really finished, as long as the author is living, I don't think (Laughs.) He does what he hopes is improvement. This (revision) is much closer to the original, although I think that (Elia) Kazan was quite right in opting for the rewrite that he asked me to do in 1954, because times were so different then. There was so much more prudery in the public mind. It wasn't nearly so permissive.

Q: I recall a recent discussion you had with John Guare in which John said he never looks back at a play once it's finished.

WILLIAMS: I found that quite remarkable. Some people write a thing with a great burst of spontaneity and it's perfect in that form. He was the author of *The House of Blue Leaves,* which I've read and which I don't think he needed to rewrite. I was very happy with that play of his. I'm always very uncertain about my own work; that's been a chief source of torment to me all the years I've been working. So I guess that's why I keep trying to improve them. I'm even nervous now about how *Cat* will be received. Fortunately, I have new work to concern myself with.

Q. When you were interviewed during the writing of what became "Out Cry," you said that it would be your last long play. Have you relented since then?

WILLIAMS: I've written a long play since then, yes. *The Red Devil Battery Sign.*

Q: Are you at liberty to discuss that?

WILLIAMS: Not much. It's very dynamic, and I think it's going to be far less personal than *Out Cry*. It will be a play that a large public can relate to easily. There's much more I can tell you, but I'm not at liberty to. . . I sound like somebody who's just come out of the Watergate trials.

Q: You've spoken of "Out Cry" as your most personal play. In what way did you mean that?

WILLIAMS: I think it went most deeply inside myself — perhaps too deeply to reach a large audience. It was a mistake to put it on Broadway.

Q: Could you expand on why the play was your most personal one?

WILLIAMS: Because it contained all the phobias and all the strains — a sense of alienation and growing panic and claustrophobia that I felt during the period that I wrote it, which was the late '60s.

Q: Aren't all your plays in a sense highly personal?

WILLIAMS: More than most people's. But I think that all organic writing is personal. If it isn't rooted in the personality and the being of the author, then it is in a sense manufactured.

Q: In the introduction to "Cat on a Hot Tin Roof" you wrote, "Of course, it is a pity that so much of all creative work is so closely related to the personality of the one who does it." Have you changed your feelings about that?

WILLIAMS: No, but I find that my work has had a tendency to become more personal as I get older.

Q: Do you feel closer to some of the later plays?

WILLIAMS: I feel intensely close to the later plays, yes. But in quite a few instances the audience has not felt as close to them.

Q: Do you think the plays will be judged less harshly as time goes by and people have had a chance to read them?

WILLIAMS: I think so.

Q. The last two plays, "Small Craft Warnings" and "Out Cry" in particular?

WILLIAMS: *Out Cry* I regarded as a major work. *Small Craft Warnings* was a short work and I don't think I invested too much of myself in that. It was originally called *Confessional;* it had an interesting idea, maybe, but I wasn't as deeply concerned with it as I was with *Out Cry.* When *Out Cry* failed it was a shattering blow to me because it had done well on the road; in fact, it had recuperated all its investment. But we hit New York, and the two news-magazines really did it in. *Time* and *Newsweek.*

Q: It would be interesting to know your appraisal of your plays.

WILLIAMS: I'm very attached to *Cat on a Hot Tin Roof* and to *Streetcar. The Glass Menagerie* seems a little far away now in the past, but I realize it's highly regarded by, you know, the people who teach playwrighting. (Laughs.) From whom I've profited not at all.

Q: Did you like the television production of "The Glass Menagerie"?

WILLIAMS: I did, very much indeed. People keep asking me how I liked Kate Hepburn. How can you help but love Kate Hepburn? She's a grand old girl. Michael Moriarty happened to come on and illuminate the thing. Well, I guess his ➡

(Continued from preceding page)

part was more luminous. And he's also an actor of extraordinary talent.

Q: In the introduction to one of your early plays you said, "There is so much to say and not enough time to say it." Looking back, do you think you managed to say a good deal of it?

WILLIAMS: One never, never, never, never says a fraction of what there is to say. I think it's like an iceberg; a tiny bit appears above the surface and so much is underneath. You get older and you know more; you know more about your craft. But you don't have the energy; you don't have the vitality of youth, to use the craft that you've learned as well. And that's the sad thing about being a writer. I once said that writers age more rapidly than circus acrobats. (Laughs.) And I think there's some truth in that. But you have to try to compensate for it by what you've learned. You can to some extent, but not totally.

Q: You once said that work was your only imperative; you could give up drinking, you could give up sex, but you have to work.

WILLIAMS: Exactly, exactly. It continues to occupy most of my concern. And I still love doing the writing. And I think I'm going to have some success with it.

Q: How much time do you spend writing now?

WILLIAMS: Three hours as a rule. Sometimes as much as five. But I used to be able to put in as much as eight or ten hours. It goes very easily for the first three hours; the rest of the day is like a shadow of those hours that you get through. It's worth it, frankly. I wouldn't have elected any other profession. As a child I wanted to be a railroad engineer. (Laughs.) But I don't think I'd be happy or good as one. I've never been any good at anything but writing.

Q: How did you discover that?

WILLIAMS: Oh, through experiments. I tried a number of jobs, quite a few, but was never good at any of them. Well, I amuse myself at painting when I'm not writing. I enjoy that, but I've had no training at it. I suppose my painting is pretty corny.

Q: Has your health been good in the last few years?

WILLIAMS: If it ain't been good, I wouldn't be living. (Laughs.) People are always asking me, "How's your health, how's your health?" and if I thought there was any genuine concern I suppose I would discuss it seriously with them. (Laughs.) My health is bearable, let's say. I have had a cardiac condition since — well, I guess it dates back to rheumatic fever as a child. And those things don't improve with age. I remember when I retired from the shoe business because of a heart attack at 24 — I spent three years in the shoe business — and I went down to live with my grandparents in Memphis. And I remember one night I went out to dinner with someone who excited me rather much, and I began to have palpitations. They scared me in those days. And the dinner guest summoned the doctor — a lady doctor — and she took quite a dim view of my condition. (Laughs.) And she said we must talk about it and have subsequent examinations the next day. The next day I went to her office and she said, "Well, I think these palpitations and these symptoms, the present ones, will be temporary, will clear up after awhile." She said, "I think you'll live to be 40." (Laughs.) And here I am 63. *Variety* says I'll be 60 on my next birthday, but I don't know how they got that figure. I guess the way I look. (Laughs.) I referred them to the Registry of Births in Columbus, Miss.

Q: Was your health the poorest it's been just before you were hospitalized in 1969?

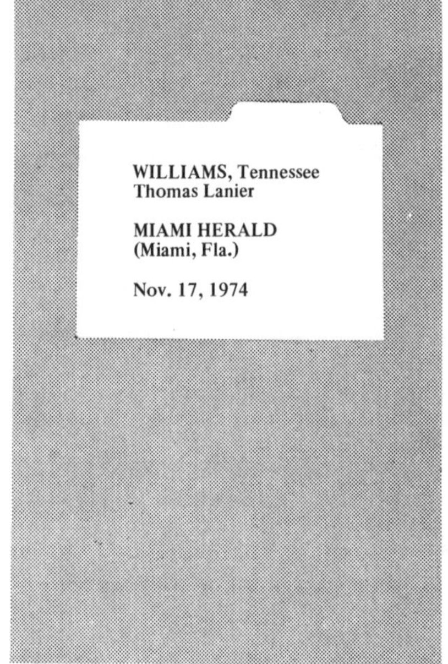

WILLIAMS, Tennessee
Thomas Lanier

MIAMI HERALD
(Miami, Fla.)

Nov. 17, 1974

WILLIAMS: Oh Lord, yes. You know, I was a patient of that notorious doctor in New York.

Q: The one they called Dr. Feelgood?

WILLIAMS: Dr. Feelgood, yes. But so many people were so greatly benefited by that doctor. But they weren't supposed to drink. Now I continued to drink while I was taking the Feelgood shots, you know. Well, I felt awfully good. (Laughs.) But they terminated with me being hauled off to the bin, you know, by my brother. It was a terrifying period in my life. I nearly died — convulsions and coronary during the cold-turkey treatment.

Q: Cold turkey for both drinking and drugs?

WILLIAMS: Both, completely. Both.

Q: Was your poor health before you were hospitalized the reason for plays that were not well-received, like "In the Bar of a Tokyo Hotel"?

WILLIAMS: *In the Bar of a Tokyo Hotel* I wrote about the time of the approach to collapse. But that's one of the plays I like. That I hope will be revived.

Q: So that was one on which you think the critical opinion was misguided?

WILLIAMS: Oh, it was really. . . calamitous, the critical opinion. In fact, *Life* magazine reviewed it saying that I was finished as a playwright. Well. . . they're finished as a magazine, and I'm still here. So you see, I've turned the tables on them. I have no malice about them. I am rather happy that I survived and they didn't.

Q: Do you think some of your other work was also undervalued? You once said that some of your best writing was in your short stories and short plays.

WILLIAMS: Yes. I think the best piece of writing I ever did was a very, very short play called *This Property is Condemned.* About a little girl and a boy — a boy flying a paper kite and the little girl walking the railroad track in the delta of Mississippi. And I think it's the best piece of writing I've ever done. And I discovered in New Orleans, another version of it which was longer. I found it in my files and I hope that it can be done in the longer form because it incorporates also the short version, except that it has a beginning inside the house and the end inside the house which is condemmed. But it only exists in first draft; it hasn't even been typed up yet.

Q: Which of the characters in your plays do you feel closest to?

WILLIAMS: Isn't it funny, I don't know. I couldn't possibly answer that question. I suppose I feel closest to the dual character in *Out Cry.*

Q: You think of the brother and sister, Felice and Clare, as a single character?

WILLIAMS: As two sides of a single character. A cousin of mine, Sidney Lanier, came to see it in Washington and he said all of us contain the animus, which is the male component, and the anima, which is the female component. And he said, those are the two characters in your play, the animus and the anima. The male and the female side of each individual. That may have been an oversimplification.

Q: You once said that Alma in "Summer and Smoke" was very much like you in that she went from puritan shackles to complete profligacy.

WILLIAMS: Oh yes. That side. . . yeah, yeah, yeah. . . puritan shackles which she broke off with great difficulty, but rather completely in the end. (Laughs.)

Q: And you feel that parallels your own life?

WILLIAMS: Yes, yes, indeed it does. I'm certainly a puritan, but an emancipated puritan. (Laughs.) You're never fully emancipated. If you're once a puritan you always remain a puritan regardless of how far out you go.

Q: In what ways have you remained a puritan?

WILLIAMS: I still have a conscience, you know. It reproaches me quite frequently. [T]

Three Happy Endings A Year

Glenna Finley

WITTE, Glenna Finley
(1925 -)

SEATTLE POST-INTELLIGENCER
(Seattle, Wash.)

Mar. 17, 1974

[See also CA-15/16]

By ARCHIE SATTERFIELD

GLENNA FINLEY writes at least three paperback romance novels a year for New American Library. She took an evening off recently and spoke to the Seattle Free Lances, a professional writers' club. Ms. Finley (Mrs. Donald Witte, of Magnolia, at home) has the floor:

"After I had sold three romances, New American Library asked me to join their stable of writers. I didn't know about that 'stable' business, but now I do know the meaning of 'indentured slavery.' I signed a contract for three books a year, 185 manuscript pages every four months. They pay me an advance on the first 100,000 copies. That's my break-even point, and when a book goes into nine paintings . . . I like that.

"I've written fourteen romances now, and the 15th is in the oven. ("The Romantic Spirit" and "When Love Speaks" are recent titles. "A Promising Affair" is due in May.)

"It gets a little confusing sometimes. We (she and her family) were in New Orleans researching settings for a book and I got the galley proofs for a book set in Scotland and another set in Morocco.

"While we were in Morocco researching 'Surrender My Love,' we heard about the wife market where men trade in their wives after a year or so and I thought: "Aha! A plot,' and my eyes lit up. Then I looked at my husband and his eyes were lit up too.

"I got the idea for 'Surrender My Love' at a Free Lances dinner in the Spaghetti Factory. I was sitting by Jim Phillips, who told me all about zoos and I thought zoos would be a good setting. So we took off visiting zoos in this country and Europe, and I was going to have the story end in the Zurich zoo. But when we got there, the darn thing was closed because of the hoof and mouth disease. (The novel ended on a train instead.)

"To this day I don't know what a Gothic novel is unless it has a governess on the cover fleeing. My books are heavier on romance than adventure. My girls are still chaste. One reader wrote that she didn't like the fact that one of my heroines had kissed the other man!

"My characters sometimes go off in strange ways, but I know about what page to bring them back into the fold.

"I try to write three pages a day, which usually takes about three hours; then I spend the other 21 thinking.

"There are several advantages to being a contract writer. You have a steady market, you can work on the cover with the artist before the book is finished, and you have the same artist for each cover because it is a series; the publisher will push your series to keep you in print.

"The main disadvantage is that you seldom have time to get away from writing.

"A friend and I took a woodworking class and every time the class met, she told me what her pet iguana had been doing. 'My God!' I thought 'A plot!' I was sorry to hear he was dead because I'd always intended to go over and shake his hand out of gratitude (for his role in "Bridal Affair." Set in Oregon, the novel is one of her most successful.)

"I have survived three executive editors and three personal editors since I started. But losing an editor is traumatic, and reminds me of a friend who went to Palm Springs for a few months. When she came back, she went to her bank, Peoples National Bank Main Branch, and all she found was a big hole in the ground. (It moved across the street while a new one is being built.)

"Sometimes I write the last two pages first; I like to write those.

"Writing is like taking a correspondence course: you have to keep up. Right now I'm 30 pages behind because I went to Canada last weekend and played."

Miss Finley agreed to let me take notes from her talk, but warned me not to expect anything like what another New American Library author said in an interview (Raina Barrett, author of "First Your Money, Then Your Clothes," ARTS, February 24).

That's all right, Glenna. She wrote about sex with love. You write about love without sex. It sort of balances out.

1,200 Owe Their Lives to Her

—Star-News Photographer Rosemary Martufi

Hiltgunt Zassenhaus, nominee for the Nobel Peace Prize.

By Ruth Dean
Star-News Staff Writer

As Adolf Hitler's psychotic tyranny was leading Germany to defeat, a young German woman was quietly conducting her own anti-Nazi resistance movement — a dangerous mission that eventually saved the lives of 1,200 Scandinavian prisners of war and belatedly brought her recognition this year as a Nobel award nominee.

Hiltgunt Zassenhaus reveals this mission for the first time in her new book, "Walls: Resisting the Third Reich — One Woman's Story" (Beacon, $7.95).

A Baltimore physician since 1952, and known to her patients as Dr. H. Margaret Zassenhaus, she first published her memoir last October in a Norwegian edition which has become a best-seller.

IT IS THOUGHT that her account may have prompted her nominatin last month for the 1974 Nobel Peace Prize, because her two sponsors, both members of the Norwegian Parliament had been in the group of POWs she rescued almost 30 years ago. She never met them, however, which fulfills the Nobel Prize requirement that the nominee have no prior association with the nominators.

Winning the prize "doesn't matter," she said in an interview, because "the moment of glory for me was long ago when I got the patients home alive."

ZASSENHAUS, Hiltgunt (1916 -)
WASHINGTON STAR–NEWS (Washington, D.C.)
Mar. 13, 1974
[See also CA-49/52]

Her story reads like a spy thriller. During a two-year period she visited all the German prisons under her official "cover" as a Scandinavian translator for the German Ministry of Justice. What wasn't included in her official duties were the bread, fruit medicines, vitamins and services of a Norwegian minister she smuggled into the prisons despite the inspection of prison wardens and, a couple of times the wary eye of the Gestapo.

She tried bluff ("everyone in Germany was afraid of everyone else"), and it worked. She always feared for her life, but a lively faith in God and her family's humanitarian example always kept her going.

It was the secret file she compiled of all the prisoners' names that saved their lives. Toward the end of the war with Germany was losing, she learned from a prison guard that Hitler had issued a secret order for the execution of all political prisoners. Through a Hamburg ship supplier who' helped her get the supplies for the POWs, she got word to Count Folke Bernadotte, then-president of the Swedish Red Cross, who successfuly negotiated the prisoners' mass release with the help of Dr. Zassenhaus's list of names.

Their release came none too soon. Only days later all political prisoners, Germans and foreigners alike, were executed, some herded onto ships which were sunk at sea.

COMING TO America was like going "to the moon," she said, but now that she's lived here more than 20 years as a naturalized citizen, she sees the Nazi experience in perspective as a history lesson for our time. That's why she wrote the book.

"It has a message for today so we won't repeat the mistakes of the past." She said she couldn't emphasize enough how important it is for every individual to stand up for his or her convictions and "get involved."

She blames Hitler's rise to power on "the silent majority who went along, because they were guilty of the most deadly fault — indifference."

DR. ZASSENHAUS is concerned present psychological attitude of the American public in the wake of Watergate and the energy crisis.

"There seems to be a feeling of great frustration, a tendency to isolation and retreating to their own backyards. I saw that in Germany toward the end of the war when people prayed that the bombs just wouldn't fall in their yard but in their neighbor's yard or in the next city.

"We talk about Nixon, about Watergate, but what are we doing about ourselves, about our own attitudes? We must get involv ed ourselves to make America a better place to live. I think the average young person should be more concerned for his country. My story tells what the individual can do — if you try.

"Remember that old saying: 'Evil can only happen as long as the good men do nothing.'"